Course   Introduction to Supply Chain

Course Number   **MGT 301**

                 COLORADO STATE UNIVERSITY - FORT COLLINS

                 MANAGEMENT

http://create.mheducation.com

ISBN-10: 1308984588   ISBN-13: 9781308984582

Contents

Credits

Preface

Over the last eight decades, the discipline of business logistics has advanced from the warehouse floor and transportation dock to the boardroom of leading global enterprises. We have had the opportunity to be actively involved in this evolution through research, education, and advising. *Supply Chain Logistics Management* encompasses the development and fundamentals of the logistics discipline within a supply chain structure. It also presents our vision of the future of business logistics and supply chain management and their role in enterprise competitiveness.

Although individually and collectively the three authors have written extensively on various aspects of logistics, the decision to initially write and subsequently revise *Supply Chain Logistics Management* represents the synthesis of many years of research, augmenting and, in many ways, supplanting earlier works of the authors published by McGraw-Hill. The union of ideas presented in this text provides an integrated supply chain framework for the study of logistics, serves to expand the treatment of supply chain management by placing it firmly in the context of integrated business strategy, and highlights the increasing importance of logistics in the supply chains supporting a global economy.

Logistics includes all the activities required to move product and information to, from, and between members of a supply chain. The supply chain provides the framework for businesses and their suppliers to jointly deliver goods, services, and information efficiently, effectively, relevantly, and in a sustainable manner to customers. *Supply Chain Logistics Management* presents the mission, business processes, and strategies needed to achieve integrated logistical management. We hope the text achieves three fundamental objectives: (1) presents a comprehensive description of existing logistical practices in a global economy, (2) describes ways and means to apply logistics principles to achieve competitive advantage, and (3) provides a conceptual approach for integrating logistics as a core competency within enterprise supply chain strategy.

For their specific suggestions regarding the manuscript, our appreciation goes to Eduardo Davila, Arizona State University–Tempe; Richard Hoffmann, Pennsylvania State University; Jeff Miller, University of Maryland–College Park; Anthony S. Roath, University of Oklahoma; Dmitriy Shaltayev, Christopher Newport University; Marjorie Smith, Mountain State University; Alvin J. Williams, University of South Alabama, and Zachary Williams, Central Michigan University, all of whom provided detailed reviews and offered numerous suggestions for improving the presentation.

We also wanted to acknowledge the staff at McGraw-Hill/Irwin for their guidance and efforts on behalf of the book: Richard Hercher, Executive Editor, Operations and Decision Sciences; Danielle Andries, Editorial Coordinator; Lisa Bruflodt, Project Manager and Jaime Halteman, Marketing Manager.

As active members of the Council of Supply Chain Management Professionals, we have been the fortunate recipients of contributions by many council members to the development of this manuscript. In particular, we wish to acknowledge the assistance of Rick Blasgen, president and CEO of the Council of Supply Chain Management Professionals, and the CSCMP staff who maintain an open door to the academic community.

Over the past 48 years, the business executives who have attended the annual Michigan State University Logistics Management Executive Development Seminar have been exposed to the basic concepts presented in the text and have given freely of their time and experience. We also acknowledge the long-standing support to Michigan State Department of Supply Chain Management, through the funding of the endowed chairs, provided by the late John H. McConnell, founder of Worthington Industries.

The number of individuals involved in teaching logistics around the world expands daily. To this group in general, and in particular to our colleagues at Michigan State University, whose advice and assistance made it possible to complete and enhance this text, we express our sincere appreciation.

Teachers receive continuous inspiration from students over the years, and in many ways the day of judgment in an academic career comes in the seminar or classroom. We have been fortunate to have the counsel of many outstanding young scholars who currently are making substantial impact on the academic and business worlds. In particular, we appreciate the input of students who have used this text in manuscript form and made suggestions for improvement. We also acknowledge the contributions of Drs. Judith Whipple and Thomas Goldsby, who participated extensively in case development and editorial support.

We wish to acknowledge the contributions of Felicia Kramer and Pamela Kingsbury, for manuscript preparation on several earlier versions of this text, and Cheryl Lundeen, who prepared many drafts of the manuscripts. Without Felicia, Pam, and Cheryl, this long-published text in its many variations would not be a reality.

With so much able assistance, it is difficult to offer excuses for any shortcomings that might appear. Any faults are solely our responsibility.

Donald J. Bowersox

David J. Closs

M. Bixby Cooper

John C. Bowersox

Preface

Purchasing and supply management has become increasingly visible in a world where supply is a major determinant of corporate survival and success. Supply chain performance influences not only operational and financial risks but also reputational risk. Extending the supply chain globally into developing countries places new responsibilities on the supplier and supply, not only to monitor environmental, social, political, and security concerns but also to influence them. Thus, the job of the supply manager of today goes way beyond the scope of supply chain efficiency and value for money spent to search for competitive advantage in the supply chain. Cost containment and improvement represent one challenge; the other is revenue enhancement. Not only must the supply group contribute directly to both the balance sheet and the income statement; it must also enhance the performance of other members of the corporate team. Superior internal relationship and knowledge management need to be matched on the exterior in the supply network to assure that the future operational and strategic needs of the organization will be met by future markets. The joy of purchasing and supply management lives in the magnitude of its challenges and the opportunities to achieve magnificent contributions.

For more than 80 years this text and its predecessors have championed the purchasing and supply management cause. Based on the conviction that supply and suppliers have to contribute effectively to organizational goals and strategies, this and previous editions have focused on how to make that mission a reality.

A great deal has happened in the supply field since the 14th edition was published. Continuing advances in MIS and technology provide new ways to improve supply efficiency and effectiveness. New security, environmental, and transparency requirements and the search for meaningful supply metrics have further complicated the challenges faced by supply managers all over the world. As a consequence, several changes and updates have been made to the 15th edition. First, the new edition provides an opportunity to incorporate the latest theory and best practice in supply chain management into the text. Wherever appropriate, real-world examples and current research are used to illustrate key points. Second, the application of information technology to supply chain processes continues to change rapidly, including the evolution of cloud-based computing. The text has been updated accordingly, including a major revision to Chapter 4. Third, there are also several important emerging issues—including sustainability, challenges of managing risk in a global supply chain, and collaboration—that are addressed in this text. Lastly, nearly one-third of the cases have been replaced with new cases that cover topics such as negotiation, outsourcing, risk management, and sustainability. Thus, the examples in the text and more than 45 real-life supply chain cases afford the chance to apply the latest research and theoretical developments in the field to real-life issues, opportunities, decisions, and problems faced by practitioners.

In this edition the focus on decision making in the supply chain has also been strengthened considerably. The chapter sequence reflects the chronological order of the acquisition process. Criteria for supply decisions have been identified in three categories: (1) strategic, (2) operational, and (3) additional. It is the third category with balance sheet and income statement considerations, all dimensions of risk, environmental, and social considerations that is growing in relevance, making sound supply decisions an even more complex challenge.

Since the sixth edition nearly 40 years ago, Michiel R. Leenders has been an author of this text. As Professor of Operations at the Ivey Business School, Mike has been one of the great leaders in the supply field for more than half a century. His accomplishments include authorship of three other procurement books, founding director of the Ivey Purchasing Managers Index, and a long list of articles and presentations at international conferences. In 2003, Mike received the International Federation of Purchasing and Materials Management's highest research honor in the form of the Hans Ovelgonne Award. Mike did not participate in this edition, although his past contributions are still evident throughout this text.

A book with text and cases depends on many to contribute through their research and writing to expand the body of knowledge of the field. Thus, to our academic colleagues our thanks for pushing out the theoretical boundaries of supply management. To many practitioners, we wish to extend our gratitude for proving what works and what does not and providing their stories in the cases in this text. Also many case writers contributed their efforts so that approximately one-third of all the cases in this edition are new.

Case contributors in alphabetical order included: Carolynn Cameron, Garland Chow, Jorge Colazo, Jenni Denniston, Dominque Fortier, Manish Kumar, Glen Luinenberg, Eric Silverberg, Dave Vannette, and Marsha Watson.

Instructor and student supplements are available on this book's website at **www.mhhe.com/johnson15e.** Instructor ancillaries are password-protected for security.

The production side of any text is more complicated than most authors care to admit. At McGraw-Hill Education Christina Kouvelis, Kaylee Putbrese, Michelle Valenti, Jane Mohr, Dheeraj Chahal and many others contributed to turn our efforts into a presentable text.

The support of Dean Bob Kennedy and our colleagues at the Ivey Business School has been most welcome.

The assistance of the Institute for Supply Management in supporting the continuous improvement of supply education is also very much appreciated.

P. Fraser Johnson

Anna E. Flynn

CHAPTER 1

21st-Century Supply Chains

Chapter Outline

The Supply Chain Revolution
Why Integration Creates Value
Generalized Supply Chain Model
Information System Functionality
Supply Chain Information System Modules
    Enterprise Integration and Administration
    Enterprise Supply Chain Operations
    Enterprise Planning and Monitoring
    Communication Technology
    Consumer Connectivity
Integrative Management and Supply Chain Processes
    Collaboration
    Enterprise Extension
    Integrated Service Providers (ISP)
Responsiveness
    Anticipatory Business Model (Push)
    Responsive Business Model (Pull)
    Postponement
    Barriers to Implementing Responsive Systems
Financial Sophistication
    Cash-to-Cash Conversion
    Dwell Time Minimization
    Cash Spin
Globalization
Summary

As recently as the 1990s, the average time required for a company to process and deliver merchandise to a customer from warehouse inventory ranged from 15 to 30 days, sometimes even longer. The typical order-to-delivery process involved order creation and transfer, which was usually via telephone, fax, electronic data interchange (EDI), or public mail; followed by order processing, which involved the use of manual or computer systems, credit authorization, and order assignment to a warehouse for processing; followed by shipment to a customer. When everything went as planned, the average time for a customer to receive items ordered was lengthy. When something went wrong, as it often did, such as inventory out-of-stock, a lost or misplaced work order, or a misdirected shipment, total time to service customers escalated rapidly.

To support this lengthy and unpredictable time to market, it became common practice to accumulate inventory. For example, duplicate inventories were typically stocked by multiple supply chain members. Despite such extensive inventory, out-of-stocks and delayed deliveries were common due in part to the large number of product and process variations.

These accepted business practices of the 20th century, as well as the distribution channel structure used to complete delivery, evolved from years of experience dating from the industrial revolution. Such long-standing business practices remained in place and unchallenged because no clearly superior alternative existed. The traditional distribution process was designed to overcome challenges and achieve benefits that long ago ceased to be important. The industrialized world is no longer characterized by scarcity. Consumer affluence and desire for wide choice of products and services continue to grow. In fact, today's consumers want a wide range of product and source options they can configure to their unique specifications. Given the rapid growth of information technology and the accessibility of the Internet, consumer desires have shifted from passive acceptance to active involvement in the design and delivery of specific products and services. Transportation capacity and operational performance have increasingly become more economical and reliable. Today's transportation is supported by sophisticated information systems that facilitate predictable and precise delivery. The capability to continuously track shipments and receive near instant notification of delayed delivery is common practice.

Massive change has occurred as a result of available information technology. During the decade of the 1990s, the world of commerce was irrevocably impacted by computerization, the Internet, and a range of inexpensive information transmission capabilities. Information characterized by speed, accessibility, accuracy, and most of all relevancy are now the norm. The Internet is a common and economical way to complete business-to-business (B2B) transactions. An increasing number of consumers are directly connected to firms via the Internet. Driven by these fundamental forces, a global economy has emerged.

What began during the last decade of the 20th century and will continue to unfold well into the 21st century is what historians are increasingly characterizing as the dawning of the **information** or **digital age.** In the information age the reality of connectivity among collaborating business organizations continues to drive a new order of relationships called **supply chain management.** Managers are increasingly improving and integrating traditional marketing, manufacturing, purchasing and logistics practices. In this new order of affairs, products can be manufactured to exact specifications and rapidly delivered to customers at locations throughout the globe. Logistical systems exist that have the capability to deliver products at precise times. Customer order and delivery of product assortments can be performed in hours. The frequent occurrence of service failures that characterized the past is increasingly being replaced by a growing managerial commitment to zero defect or what is commonly called **six-sigma** performance.[1] **Perfect orders**—delivering the desired assortment and quantity of products to the right location on time, damage-free, and correctly invoiced—once the exception, are now becoming the expectation. Perhaps most important is the fact that such high-level performance is being achieved at lower total cost and with the commitment of fewer financial resources than common in the past. All of this fundamental change in business enterprise structure and strategy is primarily being driven by information technology.

In this initial chapter, the supply chain management business model and value proposition are introduced as a growing strategic commitment of contemporary firms. The chapter reviews the development of the supply chain revolution in business practice that has

---

[1] Six-sigma performance reflects a level of achievement having an error rate of 3.4 defects per million, or 99.99966 percent perfect.

resulted in a generalized supply chain model. Next, the supply chain concept is presented in a strategic framework. The following section discusses the importance of information systems functionality and the modules that support supply chain operations. The chapter then examines integrative management, responsiveness, financial sophistication, and globalization as forces driving the emergence of supply chain logic. The overall objective of Chapter 1 is to position the logistical challenges of supporting a 21st century supply chain strategy. The supply chain is positioned as the strategic framework within which logistical requirements are identified and related operations managed.

The Supply Chain Revolution

What managers are experiencing today we choose to describe as the **supply chain revolution** and a related **logistical renaissance.** These two massive shifts in expectation and practice concerning best-practice performance of business operations are highly interrelated. However, supply chain and logistics are significantly different aspects of contemporary management.

Supply chain management consists of multiple firms collaborating to leverage strategic positioning and to improve operating efficiency. For each firm involved, the supply chain relationship reflects a strategic choice. A supply chain strategy is a channel and business organizational arrangement based on **acknowledged dependency** and **collaboration.** Supply chain operations require managerial processes that span traditional functional areas within individual firms and link suppliers, trading partners, and customers across business boundaries.

Within a firm's supply chain management, **logistics** is the work required to move and geographically position inventory. As such, logistics is a subset of and occurs within the broader framework of a supply chain. Logistics is the process that creates value by timing and positioning inventory. Logistics is the combination of a firm's order management, inventory, transportation, warehousing, materials handling, and packaging as integrated throughout a facility network. Integrated logistics serves to link and synchronize the overall supply chain as a continuous process and is essential for effective supply chain connectivity. While the purpose of logistical work has remained essentially the same over the decades, the way the work is performed continues to radically change.

The fundamental focus of this book is integrated logistics management. However, to study logistics, a reader must have a basic understanding of supply chain management. Supply chain strategy establishes the operating framework within which logistics is performed. As will be reviewed shortly, dramatic change continues to evolve in supply chain practice. Accordingly, logistics best practice, as described in this book, is presented as a work in progress, subject to continuous change based on the evolving nature of supply chain structure and strategy. Chapter 2, Logistics, examines the renaissance taking place in logistics best practice and sets the stage for chapters that follow.

At first glance, supply chain management may appear to be a vague concept. A great deal has been written on the subject without much concern for basic definition, structure, or common vocabulary. Confusion exists concerning the appropriate scope of what constitutes a supply chain, to what extent it involves integration with other companies as contrasted to integrating a firms internal operations, and how to best implement a strategy concerning competitive practices and legal constraints. For most managers, the supply chain concept has intrinsic appeal because it envisions new business arrangements offering the potential to improve competitiveness. The concept also implies a highly effective network business relationships that serve to improve efficiency by eliminating duplicate and nonproductive work. Understanding more specifically what constitutes the supply chain revolution starts with a review of traditional distribution channel practice.

To overcome challenges of commercial trading, firms developed business relationships with other product and service companies to jointly perform essential activities. Such acknowledged dependency was necessary to achieve benefits of specialization. Managers, following the early years of the industrial revolution, began to strategically plan core competency, specialization, and economy of scale. The result was realization that working closely with other businesses was essential for continued success. This understanding that no firm could be totally self-sufficient contrasted to some earlier notions of vertical integration.[2] Acknowledged dependence between business firms created the study of what became known as **distribution** or **marketing channels.**

Because of the high visibility of different types of businesses, the early study of channel arrangements was characterized by classification based on specific roles performed during the distribution process. For example, a firm may have been created to perform the value-added services called wholesaling. Firms doing business with a wholesaler had expectations concerning what services they would receive and the compensation they would be expected to pay. In-depth study of specific activities quickly identified the necessity for leadership, a degree of commitment to cooperation among all channel members, and means to resolve conflict. Scholars who conduct research in channel structure and strategy developed typologies to classify observable practice ranging from a single transaction to highly formalized continuous business relationships.

The bonding feature of channel integration was a rather vague concept that all involved would enjoy benefits as a result of cooperating. However, primarily due to a lack of high-quality information, the overall channel structure was postured on an adversarial foundation. When push came to shove, each firm in the channel would first and foremost focus on achieving its individual goals. Thus, in final analysis, channel dynamics were more often than not characterized by a dog-eat-dog competitive environment.

During the last decade of the 20th century, channel strategy and structure began to shift radically. Traditional distribution channel arrangements moved toward more integration and collaboration. Prior to reviewing the generalized supply chain model, it is important to understand why integration creates value.

Why Integration Creates Value

To explain the basic benefits and challenges of integrated management, it is useful to point out that customers have at least three perspectives of value.

The traditional perspective is **economic value.** Economic value builds on economy of scale in operations as the source of efficiency. Economy of scale seeks to fully utilize fixed assets to achieve the lowest, total landed cost. The focus of economic value is efficiency of product/service creation. Economic value is all about doing things as well as possible. The customer take-away of economic value is **high quality at a low price.**

A second value perspective is **market value.** Market value is about presenting an attractive assortment of products at the right time and place to realize effectiveness. Market value focuses on achieving economy of scope in product/service presentation. The creation of multimerchant shopping malls, large-scale mass-merchandising retail stores, and multivendor Internet fulfillment operations are all initiatives to achieve **market value.** The customer's take-away in terms of market value is **convenient product/service assortment and choice.**

Realization of both economic and market value is important to customers. However, increasingly firms are recognizing that business success also depends upon a third perspective

---

[2] Henry Ford, *Today and Tomorrow* (New York: Doubleday, Page, and Company, 1926). Reprinted by Productivity Press (Portland, OR, 1988).

TABLE 1.1
Integrative
Management Value
Proposition

Economic Value	Market Value	Relevancy Value
• Lowest total cost	• Attractive assortment	• Customization
• Economy-of-scale efficiency	• Economy-of-scope effectiveness	• Segmental diversity
• Product/service creation	• Product/service presentation	• Product/service positioning
Procurement/Manufacturing Strategy	**Market/Distribution Strategy**	**Supply Chain Strategy**

of value, referred to as **relevancy value.** Relevancy value involves customization of value-adding services, over and above basic product characteristics and physical location, that make a real difference to customers. Relevancy value means the right products and services, as reflected by market value, at the right price, as reflected by economic value, modified, sequenced, synchronized, and positioned in a manner that creates customer-specific value. In a consumer context, for example, relevancy means transforming ingredients into ready-to-eat meals. In general merchandise retailing, relevancy means transforming products into fashionable apparel. In manufacturing and assembly, relevancy is achieved by integrating specific components into products to increase functionality desired by a specific customer. The customer's take-away in terms of relevancy is a unique product/service bundle.

The simultaneous achievement of economic value, market value, and relevancy value requires total integration of the overall business process and is known as the integrative management value proposition, as illustrated in Table 1.1.

Generalized Supply Chain Model

The general concept of an integrated supply chain is often illustrated by a line diagram that links participating firms into a coordinated competitive unit. Figure 1.1 illustrates a generalized model adapted from the supply chain management program at Michigan State University.

The context of an integrated supply chain is multifirm collaboration within a framework of key resource flows and constraints. Within this context, supply chain structure and strategy results from efforts to operationally align an enterprise with customers as well as the supporting distributive and supplier networks to gain competitive advantage. Business operations are ideally integrated from initial material purchase to delivery of finished products and services to customers.[3]

Value results from the synergy among firms constituting a supply chain as a result of five critical flows: information, product, service, financial, and knowledge (see the bidirectional arrow at the top of the Figure 1.1). Logistics is the primary conduit of product and service flow within a supply chain arrangement. Each firm engaged in a supply chain is involved in performing some aspects of overall logistics. Achievement of logistical integration and efficiency across the supply chain is the focus of this text. The generalized supply chain arrangement illustrated in Figure 1.1 logically and logistically links a firm and its distributive and supplier network to customers. The message conveyed by the figure is that the integrated value-creation process must be aligned and managed from material procurement to end-customer product/service delivery in order to achieve effectiveness, efficiency, relevancy, and sustainability.

---

[3] Customers are defined as destination points in a supply chain. Customers either consume a product or use it as an integral part or component of an additional process or product. The essential point is that the original product loses its unique configuration when consumed. Business entities that purchase products from manufacturers for resale, for example, wholesalers and retailers, are referred to as *intermediate customers.*

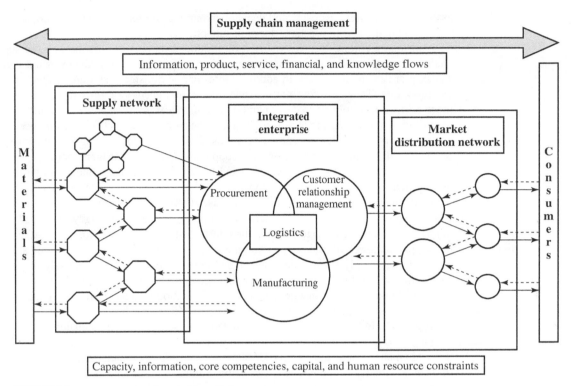

FIGURE 1.1   The Integrated Supply Chain Framework

The integrated supply chain perspective shifts traditional channel arrangements from loosely linked groups of independent businesses that buy and sell inventory to each other toward a managerially coordinated initiative to increase market impact, overall efficiency, continuous improvement, and competitiveness. In practice, many complexities serve to cloud the simplicity of illustrating supply chains as directional line diagrams. For example, many individual firms simultaneously participate in multiple and competitive supply chains. To the degree that a supply chain becomes the basic unit of competition, firms participating in multiple arrangements may confront loyalty issues related to confidentiality and potential conflict of interest.

Another factor that serves to add complexity to understanding supply chain structure is the high degree of mobility and change observable in typical arrangements. It's interesting to observe the fluidity of supply chains as firms enter and exit without any apparent loss of essential connectivity. For example, a firm and/or service supplier may be actively engaged in a supply chain structure during selected times, such as a peak selling season, and not during the balance of a year. During the 2010 Christmas season, Toys R Us added 600 temporary or pop-up express stores to accommodate demand. An estimated 10,000 positions were required to staff these stores. In total, some 45,000 employees were added across the nation to meet seasonal demand projections.

Information System Functionality

The overarching enabler of supply chain management is information technology. Supply chain technology systems initiate activities and track information regarding processes, facilitate information sharing both within the firm and between supply chain partners, and assist in management oversight and decision making. Comprehensive information systems are a combination of transaction, decision support, and communication sub-systems.

From its inception, logistics focused on product storage and flow through the supply chain. Information flow and accuracy were often overlooked because they was not viewed as being critical to customers. In addition, information transfer rates were limited to manual processes. There are four reasons why timely and accurate information has become more critical in supply chain design and operations. First, customers perceive information regarding order status, product availability, delivery tracking, and invoices as necessary dimensions of day-to-day business operations. Customers demand real-time information. Second, with the goal of managing total supply chain assets, managers realize that information can be used to reduce inventory and human resource requirements. In particular, requirements planning based on timely information can reduce inventory by minimizing demand uncertainty. Third, information increases flexibility with regard to how, when, and where resources may be utilized to achieve competitive advantage. Finally, enhanced information transfer and exchange utilizing the Internet is facilitating collaboration and redefining supply chain relationships. A common example of comprehensive information systems driving better supply chain utilization can be found in today's international shipping arena. It is common for a firm to re-direct a container mid-transit based on real time feedback from local markets. This change, enabled by information technology results in higher service levels and simultaneously improved asset utilization.

Supply chain information systems (SCIS) are the thread linking logistical activity into an integrated process. Integration builds on four levels of functionality: (1) transaction systems, (2) management control, (3) decision analysis, and (4) strategic planning. Figure 1.2 illustrates logistics activities and information required at each level. As the pyramid shape

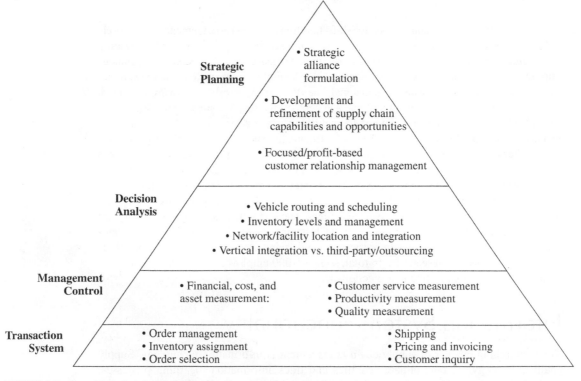

FIGURE 1.2 Supply Chain Information System Functionality

suggests, management control, decision analysis, and strategic planning enhancements require a strong transaction system foundation.

A **transaction system** is characterized by formalized rules, procedures, and standardized communications; a large volume of transactions; and an operational, day-to-day focus. The combination of structured processes and large transaction volume places a major emphasis on information system efficiency. At the most basic level, transaction systems initiate and record individual logistics activities and their outcomes. Typical transaction functionality includes order entry, inventory assignment, order selection, shipping, pricing, invoicing, and customer inquiry. For example, customer order entry represents a customer request for products into the information system. Order entry transaction initiates a second transaction as inventory is assigned to the order. A third transaction is then generated to direct warehouse operations to select the order. A fourth transaction initiates order shipment to the customer. A final transaction creates the invoice and a corresponding account receivable. Throughout the process, the firm and customer expect real-time information regarding order status. Thus, the customer order performance cycle is completed through a series of information system transactions.

The second SCIS level, **management control,** focuses on performance measurement and reporting. Performance measurement is necessary to provide feedback regarding supply chain performance and resource utilization. Common performance dimensions include cost, customer service, productivity, quality, and asset management measures. As an example, specific performance measures include transportation and warehousing cost per hundredweight, inventory turnover, case fill rate, cases per labor hour, and customer service perception.

While it is necessary that SCIS report historical system performance, it is also necessary for the system to identify operational exceptions. Exception information is useful to highlight potential customer or operational problems. For example, proactive SCIS should be capable of avoiding future inventory shortages based on forecast requirements and planned inventory. Exception reporting should also identify potential transportation, warehouse, or labor constraints. While some control measures, such as cost, are well defined, other measures, such as service and quality, may be less specific. For example, customer service can be measured internally, from the enterprise's perspective, or externally, from the customer's perspective. While internal measures are relatively easy to track, information concerning external measures is more difficult to obtain, since it involves the customer or other external partners.

The third SCIS level, **decision analysis,** focuses on software tools to assist managers in identifying, evaluating, and comparing strategic and tactical alternatives to improve performance. Typical analyses include supply chain design, inventory management, resource allocation, transportation routing, and customer segment profitability. Decision analysis SCIS should ideally include database maintenance, modeling, analysis, and reporting. Like management control, decision analysis may include operational considerations such as vehicle routing and warehouse planning. Decision analysis is also being used to manage customer relationships by determining the trade-offs associated with having satisfied and successful customers.

Strategic planning, the final SCIS level, organizes and synthesizes transaction data into a relational database that assists in strategy formation and evaluation. Essentially, strategic planning focuses on information to evaluate and refine supply chain and logistics strategy. Examples of strategic planning include the desirability and scope of strategic alliances, development and refinement of supply chain capabilities, and opportunities related to customer relationship management. The relative shape of Figure 1.3 illustrates SCIS development characteristics and justification. Development and maintenance costs include hardware, software, communications, and human resources. In the past, most systems development focused on improving transaction system efficiency. While these investments originally offered returns in terms of speed and lower operating costs, there are now fewer

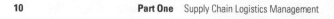

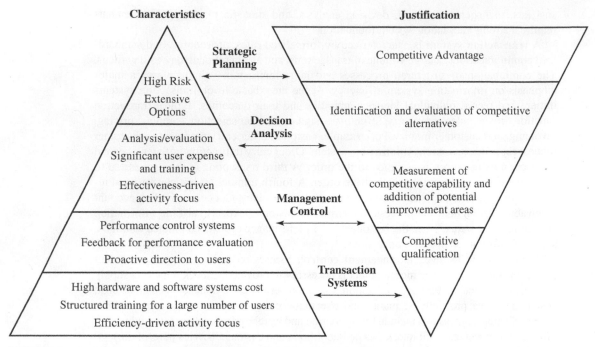

FIGURE 1.3   SCIS Usage, Decision Characteristics, and Justification

improvement opportunities. Most SCIS development and implementation is now focused on enhanced supply chain system integration and improved decision making.

Supply Chain Information System Modules

A comprehensive SCIS initiates, monitors, assists in decision making, and reports on activities required for completion of supply chain operations and planning. The major system modules and their interfaces are: (1) **Enterprise Resource Planning (ERP),** (2) communication systems, (3) execution systems, and (4) planning systems. Figure 1.4 illustrates a more application-oriented perspective. This application perspective is used to discuss each module's specific characteristics and functionality.

FIGURE 1.4
Application-Oriented
SCIS Framework

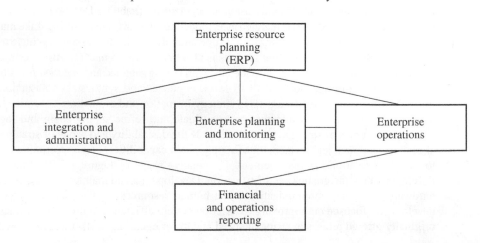

The ERP systems in Figure 1.4 are the backbone of most firms' logistics information system. This backbone maintains current and historical data and processes to initiate and monitor performance. During the 1990s, many firms began to replace self-developed functional modules (called "legacy systems") with ERP systems designed as integrated transaction modules and processes with a common and consistent database. The database includes information storage capability for both operations (i.e., product and activity based) and financial (i.e., monetary based) transactions. ERP systems facilitate integrated operations and reporting to initiate, monitor, and track critical activities such as order fulfillment and replenishment. ERP systems also incorporate an integrated corporatewide database, sometimes referred to as a data warehouse, along with appropriate transactions to facilitate logistics and supply chain planning and operations. Supply chain transactions facilitated by ERP systems include order entry and management, inventory assignment, and transportation. Beyond these supply chain applications, ERP systems typically include financial, accounting, and human resource capability. Data mining, knowledge management, and other enterprise integration applications operate using the ERP backbone to develop and organize insight regarding customers, products, and operations.

Enterprise Integration and Administration

Enterprise integration and administration are ERP modules that are not specifically supply chain applications. However, supply chain operations do have substantial interaction with these ERP components. Figure 1.5 illustrates the major enterprise integration and administration components. They are (1) general administration, (2) accounts receivable and payable, (3) financial inventory accounting, (4) general ledger, and (5) human resources.

General administration includes the various transactions to structure the firm and define transaction process flows. Supply chain operations use these modules to define reporting, functional, and organizational structures as well as to define process flows such as customer and replenishment order fulfillment. Accounts receivable and payable represent the functions for invoice collection from customers and invoice payment to suppliers. While these are typically acknowledged as accounting functions, there is a significant interaction with supply chain operations since accounts payable is influenced by materials and services acquisition and accounts receivable is influenced by delivery and invoicing of complete orders. Financial inventory accounting relates to the tracking of value-added processes through the supply chain to facilitate financial and tax reporting. The timing and location of supply chain value-added processes (e.g., production, inventory control, and packaging) can have a significant influence regarding what can be reported to the treasury (for taxation purposes) and the financial markets (for stock valuation purposes). General ledger relates to the structure of the detailed accounts for monitoring and reporting

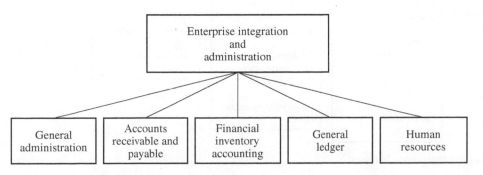

FIGURE 1.5
Enterprise Integration and Administration Components

revenues and accounts. Since supply chain involves substantial interaction with firm and external processes, the structure of the general ledger accounts significantly influences the supply chain's ability to measure, monitor, and report cost related to delivering product or serving customers. The human resource module of the ERP systems tracks personnel profiles and their activity levels. Since most firms have a large number of individuals involved in supply chain operations (e.g., manufacturing, distribution, and purchasing) and often in different global environments, the ability to track pay scales and activity levels is critical to make effective supply chain personnel decisions.

Enterprise Supply Chain Operations

Enterprise operations include the SCIS modules required to support day-to-day supply chain operations. Figure 1.6 illustrates the specific modules including: (1) customer relationship management, (2) logistics, (3) manufacturing, (4) purchasing, and (5) inventory deployment. Enterprise operations systems work in conjunction with the firm's ERP system to provide specific functionality to support supply chain operations. While some ERP systems support required supply chain functionality, others lack some functionality such as that required to support warehouse and transportation operations.

Customer accommodation systems, also known as **customer relationship management (CRM)** systems, are relatively new applications designed to facilitate information sharing between customers, sales force, and operations management. The logistics module directs and monitors logistics activities including finished goods inventory management,

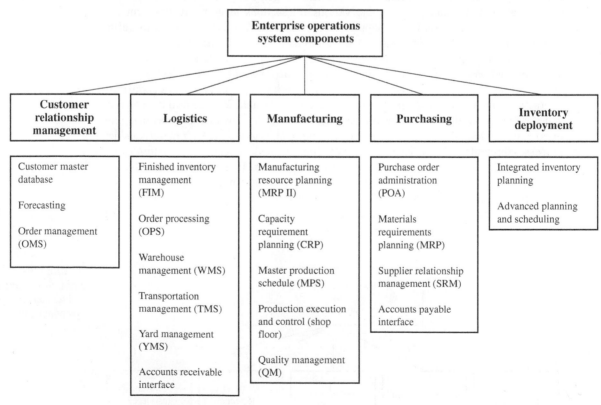

FIGURE 1.6 Enterprise Operations Modules

warehouse management, transportation management, and yard management. The manufacturing module schedules and allocates production resources and determines component requirements. The purchasing module initiates and tracks procurement activities including purchase order initiation, expediting, and supplier management. The inventory deployment system module schedules and monitors material flows to meet production and deployment requirements. Typical operational applications included in each module are listed. These applications are discussed throughout the text in conjunction with operational topics.

The traditional information technology delivery method has been for companies to operate and maintain private computer capabilities. Large mainframe computer capacity is essential to operate the varied information technology systems necessary to guide supply chain operations. This commitment to internal computing has rapidly changed in the 21st century. Increasingly firms are purchasing supply chain information technology support in the form of externally hosted systems. A wide variety of systems, such as **warehouse management (WMS)**, **transportation management (TMS)**, and **yard management (YMS)**, are available from technology application companies that specialize in providing and maintaining state-of-the-art performance systems. Typically referred to as **Software as a Service (SaaS)**, these application-specific software packages can be purchased for either internal use or on a hosted basis. When hosted by specialized service firms that provide the application using the capabilities of large computer resources, the application is referred to as **cloud computing.**

Enterprise Planning and Monitoring

Enterprise planning and monitoring are the processes and technologies that facilitate exchange of planning and coordinating information both within the firm and between supply chain partners. Figure 1.7 illustrates the major enterprise planning and monitoring components. The modules include (1) sales and operations planning, (2) supply chain visibility and event management, and (3) supply chain compliance. Since many of these activities involve interaction with other members of the supply chain, effective applications require substantial standardization with other firm functions and supply chain partners.

Sales and operations planning (S&OP), which is discussed further in Chapter 6, describes the process used to balance demand requirements and supply capabilities of the firm and its supply chain partners. While S&OP itself is a process requiring functional coordination and integration, it requires information technology to evaluate the demand, supply, and resource trade-offs. This technology is generally characterized as planning and scheduling applications. Supply chain visibility and event management tracks shipments

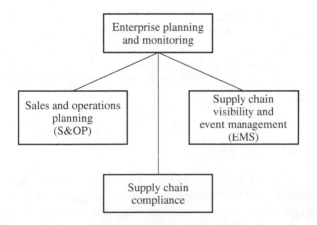

FIGURE 1.7
Enterprise Planning and Monitoring Modules

while they are in-transit and are increasingly capable of proactively suggesting changes in supply chain flows to minimize the potential of manufacturing shutdowns or service failures. Supply chain compliance systems monitor component and product flow information to make sure they comply with government and regulatory requirements for label, taxation, and security restrictions.

Communication Technology

Communication technology is the hardware and technical software that facilitates information exchange between the systems and physical infrastructure within the firm and between supply chain partners. The real-time information interchange between functions and supply chain partners facilitate coordination of inbound material, production, inventory, customer orders, and customer shipment. From a supply chain perspective, the availability of common and consistent requirements, activity, and performance information between supply chain partners enhances operational effectiveness, efficiency, relevancy, and sustainability.

Consumer Connectivity

The rapid development and deployment of the Internet has added a new dimension to the interface between firms and their customers. Both retailers and manufacturers are increasingly in direct Internet contact with the end consumers. This connectivity has developed along two main dimensions of communication—ordering and after-sale connectivity. Each has supply chain implications.

In terms of ordering, the Internet offers a way for consumers to facilitate and maintain direct contact with retailers and manufacturers. In essence this form of two-way connectivity is an expansion of traditional mail ordering. Empowered with the speed and flexibility of Internet connectivity, the interactive communications during ordering, determination of inventory status, processing time and location, and product delivery detail can be more diverse and comprehensive. For example, complete order-to-delivery tracking is a common feature. With the ease and speed of Internet connectivity, information concerning the total order to home delivery or retail pickup can be monitored.

With respect to product returns, or what is commonly called **reverse logistics,** the Internet offers a fast and accurate way to facilitate and track the product repair or replacement process. In addition, the existence of direct connectivity between the end consumer and the product manufacturer facilitates the rapid resolution of customer service issues related to product use and warranty.

In addition to information technology, the rapid emergence of supply chain relationships is being driven by four related forces: (1) integrated management and supply chain processes, (2) responsiveness, (3) financial sophistication, and (4) globalization. These forces will continue to drive supply chain structure and strategy initiatives across most industries for the foreseeable future. A brief discussion of each supply chain driver provides a foundation for understanding the challenges supply chain management places on exacting logistical performance.

Integrative Management and Supply Chain Processes

Across all aspects of business operations, attention is focused on achieving improved integrative management. The challenge to achieving integrated management results from the long-standing tradition of performing and measuring work on a functional basis. Since the industrial revolution, achieving best practice has focused managerial attention on functional specialization.[4] The prevailing belief was the better the performance of a specific function, the greater the efficiency of the overall process. For well over a century, this fundamental commitment to functional efficiency has driven best practice in organization structure, performance measurement, and accountability.

In terms of management, firms have traditionally been structured into departments to facilitate work focus, routinization, standardization, and control. Accounting practices were developed to measure departmental performance. Most performance measurement focused on individual functions. Two examples of common functional measurement are the cost per unit to manufacture and the cost per hundredweight to transport. Cross-functional measurements and allocations were typically limited to costs common to all functional areas of work, such as overhead, labor, utilities, insurance, interest, and so on.

Excellence in supply chain performance requires the simultaneous achievement of eight key processes. Table 1.2 identifies the eight key processes and provides a brief description of each. Although these integrative processes are not the exclusive domain of supply chain logistics, some critical elements of each are integral to a firm achieving high-level operational success. Therefore, supply chain structure, strategy, and continuous operational execution must be focused on achieving and continuously improving these essential eight processes. Simultaneous operational achievement of these eight processes forms the essence of achieving both operational integration and performance excellence.

The fundamental challenge of integrated management is to redirect traditional emphasis on functionality in an effort to focus on process achievement. Over the past few decades, it has become increasingly apparent that functions, individually performed best in class, do not necessarily combine or aggregate to achieve lowest total cost or highly effective processes. Integrative management seeks to identify and achieve lowest total process cost by capturing trade-offs that exist between functions. To illustrate, in terms of logistics, a firm might be able to reduce total cost to serve a customer as a result of spending more for faster, dependable transportation if the overall cost of inventory associated with the process can be reduced by an amount greater than that being spent for premium transportation. The

[4] Frederick W. Taylor, *Scientific Management* (New York: W. W. Norton, 1967).

Process	Description
Demand planning responsiveness	The assessment of demand and strategic design to achieve maximum responsiveness to customer requirements.
Customer relationship collaboration	The development and administration of relationships with customers to facilitate strategic information sharing, joint planning, and integrated operations.
Order fulfillment/service delivery	The ability to execute superior and sustainable order-to-delivery performance and related essential services.
Product/service development launch	The participation in product service development and lean launch.
Manufacturing customization	The support of manufacturing strategy and facilitation of postponement throughout the supply chain.
Supplier relationship collaboration	The development and administration of relationships with suppliers to facilitate strategic information sharing, joint planning, and integrated operations.
Life cycle support	The repair and support of products during their life cycle, including warranty, maintenance, and repair.
Reverse logistics	The return and disposition of inventories in a cost-effective and secure manner.

TABLE 1.2
Eight Supply Chain Integrative Processes

focus of integrated management is **lowest total process cost,** which is not necessarily the achievement of the lowest cost for each function included in the process.

The concept of trade-off and the goal of lowest total cost have logical appeal. While deceptively simple, managers continue to find the identification, measurement, and implementation of a process to minimize total cost a difficult task in day-to-day operations. The unavailability of focus on functional goals and the cost measures capable of quantifying cross-functional trade-offs served to stimulate development of such integrative tools as Total Cost Analysis, Process Engineering, and Activity-Based Costing (ABC).

Three important facets of supply chain logic resulted from increased managerial attention to: (1) collaboration, (2) enterprise extension, and (3) integrated service providers.

Collaboration

As discussed earlier, the history of business has been dominated by a desire to cooperate but always presented within a competitive framework. Whereas competition remains the dominant model guiding free market economies, the increasing importance of collaboration has positioned the supply chain as a primary unit of competition. In today's global economy, supply chain arrangements compete with each other for customer loyalty. Supply chains dominated by Sears Holding, Target, and Walmart are direct competitors in many markets. Similar supply chain alignments can be observed in industries ranging from entertainment to food to automobiles to chemicals. The global strategic reach of Limited Logistics Services is an example of the complexity of modern supply chain management. Garments manufactured throughout the world are delivered direct to retail stores, and are sold in all fashion seasons to worldwide consumers.

The general impetus to institutionalized collaborative working arrangements was the 1984 enactment of the National Cooperative Research and Development Act, which was expanded in scope by further legislation in 1993 and 2004.[5] This national legislation and its subsequent modification signaled fundamental change in traditional Justice Department antitrust philosophy. The basic legislation, as supplemented by administrative rulings, encouraged firms to develop collaborative initiatives in an effort to increase the global competitiveness of U.S.-based firms. Widespread realization that cooperation is both permissible and encouraged served to stimulate formation of supply chain arrangements.

While all forms of price collusion remain illegal, the collaborative legislation served to facilitate cross-organizational sharing of operating information, technology, and risk as ways to increase competitiveness. The response was a wide variety of new and innovative operating arrangements. One such development was the growing vision of enterprise extension.

---

[5] On October 11, 1984, President Reagan signed into law the National Cooperative Research Act of 1984 (Public Law 98-462) in an effort "to promote research and development, encourage innovation, stimulate trade, and make necessary and appropriate modifications in the operation of the antitrust laws." This law enables research and development activities to be jointly performed up to the point where prototypes are developed. The law further determined that antitrust litigation would be based on the rule of reason, taking into account all factors affecting competition. An extension to this act was signed into law by President Clinton on June 10, 1993. The extension, National Cooperative Production Amendments of 1993 (Public Law 103-42), allows joint ventures to go beyond just research to include the production and testing of a product, process, or service. This created a new act called the National Cooperative Research and Production Act of 1993 to replace the 1984 act. Furthermore, this new act established a procedure for businesses to notify the Department of Justice and the Federal Trade Commission of their cooperative arrangement in order to qualify for "single-damages limitation on civil antitrust liability." In 2004 President Bush signed into law the Standards Development Organization Advancement Act (SDOAA, H. R. 1086) which amended the 1993 act to include immunity for standards development organizations and thereby further validated the collaborative doctrine.

Enterprise Extension

The central thrust of enterprise extension is to expand managerial influence and control beyond the ownership boundaries of a single enterprise to facilitate joint planning and operations with customers and suppliers. The fundamental belief is that collaborative behavior to integrate processes between firms will improve impact, reduce overall risk, and greatly improve efficiency. Enterprise extension builds on two basic paradigms: information sharing and process specialization.

The **information sharing paradigm** is the widespread belief that achieving a high degree of cooperative behavior requires that supply chain participants voluntarily share operating information and jointly plan strategies. The scope of cross-enterprise collaboration should span beyond sales data to include plans detailing promotion, new product introduction, and day-to-day operations. It's important to emphasize that information sharing to support collaboration must not be limited to historical or even accurate current sales data. Of greater importance is a willingness to share information about future strategic initiatives to facilitate joint operations. The guiding principle is that information sharing is essential among supply chain participants to collectively meet customer demand faster and more efficiently.

The **process specialization paradigm** is the commitment to focusing collaborative arrangements on planning joint operations with a goal of eliminating nonproductive or non-value-adding redundancy by firms in a supply chain. The basic idea is to design the overall supply chain processes in a manner that facilitates a specific firm's competencies along with the responsibility and accountability to perform each element of essential work in a manner that maximizes overall results.

Firms participating in a supply chain have specific roles to perform within the context of shared strategic goals. Sharing information and joint planning can reduce risk related to inventory positioning. Collaboration can eliminate duplicative or redundant work, such as repetitive quality inspection, by designating and empowering a specified member of the supply chain to be fully responsible and accountable. Such extended enterprise integration introduces new challenges regarding measurement, benefit and risk sharing, trust, leadership, and conflict resolution. It is clear that the challenges of collaboration and enterprise extension constitute new managerial horizons. A third contributing force to supply chain development is the rapidly changing managerial attitude toward integrated service providers.

Integrated Service Providers (ISPs)

As noted earlier, the origins of contemporary business were grounded in functional specialization. It is not surprising that firms developed the practice of **outsourcing** work to businesses that are specialists in the performance of specific functions. The two traditional logistics service providers are transportation and warehousing specialists.

The for-hire transportation industry consists of thousands of carriers who specialize in product movement between geographic locations. Over the years, a comprehensive carrier network has emerged, providing shippers a broad assortment of services, utilizing all available forms, called **modes,** of transportation and related technology. The value proposition of for-hire transportation is based on specialization, efficiency, and scale economies. Value is generated by a carrier's capability to provide shared transportation services for multiple shippers. The transport alternatives for shippers are either to invest capital in transportation equipment and operations or to engage the services of for-hire carriers. Naturally, a large number of firms develop transportation solutions that combine benefits of these alternatives.

In addition to transportation, a large number of service companies have traditionally provided warehouse services. Traditionally called **public warehouses,** these firms provide product storage supplemented with other specialized services. Two significant benefits are gained when shippers use public warehouses. First is elimination of capital investment in warehouse buildings. The second is the ability to consolidate small shipments for combined delivery with products of other firms that use the same public warehouse. Such multishipper consolidation achieves transportation efficiency not typically available when firms ship from their own warehouses. Many firms combine private and public warehouses into go-to-market and product supply networks.

An example of integrated service provider collaboration is the distribution service offered by Kane Is Able Inc. Kane Is Able offers its distribution center clients a shared warehouse and delivery service. Small shipments from several different food manufacturing and processing companies that are being distributed to a single customer are combined into one consolidated delivery using a shared distribution process. The results of sharing infrastructure are fewer trucks, greater utilization, fewer deliveries, and handling efficiencies.

In 1980 the landscape of for-hire services in the United States changed dramatically. Within a few short months, the economic and political regulatory infrastructure of transportation in the United States shifted from economic to social regulation as a result of the passage of the Motor Carrier Regulatory Reform and Modernization Act (MCA-80) and the Staggers Rail Act.[6] These regulatory changes, as amended, served to support an open transportation market involving less government economic regulation for all forms of transportation. Over time, this trend extended worldwide to deregulate transportation in most free-market industrialized nations.

In contrast to transportation, firms engaged in public warehousing were not operationally regulated by federal or state governments. In an effort to avoid regulation most warehouse firms did not offer transportation services. However, with the deregulation of transportation, that practice soon changed. Overnight, warehousing firms began to offer transportation services. Likewise, many transport carriers began to offer customers warehouse services.

What occurred in the logistics service industry was a radical shift from single function to multifunctional outsourcing. **Integrated service providers (ISPs)** began to market a range of logistics services that included all work necessary to accommodate customers, ranging from order entry to product delivery. In many situations the foundation of transportation and warehouse services was augmented by the performance of a wide range of special services. These customized services are typically described as **value-added services (VAS).** For example, United Parcel Service (UPS) stocks Nike shoes and warmups at its Louisville warehouse and processes orders hourly. All related communication and financial administration are handled by a UPS call center. Thus, Nike has effectively outsourced basic logistics and related value-added service to UPS.

The common name used throughout industry to describe ISPs is **third-party and fourth-party service providers.** In a general sense, ISPs are commonly classified as being either **asset- or nonasset-based,** the distinction being that asset-based (third-party) firms own and operate transportation equipment and warehousing buildings. In contrast, nonasset service (fourth-party) firms specialize in providing comprehensive information services that facilitate supply chain arrangements. Such fourth-party service providers arrange services, often integrating third-party asset operators on behalf of their customers.

The 2010 U.S. third-party contract logistics market was estimated to be $160 billion.[7] The growth of integrated service providers makes both the formation and dismantling of supply chain arrangements easier. As an organization's need for speed and operational flexibility change, ISPs can be utilized as needed. Supply chain participants have the opportunity to engage the capabilities of what amounts to a virtual logistics network. Such outsourcing helps facilitate process-focused integrative management.

---

[6] Public Laws 96-296 and 96-488, respectively. These laws, as well as others briefly noted here, are discussed in greater detail in Chapter 8.

[7] "U.S. 3PL/Contract Logistics Market," Armstrong & Associates, Inc., 2009.

As discussed, the advent of collaboration, extended enterprise visioning, and the increased availability of integrated service providers combined to drive radically new supply chain solutions. The notion of shared and synergistic benefits served to solidify the importance of relationships between firms collaborating in a supply chain. The extended enterprise logic stimulated visions of increased efficiency, effectiveness, relevancy, and sustainability as a result of sharing information, planning, and operational specialization between supply chain participants. The deregulation of transportation served as a catalyst for the rapid expansion of integrated service providers. This development served to redefine and expand the scope of specialized services available to facilitate supply chain operations. In combination, these drivers helped create integrated supply chain management. They served to identify and solidify the strategic benefits of integrated management. They combined to reinforce the value of core-competence specialization and cast the challenges and opportunity of creating virtual supply chains.

Responsiveness

One could argue that the challenges and benefits of integrative management offered sufficient reason for the supply chain revolution. However, other basic drivers continue to make supply chain arrangements even more appealing. A fundamental paradigm shift in strategic thinking occurred as a direct impact of information technology. Information connectivity created the potential for developing responsive business models. To elaborate the far-reaching implications of this major development, it is useful to contrast traditional (**push**) or **anticipatory** business practice to the emerging time-based **responsive** (or **pull**) business model. The responsive business model is also referred to as **demand driven.**

Anticipatory Business Model (Push)

Since the industrial revolution, the dominant business model has required anticipation of what customers will demand in the future. Because information concerning purchase behavior was not readily available and firms loosely linked together in a channel of distribution did not feel compelled to share their plans, business operations were driven by forecasts. The typical manufacturer produced products based on market forecast. Likewise, wholesalers, distributors, and retailers purchased inventory based on their unique forecasts and promotional plans. Since the forecast results were typically wrong, considerable differences existed between what firms planned to do and what they in fact ended up doing. Such variation typically resulted in unplanned inventory. Because of high cost and risk associated with conducting business on an anticipatory basis, the prevailing relationship between trading partners was often adversarial; each firm needed to protect its own interest.

Figure 1.8 illustrates the typical stages in a single firm's implementation of the anticipatory business model: forecast, purchase materials, manufacture, warehouse, sell, and then deliver. In retail and wholesale enterprises, operations involved anticipatory purchase of inventory assortments to accommodate expected sales. The key point is that almost all

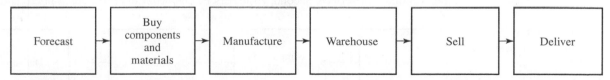

FIGURE 1.8   Anticipatory Business Model

essential work has been traditionally performed in *anticipation* of future requirements. The likelihood of misgauging customer requirements rendered the anticipatory business model highly risky. In addition, each firm in the distribution channel duplicated a similiar anticipatory process.

Responsive Business Model (Pull)

The fundamental difference between anticipatory and responsive supply chain arrangements is timing. The responsive business model seeks to reduce or eliminate forecast reliance by joint planning and rapid exchange of information between supply chain participants.

The availability of low-cost information has created **time-based competition.** Managers are increasingly sharing information to improve both the speed and accuracy of supply chain logistics. To illustrate, managers may share information to improve forecasting accuracy or even eliminate forecasts in an effort to reduce anticipatory inventory deployment. This transformation from anticipatory toward responsive business is possible because today's managers have sense and response information technology to rapidly obtain and share accurate sales data and exercise improved operational control. When all members of the supply chain synchronize their operations, opportunities exist to reduce overall inventory and eliminate costly duplicate practices. More important, customers can be provided with products they want, fast.

Figure 1.9 illustrates a responsive business model that manufactures or assembles products to customer order. The fundamental difference in responsive models is the sequence of events that drive business practice. Also notable, in comparison to Figure 1.8, are the fewer steps required to complete the responsive process. Fewer steps typically equate to less cost and less elapsed time from order commitment to delivery. The responsive sequence is initiated by a sale followed by a sequence of material purchase, custom manufacturing, and direct customer delivery.

In many ways, the responsive business model is similar to the traditional build-to-order manufacturing. The primary difference between modern responsive operations and traditional build-to-order are the time to execute and the degree of potential customization. In terms of time to execute the order to delivery, the contemporary responsive system is substantially faster than the traditional build-to-order manufacturing. It is becoming common practice to replenish retail store inventories of consumer products on a daily basis. Custom-built automobiles are being promised for delivery within ten working days, with the goal to even further reduce the order-to-delivery cycle. Such compressed order-to-delivery cycles were not even imaginable a few years ago.

Perhaps an even more appealing attribute of responsive supply chains is their potential to uniquely customize products on smaller orders than was typical of traditional build-to-order lot size manufacturing. Direct connectivity with customers via the Internet is accelerating customization. In most traditional anticipatory distribution systems, the customer is a passive participant. About the only power the customer has in the traditional process is the decision to buy or not buy. Direct connectivity of customers in a responsive process has at least three benefits. First, involvement provides comprehensive search capabilities that serve to expand the range of sources and choices a customer can consider when selecting a product or service. Second, customers can be better informed about prices and, in

FIGURE 1.9
Responsive Business
Model

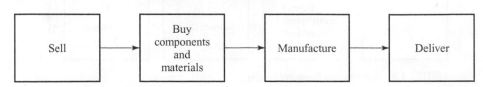

some situations, are able to drive price advantage by virtue of bids and/or auctions. Finally, information-intense responsive systems provide innovation such as a **customer choice-board** wherein customers design or customize their own product configuration.

Postponement

At the heart of time-based competition is the capability to postpone customization and the timing of logistical fulfillment. The concept of **postponement** has long been discussed in business literature.[8] However, practical examples involving postponement are directly related to advancements in information technology. Postponement strategies and practices serve to reduce the anticipatory risk of supply chain performance. As noted earlier, anticipatory arrangements require most inventory to be produced to final product state and deployed on the basis of forecasts or planned requirements. Working arrangements, which allow postponement of final manufacturing, customization, or distribution of a product until receipt of a customer order, reduce the incidence of wrong manufacturing or incorrect inventory deployment. Two types of postponement are common in highly responsive supply chain operations: (1) manufacturing, or form postponement; and (2) geographic, or logistics postponement.

Manufacturing Postponement

The global competitive climate of the 21st century is facilitating the development of new manufacturing techniques designed to increase flexibility and responsiveness while maintaining unit cost and quality. Traditional practice has focused on achieving economy of scale by planning extensive manufacturing runs. In contrast, flexible manufacturing logic is typically driven by a desire to increase responsiveness to customer requirements.

The vision of **manufacturing,** or **form, postponement** is one of products being manufactured one order at a time with no preparatory work or component procurement until exact customer specifications are fully known and purchase confirmation is received. This dream of building to customer order is not new. What is new is the expectation that flexible manufacturing can achieve such responsiveness without sacrificing efficiency. To the degree technology can support market-paced flexible manufacturing strategies, firms are to a degree freed from the risk associated with forecast-driven anticipatory operations.

In practice, manufacturing lot size economics cannot be ignored. The challenge is to quantify cost trade-offs between procurement, manufacturing, and logistics. At this point, it is sufficient to understand that the trade-off is between the cost and risk associated with anticipatory manufacturing and the loss of economy of scale resulting from introducing flexible procedures. Manufacturing lot size reduction requires a trade-off between line setup, switchover, and associated procurement expense balanced against cost and risk associated with stockpiling finished inventory. In the traditional functional style of management, manufacturing schedules were established to realize the lowest unit cost of production. From an integrative management perspective, the goal is to achieve desired customer satisfaction at the lowest total cost. This may require manufacturing postponement at some per-unit-cost sacrifice to achieve overall supply chain efficiency.

The operative goal of manufacturing postponement is to maintain products in a neutral or noncommitted status as long as possible. The ideal application of form postponement is to manufacture a standard or base product in sufficient quantities to realize economy of scale while deferring finalization of features, such as color or accessories, until customer commitment is received. Given a postponement-driven manufacturing scenario, economy

---

[8] Wroe Alderson, *Marketing Behavior and Executive Action* (Homewood, IL: Richard D. Irwin, Inc., 1957), p. 426.

of scope is introduced into the logistics equation by producing a standard or base product to accommodate a wide range of different customers. One of the first commercially viable examples of manufacturing postponement was mixing paint color at retail stores to accommodate individual customer request. Perfecting the in-store mixing process dramatically reduced the number of stockkeeping units required at retail paint stores. Instead of trying to maintain inventories of premixed color paint, retail stores stock a base paint and customize the color to accommodate specific orders. Some believe this relatively simple application of form postponement in the paint industry was a major factor facilitating the birth of the consumer-driven home improvement industry. Overnight, retail paint stores went from excessive stock-outs to being fully in stock. Plus, while consumers waited for paint to be custom color-mixed, they were exposed to a wide variety of do-it-yourself painting accessories available for purchase.

In other industries, manufacturing practice is to process and store product in bulk, postponing final packaging configuration until customer orders are received. In some situations products are processed and packed in cans with brand identification labeling being postponed until specific customer orders are received. Other examples of manufacturing postponement include the increased practice of installing accessories at automobile, appliance, and motorcycle dealerships, thereby customizing products to customer request at the time of purchase.

These manufacturing postponement examples have one thing in common: They reduce the number of stockkeeping units in logistical inventory while supporting a broad-line marketing effort and retaining mass manufacturing economies of scale. Until the product is customized, it has the potential to serve many different customers.

The impact of manufacturing postponement is twofold. First, the variety of differentiated products, moved in anticipation of sale, can be reduced, and therefore the risk of logistical operational malfunction is lower. The second, and perhaps the more important, impact is the increased use of logistical facilities to perform light manufacturing and final assembly. To the extent that a degree of specialized talent or highly restrictive economy of scale does not exist in manufacturing, product customization may be best delegated and performed near the customer destination market. This form of manufacturing postponement is often called **late customization.** The traditional mission of logistical warehouses in some industries has changed significantly to accommodate manufacturing postponement. For example, Kohler Co. does a significant amount of product customization in integrated service provider-run distribution centers.

Geographic Postponement

In many ways **geographic,** or **logistics, postponement** is the exact opposite of manufacturing postponement. The basic notion of geographic postponement is to build and stock a full-line inventory at one or a limited number of strategic locations. Forward deployment of inventory is postponed until customer orders are received. Once the logistical process is initiated, every effort is made to accelerate the economic movement of products directly to customers. Under the concept of geographic postponement, the anticipatory risk of inventory deployment is partially eliminated while manufacturing economy of scale is retained.

Many applications of geographic postponement involve service supply parts. Critical and high-cost parts are maintained in a central inventory to assure availability for all potential users. When demand occurs, orders are electronically transmitted to the central service center and expedited shipments are made directly to the forward service center, using fast, reliable transportation. The end result is highly reliable customer service with reduced overall inventory investment.

The potential for geographic postponement has been facilitated by increased logistical system capability to process, transmit, and deliver precise order requirements with a high degree of accuracy and speed. Geographic postponement substitutes accelerated delivery of precise order requirements for the anticipatory deployment of inventory to local market warehouses. Unlike manufacturing postponement, systems utilizing geographic postponement retain manufacturing economies of scale while meeting customer service requirements by accelerating direct shipments.

In combination, manufacturing and geographic postponement offer alternative ways to reduce risk associated with anticipatory distribution. Both postpone risk until customer commitments are received. The factors favoring one or the other form of postponement hinge on volume, value, competitive initiatives, economies of scale, and desired customer delivery speed and consistency. In a growing number of supply chains, both types of postponement are combined to create a highly flexible strategy.

Barriers to Implementing Responsive Systems

In reality, today's best supply chain practices do not reflect either extreme anticipatory or responsive design. Most established firms remain, to a significant degree, committed to anticipatory practices. However, responsive strategies are rapidly emerging. Perhaps the greatest barrier to adopting responsive arrangements is the need for publicly held corporations to maintain planned quarterly profits. This accountability creates expectations concerning continued sales and financial results. Such expectations often drive promotional and pricing strategies to "load the channel" with inventory to create timely sales. Conversely, it is never timely to make a major reduction in channel inventory. Efforts to lean or deload inventory to implement a more responsive operating posture require the ability to absorb a one-time sale reduction among supply chain partners. Start-up ventures are ideally positioned to implement responsive fulfillment systems because they do not face the challenge of taking inventory out of an existing channel.

A second barrier to implementing responsive operations is the need to establish and sustain collaborative relationships. Most business managers simply do not have training or experience in how to develop and implement collaborative arrangements designed to share benefits and risks. While managers generally express a high degree of belief in the long-term potential for responsive alliances, they typically confront considerable frustration concerning how to implement such supply chain arrangements.

For the foreseeable future, most firms will continue to implement strategies that combine anticipatory and responsive supply chain arrangements. The trend toward increased involvement in responsive arrangements with specific customers and suppliers will continue to expand as the full advantage of Web-based operations materializes.

Financial Sophistication

Few managers question the benefits of applying the time-based strategies discussed above to supply chain operations. However, a valid question is, How fast is fast enough? Speed simply for the sake of being fast has little, if any, enduring value.[9] The answer concerning how much speed is desirable is found in understanding the financial impact. The process of creating value dictates that faster, more flexible, and more precise ways of servicing customers are justified as long as they can be provided at competitive prices. A third force driving competitive supply chain strategy is the ability to manage in a more timely manner to achieve financially attractive working arrangements.

---

[9] George Stalk Jr. and Alan M. Webber, "Japan's Dark Side of Time," *Harvard Business Review* (July/August 1993), pp. 93–102.

The financial benefits of timely response are straightforward. Fast delivery within the supply chain translates to less inventory and reduced need for distribution facilities. Faster delivery to customers means less working capital is required to support supply chain operations. Three aspects of financial sophistication are cash-to-cash conversion, dwell time minimization, and cash spin.

Cash-to-Cash Conversion

The time required to convert raw material or inventory purchases into sales revenue is referred to as **cash-to-cash conversion.** Cash conversion is generally related to inventory turn: The higher the inventory turn, the quicker the cash conversion. A goal of supply chain design is to control and reduce order receipt-to-delivery time in an effort to accelerate inventory turns.

In traditional business arrangements, benefits related to cash-to-cash conversion have typically been enjoyed at the expense of business partners. Given typical purchase discounts and invoicing practices, it is operationally possible for firms to rapidly sell merchandise and still qualify for prompt payment discounts. To illustrate, terms of sale offering a 2 percent discount net 10-day payment (2% net 10) means that a prompt payment discount is earned if the invoice is paid within 10 days from confirmed time of delivery. Thus, if the invoice is $1000, a payment made within 10 days will earn a $20 discount. If the firm sells the product for cash before the invoice payment date, it in effect enjoys free inventory and may even earn interest by investing cash while awaiting the payment date.

In responsive systems, cash-to-cash conversion benefits can be shared by managing inventory velocity across the supply chain. This ability to manage inventory velocity from origin to final destination has the potential to achieve greater overall efficiencies than are attainable by a single firm. Coordinated operations may require that a designated firm in the supply chain serve as the principal inventory stocking location. Such practice means that risks and benefits related to inventory need to be shared by participating firms. To facilitate such arrangements, supply chain members often replace traditional discounts with **dead net pricing.**

Dead net pricing means that all discounts and allowances are factored in the selling price. Thus, incentives for timely payment are replaced by detailed performance commitments at a specified net price. Invoice payment, based on negotiated net price, is completed upon verification of physical receipt. Such payment is typically in the form of Electronic Funds Transfer (EFT), thereby streamlining both the flow of physical goods and cash among supply chain partners. Managing supply chain logistics as a continuous synchronized process also serves to reduce dwell time.

Dwell Time Minimization

Traditional distribution arrangements typically involve independent business units loosely linked together on a transaction-to-transaction basis. Such traditional business operations are driven by a series of **independent** transactions buffered by inventory. In contrast, a supply chain has the potential to function as a synchronized series of **interdependent** business units.

At the heart of supply chain operating leverage is the willingness to transfer inventory on an as-needed basis, taking advantage of as much collaboration and information as possible. Such collaboration and information can be focused on maintaining the continued flow and velocity of inventory moving throughout the supply chain. The potential of such synchronization is one key benefit of supply chain connectivity.

A significant measure of supply chain productivity is **dwell time.** Dwell time is the ratio of time that an asset sits idle to the time required to satisfy its designated supply chain

privately owned and operated, and many gas companies act as both gas distribution and contract transportation providers.

The basic nature of a pipeline is unique in comparison to other modes of transport. Pipelines operate on a 24-hour basis, 7 days per week, and are limited only by commodity changeover and maintenance. Unlike other modes, there is no empty container or vehicle to return. Pipelines have the highest fixed cost and lowest variable cost among transport modes. High fixed costs result from the right-of-way for pipeline, construction and requirements for control stations, and pumping capacity. Since pipelines are not labor-intensive, the variable operating cost is extremely low once the pipeline has been constructed. An obvious disadvantage is that pipelines are not flexible and are limited with respect to commodities that can be transported, as only products in the forms of gas, liquid, or slurry can be handled.

Experiments regarding potential movement of solid products in the form of slurry or hydraulic suspension continue. Coal slurry pipelines have proved to be an efficient and economical mode of transporting coal over long distances. Coal slurry lines require massive quantities of water, which has an environmental impact warranting further discussion and consideration.

Air

The newest but least utilized mode of transportation is airfreight. The significant advantage of airfreight lies in speed. A coast-to-coast shipment via air requires only hours contrasted to days with other modes of transport. While costly, the speed of air transport potential allows other aspects of logistics such as warehousing and inventory to be reduced or eliminated.

Air transport, despite its high profile, still remains more of a potential than a reality. Airfreight accounts for 1 percent of intercity ton-miles. Air transport capability is limited by load size, weight lift capacity, and aircraft availability. Traditionally, intercity airfreight was transported on scheduled passenger flights. While the practice was economical, it resulted in a limited capacity and flexibility of freight operations. The high cost of jet aircraft, coupled with the erratic nature of freight demand, served to limit the economic commitment of dedicated aircraft to all-freight operations.

However, the advent of premium air carriers such as Federal Express and United Parcel Air introduced scheduled global airfreight service. While such premium service was originally targeted at high-priority documents, it has expanded to include package freight. For example, premium carriers have integrated their service to include overnight parts delivery from centralized distribution centers located near their air hubs. Overnight air delivery from a centralized warehouse is attractive to firms with a large number of high-value products and time-sensitive service requirements.

The fixed cost of air transport is low compared to rail, water, and pipeline. In fact, air ranks second only to truck with respect to low fixed cost. Airways and airports are generally developed and maintained by government. The fixed costs of airfreight are associated with aircraft purchase and the requirement for specialized handling systems and cargo containers. On the other hand, airfreight variable cost is extremely high as a result of fuel, user fees, maintenance, and the labor intensity of both in-flight and ground crews.

Since airports require significant real estate, they are generally limited with respect to integration with other transport modes. However, there is substantial interest in integrating air transport with other modes and developing all-freight airports to eliminate conflict with passenger service. For example, Alliance Airport, located near Fort Worth, Texas, was designed to integrate air, rail, and truck distribution from a single location.

No particular commodity dominates the traffic carried by airfreight operations. Perhaps the best distinction is that most freight has high value and priority. When the marketing period for a product is extremely limited, such as Christmas gifts, high-fashion clothing, fresh fish, or cut flowers, air may be the only practical transportation method to support global operations. Routine logistics of products such as computers, repair parts, and medical supplies also utilize airfreight.

Modal Comparative Characteristics and Capabilities

Table 8.4 compares the fixed-variable cost structure of each mode. Table 8.5 ranks modal operating characteristics with respect to speed, availability, dependability, capability, and frequency.

Speed refers to elapsed movement time. Airfreight is the fastest of all modes. **Availability** refers to the ability of a mode to service any given pair of locations. Highway carriers have the greatest availability since they can drive directly to origin and destination points. **Dependability** refers to potential variance from expected or published delivery schedules. Pipelines, because of their continuous service and limited interference due to weather and congestion, rank highest in dependability. **Capability** is the ability of a mode to handle any transport requirement, such as load size. Water transport is the most capable. The final classification is **frequency,** which relates to the quantity of scheduled movements. Pipelines, again because of their continuous service between two points, lead all modes in frequency.

As Table 8.5 illustrates, the appeal of highway transport is in part explained by its high relative ranking across the five operating characteristics. Truck rank first or second in all categories except capability. Although substantial improvements in motor capability resulted from relaxed size and weight limitations on interstate highways and approval to use tandem trailers, it is not realistic to assume motor transport will surpass rail or water capability.

Infrastructure in Crisis

Following World War II the United States embarked on an aggressive development program that resulted in construction of 46,837 miles of interstate highways. However, by 2010 this highway system was in need of expansion and widespread repair to sustain the safe movement of commercial and private transportation.

TABLE 8.4
Cost Structure for Each Mode

- *Rail.* High fixed cost in equipment, terminals, tracks, etc. Low variable cost.
- *Truck.* Low fixed cost (highways in place and provided by public support). Medium variable cost (fuel, maintenance, etc.).
- *Water.* Medium fixed cost (ships and equipment). Low variable cost (capability to transport large amount of tonnage).
- *Pipeline.* Highest fixed cost (rights-of-way, construction, requirements for control stations, and pumping capacity). Lowest variable cost (no labor cost of any significance).
- *Air.* Low fixed cost (aircraft and handling and cargo systems). High variable cost (fuel, labor, maintenance, etc.).

TABLE 8.5
Modal Operating Characteristics*
*Lowest rank is best.

Operating Characteristics	Rail	Truck	Water	Pipeline	Air
Speed	3	2	4	5	1
Availability	2	1	4	5	3
Dependability	3	2	4	1	5
Capability	2	3	1	5	4
Frequency	4	2	5	1	3
Composite Score	14	10	18	17	16

On August 1, 2007, the collapse of a major span of interstate highway I-35W bridging the Mississippi River in downtown Minneapolis vividly called to public attention the nation's crumbling network of bridges, tunnels, and roads. The American Society of Civil Engineers estimated in 2010 that 26 percent of U.S. bridges are either structurally deficient or obsolete. The engineers estimated a need for $2.2 trillion in expenditures through 2014 to bring the infrastructure to acceptable standards.[18]

Participants in the transportation system are deeply concerned about these and other growing issues related to safety, congestion, and inadequate system capacity across all five transportation modes. Most transportation professionals agree the United States is in need of a far-reaching National Transportation Plan to facilitate both the repair and reinvention of transportation infrastructure. The 2009 American Recovery and Reinvestment Act set aside $12 billion for repairs and new infrastructure projects. However, depressed economic conditions have limited the actual expenditures. On April 15, 2010, the federal Department of Transportation (DOT) released a draft of a five-year strategic transportation plan entitled "Transportation for a New Generation."[19] This document attempts to articulate a revised national transportation policy.

Specialized Transportation Services

Transportation service can be improved by combining modes. Prior to deregulation, government policy limited carriers to operating in a single mode. Such restrictive ownership sought to promote competition between modes and limit the potential for monopoly practices. Following deregulation carriers were free to develop integrated modal services in efforts to more efficiently and effectively meet the needs of customers. The following section reviews the current range of specialized services offered by different carriers.

Package Service

Over the past several decades a serious problem existed in the availability of small-shipment transportation. It was difficult for common carriers to provide reasonably priced small-shipment service because of overhead cost associated with terminal and line-haul operations. This overhead forced motor carriers to implement a **minimum charge.** The minimum applies to all shipments regardless of shipment size or distance. As a result of the minimum charge and lack of alternatives, an opportunity existed for companies offering specialized service to enter the small-shipment or package-service market.

Package services represent an important part of logistics, and the influence of carriers in this segment is increasing because of their size and intermodal capabilities. The advent of e-commerce and the need for consumer-direct last-mile delivery have significantly increased demand for package delivery services. While package services are expanding, the services required do not fall neatly into the traditional modal classification scheme. Packages are regularly transported by using the line-haul services of rail, motor, and air. Package service provides both regular and premium services.

Numerous carriers offer delivery services within metropolitan areas. Other carriers offer package delivery service on a national and global basis. The most recognizable carriers are Federal Express (FedEx), United Parcel Service **(UPS),** and the United States Postal Service **(USPS).**

---

[18]*Bloomberg Businessweek*, November 1 and 7, 2010, p. 14.
[19]"Transportation for a New Generation," U.S. DOT Strategic Plan FY 2010–2015, USDOT, April 15, 2010.

The first widely recognized premium air package service was initiated by Federal Express in 1973. FedEx provided nationwide overnight service utilizing a fleet of dedicated cargo aircraft. Since inception, FedEx original service has expanded internationally. FedEx also currently offers LTL and TL service.

The original service offered by UPS was contract delivery of local shipments for department stores. Today, UPS offers a diverse range of package services. In fact, UPS has expanded its scope of overall operating authority by shipping packages that conform to specialized size and weight restrictions nationwide and globally for consumers and business enterprises. While UPS provides logistical services related to all types of products, specialization in small packages enables a cost-effective overnight service between most cities within 300 miles.

UPS has various capabilities and offers a range of services, including ground and premium air. Table 8.6, based on UPS promotional materials, summarizes the integrated services offered by package carriers. It is interesting to note that ground service frequently involves intermodal movement by a combination of truck and train capacity.

The United States Postal Service **(USPS)** operates ground and air parcel service. Charges for parcel have traditionally been based on weight and distance. Generally, parcels must be delivered to a post office for shipment origination. However, in the case of large

TABLE 8.6
Examples of Expanded Parcel Carrier Services

Source: Modified and condensed from United Parcel Service Web site, www.ups.com.

Freight Services	
Same Day Air	Guaranteed same day delivery for letters and packages.
Next Day Delivery	Guaranteed weekday (Saturday available), next day delivery. Ranges from early morning (8:00 A.M.) delivery to air saver (3:00–4:30 P.M.) delivery.
Second Day Delivery	Guaranteed delivery on the second business day. Services offered range from noon delivery to end of business day delivery.
3 Day Select	Guaranteed 3 day delivery to and from every U.S. address.
Ground	Low-cost ground delivery with guaranteed delivery date.
Worldwide Express	Guaranteed delivery to and from the U.S., Canada, and Europe with next day, 2 day, and time-definite deliveries.
Standard to/from Canada	Guaranteed, fully tracked, door-to-door ground delivery from the 48 contiguous states to/from all addresses in the 10 Canadian provinces. Many time-definite delivery options available.
World Ease	A worldwide consolidated clearance service that groups several shipments destined for one country into a single shipment.
Optional, Value-Added Services	
Collect on Delivery (COD)	Payment collected immediately upon delivery and delivered promptly to customer. Will exchange international monies.
Delivery Confirmation	Confirms delivery with the recipient's signature. Additional service shows digital signature of person receiving package, proof of delivery, and telephone confirmation of delivery.
Hazardous Materials	Transport hazardous materials and international dangerous goods within the continental U.S.
Hold for Pickup	Packages are delivered to the facility of choice and carrier calls the consignee by telephone for pickup.
Saturday Pickup/Delivery	Packages shipped and picked up on Saturdays.
10KG and 23KG Boxes	A fixed-rate shipping solution for express shipments up to 10 kg (22 lb) and 25 kg (55 lb).
Hundredweight Service	Contract service for multipackage shipments less than 1000 lb that are less than a pallet load sent to a single address.
Returns	Includes labels (preprinted, on demand, and mailed), and authorized return services.
Excess Value Insurance	Third-party insurance provides protection for shipments valued between $100 and $50,000.

users and when it is convenient for the Postal Service, pickup is provided at the shipper's location. Intercity transport is accomplished by purchasing air, highway, rail, and even water service from for-hire carriers. Delivery is provided to the destination by the Postal Service.

In 2006 the range of services provided by the USPS were significantly expanded as a result of the passage of the Postal Accountability and Enhancement Act **(PAEA).** The USPS has a last-mile advantage over all other package carriers in that it is structured to facilitate delivery to every household in the United States every day. Under provision of the PAEA the USPS was given flexibility in pricing. The traditional practice of charging the same price per unit of freight was modified to include commercial volume pricing, minimum value rebates, and online price breaks. In 2010 the USPS introduced a new service called "If it fits it ships." This service offers one flat rate for any shipment between two U.S. domestic locations if it fits into any of the five different box sizes. These rates are guaranteed regardless of package weight.

The importance of parcel service to the logistical system cannot be overemphasized. One of the expanding forms of marketing in the United States is direct to consumer, in which orders are placed via the Internet, telephone, or mail for subsequent home delivery. Firms that specialize in consumer fulfillment are one of the fastest growing forms of logistics service providers.

Intermodal

Intermodal transportation combines two or more modes to take advantage of the inherent economies of each and thus provide an integrated service at lower total cost. Many efforts have been made over the years to integrate different transportation modes. Initial attempts at modal coordination trace back to the early 1920s, but during the regulatory period cooperation was restrained by restrictions designed to limit monopoly practices. Intermodal offerings began to develop more successfully during the 1950s with the advent of integrated rail and motor service commonly termed **piggyback service.** This common intermodal arrangement combines the flexibility of truck for short distances with the low line-haul cost associated with rail for longer distances. The popularity of such offerings has increased significantly as a means to achieve more efficient and effective transportation.

Technically, coordinated or intermodal transportation could be arranged among all basic modes. Descriptive jargon such as piggyback fishyback, trainship, and airtruck have become standard transportation terms.

TOFC/COFC

The best known and most widely used intermodal systems are the trailer on a flatcar **(TOFC)** and container on a flatcar **(COFC).** Containers are the boxes utilized for intermodal product storage and movement between motor freight, railroads, and water transportation. Containers are typically 8 feet wide, 8 feet high, and 20 or 40 feet long, and do not have highway wheels. Trailers, on the other hand, are of similar width and height but can be as long as 53 feet and have highway wheels. As the name implies, a trailer or container is placed on a railroad flatcar for some portion of the intercity line-haul and pulled by a truck at origin and to the final destination. Line-haul cost is the expense to move railcars or trucks between cities. Since the original development of TOFC, various combinations of trailer or container on flatcar—double-stack, for instance—have increased significantly.

While the TOFC concept facilitates direct transfer between rail and motor carriage, it also has several technical limitations. The placement of a trailer with highway wheels attached, transferred to a railcar, can lead to wind resistance, damage, and weight problems.

The use of containers reduces these potential problems, as they can be double stacked and are easily transferred to water carriers. They require special equipment for over-the-road delivery or pickup.

Containership

Fishyback, trainship, and containership are examples of the oldest form of intermodal transport. They utilize waterways, which are one of the least expensive modes for line-haul movement. A comparison completed by the Maritime Administration **(MARAD)** showed that one 15-barge tow has the equivalent capacity of 225 railcars or 900 trucks.[20]

The fishyback, trainship, and containership concept loads a truck trailer, railcar, or container onto a barge or ship for the line-haul movement on inland navigable waterways. Such services are provided in coastal waters between Atlantic and Gulf ports, and between the Great Lakes and coastal points.

A variant of this intermodal option is the **land bridge** concept that moves containers in a combination of sea and rail transport. The land bridge is commonly used for containers moving between Europe and the Pacific Rim to reduce the time and expense of all-water transport. For example, containers are shipped to the West Coast of North America from the Pacific Rim, loaded onto railcars for movement to the East Coast, and then reloaded onto ships for movement to Europe. The land bridge concept is based on the benefit of ocean and rail combinations that utilize a single tariff, which is lower than the combined total cost of two separate rates.

An over $5 billion expansion of the Panama Canal is underway with completion scheduled for 2014. While not directly part of the U.S. Transport infrastructure, the new canal will have a major impact on freight movements to and from the North American continent. Once expanded, the canal will be able to handle the largest tanker and container ships in current and projected global service. The expansion will greatly increase Southwestern United States Gulf Coast ports access to Far East traffic. The expanded canal will also have transshipment capability. This new capability is expected to increase the canal's role in North/South multimodal transportation.[21]

Nonoperating Intermediaries

The overall transportation industry also includes several businesses that do not own or operate equipment. These nonoperating intermediaries broker services of other firms. A transportation broker is somewhat similar to a wholesaler in a marketing channel.

Nonoperating intermediaries find economic justification by offering shippers lower rates for movement between two locations than would be possible by direct shipment via common carrier. Because of peculiarities in the common-carrier rate structure, such as minimum freight charges, surcharges, and less-than-volume rates, conditions exist whereby nonoperating intermediaries can facilitate savings for shippers. Interestingly, there are cases where nonoperating intermediaries charge higher rates than those offered by carriers. The justification for the higher charges is based on ability to arrange faster delivery and/or more value-added services. The primary intermediaries are freight forwarders, shipper associations, and brokers.

Freight forwarders are for-profit businesses that consolidate small shipments from various customers into a bulk shipment and then utilize a common surface or air carrier

[20]U.S. Waterborne Foreign Trade Containerized Cargo, "Top 25 U.S. Ports," January–June 2004, Port Import Export Reporting Services. MARAD waterborne traffic statistics, http://www.marad.dot.gov/MARAD.

[21]Toby Gooley, "Panama Aims to Become a Crossroads of Global Trade," *DC Velocity,* October 4, 2010, and Joseph O'Reilly, "U.S. Ports Dig Panama Gold," *Inbound Logistics,* September 2010, pp. 18–22.

for transport. At destination, the freight forwarder splits the consolidated shipment into the original smaller shipments. Local delivery may or may not be arranged by the forwarder. The main advantage of the forwarder is a lower freight rate obtained from consolidation to large shipments.

Shipper associations are operationally similar to freight forwarders in that they consolidate small shipments into large movements to gain cost economies. Shipper associations are voluntary nonprofit entities where members, operating in a specific industry, collaborate to gain economies related to small-shipment purchases. Typically, members purchase product from common vendors or from sources of supply located in one area. A common practice is to order small quantities at frequent intervals to minimize retail inventory. Participation in a shipper association typically means improved speed of delivery, since a large number of different products may be purchased at one location, such as the garment district in New York City.

Brokers are intermediaries that coordinate transportation arrangements for shippers, consignees, and carriers. They also arrange shipments for exempt carriers and owner operators. Brokers typically operate on a commission basis. Brokers provide extensive services such as shipment matching, rate negotiation, billing, and tracing. The entire area of brokerage operations is highly adaptable to Internet-based transactions and is increasing in importance as a result of increased globalization.

Transportation Economics and Pricing

Transportation economics and pricing are driven by multiple factors that influence rates. The primary factors are distance, weight, and density. These important factors are discussed from a shipper's perspective.

Economy of Distance

Distance is a major influence on transportation cost since it directly contributes to variable expense, such as labor, fuel, and maintenance. Figure 8.2 illustrates the general relationship between distance and transportation cost. Two important points are illustrated. First, the cost curve does not begin at zero because there are fixed costs associated with shipment pickup and delivery regardless of distance. Second, the cost curve increases at a decreasing rate as a function of distance. This characteristic is known as the **tapering principle.**

Economy of Weight

A second factor is shipment weight. Similar to other logistics activities, scale economies exist for most transportation movements. This relationship, illustrated in Figure 8.3, indicates that transport cost per unit of weight decreases as load size increases. This occurs

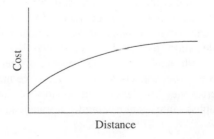

FIGURE 8.2
Generalized
Relationship between
Distance and
Transportation Cost

FIGURE 8.3
Impact of Weight on
Transportation Cost

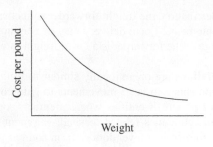

FIGURE 8.4
Impact of Density on
Transportation Cost

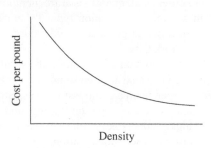

because the fixed costs of pickup, delivery, and administration are spread over incremental weight. This relationship is limited by the size of the transportation vehicle. The managerial implication is that small loads should be consolidated into larger loads to maximize scale economies.

Economy of Density

A third factor is product density. Density is the combination of weight and volume. Weight and volume are important since transportation cost for any movement is usually quoted in dollars per unit of weight. Transport charges are commonly quoted per hundredweight (CWT). In terms of weight and volume, vehicles are typically more constrained by cubic capacity than by weight. Higher-density products allow fixed transport cost to be spread across more weight. As a result, higher density products are typically assessed lower transport cost per unit of weight. Figure 8.4 illustrates the relationship of declining transportation cost per unit of weight as product density increases. In general, traffic managers seek to improve product density so that trailer cubic capacity can be fully utilized.

Other Pricing Factors

Several other factors have importance to transportation economics. Four of the more important factors are discussed. Stowability refers to how product dimensions fit into transportation equipment. Odd package sizes and shapes, as well as excessive size or length, may not fit well in transportation equipment, resulting in wasted cubic capacity. Although density and stowability are similar, it is possible to have items with similar densities that stow very differently. Items having rectangular shapes are much easier to stow than odd-shaped items. For example, while steel blocks and rods may have the same physical density, rods are far more difficult to stow than blocks because of their length and shape. Stowability is also influenced by other aspects of size, since large numbers of items may be **nested** in shipments whereas they may be difficult to stow in small quantities. For example, it is possible to accomplish significant nesting for a truckload of trash cans while a single can is difficult to stow.

Handling

Special handling equipment may be required to load and unload trucks, railcars, or ships. In addition to special handling equipment, the manner in which products are physically grouped together in boxes or on pallets for transport and storage impacts handling cost.

Liability

Liability includes product characteristics that can result in damage. Carriers must either have insurance to protect against potential damage or accept financial responsibility. Shippers can reduce their risk, and ultimately transportation cost, by improved packaging or reducing susceptibility to loss or damage.

Market

Finally, market factors such as lane volume and balance influence transportation cost. A **transport lane** refers to movements between origin and destination points. Since transportation vehicles and drivers typically return to their origin, either they must find a **back-haul** load or the vehicle is returned or **deadheaded** empty. When empty return movements occur, labor, fuel, and maintenance costs must be charged against the original front-haul movement. Thus, the ideal situation is to achieve two-way or balanced movement of loads. However, this is rarely the case because of demand imbalances in manufacturing and consumption locations. Demand location and seasonality result in transport rates that change with direction and season. Logistics system design must take such factors into account to achieve back-haul economies whenever possible.

Costing Freight

The second dimension of transport economics and pricing concerns the criteria used to allocate cost. Cost allocation is primarily a carrier concern, but since cost structure influences negotiating ability, the shipper's perspective is important as well. Transportation costs are classified into a number of categories.

Variable

Costs that change in a predictable, direct manner in relation to some level of activity are labeled **variable costs.** Variable costs include direct carrier costs associated with movement of each load. These expenses are generally measured as a cost per mile or per unit of weight. Typical variable cost components include labor, fuel, and maintenance.

Fixed

Expenses that do not change in the short run and must be paid even when a company is not operating, such as during a holiday or a strike, are **fixed costs.** The fixed category includes costs not directly influenced by shipment volume. For transportation firms, fixed components include vehicles, terminals, rights-of-way, information systems, and support equipment. In the short term, expenses associated with fixed assets must be covered by contribution above variable costs on a per shipment basis.

Joint

Expenses created by the decision to provide a particular service are called **joint costs.** For example, when a carrier elects to haul a truckload from point A to point B, there is an implicit decision to incur a **joint** cost for the back-haul from point B to point A. Either the joint cost must be covered by the original shipper from A to B or a back-haul shipper must be found. Joint costs have significant impact on transportation charges because carrier quotations must include implied joint costs based on assessment of back-haul recovery.

Common

This category includes carrier costs that are incurred on behalf of all or selected shippers. **Common costs,** such as terminal or management expenses, are characterized as overhead. These are often allocated to a shipper according to a level of activity like the number of shipments or delivery appointments handled.

Pricing Freight

This section presents the traditional pricing mechanics used by carriers. This discussion applies specifically to common carriers, although contract carriers follow a similar approach.

Class Rates

In transportation terminology, the price in dollars and cents per hundredweight to move a specific product between two locations is referred to as the **rate.** The rate is listed on pricing sheets or on computer files known as **tariffs.** The term **class rate** evolved from the fact that all products transported by common carriers are classified for pricing purposes. Any product legally transported in interstate commerce can be shipped via class rates.

Determination of common carrier class rates is a two-step process. The first step is to determine the **classification** or grouping for the product being transported. The second step is determining the rate or price based on the freight classification of the product, weight, and shipment origin/destination points.

Freight Classification

All products transported are grouped together into uniform classifications. The classification takes into consideration the characteristics of a product or commodity that influence the cost of handling or transport. Products with similar density, stowability, handling, liability, and value characteristics are grouped together into a class, thereby reducing the need to deal with each product on an individual basis. The particular class that a given product or commodity is assigned is referred to as its **rating.** A products rating is used to determine the freight rate. It is important to understand that the classification is not the price or rate charged for movement of a product. Rating refers to a product's transportation characteristics in comparison to other commodities.

Truck and rail carriers each have independent classification systems. The trucking system uses the *National Motor Freight Classification,* while rail classifications are published in the *Uniform Freight Classification.* The truck classification system has 18 classes of freight, and the rail system has 31. In local or regional areas, individual groups of carriers may publish additional classification lists.

Classification of individual products is based on a relative index of 100. Class 100 is considered the class of an average product, while other classes run as high as 500 and as low as 35. Each product is assigned an item number for listing purposes and then given a classification rating. As a general rule, the higher a class rating, the higher the transportation cost for the product. Historically, a product classified as 200 would be approximately

Item	Articles	Classes	
		LTL	**TL**
86750	Glass, leaded, see Note, item 86752:		
Sub 1	With landscape, pictorial, or religious designs, packed in boxes.	200.	70.
Sub 2	With curved, angled, or straight-line patterns, or with designs other than landscape, pictorial, or religious, in boxes.	100.	70.
86752	*Note:* The term "leaded glass" means glass either colored or clear, set in lead or in other metal.		
86770	Glass, microscopical slide or cover, in boxes.	70.	40.
86830	Glass, rolled, overlaid with aluminum strips with metal terminals attached, in boxes, crates, or Package 1339.	77.5	45.
86840	Glass, rolled, overlaid with aluminum strips, NOI, in boxes, crates, or Package 1339.	70.	37.5
86900	Glass, silvered for mirrors, not framed, backed, or equipped with hangers or fastening devices:		
Sub 1	Shock (window glass, silvered), in boxes, see Note, item 86902; also TL, in Packages 227 or 300.	86.	40.
Sub 2	Other than shock glass; also TL, in Packages 227 or 300: Bent:		
Sub 3	Not exceeding 15 feet in length or 9 feet in breadth, in boxes.	100.	70.
Sub 4	Exceeding 15 feet in length or 9 feet in breadth, in boxes.	250.	70.
Sub 5	Not bent, see Package 785:		
Sub 6	120 united inches or less, in boxes, crates, or Packages 198,	70.	40.
Sub 7	235, or 1339.		
sub 8	Exceeding 120 united inches but not exceeding 15 feet in length or 9 feet in breadth, in boxes or crates.	100.	40.
Sub 9	Exceeding 15 feet in length or 9 feet in breadth, in boxes or crates.	200.	45.
86902	*Note:* Glass, silvered for mirrors, which has been framed or backed, or equipped with large hangers or fastening devices, is subject to the classes for mirrors, NOI.		
85940	Glass, window, other than plate, with metal edging other than sash or frames, in boxes.	77.5	45.
86960	Glazing units, glass, not in sash, see Note, item 86966, in boxes, crates, or Packages 2133, 2149, or 2281.	70.	45.
86966	*Note:* Applies on units consisting of sheets of glass separated by air or vacuum, sealed at all edges with same or other materials.		
87040	Skylight, roofing, or sidewall construction material consisting of rough rolled glass, wired or not wired, and installation accessories, see Note, item 87042, in boxes or crates.	65.	35.

TABLE 8.7   National Motor Freight Classification 100-S

Source: Reprinted with permission from the American Trucking Association.

twice as expensive to transport as a product rated 100. While the actual current multiple may not be two, a class 200 rating will still result in substantially higher freight costs than a class 100 rating. Products are also assigned classifications on the basis of the weight being shipped. Less-than-truckload **(LTL)** shipments of identical products will have higher ratings than truckload **(TL)** shipments.

Table 8.7 illustrates a page from the *National Motor Freight Classification*. It contains general product grouping 86750, which is **glass, leaded.** Notice that the leaded glass category is further subdivided into specific types of glass such as *glass, microscopical slide or cover, in boxes* (item 86770). For LTL shipments, item 86770 is assigned a class 70 rating. TL shipments of the same glass items are assigned a class 40 rating, provided a minimum of 360 hundredweight is shipped.

Products are also assigned different ratings on the basis of packaging. Glass may be rated differently when shipped loose, in crates, or in boxes than when shipped in wrapped protective packing. It should be noted that packaging differences influence product density, stowability, and damage, illustrating that cost factors discussed earlier enter into the rate-determined process. Thus, a number of different classifications may apply to the same product depending on shipment size, transport mode, and product packaging.

One of the major responsibilities of transportation managers is to obtain the best possible rating for all products shipped, so it is useful for members of a traffic department to have a thorough understanding of the classification systems. Although there are differences in rail and truck classifications, each system is guided by similar rules.

It is possible to have a product reclassified by written application to the appropriate classification board. The classification board reviews proposals for change or additions with respect to minimum weights, commodity descriptions, packaging requirements, and general rules and regulations. An alert traffic department will take an active role in classification. Significant savings may be realized by obtaining an improved classification for a product or by recommending a change in packaging or shipment quantity that will reduce a product's rating.

Rate Determination

Once a classification rating is obtained for a product, the rate must be determined. The rate per hundredweight is usually based on the shipment origin and destination, although the actual price charged for a particular shipment is normally subject to a minimum charge and may also be subject to surcharges. Historically, the origin and destination rates were manually maintained in notebooks that had to be updated and revised regularly. Then rates were provided on diskettes by carriers. Today, options for selecting carriers range from Internet software that examines carrier Web sites and determines the best rates to participation in online auctions.

Origin and destination rates are organized by zip codes. Table 8.8 illustrates rates for all freight classes from Atlanta, Georgia (zip 303), to Lansing, Michigan (zip 489). The table lists rates for shipments ranging in size from the smallest LTL (less than 500 pounds; listed as L5C) to the largest TL (greater than 40,000 pounds; listed as M40M). The rate is quoted

Origin 303: Destination 489: MC 81.00: RBNO 00775E									
Rate Class	**L5C**	**M5C**	**M1M**	**M2M**	**M5M**	**M10M**	**M20M**	**M30M**	**M40M**
500	233.58	193.89	147.14	119.10	84.05	65.37	40.32	32.25	28.24
400	188.24	156.25	118.58	95.98	67.73	52.69	32.55	26.03	22.79
300	144.11	119.63	90.78	73.48	51.86	40.34	24.94	19.95	17.45
250	126.30	104.84	79.56	64.40	45.45	35.34	21.86	17.48	15.31
200	98.37	81.66	61.97	50.16	35.40	27.53	17.00	13.60	11.91
175	88.65	73.58	55.84	45.20	31.90	24.81	15.30	12.24	10.72
150	76.11	63.18	47.94	38.81	27.38	21.30	13.20	10.56	9.24
125	64.76	53.76	40.80	33.03	23.31	18.12	11.25	9.00	7.88
110	56.27	46.71	35.43	28.69	20.25	15.75	9.88	7.90	6.92
100	52.62	43.68	33.15	26.83	18.94	14.73	9.22	7.38	6.46
92	49.79	41.33	31.37	25.39	17.92	13.94	8.91	7.12	6.24
85	46.15	38.31	29.07	23.53	16.61	12.92	8.58	6.86	6.01
77	42.91	35.62	27.03	21.88	15.44	12.01	8.34	6.67	5.84
70	40.48	33.59	25.50	20.64	14.57	11.33	8.10	6.48	5.67
65	38.46	31.92	24.22	19.61	13.84	10.76	8.02	6.41	5.61
60	36.84	30.58	23.21	18.78	13.26	10.31	7.94	6.35	5.56
55	34.81	28.90	21.93	17.75	12.53	9.74	7.85	6.28	5.50
50	32.79	27.22	20.66	16.71	11.80	9.18	7.77	6.22	5.44
Weight Limits (lb)	Under 500	500– 1000	1000– 2000	2000– 5000	5000– 10,000	10,000– 20,000	20,000– 30,000	30,000– 40,000	Over 40,000

TABLE 8.8 Example of Rates from Atlanta, Georgia (zip 303), to Lansing, Michigan (zip 489)

in dollars per hundredweight. Assuming a shipment of 10,000 pounds, the rate for class 85 between Atlanta and Lansing, using this example tariff, is $12.92 per hundredweight.

Historically, the published rate had to be charged for all shipments of a specific class and origin/destination combination. This required frequent review and maintenance to keep rates current. Following deregulation, carriers offered more flexibility through rate discounts. Now instead of developing an individual rate table to meet the needs of customer segments, carriers apply a discount from class rates for specific customers. The discount depends on the shipper's volume and market competition.

An alternative to the per hundredweight charge is a per mile charge, which is common in TL shipments. As discussed previously, TL shipments are designed to reduce handling and transfer costs. Since the entire vehicle is used in a TL movement and there is no requirement to transfer the shipment at a terminal, a per mile basis offers a more appropriate pricing basis. For a one-way move, charges may vary per mile based on the market, the equipment, and the product involved. Although it is negotiable, this charge typically includes loading, unloading, and liability.

In addition to the variable shipment charge applied on either a per hundredweight or per mile basis, two additional charges are common for transportation: **minimum charges** and **surcharges.** The minimum charge represents the amount a shipper must pay to make a shipment, regardless of weight. A surcharge represents an additional charge designed to cover specific carrier costs.

Class rates, minimum charges, and surcharges form a pricing structure that, in various combinations, is applicable within the continental United States. The tariff indicates the class rate for any rating group between specified origins and destinations. In combination, the classification framework and class rate structure form a generalized pricing mechanism.

Cube Rates

Considerable attention has recently focused on development of a simplified method of transportation pricing. Typically called **cube** or **density** rates, the new approach replaces the 18 traditional freight classifications of the NMFC with five cube groupings. Under the cube concept, shippers complete a cube shipping document **(CSD),** which replaces the traditional bill of lading. To further identify freight characteristics, shippers provide the total weight of both stackable **(ST)** and nonstackable **(NST)** freight included in the shipment. Rates are then determined for the weight contained in each category of freight. The CSD offers five weight break groups. Four are weight breaks for shipments under 500 pounds. Rates for shipments over 500 pounds are based on multiples of 500 pounds with no shipment weight limit. While still emerging, cube-based rates and the associated cube shipping document offer a promising approach to reducing the complexity and improve the accuracy of traditional transportation pricing.[22]

Commodity Rates

When a large quantity of a product moves between two locations on a regular basis, it is common practice for carriers to publish a **commodity rate.** Commodity rates are special or specific rates published without regard to classification. The terms and conditions of a commodity rate are usually indicated in a contract between the carrier and shipper.

[22]For a definitive discussion of challenges related to implementing cube-based rates see "Unpacking Transportation Pricing," Peter D. Moore, Hank Mallen, Gynnette Guess, and Alan Van Boven, The University of Tennessee Center for Executive Education, 2010. For an early discussion of the potential of cube rates see Ray Bohman, "New LTL Pricing: Thinking Inside the Cube," *Logistics Management*, October 2007, pp. 21–24.

Commodity rates are published on a point-to-point basis and apply only on specified products. Today, most rail freight moves under commodity rates. They are less prevalent in motor carriage. Whenever a commodity rate exists, it supersedes the corresponding class or exception rate.

Exception Rates

Special rates published to provide prices lower than the prevailing class rates are called **exception rates.** The original purpose of the exception rate was to provide a special rate for a specific area, origin/destination, or commodity when justified by either competitive or high-volume movements. Rather than publish a new tariff, an exception to the classification or class rate was established.

Just as the name implies, when an exception rate is published, the classification that normally applies to the product is changed. Such changes may involve assignment of a new class or may be based on a percentage of the original class. Technically, exceptions may be higher or lower, although most are less than original class rates. Unless otherwise noted, all services provided under the class rate remain under an exception rate.

Since deregulation, several new types of exception rates have gained popularity. For example, an **aggregate tender rate** is utilized when a shipper agrees to provide multiple shipments to a carrier in exchange for a discount or exception from the prevailing class rate. The primary objective is to reduce carrier cost by permitting multiple shipment pickup during one stop at a shipper's facility or to reduce the rate for the shipper because of the carrier's reduced cost. To illustrate, UPS offers customers that tender multiple small package shipments at one time a discount based on aggregate weight and/or cubic volume.

A **limited service rate** is utilized when a shipper agrees to perform selected services typically performed by the carrier, such as trailer loading, in exchange for a discount. A common example is a **shipper load and count rate**, where the shipper takes responsibility for loading and counting the cases. Not only does this remove the responsibility for loading the shipment from the carrier, but it also implies that the carrier, once the trailer is sealed, is not responsible for guaranteeing case count. Another example of limited service is a **released value rate,** which limits carrier liability in case of loss or damage. Normally, the carrier is responsible for full product value if loss or damage occurs in transit. The quoted rate must include adequate insurance to cover the risk. Often it is more effective for manufacturers of high-value product to self-insure to realize the lowest possible rate. Limited service is used when shippers have confidence in the carrier's capability. Cost can be reduced by eliminating duplication of effort or responsibility.

Special Rates and Services

A number of special rates and services provided by carriers are available for use in logistical operations. Several common examples are discussed.

Freight-all-kind (FAK) rates are important to logistics operations. Under FAK rates, a mixture of different products is transported under a negotiated rating. Rather than determine the classification and applicable freight rate of individual products, an average rating is applied for the total shipment. In essence, FAK rates are line-haul rates since they replace class, exception, or commodity rates. Their purpose is to simplify the paperwork associated with the movement of mixed commodities.

Numerous special rates exist that may offer transportation savings on specific freight movements. When a commodity moves under the tariff of a single carrier, it is referred to as a **local rate** or single-line rate. If more than one carrier is involved in the freight movement, a **joint rate** may be applicable because multiple carriers are involved in the actual transportation process. Because some motor and rail carriers operate in restricted territory, it may be necessary to utilize the services of more than one carrier to complete a shipment. Utilization of a joint rate can offer substantial savings over the use of two or more local rates.

Transit services permit a shipment to be stopped at an intermediate point between initial origin and destination for unloading, storage, and/or processing. The shipment is then reloaded for delivery to the destination. Typical examples of transit services are milling for grain products and processing for sugar beets. When transit privileges exist, the shipment is charged a through rate from origin to destination plus a transit privilege charge.

For a variety of reasons, a shipper or consignee may desire to change routing, destination, or even the consignee after a shipment is in transit. This process is called **diversion and reconsignment.** This flexibility can be extremely important, particularly with regard to food and other perishable products where market demand can quickly change. It is a normal practice among certain types of marketing intermediaries to purchase commodities with the full intention of selling them while they are in transit. **Diversion** consists of changing the destination of a shipment prior to its arrival at the original destination. **Reconsignment** is a change in consignee prior to delivery. Both services are provided by railroads and truck carriers for a specified charge.

A **split delivery** is desired when portions of a shipment need to be delivered to different destinations. Under specified tariff conditions, delivery can involve multiple destinations. The payment is typically structured to reflect a rate as if the shipment were going to the most distant destination. In addition, there is typically a charge for each delivery.

Demurrage and detention are charges assessed for retaining freight cars or truck trailers beyond specified loading or unloading time. The term **demurrage** is used by railroads for holding a railcar beyond 48 hours before unloading the shipment. Trucks use the term **detention** to cover similar delays. In the case of motor carriers, the permitted time is specified in the tariff and is normally limited to a few hours.

In addition to basic transportation, truck and rail carriers offer a wide variety of **special** or **accessorial** services. Table 8.9 provides a list of frequently utilized ancillary services.

Carriers may also offer environmental services and special equipment. **Environmental services** refer to special control of freight while in transit, such as refrigeration, ventilation, and heating. For example, in the summer, Hershey typically transports chocolate confectionery products in refrigerated trailers to protect them from high temperature levels. **Special equipment charges** refer to the use of equipment that the carrier has purchased for a shipper's convenience. For example, specialized sanitation equipment is necessary to clean and prepare trailers for food storage and transit if the trailer has been previously utilized for nonfood products or commodities.

• *COD.* Collect payment on delivery.
• *Change COD.* Change COD recipient.
• *Inside delivery.* Deliver product inside the building.
• *Marking or tagging.* Mark or tag product as it is transported.
• *Notify before delivery.* Make appointment prior to delivery.
• *Reconsignment of delivery.* Redirect shipment to a new destination while in transit.
• *Redeliver.* Attempt second delivery.
• *Residential delivery.* Deliver at a residence without a truck dock.
• *Sorting and segregating.* Sort commodity prior to delivery.
• *Storage.* Store commodity prior to delivery.

TABLE 8.9
Typical Carrier
Ancillary Services

Although the brief coverage of special services is not all-inclusive, it does offer several examples of the range and type of services carriers offer. A carrier's role in a logistical system is most often far greater than providing line-haul transportation.

Transportation Management

Transportation management involves a wide variety of planning, execution, and administrative responsibilities. Firms are increasingly adopting Transportation Management Systems (TMS) as an integral part of their information technology strategy. In general, a TMS proactively identifies and evaluates transportation strategies and tactics to determine the best methods to ship products. As illustrated in Table 8.10, this includes the capability to select transport modes, plan loads, consolidate shipments, route vehicles, and efficiently use transportation capacity. The fundamental deliverables of a TMS are reduced cost and the increased ability to provide on-time delivery.

The generalized functionality of a TMS can be described in terms of five capabilities: (1) operational management, (2) consolidation, (3) negotiation, (4) control, and (5) auditing and claims administration.

Operational Management

From an operational perspective, key elements of a TMS are equipment scheduling and yard management, load planning, routing and advanced shipment notification **(ASN),** and movement administration.

Equipment Scheduling and Yard Management

One major responsibility of the traffic department is equipment scheduling and yard management. Scheduling is an important process in both common carrier and private transportation. A serious and costly operational bottleneck can result from transportation equipment waiting to be loaded or unloaded. Proper yard management requires careful load planning, equipment utilization, and driver scheduling. Additionally, equipment preventive maintenance must be planned, coordinated, and monitored. Finally, any specialized equipment requirements must be planned and implemented.

Closely related to equipment scheduling is the arrangement of delivery and pickup appointments. To avoid extensive waiting time and improve equipment utilization, it is important to preschedule dock positions or slots. It is becoming common practice to establish standing appointments for regular shipments. Some firms are implementing the practice of establishing advanced appointments at the time of order commitment. Increasingly, the effective scheduling of equipment is key to implementing time-based logistical

TABLE 8.10
Typical Transportation
Management System
Functionality

- Order consolidation
- Route optimization
- Carrier rate management
- EDI links with carriers
- Internet-based shipment tracking
- Integrated claims management
- Identify most economical mode: parcel, less-than-truckload, truckload, pool distribution, stops in transit
- Calculate best route
- Carrier selection based on cost and service including performance
- Yard management

arrangements. For example, cross-dock arrangements are totally dependent on precise scheduling of equipment arrival and departure.

Load Planning

How loads are planned directly impacts transportation efficiency. In the case of trucks, capacity is limited in terms of weight and cube. Planning the load sequence of a trailer must consider product physical characteristics and the size of individual shipments, as well as delivery sequence if multiple shipments are loaded on a single trailer.

Routing and Advanced Shipment Notification (ASN)

An important part of achieving transportation efficiency is shipment **routing.** From an administrative viewpoint, the traffic department is responsible for assuring that routing is performed in an efficient manner while meeting key customer service requirements. It is common practice for shippers to electronically provide consignees advanced shipment notification **(ASN).** While the specifics of ASN documents vary, their primary purpose is to allow adequate time to plan arrival, arrange delivery appointments, and plan to redeploy the shipment's content. How deliveries are planned must take into consideration special requirements of customers in terms of time, location, and special unloading services.

Movement Administration

Traffic managers have the basic responsibility of administering the performance of for-hire and private transportation. Effective administration requires continuous carrier performance measurement and evaluation. The advent of information connectivity has significantly improved shipment reliability. The fact that most shippers have reduced the size of their carrier base has greatly simplified administration. Effective administration requires carrier selection, integration, and evaluation.

A basic responsibility of the traffic department is to select carriers to perform for-hire transport. To some degree all firms use the services of for-hire carriers. Even those with commitment to private fleets regularly require the supplemented services of common, contract, and specialized carriers to complete transportation requirements.

Consolidation

At several different points throughout this text the importance of freight consolidation is discussed. The fact that freight costs are directly related to size of shipment and length of haul places a premium upon freight consolidation. In terms made famous by the late President Truman, *the buck stops here,* meaning traffic management is the business function responsible for achieving freight consolidation.

The traditional approach to freight consolidation was to combine LTL or parcel shipment moving to a general location. The objective of outbound consolidation was straightforward. The transportation savings in moving a single consolidated shipment versus multiple individual, small shipments were typically sufficient to pay for necessary handling and local delivery while achieving significant total cost reduction.

The shift to response-based logistics has introduced new challenges regarding consolidation. Time-based logistics tends to transpose the impact of unpredictable demand from inventory safety stock to creation of small shipments. All members of the supply chain are seeking to reduce inventory dwell time by more closely synchronizing replenishment with demand.

The result is more frequent, small orders. Not only does the increase in small shipments result in higher transportation cost, it also translates to more handling and dock congestion.

To control transportation cost when a time-based strategy is used, managerial attention must be directed to the development of ingenious ways to achieve of transportation consolidation. To plan freight consolidation, it is necessary to have reliable information concerning inventory status. It is also desirable to be able to reserve or promise scheduled production to achieve planned consolidations. To the extent practical, consolidations should be planned prior to order processing and warehouse order selection to avoid delay. All aspects of consolidation require timely and relevant information concerning planned activity.

From an operational viewpoint, freight consolidation techniques are grouped as **reactive** and **proactive.** Each type of consolidation is important to achieving transportation efficiency.

Reactive Consolidation

A reactive approach to consolidation does not attempt to influence the composition and timing of transportation movements. The consolidation effort reacts to shipments as they come and seeks to combine individual orders into larger shipments for line-haul movement. Perhaps the most visible example of effective reactive line-haul is United Parcel Service's nightly sortation and consolidation of package freight for intercity movement.

From an operational viewpoint, there are three ways to achieve effective reactive consolidation: (1) market area, (2) scheduled delivery, and (3) pooled delivery.

The most basic method of consolidation is to combine small shipments going to different customers within a geographical **market area.** This procedure does not interrupt the natural freight flow by changing the timing of shipments. Rather, the overall quantity of shipments to a market area provides the consolidation basis.

The difficulty of developing either inbound or outbound market area consolidations is the variation in daily volume. To offset the volume deficiency, three operating arrangements are commonly used. First, consolidated shipments may be sent to an intermediate break-bulk point for purposes of line-haul transportation savings. There, individual shipments are separated and forwarded to their destination. Second, firms may elect to hold consolidated shipments for scheduled delivery on specific days to given destination markets. Third, consolidation of small shipments may be achieved by utilizing the services of a third-party logistics firm to pool delivery. The last two methods require special arrangements, which are discussed in greater detail below.

A strategy of holding shipments to specific markets for delivery on selected days each week is referred to as **scheduled area delivery.** The scheduled delivery plan is normally communicated to customers in a way that highlights the mutual benefits of consolidation. The shipping firm commits to the customer that all orders received prior to a specified cutoff time will be guaranteed for delivery on the scheduled day.

Participation in **pooled delivery** typically means that a freight forwarder, public warehouse, or transportation company arranges consolidation for multiple shippers serving the same geographical market area. Integrated service providers that arrange pooled consolidation services typically have standing delivery appointments at high-volume delivery destinations. It is common, under such arrangements, for the consolidation company to also perform value-added service such as sorting, sequencing, or segregation of inbound freight to accommodate customer requirements.

Proactive Consolidation

While reactive efforts to develop transportation consolidations have been successful, two forces are driving a more proactive approach. First, the impact of response-based logistical systems is creating a larger number of small shipments. This trend toward increased smaller shipments has been intensified by the growth of e-commerce. Second, proactive consolidation reflects the desire for shippers, carriers, and consignees to participate in consolidation savings.

An important step toward achieving proactive consolidation is **preorder planning** of quantity and timing to facilitate consolidated freight movement. Simply stated, the creation of orders should not be restricted to standard buying times or inventory replenishment rules. Buyer participation in order creation can greatly facilitate proactive freight consolidation.

Significant freight consolidation opportunities also may exist if nonrelated firms can be coordinated. Commonly referred to as **multivendor consolidation,** the general idea of grouping different shippers' freight has always been integral to line-haul operations of LTL carriers. The new initiative is jointly planning warehousing and order processing across different companies to facilitate such consolidation. Creating such multivendor consolidation is a value-added service offered by a growing number of ISPs. Likewise, firms are increasingly endorsing pooling arrangements with competitors to achieve logistical efficiency.

Negotiation

For any given shipment, it is the responsibility of the traffic department to obtain the lowest possible rate consistent with service required.

The prevailing tariff represents the starting point in transportation negotiation. The key to effective negotiation is to seek win-win agreements wherein both carriers and shippers share productivity gains. As indicated several times throughout this text, the lowest possible cost for transportation may not be the lowest total cost of logistics. The traffic department must seek the lowest rate consistent with service standards. For example, if 2-day delivery is required, the traffic department seeks to select the method of transport that will consistently meet this standard at the lowest possible cost. Given the special considerations of transportation, several factors discussed throughout this section must guide rate negotiation. However, in the context of building solid carrier relationships, traffic managers must seek fair and equitable rates.

Control

Other important responsibilities under the control of transportation management are tracing, expediting, and driver hours administration. **Tracing** is a procedure to locate lost or late shipments. Shipments committed across a transportation network are bound to be misplaced or delayed from time to time. Most large carriers maintain online tracing to aid shippers in locating a shipment. The tracing action must be initiated by the shipper's traffic department, but once initiated, it is the carrier's responsibility to provide the desired information. **Expediting** involves the shipper notifying a carrier that it needs to have a specific shipment move through the carrier's system as quickly as possible and with no delays.

Driver fatigue concerns prompted the Department of Transportation's Federal Motor Carrier Safety Administration **(FMCSA)** in 2005 to alter the **hours of service (HOS)** that interstate truck drivers could operate. The changes were developed to ensure drivers were getting sufficient off-duty time to rest while at the same time increasing daily driving time for trucking companies. The changes significantly restructured working conditions for truckers. Under the new rules all breaks were counted as on-duty time. Although total driving hours were extended, the impact of the new regulation was to reduce the productive workday and reduce the effectiveness of driver teams. The new rules reduced the time a driver could rest during team movements.

TABLE 8.11
Hours of Drivers'
Service

Source: U.S. Department of
Transportation.

Hours of Service Rules
11 hours' driving
14 consecutive hours on duty
Breaks count as on-duty time.
10 consecutive and uninterrupted hours off duty
60/70 hours in 7/8 days
Drivers must take 34 hours off duty before restarting an on-duty period.

The new regulations lengthened daily driving time; counted rest, unloading, and breaks as driving time; extended the required time off between shifts; and maintained a weekly maximum for on-duty hours. An overview of the rule changes are presented in Table 8.11. The rules as modified remain under legal review.

HOS regulation is a good example of how government policy can influence transportation. In cases of private transportation, HOS administration is the direct responsibility of the traffic department. In for-hire carriers, oversight is the responsibility of carrier management.

Auditing and Claim Administration

When transportation service or charges are not performed as promised, shippers can make claims for restitution. Claims are typically classified as **loss and damage** or **overcharge/undercharge.** Loss and damage claims occur when a shipper demands the carrier pay for partial or total financial loss resulting from poor performance. As the name implies, loss and damage claims usually occur when product is lost or damaged while in transit. Overcharge/undercharge claims result when the amount billed is different from that expected and are typically resolved through freight bill audit procedures.

Agreements stipulate the proper procedure for filing claims and help define which parties are responsible. Two factors regarding claim administration are of primary importance. First, detailed attention should be given to claim administration because recoveries are achieved only by aggressive audit programs. Second, large volumes of claims are indicative of carriers that are not performing their service obligations. Regardless of the dollars recovered by claim administration, the breakdown in customer service performance resulting from loss and damage claims impacts a shipper's reputation with its customers.

A common practice in consumer goods industries is the reconciliation of actual shipment content to the advanced shipment notification (ASN). The challenge is to match actual case counts shipped and stock keeping units (SKUs) to ordered and expected amounts. This is a major problem given the increased use of cross-dock handling from distribution center receiving to retail outbound shipment. It is common practice for retailers to issue penalty chargebacks to suppliers for noncompliance to planned order content and quantity.

Auditing freight bills is an important responsibility of the traffic department. The purpose of auditing is to ensure freight bill accuracy. Transport rate complexity results in a higher error probability than in most other purchasing decisions. There are two types of freight audits. A **preaudit** determines proper charges prior to payment of a freight bill. A **postaudit** makes the same determination after payment has been made. Auditing may be either external or internal. If external, specialized freight-auditing companies are employed, utilizing personnel who are experts in specific commodity groupings. This is generally more efficient than the use of internal personnel who may not have the same level of expertise. Payment for external audit is usually based on a percentage of recovered overcharges. It is crucial that a highly ethical firm be employed for this purpose, because valuable marketing and customer information is contained in the freight bill and corporate activities may be adversely affected if sensitive information is not held in confidence.

A combination of internal and external auditing is frequently employed, depending on the value of the freight bill. For example, a bill of $600 with a 10 percent error results in a $60 recovery, but a $50 bill with a 10 percent error results in only a $5 recovery. Therefore, bills with larger recovery potential may be audited internally.

It is common practice for firms to determine and pay freight at the time a shipment is tendered to a carrier. This shifts the audit responsibility to the carrier, which must then file an undercharge claim for recovery from the shipper.

Documentation

Detailed documentation is required to perform a transportation service. With the exception of private transfer within the confines of a single firm, products are typically being sold when being transported. Thus, a change of ownership occurs during the time the transport service is performed. When for-hire carriers are used to perform the transportation, the transaction must establish clear legal responsibility of all parties involved. The primary purpose of transportation documentation is to protect all involved parties. Three primary types of transport documentation are bills of lading, freight bills, and shipment manifests.

Bill of Lading

The **bill of lading** is the basic document utilized in purchasing transport services. It serves as a receipt and documents products and quantities shipped. For this reason, accurate product description and count are essential. In case of loss, damage, or delay, the bill of lading is the basis for damage claims. The designated individual or buyer on a bill of lading is the only bona fide recipient of goods. A carrier is responsible for proper delivery according to instructions contained in the document. The information contained on the bill of lading determines all responsibilities related to timing and ownership.

The bill of lading specifies terms and conditions of carrier liability and documents responsibilities for all possible causes of loss or damage except those defined as **force majeure** (circumstances beyond anyone's control, such as a natural disaster). Figure 8.5 provides an example of a Uniform Straight Bill of Lading. Government regulations permit uniform bills of lading to be computerized and electronically transmitted between shippers and carriers.

In addition to the **uniform** bill of lading, other commonly used types are **order-notified, export,** and **government.** It is important to select the correct bill of lading for a specific shipment.

An order-notified or negotiable bill of lading is a credit instrument. It provides that delivery not be made unless the original bill of lading is surrendered to the carrier. The usual procedure is for the seller to send the order-notified bill of lading to a third party, usually a bank or credit institution. Upon customer payment for the product the credit institution releases the bill of lading. The buyer then presents it to the common carrier, which in turn releases the goods. This facilitates international transport where cross-border payment for goods may be a major consideration. An export bill of lading permits a shipper to use export rates, which may be lower than domestic rates. Export rates may reduce total cost when applied to domestic origin or destination line-haul transport. Government bills of lading may be used when the product is owned by the U.S. government.

UNIFORM STRAIGHT BILL OF LADING

Original—Not Negotiable

(To be Printed on "White" Paper)

Shipper's No. . . . .

Agent's No. . . . .

Company

RECEIVED, subject to the classifications and tariffs in effect on the date of the issue of this Bill of Lading,

at . . . . , 19 . . .

from . . . .

the property described below, in apparent good order, except as noted (contents and condition of contents of packages unknown), marked, consigned, and destined as indicated below, which said company (the word company being understood throughout this contract as meaning any person of corporation in possession of the property under the contract) agrees to carry to its usual place (of delivery at mid destination, if on its own road or its own water line, otherwise to deliver to another carrier on the route to said destination. It is mutually agreed, as to each carrier of all or any of said property over all or any portion of said route to destination, and as to each party at any time interested in all or any of said property, that every service to be performed hereunder shall be subject to all the conditions not prohibited by law, whether printed or written, herein contained, including the conditions on back hereof, which are hereby agreed to by the shipper and accepted for himself and his assigns.

(Mail or street address of consignee—For purposes of notification only.)

Consigned to . . . .

Destination . . . . State of . . . . County of . . . .

Route . . . .

Delivering Carrier . . . . Car Initial . . . . Car No. . . . .

No. Pack-ages	Description of Articles, Special Marks, and Exceptions	*Weight (Subject to Correction)	Class or Rate	Check Column	Subject to Section 7 of conditions, if this ship-ment is to be delivered to the consignee without recourse on the consign-or, the consignor shall sign the following state-ment:
					The carrier shall not make delivery of this shipment without pay-ment of freight and all other lawful charges.
					. . . . (Signature of consignor.)
					If charges are to be pre-paid, write or stamp here. "To be Prepaid."
					. . . .
					Received $ . . . . to apply in prepayment of the charges on the property described hereon.
					Agent or Cashier.
					Per . . . . (The signature here acknowl-edges only the amount prepaid.)

* If the shipment moves between two ports by a carrier by water, the law requires that the bill of lading shall state whether it is "carrier's or shipper's weight."

Note.—Where the rate is dependent on value, shippers are required to state specifically in writing the agreed or declared value of the property.

The agreed or declared value of the property is hereby specifically stated by the shipper to be not exceeding

. . . . per . . . .

Charges advanced:

$ . . . .

. . . . Shipper.   . . . . Agent.

Per . . . .   Per . . . .

Permanent postoffice address of shipper . . . .

FIGURE 8.5 Uniform Straight Bill of Lading

Freight Bill

The **freight bill** represents a carrier's method of charging for transportation services performed. It is developed by using information contained in the bill of lading. The freight bill may be either **prepaid** or **collect.** A prepaid bill means that transport cost is paid by the shipper prior to performance, whereas a collect shipment shifts payment responsibility to the consignee.

Considerable administration is involved in preparing bills of lading and freight bills. There has been significant effort to automate freight bills and bills of lading through EDI or Internet transactions. Some firms elect to pay their freight bills at the time the bill of lading is created, thereby combining the two documents. Such arrangements are based upon the financial benefits of reduced paperwork cost, and as noted earlier shift the audit responsibility to the carrier.

Shipment Manifest

The **shipment manifest** lists individual stops or consignees when multiple shipments are placed on a single vehicle. Each shipment requires a bill of lading. The manifest lists the stop, bill of lading, weight, and case count for each shipment. The objective of the manifest is to provide a single document that defines the overall contents of the load without requiring review of individual bills of lading. For single-stop shipments, the manifest is the same as the bill of lading.

Product Pricing and Transportation

Pricing is an important aspect of marketing strategy that directly impacts logistical operations. The terms and conditions of pricing determine which party has responsibility for performing logistics activities. A major trend in price strategy has been to **debundle** the price of products and materials so that services such as transportation, which were traditionally included in a delivered price, become separate and visible items. Pricing practices have a direct impact on the timing and stability of logistical operations. In this section, basic pricing structures are briefly reviewed, followed by a discussion of pricing impact areas. No attempt is made to review the broad range of economic and psychological issues related to price strategy. The focus is on the relationship between pricing, logistical operations, and transportation decisions. Pricing decisions directly determine which party in the transaction is responsible for performing logistics activities, passage of title, and liability. FOB origin and delivered pricing are the two most common methods.

FOB Pricing

The term FOB technically means **free on board** or **freight on board.** A number of variations of FOB pricing are used in practice. **FOB origin** is the simplest way to quote price. Under FOB origin the seller indicates the price at point of origin and agrees to tender a shipment for transportation loading, but assumes no further responsibility. The buyer selects the mode of transportation, chooses a carrier, pays transportation charges, and takes risk of in-transit loss and/or damage. In **FOB destination pricing,** product ownership title does not pass to the buyer until delivery is completed. Under FOB destination pricing, the seller arranges for transportation and the charges are added to the sales invoice. The firm paying the freight bill does not necessarily assume responsibility for ownership of goods in transit, for the freight cost, or for filing of freight claims. These are issues of negotiation that are critical to supply chain collaboration.

Delivered Pricing

The primary difference between FOB and **delivered pricing** is that in delivered pricing the seller establishes a price that includes transportation. In other words, the transportation cost is not specified as a separate item. There are several variations of delivered pricing.

Under **single-zone delivered pricing,** buyers pay a single price regardless of where they are located. Delivered prices typically reflect the seller's average transportation cost. In actual practice, some customers pay more than their fair share for transportation while others are subsidized. The United States Postal Service uses a single-zone pricing policy throughout the United States for first-class letters. The same fee or postage rate is charged for a given size and weight regardless of distance traveled to the destination.

Single-zone delivered pricing is typically used when transportation costs are a relatively small percentage of selling price. The main advantage to the seller is the high degree of logistical control. For the buyer, despite being based on averages, such pricing systems have the advantage of simplicity.

The practice of **multiple-zone pricing** establishes different prices for specific geographic areas. The underlying idea is that logistics cost differentials can be more fairly assigned when two or more zones—typically based on distance—are used to quote delivered pricing. Parcel carriers such as United Parcel Service use multiple-zone pricing.

The most complicated and controversial form of delivered pricing is the use of a **base-point pricing system** in which the final delivered price is determined by the product's list price plus transportation cost from a designated base point, usually the manufacturing location. This designated point is used for computing the delivered price whether or not the shipment actually originates from the base location. Base-point pricing is common in shipping assembled automobiles from manufacturing plants to dealers.

Figure 8.6 illustrates how a base-point pricing system typically generates different net returns to a seller. The customer is quoted a delivered price of $100 per unit. Plant A is the base point. Actual transportation cost from plant A to the customer is $25 per unit. Plant A's base product price is $85 per unit. Transportation costs from plants B and C are $20 and $35 per unit, respectively.

When shipments are made from plant A, the company's net return is $75 per unit, the $100 delivered price minus the $25 transportation cost. The net return to the company

FIGURE 8.6
Base-Point Pricing

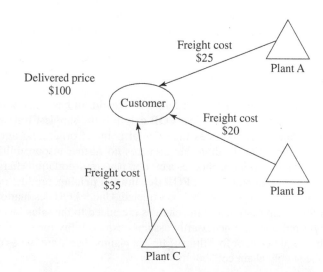

varies if shipments are made from plant B or C. With a delivered price of $100, plant B collects $5 in **phantom freight** on shipments to a customer. Phantom freight occurs when a buyer pays transportation costs greater than those actually incurred to move the shipment. If plant C is the shipment origin, the company must absorb $10 of the transportation costs. **Freight absorption** occurs when a seller pays all or a portion of the actual transportation cost and does not recover the full expenditure from the buyer. In other words, the seller decides to absorb transportation cost to be competitive.

Base-point pricing simplifies price quotations but can have a negative impact on customers and supply chain collaboration. For example, dissatisfaction may result if customers discover they are being charged more for transportation than actual freight costs. Such pricing practices may also result in a large amount of freight absorption for sellers.

Pickup Allowances

Pickup allowances are equivalent to purchasing merchandise on an FOB origin basis. Buyers are given a reduction from the standard delivered price if they or a representative pick up shipments at the seller's location and perform transportation. A buyer may also use a for-hire carrier or an integrated service provider (ISP) to perform merchandise pickup. In the food and grocery industry, which traditionally practiced delivered pricing, firms have realized significant savings by using private and for-hire carriers to pick up rather than purchase merchandise on a delivered basis.

While some confusion exists concerning how to best establish a pickup allowance, a safe rule is that a seller should provide the same allowance to all directly competitive buyers. A uniform pickup allowance is often the price incentive offered to the customer closest to the shipping point. Other common policies offer pickup allowances equivalent to the applicable common carrier rate for the shipment.

Pickup allowances offer potential benefits for both the seller and the buyer. Shippers are required to deal with fewer small shipments, thereby reducing the need for extensive outbound freight consolidation. Buyers gain control over the merchandise earlier and are in a position to achieve greater utilization of transportation equipment and drivers.

Summary

Transportation is usually the largest single cost expenditure in most logistics operations. Prior to deregulation, transportation services were standardized and inflexible, resulting in limited ability to develop a competitive advantage. As a result of deregulation, service offerings have been expanded and restrictions relaxed, allowing transportation resources to be effectively integrated into overall supply chain logistics.

This chapter introduced major principles of transportation economics. Knowledge of transportation economics and pricing is essential for effective logistics management. The primary drivers of transportation costs are distance, volume, density, stowability, handling, liability, and market factors. These drivers determine transportation prices that are presented to buyers as rates for performing specific services. Logistics managers need to have a working familiarity with the basic rate structure for line-haul and specialized transport-related services.

The fundamental responsibilities of traffic administration are operational management, consolidation, negotiation, control, auditing, and claims administration. Most transportation managers coordinate administration using a Transportation Management System

(TMS). The extent to which the administrative responsibilities discussed are performed by an internal traffic department or are provided by an integrated service provider is a matter of managerial preference.

Finally, transportation and pricing decisions are closely related. The growing practice of debundling the price of products and related services, such as transportation, has increased the involvement of logistics managers in general price administration.

Study Questions

1. Compare and contrast the transportation principles of economy of scale and economy of distance. Illustrate how they combine to create efficient transportation.
2. What is the economic justification for the rapid growth of premium package services?
3. Railroads have the largest percentage of intercity freight ton-miles, but motor carriers have the largest revenue. How do you explain this relationship?
4. The five basic modes of transportation have been available for well over 50 years. Is this the way it will always be, or can you identify a sixth mode that may become economically feasible in the foreseeable future?
5. Seven economic drivers that influence transportation cost were presented. Select a specific product and discuss how each factor impacts determination of freight rate.
6. What is the purpose of freight classification? Describe the differences between a rate and a rating. How do they relate to classification?

Challenge Questions

1. Do you believe it will be 2014 or beyond before we can be assured that the majority of all containers inbound to U.S. ports will be security screened at loading ports? What actions could you propose to rectify this dilemma?
2. What is your position on the approval of the Alliance Network's collective LTL rate making? What might be the longer-term implications of such collaboration?
3. What in your opinion will be the major impact of the Walmart decision to purchase FOB from its suppliers? The current stated objective is to reduce transportation costs on freight inbound to Walmart's distribution centers. How might the business relationship be impacted if at some future time Walmart decides to bypass its distribution centers and move merchandise direct from suppliers to its retail stores?
4. Supporters of LTL cube rates feel traditional pricing methods are overcomplicated and reduce transportation efficiency. As a newly minted logistics graduate, assume your employer asks for your evaluation of the traditional versus cubic-based LTL pricing. State your position as either a shipper or a carrier.

CHAPTER 9

Warehousing

Chapter Outline

Strategic Warehousing
  Economic Benefits
  Service Benefits
Warehouse Operations
  Handling
  Storage
Warehouse Ownership Arrangements
  Private
  Public
  Contract
  Network Deployment
Warehouse Decisions
  Site Selection
  Design
  Product-Mix Analysis
  Expansion
  Handling
  Layout
  Sizing
  Warehouse Management Systems (WMS)
  Yard Management System (YMS)
  Accuracy and Audits
  Security
  Safety and Maintenance
Summary

Warehousing incorporates many different aspects of logistics operations. Because of the many types of warehouses, the presentation does not fit the neat classification schemes used in areas such as order management, inventory, and transportation. A warehouse has traditionally been viewed as a place to hold or store inventory. However, in contemporary logistical systems, warehouse functionality is more properly viewed as mixing and modifying inventory to meet customer requirements. Storage of products is ideally held to a minimum. This chapter provides a foundation for understanding the value warehousing contributes to the logistics process. The discussion is relevant for all types of warehouses, including distribution centers, consolidation terminals, break-bulk facilities, and cross-docks. The objective is to introduce general managerial considerations related to warehousing.

Strategic Warehousing

While effective logistics systems should not be designed to hold inventory for extended times, there are occasions when inventory storage is justified on the basis of cost and service.

Storage has always been an important aspect of economic development. In the pre-industrial era, storage was performed by individual households forced to function as self-sufficient economic units. As transportation capability developed, it became possible to engage in specialization. Product storage shifted from households to retailers, wholesalers, and manufacturers. Warehouses stored inventory in the logistics pipeline, serving to coordinate product supply and consumer demand. Because the value of strategic storage was not well understood, warehouses were often considered necessary evils that added cost to the distribution process. The idea that using middlemen in the supply chain simply increases cost follows from that belief. During earlier times the need to deliver product assortments was limited. Labor productivity, handling efficiency, and inventory turnover were not major concerns. Because labor was relatively inexpensive, human resources were used freely. Little consideration was given to efficiency in space utilization, work methods, or handling. Despite such shortcomings, these initial warehouses provided a necessary bridge between production and marketing.

Following World War II, managerial attention shifted toward strategic storage. Management began to question the need for vast warehouse networks. In the distributive industries such as wholesaling and retailing, it was traditionally considered best practice to dedicate a warehouse containing a full assortment of inventory to every sales territory. As forecasting and production scheduling techniques improved, management questioned such risky inventory deployment. Production planning became more dependable as disruptions and time delays during manufacturing decreased. Seasonal production and consumption still required warehousing, but the overall need for storage to support stable manufacturing and consumption patterns was reduced.

Changing consumer demand more than offset any reduction in warehousing resulting from these manufacturing improvements. Retailers, faced with the challenge of providing consumers an increasing assortment of products, found it more difficult to maintain purchasing and transportation economics when buying direct from suppliers. The cost of transporting small shipments made direct ordering prohibitive. This created an opportunity to establish strategically located warehouses to provide timely and economical inventory replenishment for retailers. Progressive wholesalers and integrated retailers developed state-of-the-art warehouse systems to logistically support retail inventory replenishment. Thus, the focus on warehousing shifted from passive storage to strategic inventory assortment. The term **distribution center** became widely used throughout industry to capture this dynamic development in traditional warehousing.

Improvements in retail warehousing efficiency soon were adopted by manufacturing. For manufacturers, strategic warehousing offered a way to reduce holding or dwell time of materials and parts. Warehousing became integral to just-in-time **(JIT)** and stockless production strategies. While the basic notion of JIT is to reduce work-in-process inventory, such manufacturing strategies need dependable logistics support. Achieving such logistical support across a global market typically requires strategically located warehouses. Utilizing centralized parts inventory at a central warehouse reduces the need for inventory at each assembly plant. Products can be purchased and shipped to the strategically located central warehouse, taking advantage of consolidated transportation. At the warehouse, products are sorted, sequenced, and shipped to specific manufacturing plants as needed.

Where fully integrated, sortation and sequencing facilities become a vital extension of manufacturing.

On the outbound, or market-facing, side of manufacturing, warehouses can be used to create product assortments for customer shipment. The capability to receive mixed product shipments offers customers two specific advantages. First, logistical cost is reduced because an assortment of products can be delivered while taking advantage of consolidated transportation. Second, inventory of slow-moving products can be reduced because of the capability to receive smaller quantities as part of a larger consolidated shipment. Manufacturers that provide sorted and sequenced product shipments on a timely basis are positioned to achieve a competitive advantage.

An important goal in warehousing is to maximize flexibility. Flexibility is facilitated by information technology. Technology has influenced almost every aspect of warehouse operations by creating new and better ways to perform storage and handling. Flexibility is also an essential part of being able to respond to ever-changing customer demand in terms of product assortments, value-added services, and the manner in which shipments are sequenced and presented. Information technology facilitates flexibility by allowing warehouse operators to quickly react to changing customer requirements.

Strategic warehousing serves to satisfy requirements related to **local presence.** While benefits of local presence may not be as obvious as other service benefits, it is often cited by executives as a major advantage of local warehouses. The underlying belief is that a local warehouse can respond faster to customer needs than can a more distant warehouse. It is anticipated that local warehouse presence will increase market share and potentially profitability. While the local-presence factor is a frequently discussed strategy, little solid research exists to confirm or refute its benefits. In addition, more reliable transportation and technology-based order processing are closing the response time gap regardless of distance. Unless a warehouse is economically or service justified, it is unlikely that local presence will favorably influence operational results. The fact remains that a network of strategically located warehouses does provide key customers the perception they will be logistically supported.

Benefits realized from strategic warehousing are classified as economic and service. No warehousing should be included in a logistical system unless it is fully justified on some combination of cost and service. Ideally, a warehouse will simultaneously provide both economic and service benefits.

Economic Benefits

Economic benefits of warehousing occur when overall logistics costs are reduced. For example, if adding a warehouse in a logistical system reduces overall transportation cost by an amount greater than required investment and operational cost, then total cost will be reduced. When total cost reductions are achievable, the warehouse is economically justified. Four basic economic benefits are: (1) consolidation and break-bulk, (2) sorting, (3) seasonal storage, and (4) reverse logistics.

Consolidation and Break-Bulk

The economic benefits of consolidation and break-bulk are to reduce transportation cost by using warehouse capability to increase the size of shipments.

In consolidation, the warehouse receives inventory, from a number of sources, that are combined into a large single shipment to a specific destination. The benefits of consolidation are the realization of the lowest possible freight rate, timely and controlled delivery, and reduced congestion at a customer's receiving dock. The consolidation enables both the inbound movement from origin and the outbound movement to destination to be consolidated into a larger shipment, which generally results in lower transportation charges per unit and most often quicker delivery.

A break-bulk operation receives a single large shipment and arranges for delivery to multiple destinations. Economy of scale is achieved by transporting the larger shipment from origin to destination. The break-bulk warehouse or terminal sorts or splits the larger shipment into individual orders for customer delivery.

Both consolidation and break-bulk arrangements use warehouse capacity to improve transportation efficiency. Many logistical arrangements involve both consolidation and break-bulk. Figure 9.1 illustrates each activity.

Sorting

The basic benefit of sorting is to reconfigure freight as it is being transported from origin to destination. Three types of assortment—cross-docking, mixing, and assembly—are widely performed in logistical systems.

The objective of **cross-docking** is to combine inventory from multiple origins into a customized assortment to meet the needs of a specific customer. Retailers make extensive use of cross-dock operations to replenish fast-moving store inventories. Cross-docking requires precise on-time delivery from each manufacturer. As product is received and unloaded at the cross-dock, it is sorted by customer destination. In most instances, the customer has communicated precise volume requirements of each product, requested for each delivery destination. The manufacturers, in turn, may have sorted, loaded, and labeled the appropriate quantity by final destination when trailers were loaded at origin. Product is then literally moved across the dock from receiving into a truck dedicated to the delivery destination. Once outbound trucks are loaded with mixed product from multiple manufacturers, they are released for transport to destination. The high degree of precision

FIGURE 9.1
Consolidation and Break-Bulk Arrangements

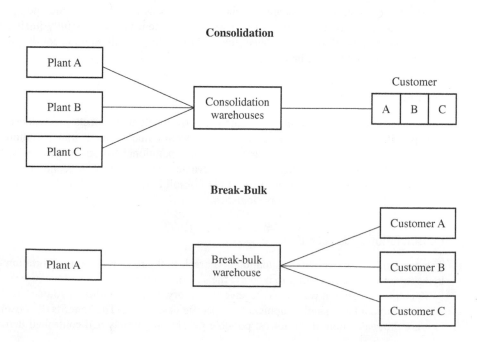

required for effective cross-docking makes successful operation highly dependent on information technology.

Meijer Superstores has developed a very effective cross-dock distribution process. On selected days, vendors are requested to arrive at a specific time with inbound merchandise deliveries at the Meijer cross-dock facility. Prior to their arrival, the participating manufacturers have received orders from Meijer buyers for specific items and quantities of merchandise based on retail store transaction data. At a designated time, all participating vendor trucks simultaneously begin unloading onto a conveyor handling device and merchandise is moved through inbound electronic scanning. This initial scan provides proof of receipt for vendor merchandise payment and assigns the scanned merchandise to a specific retail store. The merchandise is then routed to a specific store-bound trailer. As the merchandise is loaded into the trailer, it is once again electronically scanned. This second scan provides a cross-check that the appropriate merchandise is being sent to each store, and also provides accounting control information. The entire cross-dock process requires a couple of hours to complete. Trailers arriving at the cross dock at 3 P.M. are unloaded and released by 5 P.M. Outbound trailers arrive at retail stores based on required transit time and can be scheduled to be unloaded. Merchandise arriving at the retail store can be available for purchase by customers a short time after the trailer is delivered to the store. Thus products loaded out in the morning from nearby suppliers such as Kellogg or Gerber may actually be received by Meijer, moved from the cross dock to retail stores, and be purchased and in some cases even consumed on the same day.

An end result similar to cross-docking is achieved by **mixing.** However, mixing is usually performed at an intermediate location between shipment origin and destination. In a typical mixing operation, carloads or truckloads of products are shipped from origin to mixing facilities. These inbound shipments are planned to minimize inbound transportation cost. Upon arrival at the mixing warehouse, shipments are unloaded and sorted into the combination desired by each customer. In-transit mixing has been traditionally supported by special transportation rates that provide financial incentives to facilitate the process.[1] During the mixing process, inbound products can be combined with others regularly stocked at a warehouse. Warehouses that perform mixing have the net effect of reducing overall product storage in a logistical system while achieving customer-specific assortments and minimizing transportation cost.

The most common use of **assembly** is to support manufacturing operations. Products and components are assembled from a variety of second-tier suppliers at an assembly facility located in close proximity to the manufacturing plant. While manufacturing organizations have traditionally performed assembly, it has become common to utilize value-added services performed by an **integrated service provider** (ISP) to sort, sequence, and deliver components when needed in manufacturing. Like cross-docking and mixing, assembly creates a precise grouping of inventory at a precise time and location. Automotive companies have been very successful at encouraging tier one suppliers to locate in close proximity to assembly plants. For example, at Honda's Marysville, Ohio, assembly plant, a tier one supplier provides preassembled tire-wheel units direct to the auto plant for attachment to cars on the assembly line. Based on production assembly schedules, the tier one supplier preassembles the wheel and tire to match the color of the car, installs appropriate aspects of the brake assembly, and completes all quality inspection. At the appropriate time, an inflated tire-wheel unit is transported via conveyor from an adjacent building for arrival at the final assembly line for attachment to the auto. Figure 9.2 illustrates three sorting arrangements.

[1] See Chapter 8.

228   **Part Two**   Supply Chain Logistics Operations

FIGURE 9.2
Sorting Arrangements

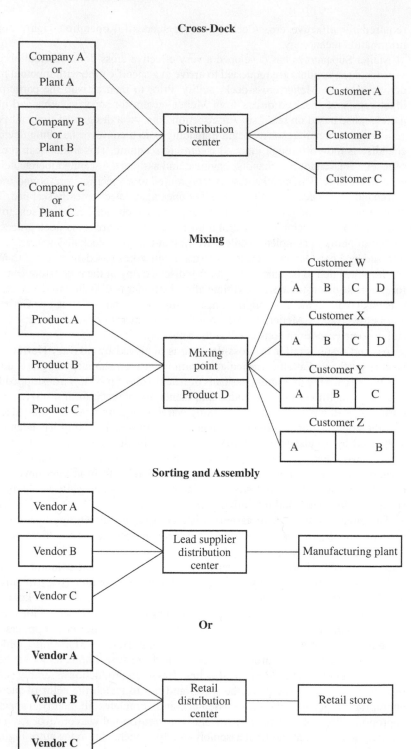

Seasonal Storage

The economic benefit of seasonal storage is to accommodate either seasonal production or demand. For example, lawn furniture and toys are typically produced year-round but are sold primarily during a very short marketing period. In contrast, agricultural products are harvested at specific times, with distribution and consumption occurring throughout the year. Both situations require inventory storage to support marketing efforts. Storage provides an inventory buffer, which allows production efficiencies within the constraints imposed by material sources and consumers.

Reverse Logistics Processing

A great deal of the physical work related to reverse logistics is performed at warehouses. Reverse logistics includes the activities to support: (1) returns management, (2) remanufacturing and repair, (3) remarketing, (4) recycling, and (5) disposal. Returns management is designed to facilitate the reverse flow of product that did not sell or to accommodate recalls. Remanufacturing and repair facilitates the reverse flow of product following its initial use for revitalization. Refurbished product can be reused or sold as appropriate. The product itself or components are then updated for sale at a discounted price. Many computer and electronics manufacturers use remanufacturing to enhance their profits after initial leases are over. Remarketers use coordination and reverse flow to position and resell product when the original user no longer needs it. The Defense Logistics Agency has a comprehensive remarketing process to facilitate transfer and sale of used equipment to other military services or governmental agencies. Recycling involves returning product following its useful life with the objective of decomposing it to its component materials so that they can be effectively reused. Metals, plastics, and precious commodities are often the focus of recycling activities. When material cannot be effectively reused, it still may require reverse logistics for appropriate disposal.

Controlled inventory consists of hazardous materials and product recalls that have potential consumer health or environmental considerations. The reclamation of controlled inventory must be performed under strict operating scrutiny that prevents improper disposal. As one might expect, varied governmental agencies, such as the Consumer Product Safety Commission **(CPS),** Department of Transportation **(DOT),** the Environmental Protection Agency **(EPA),** Food and Drug Administration **(FDA),** and the Occupational Safety and Health Administration **(OSHA),** are directly involved in disposal of controlled inventory.

Less attention has traditionally focused on reclamation of regular or non-controlled inventory. The product involved in regular inventory reclamation is typically damaged, worn out or aged beyond the recommended sell-by date. However, the merchandise involved may represent overstock inventory that can be marketed. While some unsalable product results from warehouse damage, most is returned from retail inventory or direct from consumers.

While reclamation is difficult for regular inventory, it is far more challenging for controlled inventory. In return situations, product flow lacks the orderly process characteristic of outbound movement. Reverse movement typically consists of nonuniform package sizes and varied master cartons as contrasted to outbound movement of cases and pallets. In reverse logistics packages are often broken, and product may not be packaged correctly. Return products typically require significant manual sortation and inspection to determine appropriate disposal. However, the opportunity to recover cost by reimbursement and recycling is significant. Because of the growing importance of reverse logistics some integrated service providers have developed lucrative businesses by specializing in related services.

Service Benefits

Warehouses can provide services that enhance top-line revenue growth. When a warehouse is primarily justified on service, the supporting rationale is that profits from sales improvements will more than offset added cost. It is a difficult assignment to quantify service return-on-investment because it's hard to measure. For example, establishing a warehouse to service a specific market may increase cost but should also increase market sales, revenue, and potentially gross margin. Warehouses can improve service in three ways: (1) spot-stocking, (2) full-line stocking, and (3) value-added services.

Spot-Stocking

Spot-stocking is typically used to support customer requirements. Manufacturers of highly seasonal products often spot-stock. Instead of maintaining inventory in a warehouse year-round, or shipping to customers direct from manufacturing plants, responsiveness in peak selling periods can be enhanced through temporary inventory positioning in strategic markets. Under this concept, select inventory is positioned or **spot-stocked** in a local market warehouse in anticipation of responding to customer need during the critical sales period. Utilizing warehouse facilities for spot-stocking allows inventories to be placed in a variety of markets adjacent to key customers just prior to a period of high seasonal sales. For example, agricultural fertilizer companies sometimes spot-stock near farmers in anticipation of the growing season. After the growing season, such spot-stocking would likely be reduced or eliminated.

Full-Line Stocking

The traditional use of warehouses by manufacturers, wholesalers, and retailers is to stock product inventory combinations in anticipation of customer orders. Typical retailers and wholesalers provide inventory assortments of multiple products from different manufacturers. In effect, these warehouses provide one-stop shopping capability for goods from multiple manufacturers.

The difference between spot-stocking and full-line stocking is the degree and duration of warehouse utilization. A firm following a spot-stocking strategy would temporarily warehouse a narrow product assortment in a large number of warehouses for a limited time period. The full-line stocking warehouse is more often restricted to a few strategic locations and operates year-round. Full-line stocking warehouses improve service by reducing the number of suppliers that a customer must logistically deal with. The combined assortments also make economical larger shipments possible.

Value-Added Services

The demand for highly customized service has transformed modern distribution warehouses into facilities that specialize in performing **value-added services (VAS).** A value-added service is any work that creates a greater value for customers. Value-added services typically change the physical features or configuration of products so they are presented to customers in a unique or customized manner. Table 9.1 provides a list of typical value-added services.

Warehouses can postpone final product configuration by completing packaging, labeling, and even light manufacturing. For example, vegetables can be processed and canned in **brights** at the processing plants. Brights are cans without labels. Holding inventory as brights means that product is not committed to specific customers or carton configuration

• Cross-dock/transloading	• Order fulfillment
• Customer returns	• Pick/pack
• Home delivery	• Pool distribution
• In-transit merge	• Repair/refurbish
• Kan Ban	• Returnable container management
• Kitting	• Reverse logistics
• Labeling/preticketing	• RFID tag application
• Lot control	• Sequencing/metering
• Mass customization/postponement	• Specialty packaging
• Manufacturing support	• Store support/direct store delivery (DSD)

TABLE 9.1
Value-Added Services

during initial manufacturing or processing. Once a specific customer order is received, the warehouse can complete labeling and finalize packaging. Examples of postponement range from packaging pharmaceuticals at Bristol Meyers Squibb to customizing appliances at Whirlpool.

Postponement provides two economic benefits. First, risk is minimized because customized packaging is not performed in anticipation of customer orders or to accommodate a forecast. Second, total inventory can be reduced by using inventory of the base product to aggregate demand across multiple customers' requirements. The combination of reduced risk and lower inventory can result in reduced total cost to service even if packaging performed at the warehouse is more expensive per unit than if it were completed during manufacturing.[2]

Warehouse Operations

Once the scope of a given warehouse is determined, managerial attention focuses on establishing the operation. A typical warehouse contains materials, parts, and finished goods inventory. Warehouse operations consist of handling and storage. The objective is to efficiently receive inventory, store it as required, assemble it into unique orders, and make customer shipment. This emphasis on continuous product flow requires a modern warehouse be viewed as a product mixing facility. As such, a great deal of managerial attention concerns how to design the facility to accomplish efficient handling.

Handling

A first consideration is movement continuity and efficiency throughout the warehouse. Movement continuity means that it is better for an employee using handling equipment to perform longer moves than to undertake a number of short handlings to accomplish the same overall inventory move. Exchanging products between handlers or moving goods from one piece of equipment to another wastes time and increases the potential for product damage. Thus, as a general rule, longer warehouse handling movements are preferred. Ideally, goods, once in motion, should be continuously moved until arrival at their final destination.

Scale economies justify moving the largest quantities or loads possible. Instead of moving individual cases, handling procedures should be designed to move cases grouped on pallets, slipsheets, or containers. The overall objective of handling is to eventually sort inbound shipments into unique customer assortments. The three primary handling activities are receiving, in-storage handling or transfer, and shipping.

[2]For an expanded discussion of postponement strategies see Chapter 1.

Receiving

The majority of products and materials arrive at warehouses in large-quantity truck shipments. The first handling activity is unloading. At most warehouses, unloading is performed using a combination of a lift truck, conveyors, and manual processes. When freight is floor stacked in the transportation vehicle, the typical procedure is to group products into unit loads using pallets. In some situations products are placed on conveyors to facilitate receiving. When inbound product arrives unitized on pallets or in containers, lift trucks are used to move products from the vehicle to the dock. A primary benefit of receiving unitized loads is the ability to rapidly unload and release inbound transportation equipment.

In-Storage Handling

In-storage handling consists of inventory movements performed within the warehouse. Following receipt and movement to an initial staging location, product is often moved within the facility for storage or order selection. Finally, when an order is processed it is necessary to select the required products and move them to a shipping area. These two types of in-storage handling are typically referred to as **transfer** and **selection.**

There are at least two and sometimes three transfer movements in a typical warehouse. The merchandise is initially moved from the receiving area to a remote storage location. This movement is typically achieved using a lift truck when pallets or slipsheets are used or by other mechanical means for other types of unit loads. A second internal movement may be required prior to order assembly, depending upon warehouse operating procedures. When unit loads have to be broken down for order selection, they are usually transferred from storage to an order selection or picking area. When products are large or bulky, such as appliances, this intermediate movement to a picking area may not be necessary. Such product is often selected from the storage area and moved directly to the outbound shipment staging area. The staging area is typically adjacent to the shipping dock. In order selection warehouses, the assembled customer order is transferred from the selection area to the shipping staging area. Characteristically, in-storage handling involves lower volume movements than receiving.

Order selection is one of the major handling activities within warehouses. The selection process requires that materials, parts, and products be grouped to facilitate order assembly. It is typical for one area of a warehouse to be designated as a selection or picking area to assemble orders. For each order, the combination of products must be selected and packaged to meet specific customer order requirements.

An emerging technology, radio-frequency identificator **(RFID)** holds substantial promise in the area of warehouse layout, receiving, order selection, and shipping. Because of the large number of different products processed and handled in a typical distribution center, RFID technology has great potential to improve operational efficiency. The deployment of RFID technology in warehouse design and material handling is discussed in Chapter 10.

Shipping

Shipping consists of order verification and outbound transportation equipment loading. As in receiving, firms may use conveyors or unit load handling equipment such as lift trucks to move products from the staging area into the outbound truck trailer or container. In comparison to receiving, warehouse shipping must accommodate relatively low-volume movements of a mixture of products, thus reducing the potential for economies of scale. Shipping unit loads is becoming increasingly popular because considerable time can be saved in vehicle loading. A unit load consists of unitized or palletized product. To facilitate this loading and subsequent unloading upon delivery, many customers are requesting that suppliers provide mixed combinations of product within a trailer or on a pallet. The alternative is to floor-stack cases in the transportation vehicle. Shipment content verification is typically required when product changes ownership. Verification may be limited to a simple carton count or a piece-by-piece check for proper brand, size, and in some cases serial number to assure shipment accuracy. Over-the-road trailers are typically sealed at the time they are fully loaded and ready for shipment. The seal serves to verify that the content has not been altered during transit. Certification that seals have not been tampered with has become a critical factor in post 9/11 security.[3]

Storage

In planning warehouse layout, it is essential that products be assigned specific locations, called **slots,** on the basis of individual characteristics. The most important product variables to consider in a slotting plan are product velocity, weight, and special storage requirements.

Product velocity is the major factor driving warehouse layout. High-volume product should be positioned in the warehouse to minimize movement distance. For example, high-velocity products should be positioned near doors, primary aisles, and at lower levels in storage racks. Such positioning minimizes warehouse handling and reduces the need for frequent lifting. Conversely, products with low volume are typically assigned locations more distant from primary aisles or higher up in storage racks. Figure 9.3 illustrates a storage plan based on product movement velocity.

Similarly, the storage plan should take into consideration product weight and special characteristics. Relatively heavy items should be assigned storage locations low to the ground to minimize lifting. Bulky or low-density product requires cubic space. Floor space along outside walls is ideal for such items. On the other hand, smaller items may require storage shelves, bins, or drawers. The integrated storage plan must consider individual product characteristics.

[3]See Chapter 16.

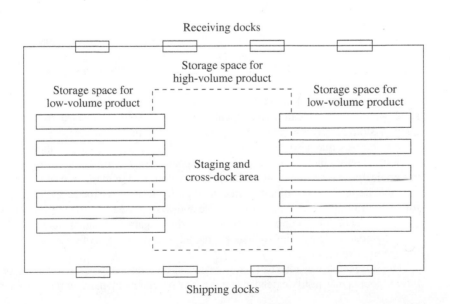

FIGURE 9.3
Storage Plan Based on Product Movement Velocity

A typical warehouse is engaged in a combination of **active** and **extended** product storage alternatives. Warehouses that directly serve customers typically focus on active short-term storage. In contrast, other warehouses may use extended storage for speculative, seasonal, or obsolete inventory. In controlling and measuring warehouse operations, it is important to differentiate the relative requirements and performance capabilities of active and extended storage.

Active Storage

Regardless of inventory velocity, most goods must be stored for at least a short time. Storage for basic inventory replenishment is referred to as active storage. Active storage must provide sufficient inventory to meet the forecasted demand of the service area. The need for active storage is usually related to the capability to achieve transportation or handling economies of scale. For active storage, handling processes and technologies need to focus on quick movement and flexibility with minimal consideration for extended and dense storage.

The active storage concept includes **flow-through** or **cross-dock distribution,** which uses warehouses for consolidation and assortment while maintaining minimal or no inventory in storage. The resulting need for reduced inventory favors flow-through and cross-docking techniques that emphasize movement and de-emphasize storage. Flow-through distribution is most appropriate for high-volume, fast-moving products where quantities are reasonably predictable. While flow-through distribution places minimal demands on storage requirements, it does require that product be quickly unloaded, de-unitized, grouped and sequenced into customer assortments, and reloaded into transportation equipment. As a result, the handling emphasis is on accurate information-directed quick movement.

Extended Storage

When inventory is held for a longer time than required for normal replenishment of customer stocks, it is referred to as **extended storage.** In some special situations, storage may be required for several months prior to customer shipment. Extended storage uses handling processes and technologies that focus on maximum space utilization with minimal need for quick access.

A warehouse may be used for extended storage for a variety of reasons. Some products, such as seasonal items, require storage to await demand or to spread supply across time. Other reasons for extended storage include erratic demand items, product conditioning, speculative purchases, and discounts.

Product conditioning sometimes requires extended storage, such as to ripen bananas. Food warehouses typically have ripening rooms to hold products until they reach peak quality. Storage may also be necessary for extended quality checks.

Warehouses may also retain products for an extended basis when they are purchased on a speculative basis. The magnitude of speculative buying depends upon the specific materials and industries involved, but it is very common in marketing of commodities and seasonal items. For example, if a price increase for an item is expected, it is not uncommon for a firm to buy ahead at the current price and warehouse the product for later use. In this case, the discount or savings have to be traded off against extended storage and inventory carrying cost. Commodities such as grains, oil, and lumber are often purchased and stored for speculative reasons.

The warehouse may also be used to realize special discounts. Early purchase or forward-buy discounts may justify extended storage. The procurement manager may be able to realize a substantial price reduction during a specific time of the year. Under such conditions the warehouse is expected to hold inventory in excess of active storage. Manufacturers of fertilizer, toys, and lawn furniture often attempt to shift the warehousing burden to customers by offering off-season warehouse storage allowances.

Warehouse Ownership Arrangements

Warehouses can also be classified based on ownership. A **private** warehouse is operated by the enterprise that owns the merchandise handled and stored in the facility. A **public** warehouse, in contrast, is operated as an independent business offering a range of for-hire services, such as storage, handling, and transportation. Public warehouse operators generally offer a menu of relatively standardized services to customers. **Contract warehousing,** which is a customized extension of public warehousing, combines the benefits of private and public warehousing. Contract warehousing is a long-term business arrangement that provides unique or tailored logistics services for a limited number of customers. The client and the warehouse provider typically share the risks associated with the operation. The important differences between contract and public warehouse operators are the anticipated length of the relationship, degree of exclusive or customized services, and shared incorporation of benefits and risks.

Private

A private warehouse is typically operated by the firm owning the product. The building, however, may be owned or leased. The decision concerning ownership or lease is primarily based on financial considerations. Sometimes it is not possible to find a warehouse for lease that fits specialized logistical requirements; for example, the physical nature of an available building may not be conducive for efficient handling, such as buildings with inappropriate storage racks or with shipping/receiving dock or support column constraints. The only suitable course of action may then be to design and arrange for new construction.

The major benefits of private warehousing are control, flexibility, cost, and a range of intangibles. Private warehouses offer substantial control since management has authority to prioritize activities. Such control should facilitate integration of warehouse operations with the balance of a firm's logistics operations.

Private warehouses generally offer more flexibility since operating policies, hours, and procedures can be adjusted to meet specific customer and product requirements. Firms with very specialized customers or products are often motivated to own and operate warehouses.

Private warehousing is usually considered less costly than public warehousing because private facilities are not operated for a profit. As a result, both the fixed and variable cost components of a private warehouse may be lower than for-hire counterparts.

Finally, private warehousing may offer intangible benefits. A private warehouse, with the firm's name on its sign, may stimulate customer perceptions of responsiveness and stability. This perception may provide marketing image in comparison to competitors.

Despite the noted benefits, the use of private warehousing is declining because of an increasing managerial interest in reducing capital invested in logistical assets. Also, the perceived cost benefit of private warehousing is potentially offset by a public warehouse's ability to gain operational economies of scale and scope as a result of the combined throughput of multiple clients.

Public

Public warehouses are used extensively in logistical systems. Almost any combination of services can be arranged on a for-hire basis for either short or long term. Public warehouses have traditionally been classified based on operational specialization such as (1) general merchandise, (2) refrigerated, (3) special commodity, (4) bonded, and (5) household goods and furniture.

General merchandise warehouses are designed to handle package products such as electronics, paper, food, small appliances, and household supplies. Refrigerated warehouses typically offer frozen or cooler capacity designed to protect food, medical, photographic, and chemical products requiring temperature control. Special commodity warehouses are designed to handle bulk material or items requiring special handling, such as tires or clothing. Bonded warehouses are licensed by the government to store goods prior to payment of taxes or import/export duties. They exert tight control over movements in and out of the facility, since documents must accompany each move. Finally, household goods or furniture warehouses specialize in handling and storing large, bulky items such as appliances and furniture. Of course, many public warehouses offer a combination of services. Public warehouses provide flexibility and shared services benefits. They have the potential to offer operating and management expertise since warehousing is their core business.

From a financial perspective, public warehousing may be able to achieve lower operating cost than private facilities. Such variable cost differential may result from lower wage scales, better productivity, and shared overhead among clients. Public warehouses typically do not require capital investment on the part of their customers. When management performance is judged according to return on investment, the use of public warehousing can be an attractive alternative. Public warehousing offers flexibility concerning size and number of warehouses, thus allowing users to respond to supplier, customer, and seasonal demands. In comparison, private warehouses are relatively fixed and difficult to change because buildings have to be constructed, expanded as necessary and sold when no longer required.

Public warehousing also have the potential to share scale economies since the combined requirements of users can be leveraged. Such leverage spreads fixed costs and may justify investment in state-of-the-art handling equipment. A public warehouse may also leverage transportation by providing consolidation of multiple-client freight. For example, rather than require both supplier A and supplier B to deliver to a retail store from their own warehouses, a public warehouse serving both clients could arrange combined delivery, thus providing reduced transportation cost for the customer.

A great many firms utilize public warehouses for customer accommodation because of the variable cost, scalability, range of services, and flexibility. A public warehouse charges clients a basic fee for in and out handling plus storage. In the case of handling, the charge is assessed on the cases or pounds moved. For storage, the charge is assessed on the cases or weight in storage over time. Special or value-added services provided by public warehouses are typically priced on a negotiated basis.

Contract

Contract warehousing combines characteristics of private and public operations. A long-term contractual relationship will typically result in lower total cost than a public warehouse. In fact many contract warehouse providers have extensive real estate investments. One integrated service provider (ISP) may own and operate facilities in multiple key manufacturing or distribution locations. Thus, one provider may be able to meet a customer's requirements in a combination of markets. At the same time, contract warehouse operations can provide benefits of expertise, flexibility, scalability, and economies of scale by sharing management, labor, equipment, and information resources across multiple clients.

Contract warehouses typically offer a range of logistical services such as transportation management, inventory control, order processing, customer service, and return merchandise processing. Contract logistics firms, typically called **integrated service providers (ISPs)**, are capable of performing the total logistics responsibility for an enterprise.

For example, Kraft Foods has increasingly utilized contract warehousing as a replacement for private and public frozen and dry grocery facilities. Since the late 1990s, Kraft has used AmeriCold Logistics, an integrated warehousing and distribution services company, to perform storage, handling, and distribution services. The arrangement has multiple benefits for both parties. The long-term contractual arrangement allows Kraft to expand its distribution network without incurring the time or cost of building expansion. Kraft is assured that there will always be space for new products, so its distribution network is protected. AmeriCold doesn't have to be concerned with selling space to Kraft. Moreover, the longer Kraft utilizes AmeriCold's services, the better the contract warehousing firm's capability to understand business needs and provide customized services.

Network Deployment

As would be expected, many firms utilize a combination of private, public, and contract facilities. Full warehouse utilization throughout a year is rare. As a managerial guideline, a typical warehouse will be fully utilized between 75 and 85 percent of the time; so from 15 to 25 percent of the time, space needed to satisfy peak requirements will not be used. In such situations, a deployment strategy may be the use of private or contract warehouses to cover the 75 percent requirement while public facilities are used to accommodate peak demand.

Developing a warehouse network strategy requires answers to two key questions. The first is how many warehouses are required. The second question focuses on which warehouse ownership types should be used in specific markets. For many firms, the answer is a combination of warehouse alternatives, differentiated by customer and product. Specifically, some customer groups may be served best from a private warehouse, while public or contract warehouses may be appropriate for others. This warehouse segmentation is increasingly popular as key customers are requiring more customized value-added services and capabilities.

Warehouse Decisions

The basic concept that warehouses provide an enclosure for material storage and handling requires detailed analysis before the size, type, and shape of the facility can be determined. This section reviews planning issues that establish the character of the warehouse, which in turn determines attainable handling efficiency.

Site Selection

The first task is to identify both the general area and then the specific warehouse location. The general area concerns the broad geography where an active warehouse makes sense from a service, economic, and strategic perspective. The general question focuses on the broader geographic area as illustrated by the need to place a warehouse in the Midwest, which generally implies having a facility in Illinois, Indiana, or Wisconsin. In contrast, a retailer such as Target or Home Depot typically selects a warehouse location that is central to a prerequisite number of retail store locations. Thus, the selection and number of retail outlets drive the support warehouse location. Network design is discussed in Chapter 12.

Once the general warehouse location is determined, a specific building site must be identified. Typical areas in a community for locating warehouses are commercial developments and outlying or suburban areas. The factors driving site selection are service availability and cost. Land cost is an important factor. A warehouse need not be located in a major industrial area. In many cities, warehouses are among industrial plants and in areas zoned for light or heavy industry. Most warehouses can operate legally under the restrictions placed upon general commercial property.

Beyond procurement cost, setup, and operating expenses such as transport access, utility hookups, taxes, and insurance rates require evaluation. The cost of essential services may vary extensively between sites. For example, a food-distribution firm recently rejected what otherwise appeared to be a totally satisfactory warehouse site because of projected insurance rates. The site was located near the end of a water main. During most of the day, adequate water pressure was available to handle operational and emergency requirements. However, a water problem was possible during two short periods each day. From 6:30 A.M. to 8:30 A.M. and from 5:00 P.M. to 7:00 P.M. the overall demand for water along the line was so great that a sufficient pressure was not available to handle emergencies. Because of this deficiency, abnormally high insurance rates were required and the site was rejected.

Several other requirements must be satisfied before a site is purchased. The site must offer adequate room for expansion. Necessary utilities must be available. The soil must be capable of supporting the structure. The site must be sufficiently high to afford proper water drainage. Additional requirements may be situationally necessary, depending upon the structure to be constructed. For these reasons and others, the final selection of the site should be preceded by extensive analysis.

Design

Warehouse design must consider product movement characteristics. Three factors to be determined during the design process are the number of floors to include in the facility, a cube utilization plan, and product flow.

The ideal warehouse design is a one-floor building that eliminates the need to move product vertically. The use of vertical handling devices, such as elevators and conveyors, to move product from one floor to the next requires time and energy, and typically creates handling bottlenecks. So, while it is not always possible, particularly in business districts where land is restricted or expensive, as a general rule distribution warehouses should be designed as one-floor operations to facilitate handling.

Warehouse design must maximize cubic utilization. Most warehouses are designed with 25- to 30-foot clear ceilings, although selected automated and high-rise handling equipment can effectively use heights over 100 feet. Maximum effective warehouse height is limited by the safe lifting capabilities of handling equipment, such as lift trucks, rack design, and fire safety regulations imposed by sprinkler systems.

Warehouse design should facilitate continuous straight product flow through the building. This is true whether the product is moving into storage or is being cross-docked. In general, this means that product should be received at one end of a building, stored as necessary in the middle, and shipped from the other end. Figure 9.4 illustrates straight-line product flow that facilitates velocity while minimizing congestion and redundant handling.

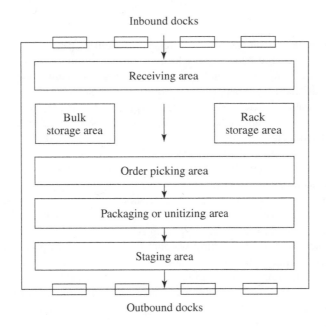

Inbound docks

Outbound docks

FIGURE 9.4
Basic Warehouse
Design

Product-Mix Analysis

An important area is the analysis of products that will be distributed through the warehouse. The design and operation of a warehouse are both dependent on the product mix. Each product should be analyzed in terms of annual demand, weight, cube, and packaging. It is also important to determine the total size, cube, and weight of the average order to be processed through the warehouse. These data provide necessary information for determining warehouse space, design and layout, handling equipment, operating procedures, and controls.

Expansion

Because warehouses are increasingly important in supply chain networks, their future expansion should be considered during the initial planning phase. It is common to establish 5- to 10-year expansion plans. Potential expansion may justify purchase or option of a site three to five times larger than required to support initial construction.

Building design should also accommodate future expansion. Some walls may be constructed of semipermanent materials to allow quick removal. Floor areas, designed to support heavy movements, can be extended during initial construction to facilitate expansion.

Handling

A handling system is the basic driver of warehouse design. As noted previously, product movement and assortment are the main functions of a warehouse. Consequently, the warehouse is appropriately viewed as a structure designed to facilitate efficient product flow. It is important to stress that the handling system must be selected early in the warehouse development process. Handling equipment and technology are discussed in Chapter 10.

Layout

The layout or storage areas of a warehouse should be planned to facilitate product flow. The layout and the handling system are integral. In addition, special attention must be given to location, number, and design of receiving and loading docks.

It is difficult to generalize warehouse layouts since they are usually customized to accommodate specific product handling requirements. If pallets are utilized, an early step is to determine the appropriate size. A pallet of nonstandard size may be desirable for specialized products. The most common pallet sizes are 40 × 48 inches and 32 × 40 inches. In general, the larger the pallet load, the lower the movement cost per pound or package over a given distance. One lift truck operator can move a large load in the same time and with the same effort required to move a smaller load. Analysis of product cases, stacking patterns, and industry practices will determine the size of pallet best suited to the operation. Regardless of the size finally selected, management should adopt one pallet size for use throughout the warehouse.

The second step in planning warehouse layout involves pallet positioning. The most common practice in positioning pallets is at 90 degree, or square, placement to the aisle. Square positioning is widely used because of layout ease. Square placement means that the pallet is positioned perpendicular to the aisle. The placement of specific products in selected pallet locations is called **slotting.** Naturally, key to an efficient layout is a well-developed slotting plan.

Finally, the handling equipment must be integrated to finalize layout. The path and tempo of product flow depend upon the handling system. To illustrate the relationship between handling and layout, two systems and their respective layouts are illustrated in Figure 9.5. These examples represent two of many possible layouts.

Layout A illustrates a handling system and layout utilizing lift trucks for inbound and inventory transfer movements. Tow tractors and inventory collection trailers are used for

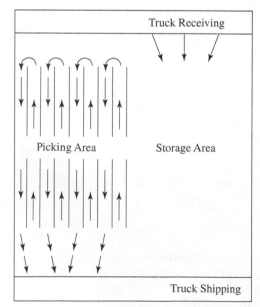

Layout A.

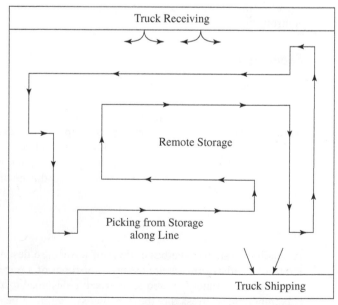

Layout B.

FIGURE 9.5   Layouts A and B

order selection. This scenario assumes that products can be palletized. This layout is greatly simplified because offices, special areas, and other details are omitted.

The floor plan of layout A is approximately square. The advocates of square design feel that it provides the best framework for overall operating efficiency. As indicated earlier in this chapter, products should be positioned in a specific area of the warehouse for order selection. Such is the case in layout A. This area is labeled the **selection,** or **picking, area.** Its primary purpose is to minimize the distance order pickers must travel when assembling an order.

The selection area is supported by a **storage area.** When products are received they are palletized and moved to the storage area. The selection area is replenished from storage as required. Within the selection area, products are positioned according to weight, bulk, and replenishment velocity to minimize outbound movement. Customer orders are assembled by an order selector using a tow tractor pulling trailers through the selection area. The arrows in layout A indicate product selection flow.

Layout B illustrates a handling system utilizing lift trucks to move product inbound and for transfer movements. A continuous towline is used for order selection. The floor plan in layout B is rectangular. In a system using a continuous-movement towline, the compact selection area is replaced by order selection directly from storage. Products are moved from receiving areas into storage positions adjacent to the towline. The orders are then selected directly from storage and placed on carts, which are pulled around the warehouse by the towline. Merchandise is stored or positioned to minimize internal movement. The weakness of the fixed towline is that it facilitates selection of all products at an equal speed and frequency. The arrows in layout B indicate major product movements. The line in the center of the layout illustrates the path of the towline.

As indicated, both layouts A and B are greatly simplified. The purpose is to illustrate the extremely different approaches managers have developed to reconcile the relationship between handling and warehouse layout.

Sizing

Several techniques are available to help estimate warehouse size. Each method begins with a projection of the total volume expected to move through the warehouse during a given period. The projection is used to estimate base and safety stocks for each product to be stocked in the warehouse. Some techniques consider both normal and peak inventory. Failure to consider utilization rates can result in overbuilding. It is important to note, however, that a major complaint of warehouse managers is underestimation of warehouse size requirements. A good rule of thumb is to allow for 10 percent additional space to account for increased volume, new products, and new business opportunities.

Warehouse Management Systems (WMS)

The development of work procedures goes hand in hand with training warehouse personnel. Most firms depend upon a warehouse management system **(WMS)** to standardize work procedures and facilitate best practice.

One of the main uses of a WMS is to coordinate order selection. Two basic methods of order selection are **discrete selection** and **wave selection,** also known as **batch selection.** In discrete selection, a specific customer's order is selected and prepared for shipment as the work assignment. Discrete order selection is often used when order content and handling selection are critical.

Wave selection can be designed and operationalized in a variety of ways. A wave can be coordinated by an area of the warehouse wherein all quantities of all products required to complete all customer orders are selected at one time. Using this type of wave selection, employees are typically assigned responsibility for a specific portion of the warehouse. Waves can also be planned around a specific shipment destination and/or carrier, for example, all UPS shipments to the East Coast. Because each employee has a thorough knowledge of a specific warehouse selection area or shipping procedure, fewer selection errors typically result using wave picking.

WMS also coordinates work procedures that are important for receiving and shipping. Established procedures for receiving and ensuring product entry into inventory records are critical. If pallets are used, the merchandise must be stacked in appropriate patterns to ensure maximum load stability and consistent case counts. Personnel working in shipping must have knowledge of trailer loading practices. In specific types of operations, particularly when merchandise changes ownership, items must be checked during loading.

Work procedures are not restricted to floor personnel. Procedures must be established for administration and maintenance. Replenishment of warehouse inventory can cause operational problems if proper ordering procedures are lacking. Normally, there is limited interaction between buyers and warehouse personnel, although such communication is improving within integrated supply chain management organizations. Buyers tend to purchase in quantities that afford the best price with little attention given to pallet compatible quantities or available warehouse space.

Ideally buyers should coordinate with warehouse personnel before commissioning large orders or introducing new products. The experience of some companies has forced management to require buyers to predetermine warehouse space assignment prior to ordering. Another potential problem is the quantity of cases ordered. The goal is to purchase in pallet-multiple quantities. For example, if a product is ideally stacked on pallets in a 50-case pattern, the buyer should order in multiples of 50. If an order is placed for 120 cases, upon arrival the cases will fill two pallets plus 20 on a third pallet. The extra 20 cases will require the warehouse cubic space typically used for a pallet of 50 and will require the same amount of handling capacity to move.

Figure 9.6 illustrates a range of activities coordinated by a typical WMS. Historical warehouse system functionality focused on receiving replenishment shipments, stock putaway, and order picking. Traditional activities are listed under **basic functionality.** Warehouses today must offer a broader range of services as they are frequently performing value-added services. They are also required to manage more inventory on a just-in-time basis. The figure illustrates typical **advanced functionality** activities. Yard management, sometimes a functionality of a firm's transportation management system **(TMS),** refers to the process of managing the vehicles and the inventory within vehicles while in the warehouse yard. Faster inventory turnover requires better visibility of inventory, even when in transportation vehicles. Labor management refers to maximizing the use of warehouse labor. Historically, warehouse labor has been quite specialized, allowing for relatively easy planning. Warehouse optimization refers to selection of the best location within the warehouse for the storage and retrieval of product to minimize time and movement. **Value-added services** refer to the coordination of warehouse activities to customize product, such as packaging, labeling, kitting, and setting up displays.

Planned cross-docking and merging is the integration of two or more parts of a customer order that have been supplied from a different source without maintaining inventory. This strategy is sometimes used in the personal computer industry to merge a processing unit and the display monitor in a warehouse just prior to delivery to the ultimate customer. Since there is no inventory of either part in the warehouse, the merging activity requires precise timing and coordination.

A final execution function is the capability to manage reverse logistics activities such as returns, repair, and recycling. Both customers and environmental interests are increasing

Chapter 9   Warehousing   **243**

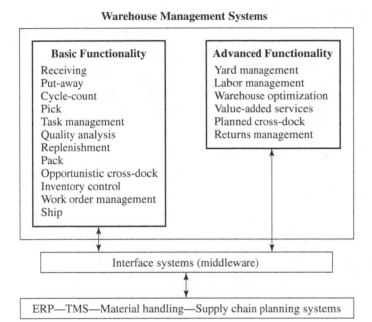

Warehouse Management Systems

Basic Functionality	**Advanced Functionality**
Receiving	Yard management
Put-away	Labor management
Cycle-count	Warehouse optimization
Pick	Value-added services
Task management	Planned cross-dock
Quality analysis	Returns management
Replenishment	
Pack	
Opportunistic cross-dock	
Inventory control	
Work order management	
Ship	

Interface systems (middleware)

ERP—TMS—Material handling—Supply chain planning systems

FIGURE 9.6
Warehouse
Management System
Functionality

Selected Functionality	Decision Support Benefits
Put-away	Improved productivity and cube utilization.
Task interleaving	Routing of fork trucks on demand as contrasted to predetermined assigned tasks, areas, or sequences.
Pick/replenishment	Direct picking from single or multiple locations including pick to assure expiration date compliance. Facilitates replenishment of pick location inventories when appropriate.
Slotting	Variable slot or product placement locator assignment to enhance space utilization.
Cross-docking	Facilitate direct receipt to shipment flow.
Inventory visibility	Tracking specific inventory lots by warehouse location as well as daily visibility of receipts. Date-specific lot control.
Work queue resolution	Identification of alternative ways to rapidly or efficiently resolve work constraints or queues.
Picking strategy	Routines to perform selected picking strategies.
Error correction	Ability to identify, resolve, and correct data errors in real time.
	Ability to identify and resolve differences in purchase orders or advanced shipment notifications (ASN) and actual quantities or product received.
Simulations	Performance of real-time decision support scenarios to assist in operational decision making.
Return goods	Facilitate processing and audit compliance for reverse logistics programs.
Cycle counts	Ability to conduct and resolve real-time inventory counts.

TABLE 9.2
WMS Functionality and
Decision Support

their demands that supply chains can accommodate reverse logistics. Table 9.2 summarizes WMS functionality and decision support benefits.

Yard Management Systems (YMS)

An important part of warehouse-related information technology is the yard management system **(YMS).** The YMS in essence couples the warehouse with inbound and outbound transportation equipment. This coordination takes the form of arranging dock appointments for receiving ordered merchandise and transportation equipment for shipping outbound. From a performance perspective, the YMS is the scheduler. For high-level transportation and warehousing efficiency, it is essential to appropriately sequence inbound and outbound warehouse activity. It is also important to maintain an accurate accountability of what merchandise and transportation equipment is in the warehouse or factory yard. Many stories exist to illustrate the dilemma of expediting an inbound product shipment due from a supplier only to have it arrive on time as scheduled and be dispatched to the warehouse yard due to no dock availability. An appropriate way to view the YMS is as the software that links and coordinates transportation **(TMS)** with the warehouse **(WMS).**

Accuracy and Audits

WMS functionality requires verification of inventory accuracy to maintain operational effectiveness. Inventory accuracy is typically maintained by annual physical inventory counts or by counting specific portions of the inventory on a planned basis. **Cycle counting** is the audit of selected inventory on a cyclic schedule. Selection of individual items to be counted and verified can be based on the dollar value of the items, storage location, frequency of movement, or turnover. Once counted, discrepancies between physical and WMS inventories are reconciled to assure continued system validity.

Audits related to inventory accuracy are only one type of audit that is typically used to maintain and improve warehouse operating efficiency. Audits are also common to maintain safety, assure compliance to security regulations, drive procedural improvement, and facilitate work changes.

Security

In a broad sense, security in a warehouse involves protection against merchandise pilferage, deterioration, and any form of operational disruption. Each form of security requires management attention.

Pilferage

In warehouse operations it is necessary to protect against theft by employees and thieves as well as from riots and terrorist-related disturbances. Typical security procedures should be strictly enforced at each warehouse. Security begins at the fence. As standard procedure, only authorized personnel should be permitted into the facility and on surrounding grounds. Entry to the warehouse yard should be controlled through a single gate. Without exception, no private automobile, regardless of management rank or customer status, should be allowed to enter the yard or park adjacent to the warehouse.

To illustrate the importance of security guidelines, the following experience may be helpful. A firm adopted the rule that no private vehicles would be permitted in the warehouse yard. Exceptions were made for two office employees with special needs. One night after work, one of these employees discovered a bundle taped under one fender of his car. Subsequent checking revealed that the car was literally a loaded delivery truck. The matter was promptly reported to security, who informed the employee not to alter any packages taped to the car and to continue parking inside the yard. Over the next several days, the situation was fully uncovered, with the ultimate arrest and conviction of seven warehouse employees who confessed to stealing thousands of dollars, worth of company merchandise. The firm would have been far better off had it provided transportation for the two special-needs employees from the regular parking lots to their work locations.

Shortages are always a major concern in warehouse operations. Many are honest mistakes that occur during order selection and shipment, but the purpose of security is to eliminate all forms of theft. A majority of thefts occur during normal working hours.

Inventory control and order processing systems help protect merchandise from being carried out of the warehouse unless accompanied by a computer release document. If samples are authorized for salesperson use, such merchandise should be maintained in a separate inventory. Not all pilferage occurs on an individual basis. Organized efforts between warehouse personnel and truck drivers can result in deliberate overpicking or high-for-low-value product substitution in order to move unauthorized merchandise out of the warehouse. Employee work assignment rotation, total case counts, and occasional complete line-item checks can reduce vulnerability to such collaboration.

A final concern is the increased incidence of hijacking over-the-road trailer loads from yards or while in transit. Hijacking is a major logistical concern. Over-the-road hijack prevention is primarily a law-enforcement matter, but in-yard theft can be eliminated by tight security provisions. Such over-the-road theft is a significant problem in developing countries. One beverage company manager reported that he budgeted to lose one truck a week to theft in his South American operation. He instructed his drivers to simply turn over the keys and walk away rather than risk their lives. Procedures and technology related to terrorist-initiated security are discussed in Chapter 16.

Damage

Within the warehouse, a number of factors can reduce a product or material to nonsalable status. The most obvious form of product deterioration is damage from careless handling. For example, when pallets of merchandise are stacked in great heights, a marked change in humidity or temperature can cause packages supporting the stack to collapse. The warehouse environment must be carefully controlled and measured to provide proper product protection. Of major concern is warehouse employee carelessness. In this respect, the lift truck may well be management's worst enemy. Regardless of how often lift truck operators are warned against carrying overloads, some still attempt such shortcuts when not properly supervised. In one situation, a stack of four pallets was dropped off a lift truck at the receiving dock of a food warehouse. Standard procedure was to move two pallets per load. The dollar cost of the damaged merchandise exceeded the average daily profit of two retail supermarkets. Product deterioration from careless handling within the warehouse is a form of loss that cannot be insured against or offset with compensating revenue.

Another major form of deterioration is incompatibility of products stored or transported together. For example, care must be taken when storing or shipping chocolate to make sure that it does not absorb odors from products it is being transported with, such as household chemicals.

Safety and Maintenance

Accident prevention is a concern of warehouse management. A comprehensive safety program requires constant examination of work procedures and equipment to locate and take corrective action to eliminate unsafe conditions before accidents result. Accidents occur when workers become careless or are exposed to mechanical or physical hazards. The floors of a warehouse may cause accidents if not properly cleaned. During normal operation, rubber and glass deposits collect on aisles and, from time to time, broken cases will result in product seepage onto the floor. Proper cleaning procedures can reduce the accident risk of such hazards. Environmental safety has become a major concern of government agencies such as OSHA and cannot be neglected by management.

A preventive maintenance program is necessary for handling equipment. Unlike production machines, movement equipment is not stationary, so it is more difficult to properly maintain. A preventive maintenance program scheduling periodic checks of all handling equipment should be applied in every warehouse.

Summary

Warehousing exists to support marketing, manufacturing and distribution efficiency. While the role of the warehouse has traditionally been to stock inventory, contemporary warehousing involves a broader value proposition in terms of economic and service benefits. Economic benefits include consolidation and break-bulk, sorting, seasonal storage, and reverse logistics. Service benefits include spot-stocking, full-line stocking, and value-added services. The perspective of warehousing is changing from a traditional storage mission to one characterized by customization, velocity, and movement.

Distribution centers and warehouses are designed to accommodate the primary activities of inventory handling and storage. Handling includes receiving inbound shipments; in-storage handling to move between different storage areas, such as long-term, bulk, and picking; and packing and staging shipments to customers. Active storage facilitates cross-docking, consolidation, break-bulk, and postponement. Extended storage activities facilitate balancing supply and demand and speculation.

Warehouses are usually classified on the basis of ownership. A private warehouse is operated by the enterprise that also owns the merchandise in the facility. A public warehouse is operated independently and offers various for-hire value-added services. A contract warehouse is a long-term business arrangement that provides tailored services for a limited number of customers. An integrated warehousing strategy often incorporates a combination of warehouse ownership options.

There are numerous managerial decisions in planning and initiating warehouse operations, including site selection, design, product-mix analysis, expansion, handling, layout, sizing, WMS, accuracy and audits, security, safety, and maintenance. Each of these activities requires considerable managerial effort to ensure facilities start up and run smoothly on a daily basis and are able to accommodate change rapidly and successfully, as necessary to meet current business demands.

Study Questions

1. Discuss and illustrate the economic justification for establishing a warehouse.
2. Why could a warehouse be described as a "necessary evil"?
3. Under what conditions could it make sense to combine private and public warehouses in a logistical system?
4. What role are warehouse operators playing in postponement strategies?
5. Discuss and illustrate the role of warehouses in reverse logistics.
6. Explain the following statement: "A warehouse should merely consist of walls enclosing an efficient handling system."

Challenge Questions

1. What do you consider to be the major benefits of the Meijer cross-dock process? What aspects of the cross-dock are you concerned about? How would you complete a cost–benefit analysis of the cross-dock operation?

2. Assume you are responsible for manufacturing production at Honda Marysville. On a given day, the tier one supplier operating the adjacent tire-wheel assembly operation feeds the incorrect tire-wheel combination to the assembly line, resulting in a blue car having wheels designed for a white car. How would you resolve this problem?

3. Assume you work for a pharmaceutical company and you are faced with an unprecedented nationwide recall. The product in question is not considered a health threat, but the recall has high profile in the public news media. How would you proceed? Be specific concerning your sequence of actions, supporting logic and public relations initiatives.

4. Canadian Tire is one of Canada's largest companies. They operate four large distribution centers which service over 470 tire retail outlets. They recently installed a YMS, which they have integrated with their WMS and TMS systems. Their expectation was improved performance in over-the-road transportation equipment utilization, driver productivity, and warehouse dock/door utilization. As a relatively new logistics employee, you have been asked to develop an evaluation system to measure operational productivity improvement. While management does not want a financial impact evaluation, they are interested in developing benchmarks to measure initial and sustainable productivity improvement. You have the job—how would you proceed?

CHAPTER 7

Inventory

Chapter Outline

Inventory decisions are both high risk and high impact throughout the supply chain. Inventory committed to support future sales drives a number of anticipatory supply chain activities. Without the proper inventory assortment, lost sales and customer dissatisfaction may occur. Likewise, inventory planning is critical to procurement and manufacturing. Material or component shortages can shut down manufacturing or force production schedule modification, added cost, and potential finished goods shortages. Just as shortages can disrupt marketing and manufacturing plans, inventory overstocks also create operating problems. Overstocks increase cost and reduce profitability as a result of added warehousing space, working capital, insurance, taxes, and obsolescence. Management of inventory resources requires an understanding of functionality, principles, cost, impact, and dynamics.

Inventory Functionality and Definitions

Inventory management involves risk which varies depending upon a firm's position in the distribution channel. The typical dimensions of inventory risk relate to time duration, depth, and breadth of commitment.

For a manufacturer, inventory risk is long-term. The manufacturer's inventory commitment begins with raw material and component parts purchase, includes work-in-process, and ends with finished goods. In addition, finished goods are often positioned in warehouses in anticipation of customer demand. In some situations, manufacturers are required to consign inventory to customer facilities. For example, many mass merchants require manufacturers to stock their products on retail store shelves and wait for payment until consumers purchase the products (i.e., consignment inventory). In effect, this practice shifts all inventory risk to the manufacturer. Although a manufacturer typically has a narrower product line than a retailer or wholesaler, the manufacturer's inventory commitment is deep and of long duration.

A wholesaler purchases large quantities from manufacturers and sells smaller quantities to retailers. The economic justification of a wholesaler is the capability to provide customers an assortment of merchandise from different manufacturers in reduced quantities. When products are seasonal, the wholesaler may be required to take an inventory position far in advance of the selling season, thus increasing depth and duration of risk. One of the greatest challenges of wholesaling is product-line expansion to the point where the width of inventory risk approaches that of the retailer while depth and duration of risk remain characteristic of traditional wholesaling. In recent years, powerful retailers have driven a substantial increase in depth and duration by shifting inventory responsibility back to wholesalers.

For a retailer, inventory management is about the velocity of buying and selling. Retailers purchase a wide variety of products and assume substantial risk in the marketing process. Retail inventory risk can be viewed as broad but not deep. Due to the high cost of store location, retailers place prime emphasis on inventory turnover. Inventory turnover is a measure of inventory velocity and is calculated as the ratio of sales for a time period divided by average inventory.

Although retailers assume a position of risk on a wide variety of products, their position on any one product is not deep. Risk is spread across more than 30,000 stockkeeping units (SKUs) in a typical supermarket. A mass retailer offering general merchandise and food often exceeds 50,000 SKUs. Faced with this breadth of inventory, retailers attempt to reduce risk by pressing manufacturers and wholesalers to assume greater and greater inventory responsibility. Pushing inventory back up the channel has resulted in retailer demand for fast delivery of mixed-product shipments from wholesalers and manufacturers. Specialty retailers, in contrast to mass merchandisers, normally experience less width of inventory risk as a result of handling narrower assortments. However, they must assume greater risk with respect to depth and duration of inventory holding.

If a business plans to operate at more than one level of the distribution channel, it must be prepared to assume the associated inventory risk. For example, a food chain that operates a regional warehouse assumes risk related to wholesale functionality over and above normal retail operations. To the extent that an enterprise becomes vertically integrated, inventory must be managed at multiple levels of the supply chain.

Inventory Functionality

From an inventory perspective, the ideal situation would be a response-based supply chain. At various points in early chapters, the practicality of implementing a fully response-based supply chain was discussed in terms of the total costs and timeliness of

TABLE 7.1
Inventory Functionality

Geographical Specialization	Allows geographical positioning across multiple manufacturing and distributive units of an enterprise. Inventory maintained at different locations and stages of the value-creation process allows specialization.
Decoupling	Allows economy of scale within a single facility and permits each process to operate at maximum efficiency rather than having the speed of the entire process constrained by the slowest.
Supply/Demand Balancing	Accommodates elapsed time between inventory availability (manufacturing, growing, or extraction) and consumption.
Buffering Uncertainty	Accommodates uncertainty related to demand in excess of forecast or unexpected delays in order receipt and order processing in delivery and is typically referred to as safety stock.

customer support. While a zero-inventory supply chain is typically not achievable, it is important to remember that each dollar invested in inventory is a trade-off to an alternative use of assets.

Inventory is a current asset that should provide return on the capital invested. The return on inventory investments is the marginal profit on sales that would not occur without inventory. Accounting experts have long recognized that measuring the true cost and benefits of inventory on the corporate profit-and-loss is difficult.[1] Lack of measurement sophistication makes it difficult to evaluate the trade-offs between service levels, operating efficiency, and inventory level. While aggregate inventory levels throughout sectors of the economy have decreased, many enterprises still carry more inventory than needed to support actual business requirements. The forces driving this generalization are understood better through a review of the four prime functions of inventory. Table 7.1 summarizes inventory functionality.

These four functions, **geographical specialization, decoupling, balancing supply and demand, and buffering uncertainty,** require inventory investment to achieve operating objectives. While logistics, as discussed in Chapter 2, has made significant progress in reducing overall supply chain inventory, inventory properly deployed creates value and reduces total cost. Given a specific manufacturing/marketing strategy, inventories planned and committed to operations can only be reduced to a level consistent with performing the four inventory functions. All inventory exceeding the minimum level represents excess commitment.

At the minimum level, inventory invested to achieve geographical specialization and decoupling can be modified only by changes in network facility location and operational processes of the enterprise. The automotive manufacturers use geographical specialization by locating the sheet metal and bumpers (auto body parts) in the colder regions since that is where many of the crashes occur due to the snow and ice. Decoupling is the separation of a manufacturing process from the selling process. For example, the manufacturing process may demonstrate significant economies of scale while sales occur at relatively low levels. In this situation, firms may use decoupling to manufacture the inventory in large-enough quantities to achieve economies of scale, even though it may be necessary to hold it as inventory prior to sale. Inventory to balance supply and demand is necessary when the timing of product supply is different than the demand pattern. For example, fruits

---

[1] Douglas M. Lambert, *The Development of an Inventory Costing Methodology* (Chicago: National Council of Physical Distribution Management, 1976), p. 3; and *Inventory Carrying Cost, Memorandum 611* (Chicago: Drake Sheahan/Stewart Dougall, Inc., 1974).

and vegetables have a relatively limited growing season, but consumers desire year-round consumption and will buy throughout the year. Another example is the seasonal demand for toys and garden supplies, where sales occur in a very short time span but production occurs all year. Balancing inventory is necessary to match the supply and demand patterns. Buffering inventory is necessary when there is uncertainty in both supply and demand. When there is uncertainty over when product will become available (supply) and when the customer requires it (demand), it may be necessary to hold buffer inventory.

Inventory committed to safety stocks represent the greatest potential for improved logistics performance. This commitment is operational in nature and can be adjusted rapidly in the event of an error or policy change. A variety of techniques are available to assist management in planning safety stock commitments. The focus of this chapter is the analysis of safety stock relationships and inventory policy development.

Inventory Definitions

In designing inventory policy, specific inventory relationships must be considered. Management must understand these relationships to establish inventory policy with respect to when and how much to order. The **inventory policy** drives inventory performance. The two key indicators of inventory performance are **service level** and **average inventory.**

Inventory Policy

Inventory policy consists of guidelines regarding what to purchase or manufacture, when to take action, and in what quantity. It also includes decisions regarding geographical inventory positioning. For example, some firms may decide to postpone inventory positioning by maintaining stock at the plant. Other firms may use a more speculative strategy of positioning product in local markets or regional warehouses. It is advantageous to use a geographic postponement strategy, centralizing the inventory position for items with high demand uncertainty or high value. Speculative positioning may be more appropriate for items that are relatively low value or that require quick accessibility by customers. Development of sound inventory policy is the most difficult dimension of inventory management.

A second policy aspect concerns inventory management practice. One approach is to independently manage inventory at each stocking facility. At the other extreme is central inventory management of all stocking locations. Centralized inventory management requires effective communication and coordination. The increased availability of information technology and integrated planning systems allows more firms to implement centralized inventory planning. Centralized inventory planning systems can reduce demand uncertainty between distribution locations.

Service Level

Service level is a performance target specified by management. It defines inventory performance objectives. Service level is often measured in terms of performance cycle time, case fill rate, line fill rate, order fill rate, or any combination of these. The **performance cycle** is the elapsed time between the release of a purchase order by a buyer to the receipt of shipment. A **case fill rate** is the percent of cases or units ordered that are shipped as requested. For example, a 95 percent case fill rate indicates that, on average, 95 cases out of 100 are filled from available stock. The remaining five cases are back-ordered or deleted. The **line fill rate** is the percent of order lines filled completely. **Order fill** is the percent of customer orders filled completely.

FIGURE 7.1
Inventory Cycle for
Typical Product

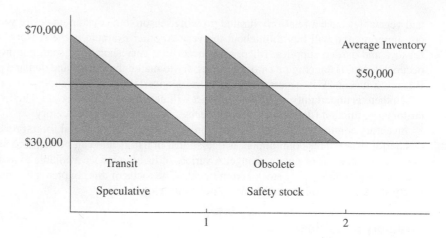

Inventory management is a major element of supply chain logistics strategy that must be integrated to achieve overall service objectives. While one strategy to achieve a high service level is to increase inventory, an alternative approach may be the use of faster or more reliable transportation and collaboration with customers and service providers to reduce uncertainty.

Average Inventory

The materials, components, work-in-process, and finished product typically stocked in the logistical system are referred to as **inventory** and the rolling mean across time is referred to as **average inventory.** From a policy viewpoint, target inventory levels must be planned for each facility. Figure 7.1 illustrates the performance cycles for one item at one location. At the maximum, the facility has in stock during the normal performance cycle $70,000 and a minimum of $30,000. The difference between these two levels, $40,000 ($70,000 − $30,000), is the order quantity, resulting in a cycle inventory of $20,000 ($40,000/2). Cycle inventory or base stock is the portion of average inventory that results from replenishment. Stock level is at a maximum following stock receipt from the supplier. Customers deplete inventory until the stock level reaches its minimum. Prior to the stock level reaching the minimum, a replenishment order is initiated so that inventory will arrive before an out-of-stock occurs. The replenishment order must be initiated before the available inventory is less than or equal to forecasted demand during the performance cycle time. The amount ordered for replenishment is termed the **order quantity.** Given this basic order formulation, average cycle inventory or base stock equals one-half order quantity.

The **transit inventory** represents the amount typically in transit between facilities or on order but not received. The **obsolete inventory** is the stock that is out-of-date or that has not experienced recent demand. Eventually, it is donated, destroyed, or sold at a loss. **Speculative inventory** is bought prior to need to hedge a currency exchange, take advantage of a special discount, or prepare for a potential work force disruption. A modern example of speculative inventory purchase occurs each year as many Asia-Pacific countries observe a multi-week celebration for Chinese New Year resulting in planned production facility closures.

The remainder of inventory in the typical logistics system is **safety stock.** Safety stock is maintained in a logistical system to protect against demand and performance cycle uncertainty. Safety stock is used only near the end of replenishment cycles when uncertainty has caused higher-than-expected demand or longer-than-expected performance cycle times. Thus, typical average inventory is **one-half order quantity plus safety stock and in-transit stock** ($70,000 − $40,000/2 + $30,000).

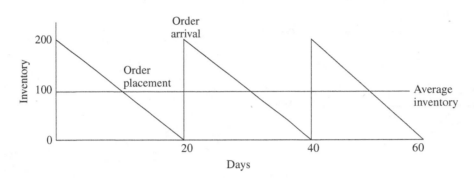

FIGURE 7.2

Inventory Relationship for Constant Sales and Performance Cycle

Average Inventory across Multiple Performance Cycles

In initial policy formulation, it is necessary to determine how much inventory to order at a specified time. To illustrate, assume the replenishment performance cycle is a constant 10 days and daily sales rate is 10 units per day. Also assume the order quantity is 200 units.

Figure 7.2 illustrates this relationship. This type of chart is referred to as a **sawtooth diagram** because of the series of right triangles. Since complete certainty exists with respect to usage and performance cycle, orders are scheduled to arrive just as the last unit is sold. Thus, no safety stock is necessary. Since the rate of sale in the example is 10 units per day and it takes 10 days to complete inventory replenishment, a sound reorder policy might be to order 200 units every 20 days. Given these conditions, common terminology related to policy formulation can be specified.

First, the **reorder point** is specified as 100 units on hand. The reorder point defines when a replenishment order is initiated. In this example, whenever the quantity on hand drops below 100, an additional order for 200 units is placed. The result of this policy is that daily inventory level ranges from a maximum of 200 to a minimum of zero over the performance cycle.

Second, average inventory is 100 units, since stock on hand exceeds 100 units one-half of the time, or for 10 days, and is less than 100 units one-half of the time. In fact, average inventory is equal to one-half the 200-unit order quantity.

Third, assuming a work year of 240 days, 12 purchases will be required during the year. Therefore, over a period of 1 year, 200 units will be purchased 12 times for a total of 2400 units. Sales are expected to equal 10 units per/day over 240 days for a total of 2400 units. As discussed above, average inventory is 100 units. Thus, **inventory turns** will be 24 (2400 total sales/100 units of average inventory).

In time, such routine operations would lead management to ask some questions concerning the arrangement. What would happen if orders were placed more frequently than once every 20 days? Why not order 100 units every 10 days? Why order as frequently as every 20 days? Why not reorder 600 units once every 60 days? Assuming that the inventory performance cycle remains a constant 10 days, what would be the impact of each of these alternative ordering policies on reorder point, average base inventory, and inventory turnover?

The policy of ordering a smaller volume of 100 units every 10 days means that two orders would always be outstanding. Thus, the reorder point would remain 100 units on hand or on order to service average daily sales of 10 units over the 20-day inventory cycle. However, average inventory on hand would drop to 50 units, and inventory turnover would increase to 48 times per year. The policy of ordering 600 units every 60 days would result

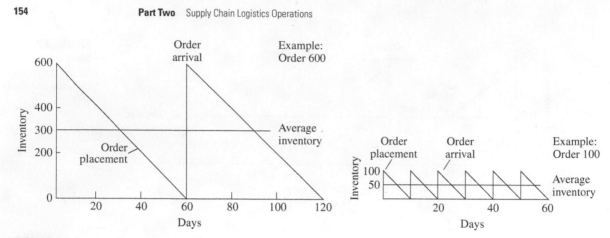

FIGURE 7.3
Alternative Order Quantity and Average Inventory

in an average base inventory of 300 units and a turnover of approximately eight times per year. These alternative ordering policies are illustrated in Figure 7.3.

The figure illustrates that average inventory is a function of the reorder quantity. Smaller replenishment order quantities do result in lower average inventory, but there are other factors such as performance cycle uncertainty, purchasing discounts, and transportation economies that are important when determining order quantity.

An exact order quantity policy can be determined by balancing the cost of ordering and the cost of maintaining average inventory. The **Economic Order Quantity (EOQ)** model provides a specific quantity balancing of these two critical cost components. By determining the EOQ and dividing it into annual demand, the frequency and size of replenishment orders minimizing the total cost of cycle inventory are identified. Prior to reviewing EOQ, it is necessary to identify costs typically associated with ordering and maintaining inventory.

Independent vs. Dependent Demand

Supply chains are typically a combination of independent and dependent demands. At the consumer level, most demand is independent as consumers do not typically let the retailer know when they are arriving to purchase product. Consumers arrive at the store and generally expect the product to be on the shelf. While retailers can forecast demand based on historical patterns, they must anticipate consumer requirements by having inventory pre-positioned at the store. This situation is often termed "just-in-case" inventory because it must be committed just in case the consumer walks into the store. At the supplier end of the supply chain, component inventory can typically be characterized as dependent. A dependent demand situation is characteristic of component parts that are assembled into final products such as for automotive or electronic manufacturers. In the dependent case, the manufacturer establishes a production schedule that is typically shared with their suppliers. Based on the production schedule, the supplier can anticipate the demand and the required delivery schedule for component parts. For example, for an automotive assembly plant with a production schedule of 1,000 cars per day, the tire supplier would know to schedule the arrival of 4,000 tires daily to meet that production schedule. In dependent demand situations, it is possible to use "just-in-time" deployment since there is no demand uncertainty once the finished product schedule is established and shared with suppliers.

Inventory Carrying Cost

Inventory carrying cost is the expense associated with maintaining inventory. Inventory expense is calculated by multiplying annual inventory carrying cost percent by average inventory value. Standard accounting practice is to value inventory at purchase or standard manufacturing cost rather than at selling price.

Assuming an annual inventory carrying cost percentage of 20 percent, the annual inventory expense for an enterprise with $1 million in average inventory would be $200,000 (20% × $1,000,000). While the calculation of inventory carrying expense is basic, determining the appropriate carrying cost percent is less obvious.

Determining carrying cost percent requires assignment of inventory-related costs. Financial accounts relevant to inventory carrying cost percent are capital, insurance, obsolescence, storage, and taxes. While cost of capital is typically based on managerial policy, expense-related taxes, insurance, obsolescence, and storage typically vary depending on the specific attributes of individual products.

Capital

The appropriate charge to place on capital invested in inventory varies widely. Capital assessments range from the prime interest rate to a percent determined by upper management. The logic for using the prime interest rate or a specified rate pegged to the prime rate is that cash to replace capital invested in inventory can be obtained in the money markets at that rate. Higher management specified capital costs are based on expected or target return on investment for capital deployed. Such target rates are typically termed **hurdle** rates.

The cost of capital may vary significantly by firm and industry. Firms that are aggressive in uses of cash will typically employ a higher cost of capital percentage. Similarly, industries with high value or short life cycle product will employ a higher cost of capital to drive lower inventories. For example, electronics or pharmaceutical firms may use high capital rates (20–30%) since they expect high returns on their development investments and their products have short life cycles, while food and beverage manufacturers may accept lower hurdle rates (5–15%) since they have longer product life cycles and relatively lower risk.

Confusion often results from the fact that senior management frequently does not establish a clear-cut capital cost policy. For supply chain logistics planning, the cost of capital must be clearly specified since it has significant impact on system design and performance.

Taxes

Local taxing authorities in many areas assess taxes on inventory held in warehouses. The tax rate and means of assessment vary by location. The tax expense is usually a direct levy based on inventory value on a specific day of the year or average inventory value over a period of time. In many cases tax exemption such as free port status is available from local and state authorities.

Insurance

Insurance cost is an expense based upon estimated risk or loss over time. Loss risk depends on the product and the facility storing the product. For example, high-value products that are easily stolen and hazardous products result in high insurance cost. Insurance cost is also influenced by facility characteristics such as security cameras and sprinkler systems that might help reduce risk. Since September 11, 2001, issues related to the risk of terrorism have become of greater concern in supply chain design.

Obsolescence

Obsolescence cost results from deterioration of product during storage. A prime example of obsolescence is product that ages beyond recommended sell-by date, such as food and pharmaceuticals. Obsolescence also includes financial loss when a product no longer has fashion appeal or no longer has any demand. Obsolescence costs are typically estimated on the basis of past experience concerning markdowns, donations, or quantity destroyed. This expense is the percent of average inventory value declared obsolete each year.

Storage

Storage cost is facility expense related to product holding rather than product handling. Storage cost must be allocated on the requirements of specific products since it is not related directly to inventory value. In public or contract warehouses, storage charges are billed on an individual basis. The cost of total annual occupancy for a given product can then be assigned by multiplying the average daily physical space occupied by the standard cost factor for a specified time. This figure can then be divided by the total number of units of merchandise processed through the facility to determine average storage cost per merchandise unit.

Table 7.2 illustrates the components of annual inventory carrying cost and typical range of component costs. It should be clear that the final carrying cost percent used by a firm is a matter of managerial policy. Decisions regarding inventory cost are important because they trade off against other logistics cost components in system design and operating decisions.

Planning Inventory

Inventory planning consists of determining when and how much to order. When to order is determined by demand and replenishment lead time average and uncertainty. How much to order is determined by the order quantity. Inventory control is the process of monitoring inventory status.

When to Order

As discussed earlier, the reorder point defines when a replenishment shipment should be initiated. A reorder point can be specified in terms of units or days' supply. This discussion focuses on determining reorder points under conditions of demand and performance cycle certainty.

TABLE 7.2
Inventory Carrying
Cost Components

Element	Average Percent	Percent Ranges
Cost of capital	10.00%	4–40%
Taxes	1.00	.5–2
Insurance	1.00	0–2
Obsolescence	1.00	.5–2
Storage	2.00	0–4
Totals	15.00%	5–50%

The basic reorder point formula is:

$$R = D \times T$$

where

R = Reorder point in units;

D = Average daily demand in units; and

T = Average performance cycle length in days.

To illustrate this calculation, assume demand of 20 units/day and a 10-day performance cycle. In this case,

$$R = D \times T$$
$$= 20 \text{ units/day} \times 10 \text{ days}$$
$$= 200 \text{ units}.$$

An alternative form is to define reorder point in terms of days of supply. For the above example, the days of supply reorder point is 10 days.

The use of reorder point formulations implies that the replenishment shipment will arrive as scheduled. When uncertainty exists in either demand or performance cycle length, safety stock is required. When safety stock is necessary to accommodate uncertainty, the reorder point formula is:

$$R = D \times T + \text{SS}$$

where

R = Reorder point in units;

D = Average daily demand in units;

T = Average performance cycle length in days; and

SS = Safety stock in units.

Computation of safety stock under conditions of uncertainty is discussed later in this chapter.

How Much to Order

Lot sizing balances inventory carrying cost with the cost of ordering. The key to understanding the relationship is to remember that average inventory is equal to one-half the order quantity. Therefore, the greater the order quantity, the larger the average inventory and, consequently, the greater the annual carrying cost. However, the larger the order quantity, the fewer orders required per planning period and, consequently, the lower the total ordering cost. Lot quantity formulations identify the precise quantities at which the annual combined total inventory carrying and ordering cost is lowest for a given sales volume. Figure 7.4 illustrates the relationships. The point at which the sum of ordering and carrying cost is minimized represents the lowest total cost. The objective is to identify the ordering quantity that minimizes the total inventory carrying and ordering cost.

Economic Order Quantity

The EOQ is the replenishment practice that minimizes the combined inventory carrying and ordering cost. Identification of such a quantity assumes that demand and costs are

FIGURE 7.4
Economic Order
Quantity

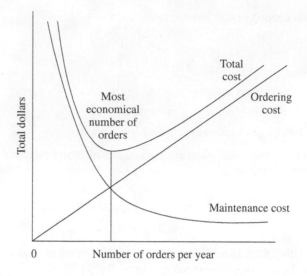

TABLE 7.3
Factors for
Determining EOQ

Annual demand volume	2400 units
Unit value at cost	$5.00
Inventory carrying cost percent	20% annually
Ordering cost	$19.00 per order

relatively stable throughout the year. Since EOQ is calculated on an individual product basis, the basic formulation does not consider the impact of joint ordering of multiple products.

The most efficient method for calculating EOQ is mathematical. Earlier in this chapter a policy dilemma regarding whether to order 100, 200, or 600 units was presented. The answer can be found by calculating the applicable EOQ for the situation. Table 7.3 contains the necessary information.

To make the appropriate calculations, the standard formulation for EOQ is:

$$EOQ = \sqrt{\frac{2C_oD}{C_iU}}$$

where

EOQ = Economic order quantity;

C_o = Cost per order;

C_i = Annual inventory carrying cost;

D = Annual sales volume, units; and

U = Cost per unit.

Substituting from Table 7.3,

$$EOQ = \sqrt{\frac{2 \times 19 \times 2400}{0.20 \times 5.00}}$$
$$= \sqrt{91,200}$$
$$= 302 \text{ (round to 300)}.$$

Total ordering cost would amount to $152 (2400/300 × $19.00), and inventory carrying cost would amount to $150 [300/2 × (5 × 0.20)]. Thus, rounding to allow ordering in multiples of 100 units, annual reordering, and inventory carrying cost have been equated.

To benefit from the most economical purchase arrangement, orders should be placed in the quantity of 300 units rather than 100, 200, or 600. Thus, over the year, eight orders would be placed and average base inventory would be 150 units. Referring back to Figure 7.4, the impact of ordering in quantities of 300 rather than 200 can be identified. An EOQ of 300 implies that additional inventory in the form of base stock has been introduced into the system. Average inventory has been increased from 100 to 150 units on hand.

While the EOQ model determines the optimal replenishment quantity, it does require some rather stringent assumptions. The major assumptions of the simple EOQ model are: (1) all demand is satisfied; (2) rate of demand is continuous, constant, and known; (3) replenishment performance cycle time is constant and known; (4) there is a constant price of product that is independent of order quantity or time; (5) there is an infinite planning horizon; (6) there is no interaction between multiple items of inventory; (7) no inventory is in transit; and (8) no limit is placed on capital availability. The constraints imposed by some of these assumptions can be overcome through computational extensions; however, the EOQ concept illustrates the importance of the trade-offs associated with inventory carrying and replenishment ordering cost.

Relationships involving the inventory performance cycle, inventory cost, and economic order formulations are useful for guiding inventory planning. First, the EOQ is found at the point where annualized order placement cost and inventory carrying cost are equal. Second, average base inventory equals one-half order quantity. Third, the value of the inventory unit, all other things being equal, will have a direct relationship with replenishment order frequency. In effect, the higher the product value, the more frequently it will be ordered.

While the EOQ formulation is relatively straightforward, there are other factors that must be considered in actual application. These factors refer to various adjustments necessary to take advantage of special purchase situations and unitization characteristics. Three typical adjustments are volume transportation rates, quantity discounts, and other EOQ adjustments.

Volume Transportation Rates

In the EOQ formulation, no consideration was given to the impact of transportation cost upon order quantity. Regardless of whether product is sold on a delivered basis or ownership is transferred at origin, the cost of transportation must be paid by supply chain participants. Collaborative efforts to order in quantities that minimize total cost are essential to sound logistical arrangements.

As a general rule, the greater the weight of an order, the lower the cost per pound of transportation from any origin to destination.[2] A freight-rate discount for larger shipments is common across all transportation modes. Thus, all other things being equal, supply chain arrangements should utilize quantities that offer maximum transportation economies. Such quantities may be larger than the EOQ purchase quantity. Increasing order size has a twofold impact upon inventory cost. Assume for purposes of illustration that the most desirable transportation rate is obtained when a quantity of 480 is ordered, as compared to the EOQ-recommended order of 300 calculated earlier. The first impact of the larger order is to increase the average base inventory from 150 to 240 units. Thus, ordering in larger quantities increases inventory carrying cost.

[2]To determine transportation rates, the unit quantity must generally be converted to weight or cube.

TABLE 7.4
EOQ Data Requirements for Consideration of Transportation Economies

Annual demand volume	2400 units
Unit value at cost	$5.00
Inventory carrying cost percentage	20% annually
Ordering cost	$19.00 per order
Small shipment rate	$1.00 per unit
Large shipment rate	$0.75 per unit

TABLE 7.5
Volume Transportation Rate Modified EOQ

	Alternative 1: $EOQ_1 = 300$	Alternative 2: $EOQ_2 = 480$
Inventory Carrying Cost	$ 150	$ 240
Ordering Cost	$ 152	$ 95
Transportation Cost	$2,400	$1,800
Total Cost	$2,702	$2,135

The second impact is a decrease in the number of orders required to satisfy annual requirements. Decreased number of orders increases the shipment size, facilitating lower per-unit transportation cost.

To complete the analysis it is necessary to formulate the total cost with and without transportation savings. While this calculation can be directly made by modification of the EOQ formulation, direct comparison provides a more insightful answer. The only additional data required are the applicable freight rate for ordering in quantities of 300 and 480. Table 7.4 provides the data necessary to complete the analysis.

Table 7.5 illustrates total cost analysis. Reducing total annual cost by purchasing 480 units five times per year rather than the original EOQ solution of 300 units eight times per year results in approximately a $570 savings.

The impact of volume transportation rates upon total cost of procurement cannot be neglected. In the example above, the equivalent rate per unit dropped from $1 to $0.75, or by 25 percent. Thus, any EOQ must be tested for transportation cost sensitivity across a range of weight breaks.

Another point illustrated in the data in Table 7.5 is the fact that rather substantial changes in the size of an order and the number of orders placed per year result in only a modest change in the total ordering and inventory carrying cost. The EOQ quantity of 300 had a total annual cost of $302, whereas the revised order quantity had a comparative cost of $335.

EOQ formulations are much more sensitive to significant changes in order cycle or frequency. Likewise, substantial changes in cost factors are necessary to significantly change the economic order quantity.

Finally, two factors regarding inventory cost under conditions of origin purchase are noteworthy. FOB (Free On Board) origin purchase means that the buyer is responsible for freight cost and risk while the product is in transit. It follows that any change in weight break leading to a shipment method with a different transit time should be considered, using the added cost or savings as appropriate in a total cost analysis.

Second, the transportation cost must be added to the purchase price to determine the value of goods tied up in inventory. Once the inventory has been received, the cost of the product must be increased to reflect the inbound transportation.[3]

---

[3]Some aspects of pricing are discussed in greater detail in Chapter 8.

Cost	Quantity Purchased
$5.00	1–99
4.50	100–200
4.00	201–300
3.50	301–400
3.00	401–500

TABLE 7.6
Example of Quantity Discounts

Quantity Discounts

Purchase quantity discounts represent an EOQ extension similar to volume transportation rates. Table 7.6 illustrates a sample schedule of discounts. Quantity discounts can be handled directly with the basic EOQ formula by calculating total cost at any given volume-related purchase price, similar to the process used in calculating transportation rate impact, to determine associated EOQs. If the discount at any associated quantity is sufficient to offset the added inventory carrying cost less the reduced cost of ordering, then the quantity discount is a viable choice. It should be noted that quantity discounts and volume transportation rates each drive larger purchase quantities. This does not necessarily mean that the lowest total cost purchase will always be a larger quantity than would otherwise be the case under basic EOQ.

Other EOQ Adjustments

A variety of other special situations may justify adjustments to the basic EOQ. Examples are (1) production lot size, (2) multiple-item purchase, (3) limited capital, (4) dedicated trucking, and (5) unitization. Production lot size refers to the most economical quantities from a manufacturing perspective. Multiple-item purchase refers to situations when more than one product are bought concurrently, so quantity and transportation discounts must consider the impact of product combinations. Limited capital describes situations with budget limitations for total inventory investment. Since the multiple product order must be made within the budget limitations, order quantities must recognize the need to allocate the inventory investment across the product line. Retailers often apply budget limitations when setting their "open-to-buy" for item categories. Dedicated trucking can influence order quantity since the truck has a fixed cost consideration.[4] Once it is decided to use a dedicated fleet to transport replenishment product, the enterprise should try to purchase in quantities that fully use available capacity. Back haul capacity availability may also justify purchasing products earlier than otherwise determined by EOQ considerations.

Another consideration when determining replenishment order quantity is unitization. Many products are stored and moved in standard units such as cases or pallets. Since these standardized units are often designed to fit transportation vehicles, there may be significant diseconomies when the EOQ does not reflect standard units. As an example, suppose that a full pallet quantity is 200 units of a specified product. Using an EOQ of 300 units would require shipments of 1.5 pallets. From a handling or transportation utilization perspective, it is probably more effective to order either one or two pallets alternately or permanently.

[4]See Chapter 8. In such situations, the cost of money invested in inventory should be appropriately charged when the goods are paid for at origin.

Managing Uncertainty

To understand basic principles, it is useful to understand inventory relationships under conditions of certainty. Formulation of inventory policy must consider uncertainty. Two types of uncertainty directly impact inventory policy. **Demand uncertainty** involves the variation in sales during inventory replenishment. **Performance cycle uncertainty** involves inventory replenishment time variation.

Demand Uncertainty

Sales forecasting estimates unit demand during the inventory replenishment cycle. Even with good forecasting, demand during replenishment cycle typically exceeds or falls short of what is planned. To protect against a stockout when demand exceeds forecast, safety stock is added to base inventory. Under conditions of demand uncertainty, average inventory represents one-half order quantity plus safety stock. Figure 7.5 illustrates the inventory performance cycle under conditions of demand uncertainty. The dashed line represents the forecast. The solid line illustrates inventory on hand across multiple performance cycles. The task of planning safety stock requires three steps. First, the likelihood of stockout must be gauged. Second, demand during a stockout period must be estimated. Finally, a policy decision is required concerning the desired level of stockout protection.

Assume for purposes of illustration that the inventory performance cycle is 10 days. History indicates daily sales range from 0 to 10 units with average daily sales of 5 units. The economic order is assumed to be 50, the reorder point is 50, the planned average inventory is 25, and sales during the performance cycle are forecasted to be 50 units.

During the first cycle, although daily demand experienced variation, the average of 5 units per day was maintained. Total demand during cycle 1 was 50 units, as expected. During cycle 2, demand totaled 50 units in the first 8 days, resulting in a stockout. Thus, no sales were possible on days 9 and 10. During cycle 3, demand reached a total of 39 units. The third performance cycle ended with 11 units remaining in stock. Over the 30-day period total sales were 139 units, for average daily sale of 4.6 units.

From the history recorded in Table 7.7, it is observed that stockouts occurred on 2 of 30 total days. Since sales never exceed 10 units per day, no possibility of stockout exists on the first 5 days of the replenishment cycle. Stockouts were possible on days 6 through 10 on the remote possibility that demand during the first 5 days of the cycle averaged

FIGURE 7.5
Inventory Relationship, Demand Uncertainty, and Constant Performance Cycle

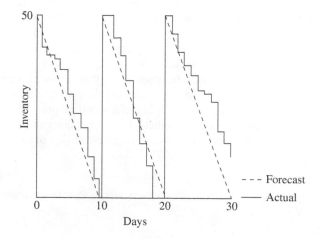

	Forecast Cycle 1		Stockout Cycle 2		Overstock Cycle 3	
Day	Demand	Accumulated	Demand	Accumulated	Demand	Accumulated
1	9	9	0	0	5	5
2	2	11	6	6	5	10
3	1	12	5	11	4	14
4	3	15	7	18	3	17
5	7	22	10	28	4	21
6	5	27	7	35	1	22
7	4	31	6	41	2	24
8	8	39	9	50	8	32
9	6	45	Stockout	50	3	35
10	5	50	Stockout	50	4	39

TABLE 7.7

Typical Demand Experience during Three Replenishment Cycles

Daily Demand (in units)	Frequency (days)
Stockout	2
0	1
1	2
2	2
3	3
4	4
5	5
6	3
7	3
8	2
9	2
10	1

TABLE 7.8

Frequency of Demand

10 units per day and no inventory was carried over from the previous period. Since during the three performance cycles 10 units were sold on only one occasion, it is apparent that the real risk of stockout occurs only during the last few days of the performance cycle, and then only when sales exceed the average by a substantial margin.[5] Some approximation is possible concerning sales potential for days 9 and 10 of cycle 2. A maximum of 20 units might have been sold if inventory had been available. On the other hand, it is remotely possible that even if stock had been available, no demand would have occurred on days 9 and 10. For average demand of 4 to 5 units per day, a reasonable appraisal of lost sales is 8 to 10 units.

It should be apparent that the risk of stockouts created by variations in sales is limited to a short time and includes a small percentage of total sales. Although the sales analysis presented in Table 7.7 helps develop an understanding of the opportunity, the appropriate course of action is still not clear. Statistical probability can be used to assist management in planning safety stock.

The sales history over the 30-day period has been aggregated in Table 7.8 as a frequency distribution. The main purpose of a frequency distribution is to observe variations around the average daily demand. Given an expected average of 5 units per day, demand exceeded average on 11 days and was less than average on 12 days. An alternative way of illustrating a frequency distribution is by a bar chart, as in Figure 7.6.

[5]In this example, daily statistics are used. An alternative, which is technically more correct from a statistical viewpoint, is to utilize demand over multiple performance cycles. The major limitation of order cycles is the length of time and difficulty required to collect the necessary data

FIGURE 7.6
Historical Analysis of
Demand History

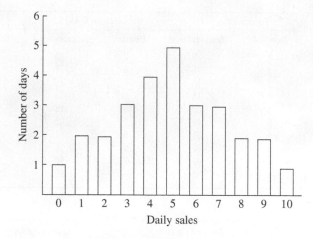

FIGURE 7.7
Normal Distribution

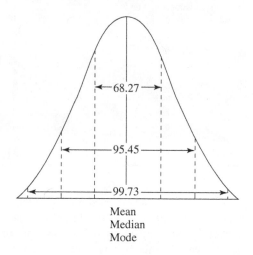

Given the historical demand frequency, it is possible to calculate the safety stock necessary to provide a specified degree of stockout protection. Probability theory is based on the random chance of a specific occurrence within a large number of occurrences. The situation illustrated uses a 28-day sample. In actual application, a larger sample size would be desirable.

The probability of occurrences assumes a pattern around a measure of central tendency, which is the average value of all occurrences. While a number of frequency distributions can be used in inventory management, the most common is the **normal distribution.**

A normal distribution is characterized by a symmetrical bell-shaped curve, illustrated in Figure 7.7. The essential characteristic of a normal distribution is that the three measures of central tendency have equal value. The **mean** (average) value, the **median** (middle) observation, and the **mode** (most frequently observed) all have the same value. When these three measures are nearly identical, the frequency distribution is **normal.**

The basis for predicting demand during a performance cycle using a normal distribution is the **standard deviation** of observations around the three measures of central tendency. The standard deviation is the dispersion of observations within specified areas under the normal curve. For the inventory management application, the observation is unit sales per day and the dispersion is the variation in daily sales. Within 1 standard deviation, 68.27

percent of all events occur. This means that 68.27 percent of the days during a performance cycle will experience daily sales within $\pm$ 1 standard deviation of the average daily sales. Within $\pm$ 2 standard deviations, 95.45 percent of all observations occur. At $\pm$ 3 standard deviations, 99.73 percent of all observations are included. In terms of inventory policy, the standard deviation provides a method of estimating the safety stock required to achieve a specified degree of out-of-stock protection.

The first step in setting safety stock is to calculate the standard deviation. Most calculators and spreadsheets calculate standard deviation, but if one of these aids is not available, another method to compute the standard deviation is:

$$\sigma = \sqrt{\frac{\sum F_i D_i^2}{n}}$$

where

σ = Standard deviation;

F_i = Frequency of observation i;

D_i = Deviation of observation from mean for observation i; and

n = Total observations available.

The necessary data to determine standard deviation are contained in Table 7.9.

The standard deviation of the data in Table 7.9 is rounded to 3 units. When setting safety stocks, 2 standard deviations of protection, or 6 units, would protect against 95.45 percent of all observations included in the distribution. However, the only situations of concern in determining safety stock requirements are observations that exceed the mean value. No problem exists concerning inventory to satisfy demand equal to or below the average. Thus, on 50 percent of the days, no safety stock is required. Safety stock protection at the 95 percent level will, in fact, protect against 97.72 percent of all possible observations. The 95 percent coverage will cover all situations when daily demand is $\pm$ 2 standard deviations of the average plus the 2.72 percent of the time when demand is more than 2 standard deviations below the mean. This added benefit results from what is typically called a **one-tail** statistical application.

Units	Frequency (F_i)	Deviation from Mean (D_i)	Deviation Squared (D_i^2)	$F_i D_i^2$
0	1	−5	25	25
1	2	−4	16	32
2	2	−3	9	18
3	3	−2	4	12
4	4	−1	1	4
5	5	0	0	0
6	3	+1	1	3
7	3	+2	4	12
8	2	+3	9	18
9	2	+4	16	32
10	1	+5	25	25
$n = 28$	$\bar{s} = 5$			$\sum F_i D_i^2 = 181$

$$\sigma = \sqrt{\frac{F_i D_i^2}{N}} = \sqrt{\frac{181}{28}} = 2.54$$

TABLE 7.9

Calculation of Standard Deviation of Daily Demand

TABLE 7.10
Calculation of Standard Deviation of Replenishment Cycle Duration

Performance Cycle (days)	Frequency (F_i)	Deviation from Mean (D_i)	Deviation Squared (D_i^2)	$F_i D_i^2$
6	2	−4	16	32
7	4	−3	9	36
8	6	−2	4	24
9	8	−1	1	8
10	10	0	0	0
11	8	+1	1	8
12	6	+2	4	24
13	4	+3	9	36
14	2	+4	16	32
				$\sum F_i D_i^2 = 200$

$$N = 50 \quad t = 10$$

$$\sigma = \sqrt{\frac{F_i D_i^2}{N}} = \sqrt{\frac{200}{50}} = \sqrt{4} = 2 \text{ days}$$

The above example illustrates how statistical probability can assist with the quantification of demand uncertainty, but demand conditions are not the only source of uncertainty. Performance cycles can also vary.

Performance Cycle Uncertainty

Performance cycle uncertainty means operations cannot assume consistent delivery. The planner should expect that actual performance cycle experience will cluster near the expected value and be skewed toward delayed delivery.

Table 7.10 presents a sample frequency distribution across multiple performance cycles. Although 10 days is the most frequent, replenishment experience ranges from 6 to 14 days. If the performance cycle follows a normal distribution, an individual performance cycle would be expected to fall between 8 and 12 days 68.27 percent of the time.

From a practical viewpoint, when cycle days drop below 10, there is not any need for safety stock. If the performance cycle were consistently below the planned performance cycle, then adjustment of expected duration would be in order. The situation of most immediate concern occurs when the duration of the performance cycle exceeds 10 days.

From the viewpoint of the probability of exceeding 10 days, the frequency of such occurrences, from the data in Table 7.10, can be restated in terms of performance cycles greater than 10 days and equal to or less than 10 days. In the example data, the standard deviation would not change because the distribution is normal. However, if the actual experience has been skewed in excess of the expected cycle duration, then a **Poisson distribution** may have been more appropriate. In Poisson frequency distributions, the standard deviation is equal to the square root of the mean. As a general rule, the smaller the mean, the greater the degree of skewness. This is true because it is not possible to have negative values for either demand or performance cycle length.

Safety Stock with Combined Uncertainty

The typical situation confronting the inventory planner is illustrated in Figure 7.8, where both demand and performance cycle uncertainties exist. Planning for both demand and performance cycle uncertainty requires combining two variables. The duration of the cycle is, at least in the short run, independent of the daily demand. However, in setting safety stocks, the joint impact of the probability of both demand and performance cycle variation

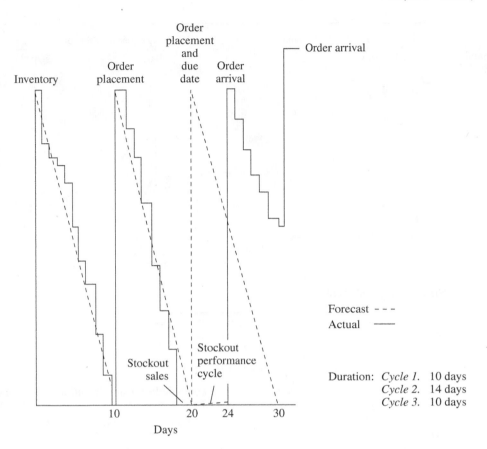

FIGURE 7.8
Combined Demand and
Performance Cycle
Uncertainty

Forecast - - -

Actual ———

Duration: *Cycle 1.*   10 days
            Cycle 2.   14 days
            Cycle 3.   10 days

must be determined. Table 7.11 presents a summary of sales and replenishment cycle performance. The key to understanding the potential relationships of the data in Table 7.11 is the 10-day performance cycle. Total demand during the 10 days potentially ranges from 0 to 100 units. On each day of the cycle, the demand probability is independent of the previous day for the entire 10-day duration. Assuming the full range of potential situations illustrated in Table 7.11, total sales during a performance cycle could range from 0 to 140 units. With this basic relationship between the two types of uncertainty in mind, safety stock requirements can be determined by either numerical or convolution procedures.

The **numerical compounding** of two interdependent variables involves multinominal expansion. This type of procedure requires extensive calculation. A direct method is to determine the standard deviations of demand and performance cycle uncertainty and then to approximate the combined standard deviation using the convolution formula:

$$\sigma_c = \sqrt{TS_D^2 + D^2 S_t^2}$$

where

σ_c = Standard deviation of combined probabilities;

T = Average performance cycle time;

S_t = Standard deviation of the performance cycle;

D = Average daily sales; and

S_D = Standard deviation of daily sales.

TABLE 7.11
Frequency
Distribution—Demand
and Replenishment
Uncertainty

Demand Distribution		Replenishment Cycle Distribution	
Daily Sales	**Frequency**	**Days**	**Frequency**
0	1	6	2
1	2	7	4
2	2	8	6
3	3	9	8
4	4	10	10
5	5	11	8
6	3	12	6
7	3	13	4
8	2	14	2
9	2		
10	1		
$n = 28$		$n = 50$	
$D = 5$		$T = 10$	
$S_s = 2.54$		$S_t = 2$	

Substituting from Table 7.11,

$$\sigma_c = \sqrt{10.00(2.54)^2 + (5.00)^2 (2)^2}$$
$$= \sqrt{64.52 + 100} = \sqrt{164.52}$$
$$= 12.83 \text{ (round to 13)}.$$

This formulation estimates the convoluted or combined standard deviation of T days with an average demand of D per day when the individual standard deviations are S_t and S_D, respectively. The average for the combined distribution is the product of T and D, or 50.00 (10.00 × 5.00).

Thus, given a frequency distribution of daily sales from 0 to 10 units per day and a range in replenishment cycle duration of 6 to 14 days, 13 units (1 standard deviation multiplied by 13 units) of safety stock is required to protect 84.14 percent of all performance cycles. To protect at the 97.72 percent level, a 26-unit safety stock is necessary. These levels assume a one-tail distribution since it is not necessary to protect against leadtime demand below average.

It is important to note that the specific event being protected against is a stockout during the performance cycle. The 84.14 and 97.72 percent levels are not product availability levels. These percentages reflect the probability of a stockout during a given performance cycle. For example, with a 13-unit safety stock, stockouts would be expected to occur during 15.86 (100 − 84.14) percent of the performance cycles. Although this percentage provides the probability of a stockout, it does not estimate magnitude. The relative stockout magnitude indicates the percentage of units stocked out relative to overall demand which depends on the number of cycles.

Still assuming the replenishment order quantity of 50 units, average inventory requirements would be 25 units if no safety stock were desired. The average inventory with 2 standard deviations of safety stock is 51 units [25 + (2 × 13)]. This inventory level would protect against a stockout during 97.72 percent of the performance cycles. Table 7.12 summarizes the alternatives confronting the planner in terms of assumptions and corresponding impact on average inventory.

Estimating Fill Rate

The fill rate is the magnitude rather than the probability of a stockout. The case fill rate is the percentage of units that can be filled when requested from available inventory.

	Order Quantity	Safety Stock	Average Inventory	
Assume constant S sales and constant T performance cycle	50	0	25	**TABLE 7.12** Average Inventory Impact Resulting from Changes in EOQ
Assume demand protection $+2\sigma$ and constant T performance cycle	50	6	31	
Assume constant S demand and $+2\sigma$ performance cycle protection	50	20	45	
Assume joint $+2\sigma$ for demand and performance cycle	50	26	51	

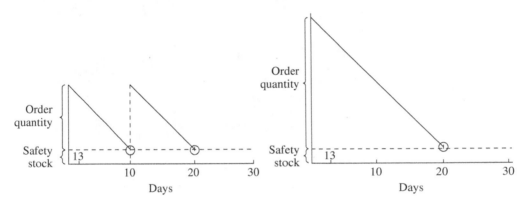

FIGURE 7.9   Impact of Order Quantity on Stockout Magnitude

Figure 7.9 graphically illustrates the difference between stockout probability and stockout magnitude. Both illustrations in Figure 7.9 have a safety stock of 1 standard deviation or 13 units. For both situations, given any performance cycle, the probability of a stockout is 31.73 percent. However, during a 20-day period, the figure on the left illustrates two instances where the stock may be depleted. These instances are at the end of the cycle. If the order quantity is doubled, the system has the possibility of stocking out only once during the 20-day cycle. So, while both situations face the same demand pattern, the first one demonstrates more stockout opportunities and potential. In general, for a given safety stock level, increasing the replenishment order quantity decreases the relative magnitude of potential stockouts and conversely increases customer service availability.

The mathematical formulation of the relationship is:

$$\text{SL} = 1 - \frac{f(k)\,\sigma_c}{Q}$$

where

SL = The stockout magnitude (the product availability level);

$f(k)$ = A function of the normal loss curve which provides the area in a right tail of a normal distribution;

σ_c = The combined standard deviation considering both demand and replenishment cycle uncertainty; and

Q = The replenishment order quantity.

To complete the example, suppose a firm desired 99 percent product availability or case fill rate. Assume the Q was calculated to be 300 units. Table 7.13 summarizes the required information.

TABLE 7.13
Information for
Determining Required
Safety Stock

Desired Service Level	99%
σ_c	13
Q	300

TABLE 7.14
Loss Integral for
Standardized Normal
Distribution

k	f(k)	k	f(k)
0.0	.3989	1.6	.0232
0.1	.3509	1.7	.0182
0.2	.3068	1.8	.0143
0.3	.2667	1.9	.0111
0.4	.2304	2.0	.0085
0.5	.1977	2.1	.0065
0.6	.1686	2.2	.0049
0.7	.1428	2.3	.0037
0.8	.1202	2.4	.0027
0.9	.1004	2.5	.0020
1.0	.0833	2.6	.0015
1.1	.0686	2.7	.0011
1.2	.0561	2.8	.0008
1.3	.0455	2.9	.0005
1.4	.0366	3.0	.0004
1.5	.0293	3.1	.0003

Since $f(k)$ is the term used to calculate safety stock requirements, the above equation must be solved for $f(k)$ using algebraic manipulation. The result is:

$$f(k) = (1 - SL) \times (Q/\sigma_c).$$

Substituting from Table 7.13,

$$f(k) = (1 - 0.99) \times (300/13)$$
$$= 0.01 \times 23.08 = .2308.$$

The calculated value of $f(k)$ is then compared against the values in Table 7.14 to find the one that most closely approximates the calculated value. For this example, the value of k that fits the condition is 0.4. The required safety stock level is:

$$SS = k \times \sigma_c$$

where

SS = Safety stock in units;

k = The k factor that corresponds with $f(k)$;

σ_c = The combined standard deviation.

So, substituting in for the example,

$$SS = k \times \sigma_c$$
$$= 0.4 \times 13 = 5.2 \text{ units}$$

The safety stock required to provide a 99 percent product fill rate when the order quantity is 300 units is approximately 5 units. Table 7.15 shows how the calculated safety stock and average inventory levels vary for other order quantities. An increased order size can be

Order Quantity (Q)	k	Safety Stock	Average Inventory
300	0.40	5	155
200	0.70	8	108
100	1.05	14	64
50	1.40	18	43
25	1.70	22	34

TABLE 7.15
Impact of Order Quantity on Safety Stock

used to compensate for decreasing the safety stock levels, or vice versa. The existence of such a trade-off implies that there is a combination of replenishment order quantities that will result in desired customer service at the minimum cost.

Dependent Demand Replenishment

With respect to dependent demand replenishment, inventory requirements are a function of known events that are not generally random. Therefore, dependent demand does not require forecasting because there is no uncertainty. It follows that no specific safety stock should be necessary to support a time-phased procurement program such as materials requirements planning **(MRP).**[6] The basic notion of time phasing is that parts and subassemblies need not be carried in inventory as long as they arrive when needed or just-in-time.

The case for carrying no safety stocks under conditions of dependent demand rests on two assumptions. First, procurement replenishment to support planning is predictable and constant. Second, vendors and suppliers maintain adequate inventories to satisfy 100 percent of purchase requirements. The second assumption may be operationally attained by use of volume-oriented purchase contracts that assure vendors and suppliers of eventual purchase. In such cases the safety stock requirement still exists for the overall supply chain, although the primary responsibility rests with the supplier.

The assumption of performance cycle certainty is more difficult to achieve. Even in situations where dedicated transportation is used, an element of uncertainty is always present. The practical result is that safety stocks do exist in many dependent demand situations.

Three basic approaches have been used to introduce safety stocks into dependent demand situations. First, a common practice is to put **safety time** into the requirements plan. For example, a component is ordered earlier than needed to assure timely arrival. A second approach is to increase the requisition by a quantity specified by some estimate of expected plan error. For example, assume that plan error will not exceed 5 percent. This procedure is referred to as **over-planning top-level demand.** The net result is to increase procurement of all components in a ratio to their expected usage plus a cushion to cover plan error. Components common to different end products or subassemblies covered by the overplanning will naturally experience greater quantity buildups than single-purpose components and parts. The third method is to utilize the previously discussed statistical techniques for setting safety stocks directly to the component rather than to the item of top-level demand.

Inventory Management Policies

Inventory management implements inventory policy. The reactive or pull inventory approach uses customer demand to pull product through the distribution channel. An alternative philosophy is a planning approach that proactively allocates or deploys inventory on the basis of forecasted demand and product availability. A third, or hybrid, logic uses a combination of push and pull.

[6]These concepts are discussed later in this chapter under Planning Methods.

Inventory Control

The managerial procedure for implementing an inventory policy is **inventory control.** The accountability of control measures units on hand at a specific location and tracks additions and deletions. Accountability and tracking can be performed on a manual or computerized basis.

Inventory control defines how often inventory levels are reviewed to determine when and how much to order. It is performed on either a perpetual or a periodic basis.

Perpetual Review

A perpetual inventory control process continuously reviews inventory levels to determine inventory replenishment needs. To utilize perpetual review, accurate tracking of all SKUs is necessary. Perpetual review is implemented through a reorder point and order quantity.

As discussed earlier,

$$\text{ROP} = D \times T + \text{SS}$$

where

ROP = Reorder point in units;

D = Average daily demand in units;

T = Average performance cycle length in days; and

SS = Safety or buffer stock in units.

The order quantity is determined using the EOQ.

For purposes of illustration, assume no uncertainty so no safety stock is necessary. Table 7.16 summarizes demand, performance cycle, and order quantity characteristics. For this example,

$$\text{ROP} = D \times T + \text{SS}$$

$$= 20 \text{ units/day} \times 10 \text{ days} + 0 = 200 \text{ units}.$$

The perpetual review compares on-hand and on-order inventory to the item's reorder point. If the on-hand plus on-order quantity is less than the established reorder point, a replenishment order is initiated.

Mathematically, the process is:

$$\text{If } I + OQ_0 \leq \text{ROP, then order } OQ,$$

where

I = Inventory on hand;

OQ_0 = Inventory on order from suppliers;

ROP = Reorder point in units; and

OQ = Order quantity in units.

TABLE 7.16
Sample Demand,
Performance Cycle,
and Order Quantity
Characteristics

Average daily demand	20 units
Performance cycle	10 days
Order quantity	200 units

For the previous example, a replenishment order of 200 is placed whenever the sum of on-hand and on-order inventory is less than or equal to 200 units. Since the reorder point equals the order quantity, the previous replenishment shipment would arrive just as the next replenishment is initiated. The average inventory level for a perpetual review system is:

$$I_{avg} = OQ/2 + SS$$

where

I_{avg} = Average inventory in units;

OQ = Order quantity units; and

SS = Safety stock units.

Average inventory for the previous example is calculated as:

$$I_{avg} = Q/2 + SS$$
$$= 300/2 + 0 = 150 \text{ units.}$$

Most illustrations throughout this text are based on a perpetual review system with a fixed reorder point. The reorder formulation assumes purchase orders will be placed when the reorder point is reached, and the method of control provides a perpetual monitoring of inventory status. If these two assumptions are not satisfied, the control parameters **(ROP and OQ)** determining the perpetual review must be refined.

Periodic Review

Periodic inventory control reviews the inventory status of an item at regular intervals such as weekly or monthly. For periodic review, the basic reorder point must be adjusted to consider the intervals between review. The formula for calculating the periodic review reorder point is:

$$ROP = D(T + P/2) + SS$$

where

ROP = Reorder point;

D = Average daily demand;

T = Average performance cycle length;

P = Review period in days; and

SS = Safety stock.

Since inventory counts occur periodically, any item could fall below the desired reorder point prior to the review period. Therefore, the assumption is made that the inventory will fall below ideal reorder status prior to the periodic count approximately one-half of the review times. Assuming a review period of 7 days and using conditions similar to those of the perpetual example, the ROP then would be as follows:

$$ROP = D(T + P/2) + SS,$$
$$= 20(10 + 7/2) + 0 = 20(10 + 3.5) = 270 \text{ units.}$$

The average inventory formulation for the case of periodic review is:

$$I_{avg} = OQ/2 + (P \times D)/2 + SS$$

where

I_{avg} = Average inventory in units;

OQ = Order quantity in units;

P = Review period in days;

D = Average daily demand in units;

SS = Safety stock in units.

For the preceding example, the average inventory is calculated as:

$$I_{avg} = OQ/2 + (P \times D)/2 + SS$$
$$= 300/2 + (7 \times 10)/2 + 0 = 150 + 35 = 185 \text{ units}$$

Because of the time interval introduced by periodic review, periodic control systems generally require larger average inventories than perpetual systems. Ideal review frequency typically depends on a combination of item volume, value, and replenishment process. Items with high volume and value should employ perpetual review to minimize inventory and stockout risk. Items which must be replenished as a group would typically be reviewed periodically since they must be ordered together anyway.

Reactive Methods

The **reactive** or **pull inventory system,** as the name implies, responds to a channel member's inventory needs by drawing the product through the distribution channel. Replenishment shipments are initiated when available warehouse stock levels fall below a predetermined minimum or order point. The amount ordered is usually based on some lot-sizing formulation, although it may be some variable quantity that is a function of current stock levels and a predetermined maximum level.

The basic perpetual or periodic review process discussed earlier exemplifies a typical reactive system. Figure 7.10 illustrates a reactive inventory environment for a warehouse serving two wholesalers. The figure shows the current inventory (*I*), reorder point (*ROP*), order quantity (*OQ*), and average daily demand (*D*) for each wholesaler. A review of the wholesaler inventory indicates that a resupply order for 200 units should be placed by

FIGURE 7.10
A Reactive Inventory
Environment

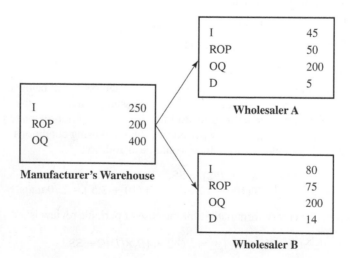

wholesaler A from the warehouse. Since current inventory is above ROP for wholesaler B, no resupply action is necessary at this time. However, more thorough analysis illustrates that the independent actions by wholesaler A will likely cause a stockout at wholesaler B within a few days. Wholesaler B will likely stock out because inventory level is close to the reorder point and the supplying warehouse center will not have enough inventory to replenish wholesaler B.

Classical reactive inventory logic is rooted in the following assumptions. First, the system is founded on the basic assumption that all customers, market areas, and products contribute equally to profits.

Second, a reactive system assumes infinite capacity at the source. This assumption implies that product can be produced as desired and stored at the production facility until required throughout the supply chain.

Third, reactive inventory logic assumes infinite inventory availability at the supply location. The combination of assumptions 2 and 3 implies relative replenishment certainty. The reactive inventory logic provides for no back orders or stockouts in processing replenishment orders.

Fourth, reactive decision rules assume that performance cycle time can be predicted and that cycle lengths are independent. This means that each performance cycle is a random event and that extended cycles don't generally occur for subsequent replenishment orders. Although reactive logic assumes no control over cycle times, many managers are, in fact, able to influence performance cycle length through expediting and alternative sourcing strategies.

Fifth, reactive inventory logic operates best when customer demand patterns are relatively stable and consistent. Ideally, demand patterns should be stable over the relevant planning cycle for statistically developed inventory parameters to operate correctly. Most reactive system decision rules assume demand patterns based on standard normal, gamma, or Poisson distributions. When the actual demand function does not resemble one of the above functions, the statistical inventory decision rules based on these assumptions will not operate correctly.

Sixth, reactive inventory systems determine each distribution warehouse's timing and quantity of replenishment orders independently of all other sites, including the supply source. Thus, there is little potential to effectively coordinate inventory requirements across multiple distribution warehouses. The ability to take advantage of inventory information is not utilized—a serious defect when information and its communication are among the few resources that are decreasing in cost in the supply chain.

The final assumption characteristic of reactive inventory systems is that performance cycle length cannot be correlated with demand. The assumption is necessary to develop an accurate approximation of the variance of the demand over the performance cycle. For many situations higher demand levels create longer replenishment performance cycles since they also increase the demands on inventory and transportation resources. This implies that periods of high demand should not necessarily correspond to extended performance cycles caused by stockouts or limited product availability.

Operationally, most inventory managers constrain the impact of such limitations through the skillful use of manual overrides. However, these overrides often lead to ineffective inventory decisions since the resulting plan is based on inconsistent rules and managerial policy.

Planning Methods

Inventory planning methods use a shared database to coordinate inventory requirements across multiple locations or stages in the supply chain. Planning activities may occur centrally to coordinate inventory allocation and delivery to multiple destinations. Planning

FIGURE 7.11
Fair Share Allocation
Example

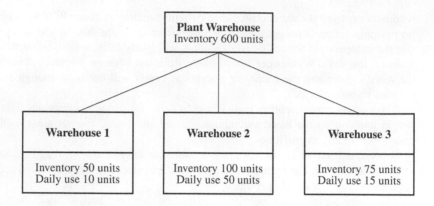

may also coordinate inventory requirements across multiple channel partners such as manufacturers and retailers. The Advanced Planning and Scheduling **(APS)** systems discussed in Chapter 6 illustrate the capability of planning applications. While APS systems computerize the process, it is important that logistics managers understand the underlying logic and assumptions. Two inventory planning methods are fair share allocation and Distribution Requirements Planning **(DRP).**

Fair Share Allocation

A simplified inventory management planning method that provides each distribution facility with an equitable distribution of available inventory is called **fair share allocation.** Figure 7.11 illustrates the network structure, current inventory level, and daily requirements for three warehouses served by a single plant warehouse.

Using fair share allocation, the inventory planner determines the amount of inventory that can be allocated to each warehouse from the available inventory at the plant. For this example, assume that it is desirable to retain 100 units at the plant warehouse; therefore, 500 units are available for allocation. The calculation to determine the common days supply is:

$$DS = \frac{AQ + \sum_{j=1}^{n} I_j}{\sum_{i=1}^{n} D_j}.$$

where

DS = Common days supply for warehouse inventories;

AQ = Inventory units to be allocated from plant warehouse;

I_j = Inventory in units for warehouse j; and

D_j = Daily demand for warehouse j.

In this example,

$$DS = \frac{500 + (50 + 100 + 75)}{10 + 50 + 15}$$

$$= \frac{500 + 225}{75} = 9.67 \text{ days}$$

The fair share allocation dictates that each warehouse should be stocked to 9.67 days of inventory. The amount to be allocated to each warehouse is determined by:

$$A_j = (DS - I_j / D_j) \times D_j$$

where

A_j = Amount allocated to warehouse j;

DS = Days supply that each warehouse is brought up to;

I_j = Inventory in units for warehouse j; and

D_j = Daily demand for warehouse j.

The amount allocated to warehouse 1 for this example is:

$$
\begin{aligned}
A_1 &= (9.67 - 50/10) \times 10 \\
&= (9.67 - 5) \times 10 \\
&= 4.67 \times 10) = 46.7 \text{ (round to 47 units)}.
\end{aligned}
$$

The allocation for warehouses 2 and 3 can be determined similarly and is 383 and 70 units, respectively.

While fair share allocation coordinates inventory levels across multiple sites, it does not consider specific factors such as differences in performance cycle time, EOQ, or safety stock requirements. Fair share allocation methods are therefore limited in their ability to manage multistage inventories.

Requirements Planning

Requirements planning is an approach that integrates across the supply chain, taking into consideration unique requirements. Requirements planning is typically classified as Materials Requirements Planning (MRP) or Distribution Requirements Planning (DRP). There is one fundamental difference between the two techniques. MRP is driven by a production schedule. In contrast, DRP is driven by supply chain demand. So, while MRP generally operates in a dependent demand situation, DRP is applicable to an independent demand environment where uncertain customer requirements drive inventory requirements. MRP coordinates scheduling and integration of materials into finished goods, and so controls inventory until manufacturing or assembly is completed. DRP takes coordination responsibility once finished goods are received in the plant warehouse.

Figure 7.12 illustrates the conceptual design of a combined MRP/DRP system that integrates finished goods, work-in-process, and materials planning. The top half of the figure illustrates an MRP system that time-phases raw material arrivals to support the production schedule. The result of MRP execution is finished goods inventory at the manufacturing site. The bottom half of the figure illustrates the DRP system that allocates finished inventory from the manufacturing site to distribution warehouses and ultimately to retail customers. DRP time-phases the movements to coordinate inventory arrivals to meet customer requirements and forecasts. The MRP and DRP systems interface at the manufacturing site. Close coordination between the two systems results in minimal need for safety stock. DRP coordinates inventory levels, schedules, and when necessary, reschedules inventory movement between levels.

The fundamental DRP planning tool is the schedule, which coordinates requirements Schedules for the same SKU are integrated to determine the overall requirements for replenishment facilities such as a plant warehouse.

FIGURE 7.12
Conceptual Design of
Integrated MRP/DRP
System

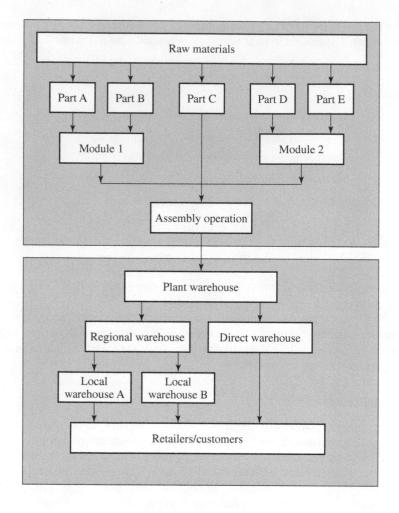

Figure 7.13 illustrates DRP planning schedules for two warehouses and a central supply facility. The schedules are developed using weekly time increments known as **time buckets.** Each bucket projects one period of activity. Although weekly increments are most common, daily or monthly increments can be used. For each site and SKU, the schedule reports current on-hand balance, safety stock, performance cycle length, and order quantity. In addition, for each planning period, the schedule reports gross requirements, scheduled receipts, and projected inventory on hand. Using the combination of requirements and projected availability, DRP determines the planned orders necessary to meet anticipated requirements. Gross requirements reflect the demand from consumers and other distribution facilities supplied by the site under review. For Figure 7.13, the gross requirements of the central supply facility reflect the cascading demands of the eastern and western warehouses. Scheduled receipts are the replenishment shipments planned for arrival at the distribution warehouse. Projected on-hand inventory refers to the anticipated week-ending level. It is equal to the prior week's on-hand inventory level less the current week's gross requirements plus any scheduled receipts. While planning approaches to inventory management offer significant benefits, they have some constraints.

Eastern Warehouse

					Weeks				
	Past due	1	2	3	4	5	6	7	8
Gross requirements		100	120	150	130	100	80	70	90
Scheduled receipts		0	0	400	0	0	0	400	0
Projected on hand	400	300	180	430	300	200	120	450	360
Planned orders		400	0	0	0	400	0	0	0

Safety stock: 100
Order quantity: 400
Leadtime: 2 weeks

Plant Warehouse

Safety stock: 100
Batch size: 600
Leadtime: 1 week

						Weeks				
	Past due	1	2	3	4	5	6	7	8
Gross requirements		400	150	0	150	550	0	0	0
Scheduled receipts		0	600	0	600	0	0	0	0
Projected on hand	600	200	650	650	1100	550	550	550	550
Planned production		600	0	600	0	0	0	0	0

Western Warehouse

					Weeks				
	Past due	1	2	3	4	5	6	7	8
Gross requirements		40	50	60	90	70	100	40	30
Scheduled receipts		0	0	150	0	150	150	0	0
Projected on hand	200	160	110	200	110	190	240	200	170
Planned orders		0	150	0	150	150	0	0	0

Safety stock: 50
Order quantity: 150
Leadtime: 1 week

Requirement ----------->

Shipment ———————>

FIGURE 7.13   Distribution Requirements Planning Example

First, inventory planning systems require accurate and coordinated forecasts for each warehouse. The forecast is necessary to direct the flow of goods through the supply chain. Ideally, the system does not maintain excess inventory at any location, so little room for error exists in a lean inventory system. To the extent this level of forecast accuracy is possible, inventory planning systems operate well.

Second, inventory planning requires consistent and reliable product movement between warehouse facilities. While variable performance cycles can be accommodated through safety leadtimes, such uncertainty reduces planning system effectiveness.

Third, integrated planning systems may be subject to system nervousness, or frequent rescheduling, due to production breakdowns or delivery delays. System nervousness leads to fluctuation in capacity utilization, rescheduling cost, and confusion in deliveries. This is intensified by the volatile operating environment characteristic of supply chain logistics. Uncertainties such as transportation and vendor delivery reliability can cause an extreme DRP nervousness.

Collaborative Inventory Replenishment

In Chapters 5 and 6 CPFR was introduced and discussed as a major collaborative effort between supply chain trading partners. Several collaborative initiatives focus only on inventory replenishment. Replenishment programs are designed to streamline the flow of goods within the supply chain. There are several specific techniques for collaborative replenishment, all of which build on supply chain relationships to rapidly replenish inventory on the basis of joint planning or actual sales experience. The intent is to reduce reliance on forecasting when and where inventory will need to be positioned to demand on a just-in-time basis. Effective collaborative replenishment programs require extensive cooperation and information sharing among supply chain partners. Specific techniques for collaborative inventory replenishment are quick response, vendor-managed inventory, and profile replenishment.

Quick Response

A technology-driven cooperative effort between retailers and suppliers to improve inventory velocity while closely matching replenishment supply to consumer buying patterns is quick response **(QR).** QR is implemented by sharing retail sales for specific products between supply chain participants to facilitate right product assortment availability when and where it is required. Instead of operating on a 15- to 30-day order cycle, QR arrangements can replenish retail inventories in a few days. Continuous information exchange regarding availability and delivery reduces uncertainty for the total supply chain and creates the opportunity for maximum flexibility. With fast, dependable order response, inventory can be committed as required, resulting in increased turnover and improved availability. Walmart's retail link system is a prime example of the power of sharing sales to facilitate QR.

Vendor-Managed Inventory

Vendor-managed inventory **(VMI)** is a modification of quick response that eliminates the need for replenishment orders. The goal is to establish a supply chain arrangement so flexible and efficient that retail inventory is continuously replenished. The distinguishing factor between QR and VMI is who takes responsibility for setting target inventory levels and making restocking decisions. In QR, the customer makes the decisions. In VMI, the supplier assumes more responsibility and actually manages an inventory category for the customer. By receiving daily transmission of retail sales or warehouse shipments, the supplier assumes responsibility for replenishing retail inventory in the required quantities, colors, sizes, and styles. The supplier commits to keeping the customer in stock and to maintaining inventory velocity. In some situations, replenishment involves cross-docking or direct store delivery **(DSD)** designed to eliminate the need for warehousing between the supplier and customer.

Profile Replenishment

Some manufacturers, wholesalers, and retailers are experimenting with an even more sophisticated collaboration known as profile replenishment **(PR).** The PR strategy extends

QR and VMI by giving suppliers the right to anticipate future requirements according to their overall knowledge of a merchandise category. A category profile details the combination of sizes, colors, and associated products that usually sell in a particular type of retail outlet. Given PR responsibility, the supplier can simplify retailer involvement by eliminating the need to track unit sales and inventory level for fast-moving products. Gerber products, a processor of baby food, uses PR with some of its key customers since it has better knowledge of product combinations that consumers will purchase than most retailers.

Many firms, particularly manufacturers, are using DRP and even APS logic to coordinate inventory planning with major customers. The manufacturers are extending their planning framework to include customer warehouses and, in some cases, their retail stores. Such integrated planning capabilities facilitate manufacturer coordination and management of customer inventories.

Collaborative planning effectively shares inventory requirements and availability between supply chain partners, thus reducing uncertainty. Table 7.17 illustrates the service and inventory impact in a simulated environment under conditions of low and high uncertainty.[7] Table 7.18 illustrates managerial considerations that drive adaptations of control logic.

Inventory Management Practices

An integrated inventory management strategy defines the policies and process used to determine where to place inventory and when to initiate replenishment shipments, as well as how much to allocate. The strategy development process employs three steps to classify products and markets, define segment strategies, and operationalize policies and parameters.

[7]David J. Closs et al., "An Empirical Comparison of Anticipatory and Response-Based Supply Chain Strategies," *International Journal of Logistics Management* 9, no. 2 (1998), pp. 21–34.

	Low Uncertainty Anticipatory	Low Uncertainty Responsive	High Uncertainty Anticipatory	High Uncertainty Responsive
Customer Service				
Fill rate percent	97.69	99.66	96.44	99.29
Inventories				
Supplier inventory	12.88	13.24	14.82	13.61
Manufacturer inventory	6.05	6.12	7.03	6.09
Distributor inventory	5.38	5.86	5.04	5.63
Retailer inventory	30.84	15.79	32.86	20.30
System inventory	55.15	41.01	59.76	45.83

TABLE 7.17
Comparative Service and Inventory Characteristics for Anticipatory versus Responsive Inventory Systems

Source: Adapted from David J. Closs et al., "An Empirical Comparison of Anticipatory and Response-Based Supply Chain Strategies," *International Journal of Logistics Management* 9, no. 2 (1998), pp. 21–34. Used with permission.

Use Planning Logic under Conditions of	Use Reactive Logic under Conditions of
Highly profitable segments	Cycle time uncertainty
Dependent demand	Demand uncertainty
Economies of scale	Destination capacity limitations
Supply uncertainty	
Source capacity limitations	
Seasonal supply buildup	

TABLE 7.18
Suggested Inventory Management Logic

Product/Market Classification

The objective of product/market classification is to focus and refine inventory management efforts. Product/market classification, which is also called **fine-line** or **ABC classification,** groups products, markets, or customers with similar characteristics to facilitate inventory management. The classification process recognizes that not all products and markets have the same characteristics or degree of importance. Sound inventory management requires that classification be consistent with enterprise strategy and service objectives.

Classification can be based on a variety of measures. The most common are sales, profit contribution, inventory value, usage rate, and item category. The typical classification process sequences products or markets so that entries with similar characteristics are grouped together. Table 7.19 illustrates product classification using sales. The products are classified in descending order by sales volume so that the high-volume products are listed first, followed by slower movers. Classification by sales volume is one of the oldest methods used to establish selective inventory policies. For most marketing or logistics applications, a small percentage of the entities account for a large percentage of the volume. This operationalization is often called the **80/20 rule or Pareto's principle.** The 80/20 rule, which is based on widespread observations, states that for a typical enterprise 80 percent of the sales volume is typically accounted for by 20 percent of the products. A corollary to the rule is that 80 percent of enterprise sales are accounted for by 20 percent of the customers. The reverse perspective of the rule would state that the remaining 20 percent of sales are obtained from 80 percent of the products, customers, etc. In general terms, the 80/20 rule implies that a majority of sales result from a relatively few products or customers.

Once items are classified or grouped, it is common to label each category with a character or description. High-volume, fast-moving products are often described as A items. The moderate-volume items are termed the B items, and the low-volume or slow movers are known as Cs. These character labels indicate why this process is often termed ABC analysis. While fine-line classification often uses three categories, some firms use four or five

TABLE 7.19
Product Market Classification (Sales)

Product Identification	Annual Sales (in 000s)	Percent Total Sales	Accumulated Sales (%)	Products (%)	Classification Category
1	$45,000	30.0%	30.0%	5%	A
2	35,000	23.3	53.3	10	A
3	25,000	16.7	70.0	15	A
4	15,000	10.0	80.0	20	A
5	8,000	5.3	85.3	25	B
6	5,000	3.3	88.6	30	B
7	4,000	2.7	91.3	35	B
8	3,000	2.0	93.3	40	B
9	2,000	1.3	94.6	45	B
10	1,000	0.7	95.3	50	B
11	1,000	0.7	96.0	55	C
12	1,000	0.7	96.7	60	C
13	1,000	0.7	97.4	65	C
14	750	0.5	97.9	70	C
15	750	0.5	98.4	75	C
16	750	0.5	98.9	80	C
17	500	0.3	99.2	85	C
18	500	0.3	99.5	90	C
19	500	0.3	99.8	95	C
20	250	0.2	100.0	100	C
	$150,000				

categories to further refine classifications. Grouping of similar products facilitates management efforts to establish focused inventory strategies for specific product segments. For example, high-volume or fast-moving products are typically targeted for higher service levels. This often requires that fast-moving items have relatively more safety stock. Conversely, to reduce overall inventory levels, slower-moving items may be allowed relatively less safety stock, resulting in lower service levels.

In special situations, classification systems may be based on multiple factors. For example, item gross margin and importance to customers can be weighted to develop a combined index instead of simply using sales volume. The weighted rank would then group items that have similar profitability and importance characteristics. The inventory policy, including safety stock levels, is then established using the weighted rank.

The classification array defines product or market groups to be assigned similar inventory strategies. The use of item groups facilitates the identification and specification of inventory strategies without requiring tedious development of individual item strategies. It is much easier to track and manage 3 to 10 groups instead of hundreds of individual items.

Segment Strategy Definition

The second step is to define the inventory strategy for each product/market group or segment. The strategy includes specification for all aspects of the inventory management process, including service objectives, forecasting method, management technique, and review cycle.

The key to establishing selective management strategies is the realization that product segments have different degrees of importance with respect to achieving the enterprise mission. Important differences in inventory responsiveness should be designed into the policies and procedures used for inventory management.

Table 7.20 illustrates a sample integrated strategy for four item categories. In this case, the items are grouped by ABC sales volume and as a promotional or regular stock item. Promotional items are those commonly sold in special marketing efforts that result in considerable demand lumpiness. Lumpy demand patterns are characteristic of promotional periods with high volume followed by postpromotion periods with relatively low demand.

Table 7.20 illustrates a management segmentation scheme based on service objectives, forecasting process, review period, inventory management approach, and replenishment monitoring frequency. Additional or fewer characteristics of the inventory management process may be appropriate for some enterprises. Although this table is not presented as a comprehensive inventory strategy framework, it illustrates the issues that must be considered. The rationale behind each element is presented on the basis of the full-line classification.

Policies and Parameters

The final step in implementing a focused inventory management strategy is to define detailed procedures and parameters. The procedures define data requirements, software applications, performance objectives, and decision guidelines. The parameters delineate

Fine-Line Classification	Service Objective	Forecasting Procedure	Review Period	Inventory Management	Replenishment Monitoring
A (Promotional)	99%	CPFR	Perpetual	Planning—DRP	Daily
A (Regular)	98	Sales history	Perpetual	Planning—DRP	Daily
B	95	Sales history	Weekly	Planning—DRP	Weekly
C	90	Sales history	Biweekly	Reorder point	Biweekly

TABLE 7.20
Integrated Strategy

values such as review period length, service objectives, inventory carrying cost percentage, order quantities, and reorder points. The combination of parameters either determines or can be used to calculate the precise quantities necessary to make inventory management decisions.

Summary

Inventory typically represents the second largest component of logistics cost next to transportation. The risks associated with holding inventory increase as products move down the supply chain closer to the customer because the potential of having the product in the wrong place or form increases and costs have been incurred to distribute the product. In addition to the risk of lost sales due to stockouts because adequate inventory is not available, other risks include obsolescence, pilferage, and damage. Further, the cost of carrying inventory is significantly influenced by the cost of the capital tied up in the inventory. Geographic specialization, decoupling, supply/demand balancing, and buffering uncertainty provide the basic rationale for maintaining inventory. While there is substantial interest in reducing overall supply chain inventory, inventory does add value and can result in lower overall supply chain costs with appropriate trade-offs.

From a supply chain logistics perspective, the major controllable inventory elements are replenishment cycle stock, safety stock, and in-transit stock. The appropriate replenishment cycle stock can be determined using an EOQ formula to reflect the trade-off between storage and ordering cost. Safety stock depends on the mean and variance of demand and the replenishment cycle. In-transit stock depends on the transport mode.

Inventory management uses a combination of reactive and planning logics. Reactive logic is most appropriate for items with low volume, high demand, and high performance cycle uncertainty because it postpones the risk of inventory speculation. Inventory planning logic is appropriate for high-volume items with relatively stable demand. Inventory planning methods offer the potential for effective inventory management because they take advantage of improved information and economies of scale. Adaptive logic combines the two alternatives depending on product and market conditions. Collaboration offers a way for parties in the supply chain to jointly gain inventory efficiency and effectiveness.

Study Questions

1. Discuss the relationship between service level, uncertainty, safety stock, and order quantity. How can trade-offs between these elements be made?
2. Discuss the disproportionate risk of holding inventory by retailers, wholesalers, and manufacturers. Why has there been a trend to push inventory back up the channel of distribution?
3. What is the difference between the probability of a stockout and the magnitude of a stockout?
4. Illustrate how fine-line inventory classification can be used with product and customer segments. What are the benefits and considerations when classifying inventory by product, customer, and customer/product?

5. Customer-based inventory management strategies allow for the use of different availability levels for specific customers. Discuss the rationale for such a strategy. Are such strategies discriminatory? Justify your position.

6. Discuss the differences between reactive and planning inventory logics. What are the advantages and risks associated with each? What are the implications of each?

Challenge Questions

1. Aggregate inventory data suggest that while overall average inventory levels are declining, the relative percentage being held by manufacturers is increasing. Explain why you think this observation is either true or false. Describe how such a shift could benefit the operations of the entire channel and how manufacturers could take advantage of the shift.

2. Consumers are expressing increased demand for product customization in the form of features, labeling, color, or packaging. What is the impact of this trend on supply chain inventory? What strategies can firms and supply chains use to mitigate this impact?

3. Many of the retailers and in some cases wholesalers are driving their suppliers to provide vendor-managed inventory and consignment inventory at no additional cost to the customer. In effect, the customer is looking to shift inventory risk and responsibility to the supplier without paying for it. Describe initiatives that the supplier can use to recoup some value when they have to follow these customer requirements.

4. You have been asked to establish an inventory carrying cost percent to supply your firm's supply chain planning initiatives. Identify and describe the carrying cost components. Review the various approaches to determine the opportunity cost component and provide the rationale for each. As part of the assignment, you must recommend which approach you would use and why. You should also identify the implications of the opportunity cost decision on supply chain design decisions.

Chapter **One**

Purchasing and Supply Management

2 Purchasing and Supply Management

Key Questions for the Supply Decision Maker

Should we

- Rethink how supply can contribute more effectively to organizational goals and strategies?
- Try to find out what the organization's total spend with suppliers really is?
- Identify opportunities for meaningful involvement in major corporate activities?

How can we

- Align our supply strategy with the organization's strategy?
- Get others to recognize the profit-leverage effect of purchasing/supply management?
- Show how supply can affect our firm's competitive position?

Every organization needs suppliers. No organization can exist without suppliers. Therefore, the organization's approach to suppliers, its acquisition processes and policies, and its relationships with suppliers will impact not only the performance of the suppliers, but also the organization's own performance. No organization can be successful without the support of its supplier base, operationally and strategically, short- and long-term.

Supply management is focused on the acquisition process recognizing the supply chain and organizational contexts. Special emphasis is on decision making that aligns the supplier network and the acquisition process with organizational goals and strategies and ensures short- and long-term value for funds spent.

There is no one best way of organizing the supply function, conducting its activities, and integrating suppliers effectively. This is both interesting and challenging. It is interesting because the acquisition of organizational requirements covers a very wide and complex set of approaches with different needs and different suppliers. It is challenging because of the complexity and because the process is dynamic, not static. Moreover, some of the brightest minds in this world have been hired as marketing and sales experts to persuade supply managers to choose their companies as suppliers. It is also challenging because every supply decision depends on a large variety of factors, the combination of which may well be unique to a particular organization.

For more than 80 years, this text and its predecessors have presented the supply function and suppliers as critical to an organization's success, competitive advantage, and customer satisfaction. Whereas in the 1930s this was a novel idea, over the past few decades there has been growing interest at the executive level in the supply chain management and its impact on strategic goals and objectives.

To increase long-term shareholder value, the company must increase revenue, decrease costs, or both. Supply's contribution should not be perceived as only focused on cost. Supply can and should also be concerned with revenue enhancement. What can supply and suppliers do to help the organization increase revenues or decrease costs? should be a standard question for any supply manager.

The supply function continues to evolve as technology and the worldwide competitive environment require innovative approaches. The traditionally held view that multiple sourcing increases supply security has been challenged by a trend toward single sourcing. Results from closer supplier relations and cooperation with suppliers question the wisdom of the traditional arm's-length dealings between purchaser and supplier. Negotiation is receiving increasing emphasis as opposed to competitive bidding, and longer-term contracts are replacing short-term buying techniques. E-commerce tools permit faster and lower-cost solutions, not only on the transaction side of supply but also in management decision support. Organizations are continually evaluating the risks and opportunities of global sourcing. All of these trends are a logical outcome of increased managerial concern with value and increasing procurement aggressiveness in developing suppliers to meet specific supply objectives of quality, quantity, delivery, price, service, and continuous improvement.

Effective purchasing and supply management contributes significantly to organizational success. This text explores the nature of this contribution and the management requirements for effective and efficient performance. The acquisition of materials, services, and equipment—of the right qualities, in the right quantities, at the right prices, at the right time, with the right quality, and on a continuing basis—long has occupied the attention of managers in both the public and private sectors.

Today, the emphasis is on the total supply management process in the context of organizational goals and management of supply chains. The rapidly changing supply scene, with cycles of abundance and shortages, varying prices, lead times, and availability, provides a continuing challenge to those organizations wishing to obtain a maximum contribution from this area. Furthermore, environmental, security, and financial regulatory requirements have added considerable complexity to the task of ensuring that supply and suppliers provide competitive advantage.

PURCHASING AND SUPPLY MANAGEMENT

Although some people may view interest in the performance of the supply function as a recent phenomenon, it was recognized as an independent and important function by many of the nation's railroad organizations well before 1900.

Yet, traditionally, most firms regarded the supply function primarily as a clerical activity. However, during World War I and World War II, the success of a firm was not dependent on what it could sell, since the market was almost unlimited. Instead, the ability to obtain from suppliers the raw materials, supplies, and services needed to keep the factories and mines operating was the key determinant of organizational success. Consequently, attention was given to the organization, policies, and procedures of the supply function, and it emerged as a recognized managerial activity.

During the 1950s and 1960s, supply management continued to gain stature as the number of people trained and competent to make sound supply decisions increased. Many companies elevated the chief purchasing officer to top management status, with titles such as vice president of purchasing, director of materials, or vice president of purchasing and supply.

As the decade of the 1970s opened, organizations faced two vexing problems: an international shortage of almost all the basic raw materials needed to support operations and a rate of price increase far above the norm since the end of World War II. The Middle East oil embargo during the summer of 1973 intensified both the shortages and the price escalation. These developments put the spotlight directly on supply, for their performance in obtaining needed items from suppliers at realistic prices spelled the difference between success and failure. This emphasized again the crucial role played by supply and suppliers.

As the decade of the 1990s unfolded, it became clear that organizations must have an efficient and effective supply function if they were to compete successfully in the global marketplace. The early 21st century has brought new challenges in the areas of sustainability, supply chain security, and risk management.

In large supply organizations, supply professionals often are divided into two categories: the tacticians who handle day-to-day requirements and the strategic thinkers who possess strong analytical and planning skills and are involved in activities such as strategic sourcing. The extent to which the structure, processes, and people in a specific organization will match these trends varies from organization to organization, and from industry to industry.

The future will see a gradual shift from predominantly defensive strategies, resulting from the need to change in order to remain competitive, to aggressive strategies, in which firms take an imaginative approach to achieving supply objectives to satisfy short-term and long-term organizational goals. The focus on strategy now includes an emphasis on process and knowledge management. This text discusses what organizations should do today to remain competitive as well as what strategic purchasing and supply management will focus on tomorrow.

Growing management interest through necessity and improved insight into the opportunities in the supply area has resulted in a variety of organizational concepts. Terms such as *purchasing, procurement, materiel, materials management, logistics, sourcing, supply management,* and *supply chain management* are used almost interchangeably. No agreement exists on the definition of each of these terms, and managers in public and private institutions may have identical responsibilities but substantially different titles. The following definitions may be helpful in sorting out the more common understanding of the various terms.

Supply Management Terminology

Some academics and practitioners limit the term *purchasing* to the process of buying: learning of the need, locating and selecting a supplier, negotiating price and other pertinent terms, and following up to ensure delivery and payment. This is not the perspective taken in this text. *Purchasing, supply management,* and *procurement* are used interchangeably to refer to the integration of related functions to provide effective and efficient materials and services to the organization. Thus, purchasing or supply management is not only concerned with the standard steps in the procurement process: (1) the recognition of need, (2) the translation of that need into a commercially equivalent description, (3) the search for potential suppliers, (4) the selection of a suitable source, (5) the agreement on order or contract details, (6) the delivery of the products or services, and (7) the payment of suppliers.

Further responsibilities of supply may include receiving, inspection, warehousing, inventory control, materials handling, packaging scheduling, in- and outbound transportation/traffic, and disposal. Supply also may have responsibility for other components of the supply chain, such as the organization's customers and their customers and their suppliers' suppliers. This extension represents the term *supply chain management,* where the focus is on minimizing costs and lead times across tiers in the supply chain to the benefit of the final customer. The idea that competition may change from the firm level to the supply chain level has been advanced as the next stage of competitive evolution.

In addition to the *operational responsibilities* that are part of the day-to-day activities of the supply organization, there are *strategic responsibilities*. *Strategic sourcing* focuses on long-term supplier relationships and commodity plans with the objectives of identifying opportunities in areas such as cost reductions, new technology advancements, and supply market trends. The Sabor case in Chapter 2 provides an excellent example of the need to take a strategic perspective when planning long-term supply needs.

Lean purchasing or *lean supply management* refers primarily to a manufacturing context and the implementation of just-in-time (JIT) tools and techniques to ensure every step in the supply process adds value, that inventories are kept at a minimum level, and that distances and delays between process steps are kept as short as possible. Instant communication of job status is essential and shared.

Supply and Logistics

The large number of physical moves associated with any purchasing or supply chain activity has focused attention on the role of logistics. According to the Council of Supply Chain Management Professionals, "Logistics management is that part of supply chain management that plans, implements, and controls the efficient, effective forward and reverse flow and storage of goods, services, and related information between the point of origin and the point of consumption in order to meet customers' requirements."[1] This definition includes inbound, outbound, internal, and external movements. Logistics is not confined to manufacturing organizations. It is relevant to service organizations and to both private- and public-sector firms.

The attraction of the logistics concept is that it looks at the material flow process as a complete system, from initial need for materials to delivery of finished product or service to the customer. It attempts to provide the communication, coordination, and control needed to avoid the potential conflicts between the physical distribution and the materials management functions.

Supply influences a number of logistics-related activities, such as how much to buy and inbound transportation. With an increased emphasis on controlling material flow, the supply function must be concerned with decisions beyond supplier selection and price. The Qmont Mining case in Chapter 4 illustrates the logistics considerations of supplying multiple locations.

Organizations are examining business processes and exploring opportunities to integrate boundary-spanning activities in order to reduce costs and improve lead times. For example, Renault-Nissan announced in 2014 that it would integrate supply chain management activities, including purchasing and logistics, with manufacturing and R&D. The company had targeted €4.3 billion in annual savings from this initiative.[2]

---

[1] Council of Supply Chain Management Professionals, http://cscmp.org/about-us/supply-chain -management-definitions, accessed February 15, 2014.

[2] M. Williams, "Renault-Nissan Could integrate SCM Functions," *Automotive Logistics*, February 5, 2014, www.automotivelogisticsmagazine.com/news/renault-nissan-could-integrate-scm-functions, accessed February 15, 2014.

Supply chain management is a systems approach to managing the entire flow of information, materials, and services from raw materials suppliers through factories and warehouses to the end customer. The Institute for Supply Management (ISM) glossary defines *supply chain management* as "the design and management of seamless, value-added processes across organizational boundaries to meet the real needs of the end customer. The development and integration of people and technological resources are critical to successful supply chain integration."[3]

The term *value chain,* a term commonly used in the strategy literature, has been used to trace a product or service through its various moves and transformations, identifying the costs added at each successive stage.

Some academics and practitioners believe the term *chain* does not properly convey what really happens in a supply or value chain, and they prefer to use the term *supply network* or *supply web.*

The use of the concepts of purchasing, procurement, supply, and supply chain management will vary from organization to organization. It will depend on (1) their stage of development and/or sophistication, (2) the industry in which they operate, and (3) their competitive position.

The relative importance of the supply area compared to the other prime functions of the organization will be a major determinant of the management attention it will receive. How to assess the materials and services needs of a particular organization in context is one of the purposes of this book. More than 45 cases are provided to provide insight into a variety of situations and to give practice in resolving managerial problems.

THE SIZE OF THE ORGANIZATION'S SPEND AND FINANCIAL SIGNIFICANCE

The amount of money organizations spend with suppliers is staggering. Collectively, private and public organizations in North America spend about 1.5 times the GDPs of the United States, Canada, and Mexico combined, totaling at least $29 trillion U.S. dollars spent with suppliers.

Dollars spent with suppliers as a percentage of total revenues is a good indicator of supply's financial impact. Obviously, the percentage of revenue that is paid out to suppliers varies from industry to industry and organization to organization, and increased outsourcing over the last decade has increased the percentage of spend significantly. In almost all manufacturing organizations, the supply area represents by far the largest single category of spend, ranging from 50 to 80 percent of revenue. Wages, by comparison, typically amount to about 10 to 20 percent. In comparison, the total dollars spent on outside suppliers typically ranges from 25 to 35 percent of revenues. The Delphi Corporation case in Chapter 13 is a good illustration of the significance of spend in a manufacturing organization. Total purchases were $17 billion compared to revenues of $28 billion.

The financial impact of the corporate spend is often illustrated by the profit-leverage effect and the return-on-assets effect.

---

[3] Institute for Supply Management, "Glossary of Key Supply Management Terms," www.ism.ws.

Profit-Leverage Effect

The profit-leverage effect of supply savings is measured by the increase in profit obtained by a decrease in purchase spend. For example, for an organization with revenue of $100 million, purchases of $60 million, and profit of $8 million before tax, a 10 percent reduction in purchase spend would result in an increase in profit of 75 percent. To achieve a $6,000,000 increase in profit by increasing sales, assuming the same percentage hold, might well require an increase of $75 million in sales, or 75 percent! Which of these two options—an increase in sales of 75 percent or a decrease in purchase spend of 10 percent— is more likely to be achieved?

This is not to suggest that it would be easy to reduce overall purchase costs by 10 percent. In a firm that has given major attention to the supply function over the years, it would be difficult, and perhaps impossible, to do. But, in a firm that has neglected supply, it would be a realistic objective. Because of the profit-leverage effect of supply, large savings are possible relative to the effort that would be needed to increase sales by the much-larger percentage necessary to generate the same effect on the profit and loss (P&L) statement. Since, in many firms, sales already has received much more attention, supply may be the last untapped "profit producer."

Return-on-Assets Effect

Financial experts are increasingly interested in return on assets (ROA) as a measure of corporate performance. Figure 1–1 shows the standard ROA model, using the same ratio of figures as in the previous example, and assuming that inventory accounts for 30 percent of total assets. If purchase costs were reduced by 10 percent, that would cause an extra benefit of a 10 percent reduction in the inventory asset base. The numbers in the boxes show the initial figures used in arriving at the 10 percent ROA performance.

FIGURE 1–1
Return-on-Assets Factors

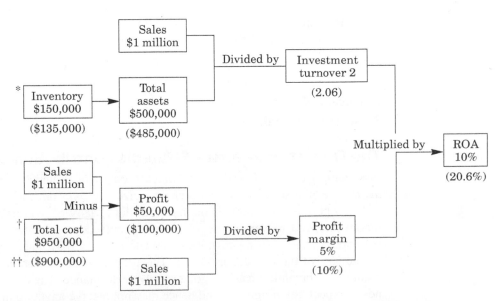

*Inventory is approximately 30 percent of total assets.
†Purchases account for half of total sales, or $500,000.
††Figures in parentheses assume a 10 percent reduction in purchase costs.

The numbers below each box are the figures resulting from a 10 percent overall purchase price reduction, and the end product is a new ROA of 20.6 percent or about an 100 percent increase in return on assets.

Reduction in Inventory Investment

Charles Dehelly, senior executive vice president at Thomson Multimedia, headquartered in Paris, France, said: "It came as quite a surprise to some supply people that I expected them to worry about the balance sheet by insisting on measuring their return on capital employed performance."[4] Mr. Dehelly was pushing for reductions in inventory investment, not only by lowering purchase price, as shown in the example in Figure 1–1, but also by getting suppliers to take over inventory responsibility and ownership, thereby removing asset dollars in the ROA calculations, but also taking on the risk of obsolescence, inventory carrying, and disposal costs. Since accountants value inventory items at the purchaser at purchased cost, including transportation, but inventory at the supplier at manufacturing cost, the same items stored at the supplier typically have a lower inventory investment and carrying cost.

Thus, it is a prime responsibility of supply to manage the supply process with the lowest reasonable levels of inventory attainable. Inventory turnover and level are two major measures of supply chain performance.

Evidently, the financial impact of supply is on the balance sheet and the income statement, the two key indicators of corporate financial health used by managers, analysts, financial institutions, and investors. While the financial impact of the supply spend is obviously significant, it is by no means the only impact of supply on an organization's ability to compete and be successful.

SUPPLY CONTRIBUTION

Although supply's financial impact is major, supply contributes to organizational goals and strategies in a variety of other ways. The three major perspectives on supply are shown in Figure 1–2:

1. Operational versus strategic.
2. Direct and indirect.
3. Negative, neutral, and positive.

The Operational versus Strategic Contribution of Supply

First, supply can be viewed in two contexts: operational, which is characterized as *trouble avoidance*, and strategic, which is characterized as *opportunistic*.

The operational context is the most familiar. Many people inside the organization are inconvenienced to varying degrees when supply does not meet minimum expectations. Improper quality, wrong quantities, and late delivery may make life miserable for the ultimate user of the product or service. This is so basic and apparent that "no complaints" is assumed to be an indicator of good supply performance. The difficulty is that many users never expect anything more and hence may not receive anything more.

[4] M. R. Leenders and P. F. Johnson, *Major Changes in Supply Chain Responsibilities* (Tempe, AZ: CAPS Research, March 2002), p. 104.

**FIGURE 1–2
Purchasing's
Operational
and Strategic
Contributions**

Source: Michiel R. Leenders and Anna E. Flynn, *Value-Driven Purchasing: Managing the Key Steps in the Acquisition Process* (Burr Ridge, IL: Richard D. Irwin, 1995), p. 7.

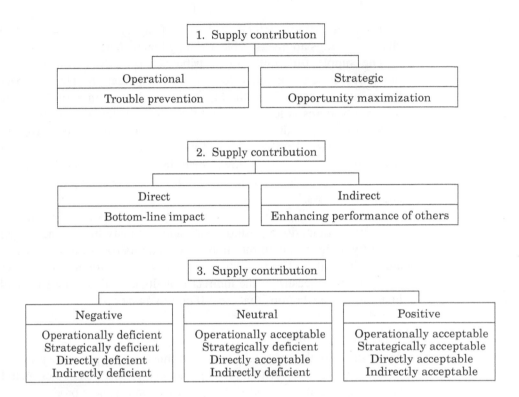

The operational side of supply concerns itself with the transactional, day-to-day operations traditionally associated with purchasing. The operational side can be streamlined and organized in ways designed to routinize and automate many of the transactions, thus freeing up time for the supply manager to focus on the strategic contribution.

The strategic side of supply is future oriented and searches for opportunities to provide competitive advantage. Whereas on the operational side the focus is on executing current tasks as designed, the strategic side focuses on new and better solutions to organizational and supply challenges. (Chapter 2 discusses the strategic side in detail.)

The Direct and Indirect Contribution of Supply

The second perspective is that of supply's potential direct or indirect contribution to organizational objectives.

Supply savings, the profit-leverage effect, and the return-on-assets effect demonstrate the direct contribution supply can make to the company's financial statements. Although the argument that supply savings flow directly to the bottom line appears self-evident, experience shows that savings do not always get that far. Budget heads, when presented with savings, may choose to spend this unexpected windfall on other requirements.

To combat this phenomenon, some supply organizations have hired financial controllers to assure that supply savings do reach the bottom line. Such was the case at Praxair, a global supplier of specialty gases and technologies. The chief supply officer and the CFO agreed that a financial controller position was needed in the supply organization to support financial analysis and budgeting. Validating cost savings and linking cost savings to the business unit operating budgets were an important part of this person's responsibilities.[5]

[5] Leenders and Johnson, *Major Changes in Supply Chain Responsibilities*, p. 89.

The appeal of the direct contribution of supply is that both inventory reduction and purchasing savings are measurable and tangible evidence of supply contribution.

The supply function also contributes indirectly by enhancing the performance of other departments or individuals in the organization. This perspective puts supply on the management team of the organization. Just as in sports, the team's objective is to win. Who scores is less important than the total team's performance. For example, better quality may reduce rework, lower warranty costs, increase customer satisfaction, and/or increase the ability to sell more or at a higher price. Ideas from suppliers may result in improved design, lower manufacturing costs, and/or a faster idea-to-design-to-product-completion-to-customer-delivery cycle. Each would improve the organization's competitiveness.

Indirect contributions come from supply's role as an information source; its effect on efficiency, competitive position, risk, and company image; the management training provided by assignments in the supply area; and its role in developing management strategy and social policy. The benefits of the indirect contribution may outweigh the direct contribution, but measuring the indirect benefits is difficult since it involves many "soft" or intangible contributions that are difficult to quantify.

Information Source

The contacts of the supply function in the marketplace provide a useful source of information for various functions within the organization. Primary examples include information about prices, availability of goods, new sources of supply, new products, and new technology, all of interest to many other parts of the organization. New marketing techniques and distribution systems used by suppliers may be of interest to the marketing group. News about major investments, mergers, acquisition candidates, international political and economic developments, pending bankruptcies, major promotions and appointments, and current and potential customers may be relevant to marketing, finance, research, and top management. Supply's unique position vis-à-vis the marketplace should provide a comprehensive listening post.

Effect on Efficiency

The efficiency with which supply processes are performed will show up in other operating results. While the firm's accounting system may not be sophisticated enough to identify poor efficiency as having been caused by poor purchase decisions, that could be the case. If supply selects a supplier who fails to deliver raw materials or parts that measure up to the agreed-on quality standards, this may result in a higher scrap rate or costly rework, requiring excessive direct labor expenditures. If the supplier does not meet the agreed-on delivery schedule, this may require a costly rescheduling of production, decreasing overall production efficiency, or, in the worst case, a shutdown of the production line—and fixed costs continue even though there is no output. Many supply managers refer to user departments as internal customers or clients and focus on improving the efficiency and effectiveness of the function with a goal of providing outstanding internal customer service.

Effect on Competitive Position/Customer Satisfaction

A firm cannot be competitive unless it can deliver end products or services to its customers when they are wanted, of the quality desired, and at a price the customer feels is fair.

If supply doesn't do its job, the firm will not have the required materials or services when needed, of desired quality, and at a price that will keep end-product costs competitive and under control.

The ability of the supply organization to secure requirements of better quality, faster, at a better price than competitors, will not only improve the organization's competitive position, but also improve customer satisfaction. The same can be said for greater flexibility to adjust to customers' changing needs. Thus, a demonstrably better-performing supply organization is a major asset on any corporate team.

A major chemical producer was able to develop a significantly lower-cost option for a key raw material that proved to be environmentally superior as well as better quality. By selling its better end product at somewhat lower prices, the chemical producer was able to double its market share, significantly improving its financial health and competitive position as well as the satisfaction of its customers.

Effect on Organizational Risk

Risk management is becoming an ever-increasing concern. The supply function clearly impacts the organization in terms of operational, financial, and reputation risk. Supply disruptions in terms of energy, service, or direct or indirect requirements can impact the ability of the organization to operate as planned and as expected by its customers, creating operational risks.

Given that commodity and financial markets establish prices that may go up or down beyond the control of the individual purchaser, and that long-term supply agreements require price provisions, the supply area may represent a significant level of financial risk. Furthermore, unethical or questionable supply practices and suppliers may expose the organization to significant reputation risk.

Effect on Image

The actions of supply personnel influence directly the public relations and image of a company. If actual and potential suppliers are not treated in a businesslike manner, they will form a poor opinion of the entire organization and will communicate this to other firms. This poor image will adversely affect the purchaser's ability to get new business and to find new and better suppliers. Public confidence can be boosted by evidence of sound and ethical policies and fair implementation of them.

The large spend of any organization draws attention in terms of supplier chosen, the process used to choose suppliers, the ethics surrounding the supply process, and conformance to regulatory requirements. Are the suppliers chosen "clean" in terms of child labor, environmental behavior, and reputation? Is the acquisition process transparent and legally, ethically, strategically, and operationally defensible as sound practice? Do supply's actions take fully into account environmental, financial, and other regulatory requirements, such as national security?

Global brands have come under increased scrutiny for their sourcing policies, accused of turning a blind eye to the labor practices of their suppliers. The collapse of a Bangladeshi factory in April 2013, killing more than 1,100 people, focused worldwide attention on poor working conditions and low pay for workers manufacturing garments for companies that included Walmart, Benetton, and Loblaws. The disaster spurred a debate about the responsibility of large retailers to ensure that their supplier factories met acceptable safety standards and paid their workers a living wage. There are an estimated 5,000 garment factories in Bangladesh, employing approximately 3.6 million workers, many of whom are paid the minimum wage of $38 a month.

Maintaining a proper corporate image is the responsibility of every team member and supply is no exception.

Training Ground

The supply area also is an excellent training ground for new managers. The needs of the organization may be quickly grasped. Exposure to the pressure of decision making under uncertainty with potentially serious consequences allows for evaluation of the individual's ability and willingness to make sound decisions and assume responsibility. Contacts with many people at various levels and a variety of functions may assist the individual in learning about how the organization works. Many organizations find it useful to include the supply area as part of a formal job rotation system for high-potential employees.

Examples of senior corporate executives with significant supply experience include Mary Barra, CEO of General Motors; Willie A. Deese, executive vice president, Merck & Co.; and Richard B. Jacobs, president of Eaton Corporation's Filtration Division.

Management Strategy

Supply also can be used as a tool of management strategy and social policy. Does management wish to introduce and stimulate competition? Does it favor geographical representation, minority interest, and environmental and social concerns? For example, are domestic sources preferred? Will resources be spent on assisting minority suppliers? As part of an overall organization strategy, the supply function can contribute a great deal. Assurance of supply of vital materials or services in a time of general shortages can be a major competitive advantage. Similarly, access to a better-quality or a lower-priced product or service may represent a substantial gain. These strategic positions in the marketplace may be gained through active exploration of international and domestic markets, technology, innovative management systems, and the imaginative use of corporate resources. Vertical integration and its companion decisions of make or buy (insource or outsource) are ever-present considerations in the management of supply.

The potential contribution of supply to strategy is obvious. Achievement depends on both top executive awareness of this potential and the ability to marshal corporate resources to this end. At the same time, it is the responsibility of those charged with the management of the supply function to seek strategic opportunities in the environment and to draw top executive attention to them. This requires a thorough familiarity with organizational objectives, strategy, and long-term plans and the ability to influence these in the light of new information. Chapter 2 discusses both potential supply contributions to business strategy *and* the major strategy areas within the supply function.

Progressive managers have recognized the potential contributions of the supply management area and have taken the necessary steps to ensure results. One important step in successful organizations has been the elevation to top executive status of the supply manager. Although titles are not always consistent with status and value in an organization, they still make a statement within and outside of most organizations. Currently, the most common title of the chief supply officer is vice president, followed by director and manager.

The elevation of the chief supply officer to executive status, coupled with high-caliber staff and the appropriate authority and responsibility, has resulted in an exciting and fruitful realization of the potential of the supply function in many companies. Chapter 3 discusses supply organizations issues in greater detail.

THE NATURE OF THE ORGANIZATION

The nature of the organization will determine how it will structure and manage its supply function. Whether the organization is public or private and produces goods or services or both, its mission, vision, and strategies, its size, number of sites, location, financial strength, and reputation will all be factors influencing its supply options and decisions. These will be addressed broadly in this first chapter and will be added to subsequently in this text.

Public or Private Organization

Public institutions, including all levels of government from municipal to state or provincial to federal, tend to be service providers but are not exclusively so and are subject to strict regulatory requirements regarding acquisition processes and policies. The public sector in many countries also includes education, health, utilities, and a host of agencies, boards, institutes, and so forth. The Wentworth Hospital case in Chapter 7 provides an example of supply in a public-sector context. This case illustrates how many purchases in the public sector can be for capital and indirect supplies, which creates challenges for supply to influence purchasing decisions that ensure best value.

A large segment of the acquisition needs of public institutions is concerned with the support of the organization's mission and maintenance of facilities and offices. Concerns over public spending deal with transparency and fairness of access to all eligible suppliers, social aims such as support of minority and disadvantaged groups, and national security. Need definition and specification are often part of the supply manager's responsibilities and are often geared to allow for multiple bidders.

That not all public organizations are alike is evident from Figure 1–3, which shows just some of the differences among public bodies.

Nongovernmental organizations (NGOs) and other nonprofit organizations would have a breakdown similar to those listed for public organizations, but might also operate internationally.

Private Organizations

Private organizations, which include companies with publicly traded stocks, tend to have fewer constraints on need definition, specification, and supplier selection. The laws of the

FIGURE 1–3
Differentiations for Supply Management in Public Organizations

Level:	Municipal ← →	State or Provincial ← →	Federal
Mission:	Social Aims ← →	Other or Combination ← →	Economic
Revenue Generation:	Limited ← →	Combination ← →	Substantial
Size:	Small ← →	Medium ← →	Large
Number of Sites:	Single ← →	Few ← →	Many

14 *Purchasing and Supply Management*

FIGURE 1–4 **Differentiations for Supply Management in Private Organizations**

Goods or Services:	Manufacturer ⟷ Combination ⟷ Services
Strategy:	Low cost ⟷ Combination ⟷ Differentiation
Size:	Small ⟷ Medium ⟷ Large
Number of Sites:	Single ⟷ Few ⟷ Many
Location:	Domestic ⟷ Few International ⟷ Many International
Financial Strength:	Weak ⟷ Medium ⟷ Strong
Reputation:	Poor ⟷ Medium ⟷ Outstanding

land (covered in Chapter 5) will establish the main ground rules for commerce. Transparency of commitments with suppliers has recently become more relevant to ensure that long-term commitments are properly disclosed in the company's financial statements. Whereas in public institutions standardization is seen as a means of fairness to suppliers, in private companies, custom specifications are seen as a means of securing competitive advantage.

Figure 1–4 shows some of the influencers that will affect supply management in private organizations. It is clear that for both public and private organizations these differences will affect supply significantly and some generalizations on supply impact follow.

Goods or Service Producers

Another major supply influence is whether the organization produces goods or services or both. Goods producers, often called manufacturers, may produce a wide range of products, both in the industrial goods category and in consumer goods. For goods producers, normally the largest percentage of total spend of the organization is on materials, purchased parts, packaging, and transportation for the goods produced. For service providers (and the range of possible services is huge), normally the largest percent of spend is focused on services and the process enabling the delivery of the services. The Erica Carson case in this chapter describes a supply decision in a large services organization, a financial institution. This case illustrates the opportunities for supply to contribute to the customer value proposition.

The following table identifies what the impact on organizational requirements is likely to be depending on whether the organization is primarily focused on manufacturing or providing a service:

Manufacturer	Service Provider
• The largest portion of needs is generated by customer needs. • The largest portion of spend with suppliers will be on direct requirements which comprise products sold to customers.	• The largest portion of needs is generated by capital, services, and other requirements enabling employees to provide the service. • In retailing the largest spend is focused on resale requirements.

Very few organizations are pure manufacturers or service providers. Most represent a mixture of both. A restaurant provides meals and drinks as well as service and a place to eat.

An insurance company provides insurance policies and claim service as well as peace of mind. An R&D organization performs research, as well as research reports, models, and prototypes. A manufacturer may supply capital goods as well as repair service and availability of replacement parts.

Wholesalers, distributors, and retailers provide resale products in smaller quantities and in more convenient locations at more convenient times than the manufacturers can provide. For these resellers the ability to buy well is critical for success.

Resource and mining organizations explore for natural resources and find ways and means of bringing these to commodity markets. Educational institutions attempt to transform students into educated persons, frequently providing them with meals, residences, classrooms, parking facilities, and, hopefully, diplomas or degrees. Health organizations provide diagnostic and repair services using a very large variety of professionals, equipment, facilities, medicines, and parts to keep their clients healthy and functioning.

It is no surprise that the nature of the organization in terms of the goods and services it provides will significantly affect the requirements of its supply chain.

The Mission, Vision, and Strategy of the Organization

Supply strategy has to be congruent with organizational strategy. Therefore, the mission, vision, and strategy of the organization are the key drivers for how the supply function will be managed and how supply decisions are made and executed. A nonprofit organization with social aims may acquire its office needs totally differently from one that competes on cost in a tough commercial or consumer marketplace. An innovation-focused organization may define flexibility quite differently from one that depends largely on the acquisition and transformation or distribution of commodities.

In the past, the supply manager was largely focused on the traditional value determinants of quality, quantity, delivery, price, and service as the five key drivers of sound supply decisions. Today's supply managers face a host of additional concerns, as corporate mission, vision, and strategies require concerns over risk, the environment, social responsibility, transparency, regulation, and innovation as well. Thus, the old adage of value for money, a guiding principle for supply managers for centuries, has become a lot tougher over the last few decades and continues to evolve. The text and cases in this book are focused on major supply decisions appropriate for the unique organization in which the supply professional is employed.

The Size of the Organization

The larger the organization, the greater the absolute amount of spend with suppliers. And the amount of the spend will be a major determinant of how many resources can be allocated to the acquisition process. Given a cost of acquisition of 1 to 2 percent of what is acquired, for a $100,000 purchase, up to $2,000 can be spent on acquisition. However, a $100 million acquisition can afford up to $2 million and a $1 billion spend up to $20 million.

Therefore, the larger the amount of spend, the greater the time and care that can and should be allocated to acquisition. Therefore, in very small organizations, the responsibility for acquisition may be a part-time allocation to one or more individuals who probably wear multiple hats. In very large organizations, supply professionals may be completely dedicated to one category of requirements on a full-time basis. And a supply group may count hundreds of professionals.

Single or Multiple Sites

An additional influence is whether the organization operates out of a single or multiple sites. The simplest situation is the single site. The supply situation becomes more complex as the number of sites increases. Transportation and storage issues multiply with multiple sites along with communication and control challenges. This is especially true for multinationals supplying multiple sites in different countries.

Financial Strength

Supply management stripped to its bare essentials deals with the exchange of money for goods and services. With the acquiring company responsible for the money and the supplier for the goods and services, the ability of the buying organization to pay will be a very important issue in the supplier's eyes. And the ability to pay and flexibility on when to pay depend on the financial strength of the organization. The stronger the buying organization is financially, the more attractive it becomes as a potential customer. A supplier will be more anxious to offer an exceptionally good value proposition to an attractive customer. And the ability and willingness to pay quickly after receipt of goods or services add valuable bargaining chips to any purchaser.

Reputation

Corporate reputation in the trade is another important factor in building a positive corporate image both for suppliers and purchasers. If supply management is defined as the fight for superior suppliers, then a strong corporate image and reputation are valuable contributors. Superior suppliers can pick and choose their customers. Superior suppliers prefer to deal with superior customers. Superior customers enhance a superior supplier's reputation. "You are known by the company you keep" applies in the corporate world just like it does in personal life. And supply managers can significantly affect their company's image by their actions and relations with suppliers.

For a long time the reputation of Fisher & Paykel (F&P) in New Zealand and Australia was such that any F&P supplier could use this as a persuasive argument for gaining additional customers in that area of the world. "If you are good enough to supply F&P, you are good enough for us" was the implication. A good buyer–supplier relationship is built on the rock of impeccable performance to contract agreements. Pay the right amount on time without hassle and deliver the right quality and quantity of goods or services on time and charge the correct price without hassle. These commitments are not as simple as they sound. Moreover, superior customers and superior suppliers add ethical treatment; advance communications on future developments in technology, markets, and opportunities for improvements as additional expectations; and are continually striving to do better.

Corporate reputations are built on actions and results, not on noble intentions. It takes time to build a superior reputation, but not much time to harm a reputation.

SUPPLY QUALIFICATIONS AND ASSOCIATIONS

In recognition that the talent in supply has to match the challenges of the profession, public and private organizations as well as supply associations have taken the initiative to ensure well-qualified supply professionals are available to staff the function.

Education

Although there are no universal educational requirements for entry-level supply jobs, most large organizations require a college degree in business administration or management. Several major educational institutions, such as Arizona State University, Bowling Green State University, George Washington University, Miami University, Michigan State University, and Western Michigan University, now offer an undergraduate degree major in Purchasing/Supply/Supply Chain/Logistics Management as part of the bachelor in business administration degree. In addition, many schools offer certificate programs or some courses in supply, for either full- or part-time students. A number of schools, including Arizona State, Michigan State, NYU Stern, and Howard University, also offer a specialization in supply chain management as part of a master of business administration degree program.

In Canada, the Ivey Business School has offered for over 60 years a purchasing and supply course as part of its undergraduate and graduate degree offerings. Other universities such as HEC, Laval, York, Queens, University of British Columbia, and Victoria have followed suit; academic interest in supply chain management is at an all-time high.

While, obviously, a university degree is not a guarantee of individual performance and success, the supply professional with one or more degrees is perceived on an educational par with professionals in other disciplines such as engineering, accounting, marketing, information technology (IT), human resources (HR), or finance. That perception is important in the role that supply professionals are invited to play on the organizational team.

Professional Associations

As any profession matures, its professional associations emerge as focal points for efforts to advance professional practice and conduct. In the United States, the major professional association is the Institute for Supply Management (ISM), founded in 1915 as the National Association of Purchasing Agents. The ISM is an educational and research association with over 40,000 members who belong to ISM through its network of domestic and international affiliated associations.

In addition to regional and national conferences, ISM sponsors seminars for supply people. It publishes a variety of books and monographs and the leading scholarly journal in the field, *The Journal of Supply Chain Management,* which it began in 1965. Additionally, ISM and its Canadian counterpart, the Supply Chain Management Association (SCMA), formally the Purchasing Management Association of Canada, work with colleges and universities to encourage and support the teaching of purchasing and supply management and related subjects and provide financial grants to support doctoral student research.

ISM launched the Certified Professional in Supply Management (CPSM) program in May 2008. The CPSM program focuses skill development in areas such as supplier relationship management, commodity management, risk and compliance issues, and social responsibility.

Since the early 1930s, ISM has conducted the monthly "ISM Report on Business," which is one of the best-recognized current barometers of business activity in the manufacturing sector. In 1998, the association initiated the Nonmanufacturing ISM Report on Business. The survey results are normally released on the second business day of each month. The Ivey Purchasing Managers Index (Ivey PMI), conducted by the Ivey Business School, is the Canadian equivalent of ISM's Report on Business, but covers the complete Canadian economy, including the manufacturing services and government sectors.

In 1986, CAPS Research (formally the Center for Advanced Purchasing Studies) was established as a national affiliation agreement between ISM and the College of Business at Arizona State University. CAPS is dedicated to the discovery and dissemination of strategic supply management knowledge and best practices. It conducts benchmarking studies, runs executive round tables and best practices workshops, and publishes research reports in a wide range of areas.

In Canada, the professional association is the Supply Chain Management Association (SCMA), formally the PMAC, formed in 1919. Its membership of approximately 8,000 is organized in 10 provincial and territorial institutes from coast to coast. Its primary objective is education, and in addition to sponsoring a national conference, it offers an accreditation program leading to the Supply Chain Management Professional (SCMP) designation.

In addition to ISM and SCMA, there are other professional purchasing associations, such as the National Institute of Governmental Purchasing (NIGP), the National Association of State Purchasing Officials (NASPO), the National Association of Educational Procurement (NAEP), and the Association for Healthcare Resource and Materials Management (AHPMM).

Several of these associations offer their own certification programs. Most industrialized countries have their own professional purchasing associations. CIPS (Chartered Institute of Purchasing and Supply) has affiliates in the United Kingdom, Australia, New Zealand, Africa and China, and Hong Kong. Other examples include the Indian Institute of Materials Management and the Japan Materials Management Association. These national associations are loosely organized into the International Federation of Purchasing and Supply Management (IFPSM), which has as its objective the fostering of cooperation, education, and research in purchasing on a worldwide basis among the 48 national and regional purchasing associations worldwide, representing approximately 250,000 supply professionals.

CHALLENGES AHEAD

There are at least six major challenges facing the supply profession over the next decade: supply chain management, measurement, risk management, sustainability, growth and influence, and effective contribution to corporate success.

Supply Chain Management

The success of firms like Walmart and Zara in exploiting supply chain opportunities has helped popularize the whole field of supply chain management. Nevertheless, significant challenges remain: While the giant firms in automotive, electronics, and retailing can force the various members of the supply chain to do their bidding, smaller companies do not have that luxury. Thus, each organization has to determine for itself how far it can extend its sphere of influence within the supply chain and how to respond to supply chain initiatives by others. Clearly, opportunities to reduce inventories, shorten lead times and distances, plan operations better, remove uncertainties, and squeeze waste out of the supply chain are still abundant. Thus, the search for extra value in the supply chain will continue for a considerable period of time.

Measurement

There is significant interest in better measurement of supply not only to provide senior management with better information regarding supply's contribution, but also to be able to assess the benefits of various supply experiments. No one set of measurements is likely to suffice for all supply organizations. Therefore, finding the set of measures most appropriate for a particular organization's circumstances is part of the measurement challenge.

Risk Management

A study at Michigan State University found that supply chain disruptions and supply chain risk are among the most critical issues facing supply chain managers.[6] Supply chains have become increasingly global and, therefore, face risks of supply interruptions, financial and exchange rate fluctuations, lead time variability, and security and protection of intellectual property rights, to name only a few. The trend to single sourcing and lean global supply chains has also created the increased risks for supply disruptions.

Supply managers need to continually assess risks in the supply chain and balance risk/reward opportunities when making supply decisions. For example, the attraction of lower prices from an offshore supplier may create longer-term high costs as a result of the need to carry additional safety stock inventories or lost sales from stock-outs. The Russel Wisselink case in Chapter 9 describes how one organization ran into problems in a low cost country sourcing program. Risk management will be covered in more detail in Chapter 2.

Sustainability

Responsibility for reverse logistics and disposal has traditionally fallen under the supply organization umbrella (see Chapters 16 and 17). These activities include the effective and efficient capture and disposition of downstream products from customers. More recently, however, pressures from government and consumer groups are motivating organizations to reduce the impact of their supply chains on the natural environment. For example, the European Union (EU) has set aggressive targets for greenhouse gas reductions and cuts to overall energy consumption, and has implemented new legislation as a result. Supply will be at the forefront of sustainability initiatives. Senior management will expect supply to work with suppliers to identify solutions for the environmental and sustainability challenges they face.

Growth and Influence

Growth and influence in terms of the role of supply and its responsibilities inside an organization can be represented in four areas as identified in a CAPS Research focus study.[7] In the first place, supply can grow in the percentage of the organization's total spend for which it is meaningfully involved. Thus, categories of spend traditionally not involving purchasing, such as real estate, insurance, energy, benefit programs, part-time help, relocation services, consulting, marketing spend with advertising and media agencies, travel and facilities management, IT, and telecommunications and logistics, have become part of procurement's responsibility in more progressive corporations.

[6] S. A. Melnyk et al., *Supply Chain Management 2010 and Beyond: Mapping the Future of the Strategic Supply Chain* (The Eli Broad College of Business at Michigan State University, 2006).

[7] Leenders and Johnson, *Major Changes in Supply Chain Responsibilities.*

Second, the growth of supply responsibilities can be seen in the span of supply chain activities under purchasing or supply leadership. Recent additions include accounts payable, legal, training and recruiting, programs and customer bid support, and involvement with new business development.

Third, growth can occur in the type of involvement of supply in what is acquired and supply chain responsibilities. Clearly, on the lowest level, there is no supply involvement at all. The next step up is a transactionary or documentary role. Next, professional involvement implies that supply personnel have the opportunity to exercise their expertise in important acquisition process stages. At the highest level, meaningful involvement, a term first coined by Dr. Ian Stuart, represents true team member status for supply at the executive table. Thus, in any major decision taken in the organization, the question *What are the supply implications of this decision?* is as natural and standard as *What are the financial implications of this decision?*

Fourth, supply can grow by its involvement in corporate activities from which it might have been previously excluded. While involvement in make-or-buy decisions, economic forecasts, countertrade, in- and outsourcing, and supplier conferences might be expected, other activities such as strategic planning, mergers and acquisitions, visionary task forces, and initial project planning might be good examples of broader corporate strategic integration.

Each of these four areas of opportunity for growth allows for supply to spread its wings and increase the value of its contributions.

Effective Contribution to Organizational Success

Ultimately, supply's measure of its contribution needs to be seen in the success of the organization as a whole. Contributing operationally and strategically, directly and indirectly, and in a positive mode, the challenge for supply is to be an effective team member. Meaningful involvement of supply can be demonstrated by the recognition accorded supply by all members of the organization.

How happy are other corporate team members to have supply on their team? Do they see supply's role as critical to the team's success? Thus, to gain not only senior management recognition but also the proper appreciation of peer managers in other functions is a continuing challenge for both supply professionals and academics.

THE ORGANIZATION OF THIS TEXT

In this first chapter are listed the more common influences for all organizations. In subsequent chapters, we will cover various decisions regarding organizational and supply strategies, organization supply processes, make or buy, the variety of organizational needs, and how to translate these into commercial equivalents. These will be followed by decisions on quality, quantity, delivery, price, and service—the traditional five value criteria—culminating in supplier selection. Suppliers are located domestically and internationally and their location will affect how supply should be managed. The legal and ethical framework for supply establishes the framework for the contract between these two parties. How to evaluate supplier performance and how to relate to suppliers is followed by a section on supply chain associated responsibilities which may or may not be part of the supply manager's assignment. This text concludes with the evaluation of the supply function, its performance reporting, and current trends in the field.

Conclusion

If the chief executive officer and all members of the management team can say, "Because of the kinds of suppliers we have and the way we relate to them, we can outperform our competition and provide greater customer satisfaction," then the supply function is contributing to its full potential.

This is the ambitious goal of this text: to provide insights for those who wish to understand the supply function better, whether or not they are or will be employed in supply directly.

Questions for Review and Discussion

1. What is the profit-leverage effect of supply? Is it the same in all organizations?
2. "Supply is not profit making; instead, it is profit taking since it spends organizational resources." Do you agree?
3. What kinds of decisions does a typical supply manager make?
4. "In the long term, the success of any organization depends on its ability to create and maintain a customer." Do you agree? What does this have to do with purchasing and supply management?
5. Is purchasing a profession? If not, why not? If yes, how will the profession, and the people practicing it, change over the next decade?
6. Differentiate between purchasing, procurement, materials management, logistics, supply management, and supply chain management.
7. In what ways might e-commerce influence the role of supply managers in their own organizations? In managing supply chains or networks?
8. In the petroleum and coal products industry, the total purchase/sales ratio is 80 percent, while in the food industry it is about 60 percent. Explain what these numbers mean. Of what significance is this number for a supply manager in a company in each of these industries?
9. How does supply management affect return on assets (ROA)? In what specific ways could you improve ROA through supply management?
10. How can the expectations of supply differ for private versus public organizations? Services versus goods producers?

References

Carter C. R.; L. M. Ellram, L. Kaufmann; C. W. Autry; X. Zhao; and T. E. Callarman, "Looking Back and Moving Forward: 50 years of the *Journal of Supply Chain Management,"Journal of Supply Chain Management* 50, no. 1, 2014, pp. 1–7.

Cavinato, J. L.; A. E. Flynn; and R. G. Kauffman. *The Supply Management Handbook.* 7th ed. Burr Ridge, IL: McGraw-Hill/Irwin, 2007.

Johnson, P. F., and M. R. Leenders, *Supply's Organizational Roles and Responsibilities,* Tempe, AZ: CAPS Research, May 2012, 118 pages.

Lambert, D. M. *Supply Chain Management: Processes, Partnerships and Performance*, Sarasota, Florida: Supply Chain Management Institute, 2004.

Leenders, M. R., and H. E. Fearon. "Developing Purchasing's Foundation," *The Journal of Supply Chain Management* 44, no. 2 (2008), pp. 17–27.

Leenders, M. R., and A. E. Flynn. *Value-Driven Purchasing: Managing the Key Steps in the Acquisition Process*. Burr Ridge, IL: Irwin Professional Publishing, 1995.

Villena, V. H., E. Revilla, and T. Choi, "The Dark Side of Buyer-Supplier Relationships: A Social Capital Perspective," *Journal of Operations Management* 29, no. 6 (2011), pp. 561–576.

Case 1–1

Denniston Spices

Amy Lin, materials planner at Denniston Spices, in Phoenix, Arizona, was faced with an important problem caused by a supplier who was implementing a new enterprise resource planning (ERP) system. It was Tuesday, April 9, 2014, and during a call the previous day from Juan Aranda, sales manager at Whittingham Foods, Amy learned that potential supply problems might occur starting in September as the new system was implemented at the Whittingham's Indianapolis plant. In order to avoid stockouts, Juan asked Amy to provide a forecast of her plant's needs for September to November by April 30th, so he could make arrangements to have product shipped to Denniston in late August.

DENNISTON SPICES

Founded in 1903 by Walter J. Denniston, Denniston Spices was a global leader in the food industry—manufacturing, marketing, and distributing a wide variety of spices, mixes, condiments, and other seasoning products to the retail, commercial, and industrial markets. Headquartered in Chicago, the company had sales revenues of $5.5 billion and sold its products in more than 100 countries worldwide. Its customers included retail outlets, food manufacturers, restaurant chains, food distributors, and food service businesses. Denniston Spices was also a leading supplier of private label items.

The Phoenix plant manufactured and distributed spices, herbs, extracts, and seasoning blends to retail and industrial customers in the southwest United States. Amy Lin was responsible for managing approximately 300 stock-keeping units (SKUs) consisting of spices and compounds, purchased from Whittingham Foods, which was the sole supplier for these products. All SKUs supplied to the Phoenix plant by Whittingham came from their Indianapolis facility.

INVENTORY CONTROL

It was company policy that each SKU had minimum safety stock inventory to protect against stockouts. Safety stock levels were set by the materials planners and typically ranged from two to four weeks. Reorder points were set at the safety stock level for each SKU plus four weeks, which reflected the lead time from Whittingham Foods for most products. Orders were constrained by minimum order quantities set by the supplier.

Forecasting and setting reasonable safety stock levels were made difficult because of variability in demand, particularly from industrial customers. Many of the Phoenix plant's industrial customers were small- and medium-sized manufacturers that ordered sporadically.

Prices for products supplied by Whittingham Foods ranged from $50 to $250 per pound, and had shelf-lives of either 90, 180, or 270 days. The major challenge in Amy's role was to balance high inventory costs and short shelf lives with the risks of stockout costs and inventory spoilage. Denniston Spices offered 10-day delivery lead times to its customers and it typically took 2 to 7 days for an order to be processed and shipped. The Phoenix plant had a customer service level target of 98 percent.

INVENTORY BUILD FOR AUGUST

The call from Juan Aranda did not come as a surprise to Amy, who had known for several weeks that Whittingham Foods was implementing a new ERP system and at some point she would need to purchase additional safety stock inventory. Whittingham Foods was as key supplier to several Denniston plants, and switching suppliers was not feasible for such a short period of time due to the costs and administrative issues related to government regulations regarding the certification of suppliers. While there was a possibility they would not experience any problems and supply would not be interrupted, Amy did not want to take any chances and had the full support of her boss, Kevin Sherman, the director of purchasing.

As a starting point, Amy collected demand data for eight SKUs during July to November period in 2012 and 2013 (see Exhibit 1). For each of the eight SKUs, she also collected information related to safety stock levels, minimum order quantities (MOQ), shelf life, and cost per pound. She purposely selected SKUs from different final products that included a range of costs and annual demand, with the objective of developing an inventory build policy for the SKUs ordered from Whittingham Foods. Amy knew that certain events in 2012 and 2013 distorted the data. For example, the company had expanded in 2013 through an acquisition and the plant increased production in order to build additional finished goods inventories as a result of a facility consolidation project in the fall of 2013.

As Amy looked at the data on her spreadsheet, she wondered if it would be possible to balance stockout risks with inventory holding and inventory spoilage costs. It was important that she develop a preliminary plan within the next week so she could get it approved by the director of purchasing and the general manager. Margins were tight and Amy knew that she had to do her best to develop a plan that controlled costs without jeopardizing customer service levels.

EXHIBIT 1   **Historical Usage for Whittingham Products**

SKU #	Year	July	Aug.	Sept.	Oct.	Nov.	Safety Stock (lb.)	MOQ (lb.)	Shelf Life (Days)	Cost ($/lb.)
W9450	2012	51	208	80	75	103	1,000	200	90	$ 90
	2013	0	325	3,060	4,770	7,024				
W9451	2012	3,251	5,794	2,492	1,830	3,052	3,600	200	90	$ 195
	2013	956	2,854	2,730	2,621	3,786				
W9452	2012	979	680	460	894	778	600	200	180	$ 65
	2013	360	336	282	325	550				
W9453	2012	189	229	271	397	420	650	200	180	$ 110
	2013	549	642	1,019	1,655	2,588				
W9454	2012	52	56	54	45	50	100	200	270	$ 235
	2013	16	76	18	0	20				
W9455	2012	7	2	0	20	0	400	200	270	$ 65
	2013	724	304	304	376	424				
W9456	2012	120	4	55	1	60	15	80	270	$ 120
	2013	16	1	43	17	15				
W9457	2012	41	157	54	117	0	320	80	270	$ 120
	2013	0	131	82	69	0				

Case 1–2

Erica Carson

"We will do it for 10 percent less than what you are paying right now." Erica Carson, purchasing manager at Wesbank, a large western financial institution, had agreed to meet with Art Evans, a sales representative from D.Killoran Inc., a printing supplier from which Wesbank currently was not buying anything. Art Evans's impromptu and unsolicited price quote concerned the printing and mailing of checks from Wesbank.

Wesbank, well known for its active promotional efforts to attract consumer deposits, provided standard personalized consumer checks free of charge. Despite the increasing popularity of Internet banking, the printing of free checks and mailing to customers cost Wesbank $8 million in the past year.

Erica Carson was purchasing manager in charge of all printing for Wesbank and reported directly to the vice president of supply.

It had been Erica's decision to split the printing and mailing of checks equally between two suppliers. During the last five years, both suppliers had provided quick and quality service, a vital concern of the bank. Almost all checks were mailed directly to the consumer's home or business address by the suppliers. Because of the importance of check printing, Erica had requested a special cost analysis study a year ago, with the cooperation of both suppliers. The conclusion of this study had been that both suppliers were receiving an adequate profit margin and were efficient and cost-conscious and that the price structure was fair. Each supplier was on a two-year contract. One supplier's contract had been renewed eight months ago; the other's expired in another four months.

Erica believed that Killoran was underbidding to gain part of the check-printing business. This in turn would give Killoran access to Wesbank's customers' names. Erica suspected that Killoran might then try to pursue these customers more actively than the current two suppliers to sell special "scenic checks" that customers paid for themselves.

were among the leading brands in the industry, and the Durham plant manufactured 20 product lines that were distributed to retail customers in North America, including grocery store chains, boutique candy shops, and convenience stores.

Garland's brands were managed by cross-functional teams with representatives from sales and marketing, operations, finance, engineering, purchasing, and distribution. Each team was governed by corporate goals for growth, profitability, and brand management, but was given significant autonomy to make strategic and tactical decisions in order to achieve their business performance objectives (BPOs).

The competitive nature of the industry placed an upper limit on prices, so margins were determined by production and supply chain efficiencies. Consequently, cost control and continuous improvement were high priorities. The company's enterprise resource planning (ERP) system generated weekly BPO reports for team members.

THE EDGEWORTH TOFFEE BRAND

Production of Edgeworth Toffee was a two-step process: manufacturing and packing. The product was manufactured in two formats. The first format was a fixed-size, retail-ready pack, which contained a half-pound of toffee. The second format was a 10-pound bulk package that was placed in stores so that customers could select the amount of toffee they wanted and self-pack the product. Production of the fixed-size format was approximately 2,500 cases a year, compared to approximately 3,000 cases a year of the bulk format. Both formats sold for $145 per case.

There were two dedicated packing lines for Edgeworth Toffee, one for each format. However, the packing lines had long outlived their useful lives, and efficiencies had declined in recent years (see Exhibit 1). Furthermore, sales of Edgeworth Toffee had been flat for the past couple of years, and

in an effort to spur consumer interest in the brand, marketing was proposing a new marketing strategy that included a face-lift for the packaging. However, the new packaging would require a different type of packing technology. John Slaughter, the representative from marketing on the Edgeworth Toffee team, felt that the introduction of new packaging combined with a new marketing campaign could deliver as much as a 20 percent increase in sales. It was unclear to Shanti whether the new marketing strategy would be enough to stimulate increased sales, or if the product was mature and a decline in demand was inevitable.

THE MANUFACTURING AND PACKING LINE REPLACEMENT OPTIONS

The accounting department set standard costs for each product line annually. Exhibit 1 provides the standard costs for Edgeworth Toffee, and Exhibit 2 shows actual operating performance data for the manufacturing and packing lines. As shown in Exhibit 2, the packing line was operating at 48 percent efficiency, and the scrap rate was nearly 10 percent. Annual maintenance costs on the packing line were approximately $18,000 per year and expected to increase by at least 25 percent in the next 12 months.

Working with Ian Haase, purchasing manager at the Durham plant and a member of the Edgeworth Toffee team, Shanti obtained an estimate of $140,000 for the cost of replacing the two packing lines for Edgeworth Toffee, including installation. It was expected that the new equipment would be able to achieve the BPO efficiency and scrap rate targets and be able to accommodate the new packaging that marketing was recommending.

Shanti also felt that it was time to examine replacement of the manufacturing line. The manufacturing and packing lines had originally been installed together more than 20 years earlier. Although efficiency of the

EXHIBIT 1   **Operating Standard Costs for Edgeworth Toffee**

	$ per case	%
Selling price	$145.00	100
Raw material	24.65	17
Packaging material	29.00	20
Labor—manufacturing	13.05	9
Labor—packing	7.25	5
Overhead & depreciation	21.75	15
Total cost	95.70	66
Margin	49.30	34

EXHIBIT 2   **Manufacturing and Packing Line Performance Statistics**

Measure	Standard (%)	Actual (%)
Manufacturing efficiency	80	76
Manufacturing scrap rate	1.2	1.5
Packing efficiency	80	48
Packing scrap rate	1.2	9.6

manufacturing line was close to the target of 80 percent, it was also showing signs of deterioration. The efficiency rate had declined to 76 percent, compared to more than 90 percent five years prior, and it had become increasingly more difficult to find replacement parts. A new manufacturing line would cost approximately $600,000 installed.

OUTSOURCING

In addition to investigating options to replace the existing manufacturing and packing lines, Shanti had also looked into outsourcing. A preliminary review indicated that there would be substantial coordination costs if only packing was outsourced; therefore, outsourcing manufacturing and packing was investigated. Ian and Shanti selected two contract manufacturers to submit proposals, Martin Contract Manufacturing (Martin) and Dasari Inc. Bids were requested from both for the existing packaging and the new packaging proposed by marketing. In order to make sure the suppliers were well informed about the manufacturing and packing processes, both were invited to tour the Durham plant, and they were provided with detailed information and related data regarding the operation of the lines.

Following a review of the proposals submitted by the suppliers, Ian and Shanti decided that Martin had the best bid. Martin quoted a cost of $68.00 for manufacturing and packing for both the current packaging and marketing's new packaging. The supplier would be responsible for raw material and packaging material costs. In addition, Garland would pay $35,000 in tooling costs up front. Martin indicated that it would need six months to ramp up production of Edgeworth Toffee.

THE TEAM MEETING

As Shanti looked at the information on her laptop that had been collected regarding manufacturing and packing of Edgeworth Toffee, she knew that something had to be done to address the declining margins of the brand as a result of increased production costs. Investing in new equipment seemed like an obvious solution; however, the capital investment would be significant and her proposal would need to exceed the company's 10 percent cost of capital rate to get approval by finance.

While reviewing the proposal by Martin, Shanti felt that some of the overhead costs at the Durham plant could be eliminated if production of Edgeworth Toffee was outsourced. The estimate provided by the accounting department was that overhead costs allocated to the brand could be reduced by approximately 30 percent if production was outsourced.

Historically, the company's strategy had been to control production of its products to ensure quality and delivery performance. Garland had an excellent reputation with it customers and the customer service level for Edgeworth Toffee was a line fill rate of 98 percent. However, if the case to outsource could be made successfully to the team on Monday, Shanti felt that senior management would approve the proposal. This was an important decision and she wanted to make a clear recommendation at the meeting on Monday, supported by a thorough analysis of both options.

Case 5–2

Marshall Insurance Company

Kara Murphy, purchasing manager with Marshal Insurance Company (Marshall), in Spokane, Washington, was evaluating a proposal submitted from David Callum, from Gilmore Printing (Gilmore). David was proposing that Gilmore take responsibility for managing all forms and printed materials inventory for the Marshall Automobile Club. Kara could see the advantages of outsourcing management of printed materials, but she remained concerned that this arrangement would not provide the service that clients and employees had come to expect. It was Thursday, June 12, and David was expecting a response from Kara on Tuesday, June 17, during a meeting scheduled for that afternoon.

MARSHALL INSURANCE COMPANY

The Marshall Insurance Company was a large, publicly held, personal lines property and casualty insurer. Founded in 1948, it had $73.5 billion in total assets. The Marshall Automobile Club (MAC) was a division of Marshall that provided roadside assistance services to its clients 24 hours a day, 365 days a year. Its more than 750,000 clients included both individuals and corporations.

MAC provided services to two customer groups, corporate clients, such as original equipment automotive manufacturers (OEMs) who provide free roadside assistance plans with new vehicle purchases, and individuals (or retail clients). Individual members could choose from a variety of plans for families that provided coverage for cars, trucks, motorcycles, and recreational vehicles. In addition to traditional roadside services, MAC offered features such as a trip planning, a travel reservation service, and trip interruption insurance.

Individual clients would join MAC through an online registration tool or by completing a form at a local Marshall office. Payment was typically made using a credit card. OEM clients sent their membership information to MAC daily in encrypted data files. Both individual and corporate client membership information was processed at the Spokane office, where membership cards were prepared and sent out along with an information kit that included a welcome letter, handbook, various promotional materials, and a keychain. Kits were customized for each client, in some cases using OEM letterhead if the member was joining as part as a new vehicle purchase plan. Anywhere from 2,000 to 3,000 kits were assembled each week, which took the time of two full-time staff. It was common to have more staff work on kit assembly in periods of strong demand. Storeroom staff were paid $900 per week plus benefits.

Kara's responsibilities included managing the 3,000 square foot storeroom, where printed materials were stored and kits were assembled. In addition to materials for distribution to new clients, other printed materials included MAC marketing brochures and promotional materials. In total, more than 250 different printed products were held in inventory. In order to take advantage of discounts from printing suppliers, MAC had four to six months of inventory for many products.

THE GILMORE PROPOSAL

During a meeting the previous week, David Callum proposed to Kara that his company take responsibility for managing forms and printed materials for MAC. The proposal indicated that Gilmore would manage relationships with printing suppliers, including inventory management, kit fulfillment, and distribution to clients. David described how they were providing this service to other large corporate clients, in a range of industries, that were interested in eliminating manual back-office operations. He indicated that the typical fee was approximately $3.00 per kit, including mailing costs. The purpose of the meeting on Tuesday was to see if there was interest from Kara in pursuing the proposal; at that time Kara would need to provide David with details regarding annual volumes and materials involved.

Kara could see the advantages of outsourcing management of the storeroom operations and kit assembly. Office space was at a premium at Marshal, and the storeroom could easily be converted to other uses. The headaches associated with ordering materials and maintaining inventory records could be eliminated.

However, Kara did have concerns. First, she was suspicious that Gilmore was looking to take over all the printing business for MAC. Although an important supplier, Gilmore was currently responsible for approximately 30 percent of the printing purchases for MAC. Under the outsourcing arrangement proposed by David, Gilmore would take over existing contracts with Marshall suppliers, but as these contracts expired, it would be up to Gilmore to decide who would do the printing.

Secondly, timely processing of client membership cards and kits was critical. The expectation was that these materials would be processed within 24 hours. Kara was worried about maintaining service levels under an outsourcing arrangement with Gilmore. Furthermore, client information was confidential, and Kara had concerns about security and ensuring that Gilmore did not use the MAC client database for other purposes, such as advertising and promoting products and services for other customers.

PREPARING FOR THE MEETING

Kara felt that the proposal from David had merit and she wanted to give it careful consideration. As she examined the information he had left with her, Kara wondered how to proceed. Were the risks worth the potential problems? What questions should she ask at the meeting on Tuesday? And were there any conditions she should place on the arrangement with Gilmore if they were to proceed?

Case 5–3

Alicia Wong

Alicia Wong, Corporate Supply Manager, Thain Foods Limited, wanted to prepare a proposal to manufacture mustard in-house. Mustard, an important ingredient in many of the company's products, was currently purchased from an outside supplier. She hoped a comprehensive proposal could be prepared in one-month's time for the CEO's approval.

130   *Purchasing and Supply Management*

GENERAL COMPANY BACKGROUND

Thain Foods Limited (TFL) had been in business for more than 30 years. Its products included a wide range of syrups, fudges, cone dips, sauces, mayonnaise, and salad dressings. Its customers were major food chains, hotels, and restaurants in North America and Europe.

TFL believed in continuous improvement to its operations. Over the last two years, it invested more than $2 million in plant facilities, the bulk of it new, state-of-the-art process equipment and process control. All production and process control functions were computerized for maximum efficiency.

TFL employed about 120 people. It had a corporate structure of CEO; president; executive vice president, domestic sales; and national account manager and used a network of food brokers who sold and promoted its products.

THE SUPPLY AREA

Alicia was responsible for supply and reported directly to the CEO. She had an inventory control officer, a buyer, and a receiver under her supervision. Purchases could be classified into five different types: labels, packaging, raw materials, commodities, and MRO supplies. Mustard was an important raw material used in many of TFL's products.

CURRENT PRACTICE: PURCHASING MUSTARD EXTERNALLY

Whenever mustard was required, the buyer e-mailed the supplier and requested that it prepare the appropriate amount to be picked up by a truck from TFL. The purchase order would be prepared before the truck left for the supplier, normally the next day. The mustard supplier used mustard seed as its raw material and blended in the other ingredients after the seed had been reduced to mustard flour. Every month TFL purchased 500 drums, or 100,000 liters, of mustard. The cost of the mustard itself was $64 per drum. Freight costs were borne by TFL and amounted to about $8 per drum. TFL operated three eight-hour shifts, five days a week. Each worker was paid about $20 per hour. It took about 10 minutes of a worker's time to handle each drum. This included pouring the mustard into the processing kettle, making sure other added ingredients mixed well, and rinsing the drums. The drums were bulky and, because they could not be used in the plant for other purposes, had to be

rinsed for a contractor who took them away. The costs of disposing of the drums in this manner were negligible. Other costs and overhead of purchasing were $0.02 per liter.

SUGGESTED CHANGE: MANUFACTURING MUSTARD IN-HOUSE

The mustard to be produced at TFL would be composed of roughly 60 percent solid, 20 percent water, and 20 percent vinegar. The solid portion was a spice blend, consisting essentially of mustard flour, salt, and other spices that could be readily bought. Water was not a problem because the city provided a reliable supply. Vinegar was already a raw material that TFL ordered in bulk regularly from suppliers. Alicia therefore believed that it was a simple matter for TFL to make the mustard for its own use. TFL only needed to buy the spice blend and add water and vinegar in the right proportions. She approached a supplier who indicated that it could make the spice blend at a delivered price of $0.15 per liter for TFL, including freight. However, it needed time for tests to ensure that the blend would be of the right quality for TFL's use. Vinegar cost TFL $0.1875 per liter delivered in 15,000 liter lots. And TFL was paying $0.025 per liter for water. Alicia also checked whether production had the time and equipment to make the mustard. Production felt that the change would not be too drastic and no additional workers would be necessary. However, it would use up more of the existing workers' time. Production calculated that the change would entail a total labor and overhead cost of about $0.105 per liter of mustard using standard cost accounting for labor time and overhead charges.

Alicia organized an information gathering and discussion session involving supply, production, quality assurance, and distribution to discuss the proposed change. The workers were keen on the idea because this meant that they would no longer have to haul and rinse the bulky drums (water and vinegar could be easily channeled to the mixing containers using existing pipes). However, quality assurance expressed concern about the quality of mustard if produced in-house. Because the mustard was an ingredient in many of TLF's products, such a change might adversely affect the quality and taste of these products.

Alicia wanted her proposal for in-house manufacture of mustard to be in the company's best interest and wondered how to proceed next.

Chapter **Eleven**

Cost Management

Chapter Outline

Strategic Cost Management
Sources of Competitive Advantage
Frameworks for Cost Management

Cost Management Tools and Techniques
Total Cost of Ownership
Target Costing
The Learning Curve or Experience Curve
Value Engineering and Value Analysis
Activity-Based Costing

Negotiation
Negotiation Strategy and Practice
*Framework for Planning and Preparing
  for Negotiation*

Conclusion

Questions for Review and Discussion

References

Cases

Key Questions for the Supply Decision Maker

Should we

- Use target pricing?
- Negotiate with our suppliers or accept their existing terms and conditions?
- Estimate total cost of ownership for all our purchases?

How can we

- Understand what it costs our suppliers to manufacture their products or deliver their services?
- Make a cost analysis on all our large-dollar purchase items?
- Achieve our objectives in a negotiation with an important supplier?

The profit leverage effect of supply (discussed in Chapter 1) lays the foundation for the role of supply in helping the firm meet strategic goals of continuous improvement, customer service, quality, and increased competitiveness. Leveraging the potential of supply requires fully exploiting all opportunities to reduce, contain, or avoid costs, resulting in the lowest total cost of ownership and, hopefully, leading the organization to becoming the low-cost producer of high-quality goods and services. Cost analysis and cost management are important whether the source of competitive advantage for a specific product or service is product leadership (higher perceived product or service differentiation and lower customer price sensitivity) or cost leadership (lower perceived product or service differentiation and higher customer price sensitivity).

Supply management can contribute to attainment of low-cost-producer status by its management of internal and external costs. Methods of streamlining the acquisition process and reducing internal costs associated with acquisition were discussed in Chapters 3 and 4. This chapter focuses on managing external costs.

As the status of the supply function in well-managed companies has increased in importance, a more professional attitude has developed in the people responsible for the operation of the function. As the professional competence of the personnel has increased, greater use has been made of the more sophisticated tools available to the business decision-making executive. Negotiation and cost management techniques are prime examples of this developing professionalism.

In the long run, companies need suppliers that provide the lowest total costs, not necessarily the lowest prices. Consequently, a focus on costs, as opposed to prices, allows purchasers to make informed decisions and identify opportunities to reduce waste in the supply chain. However, understanding "what the numbers tell us" is only part of the battle. Effective buyers also need to understand how and when to use information effectively in a negotiation setting with important suppliers and key internal stakeholders. This chapter addresses supply's role in strategic cost management, describes cost management techniques, and explains basic negotiation concepts. Cost management and negotiation represent a powerful combination for supply professionals.

Two key decisions are addressed in this chapter: (1) How can cost management and negotiation tools help identify opportunities and assure value? (2) How can we determine the supplier's costs? deliverer's cost? our own use costs? and disposal costs?

STRATEGIC COST MANAGEMENT

Strategic cost management is an externally focused process of analyzing costs in terms of the overall value chain. Cost analysis can be used to measure and improve cost performance by focusing attention on specific cost elements. Cost management systems can be designed that depend on strategic partnering to achieve competitive advantage. Cost management is a major opportunity area for strong supply leadership and management. Cost management is a continuous improvement process. The focus is essentially on applying tools and techniques to sustain cost savings year over year. Supply leaders and managers must develop a cost culture rather than a price culture with multiple internal stakeholders and externally with suppliers. Cost management should be part of the standard operating procedure in every supply management organization.

The actual cost management process in any organization depends on context. What is the strategic positioning of the organization and how sophisticated is the supply organization in terms of price and cost analysis? If little attention has been paid to spend, then the opportunities may come from spend aggregation and price-volume leverage, supply base rationalization, and better terms and condition. As supply develops expertise in cost management, attention turns to avoiding, eliminating, or reducing costs through design and redesign of products/services, and process improvements internally within the supplier's processes and in joint processes.

Sources of Competitive Advantage

Sources of sustainable competitive advantage are: (1) product or service differentiation (wherein customers have low price sensitivity), (2) low cost (wherein customers have high price sensitivity), and (3) a combination of product or service differentiation and cost leadership. While an organization may be positioned strategically in one category, it may have products or services in both. For example, a technical support center may offer customized support 365/24/7 for a relatively high price and also offer basic online diagnostics and reporting as part of a standard package. Or a fast-food restaurant chain may compete fiercely on price with value menus while also offering relatively highly priced specialty hamburgers.

Frameworks for Cost Management

Supply professionals must understand their own organization's strategic positioning (overall and by product or service) and that of their suppliers. Cost analysis and cost management approaches can then be adapted and applied appropriately. Various tools discussed in this text provide a framework for cost management. These include ABC (Pareto) analysis (Chapter 8) and portfolio analysis (Chapter 11).

ABC or Pareto Analysis and Cost Management

ABC analysis assigns items to either the A, B, or C category. A items are high-dollar items, B are medium-dollar, and C are low-dollar items. From a cost management perspective, more time and managerial attention is directed toward A items because of the percent of annual spend consumed by the purchase of these items. The supply manager would focus on understanding the supplier's cost structure to identify opportunities for either the supplier or a joint buyer-supplier initiative to eliminate, reduce, or avoid costs in any of a number of cost elements, including materials, services, labor, and overhead. Thinking about the supplier's strategic positioning, A items might be either differentiated products (customized) or low-cost commodity type items. If they are customized, then the source of cost reductions might come from decisions inside the buying organization such as specification or design changes. If the items are commodity-type items meaning they are standard off-the-shelf goods or services with substitutes available, then the cost reductions might come from inside the supplier's organization and be from its supply chain, production process, or distribution network.

Portfolio or Quadrant Analysis and Cost Management

Portfolio analysis enables a supply management team to place each major spend category on a spend map based on the risks to acquire in the marketplace and the value of the category to the organization. Figure 11–1 provides typical characteristics of each quadrant. The *x*-axis represents the assessment of risk to acquire or how easy or hard is it to acquire a specific spend category (good or service) in the marketplace. (Also see strategy development in Chapter 12). The Delphi Corporation case in Chapter 13 shows how the company uses a similar framework as part of its strategic sourcing process.

FIGURE 11–1 **Characteristics of Spend Categories**

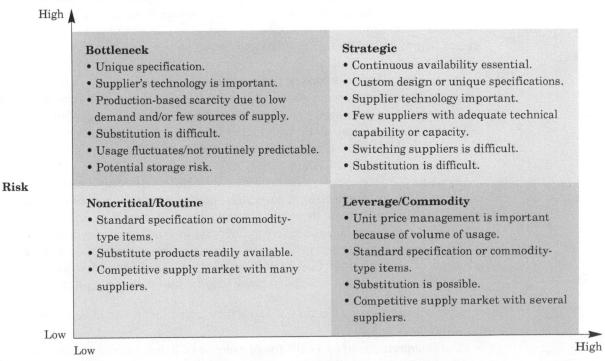

Source: Adapted from Peter Kraljic, "Purchasing Must Become Supply, Management," *Harvard Business Review, 1983.*

The analyst should locate the spot on the map that represents the best analysis of two dimensions. This is done by first analyzing and determining the point on one axis, then doing the same for the other axis, and then locating the point of intersection on the map. For example, not all leverage items behave the same. A leverage item in the upper-right corner of that quadrant is both of greater value to the organization and higher risk (harder to acquire in the marketplace) than a leverage item (good or service) located in the lower-left corner of the leverage quadrant.

Portfolio analysis provides a framework for developing strategic plans for spend categories and for applying price and cost management tools. The price analysis tools discussed in Chapter 10 are primarily used when purchasing lower risk commodity-type items of lower total value to the organization. The cost tools discussed in this chapter are primarily applied to higher-risk and higher-value purchases. A key decision in this process is the definition of value. The original intent was for value to be defined as impact on the organization. In practice, many users define value as percent of annual spend.

Commodity-type items of low value to the organization (noncritical or routine) are essentially commodities. If a supplier has positioned a good or service as a cost leader, it is essentially selling a commodity and price must be competitive. To compete aggressively on price, the supplier must focus on continually reducing its costs. For a manufacturer these might be production costs, carrying costs, and raw materials costs. For a service provider, these might be labor costs or process costs. The buyer's cost management approach might be to minimize acquisition or order process costs and rely on market competition to keep prices competitive.

Commodity-type goods and services in the leverage quadrant are both higher value (either more impact on the organization's success or higher-dollar value, depending on the definition of value) and riskier to acquire. The supply manager's goal is still to manage costs by minimizing order processing costs. Because of the higher value of these purchases, the benefits of other cost analysis tools such as total cost of ownership may be worth the cost of the process.

As goods and services become riskier to acquire while still of low to moderate value to the organization (bottleneck), the supply manager's goal may be to assure supply. Process costs related to negotiating longer-term contracts and building stronger buyer–supplier relationships may increase along with higher carrying costs if inventory is used to assure supply. Longer-term costs may be incurred to conduct value analysis to find less costly ways to deliver the same function.

Strategic goods and services are both more valuable to the buying organization and riskier to acquire. The supply manager's goals are to assure continuous supply at the lowest total cost of ownership. A more thorough understanding of internal cost structure and the supplier's cost structure may be necessary to find ways to avoid, eliminate, or reduce costs.

Price analysis, addressed in Chapter 10, examines price proposals without examining elements of cost and profit. Cost analysis reviews actual or future costs. Some supply managers believe they are not justified in going very far into suppliers' costs because:

- In many cases, suppliers do not know their costs, and it would be useless to inquire about them.

- The interpretation of cost calls for an exercise of judgment, and differences of opinion would arise even if all the numbers were available.

- Some suppliers will not divulge cost information.

- The seller's costs do not determine market prices.
- The buyer is not interested in the supplier's costs anyway; the primary concern is getting the best price consistent with quality, quantity, delivery, and service.
- If a seller offers a price that does not cover costs, either in ignorance or with full recognition of what it is doing, the matter is the seller's problem and not the buyer's.

However, unless a buyer has some idea of a supplier's costs, at least in a general way, it is difficult to judge the reasonableness of the supplier's prices. Furthermore, the position that the buyer is neither concerned with, nor responsible for, suppliers who offer merchandise below cost must recognize two things: First, good suppliers need to cover their costs to survive and prosper; and, second, prices may subsequently rise materially above cost as suppliers fight for financial survival.

The party in the strongest position in a negotiation session is the one with the best data. Recognizing the importance of cost, it is common practice for the purchaser to make the best estimate possible of the supplier's costs as one means of judging the reasonableness of the price proposed. Many larger firms have cost analysts within the supply area to assist in analyzing supplier costs in preparation for negotiation. Some companies use cost-based pricing, a cost modeling system used by purchasers to determine total cost. These cost estimates must be based on such data as are available.

COST MANAGEMENT TOOLS AND TECHNIQUES

Five cost management techniques are addressed in this section: total cost of ownership (TCO), target pricing, the learning curve, value engineering and value analysis, and activity-based costing.

Total Cost of Ownership

The purchaser should estimate the total cost of ownership (TCO) before selecting a supplier. Broadly defined, total cost of ownership for noncapital goods acquisition includes all relevant costs, such as administration, follow-up, expediting, inbound transportation, inspection and testing, rework, storage, scrap, warranty, service, downtime, customer returns, and lost sales. The acquisition price plus all other associated costs becomes the total cost of ownership. A total cost approach requires the cooperation of engineering, quality, manufacturing, and supply to coordinate requirements such as specifications and tolerances that affect the supply decision. A similar approach may be applied when describing the required service in the statement of work (SOW). Early supplier involvement also is essential to ensure cost-effectiveness.

TCO models attempt to determine all the cost elements, thereby revealing opportunities for cost reduction or cost avoidance for each cost element, rather than merely analyzing or comparing prices. The difficulty lies in identifying and tracking these cost elements and using the information appropriately to compare different suppliers.

In TCO analysis, acquisition price is merely one part of the costs associated with owning a good or procuring a service. While the most obvious reason for using TCO is to identify the actual cost of the supply decision, TCO also can be used to:

1. Highlight cost reduction opportunities.
2. Aid supplier evaluation and selection.

3. Provide data for negotiations.
4. Focus suppliers on cost reduction opportunities.
5. Highlight the advantage of expensive, high-quality items.
6. Clarify and define supplier performance expectations.
7. Create a long-term supply perspective.
8. Forecast future performance.

There are a number of methods for estimating the total cost of ownership. Each firm must develop or adopt a method of cost modeling that best fits the needs of the organization. In close buyer–supplier relationships, the seller may willingly share cost data with the buyer. In other situations, the buyer or sourcing team may have to develop its own cost model to prepare for negotiations. There are many approaches to cost modeling, from informal ones to highly sophisticated, complex computer models. Firms typically use either *standard cost models,* which are applied to a variety of supply situations, or *unique cost models,* which are developed for a specific item or situation.

One way of analyzing cost elements is demonstrated by a model developed by Ellram that refers to three cost components: (1) pretransaction costs (e.g., identifying need, qualifying sources, and adding supplier to internal systems); (2) transaction costs (e.g., purchase, inspection, and administrative costs); and (3) post-transaction (e.g., defective parts, repairs, and maintenance). The acquisition price is broken down into the individual cost elements from which the price is derived. Each of these cost elements then can be analyzed by the buyer for areas of reduction or avoidance. Cost elements are both tangible and intangible, meaning that many are difficult to estimate.

Manufacturing Cost Elements

The following section addresses the typical cost elements of a manufactured product and provides suggestions for estimating the cost of each.

The prices of *raw material* entering into the product are commonly accessible and the amounts required are also fairly well known. Material costs can be estimated from a bill of material, a drawing, or a sample of the product. The buyer can arrive at material costs by multiplying material quantities or weight per unit by raw material prices. Sometimes a material usage curve will be helpful. The purpose of the curve is to chart what improvement should occur from buying economies and lower scrap rates as experience is gained in the manufacturing process. Use of price indexes and maintenance of price trend records are standard practice. For *component parts,* catalog prices often offer a clue. *Transportation costs* are easily determined.

Overhead costs generally consist of indirect costs incurred in the manufacturing, research, or engineering facilities of the company. The buyer's own engineers should provide data on processing costs. Equipment depreciation typically is the largest single element in manufacturing overhead. It is important to know how these overhead costs are distributed to a given product. If overhead is allocated as a fixed percentage of direct labor costs and there is an increase in labor costs, overhead costs can be unduly inflated unless the allocation percentage is changed. General overhead rates can be approximated.

The growing tendency for industry to become more capital intensive has increased the relative percentage of overhead versus direct labor and materials. Because some items in the overhead, such as local real estate taxes, are attributable to the location of the supplier and others are properly seen as depreciation or investment at varying technological and economic risk levels, the analysis and allocation of these costs to individual products are particularly difficult.

Both *tooling costs* and *engineering costs* often are included as a part of general manufacturing overhead, but it is wisest to pull them out for analysis as separate items since each may account for a relatively large amount of cost. The buyer wants to know what it should cost a reasonably efficient supplier to build the tooling and own the completed tooling, what its life expectancy (number of units) is, and whether the tooling can be used with equipment other than that owned by the supplier. Only with such information can the buyer guard against being charged twice for the same tooling.

General and administrative expense includes items such as selling, promotion, advertising, executive salaries, and legal expense. Frequently there is no justification for the supplier to charge an advertising allocation in the price of a product manufactured to the buyer's specifications or after entering into a long-term buyer-supplier partnering relationship.

Direct labor estimates are not made as easily as material estimates. Even though labor costs are normally labeled direct for machine operators and assembly-line workers, in reality they tend to be more fixed than most managers care to admit. If an organization's management prefers not to lay off personnel, then inventories and overtime may be used to smooth fluctuations in demand and labor cost becomes at least semivariable and subject to allocation. The management of many organizations prefers to reduce direct labor cost by relying on contract, freelance, or temporary labor, domestic or offshore, thereby eliminating or greatly reducing the costs of salaries, wages, and benefits.

Product mix, run sizes, and labor turnover may affect labor costs substantially. The greater the mix, the shorter the lot size produced, and the higher the turnover, the greater the direct labor costs will be. These three factors alone may create substantial cost differences between suppliers of an identical end product. Geographical considerations also play a large part because differences in labor rates do exist between plant locations. Such differences may change dramatically over time, as the rapid increases in direct labor rates in Japan and Germany demonstrated in the 1950s and in China and India currently. The astute cost analyst will estimate the supplier's real labor costs, taking the above considerations into account.

Services Cost Elements

As addressed in Chapter 6 "Need Identification," services are intangible products that may or may not be bundled with a good. A service provider does not have costs of manufacturing and the accompanying carrying costs for raw materials, work-in-process, and finished goods inventory. The primary cost elements for a service provider are direct and indirect labor depending on whether the service is high or low labor intensive.

Overhead costs generally consist of indirect costs incurred in the design, development, delivery, and operational facilities of the company. The buyer's own operations should provide data on processing costs. Depending on the type of service provider, equipment depreciation may be a very small part of overhead. Labor intensity will affect the relative percentage of overhead versus direct labor.

General and administrative expense includes items such as selling, promotion, advertising, executive salaries, and legal expense. Frequently there is no justification for the supplier to charge an advertising allocation in the price of a service designed to the buyer's specifications or after forming a long-term buyer-supplier partnering relationship.

Transportation costs, in the form of Travel and Entertainment (T&E), may be high depending on the amount and geographical range of travel in support of sales and customer relationship management. These costs may be easily determined if the service provider has consolidated and manages this spend category. Or these costs may be hidden if responsibility for travel spend is highly decentralized. While travel spend is often targeted for cost reduction, starkly different perspectives on cost-cutting opportunities are likely to be offered by users and cost-cutters.

Direct labor for a service contract includes the supplier's employees whose time is directly engaged to perform an identifiable task required under the terms of the contract. This task may or may not result in a tangible output, for example an architectural drawing, depending on the nature of the service provided. If an organization's management prefers not to lay off personnel, and there are strong pressures to keep the so-called direct labor force reasonably stable and employed then overtime often is used to smooth fluctuations in demand and labor cost becomes at least semivariable and subject to allocation. Companies in the service sector are also relying more on freelance, contract, and temporary labor, domestic and offshore, to eliminate or reduce labor costs.

In high labor intensity services, the cost of managing multiple sources for the same service or the costs of switching suppliers may be very high. These costs include resolving contractual issues, knowledge-transfer costs, licensing fees, initial setup and training costs with a new supplier, and the internal resources to manage the process. These costs may be underestimated when initial sourcing decisions are made.

Services mix, length of service contract, location of service provision (supplier's site or buyer's site and onshore, near shore, or offshore) and labor turnover may affect labor costs substantially. The greater the mix, the shorter the contract term, the higher the labor rate, and the higher the turnover, the greater the direct labor costs will be. Geographical considerations also play a large part because differences in labor rates exist between locations. Labor savings is a prime driver of the trend to outsource and offshore a growing variety of services including legal, medical test reading, research analyst, and software developer. Labor differentials may change dramatically over time. Recent rapid increases in direct labor rates in certain job categories such as IT and call centers in India and China, have led to some industries moving to lower-cost sections of a country such as inner or western China or to lower-cost countries such as the Philippines, Vietnam, and Pakistan. The same thing occurred in Japan and Germany in the past. The astute cost analyst will estimate the supplier's real labor costs, taking the above considerations into account.

There are several opportunities for buyers of services to reduce, contain, and avoid cost in services contracts. These include:[1]

1. Usurping procurement leverage.
2. Hidden cost adders.
3. Cost of money.
4. Billing and calculation errors.
5. Substitution of lower-skilled staff or inputs.
6. Providing levels of service below commitment.

[1] Lisa M. Ellram, Wendy L. Tate, and Corey Billington, "Understanding and Managing the Services Supply Chain," *The Journal of Supply Chain Management* 40, no. 4 (2004), p. 17.

7. Bundling of services with other services or goods.

8. Summary invoicing.

Based on this list, many of the cost-saving, reduction, and avoidance opportunities in services come from improving operating efficiency and productivity rather than better design.

Frequently, in highly professional services the cost of the professional service may be relatively low compared to the benefit expected. For example, a good design may increase sales substantially; a good architect may be able to design a low-cost but effective structure; and a good consulting recommendation may turn around a whole organization. It often is difficult to deal with this trade-off between the estimated costs for the job versus the estimated benefits. Some supply managers are working to develop cost models for highly skilled service providers to better understand the service providers' cost structure and identify opportunities to lower costs.

Services involving largely lower- to medium-skilled people may focus more on cost minimization and efficiency. Services requiring highly skilled individuals may require the purchaser to distinguish between levels of professional skill and may require extensive ongoing communication between requisitioner and supply manager through all phases of the acquisition process. It is important to clearly define the quantity of each skill level required for successful delivery of the service and to match that skill level with the price and total cost of the project. For example, if a paralegal can perform the service at the quality level desired, then there may be no reason to pay the hourly cost of a partner in a high-level law firm.

Cost management of services often starts with demand management, also referred to as consumption management in some industries. An internal review analyzes consumption patterns to determine what, if any, changes can be made to consumption of the service. These include: eliminate the service, reduce the volume of the service, reduce the frequency of the service, change the specification; find a substitute; improve the purchasing process to eliminate maverick or off-contract buying; reduce overconsumption, rationalize the supply base; consolidate spend; and standardize the price, terms, and conditions.

Understanding the cost structure of professional service providers is important as more highly professional service providers offshore aspects of their business. For example, U.S. law firms offshore legal work, consulting firms offshore analytical work, and hospitals offshore the interpretation of medical tests. Should a client of these service providers share in the labor savings realized by these decisions? Do these offshoring decisions raise other issues about quality and costs?

Life-Cycle Costing and Capital Goods Acquisition

Life-cycle costing (LCC) is the term for TCO used in capital acquisitions. It is an appropriate decision approach to capital investments in which the price of the capital good may be dwarfed by the other costs associated with owning, operating, and disposing of the item. The philosophy behind LCC is the same as TCO. The total cost of a piece of equipment goes well beyond the purchase price or even its installed cost. What is really of interest is the total cost of performing the intended function over the lifetime of the task or the piece of equipment. Thus, an initial low purchase price may mask a higher operating cost, perhaps occasioned by higher maintenance and downtime costs, more skilled labor, greater material waste, more energy use, or higher waste processing charges. Since the low bid would favor a low initial machine cost, an unfair advantage may accrue to the supplier with possibly the highest life-cycle cost equipment.

It is the inclusion of every conceivable cost pertaining to the decision that makes the LCC concept easier to grasp theoretically than to practice in real life. Since many of the costs are future ones, possibly even 10 to 15 years hence and of a highly uncertain nature, criticisms of the exactness of LCC are well founded. Fortunately, IT solutions are available varying from simple accounting programs, which compute costs from project life cycles, to Monte Carlo simulation of the equipment from conception to disposal. The software allows for testing of sensitivity, and, when necessary, inputs can be changed readily. In one total cost of ownership study for a multimillion-dollar piece of equipment, 139 different cost elements were identified for the computer simulation of the process.

LCC is a serious and preferable alternative to emphasizing the selection of low bids, particularly in governmental purchasing. The experience with LCC has shown in a surprising number of instances that the initial purchase price of equipment may be a relatively low percentage of LCC. For example, the price paid for computers seldom accounts for over 50 percent of LCC, and most industrial equipment falls into the 20 to 60 percentage range.

However, price is often the major factor in an acquisition decision. This is easy to understand when the number and variety of cost elements and the difficulty in calculating these costs are considered. The fundamental questions about cost elements for capital goods include the following:

- Is the equipment intended for replacement only or to provide additional capacity?
- What is the installed cost of the equipment?
- What will start-up costs be?
- Will its installation create problems for plant layout?
- What will be the maintenance and repair costs?
- Who will provide repair parts and at what cost?
- Are accessories required and, if so, what will their costs be?
- What will be the operating costs, including power and labor?
- What is the number of machine-hours the equipment will be used?
- Can the user make the machine or must it be purchased?
- At what rate is the machine to be depreciated?
- What financing costs are involved?
- If the equipment is for production, what is the present cost of producing the product compared to the cost of obtaining the product from a supplier?
- If the equipment is for production, what is the projected cost of producing the product compared to the cost of obtaining the product from a supplier?

For example, in the semiconductor industry, capital equipment purchases normally represent the largest single percentage category of all purchase dollars. At Intel the goal is to tie capital equipment purchasing and equipment service to performance-based contracting. Thus, the supplier gets paid for uptime and quality output. The more the running time exceeds agreed-to output goals, the greater the rewards for the supplier. Future plans are driven by the need for continuous improvement in cost per wafer and number of wafers per year per machine. Only a few key supplier partners are included in Intel's longer-range technology road maps planning process—looking five years out. Total cost of ownership, not just the cost of the equipment itself, drives future technology decisions. Obviously, the corporate team approach is required to manage this process, and exceptionally capable individuals need to represent supply on the corporate team.

Target Costing

In target costing, a management team establishes the price at which it plans to sell its finished product, then subtracts out its normal operating profit, leaving the target cost that the organization seeks. The formula is Target Cost = Estimated Selling Price − Desired Profit. The target cost is then further subdivided into appropriate cost sectors, such as manufacturing process, overhead, materials, and services. Supply becomes responsible for working with suppliers to achieve the materials and services target. Target costing is typically used in new product development. Target pricing focuses the attention of everyone in the organization on designing costs out of products and services rather than on eliminating costs after production has begun or services have been delivered. This concept is a logical extension of the quality movement's basic premise that it makes sense to build something right the first time.

For example, if the end product is a manufactured item that will be sold for $200, and purchased goods represent 60 percent of each dollar in sales revenue, then supply would be responsible for $120 of the $200 selling price. If it is determined that a 10 percent reduction in price is desirable because of the expected impact on sales revenue, then supply would be responsible for securing a 10 percent reduction in its portion of the costs ($120) of the item, or $12. This means purchased materials, on a unit basis, should not exceed $108. This becomes the target materials cost in the pricing structure. See the example in Figure 11–2.

Target pricing results in companywide cost reductions in:

1. Design to cost, on the part of design engineering.
2. Manufacture to cost, on the part of production.
3. Purchase to cost, on the part of supply.

FIGURE 11–2
Target Pricing Example

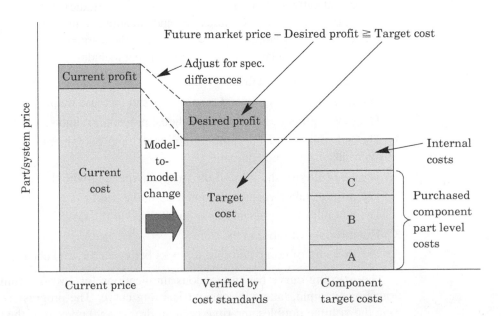

Implications for Supply Management

For supply, target pricing can be beneficial by providing a means of documenting specific price reductions needed from suppliers, demonstrating supply's contribution to the pricing goals of the firm, and documenting supply's contribution on a product-by-product basis. To be effective, target pricing works best when the customer has clout or leverage in the supply chain; when there is loyalty between buyer and seller, as in a partnering arrangement or alliance; and when the supplier also stands to benefit from the cost reductions.

The cost reductions on the part of the supplier conceivably can come from several areas: The supplier can seek reductions in overhead expenses and/or general, selling, and administrative expenses; the supplier can improve efficiencies in labor as measured by the learning curve; or the supplier can seek labor cost reductions and material cost reductions from its supply chain. This last option requires the supplier to pass down these techniques to *its* suppliers in the supply chain.

Overall, target pricing provides supply with:

1. A measurable target for supply performance.
2. A yardstick for measuring cost reductions.
3. A means of measuring the supplier's efficiency.

As with all cost analysis tools, the expected benefits from the target-costing process must exceed the costs associated with conducting the analysis. To be successful, the effort requires cross-functional team efforts, early supplier and early supply involvement, concurrent engineering, and value engineering.

The Learning Curve or Experience Curve

The learning curve provides an analytical framework for quantifying the commonly recognized principle that one becomes more proficient with experience. Its origins lie in the aircraft industry in World War II when it was empirically determined that labor time per plane declined dramatically as volume increased. Subsequent studies showed that the same phenomenon occurred in a variety of industries and situations. Although conceptually most closely identified with direct labor, most experts believe the learning curve is actually brought about by a combination of a large number of factors that includes:

1. The learning rate of labor.
2. The motivation of labor and management to increase output.
3. The development of improved methods, procedures, and support systems.
4. The substitution of better materials, tools, and equipment, or more effective use of materials, tools, and equipment.
5. The flexibility of the job and the people associated with it.
6. The ratio of labor versus machine time in the task.
7. The amount of preplanning done in advance of the task.
8. The turnover of labor in the unit.
9. The pressure of competition to do tasks better, faster, and cheaper.

The learning curve has tremendous implications for cost determination and negotiation. For example, take a 90 percent learning curve. The progress is logarithmic. Every time the volume doubles, the time per unit drops to 90 percent of the time per unit at half the volume. Suppose we wish to purchase 800 units of a highly labor-intensive, expensive product that will be produced by a group of workers over a two-year period. The 100th unit has been produced at a labor time of 1,000 hours. With a 90 percent learning curve, the labor time for the 200th unit would drop to 900 hours and the 400th unit to 90 percent of 900 hours, or 810 hours per unit.

Do service firms exhibit learning curves? Is there a significant association between experience-based knowledge and productivity increases in services? While the application of learning curve theory to services has not been well-researched, it is an interesting concept in a service economy.

It is important to recognize that the choice of learning curve, be it 95, 90, 85, or 80 percent or any other figure, is not an exact science. Normally, fairly simple tasks, like putting parts into a box, tend to have a learning curve close to 95 percent. Medium-complexity tasks often have learning curve rates between 80 and 90 percent, while highly complex tasks tend to be in the 70 to 80 percent range.

The learning curve implies that improvement never stops, no matter how large the volume becomes. The potential of the learning curve in supply management has not yet been fully explored. It is a powerful concept. Progressive discounts, shortened lead times, and better value can be planned and obtained through its use. The learning curve is used along with target costing to set progressively lower price targets for future deliveries.

Value Engineering and Value Analysis

Value methodology is a systematic approach to analyzing the functions of a product, part, service, or process to satisfy all needed quality and user requirements at optimum total cost of ownership. Value can be expressed as:

$$\text{VALUE} = \frac{\text{Function}}{\text{Cost}}$$

Function is defined in a noun-verb combination: for example, "holds liquid." The goal is to perform a function at the same or an improved level while reducing costs. The focus is on functional analysis. Unnecessary costs, those that do not provide quality, extend product or service life, or provide features desired by customers, can be avoided or eliminated.

Value engineering (VE) refers to the application of this analytical process to the design stage of a product or service; *value analysis (VA)* to the redesign of a product or service. By focusing on function and cost in the design stage, unnecessary costs can be avoided. In the redesign stage, the organization has already incurred costs that must now be reduced or eliminated. Lower total cost of ownership is achieved when a cost management focus starts in design.

Activity-Based Costing

Traditional cost accounting introduces distortions into product costing because of the way it allocates overhead on the basis of direct labor. In the past, when labor costs often were the largest cost category, this allocation made sense. However, as the cost of materials has eclipsed labor costs as the single largest cost factor, accountants have looked for other ways to allocate overhead.[2] Basically, *activity-based costing (ABC)* tries to turn indirect costs into direct costs by tracking the cost drivers behind indirect costs.

[2] The section is drawn largely from John C. Lere and Jayant V. Saraph, "Activity-Based Costing for Purchasing Managers' Cost and Pricing Determinations," *International Journal of Purchasing and Materials Management,* Fall 1995, pp. 25–21.

One of the biggest hurdles in ABC is the cost of tracking indirect costs and translating them into direct costs, compared with the benefits of being able to assign these costs to specific products more accurately. In ABC, manufacturing overhead is divided into costs that change in response to unit-level activities (in proportion to the number of units produced), batch-level activities (in proportion to the number of batches produced), and product-level activities (that benefit all units of a product). The remainder are true fixed costs and are allocated the same way as in traditional cost accounting.

It is easy for those trying to apply the ABC concept to collect too much detail and be unable to make much sense out of it. Even so, it is a powerful tool that has many implications for supply management.

Implications for Supply Management

Buyers can use activity-based costing as a tool to reduce supplier costs by:

- Eliminating nonvalue-adding activities.
- Reducing activity occurrences.
- Reducing the cost driver rate.

To accomplish these goals, buyers must collect data from suppliers on activities (specific tasks), cost drivers (a metric to measure activity), cost driver rates (rate at which cost is incurred), and units of cost driver (the amount of activity). Buyers then can determine which activities add value and should occur, and which do not add value and should be eliminated. Even if an activity is deemed value-adding, it may be possible to reduce the number of times the activity occurs, thereby reducing cost.

For example, receiving inspection may be rated as nonvalue-adding and targeted for elimination, or it may be deemed value-adding but the number of receipts requiring inspection may be reduced, thereby reducing costs. Lastly, the cost of the activity itself may be targeted as an area for improvements in efficiency through value analysis and system redesign.

Assigning cost estimates to activities is often difficult. It is essential, however, to enable comparison of activities and activity levels and to determine where improvements contribute most to organizational performance. Competing goals and objectives of different functional areas may increase the difficulty of using ABC as a decision-making tool. In the example above, receiving may use ABC to decrease incoming inspections and improve receiving department performance. Quality assurance, however, may want to increase incoming inspection to reduce acceptance rates of nonconforming product.

NEGOTIATION

Negotiation is the most sophisticated and most expensive means of price determination. Negotiation requires that the buyer and supplier, through discussion, arrive at a common understanding on the essentials of a purchase/sale contract, such as delivery, specifications, warranty, prices, and terms. Because of the interrelation of these factors and many others, it is a difficult art and requires the exercise of judgment and tact. Negotiation is an attempt to find an agreement that allows both parties to realize their objectives. It must be used when the buyer is in a single- or sole-source situation; both parties know that a purchase contract will be issued, and their task is to define a set of terms and conditions acceptable to both.

FIGURE 12–1
A Simple One-Stage Supplier Selection Decision

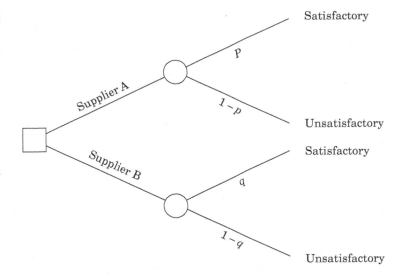

product design or engineering services to support the new product design process. The supplier should probably be local for ease of communication with the design engineers and have good technical credentials. Likewise, a janitorial service for the engineering offices would be local with good references. However, for a large printed circuit board order for a production run, price would be one key factor, and delivery should be on time, but not necessarily unusually fast. Thus, even on requirements with identical technical specifications, the weighting of the selection criteria may vary. It is this sensitivity to organizational needs that separates the good supply manager from the average. The one result every supply professional wishes to avoid is unacceptable supplier performance. This may create costs far out of proportion to the size of the original purchase, upset internal relationships, and strain supplier goodwill and final customer satisfaction.

Decision Trees

The supplier selection decision can be seen as a decision made under uncertainty and can be represented by a decision tree. Figure 12–1 shows a very simple one-stage situation with only two suppliers seriously considered and two possible outcomes. It illustrates, however, the uncertain environment present in almost every supplier choice and the risk inherent in the decision. To use decision trees effectively, the supply professional must identify the options and the criteria for evaluation and assess the probabilities of success and failure. This simple tree could apply to a special one-time purchase without expectation of follow-on business for some time to come.

The more normal situation for future repetitive purchases is shown in Figure 12–2. Whether the chosen source performs well or not for the current purchase under consideration, the future decision about which supplier to deal with next time around may well affect the present decision. For example, if the business is placed with supplier C and C fails, this may mean that only A could be considered a reasonable source at the next stage. If having A as a single source, without alternatives, is not acceptable, choosing C as the supplier at the first stage does not make any sense. If, however, the business is placed with supplier A and A fails, then the buyer has three options: Stay with A and fix things or switch to B or C.

FIGURE 12–2
Simplified Three-Stage Decision Tree for Supplier Selection

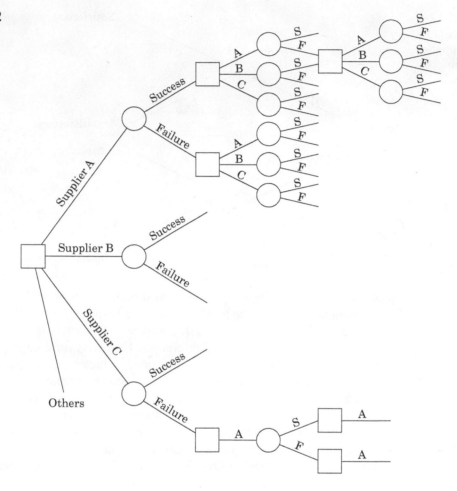

It is necessary to consider the selection decision as part of a chain of events, rather than as an isolated instance. This addition of a time frame—past, present, and future—makes the sourcing decision even more complex. However, as long as the objective of finding and keeping good sources is clearly kept in mind, the decision can be evaluated in a reasonable business context.

IDENTIFYING POTENTIAL SOURCES

There are three potential supply options for any new need/requirement of an organization. The make option or doing it in-house may be realistic for some needs but not for others. These decisions have already been discussed in Chapter 5 under make or buy, insourcing, and outsourcing. The second option is to acquire the new need from a current supplier of other requirements. Most supply professionals would prefer to pursue this option. There is already a record of past performance and communication and logistics requirements are in place.

Assuming past dealings with the current supplier have been satisfactory, the expectation would be that additional business might secure an even better value proposition on the total set of requirements supplied. Therefore, current good or superior suppliers have a right to

FIGURE 12–3   **Identification of Potential Sources for a New Need/Requirement**

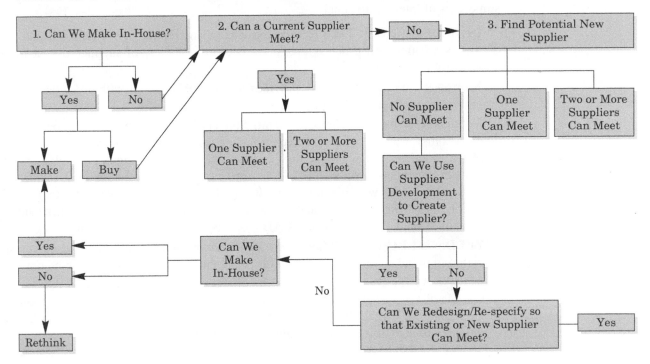

expect additional volumes of business as a reward for their performance on current and past business. Both purchaser and supplier stand to benefit from this understanding.

The third option is to engage in a search for potential suppliers, assuming the first two options were not satisfactory or the supply professional was anxious to test the market. Figure 12–3 diagrams the three options and the potential outcomes. When no suitable supplier can be found, the supply professional still has the option of using supplier development (discussed later in this chapter) or redesign or respecification to see if a suitable source can be found or developed. There is a remote chance that, despite all efforts, no solution is found. Then the supply professional and the requisitioner need to see if an alternative or substitute solution can be found.

Information Sources

The identification of potential sources is a key driver of the ultimate success or failure of the supplier selection effort. Every supply professional is always on the alert for potential new sources.

Knowledge of sources is therefore a primary qualification for any effective supply manager. Online searches, e-catalogs, and company websites are the most common tools used today. Other sources include trade journals, advertisements, supplier and commodity directories, sales interviews, colleagues, professional contacts, and the supply department's own records.

Online Sources

The Internet provides a rapidly growing and ever-changing body of information for supply professionals. The challenge is not just finding information, but identifying, sorting, analyzing, and using relevant information. The following list contains web addresses for some sites of interests to supply.

D&B www.dnb.com D&B provides basic company reports online for a fee, and company's location and products gratis. D&B offers a variety of supplier risk, loss, and viability predictors.

Kompass www.kompass.com provides a global B2B portal with a database of 11+ million companies worldwide.

Thomas Register www.thomasNet.com Supplier Discovery and Product Sourcing. The most comprehensive online resource for finding companies and products manufactured in North America. Services include online order placement, viewing and downloading millions of computer-aided design (CAD) drawings, and viewing thousands of online company catalogs and websites. It includes listings for over 610,000 qualified manufacturers, distributors, MRO providers, and custom manufacturers; 100 million products, and millions of 2D and 3D downloadable CAD modules from leading manufacturers.

Ziff Davis LLC www.ziffdavis.com Ziff Davis is an all-digital media company specializing in the technology market. This is a resource for information on e-commerce.

McRAE's Blue Book www.mcraesbluebook.com With three industrial market leaders, MacRAE'S Blue Book and the Canadian Trade Index, InfoMex Mexican Industrial Directory, the MacRAE'S Owen Media Network specializes in delivering high-value, unique company information to industrial buyers and sellers worldwide.

Catalogs

A well-managed purchasing and supply department must have catalogs (online, hard copy, or both) of the commonly known sources of supply, covering the most important materials in which a company is interested. The value of catalogs depends largely on presentation form, accessibility, frequency and extent of use. Electronic catalogs (discussed in Chapter 4) are increasingly used. The advantage of eCatalogs is that both buyers and internal customers have ready access to them and they can be customized to include the prices and other terms and conditions negotiated by the buyer with the seller. Management of eCatalog content is as serious an issue as management of hard-copy catalogs. Advances in online catalog management continue to increase the ease of access and improve the form of presentation.

The accessibility of catalog content is driven by the manner in which it is indexed and filed, a not-so-simple task even with online catalogs. Hard-copy catalogs are issued in all sorts of sizes and formats that make them difficult to handle. Proper indexing of catalogs is essential. Some companies still use microfilm files and loose-leaf binders with sheets especially printed for catalog filing; others use a form of card index. Indexing should be according to suppliers' names as well as products listed. It should be specific, definite, and easily understandable. The sort and search function of an eCatalog can make a catalog more or less user-friendly. Distributors' catalogs contain many items from a variety of manufacturing sources and offer a directory of available commodities within the distributors' fields. Equipment and machinery catalogs provide information about specifications and the location of a source of supply for replacement parts as well as new equipment. Catalogs frequently provide price information, and many supplies and materials are sold from standard list prices or by quoting discounts only. Catalogs are also used as reference books by internal customers.

Trade Journals

Trade journals also are a valuable source of information about potential suppliers. The list of such publications is very long, and the individual items in it vary in value. Yet in every field there are worthwhile trade magazines, and buyers read extensively those dealing with their own industry and with those industries to which they sell and from which they buy. These journals are utilized in two ways. The first use is to gain general information from the articles that might suggest new products and substitute materials as well as information about suppliers and their personnel. The second use is a consistent perusal of the advertisements to stay current on offerings.

Trade Directories

Trade directories are another useful source of information. They vary widely in their accuracy and usefulness, and care must be exercised in their use. Trade registers, or trade directories, are online or hard-copy volumes that list leading manufacturers, their addresses, number of branches, affiliations, products, and, in some instances, their financial standing or their position in the trade. They also contain listings of the trade names of articles on the market with names of the manufacturers and classified lists of materials, supplies, equipment, and other items offered for sale, under each of which is given the name and location of available manufacturing sources of supply. These registers are organized by commodity, manufacturer, or trade name. Standard directories include the Thomas Register (thomasnet.com), MacRAE's Blue Book (macraesbluebook.com) and Kompass publications (kompass.com).

Trade directories of minority- and women-owned business enterprises can assist purchasers with a goal or requirement to increase the percentage of contracts awarded to these firms. For example, the System for Award Management (sam.gov) simplified the U. S. federal contracting process by creating an integrated database that consolidated the capabilities of the Central Contractor Registration (CCR)/Federal Registration (FedReg), Online Representations and Certifications Application (ORCA). It is a Federal Acquisition Regulation (FAR)-mandated web-based system that streamlines the solicitation and award process for both vendor and government by collecting vendor representations and certifications of business information that is required by law for contract award. The Excluded Parties List System (EPLS) is an electronic, web-based system that identifies those parties excluded from receiving federal contracts, certain subcontracts, and certain types of federal financial and nonfinancial assistance and benefits. The EPLS keeps its user community aware of administrative and statutory exclusions across the entire government and individuals barred from entering the United States. Searches can be based on North American Industry Classification System (NAICS, pronounced NAKES) Codes, keywords, location, quality certifications, business type, and ownership race and gender. Diversity Information Resources (www.diversityinforesources.org) fosters economic development through the publication of directories of minority, women, veteran, service-disabled, Gay, Lesbian, Bisexual, and/or Transgendered (GLBT)-owned businesses, and HUBZone suppliers. A number of organizations also certify businesses as minority- and women-owned, including the Women's Business Enterprise National Council (WBENC) (wbenc.org); the National Women Business Owners Corporation (NWBOC) (nwboc.org); the National Minority Supplier Development Council (NMSDC) (www.nmsdc.org); and in the public sector, the Office of Small Disadvantaged Business Utilization (OSDBU) (www.sbu.gov/GC/OSDBU.html) which also certifies Asian, Black, Hispanic, and Native American business enterprises.

Sales Representation

Sales representatives may constitute one of the most valuable sources of information available, with references to sources of supply, types of products, and trade information generally. One challenge for supply personnel is balancing the need to meet with sales representatives with other responsibilities and time constraints. It is essential to develop good supplier relations that begin with a friendly, courteous, sympathetic, and frank attitude toward the supplier's salesperson. After contact, relevant information should be captured in a format that can be easily accessed and used effectively. Some organizations develop routing mechanisms on their web sites to alleviate the time pressure on buyers and sellers by providing information about how to do business with the organization and routing callers to the appropriate person or portal for RFQs, RFPs, and invitations to bid.

Supplier and Commodity Databases

Information from any source, if of value, should be captured. For example, an index of catalogs makes it easy to access a needed catalog. Two common databases are of suppliers and commodities. The supplier database includes information on each active supplier, including locations and contact information, open orders and past orders, supplier performance scorecards, and other pertinent information that might be of value to future decisions. Supplier databases may be managed online, in a simple computer file, or in a card file.

A commodity database classifies material on the basis of the product and includes information related to the sources from which the product has been purchased in the past, perhaps the price paid, the point of shipment, and a link or cross-reference to the supplier database. Miscellaneous information is also given, such as whether specifications are called for, whether a contract already exists covering the item, whether competitive bids are commonly asked for, and other data that may be of importance. Accompanying files dealing with sources are those relating to price and other records. Some of these have already been discussed in earlier chapters, and others will be discussed later. The information management aspects of enterprise resource planning (ERP) systems and e-procurement systems are discussed in Chapter 4.

Visits to Suppliers

Some supply managers feel that visits to suppliers are particularly useful when there are no difficulties to discuss. The supply manager can talk with higher-level executives rather than confining discussion to someone who happens to be directly responsible for handling a specific complaint. This helps to cement good relationships at all levels of management and may reveal much about a supplier's future plans that might not otherwise come to the buyer's attention. Such a visitation policy does raise certain problems not found in the more routine types of visits, such as who should make the visits, how best to get worthwhile information, and the best use of the data once obtained. Experience has indicated that the best results come from (1) developing, in advance, a general outline of the kinds of information sought; (2) gathering, in advance, all reasonably available information, both general and specific, about the company; and (3) preparing a detailed report of the findings after the visit. When the visits are carefully planned, the direct expense incurred is small compared with the returns.

Samples

In addition to the usual inquiries and a plant visit, samples of the supplier's product can be tested. This requires thinking about the "sample problem." Frequently a sales representative for a new product urges the buyer to accept a sample for test purposes. This raises questions about what samples to accept, how to ensure a fair test of those accepted, who should bear the expense of testing, and whether or not the supplier should be given the results of the test. (See "Sampling, Inspection and Testing" in Chapter 7.)

Colleagues

Frequently, internal business partners are valuable sources of information about potential sources of supply. Purchase requisitions may invite the requisitioner to identify potential sources.

References

Often buyers will include a request for references in the RFQ, RFP, or RFB/invitation to bid. To get the most useful information possible, it is the job of the interviewer to set the parameters for the interview. First, make sure that the reference is a company of similar size and objectives. Second, talk to people with firsthand knowledge of the supplier's performance. Third, ask open-ended questions that allow the reference to describe the performance of the supplier and the relationship. For example, a new customer might be asked about the implementation process: "Did it go smoothly? Tell me about a time things weren't going according to plan. How did the supplier deal with the problem or change?" A veteran customer might be asked about the supplier's actions to stay competitive or to continuously improve: "Tell me about a time when the supplier initiated an improvement that also benefited you (the customer)?" Past customers might be asked about the transition process to another supplier: "When you switched suppliers, how did the original supplier handle the transition of information? materials? and so forth?" Potential sources need to be evaluated.

Standard Information Requests

Additional information from the supplier is usually sought during the identification of potential suppliers stage and before supplier selection takes place. As described in Chapter 4, the nature of these communications takes a variety of forms.

The Request for Information (RFI)

The request for information or expression of interest serves several purposes. It signals that the supply professional has identified a supplier as a potential source of supply. It is also an opportunity for the supplier to indicate its willingness to enter into a potential business relationship. Although the content of the RFI may vary considerably from technical data to interest in receiving an invitation to bid, it is clear to both parties that the RFI does not commit either party to future business. If the information collection process could result in significant additional expense for the supplier, it is appropriate for the supply professional to offer reimbursement of some or all of these costs.

The Request for Quotation (RFQ) or Request for Bid (RFB) or Invitation to Bid or Tender

These requests represent a serious inquiry of the supplier on a specific requirement or a variety of requirements. The RFQ and its equivalents ask the supplier to declare at what price and what terms they are prepared to supply. In the public sector, it is often an organizational requirement that all requirements exceeding a certain dollar amount be put out to bid and that the lowest bidder will be awarded the contract. Bidders are required to submit their bids by a certain deadline and meet all of the conditions stated in the invitation to bid or tender.

Suppliers are invited to attend a public opening of bids and, thus, each bidder knows exactly what prices have been quoted by all bidders or to review the awards online. After the public opening, public supply professionals usually require some additional time to examine all bids for compliance with conditions and to deal with possible exceptions. Fair as this process may appear, it is still occasionally abused. Various bidders may collude to rig prices. A recent example involving road construction contracts in Montreal had a group of bidders, reported to be Mafia related, deciding on the lowest bid beforehand and who was allowed to be the lowest bidder. This resulted in an elevation of construction costs exceeding 10 percent.

In the private sector, there is no public opening of bids and the lowest bid may not be accepted if, in the opinion of the supply professional, a higher bid represents better value. Because the preparation of a bid always entails costs for the supplier and may raise expectations, it is deemed ethical practice to invite only those suppliers to bid who have a serious chance of receiving the business.

In the RFQ, RFB, and Invitation to Bid, the assumption is that requirement specifications are sufficiently descriptive and standard so that multiple suppliers can meet these requirements. Therefore, the price and terms quoted differentiate among suppliers.

The Request for Proposal (RFP)

An RFP allows more latitude to the supplier than an RFQ when it is difficult to describe a requirement, or the supply organization lacks the ability to create an RFQ or the supply professional expects that innovation or creativity in the market might result in a superior solution. The RFP permits the supplier to fit the proposal to its strengths. For the supply professional, comparison of RFPs received is considerably more difficult than an RFQ evaluation and may involve a lot of judgment. Also, the preparation of an RFP is often more expensive for the supplier than an RFQ, and the issue of reimbursement for supplier costs incurred in its preparation needs to be resolved. Moreover, if the RFP contains proprietary technical or commercial information, protection of confidentiality is critical. Often the RFP is used as the first stage of a two-stage process in which only certain suppliers are invited to quote on the business or enter into negotiations for the final round.

ADDITIONAL SUPPLIER SELECTION DECISIONS

The discussion on supplier selection in this chapter has thus far focused on the identification of potential suppliers and information about them. There are, however, additional decisions that need to be identified and five, in particular, are highlighted here:

1. Should we use a single source, dual sources, or more than two?
2. Should we buy from a manufacturer or a distributor?
3. Where should the supplier be located?
4. Relative to our organization, should the supplier be small, medium, or large?
5. If no supplier can be found, should we use supplier development?

Single versus Multiple Sourcing

Should the supply professional choose a single supplier or utilize several? The answer to this question must be the very unsatisfactory one: "It all depends."

Table 12–1 lists the main arguments for placing all orders for a given item with one supplier and Table 12–2 provides the main arguments for multiple sourcing:

TABLE 12–1
Single Sourcing

1. Prior commitments, a successful past relationship, or an ongoing long-term contract with a preferred supplier might prevent even the possibility of splitting the order.
2. The supplier may be the exclusive owner of certain essential patents or processes and, therefore, be the only possible source.
3. A given supplier may be so outstanding in the quality of product or in the service or value provided as to preclude serious consideration of buying elsewhere.
4. The order may be so small as to make it not worthwhile to divide it.
5. Concentrating purchases may make possible certain discounts or lower freight rates that could not be had otherwise.
6. The supplier will be more cooperative, more interested, and more willing to please if it has all the buyer's business.
7. When the purchase of an item involves a die, tool, mold charge, or costly setup, the expense of duplicating this equipment or setup is likely to be substantial.
8. Deliveries may be more easily scheduled.
9. The use of just-in-time production, stockless buying, or systems contracting.
10. Effective supplier relations require considerable resources and time. Therefore, the fewer suppliers the better.
11. Single sourcing is a prerequisite to partnering.

TABLE 12–2
Multiple Sourcing

1. It has been traditional practice to use more than one source, especially on the important requirements.
2. Knowing that competitors are getting some of the business may keep the supplier more alert to the need for giving good value.
3. Assurance of supply is increased. Should fire, strikes, breakdowns, or accidents occur to any one supplier, deliveries can still be obtained from the others for at least part of the needs.
4. The supply organization has developed a unique capability of dealing with multiple sources.
5. To avoid supplier dependence on the purchaser.
6. To obtain greater flexibility, because the unused capacity of all the suppliers may be available.
7. Even in situations involving close and cooperative supplier relationships, it is possible to make backup arrangements so that supplier X specializes in product Q and backs up supplier Y, who specializes in product R and backs up supplier X.
8. Strategic reasons, such as military preparedness and supply security, may require multiple sourcing.
9. Government regulations may insist that multiple suppliers, or small or minority sources, be used. If there is high risk associated with a small or single-minority source, multiple sourcing may be necessary.
10. Sufficient capacity may not be available to accommodate the purchaser's current or future needs.
11. Potential new or future suppliers may have to be tested with trial orders, while other sources receive the bulk of the current business.
12. Volatility in the supply market makes single sourcing unacceptably risky.

Genuine concern exists among supply executives about how much business should be placed with one supplier, particularly if the supplier is small and the buyer's business represents a significant portion of the seller's revenue. It is feared that sudden discontinuance of purchases may put the supplier's survival in jeopardy, and yet the purchaser does not wish to reduce flexibility by being tied to dependent sources. One rule of thumb is that no more than a certain percentage, say 20 or 30 percent, of the total supplier's business should be with one customer.

If a decision is made to divide an order among several suppliers, then the question is how to divide the business. Actual practice varies widely. One method is to divide the business equally. Another is to base the allocation on geographical coverage. Another is to place the larger share with a favored supplier and give the rest to one or more alternates. In the chemical industry, as in a number of others, it is common practice to place business with various suppliers on a percentage of total requirements basis. Total requirements may be estimated, not necessarily guaranteed, and there may not even be a minimum volume requirement. Each supplier knows what its own percentage of the business amounts to, but may not be aware who the competition is or how much business each competitor received if the number of sources exceeds two. There is no common practice or "best" method or procedure. There was renewed interest in single sourcing in conjunction with the quality movement, partnerships, and strategic sourcing. Interest in dual or multisourcing as a risk mitigation strategy is renewed each time there is an event that disrupts global supply chains. Recent events include the Great Recession, the earthquake and tsunami in Japan, and a factory fire at a Chinese factory making almost one-sixth of the world's supply of DRAM chips. The allocation of business between and among suppliers is a key component of building resilient supply chains.

Manufacturer versus Distributor

Should a supply professional deal with the manufacturer directly or through some trade channel such as a wholesaler, distributor, or even a retailer? Occasionally, various types of trade associations pressure supply professionals to patronize the wholesaler, distributor, or mill supply house. The real issue is often closely related to buying from local sources.

The justification for using trade channels is found in the value-added services rendered. If wholesalers are carrying the products of various manufacturers and spreading marketing costs over a variety of items, they may be able to deliver the product at a lower cost, particularly when the unit of sale is small and customers are widely scattered or when the demand is irregular. Furthermore, they may carry a stock of goods greater than a manufacturer could afford to carry in its own branch warehouse and therefore be in a better position to make prompt deliveries and to fill emergency orders. Also, they may be able to buy in car- or truckload lots, with a saving in transportation charges and a consequent lower cost to the buyer.

Local sentiment may be strongly in favor of a certain distributor. Public agencies are particularly susceptible to such influence. Sometimes firms that sell through distributors tend, as a matter of policy, to buy, whenever possible, through distributors.

On the other hand, some large organizations often seek ways of going around the distributor, particularly when the buyer's requirements of supply items are large, when the shipments are made directly from the original manufacturer, and when no selling effort or service is rendered by the wholesaler. Some manufacturers operate their own supply houses to get the large discount. Others have attempted to persuade the original manufacturers to establish quantity discounts—a practice not unlike that in the steel trade.

Still others have sought to develop sources among small manufacturers that do not have a widespread distribution organization. Some attempts have been made to secure a special service from a chosen distributor, such as an agreement whereby the latter would add to its staff "two people exclusively for the purpose of locating and expediting nuisance items in other lines." A similar arrangement might place a travel agent directly on the purchaser's premises to improve service or require corporate travelers to use a designated online travel booking tool. Systems contracting and stockless purchasing systems depend heavily on concentrating a large number of relatively small purchases with a highly capable distributor.

Ultimately, every participant in the value chain needs to add value. This guiding principle should apply also to the selection of nonmanufacturers in the distribution network.

Geographical Location of Sources

Where should an organization's suppliers be located—onshore or offshore? If onshore, should they be local, regional, or national suppliers? If offshore, how far offshore?

Onshore: Local, Regional, or National

Onshore sources are domestic suppliers. They may be local, regional, or national. For example, a company in Vancouver may prefer to do business with suppliers in Vancouver (local), or Western Canada (regional), or Canada (national).

While there have been varying degrees of global trade throughout history, onshore or domestic sourcing was standard operating procedure for most buyers until the mid-1980s. The difficulties and expense of communications and transportation made onshore sourcing more practical even with the labor rate differential. Historically, the advantages of local sourcing have been more dependable service: for example, shorter distances and fewer dangers of transport interruptions; knowledge of the purchaser's specific requirements and the seller's special qualifications; greater flexibility in meeting the purchaser's requirements; and equal facilities, know-how, and financial strength compared to offshore sources. Thus, there may well be sound economic reasons for preferring a local source to a more distant one. However, transformations in communications and transportation, improvements in infrastructure, education, and legal frameworks have made it easier to extend the advantages of local sourcing to offshore locations.

In just-in-time and lean production systems, proximity of the supplier's plant to that of the purchaser is vital. For example, automotive manufacturers encourage suppliers to locate plants close to automobile assembly operations. In 2012, Honda had nine manufacturing plants in the United States and spent $22 billion with U.S. suppliers, including over 500 original equipment manufacturers (OEM) in 34 states and 13,500 MRO suppliers (honda.com).

A second basis for selecting local sources rests on equally sound, although somewhat less tangible, grounds. The organization owes much to the local community. The facility is located there, the bulk of the employees live there, and often a substantial part of its financial support, as well as a notable part of its sales, may be local. The local community provides the company's personnel with their housing, schools, churches, and social life.

An argument can be made that participating in the local community, in part by doing business with or developing local suppliers, is part of corporate social responsibility.

One complication is the difficulty in defining *local*. Is *local* the buyer's city, county, or state/province? If a company has operations with employees and customers in many parts of a country, might *local* mean national? And if a company has employees and customers in many countries, does *local* mean global? Increasingly, global companies generate larger portions of their revenue and profits from offshore customers. For example, in 2013 U.S.-based Yum! Brands (KFC, Pizza Hut, and Taco Bell) reported that almost 70 percent of its profits came from outside the United States compared to 20 percent in 1997 (yum.com). To reflect the shift in growth potential, in 2014, the company reorganized into five divisions: Yum! China, Yum! India, KFC, Taco Bell, and Pizza Hut with the latter three divisions covering all other locations by brand (113 countries, including the United States).

Regional sourcing means doing business with suppliers in a geographic area, the Northeastern United States, for example. National sourcing means buying from suppliers located in the same country as the buyer. These distinctions are also blurred by trade agreements. For example, regional might also refer to countries in a regional trade pact such as NAFTA (Canada, Mexico, and the United States); or the European Union (EU) with 28 member countries; or ASEAN, a trade bloc of 10 countries, including Singapore, Thailand, Vietnam, and Indonesia, or one of the other multination trade blocs. One of the purposes of these pacts is to reduce or eliminate trade barriers and essentially to extend domestic treatment to what are physically offshore locations. To what extent do regional trade blocs blur the definition and boundaries of *region* and even *nation*?

Bilateral trade negotiations may also blur national boundaries. For example, Canada and the United States negotiate exceptions to legislation restricting federal procurement spend to domestic suppliers. There is a quid pro quo in the negotiations that enable Canadian suppliers to bid on U.S. government contracts in exchange for U.S. suppliers bidding on similarly valued Canadian federal contracts. Negotiators also seek to flow down these allowances to Canadian provincial and territorial spend and U.S. city, state, and municipality spend.

Offshore: Near Shore and Far Shore

Offshore means suppliers are located in another country. Near shore refers to a location that is closer in terms of travel time and time zones. For example, the United States, Mexico, and Canada are near shore relative to each other. Far shore entails longer transit times across more time zones: for example, the United States to countries in Asia. Offshoring is not the same thing as outsourcing. For example, most large organizations outsource the operation of in-house dining. The foodservice provider may be a local, regional, national, or an international company, but the employees are onshore.

Organizations also outsource and offshore. Many organizations have shut down in-house business processes, from call centers to legal to IT, and outsourced them to India, the Philippines, and other countries. The same is true for manufacturing and assembly. Nike, Inc. subcontracts all of its footwear production to independently owned and operated offshore suppliers. Roughly 90 percent of the parts in an iPhone are outsourced offshore, including advanced semiconductors from Germany and Taiwan, memory from Korea and Japan, display panels and circuitry from Korea and Taiwan, chipsets from Europe, rare metals from Africa and Asia, and assembly in China. Apple's iPhones are sold in 100 countries. The company has 100 local markets.

Honda, on the other hand, has an operational strategy of building products close to its customers. It owns and operates (a make decision in make or buy) offshore manufacturing facilities in the United States, Mexico, Europe, South America, China, India, New Zealand, Turkey, Thailand, and Indonesia as well as onshore facilities in Japan. When Honda first started manufacturing in the United States, most components were sourced from Japan. Today Honda of America sources the majority of inputs from U.S. suppliers.

Companies all over the world face the same question of where to source goods and services. Hon Hai Precision Industry (trade name Foxconn), a primary assembler for Apple, announced in January 2014 that it is assessing the feasibility of building a manufacturing plant in the United States to produce liquid display screens larger than 60 inches to overcome the difficulties of shipping large TV screens to the United States from Asia.

Reshoring

To a certain degree, no location decision is a final decision. The supplier location decision may change as internal organizational and external market conditions change. The cost of switching from one location to another, and from one supplier to another, must be assessed. Recently, a number of organizations have, or are considering, bringing some supply back to their home country (reshoring). For example, while call centers are still outsourced to India and, increasingly, to the Philippines, there is growth in the United States of virtual call centers using home-based agents. Caterpillar is opening a new factory in Texas to make excavators, but has also just announced that it will expand its research and development activities in China. Lenovo, a Chinese company, is bringing back computermaking to North Carolina to enhance its reputation and gain direct business benefits. The location decisions made by an organization are a critical part of organizational as well as supply strategy. (See Chapter 17 for additional discussion of this trend.)

Supplier Size

If a supply professional has the option of buying from a large, medium, or small supplier, which size of supplier should be favored? How does the size of the purchasing organization affect the decision? A matrix of relative sizes can be developed (see Figure 12–4). The size and nature of the requirement may also affect the decision, because it is general wisdom

FIGURE 12–4
Relative Purchaser and Supplier Size

Purchaser Size	Supplier Size
Small	Small Medium Large
Medium	Small Medium Large
Large	Small Medium Large

that the larger the requirement, the larger the supplier should be. Generally, smaller suppliers tend to be local for those smaller requirements where flexibility, speed of response, and availability tend to be more important than price. Larger suppliers tend to be more appropriate for high-volume requirements where technology, quality, and total cost of ownership may be critical; medium suppliers fall in between. The trouble with generalizations is that exceptions abound. Small suppliers tend to fill niches that the larger ones cannot or may have chosen not to cover. According to *Hispanic Business* magazine, the leaders of its fastest-growing 100 companies focus on a strategy of focusing on, and filling, one niche in the marketplace.

Historically, small suppliers have shown a loyalty and service deemed impossible from larger suppliers. Many larger organizations are trying to reverse this perception by developing a strong customer service focus. Small suppliers tend to depend on the management of a key owner-manager, and this person's health and attitude will affect the risk of doing business. Larger organizations tend to have greater stability and greater resources, reducing the day-to-day risk of supplier performance.

Interest in diversity of customers, employees, and suppliers has renewed interest in the large purchaser–small supplier interface and the role of education, assistance, and continuing watchfulness on the part of supply to help the supplier succeed.

SUPPLIER DEVELOPMENT/REVERSE MARKETING

In supplier selection the assumption has so far been made that at least one suitable and willing supplier already exists and that the purchaser's problem is primarily one of determining who is the best supplier. It is possible, however, that no suitable source is available and that the purchaser may have to create a source. Reverse marketing or supplier development implies a degree of aggressive procurement involvement not encountered in supplier selection. For example, it places a supply manager in a position where a prospective supplier must be persuaded to accept an order. In this no-choice context, the purchaser does not initiate supplier development as an appropriate technique or tool; it is the only alternative other than making the part or producing the service in-house.

Reverse marketing/supplier development also has a broader point of view. It defines the need for developing new or existing suppliers as follows: The purchaser is aware that benefits will accrue to both the supplier and the purchaser, benefits of which the supplier may not be aware. These benefits may be limited to the particular order at hand, or they may include more far-reaching aspects, such as technical, financial, and management processes, skills, or quality levels; reduction of marketing effort; use of long-term forecasts or permitting smoother manufacturing levels and a minimum of inventory; and so on.

It is the aggressiveness and initiative by the supply professional that makes the difference (see Figure 12–5). In the normal market context, the purchaser responds to marketing efforts. In reverse marketing, the purchaser, not the supplier, has the initiative and will predetermine prices, terms, and conditions as part of the aggressive role. Taking the initiative requires extensive research on the part of the supply professional to understand fully the organization's short- and long-term needs, operationally and strategically, and assess the supplier's capability to meet these needs so that a win-win proposal can be made. This is why the term *reverse marketing* has been chosen as a synonym for supplier development.

FIGURE 12–5
Supplier
Development
Initiative with
the Purchaser

THE MARKETING CONTEXT

Marketing initiative

Supplier ← Purchasing response ← Purchaser

THE SUPPLIER DEVELOPMENT CONTEXT

Supplier — Sales response → Purchaser

Purchasing initiative

Numerous examples show that high payoffs are possible from this supply initiative and that suppliers of all sizes may be approached in this fashion.

A further reason for reverse marketing is that there are bound to be deficiencies in the normal industrial marketing process in which the marketer traditionally takes the initiative. Even when a supplier and a purchaser have entered into a regular buyer–seller relationship, often neither party is fully aware of all the opportunities for additional business that may exist between them. This might arise because of salesperson and supply professional specialization, a lack of aggressiveness by the salesperson, or a lack of inquisitiveness by the purchaser.

If gaps are evident even where an established buyer–seller relationship exists, there must be even greater shortcomings where no such relationship has yet been established. For example, a supplier may be unable to cover its full market because of geography, limited advertising, or lack of coverage by its sales force, distributors, or agents. Most suppliers have lines of products that receive more management attention and sales push than other products also made or sold by the same company. It is always difficult to keep entirely up to date. A time lag may exist between the time of product or service introduction and the time the supply manager finds out about it. By filling these gaps through aggressiveness, the supply professional effectively strengthens this whole process.

One of the most important arguments in favor of reverse marketing not yet mentioned arises from future considerations. If the supply role is envisaged as encompassing not only the need to fill current requirements but also the need to prepare for the future, reverse marketing is valuable in assuring future sources of supply.

There are at least three outside forces that suggest the increasing necessity for purchaser initiative in the creation of future sources of supply. One of these forces is technological. The increasing rate of development of new products, materials, and processes will tend to make the industrial marketing task even more complex and more open to shortcomings. In addition to this, the increase in international trade will tend to widen supplier horizons and may create a need for purchaser aggressiveness in the development of global sources of supply. One of the most demanding and important tasks of management of a subsidiary in a less economically developed country is the problem of supplier development. Lastly, new management concerns with extracting competitive advantage from the supply chain require purchasers to be more aggressive with suppliers and to develop sources to their expectations.

For example, Honda of America developed a program to help reestablish strong, financially stable tool and die manufacturers in the United States after years of decline in the U.S. tooling industry. By helping their partners more efficiently design and manufacture their products and by providing financial support through new purchase orders, Honda helped their partners become more competitive locally and globally.[2]

EVALUATING POTENTIAL SOURCES

The evaluation of an existing supplier is substantially easier than the evaluation of a new source. Since checking out a new supplier often requires an extensive amount of time and resources, it should be done only for those suppliers that stand a serious chance of receiving a significant order. Where such a potential supplier competes with an existing supplier, the expected performance of the new source should, hopefully, be better than that of the existing one. The use of trial orders has been mentioned as a popular means of testing a supplier's capability, but it still fails to answer the question about whether the trial order should have been placed with a particular source at all. Even though a supplier may complete a trial order successfully, it may not be an acceptable source in the long run.

The evaluation of potential sources, therefore, attempts to answer one key question:

1. Is this supplier able to supply the purchaser's requirements satisfactorily, both strategically and operationally in the short and long term?

The question must be assessed on the basis of the three levels of need criteria described in Chapter 6. It is useful to repeat the three levels of need criteria and, hence, supplier evaluation and selection criteria here: level 1—strategic; level 2—traditional: quality, quantity, delivery, price, and service; and level 3—current additional: financial, risk, environmental, regulatory, social, and political. The following sections will address supplier evaluation according to these criteria.

Level 1—Strategic

Effective sourcing decisions form the basis of sound supply for any organization. These decisions should be driven by a sourcing strategy that is directly linked to organizational strategy, goals, and objectives. Many organizations have adopted the term *strategic sourcing* to capture the linkage between sourcing strategy and organizational strategy. A strategic sourcing process considers suppliers and the supply base integral to an organization's competitive advantage. It is important to define clearly the term *strategic* and establish what makes a purchase or a supplier strategically important to the organization. Typically, a strategic purchase is one that is mission critical. The good or service has the potential to either help or hinder the attainment of the organization's mission. Categorizing purchases into strategic and nonstrategic buckets is a first step in the strategic sourcing process. This type of categorization drives the decisions throughout the sourcing and selection process, including the allocation of resources to any specific buy. Without this categorization, the

---

[2] www.honda.com/newsandviews/local_news_content/[5032]_Honda_in_America.pdf.

supply manager or sourcing team may overinvest resources, time, and attention in tactical or operational purchases and underinvest in strategic ones.

Linking Sourcing with Strategy

From various sources of information, the supply professional is able to make up a list of available suppliers from whom the necessary items can be acquired. The first level of analysis is finding out which suppliers might be able to meet the buying organization's requirements. The second level of analysis is determining which of these the supply manager or sourcing team is willing to consider seriously as a source. For items that are high risk and high value, the investigation may be drawn out and extensive, requiring the collaboration of supply, internal users, and technical experts such as engineering, operations, quality control, systems, and maintenance on a formal or informal team. The cost of analysis greatly outweighs the advantages for items that are inexpensive and consumed in small quantities.

It is not possible to separate risk assessment from strategy development. Therefore, risk assessment and strategy development are discussed jointly as level 1 valuation criteria. Although the same argument can be applied for the other level 2 and 3 criteria, they will be discussed later.

Risk Assessment

Every organization's management makes decisions about the risks it is willing to take in light of the expected returns. It takes actions to avoid, mitigate, transfer, insure against, limit, or explicitly assume risk. For the supply manager, it is essential to consider each decision in the context of the organization's risk profile.

Research into risk assessment behavior of supply professionals shows that the perceived risk of placing business with an untried and unknown supplier is high. Likewise, the perceived risk associated with routine, repetitive purchases is much less than the risk of new or less standard acquisitions. In general, the risk is seen to be higher with unknown materials, parts, equipment or services, or suppliers and with increased dollar amounts. Commodity managers can take a number of actions to avoid, mitigate, transfer, limit, or insure against risk. For example, a supply professional may attempt to transfer risk by asking for advice, such as engineering judgment, or by seeking additional information, including placing a trial order, or hedging in the commodities market. He or she may require bid bonds, performance bonds, or payment bonds to insure against risk, or avoid risk by not doing business with suppliers in certain countries, or mitigate risk by dual or multiple sourcing rather than single sourcing. It is possible to limit risk by negotiating payment terms that allow progress payments when certain milestones are met, but withholds a percentage of the payment until completion and acceptance of the service provided. When a supply professional takes an action such as selecting a supplier, or switching suppliers, or agreeing to certain terms and conditions, he or she should take these actions with the explicit understanding of both the risk at which the decision puts the organization, the return expected, and the balance between the two.

Loss Exposure.   There are selective buying situations in which the specifications may well expose the buying organization to risk. Robert S. Mullen, director of purchasing at Harvard University, cited the instance of a purchase of fireproof mattresses, costing only about $1,000 more in total to avoid a multimillion dollar suit in case of student injury or death.

Environmental risks represent another category. For example, more oil spills and fires have occurred with the increase in rail transport of crude oil. Pre-2011 tank cars, which are minimally reinforced and more easily punctured, are carrying Bakken crude oil, which has a lower flash point (point at which vapors could ignite). Recovery costs from the 2013 train derailment and spill in Quebec alone were estimated to exceed $200 million. The estimated cost to retrofit the fleet is $1 billion plus the loss of inventory when demand is high. The rail industry supports tougher safety requirements for new and existing tank cars, including thicker shells, puncture-resistant shields, and stronger valve fittings to prevent spills and fires if the cars should derail. Since railway companies rarely own railway cars, the costs will initially fall on the tank car lessors, including GATX Corporation and General Electric Railcar Services Corp., and tank car manufacturers. Ultimately, shippers will bear the expenses, and the costs of moving crude by rail will increase.

Another form of loss exposure is related to the possibility of pilferage. The attractiveness of the requirements to consumers and the ease of resale may be reasons for theft. An alert purchaser can significantly cut down on losses by purchasing in smaller quantities, insisting on tamper-proof packaging, choosing the appropriate transportation mode, following the advice of security experts, and making sure that quantities are carefully controlled throughout the acquisition and disposal process.

Strategy Development

Risk assessment is a key step in strategy development. Supply risks can be assessed in several ways. Pareto analysis (see Chapter 6), which compares dollar volume to variables such as percent of suppliers, percent of inventory, and number of orders, focuses strategy development on high-dollar purchases. Portfolio analysis typically includes supply market risks in the assessment and focuses attention on the value-generating capability of a purchase in light of the risks of acquiring the purchase in the marketplace. While there are numerous two-by-two matrices in existence, Figure 11–1 is a classic example of this approach. From this analysis of value and market risk, the actual goods and services purchased by an organization can be placed in the appropriate spot in the appropriate quadrant, broad strategies developed by quadrant, and specific commodity strategies for each commodity in a quadrant; and decisions can then be made about the most appropriate sourcing strategy and tools for each category. The Delphi Corporation case in Chapter 13 provides an illustration of how a large automotive parts supplier uses a similar framework to assess the risk/volume trade-off as part of their strategic sourcing process.

Noncritical and leverage purchases share the same market risk, between low and medium, which means there are multiple suppliers and market forces keep prices competitive. Since the items are fairly standard, quality is comparable and substitutes are available. Therefore, convenience, ease of acquisition, low acquisition costs, and delivery systems may be the most important decision criteria. As the required volume of standard items increases, leverage opportunities increase and price per unit becomes a critical variable. Volume gives the buying organization more power in the marketplace, and the supply manager focuses on developing strategies to leverage volume and scale. The supply manager may develop a strategy to move items from the noncritical to the leverage category by bundling items differently, standardizing purchases, or consolidating the supply base.

These moves push the item to the right on the value or x-axis and result in price savings from increasing volume. These initiatives usually focus attention on internal processes and business relationships as supply managers develop the means to analyze and consolidate spend that is often dispersed throughout the organization.

The items in the leverage category merit special attention because they represent the "low hanging fruit" that companies pick when they begin to focus attention on purchasing and supply management. Many of the eBusiness tools discussed in Chapter 4 are especially appropriate in managing leverage purchases. By reducing the supply base to as few as the risk profile indicates is appropriate, the supply manager can generate price savings that free up cash for other uses such as reallocating to support or generate revenue growth.

Bottleneck purchases, which are medium to high risk to acquire, represent a difficult category to manage because of the uniqueness built into the specification. Interestingly, often it is the decisions made by members of the buying organization that elevate the risk. The more unique or customized the good or service, the more difficult it is to acquire. One of supply's objectives discussed in Chapter 2 was to standardize wherever possible. The challenge of fulfilling this objective is felt most strongly when managing bottleneck purchases. For example, an organization wants to develop supply management training for its global supply group of 2,500 people located in 25 countries across multiple time zones, cultures, and languages. If the company sends out an RFP to solicit proposals and requires highly customized courses, there will be few providers with the capabilities to do the job, and the proposals and quotes will reflect this complexity. If the internal training design team can develop a statement of work that clearly delineates the standard course content from the customized content, they will in effect reduce the risk (and cost) of acquisition. The challenge for the manager of bottleneck goods and services is as much an internal challenge as an external one. The supply manager must work with internal business partners to determine the appropriate level and type of customization required to satisfy the needs and wants of the final customer. Any uniqueness that is not valued by the final customer is waste and should be eliminated. This is a high-risk decision because the cost of building in unnecessary uniqueness can be quite high, and the cost of eliminating a unique characteristic that the final customer truly values and will pay for may be even more costly. The tools to extract value from this category include cross-functional and cross-organizational teams, value analysis, total cost modeling, and customer relationship management. For example, automotive manufacturers have successfully standardized many parts across both make and model of cars without harming the perceptions of buyers or the company's pricing strategy. Bottleneck purchases represent cost reduction or savings opportunities that require concerted cross-functional and often cross-organizational effort to realize.

Strategic purchases represent both the greatest risk and the greatest reward opportunity for an organization and its supply network. Strategic purchases share the same characteristics of bottleneck purchases in that they often are highly customized or possess some characteristic that limits the number of viable suppliers. The difference is that strategic purchases have the greatest potential to help or hurt attainment of the organization's mission. For example, if the mission of the organization is summed up in a phrase such as "Select and Use," then any purchase that drives a potential customer to select and use a product might be considered strategic. This might include the ingredients in a detergent or the artwork on the packaging, but not the office supplies used in general operations. The acquisition of strategic purchases and management of strategic spend historically have been handled by many people outside of the supply organization. For example, jet fuel for an airline or energy supplies for certain manufacturing concerns may represent both high-dollar and high-value purchases, and those with primary ownership of these purchase categories were business specialists with technical rather than supply management skills. The trend is toward joint ownership of strategies, goals, objectives, metrics, and accountability for these purchases. Supply brings expertise such as supply base knowledge, negotiating skill, contract development and management skill, and the ability to build and manage a long-term relationship to complement the technical knowledge of the internal business partner. The tools and techniques applied to strategic purchases include total cost modeling, value analysis and engineering, cross-functional teams, and strategic alliances. Many of the efficiency tools and process improvements described in this text free up time for supply personnel to focus resources and human talent on the acquisition and management of strategic purchases.

Another strategic option is the potential to use supply expertise and leverage in the market of the buying organization to purchase goods and services for suppliers, customers, or other supply chain members. Typically, this is the acquisition of direct materials, parts, and/or packaging for first-tier suppliers, giving the supply professional cost and quality control.

In certain industries in which purchasers are much larger companies than suppliers, the supply professional may have the power to direct small suppliers to use specific sources of supply. Under this kind of arrangement the supplier receives a processing fee and an administrative margin. Automotive suppliers of stampings commonly work under this kind of arrangement for steel supply.

Level 2—Traditional

Applying the traditional level 2 evaluation criteria of quality, quantity, delivery, price, and service is still a fundamental assessment task in evaluating potential suppliers. For a manufactured good, these are typically evaluated on the basis of the technical, engineering, manufacturing, and logistics strengths of potential suppliers. For a service, these are typically evaluated on the basis of service design, operations, and delivery strengths of the potential suppliers.

Technical, Engineering, Manufacturing, and Logistics Strengths

Technical and engineering capability, along with manufacturing strength, impinges on a number of supply concerns. The most obvious factor is the quality capability of the supplier. It is possible, however, that a company capable of meeting current quality standards may still lack the engineering and technical strengths to stay current with technological advances. Similarly, manufacturing may lack capacity, or the space to expand, or the flexibility to meet a variety of requirements. Presumably, the reason for selecting one supplier over another is that of greater strengths in areas of importance to the purchaser. The evaluation of the supplier, therefore, should focus not only on current capability, but also on the supplier's future strengths. Only in very large organizations might the supply group have sufficient technical strength to conduct such supplier evaluations on its own. Normally, other functions such as engineering, manufacturing, internal users, or quality control provide expert assistance to assess a potential supplier on technical and manufacturing strengths.

Should the supplier be a distributor, the stress might be more on logistics capability. The nature of the agreements with the distributors' supplying manufacturers, their inventory policies, systems capability and compatibility, and ability to respond to special requirements would all be assessed, along with technical strengths of the personnel required to assist the supply professional to make the right choices among a series of acceptable options. A number of distributors have developed strong supplier-/vendor-managed inventory programs, permitting organizations the option of outsourcing the total MRO supply function and reducing the total supply base significantly.

Service Design, Operations, and Delivery

Service design, operations, and delivery impinge on a number of supply concerns. First, the quality capability of the supplier is determined to a large extent on its ability to design services that meet the quality standards of the users as defined in the statement of work (SOW). Just as with manufacturing, a service provider may not have the capability to meet future quality standards either because the supplier is not able to attract and retain high-quality employees or it fails to upgrade its technology. For example, there is a persistent gap between shippers' IT expectations and third-party logistics providers' capabilities. While some of this is because 3PLs are slow to upgrade their IT, some of it is also because shippers lack adequate information about their supply chains. Similarly, a supplier's service operations and service delivery system may lack the capacity to expand or the flexibility to meet a variety of requirements. For example, a management consulting company may need to have a presence in specific countries with staff fluent in specific languages and cultures for the buying organization's current and future operations. Presumably, one service provider is selected over another because its strengths match the buyer's needs. The evaluation of the supplier, therefore, should focus not only on current capability, but also on the supplier's future strengths. Normally, for services, other functions such as internal users and budget owners provide expert assistance to assess a potential service supplier on its capabilities. For example, the human resources department, legal, and compliance may be on a team with supply for purchases of services related to benefits.

Management and Financial Evaluation

As the tendency toward greater reliance on single sources for a longer period of time continues, along with greater interest in lean operations, lean supply, and strategic sourcing, a potential supplier's management strengths take on added significance. From the supply point of view, the key question is this: Is the management of this supplier a corporate strength or a weakness? This will require a detailed examination of the organization's mission, values and goals, its structure, qualifications of managers, management controls, the performance evaluation and reward system, training and development, information systems, and policies and procedures. It is also useful to have an explanation about why the supplier's management believes it is managing well and an indication of its most notable successes and failures. A functional assessment of strengths and weaknesses in areas like marketing, supply, accounting, and so on will substantiate the overall picture. For example, in a contract in which the supplier spends a substantial percentage of total volume on raw materials and parts with suppliers or subcontractors, the supply group of the buying organization would be best suited to evaluate the supplier's procurement system, organization, procedures, and personnel. This is especially important when assessing supply chains that consist of multiple tiers of suppliers.

Supplier documentation and personal visits by the sourcing team are typically required. For large contracts in large organizations, the sourcing team's formal report detailing the management strengths and weaknesses of potential suppliers will be the deciding factor in the selection process.

The financial strengths and weaknesses of a supplier affect its capability to respond to the needs of customers. The supply professional must determine the extent of the financial assessment appropriate for each purchase. As discussed earlier in this chapter, the critical question is this: Is the product or service strategic? If so, then the supplier is strategically important and a full financial analysis is necessary. While short-term alternatives may lessen the risks, the strategic nature of the purchase indicates the need for complete understanding of the long-term risks and opportunities from the supplier's financial situation. Many supply managers focus on early warning systems to alert them to changes in the financial situation of key suppliers that may affect the buying organization. This allows them to step in and work with the supplier or strengthen their contingency plans if the supplier's situation worsens.

There are often substantial opportunities for negotiation if the purchaser is fully familiar with the financial status of a supplier. For example, the offer of advance payment or cash discounts may have little appeal to a cash-rich source but highly attractive to a firm short of working capital. A supplier with substantial inventories may be able to offer supply assurance and a degree of price protection at times of shortages that cannot be matched by others without the materials or the funds to acquire them.

Individual financial measures that may be examined include, but are not limited to, credit rating, capital structure, profitability, ability to meet interest and dividend obligations, working capital, inventory turnover, current ratio, and return on investment. Presumably, financial stability and strength are indicators of good management and competitive ability. Financial statements, therefore, are a useful source of information about a supplier's past performance. Whether the supplier will continue to perform in the same manner in the future is an assessment the purchaser must make, taking all available information, including the financial side, into account. Some of the financial ratios that a buyer may want to take a look at include profit and loss, inventory turnover, account receivables turns, and current ratio. This information is available from a variety of sources including Dun & Bradstreet (www.dnb.com) and Hoovers (www.hoovers.com). For privately held companies, the buyer may have difficulty accessing sufficient financial information depending on the buyer's strength in the relationship.

There is general agreement among supply executives that a supplier's management capability and financial strength are vital factors in source evaluation and selection. Even after a satisfactory evaluation of management, financial, and technical strengths of a supplier has been completed, the question remains about what weight should be accorded to each of the various dimensions. Also, should the supply manager take the initiative in insisting that the supplier correct certain deficiencies, particularly on the management or financial side?

Many examples exist that illustrate the need for supplier strength. These are normally related to the long-term survival of the company. Small suppliers are frequently dependent on the health, age, and abilities of the owner-manager. Every time this individual steps into an automobile, the fate of the company rides along. The attitudes of this individual toward certain customers may be very important in supply assurance.

Most long-term and significant supplier–buyer relationships are highly dependent on the relationships and communication channels built by the respective managers in each organization. Unless each side is willing and able to listen and respond to information supplied by the other side, problems are not likely to be resolved to mutual satisfaction.

Level 3—Current Additional

In the following section, the current additional criteria which includes financial considerations, environmental impact, innovation, regulatory compliance, and social and political factors will be addressed. All of these potentially impact the strategic aspects of supply, and risk has already been discussed in that context.

Financial Considerations

Financial considerations other than price may impact the supplier selection decision. The financial health of the supplier has already been discussed as part of the normal supplier assessment process when the prime concern is the supplier's viability as an ongoing enterprise in the long term.

In this additional context an opportunistic perspective is used to find potential ways of strengthening the purchasing organization's financial statements beyond obtaining a lower price. For example, is it possible to have the supplier manage and own inventories so that they do not show up on the financial statements of the purchasing organization? Can capital purchases be timed to achieve tax savings? Can judicious use of international finance experts facilitate global supply agreements in terms of trade credit, payment, guarantees, and inventory financing?

Environmental Impact

Sustainability is the ability to achieve economic prosperity while protecting the natural systems of the planet and providing a higher quality of life for present and future generations. To accomplish this, decision makers must consider the role of four types of capital: financial capital (cash, investment, and monetary instruments), manufactured capital (infrastructure, machines, tools, and factories), human capital (labor and intelligence, culture, and organization) and natural capital (resources, living systems, and ecosystem services). Supply managers play a key role in an organization's sustainability initiatives in product or service design, sourcing and contracting, and asset or investment recovery. Consequently, supply's role in helping to achieve this goal needs to be examined carefully.

The first issue is, How can our organization design products and services that directly or indirectly contribute to sustainability? The second issue is, How can our organization purchase materials, products, or equipment that directly or indirectly contributes to sustainability? How can the supply group raise sustainability questions when others in the organization fail to do so? The third issue is, How can we purchase from sources, domestic or international, that we know are committed to sustainability and sound practices? These are not easy questions answered glibly out of context. It is possible to evade the issue by putting government in the control seat, saying, "As long as government allows it, it must be all right." A practical consideration is that government may shut down a polluting supplier with little notice, endangering supply assurance.

Environmental supply chain strategies range from merely trying to avoid violations to including environmental considerations from the design stage forward. The preferred hierarchy is (1) source reduction—design or use less, (2) reuse—multiple use of same item such as a package or container, (3) recycle—reprocess into raw material, (4) incinerate—at least extract energy, but create CO_2 pollution at a minimum, (5) landfill—require space and transportation to store with potential impact on land and water. The introduction of gas-electric hybrid vehicles and the development of fuel cell technology are examples of source reduction initiatives. "Designing for recycling" requires manufacturers of appliances and automobiles to design products for ease of disassembly to allow for recovery of useful materials. In the automobile industry, this represents a particularly difficult challenge. Much of the weight-reduction emphasis to improve government-required fuel ratings has come about by the substitution of lightweight, but difficult to retrieve and recycle, plastics for heavier but easily recycled metal parts.

Suppliers can aid substantially in addressing these priorities to minimize the environmental impact of purchasers' and their customers' requirements. In many organizations, supply's role as an information link between environmentally affected individuals, internal functions, and suppliers in the handling of waste and hazardous materials has been established already. Government regulations stipulate precautions for the use, transport, storage, and disposal of hazardous materials. For example, in the United States, the Department of Transportation, the Occupational Safety and Health Administration, and the Environmental Protection Agency all have regulations pertaining to hazardous goods. In Canada, there are federal and provincial regulations related to hazardous goods.

There are many organizations and programs available to support the efforts of supply managers. For example, since 1982, Rocky Mountain Institute (RMI) has worked with corporations, governments, communities, and citizens to help solve problems, gain competitive advantage, increase profits, and create wealth through the more productive use of resources. RMI's Research & Consulting team helped a semiconductor manufacturer improve its buildings and equipment in ways that also radically reduced energy costs and carbon emissions; showed urban planners how to spur economic development through better building design and water infrastructure; and helped conceive a successful floor-covering service utilizing resource-efficient, closed-loop industrial processes with an innovative business model.

The U.S Environmental Protection Agency (www.epa.gov) offers programs and tools that contribute to sustainability in the areas of planning and practices, scientific tools and technology, and measuring progress. Its publications, *Sustainable Materials Management* and *The Lean and Green Supply Chain: A Practical Guide for Material Managers and Supply Chain Managers to Reduce Costs and Improve Environmental Performance,* illustrate the efficiency-enhancing opportunities that arise when companies incorporate environmental costs and benefits into mainstream materials and supply chain management decision making. The Office of Policy (OP) works with participating trade associations; EPA programs; and regions, states, and other groups to find sensible solutions to sector-specific problems. The U.S. National Recycling Coalition (www.nrcrecycles.org) represents all the diverse interests committed to the common goal of maximizing recycling to achieve the benefits of resource conservation, solid waste reduction, environmental protection, energy conservation, and social and economic development.

Internationally, the ISO 14000 certification, developed along the lines of ISO 9000, is a process for certifying the environmental management system of an organization. Benefits of certification may include reduced cost of waste management, savings in consumption of energy and materials, lower distribution costs, and improved corporate image among regulators, customers, and the public.

Strategic supply management is all about maximizing opportunities and minimizing risks. In the area of environmental impact and sustainability, there are many opportunities for supply managers who are at the forefront of environmental awareness. By being ahead of, rather than behind, legislative requirements, supply managers may find that opportunities to tap government financial support and public recognition for innovative experiments may exist. The simple fact is that almost every supplier selection decision is likely to be impacted by environmental considerations.

Innovation

Assessing a supplier's potential for innovation requires evidence of continuing improvement and managerial and technical competence. Also references from existing customers are relevant in this regard. Where innovation is a strategic issue, the skills required to assess a supplier's potential go well beyond those of the typical supply professional. Strategic innovation acquisition may involve mergers and acquisitions, patents, licensing, and contracts. These specialized areas are well beyond the scope of this text. Suffice it to say here that even the more common innovation initiatives of continuous improvement, suggestions from both purchaser and supplier involving each other's operations, and a conviction that the status quo is not acceptable for the future are vital to effective innovation.

Regulatory Compliance

The supply professional does not want supply arrangements to be sidetracked because of a lack of supplier attention to regulatory compliance. Therefore, it is appropriate to assess a potential supplier in terms of compliance. What evidence can the supplier provide to assure the supply professional that compliance will not become a future issue? The lack of citations can be seen as one sort of evidence. So can the speed of correction in case of citations. The very broad range of regulations regarding trade, employee treatment, financial dealings, the environment, international business, workplace safety and health, and so forth requires a comprehensive approach to compliance valuation.

Social and Political Factors

Noneconomic factors may have a significant bearing on sourcing decisions. These include social and political concerns. In a CAPS Research study, Carter and Jennings defined the supply manager's involvement in the socially responsible management of the supply chain as "a wide array of behaviors that broadly fall into the category of environmental management, safety, diversity, human rights and quality of life, ethics, and community and philanthropic activities."[3]

---

[3] Craig R. Carter and Marianne M. Jennings, *Purchasing's Contribution to the Socially Responsible Management of the Supply Chain* (Tempe, AZ: Center for Advanced Purchasing Studies, 2000), p. 7.

Social.   Most organizations recognize that their existence may affect the social concerns of society. Some social problems can be addressed through supply policy and actions. For example, it is possible to purchase certain services or goods from social agencies employing recovering addicts, former prisoners, or the physically and mentally handicapped. It is possible to purchase from suppliers located in low-income areas or certain geographical areas of high unemployment. Government legislation requiring suppliers on government contracts to place a percentage of business with designated service-disabled veteran-, minority-, or woman-owned businesses has forced many purchasers to undertake searches for such suppliers. Many supply managers have initiated assistance and educational programs to make their minority sourcing programs work. For example, the secretary of the Department of Energy (DOE) established a mentor-protégé program in which prime contractors help energy-related small minority businesses increase their capabilities in return for subcontracting credit and other incentives. In one sense these early reverse marketing efforts provided useful insights into the process of developing partnerships with larger suppliers as well.

Companies in the private sector often engage in these actions voluntarily out of a sense of corporate social responsibility and to gain strategic advantage. For example, Ford, General Motors, and Toyota Motor North America have positioned supplier diversity as a strategic advantage because they see the connection between from whom they buy and to whom they sell. By helping to develop the economy of the ethnic community through its supplier development programs it is also increasing the purchasing power of the community's members.

There are problems and opportunities when exercising purchasing power in the social area. Balancing the often conflicting goals of the organization (lowest total cost with social responsibility) and assessing and mitigating the risks presented by supplier diversity programs adds a level of complexity to what may already be a complex sourcing decision. Most supply managers agree that the "deal" must make good business sense. There are a number of resources and publications available to link buyers and minority and women business owners including the following:

- The U.S. Small Business Administration (SBA) (www.sba.gov).
- The National Minority Supplier Development Council and its regional Purchasing Councils, (www.nmsdc.org).
- *Minority Business Entrepreneur (MBE)* magazine, www.mbemag.com.
- *Hispanic Business* magazine, www.hispanicBusiness.com.

Political.   The basic question in the political area is, Should the acquisition area be seen as a means of furthering political objectives? Public agencies have long been under pressure of this sort. "Buy local" is a common requirement for city and state purchasing officials. "Buy American" is a normal corollary requirement. The attempt by the Canadian government to spread purchases across the country, approximately in line with population distribution, is another example. For military purposes, the U.S. government has a long-standing tradition of support and development of a national supply base to afford security protection in the case of conflict and, recently, to reward other countries for their support of U.S. initiatives.

The question always arises about how much of a premium should be paid to conform with political directives. Should a city purchasing agent buy buses from the local manufacturer at a 12 percent premium over those obtainable from another state or other country? The debate over offshore outsourcing has raised the political stakes, and many public entities are passing legislation to prevent offshore outsourcing that results in a loss of jobs domestically. Politics aside, whether this behavior is good for the economy in the long run is an ongoing debate.

For private industry, political questions are also present. Should the corporation support the political and economic aims of the governing body? Governments have little hesitation on large business deals to specify that a minimum percentage should have domestic content. In the aerospace and telecommunications industry, for example, international orders are often contingent on the ability to arrange for suitable subcontracting in the customer's home country. It is interesting that governments have no fear to tread where private industry is forbidden to walk. Multinationals often find themselves caught in countries with different political views. U.S. companies for over 50 years have not been allowed to trade with Cuba, yet their subsidiaries in other countries face strong national pressure to export to Cuba the same products that the U.S. parent is not allowed to sell from U.S. soil. The same holds for purchasing from countries with whom trade is not encouraged by the government. American subsidiaries frequently find themselves caught between the desire of the local government to encourage local purchases and the U.S. government, which encourages exports from the parent company or its suppliers. The growing role of government in all business affairs is likely to increase difficulties of this kind in the future. Their resolution is far from easy and will require a great deal of tact and understanding.

Chapter 17 also covers the role of supply in corporate social responsibility.

Level 3 Criteria Conclusion

The supplier's performance according to level 3 criteria has become a matter of considerable concern in supplier selection. What environmental programs does the supplier have in place to assure compliance with current environmental regulations? What plan does the supplier have to meet future requirements, and what is management's attitude towards the environment? What is the supplier's attitude to corporate social responsibility? In the early 1990s, Nike's share value was significantly discounted because it was found to be using shoe manufacturers in underdeveloped countries where child labor and poor working conditions were prevalent. Starting in 1996, in response to weak demand and unrelenting criticism, Nike upgraded factory and employee standards, started a nonprofit to conduct audits, and began publishing audit data, including conditions and pay in its factories. Thus, suppliers do affect the reputation of the purchasing organization and the potential reputational risk is high.

The belief that in any organization, customers, employees, and suppliers should be treated equally leads to the conclusion that organizations with similar values make for good customers and suppliers of each other. This shows up in leadership, attitude towards innovation and continuing improvement, concern for the environment and society, as well as employee, customer, and supplier satisfaction. Although the full evidence of compatibility may not be forthcoming until well after a trading relationship has been established, significant clues can be extracted in face-to-face meetings between corporate leaders, examination of corporate publications, and reactions from customers.

RANKING POTENTIAL SUPPLIERS

During the first two stages of the acquisition process, need identification and description, it is important to establish which of the three levels of selection criteria are most relevant for this particular requirement. This will not only assist in identifying potential suppliers but also in evaluation of bids and ultimate supplier selection. Because many purchasing organizations use formal supplier performance evaluations for existing and new suppliers, the criteria used for selection and subsequent actual performance should be similar.

Letting suppliers know how bids will be evaluated and what weights will be used to compare competitive bids is considered good practice. Thus, in the traditional context, quality might be assigned 60 points, price 30 points, and delivery 10 points for a particular purchase. Even in such a simple three-factor, no strategy, or level 3 consideration, judgment is required to establish these weightings and how to assign points for differing bids.

The Caledon Concrete Mixers case in Chapter 7 illustrates an example of a company that uses a supplier evaluation system that weights different aspects of supplier bids using a point system. If more than one potential supplier is available, the supply professional's ranking of each supplier in relation to one another and the selection interview will determine the best available source. Almost all of the cases in this text require this kind of judgment.

A recent multimillion dollar purchase of paper at the World Bank resulted in supply's rethinking of how to measure the environmental impact of this requirement. This resulted in a new set of seven environmental evaluation criteria: fiber type, transportation pulp to mill and mill to Bank, chemical processing, certifications when sourcing, energy source at the mill, packaging, and compliance and other sustainability considerations. A low environmental score disqualified potential suppliers, even though their traditional offering in terms of quality, quantity, delivery, price, and service would have been deemed acceptable in prior years. In the supplier ranking scheme of 100 points, 70 points were assigned to the technical environmental evaluation criteria mentioned above. A total of 30 points was assigned to total annual cost, with the full 30 points given to the lowest bidder. The highest points assigned on the technical side were below 40, suggesting either lots of further improvement potential for the future or the need for a recalibration of point assignment.

The next chapter on supplier evaluation and relationships describes ranking systems. Therefore, the coverage in this chapter is brief.

Conclusion The most critical decision for the supply professional deals with the selection of suppliers. Based on his or her understanding of the organization's strategic and operational needs, short and long term, the supply manager has to find the best way of matching the marketplace to these needs. Finding potential suppliers and gathering relevant information about them are standard tasks prior to supplier selection. Options of in-house, existing supplier, and new supplier need to be considered as well as single and multiple sourcing, dealing with manufacturers or distributors, domestic or offshore supplier, and small or large supplier. Whether supplier development should be used operationally or strategically is also a consideration. Evaluating potential sources according to the three levels of acquisition criteria requires a disciplined and reasoned approach. There is always a risk that actual supplier performance will not match expectations and risk management is intricately linked with the supplier selection decision.

Questions for Review and Discussion

1. Why might a supply manager prefer to look for a new supplier rather than place additional business with an existing supplier? Why not?

2. What challenges do you see in assessing a supplier's environmental performance?

3. Why is the trend toward single sourcing? What are the disadvantages to this trend?

4. What are standard supply risks? How might they be mitigated?

5. Why might it be preferable to buy from a distributor or wholesaler rather than directly from the manufacturer?

6. What are the advantages of purchasing from large, global sources?

7. When might it be appropriate to conduct a formal, rather than an informal, supplier evaluation?

8. What are the similarities and differences between evaluating new and existing sources of supply?

9. Why is supply focusing more attention on a supplier's management as part of the evaluation process? How might this evaluation be conducted?

10. How might social or political issues impact a supplier selection decision?

References

Carter, C. R.; and M. M. Jennings. *Purchasing's Contribution to the Socially Responsible Management of the Supply Chain.* Tempe, AZ: CAPS Research, 2000.

EPA. *Sustainable Materials Management.* Washington:D.C.: EPA, 2009, www.epa.gov/wastes/conserve/smm/pdf/vision2.pdf

Flynn, A. E. "Knowledge-Based Supply Management." Chap. 7. In *The Purchasing Handbook.* 7th ed., eds. J. L. Cavinato; A. E. Flynn; and R. G. Kauffman. New York: McGraw-Hill, 2006.

Gottfredson, M.; R. Puryear; and S. Phillips. "Strategic Sourcing: From Periphery to the Core." *Harvard Business Review* 83, no. 2 (2005), pp. 132–139.

Nelson, D. P. E. Moody; and J. R. Stegner. *The Incredible Payback: Innovative Sourcing Solutions That Deliver Extraordinary Results.* New York: AMACON, 2006.

Sako, M. "Supplier Development at Honda, Nissan and Toyota: Comparative Case Studies of Organizational Capability Enhancement." *Industrial and Corporate Change* 13, no. 2 (2004), pp. 281–308.

Thornton, L. M.; C. W. Autry; D. M. Gligor; and A. B. Brik. "Does Socially Responsible Supplier Selection Pay Off for Customer Firms? A Cross-Cultural Comparison." *Journal of Supply Chain Management* 49 (2013), pp. 66–89.

Case 12–1

Loren Inc.

On June 15, Brent Miller, raw materials buyer, had to prepare his recommendation for Loren's annual hexonic acid requirements. Four suppliers had submitted substantially different bids for this annual contract to commence August 1. Brent knew his recommendation would involve a variety of policy considerations and wondered what his best option would be.

COMPANY BACKGROUND

Loren (Canada) was the Canadian subsidiary of a larger international chemical company. The company sold both consumer and industrial products and had over the years established an excellent reputation for quality products and marketing effectiveness. This was evidenced by a substantial growth in total sales and financial success. Total Canadian sales were approximately $800 million and after-tax profits were $40 million. Raw material and packaging costs were about 50 percent of sales.

PURCHASING

Brent Miller, a recent graduate of a well-known business school, knew that purchasing was well regarded as a function at Loren. The department was staffed with 12 well-qualified persons, including a number of engineering and business graduates at both the undergraduate and master levels. The department was headed by a director who reported to the president. It was organized along commodity lines, and Brent Miller had recently been appointed raw materials buyer reporting to the manager of the chemicals buying group. The hexonic acid contract would have to be approved by his immediate supervisor and the director of the department.

Brent was aware that several Loren purchasing policies and practices were of particular importance to his current hexonic contract decision. The purchasing department had worked very hard with suppliers over the years to establish a single-bid policy. It was felt that suppliers should quote their best possible offer on their first and only quote, and all suppliers should be willing to live with the consequences of their bid. Long-term supplier relations with the best possible long-term opportunities were considered vital to the procurement strategy. Assured supply for all possible types of market conditions was also of prime concern. Multiple sources were usually favored over single sources where this appeared to be reasonable and where no strong long-term price or other disadvantages were expected. Frequent supplier switching would not be normal, although total volumes placed with suppliers might change depending on past performance and new bids. Brent recognized that any major departure from traditional practice would have to be carefully justified. Exhibit 1 shows the four prime objectives of the purchasing department and Exhibit 2 contains excerpts from the company's familiarization brochure for new suppliers.

EXHIBIT 1
Purchasing Objectives

The basic objectives for the Loren purchasing department are:

A) *Assurance of Material Availability.* The major objective of purchasing must be the guarantee of sufficient supply to support production requirements.

B) *Best Value.* Loren recognizes that value is a combination of price, quality, service, and that maximum profitability can only be obtained through the purchase of optimal value on both short- and long-term basis.

C) *An Ethical Reputation.* All dealings must respect all aspects of the law and all business relationships must be founded on a sound ethical approach.

D) *Gathering of Information.* Purchasing involves a constant search for new ideas and improved products in the changing markets. A responsibility also exists to keep the company informed on industry trends including information on material supply and costs.

EXHIBIT 2 **Excerpts from Brochure for New Suppliers**

The purpose of the information contained herein is to give our suppliers a better understanding of certain policies and practices of Loren. We believe it is important that we understand our suppliers and, in turn, that they understand us. As you know Loren believes in free enterprise and in competition as the mainspring of a free enterprise system. Many of our basic policies stem from a fundamental belief that competition is the fairest means for Loren to purchase the best total value. However, the policies and practices we want to outline here for you relate to Loren's business ethics and the ethical treatment of suppliers. In brief, fair dealing means these things to us:

1. We live up to our word. We do not mislead. We believe that misrepresentations, phantom prices, chiseling, etc., have no place in our business.

2. We try to be fair in our demands on a supplier and to avoid unreasonable demands for services; we expect to pay our way when special service is required.

3. We try to settle all claims and disputes on a fair and factual basis.

4. We avoid any form of "favored treatment," such as telling a supplier what to quote to get our business or obtaining business by "meeting" an existing price. In addition, all suppliers that could qualify for our business are given identical information and an equal opportunity to quote on our requirements.

5. We do not betray the confidence of a supplier. We believe that it is unethical to talk about a supplier with competitors. New ideas, methods, products, and prices are kept confidential unless disclosure is permitted by the supplier.

6. We believe in giving prompt and courteous attention to all supplier representatives.

7. We are willing to listen to supplier complaints at any level of the buying organization without prejudice concerning the future placement of business.

We also do not believe in reciprocity or in "tie-ins" which require the purchase of one commodity with another.

  We believe that supplier relationships should be conducted so that personal obligations, either actual or implied, do not exist. Consequently, we do not accept gifts and we discourage entertainment from suppliers. Similarly, we try to avoid all situations which involve a conflict of personal interest.

HEXONIC ACID—RECENT MARKET HISTORY

Loren expected to use approximately 3,000 tons of hexonic acid in the following year. Requirements for the past year amounted to 2,750 tons and had been supplied by Canchem and Alfo at 60 and 40 percent, respectively.

  Hexonic acid was a major raw material in a number of Loren products. Its requirements had grown steadily over the years and were expected to remain significant in the years to come. The availability of this material in the marketplace was difficult to predict. The process by which it was produced yielded both hexonic and octonic acids and the market was, therefore, influenced by the demand for either product.

  Two years previously there had been major shortages of hexonic acid due to strong European and Japanese demand. Furthermore, capacity expansions had been delayed too long because of depressed prices for hexonic and octonic acid over the previous years. During this period of shortage, both of Loren's suppliers, Alfo and Canchem, were caught by the market upsurge. Alfo had just shut down its old Windsor plant and had not yet brought its new Quebec City plant up to design capacity. At the same time, Canchem was in the midst of converting its process to accommodate recent chemical improvements, and they, too, found themselves plagued with conversion problems. Both companies were large multiplant companies in Canada and had supplied Loren for many years. The parent companies of both Alfo and Canchem had been faced with too high a demand in the United States to be able to afford any material to help meet the Canadian commitments of their subsidiaries. As a result, both Canadian suppliers were forced to place many of their customers on allocation. However, through considerable efforts both were able to fulfill all of Loren's requirements. The increased prices charged throughout this period

EXHIBIT 3
Hexonic
Acid—Purchase
History

Period	Total Volume Purchased	Canchem Percent Delivered/Cost	Alfo Percent Delivered/Cost
Three years ago	1,800 tons	50% $828 / ton	50% $828 / ton
Two years ago	2,200 tons	50% $1,176 / ton	50% $1,084 / ton
Last year	2,750 tons	60% $1,384 / ton	40% $1,296 / ton

fell within the terms of the contracts and were substantially lower than those that would have been incurred if Loren would have had to import offshore material. Quotations on such imports had revealed prices ranging from $1,920 to $2,880 per ton.

The past year was relatively stable with both producers running almost at capacity. Loren again had contracted its requirements with Alfo and Canchem, both of whom continued to perform with the same high quality and service to which Loren had become accustomed over the years.

For the past year, Brent's predecessor had recommended a split in the business of 60 percent to Canchem and 40 percent to Alfo based on a number of factors. Important to the decision at the time was the start-up of the new Alfo plant. Alfo's quotation of $1,292 per ton delivered offered a lower price per ton than Canchem's at $1,384 per ton, but it had been uncertain whether the new plant would be able to guarantee more than 40 percent of Loren's hexonic acid requirements. Currently, however, Alfo had brought their plant up to capacity and could certainly supply all of the 3,000 tons required, if called on (see Exhibit 3 for a recent history of hexonic acid purchases).

Brent thought that recently the hexonic acid cycle had turned around. Hexonic acid demand had eased and now it was octonic acid that was in high demand by the booming paint industry. Recent plant expansions by a number of suppliers had been completed. The overall result seemed to be a building of excess hexonic acid inventories. Brent believed this would be reflected in a buyer's market in the coming year and looked forward to aggressive quotes from all potential sources.

MEETINGS WITH HEXONIC ACID SUPPLIERS

An important part of the buyer's job at Loren was to become an expert in the materials purchased. Among other things, this meant keeping an open ear to the market and building strong relationships with suppliers. It was the buyer's responsibility to assure that all information between buyer and seller would be completely confidential.

The director of purchasing believed it was important to build a reputation so that suppliers could trust Loren purchasing personnel. On May 14, Brent sent out the hexonic acid inquiry to the four suppliers he believed had a chance of quoting competitively on the needs of the Hamilton plant. The two current Canadian suppliers, Alfo and Canchem, were included as well as two American companies. The deadline for bids was June 7 at 4 p.m. Brent knew that on receipt of the inquiry, supplier sales representatives would be eager to discuss it. Actually, he had two contacts before the inquiry was sent out.

MEETING WITH ALFO

Mr. Baker, sales representative of Alfo, met with Brent on April 20. He said that Alfo had unfilled capacity at its new Quebec City plant and he appeared eager to receive an indication of Loren's future hexonic acid requirements. Mr. Baker informed Brent that he was aware of low-priced hexonic acid on the European market, but also made sure to emphasize that it would be uncompetitive in the Canadian market after the cost of duty and freight were added. Brent said it was a published fact that inventories were building in the United States as other hexonic acid users showed signs of easing their demands.

The meeting ended with the assurance from Brent that Mr. Baker would again receive an invitation to quote on the next period's business.

PHONE CALL BY MICHIGAN CHEMICAL

Mr. Wallace, sales representative of Michigan Chemical, assured Brent over the telephone on April 30 that his company would be a contender this year. He said that Michigan Chemical would be represented by their Canadian distributor, Carter Chemicals Ltd., located in Niagara Falls, Ontario. Brent remembered that Michigan Chemical had a good record with Loren (U.S.). According to the U.S. raw materials buying group, Michigan Chemical had supplied close to 99 percent of its commitment in the recent period of shortage. Brent emphasized to Mr. Wallace over the telephone that the present suppliers held the advantage and that he would have to offer better value in order for Loren to swing any business away from them. Brent said at the end of the call that Michigan Chemical would receive an inquiry and that their quote would be seriously considered.

MEETING WITH CANCHEM

On June 3, Mr. Aldert, sales representative for Canchem, personally brought in his company's quotation and presented the terms to Brent with a distinct air of confidence. Mr. Aldert explained that although his delivered price of $1,384 per ton was the same as that which Loren was currently paying for delivered Canchem material, it remained a competitive price. Brent could not help showing his disappointment to Mr. Aldert, and he said that he had expected a more aggressive quote. However, he assured Mr. Aldert that every consideration would be given to Canchem once all the quotations were in by the June 7 deadline.

MEETING WITH AMERICAN CHEMICAL INC. (AMCHEM)

On the morning of June 7, two representatives from AMCHEM delivered their hexonic acid quotation and explained its contents to Brent. AMCHEM had recently completed a plant expansion at its Cleveland plant and clearly had the ability to supply many times Loren's total requirements. Brent thought the quote of $1,204 per ton appeared attractive and noted that the price per ton depended on the specific volume allocated to AMCHEM. The price of $1,204 applied to an annual volume to 1,050 tons. For a volume of 2,250 tons per year, the delivered price would be lowered to $1,192.

When the representatives had left, Brent searched the hexonic acid material file for any information about past dealings with AMCHEM. He found that Loren had been supplied with AMCHEM hexonic acid seven years previously. At that time, AMCHEM apparently had quoted a price below Canchem and Alfo and, as a result, had been allocated a portion of the business. This had the result of sparking aggressiveness into the two Canadian suppliers during the next inquiry. Both fought to gain back the tonnage that had been taken away from them. Apparently, neither Canchem nor Alfo had been aware who their competitor was at the time.

Brent also telephoned the purchasing department of Loren (U.S.) in an effort to draw any information about their experience with AMCHEM. Supplier information like this flowed quite freely within the corporation on a need-to-

know basis. The U.S. buyer informed Brent that AMCHEM did at one time supply the parent with hexonic acid and that quality and service were excellent. However, he did caution Brent that during the recent period of shortage, AMCHEM did place Loren (U.S.) on allocation and as a result fell short of its commitment by a considerable extent.

MEETING WITH ALFO

Mr. Baker, sales representative of Alfo, presented his company's quote to Brent at 3 p.m., the afternoon of June 7. He explained that the contractual terms and $1,296 delivered price offered were the same as those under the current contract with Alfo. Brent thanked Mr. Baker for his quotation and told him he would be informed in late June when a decision had been made.

QUOTATION BY CARTER CHEMICAL

The quotation from Carter Chemical arrived in the afternoon mail on June 7. The $1,268 per ton FOB destination quote was a pleasant surprise to Brent. He thought that Michigan Chemical had been right when they had said that their distributor would make an aggressive offer. Brent now had received two quotes that offered a better laid-down cost than the two current suppliers.

VISIT OF CANCHEM

At 3:45 p.m. on June 7, Brent received another visit from Mr. Aldert of Canchem, who had apparently been disheartened after his earlier meeting on June 3. He had gone back to his management, for he now had a new quotation prepared. His new quote offered Loren hexonic acid on a three-year contract for $1,192 per ton. With freight included, this price appeared to be equal to the lowest bid that had been received. Brent realized that he had probably inspired Mr. Aldert to resubmit his quotation by the feedback he had given him during their June 3 meeting. With this in mind, Brent was wary of accepting this quotation for fear he would be setting a bad precedent. He told Mr. Aldert that he might not be in a position to accept his bid, but would let him know subsequently. The following day Brent discussed the situation with his superior, Mr. Williams. Mr. Williams retraced the steps Brent had gone through. It had been normal practice at Loren to open quotes as they were received. It had also been standard policy not to give suppliers any feedback on their quote until all quotes had been received. Mr. Williams told Brent to think the situation over in his own mind and to make a recommendation on

A more recent example is Korean dominance in the dynamic random access memory (DRAM) market. With increasing Taiwanese and Chinese sales growth, other memory suppliers are forming alliances to compete. Because there are many more Taiwanese and Chinese companies that can invest in such a capital-intensive industry, Korean manufacturers may have difficulty maintaining long-term leadership despite superior technology and operational excellence.

D. The international supplier may be concentrating on certain *products, and pricing* export products at particularly attractive levels to gain volume. One practice is dumping, which occurs when a product is sold in another country for less than either (a) the price in the domestic market, or (b) the cost to make the product. Dumping is illegal in some countries for certain products because the government wants to protect the domestic producer from what is perceived as unfair competition. While there are many attempts to prevent dumping practices, control of this is complex and has never been particularly effective. Some countries and regions have developed infrastructures and supply networks that support the efficient production of certain goods; for example, integrated circuits, computers, and computer parts in Malaysia; clothes and shoes in China; and wire and cable assemblies in Mexico.

Industry clusters may develop in a country. For example, the Monterrey, Mexico, industrial cluster has attracted many of the world's top manufacturers of industrial, commercial, and home refrigeration, heating, and air conditioning equipment. LG has been there since 1988. It has also attracted parts and components suppliers. The largest producer of precision copper tube, China's Golden Dragon Precise Copper Tube Group, is there. A second cluster is growing around the aerospace industry and a third around automobile manufacturing.[4]

The Trojan Technologies case at the end of this chapter illustrates how a company wants to achieve cost savings through a low-cost country sourcing plan. The challenge for Joyce Guo in the case is to develop a global sourcing process and decide which parts are best suited for sourcing in Asia.

3. *Government Pressures and Trade Regulations*

North American firms produce many goods that are sold (exported) around the world. The United States exported $1.59 trillion in goods and $683 billion in services in 2013.[5] Canadian exports reached $477.3 billion.[6] It makes sense to consider buying from suppliers in customer countries. Many executives accept the social responsibility to help develop the economies of the countries in which they operate.

Additionally, many nations insist as a condition of sale of a major product—for example, aircraft—to their country that the seller agree to buy a specified value of goods or services in that country. These types of arrangements, called *offset agreements*, are covered in more detail later in this chapter.

Also, trade incentives or restrictions may influence decisions about source location. For example, China's market share of textiles increased rapidly after the United States lifted

---

[4] Adam Thomson, "Investors Shrug Off Mexican Drugs Violence, *The Financial Times*, July 29, 2011.

[5] U.S. Census Bureau, U.S. Bureau of Economic Analysis, *U.S. International Trade in Goods and Services: Annual Summary, 2013*, www.bea.gov

[6] www.statcan.gc.ca/

quotas on textile imports. Decision makers must consider various combinations of sourcing locations and destinations for inputs (goods and services) and products in relation to bilateral trade agreements to identify savings opportunities.

4. *Quality*

While the quality level of the offshore sources generally is not higher than that of domestic suppliers, on some items it is more consistent. This is due to several factors, such as newer, better capital equipment; better quality control systems; and the offshore supplier's success in motivating its workforce to accept responsibility for doing it right the first time (the zero-defects concept). Also, some firms buy globally to round out their product line, with domestic suppliers furnishing "top-of-the-line" items and international suppliers filling in some of the "low-end" holes, and vice versa.

5. *Faster Delivery and Continuity of Supply*

Because of limited domestic capacity, in some instances the offshore supplier can deliver faster than the domestic supplier. The offshore supplier may even maintain an inventory of products in North America, available for immediate shipment.

Some countries have made investments in infrastructure (roads, ports, and power) that support strong supply lines. For example, China invests heavily in the rapid development and expansion of infrastructure.

Cycle time can also be compressed by automating compliance processes. For example, with Importer Security Filing—"10 + 2"—now in effect in the United States, companies must be prepared to deliver customs paperwork electronically. Electronic filing is now a requirement for the efficient reporting and archiving of all trade transactions, including third-party ones. This expedites cross-border trade and reduces or eliminates the time and cost of shipping and warehousing paper files.

Also, a Global Trade Management (GTM) IT system enables a virtual network of partners including suppliers and government agencies. A GTM speeds up compliance requirements such as product screening and foreign trade zone support. They enable faster information gathering and more data transparency. With the availability of Software as a Service (SaaS), these solutions are more affordable (see Chapter 4).

6. *Better Technical Service*

If the offshore supplier has a well-organized distribution network in North America, better supply of parts, warranty service, and technical advice may be available than from domestic suppliers. Offshore suppliers in locations with a large pool of people fluent in American English and Latin American Spanish along with technical knowledge may also provide superior call center and customer service experiences.

7. *Technology*

Increasingly, as domestic and offshore organizations specialize, technological know-how in specific lines varies. Particularly in the case of capital equipment, such as for the primary metals industry (steel and aluminum), offshore suppliers may be more advanced technologically than their North American counterparts.

On the services side, communications technology advancements and the availability of technologically sophisticated workers at lower wage rates than their domestic counterparts make offshoring attractive for software development, engineering and accounting services, technical support, customer support center operations, and some legal and medical services. For example, India has advantages in industries that rely on *soft* infrastructure (intangible assets) and excels at software and biotechnology.

Often governments encourage the development of *technology clusters or corridors.* India, China, and Mexico do this, but in different ways. These areas attract investment and create employment. They may include co-located science or business parks as well as colleges or training centers. They become magnets for outsourced IT work, including IT, business processes, automotive, and aerospace, which can lead to overstressed infrastructure, escalating real estate costs, and a shortage of skilled professionals.

8. *Marketing Tool*

To sell domestically made products in certain countries, it may be necessary to agree to purchase specified dollar amounts from suppliers in those countries. (See countertrade later in this chapter.)

9. *Tie-in with Offshore Subsidiaries*

Many firms operate manufacturing, distribution, or natural resource-based companies in other countries. A conscious decision may be made, particularly in the case of emerging markets and the least-developed economies, to support the local economy by purchasing there for export to the home country.

10. *Competitive Clout*

Competition tends to pressure the domestic supplier to become more efficient, to the long-term benefit of both the supplier and the buyer. Purchasers use imports or the threat of imports as a lever to pressure concessions from domestic suppliers.

Partnering with an offshore supplier may also improve competitiveness of both when neither nation is able to dominate both invention and low-cost manufacturing. There are hybrid organizations in the clean energy sector. For example, Missouri-based Peabody Energy purchased a stake in GreenGen, a Chinese high-tech, low-emissions coal-fired plant slated for a 2011 opening. In return, Peabody obtains data from, and lends expertise to, a cutting-edge Chinese power plant.

Potential Problem Areas

While it is not possible in this chapter to give a complete discussion of all the potential problem areas faced in global sourcing and the methods for minimizing the impact of each, the major ones can be highlighted. The same principles of effective supply discussed throughout this book apply to global supply, but some unique problems arise when dealing across country boundaries.

Seventeen potential problem areas are highlighted. The astute buyer will recognize that he or she must consider the total cost of ownership, not just the initial purchase price, when evaluating an offshore source.

1. *Source Location and Evaluation*

The key to effective supply is selecting responsive and responsible suppliers. Globally, this is sometimes difficult because obtaining relevant evaluation data is both expensive and time consuming. However, the methods of obtaining data on international suppliers essentially are the same as for domestic suppliers (discussed in Chapter 12). In addition to gathering background data (discussed later in this chapter under "Information Sources for Locating and Evaluating Suppliers"), certainly the best method of obtaining detailed data is an on-site supplier visit. Because a visit to a supplier(s) in another country is expensive and time consuming, it must be well planned. If the dollars and risk involved are great, the on-site visit is a necessity. Firms doing a great deal of international buying will make frequent visits to offshore sources; for example, in a firm buying millions of dollars' worth of electronics equipment, the responsible supply manager spends a significant percent of his or her time in the Far East visiting and negotiating with potential or actual suppliers.

There are alternatives to personal on-site visits, such as the use of consultants and local third-party purchasing organizations. The Internet has made information on potential sources more readily available, and e-mail, text messaging, and web meetings represent cost-effective methods of communication.

2. Lead Time and Delivery

Improvements in transportation and communications have reduced the lead time for offshore purchases. However, there are four areas in which the buyer should anticipate additional lead time:

A. Establishing credit for a first-time international buyer often involves obtaining a letter of credit, which is a document that assures payment.

B. Even with improvements in transportation, the buyer may still experience delays, particularly with inland carriers in the supplier's country.

C. Delays in domestic customs are also possible. Proper documentation and customs bonds help expedite shipments through customs. The customs bond allows goods to be released after inspection and lets the buyer pay duties later. Delays due to increased security or security-related emergencies should also be anticipated.

D. The time goods are in port, for both outbound and inbound, also depends on the number of ships in line for unloading, hours of port operations, and additional security measures.

Selecting the mode of transport is an important decision in international sourcing because of long supply lines and greater risk of loss or damage. High-value, low-weight items may move by airfreight, and delivery time may be almost as short as from domestic suppliers. High-weight items that are costly to transport should move by ocean shipment. Lead time may be several weeks.

For high-bulk, high-weight, low-value commodities, such as steel, the buying firm must do a much longer-range planning job (which is possible in most firms) and must notify the offshore supplier promptly of any schedule changes. Also, the selection of the transportation carrier must be done with great care. To compensate for transport uncertainty, the buyer may insist that the supplier maintain a safety stock inventory in North America. Some type of performance bond also might be required.

Most large transportation services companies and international freight forwarders have information systems that allow shippers to track and trace shipments. Such information can be useful in inventory planning and can help identify potential problems, such as stockouts or production shortages.

3. Expediting

Expediting is the process of speeding up production or delivery. Because of distance, expediting an offshore supplier's production/shipment is more difficult. This places a premium on knowing a supplier's personnel and ensuring that they are responsive. Some firms also arrange to have an expediter on contract in the offshore country or to use personnel from a company-owned subsidiary closer to the supplier to assist with expediting problems.

4. Political, Labor, and Security Problems

Depending on the country in which the supplier is located, the risk of supply interruption due to governmental problems—for example, change in government or trade disputes—may be quite high. Disruptions may also be caused by unsafe buildings and equipment, poor working conditions, violation of child labor laws, strikes, or environmental events. Often these events are related to weak or nonexistent health, safety, and environmental laws and regulations, noncompliance with existing laws and regulations, or corruption.

The heightened risk of supply chain disruptions from terrorist acts, counterfeit goods, or unsafe products increases the time and cost of offshore sourcing. Every importer and exporter must have the knowledge and records about its products, where they were sourced, and how they were transported, because governments continue to increase their requirements for safety standards and compliance reporting. The cost of correction for a product recall or scandal, including the cost of brand or image degradation, can be huge.

Risk management strategies and contingency planning are of even greater importance in the global economy. The supply manager must assess risks, establish a monitoring system, and communicate in time to implement a contingency plan.

5. Hidden Costs

When comparing an offshore source with a domestic source, it is easy to ignore some of the costs in the offshore purchase. The buyer must compare total cost of ownership before opting for an offshore supplier. The following checklist of cost factors provides some examples of hidden costs.

- Currency exchange premiums.
- Commissions to customs brokers.
- Terms of payment costs and finance charges: letter of credit fee, translation costs, exchange rate differentials.
- Foreign taxes imposed.
- Import tariffs.
- Extra safety stock/buffer and transit inventory, plus inventory carrying costs due to longer lead times.
- Extra labor for special handling.
- Obsolescence, deterioration, pilferage, and spoilage.
- Additional administrative expenses.
- Packaging and container costs.
- Business travel.
- Fees for freight forwarders, consultants, or inspectors.

- Marine insurance premium.
- Customs documentation charges.
- Transportation costs, including from manufacturer to port, ocean freight, from port to company plant, freight forwarder's charges, port handling charges, warehouse costs.
- Additional security measures.

6. Currency Fluctuations

Should payment be made in the buyer's currency or that of the country in which the purchase is made? If payment is to be made in a short period of time, the currency exchange rate may be less of a problem. However, if payment is not due for several months or if the supply relationship lasts for a long time, the exchange rates could change appreciably, making the price substantially higher or lower than at the time the agreement was originally signed.

Most significant world exchange rates float freely, and sometimes change rather rapidly, due to economic, political, and psychological factors. This means that the buyer, when contracting, also must make a forecast of how the exchange rates likely will move between now and the time of payment. In addition, certain countries sometimes impose restrictions and controls on the use of their currency. This requires that the buyer have a good source of financial advice. For example, the ongoing discussions between the United States and China over Chinese currency valuation have the potential to impact supply decisions.

Probably the most conservative approach is to price in U.S. dollars, for the buyer then knows exactly what the cost will be, but this denies the advantage of a lower price if the dollar increases in exchange value between the time the contract is written and the time when payment is made. Various approaches are possible, such as pricing in the supplier's currency with a contractual limit to the amount of exchange rate fluctuation permitted, up or down. Or the really knowledgeable buyer may protect against an unfavorable rate change by dealing in foreign currency options. It is important that supply cooperate closely with finance to assure that the corporation manages its currency risks and cash flows effectively.

7. Payment Methods

The method of payment often differs substantially in international sourcing than in domestic. In some instances, the offshore supplier may insist on cash with the order or before shipment.

Suppliers with whom the buyer has established a long-term relationship may be willing to ship on open account. But the seller may insist that title to goods does not pass until payment is made. The instrument used in this case is a *bill of exchange (draft)*, which the seller draws on the buyer and to which it attaches the shipping document before handing it to its bank for collection. The bank, in turn, sends the documents to a bank in the buyer's country, together with instructions covering when the documents are to be released to the buyer—normally at time of presentation—a *sight draft*.

Commercial letters of credit (CLCs) are the most actively used structured payment instruments in global trade. Their purpose is to provide secure, efficient, and prompt payment. The CLC is drawn by the buyer's bank at the buyer's request, and guarantees that the bank will pay the agreed-on amount when all prescribed conditions, such as satisfactory delivery, have been completed. Discrepancies in the complying documents provided by the seller may result in lengthy delays in payment and create misunderstandings between buyer and seller.

8. *Quality*

It is extremely important that there be a clear understanding between buyer and seller of the quality specifications. Misunderstandings can be quite costly, due to the distances and lead times involved. Also, there could be a problem in interpretation of drawings and specifications. In addition, it is important that both buyer and seller agree on what quality control/ acceptance procedures are to be used.

As more services are offshored, all the challenges of defining and assuring quality services are increased by distance, language, and cultural diversity. A clear and unambiguous statement of work (SOW) is the foundation of quality services. For an example of purchasing services on a global basis, see the Marc Biron case at the end of this chapter. In the case, Marc Biron has been asked to manage the global marketing spend for a large financial services firm.

9. *Warranties and Claims*

In the event of rejection for quality reasons, what are the responsibilities of both parties? Due to distances, return and replacement of items is complex and time consuming. Are there provisions for the buyer reworking the items? Who pays for rework, and how are rework costs calculated? These areas should be agreed to in advance of the purchase.

For services, it may be even more difficult to resolve differences over perceived quality levels with an offshore supplier than a domestic one. Clearly defined expectations are a critical success factor in services contracts.

10. *Tariffs and Duties*

A *tariff* is a schedule of duties (charges) imposed on the value of the good imported (or, in some cases, exported) into a country. While, theoretically, the world is moving to eliminate tariffs through the various World Trade Organization agreements, tariffs still exist. The buyer must know which tariff schedule(s) applies and how the duties are computed. Additionally, the contract should make it clear who pays the duty—buyer or seller.

A *Certificate of Origin,* issued by a proper authority in the exporting country, is the document used to certify the origin of materials or labor in the manufacture of the item. It is used to obtain preferential tariff rates, when available. For example, the North American Free Trade Agreement (NAFTA) has rules relating to origin. The United States has adopted the Harmonized Tariff Schedule to provide a uniform, updated international coding system for goods moving in international trade.

The cost of noncompliance with import regulations can be staggering. In a case where containers are marked with incorrect country of origin, the costs can include delayed receipt of goods, charges for freight forwarders or attorneys to get the goods released from customs, remarking, storage, and time to fix the problem. For more serious offenses, fines may apply, legal action may be required, and seizure, and possibly forfeiture, of goods may occur.

11. Administration Costs

Global supply requires additional documentation, mainly for duty and customs, logistics activities, payment, and financial transactions. Even with developments such as electronic funds transfers and Internet-based communications systems, the administrative costs in international buying pose a major problem.

12. Legal Issues

If potential legal problems are a risk in domestic buying, they are several times greater in international buying. If delivery time is critical, a penalty or liquidated-damages clause for late delivery may be advisable. Also, a performance bond may be required or a bank guaranty to ensure payment in case of specified nonperformance. Litigation is time consuming and expensive; therefore, it is increasingly common to agree to settle international trade disputes by international arbitration.

The UN Convention on Contracts for the International Sale of Goods (CISG) went into effect January 1, 1988. The CISG applies only to the sale of goods and does not apply to services. As of September 26, 2013, 80 countries, including Canada, Mexico, the United States, China, Germany, and Japan had adopted the CISG. The goal of the CISG is to create a uniform international law for the sale of goods. There are several key differences between the Uniform Commercial Code (UCC) and the CISG, and purchasers should be aware of them:

A. Under the UCC, the terms of a contract may vary in the acceptance from the proposed contract, and a contract still may exist. Under the CISG, however, no contract is created if the terms of acceptance differ from the proposed terms.

B. Under the UCC, the statute of frauds requires a written agreement if the value of the goods exceeds $500. Under the CISG there is no dollar limit.

C. Under the UCC, there are implicit warranties, such as warranty of merchantability, and a warranty of fitness for purpose. Under the CISG, there are additional warranties.

Purchasers should consider carefully the laws under which an international contract is governed. If trading with a company in a country where the CISG has been adopted, the CISG governs the contract and the buyer should understand the differences between the CISG and the UCC. CISG allows the parties to "opt out" and agree on other relevant law to govern the contract. However, unless another body of law specifically is stated and agreed upon, the CISG will apply automatically if both nations have adopted the CISG. Likewise, if the other party is from a country that has not adopted the CISG and wants to have its domestic law apply, the U.S. purchaser may try to get agreement on using the CISG instead.

Rotterdam Rules.   The United Nations Convention on Contracts for the International Carriage of Goods Wholly or Partly by Sea, known as the Rotterdam Rules, has been signed by 21 nations (including the United States) representing over 25 percent of 2008 world trade volume. Ratification by parliamentary and legislative bodies of 20 countries puts them into force.

The rules establish a uniform and modern global legal regime governing the rights and obligations of stakeholders in the maritime transport industry under a single contract for door-to-door carriage. The convention builds upon and provides a modern alternative to earlier conventions governing the international carriage of goods by sea, as well as codifying important industry practice. The rules provide a legal framework that accounts for the many technological and commercial developments in maritime transport, including the growth of containerization, the need for door-to-door transport under a single contract of carriage, and the development of electronic commerce.

Services.   There is no international common law of contracts. The choice of law will depend on the countries represented in the deal. The supplier is likely to want to apply the laws of its country; the U.S. courts may prefer U.S. federal laws. The two (or more) parties may agree to defer to U.S. state law. Or the parties to the agreement may agree to apply the UN CISG if it is a mixed contract and the services portion does not form the preponderance of the contract.

The parties should agree on what laws apply, where a dispute will be resolved, and in what language. As with domestic services purchasing, the statement of work (SOW) is critical to forming a contract that guides performance of supplier and buyer. Also, service specific clauses should be included in the contract to clearly define risks and reward allocation between buyer and supplier.

Other U.S. laws affecting international transactions are the Exxon-Florio Amendment to the Omnibus Trade Competitiveness Act, the International Traffic-in-Arms Regulations (ITAR), antiboycott legislation, and the Foreign Corrupt Practices Act.

13. Logistics and Transportation

Logistics presents some of the biggest problems for buyers involved in international sourcing. The trend toward integrated logistics on the domestic side is mirrored by a similar move in global supply. Integrated logistics refers to the coordination of all the logistics functions—the selection of modes of transportation and carriers, inventory management policies, customer service levels, and order management policies. Logistics companies that provide a wider base of services, thereby allowing firms to coordinate logistics functions, should enable more cost-effective and competitive international sourcing.

Many firms outsource logistics activities to third-party logistics (3PL) providers. Deregulation and globalization have resulted in a series of mergers and alliances in the third-party logistics industry as service providers attempt to provide a global presence for their major customers. International freight forwarders are increasingly diversified, offering a number of value-added services, such as payment of freight charges, tracing and expediting, making routing recommendations, issuing export declarations, and preparing certificates of origin. The growth of one-stop service providers is likely to continue and appears to be in congruence with intermodalism (e.g., air-sea, rather than all air) and outsourcing.

14. Language

Words mean different things in different cultures. An American word (legitimate or slang) may have a different connotation in the United Kingdom or in South Africa (both English-speaking countries). Consider then the difficulties of communicating with someone who does not speak your language, when everything must go through a translator. Often, the buyer may not even know what connotations the words used by the translator have.

Because of these language difficulties, some firms insist that a supply manager who is going to have repeated dealings with suppliers whose native language is different from theirs be multilingual or take a language course. The buyer still will have to use an interpreter, but may be a bit more comfortable. Language difficulties may be compounded by the prevalent use of electronic communications such as e-mail and texting. Writing in a second or third language may prove even more difficult than face-to-face communication.

15. *Communications*

Many supply managers worldwide are used to instant communication when dealing with their domestic supply network partners. Communicating with offshore suppliers is easier than ever with online video conferencing such as Cisco WebEx and Skype, which are cheap, easy to set up, and accessible by most Internet connections. Text messaging, instant messaging, e-mail, phone, and fax all help make communication fast, inexpensive, and reliable. Texting, which is widely used globally for personal communication, is increasingly used in business dealings. Security, confidentiality, reliability, and speed are critical. Some organizations use service level agreements (SLAs) to define reliability and quality parameters.

Still, global supply can involve problems with communication. These relate to time zone differences and problems with the communication network itself. When dealing with suppliers several time zones away, purchasers cannot simply pick up the phone and talk with their supplier any time of the day or night. Because of the time differences, some communication must be done in the evening or early hours of the morning. Furthermore, long-distance telephone calls add to the costs of global supply. Poor reliability of communication networks in some regions of the world also may create difficulties in some circumstances. Proximity to the supplier may be an advantage if the supplier and buyer are in the same time zone. For example, the majority of Mexican cities are in the same time zone as Chicago. On-site visits are easier because there are frequent direct flights from multiple U.S. cities. Language is less of a barrier because many Mexican managers speak English, and more people from the States are conversant in Spanish. These considerations must be factored into the sourcing analysis, especially the total cost analysis.

16. *Cultural and Social Customs*

Even in North America, business customs vary from area to area: for example, Boston or New York City compared with Houston or Birmingham or Monterrey with Mexico City. Certainly business/social customs vary even more widely in other countries. Good purchasers do not focus only on the economic transaction but also on the noneconomic needs of their supply network partners. Furthermore, problems caused by cultural misunderstandings can lead to higher supply chain costs. Therefore, purchasers need to have cross-cultural skills and must adjust to their suppliers' customs if they are to be effective in communicating and negotiating with suppliers.

In general, learn about the history, culture, and customs of the country you are traveling to, paying close attention to simple actions and behaviors that are considered rude or inappropriate. Many cultures are more formal than U.S. culture, so start out using last names and formal titles. Get cultural advice from professionals or colleagues familiar with the country. Make sure your interpreter understands the issues you will be discussing. Even if your counterparts speak your native language, remember to speak slowly, avoid jargon, and use graphics to illustrate points. Document decisions and key points of discussions. Be prepared to spend time getting to know people as part of the negotiation process. Even as business practices become more homogenized across cultures, adapting to cultural norms may improve the chances of a successful business relationship.

17. Ethics and Social Responsibility

Because of perceived problems involving U.S. firms dealing with offshore customers or suppliers, Congress passed the Foreign Corrupt Practices Act (FCPA) in 1977. Basically, this law prohibits U.S. firms from providing or offering payments to officials of foreign governments to obtain special advantages. The FCPA distinguishes between transaction bribes and "variance" or "outright" purchase bribes.

The FCPA does allow transaction bribes or facilitating payments ("grease") to persuade foreign officials to perform their normal duties, such as getting a phone installed or processing papers. The types of actions that might trigger an investigation into outright or variable bribes are payments of large commissions, payments to individuals who do not render substantial services, and payments made in cash and labeled miscellaneous. If the North American supply professional has little experience with a particular environment, it is essential that he or she become familiar with the FCPA, the Omnibus Trade Act of 1988, and individual country customs.

As more companies commit to, and report on, their corporate social responsibility, formal monitoring and measurement are required for global trade and supply chain practices. Companies want to ensure their goods are manufactured with appropriate testing and without the use of child labor or other unethical practices. Environmental impact is also of increasing importance in supply chain design and management. Supply chain visibility and accountability are increasingly important to importers. (See Chapter 17.)

SELECTING AND MANAGING OFFSHORE SUPPLIERS

Selecting and managing offshore suppliers requires an organizational infrastructure that can compensate for the challenges of offshore sourcing and optimize the opportunities of a globally networked supply base. Decisions must be made about (1) the structure of the global sourcing group, (2) the role of third-party intermediaries, and (3) how potential sources will be identified and researched.

Global Sourcing Organizations

The structure of a global supply organization is influenced by the location of key suppliers and company operations and the overall corporate organizational structure. Companies with a decentralized organization structure give business unit and/or local supply staff responsibility for international supply. In a centralized or hybrid structure, global supply activities can be coordinated through several organizational models, including (1) regional purchasing offices, (2) a global commodity management organization, and (3) international purchasing offices (IPO).

Regional Purchasing Offices

One approach is to create regional purchasing offices, such as the approach taken by Unisys. The global supply organization at Unisys has a chief purchasing officer for each of its four regions—the United States; Europe, the Middle East, and Africa; Asia and the Pacific; and Latin America and the Caribbean—each reporting to the corporate vice president of global procurement. Furthermore, the structure in each region is identical. The vice president of global procurement believed that some procurement activities, such as customer sales support, process management, and supplies and services, required close geographic proximity.

However, commodity management represented one area where geographic location was not always important. While it was necessary to negotiate local and regional supply agreements for many commodities, responsibility was divided between the European and U.S. commodity purchasing organizations for its global suppliers. Discussions between the corporate vice president of global procurement and the commodity management directors for the United States and Europe led to consensus regarding lead responsibility for global commodities. Such decisions were based on supplier location, previous experience of the United States and European purchasing staff with the commodities in question, and staff availability.[7]

Global Commodity Management Organization

Another approach is the creation of a global commodity management organization. This makes sense when there are a large number of common requirements across facilities or business units and the supply base is not always located in the same geographic area as the buying company's operations. The global commodity managers are responsible for identifying world-class suppliers for important requirements common to the company's global operations. Meanwhile, local supply managers are allowed to focus on identifying capable local suppliers for requirements unique to their operation.

For example, French electronics and media services company Thomson (known as the RCA brand in North America), which had its main operations in North America and Europe, relied heavily on suppliers in Asia. Given the large number of common requirements and suppliers, along with the geographical spread of manufacturing and laboratory facilities, the vice president of worldwide sourcing deemed it essential to increase the staffing of global commodity management. Therefore, a number of global commodity coordinators positions were created, each assigned worldwide responsibility for a specific group of common requirements.[8]

International Purchasing Office (IPO)

A third approach to global sourcing is the creation of international purchasing offices (IPOs). International purchasing offices can be focused on the basis of commodities, such as important raw materials, or on the basis of projects, such as large capital projects. Typically, IPOs are used when the company does not have a presence in the same geographic region where important suppliers are located. The logic of establishing IPOs is that the local presence of supply personnel can provide better access to suppliers and lower total costs. IPOs facilitate activities such as local sourcing and review, supplier development, materials management, quality control, and payment and can employ local personnel

[7] M. R. Leenders and P. F. Johnson, *Major Changes in Supply Chain Responsibilities* (Tempe, AZ: CAPS Research, 2002).

[8] Ibid.

thoroughly familiar with the language, culture, and way of doing business in that country or geographic area.

For example, when John Bradshaw became vice president of global procurement at Godiva Chocolatier in New York in 2007, he changed the name of purchasing to procurement and took the organization global. He assigned individuals to work in procurement in offices in regions where Godiva had operations—Brussels, Hong Kong, Tokyo, and Shanghai.[9]

Intermediaries

Should purchases be made direct from the supplier or through an intermediary? This depends on factors such as how much specialized international buying knowledge is available in the supply department and the volume and frequency of sourcing expected. Many firms use intermediaries for some or all of their global purchasing. The following list describes some of the options available.

Import brokers and agents.   For a fee (usually a percentage of purchase value—and it can be as high as 25 percent), the broker or agent will assist in locating suppliers and handling required documentation. In most situations, title passes directly to the buying organization. The buyer, of course, must make sure the fee is reasonable with regard to the services performed.

Import merchant.   The import merchant makes a contract with the buyer and then buys the product in its name from the offshore supplier, takes title, delivers to the place agreed on with the buyer, and then bills the buyer for the agreed-on price. The buyer pays a fee (buried in the price paid) for the buying services provided.

Seller's subsidiary.   Purchasing from the North American subsidiary of an offshore supplier is a common approach. The subsidiaries provide the benefits of having a better location (right time zone), conducting business in English, and accepting payments in U.S. dollars. They also may provide credit terms.

Sales representatives.   Some companies hire sales agents to represent them in various regions of the world. Typically, sales representatives handle low-volume-value contracts and are paid a commission by the supplier that is included in the price of the goods.

Trading company.   A trading company is typically a large firm that normally handles a wide spectrum of products from one or a limited number of countries. Trading companies are used extensively by Japanese firms to move products into North America. The advantages to the buyer of using a trading company are (1) convenience; (2) efficiency; (3) often lower costs, due to volume; (4) reduced lead times because it often maintains inventory in North America; and (5) greater assurance of the product meeting quality specifications because the trading company inspects in the producing country before shipment. But, as with any supplier, the buyer should assess the trading company carefully.

[9] S. Avery, "Godiva Transforms Purchasing into Global Procurement," *Purchasing*, January 14, 2010, www.purchasing.com/article/443489-Godiva_transforms_purchasing_into_global_procurement.php

In global sourcing, the task of locating and evaluating potential suppliers, and selecting and managing chosen suppliers is more difficult than in domestic source selection. Also, decisions must be made about how to organize the supply process/function for efficient and effective global sourcing.

Information Sources for Locating and Evaluating Offshore Suppliers

Similar types of information sources are available to the global buyer as the domestic buyer. They are as follows:

1. The *Internet* can be used to gain access to websites for companies and government organizations. Most large and medium-sized companies have websites that describe their main products and services. Many governments have extensive websites that provide a variety of information, such as trade statistics and assistance for importing and exporting goods and services.

2. A number of *government sources* are available. The U.S. Department of Commerce can supply current lists of names and addresses of offshore suppliers, by general types of products produced. The district offices, located in most major U.S. cities, can be helpful in obtaining this information.

Almost all countries of the world maintain an embassy in Washington, D.C. The major industrial nations (and many of the lesser economically developed countries) maintain trade consulates in the United States and Canada (typically in Washington, D.C., or Ottawa, but many also have an office in other major cities, such as New York, Toronto, Miami, New Orleans, Chicago, San Francisco, or Los Angeles). Their role is to promote exports from their country so they will supply names of suppliers and background information.

3. The *chambers of commerce* located in major cities in the United States, Canada, and around the world will help buyers locate sources. The International Chamber of Commerce has contacts through its country branches around the world and will supply leads to possible sources.

4. Typically, the *supply department* of a company with experience in offshore sourcing is willing to share that information with other buyers, providing they are not direct competitors. The *local associations* of the Institute for Supply Management (ISM) and the Supply Chain Management Association of Canada (SCMA) often can facilitate such an information exchange. Many countries have comparable purchasing, supply, and supply chain organizations that might be of assistance. The International Federation of Purchasing and Supply Management (IFPSM), made up of member nation associations, maintains a list of contacts in many countries. These are buyers and supply managers who have agreed to supply to buyers in other nations information on suppliers in their own countries.

5. There are a variety of *supply chain partners* that can help locate sources. Current domestic suppliers often are in a position to supply information and leads on noncompetitive suppliers. Almost all major banks have an international trade department. In addition to supplying information on currency, payment, documentation procedures, and governmental approval procedures, a bank's international trade department can assist in locating potential sources.

Customers also can assist with locating international suppliers. This source of information can be especially useful when the customer also has international operations or markets for its products.

6. Every major industrial country has at least one *supplier locator directory*, similar to the commonly used *Thomas Register* (thomasnet.com) for North American manufacturers. The foreign trade consulate or embassy of any nation should be able to refer you to the appropriate directory for their country. Dun & Bradstreet (D&B) also has offices in many countries and can supply a D&B report on many firms.

7. *Importers and foreign trade brokers* stay informed about developments in the supply base of the countries with which they deal, and they can give the buyer a great deal of useful information.

The evaluation of a specific supplier's capabilities is more difficult than locating the supplier. Two key sources of evaluation information are the shared experiences of other supply people, which usually can be obtained simply by asking, and the supplier visit, which was discussed earlier in this chapter.

If a supplier visit is not made, the buyer should at least ask the potential supplier for information such as (1) a list of present and past North American customers, (2) payment procedures required, (3) banking reference, (4) facilities list, (5) memberships in quality specification-setting associations, and (6) basic business information, such as length of time in business, sales and assets, product lines, and ownership.

INCOTERMS

Shipping terms and responsibilities are more complex in international sourcing than in domestic transportation. The International Chamber of Commerce has created Incoterms (International Commercial Terms) as a uniform set of rules to clarify the costs, risks, and obligations of buyers and sellers in an international commercial transaction. Incoterms provide globally accepted definitions that avoid disputes over what the terms mean. They determine who pays the freight, who pays the carrier, who handles the import clearance and export clearance, and two of the terms address insurance. Almost any international purchase or sale contains a reference to Incoterms.

These rules were first published in 1936 and are modified periodically. The most current version is Incoterms 2010. The latest revisions reclassified the rules into two classes (rules for any mode of transport and rules for sea and inland waterway transport only), applied the rules to domestic and international trade, developed two terms to replace four from the 2000 rules, clarified that only the first seller will be responsible for shipping the goods when commodities are sold multiple times during transit, clearly allocated terminal handling charges to avoid potential double exposure for the buyer, allocated insurance responsibility and security-related obligations, allowed electronic communication in lieu of paper where agreed or customary, and reiterated that parties should refer to Incoterms 2010 (or whichever version is preferred) expressly in their sales contract.[10]

The 13 Incoterms have been grouped into two categories:[11]

[10] S. Shepherd and T. Graham. *New Incoterms 2010: A Summary of the Principal Changes to Incoterms 2000*, www.ince.law.com, 2011.

[11] Edward G. Hinkelman, Dictionary of International Trade, 10th ed., Novato, CA: World Trade Press, 2012.

Rules for Any Form of Transport

1. EXW: Ex Works (*named place*). The seller/exporter makes the goods available at his or her premises and the buyer assumes all costs and risks from the seller's "named place" of business. The seller does not clear the goods for export and does not load the goods for transport. This arrangement places the greatest responsibility on the buyer, who assumes all risks from the time when the seller has made the goods available.

2. FCA: Free Carrier (*named place*). The seller clears the goods for export and delivers them to the carrier specified by the buyer at the named location, where the buyer takes possession. The "named place" is domestic to the seller and the carrier can be a shipping line, an airline, a trucking firm, a railway, or an individual or firm that undertakes to procure carriage by any of these methods of transport, including intermodal, such as an international freight forwarder. The buyer assumes all risk of loss or damage from the time the goods have been delivered to the carrier.

3. CIP: Carriage and Insurance Paid (*named place of destination*). The seller clears the goods for export, delivers them to the carrier, and is responsible for paying for carriage and insurance to the named port of destination. The seller is also responsible for the costs of unloading, customs clearance, duties, and other costs if included in the cost of carriage, such as in small package delivery.

4. CPT: Carriage Paid To (*named place of destination*). The seller clears the goods for export and delivers them to the carrier and is responsible for paying carriage to the named port of destination. The seller is also responsible for the costs of unloading, customs clearance for import, and duties where such costs are included in the cost of carriage, such as small package courier. The buyer is responsible for all additional costs, such as procuring and paying for insurance coverage.

5. DDP: Delivered Duty Paid (*named place of destination*). The seller clears the goods for export and is responsible for making them available to the buyer at the named place of destination, including customs clearance for import. Therefore, the seller assumes all responsibilities for all costs associated with transportation to the named place of destination, including duties and other costs payable upon import. The buyer is responsible for unloading. DDP can be used for any mode of transport and the buyer assumes all risks from the time the goods have been made available at the "named place of destination."

6. DAT: Delivered at Terminal (*named place of destination*). The seller covers all transport costs and assumes all risks until the goods, having been unloaded from the arriving means of transport, are placed at the buyer's disposal at a named terminal at the named port or place of destination. DAT requires the seller to clear the goods for export where applicable, but the seller has no obligation to clear the goods for import, pay any import duty, or carry out any import customs formalities. DAT addresses the case of containers that might be unloaded and then loaded into a container stack at the terminal, awaiting shipment.

7. DAP: Delivered at Place (*named place of destination*). The seller clears the goods for export and is responsible for making them available to the buyer on the arriving vehicle at the named place of destination. The buyer is responsible for unloading and

clearing the goods for import. The buyer assumes all risks from the time the goods have been made available at the place of destination.

Rules for Sea and Inland Waterway Transport Only

1. FAS: Free Alongside Ship (*named port of shipment*). The seller clears the goods for export and places them alongside the vessel for loading. The buyer takes possession at the dock of the port of export.

2. FOB: Free on Board (*named port of shipment*). The seller clears the goods for export and is responsible for the costs and risks of delivering the goods on board at the named port of export. Title passes once the goods are on board. It should not be confused with the conventional North American term *F.O.B.*

3. CFR: Cost and Freight (*named port of destination*). The seller is responsible for clearing the goods for export, delivering the goods on board at the port of shipment, and paying the costs to transport the goods to the named port of destination. The buyer assumes responsibility for risk of loss or damage and additional transportation costs once the goods are on board at the port of shipment.

4. CIF: Cost, Insurance, and Freight (*named port of destination*). The seller clears the goods for export, is responsible for delivering the goods on board at the port of shipment, pays the costs associated with transport of the goods to the port of destination, and procures and pays for marine insurance in the buyer's name for the shipment. The buyer assumes responsibility for risk of loss or damage once the goods are on board at the port of shipment. The seller also contracts for insurance cover against the buyer's risk of loss of or damage to the goods during the carriage. The seller is required to obtain insurance only on minimum cover. For more coverage, the buyer will need to either agree with the seller or purchase its own extra insurance.

It is possible, and in some cases desirable, to agree to add wording to the Incoterms that specifies buyer, seller, and carrier responsibilities. For example, agreeing to DDP terms obligates the seller to pay for import duties, but using the term "DDP VAT Unpaid" means that the seller is not responsible for paying value-added taxes.[12]

Incoterms do not (1) apply to contracts for services; (2) define contractual rights and obligations other than for delivery; (3) specify details of the transfer, transport, and delivery of the goods; (4) determine how title of the goods will be transferred; (5) protect either party from risk of loss; (6) cover the goods before or after delivery; or (7) define the remedies for breach of contract.[13]

In addition, packaging and insurance decisions in international supply are much more complex than in domestic buying situations. Although it is the responsibility of the seller to provide packaging, it is important that the buyer and seller agree on arrangements for packaging in the contract. Although many Incoterms do not obligate either the buyer or the seller to procure insurance, both parties should recognize the risks and make arrangements for suitable coverage.

---

[12] Ibid.

[13] Ibid.

TOOLS FOR GLOBAL SUPPLY

There are a number of tools available to the supply manager when sourcing globally. These include (1) countertrade, (2) foreign trade zones (FTZ), (3) bonded warehouses, temporary importation bonds (TIBs), and duty drawbacks.

Countertrade

Countertrade is a fancy term for a barter agreement, but with some twists. Barter has been around for years and takes place when payment between buyer and seller is made by the exchange of goods rather than cash. U.S. firms, in times of shortage, often swap merchandise; for example, a utility trades fuel oil to another utility in exchange for copper cable, as a matter of expediency. However, the complexities of international trade, particularly with developing countries, have brought some new variations, with supply right in the middle of the action. There are five principal variations of countertrade.

Barter/Swaps

Barter involves the exchange of goods instead of cash. Typically, barter takes place when a country, which is short of hard currency, agrees to exchange its product for another country's product. This normally is a rather clean transaction, for the firms (countries) are exchanging equivalent dollar values. If goods of the same kind—for example, agricultural items or chemicals—are exchanged to save transportation costs, the arrangement is called a *swap*.

In a mixed barter, the seller ships product of a certain value—for example, motors—and agrees to take payment in a combination of cash and product—for example, wheat. It then is up to supply to resell the product for cash or to barter it to someone else. A commodity that changes hands twice is referred to as a *two-corner trade*. If it changes hands three times, it is a *three-corner deal*. Supply often gets involved in situations where working out the particular barters or swaps is both difficult and time consuming.

Offset Arrangements

Offsets are distinguished by the condition that one part of the countertrade be used to purchase government and/or military-related exports. Under these agreements, in order to make the sale, the selling company agrees to purchase a given percentage of the sales price in the customer country. The negotiation usually starts at 50 percent and then goes up or down from there. Whatever the figure agreed to, it then is up to supply to figure out how it can spend the specified amount for worthwhile goods or products. In some instances, the goods purchased later are resold, putting the supply department largely in the role of a trading company. Such resale occurs when supply cannot locate a supplier of suitable, needed merchandise in the customer country and simply makes a purchase of goods (that hopefully later will be salable) to complete the deal. Even if specific deals are unprofitable, firms engaging in countertrade usually are looking for long-term, meaningful, and mutually advantageous relationships with the other country.

When other countries buy North American–produced merchandise, they often push hard for offsets to gain access to technology, to get U.S. dollars, to increase employment, and/or to help maintain political stability by protecting jobs and domestic producers.

Counterpurchase

Counterpurchase agreements require the initial exporter to buy (or to find a buyer for) a specified value of goods (often stated as a percentage of the value of the original export) from the original importer during a specified time period.

Buyback/Compensation

In buyback agreements, the selling firm agrees to set up a producing plant in the buying country or to sell the country capital equipment and/or technology. The original seller then agrees to buy back a specified amount of what is produced by the plant, equipment, or technology. Buyback agreements can span 10 or more years.

Switch Trade

In switch trades, a third party applies its "credits" to a bilateral clearing arrangement. The credits are used to buy goods and/or services from the company or country in deficit. Usually a broker or trading house handles the switch.

Countertrade is used in situations where a country has a shortage of foreign exchange or a shortage of credit to finance its desired trade flows, wishes to diversify its foreign exchange earnings, or is encouraging the development of the domestic economy by promoting labor-intensive exports. The number of countries participating in countertrade has increased steadily and includes most of the United States' main trading partners, such as Canada, the United Kingdom, and China.

The World Trade Organization, the International Monetary Fund and governments, including the United States, Germany, and the UK, generally view countertrade as contrary to an open free-trading system. The U.S. government, however, does not oppose participation by U.S. companies. The Bureau of Industry and Security (BIS) reports annually to Congress on the impact of offsets in the defense trade on defense preparedness, industrial competitiveness, employment, and U.S. trade. U.S. firms entering into foreign defense sales contracts must report all offset transactions in excess of $5 million in contracts for the sale of defense articles or services, and offset transactions completed that were valued in excess of $250,000.

The exact value of international countertrade transactions is not known—secrecy surrounding the transactions typically prevents collection of these data. However, in 2011, U.S. firms reported 745 offset transactions (transactions conducted to fulfill offset agreement obligations) with 31 countries with an actual value of $4.01 billion, and an offset credit value of $5.18 billion.[14]

Countertrade is also used in civilian government procurement projects, such as the sale of civilian aircraft, telecommunications, and technology systems. In the competitive global marketplace, the ability to meet countertrade requirements in a cost-effective manner offers a competitive advantage. Supply has a legitimate role in managing countertrade arrangements and should be involved early in the process. Supply can provide feedback on cost implications, the status of the countertrade market, sourcing information, and the availability of suppliers and opportunities for barter.

Unfortunately, supply is not always involved in the decision to engage in countertrade, but becomes involved after the decision has been made, at the stage where potential

---

[14] U.S. Department of Commerce, Bureau of Industry and Security, *Offsets in Defense Trade, Sixteenth Study,* December 2012, p. i.

counterpurchases are being evaluated. Given the risks of countertrade—the possibility of poor-quality goods and services, the development of unprofitable deals, and the acceptance of goods and services that do not match marketing channels—the supply function should be consulted in the proposal evaluation stage.

Often, countertrade obligations present complex problems for supply managers. However, they may also provide the opportunity to develop lower-cost sources of supply in the world marketplace.

Because countertrade is a "way of life" for many supply professionals, several guidelines are suggested:

1. Decide whether countertrade is a viable alternative. If a company does not have the organization to do the international sourcing required, it might contract with a third-party service provider to manage the process or refuse to participate.
2. Build the cost of countertrade into the selling price.
3. Know the country—its government, politics, and regulations.
4. Know the products involved and what is available.
5. Know the countertrade negotiation process—offset percentage, penalties, and time period.

The Global Offset and Countertrade Association (G.O.C.A.) (formerly the American Countertrade Association—ACA) includes over 100 globally based companies engaged in countertrade and offset. The purpose of G.O.C.A. is to promote trade and commerce between companies and their foreign customers through a greater understanding of countertrade and offset (www.globaloffset.org).

Foreign Trade Zones

Foreign trade zones (FTZ) are special commercial and industrial areas in or near ports of entry, designed to avoid, postpone, or reduce duties on imported goods. Foreign and domestic merchandise, including raw materials, components, and finished goods, may be brought in without paying customs duties. FTZs are the U.S. version of what are known internationally as free trade zones. Merchandise brought into these zones may be stored, sold, exhibited, repacked, assembled, sorted, graded, cleaned, or otherwise manipulated prior to reexport or entry into the national customs territory.

U.S. FTZs are restricted-access sites in or near ports of entry. They are licensed by the Foreign Trade Zone Board and operate under the supervision of the U.S. Customs and Border Protection Service. Zones are operated under public utility principles to create and maintain employment by encouraging operations in the United States that might otherwise have been carried on abroad.

There are two categories of FTZs: general-purpose zones and subzones.

General purpose zones handle merchandise for many companies and are typically sponsored by a public agency or corporation, like a port authority.

Subzones are special-purpose zones, usually located at manufacturing plants. Subzones are usually preexisting manufacturing sites that operate under the guarantee of a local general-purpose site. There are no legal differences in the types of activities that can be undertaken at zones or subzones. According to government data, the value of shipments into zones was $732 billion in 2012. This has been the pattern for 15 years. In 2012 there were 174 FTZs, with 276 active manufacturing/production operations.[15]

Each FTZ differs in character depending upon the functions performed in serving the pattern of trade peculiar to that trading area. The six major functions that may be conducted within a zone are the following:

Manufacturing. Manufacturing involving foreign goods can be carried on in the zone area. Foreign goods can be mixed with domestic goods and, when imported, duties are payable only on that part of the product consisting of foreign goods. In some circumstances, the final assembled product may qualify for reduced duties, or might have no duties imposed if it has more than 50 percent U.S. content of labor or components. Such merchandise can be classified as "American made" for purposes of export under NAFTA. Besides reduced duties, there is a saving on interest, because duty payments are not due until the merchandise leaves the FTZ and enters the United States.

Transshipment. Goods may be stored, repacked, assembled, or otherwise manipulated while awaiting shipment to another port, without the payment of duty or posting a bond.

Storage. Part or all of the goods may be stored at a zone indefinitely. This is especially important for goods being held for new import quotas or until demand and price increase.

Manipulation. Imported goods may be manipulated, or combined with domestic goods, and then either imported or reexported. Duty is paid only on imported merchandise.

Refunding of duties, taxes, and drawbacks. When imported merchandise that has passed through customs is returned to the zone, the owner immediately may obtain a 99 percent drawback of duties paid. Likewise, when products are transferred from bonded warehouses to foreign trade zones, the bond is canceled and all obligations in regard to duty payment and time limitations are terminated. Also, exporters of domestic goods subject to internal revenue taxes receive a tax refund when products move into a foreign trade zone.

Exhibition and display. Users of a zone may exhibit and display their wares to customers without bond or duty payments. They can quote firm prices (because they can determine definite duty and tax rates in advance) and provide immediate delivery. Duty and taxes apply only to goods that enter customs territory.

If the company has large offshore suppliers or is contemplating importing substantial amounts of dutiable products, savings can be realized on duties or drawbacks, and on the cost of shipping both imported materials to plants in the hinterland and manufactured products back to the same port for export. The functions actually performed in any zone depend on the inherent nature of the trading and commercial community and demands made by users of zone facilities.

Avoiding, postponing, or reducing duties on imported goods makes them more competitive in the U.S. marketplace and creates economic benefits for the local community through job creation. The potential disadvantages of the FTZ are (1) the additional labor costs and operating and handling costs associated with its use and (2) the uncertainty of its long-term use due to changes in international trade agreements that are reducing and eliminating import duties.

---

[15] U.S. Department of Commerce, *74th Annual Report of the Foreign-Trade Zones Board,* 2012.

Maquiladoras

Mexico's maquiladoras are examples of the foreign trade zone concept or industrial parks. Non-Mexicans can own the maquila, or plant, in the maquiladora in order to take advantage of low Mexican labor costs. Maquilas are best suited to labor-intensive assembly. Parts and supplies enter Mexico duty free, and products exported to the United States are taxed only on the value added in Mexico. According to the maquiladoras's industry association (index.org.mx), exports and foreign investment each grew by more than 50 percent between 2009 and 2012, to $196 billion and $7.4 billion, respectively. Employment, which fell sharply after the global financial crisis, rebounded by 25 percent to just over $2 million, slightly above the average for 2007–08.[16]

Much assembly work was shifted to lower-cost countries such as China. As the wage differential decreases, companies from the United States and elsewhere are looking to the maquilas to do more sophisticated manufacturing and product design. Since the maquilas originally did assembly, there is a limited supply base in proximity to the maquilas. Industry clusters in automotive and aerospace are growing.

Bonded Warehouses

Bonded warehouses are utilized for storing goods until duties are paid or goods are otherwise properly released. Ownership is approved by the Treasury Department. They are under bond or guarantee for the strict observance of the revenue laws of the United States. The purpose of bonded warehousing is to exempt the importer from paying duty on foreign commerce that will be reexported or to delay payment of duties until the owner moves the merchandise into the host country. Goods can be stored for three years. At the end of the period, if duty has not been paid, the government sells the goods at public auction.

All merchandise exported from bonded warehouses must be shipped in the original package unless special permission has been received from the collector of customs. Any manufacturing must be conducted under strict supervision and the resulting items must be reexported.

Temporary Importation Bond (TIB) and Duty Drawbacks

A temporary importation bond (TIB) permits certain classes of merchandise to be imported into the United States. These are articles not for sale, such as samples, or articles for sale on approval. A bond is required, usually for an amount equal to twice the estimated duty. While there is a fee for the TIB, the net effect is that no duty is paid on the merchandise, provided it is reexported. The TIB is valid for one year, with two one-year extensions possible. However, if the goods are not exported on time, the penalty can be twice the normal duty, which is why the TIB must be for twice the normal duty.

Duty drawback permits a refund of duties paid on imported materials that are exported later. The buyer enters into a duty drawback contract with the U.S. government, imports the material for manufacture, and pays the normal duty. If the final manufactured or processed product is exported within five years of import, duty drawback can be obtained. There are three main types of duty drawback: direct identification drawback, substitution drawback, and rejected merchandise drawback. Provisions for duty refunds differ slightly under each type.

---

[16] "Mexico's Maquiladoras: Big Maq Attack," *The Economist* (October 26, 2013).

REGIONAL TRADING AGREEMENTS

Efforts to eliminate trade barriers result in bilateral, regional, and global trade agreements. Supply managers should know who the major trading partners with their countries are, what trade agreements are in place, and what opportunities exist in emerging economic markets.

Several major regional trading agreements are described in the following sections. Data on trading patterns of the majority of the countries in the world or regional trading blocks are available from the World Trade Organization (wto.org). The WTO hosts an interactive database of international trade statistics from 1948 to the present.

North American Free Trade Agreement (NAFTA)

In 1994, the North American Free Trade Agreement (NAFTA) took effect for the United States, Canada, and Mexico to eliminate tariffs and nontariff barriers to trade of goods and services. The final NAFTA provisions were implemented on January 1, 2008. NAFTA created a free trade area of 444 million people producing $17 trillion worth of goods and services. Canada and Mexico are the two largest importers of U.S. exports and the second and third largest suppliers to the United States. They purchase nearly one-third of U.S. merchandise exports. U.S. exports of goods and services to Canada and Mexico have tripled since NAFTA entered into force and U.S. imports from Canada and Mexico have also risen substantially.[17] Since the agreement, merchandise trade between the NAFTA countries has grown dramatically.

Actions that would build upon NAFTA include improved cooperation in the trade of intermediate goods and supply chains; improved border infrastructure to reduce the disruptions in production chains caused by post–9-11 security that cause unpredictable and extended delays; and the possibility of creating a customs union, a free trade area with a common set of external tariffs.

Buyers must adhere to NAFTA's rules of origin for products eligible for preferential reduced tariff rates. Other goods are taxed as if they were from any other country. Filling out and filing the certificate of origin is a major problem for many importers and a cost driver because of inconsistent and product-specific rules and documentation. Purchasers can file an annual blanket certificate if they anticipate buying the same goods more than once a year. Common external tariffs would enable the NAFTA countries to eliminate the agreement's rules of origin.[18]

The European Union (EU)

Efforts to increase cooperation economically and politically began in Europe after World War II. In 1993 four freedoms were agreed to: freedom of movement of goods, services, people, and money. In 2002, the euro became the sole currency of the EU member states, allowing easier price comparisons and lower foreign currency transaction costs. Currently the debate is over whether or not a European constitution is needed, and if so, what form it should take.

---

[17] U.S. Census Bureau, Foreign Trade Division, and U.S. Department of Commerce, Bureau of Economic Analysis.

[18] www.ustr.gov/trade-agreements/free-trade-agreements/north-american-free-trade-agreement-nafta.

As of 2013, the EU included 28 member states, 24 official and working languages, a total population of more than 500 million people, and EU GDP in 2012 of €12,945,402 million. With just 7 percent of the world's population, the EU's trade with the rest of the world accounts for around 20 percent of global exports and imports.[19]

ASEAN

The Association of South East Asian Nations (ASEAN) was established in 1967. Today it includes 10 South East Asian countries (Brunei Darussalam, Cambodia, Indonesia, Lao PDR, Malaysia, Myanmar, Philippines, Singapore, Thailand, and Vietnam). The ASEAN Free Trade Area (AFTA) was created in January 1992 to eliminate tariff barriers. ASEAN has a 2015 target to integrate the ASEAN economies into a single production base creating a regional market of 592 million people. ASEAN had a combined GDP of US$1.492 billion in 2009.[20]

Mercosur

Mercosur (El Mercado Común del Sur) was established in 1991 and encompasses Argentina, Brazil, Paraguay, Uruguay, Venezuela, and Bolivia in a customs union. As associate members, Chile, Colombia, Ecuador, Peru, Guyana, and Surinam can join free trade agreements but are not part of the customs union. Often referred to as the Common Market of the South, Mercosur is four times as big as the EU in area, encompasses more than 275 million people, and accounts for more than three-quarters of the economic activity on the continent (2011 combined GDP of US$3.3 trillion).[21]

Andean Community

The Andean Community (Spanish: Comunidad Andina de Naciones or CAN) includes Bolivia, Colombia, Ecuador, and Peru. CAN originated in 1969 with the ultimate aim to create a Latin American common market. A free trade area was established in 1993 and a common external customs tariff in 1994. CAN has a combined population of 103 million and a GDP in 2010 of US$902.8 billion.

CAN and Mercosur, the two main South American trading blocs, agreed in 2008 to form the Union of South American Nations (unasur.org). In 2012, the EU signed a trade agreement with Colombia and Peru and continues to consider expanding it to Ecuador and Bolivia.[22]

China's Trade Agreements

According to the China FTA Network (http://fta.mofcom.gov.cn), the Chinese Government sees Free Trade Agreements (FTAs) as a way to further open up to the outside world, to speed up domestic reforms, to integrate into global economy, to strengthen economic cooperation with other economies, and to supplement the multilateral trading system. China has 14 FTA partners, including ASEAN, Pakistan, Chile, and New Zealand, comprising 31 economies. The Chinese government has also created a mechanism for collectively interacting with groups of nations. In 2000, the Forum on

[19] www.europa.eu

[20] www.aseansec.org

[21] www.mercosur.int

[22] www.comunidadandina.org

China-Africa Cooperation (FOCAC) with 54 African countries was created. In 2014, the Community of Latin American and Caribbean States (CELAC) agreed to create a mechanism for collectively interacting with China.

The World Trade Organization (WTO)

The WTO was formed on January 1, 1995 following the Uruguay Round of trade negotiations. It replaced the General Agreement on Trade and Tariffs (GATT), which had been in existence since 1947.

In 2013, the WTO had 159 member countries, which account for more than 90 percent of world trade. Its overriding objective is to help trade flow smoothly, freely, fairly, and predictably. The WTO accomplishes this objective by administering trade agreements, acting as a forum for trade negotiations, handling trade disputes, monitoring national trade policies, assisting developing countries in trade policy issues, and cooperating with other international organizations. While GATT dealt mainly with trade in goods, WTO also has new agreements on trade in services and intellectual property rights.[23]

EMERGING MARKETS

Although there is no common definition of an emerging market, generally speaking it refers to countries undergoing a high growth rate and rapid economic liberalization. One assessment of emerging markets is the MSCI Emerging Markets Index (msci.com). In early 2014, emerging markets by region were the Americas (Brazil, Chile, Columbia, Mexico, and Peru); Europe, the Middle East, and Africa (Czech Republic, Egypt, Greece, Hungary, Poland, Russia, South Africa, Qatar, Turkey, and the United Arab Emirates); and Asia (China, India, Indonesia, Korea, Malaysia, Philippines, Taiwan, and Thailand). These, and other emerging economies, represent huge opportunities for sourcing and supply management.

How does a supply manager identify and assess the risks and opportunities of any particular emerging market? What questions should be asked? and Where can the answers be found? There are many resources at the national and international level to assist supply professionals engaged in global trade. These include departments in the United Nations, the World Bank, the International Monetary Fund, and the World Trade Organization. GlobalEdge (globaledge.msu.edu) at Michigan State University is an excellent source of global business knowledge. Three resources published annually that provide a good starting point for gaining a better understanding of global opportunities and challenges are *The Global Competitiveness Report, The World Factbook,* and *The Corruption Perceptions Index.* A fourth resource, the *Bribe Payers Index,* is updated every few years.

The *Global Competitiveness Report* published by the World Economic Forum defines competitiveness as the set of institutions, policies, and factors that determine the level of productivity of a country. Every country is measured on 12 pillars of competitiveness: institutions, infrastructure, macroeconomic stability, health and primary education, higher education and training, goods market efficiency, labor market efficiency, financial

[23] www.wto.org

424 *Purchasing and Supply Management*

market sophistication, technological readiness, market size, business sophistication, and innovation.[24]

The *World Factbook*, produced by the U.S. Central Intelligence Agency, contains all vital information and statistics for most countries around the world, including geography, people, government, economy, communications, transportation, transnational issues, and military.

Transparency International (transparency.org) produces numerous reports on global transparency. The annual *Corruption Perceptions Index* measures the perceived levels of public-sector corruption in 177 countries based on expert opinion. Countries are scored from 0 (highly corrupt) to 100 (very clean). On the 2013 index, 69 percent of countries score less than 50, with wide regional differences. Transparency International advocates stricter implementation of the UN Convention against Corruption, the only global initiative that provides a framework for putting an end to corruption.

The organization also produces the *Bribe Payers Index,* which is based on the views of business executives about countries they have a business relationship with as a supplier, client, partner, or competitor. The index ranks the likelihood of companies from 28 leading economies to win business offshore by paying bribes. These indexes provide indicators of the business climate that may be factored in the assessment of risk and total cost of doing business in various countries. Determining the risks and opportunities in a country requires a level of knowledge and analysis beyond what is required for domestic sourcing. Assessments in these reports and surveys may aid supply decision makers in identifying opportunities and risks in emerging economies.

Conclusion

In our global economy, it is nearly impossible for most companies to rely on the domestic supply base for 100 percent of purchased goods and services. For many organizations, global supply management has become a reality, as they are forced to seek out world-class suppliers to maintain their competitive position. The benefits of global procurement extend beyond simple price and cost advantages. Firms may purchase products and services abroad to gain access to better technology, secure items not available domestically, or purchase better-quality products.

While managing a global supply network can represent an important opportunity, it does provide a number of significant challenges. Consequently, the capability of managing global supply chains effectively can be a source of competitive advantage.

[24] K. Scwab, *The Global Competitiveness Report 2013–2014* (Geneva: World Economic Forum, 2013), pp. 1–9.

Questions for Review and Discussion

1. What are the factors/forces that have caused the increase in global trade? What changes do you think will occur in the next 10 years?

2. Why have North American firms outsourced and offshored the manufacture of goods and delivery of services?

3. What do firms see as the principal advantages to be gained when they buy globally? What are the principle disadvantages?

4. How can the buying firm minimize the problem areas connected with global buying? Which do you feel are most serious?

5. How can the buyer best get a list of potential international sources? Evaluate potential suppliers?

6. What are the pros and cons of buying direct versus using some form of intermediary?

7. What are the forms of countertrade, and what problems do they cause for the buyer? How can the buyer help make countertrade work?

8. How can the buyer make effective use of foreign trade zones?

9. What advantages are there for buyers affected by the North American Free Trade Agreement (NAFTA)? What is a certificate of origin? Why does the buyer need to be concerned with this?

10. What are Incoterms? What factors should be considered when selecting an Incoterm?

References   Daniels. J. D.; L. H. Radebaugh; and D. P. Sullivan. *International Business: Environments and Operations.* 14th ed. Upper Saddle River, NJ: Prentice Hall, 2012.

Fishman, T. C. *China Inc.* New York: Scribner, 2005.

Hinkelman, E. G. *Dictionary of International Trade.* 10th ed. Novato, CA: World Trade Press, 2012.

Kamann, D. J., and V. Van Nieulande. "A Four-Filter Method for Outsourcing to Low-Cost Countries." *Journal of Supply Chain Management* 46 (2010), pp. 64–79.

Leenders, M. R., and P. F. Johnson. *Major Changes in Supply Chain Responsibilities.* Tempe, AZ: Center for Advanced Purchasing Studies, 2002.

Oshri, I.; J. Kotlarsky; and L. Willcocks. *The Handbook of Global Outsourcing and Offshoring.* 2nd ed. London: Palgrave Macmillan, 2011.

"Reshoring Manufacturing: Coming Home." *The Economist*, January 19, 2013.

Schwab, K., et al. *The Global Competitiveness Report, 2013–2014.* Geneva: World Economic Forum, 2013.

The *World Factbook* 2013–14. Washington, D.C.: Central Intelligence Agency, 2013. https://www.cia.gov/library/publications/the-world-factbook/index.html.

The 2013 Corruption Perceptions Index. Transparency International, http://cpi .transparency.org/cpi2013/

World Trade Organization. *Global Competitiveness Report 2013–2014*, www.weforum.org /issues/global-competitiveness

World Trade Organization. *International Trade Statistics 2008.* www.wto.org.

World Trade Organization Interactive Statistics Database. www.wto.org/english/res_e /statis_e/statis_e.htm

Case 14–1

Trojan Technologies

As Joyce Guo, senior buyer at Trojan Technologies Inc. in London, Ontario, Canada, finished her presentation, Randy Haill, materials manager, made the following comments to her:

> It appears there is a lot of opportunity and I want to proceed to the next step. Joyce, I need you to lay out an implementation plan for low-cost region sourcing that we can take to the president for his approval. Our plan will have to include the sourcing process, a schedule and timeline for implementation, a budget and the expected savings. We will also have to identify the risks and our contingency plans. Get to work on this and let's meet Friday morning next week to follow-up.

It was Thursday, February 23 and, as Joyce packed up her laptop and notes, she recognized that she had a lot more work to do before her meeting with Randy the following week.

TROJAN TECHNOLOGIES

Trojan Technologies Inc. (Trojan) was a leading water treatment technology company with the largest installed base of ultraviolet water treatment systems in operation around the world. Trojan specialized in the design, manufacture, and sale of pressurized and open-channel, ultraviolet disinfection and water treatment systems for industrial, municipal, commercial, and residential applications. Trojan's head office was in London, Ontario, Canada. The company had sales of $140 million and employed approximately 400 people in offices around the world, and served its customer base through an extensive network of dealers and representatives.

Trojan was owned by Danaher Corporation (Danaher), which had acquired the company in 2004. Danaher was a diversified global manufacturer, with businesses in professional instrumentation, industrial technologies, and tools and components. Sales revenues were $6.8 billion with a net profit of $746 million, and Danaher employed approximately 37,000 people. Management used its Danaher Business System (DBS) of continuous improvement to guide and measure operations and business activities.

Trojan's current product line consisted of 10 systems across its five markets: (1) residential water treatment, (2) municipal drinking water, (3) municipal wastewater, (4) environmental contaminant treatment, and (5) industrial process. Systems for commercial and government customers ranged from approximately $50,000 to more than $1 million. These systems, which typically had a product life cycle of 7 to 10 years before being replaced with a new design, were designed and manufactured at the London facility, and modified to meet individual customer requirements. In a typical year, Trojan manufactured 500 to 600 systems for its commercial and government customers.

THE PURCHASING ORGANIZATION

Trojan's purchasing organization had seven buyers responsible for six commodity groups:

1. Lamps, quartz sleeves, and ballast.
2. Electrical parts and panels.
3. Stainless steel fabrication parts.
4. Machined and plastic parts.
5. Hydraulic parts and sensors.
6. MRO.

Purchases in the first two commodity groups accounted for approximately 60 percent of Trojan's $45 million spend on direct materials. However, most of these components were high-technology items and were locked up in strategic sourcing agreements. The remaining 40 percent comprised approximately 400 SKUs that were sourced primarily to North American suppliers.

THE LOW-COST REGION SOURCING PROJECT

Following its acquisition of Trojan, Danaher implemented several new initiatives aimed at improving corporate performance. One area targeted was global sourcing—an initiative Randy was asked to champion.

Randy turned to Joyce to lead a project investigating potential opportunities at Trojan for global sourcing and to recommend what action, if any, the company should take. Joyce had joined Trojan, approximately one year prior following completion of her MBA at the Richard Ivey School of Business, as senior buyer for stainless steel fabrication parts. With her background as a purchasing manager for a state-owned enterprise in China before returning to school

EXHIBIT 1
**Parts List
of Potential
Candidates
for Global
Sourcing**

Part Number	Description	Piece Price ($)	Annual Volume
PJ - 224	Stainless Steel Tray	13.31	2,000
PJ - 245	Stainless Steel Tray	6.11	10,000
ML - 092	Metal Disk	2.37	72,000
ML - 667	Clamp	1.65	15,000
RK- 376	Spring	1.07	20,000
LM - 144	O-Ring	0.18	20,000
GA - 136	Quartz Sleeve	27.62	15,000
GA- 208	Quartz Sleeve	18.57	18,000
GA - 659 - 1	Quartz Sleeve	6.19	700
GA - 659 - 2	Quartz Sleeve	5.85	1,000
GA - 659 - 3	Quartz Sleeve	8.66	11,000
GA - 024	Quartz Sleeve	27.62	2,000
RR - 061	Ceramic Disk	1.87	70,000
JH - 625	Machined Collar	139.15	500
DM - 354 - 01	Weldment	52.03	6,000
DM - 354 - 02	Weldment	63.03	1,000
TB - 024 - 01	Wire Harness	9.47	2,500
TB - 024 - 02	Wire Harness	13.27	2,500
TB - 024 - 03	Wire Harness	17.15	2,500
TB - 024 - 04	Wire Harness	21.37	2,500
PB - 554	PS 120/130V 50W	46.20	250
ML - 174	Metal Bracket	15.95	1,050

at Ivey, Randy felt that Joyce had the perfect credentials to lead the low-cost region sourcing project.

In her report to Randy on February 23, Joyce indicated that

- Trojan's global sourcing was not part of the company's purchasing strategy. Presently, international purchases were limited only to those components that were otherwise not available to North America.

- By not engaging in global sourcing, Trojan was missing potential opportunities for lower costs, higher quality, and improved product availability.

- Companies using global sourcing had been able to reduce costs substantially for some products and services.

- Several Danaher businesses sourced components globally and the company had set up an international purchasing office in China, staffed by five people: a sourcing manager, a buyer, and three engineers.

- China appeared to offer Trojan the best opportunities for low-cost sourcing, and Joyce suggested that the company start its global sourcing initiative there.

As part of her report to Randy, Joyce also identified a preliminary list of purchased components that she considered potential candidates for global sourcing that were not part of strategic sourcing agreements (see Exhibit 1).

IMPLEMENTATION PLAN

In preparation for her meeting with Randy, Joyce wanted to prepare a thorough plan for implementing low-cost region sourcing. Joyce expected that if the project went ahead, Randy would put her in charge and she wanted to make sure it would be a success.

As a starting point, Joyce wanted to create a process that Trojan would use for low-cost region sourcing. She expected that people from the engineering and quality departments would be involved, and Joyce wanted to identify the specific steps that would be used to source each component. Joyce wanted to identify the approximate time to complete each step in order to estimate the sourcing cycle time.

Starting the low-cost region sourcing process would require clear criteria on which to select components and evaluate their suitability. Joyce wanted to establish guidelines for components that could be used to identify parts that provided the greatest opportunity and probability for success.

A major consideration for Joyce was setting expectations for cost reductions that Trojan could achieve through low-cost region sourcing. Based on the information that she collected so far, Joyce found that while global sourcing provided opportunities for substantial reductions in piece prices, there were also additional costs. For example, Trojan would have to pay 8 percent duties for products imported from China. She also learned that, based on the experience of other Danaher businesses, inventories could increase by 25 percent and transportation premiums averaged 5 percent. In addition, Joyce believed that there would be other administrative and travel costs she would need to budget.

Not only would Joyce have to provide an estimate to Randy concerning what Trojan could save each year through low-cost region sourcing, but also set guidelines regarding when piece price reductions justified the costs and efforts to switch suppliers. In preparing her cost savings estimate, Joyce would have to take into account that Trojan's standard costs were adjusted each January the 1st. Consequently, savings could only be claimed for the year in which purchases were made.

A final concern was risk management and contingency planning. Trojan was enjoying strong sales growth and Joyce wanted to avoid supply shortages or quality problems. Consequently, Joyce wanted to establish appropriate policies that would address low-cost region sourcing supply risks.

Case 14–2

Marc Biron

MARC BIRON

"I want you to see how supply can add value to our global marketing spend. You've got a couple of months to come back to me with a plan." Marc Biron, supply manager at BCI, one of the world's largest financial institutions, headquartered in Paris, France, pondered the new assignment just given to him by Pierre Jardin, the vice president of supply at BCI.

BCI

BCI, started as a small commercial bank over a hundred years earlier, had grown over the years to offer a large variety of financial services, including commercial and retail banking, asset management, and retail and wholesale insurance. Over the past two decades BCI had expanded its international presence significantly by acquisition of regional financial institutions in all major countries around the world. With revenues in excess of $200 billion a year, BCI was considered a major global giant in the industry.

SUPPLY AT BCI

Until five years ago, supply at BCI had been decentralized with each local or regional business unit responsible for managing its own supply requirements. A review of supply by a major consulting firm pointed out that a centralized supply function might be able to achieve considerable savings by consolidating world requirements and bringing professional supply expertise to the acquisi-

tion of BCI requirements. For example, the consultants pointed out that in their estimate IT expenditures with suppliers might exceed $6 billion per year and that major improvements in process and spend should be possible. BCI's senior management board followed the consultant's advice and hired Pierre Jardin, who had managed the supply function at one of BCI's competitors, to establish a central procurement organization. Pierre had personally started on the IT spend in Europe, while building up a group of supply professionals at head office. In the first two years, Pierre had succeeded in saving about $1 billion on Europe's IT spend with suppliers, and he then hired Marc Biron to take over IT acquisition. Having spent three years in IT supply worldwide, Marc had learned how each of the international business units operated. He was also well aware that business unit managers prized their local independence and were wary of head office involvement in their units. Nevertheless, Marc was successful in negotiating IT supply contracts that provided an additional $1 billion in annual savings.

THE NEW BCI PRESIDENT

Two years ago, a new president took over at BCI. With a strong marketing background, the new president insisted on worldwide brand recognition for BCI, with all business units displaying the corporate logo in all of their communications, promotion, and advertising. In addition, a major increase in marketing spend was initiated to grow the brand. For the first two years, there was no supply involvement in any country on the media spend as local and regional marketing managers had free reign on how to spend their budgets.

MARC BIRON'S ASSIGNMENT

Pierre Jardin had made reasonable progress in improving BCI's spend with suppliers for certain categories. In addition to the IT spend on hardware, software, and IT services, he had made progress in increasing supply involvement in corporate travel, furniture, and paper purchases. In each category, resistance from local managers with strong preference for local and, in many cases, multiple suppliers had been strong.

Aware that marketing's spend was large, although Pierre did not know the exact amount, he decided that this category might represent an opportunity for the supply function. Not only might BCI achieve considerable savings, but here was a category spend where, even in those business units that had a local supply manager, there had been no supply involvement at all historically. Therefore,

working with and through local supply managers was not even an option.

Although Pierre was reluctant to pull Marc Biron out of his IT assignment, he felt that Marc had the international experience, skills, and personality to tackle marketing's spend as a category. He, therefore, called Marc into his office and explained why he wanted Marc to drop his IT work and take on the marketing spend challenge. He gave Marc two months to come up with a plan.

THE MARKETING SPEND

Marc Biron had no marketing spend experience. He agreed with Pierre that this category was one of BCI's largest spends and if IT experience was any indicator, potentially an area of major savings opportunities. He knew that this was a major test for him and that success in this task would impact favorably on his future career. On the other hand, finding a successful way of gaining meaningful involvement for supply in this category would be difficult. He wondered how he should use the next two months that Pierre had granted him to come up with a plan and what that plan would be.

Case 14–3

Sarin Pharmaceuticals Ltd.

Alan Mannik, director of procurement for the Sarin Pharmaceuticals Ltd. (Sarin) Animal Health Division plant in Vancouver, British Columbia, was planning for the transfer of eight products from the company's plant in France. He had a conference call with Francois Simpson from the Sarin facility in Arras, France, on June 11 to discuss details of the transfer. It was Monday, June 2, and Alan needed to prepare for the meeting, which was set up to review purchasing transition issues. He was particularly concerned with the supply of raw materials and packaging.

SARIN PHARMACEUTICALS LTD.

Founded in 1865, Sarin was headquartered in New York and had a reputation for excellence and innovation in the discovery, development, and manufacturing of medicines for people and animals. In the most recent year, company revenues were $12 billion, with net income of $1.4 billion. The company employed more than 45,000 people who worked in 60 countries.

Sarin was organized into four segments: pharmaceuticals, vaccines, consumer health, and animal health. The Pharma-

ceutical Division accounted for approximately 70 percent of company revenues, while the Vaccine, Consumer Health, and Animal Health Divisions represented 13 percent, 10 percent, and 7 percent of Sarin's revenues respectively. The Pharmaceutical Division developed and manufactured medicines for the treatment of a variety of serious and chronic diseases, such as cancer, epilepsy, and heart disease. The Vaccine Division produced pediatric and adult vaccines to prevent a range of infectious diseases, including hepatitis A and B, polio, and influenza. The Consumer Health Division focused on a wide range of consumer health products in the areas of skin care, wellness, oral care, and nutrition. The smallest division, Animal Health, developed and produced medicines for livestock, poultry, and pets.

Sarin focused on its strategic mission of discovering, developing, and bringing to market health care products in an effective manner that fulfilled unmet medical needs. As a result, the company had recently divested a number of operations that did not align with the company's strategy. A number of businesses that complemented Sarin's strategy had recently been acquired, and

price may have dropped and the buyer could now buy the goods for less money. Either way, the buyer no longer wants the goods.

To justify cancellation, the buyer becomes extremely watchful of deliveries and rejects goods that arrive even a day late. Inspection is tightened, and failure to meet any detail in the specifications is seized on as an excuse for rejection. Such methods should never be followed by a good supply officer. Longer term these practices undermine the credibility of the supply organization.

Cancel due to Market Change

Second, the buyer cancels because of a clause in purchase contracts that seeks to guarantee against price decline. If goods are subject to price fluctuations, it is in the interest of the buyer to be protected against unreasonable price changes.

Open Price

Occasionally a long-term contract is drawn up that leaves the determination of the exact price open until deliveries are called for. To meet these conditions, a clause such as the following may be incorporated in purchase contracts:

> Seller warrants that the prices stated herein are as low as any net prices now given by seller to any customer for like materials, and seller agrees that if at any time during the life of this order seller quotes or sells at lower prices similar materials under similar conditions, such lower prices shall be substituted for the prices stated herein.

These stipulations against price decline are not confined to purchase agreements. Under some circumstances the buyer may receive price reductions on the seller's initiative. An example of this type of clause is the following:

> Should the purchaser at the time of any delivery, on account of this contract, be offered a lower price on goods of equal quality and in like quantity by a reputable manufacturer, it will furnish the seller satisfactory proof of same, in which event the seller will either supply such shipment at the lower price or permit the buyer to purchase such quantity elsewhere, and the quantity so purchased elsewhere will be deducted from the total quantity of this contract. Should the seller reduce its prices during the terms of this contract, the buyer shall receive the benefit of such lower prices.

Such clauses are legally enforceable and frequently work to the buyer's advantage. However, the administrative problems of enforcement mean these clauses are often ignored.

Cancellation of Orders and Breach of Contract

Both buyers and sellers are expected to adhere to the terms of a contract. Occasionally one or the other seeks to cancel the contract. Ordinarily this is a more serious problem for the seller than it is for the buyer.

Seller Cancels

Occasionally a seller may wish to avoid complying with the terms of an agreement such as refusing to manufacture the goods or delaying the delivery beyond the period stipulated in the agreement. The rights of the purchaser under these circumstances depend on the conditions surrounding the transaction. The seller is likely to be able, without liability, to delay delivering purchased goods when the buyer orders a change in the original agreement that may delay the seller in making delivery.

The purchaser may refuse to accept (without obligation) a later delivery if the seller fails to meet the contracted delivery date. However, it may be difficult to secure what the buyer might consider reasonable damages for the breached sales contract. The courts have difficulty establishing guiding rules for the jury to use in estimating the damages justly allowed a buyer who sustains financial losses resulting from a seller's failure to fulfill a contract of sale.

Damages

If there is a general rule (Section 2-713), it is that the allowable damages are measured by the difference between the original contract price and the market value of the merchandise at the time for tender under the contract and at the place where the goods should have been delivered, together with any incidental and consequential damages provided in Section 2-715, but less expenses saved in consequence of the seller's breach.

However, in a very strong seller's market, where the breach of contract by the seller is related to failure to deliver on a promised date or even to abide by the agreed price, the practical alternatives open to the buyer are almost nil. The buyer still wants the goods and may be unable to acquire them from any other supplier on time or at any better price.

Actually, this is true even where the contract provides the buyer the option to cancel. The purchaser wants goods, not damages or the right to cancel. Since the chances of getting the goods as promptly from any other supplier are slight, the buyer is likely to work with the original supplier to ensure delivery. If the supplier acted in bad faith on price or delivery, the buyer may work harder to find an alternate supplier.

Buyer Cancels

Sometimes the buyer attempts to cancel a contract. Sellers often include a clause: "This contract is not subject to cancellation." The inclusion of such a clause has little practical effect, unless it is intended to indicate to the purchaser that if he or she attempts to cancel, a suit for breach of contract may be expected.

The Rocky Plains Brewing case at the end of this chapter describes a situation in which the buyer has canceled a contract with a supplier of labels and the supplier retaliates by threatening to withhold shipments, which would potentially shut down production. Mike Pearson, packaging materials manager for Rocky Plains Brewery, has to decide how to resolve the supply problem and avoid production interruptions.

COMMON LAW AND THE PURCHASE OF SERVICES

The UCC does not address contracts for services. Common law governs the purchase of services. This includes (1) contracts solely for services and (2) contracts wherein services and goods are bundled and the service portion equals more than 50 percent of the value of the contract.

Origins of Common Law

Common law originated in England and became the foundation of U.S. law in the original 13 colonies. It is not based on written rules of law. It is based on the law of the courts as expressed in judicial decisions. Common law develops over time as courts make decisions on a case-by-case basis, developing what is known as "case law."

When deciding cases, judges look to prior judicial decisions for established precedents. They make adaptations only to account for changing conditions and societal needs. Judicial precedents derive their force from the doctrine of *stare decisis* (Latin for "stand by the decided matter"). Courts cite *stare decisis* when an issue has been previously brought to the court and a ruling already issued. Generally, courts will adhere to the previous ruling, though this is not universally true.

The common law system has both flexibility and stability. *Flexibility* comes as changing conditions make decisions inapplicable except as analogy. Then the courts turn to other English-speaking (common law) judicial experiences. *Stability* derives from general acceptance of certain authoritative materials. When the courts fail to address changing conditions, statutes are enacted that supersede common law. Typically, however, in statutory interpretation, the courts have recourse to the doctrines of common law.

Implications for Supply Managers

Supply managers who contract for services must understand that while common law provides them with general guidelines for contracting for services, it does not offer much in terms of performance obligations. Because the parties to a service contract cannot refer to a set of rules to govern performance, they must ensure that each and every performance requirement and expectation is clearly defined in the contract. Many service contracts start with a performance-based specification (statement of work). The process of writing the specification should lead to the development of clear performance obligations in the contract.

Contracting for Services

The purchase agreement for services usually is called a service contract or contract for services. It may be short or long term, a standard or custom document. Services lend themselves to a large variety of contract types, including fixed price, unit price, cost-plus-percentage-fee, cost-plus-fixed-fee, or incentive contracts.

Many professional service providers try to use standard contracts agreed to by their professional association. Frequently, the associations even have guidelines about appropriate fee structures and contracts for a particular kind of work. However, a purchaser is not compelled to accept these contracts as they are.

Most organizations develop a wide range of contracts, each with its own service-specific language. Thus, a security service contract will appear totally different from a contract for corporate maintenance, food service, or marketing consulting. Suppliers in each service area will suggest the use of their own contracts. In the case of low-value services, using such a standard contract may be the simplest and least expensive solution. For many professional services a custom contract may be needed to adequately address key issues.

Types of Services Contracting Methods

Several types of contracting methods are used in services purchasing. These include service level agreements (SLA), milestone deliverables, time and materials (T&M), volume of service (VoS), cost, and cost plus. Each is described in the following section.

> *Service Level Agreement (SLA):* An SLA is a document that details the means, method, organization, and processes along with material requirements.

Milestone Deliverables: This method requires that specific activities be completed by a prescribed date, or that the supplier(s) prepare and deliver to the buyer documentation that reports on the current status of ongoing projects or activities. The requirements for providing milestone deliverables are detailed in the contract.

Time & Materials (T&M): Acquiring services on the basis of (1) direct labor hours at specified fixed hourly rates that include wages, overhead, general and administrative expenses, and profit; and (2) materials at cost, including, if appropriate, material handling costs as part of material costs.

Volume of Service (VoS): Generally imbedded in Service Level Agreements and related contracts, the volume of service refers to the predetermined services that will be provided over a specified period of time. Volume of service agreements may be more project oriented, wherein the buyer can specify the number of temporary workers needed to satisfy the needs of the project. The scope of work and level of services are usually structured for periods of one year or longer.

Cost and Cost Plus: These are cost reimbursement types of contracts that provide for payment of allowable incurred costs, to the extent prescribed in the contract. These contracts establish an estimate of total cost for the purpose of obligating funds and establishing a ceiling that the supplier(s) may not exceed (except at their own risk) without the approval of the buyer. Cost reimbursement type contracts are generally used when a reasonable basis for firm contract pricing may not exist.

Aligning Commercial and Legal Agreements

One of the key decisions this chapter addresses is, How can the supply manager assure that the legal agreement accurately reflects the commercial agreement? For services, this is especially difficult because of their intangibility. Efforts to link the provisions of the statement of work to the contractual provisions force both the buyer and the seller to clarify expectations, develop specific language, and appropriate metrics.

Service Level Agreements (SLAs) and Contractual Provisions

A service level agreement includes each important aspect of the service and the metrics used to determine level of performance of the service provider. SLAs are frequently used for repetitive services such as software or equipment maintenance, call centers, and professional services.

Linking the SLA provisions with contract clauses helps align the commercial agreement with the legal agreement. The goal is to drive performance. The buying organization must clarify its expectations of service performance and distill these expectations into measurable performance targets. Likewise, the selling organization (the services provider) must clarify its performance assertions and distill these into measurable deliverables.

The first step is to define variables and metrics. Variables are the indicators of performance. For example, response time may be a variable of interest. The metric is the definition of acceptable response time. For example, the supplier commits to having a service technician on-site within two hours of a service request 98 percent of the time. This service level can then be incorporated into contract clauses to strengthen the contract by avoiding ambiguity.

The resulting contract should capture accurately the expected performance of both parties and drive behavior toward achieving that performance. It will also clarify the actions that will be taken if either party fails to live up to its commitment. Again, it is worth remembering that both buyers and sellers prefer to use the courts as the last, not the first, resort. A strong services contract is a good court avoidance measure.

Typical Provisions in a Services Contract

The specific provisions in a service contract vary depending on whether the service is strategic or nonstrategic and repetitive or nonrepetitive spend, and whether it is a short- or long-term agreement, and with the nature and location of the service provided.

There are a number of provisions that are typical in contracts for many types of services (see Figure 15–1). Several items are discussed in the following section.

Terms and Conditions of Services Contracts

The terms and conditions of a services contract, like that of a contract for goods, are designed to clearly and unambiguously describe the quality, quantity, delivery, price/cost, and service agreed to by both parties. It should specifically address the price, changes to price,

FIGURE 15–1

A Typical Table of Contents for a Generic Service Contract

Source: P. O'Reilly, D. H. Garrison, and F. Khalil, "Service Contracts" in *NAPM InfoEdge*, May 2001.

1. Definitions and Rules of Construction
2. Scope of Services [refers to the Statement of Work]
3. Term of Agreement
4. General Provisions
4.1. Entire Agreement
4.2. Notices
4.3. Governing Law
4.4. Confidentiality
4.5. Audit Rights
4.6. Access
4.7. Severability
4.8. Media Releases
4.9. Right to Engage in Other Activities
5. Service Level Agreements
5.1. Service Levels in General
5.2. Periodic Reviews and Revisions to Service Levels
5.3. Measurement and Monitoring Tools for Service Levels
6. Termination
6.1. Termination by Buyer for Cause
6.2. Termination by Supplier for Cause
6.3. Termination for Convenience
6.4. Service Level Termination Event
7. Charges
8. Invoicing and Payment
9. Personnel Matters

9.1. Key Supplier Personnel
9.2. Limitations on Transfers of Key Supplier Personnel
9.3. Replacement of Supplier Personnel
9.4. Qualifications of Supplier Personnel
9.5. No Solicitation of Employees of Other Party
10. Buyer Responsibilities
11. Supplier's Representatives and Warranties
11.1. Supplier Warranties and Additional Covenants
11.2. Disclaimer of Warranties
12. Indemnities
13. Limitation of Liability
14. Request for Renegotiation
15. Documents Incorporated by Reference
16. Appendices
16.1. Scope of Services [Statement of Work]
16.2. Service Level Agreements/Performance Credits
16.3. Charges, Measures of Utilization, and Financial Responsibilities
16.4. Travel Guidelines and Policy
16.5. Technology Standards
16.6. Reporting and Meeting Requirements
16.7. Approved Subcontractors
16.8. Procedures Manual

actions if market prices fluctuate or how price will be determined as well as bonus or incentive arrangements, the payment schedule including discounts or interest for late payment, delivery time (may be start and stop time, frequency, etc.), and location of service delivery. Quality is often addressed in service level agreements discussed later in this section.

A detailed discussion of each provision is outside the scope of this book. However, several provisions that are typically addressed in service contracts for all types of services are discussed in detail in the following sections.

Request for Renegotiation

A renegotiation clause may require both parties to agree to renegotiate in good faith if any party believes that compensation or other requirements of the agreement no longer meet the essential purpose of the contract. In a long-term agreement, if business conditions change or if one party might be taking advantage of the other party, this clause might be useful. Rights under this provision should be mutual. The provision only requires that the parties come to the bargaining table and negotiate in good faith.

Dispute Resolution

Alternative dispute resolution clauses may help parties in a dispute reach resolution without resorting to the courts. These methods are discussed later in this chapter.

Termination for Cause

This provision defines what constitutes a default that is sufficient cause for the buyer to terminate the contract. It may also describe the rights the supplier has under the contract to correct the cause. Service level agreements may be used to specifically identify events that will trigger termination with cause. A Service Level Termination Event clause might read, *"A Service Level Termination Event will occur if Seller fails to meet any Service Level for two consecutive months or six times in any twelve-month period. A Service Level Termination Event will be considered as a termination under the Termination for Cause provision of this Agreement."*

Termination for Convenience

A Termination for Convenience clause is common in government contracts and increasingly in private contracts. If a prime contract contains the clause, so should any related subcontracts. Also, there should be complimentary payout amounts under both the prime and subcontract provisions.

Determining if a termination was improper has typically rested on determining if it was made in bad faith or constituted a clear abuse of discretion. If the termination for convenience clause is exercised in bad faith, the termination may be a breach of contract. For example, if an owner chooses to exercise the termination for convenience clause when work was 90 percent complete to avoid paying the balance of the profit on the remaining contract work, the termination could be held to be a bad faith termination and constitute a breach of contract.

However, it is difficult to prove bad faith or clear abuse of discretion. Court rulings have restricted the use of the bad faith or discretion test starting with a 1982 case in which it was ruled that the clause could not be used to avoid paying anticipated profits unless there was a change of circumstances that warranted the use of the clause.

Clauses Related to On-Premise Service Delivery

Several clauses may be needed to address issues that might arise if the service occurs on the purchaser's premises. For example, in construction or installation services, clauses may cover security, access, nature of dress, hours of work, applicability of various codes for health and safety, what working days and hours are applicable, and what equipment and materials are to be provided by whom.

Clauses Related to Professional Services

More organizations are outsourcing (and offshoring) professional services, including legal, engineering, software development, medical, and so on. Certain clauses are typically included in these professional services contracts.

For example, when contracting for consulting services, the contract might include a key personnel clause, warranty clause, an independent contractor clause, a work product clause, and a nondisclosure clause.

Key Personnel. This is included if the success of the service depends on specific individuals. This provision (1) allows the customer to approve of key personnel assigned to the project, (2) requires that the supplier keep the specified key personnel assigned as needed (e.g., full time) to the project, and (3) gets the customer's approval before transferring key personnel.

Warranty Clause. Depending on the clarity of functional requirements and the availability of objective criteria for assessing performance, the buyer may be able to negotiate a warranty for the service provider's work. If the work is unacceptable, the clause may require the consultant to redo it at no additional charge until it is acceptable. If the functional requirements are vague, the service provider probably will not agree to this clause.

Independent Contractor Clause. To protect the buying organization, it is important to meet the IRS requirements for hiring an independent contractor and to include a clause stating that the contractor is independent and therefore responsible for filing his or her own taxes.

Work Product Clause. This assigns the ownership of the work product to the buying organization. While large service providers may not be willing to agree to this, many smaller ones will. Even if ownership does not pass to the buying organization, the contract should require documentation of the work product to avoid future problems.

Indemnification. To indemnify means to secure against future loss, damage, or liability. An indemnification clause is used to protect the buyer against all claims, costs, and expenses that arise from the supplier's breach of its obligations. This includes claims of patent, copyright, or trademark infringement against the supplier.

Nondisclosure Clause. The contractor should be contractually obligated to keep the buying organization's information confidential. For example, consultants sell their services to many companies, some of whom may be competitors, and this clause can provide a remedy short of going to court.

Subcontractor Clause. This clause either allows or disallows the use of subcontractors. If allowed, the buyer may retain approval before subcontractors are selected. As more services are offshored, the buyer may wish to expand or restrict the supplier's use of offshore subcontractors.

Errors When Drafting Services Contracts

The most common error when drafting contracts for services is vagueness. This follows somewhat naturally from the intangible nature of many services and the difficulty in clearly and unambiguously describing some service requirements.

Vagueness may apply to any area listed in Figure 15–1. Because most of the quality and cost are driven in during the need recognition and description stages of the acquisition process, these are the areas to focus on in services acquisition. The buying team should develop a clear and unambiguous scope of work, measurable performance specifications (included in service level agreements), and clear accountability for buyer and supplier.

Improving the ability to draft effective statements of work and services contracts may be one of the greatest opportunity areas for supply management.

SOFTWARE CONTRACTS

"Software is characterized by novel speed, copying, and storage capabilities, and new inspection, monitoring, and quality challenges," according to the American Law Institute. Consequently, "the law governing the transfer of hard goods is inadequate to govern software transactions."

Compounding these inherent challenges are the differences in licensing open source software and commercial software and the growth in cloud computing. A study identified six major issues when negotiating contracts for cloud computing:

1. exclusion or limitation of liability and remedies, particularly regarding data integrity and disaster recovery;
2. service levels, including availability;
3. security and privacy, particularly regulatory issues under the European Union Data Protection Directive;
4. lock-in and exit, including term, termination rights, and return on data on exit;
5. providers' ability to change service features unilaterally; and
6. intellectual property rights.[1]

The Principles of the Law of Software Contracts was approved by the American Law Institute (ALI) in 2009. The principles are meant to clarify the ambiguity created by conflicting legal decisions and the application of multiple laws to software licenses, such as intellectual property law (including, most importantly, copyright), Article 2 of the Uniform Commercial Code, and various consumer laws (especially warranty acts). The principles address issues including contract formation, the relationship between federal intellectual property law and private contracts governed by state law, the enforcement of contract terms governing quality and remedies, the meaning of breach, indemnification against infringement, automated disablement, and contract interpretation.

There is concern in the software industry about provisions in the principles, especially in two areas: (1) perceived limitations on negotiating the terms of software licenses for business, and (2) the "nondisclaimable warranty" and hidden material defects in software, where the definitions of hidden and defects may be unclear.

[1] W. K. Hon, C. Millard and I. Walden. "Negotiating Cloud Contracts: Looking at Clouds from Both Sides Now," *Stanford Technology Law Review*, 16 Stan. Tech. L. Rev. 79 (2012).

Software licensors need to deal with the likelihood that the courts will be influenced by the principles and need to review their agreements and processes. Supply managers responsible for software contracts should also be aware of how the principles influence case law, statutes, or interpretations of UCC Article 2, and the impact court rulings have on their approach to negotiations and contract formation.

E-COMMERCE AND THE LAW

The growth of e-commerce has led to both hope and despair in many quarters. Some fear that it will lead to a greater divide between the haves and have-nots, both between and within nations. Many companies, governments, and nongovernmental organizations are focused on broadening access to technology. This means integrating technology into people's lives by making it available and equipping people with the tools to use it.

Many policy makers believe that e-commerce will lead to wider economic growth and have endorsed general principles focusing on facilitating the market-driven development of electronic commerce. For example, in the late 1990s a number of joint statements (e.g., United States-EU, United States-Japan) were issued in support of electronic commerce as an engine of growth.

The growth of e-commerce also raised the question of whether or not existing laws sufficiently address the legal ramifications of e-commerce. The governments of many countries as well as the World Intellectual Property Organization (wipo.int), the UN Commission on International Trade Law (UNCITRAL) and the European Union have focused on the legal aspects.

In some countries, it is believed that a legal structure must be developed first before the government allows and encourages the spread of e-commerce. In other countries, such as the United States, e-commerce was quickly adopted by many businesses and the law came later.

Electronic Signatures

One critical issue in e-commerce transactions is the legality of electronic or digital signatures for contractual purposes. The term *digital signature* is used generically to mean electronic authentication of documents.

The United Nations Commission on International Trade Law (UNCITRAL) provided the Model Law on Electronic Signatures in 2001. Most countries, including Canada, Japan, China, India, Brazil, the Russian Federation, Malaysia, and the United States, have electronic signature laws, though they vary in complexity. The European Union Signature Directive provides an in-depth legal framework for electronic signatures and their validity inside and between EU countries. Each of the 28 member countries must incorporate this into their legislation, so additional layers of complexity are added by some countries. Electronic signatures may not apply across borders. Applicability with specific trading partners should be verified.

The U.S. E-Sign Act

In the United States, most states have passed legislation on electronic signatures. The passage of the Electronic Signatures in Global and National Commerce Act, Public Law No. 106–229 (E-Sign Act) in June 2000 was an attempt to develop uniform rules across the country.

The E-Sign bill was introduced to regulate interstate commerce by electronic means by permitting and encouraging the continued expansion of electronic commerce through the operation of free market forces and for other purposes. This statute grants online legal or financial agreements signed with a digital signature or chain of electronic code equivalent legal status with handwritten signatures and paper documents. It also included electronic recordkeeping provisions. As discussed earlier in this chapter, the UCC has been amended to reflect the legality of electronic signatures and records.

The important features are (1) technology neutrality and (2) party autonomy. Technology-neutral standards prevent governments from legislating a specific type of technology. Parties entering in electronic contracts can choose the IT system to use to validate an online agreement. Party autonomy is the right of businesses to "freedom of contract" in determining the terms and conditions specified in a transaction.

U.S. Uniform Electronic Transactions Act

The Uniform Electronic Transactions Act (UETA) was approved and recommended for enactment by the National Conference of Commissioners on Uniform State Laws in July 1999. UETA validates the use of electronic records and electronic signatures. Forty-seven states, the District of Columbia, Puerto Rico, and the Virgin Islands have adopted UETA. Illinois, New York, and Washington have not adopted the uniform act, but have statutes pertaining to electronic transactions.

The federal E-Sign Act allows a state to preempt the act if it has enacted UETA. UETA and the E-Sign Act bear many similarities and in some situations the language of UETA was borrowed by the authors of the E-Sign bill. However, there are differences. UETA is more comprehensive than E-Sign and addresses some topics differently. UETA contains provisions for the following issues that are not dealt with in the E-Sign Act:

- *Attribution.* An electronic record or signature is attributed to a person if it was an act of that person.
- *Effect of other state law.* UETA recognizes that an electronic signature is just as effective, valid, and enforceable as paper. However, questions of authority, forgery, and contract formation are determined by other state law.
- *Effect of party agreement.* The parties to the contract are free to enter into agreements concerning their use of electronic media.
- *Send and receive.* UETA ties the determination of when an electronic record is sent or received to the communications systems used by the parties to the contract.
- *Effect of change or error.* E-Sign does not contain provisions for dealing with mistakes in electronic communications, while UETA does contain such provisions for breaches in security procedures and mistakes made by an individual dealing with an electronic agent. Unless otherwise specified, the rules of mistake apply.
- *Admissibility.* UETA specifies that electronic records cannot be excluded as evidence solely because they are in electronic format.[2]

---

[2] Patricia Brumfield Fry, "A Preliminary Analysis of Federal and State Electronic Commerce Laws," UETA Online, www.nccusl.org/update/whatsnew-article1.asp

INTELLECTUAL PROPERTY LAWS

In the Knowledge Age, more and more wealth is derived from intellectual capital. According to the World Intellectual Property Organization (wipo.int), intellectual property (IP) refers to creations of the mind: inventions, literary and artistic works; designs; and symbols, names and images used in commerce. IP is protected in law through patents, copyright, industrial designs, and trademarks. Intellectual property is divided into two categories.

Industrial property includes inventions (patents), trademarks, industrial designs, and geographic indications of source. *Copyright* includes literary and artistic works such as novels, poems, and plays; films; musical works; artistic works such as drawings, paintings, photographs, and sculptures; and architectural designs. Rights related to copyright include those of performing artists in their performances, producers of sound recordings, and those of broadcasters in their radio and television programs.

Emerging Global Issues in Intellectual Property Rights

According to the World Intellectual Property Organization (WIPO), the emerging issues in intellectual property range from the Internet to health care to nearly all aspects of science and technology and literature and the arts. The legal issues of who actually owns intellectual capital are of great concern globally. New technology enables the rapid and widespread duplication and transfer of information. However, should access give unlimited rights when intellectual property interests are involved? What is fair use? Does existing domestic and international law adequately address the challenges caused by new technology?

WIPO is an international organization dedicated to promoting the use and protection of intellectual property. Headquartered in Geneva, Switzerland, WIPO is one of the 16 specialized agencies of the United Nations. It has 186 nations as member states and administers 23 international treaties dealing with different aspects of intellectual property protection. The World Trade Organization also has agreements on trade in services and intellectual property rights.

WIPO research has dealt with intellectual property issues related to access to drugs and health care, small and medium-sized enterprises, electronic commerce programs and activities, Internet domain disputes, genetic resources, and traditional knowledge and folklore.

Copyright Law

The U.S. Copyright Act is federal legislation enacted by Congress to protect the writings of authors. As technology has changed, the term "writings" has expanded and the Copyright Act now reaches architectural design, software, the graphic arts, motion pictures, and sound recordings.

A copyright gives the owner the exclusive right to reproduce, distribute, perform, display, or license his or her work. The owner also receives the exclusive right to produce or license derivatives of his or her work with limited exceptions for types of "fair use," such as book reviews. A Copyright is a form of protection provided to the authors of "original works of authorship" including literary, dramatic, musical, artistic, and certain other intellectual works, both published and unpublished. The 1976 Copyright Act generally gives the owner of copyright the exclusive right to reproduce the copyrighted work, to prepare derivative works, to distribute copies or phonorecords of the copyrighted work, to perform the copyrighted work publicly, or to display the copyrighted work publicly.

To be covered by copyright, a work must be original and in a concrete "medium of expression." Under current law, works are covered whether or not a copyright notice is attached and whether or not the work is registered. The Copyright Office of the U.S. Library of Congress administers the act. One hundred sixty-seven countries have ratified the Berne Convention, the leading international treaty dealing with copyright, which is administered by WIPO.[3]

Patents

A patent is a property right that provides the inventor/developer the sole rights of making, using, and selling the item in question—and denying others the right to also do so, unless the inventor decides to sell the patent rights. An invention must be novel, useful, and not of an obvious nature.

Patents are granted by national (e.g., the U.S. Patent and Trademark Office) or regional (e.g., the European Patent Office) government agencies for rights within that jurisdiction. The Patent Cooperation Treaty (PCT), administered by WIPO, is an international treaty between 148 countries that makes it possible to seek patent protection simultaneously in member countries by filing a single "international" patent application instead of filing several separate national or regional patent applications. The granting of patents remains under the control of the national or regional patent offices. The PCT assists applicants internationally, helps patent offices with granting decisions, and facilitates public access to relevant technical information. Applications may be filed electronically through e-PCT. The PCT is used by the world's major corporations, research institutions, and universities. For example, LG Electronics has filed more than 8,000 applications since the Republic of Korea joined the PCT in 1984. LG is among the top PCT filers worldwide.

Types of Inventions.   *Utility patents* are issued for four general types of new and useful inventions/discoveries: (1) machines, (2) manufactures, (3) compositions of matter, and (4) processes. Changing technology has led to an ever-expanding understanding of what constitutes a human-made product. This has led to additions to the Patent Act for design and plant patents.

Patent Infringement and Liability.   In the United States, *utility patents* are normally issued for a nonrenewable period of 20 years, measured from the date of application. *Design patents* last 14 years from the date the patent is granted. There is an implicit warrant that a supplier's regular products do not infringe against the patent rights of any third party. A contractual clause may transfer this responsibility to the buyer.

When the buyer orders goods to be assembled, prepared, or manufactured to the buyer's specifications, then the buyer warrants that there is no infringement of patent or trademark. If there is a charge of infringement of a patent or trademark, the buyer may be liable to legal action. There is a tacit representation on the part of the buyer that the seller will be safe in manufacturing according to the specifications, and the buyer then is obliged to indemnify the seller for any loss suffered (UCC Section 2-312).

If a charge of patent infringement is made against the buyer, the supplier should be notified promptly so that the charge can be defended, or settlement made, in a timely manner. Also, if a seller attempts to include a patent disclaimer clause in the sales contract, the

---

[3] World Intellectual Property Organisation (WIPO), www.wipo,int/treaties/en/ip/berne/

buyer should be extremely cautious in accepting such a clause, since there may be costly litigation if patent infringement has occurred.

Protection Clause.   Sometimes a buyer contracts with a supplier to manufacture an item, to the buyer's specifications, that includes a new idea, process, or product that has not yet been awarded patent protection. This often happens in high-technology industries. To guard against losing the right to the new development and possible subsequent financial rewards, the buyer includes a protection clause in the contract.

Recent Developments.   The 2011 Leahy-Smith *America Invents Act* (AIA) made major changes to U.S. patent law. Some changes relate to patenting business methods such as tax strategy, and others were designed to reduce litigation. The two changes with the broadest impact were the following:

1. The United States converted from a first-to-invent system to a first-to-file system, which is used by most countries. This simplifies and reduces the cost of disputes when multiple applications are filed for similar inventions. However, it favors large organizations with the resources to file early for a patent and then refile if required after final design versus smaller companies that typically file after they know an invention works.
2. A "prior commercial user" defense was established for inventors who commercially use certain inventions at least one year before another inventor files a patent on the same invention or discloses it publicly. This protects inventions that a company uses, but does not want to patent such as an invention that is invisible to the customer.

Trademarks

A trademark is a logo, brand name, or design that is new or distinctive enough to market or represent a company or its goods and services. It protects the owner of the mark by ensuring the exclusive right to use it to identify goods or services, or to authorize another to use it in return for payment. The protection period varies but a trademark can be renewed indefinitely for a fee. Trademark protection is enforced by the courts, which in most systems have the authority to block trademark infringement.

The trademark system facilitates global trade. It promotes initiative and enterprise worldwide by rewarding the owners of trademarks with recognition and financial profit. If enforced, it also hinders unfair competitors, such as counterfeiters, from using similar distinctive signs to market inferior or different products or services.

The manufacture and sale of counterfeit goods is a problem in some industries. In some, such as aerospace, counterfeit parts of inferior design, material, and manufacture may cause loss of life. In others, such as shoes, clothing, and accessories, the loss is a degradation of brand as well as financial losses. The lack of international intellectual property laws exacerbates this situation. What is illegal in one country is a perfectly acceptable sector of the economy in another.

Counterfeiting has been affecting trade for 2,000 years and most countries have been involved at one time or another: from the British cotton mills in Manchester forging American trademarks, to the U.S. textile industry copying the English water-spinning frame, to Korean's hawking high-end handbags, to the Chinese copying almost everything. Counterfeiting typically occurs in developing economies with a low-cost manufacturing base, weak IP laws, and limited enforcement. Intellectual property laws develop with the economy and harmonize over time nationally and internationally through bilateral and multilateral agreements.

China, for example, first introduced modern copyright, patent, and trademark laws in the late 1970s. Under pressure from the United States, China updated IP laws in the 1980s, the 1990s, and again in 2001 prior to joining the World Trade Organization (WTO). While China now has a multipronged approach to enforcement, two obstacles remain: (1) an administrative and judicial inability or unwillingness to enforce IP laws and (2) an overall lack of administrative and judicial transparency. As Chinese companies grow and innovate, they too want to protect their IP and many predict that Chinese IP laws and enforcement will strengthen.

The Anti-Counterfeiting Trade Agreement (ACTA) signed in 2011 by Australia, Canada, Japan, Korea, Morocco, New Zealand, Singapore, and the United States is an example of a multilateral trade agreement related to IP. The purpose of the ACTA is to strengthen the international legal framework for effectively combating global proliferation of commercial-scale counterfeiting and piracy. The agreement calls for strong legal frameworks and provides innovative provisions to deepen international cooperation and to promote strong intellectual property rights (IPR) enforcement practices. Representatives of the European Union, Mexico, and Switzerland, the remaining negotiating parties, confirmed their preparations to sign the agreement as soon as practicable. The agreement will enter into force following the deposit of the sixth instrument of ratification, acceptance, or approval.

Industrial Design

An industrial design is the ornamental or aesthetic aspect of an article. This includes its three-dimensional features, such as the shape or surface of an article, or two-dimensional features, such as patterns, lines, or color. Industrial designs are applied to a wide variety of products of industry and handicraft such as clinical and medical instruments, luxury items, housewares, electrical appliances, vehicles, and architectural structures. To be protected under most national laws, an industrial design must appeal to the eye. It does not protect any technical features of the article to which it is applied.

Geographical Indication

A geographical indication is a sign used on goods from a specific geographical origin that possess qualities or a reputation due to its origin. It may be used for a variety of agricultural products, such as "Tuscany" for olive oil produced in a specific area of Italy, or "Roquefort" for cheese produced in France, or "Champagne" for sparkling wine produced in that region of France. Yes, that is why California bubbly is called sparkling wine, not champagne.

PRODUCT LIABILITY

From lead paint on toys to e-coli on spinach to melamine in milk and pet food, keeping products safe for consumers is an ongoing challenge across industries and countries. Product liability refers to the liability of any or all parties along the manufacturing supply chain for damage caused by that product. This includes the manufacturer of component parts, an assembling manufacturer, the wholesaler, and the retail store owner. Liability suits have been filed over inherent defects in products that harmed consumers.

Product safety and product liability considerations have become more important for several reasons: (1) Lawsuits, large settlements, and greater public awareness have occurred when government regulations and oversight increase and judicial interpretations of the existing laws favor plaintiffs; (2) a reduction or elimination of either regulations or oversight leads to lax control within and among supply chains, resulting in large product recalls; (3) the growth of global supply chains and the inherent difficulties of managing all aspects of safety and quality across borders and across legal and regulatory systems increase the risk of harm to consumers.

The definition of product liability has expanded from tangible goods to include intangibles (gas), naturals (pets), real estate (house), and writings (navigational charts). The move to create a body of law covering software is largely focused on liability issues. The supply managers' role and responsibility increases as firms attempt to reduce the financial threat of product and service liability problems.

Claims can be based on negligence, strict liability, or breach of warranty of fitness.

Strict Liability

Product liability is generally considered a strict liability offense. This means that the defendant is liable when it is shown that the product was defective. No amount of care on the part of the manufacturer exonerates it from its legal liability if it is demonstrated that the product was defective.

There are three types of relevant product defects: design defects, manufacturing defects, and defects in marketing. *Design defects* occur when a product may perform its function but is inherently dangerous due to a design flaw. *Manufacturing defects* occur during the construction or production of the item. *Marketing defects* result from improper instructions and failures to warn consumers of latent dangers in the product.

The United States does not have a federal products liability law. State statutes apply. However, the U.S. Department of Commerce promulgated a Model Uniform Products Liability Act (MUPLA) for voluntary state use. The law of products liability is found mainly in common law (case law) and in Article 2, Sections 314–315, of the UCC, which deal with implied and express warranties of merchantability.

Implications for Supply.   Part of the strategic role of supply managers is to minimize organizational risk. Taking a more active role in designing for procurability and sustainability is one way for supply managers to be more strategic. Considering potential risks and associated costs throughout the life of a product can help the organization avoid product liability suits. In the sourcing, evaluating, selecting, contracting, and receiving stages, there are opportunities to recognize and deal with potential product liability. The earlier in the process this is done, the lower the cost to financials and reputation or brand. This requires close internal relationships with design, engineering, quality control, manufacturing, and marketing to ensure that the organization is not being unreasonably exposed to product liability lawsuits. It also requires a close relationship and involvement with top management to ensure that the costs of failure are fully understood and included in organizational risk management.

The increased application of strict liability tests and the lack of federal product liability laws mean that an organization may assume greater liability based on the actions of the purchaser. Supply managers must ensure defect-free materials and components capable of performing a full range of applications and uses, in compliance with relevant standards, tests, and criteria for product safety.

ALTERNATIVE DISPUTE RESOLUTION

If legal action is the last resort in disputes with suppliers, alternative dispute resolution (ADR) may be seen as the next to the last resort. ADR is any means of settling disputes outside of the courtroom, including arbitration, mediation, early neutral evaluation, and conciliation. Packed court dockets, the rising cost of litigation, and time delays encourage the use of ADR. Some programs are voluntary; others are mandatory. All provide an opportunity to reach negotiated settlements and maintain working professional relationships.

Title 9 of the U.S. Code establishes federal law supporting arbitration based on Congress's plenary power over interstate commerce. Where it applies, its terms prevail over state law. There are also numerous state ADR laws. Thirty-five jurisdictions have adopted the Uniform Arbitration Act as state law, and in similar form in 14 others. Thus, the arbitration agreement and the arbiter's decision may be enforceable under state and federal law. In 1970, the United States joined the UN Convention on the Recognition and Enforcement of Foreign Arbitral Awards.

The two most common forms of ADR are arbitration and mediation.

Commercial Arbitration

Regardless of the type of contract, disputes will arise. While annoying, these disputes usually cost too much in time and money to go to court. Most are settled by buyers and sellers through negotiation. Arbitration clauses are included in contracts to avoid litigation when a negotiated agreement cannot be reached. An impartial arbitrator, or panel of arbitrators, listens to the evidence and renders a judgment. Both parties have agreed in advance to accept without appeal. This is less costly and time consuming than court action. Arbitration is a simplified version of a trial involving no discovery and simplified rules of evidence.

To select an arbiter, both sides may agree on one, or each side may select one arbitrator and the two arbitrators elect the third to comprise a panel. Arbitration hearings usually last only a few hours and the opinions are not public record. Arbitration has long been used in labor, construction, and securities regulation; and its use is growing in other business disputes.

Standard arbitration clauses exist that are valid, irrevocable, and enforceable under arbitration laws of certain states. For matters under the jurisdiction of the federal courts, there is the Federal Arbitration Law. Even in states without such laws, it is possible to demand arbitration if provision is made in the contract, and if there is a statute making "*future* disputes" the subject of binding arbitration agreements.

Arbitration clauses in contracts are a reasonable measure of protection against costly litigation. The following questions will help ensure that the clause is sound:

1. Is the clause in the proper form under the appropriate arbitration laws? Unless properly drawn, it may not be legally valid, irrevocable, and enforceable.

2. Does the clause fully express the will of the parties or is it ambiguous? If it is uncertain in its terms, the time and expense involved in determining the scope of the clause and the powers of the arbitrators under it may destroy its value or increase costs.

3. Does the clause ensure the appointment of impartial arbitrators? If a person serving as arbitrator is an agent, advocate, relative, or representative of a party, or has a personal interest in the matter being arbitrated, the award rendered may be vacated by the court on the ground of evident corruption or partiality on the part of an arbitrator.

4. Does the clause provide adequately, by reference to the rules of an association or otherwise, for a method of naming arbitrators, thus safeguarding against deadlocks or defaults in the proceedings? If not, the actual hearing of the dispute may be unduly delayed, and the practical value of the arbitration defeated.

Mediation

Mediation is a less formal alternative to litigation than arbitration. Mediators are individuals trained in negotiations. They bring opposing parties together and attempt to work out a settlement or agreement that both parties accept or reject. Mediation is used for a wide range of case types.

Internal Escalation

A third form of alternate dispute resolution is internal escalation. It may be agreed by both buyer and seller that if a dispute arises, the first round of resolution will fall to the purchaser and sales representative. If they cannot resolve the matter, their supervisors will get together and so on, with the final round between the top executives of both organizations. Only if they fail to agree will other forms of dispute resolution be pursued.

REGULATORY REQUIREMENTS

There are a wide range of regulations that affect business. Some are industry specific and some apply across industries. Three are addressed here: Dodd-Frank, the Sarbanes-Oxley Act, and Environmental Regulations.

The Dodd-Frank Act and Conflict Minerals

Conflict minerals, as defined in Section 1502(e)(4) of the Dodd–Frank Wall Street Reform and Consumer Protection Act (2010), include tantalum, tin, tungsten, and gold or any other mineral or derivative determined by the U.S. Secretary of State to be financing conflict in the Democratic Republic of the Congo (DRC) or an adjoining country. Adjoining countries share an internationally recognized border with the DRC and include Angola, Burundi, Central African Republic, Republic of the Congo, Rwanda, South Sudan, Tanzania, Uganda, and Zambia. Conflict minerals are used in a wide range of products, including mobile phones, computers, digital cameras, video game consoles, jewelry, light bulbs, pipes, electronic circuits, and automobiles.

U.S. publicly traded companies are required to confirm annually that their supply chains are free of conflict minerals and to provide a description of the measures taken to exercise due diligence on the conflict minerals' source and chain of custody. Due diligence must follow a nationally or internationally recognized framework. The OECD's "Due Diligence Guidance for Responsible Supply Chains of Minerals from Conflict-Affected and High-Risk Areas" is currently the only recognized framework available for use.

According to the OECD Due Diligence Guidance, the mineral supply chain refers to the system of all the activities, organizations, actors, technology, information, resources, and services involved in moving the mineral from the extraction site downstream to its incorporation in the final product for end consumers. The process of bringing a raw mineral to the consumer market involves multiple actors and generally includes the extraction, transport, handling, trading, processing, smelting, refining and alloying, and manufacturing and sale of end product.

The OECD guidance recommends five key steps to establish a due diligence program to prevent and detect sourcing of conflict minerals:

1. Establish strong company management systems.
2. Identify and assess risk in the supply chain.
3. Design and implement a strategy to respond to identified risk.
4. Carry out independent third-party audit of the supply chain (e.g., audit high-risk suppliers or smelters).
5. Report on supply chain due diligence internally to management.

Compliance will likely require a cross-functional team, including representatives from sales, purchasing/procurement, legal, senior management, customer service, engineering, investor relations, quality and environmental, and health and safety functions. The amount of time required for a due diligence program depends on the size of the supply chain; volume of conflict minerals being used; the cost, accessibility, availability, and quality of alternate supply sources or materials; the stockpile of minerals already in the supply chain; and the company's commitment to the effort.

The SEC standards are focused on reasonable design and good faith effort because the rule requires cooperation by a company's suppliers, and it may be difficult to force supplier cooperation. The Reasonable Country of Origin Inquiry (RCOI) should include an understanding of the issuer's supplier/sub-supplier population, a framework or process for evaluating responses from suppliers, and sufficient knowledge of the issuer's supply chain to be able to identify potential red flags in suppliers' responses. Companies may need to work with industry/trade organizations, negotiate cooperation into contracts, or use their buying power leverage to force the issue. This may be difficult for smaller companies with less leverage. Suppliers may move toward compliance in response to the broad applicability of the rule.

In its eighth *Supplier Responsibility 2014 Progress Report*, issued in January 2014, Apple announced that it would cease using conflict minerals. It reported that its entire supply of tantalum, a rare metal used in the production of capacitors, is provided by certified conflict-free smelters. Apple's approach is to verify a critical mass of suppliers to influence demand while also supporting verified supply lines and economic development in the region. However, conflict-free smelter certification programs are not well developed. The Global e-Sustainability Initiative (GeSI) and the Electronic Industry Citizenship Coalition (EICC) updated their Conflict-Free Smelter program to incorporate the OECD guidelines. Participating companies must implement the OECD guidelines, conduct a third-party review of their supply chains to verify compliance, and obtain documentation from smelters about the mines of origin for all materials supplied.

In March 2014, the EU proposed voluntary rules to prevent European companies from importing conflict minerals. The rationale is that U.S. legislation has led many U.S. companies to stop sourcing these minerals in Africa rather than going through the onerous certification process. The biggest hindrance according to the EU's trade commission is that only about 20 percent of smelters and 40 percent of refiners conduct due diligence with their supply chain. The EU imports about 25 percent of the global trade in tin, tungsten, and tantalum and about 15 percent of gold.[4]

---

[4] C. Oliver, K. Manson, and J. Wilson, "EU Plans Voluntary Rules on Conflict Mineral Imports," *Financial Times,* March 5, 2014.

The Sarbanes-Oxley Act

The Sarbanes-Oxley Act (2002) is the public company accounting reform and investor protection act. Several sections of the act might impact supply management.

Section 401a requires off-balance-sheet transactions and obligations to be listed. For supply management this might include long-term purchase agreements such as multiyear supplier-managed inventory programs, cancellation and restocking charges, and lease agreements.

Section 404 requires the creation and maintenance of viable internal controls that the SEC has ruled include policies, procedures, training programs, and other processes beyond financial controls. For supply management this might include insecure and unreliable communications such as e-mails used to communicate with trading partners, poor purchase commitment visibility, and inventory write-offs.

Section 409 requires timely reporting of material events that impact financial reporting. Supply events that might meet the threshold of materiality include late supplier deliveries, ERP system crashes that disrupt shipments, and poor inventory accuracy.

Environmental Regulations

Why are environmental issues of concern to supply managers, especially U.S. supply managers? For one thing, the people of the United States consume approximately 25 percent of the world's resources despite representing less than 5 percent of the world's population. China's explosive growth has, like most industrial revolutions, come with severe environmental problems. Both business and government leaders should consider the impact of these numbers.

The U.S. and Canadian governments have enacted a number of important regulations, and many of these affect the supply function. Important among these regulations in the United States are four pieces of federal legislation: (1) the Resource Conservation and Recovery Act, (2) the Toxic Substances Control Act, (3) the Comprehensive Environmental Response, Compensation and Liability Act, and (4) the Clean Air Act. In Canada, the major pieces of environmental legislation are the Environmental Protection Act and the Water Resources Act.

Among the implications of government environmental legislation for supply is that

1. Purchasers contracting for waste disposal may want to (*a*) ensure that a disposal supplier is competent and reputable and has an EPA permit, (*b*) require the supplier to warrant that employees are trained in handling the specific waste, and (*c*) insist on the right to inspect the facility and the EPA permit.

2. Purchasers should require suppliers to warrant that any chemical or chemical mixture they provide is listed by the EPA.

3. Purchasers must track the amount and type of chemicals that enter and leave the plant and consult the Material Safety Data Sheets (MSDS).

4. Purchasers can choose environmentally friendly products; establish criteria for supplier selection that limit purchases from suppliers that sell damaging products; and be alert to alternatives, substitutes, or new technology that may help their companies meet the goals of government legislation.

The U.S. government provides details of its major environmental laws on the Environmental Protection Agency (EPA) website (www.epa.gov).

Environmentally Preferable Purchasing

Recognizing that the U.S. government is one of the largest consumers of goods and services in the world, the EPA developed the Environmentally Preferable Purchasing (EPP) program. EPP requires all federal procurement officials to assess and give preference to products and services that are environmentally preferable. A database of environmental attribute information for a wide range of products exists. Although developed for federal agency procurement, commercial purchasers may find the information useful.

Environmentally Preferable Purchasing (EPP) helps the federal government "buy green" and use the federal government's buying power to stimulate market demand for green products and services. This site can help green vendors, businesses of all sizes, and consumers to

- Find and evaluate information about green products and services.
- Identify federal green buying requirements.
- Calculate the costs and benefits of purchasing choices.
- Manage green purchasing processes (www.epa.gov/epp).

Voluntary Compliance Programs

The EPA is developing a more comprehensive program designed to hold down the costs of environmental continuous improvement. The goals are to develop an industry-by-industry approach, coordinate rule making, simplify recordkeeping and reporting requirements, permit streamlining, and review enforcement/compliance objectives. Toward those goals, the EPA has developed a wide range of voluntary compliance programs (www.epa.gov/compliance/incentives).

ETHICS

Ethics comes from a Greek work *ethika,* which means "character" or "custom." It relates to the principles or standards of human conduct, sometimes called *morals* (Latin *mores,* "customs"). Ethics, as a branch of philosophy, is considered a normative science. It is concerned with norms of human conduct. Each individual makes decisions out of an ethical framework. Each organization creates an ethical framework as part of its organizational culture that drives and constrains behavior.

Numerous factors influence ethics, including family, education, religion, peers, gender, age, socioeconomic status, culture, and experience. When a group of diverse people is brought together in one organization, it is important to consciously create an ethical culture. This culture is documented by the standards of conduct in a code of ethics. It is brought to life by the attitude, behavior, and practices of company leaders as well as each individual in the organization. This is especially true when ethical challenges occur. It is reinforced by the procedures put in place to monitor ethical behavior and by the language used in the course of doing business.

Purchasing represents the exchange of money for goods and services. Often, a very large amount of money is involved in this exchange. It is, therefore, vital that the transactions associated with this process be carried out at the highest ethical level. Unfortunately, temptation is always present where large amounts of money are involved. Sometimes suppliers will go to considerable lengths to secure business and resort to unethical practices, such as bribes or large gifts. Sometimes unscrupulous purchasers take advantage of their privileged position to extract personal rewards that are unethical as well as illegal.

Clearly, both suppliers and purchasers are responsible for ensuring that unethical conduct is not tolerated. Both the Supply Chain Management Association (SCMA) of Canada and the U.S.-based Institute for Supply Management (ISM) have codes of ethics and principles and standards of purchasing practice that guide the professional behavior of their members. (See Figure 15–2 and 15–3.)

International Federation of Purchasing and Supply Management (IFPSM) is the union of 48 National and Regional Purchasing Associations worldwide. About 250,000 supply

FIGURE 15–2   **Excerpts from SCMA Code of Ethics**

SCMA CODE OF ETHICS

A. Standards of Conduct

Members will conduct themselves in a manner that a reasonable and informed third party would conclude as being appropriate to a professional in supply chain management.
1. *Avoidance of conflicts of interest.* Members should exercise professional judgment and discretion in order to avoid any apparent or actual conflict of interest when performing their duties.
2. *Protection of confidential or sensitive information.* Where a member has been privy to confidential or sensitive information, it is their responsibility to ensure that it remains so.
3. *Business relationships.* Members should maintain relationships with suppliers and third parties in a manner that contributes to and promotes fair competition in the market and protects the interests and reputation of his or her employer.
4. *Gifts, gratuities, and hospitality inducements.* When permitted by employing organizations, members must ensure that the objectivity of their decisions is not compromised or unduly influenced by the acceptance of gifts, gratuities, or hospitalities of any kind.
5. *Environmental and social responsibilities.* Members shall exercise their responsibilities in a manner that promotes and provides opportunities for the protection and preservation of the natural environment.

B. Professional Principles

Members will perform their roles and duties based on the following principles of professional practice:
1. *Professional competency.* To maintain their professional competency by staying informed of, and complying with, the best supply chain management practices, and for SCMP designation members to retain their professional certification in good standing.
2. *Professionalism.* To provide professional advice to their employer or any other impacted party to the best of their knowledge, recognizing that any final decision is the prerogative of the senior authority within the employing organization; to act with courtesy and due consideration in dealings with other professional members and in all business relationships.
3. *Honesty and integrity.* To maintain an unimpeachable standard of integrity and honesty in all their business relationships both inside and outside the organizations in which they are employed.
4. *Responsible management.* To optimize, without prejudice, the use of resources for which they are responsible so as to provide the maximum value as defined by the organizations they represent.
5. *Serving the public good.* To use their position to advance the interests and well-being of society; to denounce all forms of business practice which may compromise value or bring discredit to the organization and/or society.
6. *Compliance with legal obligations.* Members must not engage in or condone any activity or attempt to circumvent the clear intention of the law.

FIGURE 15–3   ISM Principles and Standards of Ethical Supply Management Conduct

INTEGRITY IN YOUR DECISIONS AND ACTIONS
VALUE FOR YOUR EMPLOYER
LOYALTY TO YOUR PROFESSION

From these principles are derived the ISM standards of supply management conduct:

STANDARDS

1. **Impropriety.** Prevent the intent and appearance of unethical or compromising conduct in relationships, actions, and communications.
2. **Conflicts of Interest.** Ensure that any personal, business or other activity does not conflict with the lawful interests of your employer.
3. **Influence.** Avoid behaviors or actions that may negatively influence, or appear to influence, supply management decisions.
4. **Responsibilities to Your Employer.** Uphold fiduciary and other responsibilities using reasonable care and granted authority to deliver value to your employer.
5. **Supplier and Customer Relationships.** Promote positive supplier and customer relationships.
6. **Sustainability and Social Responsibility.** Champion social responsibility and sustainability practices in supply management.
7. **Confidential and Proprietary Information.** Protect confidential and proprietary information.
8. **Reciprocity.** Avoid improper reciprocal agreements.
9. **Applicable Laws, Regulations, and Trade Agreements.** Know and obey the letter and spirit of laws, regulations, and trade agreements applicable to supply management.
10. **Professional Competence.** Develop skills, expand knowledge, and conduct business that demonstrates competence and promotes the supply management profession.

Adopted: 01/2012

professionals are members of these associations. The IFPSM facilitates the development and sharing of the practice of the purchasing and supply management profession through its network of member organizations. The IFPSM has adopted a Code of Ethics. (See Figure 15–4.)

Most large organizations deal specifically with standards of behavior of supply personnel and their relationships with suppliers in their policies and procedures. Many organizations are moving to a congruent position that equates the treatment of customers, employees, and suppliers as identical. Simply stated, "Every customer, employee, and supplier of this organization is entitled to the same level of honesty, courtesy, and fairness." Buyers are urged to behave in a manner that reflects the organization's wishes.

Several areas help establish and maintain the reputation of the supply group and the organization. These are perceptions, conflict of interest, gifts and gratuities, relationships with suppliers, and reciprocity.

Perceptions

Perception is often as important as reality. If a buyer's action is perceived by others to be inappropriate, then both the buyer's and the buying organization's reputations may be harmed. Because of this danger, everyone in supply must think about how an action will appear to others.

FIGURE 15–4   **IFPSM Code of Ethics**

Precepts

Members shall not use their authority or office for personal gain and shall seek to uphold and enhance the standing of the purchasing and supply management profession and the Federation by:

A. Maintaining an unimpeachable standard of integrity in all their business relationships both inside and outside the organizations in which they are employed;

B. Fostering the highest standards of professional competence amongst those for whom they are responsible;

C. Optimizing the use of resources for which they are responsible so as to provide the maximum benefit to their employers;

D. Complying with the letter and the spirit of:
   I. The laws of the country in which they practice;
   II. The Federation's 'guidance' on professional practice as outlined below and as may be issued by the Federation from time to time; and
   III. Contractual obligations.

E. Rejecting and denouncing any business practice that is improper; and

F. Enhancing the proficiency and stature of the profession by acquiring and maintaining current technical knowledge.

Guidance

In applying these precepts, members should follow the guidance set out below:

A. Declaration of interest. Any personal interest which may impinge or might reasonably be deemed by others to impinge on a member's impartiality in any matter relevant to their duties should be declared to their employer.

B. Confidentiality and accuracy of information. The confidentiality of information received in the course of duty must be respected and should not be used for personal gain; information given in the course of duty should be true and fair and not designed to mislead.

C. Competition. While considering the advantages to the member's employer of maintaining a continuing relationship with a supplier, any arrangement which might, in the long term, prevent the effective operation of fair competition, should be avoided.

D. Business gift. To preserve the image and integrity of both the member and the employer, business gifts should be discouraged. Gifts, other than items of very small intrinsic value, should not be accepted.

E. Hospitality. Moderate hospitality is an accepted courtesy of a business relationship. However, the recipients should not allow themselves to reach a position whereby they might be or might be deemed by others to have been influenced in making a business decision as a consequence of accepting such hospitality. The frequency and scale of hospitality accepted should not be significantly greater than a recipient's employer, through the recipient's expense account, would be likely to provide in return.

F. When in doubt of what is acceptable in terms of gifts and hospitality, the offer should be declined or advice sought from the member's superior.

Source: www.ifpmm.org/About/Ethics.cfm

Conflict of Interest

Conflict of interest touches on the issue of perception. There are situations where two parties cannot agree on the existence of a conflict. Often, the person involved truly believes that he or she can remain objective despite having conflicting interests. It may never be proven otherwise, but others may perceive that the business interest was sacrificed for personal interest.

For example, a supply professional may be in a decision-making position that involves a friend or family member's business. No matter how thorough a job the person does, some observers will always believe the business was won on personal and not professional relationships.

Gifts and Gratuities

Supply personnel can avoid ethical entanglements through conscious behavior. Whether or not to accept entertainment, gifts, and gratuities is related to perceptions. Many purchasers argue that their decisions are not swayed by a free lunch. Others argue that even if the buyer knows the entertainment did not influence the decision, others (especially rejected bidders and personnel in other functions) may not be so sure.

There is also concern that any perceived imbalance in a relationship will subconsciously motivate the parties to move to parity. For example, after accepting several dinner invitations, most people feel a sense of obligation to return the favor. How does one know for sure that one can remain objective after receiving gifts and entertainment from a salesperson?

Targets of Unfair Influence.   Supply personnel are not the only targets of attempts to influence decisions unfairly. Executives, managers, supervisors, and others in production, marketing, information systems, engineering, or elsewhere may be targeted. Anyone with direct responsibility for, or large influence on, decisions about procurement may be approached. Even when the buyer is not directly influenced, the buyer's task is affected. If undue influence is considered a serious issue, all employees can be prohibited from receiving any gift, no matter how trivial, from any supplier, actual or potential.

In some organizations nonsupply personnel are allowed to receive or extend entertainment and gifts and supply personnel are not. This policy may undermine the integrity of the supply process. Sales representatives focus their attention on nonsupply personnel who they believe can influence the decision. An astute sales representative can quickly determine who the real decision maker is and how serious the buying organization is about following its own processes. The impact on total cost of ownership is often overlooked by those who argue that there is no harm done in accepting gifts and entertainment.

The Sales Perspective.   A salesperson's job is to influence and persuade decision makers. This can be done most effectively by knowing the product or service and the potential customer's needs and wants and presenting proposals that represent good value. People learn about others and their situation by spending time with them. They also build a relationship and a foundation of trust. The easiest way is to spend time together in a social setting.

Maintaining a Professional Relationship.   The challenge is finding ways to foster the development of trust and mutual understanding of the goals and objectives of each other's organization while maintaining a professional relationship. In buyer–supplier partnerships or strategic alliances, this issue is even more pronounced. Now the supplier may be a single source in a long-term deal that brings together people from the two organizations on a regular, sometimes daily, basis. Special attention is required to ensure that the business focus is maintained.

How, then, shall the supply manager deal with the problem of excessive entertainment and gifts in any one of its varied and subtle forms? This practice is designed to influence the decision maker by creating a sense of obligation through gifts, entertainment, and even open bribery. It is, of course, often difficult to distinguish between legitimate expenditures by suppliers in the interest of goodwill and illegitimate expenditures made in an attempt to place the buyer under some obligation to the supplier. In these borderline cases, only a clearly written code of conduct and ordinary common sense can provide the answer.

The code of ethics of most supply professional associations strongly condemns gratuities beyond token gifts of nominal value. However, every year a small number of cases is uncovered of individuals who do not abide by this code, thereby placing the whole profession under suspicion.

Part of the blame must clearly lie with those who use illegal enticements to secure business. For example, a salesperson calls on a purchaser and extends an invitation to lunch so they may discuss a transaction without losing time or as a matter of courtesy. Such action is presumed to be in the interests of goodwill, although the cost of the lunch must be added to the selling price. An attractive but inexpensive gift may be given by the supplier's company to adorn the desk of the buyer. The supplier's name appears on the gift, and therefore it is construed as advertising. The sales representative may send a bottle of wine or sporting event tickets after a deal has been completed.

The custom of giving simple gifts may develop into providing much larger ones. It is difficult to draw the line between these different situations. In some organizations, the supply manager or buyer frequently refuses to allow salespeople to pay for luncheons or insists on paying for an equal number.

Commercial Bribery

Aside from its economic aspects, commercial bribery is the subject of many legal cases. Fundamentally, the rulings on commercial bribery rest on the doctrine of agency. The agent is recognized by law as keeping a fiduciary position. Any breach of faith on the part of the agent is not permitted. Therefore, the agent's acceptance of a bribe to do anything in conflict with the interests of its principal is not permitted by law.

The evils of commercial bribery are more far-reaching than first imagined. Although originating with only one business, it may quickly become an industry practice. No matter how superior the quality of goods or how low its price, a producer will have difficulty competing with businesses that practice bribery. The behavior of the buyer who accepts bribes will change. He or she will likely pay higher prices than normal. Defects in workmanship or quality are likely to be hidden. Materials from other manufacturers may be deliberately damaged or destroyed. The total cost of ownership rises as a result of commercial bribery.

Even though bribery is outlawed in almost every country in the world, it often flourishes, legally or not. The spectacular revelations about the bribery involved in the UN-sponsored oil for food program in Iraq were a sad reminder of the pervasiveness of such practices.

In the last 10 years, both international organizations and individual countries have passed and begun to enforce antibribery and anticorruption laws. Multiple laws and jurisdictions bring greater transparency to employees' actions and greater force behind refusals to engage in bribery in countries where it has been prevalent. However, it also adds complexity in terms of knowing and abiding by the applicable laws.

In the United States, enforcement of the Federal Corrupt Practices Act (FCPA) has increased dramatically as have the assessed penalties. Money laundering, fraud and tax issues, and enforcement around exports to banned countries are also receiving increased enforcement action. Similarly, new regulations that govern private business, including hedge funds and financial products like derivatives, could extend to foreign activities.

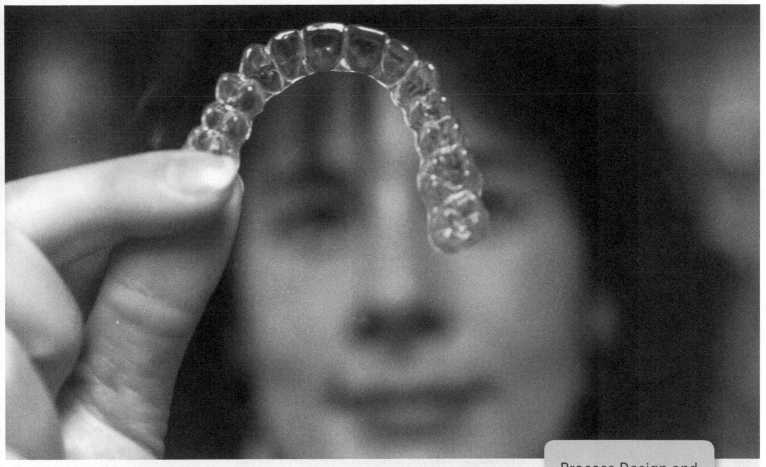

© Hugh Grannum/KRT/Newscom

Process Design and Process Technologies Are the Key to Success for Invisalign.®

Process design and new process technologies are enabling companies to make customized products quickly and cost effectively, sometimes dramatically changing an industry. One example of how process design created radical change is in the field of orthodontics. If you had metal bracket and wire braces you may recall frequent trips to the orthodontist for wire tightening, giving up foods such as popcorn and apples, and feeling self-conscious when smiling.

This all changed when Align Technology, Inc., developed and introduced the Invisalign® system. This system uses a series of factory-produced clear plastic, removable "aligners" that are custom designed for each patient's needs. The Invisalign® system, made possible by advances in information technology and manufacturing technologies such as 3D printing and robotics, may make metal braces a thing of the past.

The Invisalign® process begins when the dentist takes a digital scan of the patient's teeth. The scan is then electronically transmitted to Align Technology's technicians who use proprietary software to create an individualized treatment plan. After the dentist approves the plan, the digital scans are used to "3D print" molds that are used to form the correct shapes for the plastic aligners. Up to 80,000 custom designed aligners are made per day using a highly automated assembly line. Robots complete tasks with precision and accuracy. Radio frequency identification (RFID) tracking ensures that each patient receives the correct aligners. Even the packaging process is totally automated. The design of each step from the dentist's office through manufacturing guarantees that each patient receives a high quality, cost-effective treatment to create a perfect smile.

Whether an operation is manufacturing-oriented, service-oriented, or some combination of the two, the capabilities contained within its supply chain drive its ability to compete on quality, time, cost, or flexibility. This chapter describes some of the key decisions about manufacturing and service structures that determine an organization's operations and supply chain capabilities. For example, the Invisalign® process is designed for high quality, flexibility, and efficiency. This chapter focuses on three process structure decision areas—process selection, operations layout, and technology selection—that are key to achieving these goals.

PROCESS STRUCTURES

Managers must design processes based on *what kind* of work needs to be done. Different process structures provide different capabilities. Process structure determines how inputs, activities, flows, and outputs of a process are organized. Within a supply chain, each organization must select the process structures that are appropriate considering its competitive priorities of quality, timeliness, cost, flexibility, and innovation.

Product-Process Matrix

LO5-1 Compare and contrast the seven process structures: project, job shop, batch, repetitive process, continuous process, mass customization, and cellular manufacturing.

To better link a product's life cycle and marketing decisions with operations capabilities, Hayes and Wheelwright developed the **product-process matrix**. They observed that processes progress through a life cycle just as products do. Although developed for manufacturing, the product-process matrix also describes many service processes. To achieve high performance, a firm's process structure must be aligned with its competitive priorities and marketing strategies.

product-process matrix
Categorizes processes into structures based on output volume and variety.

The matrix shows five process structures along the diagonal based on output volume and variety: project, job shop, batch, repetitive process, and continuous process (see Figure 5-1). Often within a single company, different process structures are used for different products. An entire supply chain typically has each of these process structures. For example, the glass for a car's windshield is made using a continuous process, seats are made using a batch process, and the car is made using a repetitive process. Let's examine the characteristics of each of the process structures, as summarized in Table 5-1.

FIGURE 5-1   Product-Process Matrix

Source: Adapted from R. Hayes and S. Wheelwright, *Restoring Our Competitive Edge: Competing Through Manufacturing* (New York: John Wiley & Sons, 1984).

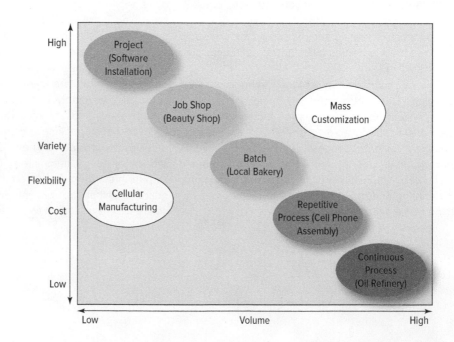

TABLE 5-1   Comparison of Process Types

Process Type	Output Characteristics	Example	Process Characteristics
Project	Unique One of a kind	Custom home Designing a video game	Unique sequencing High complexity Employees and equipment must be flexible Activities are often outsourced to specialists
Job shop	Customized, low volume	Auto repair Beauty salon	High variety of inputs and process flows Job sequencing is challenging High work-in-process inventory Highly skilled, flexible workers General-purpose equipment
Batch	Moderate volume and variety	Bakery Automotive parts Cinema	Dominant flow patterns Some common inputs Setup time can be high Moderately flexible employees and equipment
Repetitive process	Standard products with a range of options	Appliances Automobiles Buffet restaurant	All products follow the same sequence Standard methods and materials are used Low-skilled workers specialize in completing a limited number of activities
Continuous process	Commodities with high volume, little variety	Aluminum cans Laundry detergent Gasoline	Products follow sequence Operations often run 24/7 Line stoppages are very costly Highly specialized equipment Low-skilled operators

Project

A **project** produces a unique, "one of a kind" output. Examples of projects include building a custom home, designing a video game, or planning a wedding. Because the outputs are customized, the customer is highly involved in the design process. The type, sequencing, and complexity of activities change from project to project, so employees and equipment must be flexible. To maximize flexibility, a project manager plans and organizes the project, and activities are often outsourced to suppliers. For example, a wedding planner consults with a bride and groom to determine their preferences for flowers, music, photography, and food. The planner then hires and manages the florist, musicians, photographers, and caterers.

project A one-time or infrequently occurring set of activities that create outputs within prespecified time and cost schedules.

relationships

Job Shop

Automobile dealers' service shops, beauty salons, and department stores use **job shop** process structures, in which outputs are customized and produced in low volumes. Products are typically made to order for a specific customer. Each order or "job" can involve different inputs and a different sequencing of activities and thus have different flows through the process.

job shop A flexible process structure for products that require different inputs and have different flows through the process.

Because of the high variety of inputs and activities, planning and scheduling jobs can be challenging. Products can spend a lot of time waiting to be worked on, resulting in high work-in-process inventory and the need for expediting.

Because of the differences from order to order, the equipment used in a job shop is general purpose, and employees must be skilled and flexible enough to handle a wide range of tasks. Job shops are typically more labor-than capital-intensive. Equipment and employees capable of doing similar activities are typically located together in departments or groups.

Batch Process

batch process A process in which goods or services are produced in groups (batches) and not in a continuous stream.

A local bakery that produces cookies, cakes, and pies uses a **batch process** structure. Many interior parts for automobiles such as the center console are made using batch processes. Cinemas offer movies in batches. A batch process structure works well when products have moderate levels of volume and variety. A batch structure is a good choice for products that have basic models with several different options.

Although there may be some differences between the flow patterns of each batch, there are dominant flow patterns. Equipment and employee flexibility are important, but the range of flexibility needed is less than with projects or job shops. Cleaning and setup are usually required between each batch, reducing the available capacity and increasing costs. However, some companies have found creative ways to eliminate cleaning and setup. The "mystery" flavor of Spangler Candy Co.'s Dum Dum Pops is created by the mixing of flavors between batches. By eliminating the need to clean the equipment between batches, Spangler effectively reduces costs and increases productive time.

Repetitive Process

repetitive process A process in which discrete products flow through the same sequence of activities.

When there are many customers who want a similar product, such as automobiles, appliances, cell phones, or lunch at a buffet restaurant, a **repetitive process** structure is used. Some standard options such as a range of colors, features, or menu items are offered, but the range of choices is limited and determined by marketing in advance of the customer's order.

Products made using a repetitive process are typically made to stock. Discrete products flow through the same sequence of activities, and equipment can be specialized to each specific task. Operations managers usually focus on developing standard methods and procedures to continuously improve quality and reduce costs.

Employees who work on the line may not be highly skilled, but they become very efficient in completing one small task. For example, in assembling a car, one employee may install the front seats. Because employees can become bored preforming the same activity repeatedly, job rotation is often used to lessen this problem.

Continuous Process

continuous process A single-flow process used for high-volume nondiscrete, standardized products.

Standard, nondiscrete products such as gasoline, chemicals, laundry detergent, aluminum cans, and cereal are produced using **continuous processes**, in which products always flow through the same sequence of production steps. Check and mail processing are examples of continuous processes. These made-to-stock products offer customers very little variety and are considered as commodities. Differentiation typically occurs at the end of the production process. For example, laundry detergent comes in different sizes or aluminum cans are printed with different labels.

These processes use highly specialized, automated equipment, which often runs 24 hours a day, seven days a week. Economies of scale reduce unit cost, but it is very costly to stop or change the product because the specialized equipment

activity

student

Companies focusing on different competitive priorities can use different process structures for the same type of product. For example, a company that produces off-the-rack clothing uses a different process structure than a company that produces custom-tailored clothing. Identify a product and competitors who are using different competitive priorities. What position on the product-process matrix would you expect for each?

is expensive. Low-skilled employees monitor equipment while highly skilled engineers and maintenance employees work to minimize downtime and improve processes.

Mass Customization

When the product-process matrix was developed in the 1970s, the processes on the diagonal were thought to lead to the best performance. Today, changes in management practices and technologies have created more options. One way to get the cost advantages of high-volume continuous and repetitive processes while increasing variety is **mass customization**. The process used for the Invisalign® system is an example of mass customization. In other cases customers "design" products by choosing from a range of options. For example, using the NIKEiD website, customers can choose the style, color, and material for shoes with delivery in four weeks or less.

© Cultura Creative (RF)/Alamy Stock Photo

Process flexibility is essential for mass customization. Different approaches can be used to create flexibility. Mass customization can occur when products are assembled from standard modules that are stored in inventory, reducing the elapsed time from order to delivery. The exact product configuration is postponed until a customer order is received. Companies also use technologies such as **3D printing** (or *additive manufacturing*) or **flexible manufacturing systems (FMS)** to produce a wider range of products in a wider range of volumes than is economically feasible using conventional equipment.

The Internet and other technologies facilitate mass customization. For example, customers can design their own high school or college class rings at Jostens by choosing band style, metal, stone, and carvings. In doing so, each customer can trade off features and price. Mars Inc. used the Internet and new printing technology to mass customize M&Ms and create a whole new market segment, as discussed in Get Real: "Personalized M&Ms".

3D printing has the potential to increase the use of mass customization and radically change what we know about process structures. 3D printing creates objects by laying down successive thin layers of a material to build the product based on 3D modeling software. Objects can be made from a wide range of materials, including plastics, metals, ceramics, and even chocolate. Products such as jet engine parts, hearing aids, and pasta are being made using 3D printing. Advances in technology, especially in the types of materials that can be printed, will expand use of this technology. Compared to traditional manufacturing processes, 3D printing:

- Is highly flexible.
- Can eliminate the need for producing parts and assembly by printing products in one piece.
- Uses relatively low-cost equipment.
- Can be made close to the customer, reducing inventory and transportation.

mass customization Uses advanced technologies to customize products quickly and at a low cost.

3D printing Also called *additive manufacturing*, this process makes products by putting down successive layers of thin material such as plastic, metal, ceramics, or food.

Flexible manufacturing systems (FMS) Combine automated machines, robots, and material handling systems that are all controlled by a single computer.

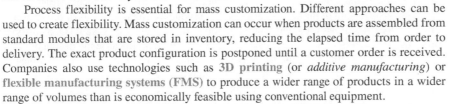

activity

student

Do some research to identify a product that is made using 3D printing. How have the operations and supply chain changed as a result of moving to the new manufacturing process?

Cellular Manufacturing

At the other end of the product-process matrix, the flexibility of job shop and batch production is retained but costs are lowered through use of **cellular manufacturing**. The complexity of job shop and small batch production environments can be reduced and efficiency increased by producing products that have similar processing characteristics using small assembly lines referred to as *cells*. The cellular approach also works well in

cellular manufacturing The production of products with similar process characteristics on small assembly lines called *cells*.

services where information or customer needs can be grouped by their similar processing characteristics. The cellular process structure will be discussed in more detail later in this chapter, in the section titled "Operations Layout."

Aligning Process Structure and Market Orientation

Different process structures involve different decisions about whether a product should be designed and produced *before* a customer order is placed or *after* the order is placed. This decision determines how the firm competes in the marketplace. There are four different marketing orientations; each delivers a different level of service in terms of lead time and customization. To be effective, an organization's process structure must fit with its marketing orientation.

engineer to order (ETO). Unique, customized products.

Products that firms **engineer to order (ETO)** are designed for individual customers and generally have long lead times. Examples include a custom-built house, a cruise ship, specialized industrial equipment, and a customized employee training program. Because each ETO product requires an entirely new design, a customer must place an order before work begins. Firms that anticipate orders often carry raw materials inventory to reduce lead times. Products that are ETO typically use either project or job shop process structures.

make to order (MTO) Products that have similar designs but are customized during production.

The basic design of **make to order (MTO)** products covers the needs of broad groups of customers but allows for some customization during production. Like ETO, a customer order triggers activities at the very early stages of production. Because the design does not start from scratch, the lead time for MTO is less than for ETO. A jet airplane, a meal at an elegant restaurant, a haircut, and a trip to the emergency room are examples of MTO operations. MTO products typically use job shop, batch, and cellular process structures.

assemble to order (ATO) Products that are produced from standard components and modules.

The designs of the components and modules in **assemble to order (ATO)** products are standardized and do not change with customer orders. However, the components and modules can be assembled in different ways to create end product configurations that meet individual customer needs. Raw materials and components are produced and stored in inventory, but final assembly is postponed until the customer places an order. For example, paint stores mix coloring agents with a white base paint after the customer places an order, to provide many color options. Subway Restaurants assemble sandwiches to order from

GET REAL

Personalized M&Ms

Who would have thought that a mature candy brand introduced in 1941 would be a candidate for mass customization? Standard M&Ms are produced using a continuous process and are packaged for distribution through grocery stores and other retail outlets all over the world.

Engineers at Mars developed a breakthrough in printing technology that enabled the introduction of personalized M&Ms in 2005. Now, customers can even put their own faces on M&Ms after uploading their own images at my.m&ms.com.

Personalized M&Ms follow the same continuous process as standard M&Ms, until the printing process. Then, the customer's choice of M&M colors are printed using the images provided by the customer. The M&Ms are then filled into packages selected by the customer and sent directly to the customer's home or business address. However, based on the price per ounce, you may not want to have these for an everyday snack.

© McGraw-Hill Education/Editorial Image, LLC, photographer

prepared ingredients, including freshly baked bread. Repetitive processes are used for ATO products, and many firms have developed mass customization processes for their ATO products.

Groceries, retail clothing, electronics, and cars are examples of **make to stock (MTS)** products. So that products are immediately available, finished products are made in advance of customer orders and held in inventory. Thus, firms must make products based on forecasts of customer demand. MTS items are typically standardized, mature products. Repetitive assembly lines and continuous processes are typically used for MTS products.

> **make to stock (MTS)** Finished goods that are held in inventory in advance of customer orders.

UNIQUE ASPECTS OF SERVICE PROCESSES

Although the product-process matrix can be used to describe services, it does not address the fact that customers often participate in service processes. **Customer contact** refers to the presence of the customer in a service process. Services range from those with high customer contact, such as a haircut, to those with low customer contact, such as package delivery. Contact with the customer creates unique challenges in designing, controlling, and operating service processes. Thinking back to the opening vignette, customer contact occurs at the dentist's office and is a critical step in the Invisalign® process. However, because Invisalign® aligners are made at a factory, customer contact is lower than for traditional braces, which are fitted and adjusted at the dentist's office.

> **customer contact** The presence of the customer in a process.

Service Process Matrix

Building on the concept of the product-process matrix, Schmenner developed the **service process matrix** shown in Figure 5-2 that categorizes services based upon the degree of customization/customer interaction and labor/capital intensity involved. Services in the same industry can compete in different ways by adopting process structures specified in this matrix.

> **service process matrix** Categorizes service processes based upon the degree of customization/customer interaction and labor/capital intensity.

Professional Services.

Lawyers, doctors, consultants, and accountants interact closely with clients to deliver customized services. Professional services tend to be time-consuming and costly because providers are highly skilled and educated. However, by reducing the degree of customization, some firms have reduced time and costs. Retailers such as Target, Walmart, and CVS have in-store medical clinics staffed with nurse practitioners. These clinics treat minor ailments quickly and at a much lower cost than a traditional family doctor.

> **LO5-2** Compare and contrast the goals and challenges associated with a service factory, a mass service, a service shop, and a professional service.

Service Factory.

Trucking companies, airlines, and hotels are examples of service factories. Customer contact, customization, and labor intensity are low while investment in facilities and equipment

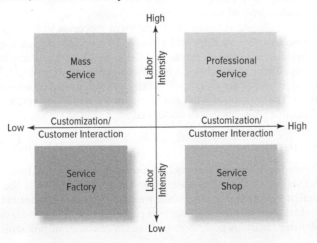

FIGURE 5-2   Service Process Matrix

Source: Adapted from R. W. Schmenner, "How Can Service Businesses Survive and Prosper?" *Sloan Management Review* 27, no. 3 (1986), pp. 21–32.

is high. A range of standard services is offered to customers who tend to value low price above all else. Operations managers in service factories are mainly concerned with utilizing equipment and facilities to a maximum extent, because these fixed assets account for the majority of operating costs. Matching capacity and demand to keep equipment and facilities busy is important to both competitiveness and profitability.

Service Shops.

Automobile repair shops and hospitals are examples of service shops, which have a high degree of capital intensity and high customer interaction/customization. Keeping up-to-date on new technology and scheduling to ensure effective utilization of technology are key operations issues. For example, auto repair shop operations typically have large spikes in demand on Mondays, making scheduling a challenge. Some organizations have specialized to reduce the variety of services offered, thus moving from service shops to mass services (described next). For example, muffler replacement and oil changes are mass services.

> ## activity
> **student**
>
> Think of the last service you purchased. What category of service was it? Can you suggest changes in product features or delivery technologies that would move the service to another category? What could be the advantages of such a change?

Mass Services. Mass services, such as retail banks, gas stations, and other retail outlets, meet the standard needs of a large volume of customers. These services have low customer interaction/customization and high labor intensity. Through automation, some mass services have reduced costs and improved customer service availability. Using ATMs, the Internet, or mobile apps, customers can do routine banking activities 24/7. Using the self-checkout at a grocery or superstore reduces the wait time for customers and requires fewer cashiers. Many mass services have been automated through Internet technologies.

Managing Front-Office and Back-Office Processes

front-office processes Processes that have contact with the customer.

back-office processes Processes that are not seen by the customer.

global

While some processes within a company require customer involvement and interaction, others do not. Processes involving customer contact are referred to as the **front-office processes**. Those that are behind the scenes are called **back-office processes**. In a formal restaurant, the front office is the dining room where the host and servers interact with the customer, and the back office is the kitchen. Clearly, front-office and back-office processes require different employee skill sets, equipment, and physical layouts.

Depending upon the nature of the service, front-office and back-office processes can be decoupled or separated from each other. With decoupling, each process can be managed separately, creating opportunities for efficiency gains. For example, consistent quality and economies of scale occur when back-office operations from different locations are combined. Fast-food chains prepare ingredients at a centralized location, with final preparation taking place in each individual restaurant's kitchen.

The ability to decouple services allows different processes to be done by different supply chain members who are dispersed globally. Decoupling through use of the Internet allows a physician in India to analyze an MRI to diagnose the illness of a patient in the United States. These approaches do not always work out as planned, however. For example, the outsourcing of activities such as call centers has resulted in complaints about customer service. The decision of what and how to decouple service operations should be driven by competitive priorities and customer needs.

Service Blueprinting

service blueprinting An approach similar to process mapping that analyzes the interface between customers and service processes.

Service blueprinting is a tool that focuses on understanding the interfaces between customers and service providers, technology, and other key aspects of the process. The approach is similar to process mapping, which we described in the supplement to Chapter 3. A cross-functional team identifies the service process to be blueprinted, documents the process step-by-step, analyzes process enhancements or causes of problems, implements improvements, and monitors the results. However, service blueprinting differs from process mapping in that it focuses on the following elements that are particular to services:

- *Customer actions* include all of the steps that customers take as part of the service delivery process.
- *Front-office/visible contact employee actions* are the actions of frontline contact employees that occur as part of a face-to-face encounter with customers.
- *Back-office/invisible contact employee actions* are nonvisible interactions with customers, such as telephone calls, as well as other activities employees undertake to prepare to serve customers.
- *Support processes* are all activities carried out by employees who do not have direct contact with customers, but whose functions are crucial to the service.
- *Physical evidence* represents all of the tangibles that customers see or collect during their contact with a company.

For example, at a retail clothing store, customer actions include looking at clothing, selecting clothing, trying on clothing, and making a purchase. The visible part of the store includes the clothing displays and dressing rooms. Behind the scenes would be receiving and storage. Physical evidence would include the store décor, the displays, and the merchandise.

In addition to evaluating existing services, blueprinting can help a new service design team identify the critical aspects of the process and find opportunities for innovation. The service blueprint itself is a tangible, visual document that lays out where and how customers and companies interact. Good blueprints require inputs from all supply chain members, including customers. Figure 5-3 shows a service blueprint for a hotel stay.

activity

student

Select a service on campus and create a service blueprint for this service. How did the service blueprint help you to understand the process? What process improvements do you recommend?

FIGURE 5-3   Service Blueprint for a Hotel Stay

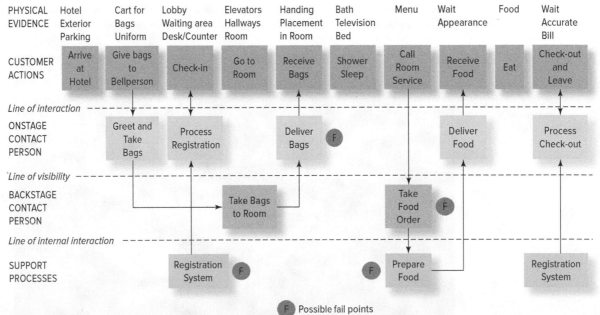

Sources: http://knowledge.wpcarey.asu.edu/article.cfm?articleId=1546; and M. J. Bitner, A. L. Ostrom, and F. N. Morgan, "Service Blueprinting: A Practical Technique for Service Innovation," *California Management Review* 50, no.3 (Spring 2008), p. 66.

Service blueprinting of a houseboat resort in Lake Powell, Arizona, showed key reasons why guests were not returning: they were doing a lot of work during their vacations. Guests had to shop for groceries and supplies and then carry these items, along with luggage, onto their boats. To remedy these problems, resort managers added a series of new services, including grocery buying and onboard chefs. As a result, the company experienced a 50 percent drop in complaints, while repeat business jumped 12 percent.

OPERATIONS LAYOUT

LO5-3 Describe how each of the operations layouts—fixed-position, functional, product, and cellular—is designed to meet the demands placed upon it.

The type of process structure selected influences the physical layout of the operation, including arrangement of the equipment, employees, inventory, and aisles for movement. When managers decide to build a new facility, develop a new product, implement new process technology, or modify processes to accommodate changes in demand, they must make layout decisions. Layout has a major impact on performance, especially cost, time, and flexibility. There are four basic types of layouts: fixed-position, functional, product, and cellular.

Fixed-Position Layout

fixed-position layout The layout used when the product cannot be moved during production.

When a product cannot be moved during its production, a **fixed-position layout** is used. Fixed-position layouts are typically used for projects involving large products such as homes, buildings, bridges, large ships, airplanes, and spacecraft.

With a fixed-position layout, all of the resources and inputs must come together at the product's location. During a visit to your family physician, a fixed-position layout is used because the nurse, doctor, and any needed treatments are brought to you.

One of the supply chain challenges associated with a fixed-position layout is ensuring that the right people, equipment, and materials all arrive at the work site at the right time. Scheduling is very complex, and project management software tools are often used to manage the process.

Functional Layout

functional layout A layout that groups together similar resources.

Multiple copies of similar resources are grouped together in a **functional layout** (sometimes called a *departmental* layout). Fitness centers and beauty salons use a functional layout. Retailers such as Macy's use a functional layout with different departments for shoes, jewelry, women's clothing, men's clothing, and cosmetics. In manufacturing, one area of

In a functional layout, workers weld parts on a door frame at the Volvo truck assembly line in Dublin, Virginia.
© Steve Helber/AP Images

a plant may do stamping, another welding, and a third assembly. Job shops and batch processes often use a functional layout where work centers using the same types of equipment are grouped together. For example, in a salon the bowls for hair washing are grouped together as are the workstations for doing nails.

There are several benefits to using a functional layout. By grouping general-purpose equipment together, a functional layout offers many different routes for a given job or customer so each has a unique flow through the process. A problem occurring at a single workstation does not usually stop production, because other similar workstations are located nearby. Learning and collaboration increases because employees with similar skills work together.

The functional layout also has several drawbacks. Because each job or customer takes a unique route through the process, scheduling, planning, and control are difficult. Processing times and work-in-process inventory tend to be high as jobs or customers wait to be processed in different departments. Consider the time you spend traveling and waiting when shopping at multiple stores within a shopping mall. Also, a significant amount of time is usually needed to clean and set up workstations when changing from one job or customer to another. In manufacturing, materials handling costs are high when jobs are moved from department to department.

In designing functional layouts, a common goal is to arrange the departments so that the time and cost of moving materials and people are minimized. To select a low-cost layout, managers compare the estimated number and cost of interdepartmental movements for all possible layouts. The complexity of this calculation increases rapidly with the number of departments involved in the decision, so facility layout software is typically used to determine functional layouts.

In retail layouts, an additional goal is usually to increase sales. Big box retailers look for ways to overcome the drawbacks of functional layouts. In large stores, customers grow tired of going from department to department looking for the items they need. Some retailers such as Target have rearranged merchandise by purchase type rather than by item type. For example, all the key items that new parents might need, such as baby clothes, diapers, and strollers, are located in the same department.

Product Layout

A **product layout** arranges resources according to a regularly occurring sequence of activities in the process. An automotive assembly line, Invisalign®, a Taco Bell kitchen, a buffet line, and an insurance claims office all use product layouts. Repetitive processes and continuous processes typically use a product layout. Product layouts minimize processing times and simplify planning, scheduling, and control because work centers are positioned in a sequence that mirrors the steps needed to assemble the product or serve the customer.

product layout A layout where resources are arranged according to a regularly occurring sequence of activities.

In a product layout, the flow of products or customers is visible and easy to trace. Operations managers sometimes use kanban systems, which are lean tools, to pull material from one workstation to the next just when it is needed. This approach minimizes the inventory of parts and components needed to support the process. In high volume situations, workstations are often linked by conveyors so that products can be automatically transported from one workstation to the next.

Lack of flexibility and low work variety for employees are drawbacks to product layouts. Because activities are linked, a problem at any single workstation can cause the entire line to stop. Think about your frustration when you are behind an indecisive person in a buffet line. This is one reason why automotive assemblers demand on-time

Automobile assembly lines use a product layout.
© Ralph Orlowski/Getty Images

delivery and high quality from their suppliers. A quality problem with any supplied part can shut the entire assembly line down. At an automobile assembly plant, this can cost tens of thousands of dollars per minute.

Line Balancing in Product Layouts

line balancing Used to assign tasks so that idle time and the number of workstations are minimized.

In designing a product layout, the goal is to have a smooth, continuous flow through the process. **Line balancing** is used to assign individual tasks to workstations for a desired output rate. Idle time and the number of workstations are minimized to increase efficiency. In Example 1 below, we review a simple example of line balancing that involves assembling a sausage and pepperoni pizza. In manufacturing, most line balancing problems will be much more complex than this example.

Example 1

precedence relationships Presents the order in which tasks must be completed.

First, identify the time required to complete each task and the order in which the tasks must be done—the **precedence relationships** (Table 5-2). Some tasks physically cannot be done until others are completed. For example, the dough must be formed before it is topped with sauce. However, either sausage or pepperoni can be added after the cheese. Both sausage and pepperoni must be added before the pizza is packaged. Visually, Figure 5-4 shows the precedence relationships.

takt time The maximum allowable cycle time at each workstation based on customer demand.

cycle time The time that it takes to process one unit at an operation in the overall process.

Next, determine the maximum total task time allowable at each workstation based on customer demand, referred to as **takt time**. The time that it takes to process a unit at a workstation is the workstation's cycle time. To ensure that a process can meet customer demand, the **cycle time** at each workstation in a process cannot exceed the takt time. If customer demand changes, the takt time should be recalculated and the assembly line rebalanced as necessary.

(5.1) Takt time *(T)* = (Available production time in a time period)/(Output needed in that time period to meet customer demand)

In our example, the time period is one 8-hour shift per day, so 480 minutes of production time are available. The customer demand for sausage and pepperoni pizzas is 200 pizzas per day. Thus, the cycle time for each workstation must be less than or equal to 2.4 minutes.

Takt time *(T)* = (8 hours/shift × 60 minutes/hour)/200 pizzas = 2.4 minutes per workstation

FIGURE 5-4   Precedence Diagram for Sausage and Pepperoni Pizza Assembly

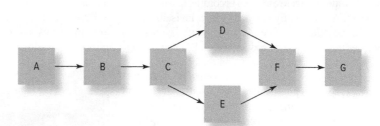

TABLE 5-2   Precedence Relationships for Sausage and Pepperoni Pizza Assembly

Task		Predecessors	Time (minutes)
A	Shape the dough to form the crust	None	2
B	Add the pizza sauce	A	1
C	Add the cheese	B	2
D	Add the sausage	C	0.75
E	Add the pepperoni	C	1
F	Package the pizza	D, E	1.5
G	Label the package	F	0.5
		Total Time	8.75

The next step is to determine the theoretical minimum number of workstations. This would be the minimum possible number of stations; the balanced line may have more stations. When determining the number of stations, *round up* to the next whole number, otherwise there will not be enough time to make all the products to meet customer demand.

(5.2)   Theoretical number of stations (N) = (Total of all task times)/(Takt time)

For the pizza example:
$$N = (2 \text{ min.} + 1 \text{ min.} + 2 \text{ min.} + .75 \text{ min.} + 1 \text{ min.} + 1.5 \text{ min.} + .5 \text{ min.})/(2.4 \text{ min. per station})$$
$$= 3.7, \text{ so round up to 4 workstations}$$

Assign as many tasks as possible to each workstation such that the sum of the task times is not greater than the takt time, which is 2.4 minutes in our example. Remember, when assigning tasks to workstations, you cannot violate the precedence relationships. For example, A must be completed before you can begin work on B.

When balancing a line, sometimes more than one task can be assigned, so you must decide which task to assign first. For example, once the pizza is topped with cheese, you can next add either sausage or pepperoni. To make this decision, you can use rules or guidelines that lead to a good, but not necessarily the best, solution. Two commonly used rules are to first enter:

1. The task with the longest operating (task) time.
2. The task with the most number of followers.

In our example, we use the longest operating time rule to assign tasks. Because both tasks D and E can be assigned after C, using the longest operating time rule, we add the pepperoni first (Task E) (see Table 5-3). If one rule results in a tie between two tasks, the other rule is typically used to decide which task to assign.

With a complex process there may be several different ways to balance the line, so select the alternative that provides the highest efficiency.

(5.3)   Efficiency = [Sum of all task times/(Actual work stations × takt time)] × 100

$$\text{Efficiency} = [(2 \text{ min.} + 1 \text{ min.} + 2 \text{ min.} + .75 \text{ min.} + 1 \text{ min.} + 1.5 \text{ min.} + .5 \text{ min.})/(5 \text{ stations} \times 2.4 \text{ min./station})] \times 100 = 73\%$$

As with the functional layout, as the number of tasks increases so does the complexity of the line balancing problem. Bottlenecks, as described in Chapter 3, are constraints that have lower output than other workstations on the line, slow the process, and reduce efficiency. To improve efficiency, reduce time at the bottleneck workstation. For example, perhaps split tasks into smaller work elements, change technology to reduce the time required, or deploy more workers at the bottleneck.

TABLE 5-3   Workstation Assignments for Pizza: Balanced Using the Longest Task Time

Workstation	Tasks in Order	Workstation Time (minutes)	Idle Time (minutes)
1	A	2	0.4
2	B	1	1.4
3	C	2	0.4
4	E, D	1.75	0.65
5	F, G	2	0.4

Cellular Layout

In situations with mid-range volume and variety, a cellular layout combines the flexibility of a small, focused job shop with the efficiency of a repetitive line. A cellular layout arranges workstations to form a number of small assembly lines called *work cells*. Workstations within each individual work cell are arranged using product layout principles. The first step in designing a cellular layout is to use group technology to identify products that have similar processing requirements, called **product families**. Product families may have similar shapes, sizes, process flows, or demand. Each work cell can be dedicated to make a product family.

product families Groups of products that have similar processing requirements.

Workers are typically dedicated to a cell and are trained in all of the activities within a cell, increasing process flexibility. As they become intimately familiar with the product and demand requirements of the cell, the workers as a team identify opportunities for improvement and take on larger roles, including planning, maintenance, and quality inspection.

Cells can make job shops or batch processes more efficient or increase the flexibility of repetitive processes. Processing time, inventory, material flow distance, and setup times are reduced, and scheduling is less complex than with functional layouts. For example, cellular manufacturing and other lean practices helped the La-Z-Boy furniture plant in Dayton, Tennessee, drastically reduce the time needed to produce and deliver a custom order. Similarly, insurance firms and banks have increased efficiencies by grouping together workers and activities that were formerly isolated into different departments.

Converting a product layout into cells creates more options in how products might be routed from cell to cell, increasing flexibility. When converting a product layout to a cellular layout, managers must determine where customization will be added to the product line. This indicates where the line should be broken, what activities should be included in each cell, and how the cells should relate to each other. Product, functional, and cellular layouts are shown in Figure 5-5. Each shape represents a different type of activity.

FIGURE 5-5 Product, Functional, and Cellular Layouts

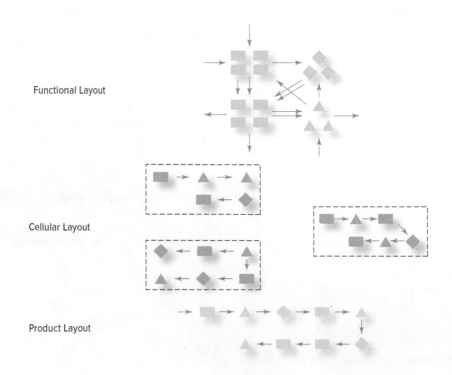

Functional Layout

Cellular Layout

Product Layout

CAPABILITY ENABLING TECHNOLOGIES

Technology has a major impact on operations and supply chains, so deciding how to use technology to enhance value for customers is an important managerial decision. Table 5-4 shows some of the technologies that are used in operations and supply chain management. Technology can reduce variation, increase efficiency, and improve safety by replacing human involvement and decision making with process automation. Advances in information technology and communications have dramatically improved operational processing, data management, visibility, and coordination across global supply chain networks. New capabilities can also be created through the use of technology, with opportunities to increase customer satisfaction or create entirely new business models—as was the case for Instagram, Uber, and Airbnb.

LO5-5 Explain how technology is used in the supply chain and the benefits and drawbacks of process automation.

Information Sharing

Quickly and accurately sharing information within the supply chain is essential for making good business decisions. Processing, communication, decision-making and integrative technologies provide the capabilities needed for information sharing. In the planning

TABLE 5-4   Types of Supply Chain Operational Technologies

Type of Technology	Capabilities	Examples
Decision support systems	Provide computing power and data management to make higher-quality decisions faster.	• Advanced planning systems • Supply chain network design • Transportation management systems (TMS) • Warehouse management systems (WMS) • Manufacturing execution systems (MES)
Processing technologies	Automate material and data processing to provide 24/7 resource availability, faster processing, greater consistency, and lower cost.	• Computer-aided design • 3D printing • Industrial robots • Drones • Flexible manufacturing systems (FMS) • Automated storage and retrieval systems (AS/RS) • Point of sale (POS) bar code scanners • Radio frequency identification (RFID) • E-procurement
Communications technologies	Create greater connectivity and speed flow of richer forms of information.	• The Internet • Mobile apps and wearables • Communication satellites • Fiber optic cables • Radio frequency data communications (RFDC)
Integrative technologies	Combine data management, communications, decision support, and processing capabilities.	• Cloud computing • Internet of Things (IoT) • Enterprise resource planning (ERP) • Product life cycle management (PLM) • Customer relationship management (CRM) • Supplier relationship management (SRM) • Collaborative planning, forecasting, and replenishment (CPFR)

phase, companies work with key customers and suppliers using collaborative planning, forecasting, and replenishment (CPFR) to ensure that they understand what products need to be made and when.

As sales are made in retail stores, sales and inventory information is automatically captured by point of sale (POS) bar codes, RFID scanners, or sensors. The data are then conveyed through the Internet to the company's enterprise resource planning system (ERP), which may be in the cloud. Inventory records are updated and, when needed, replenishment orders are generated and communicated to suppliers. The company and its suppliers may use manufacturing execution systems (MES) for their internal operations. Inventory replenishment orders that are sent from warehouses to the retail stores are scheduled and monitored using warehouse management systems (WMS) and transportation management systems (TMS). These decision support systems optimize the sequencing and routing of material flows throughout the distribution network.

Process Automation

Using technology to automate processes can increase productivity, reduce direct labor costs, and reduce variation, thereby improving quality, increasing worker safety, and improving customer service. Example automation technologies include mobile apps, robots, drones, and the Internet of Things (IoT).

Mobile apps increase convenience for customers and automate customer contact for many services. When you use an app to order a pizza, schedule a service appointment for your car, or check in for a flight, you do not have to wait for a person to assist you. This increases flexibility for you and reduces the number of customer contact employees needed by the company. In some cases, mobile apps are changing and replacing entire processes. When checking in to a Hilton hotel, for example, customers select their room and get an electronic "key" with a mobile app, allowing them to bypass the registration desk altogether.

For years robots have helped manufacturing plants to be safer and more efficient and produce higher quality products. For example, Ford Motor Company has over 20,000 robots in its factories worldwide doing everything from hazardous jobs like welding and painting, to lifting and moving heavy parts, installing windshields, and even performing quality inspections. Distribution centers also use robots extensively to pick and move products. Advances in technology are allowing "collaborative" robots to safely work side-by-side with humans. As the technology improves and the costs of robots decrease, we are likely to see more applications across a range of industries, as shown in the Get Real: Robots box below.

Drones, or unmanned aerial vehicles (UAV), are likely to bring new delivery capabilities to the supply chain. The flexibility and low cost of drone delivery make it attractive to postal services and carriers such as UPS, FedEx, and DHL. In 2015, Amazon filed a patent application for a drone delivery process in which customers can place orders using mobile devices, with order fulfillment and delivery within 30 minutes. Although there are still many regulatory, safety, and technical hurdles to overcome prior to full commercialization, drones will certainly have an impact on operations and supply chains.

The Internet of Things (IoT) allows products and machines to connect to the Internet and share data with other devices. A simple example is a washing machine that sends a text to your phone when the clothes are ready for the dryer. A more complex example is a self-driving car.

In operations and supply chains, the IoT is allowing manufacturers to gather data on product performance and make automatic changes in the process. Data can be used to optimize current products and processes, design new products, and improve customer service. For example, Diebold uses the IoT to monitor ATMs and provide maintenance before an ATM stops working, thus reducing downtime for its banking customers. Applications of the

©Andreas Rentz/Getty Images

Robots: Coming to a Pharmacy Near You?

Although robots have long been used in manufacturing, we are starting to see some surprising new applications in services. Large hospitals and pharmacies are starting to invest in robots that can fill prescriptions to increase patient safety, fill speed, and efficiency.

The University of California San Francisco Medical Center invested $15 million in a robotic system that fills prescriptions based on a doctor's electronic prescription. Compared with the traditional process previously used by the University, which had error rates of almost 3 percent, the robot fills prescriptions with remarkable accuracy. So far, it has made only one error in the six million prescriptions filled. Given that drug errors can cause injury or death, improved accuracy can be life-saving. An added benefit to the hospital is that pharmacists can now spend their time working more effectively with patients and doctors to develop treatment plans. To see the robot in action, access the following link and check out the video:

http://www.npr.org/sections/money/2015/05/27/407737439/watch-robots-transform-a-california-hospital

© 67photo/Alamy Stock Photo

IoT are currently in their infancy, but the potential for operations and supply chain management seems endless.

Despite the many benefits, there are also drawbacks to process automation. Purchasing, installing, and maintaining automation technology usually requires a high capital investment, increasing an organization's fixed costs. Limits on an organization's ability to obtain credit to finance these investments may impact its ability to automate processes. Because of the high investment, companies are sometimes reluctant to change technologies, even though they should to stay competitive.

The impact of process automation on labor should also be considered. Low wage jobs are often eliminated, but managing and maintaining automated systems requires highly skilled IT professionals, process engineers, and maintenance employees, increasing indirect labor or outsourcing costs. In some cases, customers may have concerns with the quality of a more highly automated process. For example, consider when you have to talk to an automated call center system rather than a person. When deciding to automate processes, the benefits need to be balanced against the drawbacks.

CHAPTER SUMMARY

This chapter describes some of the key decisions relating to manufacturing and service process structures and how they impact an organization's capabilities.

1. The product-process matrix classifies processes based on output volume and variety. The process types are: project, job shop, batch, repetitive process, and continuous process. Two contemporary process structures are mass customization and cellular manufacturing.

2. Services can be categorized based on customization/customer interaction and labor/capital intensity. A framework shows four classifications: professional service, service factory, service shop, and mass service.

3. The front office of a service process that is in contact with the customer has different requirements than the back office of a process that is not visible to the customer. Decoupling often increases efficiency in both the front-office and the back-office processes.

4. Layout is the physical arrangement of resources in a process. The type of layout is closely related to the type of process. Layout types are product, functional, cellular, and fixed-position.

5. Advances in technologies have enabled new business models and supply chain improvements. Process automation can reduce variation, increase efficiency, increase safety, reduce direct labor costs, and increase customer satisfaction. However, automation requires a high capital investment and highly skilled technical support, may not be able to adapt to major product changes, and in some cases may reduce customer satisfaction.

KEY TERMS

assemble to order (ATO) 148	flexible manufacturing system (FMS) 147	product families 156
back-office processes 150	front-office processes 150	product layout 153
batch process 146	functional layout 152	product-process matrix 144
cellular manufacturing 147	job shop 145	project 145
continuous process 146	line balancing 154	repetitive process 146
customer contact 149	make to order (MTO) 148	service blueprinting 150
cycle time 154	make to stock (MTS) 149	service process matrix 149
engineer to order (ETO) 148	mass customization 147	takt time 154
fixed-position layout 152	precedence relationships 154	3D printing (additive manufacturing) 147

DISCUSSION QUESTIONS

1. Airlines allow customers to purchase tickets, select seats, and check in using mobile apps. How does this process differ from a check-in process at an airline ticket counter?

2. Think of two companies in the same industry that use different process structures. Why is this the case? Is one process structure a better choice than the other? Why, or why not?

3. Consider several members of the supply chain of a company that makes plastic toy cars and trucks. Which of the processes described in the product-process matrix is likely to be used by the following supply chain members? Why?
   a. The company that assembles the toys.
   b. The company that produces the parts that go into the toys.
   c. The company that produces the plastic.

4. Provide an example of how technology has made it possible to use processes that are not on the diagonal of the product-process matrix.

5. Are some process structures inherently safer or more environmentally friendly than others?

6. In which of the service categories would you put a large state university? Why? Would a small private university be in the same category? Why, or why not?

7. Some upscale restaurants have their kitchens visible to their customers, changing the traditional view of front-office and back-office processes. What are the benefits and drawbacks to this approach?

8. Think about three of your favorite fast-food restaurants. What type of layout is used in the food preparation area of each? Are these layouts a good fit with the organization? Why, or why not? Should the layout be changed and, if so, how?

9. Provide an example of a type of technology that enhances customer service and a type of technology that reduces customer service. Why is this the case?

10. Postal services and logistics companies are experimenting with delivery using drones. What are the benefits and drawbacks of this application of technology?

SOLVED PROBLEMS

1. Using the information in Table 5-5, balance the assembly line for the Tourist T-Shirt Company. The operations run continuously for eight hours per day. Each day, 80 t-shirts must be produced to meet customer demand.
   a. Draw the precedence diagram.
   b. What is the takt time?
   c. What are the theoretical number of workstations?
   d. Assign tasks to workstations using the longest operating time rule.
   e. What is the efficiency of the balanced line?

TABLE 5-5   Precedence Relationships for Making a T-Shirt

Task		Predecessors	Time (minutes)
A	Put the pattern on the material	None	5
B	Cut out the pattern	A	3
C	Hem the neck slit opening	B	2
D	Sew the sleeve seams	B	1
E	Hem the sleeves	D	2
F	Sew the side seams of the tunic	C	3
G	Sew the sleeves to the tunic	E, F	4
H	Hem the bottom of the shirt	F	5
		Total Time	25

Solution:

a. Precedence diagram.

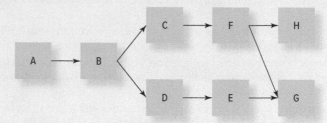

b. Takt time (T) = Production time per day/Output needed per day

   Takt time (T) = (8 hours/shift × 60 minutes/hour)/(80 T-shirts/day) = 6 minutes/ workstation

c. Theoretical minimum number of stations (N) = Total of all task times/Takt time.

   N = (25 minutes)/(6 min./station) = 4.2, so 5 stations

d. The tasks are assigned to each station in order of precedence, assigning as many tasks as possible to each station. When you can choose among multiple tasks, for example, C or D, choose the task with the longest operating time.

Workstation	Tasks in Order	Workstation Time (Min.)	Idle Time (Min.)
1	A	5	1
2	B, C, D	6	0
3	F, E	5	1
4	H	5	1
5	G	4	2

e. Efficiency = [Sum of all task times/(Actual workstations × Takt time)] × 100

   Efficiency = [(25 minutes)/(5 stations × 6 min./station)] × 100 = 83%

PROBLEMS

1. An assembly line currently has five workstations, and the time required for each is shown below.

   a. What is the current cycle time?
   b. What is the efficiency of the process?
   c. Customer demand is 80 units per hour. What is the hourly production rate of the current process?
   d. What does the cycle time need to be to be able to meet demand (i.e., what is the takt time)?
   e. What changes to the process are needed?

2. An insurance company uses the following tasks to process paperwork. Forty claims need to be processed in an *eight-hour workday*.

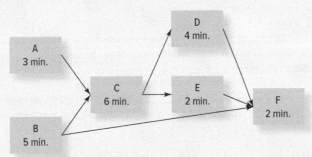

   a. What is the takt time?
   b. What is the theoretical number of workstations?
   c. Assign the tasks to the workstations to balance the line using the longest operating time rule.
   d. What is the efficiency of the balanced line?

3. Swoosh Snowboard Company must set up an assembly line for snowboards. Forecasts show that 600 units per day should be produced. The plant operates *two eight-hour shifts each day* and runs the line continuously during both shifts. The tasks required, task times, and precedence relationships are as follows:

Task	Time (seconds)	Predecessors
A	40	–
B	27	A
C	30	A
D	35	–
E	30	B
F	40	D
G	55	C, E, F
H	39	G

   a. Draw the precedence diagram.
   b. What is the takt time?

   c. What is the theoretical number of workstations?
   d. Assign the tasks to the workstations to balance the line using the longest operating time rule.
   e. What is the efficiency of the balanced line?

4. The Carry-on Luggage Company must set up an assembly line for a wheeled carry-on bag. Forecasts show that 60 units per hour should be produced. The tasks required, task times, and precedence relationships are as follows:

Task	Time (seconds)	Predecessors
A	30	–
B	50	A
C	25	A
D	10	B
E	25	B
F	15	B
G	10	C, E, F
H	30	D, G

   a. Draw the precedence diagram.
   b. What is the takt time?
   c. What is the theoretical number of workstations?
   d. Assign the tasks to the workstations to balance the line using the longest operating time rule.
   e. What is the efficiency of the balanced line?

5. Wild Widget must set up an assembly line for widgets. Forecasts show that 50 units per hour should be produced. The tasks required, task times, and precedence relationships are as follows:

Task	Time (seconds)	Predecessors
A	10	–
B	30	A
C	15	A
D	35	C, B
E	25	D
F	10	D
G	35	E, F

   a. Draw the precedence diagram.
   b. What is the takt time?
   c. What is the theoretical number of workstations?
   d. Assign the tasks to the workstations to balance the line using the longest operating time rule.
   e. What is the efficiency of the balanced line?
   f. If demand decreased to 40 units per day, what changes would be needed, if any?

6. Golf Carts Inc. must set up an assembly line for golf carts. Forecasts show that 10 units per day should be produced. The plant operates *one eight-hour shift each day* and runs the line continuously during the shift. The tasks required, task times, and precedence relationships are as follows:

Task	Time (minutes)	Predecessors
A	12	–
B	10	–
C	16	–
D	24	A, B
E	14	C
F	30	D
G	15	E, F

a. Draw the precedence diagram.
b. What is the takt time?
c. What is the theoretical number of workstations?
d. Assign the tasks to the workstations to balance the line using the longest operating time rule.
e. What is the efficiency of the balanced line?
f. If demand increased to 12 units per day, what changes would be needed, if any?

7. Williams Motor Manufacturing assembles small motors for sale to major appliance manufacturers around the world. Average demand for its best-selling motor is 600 units per day. The assembly line operates continuously during a *single eight-hour shift*. The tasks required, task times, and precedence relationships are:

Task	Time (seconds)	Predecessor
A	12	–
B	22	–
C	20	–
D	20	A
E	18	C
F	30	B, D
G	17	E
H	25	F, G
I	20	H

a. Draw the precedence diagram.
b. What is the takt time?
c. What is the theoretical number of workstations?
d. Assign the tasks to the workstations to balance the line using the longest operating time rule.
e. What is the efficiency of the balanced line?
f. If demand increased to 650 motors per day, what changes would be needed, if any?

8. A company that assembles high fidelity headphones needs to design an assembly line for one of its new products. The tasks needed and their relationships are shown in the following figure. To meet demand, the company must produce 80 headphones an hour.

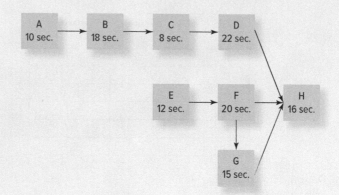

a. What is the takt time?
b. Design the line by assigning the tasks to the workstations to balance the line using the longest operating time rule.
c. Redesign the assembly line by assigning the tasks to the workstations to balance the line using the most number of followers rule. If a tie is encountered, use the longest operating time rule to decide which task to enter.
d. Which approach to line balancing results in the most efficient assembly line?

9. The Office Interiors Company has developed a new, modern office chair. Initial sales forecasts are for 50 chairs per day. The assembly operations will run for *two eight-hour shifts*. The process engineer and operations manager are working together to balance the line to make the new chair as efficiently as possible. The process engineer suggests using the longest operating time rule while the operations manager suggests using the most number of followers rule to design the line. If there is a tie, use the other rule to break the tie. Based on the processing information, which approach do you recommend? Why?

Task	Time (Minutes)	Predecessor
A	7	–
B	12	A
C	6	B
D	13	–
E	8	C, D
F	10	–
G	4	F
H	10	E, G

CASE

Coffee Roasters

Once considered a commodity product, many small boutique coffee companies are luring customers with promises of high quality and unique flavors. How do the processes used by the small companies compare with those of the major coffee processors? Coffee producers purchase green coffee beans, which have been processed through several steps. At the manufacturer, green coffee beans are screened to remove debris, and then roasted for up to 30 minutes. A roaster is typically a rotating drum in which the beans are heated. The length of time spent in the roaster impacts coffee flavor. The longer the time spent in the roaster, the richer the coffee flavor. Following roasting, beans are sprayed with water, cooled, and screened to remove any remaining debris. Once roasted, coffee is ground to the size required for the brewing process and packaged.

Ohori's Coffee is an example of a boutique coffee company. Established in 1984, Ohori's Coffee is located in Santa Fe, New Mexico. This privately owned business microroasts 32 types of coffee from Africa, the Saudi peninsula, Indonesia, the Pacific Rim, and North and South America. In batch sizes of 30 pounds or less, coffee beans are roasted in natural gas-fired rotating drum roasters carefully monitored by highly skilled "master roasters." To maintain quality, Ohori's depends on humans, not computer controls in the roasting process. Online and in its Santa Fe location, Ohori's sells whole beans and 10 different grinds ranging from Percolator to Turkish style. (Source: http://ohoriscoffee.com.)

Folgers Coffee was purchased from Procter & Gamble in 2008 by the J. M. Smucker Company in a deal reportedly worth $3.3 billion. Folgers Coffee accounts for over 30 percent of the U.S. packaged coffee market, with over $2 billion in sales. Sales growth is estimated to be 2–3 percent per year.

Folgers's largest roasting and blending facility is in New Orleans, with 550 employees. It also has manufacturing operations in Kansas City, Missouri, and Sherman, Texas. The distribution center for Folgers is near New Orleans in Lacombe, Louisiana. Its coffee is sold in a single grind type. The company sells three Classic blends, seven blends in its Coffee House product line, five types of flavored ground coffee, and 10 flavors of Folgers Gourmet Selections.

Folgers has introduced an enhanced roasting process for its Classic products. The coffee beans are preconditioned to reduce moisture and improve consistency before the final roasting. (Source: www.folgers.com.)

Think about the production processes used by Ohori's and Folgers.

Questions

1. Using the product-process matrix, which processes are likely to be used by Ohori's and Folgers? Why?

2. Explain how the choice of process supports each organization's competitive priorities.

3. Is the operations layout likely to be the same or different at Ohori's and Folgers? Why?

4. What changes would Folgers need to make to compete directly with Ohori's? Why?

CASE

Sonnie's Gourmet Sandwich Café

Sonnie's Gourmet Sandwich Café, a popular new fast casual restaurant, serves high-quality, made-to-order sandwiches. Located in a local outdoor shopping center, parking in front of Sonnie's is limited. However, there are many parking spaces available behind the café within a five-minute walk. The café has an inviting, bright, and open interior with deli cases, blackboards listing specials, and oak tables and chairs.

The café's popularity at lunch is a concern for Sonnie. During the prime lunch time between 11:30 a.m. and 1:30 p.m. Monday through Friday, the waiting line is often out the door. On average Sonnie would like to serve 40 customers per hour at lunch. Working professionals, who typically spend more than other customers at lunch, are on busy schedules and do not have time to wait in line. Sonnie estimates that currently some customers go to other restaurants because of the line.

The menu at Sonnie's includes nine standard sandwiches such as roast beef, pastrami and rye, and a BLT. Many customers choose to build their own sandwiches, selecting from eight types of bread, 25 meats, 12 cheeses, and 20 different vegetables. Sandwiches are served with chips or a choice of four types of salad.

Order Placement

When customers enter the café, they walk past a large deli counter displaying meats and cheese on their left and stop in front of a counter to place their orders. An employee greets the customer, asks for each customer's name, then takes his or her order by filling out a two-part paper form. Because of the number of choices, customers take, on average, 1 minute and 20 seconds to place their orders. However, those ordering standard sandwiches complete the order in about 1 minute. The employee gives the top part

of the order form to the customer (10 seconds) to take to the cashier and the other is handed to the next employee in line, who starts working on the order. The employee who took the order then fills the customer's beverage order and hands it to the customer (30 seconds). The customer then walks about 15 feet to the cashier and pays, which on average takes 1 minute and 30 seconds. Then the customer selects a table and waits for his or her name to be called when the order is complete.

Order Fulfillment Process

Three employees work in the food preparation area, which uses a product layout. The first employee in the food preparation line puts the choice of side on a plate (35 seconds) and then assembles the sandwich from presliced bread, meat, and cheese, a task that takes about 1 minute and 20 seconds. The sandwich is handed off to the next employee, who adds toppings and sauces (45 seconds) and slices the sandwich (10 seconds). The last employee checks the order for accuracy (15 seconds), moves the sandwich to the pick-up area, and calls the customer by name (20 seconds).

Questions

1. Compared to a fast-food restaurant such as McDonald's, where would Sonnie's sandwich shop be placed on the service process matrix? What challenges and opportunities does this position create relative to McDonald's? Why?

2. How many customers is the current process able to accommodate per hour?

3. Use line balancing and service blueprinting to redesign the process at Sonnie's. What changes do you recommend? Why?

SELECTED
READINGS & INTERNET SITES

Berman, B. "Should Your Firm Adopt a Mass Customization Strategy?" *Business Horizons* 45, no. 4 (2002), pp. 51–61.

Bitner, M.; A. Ostrom; and F. Morgan. "Service Blueprinting: A Practical Technique for Service Innovation." *California Management Review* 50, no. 3 (2008), pp. 66–94.

Chase, R. B., and D. A. Tansik. "The Customer Contact Model for Organizational Design." *Management Science* 29, no. 9 (1983), pp. 1037–50.

D'Aveni, R. "The 3D Printing Revolution." *Harvard Business Review* 93, no. 5 (2015), pp. 40–48.

Hayes, R., and S. Wheelwright. "Link Manufacturing Process and Product Life Cycles." *Harvard Business Review* 57, no. 1 (1979), pp. 133–40.

Hayes, R., and S. Wheelwright. *Restoring Our Competitive Edge: Competing Through Manufacturing.* New York: John Wiley & Sons, 1984.

Lummus, R.; R. Vokurka; and L. Duclos. "The Product-Process Matrix Revisited: Integrating Supply Chain Trade-offs." *SAM Advanced Management Journal* 71, no. 2 (2006), pp. 4–10, 20, 45.

Marsh, R. "Amazon Drone Patent Application that Comes to You with One Click." CNN Politics, May 12, (2015), http://www.cnn.com/2015/05/12/politics/amazon-patent-drone-delivery/

McKenzie, S. "Rise of Robots: The Evolution of Ford's Assembly Line."(2015) http://money.cnn.com/gallery/technology/2015/04/29/ford-factory-assembly-line-robots/index.html

Minter, S. "2012 IW Best Plants Winners: La-Z-Boy Never Rests on Continuous Improvement." *Industry-Week,*" (Jan. 17, 2013) http://www.industryweek.com/iw-best-plants/2012-iw-best-plants-winner-la-z-boy-never-rests-continuous-improvement

Porter, M. E. and J. E. Heppelmann. "How Smart, Connected Products Are Transforming Competition." *Harvard Business Review* 92, no. 11 (2014), pp. 64–88.

Safizadeh, M., and L. Ritzman. "An Empirical Analysis of the Product-Process Matrix." *Management Science* 42, no. 11 (1996), pp. 1576–95.

Sampson, S., and C. Froehle. "Foundations and Implications of a Proposed Unified Services Theory." *Production and Operations Management* 15, no. 2 (2006), pp. 329–43.

Schmenner, R. "How Can Service Business Survive and Prosper?" *Sloan Management Review* 27, no. 3 (1986), pp. 21–32.

Schmenner, R. "Service Businesses and Productivity." *Decision Sciences* 35, no. 3 (2004), pp. 333–47.

Selladurai, R. "Mass Customization in Operations Management: Oxymoron or Reality?" *Omega* 32, no. 4 (2004), pp. 295–301.

Sohel, A., and R. Schroeder. "Refining the Product-Process Matrix." *International Journal of Operations and Production Management* 22, no. 1 (2002), pp. 103–25.

Solomon, M. "Your iPhone as Hotel Room Key: Hilton Shakes up Hospitality Industry." *Forbes* (July 31, 2014), http://www.forbes.com/sites/micahsolomon/2014/07/31/hilton-shakes-hospitality-industry/

Verma, R. "An Empirical Analysis of Management Challenges in Service Factories, Service Shops, Mass Services, and Professional Services." *International Journal of Service Industry Management* 11, no. 1 (2000), pp. 8–25.

Verma, R., and K. Boyer. "Service Classification and Management Challenges." *Journal of Business Strategies* 17, no. 1 (2000), pp. 5–24.

Hilton Worldwide http://news.hiltonworldwide.com/index.cfm/news/hilton-worldwide-truly-opens-doors-company-to-roll-out-mobile-room-keys-in-2015-at-hundreds-of-us-hotels-across-four-brands

Invisalign
www.invisalign.com

Jostens
www.jostens.com

Martha Stewart
www.marthastewart.com/article/mandm-factory-tour

My M&Ms
www.mymms.com

NPR news article
http://www.npr.org/sections/money/2015/05/27/407737439/watch-robots-transform-a-california-hospital

Spangler Candy
www.spanglercandy.com

12

Demand Planning: Forecasting and Demand Management

LEARNING OBJECTIVES *After studying this chapter, you should be able to:*

LO12-1 Explain the role of demand planning in operations management, in the firm, and in the supply chain.

LO12-2 Differentiate between demand planning, demand forecasting, and demand management activities.

LO12-3 Describe various qualitative and quantitative demand forecasting procedures.

LO12-4 Develop forecasts using moving average, exponential smoothing, and linear regression models.

LO12-5 Evaluate and select forecasting models using various measures of accuracy and bias.

LO12-6 Explain how certain improvements to both product design and operations across the supply chain can make demand planning easier.

© Kiichiro Sato/AP Images

Demand Forecasting Excellence Gives Longaberger an Advantage

The Longaberger Company (www.longaberger.com) is known primarily for its high-quality baskets—still handmade, just like when the company was born in 1918. In recent years Longaberger has experienced phenomenal growth; quite a feat considering the challenges of competing in the home decorating industry. Demand planning in general, and sales forecasting in particular, are usually quite tough for a fast-growing company with a complex set of continually changing product lines. Since these are "fashion" items subject to changing trends and customer tastes, it is often difficult to judge which products will be fast sellers and which will be slow. Moreover, keeping track of pricing changes and promotional programs can be a complex planning task.

Forecasting processes at Longaberger must consider many different factors, including the growth strategy of the company, seasonal and holiday demand patterns, and both regular and irregular promotional events. The forecasting approach used at Longaberger addresses these factors by integrating three sources of information: historical sales trends and seasonal patterns; economic data quantifying market, sales, and environmental conditions; and the qualitative judgmental expertise of managers.

For Longaberger, the key to forecasting success has not been to simply pick the "right" statistical analysis method, but rather to develop an integrated system of techniques to help managers accurately plan for future demand. Forecasts generated by the system drive all kinds of production, procurement, and capacity management plans. Ultimately, the accuracy and insights provided by the demand planning system have been instrumental in helping the Longaberger Company give customers the products they want, when they want them.

DEMAND PLANNING: AN OVERVIEW

Almost all operational planning activities start with some estimate of what customers' demands will be. In order to develop demand estimates, every company has to forecast both the quantity and timing of demands, and many companies can also influence or "manage" customers' demand patterns through product pricing and through other means. These two activities, demand forecasting and demand management, are collectively known as *demand planning*.

Demand planning is the combined process of forecasting and managing customer demands to create a planned pattern of demand that meets the firm's operational and financial goals. **Demand forecasting** is a decision process in which managers predict demand patterns, whereas **demand management** is a proactive approach in which managers attempt to influence patterns of demand. Usually, demand management involves the use of pricing and promotional activities.

By doing a good job of demand planning, operations managers can more effectively plan for the amount of productive capacity and other resources their business will need, both in the short term and in the long term. Demand planning also helps operations managers know what customers they should serve and at what levels of service. Demand planning is especially difficult when products have highly varying and uncertain demand patterns. Precisely because it is so difficult, companies like Longaberger have built competitive advantages as a result of their superior abilities.

The Role That Demand Planning Plays in Operations Management

Demand planning drives almost all other activities in operations management. For many tangible products, making products to order is not an option. The lead time required is longer than customers are willing to wait. For example, you probably would not be willing to wait for a company to build a toaster oven from scratch for you. Consequently, managers have to anticipate demand and plan what materials and resources they will need well in advance of actual orders. In order to make these production plans, managers need to make good predictions of the quantities of products that will be demanded at a given time and place. Accurate planning information has many benefits, and there are severe costs to being wrong. The costs of making forecasts that are too high include money lost in holding inventory that is never sold, lost capacity that is spent making products that no one wants to buy, lost wages spent paying workers who are not needed, and so on. These costs are borne by firms throughout the supply chain, but they are also passed on to customers in the form of higher prices. Similarly, costs of making forecasts that are too low include lost sales and lower product availability for customers.

Planning Activities

Figure 12-1 illustrates how demand forecasting and demand management activities relate to one another and to other operational planning activities. Forecasting activities integrate information gathered from the market, from internal operations, and from the larger business environment to make predictions about future demand. This information includes past demand, past forecasts and their associated errors, business and economic metrics, and the judgments of experts. In addition, the forecasting system uses demand management plans that specify the firm's pricing strategies and promotional plans. By combining all of these factors, the forecasting system creates new forecasts of future demand. The demand management system in turn uses these forecasts as inputs for future demand management planning. In addition, the forecasts and demand management plans are passed on to materials and capacity planning and scheduling systems. These systems are used to manage resources and operating processes.

		Actual Demand (a)	Average Demand Estimate (from regression) (b)	Seasonal Index SI = a/b	Three Week Average Indexes
Week 2	Thursday	147.2	173.8	0.85	
	Friday	214.2	177.9	1.20	
	Saturday	190.0	182.0	1.04	
	Sunday	202.1	186.1	1.09	
	Monday	159.0	190.1	0.84	
	Tuesday	178.7	194.2	0.92	
	Wednesday	160.0	198.3	0.81	
Week 3	Thursday	181.5	202.4	0.90	
	Friday	212.8	206.5	1.03	
	Saturday	249.4	210.6	1.18	
	Sunday	242.9	214.7	1.13	

TABLE 12-5   Calculating Seasonal Indexes Using Average Demand per Cycle as the Base

		Actual Demand (a)	Average Demand for Week (b)	Seasonal Index SI = a/b	Three Week Average Indexes
Week 1	Monday	123.6		0.78	Average SI for Mondays = 0.82
	Tuesday	135.0		0.85	Average SI for Tuesdays = 0.84
	Wednesday	160.0		1.01	Average SI for Wednesdays = 0.89
Week 1	Thursday	140.4	159.1	0.88	Average SI for Thursdays = 0.89
	Friday	187.9		1.18	Average SI for Fridays = 1.18
	Saturday	195.0		1.23	Average SI for Saturdays = 1.21
	Sunday	171.8		1.08	Average SI for Sundays = 1.17
	Monday	145.9		0.87	
	Tuesday	130.0		0.77	
	Wednesday	145.0		0.86	
Week 2	Thursday	147.2	167.8	0.88	
	Friday	214.2		1.28	
	Saturday	190.0		1.13	
	Sunday	202.1		1.20	

(continued)

(continued)

		Actual Demand (a)	Average Demand for Week (b)	Seasonal Index SI = a/b	Three Week Average Indexes
	Monday	159.0		0.80	
	Tuesday	178.7		0.90	
	Wednesday	160.0		0.81	
Week 3	Thursday	181.5	197.8	0.92	
	Friday	212.8		1.08	
	Saturday	249.4		1.26	
	Sunday	242.9		1.23	

Note that the seasonal indexes in Tables 12-4 and 12-5 are not exactly the same, but they are fairly close. Using the average demand in each cycle as the base for calculating the seasonal index can be thought of as a looser approximation method than the regression approach. In practice, however, either approach can be effective.

The next step is to use the average seasonal indexes to adjust the future forecasts. For example, regression-based forecasts (the average demands) for the next two weeks (weeks 4 and 5) would be adjusted as shown in Table 12-6. Note that we could use a method other than regression for generating the base demand; it is up to the forecaster to decide what method best approximates trends or other demand patterns that exist before seasonal impacts.

TABLE 12-6   Seasonal Adjustments for Forecasts

		Forecasted Base Demand (from regression) (a)	Seasonal Index (b)	Adjusted Forecast a × b
	Monday	218.7	0.89	194.6
	Tuesday	222.8	0.90	200.5
	Wednesday	226.9	0.93	211.0
Week 4	Thursday	231.0	0.90	207.9
	Friday	235.1	1.16	272.7
	Saturday	239.2	1.17	279.9
	Sunday	243.3	1.10	267.6
	Monday	247.4	0.89	220.2
	Tuesday	251.4	0.90	226.3
	Wednesday	255.5	0.93	237.6
Week 5	Thursday	259.6	0.90	233.6
	Friday	263.7	1.16	305.9
	Saturday	267.8	1.17	313.3
	Sunday	271.9	1.10	299.1

Figure 12-7 shows the forecasts for weeks 3, 4, and 5 of the time series. Compare this to the forecasts shown in Figure 12-5. The seasonally adjusted forecasts clearly do a better job of matching seasonal shifts in the demand pattern. Note that the forecasts presented in Figure 12-5 lag the shifts by at least one period.

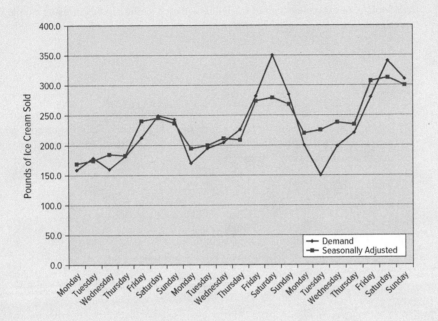

FIGURE 12-7
Seasonally Adjusted Forecasts

Causal Models

Where time series models use only past demand values as indicators of future demand, causal models use other independent, observed data to predict demand. These models concentrate on external factors that are thought to *cause* demand. For example, the amount of household disposable income in an economy might be a good leading indicator of the sales of luxury items, such as sailboats.

As mentioned earlier, regression analysis is the most commonly used method for estimating relationships between leading indicators and demand. In fact, the technique can be extended to include multiple indicators in a multiple regression analysis. In this approach, a forecaster would gather past data describing demand and multiple independent indicators considered important as predictors of demand. The regression analysis computes the coefficients (indicator weights), forming an equation that best describes the past relationships between the predictors and the actual demand data. The resulting equation is then used to forecast future values of demand, based on observed values of the leading indicators. For example, we might see the following multiple regression equation used to forecast sailboats sales:

$$\text{Sales forecast} = B + b_d(D) + b_a(A) + b_f(F) + b_s(S)$$

where:

    B = Base sales (computed y-intercept)
    D = Disposable personal income
    A = Advertising expenditures
    F = Fuel prices
    S = Sales from prior year

Each of the indicator weights (values of b) is computed by a regression method. Each value of b represents the incremental contribution of the corresponding leading indicator to the sales forecast.

Simple Linear Regression: Causal Modeling

Let's look at an example of causal modeling with one leading indicator using simple linear regresssion.

EXAMPLE 12-7

Suppose that you manage a small ice cream shop. People tend to buy ice cream on hot days, so you suspect that each day's high temperature might be a good predictor of ice cream sales. Table 12-7 provides daily sales and temperature data for three weeks of shop operations.

TABLE 12-7   Ice Cream Shop Sales and Daily High Temperatures

		High Temperature (degrees F)	Sales (lb.)		
		t	d_t	$t * d_t$	t^2
Week 1	Monday	70	123.6	8652.0	4900.0
	Tuesday	78	135.0	10530.5	6084.0
	Wednesday	75	160.0	12000.0	5625.0
	Thursday	60	140.4	8424.0	3600.0
	Friday	66	187.9	12401.4	4356.0
	Saturday	75	195.0	14625.0	5625.0
	Sunday	82	171.8	14087.6	6724.0
Week 2	Monday	75	145.9	10942.5	5625.0
	Tuesday	60	130.0	7800.0	3600.0
	Wednesday	63	145.0	9135.0	3969.0
	Thursday	64	147.2	9420.8	4096.0
	Friday	75	214.2	16065.0	5625.0
	Saturday	81	190.0	15390.0	6561.0
	Sunday	83	202.1	16774.3	6889.0
Week 3	Monday	78	159.0	12402.0	6084.0
	Tuesday	85	178.7	15189.5	7225.0
	Wednesday	85	160.0	13600.0	7225.0
	Thursday	82	181.5	14883.0	6724.0
	Friday	85	212.8	18088.0	7225.0
	Saturday	87	249.4	21697.8	7569.0
	Sunday	87	242.9	21132.3	7569.0
	Total			283240.2	122900.0
	Average	76.0	174.9		

Using the linear regression formulae with temperature as the leading indicator variable, the slope and the intercept are:

$$b = [283240.2 - (21)(76.0)(174.9)]/[122900 - (21)(76.0)^2] = 2.6 \text{ per degree F}$$

$$a = (174.9) - (2.6)(76.0) = -21.1$$

The trend results indicate that the ice cream shop should expect to sell an additional pound of ice cream each time the high temperature for a day rises by 2.6 degrees F. Suppose that the forecast is for a warming trend over the next three days with high temperatures of 82, 84, and 87 degrees, respectively. Using the causal regression model, the forecasted sales for the shop would be given as follows:

$$F_t = a + bt = -21.1 + 2.6*82 = 190.5 \text{ pounds}$$

$$F_t + 1 = a + bt = -21.1 + 2.6*84 = 195.6 \text{ pounds}$$

$$F_t + 2 = a + bt = -21.1 + 2.6*87 = 203.4 \text{ pounds}$$

Simulation Models

Simulation models are sophisticated mathematical programs that offer forecasters the ability to evaluate different business scenarios that might yield different demand outcomes. This evaluation helps forecasters to better understand how different variables and drivers of demand relate to one another.

A relatively simple simulation-based approach is known as **focused forecasting**. Focused forecasting combines common sense inputs from frontline personnel (such as sales managers) with a computer simulation process. The focused forecasting process asks managers to suggest rules of thumb that should be followed when developing forecasts. For example, one rule might be, "We will probably sell 10 percent more product this month than we did in the same month last year." These types of rules are embedded in a simulation model, and their usefulness is then tested by estimating how effective they collectively would have been in predicting demand data from the past. The forecaster then makes new forecasts using the combination of rules that would have provided the best forecasts for the past demands. Managers from different functional areas adjust the forecasts as they see fit. This approach has delivered better results than those provided by exponential smoothing or other time series–based models. However, the focused forecasting approach requires more preparation and user involvement.

simulation models Sophisticated mathematical programs that offer forecasters the ability to evaluate different business scenarios that might yield different demand outcomes.

focused forecasting A combination of common sense inputs from frontline personnel and a computer simulation process.

Artificial Intelligence

Artificial intelligence is a broad term that describes learning and decision making capability exhibited by machines or software. In the world of forecasting, artificial intelligence can be considered a next generation approach that combines time series analysis, causal modeling, simulation, and focused forecasting techniques. However, instead of requiring manager inputs (as focused forecasting does), learning algorithms that are embedded in forecasting software are able to develop rules and heuristics on their own. Artificial intelligence systems are linked to sources of data (e.g., the Internet, company sales, planning and transaction systems, and external data feeds) that they constantly scour for relevant information.

artificial intelligence Refers to learning and decision making capability that stems from software algorithms.

activity

student

Interview one or two small business managers. Ask them to describe their demand forecasting processes.

By constantly analyzing correlations between massive amounts of diverse data and demand values, the software "learns" how to weight and adapt various inputs that represent drivers of demand. Artificial intelligence systems combine massive search capability, computational power, and learning algorithms to produce more accurate demand forecasts. The nearby Get Real box describes how Lennox Industries recently implemented such a system.

GET REAL

Lennox Uses Artificial Intelligence to Improve Its Demand Planning

Lennox Industries is a global producer and service provider for heating and air conditioning equipment. The company maintains over 250,000 SKU-locations throughout its growing global network. Lennox recently launched an initiative to improve its inventory and service levels while more than doubling the number of locations in its distribution and service network.

As an important component of the initiative, Lennox purchased the SO99+ forecasting system from ToolsGroup, a demand planning vendor. By integrating the SO99+ system with its enterprise resource planning (ERP) and other information systems, Lennox enabled the artificially intelligent system to automatically adjust demand predictions minute by minute as point of sale (POS) data are automatically loaded. Further, the platform can monitor social media and incorporate positive and negative product or brand mentions in order to augment demand forecasting. The system continuously updates its demand prediction algorithms by making corrections based on updates of data describing demand drivers and actual sales.

The company attributes the following improvements to its forecasting system implementation:

- Reduced inventory by 20 percent, despite a 250 percent increase in physical locations.
- Improved same-day delivery to 40 percent and increased orders that can be delivered the next morning from 35 percent to 98 percent.

- Reduced distribution costs as a percentage of sales by more than 15 percent.
- Improved service levels by 20 percent, with a 15 percent increase in fill rate.

Companies like Lennox are particularly good candidates for sophisticated forecasting systems. Lennox's customers demand high levels of service, and the company makes a wide range of products and replacement parts that have highly seasonal and unpredictable demands.

© lisafx/iStock/Getty Images

LO12-5 Evaluate and select forecasting models using various measures of accuracy and bias.

forecast accuracy The measurement of how closely the forecast aligns with the observations over time.

forecast bias The tendency of a forecasting technique to continually overpredict or underpredict demand. Also called *mean forecast error*.

ASSESSING THE PERFORMANCE OF THE FORECASTING PROCESS

The primary measure of forecasting performance is forecast error. As we noted earlier, forecast error is defined as the actual demand value minus the forecasted demand value for a given time period. Thus, a positive forecast error indicates an overly pessimistic forecast; a negative value indicates an overly optimistic forecast. Forecast errors can be examined to determine two primary aspects of forecast performance over time: *forecast accuracy* and *forecast bias*. **Forecast accuracy** measures how closely the forecast aligns with the observations over time. Every error, whether the forecast was too high or too low, reduces accuracy. **Forecast bias**, on the other hand, is simply the average error. Forecast bias indicates the tendency of a forecasting technique to continually overpredict or underpredict demand.

Forecast bias is the average forecast error over a number of periods:

$$\text{(12.12)} \qquad \text{Bias} = \text{Mean forecast error (MFE)} = \frac{\sum_{t=1}^{n} (d_t - F_t)}{n}$$

A positive forecast bias indicates that over time forecasts tend to be too low; a negative bias indicates that forecasts tend to be too high.

Forecast bias makes intuitive sense, and it is simple to calculate. However, it does not always allow easy comparisons across products when the average demands are different. Suppose that your company sells two different products, gadgets and widgets, at the rate of about 1,000 per month and 10 per month, respectively. Now suppose that the bias for each of the products over the past few months using both metrics is equal to 5. This means that, on average, the forecasts for each of these two products were below demand by about five units each month. Does this mean that both forecasting models are performing equally well? Certainly not! A bias of 5 units on 1,000 units of sales is outstanding performance, whereas a bias of 5 units on 10 units of sales is relatively poor performance.

For comparability's sake, forecasters often compute average error (bias) on a percentage basis. This metric is known as **mean percent error (MPE)** and is calculated as:

> **mean percent error (MPE)** Average error represented as a percentage of demand.

$$\text{(12.13)} \qquad \text{Mean percent error (MPE)} = \frac{\sum_{t=1}^{n} \frac{d_t - F_t}{d_t} * 100}{n}$$

Remember that both average forecast error and mean percent error are good indicators of bias, but they do not necessarily provide good indications of forecast *accuracy*. A measure of forecast accuracy seeks to indicate the overall errors, regardless of the direction of the errors. Forecasts that are too low or too high are both undesirable. The simplest measure of forecast accuracy is known as **mean absolute deviation (MAD)** (or the *mean absolute error*). This measure provides the average size of forecast errors, irrespective of their directions. It is computed as:

> **mean absolute deviation (MAD)** The average size of forecast errors, irrespective of their directions. Also called *mean absolute error*.

$$\text{(12.14)} \qquad \text{Mean absolute deviation (MAD)} = \frac{\sum_{t=1}^{n} |d_t - F_t|}{n}$$

EXAMPLE 12-8

Table 12-8 shows the calculation of bias or mean forecast error (MFE) and MAD for two different forecasting models. While the bias for model 2 is slightly higher than that of model 1, model 2 is preferred to model 1 because its MAD is far smaller (9.3 as compared to 50). A forecasting manager can use this approach to test many different model parameters and then select the model that yields the lowest errors.

TABLE 12-8   Computing Bias (MFE) and MAD

Period	Actual Demand	Forecast Model 1	Forecast Error	Absolute Error	Forecast Model 2	Forecast Error	Absolute Error
1	100	150	−50	50	104	−4	4
2	100	50	50	50	93	7	7
3	100	150	−50	50	88	12	12
4	100	50	50	50	102	−2	2

(continued)

(continued)

Period	Actual Demand	Forecast Model 1	Forecast Error	Absolute Error	Forecast Model 2	Forecast Error	Absolute Error
5	100	150	−50	50	90	10	10
6	100	50	50	50	107	−7	7
7	100	150	−50	50	89	11	11
8	100	50	50	50	83	17	17
9	100	150	−50	50	110	−10	10
10	100	50	50	50	113	−13	13
		Average	0	50		2.1	9.3
			MFE	MAD		MFE	MAD

We should note that for normally distributed forecast errors, 1 MAD equals 0.80 standard deviations (or 1.25 MAD equals 1 standard deviation). We will return to this point later.

For purposes of comparability across products, forecasters sometimes adjust the MAD to create a related metric, the **mean absolute percentage error (MAPE)**. The MAPE indicates how large errors are relative to the actual demand quantities. Computationally, the MAPE is determined as follows:

mean absolute percentage error (MAPE) The MAD represented as a percentage of demand.

(12.15) $$\text{Mean absolute percentage error (MAPE)} = \frac{\sum_{t=1}^{n} * 100\frac{|d_t - F_t|}{d_t}}{n}$$

Though intuitively appealing, measures like MAD and MAPE are sometimes inadequate as measures of forecast accuracy in that they do not recognize that forecasts that are really far off the mark may be more harmful to the user than forecasts that miss the actual demand by a small amount. To deal with this issue of sensitivity to the magnitude of the errors, researchers developed the **mean squared error (MSE)**.

mean squared error (MSE) A more sensitive measure of forecast errors that approximates the error variance.

(12.16) $$\text{Mean squared error (MSE)} = \frac{\sum_{t=1}^{n} (d_t - F_t)^2}{n-1}$$

Because of the squared term, the MSE gives exponentially more weight to larger and larger errors. The MSE equation looks like the formula for the variance of the forecast errors. However, there are some important differences. The variance of errors would use the actual forecast errors and the mean of the forecast errors.

(12.17) $$\text{Forecast error variance} = \frac{\sum_{t=1}^{n} (e_t - \bar{e})^2}{n-1}$$

where
    e_t = the forecast error for period t
    $\bar{e}$ = the mean forecast error

At the same time, the MSE usually does give a decent *approximation* of the variance of forecast errors. Thus, the square root of MSE provides a good approximation of the standard deviation. For this reason, forecasters often track the **root mean squared error (RMSE)**, or

root mean squared error (RMSE)
Gives an approximation of the forecast error standard deviation.

(12.18)   Root mean squared error (RMSE) = $\sqrt{\text{MSE}}$

EXAMPLE 12-9

To compare the measures of forecast accuracy, let's apply them to the data presented in Table 12-9. Here, we calculate the MAD to be 6.7 and the RMSE to be 8.3. As was mentioned earlier, the MAD value is typically 80 percent of the value of the standard deviation of error. Dividing the MAD by 0.80 yields 8.4. Thus, both the adjusted MAD and RMSE provide good rough approximations to the actual standard deviation of forecast errors, which in this case is 8.2.

TABLE 12-9   Assessing Forecast Accuracy: A Comparison of MAD, RMSE, and Standard Deviation

Period	Actual	Forecast	Forecast Error (Actual− Forecast)	Absolute Error |Actual− Forecast|	Error Squared
1	345	340	5	5	25
2	328	341	−13	13	156
3	335	339	−4	4	18
4	330	339	−9	9	78
5	334	338	−4	4	16
6	340	338	2	2	6
7	338	338	0	0	0
8	328	338	−10	10	96
9	345	337	8	8	67
10	350	338	12	12	153
			8.2	6.7	8.3
			STD DEV	MAD	RMSE

Tracking Forecast Error Acceptability

Forecasters generally use forecasting metrics such as MAD and MSE to quickly and continuously evaluate forecasting models, sometimes for thousands of different products at a time. In this environment, metrics are often used to identify exceptional cases that require adjustments to model parameters. Managers need a simple test for determining when the forecast error is unacceptable. One way to test the forecast error is to develop a control chart in which forecast errors are plotted and compared to expected upper and lower control limits.[2] Such a control chart is illustrated in Figure 12-8. Several statistical tests can be done to determine with some level of confidence whether or not forecast errors are exhibiting new and unacceptable patterns.

---

[2]The logic and steps for building such a control chart are presented in the Chapter 3 Supplement.

422 **chapter 12** Demand Planning: Forecasting and Demand Management

FIGURE 12-8 Tracking
Signal Control Chart

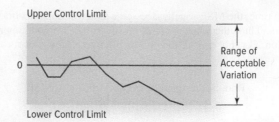

Upper Control Limit

0

Range of
Acceptable
Variation

Lower Control Limit

tracking signal The ratio of a
running total of forecast error to
MAD that indicates when the pattern of forecast error is changing
significantly.

In lieu of these rather sophisticated tests, managers often opt for a simpler metric known as the **tracking signal**. The tracking signal records the ratio of a running total of forecast error to MAD. Mathematically, this signal is expressed as

(12.19)
$$\text{Tracking signal} = \frac{\sum_{t=1}^{n}(d_t - F_t)}{MAD_{t=1 \to n}}$$

The tracking signal is essentially a comparison of forecast bias (sum of errors, rather than MFE) to forecast accuracy (MAD) over n periods. By tracking this metric over successive periods of time, managers can observe whether undesirable trends or highly biased errors are occurring. For example, managers might program a computer to compute the tracking signal each month using the most recent six months of data. If the tracking signal exceeds some control limit value, say $+/-3$, then the computer would send an alert to the forecaster. Tracking signal control limits are typically set somewhere between $+/-3$ and $+/-8$. A smaller limit gives a more sensitive indicator and would probably be used for high volume or high revenue items.

adaptive forecasting A technique
that automatically adjusts forecast
model parameters in accordance
with changes in the tracking signal.

Once a tracking signal control limit is exceeded, forecasters take action by changing the forecasting approach or model parameters. In **adaptive forecasting**, the smoothing coefficients in exponential smoothing models are automatically adjusted as a function of the tracking signal (a larger tracking signal creates a larger smoothing coefficient). Such automatic correction for unpredictable data can simplify the life of the manager, but when a particular demand forecast routinely misstates actual results, it warrants some sort of management intervention. For example, when the tracking signal frequently exceeds control limits, this suggests that something in the underlying process that drives demand has fundamentally changed and needs to be investigated. This investigation should include some assessment of the real effects of poor forecasts on organization operations. For example, consistently low forecasts may suggest that the popularity of the product has grown. Managers may also decide to raise the safety stock level to keep more inventory as a buffer against the continuing uncertainty.

Past patterns of forecast errors can give managers hints about the processes that generate both demand and errors. Such knowledge can help managers focus resources to develop sales plans and eliminate the causes of undesirable errors. Hence, forecasters should review the model and the parameters of a forecasting tool that fails to capture actual demand accurately.

Situational Drivers of Forecast Accuracy

global

All forecasters want to develop accurate forecasts. However, some demand forecasting situations create greater challenges than others. The following "rules" give an indication of how situational characteristics tend to affect forecast accuracy:

Rule 1: Short-term forecasts are usually more accurate than long-term forecasts. It is almost always easier to predict what will happen tomorrow than it is to predict what will happen next week or next year (think about predicting the weather, for example). As the time horizon for forecasting increases, more and more potentially unknown factors can affect demand.

Rule 2: Forecasts of aggregated demand are usually more accurate than forecasts of demand at detailed levels. Aggregate forecasts benefit from a cancellation of errors that exist in item-level forecasts. For example, suppose you are tasked with forecasting demand for products A1 and A2. If your forecasts are unbiased, each forecast has a 50 percent chance of being either too high or too low. However, the chance that forecasts for both products are simultaneously too high (or simultaneously too low) is less than 50 percent (it is only 25 percent if the product demands are independent). Considering a larger number of products, there is a good chance that forecasts for some products will be too high and forecasts for other products will be too low. Thus, when the individual product forecasts are combined, the aggregate forecast is overall more accurate, because some of the negative errors are cancelled out by some of the positive errors. This same logic applies when you attempt to forecast aggregate demand directly (as opposed to summing up individual forecasts). The random forces that affect demand for individual products tend to be inconsistent across all products. The effects cancel one another. Thus, aggregate demand is more stable and predictable. This aggregation benefit also applies to geographic aggregation. For a single product, an overall global demand forecast is typically more accurate than forecasts of demand in any specific geographic region.

Rule 3: Forecasts developed using multiple information sources are usually more accurate than forecasts developed from a single source. Many different market forces may drive demand for a given good or service. It is difficult for any single source of information (historical demand data, executive judgments, sales force estimates, and so on) to comprehend all of these forces. In addition, any single source is potentially biased. Consequently, a forecast created by combining information from multiple different sources is likely to reflect a more complete and unbiased picture of actual demand patterns. It is unlikely that all sources will be "wrong" in the same direction.

DEMAND MANAGEMENT

Forecasting is essentially a reactive approach that considers fluctuations in demand to be mostly outside the firm's control. Rather than simply forecasting and reacting to changes in demand, however, business executives would prefer to influence the timing, pattern, and certainty of demand to whatever extent they can. They do this through demand management activities that adjust product characteristics including price, promotion, and availability. The purpose is to influence product demand to achieve sales objectives and to accommodate the supply chain resources and capacities that the firm has in place.

Demand management is especially important when customers' demands fluctuate in an unpredictable way. These fluctuations cause operational inefficiencies all across the supply chain, including:

1. Requiring extra resources to expand and contract capacity to meet varying demand.
2. Backlogging (delivering later than originally promised) certain orders to smooth out demand fluctuations.
3. Customer dissatisfaction with the system's inability to meet all demands.
4. Buffering the system through the use of safety stocks (excess inventories), safety lead time (lead times with a cushion), or safety capacity (excess resources).

To be effective, demand management requires coordination of many sources of demand information. Different people working throughout the organization and the supply chain may individually see only parts of the overall demand picture. Demand management planning often crosses organizational boundaries in the supply chain. It requires sales, marketing, supply management, and operations personnel, as well as suppliers and intermediate customers, to work together in planning strategies for developing and fulfilling orders. Sales and marketing personnel need to be aware of the costs and constraints of operations in order to make good pricing and product availability decisions. Furthermore,

relationships

operations managers must understand customer requirements regarding acceptable lead times, as well as priorities associated with different customer orders.[3]

Managers try to manage demand by using variants of three basic tactics:

1. *Influence the timing or quantity of demand through pricing changes, promotions, or sales incentives.* These moves are usually intended to increase demand during the low periods and to reduce or postpone demand during the peak periods. For example, automobile manufacturers sometimes offer promotional packages including zero percent financing or rebates to stimulate purchases. Many service operations such as hotels, airlines, and theaters use these approaches because their services cannot be inventoried.

2. *Manage the timing of order fulfillment.* In some situations, it is possible to negotiate with customers regarding when they will take delivery of their products. Information systems can be used to inform customers of the availability of certain products, including the expected delivery date. Different customers might be quoted different delivery dates depending on their importance to the business. In some services, customers are encouraged to choose when they will order, based on expected lead times. For example, amusement parks such as Disney World use this tactic when they place signs at points in a waiting line telling you how long you can expect to wait from that point.

3. *Substitute by encouraging customers to shift their orders from one product to another, or from one provider to another.* Suppose you are ordering a new computer, but the model with the features you desire is not readily available. You might be willing to take a near substitute, or perhaps an upgraded model, if you can get it immediately or at a lower price. Dell, a computer manufacturer, is famous for "selling what it has." Dell's information systems enable sales representatives to know exactly which products are immediately available, and marketing managers price products dynamically to move those items that are in stock.

Characteristics of the product, customers' lead-time expectations, and the operations environment all influence how the above tactics are employed in a demand management process. However, in every case the ultimate goal of demand management is to match demand and operational capacity in order to attain the business's competitive objectives.

IMPROVING THE CONSTRAINTS ON DEMAND PLANNING

LO12-6 Explain how certain improvements to both product design and operations across the supply chain can make demand planning easier.

Many business firms today are redesigning operations across their supply chains to facilitate more effective demand planning and order fulfillment. Improvement initiatives are aimed at changing information sharing systems, manufacturing and service processes, supply chain relationships, and even the product design itself, so that companies can reduce both the magnitude and the impact of forecast errors on their operations.

Improving Information Breadth, Accuracy, and Timeliness

The fashion-driven clothing industry vividly demonstrates the important role of information in demand planning. Predicting the sales of a new line of merchandise is difficult. Once the firm launches a product line, it needs quick information about the market's response to the new goods. Information systems that rapidly collect and distribute accurate sales information are important in the fashion industry and in many other industries as well. Quick sales data collection is important because current data are more relevant for forecasting future sales. Initial forecasts made at product launch can be hugely improved by incorporating

---

[3]Chapter 13, "Sales and Operations Planning," discusses in detail the coordination of demand management with operational constraints.

early sales data. In addition, rapid access to customer sales information, coupled with an operations system capable of rapid response, decreases a firm's reliance on forecasting, because the firm doesn't have to forecast as far into the future. The Get Real box describing Destination Maternity Corporation provides a good example of the impact of information accuracy and timeliness.

The Role of "Big Data" in Improving Information

The growth of available data in today's world is astounding. More information is created on the Internet each year than the total that existed five years previously. Similarly, data housed in corporate and social databases is growing exponentially. Each one of us creates more than 2–5 MB of data that is captured by our devices each day. And, consider this: There are more than three times as many interconnected devices as there are people on the planet!

These trends have given rise to the term **big data**, which refers to the voluminous amounts of information that are easily accessible through interconnected systems today. These data include highly structured forms (such as transaction data, location data, and descriptive data) as well as unstructured forms (such as e-mail and blog texts, social media, and Internet click streams). Devices are also creating and capturing massive amounts of sensor data (such as temperature, GPS, data from wearable technology, and RFID and barcode data) and other types of data (for example, videos, digital images, and voice data).

big data Large amounts of data made available through sensors and interconnected systems.

GET REAL

Destination Maternity Corporation

Destination Maternity Corporation (originally known as Mothers Work, Inc.) is a leading designer, manufacturer, and marketer of maternity fashion in the United States, with over 900 locations nationwide.

Since the time of its initial public offering in March 1993, Destination has increased its store base by over 1,300 percent and grown financially to more than 10 times its original size. A critical success factor has been the company's ability to gather extensive point-of-sale information at each store. Managers have developed an information system with the following capabilities:

- Capture all customer information and create a buying history.
- Run individual mailing lists by due date.
- Receive alerts about any operational errors that may have occurred the previous day.
- Review all orders on the way to their stores.
- Make customer-unique price tickets.
- Send and receive digital photos.
- Provide sales trend information.

The system also provides such features as custom profiles for each store, daily inventory replenishment, and daily updated selling information for each style. Complementing the information system are the company's fast-turn, in-house design and quick-response, material sourcing and replenishment processes:

- Real-time tracking of sales.
- Two-day replenishment of items from warehouses.
- Two- to three-week design cycle.

- Two-week manufacturing cycle.
- One- to four-month cycle for overseas sourcing.

These process times are far shorter than the typical cycles for average fashion merchandisers. By coupling current and accurate information with a very responsive supply chain, Destination has been able to avoid lost sales while maximizing in-store inventory turns and sales per square foot. Destination provides an excellent example of how improving the constraints that otherwise limit the effectiveness of the demand planning system can yield big operational and financial benefits.

© David Brabyn/Corbis

Source: Information taken from http://Motherswork.com/.

The availability of all these types of data provides a huge opportunity for making improvements in demand planning, as well as other planning and decision making in supply chain operations management. Imagine, for example, the improved demand forecasts that a consumer goods company could achieve if its planners had real-time access to consumer purchases, eating habits, entertainment choices, and the like. Such data exist and are being extensively analyzed by companies and their consulting partners. In industrial environments, data created by sensors, robots, and computers are being analyzed to better predict purchases of equipment and business-to-business services.

Overall, the growing availability of big data, along with systems that can analyze and interpret big data, offers the promise of more robust and accurate demand planning. Such systems make planning more effective because broader sets of data mean that more complete sets of demand influences can be captured, real-time sensors make data more current, and automated data capture makes data more accurate.

Reducing Lead Time

As we noted earlier in the chapter, it is a basic fact of forecasting that the longer the time period over which you have to forecast, the greater the forecast error. A forecast of demand for two years from now is far less accurate than a forecast of demand for next month. In most cases, the number of periods that managers have to forecast into the future is determined by the order-to-delivery (OTD) lead time provided by the supply chain, or the time required to source, make, and deliver the product. Thus, reducing lead time improves forecast accuracy, because shorter lead times require shorter-term forecasts.

Speeding up or eliminating process steps that are redundant, unnecessary, or poorly executed reduces lead time. Opportunities for improvement usually extend beyond the firm throughout the supply chain. The Get Real box about Calyx and Corolla gives an example of extreme lead-time reduction facilitated by the company's redesign of the supply chain. If lead times are reduced sufficiently, operations managers can move from a build-to-stock (build-to-forecast) process to a build-to-order process where little forecasting is required.

Redesigning the Product

For a firm offering a wide range of products, forecasting is especially challenging. Consider the problems faced by Hewlett-Packard when it comes to printers, which are consumed around the world in regions that have different power requirements and languages.

GET REAL

Calyx and Corolla Delivers Freshness by Redesigning the Supply Chain

Calyx and Corolla sells flowers from growers located around the world to customers located around the world. The company promotes itself as "the flower lover's flower company™" as it competes primarily through "freshness." Calyx and Corolla promises that its flowers will last 5 to 10 days longer than most others. How is it able to deliver on this promise? Most traditional florists must deal with a long supply chain. Growers grow the flowers. Distributors buy them and sell them to regional sellers, who in turn sell them to local florists. At each stage, the flowers are produced or purchased based on the party's forecast of demand.

A typical flower can last about 19 days, once it has been cut. The traditional supply chain consumes about 10 to 11 days of this time. The founders of Calyx and Corolla redesigned the supply chain to reduce lead time by working directly with the growers. Orders received from customers (in response to printed catalogs or the Internet) are placed by Calyx and Corolla directly with the growers, who then cut, package, and ship the flowers directly to the customer via FedEx. Consequently, flowers delivered this way spend three days or less in the supply chain. The benefit for the customer is that they arrive at their destination fresher, and they also last longer. The benefit for Calyx and Corolla is that it only needs to forecast demand for three to four days into the future in order to arrange for sufficient product and transportation capacities. Its competitors have to forecast demand for several weeks into the future.

As described in the nearby Get Real box, ultimately HP responded by developing *postponable products*. A **postponable product** is one that can be configured to its final form quickly and inexpensively once actual customer demand is known. In this operations system, only components, not finished goods, are stocked near sources of demand. The components are then assembled into finished product configurations once the actual demand materializes.

postponable product A product designed so that it can be configured to its final form quickly and inexpensively once actual customer demand is known.

The postponable product approach largely eliminates the need for large and complex forecasting systems, as only the demands for the relatively few individual components are forecasted, not the demands for the many different end-item configurations. The keys to this approach are redesign of the product and redistribution of production resources so that the products can be easily configured close to the source of demand. Electronics firms such as HP often use this approach. So do private-brand producers of grocery products (e.g., canned beans, corn, peas). The grocery producers stock unlabeled cans and then print the labels and make cartons for specific brands only after actual orders are received.

Collaborating and Sharing Information

The need for forecasting partially arises from a lack of information sharing across stages of the supply chain. Suppliers make assumptions about the actions of their customers, and vice versa. Many firms today use both formal and informal approaches to share planning information with their suppliers and customers, including forecasts of product demand and planned product promotions, as well as production plans and capacity limitations. The planning partners then make commitments to a collaboratively established overall sales and production plan, taking into account the demands and constraints of the various organizations involved. This approach reduces the risks associated with forecast errors; it reduces the inventories that supply chain players typically hold to guard against such risks; and it improves customer service levels by reducing lead times.

GET REAL

HP Improves the Constraints on Forecasting through Postponement

While the "guts" of a printer are basically the same regardless of where they are sold, instruction manuals, power supplies, and cables have to be made differently to accommodate differences in language and power grids in various countries. Initially, HP forecasted each country's demand for printers and then stocked all printer variants according to the forecasts. However, forecasts were never accurate enough to make this approach work—inventories were high, expediting was common, and customer service was low.

To solve this problem, HP decided to produce and stock only the generic printer bases, along with separate power supplies, cables, and instruction manuals, in regional warehouses around the world. The warehouses act as both storage locations and light assembly plants. Once an order is received for a printer in Germany, for example, the order is sent to the nearest regional warehouse. There, a generic printer base is withdrawn from stock and paired with the appropriate power supply, cable, and instruction manual. The entire system is then tested and packed in country-specific packaging.

Forecasts for printer bases and components are more accurate than forecasts for final product variants. At HP, this approach has

reduced total landed cost (manufacturing, shipping, and inventory) by 25 percent. In addition, HP has reduced total inventories by 50 percent while simultaneously increasing customer order fill rates significantly.

© Deepak G. Pawar/The India Today Group/Getty Images

"Smartek" chips stacked and ready for final assembly in HP printers in manufacturing plant.

428   chapter 12   Demand Planning: Forecasting and Demand Management

collaborative planning, forecasting, and replenishment (CPFR)
A method by which supply chain partners periodically share forecasts, demand plans, and resource plans in order to reduce uncertainty and risk in meeting customer demand.

One systematic process for improving collaboration and information sharing in the supply chain is known as **collaborative planning, forecasting and replenishment (CPFR)**. The CPFR process requires buyers and sellers to collaboratively develop their demand plans and then to collaboratively adjust and execute those plans, with the goal of meeting customer demand with minimal inventories, lead times, and transaction costs.

To engage in CPFR, supply chain partners must first come to an understanding regarding their relationship and the roles they will play. Included in this mutual understanding are definitions of the accounts and operational processes involved and jointly developed business goals. Figure 12-9 illustrates one common version of the CPFR process, which typically consists of four collaborative activities:

- *Market planning.* The partners collaboratively discuss such issues as the introduction of new products, store openings/closings, changing inventory policies, and product promotions.
- *Demand and resource planning.* Customer demand and shipping requirements are forecasted.
- *Execution.* Orders are placed, delivered, received, and paid for. This includes preparation of shipments and recording of sales. Since logistics/distribution is critical, third-party logistics providers may be included in the CPFR effort.
- *Analysis.* Execution is monitored and key performance metrics are collected with the goal of identifying opportunities for future improvement.

FIGURE 12-9   The CPFR Approach

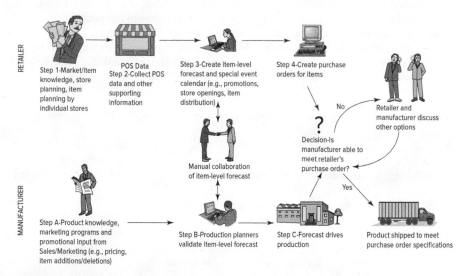

CHAPTER SUMMARY

Demand planning is a process that every firm must develop in order to deal with variability and uncertainty of product demand. This chapter discussed two fundamental elements of demand planning: demand forecasting and demand management. The following points and issues were raised:

1. The choice of a forecasting process depends on conditions in the operating environment, including the time horizon for management decisions, the level of detail that the user of the forecast needs to support decisions, the number of products for which the process must generate forecasts, the decision makers' emphasis on control or planning needs, the constancy of forecasted events, and the firm's current methods for developing forecasts.

2. Forecasting methods fall into two categories: judgment-based and statistical model–based methods. Judgment-based approaches gather inputs through grassroots methods, executive judgment, focused forecasting, historical analogy, market research, and the Delphi method. These techniques are appropriate in those situations where past data are either unavailable or no longer appropriate. They are also appropriate for forecasting technological innovations (another use of forecasting). Statistical model–based forecasting approaches try to extend the past by decomposing historical time series data and other causal factors into seasonal, trend, and other components to reveal the residual effects of unique, current forces on demand. Operations managers may develop naive forecasts or employ much more sophisticated methods.

3. Both accuracy and bias should be considered in the evaluation of forecasting errors. Mean forecast error (MFE) and mean percentage error (MPE) are good at measuring bias, while metrics such as mean absolute deviation (MAD), mean squared error (MSE), root mean squared error (RMSE), and mean absolute percentage error (MAPE) are used to monitor forecast accuracy. Managers often set up tracking signals for forecasting systems so that they can be notified when forecast errors become unusually large. This type of monitoring of forecasting performance leads to continuous updating and improvement of forecasting models.

4. Demand management involves varying the price, promotion, or availability of the product or service in order to increase, decrease, or shift the pattern of expected demand.

5. By improving supply chain constraints, operations managers can make the system more responsive to actual demand and less sensitive to forecast error. This can be done by improving information systems, reducing lead times (by changing the underlying processes and systems), redesigning the product to facilitate product postponement, and sharing information and collaborating with other supply chain partners.

6. Technology advances such as big data and artificial intelligence are improving demand planners' abilities to incorporate broader sets of considerations (and therefore less bias) into forecasts. These systems also provide more accurate and timely access to relevant information.

KEY TERMS

adaptive forecasting   422

artificial intelligence   417

autocorrelation   400

big data   425

collaborative planning, forecasting, and replenishment (CPFR)   428

Delphi method   403

demand forecasting   398

demand management   398

demand planning   398

executive judgment   402

exponential smoothing   407

focused forecasting   417

forecast accuracy   418

forecast bias   418

forecast error   400

grassroots forecasting   402

historical analogy   403

marketing research   403

mean absolute deviation (MAD)   419

mean absolute percentage error (MAPE)   420

mean percent error (MPE)   419

mean squared error (MSE)   420

moving average   405

naive model   405

postponable product   427

regression analysis   410

root mean squared error (RMSE)   421

seasonal index   411

seasonality and cycles   400

shift or step change   400

simulation models   417

smoothing coefficient   407

stable pattern   400

time series analysis models   404

tracking signal   422

trend   400

weighted moving average   406

DISCUSSION
DISCUSSION QUESTIONS

1. Think of four instances in your life when you confronted sellers' demand management practices. As a value-conscious customer, do you think that each of the four sellers served you well?

2. Your boss wants you to explain the term *exponential smoothing*. How do you reply?

3. Someone in your organization suspects a causal relationship between statistics on corrugated board shipments reported in *BusinessWeek* and your company's usage of corrugated board. How would you test this assertion? If you were to verify the relationship, how could you use it in your business?

4. In what way is an exponential smoothing model really a moving average model?

5. Your boss has less training than you have in business statistics. She asks you to explain the logic of the least squares regression method for determining a trend line. What will you tell her?

6. Your firm is considering reducing staff, and your forecasting department has been mentioned as a prime candidate for this treatment. Outline a brief memo to defend the value of your department's services to the firm. How could you quantify your claims?

7. Assume that you are the regional operations manager responsible for 27 Burger Queen restaurants. What types of demand forecast models do you think you would need for your short-term planning? What decisions would each forecast support? Identify the users of each forecast.

8. As the regional manager of 27 Burger Queens, you are thinking about expanding the number of outlets in your area. What types of forecasts would you want to create in order to support your decision?

9. What arguments would you use in order to justify tightening the limits used on a tracking signal control chart? What arguments would you use for loosening the limits?

10. Describe the likely effects of the following business trends on demand forecasting processes:
    a. Fast-to-market product design.
    b. Division of many markets into isolated niches.
    c. The Internet.
    d. More powerful and cheaper computers and forecasting software packages.

    How would you modify your firm's demand management or demand forecasting processes in response to these trends?

SOLVED
SOLVED PROBLEMS

1. Vinod Malhotra is trying to decide how many wait staff he will need to support his restaurant operations for the next month. First he needs to identify a suitable forecasting model to estimate next month's demand. He is considering three alternative models:

    Model 1: Four-month moving average
    Model 2: Four-month weighted moving average with weights = .1, .2, .3, .4
    Model 3: Exponential smoothing with $\alpha = 0.7$

    Based on past performance, which model should Vinod use?

Solution:

To evaluate the three competing forecasting models, we need to compare the errors that would have been produced if they had been used in the past. The table below shows the forecasts created by each model using eight months of past demand.

Month	Actual Demand	Model 1 Forecast	Error	Abs Error	Model 2 Forecast	Error	Abs Error	Model 3 Forecast	Error	Abs Error
1	1940									
2	2250									
3	2301									
4	2630									
5	2264	2280.3	−16.3	16.3	2386.3	−122.3	122.3	2630.0	−366.0	366.
6	2736	2361.3	374.8	374.8	2379.8	356.2	356.2	2373.8	362.2	362.
7	2503	2482.8	20.3	20.3	2529.7	226.7	26.7	2627.3	−124.3	124.
8	2422	2533.3	−111.3	111.3	2537.8	−115.8	115.8	2540.3	−118.3	118

In order to complete the table, forecasts will be needed for each month. As an example, the calculations are shown below for forecasting demand for month 8:

Model 1: $F_8 = (2630 + 2264 + 2736 + 2503) / 4 = 2533.3$

Model 2: $F_8 = (0.1) 2630 + (0.2) 2264 + (0.3) 2736 + (0.4) 2503 = 2537.8$

Model 3: $F_8 = (0.7) 2503 + (1 − 0.7) 2627.3 = 2540.3$

Calculations of bias and MAD:

Model 1: Bias $= (−16.3 + 374.8 + 20.3 − 111.3) / 4 = 66.9$;

MAD $= (16.3 + 374.8 + 20.3 + 111.3) / 4 = 130.6$

Model 2: Bias $= (−122.3 + 356.2 − 26.7 − 115.8) / 4 = 22.9$;

MAD $= (122.3 + 356.2 + 26.7 + 115.8) / 4 = 155.3$

Model 3: Bias $= (−366.0 + 362.2 − 124.3 − 118.3) / 4 = −61.6$;

MAD $= (366.0 + 362.2 + 124.3 + 118.3) / 4 = 242.7$

Conclusion: Vinod would probably be advised to use model 2, the weighted moving average model, as it has provided the lowest amount of bias in the past. Though the MAD for this model is slightly worse than that for model 1, the bias is significantly better. Vinod might want to try some other model parameters to see if he can develop an even more accurate model.

2. Suppose that an electronics company has the monthly sales shown below. It wants to develop forecasts using a time series regression model and a trend enhanced exponential smoothing model using $\alpha = 0.30$ and $\partial = 0.40$, and then seasonally adjust these two models using the regression forecasts as the base for calculating the seasonal indexes. Finally, it wants to determine which forecasting model fits the data better and use this model to predict sales for the next six months.

Month	1	2	3	4	5	6	7	8	9	10	11	12
Sales ($1,000,000)	16	20	35	18	24	33	21	23	51	35	36	64

Solution:

The parameters for the regression model are calculated in Table 12-10.

TABLE 12-10   Regression Parameter Calculations

Month	Sales		
t	d_t	$t * d_t$	t^2
1	16	16	1
2	20	40	4
3	35	105	9
4	18	72	16
5	24	120	25
6	33	198	36
7	21	147	49
8	23	184	64
9	51	459	81
10	35	350	100
11	36	396	121
12	64	768	144
Total		2855	650
Average	6.5	31.3	

Using the linear regression formulae, the slope and the intercept are:

$$b = [2,855.1 - (12)(6.5)(31.3)]/[650 - (12)(6.5)^2] = 2.9 \text{ per period}$$
$$a = (31.3) - (2.9)(6.5) = 12.6$$

Regression-based estimates for each time period are calculated as:

Month 1 forecast $= 12.6 + 2.9(1) = 15.5$
Month 2 forecast $= 12.6 + 2.9(2) = 18.4$

Table 12-11 shows the regression forecast values for all 12 months.

The trend enhanced exponential smoothing model forecasts are calculated as follows. Since no starting values are provided, we choose the actual sales in month 1 as the initial base demand value and the slope from the regression model as the initial trend value. The forecasts are:

Month 1 forecast $= F_{t+1} + T_{t+1} = 16 + 2.9 = 18.9$
Month 2:

Base forecast $= FIT_t + \alpha(d_t - FIT_t) = 18.9 + 0.3(16 - 18.9) = 18.0$
Trend forecast $= T_t + \beta(F_{t+1} + FIT_t) = 2.9 + 0.4(18.0 - 18.9) = 2.5$
Month 2 forecast $= F_{t+1} + T_{t+1} = 18.0 + 2.5 = 20.5$

Table 12-11 shows the trend enhanced exponential smoothing forecast values for all 12 months.

To seasonally adjust these forecasts we need to first estimate the seasonal indexes. As shown in Table 12-11, this is done by simply dividing the sales in each month by the base sales provided by the regression forecast. By examining the indexes, it is clear that a quarterly demand pattern exists, with most sales occurring in the third month of each quarter. We average the seasonal indexes across the four quarters represented in the data, and then use these values to adjust the regression and trend enhanced forecasts, as shown in Table 12-11.

TABLE 12-11   Forecasts for the Solved Problem

Month	Sales (a)	Regression Forecasts (b)	Trend Enhanced ES Forecasts (c)	Seasonal Indexes = a / b	Average Seasonal Indexes (d)	Season Adjusted Regression Forecasts d × b	Season Adjusted Trend Enhanced ES Forecasts d × c
1	16	15.5	18.9	1.03	SI for first month = (1.03 + 0.75 + 0.64 + 0.85)/4 = 0.82	0.82(15.5) = 12.7	0.82(18.9) = 15.4
2	20	18.4	20.5	1.09		0.86(18.4) = 15.8	0.86(20.5) = 17.6
3	35	21.3	22.8	1.65	SI for second month = (1.09 + 0.89 + 0.65 + 0.81)/4 = 0.86	1.36(21.3) = 28.9	1.36(22.8) = 31.0
4	18	24.1	30.4	0.75		19.7	24.8
5	24	27.0	29.1	0.89		23.2	25.0
6	33	29.9	29.4	1.10	SI for third month = (1.65 + 1.10 + 1.32 + 1.36)/4 = 1.36	40.6	39.9
7	21	32.8	32.7	0.64		26.7	26.7
8	23	35.6	30.1	0.65		30.6	25.8
9	51	38.5	27.9	1.32		52.3	37.9
10	35	41.4	37.6	0.85		33.8	30.7
11	36	44.3	39.3	0.81		38.0	33.7
12	64	47.1	40.4	1.36		64.0	54.8

Now we can compare the forecasts provided by both seasonally adjusted models. Table 12-12 compares the bias, MAD, MAPE, and MSE for each of the forecast models.

TABLE 12-12   Comparison of Forecasting Errors

		Seasonally Adjusted Regression				Seasonally Adjusted Trend Enhanced ES			
Month	Sales	Forecast	Forecast Error	Absolute Error	% Absolute Error	Forecast	Forecast Error	Absolute Error	% Absolute Error
1	16	12.7	3.3	3.3	21%	15.4	0.6	0.6	4%
2	20	15.8	4.2	4.2	21%	17.6	2.4	2.4	12%
3	35	28.9	6.1	6.1	17%	31.0	4.0	4.0	11%
4	18	19.7	−1.7	1.7	9%	24.8	−6.8	6.8	38%
5	24	23.2	0.8	0.8	3%	25.0	−1.0	1.0	4%
6	33	40.6	−7.6	7.6	23%	39.9	−6.9	6.9	21%
7	21	26.7	−5.7	5.7	27%	26.7	−5.7	5.7	27%
8	23	30.6	−7.6	7.6	33%	25.8	−2.8	2.8	12%
9	51	52.3	−1.3	1.3	3%	37.9	13.1	13.1	26%
10	35	33.8	1.2	1.2	4%	30.7	4.3	4.3	12%
11	36	38.0	−2.0	2.0	6%	33.7	2.3	2.3	6%
12	64	64.0	0.0	0.0	0%	54.8	9.2	9.2	14%
	Average		Bias = − 0.9	MAD = 3.5	MAPE = 14%		Bias = 1.1	MAD = 4.9	MAPE = 16%

TABLE 6-2   Functional Influences on Product Quality

Functional Personnel	Decisions and Activities with Potential Impacts on Product Quality
Marketing Managers	Choices of markets to pursue and product features to offer
	Design of advertising and other programs that communicate product attributes to customers
	Development of new product testing programs
Sales Managers	Setting of sales targets
	Interactions with customers
	Interpretations of customers' needs and desires
Product Engineers	Design of product specifications, service elements, dimensional tolerances, etc.
	Design of product prototyping procedures
Process Engineers	Design of manufacturing and service processes
	Choices of technology and associated capabilities and capacity limits
	Design of quality assurance tests and procedures
Finance and Accounting Managers	Setting of restrictions for equipment purchases
	Establishing goals for utilization of facilities and working capital
	Design of measures used to assess efficiency and productivity
Human Resources Managers	Design of hiring criteria and training and development programs
	Setting of compensation schemes and incentives
Manufacturing and Service Operations Managers	Design and execution of processing procedures
	Design of work policies
	Interactions with customers
	Management of facilities and equipment
	Scheduling of work
Supply Managers	Description of purchase requirements
	Selection of suppliers
	Establishment of contracts and associated incentives and penalties
	Management of and interactions with suppliers
Logistics Managers	Selection of transportation providers
	Development of tracking and other information systems
	Design of packaging, storage, and material handling processes
	Management of and interactions with transportation providers

while Juran emphasized the tactical/operational side of quality. These leaders advocated merging certain core management values with statistical techniques and other management tools. The resulting "total quality management," or TQM, approach helped to transform Japan's economy, making it an industrial powerhouse. Since then, this approach has spread

GET REAL

Food Safety in Global Supply Chains—A Real Challenge

sustainability   global

The Centers for Disease Control and Prevention estimate that one in six U.S. residents suffer from food poisoning each year. Quality problems in our food supply are often in the news. Rather than becoming less frequent, recent trends suggest that food safety problems are occurring even more often. In fact, many of the largest food recalls in history have occurred since 2007:

Menu Foods Pet Food—In 2007 Menu Foods Inc. recalled several brands of dog and cat food because they contained melamine, an industrial chemical used in the making of plastics.

Hallmark/Westland Meat Packing—In 2008, an investigation into slaughter practices resulted in the recall of 143 million pounds of beef, much of it destined for school lunch programs.

Peanut Corporation—This company shipped products containing salmonella a dozen times between 2007 and 2008. The shipments were later linked to eight deaths, and they sickened over 600 people in 46 states and in Canada.

Wright County/Hillandale Farms—Salmonella was the cause of a 2010 recall of over a half billion fresh eggs. The Centers for Disease Control noted over 1,900 reports of illness connected with the outbreak.

Cargill—In 2011 Cargill recalled over 35 million pounds of ground turkey due to contamination. The contaminated meat was responsible for one death and the sickening of over 75 people.

Blue Bell—In 2015 Blue Bell Ice Cream recalled over 8 million gallons of ice cream because of listeria contamination linked to at least 3 deaths and the reported illness of hundreds.

Chipotle Mexican Grill—In 2015 an E. coli outbreak sickened dozens of customers across six U.S. states. The quality failure led to the closure of 43 restaurants for almost two weeks and caused Chipotle managers to decrease sourcing from local producers. This approach had been an important selling point for the chain.

While there are likely many root causes to these quality failures, a growing concern is the lack of traceability of products as food manufacturers in industrialized countries increasingly source their ingredients from distant, low-cost countries. Many of these countries do not have the same sanitary standards for production, especially in the case of seafood and fresh produce. Sourcing products and ingredients internationally provides cost savings and the ability to source products all year long. On the other hand, the global supply chain adds complexity to an already complex system of food safety, quality, and logistics.

---

to the United States and the rest of the world. Table 6-3 summarizes the contributions of the major quality gurus. Note the similarities and differences in the core values of these leaders.

TQM: A "TOTAL" VIEW OF QUALITY

total quality management (TQM) An integrated business management strategy aimed at embedding awareness of quality in all organizational processes.

Total quality management (TQM) is an integrated business management strategy aimed at embedding awareness of quality in all organizational processes. The word *total* in total quality management has several important connotations. First, a product's quality is ultimately determined by the customer's acceptance and use of the product. Accordingly, any discussion of product quality issues should always start with a focus on all of the attributes, the total package that targeted customers will care most about. Second, quality management is a total, organizationwide activity, rather than a technical task. Quality assurance is not simply the responsibility of product inspectors. Every employee in a company has a stake in product quality, and almost everyone has some direct or indirect influence on it. Third, quality improvement requires a total commitment from all employees. A quality product results from good design combined with effective production and delivery methods. Because almost everyone in a company has some role either directly or indirectly related to design, production, or delivery, commitment to high quality is required of everyone in the firm. To make good decisions, people from all affected functions should be involved. Consequently, TQM has a heavy emphasis on decision making in cross-functional teams.

TABLE 6-3 Contributions of Quality Management Thought Leaders

Deming	Juran	Crosby	Imai
All employees are responsible for quality	Quality has many dimensions	Quality is free; zero defects is an appropriate goal	Kaizen system of continuous improvement
Variability is the source of most problems	Quality management is change management	Focus on incremental and continuous change	Need a process-oriented view
The customer is the final arbiter of quality	Cost of quality analysis highlights need for change		Frontline workers have important insights
			Worker training and development are key
Deming's 14 Points	Juran's Universal Breakthrough Sequence	Crosby's 14 Steps for Quality Improvement	Imai's Kaizen Steps
1. Create consistency of purpose for continual improvement of goods and services.	1. Proof of Need. Create awareness by showing the costs of not changing.	1. Management commitment. Make quality a high priority for the firm.	1. Standardize an operation.
2. Adopt the new philosophy for economic stability.	2. Project Identification. Pick an initial project that has the highest, most visible payoffs.	2. Quality improvement teams. Cross-functional teams guide and achieve improvements.	2. Measure the standardized operation.
3. Cease dependency on inspection to achieve quality.	3. Organize for Improvement. Put in place the resources, top management, employees, and work policies needed to ensure success.	3. Quality measurement. Clear measures that relate to individual activities.	3. Gauge measurements against requirements.
4. End the practice of awarding business on price tag alone.	4. Diagnostic Journey. Identify and understand the critical few problems and their causes.	4. Cost of quality evaluation. Assess prevention, appraisal, and failure costs.	4. Innovate to meet requirements and increase productivity.
5. Improve constantly and forever the system of production and service.	5. Remedial Action. Identify and implement necessary corrective actions.	5. Quality awareness. Formal programs for creating awareness.	5. Standardize the new, improved operations.
6. Institute training on the job.	6. Resistance to Change. Overcome resistance by encouraging wide participation and by giving people sufficient time to understand and accept the changes.	6. Corrective action. Teams identify, study, and resolve problems.	6. Continue cycle *ad infinitum.*
7. Adopt and institute modern methods of supervision and leadership.	7. Holding Onto the Gains. Prevent a return to the "old" ways of doing things by establishing new standards, increasing training, and developing new control systems.	7. Zero defects planning. Move from correcting problems to totally eliminating them.	
8. Drive out fear.		8. Employee education. Employees at all levels trained to fulfill their proper roles.	
9. Break down barriers between departments and individuals.		9. Zero defects day. Event to signal a new, higher standard of performance.	
10. Eliminate the use of slogans, posters, and exhortations.		10. Goal setting. New goals to guide performance and to keep quality in the forefront.	
11. Eliminate work standards and numerical quotas.		11. Error cause removal. Moves from correcting problems to removing the underlying causes.	
12. Remove barriers that rob the hourly worker of the right to pride in workmanship.		12. Recognition. Appreciation of employees whose actions have helped the firm achieve its quality objectives.	
13. Institute a vigorous program of education and retraining.		13. Quality council. Team leaders meet regularly to share experiences and plans.	
14. Define top management's permanent commitment to ever-improving quality and productivity.		14. Do it all over again! Repeat the steps at a higher level.	

LO6-4 Perform a cost of quality analysis.

cost of quality (COQ) A framework for quantifying the total cost of quality-related efforts and deficiencies.

prevention costs Costs associated with efforts to prevent product defects and associated failure and appraisal costs.

appraisal costs Costs resulting from inspections used to assess quality levels.

internal failure costs Costs associated with quality failures uncovered before products are delivered to customers.

external failure costs Costs associated with quality failures uncovered after products reach customers.

Recognizing the Total Impacts of Quality Performance

In addition to affecting sales and other direct measures of business performance, poor product quality can have hidden or indirect effects. For example, poor quality can affect inspection, rework, and warranty costs—elements often buried in a company's overhead expenses. A focus on quality management demands that the total costs and benefits of quality performance be first understood by everyone in the organization. This usually requires a quite involved and far-reaching analysis, known as a **cost of quality (COQ)** analysis, to help clarify the cost impacts of poor conformance quality. COQ identifies and assesses four major cost categories:

- **Prevention costs** result from efforts to prevent product defects (nonconforming products) and from efforts needed to limit both failure and appraisal costs. Such costs include resources spent on planning, new-product reviews, investments in more capable processing equipment, training, process control, and quality improvement projects.

- **Appraisal costs** result from inspections used to assess products' quality levels. Such costs include resources spent on incoming material inspections, product and process inspections, inspection staff salaries, test equipment, and development of test procedures.

- **Internal failure costs** result from defects that are found in products prior to their shipment to customers. These costs include scrapped materials, salvage and rework, excess material inventories, and other costs of correction.

- **External failure costs** result from defects that are found only after products reach customers. These costs include complaint settlements, loss of customer goodwill and future sales, returned materials, warranty work, and field service or repairs.

Fill level tolerances, by law, are very narrow when it comes to permissible underfilling. However, business profitability demands that overfill be kept to a minimum, too. Machine vision systems can check fill level to verify minimum product requirements and alert lineworkers when overfill results in excessive product giveaway.

Courtesy of Omron

Prevention costs are the costs of activities aimed at eliminating the potential causes of product defects, or failures, while appraisal costs are the costs of activities aimed at ensuring that defective products are identified and not delivered to customers. Failure costs include both the internal costs of defects found inside the company and the external costs of defects found by customers.

It is important to note that, as a product progresses from one stage to the next in the supply chain, a defect found in later stages is much more costly than a defect found in earlier stages. In later stages more resources have been invested in the product, and there is sometimes less ability to rework the product. Costs are highest when a defect is uncovered by the customer. Repair costs are relatively large, but often, and more importantly, the costs of lost sales and tarnished product image can be very large.

Some of the costs contained in these four categories are identifiable in expense reports, yet others are hidden in overhead and other administrative accounts. For example, it may be difficult to establish the percentage of production engineering and management salaries (an overhead expense) that is attributable to solving quality problems. Similarly, some percentage of safety stock inventories may be needed to cover quality problems, but this is rarely explicitly identified.

A thorough COQ analysis usually requires quite a bit of digging, in addition to the cooperation of accounting and operations personnel. They often find that the cost

GET REAL

Cost of Quality Analysis Applies to Both Services and Manufacturing

The following table provides recent cost of quality data for two different companies. The left side of the table provides costs as a percentage of revenues for a hotel restaurant; the right side shows average costs of quality across 11 manufacturing plants owned by a single large company.

Comparing these two analyses points out some interesting differences in how services and manufacturing firms may apply

the cost of quality approach. First, note that total costs of quality range from about 7 percent to 16 percent of revenues. These are fairly typical values. For a large company, costs of quality at this level could amount to hundreds of millions or even billions of dollars! In both cases, the total costs of quality went down from year 1 to year 2, especially for the restaurant, where total costs decreased from 16 percent of revenues to 12 percent of revenues.

Comparing Costs of Quality for a Hotel Restaurant and Manufacturing Plants

Hotel Restaurant	Percentage of Revenues		Manufacturing Plant	Percentage of Revenues	
	Year 1	Year 2		Year 1	Year 2
Prevention costs:			*Prevention costs:*		
Design menu	0.70%	1.12%	Design engineering	0.38%	0.27%
Equipment maintenance	0.30%	0.70%	Preventive repair / maintenance	0.43%	0.31%
Training	0.75%	1.76%	Training	0.13%	0.14%
Vendor evaluation	0.25%	0.42%	Process engineering	0.32%	0.38%
			Quality engineering	0.70%	0.91%
Total prevention costs	2.00%	4.00%	Total prevention costs	2.00%	2.00%
Appraisal costs:			*Appraisal costs:*		
Inspection of production	0.90%	0.65%	Manufacturing inspection	0.41%	0.32%
Product-testing (equipment)	1.15%	0.56%	Design analysis	0.24%	0.17%
Product-testing (labor and material)	1.70%	0.63%	Product acceptance	0.77%	0.63%
Incoming products inspection	0.25%	0.40%	Receiving inspection	0.24%	0.22%
			Lab audit	0.42%	0.40%
Total appraisal costs	4.00%	2.00%	Total appraisal costs	2.00%	1.70%
Internal failure costs:			*Internal failure costs:*		
Scrap	2.20%	1.30%	Scrap	2.84%	2.43%
Rework	1.50%	0.85%	Rework	0.58%	0.42%
Breakdown maintenance	0.80%	0.35%	Process engineering	0.15%	0.18%
Total internal failure costs	4.50%	2.50%	Total internal failure costs	3.57%	3.03%
External failure costs:			*External failure costs:*		
Returned meals (room service)	0.70%	1.10%	Returned material	0.20%	0.29%
Customer support	0.50%	0.20%	Marketing	0.05%	0.05%
Discount due to defects	1.80%	0.70%	Process engineering	0.07%	0.08%
Lost sales	2.50%	1.50%	Repair	0.02%	0.01%
			Travel	0.03%	0.03%
Total external failure costs	5.50%	3.50%	Total external failure costs	0.37%	0.46%
Total cost of quality	16.00%	12.00%	Total cost of quality	7.98%	7.24%
			Defect rate (per million units)	3.307	1,332

Sources: C. Ramdeen; J. Santos; and H. K. Chatfield, "Measuring the Cost of Quality in a Hotel Restaurant Operation," *International Journal of Contemporary Hospitality Management* 19, no. 4 (2007), pp. 286–95; and Venky Nagar and Madhav V. Rajan, "The Revenue Implications of Financial and Operational Measures of Product Quality," *The Accounting Review* 76, no. 4 (2001), pp. 495–513.

Continued

Restaurant managers attributed this improvement to the increased investments that they made in prevention—note that they spent twice as much on prevention in year 2. This supports the quality management principle that prevention is better than cure.

A second difference is in the kinds of costs tracked by the restaurant versus the manufacturing plants. While the four cost of quality categories are used by just about everyone in business, most companies need to include or exclude specific costs in accordance with the nature of their business. For example, the manufacturing plants include more engineering-related costs. Also note the differences in drivers of total costs. External failure costs make up a much larger share of the total costs of quality in the restaurant than they do in the manufacturing plants. This attests to the fact that it is much more difficult to provide remedies for service failures than for failures in tangible goods—it is hard to "repair" bad service! External failure costs can vary a great deal across different manufactured products too, depending on their durability and warranty policies.

relationships

of poor quality is surprisingly large! Once a COQ analysis has been used to quantify the monetary impact of quality on their company's performance, managers are typically highly motivated. The COQ analysis points out the magnitude of the opportunity and gives managers a stronger basis for financially justifying investments in quality improvement initiatives.

An Inverted View of Management

A focus on quality management turns a conventional view of management on its head. Traditional management views make sharp distinctions between managers and workers, often elevating the importance of managers. That is, the workers are present to support the activities of management. This view is illustrated by the pyramid shown on the left-hand side of Figure 6-1. The base of the pyramid consists of frontline workers who interact routinely with customers and operational processes, so they deal with the daily problems and difficulties of running the business. In doing so, frontline workers can be seen as supporters of smaller and smaller layers of management. In this view of the organization, managers are thought to be the decision makers and "owners" of operating processes and, therefore, they are seen to have primary responsibility for product quality.

A progressive quality management approach challenges this view, arguing that it is the workers on the front lines of business who should actually have primary "ownership" of operating processes. Further, managers should support workers, not the other way around. Frontline workers have the closest contact with customers and operational processes; therefore, they ultimately determine the quality level that the firm offers and how customers view the firm. In addition, they know more than anyone about the firm's problems and the best ways to solve them. Total quality management advocates believe that the entire organization should support the frontline workers, as the right-hand side of Figure 6-1 illustrates. This idea of elevating and empowering frontline workers is a core value of total quality management.

What does employee *empowerment* actually mean? Several elements are required. First, frontline workers must be given both the responsibility and authority to make decisions. This is sometimes the hardest change for both managers and frontline workers to accept. Both groups have to clearly define and recognize the enlarged scope of decisions for which frontline workers are responsible, and then managers have to relinquish control and actively encourage these frontline workers to take charge. Measurement and incentive systems may also need to be changed to motivate frontline worker involvement.

Second, frontline workers need to have the knowledge required to make good decisions. Empowerment usually requires education and cross-training (job rotation) of employees on all technical issues related to their job environments. Equally important, employees need training on quality management concepts and in the use of problem-solving tools. If frontline workers are to set appropriate priorities and make good business decisions, they also need an understanding of the organizational strategy and current objectives.

Finally, frontline workers must have the resources required to make quality improvements. Such resources usually include data, tools and systems, money for investments, and time.

Traditional Organizational Structure	Direction of Support	TQM Organizational View

FIGURE 6-1 Traditional versus Quality Management View of Organizational Structure

Process-Oriented Focus on Prevention and Problem Solving

Quality management is based on the idea that products are outcomes of processes. All organizations, functions, and activities involved in the design, production, and delivery of a product, good, or service should be viewed collectively as parts of a process. This extended process view includes suppliers and customers, making quality management principles very consistent with the overall supply chain management perspective. Quality problems are often only solvable through the involvement of suppliers, because their inputs may be related to problem causes. Suppliers can also help determine the costs and feasibility of changes required to address quality problems. As stated above, it is almost always more efficient to solve problems at the earliest stage possible in the supply chain, rather than trying to find a remedy or workaround at some later stage. Involving customers can clarify requirements needed to define acceptable levels of quality.

In TQM, problem prevention is emphasized, as opposed to fixing problems after they occur. It is better to eliminate the causes of problems than it is to find and sort out defective products before they go to customers. In the long term, prevention is almost always cheaper than correction. Sometimes managers refer to this prevention-oriented approach as *quality at the source* as opposed to *quality through inspection*. Furthermore, problem solving is most effective when decisions are based on the analysis of actual data, as opposed to conjectures or opinions. The supplement to this chapter illustrates a number of analytical tools that have been developed to collect and analyze data. Use of these tools along with a data-led, or fact-based, approach helps managers to detect and solve problems in processes.

Variability in repeated activities is often the major source of problems in operations processes. For example:

- Variability in the time it takes to complete a task often disrupts work flows.
- Variations in a purchased material characteristic, such as in the diameter of a ball bearing, can cause unreliability in product performance.
- Variations in marketing promotions can cause large swings in product demand, which make production processes less stable.

Variability causes unpredictability, which increases uncertainty and reduces control over processes and outputs. Thus, an important task in quality management is to continually find and eliminate sources of unwanted and uncontrolled variability. Later in this chapter we will discuss the Six Sigma program for quality management, an approach that builds upon this idea.

Viewing Quality Management as a Never-Ending Quest

Because products and processes are continually changing, and because perfection (zero defects) is deemed to be an appropriate goal, continuous process improvement should be a part of every person's job. A widely used improvement process known as Kaizen, or Continuous Improvement, is based on the notion that the long-term survival and success of any organization occurs only when everyone in the firm actively pursues opportunities to identify and implement improvements every day. Chapter 3 discussed the practice of Kaizen for process improvement. Pursuit of small improvements keeps people thinking about the process and its current operation. Furthermore, small improvements are often gained without needing large investments of capital. In many cases, these improvements can be gained with little or no required investment.

Building an Organizational Culture around Quality

relationships

An organizational culture is reflected in the values and behavioral norms that guide the decisions and interactions of people within an organization. Culture is shaped by the actions of the organization's leaders, by the environment, and by the collective experiences of the people in the organization. For example, think about the values and norms that exist among members of a sports team. Team members' goals and beliefs are shaped by what the coach says and does, but they are also shaped by what their teammates say and do. Experiences also play a role. Consider the effects on team culture that result from a series of close wins or losses. Close wins can build a sense of confidence and a winning spirit. Close losses can be disheartening.

Managers have to recognize that their actions, more than their words, help to shape culture. At the same time they have to recognize that they are not completely in control of the firm's culture. Both past experiences and external forces, such as the economic environment, labor union influences, and governmental controls, can have big impacts.

The culture within an organization can have tremendous effects on the success or failure of quality improvement initiatives. History contains many cases of companies whose quality initiatives were rendered ineffective by an incompatible culture. Most often cultural barriers to change are created by perceived inequities that have created a mistrust of management, or by incentive systems that motivate behaviors at odds with the values of quality management (e.g., when management pays for output irrespective of its quality).

It is critical for managers to continually assess their organizations and identify the dynamics of culture that may be creating values and norms of behavior that are supportive, or damaging, for quality management initiatives. Through communications, actions, measures, rewards, and incentives, managers should seek to build the values of total quality management into their corporate culture. Table 6-4 lists the values we have discussed in this section, along with some

TABLE 6-4   TQM Values and Success Factors

Values that Characterize TQM	Factors Affecting the Success of TQM
• Holistic view of product quality and its impacts	• Strong, charismatic leadership
• Emphasis on customer requirements	• Trust between labor and management
• Extended process view of operations	• Crisis situation or compelling reason for change
• Emphasis on prevention rather than inspection	• Adequate resourcing of training and improvement projects
• Disdain for variability	• Clear, well-communicated, uncomplicated change process
• Data-based decision making (vs. opinion-based)	• Unquestionable success of early efforts
• Employee empowerment	
• Top management support	
• Supplier involvement	
• Continuous improvement	

of the factors that have contributed to the creation of a TQM culture. Note that the success factors are not guarantees of success, but their absence will hinder successful implementation.

The core values of quality management are fleshed out in various quality improvement methodologies, certification standards, and awards criteria. In the following sections, we describe several methodologies and standards that you are likely to encounter, namely:

- Plan-Do-Check-Act Cycle
- Six Sigma Approach to Quality Improvement
- ISO 9000 Series: An International Quality Standard

GUIDING METHODOLOGIES FOR QUALITY MANAGEMENT

Plan-Do-Check-Act Cycles (Deming Wheel)

A popular methodology used to guide problem identification and solution is the **plan-do-check-act cycle (PDCA)**, also known as the *Deming Wheel* or *Deming Cycle* (in honor of W. Edwards Deming). The PDCA cycle (see Figure 6-2) describes the sequence used to solve problems and improve quality continuously over time.

The PDCA cycle consists of four separate but linked activities:

- *Plan.* Identify a problem by studying the current situation to detect a gap between it and the desired future situation. Identify actions to improve the situation (i.e., close the gap). Formulate a plan for closing the gap (e.g., a plan for reducing the number of defects coming from a specific process).
- *Do.* Having formulated a plan, implement it.
- *Check.* Use performance metrics to monitor and inspect the results. Identify unplanned problems elsewhere in the system or previously hidden problems uncovered by the changes.
- *Act.* Review information collected in the check step and take corrective actions to prevent reoccurrence of problems. Institutionalize changes (through revised procedures and associated training) as a starting point for the next PDCA cycle.
- The PDCA method is simple, giving all employees the impetus and guiding structure for attacking problems on a daily basis. Workers at all levels can be trained in the PDCA process and in the use of the quality tools referenced above.

Six Sigma: A Systematic Approach to Quality Management

In addition to general methods for quality improvement that can be applied by all workers, companies often need to organize specific quality improvement projects. The **Six Sigma**

plan-do-check-act cycle (PDCA)
A process for improving quality that describes the sequence used to solve problems and improve quality continuously over time; also known as the *Deming Wheel* or *Deming Cycle*.

Six Sigma A management program that seeks to improve the quality of process outputs by identifying and removing the causes of defects and variation in the various processes.

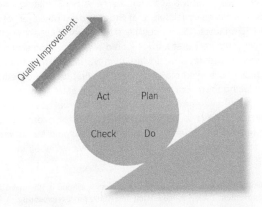

FIGURE 6-2
PDCA in Action

program for quality and process improvements has been adopted by many of the larger firms around the world. Six Sigma is a management approach that seeks to improve the quality of process outputs by using projects to identify and remove the causes of defects and variation in the various processes.

The term *sigma* refers to the Greek symbol, σ, that represents the standard deviation of values for the output of a process. The standard deviation is an indicator of process variability (inconsistency). In statistics, standard deviation is a measure of the variability or dispersion of a population, a data set, or a probability distribution. A low standard deviation indicates that the data points tend to be very close to the same value, typically the mean, while high standard deviation indicates that the data are spread out over a large range of values. As standard deviation increases, there is greater uncertainty about the exact outcome. As previously noted in this chapter, variability is regarded as a source of quality failures. A primary objective of the Six Sigma method is to design and improve products and processes so that sources of variability are reduced.

That explains the *sigma* in Six Sigma, but what about the *six*? One of the issues in quality improvement is deciding how far variability reduction efforts should go. In a Six Sigma approach, the goal is to achieve a process standard deviation that is 12 times smaller than the range of outputs allowed by the product's design specification. In this case, the design specification encompasses *six* process output standard deviations on each side of its center point.[1] Consider Example 6-1 below.

Curious students often ask, "Why is *six* sigma the goal? Why not *five* sigma, or *seven* sigma?" Good question. Early developers of the Six Sigma approach at Motorola originally chose six sigma as an appropriate goal because of the nature of their products and manufacturing processes. A six sigma rated process, where upper and lower product specifications are set 12 standard deviations apart, will produce at most only 3.4 product defects per million outputs. Is this goal suitable for other products? It all depends on the costs of quality. If the costs of failure outweigh the costs of prevention and appraisal, then pursuing greater levels of conformance (more "sigmas") is probably justified. However, for some products there is a point at which the size of potential failure cost savings does not justify the investments required to achieve them. For example, Six Sigma quality is arguably not justified for a product such as an inexpensive ballpoint pen, because the internal and external failure costs are low once a reasonable level of quality has been achieved. On the other hand, Six Sigma quality may be too low a goal for products such as drugs and medical devices, where the cost of a single failure can be very high (someone's life!).

standard deviation A measure of the variability or dispersion of a population, data set, or distribution.

EXAMPLE 6-1

You operate a trucking company that delivers products to distribution centers for a large retailer such as Walmart. Distribution centers are very busy places. Consequently, they schedule deliveries in very tight windows of time. Walmart often requires that deliveries arrive within a 15-minute window, that is, no more than 7.5 minutes before or after a scheduled time. A Six Sigma approach would seek to make truck arrivals so consistent that the standard deviation of arrival times is no more than 1.25 minutes (15 minutes/12). If this level of consistency were achieved, it would be highly unlikely that a truck would ever arrive too early or too late.

How would you reduce driving time variability this much? The Six Sigma approach provides a systematic process for first identifying sources of variability and then reducing them. For example, you might start by thinking of all the possible causes of early and late arrivals (weather, traffic, breakdowns, and so on). Then you would brainstorm ways to prevent these causes or overcome them. If variability cannot be reduced sufficiently, another option would be to widen the specifications; that is, to negotiate wider delivery windows with Walmart.

---

[1]This relationship between product specification and process variation is illustrated in the supplement to this chapter, "Quality Improvement Tools," in the section describing process capability.

TABLE 6-5   How Quality Relates to Sigma

Sigma Level	Defects per Million Units
2σ	308,770
3σ	66,810
4σ	6,209
5σ	233
6σ	3.4

The Classical View of Quality "99.9% Good" (4.6σ)	The Six Sigma View of Quality "99.99966% Good" (6σ)
• 20,000 lost articles of mail per hour.	• Seven lost articles of mail per hour.
• Unsafe drinking water almost 15 minutes each day.	• One minute of unsafe drinking water every seven months.
• 5,000 incorrect surgical operations per week.	• 1.7 incorrect surgical operations per week.
• 2 short or long landings at most major airports daily.	• One short or long landing at most major airports every five years.
• 200,000 wrong drug prescriptions each year.	• 68 wrong drug prescriptions each year.
• No electricity for almost 7 hours each month.	• One hour without electricity every 34 years.

Table 6-5 shows the levels of quality associated with other sigma levels, along with some of the quality levels seen in our everyday lives. In truth, very few business operations ever attain a Six Sigma level of quality. More important than the absolute goal are the quality improvement processes that comprise a Six Sigma program.

DMAIC: The Six Sigma Process

At the heart of the Six Sigma approach is a five-step process: define, measure, analyze, improve, and control (DMAIC). Figure 6-3 describes the **DMAIC** process. For any given good or service, members of a cross-functional team usually work through these steps together to complete a quality improvement project. The focus of the DMAIC improvement process is initially on the product outcome; then it shifts to the underlying processes needed to produce and deliver the product.

As project teams work through the DMAIC process, they focus on several objectives:

1. Each *critical-to-quality* (CTQ) characteristic should be defined from a customer's perspective and in a way in which it can be measured as objectively as possible.
2. It is important to determine and consider the future market and technology strategies for the product, as well as the strategies for the processes that are involved in delivery of the CTQ characteristics.
3. The quality improvement tools described in the supplement to this chapter are especially useful in the analyze, improve, and control steps of the process.
4. If the data do not already exist, the project team needs to develop a way to measure important outcomes on a frequent and regular basis.

activity

student

For a candy such as M&Ms, identify the important critical-to-quality characteristics. How would you measure these characteristics objectively? Which of these measures pertain to the physical product itself? Which of these measures relate to the packaging or the services surrounding the good?

DMAIC An acronym for the five steps at the heart of the Six Sigma process: define, measure, analyze, improve, and control.

LO6-5 Apply the Six Sigma DMAIC approach to quality improvement.

FIGURE 6-3   The DMAIC Process

Source: Dynamic Diagrams, 2009.

How does **Six Sigma** work?

1. DEFINE
A cross-functional team uses inputs describing customer's needs and product functionality requirements to define Critical-to-Quality (CTQ) characteristics of the product or service. CTQs represent the few characteristics that have the greatest impacts on customers' perceptions of quality, thus requiring priority and focus for related operational processes.

BEFORE SIX SIGMA

Business process towards desired end product requirements

2. MEASURE
The team identifies specific processes that create or influence CTQs, and measures current levels of quality (defects) for each CTQ, considering allowable tolerances for variation in each CTQ outcome.

3. ANALYZE
The team performs data-based analyses to uncover important root causes of process variations that lead to CTQ defects.

process range

acceptable range

Key process variable introducing highest likelihood of variation

4. IMPROVE
The team designs and implements process improvements that reduce variabilities, thereby increasing the probability that CTQs will be delivered within allowable ranges.

5. CONTROL
The team installs monitoring and adjustment systems or procedures to insure that process variations remain minimized, and that CTQ variables remain within allowable output ranges.

AFTER SIX SIGMA — Less Variation

Business process towards desired end product requirements

5. The lessons learned from the process should be documented, and the final problem solution should be implemented in all applicable areas.

The nearby Get Real box provides an example of how DMAIC can be successfully used to resolve quality problems.

Design for Six Sigma

The DMAIC process is usually aimed at improving existing products and their supporting operational processes. A similar approach has been developed to guide design decisions made in the creation of new products. **Design for Six Sigma (DFSS)** is an approach in which a cross-functional team designs products and processes in a way that balances customer requirements with the constraints and capabilities of the supporting manufacturing and service processes. The primary difference between DFSS and DMAIC is that DFSS takes place in the development phase, whereas DMAIC usually takes place after a new product has been launched. DFSS makes use of design engineering tools that may be used to simulate and evaluate different product/process design scenarios, whereas DMAIC ideally works with actual product and operational data. Other "design-for" processes and tools similar to DFSS are described in Chapter 4.

Design for Six Sigma (DFSS)
A design approach that balances customer requirements with the constraints and capabilities of the supporting manufacturing and service processes.

GET REAL

Applying DMAIC to Cough Drops

A British food company used DMAIC to improve operations in its cough drop production line, which suffered high rates of machine downtime, scrap and rework, and chronically late order deliveries.

- *Define:* The project team mapped out the production process, identified a probable cause of their defined problem—variability in the size of the cough drops—and calculated the costs associated with this problem. Too much variance in the size of a cough drop may seem incidental, but larger tablets were more likely to chip and introduce abrasive sugar dust into the machinery, causing breakdowns. That problem, along with slowdowns in packaging and the added maintenance, was estimated to cost £485,000 (783,000 USD) per year.
- *Measure:* The cough drop team found that the existing measuring techniques were not precise enough, so they did their own process measurements. They found that the process was not within specifications: Almost 20 percent of the cough drops were too large, while almost none were too small.
- *Analyze:* The team measured the accuracy of the syrup base extrusion system and found it to be accurate. They then determined that air bubbles forming in the tablets somewhere in the process were the culprit. The team investigated possible process steps where air could enter the product, finally settling on three possible steps.
- *Improve:* The team experimented with changes in product temperature, machine lubrication, and other factors to prevent air bubbles from forming. Implementing these changes caused cough drop variability to fall within

process specifications. Even so, the team noted that the process was still fairly low in capability. They suggested adding an additional wrapping line with wider tolerances for larger tablets.
- *Control:* The process changes included training for personnel and the installation of new monitoring systems to ensure that the variability improvements were maintained.

The financial impact of this project was dramatic. By decreasing the variability and increasing the wrapping tolerance for larger sizes, the company was able to save £290,000 (470,000 USD) per year in waste, maintenance, downtime, and late orders. The cost of the DMAIC project team was only £13,000 (21,000 USD), while the return on investment was 2,230.8 percent!

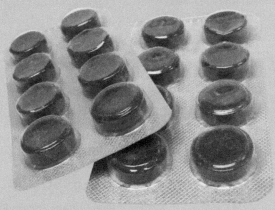

© Stockbyte/Punchstock

Implementing Six Sigma

Organizations often view Six Sigma as an improvement program aimed at gaining greater consistency and efficiency throughout the organization. The most common approach for implementing Six Sigma is to start by training key leaders in the organization in quality management philosophies and tools. Then these initial leaders train others, who then train others, and so on. Usually there are two to three levels of training targeted for various employees in the organization. Persons completing the levels of training are given names taken from the Asian martial arts tradition. For example, persons who complete the highest levels of training are called Black Belts, or even higher-level Master Black Belts. Black Belt personnel have usually completed at least several quality improvement projects. Master Black Belts may even work full-time in training others in Six Sigma processes. Employees who complete the basic level of training are often called Green Belts.

To achieve Green Belt status, employees usually must complete a project that applies the Six Sigma process to a product in their own area of work. These projects often must satisfy certain operational or financial performance goals (e.g., the project will achieve a 25 percent reduction in lead times, or the project will generate a minimum 25 percent return on investment). The cost savings from such projects can be used to pay back the costs of training for the Six Sigma program. Numerous companies have shown tremendous benefits from implementing Six Sigma. A recent study showed that a medium-sized firm that adopts Six Sigma should expect to add \$35 – \$40 million in profit each year![2]

LO6-6 Compare and contrast various quality standards and certification programs.

CERTIFYING PROGRESS IN QUALITY MANAGEMENT

The TQM and quality initiatives we have discussed up to this point are company specific; process improvements vary from company to company. Operations managers often want to know how their operational quality processes compare to others. In addition, prospective customers often want assurances that a given supplier has achieved a high level of quality performance. Certifications such as the ISO 9000 help to provide universal standards that managers and customers can use to gauge a company's quality progress.

ISO 9000: An International Quality Standard

ISO 9000 A set of internationally accepted standards for business quality management systems.

ISO 9000 defines a set of internationally accepted standards for business quality management systems. It was initially developed by the International Organization for Standardization to facilitate international trade. Since its inception in 1987, the standard has been revised several times. The newest version is referred to as the ISO 9000:2015 standard. National bodies from over 120 countries support this standard.

As a standard, ISO 9000 is applicable to all forms of organizations, irrespective of size or product offerings. Certifications have been attained by banks, consulting operations, manufacturing plants, software development firms, tourism operations, and even universities. The essential purpose of ISO 9000 is to ensure that operating processes are well documented, consistently executed, monitored, and improved. ISO 9000 certification provides essentially the same function for business processes as financial accountants provide when they audit a company's financial transactions.

Attaining ISO 9000 Certification

Over one million organizations have been independently certified to ISO 9000. To attain certification, an organization must be audited by an external, authorized party. Certification states that the firm's processes meet the requirements in the ISO 9000 standards. Typically, an organization first conducts an internal audit to determine whether its processes are consistent with the standards. Then, it contracts with a registrar (an external and independent body)[3] to perform a formal audit. Attaining ISO 9000 certification is usually quite demanding and time-consuming. The process can take anywhere from three months to two years, depending on the initial level of compliance of the firm's systems. If the organization passes the audit, its certification is recorded by the registrar.

The standard itself consists of five sections. Table 6-6 provides a brief description of each section. The standard emphasizes many of quality management's core values.

- First, it is customer-oriented, with a great emphasis placed on defining, meeting, and achieving customer satisfaction.
- Second, it emphasizes the role of leadership in engaging people to make improvements on a regular basis.
- Third, it recognizes the importance of a process-oriented approach, including the definition, measurement, and documentation of processes.

---

[2]M. Swink and B. Jacobs, "Six Sigma Adoption: Operating Performance Impacts and Contextual Drivers of Success," *Journal of Operations Management* 30, no. 6 (2012), pp. 437–53.

[3]It is possible to self-certify a system to be ISO 9000 compliant. However, such an action does not carry the weight and credibility of external certification.

TABLE 6-6   The ISO 9001: 2015 Certification Structure

Section		Focus/Description
4		**Context of the organization**
	4.1	Understanding the organization and its context.
	4.2	Understanding the needs and expectations of interested parties.
	4.3	Determining the scope of the quality management system.
	4.4	Quality management system and its processes.
5		**Leadership**
	5.1	Leadership and commitment.
	5.2	Policy.
	5.3	Organizational roles, responsibilities, and authorities.
6		**Planning**
	6.1	Actions to address risks and opportunities.
	6.2	Quality objectives and planning to achieve them.
	6.3	Planning of changes.
7		**Support**
	7.1	Resources.
	7.2	Competence.
	7.3	Awareness.
	7.4	Communication.
	7.5	Documented information.
8		**Operation**
	8.1	Operational planning and control.
	8.2	Requirements for products and services.
	8.3	Design and development of products and services.
	8.4	Control of externally provided processes, products, and services.
	8.5	Production and service provision.
	8.6	Release of products and services.
	8.7	Control nonconforming outputs.
9		**Performance evaluation**
	9.1	Monitoring, measurement analysis, and evaluation.
	9.2	Internal audit.
	9.3	Management review.
10		**Improvement**
	10.1	General
	10.2	Nonconformity and corrective action.
	10.3	Continual improvement.

- Fourth, it places a high priority on evidence-based decision making.
- Finally, the standard emphasizes the importance of managing inter- and intraorganizational relationships.

In general, the standard is fairly flexible in that it tells management *what* to do, but not necessarily *how* to do it.

Businesses are motivated to seek ISO 9000 certification for several reasons. Increasingly, firms are required to be certified to sell products in most major markets. Virtually every major industrial nation in the world has accepted these standards. Certification at least gives the appearance that a company will be a reliable supplier. Beyond appearances, ISO 9000-certified firms benefit from internal improvements as a result of the certification. To pass the audit, employees usually must reexamine and critically challenge their practices. The certification process can also improve communication links between functional areas within the firm. It forces people to forge agreements on important issues such as the firm's definition of quality and its identification of its target market. The success with ISO 9000 has caused the ISO organization to extend the focus of business issues covered by such standards. For example, in 1996 ISO introduced the ISO 14000 standard for environmental systems. This standard is discussed in greater detail in Chapter 16.

Industry Interpretations of ISO 9000

While the guidelines in ISO 9000 can be applied just about anywhere, each organization needs to carefully interpret them for their context. In some cases industry groups have created interpretations for their specific requirements. Table 6-7 shows some examples of common interpretations of ISO 9000.

TABLE 6-7   Industry-Specific Interpretations of ISO 9000

Standard	Industry
TickIT	Information technology industry (specifically software development)
AS9000	Aerospace manufacturers (e.g., AlliedSignal, Allison Engine, Rockwell-Collins, Boeing, Lockheed-Martin)
ISO/TS 16949	American and European automotive manufacturers
TL 9000	Telecom consortium (QuEST forum)
ISO 13485	Medical industry
ISO/IED 90003	Computer software
ISO/TS 29001	Petroleum, petrochemical, and natural gas industries.

CHAPTER SUMMARY

In this chapter we have explored the concept of quality management by tracing its origins and philosophical elements and describing how its core values have been fleshed out in quality standards and improvement programs today. We can summarize the important points of this chapter as follows:

1. Quality management strives to achieve a sustainable competitive advantage by focusing company actions on customer satisfaction, employee empowerment, and powerful management and statistical tools to achieve superior quality.

2. It is important to integrate quality management into the firm's strategic activities by ensuring that the voice of the customer is heard. The Six Sigma approach to quality is a corporatewide system to integrate the elements of the customer, strategy, value, processes, statistical tools, and metrics. This approach has been successfully implemented in many firms.

3. Formal certification to quality standards such as ISO 9000 indicates that a firm has passed a rigorous audit to confirm that its major processes have been documented, that everyone associated with those processes understands correct procedures, and that people routinely follow these procedures. ISO 9000 seems likely to make certification a near-universal order qualifier in important markets around the world.

4. Quality management in face-to-face services must take into consideration the interpersonal interactions of service providers and customers. Sometimes customers' perceptions of quality vary widely as they are potentially influenced by many different aspects of the operating system.

5. Regardless of the form of quality improvement program that a firm pursues, the core values of total commitment, cross-functional decision making, continuous improvement, and data-based decision making are the critical aspects to making quality improvement a success.

KEY TERMS

appraisal costs 178	external failure costs 178	quality management 173
conformance quality 173	internal failure costs 178	Six Sigma 183
cost of quality (COQ) 178	ISO 9000 188	standard deviation 184
design for Six Sigma (DFSS) 186	plan-do-check-act cycle (PDCA) 183	total quality management (TQM) 176
design quality 172	prevention costs 178	
DMAIC 185	product quality 172	

DISCUSSION QUESTIONS

1. Pick a product (good or service) that you are interested in consuming sometime in the near future (for example, a textbook, apartment rental, cell phone, etc.). Analyze the offerings of two competing firms. How do the products compare on various dimensions of quality? From these differences, what can you infer about each company's strategy and the customers that they seem to be targeting?

2. Employee empowerment is an essential element of quality management, especially in services. From your own experience, cite instances where a service provider empowered its employee to go the extra mile to delight you. Then indicate an instance where the opposite happened.

3. You have been appointed head of quality control for your organization (either a firm you have worked for or your college). During the first month, you interview disciples

of Deming, Juran, and Crosby. Each seems to be equally affable and competent. Which consultant would you hire for your organization? Why?

4. It has been said that quality management is really a "people" system, more than a technical system. If this is true, what conditions must first be in place for a firm to be successful with quality management? What are the possible repercussions for the firm if the employees aren't committed to the quality management program?

PROBLEMS

1. Given the following cost information for Company XYZ, calculate:
   a. Total appraisal cost
   b. Total prevention cost
   c. Total cost of internal failures
   d. Total cost of external failures
   e. Total cost of quality

Cost item	Total for the Year
Quality assurance	$450,000
Equipment maintenance	$205,000
Product redesign	$310,000
Product warranty and repair	$550,000
Product testing and inspection	$372,000
Training	$250,000
Process improvement/Kaizen	$120,000
Material scrap	$230,000
Rework labor	$426,000
Incoming materials inspection	$323,000
Customer support (after sale)	$150,000
Travel to suppliers/process certification	$ 75,000
Travel to customers/problem solving	$ 80,000

2. Rachel loves to bake cookies, but she has an old oven that has trouble maintaining a constant temperature. If the acceptable temperature range for making the cookies is 350 plus or minus 5 degrees, what is the allowable standard deviation in the temperature of her oven in order to achieve a Six Sigma level of quality?

3. Six Sigma quality (3.4 defects per million units produced) is probably a bit much to ask of Rachel's old oven (see problem 2).

   a. What would the standard deviation in the temperature of her oven need to be if she settled for a "Three Sigma" level of quality?
   b. If her oven exactly meets a "Three Sigma" quality level, what percentage of the time would her oven be operating at a temperature outside the acceptable range? (*Hint:* See Table 6-5.)

4. Suppose that the Dallas School District wants to achieve Six Sigma quality levels of performance in delivering students to school. It has established a 20-minute window as an acceptable range within which buses carrying students should arrive at school.

   a. What is the maximum allowable standard deviation of arrival times required in order to achieve this standard of quality?
   b. If the school district achieves this standard, about how many times out of a million deliveries will a bus deliver students either too early or too late?

CASE

Aqua-Fun

Roberta Brown sat at her desk and looked through the pre-liminary slide deck she had prepared. This presentation had to be good. In two weeks she would be giving the presentation to the top management team of Aqua-Fun. The goal: To secure their commitment to a new program aimed at improving quality. Improvements were to come through a new (to Aqua-Fun) corporatewide program to implement Six Sigma. Involvement in this program was the principal reason that Roberta had been hired by Eric Tremble, the vice-president of operations/supply chain management at Aqua-Fun, some six months earlier.

Demand for Aqua-Fun's products had grown from an emerging interest in home swimming pools over the past few decades. During that time, the founders of Aqua-Fun recognized that there was a need for good quality, fun water toys and swimming pool accessories. Since then, Aqua-Fun had grown to its current state of $195 million in annual sales, employing some 650 employees. The secret to its growth: A fair price, reliable products, and the ability to design and introduce interesting and fun new toys and accessories quickly. However, in the last two years, there was evidence that Aqua-Fun's reputation was suffering. Sales growth had slowed, and, as some of the accessories (such as pool auto-matic cleaners) became more sophisticated, warranty claims had grown dramatically. Top management's best estimate of the costs of dealing with poor quality in the field was about $6.7 million. However, Eric Tremble was convinced that Aqua-Fun's managers did not fully comprehend the total costs associated with managing quality and quality failures.

Before joining Aqua-Fun, Roberta Brown had worked for two years in a firm that had successfully improved quality, reduced costs, and increased revenues by imple-menting a companywide Six Sigma program. Roberta had been part of the Six Sigma planning and deployment team; she had gone through Green and Black Belt training; and she had successfully carried out three high visibility Six Sigma projects. Now, she was being asked to introduce a similar approach at Aqua-Fun. For both Aqua-Fun and Roberta, the time seemed right for Six Sigma.

The Presentation

Critical to this presentation was Roberta's COQ analysis (shown in the table following). She worried that the analy-sis was missing important cost categories. She was also unsure regarding which costs should be included. Items with question marks "????" in the COQ were items that she either did not have data for or was unsure about includ-ing. For example, she wasn't sure how the marketing man-agers would feel about including marketing research as a category in the COQ, though she knew that this was a large expense for the company, well above $10 million per year. Other missing categories could be quite substantial as well. Besides, Roberta still felt that there might be even more "hidden" costs of quality not captured in the analysis.

As Roberta reviewed the presentation, she noted points that she wanted to make and questions she still needed to answer:

- Aqua-Fun had tended to underestimate the true costs of quality. For example, the external failure cost estimate of $6.7 million neglected lost sales and damaged customer goodwill that might occur from poor quality products.

- The initial costs of training for a Six Sigma program (between $20,000 and $30,000 per Green Belt and $40,000–$50,000 per Black Belt) were high. In typical Six Sigma implementations, companies trained 2 to 5 percent of employees as Black Belts and they trained 50 to 100 percent of employees as Green Belts.

- There were significant benefits to be gained by such investments. Other firms had achieved 10 to 20 percent reductions in the COQ each year for the first few years of the Six Sigma program.

- To be successful, this program had to be corporate-wide. It had to involve everyone from top managers to the people working on the floor. It had to involve not only operations, purchasing, logistics, and supply chain areas but also finance, personnel, training, mar-keting, engineering, and accounting.

Questions

1. Review the COQ Analysis. Should marketing research and other similar cost categories be included? What other cost categories should be included? Where should Roberta go to get estimates for these other costs? Who else might need to be involved?

2. If Aqua-Fun implements Six Sigma, what costs might be expected to go up, at least in the short term? What costs should be expected to go down? Can this pro-gram be financially justified? How?

3. Thinking about the core values of quality manage-ment, what factors should Roberta encourage the man-agement team to consider as they design a Six Sigma implementation?

	Estimated Annual Cost ($)	Total Category Cost ($)
I. Prevention costs		9,507,000
A. Marketing/customer/user		
1. Marketing research	????	
2. Customer/user perception surveys/clinics	????	
B. Product/service/design development		
1. Design quality progress reviews	1,300,000	
2. Design support activities	900,000	
3. Design qualification and test	3,600,000	
C. Purchasing		
1. Supplier reviews, ratings, and certifications	564,000	
2. Purchase order tech data reviews	260,000	
3. Supplier quality planning	????	
D. Operations (manufacturing or service)		
1. Operations process validation (planning and equipment design)	750,000	
2. Operations support quality planning	25,000	
3. Operator quality education	95,000	
4. Operator SPC/process control	623,000	
E. Quality administration		
1. Administrative salaries and expenses	1,330,000	
2. Quality program planning and reporting	????	
3. Quality education	25,000	
4. Quality improvement projects	20,000	
5. Quality audits	15,000	
6. Other prevention costs	????	
II. Appraisal costs		8,612,000
A. Purchasing appraisal costs		
1. Receiving or incoming inspections and tests	2,260,000	
2. Measurement equipment (annualized cost)	856,000	
3. Qualification of supplier product	????	
4. Source inspection and control programs	????	
B. Operations (manufacturing or service) appraisal costs		
1. Planned operations inspections, tests, audits	3,950,000	
2. Inspection and test materials	225,000	
3. Process control measurements	325,000	
4. Laboratory support	145,000	
5. Outside endorsements and certifications	????	
C. External appraisal costs		
1. Field performance evaluation	-	
2. Special product evaluations	75,000	
3. Evaluation of field stock and spare parts	776,000	
D. Review of tests and inspection data	????	
E. Miscellaneous quality evaluations	????	

	Estimated Annual Cost ($)	Total Category Cost ($)
III. Internal failure costs		12,639,000
A. Product/service design failure costs (internal)		
1. Design corrective action	1,230,000	
2. Rework due to design changes	560,000	
3. Scrap due to design changes	3,650,000	
B. Purchasing failure costs		
1. Purchased material reject disposition and rework costs	1,330,000	
2. Purchased material replacement costs	230,000	
3. Supplier corrective action	????	
4. Uncontrolled material losses	????	
C. Operations (product or service) failure costs		
1. Material review and corrective action costs	356,000	
2. Operations rework and repair costs	1,700,000	
3. Re-inspection/retest costs	23,000	
4. Extra operations	????	
5. Scrap costs (operations)	3,560,000	
6. Downgraded end product or service	????	
7. Internal failure labor losses	????	
D. Other internal failure costs	????	
IV. External failure		6,695,000
A. Complaint investigation/customer or user service	845,000	
B. Returned goods	1,200,000	
C. Recall costs	650,000	
D. Warranty claims	3,250,000	
E. Liability costs	750,000	
F. Customer/user goodwill/lost sales	????	
G. Other external failure costs	????	
	Total COQ	$ 37,453,000

CASE

A Comment on Management Attitude

I visited my old pal Dinsmore recently. He had called to let me know that he had taken over as general manager of the Flagship hotel about six months ago, and he thought that I might be interested in seeing a real hotel from the inside. He also indicated that I might learn something about the hotel business.

When I drove up to the front door, a steady rain kept me inside the car for 10 to 15 minutes. During that time, I noticed that the doorman was peering at me from inside the lobby. Sensing that the rain was not going to quit, I made a dash for the doors and pushed my way in, dripping on the carpet in the process. The doorman told me that I could only leave the car there for about 10 minutes because it was a no-parking zone, but that the hotel garage in the next block would be glad to store it for me. He offered to lend me his umbrella in order to unload the trunk.

Accepting his offer, I retrieved my suitcase and clothes bag and dropped both at the front desk. Announcing myself as Mr. Dinsmore's guest didn't seem to make much of an impression on the clerk, who was chatting with the cashier. She seemed a little irritated at my interference.

There was no reservation for me, but they said they could fix me up since I had said the general manager had invited me. After only three rings of the "front" bell, the bellhop came to lead me to my room, which, as it turned out, wasn't made up. He commented that it was only 3 o'clock and the room would probably be fixed up by the time I returned from my business. I tipped him, dropped my bags, and remembered the car.

It wasn't necessary to worry because the police had just towed the vehicle away. The doorman said that he had waved to the tow truck but they hadn't been able to see him for the rain. He assured me that I could pick up the car in the morning with no problem. A cab could take me to the police lot, and the fine was only $25 plus the towing charge. The garage charged $6. He noted that it was interesting how they could move a car like that without having the key. He said they would make good thieves.

I found Dinsmore's office on the third floor. One of the elevators wasn't working so I took the brisk walk up the stairs. His secretary nodded and suggested that I move some magazines off that bench and sit down as "Elmer" would be with me as soon as he got off the telephone. She went back to her book.

After a few minutes, she seemed to notice my presence again and offered me some coffee from the percolator in the corner of the reception room. (She didn't like the hotel coffee, and neither, apparently, did Elmer.) I accepted with thanks, telling her I was still damp, having not been able to shower and change because the room was not prepared. She said I really shouldn't expect much else because, although checkout time was noon, they didn't like to push their guests out on rainy days like this. I said I thought that was very considerate of them.

I asked about my automobile, and she repeated the information I already had about the $25 fine and towing charges. Happens all the time, she indicated. The police have no class.

Dinsmore emerged from his office and greeted me effusively. Now, he told me, I was going to see how a hotel should be run. He took me into his office, cleared some reports off a chair, and offered me a cigar. After remarking on my trip, and how fortunate it was of him to catch me in an off moment, he asked me how I liked the place so far.

I told him about the car, the doorman, the room clerk, the room, the bellhop, and the elevator. He told me how to get the car back and dismissed the other incidents as growing pains.

Then, lowering his voice, he asked me if I would mind checking out the restaurant for him. He would pay, naturally. But he wasn't sure if the restaurant manager was really operating the place right. She didn't seem to get along with the other department heads and barely spoke to Elmer. Something funny is going on, he thought. Also, the hotel occupancy had been dropping steadily. He was sure that this had something to do with the food.

Then, straightening his tie, rolling down his sleeves, and putting on his favorite old hunting jacket, he took me on a tour of the hotel. He emphasized that I had only seen the front side of hotels in my travels. He was going to show me the real guts.

In the maid's room, nine or ten women were involved in a discussion with the housekeeper about their assignments. Those of the lower floors had to wait until the vacuum cleaners were available from the upper floors, so naturally everyone wanted to work on the upper floors. Dinsmore suggested that they might vacuum every other day; then they could share the machines on a rotating basis. The maids thought that this was a great idea, although the housekeeper didn't seem too pleased.

Dinsmore remarked to me about the lack of some people's decision-making ability. He sighed that he had to make more and more decisions each day because his staff seemed reluctant to take the initiative.

We toured all the floors. I mentioned the number of room service trays that seemed to be standing in the hall. Dinsmore said that this was a normal part of the hotel scene. The guests didn't mind because it reminded them that room service was available.

The cigar and newspaper stand looked like it belonged in the subway. The old man behind the counter offered some stale alternatives to the cigars I requested. He was very pleasant about it. Only a few magazines could be seen. "Guests don't go in for magazines anymore," Dinsmore told me. With a nudge, he reminded me that I didn't understand the hotel business.

The restaurant seemed to belong to a different world. It was packed. The maitre d' rushed over, bowed, seated us at a window, and took our drink orders. An atmosphere of quiet efficiency seemed to blanket the room. Two drinks appeared before us while attractive menus were deftly placed to our left. Elmer didn't seem happy. The restaurant, he told me, was a concession left over from the previous owners. He was trying to buy out the leases so he could turn it into a real moneymaker. At present, it made only about 10 percent net. I mentioned that most hotels lose money on their restaurants. He countered by showing me how many people were there even on that rainy day. He insisted that raising the prices while cutting back on the help was bound to increase the take.

The next morning, I retrieved my car, placed it firmly in the hotel garage, and returned for a farewell meeting with Dinsmore. He asked my opinion concerning his stewardship. He commented on the failing standards of today's workers, noted that he had ever-increasing difficulty in getting people who wanted to do quality work, and bemoaned the fact that the big grand hotels like his were losing out to the motels.

Questions

1. How would you rate Dinsmore's hotel? What evidence would you provide to support your position?

2. What are some of the most interesting examples of quality found in the case? How does Dinsmore view these examples? How would you, as the customer, view these same instances?

3. What do you think of Dinsmore's handling of the dispute involving the vacuums?

4. What would you recommend to Dinsmore about the manager of the restaurant?

5. If you were hired as a consultant by the owners of this hotel, what would you do? Why?

SELECTED READINGS & INTERNET SITES

Antony, J. "Six Sigma for Service Processes." *Business Process Management Journal* 12, no. 2 (2006), pp. 234–48.

Breen, M.; B. Jud; and P. E. Pareja. *An Introduction to ISO 9000.* Dearborn, MI: Society of Manufacturing Engineers, Reference Publication Division, 1993.

Breyfogle III, F. W.; J. M. Cupello; and B. Meadows. *Managing Six Sigma: A Practical Guide to Understanding, Assessing, and Implementing the Strategy That Yields Bottom-Line Success.* New York: John Wiley & Sons, Inc., 2001.

Crosby, P. B. *Quality Is Free.* New York: McGraw-Hill, 1979.

Deming, W. E. *Out of Crisis.* Cambridge, MA: MIT Center for Advanced Engineering Study, 1986.

Furterer, S., and A. K. Elshennawy, "Implementation of TQM and Lean Six Sigma Tools in Local Government: A Framework and a Case Study." *Total Quality Management & Business Excellence* 16, no. 10 (December 2005), p. 1179.

Garvin, D. A. *Managing Quality.* New York: Free Press, 1988.

Goetsch, D. L., and S. B. Davis. *Quality Management,* 5th ed. Englewood Cliffs, NJ: Prentice Hall, 2005.

Hoyle, D. *ISO 9000 Quality Systems Handbook,* 5th ed. New York: Butterworth-Heinemann, 2005.

Imai, M. *Kaizen: The Key to Japan's Competitive Success.* New York: Random House, 1986.

Juran, J. M., and F. M. Gryna, Jr. *Quality Planning and Analysis.* New York: McGraw-Hill, 1980.

Kotter, J. P. "Leading Change: Why Transformation Efforts Fail." *Harvard Business Review* 85, no. 1 (January 2007), p. 96.

Pyzdek, T. *The Six Sigma Handbook: A Complete Guide for Greenbelts, Blackbelts, and Managers at All Levels,* 2nd ed. New York: McGraw-Hill, 2003.

Stevenson, W. J., and A. E. Mergen. "Teaching Six Sigma Concepts in a Business School Curriculum." *Total Quality Management & Business Excellence* 17, no. 6 (July 2006), pp. 751–56.

Swink, M., and B. Jacobs, "Six Sigma Adoption: Operating Performance Impacts and Contextual Drivers of Success," *Journal of Operations Management* 30, no. 6 (2012), pp. 437-53.

Yeung, A. C. L. "Strategic Supply Management, Quality Initiatives, and Organizational Performance." *Journal of Operations Management* 26, no. 4 (2008), pp. 490–502.

American Society for Quality
www.asq.org

ISO—Organization for Standardization
www.iso.org

Macolm Baldrige National Quality Award information
www.nist.gov

Chapter Supplement: Quality Improvement Tools

LEARNING OBJECTIVES   *After studying this supplement, you should be able to:*

LO6S-1 Apply quality management tools for problem solving.

LO6S-2 Identify the importance of data in quality management.

OVERVIEW

Quality management programs make managers and employees better problem solvers by giving them the tools and procedures required to measure and improve processes, identify potential problems, and describe these problems to others. These tools can help managers determine whether processes are "under control," that is, whether they are capable of producing outcomes within the specifications needed to make products acceptable to customers. In this supplement, we use an example to illustrate the applications of important quality management tools, highlighting the types of problems they are designed to solve. While this supplement focuses on quality issues, these tools are universal and applicable to almost any process setting.

STANDARD PROBLEM SOLVING APPROACH

Chapter 6 introduced two problem solving approaches: (1) the Six Sigma improvement process known as DMAIC (define, measure, analyze, improve, and control) and (2) the plan-do-check-act (PDCA) cycle. Both approaches are good at standardizing improvement processes and giving everyone in the organization a common language for describing problems and related improvement efforts. A standard problem solving process also ensures that all employees use systematic, data-driven methods. While problem solving processes may vary from company to company, most follow the same fundamental steps represented in the DMAIC process and the PDCA cycle. Most of the tools described in this supplement deal with the measure, analyze, improve, and control steps of the DMAIC, or alternatively, steps P, D, and C of the PDCA cycle.

LO6S-1 Apply quality management tools for problem solving.

LO6S-2 Identify the importance of data in quality management.

QUALITY IMPROVEMENT TOOLS

The major goal of quality improvement is to move from uncovering the *symptoms* of a problem to determining the underlying root *causes* of a problem in a structured and logical manner. In this process, quality management decisions should be based on data whenever possible. Data fall into one of two categories: variable data or attribute data. **Variable data** measure quantifiable conditions such as speed, length, weight, temperature, density, and so forth. **Attribute data** measure qualitative characteristics of a process output (pass/fail, go/no go, good/bad). All variable data can be transformed into attribute data. However, it is not possible to transform attribute data into variable data.

variable data Data that measure quantifiable or numerical conditions.

attribute data Data that measure qualitative dimensions or conditions.

Consider the following example. To ensure safety, amusement parks have minimum height requirements for riders of roller coasters. At the Cedar Point amusement park, guests must be at least 52 inches tall to ride the Top Thrill Dragster.® The park could measure and record the actual height of each guest, gathering variable data. Instead, only those guests whose height is in question are measured. Their height is compared with a standard set at 52 inches; each guest is either tall enough to ride or not. Thus, Cedar Point is measuring an *attribute,* as opposed to a *variable.*

The various quality tools are just that—tools. They are used to address a specific question and to help managers understand what is taking place in operational processes. Table 6S-1 gives a summary of the tools and their usages.

Pear Computers: Using Quality Tools to Improve Performance

Pear Computers is a small Midwestern manufacturer of personal computers and data collection devices specifically targeting usages in the medical and dental fields. Pear has been successful in serving the needs of this market and in fending off the forays of larger computer makers such as Dell, Lenovo, and HP by relying on a strategy that emphasizes constant innovation, flexible product configurations, on-time delivery, and extremely high levels of quality.

TABLE 6S-1   Quality Improvement Tools

Quality Tools	Typical Usage
Histogram	To uncover underlying patterns (range and frequency) in data variability.
Cause-and-effect analysis	To uncover possible contributors to an observed problem; to facilitate group brainstorming.
Check sheets	To identify the frequency and location of problem causes.
Pareto analysis	To identify the most critical (relatively frequent) causes of problems.
Scatter diagrams	To determine if two variables are related to each other (whether the two variables move together in some predictable manner).
Process flow analysis	To graphically display and analyze the steps in a process.
Process capability analysis	To predict the conformance quality of a product by comparing its specification range to the range of its process variability.
Process control charts	To monitor process outputs and determine whether a process is operating according to normally expected limits.
Taguchi method/design of experiments	To evaluate and understand the effects of different factors on process outputs.

Recently, however, quality has slipped. Given where Pear Computers are used (often, literally life-and-death situations), this issue has become a major management concern. Increased final inspections have revealed that an unacceptably high number of computers are leaving final assembly DOA (dead on arrival—not working properly). Some computers have refused to boot up; others begin the start-up procedure only to stop and restart continuously without finishing the boot-up. Still others have started up and then become frozen at the start-up screen. Bob Feller, the operations manager in charge of the assembly line, has been charged with the task of eliminating these problems and ensuring that Pear delivers a computer that its customers can rely on.

Histograms

histogram A graphical representation of the distribution of values.

Variance exists in every activity or process. A **histogram** graphically displays a distribution of the values of the data of one variable to show the extent and type of variance. To create a histogram, one needs at least 30 observations, but more are better. Also, the analyst must determine the number of ranges or categories for grouping the data. The number of ranges is typically between 5 and 20, increasing with the number of observations.

Figure 6S-1 shows examples of histograms (each number identifies the frequency of occurrence of a given outcome). Histograms help problem solvers recognize and understand three critical traits of distributions:

- *Center:* The theoretical or desired mean (μ) should fall at the center of the distribution. Any gap between the observed mean and μ may indicate bias—a consistent tendency to exceed or fall short of a target.
- *Width:* The range (the difference between the highest and lowest values) is shown graphically by a histogram. The width indicates the unpredictability of the process (i.e., the wider the distribution, the less predictable it is).
- *Shape:* The overall shape of a distribution can indicate the degree of variability in outcomes and the types of factors that may be influencing the overall distribution.

Examine the five different distributions shown in Figure 6S-1. Most students are familiar with the first, normal, bell-shaped distribution. However, the other four distributions

TABLE 6S-7   Values for Setting Control Limit Lines

n = Number in Each Sample	$A_2 = \bar{x}$ Limits for 99.7% (3 sigma)	$D_4 = R$ Upper Limit	$D_3 = R$ Lower Limit
2	1.88	3.27	0
3	1.02	2.58	0
4	0.73	2.28	0
5	0.58	2.12	0
6	0.48	2.00	0
7	0.42	1.92	0.08
8	0.37	1.86	0.14
9	0.34	1.82	0.18
10	0.31	1.78	0.22
11	0.29	1.74	0.26
12	0.27	1.72	0.28
13	0.25	1.69	0.31
14	0.24	1.67	0.33
15	0.22	1.65	0.35
16	0.21	1.64	0.36
17	0.20	1.62	0.38
18	0.19	1.60	0.39
19	0.19	1.61	0.40
20	0.18	1.59	0.41

R control chart:

(6s.9) $$\text{Central line} = \bar{R}$$

(6s.10) $$\text{Lower control limit (LCL)} = D_3\bar{R}$$

(6s.11) $$\text{Upper control limit (UCL)} = D_4\bar{R}$$

Table 6S-8 gives the control chart parameters for the data in Table 6S-6. The control charts are shown in Figure 6S-9. By convention, the centerline appears as a solid line and the control limits appear as broken or dashed lines.

7. *Plot new $\bar{x}$ and R values on the control charts.* With the centerline and control limits established, the control charts are ready to be used.

TABLE 6S-8   Control Limits Calculated for the Example Control Chart

Data Points	$\bar{X}$ Chart	R Chart
Central Line	12.14 ms	0.69
Lower Control Limit (LCL)	12.14 − 0.577*0.69 = 11.74	0
Upper Control Limit (UCL)	12.14 + 0.577*0.69 = 12.54	2.115*0.69 = 1.459

FIGURE 6S-9 $\overline{X}$ and R Chart for the Example Data

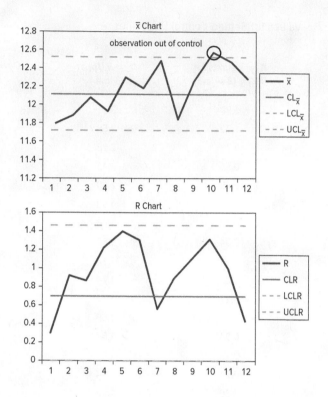

After installing the new control charts on the hard disk production line, Bob Feller recorded the 12 sample means and ranges in Table 6S-9. When they were plotted (Figure 6S-9), Bob noticed that the sample mean for batch 10 was outside of the upper control limit. In practice, this would have triggered an immediate reaction—production would have been stopped with the goal of identifying the reasons for the problem. In flagging

TABLE 6S-9   Sample Means and Ranges for Hard Disk Drives

Sample	Sample Mean $\overline{X}$	Sample Range (R)
1	11.82	0.30
2	11.90	0.92
3	12.10	0.86
4	11.95	1.23
5	12.32	1.40
6	12.20	1.30
7	12.50	0.56
8	11.86	0.89
9	12.30	1.10
10	12.60	1.32
11	12.49	1.01
12	12.30	0.42

the out-of-bounds value for sample 10, Bob also realized something important: This value was a symptom; it indicated that something was wrong, but it did not tell Bob *what* was wrong. For Bob to uncover the underlying root causes, he and the team responsible for the hard disk production line would have to make use of tools such as the cause-and-effect diagram (previously discussed) in order to uncover possible root causes.

p Attribute Control Chart

$\bar{x} - R$ charts analyze samples of data for continuous variables. In some cases, the observed data are attributes. Such cases occur when we are dealing with pass/fail, live/die, or good/bad outcomes. In these cases, managers are usually interested in determining if the proportion of nonconforming product is stable and if the process generating such products is under control. To answer these questions, we use a *p* **attribute control chart**.

Consider the data presented in Table 6S-10. Bob Feller has been informed that the research team at Pear Computers has introduced the Mercury HD 6900, a new video graphics board for its top end computers. Since this product is new, Bob decides to construct a *p* attribute control chart. He is interested in whether the process can produce fewer than 5 percent defects, a minimum standard considered acceptable at Pear.

p attribute control chart A technique used to assess if the proportion of nonconforming product is stable. Applied to attribute data.

TABLE 6S-10   Reject Rate Analysis for Mercury HD 6900

Batch	Sample Size	Defective	Fraction Defective
1	100	5	.05
2	100	6	.08
3	100	2	.02
4	100	4	.04
5	100	6	.06
6	100	2	.02
7	100	3	.03
8	100	7	.07
9	100	1	.01
10	100	3	.03
11	100	2	.02
12	100	4	.04
13	100	4	.04
14	100	1	.01
15	100	1	.01
16	100	3	.03
17	100	2	.02
18	100	4	.04
19	100	5	.05
20	100	2	.02
Totals	2000	67	Average .0335

To carry out this analysis, Bob uses the following procedure:

1. *Collect and organize the data under normal operating conditions:* Table 6S-10 shows the data that were collected when the production line was running normally and presumably under control. Note that we are using constant sample sizes.

2. *Compute control limits and construct the chart:* To calculate the $\bar{p}$ and control lines, we use the following equations:

(6s.12) $\bar{p} = \text{(Number of Defects/Total Parts Inspected)}$

(6s.13)   Upper control line $= \text{UCL} = \bar{p} + 3\sqrt{\bar{p}(1-\bar{p})/n}$

(6s.14)   Lower control line $= \text{LCL} = \bar{p} - 3\sqrt{\bar{p}(1-\bar{p})/n}$

where $n =$ sample size. If the sample size varies from batch to batch, then an average sample size can be used.

Note that here, the 3 is the control limit. In this example, we have essentially specified the mean ($(\bar{p}) +/-3\sigma$). The value of 3 can be changed to increase or decrease this interval.

For the Mercury HD 6900 data:

$$\bar{p} = 67/2000 = 0.0335$$

$$\text{UCL} = 0.0335 + 3\sqrt{0.0335\,(1-0.0335)/100} = 0.0335 + 0.0540 = 0.0875$$

$$\text{LCL} = 0.0335 - 3\sqrt{0.0335\,(1-0.0335)/100} = 0.0335 - 0.0540 = \sim 0$$
(we cannot have a negative LCL)

3. *Create the control chart and begin monitoring results:* The parameters computed in the preceding step create a *p* chart with which Bob can monitor and control future production batches.

Table 6S-11 shows data for 20 samples that Bob drew from production after creating the control chart, and Figure 6S-10 plots the number of defects from each sample. The chart shows that the process is under control (i.e., no samples are outside the control limits). However, the defects seem to exhibit *cycling*. That is, there seems to be a pattern of the defects going up and down in a consistent pattern. This is not the kind of random behavior that one would expect from a process. Bob should initiate an effort to uncover root factors contributing to this outcome (applying a technique such as cause-and-effect diagrams). Cycling indicates that something systematic (rather than random) is affecting the underlying processes.

Interpreting Control Charts

A process is out of control whenever the sample means or range values appear outside the control lines. This signals managers or workers to stop the process to identify and correct the underlying problems that caused a change in the process. Control charts may also

FIGURE 6S-10 *Np* Control Chart for the Mercury HD 6900, Sample Evaluation

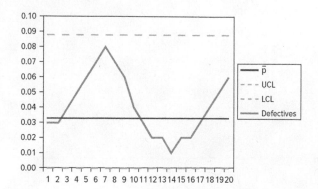

TABLE 6S-11   Sample Data Collected

Sample Number	Sample Size	Number Defective
1	100	3
2	100	3
3	100	4
4	100	5
5	100	6
6	100	7
7	100	8
8	100	7
9	100	6
10	100	4
11	100	3
12	100	2
13	100	2
14	100	1
15	100	2
16	100	2
17	100	3
18	100	4
19	100	5
20	100	6

indicate a need for intervention in the process in four conditions: trends, runs, hugging, and periodicity.

Trends. A control chart indicates a trend when successive points seem to fall along a line moving either upward or downward. A trend in control chart data indicates some continuing change in the process. This signal may warrant intervention before the trend line crosses control limits.

Runs. Truly random variations should not form any pattern in the distribution of data around the central lines. A run of points above the central line followed by a run of points below indicate systematic changes in the process that require attention.

Hugging. Hugging occurs when various points appear so closely grouped around the central line that they seem to show no variation. Hugging usually indicates some external intervention in the process to limit or eliminate variation (thus masking the problems). This intervention might be the action of some employee who wants the process to look good. With hugging you cannot judge whether the process is really operating under control or if some outside force is taking unusual measures to produce acceptable results.

Periodicity. If the plotted points show the same pattern of change over equal intervals, it is called *periodicity*. It looks much like a uniform roller coaster of the same size ups and downs around the centerline. This process should be watched closely as something is causing a defined uniform drift to both sides of the centerline.

Taguchi Methods/Design of Experiments

One of the first quality researchers to recognize the importance of linking product design to process improvement was Professor Genichi Taguchi, director of the Japanese Academy of Quality and four-time recipient of the Deming Prize. He recognized that managers could eliminate the need for mass inspection by building quality into both the products and the processes at the design stage.

Taguchi methods Statistical methods for improving the design of a product and the processes used to produce it.

Taguchi developed a straightforward, well-integrated system (now called the **Taguchi methods**) for improving the design of both a product and the process used to produce it. The objective of this system is to identify easily controllable factors and their settings to minimize variation in product features while keeping the mean values (or "response") of these features on target. Taguchi developed a methodology for designing experiments than can help managers identify the optimal settings of product specifications and process controls. One result of identifying these settings is that a product can be made robust with respect to changes in its operating and environmental conditions. Ultimately, this results in more stable, "process capable" designs. In other words, by focusing on both the product and the process and using well-developed designs, managers can develop products and processes that are properly centered and have performance distributions with reduced spread.[2]

Other Quality Control Tools

This supplement has provided only a brief introduction to the wide range of quality control tools that are available to operations managers. In addition to the tools discussed, there are other tools that you might want to explore either in other courses or by reading about them. Other important tools include:

1. Acceptance sampling.
2. Operating characteristics curves.
3. Taguchi loss functions.
4. CTQ tree (critical to quality—a tool used to decompose broad customer requirements into more easily quantified requirements).
5. Quality storyboards (a visual method for displaying a quality control story that helps the personnel go from plan and problem definition to actions).

---

[2]For more information on this system, see N. Logothetis, *Managing for Total Quality* (Englewood Cliffs, NJ: Prentice Hall, 1992), Chapters 11–14.

SUPPLEMENT SUMMARY

1. Effective quality management is data-driven. Data can be quantitative variable data, such as length and width, or it can be attribute data (e.g., good/bad). The appropriate data analysis tool depends upon the type of data.
2. Tools such as the histogram, check sheet, and Pareto analysis are graphical techniques that help to identify and prioritize problems.
3. Cause-and-effect diagrams and scatter diagrams are used to explore relationships and understand underlying causes of problems.
4. Process capability indicates if a process is able to meet the customer's quality requirements. Process control is used to monitor whether a process has changed. Taguchi's system for the design of experiments can be used to identify the settings of process factors that make a process capable.

KEY TERMS

attribute data   199

cause-and-effect
diagram   202

check sheets   203

C_p 207

C_{pk} 207

histogram   200

p attribute control
chart   215

Pareto analysis   204

process capability
analysis   206

process control
chart   210

process flow
diagram   206

scatter diagram   205

Taguchi methods   218

variable data   199

$\bar{x} - R$ chart   211

SOLVED PROBLEMS

1. Given the information presented in Figure 6S-11, calculate the process capability.

Solution:

$C_p = S/P = (20 - 10)/(16 - 10) = 10/6 = 1.667$
$K = \text{abs } [D - \overline{X}] / (S/2) = \text{abs } [15 - 13] / 5 = 0.40$
$C_{pk} = (1 - K) \, C_p = (0.4)/1.667 = 1.00$

2. You have been given the following data for a production process that is responsible for filling bags of flour.

Production specifications:	$10.00 \pm .20$ pounds
Process standard deviation (σ):	0.05 pounds
Process distribution centered at:	10.10 pounds
Specification width (S):	$10.20 - 9.80 = .40$
Process width (P):	we need 99% or 3σ on each side or $10.10 - .15 = 9.55$
	$10.10 + .15 = 10.25$
	$10.25 - 9.55 = .30$

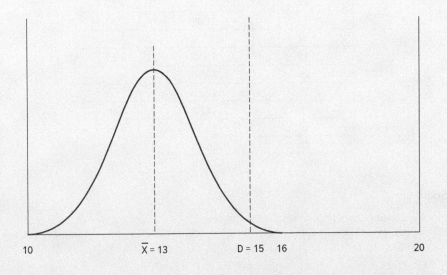

FIGURE 6S-11
Calculating C_{pk}

10    $\overline{X} = 13$ $D = 15$ 16   20

With these data, you have been asked by management to determine the answers to two questions:

- Is the process capable?
- If it is not, then what has to be done to bring the process back in control (i.e., make it capable again)?

Solution:

$C_p = S/P = .40/.30 = 1.333$

Based on the C_p value alone, the process is capable . . . but barely.

$K = |D - \overline{X}| / (S/2) = |10.00 - 10.10| / (.40/2) = .10 / .20 = .5$
$C_{pk} = (1 - K) * C_p = .5 * 1.333 = .667$

This indicates that the process is not capable. The first step for management is to recenter the production process. That is, the center of the production process must be shifted from 10.10 to 10.00. This action, while improving things, is not enough. The next is to reduce the variance of the process. The two actions, when combined, should result in a process that is now capable.

3. You have been given the following data taken from 20 samples, where each sample consists of five observations. You have been asked to calculate the limits for the $\overline{x} - R$ charts.

Sample Number	Sample Mean ($\overline{x}$)	Range (R)
1	12.25	4.50
2	12.75	5.00
3	10.63	0.50
4	15.88	1.00
5	12.00	4.00
6	14.75	4.00
7	13.25	3.00
8	13.48	8.00
9	15.50	3.00
10	15.25	7.00
11	15.75	5.00
12	13.13	4.50
13	11.88	3.00
14	15.00	6.00
15	14.30	4.50
16	14.50	6.00
17	17.65	9.00
18	14.88	3.50
19	12.63	4.00
20	16.88	4.00
Means	14.15	4.45

Solution:

Calculating the control limits for the $\overline{x}$ chart:
Upper control limit $= \overline{x} + A_2 * \overline{R} = 14.15 + 0.58 * 4.45$ (0.58 taken from table where $n = 5$) $= 16.73$

Lower control $= \bar{x} + A_2 * \bar{R} = 14.15 - 0.58 * 4.45 = 11.57$

Note: As long as $\bar{x}$ remains between 11.57 and 16.73, these data are under control. Calculating the control limits for R charts:

Upper control $= D_4 * \bar{R}$ (where D_4 taken from table) $= 2.11 * 4.45 = 9.39$

Lower control $= D_4 * \bar{R} = 0 * 4.45 = 0.0$

Note: As long as R remains between 0 and 9.39, then the sample is under control.

4. Dick Ross, the plant manager for ABC Housing Tiles, was concerned about the on-time delivery performance of one of his departments. This department manufactures bathroom tiles specifically for large "big box" home improvement stores (such as Home Depot, Menards, Lowe's, and Rona [Canada]). The buyers from these various customers were sending strong signals that they expected consistent on-time delivery (with future pressure to be on improving the level of on-time delivery).

Solution:

To help assess whether the department's on-time delivery was consistent, Dick collected two years' worth of information for calculating the parameters of the p control chart. The data are summarized as follows:

Month	Period	Sample	On-Time	p
January	1	250	230	0.921
February	2	250	229	0.916
March	3	250	229	0.918
April	4	250	228	0.915
May	5	250	228	0.912
June	6	250	230	0.923
July	7	250	226	0.905
August	8	250	223	0.892
September	9	250	228	0.913
October	10	250	226	0.905
November	11	250	227	0.908
December	12	250	228	0.912
January	13	250	228	0.912
February	14	250	233	0.932
March	15	250	230	0.921
April	16	250	227	0.911
May	17	250	229	0.918
June	18	250	224	0.896
July	19	250	226	0.905
August	20	250	230	0.923
September	21	250	227	0.910
October	22	250	227	0.908
November	23	250	229	0.916
December	24	250	228	0.914
Averages		250	227.92	0.913

Using this information, he calculated the overall $\bar{p} = 0.913$

He also calculated the UCL and LCL:

$$\text{LCL} = 0.913 - 3 \times \sqrt{\frac{0.913(1 - .913)}{250}} = 0.913 - 0.054 = 0.859$$

$$\text{UCL} = 0.913 + 3 \times \sqrt{\frac{0.913(1 - .913)}{250}} = 0.913 + 0.054 = 0.967$$

He also did a quick plot to see if these 24 months were really stable (they are; you can do it yourself to check). With these control parameters, he next took the on-time delivery data for the current 12 months (see the following table):

Month	Period	Sample	On-Time	p
January	25	250	224	0.896
February	26	250	229	0.916
March	27	250	235	0.940
April	28	250	220	0.880
May	29	250	221	0.884
June	30	250	234	0.936
July	31	250	223	0.982
August	32	250	230	0.920
September	33	250	231	0.924
October	34	250	233	0.932
November	35	250	233	0.932
December	36	250	235	0.940

These data are plotted on the following control chart:

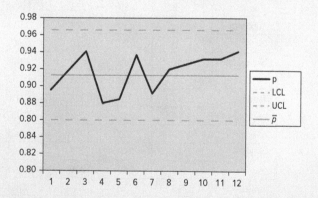

In reviewing these data, Dick noted that the process was under control. However, beginning in August there was an upward trend. Such a trend is problematic as it indicates that a systematic change is taking place. Dick took note of this so he could talk with the area supervisor. These data told Dick that his process delivers on time about 92 percent of the time. However, the data did not tell him how late the late orders were. This would require further analysis.

5. You are responsible for the production of *Always Bright* bicycle flashers (the lights that we put on our bicycles to ensure that drivers see us). Recently, top management has noted that customers have been complaining about the quality of these products. Consequently, you decide to collect some data so that you can better understand the problem. You collect production data and rejects over a one-week period

(see following table). A "✓" indicates a defect. You have decided to organize the data by type of defect and by time of day (you have a feeling that some of the problems might be worse at certain times of the day).

Orders	7 a.m. – 9 a.m.	9 a.m. – 11 a.m.	11 a.m. – 1 p.m.	1 p.m. – 3 p.m.	3 p.m. – 5 p.m.	Sum
Insufficient plating	✓✓✓✓✓✓✓		✓		✓✓✓✓✓	15
Inability to meet heat specs	✓✓✓✓✓	✓✓✓✓✓✓✓✓✓	✓✓✓✓✓✓✓✓✓	✓✓✓✓✓✓✓✓	✓✓✓✓✓✓✓	42
Scratched lens	✓✓✓✓✓✓✓✓	✓✓	✓✓✓✓	✓✓✓	✓✓✓✓✓✓✓✓✓✓	28
Failed leak test	✓✓	✓✓	✓	✓✓✓	✓✓	12
Glue on lens			✓✓✓	✓✓✓	✓	7
Cracked body	✓	✓✓		✓✓		5
	27	16	18	20	28	109

Solution:

1. Carry out a Pareto analysis on the types of defects irrespective of time of day.

   Here, we would first organize the data in terms of number of occurrences going from most frequent to least frequent.

Defect Type	Number	Percentage	Cumulative Percentage
Inability to meet heat specs	42	38.53	38.53
Scratched lens	28	25.69	64.22
Insufficient plating	15	13.72	77.98
Failed leak test	12	11.01	88.99
Glue on lens	7	6.42	95.41
Cracked body	5	4.59	100.00

What this analysis tells us is that were we to focus on the first three items, we would account for about 78 percent of all defects. This is where we should start. This can be graphically summarized as a histogram:

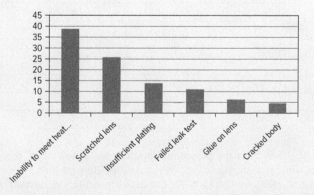

2. Does the time of the day have any impact?

   Yes, for insufficient plating and scratched lenses (both are more likely to occur before 9 a.m. or after 3 p.m.) and glue on lens (which is most likely to occur from 11 a.m. to 3 p.m.). These observations might be good candidates for CEDs.

class had paid the most to travel on the Titanic's maiden voyage (in some cases paying in excess of $100,000 in today's dollars). These people were closest to the lifeboats. They represented some of the most important people in 1912 society—John Jacob Astor IV and his wife Madeleine Force Astor, industrialist Benjamin Guggenheim, Macy's owner Isidor Straus and his wife Ida, Denver millionaire Margaret "Molly" Brown (who became known later on as the "Unsinkable Molly Brown"), Sir Cosmo Duff Gordon and his wife Lucy, and silent film actress Dorothy Gibson. In contrast, the third class was located the furthest away from the lifeboats. Also, as a result of the U.S. immigration requirements, the gates that would have given the third class passengers access to the lifeboats were locked when Titanic left Southampton.

You have been asked to study the passenger list for Titanic and to determine if the premises stated in the previous paragraph really did occur. Specifically, consider the following:

1. Using the Excel Spreadsheet, Titanic.xlsx on the text website (www.mhhe.com/swink3e), analyze the data to determine what type of passenger would be most likely to survive and least likely to survive.

2. Read about the Titanic and develop a CED to explain why so many people died on this ship. To help you in doing this assignment, you may want to read the note entitled, "RMS Titanic—Did you know??")

RMS Titanic—Did you know??

On April 14, 1912, RMS Titanic, while on her maiden voyage, struck an iceberg and sank. Up until this point, this was the single, most tragic maritime disaster in modern times (by the way, this loss has since been eclipsed—see if you can uncover the single, most tragic maritime disaster and why it occurred). To many, this event was unthinkable. After all, RMS Titanic was "unsinkable." This was not an idle claim, but the result of several modern innovations built into the Titanic, namely:

- *Double-hulled construction* – RMS Titanic was the first ship to use a double-hulled construction–with one hull constructed within another. The promise of this form of construction was that it made the Titanic less susceptible to sinking due to a punctured hull. Any puncture would have to go through two hulls–not one.
- *Electronic bulkheads* – The bulkheads, critical to locking compartments and keeping out water–were designed to be initiated electronically. The promise of this approach–speed and assuredness of closure.
- *The largest number of lifeboats on any ship* – The RMS Titanic carried lifeboats (both rigid and collapsible) for 1,168 passengers. This number was far in excess of the number mandated by the Maritime Commission.

- *Ability to stay afloat if up to five of her compartments were breached* – Based on past disasters, the designers were aware that a ship such as RMS Titanic might experience severe problems if multiple compartments were to be breached. Consequently, the Titanic was designed to float even if up to five compartments were to be breached. This was the most of any ship at the time.
- *The latest in Marconi wireless technology* for sending and receiving wireless messages.

Yet, late on April 14, 1912, at 11:40 p.m., RMS Titanic struck an iceberg. By 2:20 a.m., April 15, 1912, RMS Titanic had broken apart and was gone. People wanted to know why. The following are some (but not all) of the factors contributing to this disaster and its high loss of life:

- *Coal strike.* The departure of the RMS Titanic was delayed by some two weeks due to a British coal strike. The Titanic was delayed while sufficient coal stocks were accumulated for its maiden voyage. This had two major impacts. First, the delay put Titanic's crossing at a time when the ice floes in the mid-Atlantic were known to be worse. Second, since the ship was late, it increased the pressure for a quick voyage across the Atlantic.
- *A lost key in Queenstown.* When Titanic departed from Queenstown Ireland, on its way to New York, the crew was unable to access the binoculars needed for scouting or seeing icebergs in the distance. The reason: The key to the cabinet holding the binoculars had been left behind in Queenstown.
- *Weather conditions.* The night of April 14, 1912, was unusual in that it was perfectly still and calm–there were no waves on the ocean. Consequently, waves and wave splashes (one way that many crew located in the crow's nest could identify icebergs in the distance) were totally absent.
- *Moonless night.* Not only was the night calm, but it was also completely dark, thus further reducing the ability of the crew to spot icebergs in the distance.
- *The Blue Riband Award.* This was an award given to the ship that could record the fastest crossing of the Atlantic. Titanic was the most elegant of ships ever built but it was not the fastest (the Lusitania, which was built with Royal Navy funds, was inherently faster). However, Captain Smith, the commander of the Titanic, wanted to win this award. Consequently, he was pushing for a quick voyage.
- *Maiden voyage.* This was the first crossing for the Titanic, which meant that the crew had not worked with each other and they were still getting familiar with the ship.
- *No lifeboat drill.* Because of a late departure from Cherbourg (and an almost-collision with another ship) and another late departure from Queenstown, it was decided that there had been enough confusion for one day and the lifeboat drill was never carried out.

Consequently, many passengers did not know what to do if there was a problem. For example, they did not know where to go for their boats, where to find their lifeboat jackets, and how to get to the lifeboats. This last issue was a major one given the size of the Titanic.

- *Location of the lifeboats.* Most of the lifeboats were located amidships, on top of the ship. This, ironically, was where the first class passengers were located. However, most of the passengers were third class or steerage. These passengers were located either at the bow or stern.

- *The wireless system.* Critical to the safety of the Titanic was its wireless system. However, the wireless system was owned by the Marconi Company and manned by Marconi employees. These employees were paid on the number of messages that they sent. On April 12, Titanic was approaching New York and consequently many of its passengers wanted to send messages telling their friends and relatives that they were coming; the wireless office was simply overwhelmed with wireless volume.

- *Shut up.* The SS California had just traversed the same ice field that Titanic was about to enter. She (ships are always called *she*) found the ice field to be very dangerous. To cross it, the California had to move during the day at reduced speeds. In the evening, when the California found out that Titanic was entering the ice field, the radio operator repeatedly sent messages warning the Titanic of the potential danger ahead. The radio operators, because of the volume of work, found these messages irritating because they interrupted their ability to send out messages. One of the Titanic operators was so irritated that he sent a message to the California telling the operator to "shut up." The California operator, upon receiving this message, shut down his set (thus preventing him from receiving any other messages from Titanic until morning) and went to bed.

- *State of the water.* During early and mid-April, temperatures in the mid-Atlantic are very cold. Water temperature at night, for example, is about 40 degrees Fahrenheit (or less). At such temperatures, any person in the water for 15 to 30 minutes is likely to die from cardiac arrest and hypothermia.

- *Time delay.* From the time that the Titanic struck the iceberg until its passengers were being asked to move to their lifeboats, about an hour elapsed. Since the Titanic took less than three hours to sink, this was a critical loss of time.

- *Passenger reactions.* In many cases, the passengers could not understand the urgency. First of all, they were being asked to leave their warm rooms and to go outside where the night time temperatures were very cold. Second, many could not believe that there was a problem with the Titanic–after all, she was "unsinkable." Third, many of the crew, in asking the passengers to go to their lifeboat stations, did not convey the magnitude of the problem.

(Consider the following: Ismay from White Star, who was on the ship, and Edward Smith, the captain, both knew that the Titanic was doomed from the reports since six compartments were affected. This was one more than the five maximum that Titanic was designed to handle).

- *Immigration and naturalization practices.* Most of the passengers on the Titanic were traveling in third class; these passengers were coming to America to start a new life. In contrast, the passengers in first and second class were visiting. American Immigration practice was to secure (by lock) all access to third class. This was done to prevent any illegal immigration. However, when the Titanic struck the iceberg, the gates to third class remained locked.

- *Gates to third class compartments.* The crew did not open the gates to the third class compartments. When the Titanic struck the iceberg, the crew immediately went and manned their stations at the lifeboats; no one was formally tasked with the assignment of securing the key to third class and opening the gates.

- *The attitudes of the people.* Many of the people, especially those in third class, were used to being told what to do on the ship. When the Titanic struck the iceberg, many of these people (often families with young children) waited in their rooms for instructions.

- *The lack of lifeboats.* Simply put, the Titanic had too few lifeboats for its passengers and crew.

- *Lack of loading instructions.* Every officer in charge of a lifeboat had his own procedure and approach for loading and launching lifeboats. Some, like First Officer Charles Lightoller, only allowed women and children; others allowed men as long as they were from a reputable yachting club (not rowing club, but sailing large boats) and still others took the attitude of "first-come-first-served." In addition, some lifeboats were launched partially full while others were loaded to capacity.

- *Picking up survivors in the water.* Some lifeboats refused to pick up survivors because of fears of tipping over while others actively picked up survivors. Margaret (Molly) Brown of Denver was shocked when she learned that the person in charge of her boat refused to pick up any survivors even though the boat had the capacity to carry more passengers. Consequently, she convinced the other passengers of the need to save those in the water. They did so by threatening the boat captain with harm if he did not comply. That is why Molly Brown became known as the Unsinkable Molly Brown.

- *Rewards.* The Titanic carried a larger number than normal crew list. This was due in part to the practice of Harland and Wolfe of Belfast (the ship builders) to reward the good construction workers with berths on the Titanic for the maiden voyage (where they would be responsible for repairing any problems encountered). Nearly all of these people died when the Titanic went down.

CASE

The Bully Boy Bagging Line

Things were not going well at Bully Boy Products (BBP). BBP was a regional producer of organic fertilizer, potting soil, growing loam, and various gardening products for the discriminating gardener. It had been founded in 1976 when two agriculture students had decided that something had to be done to provide better supplies for gardeners. As one of the founders said, "Living better chemically may be great for chemicals but it has no place when it comes to gardening supplies."

Since its founding, BBP had grown by always remembering its core competencies—quality, variety, and innovative organic groups. As a result of this growth, the managers of BBP decided in 2011 to expand its production facilities, including installation of a new automated bagging line. This system was designed to provide quick product changeovers, something critical to BBP given its wide and ever-changing product line. The bagging system was brought online at the start of 2012. After four weeks of debugging, the system was thought to be ready for full-scale production. Yet, as soon as it started up, problems became evident. These problems took a variety of forms: bagging seams were poorly made at the top; some bags were overfilled, while other bags were underfilled; and some bags experienced various forms of rips (the most common form of defect). Whenever a bagging problem occurred, the standard operating procedure was to stop, clear the problem, write up the issue, and then restart production. Top management had decided that the situation in the bagging line was no longer acceptable—something had to be done. To that end, they asked Lisa Vickery to determine whether the bagging problems were random or systematic in nature.

Lisa reviewed the production on the firm's large-bag packaging line. There seemed to be much more variation in quality than she would normally expect. After calling for a summary of the data from production control, she received the BullyBoyBag.xlsx data (www.mhhe.com/swink3e) collected over the last 16 workweeks.

1. What do these data tell you?
2. Which tools did you use to determine what is happening? (*Hint*: Consider looking at the impact of staffing and day of the week.)
3. What management actions are appropriate? What would you recommend to Lisa Vickery?

SELECTED READINGS & INTERNET SITES

AT&T. *Statistical Quality Control Handbook,* 11th ed. Charlotte, NC: Delmar Publishing, 1985.

Deming, W. E. *Out of Crisis.* Cambridge, MA: MIT Center for Advanced Engineering Study, 1986.

Garvin, D. A. *Managing Quality.* New York: Free Press, 1988.

Gitlow, H.; S. Gitlow; A. Oppenheim; and R. Oppenheim. *Tools and Methods for the Improvement of Quality.* Homewood, IL: Irwin, 1989.

Ishikawa, K. *Guide to Quality Control.* White Plains, NY: Quality Resources, 1982.

Ishikawa, K. *What Is Total Quality Control? The Japanese Way.* Englewood Cliffs, NJ: Prentice Hall, 1985.

Juran, J. M., and F. M. Gryna, Jr. *Quality Planning and Analysis.* New York: McGraw-Hill, 1980.

Nelson, L. S. "Technical Aids." *Journal of Quality Technology* 16, no. 4 (October 1984), pp. 238–39.

American Society for Quality (ASQ)
www.asq.org

Six Sigma
www.isixsigma.com

8

Lean Systems

LEARNING OBJECTIVES   *After studying this chapter, you should be able to:*

LO8-1 Explain how the lean system approach improves value for internal operations and across the supply chain.

LO8-2 Describe the cultural changes, tools, and techniques needed to implement a lean approach.

LO8-3 Recognize the strengths and limitations of lean systems.

LO8-4 Apply the concept of lean systems to product design.

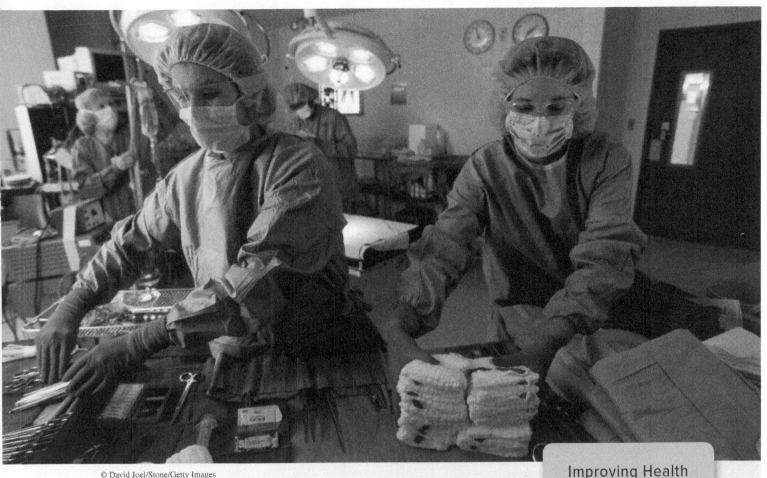

© David Joel/Stone/Getty Images

Improving Health Care through the Application of Lean Tools[1]

I magine managing the operating room (OR) staff of a 250-bed community, not-for-profit medical center. How do you get more surgeries done per day without spending more money? In studying the problem directly through the use of **gemba kaizen**, in which managers and employees are obligated to see the problems and issues in person rather than relying on reports, a process improvement team discovered that capacity was being wasted through excessively long setups. It simply took too much time to change over operating rooms between surgical cases in the 11-OR-suite inpatient surgery department. Every minute saved in operating room changeover time could be used for more surgery or for ensuring better patient quality. Adding capacity in this way would help the staff improve both patient care and physician satisfaction.

To reduce changeover time, the team applied various lean tools such as process mapping, SMED (single minute exchange of dies—a process for setup reduction), and work standardization. The staff worked to streamline processes by identifying and moving work steps that had been internal to the changeover and making these steps external (i.e., identifying steps that could be done simultaneously with other activities). Visual indicators such as color coding were used to clarify the process and to standardize the OR changeover process. These and other changes were achieved through a four-day Kaizen Event. The impact: a 60 percent reduction of operating room changeover time. As a result, patient care has improved; nurses are more satisfied; and doctors feel that they have more time to focus on patient care rather than facility issues.

_____

[1] http://leanhealthcareperformance.com/leancasestudies.html

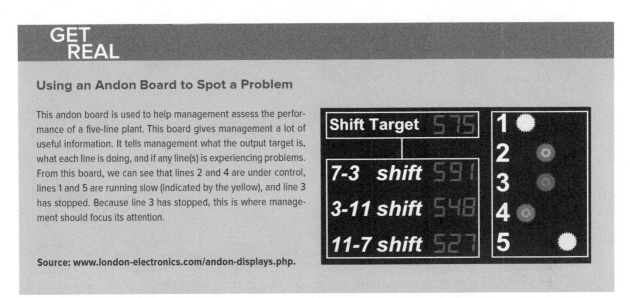

GET REAL

Using an Andon Board to Spot a Problem

This andon board is used to help management assess the performance of a five-line plant. This board gives management a lot of useful information. It tells management what the output target is, what each line is doing, and if any line(s) is experiencing problems. From this board, we can see that lines 2 and 4 are under control, lines 1 and 5 are running slow (indicated by the yellow), and line 3 has stopped. Because line 3 has stopped, this is where management should focus its attention.

Source: www.london-electronics.com/andon-displays.php.

assess different options for performance, and develop and document the implemented process changes. This highly focused effort emphasizes fast action improvements, verifiable measures of improvement, and disciplined documentation of the ideas to be used in future improvement efforts.

Critical to the success of the Kaizen Event is **gemba kaizen**, briefly mentioned at the beginning of this chapter. The term *gemba* (meaning "actual place") emphasizes the notion that managers and employees are obligated to see the problems and issues in person, rather than relying on reports. They must travel to where the problems are taking place. This may sound expensive, but a lean systems belief is that these expenses will pay off in terms of faster and higher-quality problem solving. More information about Kaizen Events is found in Chapter 3, "Managing Processes and Capacity."

> **gemba kaizen** Managers and employees are obligated to see the problems and issues in person rather than relying on reports.

Process Analysis/Value Stream Mapping

Process analysis/value stream mapping is a graphic mapping technique (as discussed in Chapter 3 and the Chapter 3 Supplement) that helps managers understand the material and information flows as a product makes its way through the process. Value stream mapping also considers factors such as capacity, quality, and variability. One of the major metrics/outputs of a value stream mapping exercise is to identify the percentage of the total lead time that is value-adding.

> **process analysis/value stream mapping** A graphical technique that helps managers understand material and information flows as a product makes its way through the process.

Value stream mapping generates two different process maps. The first is the "current state" map, which describes the value stream as it currently exists. Figure 8-5 presents an example of such a map. The second is the "future state" map. This map lays out the revised process designed to increase the percentage value metric by identifying and eliminating any non–value-adding steps in the process.

Poka-Yoke

To produce perfect quality the first time and every time, managers and workers must develop processes and systems that make performing tasks correctly every time easy and inevitable. The Japanese term **poka-yoke** (also known as *fail-safing* or *mistake-proofing*) indicates an emphasis on redesigning processes in such a way as to make mistakes either impossible or immediately apparent to the worker. For example, before giving medicines or blood, a nurse checks bar codes on the item and on the patient's bracelet to ensure that the patient is receiving the right treatment.

> **poka-yoke (foolproofing)** An emphasis on redesigning processes in such a way as to make mistakes either impossible or immediately apparent to the worker.

FIGURE 8-5   Value Stream Mapping: An Example of a Current State Map

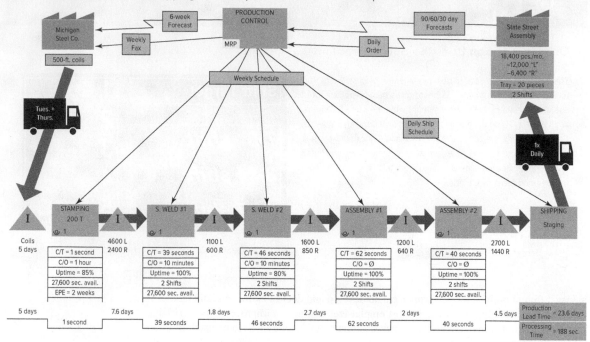

sustainability

5-S program A systematic program for effective housekeeping in operational processes.

5-S Program

Effective housekeeping is an important discipline in lean systems. It prevents wastes of waiting and inventory by reducing the chances of lost tools, equipment breakdowns, and damaged goods. One popular housekeeping program is known as the **5-S program**. The term *5-S* refers to the first letters of the five Japanese words that describe the five major activities. Table 8-4 shows the Japanese words along with their English counterparts and

TABLE 8-4   Major Activities of the 5-S Program (and Its Variants)

5-S Elements (Japanese)	5-S Elements (English)	The 5-C Campaign	Intent
Seiri	Sort	Clear out	Red tag suspected unnecessary items. After a monitoring period, throw out unnecessary items.
Seiton	Straighten	Configure	Put everything in an orderly fashion so that it can be located—"a place for everything and everything in its place." This is frequently done using "footprinting," which creates a painted outline for each item.
Seiso	Scrub	Clean and check	Clean everything and eliminate the sources of dirt.
Seiketsu	Systematize	Conform	Make cleaning and checking routine. Set the standard, train and maintain.
Shitsuke	Standardize	Custom and practice	Standardize the previous four steps into one process and continuously improve it. Use visual control through performance boards, checklists, and graphs.

a *5-C* equivalent program that is used in some companies. Some managers have added a sixth S to the list of 5-S activities—Safety. Safety has always been an important part of social responsibility for operations managers.

Simplification/Standardization

In lean systems, **simplification and standardization** are means used to reduce lead time and process variances of all sorts. *Simplification* focuses on eliminating non–value-added activities in a process. *Standardization* is aimed at clarifying and documenting the steps in a process so that they are executed exactly the same way every time by every worker.

simplification and standardization An emphasis on eliminating non–value-adding process steps and executing process steps in exactly the same way each time by every worker.

LEAN SYSTEMS: RANGE OF APPLICATION

Table 8-5 describes the level of adoption and application of the lean approach in a number of different business environments. Lean has been applied in many manufacturing companies across many industrial settings. It has become the dominant manufacturing paradigm around the world. Service companies have also adopted a *lean services* approach, especially for services that involve the repeated processing of similar jobs, such as logistics services, airlines, banks, insurance firms, call centers, software development, hospitals, and law offices. Tools such as 5-S, visual control, pull systems, and poka-yoke (mistake-proofing) have been successfully applied in service environments.

Applying Lean Systems within the Firm

The application of lean systems needs to move beyond the shop floor in order to produce maximum benefits. In the most successful firms, all functions have adopted lean principles. The lean approach requires tight coordination of marketing, sales, and operations to increase communication and decrease order processing lead times. Some firms have achieved this coordination by creating integrated product teams responsible for marketing, sales, design, production, and distribution. Importantly, marketing managers must reassess promotional programs and sales incentives that can create large swings (high variance) in demand, as these shifts are inconsistent with the lean approach.

Human resources practices for recruitment and selection, training, and performance evaluation and compensation must reflect the goals of lean. Though the lean approach tends to empower workers, not all potential workers desire to work in a lean environment. Recruitment and selection must strive to hire engaged, self-motivated employees who have a strong interest in solving problems through process innovation. Employees must also be able to work effectively with others in teams. In addition, the design of training programs needs to be driven by lean objectives.

relationships

TABLE 8-5   The Extent of Lean Systems Applications

Operational Setting	Level of Lean Systems Application
In manufacturing	Heavy adoption
In services	Growing adoption
Within firms	Heavy adoption and application
Across supply chains	Growing application
In execution activities	Mature application
In design activities	Early application
In stable business environments	Optimal application
In moderately dynamic business environments	Application with some buffers
In turbulent business environments	Very limited application

LO8-3 Recognize the strengths and limitations of lean systems.

Applying Lean Systems Across the Supply Chain

Managers have also extended lean concepts to supply chain management. However, applications of the lean approach across the supply chain have experienced a mix of benefits and problems. In stable environments, lean can enhance the performance of the supply chain by reducing lead times (thus making the supply chain more responsive to customer demands), improving quality, reducing cost, and improving customer service. Many companies have deployed lean techniques jointly with their suppliers and customers, including Toyota, John Deere, Honda, Harley-Davidson Motorcycles, Nissan, Dell, Apple, Hewlett-Packard, Nike, SYSCO (food products), Cisco (IT), Gap/Limited (clothing), Walmart, and Boeing.

Lean supply chains strive to eliminate the need for inventory, lead time, and capacity buffers. This is best achieved if suppliers and customers work together as partners in streamlining the system. Visibility plays an important role. Partners must work together to develop an environment where suppliers can "see" into their customers' operations, and vice versa. This visibility enables the partners to better understand each other's needs and capabilities, so they can be more responsive with higher quality. Finally, lean supply chains require close coordination of processes and tight integration of the transportation system to ensure the constant flow of materials and information between supply chain partners. Applying lean principles to supply chain relationships leads to the following prescriptions:

global

- Buy to achieve the lowest total cost (as compared to the lowest unit price).
- Keep distances between partners short (in the case of Toyota, this has been restated as "buy in the country where manufacturing is performed").
- Minimize the number of suppliers.
- When a problem occurs, treat the problem as a symptom and focus on what in the supply chain processes could have contributed to the emergence of that problem.
- Work with your suppliers and not against them; the firm is only as strong as the weakest supplier.

The lean supply chain produces benefits, yet it can also open up risks. Since lean supply chains are more tightly linked and have reduced buffers (in the form of excess capacity, inventory, and lead time), a problem that takes place anywhere in the supply chain can quickly and negatively affect the entire supply chain. A strike at a supplier's plant could starve the rest of the supply chain; a hurricane that destroys roads and rails can prevent shipments; a lightning storm can disrupt communications, preventing a critical order from being scheduled. Being lean can make a company more susceptible to these types of events. Additional examples are presented in Table 8-6. When protection from buffers is reduced to the lowest levels, the resulting supply chain becomes fragile; that is, when a breakdown occurs, then the supply chain stops performing. This concept is also discussed in Chapter 10, "Sourcing and Supply Management."

Applying Lean Systems to Product Innovation

LO8-4 Apply the concept of lean systems to product design.

Lean concepts can also be applied to product and process engineering and innovation. Choices made in product and process design have huge effects on the potential to achieve lean objectives. Engineers must ensure that product designs exploit any possible commonalities in processing methods or components, as these commonalities reduce the need for setups.

lean design The application of lean principles and tools to the task of designing products.

Lean design applies lean principles and tools to the task of designing products. Lean design has three major goals:

- Design products that exactly meet customers' needs (i.e., to generate real value).
- Design products that support corporate strategic objectives and that meaningfully differentiate the firm and its products from those offered by the competition.
- Design products that reduce/minimize the opportunities for waste.

Just as lean thinking seeks to reduce waste in operations, lean design seeks to reduce opportunities for product design waste. Table 8-7 lists some of the types of waste that can be reduced in lean design.

TABLE 8-6   Types of Events Causing Problems for Lean Supply Chains

Category of Event	Examples	Real World
Operational/Technological	Forecast errors Capacity constraints IT disruptions	Nike—A glitch in planning software in 2000 caused a shortage of Air Jordans. Boeing 787, 2008—A new lean process allowed very little time for startup issues and other problems.
Social	Labor strikes Sabotage	A strike at West Coast ports in 2002 starved many manufacturing plants and retail stores.
Natural/Hazard	Fire, flood, monsoon, earthquake	Japan—On March 12, 2011, an earthquake and tsunami severely impacted production and supply (especially in the computer industry). Thailand—In March/April 2011, severe flooding delayed deliveries to companies such as Nikon, Sony, and Seagate.
Economy/Competition	Interest rate fluctuations Bankruptcy of supply partners	In 2008, logistics firms encountered problems due to increasing fuel prices.
Legal/Political	Lawsuits, wars, border customs, regulations	Mattel Toys and lead paint in toys—In November 2007, lead was found in the paint used on Fischer-Price, Barbie, Polly Pockets, Batman, and Cars toys; too little time was allowed to respond to problems.

TABLE 8-7   Reducing the Opportunity for Product Design Waste

Seven Wastes in Product Design	What Does It Mean?
Complexity	Many different processes; high quantity required to deliver the product's value both on the factory floor and in the customer's use.
Precision	Product design requires precision at the outer limits of our ability to produce the product or the customer's ability to use it.
Variability	Product specifications make it difficult to control processes on the factory floor, within our supply base, or in the customer's domain.
Sensitivity	Product design results in a situation where the resulting product can be easily flawed or damaged during factory operations (either internally or within the supply base) or in the customer's domain.
Immaturity	The use of the solution found within the product design has not been previously validated for a specific application (we are not sure whether the solution offered by the product design is either valid or valued by the customer).
Danger	The use of the product design may unintentionally expose users or the environment to potentially dangerous impacts.
High skill	The product design requires processes or components that demand high degrees of training and experience (either within our internal factory or within our suppliers' operations).

Product innovation can be radical or incremental. Radical innovations sometimes make existing business models and products obsolete. For example, innovations such as the ballpoint pen, compact discs, jet engines, digital photography, and antibiotics all made their predecessors obsolete. Lean design approaches are most compatible with incremental innovation.

To be successful, radical innovation depends on unfettered idea generation with lots of exploration and testing. Employees are encouraged to generate as many new ideas as possible using new and different approaches and processes (something that runs counter to the strong emphasis on standardization found in lean systems). Furthermore, radical innovation demands the presence of slack—excess and unused resources. Slack is needed to free up time for outside-the-box idea generation, for debugging, to absorb the impact of innovation failures (not every idea works), and for pursuing unexpected opportunities. The radical innovation approach can be seen as "wasteful" from a lean perspective, because a primary goal of lean is to reduce slack.

Recognizing that a lean environment may not be consistent with the needs and demands of radical innovation raises an important fact of operations management. Not every system, such as lean systems and total quality management systems, works well in all settings. The task facing every operations manager is to identify the demands that must be satisfied and pick the system that works best in that setting.

CHAPTER SUMMARY

Lean systems and techniques have now become integral to operations and supply chain management in many industries. In this chapter, we have examined many of the concepts, management tools, and developments associated with these systems. The following are some of the major issues raised in this chapter:

1. Lean systems is a corporatewide approach that works to continuously identify, control, and eliminate all sources of waste both within the firm and across the supply chain. This requires that variance at all levels of the firm be eliminated.

2. The lean approach has seven major objectives: produce only what customers want, at the rate that customers want it, with only the features that customers want, with perfect quality, with minimum lead times, without wasting resources, and with methods that support people's development.

3. Workers implementing lean systems use many tools to reduce variance and waste. These tools work together synergistically and are highly consistent with quality improvement tools.

4. In order to be most successful, firms should expand lean thinking and the lean culture across functions within the firm and with partners across the supply chain.

5. The lean approach is not universally applicable. It is less successful in turbulent business environments, and it is not conducive to radical innovation.

KEY TERMS

andons (trouble
    lights) 294

employee
    empowerment 289

5-S program 296

focused factory 290

gemba kaizen 295

group technology
    (GT) 290

heijunka 292

inventory waste 287

jidoka 294

just-in-time (JIT) 282

Kaizen Event 294

kanban (pull)
    scheduling 291

lean design 298

lean system culture 289

lean systems
    approach 283

level, mixed-model
    scheduling 292

poka-yoke
    (foolproofing) 295

process analysis/value
    stream mapping 295

processing waste 287

pull system 288

push scheduling 292

quality at the source 293

setup reduction 293

seven basic types of
    waste 286

single minute exchange of
    dies (SMED) 293

simplification and
    standardization 297

statistical process control
    (SPC) 293

stop-and-fix (or line-stop)
    systems 294

TAKT time flow
    balancing 291

total productive maintenance
    (TPM) 290

Toyota Production System
    (TPS) 282

transportation (move)
    waste 287

visual control 293

waste from product
    defects 287

waste of motion 287

waste of
    overproduction 287

waste of waiting 287

DISCUSSION QUESTIONS

1. While Taiichi Ohno was impressed by certain aspects of the Ford Production System, he was bothered by other aspects. These included: large, special-purpose equipment; a focused, specialized workforce; and an ever-driving emphasis on cost efficiency. Why are these aspects inconsistent with lean?

2. Figure 8-4 illustrates the analogy of a boat hitting rocks as the water level falls. Why is water a good analogy for inventory? Is the sequence in which rocks are encountered a good way to prioritize inventory reduction activities? How might this prioritization scheme differ from one used in an accounting department?

3. Why is achievement of the following goals critical to the success of lean systems?
    a. Setup time and cost reduction.
    b. A relatively stable shop load.
    c. Employee empowerment.
    d. Statistical quality control.
    Give an example of how each area contributes to the success of a lean system.

4. You work in the marketing department of a firm that sells mountain bicycles and related gear. Its manufacturing division has decided to wholeheartedly adopt the lean systems philosophy. Will this affect your ability to delight your customers? Make a list of the potential pluses and minuses of this lean systems decision.

5. Discuss how lean systems might apply to a fast-food hamburger stand. How will it have to be modified to deal with daily demand variation?

6. Using the discussion of lean design, consider the design of an iPod competitor. Give examples of each of the following design wastes:
   - Complexity
   - Precision
   - Immaturity
   - Danger
   - High skill

7. What would happen if you tried to introduce a new strategy based on radical innovation into an organization in which the lean culture has been wholeheartedly adopted?

8. How would a restaurant use the 5-S program? How would an operating room use this program?

9. Why should you *not* include setup times when calculating the TAKT times?

10. What is the relationship between bottlenecks and TAKT time?

11. One lean systems' consultant has stated that, "Without standardization, there can be no improvement." Explain the reasoning behind this statement.

12. Can lean systems enhance a worker's quality of life? Discuss the pros and cons from an employee's point of view.

13. Where would you most successfully apply lean systems principles, during the introductory or growth stages of the product life cycle?

14. Can a supply chain ever be *too* lean? What would happen to the supply chain if an unexpected disruption/interruption were to occur? How might you as a supply chain manager reduce the effects of such an unexpected disruption, while staying consistent with the lean approach?

15. Imagine that your customer base is located in North America and your suppliers are located in China. Is it possible to implement lean supply chain management under such conditions? What are the challenges now facing the firm?

CASE

Good Guy Hospital Supply

Good Guy Hospital Supply (GGHS) was founded in the 1960s to serve the hospital and nursing home industry. Since then, its sales have grown an average of 26 percent per year, through both geographical expansion and increased existing-market penetration. Key to GGHS's success is service. It prides itself that it is able to fill 99.4 percent of all requests within 24 hours, and many requests actually are delivered more quickly. Recently, GGHS's quality service coordinator developed a plan to improve service levels. The new system uses a just-in-time approach to the medical supply needs of GGHS's clients. GGHS's clients had been using personal computers in their hospital medical supply stockrooms to place GGHS orders. While these clients could still purchase from other supply houses, the GGHS order entry system made it much easier for the clerical staff to place an order with GGHS. The new JIT plan, however, eliminates supplies going through GGHS's clients' medical supply stockrooms. Now the medical facility's staff and GGHS will determine the type and desired level of supplies at each stocking point. GGHS plans to place supplies at each of these stocking points; and a GGHS sales representative will tour the medical facility, identify items that have been used, and immediately restock them using inventory in the sales representative's van. Using bar coded stock and a mobile sales register, GGHS will give the hospital a detailed invoice for the items consumed each day. These reports will be designed to support each facility's medical cost control system.

GGHS's quality service coordinator argues that the increased distribution costs of this proposed system will be offset by increased product and service pricing and by the increased share of each hospital's business and that GGHS will become the vendor of choice for all items covered by its system. She argues that the hospitals will find this system attractive because it will greatly reduce their costs for stocking, ordering, and distributing medical supplies within the medical facility.

Questions

1. Is Good Guy's plan an appropriate application of JIT? Why, or why not?

2. Identify each of the stakeholders in this situation. What will each give up and get if the proposed system is accepted by GGHS's clients?

CASE

Purchasing at Midwestern State University

Jane Polski, the newly hired director of university purchasing, took one final look at the report from her purchasing manager, removed her glasses, and rubbed the bridge of her nose. Surely, she thought, things could not be that bad. According to the report, which she had commissioned, the centralized ordering process at Midwestern State University was simply "out of control." Various academic departments that placed orders through the purchasing system had complained that orders were often lost. Furthermore, the amount of time that it took for an order to be filled was difficult to predict. For example, the chemistry department had placed an order for two identical mass spectrometers, separated by three weeks. The first one took two weeks to arrive; seven months later the second order was still unfilled. Orders were often incorrectly entered. When this occurred, if the ordering department did not want to accept the incorrect order and if the item could not be returned (something that often happened because the items ordered were unique), the purchasing department was obligated to assume responsibility for the ordering error. A separate budget category had been set up for this problem (last year, it accounted for over 10 percent of total costs). Once a year, the purchasing department sold off all the misordered items—often at a significant loss. Finally, university personnel complained that, when they called the purchasing department to identify the status of an order, no one seemed to know how to locate it.

This was bad, and Jane knew that she had to do something—that was one reason that she was hired—to significantly improve operations within the purchasing department. Midwestern University had grown tremendously in the number of programs it offered. It had been decided some 40 years ago to centralize purchasing activities in one department (previously, each unit managed its own purchases). The reason for this decision was to reduce costs and improve operating and acquisition efficiencies. The current department was staffed by some 40 buyers, planners, and clerks. Most of these people had little or no prior professional purchasing experience. Furthermore, many had little more than a high school education. Most of them saw their jobs as consisting mainly of simply placing orders. With the growth in technology and the rapid changes taking place in academic research, placing orders efficiently was becoming more difficult. Systems that had worked before were not working well now.

Jane had commissioned a series of purchasing team meetings aimed at identifying areas of possible improvement. As she reviewed the report, she noted the following issues uncovered by the team:

- The department had more than 6,000 different forms. Many of the forms were developed by individual buyers for their own uses.

- The forms were difficult to complete since critical terms were often undefined and were thus interpreted in different ways.

- The department lacked a standard approach to processing orders. Workers often felt that they had many "exceptional" items to purchase that required special processing. These exceptions were not well documented.

- Except for notification of when the orders were filled, there was little contact with the customers once the request for an order was submitted.

- Department performance was evaluated in terms of utilization and cost—the percentage of the staff time devoted to receiving and processing orders.

- Every buyer processed orders differently. For example, one buyer tended to place all orders on the last day of the week, while another worked on each order to completion as soon as it arrived.

- Orders were typically worked on in the order received without any consideration of urgency or importance.

There were other issues, but Jane knew that she had enough to start devising a plan for change. The question was, where to start?

Questions

Jane is considering the application of lean services in this department. To help her, she needs the following questions addressed:

1. What should the desired outcome (objective) for this department be? How does the purchasing department create value?

2. Purchasing personnel feel that since Midwestern State University is a public, rather than private, institution, they really do not deal with customers. What is your assessment of this view? Why?

3. What measures should be used to evaluate the performance of this department?

4. Evaluate the suitability of lean services in this department.

5. What lean tools and procedures would you suggest Jane introduce into this department? Why?

CASE

Western Telephone Manufacturing

It was a tough year for Western Telephone Manufacturing (WTM) of Canton, Michigan. Until this year, WTM had been the darling of Wall Street. This company had become one of the first to wholly embrace the concepts of Six Sigma and Total Quality Management. Management had invested significantly in Six Sigma. Every employee had been trained in the tools and application of Six Sigma; an internal consulting group (Operational Services, or the OS Group, as it was referred to internally) was established to support these efforts. Furthermore, management had decided to complement its Six Sigma efforts with the implementation of lean principles and practices.

As a result, WTM had transformed itself completely over a 15-year period. Prior to the "journey" (how people at WTM referred to the process of implementing Six Sigma and Lean), quality was poor (field reports indicated that between 10 to 12 percent of all telephones produced failed in the field on initial usage by the customer, as compared to 2 to 4 percent failure rates for the competition); lead times were long (about 20 percent longer than the competition); and costs were high (a WTM telephone cost about 12 percent more than the competition). Eventually, WTM became the leader in cost control, quality (with failure rates running less than 1 percent per million), and lead times. At the heart of this quality storm was the Messiah of Six Sigma, Ted Hendrix, who also happened to be WTM's CEO.

To understand WTM's, success, all that was needed was a simple visit to any one of its manufacturing operations. Everywhere you would see posters encouraging employees to do a better job:

- Without standardization, there is no opportunity for improvement.
- First time, every time, right—that is the goal.

- You are at the heart of Quality.
- Our customers want products that work; not products that fail.
- Attack slack.
- Attack waste in every form that it appears.
- Perfect Quality—not simply a goal but what the customer expects.

Consistent with this emphasis, Ted had instituted a program that measured and monitored cost savings closely and regularly. To be promoted at WTM, it was widely recognized that you had to participate in the various programs, and you had to show that you could identify and implement projects that reflected the Six Sigma goals and that generated verifiable and significant cost savings ($25,000 over a one-year period for a Green Belt and $100,000 over a one-year period for a Black Belt). All management candidates for promotion had to generate at least 10 quarters of above average performance (i.e., actual costs were less than standard costs by a minimum of 10 percent).

Ted Hendrix was known for the quirky things he did to ensure that everyone at WTM knew the importance of Six Sigma and Lean. It was not unusual for Ted to show up in a plant where he would recognize an employee for efforts "above and beyond the call of duty." Such employees were designated as "Six Sigma Samurai." They also received a free one-week vacation for themselves and their families to anywhere in the United States, a check for $1,000 (for spending money), and a Japanese samurai sword (a Katana). Their pictures would be taken and posted in the Six Sigma Hall of Fame at corporate headquarters. Finally, and most importantly, they could expect to be on the fast track for promotion.

Until two years ago, this approach appeared to be working: WTM stock prices were above the industry average;

many business magazines had printed feature articles about WTM; cases on WTM and its journey with Six Sigma had been written and published by prestigious business schools. Then, technological innovation hit WTM. Wireless systems, Skype, cellular systems, and cloud computing were causing companies like WTM to rethink the role played by their systems—a role that was continuously changing as new technology emerged.

After hiring a major consulting company to carry out a project focusing on the future of the telephone receiver and then receiving its report, Ted Hendrix had decided that for WTM to survive into the next 20 years, the emphasis on quality had to be replaced by an emphasis on product and technological innovation and responsiveness. Innovation, Ted had decided, was the new mantra for WTM.

Consequently, Ted went around to the various plants to discuss the need for innovation. He spent time with plant management and with the employees discussing why cost and quality were no longer enough and why innovation was so important. With the support of the board of directors and his top management team, Ted made a number of highly visible changes at WTM:

- Extensive training in product innovation was carried out.
- Employees were exposed to presentations from such well-known innovation companies as GE Transport, Procter & Gamble, 3M, Apple, and Netflix.
- A new program of grants aimed at encouraging investment in innovation (and known as the WTM Innovation Grant, or WIG) was introduced.
- A new Research and Development Center was introduced at Michigan State University. This center was to work with certain faculty in North America with the goal of introducing truly new and radical innovations in telephone technology.
- Changes were made in the performance measurement scheme. Specifically, a new metric, percentage of revenue generated from products less than three years old, was introduced.

Finally, Ted tried to ensure that everyone understood the new mantra at WTM. It was no longer "Lean and Mean" but rather "Fast and New." After calling numerous consultants to review the changes made, Ted felt that WTM was now poised to become the innovator in this business.

Reality, however, has not fulfilled management expectations. Specifically, the personnel, who have always felt comfortable with Six Sigma and Lean, were distressed by the new emphasis on innovation. New, innovative products were experiencing in-field failure rates around 5 percent—well in excess of the current failure rates of less than 0.0001 percent. When WTM delayed the launch of these products so that it could drive out the root causes of the failure, it was often beaten to the market by competitors. Consequently, WTM had to be satisfied with accepting lower prices (even though its development costs were just as high as those of the competition). Employees felt comfortable with the predictability of Lean and Six Sigma; they were frustrated by the lack of predictability of innovation. Telephones that everyone at WTM thought were going to be winners often turned up being losers. Finished goods inventory went up; costs were also beginning to creep up. When a winner did occur, WTM often found itself unable to respond fast enough to the increase in demand.

In frustration, the workers at one plant went on strike. Their grievance was that management was now preventing them from doing their jobs with this new emphasis on innovation. Corporatewide grumbling with this new shift in strategy was also heard; many argued that there were still numerous opportunities for Six Sigma and Lean to do their magic; the emphasis on innovation, consequently, was seen as being premature.

As Ted Hendrix surveyed the state of WTM, he was not assured by what he saw. He saw a company experiencing real difficulties in bringing new technology to the market. What really frustrated Ted was that he knew that WTM was making great strides in developing just the technology demanded by the marketplace—only to have the advantage offered by this new technology lost once the product was released for production.

The challenge facing WTM and Ted Hendrix was to make WTM as successful with innovation as it once was with quality and cost control. Given recent changes in the firm's stock price, it appeared that Wall Street was betting against WTM.

Questions

1. Describe the culture developed at WTM as a result of the movement to Six Sigma and Lean.

2. What type of culture is most appropriate for the successful introduction of a strategy based on innovation?

3. To what extent is the current culture consistent with the requirements of an innovation strategy? Why?

4. Given expected failure rates of 5 percent in really new products, how should a firm like WTM respond? Why is this response so different from what was observed?

5. What recommendations would you make to Ted Hendrix?

TABLE 13-5   Sodas Galore Level Production Plan

					Workers		
					Required		
			Overtime or		(4,000 cases/		Fire/
		Regular	Subcontract	Ending	worker)	Hire	Lay Off
Month	Demand	Production	Production	Inventory*			
Jan.	24,000	40,000	0	21,000	10	2	0
Feb.	32,000	40,000	0	29,000	10	0	0
March	32,000	40,000	0	37,000	10	0	0
April	48,000	40,000	0	29,000	10	0	0
May	60,000	40,000	0	9,000	10	0	0
June	44,000	40,000	0	5,000	10	0	0
Total	240,000	240,000	0	130,000		2	0

Beginning inventory = 5,000; Beginning workers = 8

*Ending inventory in any month = Ending inventory in previous month + Current month production − Demand. For example, January ending inventory = 5,000 + 40,000 − 24,000 = 21,000.

EXAMPLE 13-2

Table 13-6 provides the data necessary to determine the total cost of option 1 at Sodas Galore, adjusting the size of the workforce to the amount of demand each month.

TABLE 13-6   Chase Plan: Adjust Workforce Size

					Workers		
					Required		Fire/
			Overtime or		(4,000 cases/		Lay
		Regular	Subcontract	Ending	worker)	Hire	Off
Month	Demand	Production	Production	Inventory			
Jan.	24,000	24,000	0	5,000	6	0	2
Feb.	32,000	32,000	0	5,000	8	2	0
March	32,000	32,000	0	5,000	8	0	0
April	48,000	48,000	0	5,000	12	4	0
May	60,000	60,000	0	5,000	15	3	0
June	44,000	44,000	0	5,000	11	0	4
Total	240,000	240,000	0	30,000		9	6

Beginning inventory = 5,000; Beginning workers = 8

The total cost of adjusting the workforce size to accomplish the chase plan is:

Total cost = Regular production cost + Inventory cost + Hiring/firing cost
= 240,000 cases ($.80) + 30,000 cases ($.30) + 9 hire ($1,000) + 6 fire/layoff ($1,500)
= $192,000 + $9,000 + $9,000 + $9,000
= $219,000

Notice that no inventory other than that required to meet current demand is created or used during the chase plan. The only carrying cost is due to the safety stock requirement.

To evaluate options 2 and 3 for the chase plan, we need to estimate the costs of maintaining a workforce large enough to meet the minimum monthly demand, supplementing output with either overtime or subcontracted labor in months when demand is greater than the minimum. These options are described in Example 13-3.

EXAMPLE 13-3

Table 13-7 below describes the options for supplementing capacity with either overtime or subcontract labor.

For this plan, it is assumed that the workforce is stable at six workers, which means that you must also include the cost of initially laying off or firing two workers (since the initial assumption was that eight workers are employed).

The total cost of a chase plan using overtime is:

Total cost = Regular production cost + cost + Inventory cost +
       Hiring/firing cost
    = 144,000 cases ($.80) + 96,000 cases ($1.20) + 30,000 cases ($.30)
    + 2 fire ($1,500)
    = $115,200 + $115,200 + $9,000 + $3,000 = $242,400

The total cost of a chase plan using a subcontractor to supplement regular production is:

Total cost = Regular production cost + Subcontract cost + Inventory cost +
       Hiring/firing cost
    = 144,000 cases ($.80) + 96,000 cases ($1.15) + 30,000 cases ($.30)
    + 2 fire ($1,500)
    = $115,200 + $110,400 + $9,000 + $3,000 = $237,600

TABLE 13-7   Chase Plan: Use Overtime or Subcontract Labor

					Workers		
			Overtime or		Required		Fire/
		Regular	Subcontract	Ending	(4,000 cases/		Lay
Month	Demand	Production	Production	Inventory	worker)	Hire	Off
			Beginning inventory = 5,000; Beginning workers = 8				
Jan.	24,000	24,000	0	5,000	6	0	2
Feb.	32,000	24,000	8,000	5,000	6	0	0
March	32,000	24,000	8,000	5,000	6	0	0
April	48,000	24,000	24,000	5,000	6	0	0
May	60,000	24,000	36,000	5,000	6	0	0
June	44,000	24,000	20,000	5,000	6	0	0
Total	240,000	144,000	96,000	30,000		0	2

Hybrid Plans

Usually, the actual production plan combines some aspects of level production and building inventory with aspects of chase, or it varies the production rate during each period to match production and demand. In either case a company may face some of the constraints mentioned earlier or simply may have policies related to the use of personnel.

EXAMPLE 13-4

Suppose Sodas Galore has an established policy of maintaining a stable workforce. It is believed that constantly adjusting workforce size is not practical, and there is a desire to keep morale high among the permanent employees by allowing them the opportunity to earn some overtime pay. After much internal discussion, the company decides to maintain a permanent workforce of eight production workers. Therefore, in periods of relatively low demand, the company will allow inventory to build. In periods of higher demand, the inventory will be used to satisfy as much demand as possible and overtime or subcontract production will be used to satisfy remaining demand. The costs associated with this hybrid plan are presented in Table 13-8.

TABLE 13-8   Sodas Galore: A Hybrid Solution

					Beginning inventory = 5,000; Beginning workers = 8		
Month	Demand	Regular Production	Overtime or Subcontract Production	Ending Inventory	Workers Required (4,000 cases/ worker)	Hire	Fire/ Lay Off
Jan.	24,000	32,000	0	13,000	8	0	0
Feb.	32,000	32,000	0	13,000	8	0	0
March	32,000	32,000	0	13,000	8	0	0
April	48,000	32,000	8,000	5,000	8	0	0
May	60,000	32,000	28,000	5,000	8	0	0
June	44,000	32,000	12,000	5,000	8	0	0
Total	240,000	192,000	48,000	54,000		0	0

The total cost of this hybrid aggregate plan is:

Total cost = Regular production cost + Overtime cost + Inventory cost

= (192,000 cases)($.80/case) + (48,000 cases)($1.20/case) + 54,000 cases ($.30)

= $153,600 regular production + $57,600 overtime production + $16,200

= $227,400

Comparing Aggregate Production Plans

Table 13-9 compares the costs related to the five alternative aggregate plans for Sodas Galore. Given the various planning assumptions used in this exercise, the plan that results in the lowest total cost is the chase plan with monthly hiring and firing.

In evaluating these plans, we should consider the assumptions we have made. For example, we have assumed that newly hired workers are just as productive as experienced workers. For that matter, it was also assumed that workers are in fact available. Worker availability can be a serious issue for a firm that has a reputation of frequently hiring and then laying off employees. The overtime example assumes that the existing workforce is capable of working enough overtime hours to meet the total demand. There are often limitations to the amount of overtime that the workforce can handle. Moreover, workers may become less productive the longer they work. We also assumed that the operation has a make-to-stock (MTS) orientation. Since make-to-order (MTO) and assemble-to-order

TABLE 13-9   Comparison of Five Plans at Sodas Galore

Aggregate Plan	Reg. Prod. Cost	Overtime Cost	Subcontr. Cost	Inventory Cost	Hire Cost	Fire/Lay Off Cost	Total
Level	$192,000	0	0	$39,000	$2,000		$2...
Chase— Hire/Layoff	$192,000	0	0	$ 9000	$9,000	$9,000	$2...
Chase— Overtime	$115,200	$115,200	0	$ 9000	0	$3,000	$24...
Chase— Subcontract	$115,200	0	$110,400	$ 9000	0	$3,000	$2...
Hybrid	$153,600	$ 57,600	0	$16,200	0	0	$2...

(ATO) operations do not build finished goods inventory ahead of demand, they follow something closer to a chase strategy.

There are, of course, many other possible hybrid solutions to the Sodas Galore planning situation. It is likely that a hybrid solution exists that is less costly than the pure chase plan. Sometimes operations may employ more workers than are actually needed in low demand periods just to avoid other hidden costs or risks associated with hiring/firing, overtime, and/or subcontracting (such as labor strikes, quality problems, and so on). A manager could easily set up a spreadsheet on a personal computer in order to quickly evaluate many different scenarios. If used interactively, this methodology can be effective at generating a solution that all major functions can agree on. In addition, the interactive process allows managers to see the effect of the changes as they are made, which can uncover unrealistic cost assumptions and unworkable situations. This is especially important when all of the constraints haven't been identified up front. Dialogue between managers and eventual agreement on a good production plan could actually be better than an optimal plan that is forced on everyone.

Sophisticated modeling techniques such as linear programming, integer programming, and others can be applied to the aggregate production planning process. These techniques require precise specification of assumptions, constraints, costs, and objectives in a mathematical format. For those who are interested in the more sophisticated models, the supplement to this text demonstrates an optimal solution using linear programming and spreadsheet modeling.

AGGREGATE PLANNING FOR SERVICE INDUSTRIES

As mentioned earlier, S&OP and aggregate planning are just as critical in service industries as in manufacturing. In some ways such planning is even more critical because there is no ability to build inventory in anticipation of demand. When supply and demand do not match, the impact is almost always on human resources.

Yield Management

Because of the inability to inventory demand, service companies often make extensive use of the demand management tactics discussed in Chapter 12. Consider, for example, how airlines and hotels change prices almost constantly in an attempt to fill flights or rooms. These companies use a process called **yield management**, which adjusts prices as demand occurs (or does not occur) for a service (such as seats on a specific scheduled flight or hotel rooms for a specific night).

The purpose of yield management is to shape demand in a way that yields greater revenues or profits. For example, in Michigan, there is a wonderful vacation spot known as

EXAMPLE 13-4

Suppose Sodas Galore has an established policy of maintaining a stable workforce. It is believed that constantly adjusting workforce size is not practical, and there is a desire to keep morale high among the permanent employees by allowing them the opportunity to earn some overtime pay. After much internal discussion, the company decides to maintain a permanent workforce of eight production workers. Therefore, in periods of relatively low demand, the company will allow inventory to build. In periods of higher demand, the inventory will be used to satisfy as much demand as possible and overtime or subcontract production will be used to satisfy remaining demand. The costs associated with this hybrid plan are presented in Table 13-8.

TABLE 13-8   Sodas Galore: A Hybrid Solution

					Workers		
			Overtime or		Required		Fire/
		Regular	Subcontract	Ending	(4,000 cases/		Lay
Month	Demand	Production	Production	Inventory	worker)	Hire	Off
Jan.	24,000	32,000	0	13,000	8	0	0
Feb.	32,000	32,000	0	13,000	8	0	0
March	32,000	32,000	0	13,000	8	0	0
April	48,000	32,000	8,000	5,000	8	0	0
May	60,000	32,000	28,000	5,000	8	0	0
June	44,000	32,000	12,000	5,000	8	0	0
Total	240,000	192,000	48,000	54,000		0	0

Beginning inventory = 5,000; Beginning workers = 8

The total cost of this hybrid aggregate plan is:

Total cost = Regular production cost + Overtime cost + Inventory cost
  = (192,000 cases)($.80/case) + (48,000 cases)($1.20/case) +
    54,000 cases ($.30)
  = $153,600 regular production + $57,600 overtime production +
    $16,200
  = $227,400

Comparing Aggregate Production Plans

Table 13-9 compares the costs related to the five alternative aggregate plans for Sodas Galore. Given the various planning assumptions used in this exercise, the plan that results in the lowest total cost is the chase plan with monthly hiring and firing.

In evaluating these plans, we should consider the assumptions we have made. For example, we have assumed that newly hired workers are just as productive as experienced workers. For that matter, it was also assumed that workers are in fact available. Worker availability can be a serious issue for a firm that has a reputation of frequently hiring and then laying off employees. The overtime example assumes that the existing workforce is capable of working enough overtime hours to meet the total demand. There are often limitations to the amount of overtime that the workforce can handle. Moreover, workers may become less productive the longer they work. We also assumed that the operation has a make-to-stock (MTS) orientation. Since make-to-order (MTO) and assemble-to-order

TABLE 13-9   Comparison of Five Plans at Sodas Galore

Aggregate Plan	Reg. Prod. Cost	Overtime Cost	Subcontr. Cost	Inventory Cost	Hire Cost	Fire/Lay Off Cost	Total Cost
Level	$192,000	0	0	$39,000	$2,000		**$233,000**
Chase— Hire/Layoff	$192,000	0	0	$ 9000	$9,000	$9,000	**$219,000**
Chase— Overtime	$115,200	$115,200	0	$ 9000	0	$3,000	**$242,400**
Chase— Subcontract	$115,200	0	$110,400	$ 9000	0	$3,000	**$237,600**
Hybrid	$153,600	$ 57,600	0	$16,200	0	0	**$227,400**

(ATO) operations do not build finished goods inventory ahead of demand, they follow something closer to a chase strategy.

There are, of course, many other possible hybrid solutions to the Sodas Galore planning situation. It is likely that a hybrid solution exists that is less costly than the pure chase plan. Sometimes operations may employ more workers than are actually needed in low demand periods just to avoid other hidden costs or risks associated with hiring/firing, overtime, and/or subcontracting (such as labor strikes, quality problems, and so on). A manager could easily set up a spreadsheet on a personal computer in order to quickly evaluate many different scenarios. If used interactively, this methodology can be effective at generating a solution that all major functions can agree on. In addition, the interactive process allows managers to see the effect of the changes as they are made, which can uncover unrealistic cost assumptions and unworkable situations. This is especially important when all of the constraints haven't been identified up front. Dialogue between managers and eventual agreement on a good production plan could actually be better than an optimal plan that is forced on everyone.

Sophisticated modeling techniques such as linear programming, integer programming, and others can be applied to the aggregate production planning process. These techniques require precise specification of assumptions, constraints, costs, and objectives in a mathematical format. For those who are interested in the more sophisticated models, the supplement to this text demonstrates an optimal solution using linear programming and spreadsheet modeling.

AGGREGATE PLANNING FOR SERVICE INDUSTRIES

As mentioned earlier, S&OP and aggregate planning are just as critical in service industries as in manufacturing. In some ways such planning is even more critical because there is no ability to build inventory in anticipation of demand. When supply and demand do not match, the impact is almost always on human resources.

Yield Management

Because of the inability to inventory demand, service companies often make extensive use of the demand management tactics discussed in Chapter 12. Consider, for example, how airlines and hotels change prices almost constantly in an attempt to fill flights or rooms. These companies use a process called **yield management**, which adjusts prices as demand occurs (or does not occur) for a service (such as seats on a specific scheduled flight or hotel rooms for a specific night).

The purpose of yield management is to shape demand in a way that yields greater revenues or profits. For example, in Michigan, there is a wonderful vacation spot known as

yield management A process that adjusts prices as demand for a service occurs (or does not occur).

Mackinac Island, home of the Grand Hotel. As you might expect, demand for hotel rooms on the island is greatest during the summer. Consequently, room rates fall in September and remain low until the end of May. Airlines routinely practice yield management by adjusting prices and travel restrictions to maximize revenues on each flight. Their computer systems periodically compare the expected revenue of offering a seat on a flight at the normal fare against the expected revenue from offering it at a discount. As the date of the flight approaches, the airline increases the ticket's price.

Yield management can involve very sophisticated mathematical models that simulate customer behaviors under different scenarios. Complex computer programs have been developed in certain industries to continuously analyze demand versus available capacity and make the price adjustments. Effective yield management requires extensive analysis of past demand so that typical demand patterns and trends are clear. It also requires continuous tracking of actual demand for the service. The Get Real box on yield management in the hotel industry provides more insight into this practice.

GET REAL

Yield Management in the Hotel Industry

Hotels pose an interesting problem when it comes to maximizing revenue. Why? Because fundamentally, like any service, they are a perishable product. You cannot store an unused hotel room until it is needed; if you have an empty hotel room that is unused, then it loses value and revenue every day that it is unsold. So how you deal with this challenge?

In the past, the price was to offer discounts to encourage people to come to your hotel or to extend their stays. Yet, today, we realize that such approaches are often ineffective. They are not linked to the customer's preference; they treat every customer as being the same. How do we deal with this challenge? The answer is a new development—yield management.

Yield management (also called *revenue management*) provides a means to maximize revenue from a perishable, fixed product such as a hotel or an airline. Yield management is a variable pricing strategy that is based on understanding, anticipating, and influencing customer behavior to maximize revenue from such assets. It seeks to "sell" the product to the "right" customer at the right time for the right price.

In principle, yield management tactics are fairly straightforward. In practice, applying yield management is complex. It is also multi-disciplinary in that it blends elements of market, operations, supply chain, and financial management. Yield management recognizes that what is important to one customer is not necessarily important to another. It also recognizes that some activities cannot be eliminated or temporarily stopped—a pool cannot be shut down because only a handful of guests use it; front desks must be staffed around the clock because that is what most customers expect.

In the hotel industry, yield management seeks to offer those benefits that specific customers want in order to encourage them to book a room or extend the length of their stay. For example, costs associated with a hotel's breakfast buffet, including food preparation and waste disposal, will exist whether the hotel is fully or sparsely occupied on any given day. A "free breakfast" offering

© Jupiterimages/Getty Images

during slow periods can encourage more guests to stay at your hotel, improving overall revenue with only a marginal effect on food and beverage costs. Likewise, offering complimentary phone and Internet use to corporate users as part of the negotiated rate is another way of offering certain customer segments with access to assets that they value but that are essentially fixed costs for the hotel. Thus, hotels are now better able to target and lure in specific customers—and as a result, the customers and the hotel both win!

Source: Excerpted from S. Sampson, "Yield Management in 2009: How to Keep Your Hotel Up and Running in a Downturn," *Hospitality Trends,* **March 10, 2009. Copyright (c) 2009 Shannon Sampson. Reprinted with permission.**

An Example of a Service Aggregate Plan

Ultimately, most service businesses have to develop aggregate plans based on human resource requirements. The process is not greatly different from that already discussed, except that there is no inventory to be considered. Instead, demand for services is often stated in terms of the amount of service labor required rather than the amount of product required.

 LO13-6 Explain the differences in aggregate planning in services versus manufacturing industries.

EXAMPLE 13-5

Suppose Nile Inc., an Internet retailer, needs to develop an aggregate plan for its warehouse operation. Demand in the warehouse is stated in terms of the number of labor hours required each quarter to pick, pack, and ship customers' orders. Because the business is seasonal, demand is expected to be as follows:

Quarter 1: 15,000 labor hours
Quarter 2: 12,000 labor hours
Quarter 3: 10,000 labor hours
Quarter 4: 18,000 labor hours

Full-time employees work 500 hours per quarter, and their total compensation (including benefits) is $10.00 per hour. A worker can work overtime, up to a maximum of 100 hours per quarter, for $15.00 per hour. If, however, a full-time employee is not busy for 500 hours, the employee is still paid for those hours.

Part-time workers can be hired as needed, as long as each works no more than 400 hours per quarter (there is no minimum requirement of hours for a part-time employee). Part-time workers earn $8.00 per hour. The company currently employs 20 workers. The hiring and firing cost for a part-time employee is $1,000 for each hire or fire.

In this case, a level plan would require maintaining a stable workforce, meaning that the number of full-time employees must be able to fulfill the maximum demand. The level plan is shown in Table 13-10. Because the maximum number of hours a full-time employee can work is 600 hours per quarter (regular 500 hours plus 100 overtime hours), the level number of workers required is 18,000 hours maximum/600 = 30 workers. Keep in mind that these 30 workers will have 15,000 hours of regular time pay each month regardless of the number of hours actually worked. A total of 10 workers must be hired immediately to meet the first quarter demand.

$$\begin{aligned} \text{Cost of level plan} &= \text{Regular pay} + \text{Overtime pay} + \text{Hiring cost} \\ &= (60{,}000 \text{ hours}) (\$10.00/\text{hour}) + (3{,}000 \text{ hours}) (\$15.00/\text{hour}) \\ &\quad + 10(\$1{,}000) \\ &= \$655{,}000 \end{aligned}$$

TABLE 13-10   Level Plan for Nile Inc.

Quarter	Demand (hours)	Regular Hours Paid	Overtime Hours Paid	Number of Hires
1	15,000	15,000	0	10
2	12,000	15,000	0	0
3	10,000	15,000	0	0
4	18,000	15,000	3,000	0
Total		60,000	3,000	10

(continued)

(continued)

There are several possible variations on a chase plan for Nile Inc. We will evaluate a pure chase plan. In this instance, the permanent workforce will be large enough to only meet the minimum demand requirement of 10,000 hours, working the regular hours (500 hours). Thus, the permanent workforce is 20 workers. This results in a maximum of 2,000 hours of overtime available. The permanent workforce will always work the maximum possible before part-time workers are used. Finally, since you can't hire part of a person, when part-timers are hired, you must incur the full hiring cost even though the person may not work the maximum of 400 hours that part-timers are allowed to work. Table 13-11 shows the results of this plan.

Cost of plan = Regular pay + Overtime pay + Part-time pay + Hire/fire costs
= (40,000 hours)($10.00) + (6,000 hours)($15.00) + (9,000)($8.00)
+ (31 hire/fire)($1,000)
= $593,000

TABLE 13-11   Chase Plan for Nile Inc.

Quarter	Demand	Regular Hours Paid	Overtime Hours Paid	Part-Time Hours	Part-Time Workers Needed	Hire	Fire
1	15,000	10,000	2,000	3,000	7.5 = 8	8	0
2	12,000	10,000	2,000	0	0	0	8
3	10,000	10,000	0	0	0	0	0
4	18,000	10,000	2,000	6,000	15	15	0
Total		**40,000**	**6,000**	**9,000**		**23**	**8**

activity

student

Rework the Nile Inc. chase plan assuming that the permanent workforce is 17 workers. How does your answer differ from the chase plan illustrated in Table 13-11?

As in the planning for Sodas Galore, there are again many alternatives that might be considered for Nile Inc., depending upon assumptions concerning how the labor force might actually be utilized. For example, the chase plan would be different if Nile Inc. were to decide that the permanent workforce only needs to be large enough to meet minimum demand by working maximum hours (in this case, 600 total hours). Thus, the permanent workforce would consist of only 10,000 hours/600 = 16.67, or rounded up, 17 workers. All other aspects of the plan would be different from those shown.

CHAPTER SUMMARY

This chapter has dealt with the sales and operations planning process, with specific emphasis on aggregate production planning. The major issues discussed in the chapter were as follows:

1. All firms experience difficulty in balancing supply and demand.
2. Sales and operations planning is a cross-functional process that brings representatives from sales, marketing, manufacturing, purchasing, and logistics together to develop plans for most efficiently and effectively meeting expected customer demand.

3. The sales and operations planning process results in two plans: a sales plan, which attempts to influence demand to match supply, and an aggregate production plan (APP), which attempts to match supply to demand.

4. Sales and operations planning should be a dynamic process conducted frequently during the year to update plans as new information becomes available.

5. The relevant costs in aggregate production planning are inventory holding cost, regular production cost, overtime cost, temporary workforce cost, firing/layoff cost, backorder/lost sales cost, and subcontracting cost.

6. The three basic aggregate production strategies are level production, chase, and mixed strategies. The alternatives should be compared to determine which one provides the lowest total cost.

7. Service industries have aggregate planning approaches similar to manufacturing. The major difference is that there is no inventory to consider.

KEY TERMS

aggregate production plan 448	mixed or hybrid strategy 451	sales and operations planning (S&OP) 444
chase strategy 449	rolling planning horizons 447	yield management 457
level production strategy 449		

DISCUSSION QUESTIONS

1. What is the value of the S&OP process to an organization? Why should it be a dynamic process rather than a one-time annual event?

2. Explain in your own words the typical differences in objectives for production managers and sales managers.

3. Do you think chase strategies might be more appropriate in some industries than in others? Give some examples and explain why.

4. What are the key cost advantages of a level production strategy over a chase strategy? What are the key cost advantages of a chase strategy over a level production strategy?

5. Suppose your firm is using a level production planning approach to manage seasonal demand. Your production manager is evaluated on lowest production cost but the logistics manager is evaluated on the amount of inventory the firm holds. Explain the issues.

6. Explain why the following is not necessarily a true statement: "If a company is chasing demand, then it is overinvesting in balance sheet assets because inventories will be high."

7. If most aggregate production planning problems include assumptions and ignore many needs of the company that are difficult to quantify, then what is the benefit of the process?

8. In most companies that are considered to be successful users of the S&OP process, the resulting plans and commitments are treated, essentially, as "quasi-contracts." That is, the agreement reached between the various parties cannot be unilaterally broken or changed by any party. To change the schedule requirements participation of all the parties. They must agree to the changes before they can be implemented. What are the implications of a position as it pertains to how the firm and its functional areas deal with changes?

SOLVED PROBLEM

Neal Industries manufactures blue jeans for the teen market. The S&OP team has agreed upon a demand forecast for the following year, as shown below. Given the planning information, determine the cost of a level production plan and a plan to chase demand by adjusting the size of the workforce each month. The company begins with 1,000,000 jeans in safety stock and desires to maintain this level consistently (and end with this level).

Quarter	Demand
1	6,000,000
2	9,000,000
3	15,000,000
4	10,000,000

Current workforce	400 workers
Average output per worker	20,000 jeans per quarter
Inventory holding cost	$.10/pair per quarter
Regular wage rate	$16.00 per hour
Regular production hours	500 hours per quarter
Hiring cost	$300 per worker
Firing/layoff cost	$200 per worker
Beginning inventory	1,000,0000

Solution

The total demand for the year is 40,000,000 jeans. Therefore, the average demand per quarter is 10,000,000 jeans, and 10,000,000 jeans is the level production rate.

The average worker produces 20,000 jeans per quarter. Therefore the current workforce can produce 8,000,000 jeans per quarter. To produce 10,000,000 per quarter using a level production plan will require the addition of 100 workers (2,000,000 jeans/20,000 jeans per worker).

An average worker earns $8,000 per quarter (500 hours × $16.00 per hour) and produces 20,000 jeans. Therefore, the regular production (labor) cost is $0.40 per unit.

Beginning Workers = 400 Beginning Inventory = 1,000,000						
Quarter	Demand	Production	Ending Inventory	Workers Required	Hire	Fire
1	6,000,000	10,000,000	5,000,000	500	100	0
2	9,000,000	10,000,000	6,000,000	500	0	0
3	15,000,000	10,000,000	1,000,000	500	0	0
4	10,000,000	10,000,000	1,000,000	500	0	0
Total	40,000,000	40,000,000	13,000,000		100	0

The total cost of the level production plan for Neal Industries is $0.40/unit (40,000,000 jeans) + $0.10/unit (13,000,000 jeans) + 100 hires ($300) = $16,000,000 + $1,300,000 + $30,000 = $17,330,000.

A plan to chase demand has the following results:

Quarter	Demand	Production	Ending Inventory	Workers Required	Hire	Fire/ Lay Off
1	6,000,000	6,000,000	1,000,000	300		100
2	9,000,000	9,000,000	1,000,000	450	150	0
3	15,000,000	15,000,000	1,000,000	750	300	0
4	10,000,000	10,000,000	1,000,000	500		250
Total	40,000,000	40,000,000	4,000,000		450	350

The total cost of this plan is:

$0.40/unit (40,000,000 jeans) + $0.10/unit (4,000,000 jeans) + 450 hires ($300) + 350 fires (200) = $16,000,000 + $400,000 + $135,000 + $70,000 = $16,605,000

The level production plan costs $725,000 more than this chase plan.

PROBLEMS

1. For the Sodas Galore problem discussed in the chapter, assume that employees negotiate an increase in the regular production wage rate to $24.00 per hour and $36.00 per hour for overtime. Rework all aspects of the problem using the new wage rates.

2. Using the existing data in the solved problem (Neal Industries), assume that the overtime production wage rate is $24.00 per hour. Compute the cost of a chase plan using a stable workforce of 300 workers.

3. The Johnson Company manufactures expensive medical diagnostic equipment. It plans to meet all of its projected demand (given below for the next year by quarter). The firm plans to use a constant production rate of 300 units/quarter. Production costs are $20,000 per unit and holding costs are $2,000 per quarter per unit.

Quarter	1	2	3	4
Demand	200	300	400	300

What is the cost of this production plan?

4. The current aggregate demand requirements for a firm are shown below for the next six months:

Month	May	June	July	Aug	Sept	Oct
Demand	120	100	100	100	130	150

The firm always plans to meet all demand. The firm currently has 120 workers capable of producing 120 units in a month (1 unit/worker). The workforce can be increased (at a cost of $500 per worker) or decreased (at a cost of $1,000 per worker). Inventory holding cost is $100 per unit per month. The firm currently has 40 units of inventory on hand, and it would like to have 40 units available at the end of each month. Regular production cost is $3,000 per unit.

   a. What should the aggregate plan be if the inventory holding cost is to be minimized?
   b. What is the cost of this plan?

5. A firm must plan production for the next six months. Each unit costs $250 to produce and has an inventory holding cost of $10 per unit per month based on ending inventory levels. The cost to hire a worker is $100, and the cost to fire a worker is $200 per worker. Each worker produces 10 units per month. There are 20 persons on the payroll

at the beginning of the first month. The company currently has 100 units of inventory in stock, and it wants to hold these as safety stock.

Month	1	2	3	4	5	6
Demand	300	300	300	300	400	500

a. From the information given above, what level production rate will meet demand for the next six months?

b. Given the production rate determined in (a), what is the maximum end-of-period inventory experienced at some time during the six months? What is the cost of a level production plan?

c. From the information given above, what is the total cost of a chase (hire and fire only) production plan?

6. JokersRWild makes playing cards in several different styles, but a "standard" deck of cards is used for planning purposes. The average worker at JokersRWild can make 10,000 decks of cards per month at a cost of $1.00 per deck during regular production and $1.30 during overtime. The company currently employs 25 workers. Experience shows that it costs $500 to hire a worker and $500 to fire a worker. Inventory carrying cost is $.25 per deck per month. Given the following demand estimate, develop a six-month production plan based on (a) level production, (b) chase using overtime (no workers will be fired and inventory increases if necessary), and (c) chase by changing workforce level. The beginning inventory is 50,000, and at least that amount is desired each month.

Month	January	February	March	April	May	June
Demand	200,000	150,000	200,000	400,000	550,000	250,000

7. Trexoid Inc. makes a popular video game console. Demand varies each month, with highest demand coming in the last quarter of the year. Regular production costs are $120 per unit and inventory carrying cost is $5 per unit per quarter. Overtime production cost is $150 per unit. Assume that the 10 current Trexoid employees can produce 50,000 units per quarter in regular production and can work enough overtime hours to produce the amount required if a chase plan is employed. On the other hand, hiring cost is $5,000 per employee and firing cost is $10,000 per employee. Trexoid currently has zero inventory on hand, and it would like to have zero inventories at the end of the year. Forecasted demand is as follows:

Quarter 1	30,000 units
Quarter 2	20,000 units
Quarter 3	70,000 units
Quarter 4	120,000 units

What would you suggest to Trexoid management?

8. Appliances Inc. is preparing an aggregate production plan for washers for the next four months. The company's expected monthly demand is given below in the chart. The company will have 500 washers in inventory at the beginning of the month and desires to maintain at least that number at the end of each month. Below are other critical data:

Production cost per unit = $300
Inventory carrying cost per month per unit = $50 (based on ending month inventory)
Hiring cost per worker = $1,000
Firing cost per worker = $2,000
Beginning number of workers = 10
Each worker can produce 100 units per month.

Level Plan

Month	Demand	Regular Production	Ending Inventory	Workers Required	Hire	Fire
1	4,000					
2	6,000					
3	3,000					
4	7,000					
Total	20,000					

Chase Plan

Month	Demand	Regular Production	Ending Inventory	Workers Required	Hire	Fire
1	4,000					
2	6,000					
3	3,000					
4	7,000					
Total	20,000					

Complete the tables and determine the cost of the two plans.

9. Togo makes riding lawn mowers and tractors. The company's expected quarterly demand is given below in the chart. The company will have 300 mowers in inventory at the beginning of the quarter and desires to maintain at least that number at the end of each quarter. Other critical data include:

Production cost per unit = $200
Inventory carrying cost per quarter per unit = $60 (based on ending quarter inventory)
Hiring cost per worker = $500
Firing cost per worker = $750
Beginning number of workers = 40

Each worker can produce 100 units per quarter.

Level Plan

Quarter	Demand	Regular Production	Ending Inventory	Workers Required	Hire	Fire
1	5,000					
2	9,000					
3	7,000					
4	9,000					
Total	30,000					

Chase Plan

Quarter	Demand	Regular Production	Ending Inventory	Workers Required	Hire	Fire
1	5,000					
2	9,000					
3	7,000					
4	9,000					
Total	30,000					

Complete the tables and calculate the cost of the two plans.

10. Jones Inc. is preparing an aggregate production plan for next year. The company expects demand to be 1,000 units in quarter 1; 2,000 units in quarter 2; 4,000 units in quarter 3; and 3,000 units in quarter 4. The company will have 100 units in inventory at the beginning of the year and desires to maintain at least that number at the end of each quarter as safety stock. Other information includes:

    Regular production labor cost = $100 per unit
    Overtime production cost per unit = $150
    Inventory carrying cost = $25/unit/quarter based on quarter-ending inventory
    Hiring cost = $2,000 per worker
    Firing/layoff cost = $3,000 per worker
    Beginning number of workers = 15
    Each worker can produce 100 units per quarter.

    a. What is the total cost of a level plan?
    b. What is the total cost of a chase plan utilizing hiring and firing?
    c. Suppose Jones management is reluctant to constantly change the workforce by hiring and firing. The company decides to hire seven additional workers at the beginning of the year. The company will build inventory in low-demand months and use it in high-demand months. In addition, if necessary, overtime will be used to meet demand requirements if there is not sufficient inventory available. What is the total cost of this plan?

11. Dale's Dance Studio currently has three full-time instructors who are each paid $2,500 per month. A dance instructor can work a maximum of only 100 hours per month because instruction normally takes place at night. Instructors receive $2,500 even if they do not work 100 hours, however. Part-time instructors can be hired at a cost of $40 per hour. Dale's has forecasted that demand for the next six months will be as follows:

Month	1	2	3	4	5	6
Hours	380	280	450	420	520	390

    Should Dale hire more full-time instructors or rely on part-time instructors to meet demand?

12. Make-Believe-You is a company that produces "cosplay" costumes for those people who want to live like their favorite action heroes. Currently, out of its catalog of hundreds of costumes, Make-Believe-You has identified six costumes that are demanded on a regular basis (with the following traits) and that are made in the same system:

Model	# Hours	Price	% of Sales
Harley Quinn	4.2	285	32
Guardians of the Galaxy – Star Lord	4.9	345	21
Star War – Storm trooper	5.1	395	17
Lord of the Rings – Gandalf	5.2	425	14
Batman - Dark Knight	5.4	525	10
Iron Man – from Iron Man 3/Avengers	5.8	725	6

Make-Believe-You also has developed the following agreed-upon forecast for overall demand:

Month	Predicted Demand (aggregate units)
January	220
February	280
March	460
April	190
May	310
June	145
July	110
August	225

Management has decided that it would like to begin with 200 units at the end of December and end with 100 units on hand at the end of August.

a. Using these data, identify the monthly production levels using a chase strategy.

b. Using the data in your solution to the previous question, develop an aggregate plan using a constant workforce. (*Hint:* Convert the individual units into aggregate units using a summed weighted approach. For example, Iron Man contributes 5.8*.06 = 0.35 hours of demand for capacity, while Harley Quinn contributes 4.2*.32 = 1.34 hours of demand for capacity. Use the same approach for each item to determine the overall aggregate demand for capacity.)

c. Review your answers to the previous questions.

1. Under what conditions would you go with a chase strategy even though the costs might be lower with a level strategy?

2. What actions can you introduce to improve the quality of your aggregate planning?

CASE

Med-Chem Products: Hospital Division

The following case is based on one of the coauthor's experiences with an actual company and its management.

Fiona Richey knew that she had been given the opportunity of a lifetime. She had just been hired to be an internal troubleshooter and consultant by the Hospital Division of Med-Chem Products. This was quite a feat. After all, she had graduated about four years ago with an undergraduate degree in Operations Management and Logistics from a large midwestern university. During that time, she had developed a reputation for being a good team player, a creative thinker, and someone who got things done quickly (and correctly). That was one of the major reasons that Med-Chem had hired her. Originally, she had been working for a supplier to Med-Chem. About six months ago, she was approached by one of the managers of Med-Chem, with a very attractive job offer.

Even though she had been at Med-Chem for only four weeks, she had begun to get a feel for the division, its products, its operating plans and procedures, and its problems. During this time, she had not been given any major projects. Rather, she was told to get to know people and to look around. As a result, she was ready and eager when Todd Hall, the division director, called her and gave her the first real assignment, and what an assignment. At this time, over coffee, Todd told Fiona that he had been concerned about the current planning system that was in place. He seemed to be finding out about problems after they occurred. The marketing and operations groups within the division always seemed to be making after-the-fact corrections to the plans that they each had generated. More important, no one in the division seemed to feel any responsibility for the plans. Whenever things went wrong, everyone took the position of blaming everyone else. What Todd wanted Fiona to do was twofold: he wanted her to review the current system and to prepare a critique of it. In addition, he wanted her to recommend changes. Fiona knew that she had to do well on this project.

The Hospital Division of Med-Chem

Med-Chem was a Fortune 100 drug and chemical manufacturer, headquartered in Germany and with divisions and plants located worldwide. The Hospital Division was a division of this company. In the United States, it was headquartered in Atlanta, Georgia. This division manufactured a line of pharmaceuticals and testing equipment for use in hospitals, emergency rooms, nursing homes, and so on. Within this division, there were two major groups: marketing and operations.

Marketing was responsible for three major activities: sales, distribution, and forecasting. Of these three, forecasting was considered to be the most important. The products offered by this division were essentially make-to-stock. As a result, it was important that the right amounts be in stock at any point in time. As the marketing people had told Fiona, forecasting was a nightmare task. First, Med-Chem had a very broad product line, consisting of some 5,000 items. In addition, not all of the products were equally important. The group had adopted the product model developed by the Boston Consulting Group when describing the products. According to this model, the various products could be assigned to one of four categories. The first category was that of a *star*. A star product was one that was seen as being important. A product could be important because of a high contribution margin, its unique position in the marketplace, or because it helped to enhance the reputation of the division (for being a leader in this product). These were products that management always wanted to ensure were delivered at or near 100 percent of actual demand. About 10 percent of the products fell into this category. Next came the *cash cows*. These products, about 35 percent of the current catalog, were highly stable, highly predictable in nature. They generated a very good revenue stream. Management never wanted to stock out of these items. The third group was comprised of the *question marks* (25 percent). In general, these were new products or ones that had not yet established their value in the marketplace. The final category, *dogs*, were products that were considered low performers. Typically, such product lines were old, were positioned in segments where the competition was severe, had very low contribution margins, or were not unique (i.e., there were a number of equally effective generic substitutes available). Many dogs were

kept because marketing felt that they helped to round out Med-Chem's product offerings. For all four groups, marketing rarely informed operations of large orders by major customers or its attempts to stimulate ordering through special promotions or discounts. Marketing was allowed to change the forecasts at any point, up to and including the point at which the products were scheduled to be shipped.

Operations was responsible for building the products required by marketing. At present, operations personnel viewed this as a major problem because of marketing's constant modifications to the forecasts and the lack of any data concerning actual sales occurring in the marketplace. After talking with some of the plant managers, Fiona knew that their primary objective was to minimize the total production cost, including the cost of holding inventory. With the frequent production changes dictated by changes in the forecasts, operations personnel found themselves expediting orders and undertaking dramatic production changes. If left alone, Fiona knew that operations would schedule operations to reduce cost.

Med-Chem's Current Planning System

The current system at Med-Chem had been in place for as long as anyone could remember. This system did not differentiate between the performance of marketing and the performance of operations. Everyone agreed that all the information needed by management to reduce the problems existed but no one really knew how to proceed. As Todd told Fiona before she left, there had to be a better way of planning at Med-Chem.

Questions

1. Describe the current system in use as it applies to the operations personnel and marketing personnel. To what extent does this system help or hinder Med-Chem's ability to achieve its objectives? Why?

2. For marketing and operations, what are the critical activities that they must do well for Med-Chem to be successful in the marketplace?

3. What general recommendations would you make to Todd regarding the current situation?

CASE

Fitch and Hughes, P.C.

Fitch and Hughes, P.C., is a small law firm specializing in family law, wills, estates, and trusts. The firm, begun in 1980 by Jason Fitch and George Hughes, currently has

three attorneys who are shareholders and three associate attorneys. The firm is managed by George Hughes since the retirement of his cofounder of the firm, Jason Fitch.

476   chapter 14   Materials and Resource Requirements Planning

FIGURE 14-4   MPS for the BBQ Grill Gift Set

Part Name: BBQ grill gift set								
	April				May			
MPS Beginning inventory = 10	Week 1	Week 2	Week 3	Week 4	Week 5	Week 6	Week 7	Week 8
Forecast	35	20	25	40	50	40	30	30
Actual customer orders	40	30	30	25	25	20	10	0
Projected on-hand inventory	0	0	0	0	0	0	0	0
Available to promise	0	0	0	15	25	20	20	30
MPS	30	30	30	40	50	40	30	30

period is negative, more end items are needed. Look at Figure 14-4. In week 1, the number of actual customer orders (40) exceeds the forecast of 35. So, the number of additional items needed is the beginning on-hand inventory of 10 minus the customer orders of 40; this equals negative 30. If we order 30 BBQ gift sets to be built in week 1, this will leave 0 projected on-hand inventory for week 2.

Some part of the production planned in the MPS may be committed to specific customers that have placed firm orders. The remaining planned production is **available to promise** to other customers as orders arise. The number of items that are available to promise are communicated to sales and marketing personnel so that they can arrange feasible delivery times and quantities for customers that wish to place new orders. For example, Figure 14-4 shows that in week 4, there are 15 units available to promise because only 25 of the 40 units in the MPS have been committed to actual customer orders.

The MPS does not consider whether the critical resources needed to complete the end items according to schedule are available during the planning horizon covered by the MPS. Recall that the aggregate production plan considers resources, but it does so using larger time buckets than the ones used in the MPS. Critical resources might include space, labor, equipment, suppliers, and even money. **Rough-cut capacity planning** estimates the availability of the critical resources needed by the MPS. If the resources are not available, then the MPS or the resource levels must change. For example, you could change the MPS by increasing the delivery time for some customers, acquiring critical resources, or diverting resources from other products. Some planning software systems calculate "capable to promise," which considers capacity when determining if new customer orders can be met.

available to promise The part of planned production that is not committed to a customer.

rough-cut capacity planning An estimation of the availability of the critical resources needed to support the MPS.

Bill of Materials (BOM)

bill of materials (BOM) A detailed description of an "end item" and list of all of its raw materials, parts, and subassemblies.

The **bill of materials (BOM)** is a detailed description of an "end item" along with a list of all of its raw materials, parts, and subassemblies. The BOM is essentially a "recipe" for the product; it shows the number of each type of component that is required to make *one unit* of the end item. The BOM also shows the sequence of assembly. The BOM is created when a new product is developed. Product engineering managers are responsible for making updates to the BOM.

The BOM is shown as an indented list, a parts list (see Figure 14-5), or a product structure diagram, also called a *product structure tree* (see Figure 14-6). In our example, the BBQ grill gift set is the end item, shown as level 0 in the BOM. Each set consists of four "level 1" inputs: a tote bag, a fork, a spatula, and tongs. The dependent demand for the level 1 items is driven by the needs of the level 0 item. Similarly, the demand for the level 2 items is driven by the needs of the level 1 items, and so on. The BBQ grill gift set (level 0)

LO14-2 Conduct MRP planning for items at multiple levels in the bill of materials (BOM).

Indented Bill of Materials	Parts List
Boxed BBQ grill gift set	Boxed BBQ grill gift set
* Tote bag (1)	Tote bag (1)
* Fork (1)	Fork (1)
** Metal fork (1)	Spatula (1)
*** Steel sheet (1)	Tongs (1)
** Handle A (1)	
*** Wood block (1)	Fork
** Rivet (2)	Metal fork (1)
** Leather tie	Handle A (1)
* Spatula (1)	Rivet (2)
** Metal spatula (1)	Leather tie
*** Steel sheet (1)	
** Handle A (1)	Spatula
*** Wood block (1)	Metal spatula (1)
** Rivet (2)	Handle A (1)
** Leather tie	Rivet (2)
* Tongs (1)	Leather tie
** Metal tong (1)	
*** Steel sheet (1)	Tongs
** Handle B (2)	Metal tong (1)
*** Wood block (2)	Handle B (2)
** Rivet (8)	Rivet (8)
	Metal fork
	Steel sheet (1)
	Handle A
	Wood block (1)
	Metal spatula
	Steel sheet (1)
	Metal tong
	Steel sheet (1)
	Handle B
	Wood block (2)

FIGURE 14-5 Indented Bill of Materials (BOM) and Parts List

can be thought of as the "parent" of the tote bag, fork, spatula, and tongs. These items are components, or "children," of the gift set.

The trends toward modular products and toward purchasing subassemblies from suppliers rather than making them in-house reduce the number of levels in a product's BOM, making it flatter. For example, the tote bag is purchased as a finished item from a supplier. For this reason, its children (raw materials,

student activity

Select an item such as a chair or desk and develop a product structure BOM.

FIGURE 14-6　Product Structure Bill of Materials (BOM)

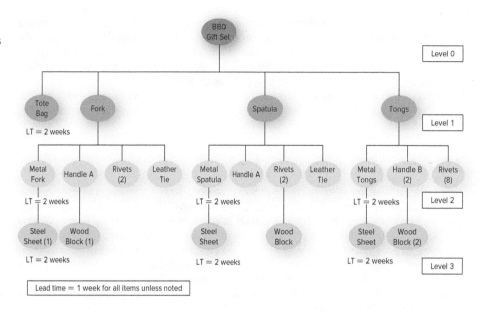

parts, and subassemblies) are not shown in the company's BOM. These raw materials, parts, and subassemblies are shown on the supplier's BOM for the tote bag.

Inventory Records

inventory status file A file that contains detailed inventory and procurement records.

Inventory records are contained in an **inventory status file**. Each inventory record includes:

- The item number.
- Description of the item.
- The lead time to order and receive the item from a supplier or to produce it internally.
- The preferred order quantity (lot size).
- Safety stock quantity.
- Other information such as cost or process descriptions.
- Quantity of on-hand inventory.
- Amount of inventory committed to a use.

scheduled receipts The quantity that has been ordered but not yet received.

- **Scheduled receipts** (the quantity that has been ordered but not yet received).

One of the key managerial decisions in MRP is the order quantity, or production lot size. Operations managers consider carrying costs, ordering costs, product costs, and stock-out costs when deciding upon the appropriate lot-sizing strategy. For purchased items, suppliers typically set the lot sizes. Consider the choices at your local grocery store for purchasing milk—typically one gallon, one quart, or a single serving. Some of the typical lot-sizing strategies are:

lot-for-lot (L4L) An order for the exact amount needed.

- **Lot-for-lot (L4L)**. An order is placed for exactly the amount that is needed in each period. L4L minimizes carrying costs, but maximizes setup or ordering costs.

fixed order quantity (FOQ) An order for the same amount each time.

- **Fixed order quantity (FOQ)**. The same amount is ordered each time. For example, the economic order quantity (EOQ) (discussed in Chapter 7) might be used. A slight variation of FOQ is *multiples of FOQ*, where purchased items may be available only in a fixed order quantity, such as a carton of 10 items. In this case, if 14 items were needed, the order quantity would be two cartons of 10 (20 items) rather than 14.

periodic order quantity (POQ) An order for an amount that covers a fixed period of time.

- **Periodic order quantity (POQ)**. An amount that covers the requirements for a fixed number of future periods is ordered. For example, enough is ordered to cover two periods' worth of net requirements each time an order is placed.

Use of fixed order quantities, multiple fixed order quantities, and periodic order quantities can create "lumpy" orders rather than a smooth continuous flow of materials. These lot-sizing rules can minimize ordering or setup costs for the firm. However, spikes in orders become accentuated and more dramatic as orders flow upstream in the supply chain to direct suppliers, and then to their suppliers, contributing to the bullwhip effect. When this effect occurs, inventory can fluctuate dramatically, going from excesses to stockouts. Coordination and information sharing among supply chain members help to reduce this effect and its associated costs.

relationships

MRP PROCESS

MRP calculations are done using computer software. However, managers need to know the mechanics in order to make good decisions using MRP outputs. Let's work through the MRP process using the BBQ grill gift set as an example. The planning process always starts with the level 0 items in the BOM and then continues down each successive level. The planning logic determines when items are needed and then works backward to determine when to place orders. As we go step-by-step through the process we will define the key items that are shown in an MRP record (see Figure 14-7).

Gross requirements refers to the total amount of an end item (finished good, subassembly, or part) that is required by *all* of its parents during each period. This must include end items that are used as replacement parts, interplant transfers, or service items. Start with the MPS for the BBQ grill gift set. The production schedule for the MPS creates the gross requirements in the MRP record for each week, as shown in Figure 14-8.

gross requirements The total amount of an end item that is required.

As discussed earlier, *scheduled receipts* are the total quantity of items from orders placed in the past and due to be delivered by the beginning of the period in which the quantity is shown. The scheduled receipts of 30 BBQ grill gift sets in week 1 (see Figure 14-9) were ordered one week ago. Note that the *order* is not shown on the current record form, just the *delivery*. The order placement was on last week's version of the record form, because the lead time for the gift sets is one week.

The next step in the process is to determine how many additional units, if any, are needed to meet the week's gross requirements. This calculation is called **requirements explosion**, and it determines the *net requirements* (see Figure 14-10). **Net requirements** are the minimum quantity required in the period based on gross requirements minus the sum of scheduled receipts and available inventory at the end of the last period (which is the inventory available at the start of the current period). When safety stock is needed, the net

requirements explosion The determination of how many additional units are needed.

net requirements The minimum amount needed in the period.

FIGURE 14-7   Example of an MRP Record

				Part Name:				
MRP Record **Lead time =** **On-hand inventory =** **Safety stock =** **Order quantity:**	**Week** **1**	**Week** **2**	**Week** **3**	**Week** **4**	**Week** **5**	**Week** **6**	**Week** **7**	**Week** **8**
Gross requirements								
Scheduled receipts								
Available inventory								
Net requirements								
Planned order receipts								
Planned order releases								

FIGURE 14-8   Gross Requirements for the BBQ Grill Gift Set

Part Name: BBQ grill gift sets								
	April				May			
MPS Beginning inventory = 10	Week 1	Week 2	Week 3	Week 4	Week 5	Week 6	Week 7	Week 8
Forecast	35	20	25	40	50	40	30	30
Actual customer orders	40	30	30	25	25	20	10	0
Completed end items	(30)	30	30	40	50	40	30	30

Part Name: BBQ grill gift sets								
MRP Record Lead time = 1 week On-hand inventory = 0 Safety stock = 0 Order quantity: L4L	Week 1	Week 2	Week 3	Week 4	Week 5	Week 6	Week 7	Week 8
Gross Requirements	(30)	30	30	40	50	40	30	30

FIGURE 14-9   Scheduled Receipts for the BBQ Grill Gift Set

Part Name: BBQ grill gift sets								
MRP Record Lead time = 1 week On-hand inventory = 0 Safety stock = 0 Order quantity: L4L	Week 1	Week 2	Week 3	Week 4	Week 5	Week 6	Week 7	Week 8
Gross Requirements	30	30	30	40	50	40	30	30
Scheduled Receipts	(30)							

Ordered last week.

requirements are calculated based on the gross requirements plus safety stock minus the sum of scheduled receipts and available inventory at the end of the last period (the starting inventory of current period). Of course, if the total of available inventory plus scheduled receipts is greater than the gross requirements, then the net requirements is zero. Available inventory is the inventory quantity that is available *at the end* of a period (see equation 14.1).

(14.1)   Available inventory = Available inventory at the start of the period + Scheduled
receipts + Planned order receipts − Gross requirements

FIGURE 14-10   Net Requirements for the BBQ Grill Gift Set

MRP Record Lead time = 1 week On-hand inventory = 0 Safety stock = 0 Order quantity: L4L	**Part Name: BBQ grill gift sets**							
	Week 1	Week 2	Week 3	Week 4	Week 5	Week 6	Week 7	Week 8
Gross requirements	30	30	30	40	50	40	30	30
Scheduled receipts	30							
Available inventory								
Net requirements		30	30	40	50	40	30	30

The next step is to calculate the planned order receipts for each week. The quantity that is planned to arrive at the *beginning* of a period is the **planned order receipt**. These arrivals come from orders that are planned to be placed at the designated time in the future. In this example, because we use a L4L policy, the planned order receipts exactly equal the net requirements, as shown in Figure 14-11.

The last step is to determine *when* to place the order. A **planned order release** is the quantity of an item that is planned to be ordered in the period. Because of the rolling time horizon of MRP records, when an order is placed (released), it shifts from being a *planned* receipt to being a *scheduled* receipt. To determine the planned order release for each period, count backward from the planned order receipt using the lead time. In the example, the planned order releases are scheduled one week before the planned order receipts, as shown in Figure 14-12.

planned order receipt The amount that is planned to arrive at the beginning of a period.

planned order release The amount of an item that is planned to be ordered in a period.

FIGURE 14-11   Planned Order Receipts for the BBQ Grill Gift Set

MRP Record Lead time = 1 week On-hand inventory = 0 Safety stock = 0 Order quantity: L4L	**Part Name: BBQ grill gift set**							
	Week 1	Week 2	Week 3	Week 4	Week 5	Week 6	Week 7	Week 8
Gross requirements	30	30	30	40	50	40	30	30
Scheduled receipts	30							
Available inventory								
Net requirements		(30)	30	40	50	40	30	30
Planned order receipts		(30)	30	40	50	40	30	30

FIGURE 14-12   Planned Order Releases for the BBQ Grill Gift Set

MRP Record Lead time = 1 week On-hand inventory = 0 Safety stock = 0 Order quantity: L4L	Part Name: BBQ grill gift set							
	Week 1	Week 2	Week 3	Week 4	Week 5	Week 6	Week 7	Week 8
Gross requirements	30	30	30	40	50	40	30	30
Scheduled receipts	30							
Available inventory								
Net requirements		30	30	40	50	40	30	30
Planned order receipts		(30)	30	40	50	40	30	30
Planned order releases	(30)	30	40	50	40	30	30	

After the planned order releases for the BBQ grill gift sets are known, the planning process continues through the BOM for each component, level by level. Look back at Figures 14-5 and 14-6, which show the BOM for the BBQ grill gift set. The next step would be to develop MRP records for the level 1 items: the tote bag, the fork, the spatula, and the tongs. Once the MRP records for the level 1 items are complete, then MRP records are developed for the level 2 items: the metal fork, the metal spatula, the metal tongs, handles A and B, the rivets, and the leather ties. Similarly, after the level 2 records are complete, MRP records for the level 3 items are calculated. This process, called an MRP "explosion," continues until the planning is complete for all levels of the BOM.

Let's walk through the calculation steps for the tote bag. Then we'll show the MRP records for the fork and spatula and develop the gross requirements for handle A, which has the fork and spatula as parents. Tote bags are purchased in cartons of 100 bags each from a supplier in China, and the lead time is two weeks with shipment by air. Because of the risk of delays, one carton (100 bags) is held as safety stock. If the available inventory drops below the safety stock level of 100, the MRP process calculates the net requirements needed to bring the inventory level back up to a minimum of 100.

First determine the tote bag's gross requirements by asking who its parents are. Because the tote bag is only used in the BBQ grill gift set and no replacement bags are purchased, the gross requirements come *only* from the planned order releases for the BBQ grill gift set. Note in Figure 14-13 that the numbers in the gross requirements line for tote bags are identical to the numbers in the planned order releases line for the BBQ grill gift set. If tote bags were used in multiple products, the planned order releases for *all* of its parents would be combined to determine its gross requirements.

Next, calculate the net requirements and associated orders. The scheduled receipt of 100 in week 1 covers the gross requirements for the first three weeks, so the first net requirement occurs in week 4. In week 4, the net requirement is 50 bags. Schedule a planned order release of 100 bags, which is the lowest order quantity possible. Because of the two-week lead time, the order must be released in week 2 so that it can be received in week 4. This same logic is used to complete the rest of the record, as shown in Figure 14-13.

Continue with the MRP records for the fork and spatula (see Figure 14-14). The gross requirements for each come from the planned order releases from the BBQ grill gift set. Let's develop the MRP record for one level 2 item: handle A, as shown in Figure 14-15.

FIGURE 14-13   MRP Requirements for Tote Bags

Part Name: BBQ grill gift set

MRP Record
Lead time = 1 week
On-hand inventory = 0
Safety stock = 0
Order quantity: L4L

	Week 1	Week 2	Week 3	Week 4	Week 5	Week 6	Week 7	Week 8
Gross requirements	30	30	30	40	50	40	30	30
Scheduled receipts	30							
Available inventory								
Net requirements		30	30	40	50	40	30	30
Planned order receipts		30	30	40	50	40	30	30
Planned order releases	(30)	30	40	50	40	30	30	

Part Name: Tote bag

MRP Record
Lead time = 2 weeks
On-hand inventory = 100
Safety stock = 100
Order quantity:
Multi = 100

	Week 1	Week 2	Week 3	Week 4	Week 5	Week 6	Week 7	Week 8
Gross requirements	(30)	30	40	50	40	30	30	
Scheduled receipts	100							
Available inventory 100	170	140	100	150	110	180	150	
Net requirements				50		20		
Planned order receipts				(100)		(100)		
Planned order releases		(100)		(100)				

The gross requirements for handle A come from the planned order releases from its parents (fork and spatula). The BOM (Figures 14-5 and 14-6) shows that one handle each is needed for the fork and the spatula. There are no other sources of demand for handle A. Notice that there is beginning on-hand inventory of 60 units. When needed, handle A is always produced in fixed order quantity (FOQ) lot sizes of 100.

To complete the entire materials requirements plan, MRP calculations would be done for all of the remaining level 2 items and then all of the level 3 items in the BOM. Some organizations use MRP for planning the higher level items in the BOM but use kanban (pull) systems to replenish the lower level items.

FIGURE 14-14 MRP Records for the Fork and the Spatula

Part Name: Fork

MRP Record
Lead time = 1 week
On-hand inventory = 0
Safety stock = 0
Order quantity: L4L

	Week 1	Week 2	Week 3	Week 4	Week 5	Week 6	Week 7	Week 8
Gross requirements	30	30	40	50	40	30	30	
Scheduled receipts	30							
Available inventory								
Net requirements		30	40	50	40	30	30	
Planned order receipts		30	40	50	40	30	30	
Planned order releases	30	40	50	40	30	30		

Part Name: Spatula

MRP Record
Lead time = 1 week
On-hand inventory = 0
Safety stock = 0
Order quantity: L4L

	Week 1	Week 2	Week 3	Week 4	Week 5	Week 6	Week 7	Week 8
Gross requirements	30	30	40	50	40	30	30	
Scheduled receipts	30							
Available inventory								
Net requirements		30	40	50	40	30	30	
Planned order receipts		30	40	50	40	30	30	
Planned order releases	30	40	50	40	30	30		

MRP OUTPUTS AND USE

MRP outputs include primary and secondary reports. The primary reports are schedules of the planned order releases that trigger purchases and the production of items in the proper time frame. Secondary reports provide cost, inventory, and schedule attainment information that helps managers judge how well the operation is performing. If a major difference between actual performance and the MRP plan occurs, then an exception report is generated.

nervousness Inconsistencies in the plan caused by changes to the MPS.

Once set, numerous changes made to the MPS can cause **nervousness** throughout the system. Significant MPS changes can modify the timing and quantities of orders for raw

FIGURE 14-15   MRP Record for Handle A

MRP Record Lead time = 2 weeks On-hand = 60 Safety stock = 0 Order quantity: FOQ = 100	Week 1	Week 2	Week 3	Week 4	Week 5	Week 6	Week 7	Week 8
Part Name: Handle A								
Gross requirements	(60)	80	100	80	60	60		
Scheduled receipts		100						
Available inventory 60	0	20	20	40	80	20		
Net requirements			80	60	20			
Planned order receipts			100	100	100			
Planned order releases	100	100	100					

60 = 30 forks + 30 spatulas

materials, parts, and subassemblies, making suppliers' planning very difficult. As a result, users may not trust the MRP plan.

MRP assumes that parts produced or received from suppliers are defect-free and delivered as scheduled. This is especially important if an L4L lot-sizing strategy is used. Thus, quality management is critical within the firm and by its suppliers. If quality and delivery performance are not perfect, then safety stock or increased lead times are required. These increase cost and decrease the effectiveness of the planning process.

DISTRIBUTION REQUIREMENTS PLANNING (DRP)

Distribution requirements planning (DRP) calculates the positioning and replenishment of *finished goods inventories* throughout the distribution network using logic similar to MRP. DRP is typically a module in enterprise resource planning (ERP) system software. Distribution networks can be very complex, with multiple levels of distribution centers and thousands of retailers (think about Conair, for example). Thus, planning and coordination across the supply chain can be difficult. The output of DRP is used for input into operations and logistics planning processes.

Similar to MRP, inventory replenishment decisions are based on a time-phased schedule considering forecasts and actual orders. The DRP process starts by combining forecasts and firm orders, ideally at each customer or the contact point as close as possible to the customer, such as the retailer or regional distribution center. Forecasts and actual orders at the customer or contact points are added to create the independent demand for the finished goods, and planned order receipts are determined for each of these locations for the planning horizon. Looking back at Figure 14-1, forecasts and actual orders create the planned order releases for the seven retailers. For Retailers 1, 2, and 3, these planned order releases are combined to form gross requirements for the Western Region distribution center, while those for Retailers 4, 5, 6, and 7 form the gross requirements for the Eastern Region distribution center.

distribution requirements planning (DRP) Determination of replenishment and positioning of finished goods in the distribution network.

LO14-3 Explain how distribution requirements planning (DRP) is used.

As with MRP, the planning horizon must extend far enough into the future so that replenishment orders can be scheduled in plenty of time to make the required shipments. For each future week at each customer location, the gross requirements estimate is compared with the amount of inventory projected to be on-hand at that location. If the projected inventory available is less than the estimated gross requirements, a replenishment order is planned for the net requirements.

The next step is to compare the schedule of gross requirements at each distribution center against its projected on-hand inventory for each week into the future. This comparison creates net requirements and planned orders, and these orders are consolidated to make gross requirements for the next upstream source of supply, while considering required lead times. The process continues to consolidate requirements and orders across all stages in the distribution network up to the production plant that makes the finished goods. The result is a week-by-week plan of demands placed on the plant that ultimately reflects the forecasted independent demands taking place at each of the customer locations. At this point, MPS and MRP processes take over.

UNDERSTANDING CAPACITY REQUIREMENTS PLANNING (CRP)

LO14-4 Conduct capacity requirements planning (CRP) using an infinite loading approach.

DRP and MRP focus on material feasibility—can we get the right amount of material at the right time? To meet customer needs, an operation also needs sufficient capacity of key resources. A load is the amount of work given to a worker, machine, work center, or facility during a specific period of time. To make sure a plan is feasible, the load is compared to the capacity, which is the output that can be done during a period of time.

Though rough-cut capacity planning suggests an MPS is feasible, after development of an MRP plan, a more detailed assessment of capacity is needed to ensure this is still the case. MRP does not compare the planned orders to the available capacity in the supply chain. Most MRP plans assume **infinite loading**; that is, they assume an infinite amount of capacity is available, which is not realistic. **Capacity requirements planning (CRP)** determines if all the work centers involved have the capacity to implement the MRP plan. The CRP process uses planned order releases and scheduled receipts to estimate work center loads. A **load profile** compares weekly load needs against a profile of actual capacity.

infinite loading The assumption that there is an infinite amount of capacity available.

capacity requirements planning (CRP) An estimate of the capacity needed at work centers.

load profile A comparison of production needs to actual capacity.

Figure 14-16 shows available capacity and a load profile for the spatula. The planned order releases are from the spatula's MRP record (Figure 14-14). The CRP table in Figure 14-16 estimates the number of production hours needed to make the spatulas, based on a machine rate of 30 minutes per spatula. The available machine capacity is 20 hours per week. The table and load graph show that the process will be overloaded in week 3, when the load of 25 hours exceeds the available capacity of 20 hours. The load exactly equals capacity in weeks 2 and 4. Underloading occurs in weeks 1, 5, and 6.

Having too much or too little capacity can be problematic. When underloading occurs, the extra capacity could be used to build anticipation inventory, but this increases costs. If underloading is an ongoing problem, the firm should find new business or develop new products to use the capacity or reduce the capacity. If there is not enough capacity to meet the production requirements, the use of overtime or outsourcing some operations are options, but costs increase. Alternatively, you can increase delivery lead times or create a backlog of orders, but this may reduce customer satisfaction and sales. If capacity is available earlier, goods can be made in advance and held in inventory until needed. Because of the differences between the load and available capacity for the spatula, managers must decide to change capacity or to change the MPS. One alternative would be to produce 10 of the units needed in week 3 in week 1, when capacity is available, and hold these units in inventory. A cross-functional team including operations, sales, marketing, finance, supply, and engineering should decide upon the best approach to manage capacity to meet the company's objectives.

FIGURE 14-16   Capacity Requirements for Spatulas

| | Part Name: Spatula | | | | | | | |
Processing Time = 30 minutes per unit	Week 1	Week 2	Week 3	Week 4	Week 5	Week 6	Week 7	Week 8
Planned order releases	30	40	50	40	30	30		
Processing load (hours)	15	20	25	20	15	15		
Available capacity (hours)	20	20	20	20	20	20		

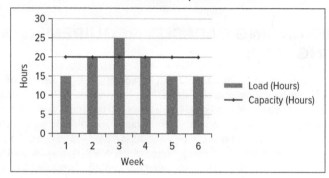

Load Profile for Spatulas

ADVANCES IN PLANNING SYSTEMS

The logic of requirements and resources planning has been around for a long time. The U.S. Army's ordering system used in World War II was essentially a manual MRP system. In the past few decades, however, the benefits of DRP, MRP, and CRP processes have become more fully realized because of the dramatic increase in computer power and the availability of low-cost MRP software. Today, the planning for very complex operations can be done using fairly low-cost requirements planning software systems.

Over the years, requirements planning systems have evolved. Initially, the focus of MRP was on manufacturing planning and scheduling. However, managers soon recognized that the output from MRP would be useful for planning in other functions such as accounting, purchasing, marketing, sales, finance, distribution, and engineering. MRP evolved into manufacturing *resource* planning, or MRP II, which considers a wider range of cross-functional issues. MRP II also has the capability to simulate the impacts of different plans. This was a precursor of the enterprise resource planning (ERP) systems that have been adopted by many firms. Recent advances in requirements and resources planning systems being implemented today include: (1) enterprise resource planning (ERP) systems, (2) advanced planning and scheduling (APS) systems, and (3) extended planning across the supply chain using demand-driven MRP. APICS—a professional organization for supply chain and operations managers—is an excellent source of information on the latest trends and directions in materials and resources planning across the supply chain.

Enterprise Resource Planning (ERP)

Rather than existing as independent, stand-alone systems, DRP, MRP, and CRP are usually embedded as integral parts of an **enterprise resource planning (ERP)** system. An ERP system consolidates all of the business planning systems and related data throughout a

enterprise resource planning (ERP) system Software that consolidates all of the business planning systems and data throughout an organization.

LO14-5 Describe how materials requirements and resource planning functions work together within an enterprise resource planning (ERP) system.

company, so the planning processes across all business functions can be integrated and consistently applied. The goal of ERP systems is to allow business processes to function seamlessly and in unison. Companies such as SAP and Oracle are the leading providers of ERP software and cloud-based applications.

A typical ERP includes the functionality of many requirements and resource planning systems, including sales, billing, accounting, finance, human resource management, and project management, along with the supply chain planning systems discussed in this chapter. Before ERP, these different planning functions were done using "legacy" software systems that were developed and used within each function, such as accounting, operations, and human resources, but were not linked or compatible with one another. As a result, data needed by other legacy systems (say, operations data were needed by accounting) had to be manually transformed via spreadsheets or databases, thus wasting time and creating errors. By allowing all business data to be in one ERP system, planning and coordination across business functions is easier, time is saved, and errors are reduced. All types of companies can gain benefits from an ERP system. An ERP system helped Red Door Spas reduce costs, improve customer service, and make better business decisions, as discussed in the nearby Get Real box.

Although they were initially focused within an organization, ERP systems and add-on software are being used to integrate companies with their customers and suppliers. In the same ways that ERP helps companies share data and planning across internal functions, expanded ERP helps a company share data and planning with its suppliers and customers. However, ERP systems are not without drawbacks. ERP software is written to meet the needs of many different companies. Thus, companies either need to modify their business processes to fit the software or spend a lot of time and money customizing the software to fit their particular needs. This involves high costs, long implementation times, highly complex software, and a lack of flexibility. Mergers and acquisitions can be especially challenging, for example. When companies have different ERP systems, data must be combined into a single system and processes must be standardized.

GET REAL

ERP Improves Performance at Elizabeth Arden Red Door Spas

ERP systems are not just for manufacturing. Elizabeth Arden Red Door Spas has 30 locations designed to provide the ultimate in pampering through salon and spa services. The management team was planning to add locations both within the United States and internationally. However, its human resource, finance, and logistics systems were not integrated, making decision making difficult. In 2006, to give its business performance a makeover, Red Door Spas replaced its legacy business systems with an ERP system by SAP. The system made it easier to track orders. Inventory at its salons and distribution center dropped, reducing costs. Employees could spend more time with customers and less time on administrative tasks. More importantly, the ERP system provided more consistent data that could be used for making better business decisions.

© ZUMA Press/Newscom

Advanced Planning and Scheduling (APS)

Conventional requirements planning systems were sequential and iterative in nature, and today many still are. In this chapter, we have described a process in which distribution requirements planning (DRP) output feeds the master production schedule (MPS), which feeds materials requirements planning (MRP), which feeds capacity requirements planning (CRP). Problems identified in the CRP process must be remedied by a revision to the MPS, and the process repeats itself until a feasible solution is found. This approach, which emerged in the past because of the lack of computer power and connectivity across legacy data systems, is fundamentally inefficient.

Imagine a planning process that simultaneously considers materials requirements along with resource capacity constraints. In this process a plan could be developed that optimizes all related costs, for example, inventory, labor, capital, and other costs. This level of joint optimization is the goal of **advanced planning and scheduling (APS) systems**, which are often included in ERP systems. APS systems use the same fundamental explosion logic of MRP. However, they integrate materials and capacity planning into one system. APS is possible because of vast improvements in computing power coupled with the development of sophisticated mathematical algorithms that help to solve very complex scheduling problems. The result is better plans that are generated much faster.

Requirements and resource planning systems have achieved a high level of acceptance because of the important advantages that they offer to a firm. As multiple firms work together to adopt and share compatible planning systems, the supply chain can experience significant benefits. Planning systems that are extended across supply chain partners provide greater visibility into the current status and into plans for the future. By anticipating supply and demand conditions into the future, APS systems help managers to identify and avoid problems and quickly evaluate alternatives. Supply chain partners can jointly plan their operations using what-if analyses. APS systems evaluate different scenarios of changes in customer demand and material delays. This analysis helps supply chain partners to identify options and create contingency plans.

Supply chain partners who work to coordinate and share planning systems typically see tremendous reductions in order fulfillment lead times, large improvements in information accuracy, reductions in inventory, and lower costs. Demand-driven MRP goes beyond a single organization to extend planning across the entire supply chain. Understanding leadtimes, variations in supply and demand, bottleneck operations, and flexibility across the entire supply chain leads to better decisions. For example, decisions about where inventory should be held within the supply chain can increase responsiveness while reducing costs.

LO14-6 Explain how advanced planning and scheduling (APS) systems improve the requirements and resource planning processes.

advance planning and scheduling (APS) systems Systems that integrate materials and capacity planning into one system.

CHAPTER SUMMARY

This chapter defined dependent demand and described materials and resource planning processes.

1. Dependent demand refers to the demand for raw materials, parts, and subassemblies needed to make end items.
2. Inputs to MRP include the master production schedule (MPS) for the end items, the bill of materials (BOM), which shows what components are needed, and inventory records.
3. The key steps in the MRP process include calculating the gross requirements, determining net requirements, establishing the timing for planned order receipts, and offsetting to determine planned order releases.

4. MRP outputs include primary reports used for operations planning and secondary reports used for performance measurement and process improvement.

5. Distribution requirements planning (DRP) uses the logic of MRP to determine the positioning and replenishment of finished goods inventories (independent demand) within a distribution network.

6. Plans developed by MRP may not be feasible unless there is adequate capacity available within the supply chain. With basic MRP, an additional step, capacity requirements planning (CRP), is used to determine if the plan developed by MRP is feasible.

7. Advances in computer technology are streamlining the planning process by combining materials and capacity planning into advanced planning and scheduling (APS) systems that are part of ERP systems.

KEY TERMS

advanced planning and scheduling (APS) systems 489

available to promise 476

bill of materials (BOM) 476

capacity requirements planning (CRP) 486

cumulative lead time 475

dependent demand 472

distribution requirements planning (DRP) 485

enterprise resource planning (ERP) systems 487

fixed order quantity (FOQ) 478

gross requirements 479

independent demand 472

infinite loading 486

inventory status file 478

load profile 486

lot-for-lot (L4L) 478

master production schedule (MPS) 475

materials requirements planning (MRP) 473

nervousness 484

net requirements 479

periodic order quantity (POQ) 478

planned order receipt 481

planned order release 481

planning horizon 475

requirements explosion 479

rough-cut capacity planning 476

scheduled receipts 478

time bucket 475

DISCUSSION QUESTIONS

1. Why are spare parts and service parts considered to be independent demand, rather than dependent demand?

2. Why is collaboration within an organization and the supply chain important when using DRP and MRP?

3. The planning process involves a rolling time horizon. What does this mean to a planner?

4. What is the relationship between cumulative lead time and changes in the MPS? Why?

5. What types of companies are likely to benefit the most from using MRP? Why?

6. What problems can MRP create for suppliers as you go upstream in the supply chain? Why?

7. As an organization increases its level of outsourcing, what is the impact on its bill of materials? Why?

8. How do L4L, FOQ, and POQ ordering policies impact setup/ordering costs and inventory costs? Why?

9. What impact will a supplier's quality and delivery problems have on a company using MRP? Why?

10. In what ways are DRP and MRP similar and how are they different?

11. How have advances in computer technology changed the planning process? Why? What changes do you expect in the future?

SOLVED PROBLEMS

The Comfort Chair Company makes furniture that is used in waiting rooms for doctors' offices. Its most popular model is an upholstered chair that comes in two colors of fabric: blue and burgundy. The BOM, provided as a product structure diagram, is shown in Figure 14-17. All of the components are the same for the blue and burgundy chairs, with the exception of the fabric. Using this information, answer questions 1, 2, and 3.

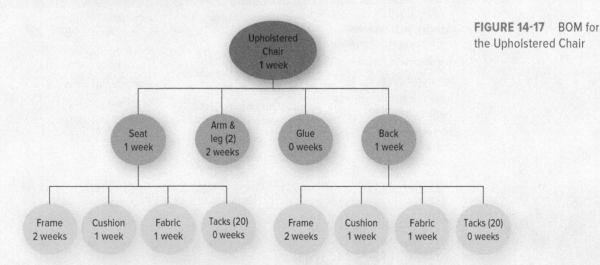

FIGURE 14-17 BOM for the Upholstered Chair

1. What is the cumulative lead time for the chair, and why is this important?

Solution:

The cumulative lead time is four weeks. The longest path is one week (upholstered chair) plus one week (seat or back) plus two weeks (frame). Thus, the planning horizon for the MPS must be at least four weeks to provide enough time to produce the chairs.

2. Given the MRP for the blue and the burgundy chairs, complete the MRP for the arm and leg assembly. Assume that the gross requirements for the arm and leg assembly depend only upon the blue and burgundy chairs.

Part Name: Blue upholstered chair

Lead time: 1 week Order quantity: L4L	Week 1	Week 2	Week 3	Week 4	Week 5	Week 6	Week 7	Week 8
Gross requirements			50	50	50	50	50	50
Scheduled receipts								
Available inventory								
Net requirements			50	50	50	50	50	50
Planned order receipts			50	50	50	50	50	50
Planned order releases		50	50	50	50	50	50	

Part Name: Burgundy upholstered chair

Lead time: 1 week Order quantity: L4L	Week 1	Week 2	Week 3	Week 4	Week 5	Week 6	Week 7	Week 8
Gross requirements		25		20	20	20	20	20
Scheduled receipts								
Available inventory								
Net requirements		25		20	20	20	20	20
Planned order receipts		25		20	20	20	20	20
Planned order releases	25		20	20	20	20	20	

Part Name: Arm and leg assembly

Lead time: 2 weeks Order quantity: Multi = 100	Week 1	Week 2	Week 3	Week 4	Week 5	Week 6	Week 7	Week 8
Gross requirements	50	100	140	140	140	140	140	
Scheduled receipts	100	100						
Available inventory 0	50	50	10	70	30	90	50	
Net requirements			90	130	70	110	50	
Planned order receipts			100	200	100	200	100	
Planned order releases	100	200	100	200	100			

Solution:

The gross requirements for the arm and leg assembly come from both the blue and the burgundy chairs. Because each chair requires two arm and leg assemblies, planned order release quantities from the upholstered chairs must be doubled.

3. If it takes 45 minutes to assemble each upholstered chair, and there is one worker in the assembly department who works 40 hours per week, can the MPS for week 4 be met for both the blue and burgundy chairs? Why, or why not?

Solution:

The time required for each chair is 45 minutes/60 minutes = .75 hours. The requirements to complete 50 blue chairs and 20 burgundy chairs in week 4 is 70 chairs × .75 hours = 52.5 hours. This exceeds the available capacity with one worker.

4. The Organic Juice Co. produces a line of fresh, natural organic juices. Given the MPS and BOM for one type of juice, Passion Swirl, complete the MRP schedules for the components: orange juice, passion fruit juice, and mango juice. There are 128 fluid ounces per gallon.

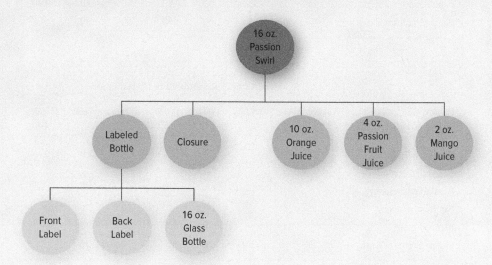

MPS

Item	Week 1	Week 2	Week 3	Week 4	Week 5	Week 6	Week 7	Week 8
Passion Swirl Number of 16 oz. bottles	2,000	2,000	2,500	2,500	2,500	3,000	3,000	3,000

Item	Orange Juice	Passion Fruit Juice	Mango Juice
Lot size rule	Multiples FOQ = 120 gallons	Multiples FOQ = 50 gallons	Multiples FOQ = 50 gallons
Safety stock	50 gallons	10 gallon	10 gallons
Beginning inventory	80 gallons	10 gallons	40 gallons
Lead time	2 weeks	3 weeks	2 weeks

Solution:

MRP can be used to determine the schedule for continuous products, as is the case in this example. To determine the gross requirements, take the MPS quantity for a period and multiply it by the number of ounces that are in the product. In week 1, for example, 2,000 16-ounce bottles of Passion Swirl are needed. Because there are 10 ounces of orange juice in each bottle of Passion Swirl, the total number of bottles, 2,000, is multiplied by 10 ounces to get the gross requirements of 20,000 ounces. The order quantity for each of the juices is in gallons, so the total number of ounces required must be divided by the number of ounces in a gallon (128 ounces/gallon) to get the gross requirements in gallons as shown in the MRP records. Repeat for the remaining periods. Use a similar approach for passion fruit juice and mango juice.

After the gross requirements are determined, complete the MRP schedule using the same approach as for discrete products. In this example, for orange juice, 50 gallons of safety stock are required. This means that the inventory level should always be 50 or more gallons. Take a look at week 3 to see how the net requirements are calculated when safety stock is used. The gross requirements of 195.3 gallons plus the safety stock of 50 gallons make up the total requirements of 254.3 gallons in week 3. At the beginning of week 3 there are 127.4 gallons available in inventory. The net requirements in week 3 are 117.9 gallons (254.3 –127.4 gallons).

MRP Record				Material Name: Orange Juice				
Lead time = 2 weeks On-hand = 80 gallons Safety stock = 50 gallons Order quantity: Multiples FOQ = 120 gallons	Week 1	Week 2	Week 3	Week 4	Week 5	Week 6	Week 7	Week 8
Gross requirements (gallons)	156.3	156.3	195.3	195.3	195.3	234.4	234.4	234.4
Scheduled receipts	240	120						
Available inventory 80 gallons	163.7	127.4	52.1	96.8	141.5	147.1	152.7	158.3
Net requirements			117.9	193.2	148.5	142.9	137.3	131.7
Planned order receipts			120	240	240	240	240	240
Planned order releases	120	240	240	2400	240	240		

MRP Record				Material Name: Passion Fruit Juice				
Lead time = 3 weeks On-hand = 10 gallons Safety stock = 10 gallon Order quantity: Multiples FOQ = 50 gallons	Week 1	Week 2	Week 3	Week 4	Week 5	Week 6	Week 7	Week 8
Gross requirements (gallons)	62.5	62.5	78.1	78.1	78.1	93.8	93.8	93.8
Scheduled receipts	100	50	100					
Available inventory 10 gallons	47.5	35	56.9	28.8	50.7	56.9	13.1	19.3
Net requirements				31.2	59.3	53.1	46.9	90.7
Planned order receipts				50	100	100	50	100
Planned order releases	50	100	100	50	100			

MRP Record					Material Name: Mango Juice			
Lead time = 2 weeks On-hand = 40 gallons Safety stock = 10 gallons Order quantity: Multiples FOQ = 50 gallons	Week 1	Week 2	Week 3	Week 4	Week 5	Week 6	Week 7	Week 8
Gross requirements (gallons)	31.3	31.3	39.1	39.1	39.1	46.9	46.9	46.9
Scheduled receipts	50							
Available inventory 40 gallons	58.7	27.4	38.3	49.2	10.1	13.2	16.3	19.4
Net requirements			21.7	10.8		46.8	43.7	40.6
Planned order receipts			50	50		50	50	50
Planned order releases	50	50		50	50	50		

PROBLEMS

1. Using the BOM shown below, how many of part E will be needed if 20 units of end item A are needed? How many of part C will be needed?

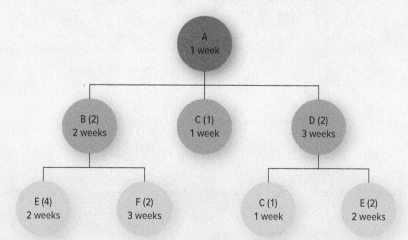

2. Based on the BOM in problem 1, what is the cumulative lead time for end item A? How will this information be used?

3. Develop an indented BOM for the product structure tree in problem 1.

4. Based on the BOM shown below, how many units of part F will be needed if 15 units of end item A are needed? If the company decided to purchase part D from suppliers, how would the BOM change? Assuming part D is purchased, how many units of part F are needed to make 15 units of end item A?

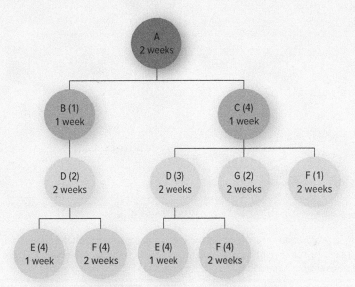

5. Based on the BOM in problem 4, what is the cumulative lead time for end item A?
6. Develop an indented BOM for the product structure tree shown in problem 4.
7. Based on the BOM shown below, how many of part D will be needed if 100 units of end item A are needed? How many of part F will be needed?

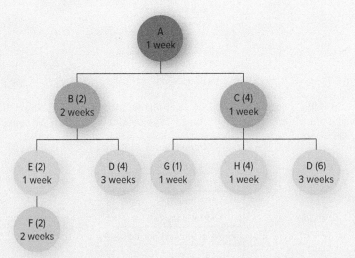

8. Using the information in problem 7, develop an indented BOM.
9. Based on the BOM shown below, how many of part J will be needed if 40 units of end item A are needed? Managers have decided to outsource part G. Revise the BOM for

end item A, assuming that item G is now purchased from a supplier. How many of part J will now be needed if 40 units of end item A are needed?

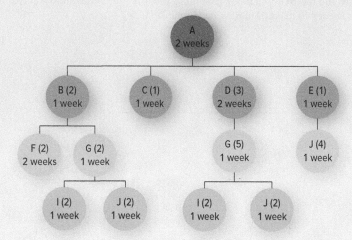

10. Draw a product structure tree for the baking pan using the BOM shown below. If there are plans to make 100 baking pans, how many handles are needed? How many bolt and nut sets are needed?

Baking Pan
* Pan (1)
** Pan shell (1)
** Handles (2)
** Bolt and nut set (4)
* Lid (1)
** Lid subassembly
***Glass (1)
***Steel rim (1)
** Handle (1)
** Bolt and nut set (2)

11. Draw a product structure tree for the patio planter using the BOM below. If there are plans to make eight patio planters, how many bolt and nut sets will be needed?

Patio Planter
* Planter box assembly
** Base assembly (1)
*** Base (1)
*** Rolling casters (4)
*** Bolt and nut set (4)
** Side assembly
*** Side panels (4)
*** Corner braces (8)
** Bolt and nut sets (4)
* Top (1)
* Bolt and nut sets (4)

12. Complete the MRP record for a bicycle frame using an L4L lot-sizing strategy. Considering the lead time, where should scheduled receipts be shown? Repeat using a fixed order quantity of 100 frames. Again, show scheduled receipts. Compare and contrast the results. What are the benefits and drawbacks to each approach?

MRP Record			Part Name: Bicycle frame					
Lead time = 2 weeks On-hand = 0 Safety stock = 0 Order quantity: L4L	Week 1	Week 2	Week 3	Week 4	Week 5	Week 6	Week 7	Week 8
Gross requirements	70	50	80	80	70	60	80	80
Scheduled receipts								
Available inventory								
Net requirements								
Planned order receipts								
Planned order releases								

MRP Record			Part Name: Bicycle frame					
Lead time = 2 weeks On-hand = 0 Safety stock = 0 Order quantity: FOQ = 100	Week 1	Week 2	Week 3	Week 4	Week 5	Week 6	Week 7	Week 8
Gross requirements	70	50	80	80	70	60	80	80
Scheduled receipts								
Available inventory								
Net requirements								
Planned order receipts								
Planned order releases								

13. Complete the MRP record for a bicycle seat.

MRP Record			Part Name: Seat					
Lead time = 1 week On-hand = 40 Safety stock = 20 Order quantity FOQ = 100	Week 1	Week 2	Week 3	Week 4	Week 5	Week 6	Week 7	Week 8
Gross requirements	70	50	80	80	70	60	80	80
Scheduled receipts								
Available inventory								
Net requirements								
Planned order receipts								
Planned order releases								

14. Based on the BOM and the MPS for end item A shown below, complete the MRP schedule for items A, C, D, and E.

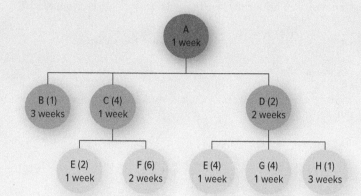

MPS

Item	1	2	3	4	5	6	7	8
A	60	20	50	120	100	50	80	40

Item	A	C	D	E
Lot size rule	L4L	L4L	L4L	Multiples FOQ = 500
Safety stock	0	0	0	100
Beginning inventory	0	0	0	300

15. Given the BOM and MPS for end items A and B shown below, complete the MRP schedules for items A, B, C, D, and E.

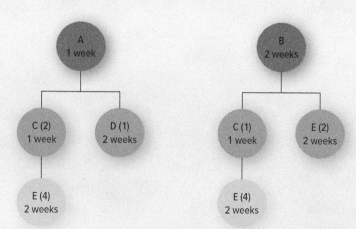

SECTION 5 SPECIAL OCCUPANCIES, AREAS, AND EQUIPMENT

Illustrated Guide to the National Electrical Code offers an exciting new approach to understanding and applying the provisions of the *National Electrical Code.** Unlike the *Code*, this text gathers and presents detailed information in a format, such as one-family or multifamily dwellings, based on "type of occupancy." *Code* specifications applicable to a given type of occupancy are logically organized in easy-to-read units and graphically enhanced by numerous technical illustrations. Going an extra step, the occupancy-specific material is subdivided into specific rooms and areas. Information relevant to more than one type of occupancy is organized into independent units for easier reference. For instance, items such as raceways and conductors are covered in Unit 5 but are related to every type of occupancy.

Students who wish to acquire a comprehensive grasp of all electrical codes will want to study this text section by section and unit by unit. Practicing electricians who have specialized in one type of occupancy and who wish to understand an unfamiliar segment may want to focus on those new areas. For example, an electrician who has been wiring commercial facilities for a number of years wants to wire a new house. Being unfamiliar with the codes concerning residential wiring, this individual can turn to Section 2, "One-Family Dwellings." Here, everything from receptacle placement to the placement of the service point is explained. Section 2 is made up of four units: Units 6 through 9. Unit 6, "General Provisions," contains general requirements for one-family dwellings, both interior and exterior. Unit 7, "Specific Provisions," addresses more complex issues, requiring additional provisions for specific areas such as kitchens, hallways, clothes closets, bathrooms, garages, basements, etc. Unit 8, "Load Calculations," simplifies the standard as well as optional load calculation methods for one-family dwellings. Unit 9, "Services and Electrical Equipment," is divided into five sub headings: Service-Entrance Wiring Methods; Service and Outside Wiring Clearances; Working Space around Equipment; Service Equipment and Panelboards; and Grounding.

The "what," "when," "where" adoption of the provisions of the *NEC* is under the discretionary control of state and local jurisdictions. State and local jurisdictions also have the liberty of appending additional codes, which in many cases may be more stringent than those outlined by the *NEC*. The *Code* may be adopted in whole or in part. For example, while some local codes do not allow the use of nonmetallic-sheathed cable for residential or commercial wiring, others allow its use in residential but not in commercial wiring applications. To ensure compliance, obtain a copy of any additional rules and regulations for your area.

This guide's objective is to provide the information needed to complete your project—without the necessity of learning the *NEC* from cover to cover. *Illustrated Guide to the National Electrical Code* will bring your project to life as quickly and as accurately as any text on the market today. In the electrical field, as in any career, the learning experience never ends. Whether you are an electrician's apprentice, a master electrician, or an electrical inspector, *Illustrated Guide to the National Electrical Code* has something for you. We believe you will find it to be a valuable addition to your reference library. In fact, you may want to include it in your toolbox or briefcase!

Take note that this guidebook was completed after all the normal steps in the National Fire Protection Association (NFPA) 70 review cycle—Proposals to Code-Making Panels, review by

National Electrical Code and *NEC* are registered trademarks of the National Fire Protection Association, Inc., Quincy, MA 02169.

Technical Correlating Committee, Report on Proposals, Comments to Code-Making Panels, review by Technical Correlating Committee, Report on Comments, NFPA Annual Meeting, and ANSI Standards Council—and before the actual publication of the 2011 edition of the *NEC*. Every effort has been made to be technically correct, but there is always the possibility of typographical errors or appeals made to the NFPA Board of Directors after the normal review cycle that could change the appearance or substance of the *Code.*

If changes do occur after the printing of this book, they will be included in the Instructor's Guide and will be incorporated into the guidebook in its next printing.

Note also that the *Code* has a standard method to introduce changes between review cycles, called "Tentative Interim Amendment," or TIA. These TIAs and correction of typographical errors can be downloaded from the NFPA Web site, www.nfpa.org, to make your copy of the *Code* current.

SUPPLEMENTS:

An Instructor Resource CD is available for this text. It contains an Instructor's Guide, unit presentations in PowerPoint, and a computerized test bank. ISBN 1-4354-9812-7

ABOUT THE AUTHOR

For eighteen years, Charles R. Miller owned and operated a successful commercial electrical contracting company (Lighthouse Electric Co., Inc.) in Nashville, Tennessee. Throughout those years, he prided himself on solving problems abandoned by less-skilled or less-dedicated technicians. In 1988, he began operating a second company, dedicated to electrical-related training and known as Lighthouse Educational Services. Mr. Miller teaches custom-tailored classes and seminars covering various aspects of the *National Electrical Code* and NFPA 70E. Countless numbers of students have taken advantage of his extensive experience in electrical contracting; regulatory exams (current electrical codes); electrical-related business and law; and electrical safety–related work practices. Class and seminar attendees have included individuals employed by companies such as Ford, Textron, the Aerostructures Corporation, Aladdin Industries, Lorillard Tobacco Company, Smith & Wesson; by academic institutions such as Tennessee State University, Vanderbilt University, and Purdue University; and governmental agencies including the National Aeronautics and Space Administration (NASA).

In 1999, Charles started writing and illustrating the "Code In Focus" column in *Electrical Contractor* magazine. His attention-to-detail illustrations and writing style make this one of the top, if not the top, read columns in the monthly magazine. Charles Miller started writing for NFPA in 2003. Titles include *Pocket Guide to Residential Electrical Installations, Pocket Guide to Commercial and Industrial Electrical Installations, NFPA's Electrical References, NFPA's Pocket Electrical References,* and *The Electrician's Exam Prep Manual.* Besides teaching, writing, and illustrating, Charles cohosted a home improvement radio talk show in Nashville, Tennessee, for more than three years.

Charles Miller has dedicated over 5000 hours to making *Illustrated Guide to the National Electrical Code* a reality. His unsurpassed attention to detail is evident on every page. Since this book's inception, every day's waking hours have been consumed with careful planning and execution of content and design. His unwavering commitment to quality, from the first page in Unit 1 to the last page in Unit 19, has produced a technically superior, quintessentially user-friendly guide.

Acknowledgments

I would like to say "thank you" to my children, Christin and Adam, for being patient and understanding during the extremely long hours and endless days working on this text. My mother, Evelyn Miller, gets a special "thank you" and "I love you" for a lifetime of support and encouragement. She called every day to check on me and quite often sent encouraging greeting cards that always came at just the right time. "Thank you" to my wife, Linda, for all your love and support as I spend long hours writing and illustrating.

Thank you to the Editor at Cengage Learning, Stacy Masucci, for the privilege of writing for such a professional publishing company. I also would like to thank the entire Cengage Learning project team, comprising all those listed on the copyright page at the front of this book.

Last, but not least, the author and Cengage Learning would like to thank the following reviewers for their contributions:

Gary Daggett
Master Electrician

Kevin Weigman
Northeastern Wisconsin Technical College

Marvin Moak
Hinds Community College

Special thanks to my good friend Don Hursey for his thorough review of *Code* content to ensure compliancy with the 2011 edition of the *NEC*.

Applicable tables and section references are reprinted with permission from NFPA 70-2011, *National Electrical Code*, copyright © 2011, National Fire Protection Association, Quincy, MA 02169. This reprinted material is not the complete and official position of the NFPA on the referenced subject, which is represented only by the standard in its entirety.

FOUNDATIONAL PROVISIONS

UNIT 1

Introduction to the National Electrical Code®

Objectives

After studying this unit, the student should:

▶ be able to give a brief account of electricity in its infancy.

▶ be able to identify the catalyst that brought about the *National Electric Code (NEC)*.

▶ understand how the *NEC* began and its purpose.

▶ understand how changes to the *Code* evolve.

▶ be familiar with the terminology, presentation, and format of the *NEC*.

▶ know what type of information is found in the *NEC* (its layout).

▶ understand the *NEC*'s concern with equipment and material standards.

▶ be able to recognize various trademark logos that denote listed and labeled products.

▶ comprehend the role of nationally recognized testing laboratories (NRTL) and the National Electrical Manufacturers Association (NEMA) as well as the expanded role of the National Fire Protection Association (NFPA).

▶ be familiar with this book's layout, text conventions, and illustration methods.

▶ be advised on how to study the *Illustrated Guide to the NEC*.

▶ be aware that electrical requirements in addition to the *NEC* may exist, and if so, that compliance is required.

THE *NATIONAL ELECTRICAL CODE*

Just as an extensive education is required for doctors to perform the duties of their chosen field, a working knowledge of the *NEC* is a necessity for anyone practicing a profession in the electrical industry. The *NEC* provides the standards by which all electrical installations are judged. Although other requirements, such as local ordinances and manufacturer instructions, must be applied, the *NEC* is the foundation on which successful installations are built. It is the most widely recognized and used compilation of technical rules for the installation and operation of electrical systems in the world today. Because of its widespread effect on the industry, it is important to understand the history of the *NEC*.

The Beginning

In 1882, New York City was home to the first central-station electric generating plant developed by Thomas A. Edison. The Pearl Street Station began operation at 3:00 P.M. on Monday, September 4. Fifty-nine customers had reluctantly consented to have their houses wired on the promise of three free months of electric light. They were given the option of discarding the service if it proved to be unsatisfactory. But this new way of lighting was more than satisfactory . . . it was a sensation. The number of customers tripled in only four months. And, as they say, the rest is history. The new industry swept the nation: New construction included the installation of electricity, and property owners demanded that existing structures be updated as well. New materials and equipment were developed and manufactured, and methods for installing and connecting these items to the electrical source were devised. For more than a decade, manufacturers, architects, engineers, inventors, electricians, and others worked independently to develop their contributions to the new technology. By 1895, there were as many as five different electric installation codes in use, and no single set of codes was accepted by all. To further complicate matters, there was an unexpected hazard darkening the prospects of this new industry.

Purpose and History of the *NEC*

Electrically caused fires were becoming commonplace and, by 1897, the problem was reaching epidemic proportions. A diverse group of knowledgeable, concerned individuals assembled to address this critical issue. The need for standardization was apparent. The consensus of more than 1200 individuals produced the first set of nationally adopted rules to govern electrical installations and operations—the *National Electrical Code*.

The *NEC* states its purpose as . . . *the practical safeguarding of persons and property from hazards arising from the use of electricity*. This objective has remained constant throughout the *NEC*'s existence, and the principles it contains continue to grow and change with the dynamic electrical industry.

Code Changes

The *NEC* is regularly revised to reflect the evolution of products, materials, and installation techniques. Since 1911, the National Fire Protection Association (NFPA) of Quincy, Massachusetts, has been responsible for the maintenance and publication of the *NEC*. The 2011 edition, which contains hundreds of reworded, as well as new, regulations, represents the diligent work of nineteen code-making panels, composed strictly of volunteers from all professions within the electrical industry.

These panels are complemented by a host of private individuals who submit proposals or comment on proposals already submitted for changes to the *NEC*. Anyone who wishes to participate can contact the National Fire Protection Association, 1 Batterymarch Park, Quincy, MA 02169-7471, and request a free booklet, "The NFPA Standards-Making System." The current edition of the *NEC* provides a form in the back of the book for submitting code change suggestions, a copy of which is reproduced on the next page for your reference. Forms are also available online at www.nfpa.org.

Now let us examine what is inside the *NEC* and how we can go about understanding it.

FORM FOR PROPOSAL FOR 2014 NATIONAL ELECTRICAL CODE

INSTRUCTIONS — PLEASE READ CAREFULLY

Type or print **legibly** in **black** ink. Use a separate copy for each proposal. Limit each proposal to a **SINGLE** section. All proposals **must be received by NFPA by 5 p.m., EST, Friday, November 4, 2011,** to be considered for the 2014 National Electrical Code. Proposals received after 5:00 p.m., EST, Friday, November 4, 2011, will be returned to the submitter. If supplementary material (photographs, diagrams, reports, etc.) is included, you may be required to submit sufficient copies for all members and alternates of the technical committee.

For technical assistance, please call NFPA at 1-800-344-3555.

FOR OFFICE USE ONLY

Log #:

Date Rec'd:

Please indicate in which format you wish to receive your ROP/ROC ☐ electronic ☐ paper ☐ download
(Note: If choosing the download option, you must view the ROP/ROC from our website; no copy will be sent to you.)

Date _____ Name _____ Tel. No. _____

Company _____ Email _____

Street Address _____ City _____ State _____ Zip _____

***If you wish to receive a hard copy, a street address MUST be provided. Deliveries cannot be made to PO boxes.*

Please indicate organization represented (if any) _____

1. **Section/Paragraph**

2. **Proposal Recommends (check one):** ☐ new text ☐ revised text ☐ deleted text

3. **Proposal (include proposed new or revised wording, or identification of wording to be deleted):** [Note: Proposed text should be in legislative format; i.e., use underscore to denote wording to be inserted (inserted wording) and strike-through to denote wording to be deleted (deleted wording).]

4. **Statement of Problem and Substantiation for Proposal:** (Note: State the problem that would be resolved by your recommendation; give the specific reason for your Proposal, including copies of tests, research papers, fire experience, etc. If more than 200 words, it may be abstracted for publication.)

5. **Copyright Assignment**

   (a) ☐ I am the author of the text or other material (such as illustrations, graphs) proposed in the Proposal.

   (b) ☐ Some or all of the text or other material proposed in this Proposal was not authored by me. Its source is as **follows:** (please identify which material and provide complete information on its source)

I hereby grant and assign to the NFPA all and full rights in copyright in this Proposal and understand that I acquire no rights in any publication of NFPA in which this Proposal in this or another similar or analogous form is used. Except to the extent that I do not have authority to make an assignment in materials that I have identified in (b) above, I hereby warrant that I am the author of this Proposal and that I have full power and authority to enter into this assignment.

Signature (Required) _____

PLEASE USE SEPARATE FORM FOR EACH PROPOSAL

Mail to: Secretary, Standards Council · National Fire Protection Association
1 Batterymarch Park · Quincy, MA 02169-7471 OR
Fax to: (617) 770-3500 OR Email to: proposals_comments@nfpa.org

8/5/2010-C

NEC Terminology, Presentation, and Format

Tables present a requirement's multiple application possibilities.

Table 210.21(B)(3) Receptacle Ratings for Various Size Circuits

Circuit Rating (Amperes)	Receptacle Rating (Amperes)
15	Not over 15
20	15 or 20
30	30
40	40 or 50
50	50

Diagrams, or figures, are used to further clarify *NEC* applications.

Receptacles   Caps

125-V, 20-A, 2-pole, 3-wire, grounding type

20-A, 125-V, 2-pole, 3-wire, grounding type

125-V, 15-A, 2-pole, 3-wire, grounding type

30-A, 125-V, 2-pole, 3-wire, grounding type

50-A, 125/250-V, 3-pole, 4-wire, grounding type

Figure 551.46(C) Configurations for grounding-type receptacles and attachment plug caps used for recreational vehicle supply cords and recreational vehicle lots.

Dictionary-style header—The left header shows the first section referenced and the right header shows the last section referenced.

Exceptions appear in *italics* and explain when and where a specific rule does not apply.

Sections are numerical listings where the *Code* requirements are located.

Parts (subheadings) are used to break down articles into simpler topics. (Not all articles have subheadings.)

Bullets (solid black circles) indicate areas where one or more complete paragraphs have been deleted since the last edition.

Informational Notes contain explanatory material such as references to other standards, references to related sections of the *Code*, or information related to a *Code* rule. These are informational only and do not require compliance »90.5(C)«.

NFPA document number followed by a page number.

CAUTION

Be advised that the local authority having jurisdiction has the ability to amend the *Code* requirements. Consult the proper authority to obtain applicable guidelines.

Highlighted text within sections indicates changes, other than editorial, since the last *NEC* edition. Vertical lines are placed in outside margins to identify large blocks of changed or new text and for new tables and changed or new figures.

Normal black letters are used for basic *Code* definitions and explanations.

Mandatory rules use the terms "shall" or "shall not" and require compliance »90.5(A)«.

Permissive rules contain the phrases "shall be permitted" or "shall not be required." These phrases normally describe options or alternative methods. Compliance is discretionary »90.5(B)«.

210.12   **ARTICLE 210—BRANCH CIRCUITS**

concrete for the portion of the branch circuit between the branch-circuit overcurrent device and the first outlet, it shall be permitted to install an outlet branch-circuit type AFCI at the first outlet to provide protection for the remaining portion of the branch circuit.

Exception No. 3: Where an individual branch circuit to a fire alarm system installed in accordance with 760.41(B) or 760.121(B) is installed in RMC, IMC, EMT, or steel-sheathed cable, Type AC or Type MC, meeting the requirements of 250.118, with metal outlet and junction boxes, AFCI protection shall be permitted to be omitted.

(B) Branch Circuit Extensions or Modifications — Dwelling Units. In any of the areas specified in 210.12(A), where branch-circuit wiring is modified, replaced, or extended, the branch circuit shall be protected by one of the following:

(1) A listed combination-type AFCI located at the origin of the branch circuit

(2) A listed outlet branch-circuit type AFCI located at the first receptacle outlet of the existing branch circuit

210.18 Guest Rooms and Guest Suites. Guest rooms and guest suites that are provided with permanent provisions for cooking shall have branch circuits installed to meet the rules for dwelling units.

II. Branch-Circuit Ratings

210.19 Conductors — Minimum Ampacity and Size.

(A) Branch Circuits Not More Than 600 Volts.

(1) General. Branch-circuit conductors shall have an ampacity not less than the maximum load to be served. Where a branch circuit supplies continuous loads or any combination of continuous and noncontinuous loads, the minimum branch-circuit conductor size, before the application of any adjustment or correction factors, shall have an allowable ampacity not less than the noncontinuous load plus 125 percent of the continuous load.

Exception: If the assembly, including the overcurrent devices protecting the branch circuit(s), is listed for operation at 100 percent of its rating, the allowable ampacity of the branch circuit conductors shall be permitted to be not less than the sum of the continuous load plus the noncontinuous load.

> Informational Note No. 1: See 310.15 for ampacity ratings of conductors.
>
> Informational Note No. 2: See Part II of Article 430 for minimum rating of motor branch-circuit conductors.
>
> Informational Note No. 3: See 310.15(A)(3) for temperature limitation of conductors.

70–52

Formal Interpretations

Section 90.6 states: *To promote uniformity of interpretation and application of the provisions of this Code, formal interpretation procedures have been established and are found in the NFPA Regulations Governing Committee Projects.* (The NFPA Regulations Governing Committee Projects are in the NFPA Directory. Contact NFPA for a copy of this annual publication.)

The *NEC* Layout

The table of contents in the *NEC* provides a breakdown of the information found in the book. Chapters 1 through 4 contain the most-often used articles in the *Code,* because they include general, or basic, provisions. Chapter 1, while relatively brief, includes definitions essential to the proper application of the *NEC.* It also includes an introduction and a variety of general requirements for electrical installations. More general requirements are found in Chapters 2, 3, and 4, addressing Wiring and Protection, Wiring Methods and Materials, and Equipment for General Use. Special issues are covered in Chapters 5 through 7. Chapter 5 contains information on Special Occupancies; Chapter 6, Special Equipment; and Chapter 7, Special Conditions. The contents of these chapters are applied in addition to the general rules given in earlier chapters. Chapter 8 covers Communications Systems and is basically independent of other chapters, except where cross-references are given. The final chapter, Chapter 9, contains Tables and Examples. Each chapter contains one or more articles, and each article contains sections. Sections may be further subdivided by the use of lettered or numbered paragraphs. The *Code* is completed by Annexes A through I, an index, and a proposal form.

WIRING SYSTEM PRODUCT STANDARDS

In addition to installation rules, the *NEC* is concerned with the type and quality of electrical wiring system materials. Two terms are synonymous with acceptability in this area: **labeled** and **listed.** Their definitions, found in Article 100, are very similar. Similarities within these definitions include: (1) an organization that is responsible for providing the listing or labeling, (2) that these organizations must be acceptable to the authority having jurisdiction, (3) that both are concerned with the evaluation of products, and (4) that both maintain periodic inspection of the production (or manufacturing) of the equipment or materials which have been listed or labeled. A manufacturer of labeled equipment (or material) must continue to comply with the appropriate standards (or performance) under which the labeling was granted. "Listed" also means that the equipment, materials, or services meet appropriate designated standards or have been tested and found suitable for a specified purpose. This information is compiled and published by the organization. The Informational Note under "Listed" states that each organization may have different means for identifying listed equipment. In fact, some do not recognize equipment as listed unless it is also labeled. Listed or labeled equipment must be installed and used as instructed » *110.3(B)* «.

The organizations described in the following directly affect the *Code* as it relates to equipment and material acceptability and play a role in developing and maintaining the standards set forth in the *NEC.*

Nationally Recognized Testing Laboratories

Prior to 1989, there were only two organizations perceived as capable of providing safety certification of products that would be used nationwide. Because there were only two, innovative technology was slow to be tested and approved. When Congress created the Occupational Safety and Health Administration (OSHA) in the early 1970s, OSHA was directed to establish safety regulations for the workplace and for the monitoring of those regulations. OSHA adopted an explanation from the *NEC* and included it in the *Code of Federal Regulations.* In part, it reads: "an installation or equipment is acceptable to the Assistant Secretary of Labor . . . if it is acceptable or certified, or listed, or labeled, or otherwise determined to be safe by a nationally recognized testing laboratory. . . ."

Testing by a nationally recognized testing laboratory (NRTL) was specified in the Code of Federal Regulations, but requirements for becoming an NRTL had not yet been identified. Although OSHA introduced "Accreditation of Testing Laboratories" in 1973, the process through which a laboratory would receive accreditation was still missing. Cooperative efforts produced the OSHA regulation finalized in 1988, and called "OSHA Recognition Process for Nationally Recognized Testing Laboratories."

OSHA's NRTL program greatly benefits manufacturers by providing a system that certifies that a product meets national safety standards. Just as important, the door was opened for a greater number of laboratories to provide certification, and manufacturers are now better able to meet the demands of today's highly competitive market.

The aim of NRTLs is to ensure that electrical products properly safeguard against reasonable, identifiable risks. An extensive network of field personnel conduct unannounced inspections at manufacturing facilities that use the laboratory's "seal of approval." Some of the better-known trademarks of testing laboratories are shown below:

© Cengage Learning 2012

Some of the labels that appear on evaluated and certified electrical products, such as the ones that follow, carry the trademarks of the testing laboratory or the laboratory's standards being used for comparison.

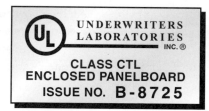 

 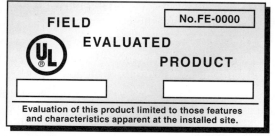

© Cengage Learning 2012

MET Laboratories

MET Laboratories, Inc., working with the Department of Labor as well as other agencies, served as a working example for the accreditation process for independent testing laboratories. In fact, MET became the first U.S. laboratory to successfully complete the process (1989), and thus became the first NRTL licensed by OSHA.

MET field inspectors interact with local electrical inspectors throughout the country to ensure product acceptance by all federal and state regulatory officials. The MET label is accepted by all fifty states, the federal government, and major retailers.

Underwriters Laboratories, Inc.

Prior to the formalization of NRTLs in 1989, electrical product standards were primarily written by Underwriters Laboratories, Inc. (UL), who also performed certification testing. Standards written by UL are still widely used. The appearance of the UL logo on a label indicates that the product complies with the UL standard. It does not mean, necessarily, that UL did the product testing. Although one of many NRTLs, Underwriters Laboratories is perhaps the most widely recognized and respected testing laboratory in operation today. Founded in 1894, UL is a not-for-profit corporation whose mission is to bring safer products to the marketplace and to serve the public through rigorous product safety testing. This organization offers a wide range of services, which include, but are not limited to, product listing, classification, component recognition, field certification, field engineering, facility registration, inspection, fact-finding, and research. As one can see from this list, UL plays a major role in guiding the safety of the electrical industry.

Intertek Testing Services

Select laboratories of Intertek Testing Services (ITS) have passed OSHA's stringent NRTL accreditation procedures and thereby have earned the right to issue product approvals and list products using the familiar ETL listed and CE marks. ITS has been conducting performance and reliability tests to nearly 200 safety standards applicable to workplace-related products since 1896. Intertek's comprehensive program includes testing, listing, labeling, and quarterly follow-up inspections. While recognized internationally by its many listed marks, the ETL listed mark is accepted throughout the United States, by all jurisdictions for electrical products, when denoting compliance with nationally recognized standards such as Wyle Laboratories (WL), International Electrotechnical Commission (IEC), UL, Canadian Standards Association (CSA), and FM Approvals (FM).

National Electrical Manufacturers Association

Founded in 1926, National Electrical Manufacturers Association (NEMA) comprises companies that manufacture equipment for all facets of electrical application, from generation through utilization. Its expansive objectives include product quality maintenance and improvement, safety standards for product manufacture and usage, and a variety of product standards, such as ratings and performance. NEMA contributes to the development of the *National Electrical Safety Code* as well as the *NEC*.

National Fire Protection Association

The NFPA, more than a century old, dedicates itself to safety standards, gathering statistical data, conducting research, providing crucial information on fire protection, prevention, and suppression methods, and much more. Boasting an internationally diverse membership of more than 75,000, this leading nonprofit organization publishes over 300 widely recognized consensus codes and standards, including the *NEC*. In addition, the NFPA is involved in training and education. Its primary pursuit is to protect lives and property from the often catastrophic hazards of fire.

THIS BOOK

The *Illustrated Guide to the NEC* is designed to teach through visualization. If a picture is truly worth a thousand words, this book should provide a more in-depth look at the *National Electrical Code* than can be found in any other single publication. Its highly detailed illustrations are complemented with concise, easy-to-understand written information. Not intended as a how-to book, the *Illustrated Guide to the NEC* instead strives to translate difficult material into simpler, straightforward principles. Once the reader understands how the *Code* translates in a specific area, the same techniques can be applied throughout.

Its Layout

Not only is the presentation of material in this text different from others on the market, but the organization of information also offers a new approach. After covering the fundamental provisions in the balance of Unit 1, this text proceeds to address code requirements by type of occupancy. Comprehensive information is given for one-family dwellings, multifamily dwellings, commercial locations, and special occupancies. To accomplish this task, information has been gathered logically from throughout the *Code* book and concentrated in one section, under the appropriate occupancy. Each occupancy type is broken down into its finite components, and each component is thoroughly discussed and illustrated (see table of contents).

Text Conventions

General text is grouped in small areas surrounding an illustration. **Notes** provide additional information considered relevant to the point being discussed. **Cautions** indicate that particular care is needed during application. **Warnings** indicate potential danger and are intended to prevent misunderstanding of a given rule.

Terms *Luminaire* and *Lighting Fixture*

The word *luminaire* is the international term for *lighting fixture*. As defined in Article 100, a luminaire is a complete lighting unit consisting of a light source such as a lamp or lamps, together with the parts designed to position the light source and to connect it to the power supply. It may also include parts to protect the light source, ballast, or distribute the light. A lampholder itself is not a luminaire. Starting with the 2002 edition, *luminaire* became the main term and *fixture* or *lighting fixture* followed in parentheses. In the 2008 edition, *fixture* and *lighting fixture* were removed and do not follow the term *luminaire*. Throughout this text, *fixture* and *lighting fixture* have also been omitted.

Studying This Text

As the title implies, frequent references are made to the *National Electrical Code*. Keep a copy of the latest edition of the *Code* close at hand. Any confusion about terminology not cleared up by the "Definitions" section of this text may be explained by consulting the *Code's Article 100—Definitions* section. Whenever direct references are made to the *Code,* benefits will be gained by taking the time to read the suggested article or section. The *Illustrated Guide to the NEC* is not intended, in any way, to replace the *Code*. Each unit's "Competency Test" requires a thorough understanding of related *NEC* subject matter. Use of this text alone is insufficient to successfully complete the test. It is, however, intended as an indispensable supplement to the *NEC*.

Note that when comparing calculations made by both the English and metric systems, slight differences will occur due to the conversion method used. These differences are not significant, and calculations for both systems are, therefore, valid.

ADDITIONAL ELECTRICAL REQUIREMENTS

Local Ordinances

The importance of local (state, city, etc.) electrical codes cannot be overemphasized. Local agencies can adopt the *NEC* exactly as written or can amend the *Code* by incorporating more or less stringent regulations. While the *NEC* represents the minimum standards for safety, some jurisdictions have additional restrictions. Obtain a copy of additional requirements (if any) for your area.

Engineers or architects who design electrical systems may also set requirements beyond the provisions of the *NEC*. For example, an engineer might require the installation of 20-ampere circuits in areas where the *NEC* allows 15-ampere circuits. Requirements from engineers or architects are found in additional documents, such as the following.

Plans and Specifications

If plans and specifications are provided for a project by knowledgeable engineers or architects, this information must be considered and, if need be, compared to the requirements set forth by the *NEC*. It is unlikely that the plans or specifications provided by competent professionals will conflict with or contradict the *Code*. Nonetheless, it is best to be diligent in applying the governing principals of the *NEC*.

Manufacturer Instructions

Some equipment or material may include instructions from the manufacturer. These instructions must be followed. For example, baseboard heaters generally include installation instructions. The *NEC* does not prohibit the installation of receptacle outlets above baseboard heaters, but the manufacturer's instructions may prohibit the installation of its heater below receptacles.

CONCLUSION

While this unit briefly discusses the history of the *National Electrical Code*, it is not possible to do justice to the importance of the *Code* in a few short pages. With only a glimpse into its history and present-day supporting structure, this text moves on to the task of understanding the contents of the *Code*. The *Illustrated Guide to the NEC* presents visually stimulating information in an occupancy-organized, concise format. To begin the journey through the 2011 edition of the *National Electrical Code*, simply turn the page, read, look, and understand.

Guarded

Guarded is defined as covered, shielded, fenced, enclosed, or otherwise protected by means of suitable covers, casings, barriers, rails, screens, mats, or platforms effectively removing the likelihood of approach or contact by persons or objects »*Article 100*«.

Ⓐ Panelboards having doors or covers are considered guarded.

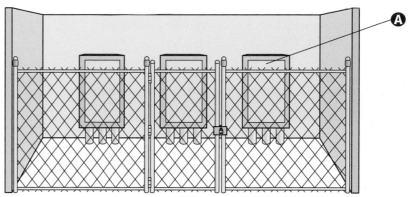

© Cengage Learning 2012

In Sight From (Within Sight From, Within Sight)

Ⓐ The *NEC* terms *in sight from, within sight from,* or *within sight,* etc., applied to equipment indicate that the specified items of equipment are visible and are not more than 50 ft (15 m) apart »*Article 100*«.

Ⓑ A motor disconnecting means must be located in sight from the motor location as required by 430.102(B).

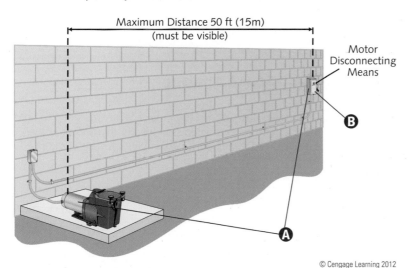

© Cengage Learning 2012

Lighting Outlet

Ⓐ An outlet intended for the direct connection of a lampholder or luminaire is called a lighting outlet »*Article 100*«.

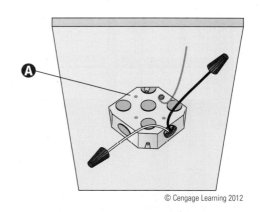

© Cengage Learning 2012

Location, Damp

Ⓐ Damp locations are those subject to moderate degrees of moisture. Exterior partially protected locations under canopies, marquees, roofed (open) porches, and similar sites are considered damp locations as well as interior locations such as some basements, barns, and cold-storage warehouses »*Article 100*«.

© Cengage Learning 2012

Location, Dry

Ⓐ Dry locations are those not normally subject to moisture, except on a temporary basis such as a building under construction ≫ *Article 100* ≪.

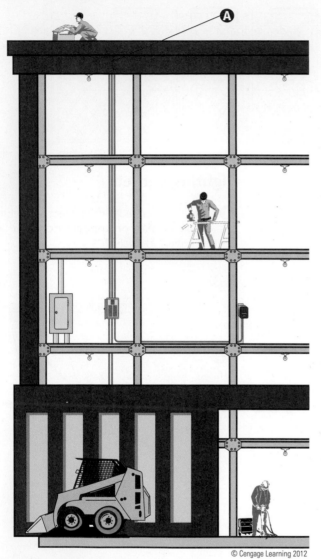

© Cengage Learning 2012

Location, Wet

Ⓐ Installations in any of the following categories are wet locations: underground, within concrete slabs, in masonry (directly contacting the earth), in areas subject to saturation (water or other liquids), and in locations unprotected from weather ≫ *Article 100* ≪.

Luminaire

A luminaire is a complete lighting unit consisting of a light source such as a lamp or lamps, together with the parts designed to position the light source and to connect it to the power supply. It may also include parts to protect the light source, ballast, or distribute the light. A lampholder itself is not a luminaire.

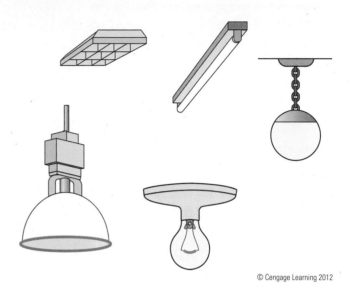

© Cengage Learning 2012

Multioutlet Assembly

Ⓐ A surface, flush, or freestanding raceway designed to hold conductors and receptacles (assembled in the field or at the factory) is called a multioutlet assembly ≫ *Article 100* ≪.

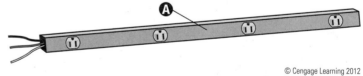

© Cengage Learning 2012

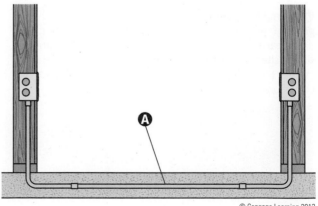

© Cengage Learning 2012

Neutral Conductor and Neutral Point

A neutral conductor is defined as the conductor connected to the neutral point of a system that is intended to carry current under normal conditions »*Article 100*«.

The neutral point is the common point on a wye-connection in a polyphase system or midpoint on a single-phase, 3-wire system, or midpoint of a single-phase portion of a 3-phase delta system, or a midpoint of a 3-wire, direct-current system »*Article 100*«.

Ⓐ The neutral point is the common point on a wye-connection in a polyphase system.

Ⓑ The neutral point is the midpoint on a single-phase, 3-wire system.

Ⓒ The neutral point is the midpoint of a single-phase portion of a 3-phase delta system.

Ⓓ The neutral point is the midpoint of a 3-wire direct-current system.

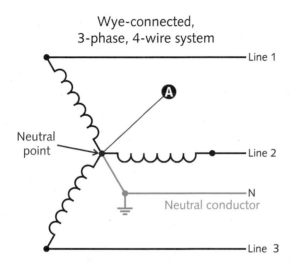

Wye-connected,
3-phase, 4-wire system

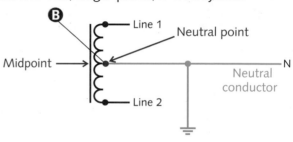

120/240 volt, single-phase, 3-wire system

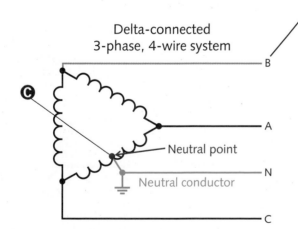

Delta-connected
3-phase, 4-wire system

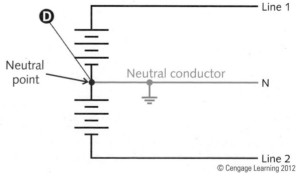

3-wire direct-current system

© Cengage Learning 2012

NOTE

At the neutral point of the system, the vectorial sum of the nominal voltages from all other phases within the system that utilize the neutral, with respect to the neutral point, is zero potential »*Informational Note to neutral point in Article 100*«.

WARNING

Neutral conductors must be identified in accordance with the requirements in 200.6.

Outlet

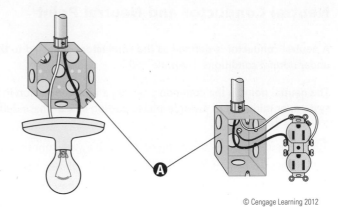

A A point in a wiring system from which current is taken to supply utilization equipment is known as an outlet ≫*Article 100*≪.

© Cengage Learning 2012

Overcurrent Protective Device, Branch-Circuit

A branch-circuit overcurrent protective device is a device capable of providing protection for service, feeder, and branch circuits and equipment over the full range of overcurrents between its rated current and its interrupting rating. Branch-circuit overcurrent protective devices are provided with interrupting ratings appropriate for the intended use but no less than 5000 amperes ≫*Article 100*≪.

© Cengage Learning 2012

Plenum

A The space above a suspended ceiling used for environmental air-handling purposes is an example of **other space used for environmental air** as described in 300.22(C).

B A compartment or chamber having one or more attached air ducts and forming part of the air distribution system is known as a plenum ≫*Article 100*≪.

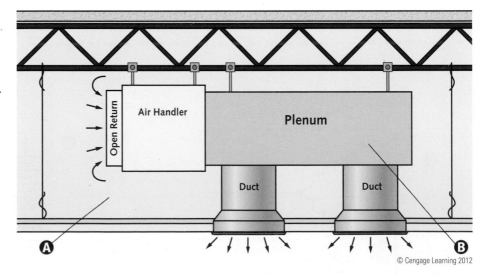

© Cengage Learning 2012

Receptacle

A A contact device installed at an outlet for the connection of an attachment plug is a receptacle ≫*Article 100*≪.

B A single receptacle is a single contact device with no other contact device on the same yoke ≫*Article 100*≪.

C A multiple receptacle is a single device consisting of two or more receptacles ≫*Article 100*≪.

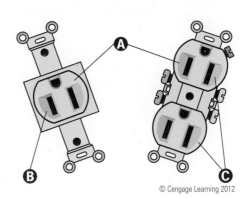

© Cengage Learning 2012

Separately Derived System

A Article 450 contains provisions for transformers.

B A separately derived system is a premises wiring system whose power is derived from a source of electric energy or equipment other than a service. A separately derived system has no direct connection from circuit conductors of one system to circuit conductors of another system, other than connections through the earth, metal enclosures, metallic raceways, or equipment grounding conductors ≫*Article 100*≪.

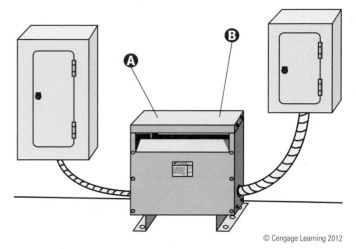

© Cengage Learning 2012

> ### NOTE
>
> An alternate ac power source, such as an on-site generator, is not a separately derived system if the grounded conductor is solidly interconnected to a service-supplied system grounded conductor ≫*250.30 Informational Note No. 1*≪.

Service

A The conductors and equipment that deliver energy from the serving utility to the wiring system of the premises are called the service ≫*Article 100*≪.

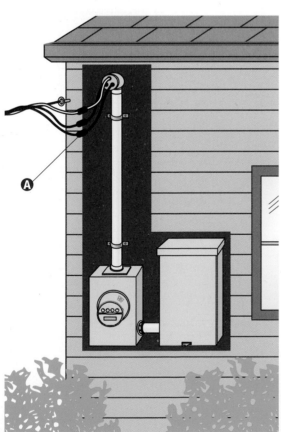

© Cengage Learning 2012

> ### NOTE
>
> Conductors and equipment are also defined as a service where receiving power underground.

Service Conductors

A The conductors from the service point to the service disconnecting means are known as service conductors ≫*Article 100*≪.

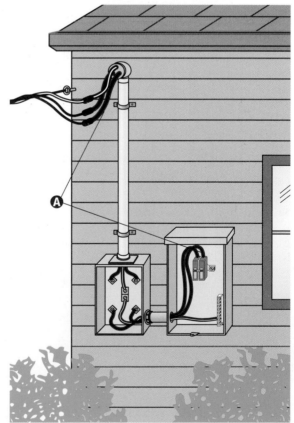

© Cengage Learning 2012

> ### NOTE
>
> Overhead service conductors are the overhead conductors between the service point and the first point of connection to the service-entrance conductors at the building or other structure ≫*Article 100*≪.

Service Drop

Ⓐ The overhead conductors between the utility electric supply system and the service point ≫ *Article 100* ≪.

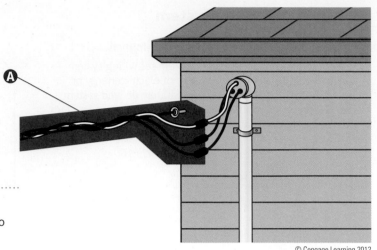

© Cengage Learning 2012

Service Equipment

Ⓐ Service equipment is that equipment (usually circuit breaker[s], switch[es], fuse[s], and accessories) necessary to constitute the main control and cutoff that is connected to the load end of service conductors ≫ *Article 100* ≪.

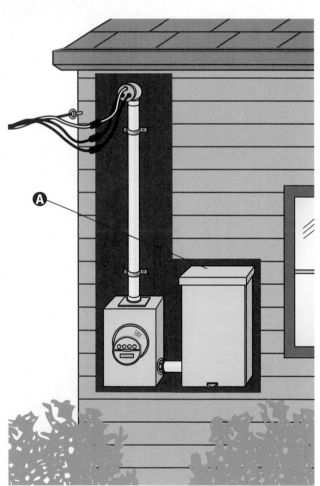

© Cengage Learning 2012

Service Lateral

Ⓐ The service lateral is the underground conductors between the utility electric supply system and the service point ≫ *Article 100* ≪.

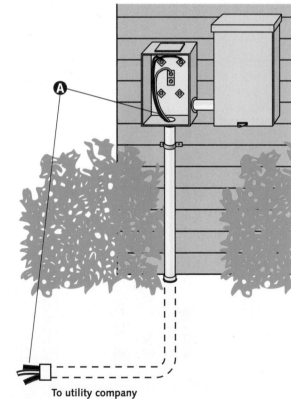

To utility company

© Cengage Learning 2012

NOTE

Underground service conductors are defined as the underground conductors between the service point and the first point of connection to the service-entrance conductors in a terminal box, meter, or other enclosure, inside or outside the building wall. In accordance with the informational note under the definition of underground service conductors, where there is no terminal box, meter, or other enclosure, the point of connection is considered to be the point of entrance of the service conductors into the building ≫ *Article 100* ≪.

Service Point

Ⓐ The service point is the point of the connection between the facilities of the serving utility and the premises wiring ≫ *Article 100* ≪.

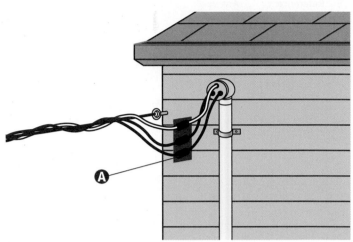

© Cengage Learning 2012

Special Permission and Authority Having Jurisdiction

Ⓐ Special permission is the written consent of the authority having jurisdiction (AHJ) ≫ *Article 100* ≪.

Ⓑ The AHJ for enforcing the *NEC* may grant exception for the installation of conductors and equipment (not under the exclusive control of the electric utilities) used to connect the electric utility supply system to the service conductors of the premises served (provided such installations are outside a building or structure, or terminate inside nearest the point of entrance of the service conductors) ≫ *90.2(C)* ≪.

Ⓒ AHJ is the organization, office, or individual responsible for enforcing the requirements of a code (or standard), or for approving equipment, materials, an installation, or a procedure ≫ *Article 100* ≪.

© Cengage Learning 2012

Summary

- Conductors within junction boxes must be accessible without damaging the construction or finish of the building or structure.
- Certain equipment, such as the service disconnecting means, must be readily accessible.
- The term *appliance* denotes more than just kitchen equipment.
- Branch circuits are divided into four categories: appliance, general purpose, individual, and multiwire.
- General purpose branch circuits may feed lights and receptacles or any combination thereof.
- An individual branch circuit feeds only one piece of equipment.
- The terms *bonded* and *grounded* are not interchangeable.

- A multiwire branch circuit must have a means to simultaneously disconnect all ungrounded (hot) conductors.
- A load having the maximum level of current sustained for three hours or more is a continuous load.
- *Equipment* is a general term encompassing a wide variety of items.
- A grounded conductor and a grounding conductor have different functions.
- A grounded conductor is not necessarily a neutral conductor.
- One duplex receptacle is not defined as a single receptacle.
- Special permission is the written consent of the AHJ.

Unit 2 Competency Test

NEC Reference   Answer

_____   _____   1. A(n) _____ branch circuit supplies two or more receptacles or outlets for lighting and appliances.

_____   _____   2. An electric circuit that controls another electric circuit through a relay is referred to as a(n) _____.

_____   _____   3. A(n) _____ branch circuit consists of two or more ungrounded conductors having a potential difference between them, and a grounded conductor having equal potential difference between it and each ungrounded conductor of the circuit and that is connected to the neutral or grounded conductor of the system.

_____   _____   4. An intermittent operation in which load conditions are regularly recurrent is the definition of _____.

_____   _____   5. The _____ is the connection between the grounded circuit conductor and the equipment grounding conductor at the service.

_____   _____   6. A(n) _____ is used to connect the system grounded conductor or the equipment to a grounding electrode or to a point on the grounding electrode system.

_____   _____   7. Rainproof, raintight, or watertight equipment can fulfill the requirements for _____ where varying weather conditions other than wetness, such as snow, ice, dust, or temperature extremes, are not a factor.

_____   _____   8. The purpose of the *NEC* is the practical safeguarding of _____ from hazards arising from the use of electricity.

_____   _____   9. A(n) _____ is a manually operated device used in conjunction with a transfer switch to provide a means of directly connecting load conductors to a power source and of disconnecting the transfer switch.

_____   _____   10. A type of surface, flush, or freestanding raceway, designed to hold conductors and receptacles, assembled in the field or at the factory is called a(n) _____.

_____   _____   11. A raceway encased in 4 in. (102 mm) of concrete on the ground floor (in direct contact with the earth) shall be considered a(n) _____ location.

_____   _____   12. A(n) _____ may consist of one or more sensing elements integral with the motor-compressor and an external control device.

_____   _____   13. An enclosure designed either for surface or flush mounting and provided with a frame, mat, or trim in which a swinging door or doors are or can be hung is called a(n) _____.

_____   _____   14. A(n) _____ is a shaftway, hatchway, well hole, or other vertical opening of space in which an elevator or dumbwaiter is designed to operate.

_____   _____   15. A multiwire branch circuit can supply:

    I. 120/240 volts to only one piece of utilization equipment

    II. 120/240 volts where all ungrounded conductors are opened simultaneously

      a) I only   b) II only   c) either I or II   d) neither I nor II

_____   _____   16. An overcurrent protective device with a circuit opening fusible part that is heated and severed by the passage of overcurrent through it is the definition of a(n)_____.

_____   _____   17. _____ is a string of outdoor lights suspended between two points.

_____   _____   18. Name two items that must be present when defining an area as a bathroom.

NEC Reference   Answer

_____   _____   19. A continuous load is where the _____ current is expected to continue for three hours or more.

         a) 80%   b) average   c) maximum   d) 125%

_____   _____   20. Solidly grounded is defined as connected to ground without inserting any _____ or impedance device.

_____   _____   21. A(n) _____ is a point on the wiring system at which current is taken to supply utilization equipment.

_____   _____   22. Circuit conductors between the final overcurrent device protecting the circuit and the outlet(s) is called a(n) _____.

_____   _____   23. _____ enclosures are constructed or protected so that exposure to a beating rain will not result in the entrance of water under specified test conditions.

_____   _____   24. Continuous duty is an operation at a substantially constant load for _____.

         a) 1 hour or more   b) 1½ hours or more

         c) 3 hours or more   d) an indefinitely long time

_____   _____   25. Ampacity is defined as the current in amperes that a conductor can carry continuously under the conditions of use without exceeding _____.

_____   _____   26. When a disconnecting means must be located within sight from a motor, the disconnect must be visible and not more than _____ ft from the motor.

_____   _____   27. A building containing three dwelling units is called a(n) _____.

Enclosures (without Device, Luminaires, or Lampholders) Supported by Raceways

A An enclosure that contains no devices **or** supports no luminaires can be supported by entering raceways when *all* of the following conditions are met: (1) the enclosure does not exceed 100 in.³ (1650 cm³) size; (2) the enclosure has threaded entries or hubs identified for the purpose; (3) the enclosure is supported by two or more conduits threaded wrenchtight into the enclosure or hubs; and (4) each conduit is secured within 36 in. (900 mm) of the enclosure, unless all entries are on the same side »314.23(E)«.

B Only rigid or intermediate metal conduit with threaded ends are permitted in 314.23(E).

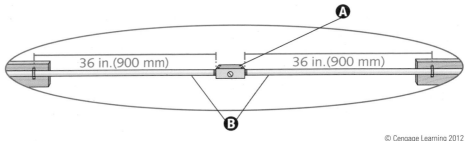

© Cengage Learning 2012

Enclosures (with Devices, Luminaires, or Lampholders) Supported by Raceways

A An enclosure that contains devices (other than splicing devices) or supports luminaires, lampholders, or other equipment can be supported by entering raceways when *all* of the following conditions are met: (1) the enclosure does not exceed 100 in.³ (1650 cm³) in size; (2) the enclosure has threaded entries or hubs identified for the purpose; (3) the enclosure is supported by two or more conduits threaded wrenchtight into the enclosure or hubs; and (4) each conduit is secured within 18 in. (450 mm) of the enclosure »314.23(F)«.

B An outlet box can support a luminaire weighing 50 pounds (23 kg) or less, unless the box is listed and marked for a weight equal to or greater than the luminaire »314.27(A)(2)«.

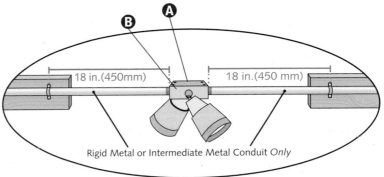

Rigid Metal or Intermediate Metal Conduit *Only*

© Cengage Learning 2012

Enclosures with Conduit Entries on One Side

A An enclosure can be supported by conduits entering on the same side when *all* of the following conditions are met: (1) the enclosure does not exceed 100 in.³ (1650 cm³) in size; (2) the enclosure has threaded entries or hubs identified for the purpose; (3) the enclosure is supported by two or more conduits threaded wrenchtight into the enclosure or hubs; and (4) each conduit is secured within 18 in. (450 mm) of the enclosure »314.23(E)«.

B Unused cable or raceway openings, other than those intended for the operation of equipment, those intended for mounting purposes, or those permitted as part of the design for listed equipment, must be closed so that the protection provided is at least equal to that provided by the wall of the equipment »110.12(A)«.

C Boxes must be supported within 18 in. (450 mm), whether or not they contain devices or support fixtures, if all the conduits enter on the same side, unless the requirements of 314.23(F) Exception No. 2 are met.

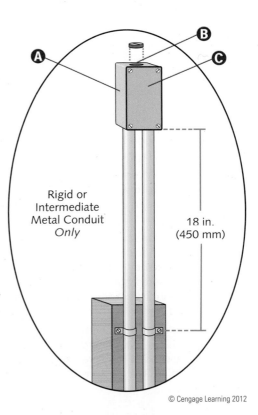

Rigid or Intermediate Metal Conduit *Only*

18 in. (450 mm)

© Cengage Learning 2012

NOTE

Boxes shall not be supported by one conduit unless the requirements of **314.23(F) Exception No. 2** are met.

Support for Conduit Bodies

(A) Any size conduit body not containing a device(s), luminaire(s), lampholder(s), or other equipment can be supported by rigid metal, intermediate metal, or rigid nonmetallic conduit or electrical metallic tubing, provided the conduit body's trade size is no larger than the largest trade size of the supporting raceway ≫314.23(E) Exception≪. Within this section, no consideration is given to splicing devices.

(B) Conduit body support must be rigid and secure ≫314.16(C)(2)≪.

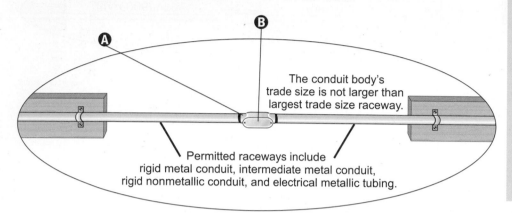

The conduit body's trade size is not larger than largest trade size raceway.

Permitted raceways include rigid metal conduit, intermediate metal conduit, rigid nonmetallic conduit, and electrical metallic tubing.

NOTE

A raceway supported conduit body that contains a device(s), luminaire(s), lampholder(s), or other equipment must be supported by either rigid metal or intermediate metal conduit only. The trade size of the conduit body must not be larger than the largest trade size of the supporting raceway ≫*314.23(F) Exception No. 1*≪.

The only conduit body not requiring two support raceways is a conduit body constructed with only one conduit entry ≫*314.23(E) Exception*≪.

Supporting Luminaires Using Lengths of Conduit Longer than 18 in.

(A) Section 314.23(F) Exception No. 2 permits unbroken length(s) of rigid or intermediate metal conduit to support a box used for luminaire or lampholder support or to support a wiring enclosure within a luminaire where all of the following conditions are met:

(B) The length of conduit extending beyond the last point of securely fastened support does not exceed 3 ft (900 mm).

(C) A luminaire supported by a single conduit does not exceed 12 in. (300 mm), in any direction, from the point of conduit entry.

(D) The weight supported by any single conduit shall not exceed 20 pounds (9 kg).

(E) At the luminaire end, each conduit (if more than one) is threaded wrenchtight into the box or wiring enclosure or into hubs identified for the purpose.

(F) Where accessible to unqualified persons, the luminaire's lowest point is at least 8 ft (2.5 m) abovegrade (or standing area) and at least 3 ft (900 mm) [measured horizontally to the 8 ft (2.5 m) elevation] from windows, doors, porches, fire escapes, or similar locations.

(G) The unbroken conduit before the last point of support is 12 in. (300 mm) or greater and that portion of the conduit is securely fastened not less than 12 in. (300 mm) from its last point of support.

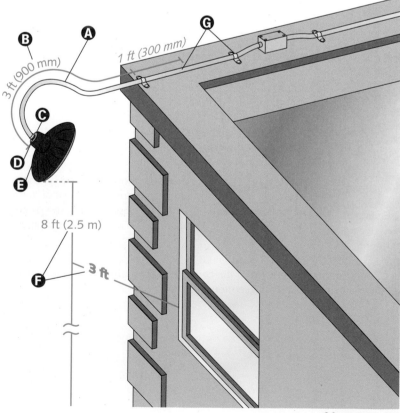

Strain Relief for Flexible Cords

Ⓐ Multiconductor cord or cable used to support a box must be protected in an approved manner so that the conductors are not subjected to strain. A strain-relief connector threaded into a box with a hub would be acceptable ≫*314.23(H)(1)*≪.

© Cengage Learning 2012

Luminaire Hanger

Ⓐ Section 314.27(B) requires an independent support, such as a luminaire hanger, for luminaires that weigh more than 50 pounds (23 kg) unless the box is listed.

Ⓑ When raceway fittings are used to support luminaire(s), they must be capable of supporting the combined weight of the luminaire assembly and lamp(s) ≫*410.36(E)*≪.

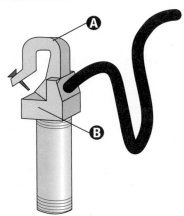

© Cengage Learning 2012

Conduit Stems Supporting Luminaires

Ⓐ An outlet box used exclusively for lighting shall be designed or installed so that a luminaire or lampholder may be attached. Boxes must be able to support a luminaire weighing at least 50 pounds (23 kg). A luminaire that weighs more than 50 pounds (23 kg) shall be supported independently of the outlet box, unless the outlet box is listed and marked for the maximum weight to be supported ≫*314.27(A)(2)*≪.

Ⓑ Stems longer than 18 in. (450 mm) shall be connected to the wiring system with flexible fittings suitable for the location. At the luminaire end, the conduit(s) shall be threaded wrenchtight into the box or wiring enclosure or into hubs identified for the purpose ≫*314.23(H)(2)*≪.

Ⓒ A box supporting lampholders, luminaires, or wiring enclosures within luminaires used in lieu of boxes in compliance with 300.15(B) must be supported by rigid or intermediate metal conduit stems ≫*314.23(H)(2)*≪.

Ⓓ A luminaire supported by a single conduit shall not exceed 12 in. (300 mm) in any horizontal direction from the point of conduit entry ≫*314.23(H)(2)*≪.

CAUTION

Any point of a luminaire supported by a single conduit must be at least 8 ft (2.5 m) abovegrade (or standing area) and at least 3 ft (900 mm) (measured horizontally to the 8 ft [2.5 m] elevation) from windows, doors, porches, fire escapes, or similar locations, unless an effective means to prevent the threaded joint from loosening (such as a set screw) is used ≫*314.23(H)(2)*≪.

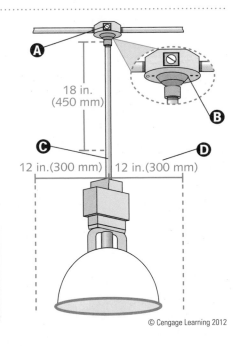

18 in. (450 mm)

12 in.(300 mm)   12 in.(300 mm)

© Cengage Learning 2012

Device Boxes Supporting Luminaires or Lampholders

Ⓐ A wall-mounted luminaire or lampholder weighing no more than 6 pounds (3 kg) can be supported by boxes (such as device boxes) not specifically designed to support luminaires or lampholders, provided the luminaire or its supporting yoke, or the lampholder, is secured to the box with at least two No. 6 or larger screws. Plaster rings, secured to other boxes, are also acceptable ≫*314.27(A) Exception*≪.

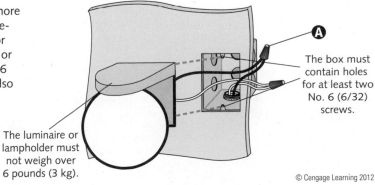

The luminaire or lampholder must not weigh over 6 pounds (3 kg).

The box must contain holes for at least two No. 6 (6/32) screws.

© Cengage Learning 2012

Mounting Nonmetallic Boxes

Ⓐ Supporting screws for nonmetallic boxes must be mounted outside of the box, unless the box is constructed in a manner that prevents contact between the conductors in the box and the supporting screws ≫ *314.43* ≪.

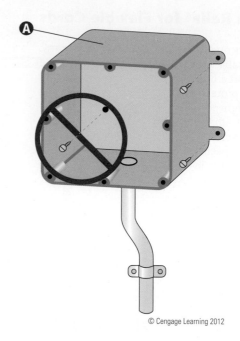

© Cengage Learning 2012

Luminaire Outlet Boxes

Ⓐ Boxes used at luminaire or lampholder outlets in a ceiling must be designed for the purpose and shall be required to support a luminaire weighing a minimum of 50 pounds (23 kg). Every box used exclusively for lighting must be designed and installed so that a luminaire may be attached ≫ *314.27(A)(2)* ≪.

Ⓑ An outlet box can support a luminaire weighing no more than 50 pounds (23 kg), unless the outlet box is listed and marked for the weight to be supported ≫ *314.27(A)(2)* ≪.

Ⓒ Inspection of the connections between luminaire conductors and circuit conductors must be possible without having to disconnect any part of the wiring (unless the luminaires are connected by attachment plugs and receptacles) ≫ *410.8* ≪.

> **NOTE**
>
> Typically, two No. 8 (8/32) screws are used to attach a luminaire or its supporting yoke to an outlet box.

> **NOTE**
>
> Boxes used at luminaire or lampholder outlets in a wall shall be designed for the purpose and shall be marked to indicate the maximum permitted weight (with luminaire) that may be supported by the box in the wall.

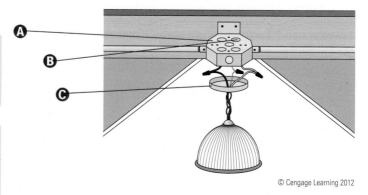

© Cengage Learning 2012

Ceiling-Suspended (Paddle) Fan Boxes

Ⓐ An outlet box shall not be used as the sole means of support for a ceiling-suspended (paddle) fan unless the box is (1) listed, (2) marked by the manufacturer as suitable for the purpose, and (3) supporting a ceiling-suspended (paddle) fan weighing 70 pounds (32 kg) or less. For outlet boxes or outlet box systems designed to support ceiling-suspended (paddle) fans weighing more than 35 pounds (16 kg), the required marking must include the maximum weight that can be supported ≫ *314.27(C)* ≪.

Ⓑ Ceiling-suspended (paddle) fans must be supported independently of an outlet box, unless the listed outlet box or outlet box system is identified for the use and installed in accordance with 314.27(C). ≫ *422.18* ≪.

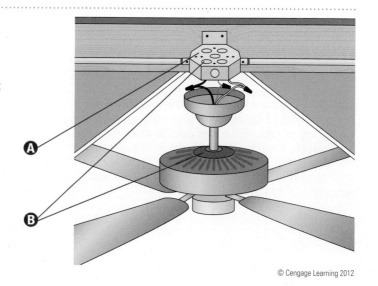

© Cengage Learning 2012

JUNCTION AND PULL BOX SIZING

Straight Pull—Two Raceways

Section 314.16 is used to determine box size requirements for 6 AWG and smaller conductors. Calculations are based on the sizes and numbers of *conductors*. Section 314.28 is used to determine the box size requirements for 4 AWG and larger conductors (under 600 volts). Calculations here are based on the sizes and numbers of *raceways*.

A Box calculations for 4 AWG and larger conductors (under 600 volts) are performed based on the size and numbers of raceways ≫ *314.28* ≪.

B Boxes or conduit bodies containing straight pulls are sized according to the largest raceway entering the box. The length must be at least eight times the trade size (metric designator) of the largest raceway ≫ *314.28(A)(1)* ≪.

N O T E

Use the trade dimension that is applicable to the installation. For example, if millimeters or centimeters are needed to size the junction or pull box, use the metric designator in millimeters instead of the trade size in inches. A junction box is needed for a straight pull with two metric designator 53 raceways. (A 2-in. trade size raceway has a metric designator of 53 mm.) Calculate the minimum length by multiplying the metric designation by eight (53 mm × 8 = 424 mm = 42.4 cm). The minimum size pull box required is 424 mm or 42.4 cm.

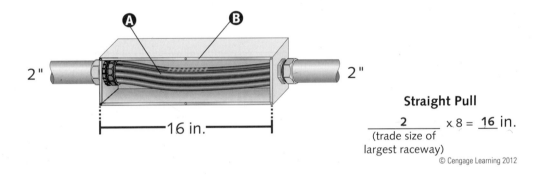

Straight Pull

$$\frac{2}{\text{(trade size of largest raceway)}} \times 8 = \underline{16}\text{ in.}$$

© Cengage Learning 2012

WIDTH AND DEPTH OF THE BOX

A The box width must be large enough to provide proper installation of the raceway or cable, including locknuts and bushings.

B The box depth must be large enough to provide proper installation of the raceway or cable, including locknuts and bushings.

C No requirement specifies the depth of the box, unless a raceway enters the back of the box.

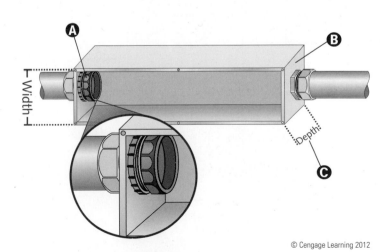

© Cengage Learning 2012

Straight Pull—Multiple Raceways

Ⓐ The length must be at least eight times the trade size (metric designator) of the largest single raceway. No extra space is required for additional raceways when calculating the minimum length of straight pulls. However, additional space is needed for the width of additional raceways, including locknuts and bushings ⟫*314.28(A)(1)*⟪.

Ⓑ Conduit bodies and boxes (junction, pull, and outlet) must be installed so that the wiring they contain can be made accessible without removing any part of the building ⟫*314.29*⟪.

> **CAUTION**
>
> Except as permitted in 250.112(l), all metal boxes shall be grounded and bonded in accordance with Parts I, IV, V, VI, VII, and X of Article 250 as applicable ⟫*314.4*⟪.

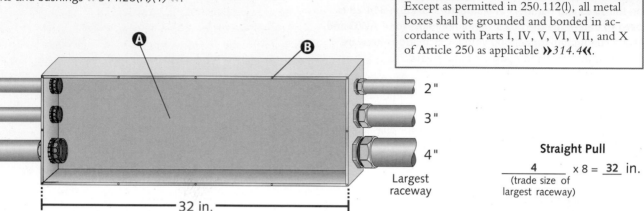

Straight Pull

$$\frac{4}{\text{(trade size of largest raceway)}} \times 8 = \underline{32}\ \text{in.}$$

© Cengage Learning 2012

Angle Pull (or Splices)—Multiple Raceways

Ⓐ Where splices or where angle or U pulls are made, the distance between each raceway entry into the box and the opposite wall must be at least six times the trade size (metric designator) of the largest raceway in a row. This distance is increased for additional raceway entries (in the same row on the same wall of the box) by the sum of the diameters of all other raceway entries ⟫*314.28(A)(2)*⟪.

Ⓑ To calculate the dimension of a box with angle pulls, start with one wall where the raceways enter the box, and find the distance to the opposite wall of the box. The path of the conductors is irrelevant to this calculation.

Ⓒ Pick one wall and multiply the largest raceway (trade diameter) by 6. Add to that number the trade diameter of all other raceway(s) in the same row, on the same side of the box.

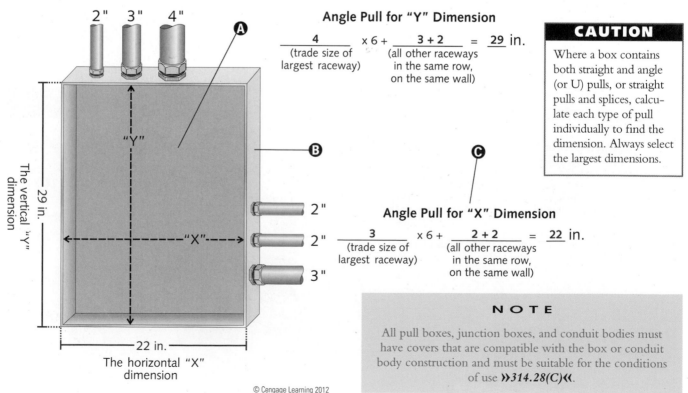

Angle Pull for "Y" Dimension

$$\frac{4}{\substack{\text{(trade size of} \\ \text{largest raceway)}}} \times 6 + \frac{3+2}{\substack{\text{(all other raceways} \\ \text{in the same row,} \\ \text{on the same wall)}}} = \underline{29}\ \text{in.}$$

Angle Pull for "X" Dimension

$$\frac{3}{\substack{\text{(trade size of} \\ \text{largest raceway)}}} \times 6 + \frac{2+2}{\substack{\text{(all other raceways} \\ \text{in the same row,} \\ \text{on the same wall)}}} = \underline{22}\ \text{in.}$$

> **CAUTION**
>
> Where a box contains both straight and angle (or U) pulls, or straight pulls and splices, calculate each type of pull individually to find the dimension. Always select the largest dimensions.

> **NOTE**
>
> All pull boxes, junction boxes, and conduit bodies must have covers that are compatible with the box or conduit body construction and must be suitable for the conditions of use ⟫*314.28(C)*⟪.

© Cengage Learning 2012

Raceways Enclosing the Same Conductors

The distance between raceway entries enclosing the same conductor shall not be less than six times the trade size (metric designator) of the largest raceway ❯❯*314.28(A)(2)*❮❮. This provision is applicable even if the raceway entries are on different walls.

A Because no other raceways enter on the same wall of the box, no additional raceway diameters are added.

B The minimum dimension required for this box is 12 in. × 12 in. The distance between the raceway entries must not be less than six times the trade size of the larger raceway. Because each raceway is located in the center of the wall of the box, the distance between the raceway entries is less than 12 in. Therefore, this installation is not permitted.

C This 12 in. × 12 in. junction (or pull) box is permitted if the raceways can be installed so the distance between the raceway entries is at least 12 in. Because the distance between the raceway entries is 12 in., this installation is permitted.

Angle pull for "X" Dimension

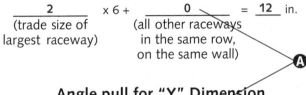

$$\frac{2}{\text{(trade size of largest raceway)}} \times 6 + \frac{0}{\text{(all other raceways in the same row, on the same wall)}} = \underline{12} \text{ in.}$$

A

Angle pull for "Y" Dimension

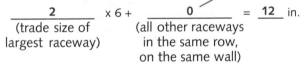

$$\frac{2}{\text{(trade size of largest raceway)}} \times 6 + \frac{0}{\text{(all other raceways in the same row, on the same wall)}} = \underline{12} \text{ in.}$$

Raceways Enclosing the Same Conductors

$$\frac{2}{\text{(trade size of larger raceway)}} \times 6 = \underline{12} \text{ in.}$$

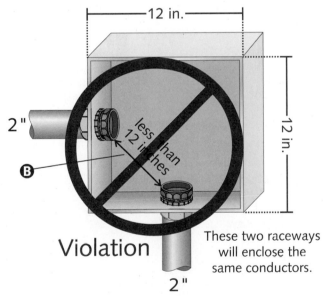

⎯ 12 in. ⎯

2"

less than 12 inches

12 in.

B

Violation

2"

These two raceways will enclose the same conductors.

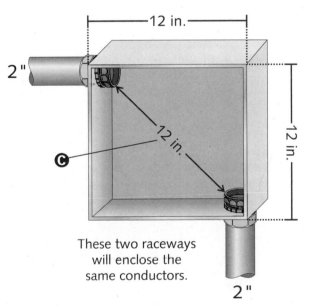

⎯ 12 in. ⎯

2"

12 in.

12 in.

C

2"

These two raceways will enclose the same conductors.

Conductors in these boxes will be larger than 6 AWG.

© Cengage Learning 2012

Angle Pull—Multiple Rows

Ⓐ Where multiple rows of raceways enter a box, calculate each row separately. Use the single row that provides the maximum distance ≫ *314.28(A)(2)* ≪.

Ⓑ Create an imaginary divider line separating each row.

Ⓒ Perform each row calculation as if in a separate box.

Angle Pull for "Y" Dimension (Back Row)

$$\underset{\substack{\text{(trade size of}\\\text{largest raceway)}}}{4} \times 6 + \underset{\substack{\text{(all other raceways,}\\\text{in the same row,}\\\text{on the same wall)}}}{3\frac{1}{2} + 3\frac{1}{2}} = \underline{31} \text{ in.}$$

Angle Pull for "Y" Dimension (Front Row)

$$\underset{\substack{\text{(trade size of}\\\text{largest raceway)}}}{3\frac{1}{2}} \times 6 + \underset{\substack{\text{(all other raceways,}\\\text{in the same row,}\\\text{on the same wall)}}}{3 + 3 + 2\frac{1}{2} + 2\frac{1}{2}} = \underline{32} \text{ in.}$$

Angle Pull for "X" Dimension (Back Row)

$$\underset{\substack{\text{(trade size of}\\\text{largest raceway)}}}{4} \times 6 + \underset{\substack{\text{(all other raceways,}\\\text{in the same row,}\\\text{on the same wall)}}}{4 + 4} = \underline{32} \text{ in.}$$

Angle Pull for "X" Dimension (Front Row)

$$\underset{\substack{\text{(trade size of}\\\text{largest raceway)}}}{3\frac{1}{2}} \times 6 + \underset{\substack{\text{(all other raceways,}\\\text{in the same row,}\\\text{on the same wall)}}}{3 + 3 + 2 + 2} = \underline{32} \text{ in.}$$

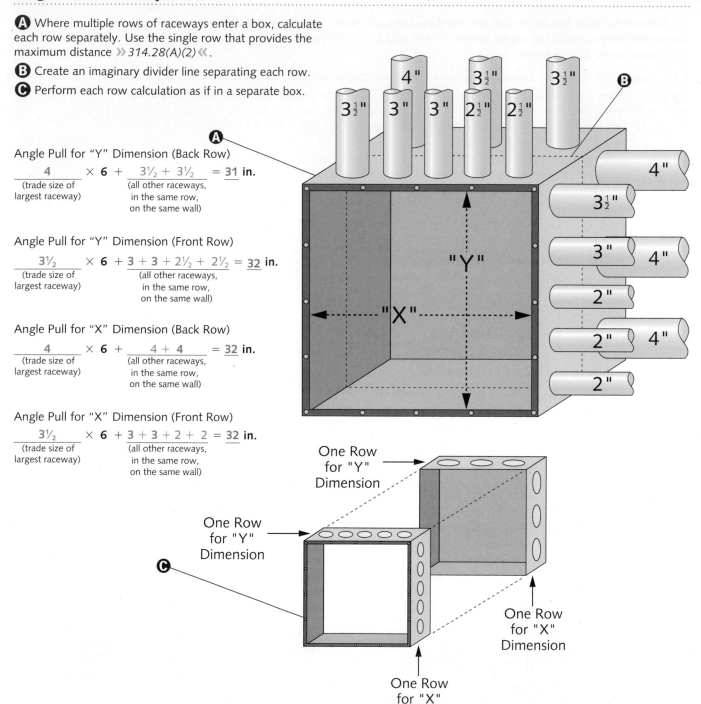

NOTE

In pull or junction boxes having any dimension over 6 ft (1.8 m), all conductors shall be cabled (or racked) in an approved manner ≫ *314.28(B)* ≪.

U Pull—Two Raceways

Ⓐ Use the angle pull method to calculate U pulls. A box with conduit entries only on one wall has a minimum distance to the opposite wall. Multiply the largest raceway by six and add the sum of the trade size (metric designator) of the other raceway(s) entering the same wall ≫*314.28(A)(2)*≪.

Ⓑ The minimum box width must include 12 in. between raceways plus the thickness of the two raceways (including enough area to provide proper installation of locknuts and bushings).

Ⓒ The distance between raceways enclosing the same conductor(s) must be at least six times the trade size (metric designator) of the largest raceway ≫*314.28(A)(2)*≪.

> ### NOTE
>
> Insulated circuit conductors (4 AWG and larger) entering a cabinet, box, enclosure, or raceway from another raceway must be fitted with a substantial, smoothly rounded insulating surface, except where the conductors are insulated from the fitting or raceway by a securely fastened-in-place material (such as a plastic bushing) ≫*300.4(G)*≪.

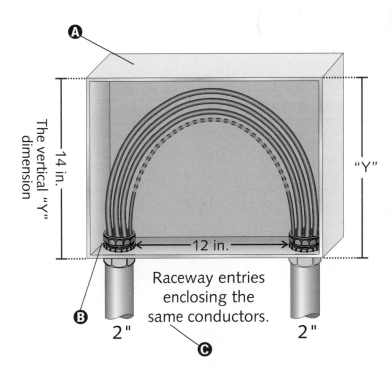

Raceway entries enclosing the same conductors.

U Pull for "Y" Dimension

$$\frac{2}{\text{(trade size of largest raceway)}} \times 6 + \frac{2}{\substack{\text{(all other raceways} \\ \text{in the same row,} \\ \text{on the same wall)}}} = \underline{14} \text{ in.}$$

Raceways Enclosing the Same Conductors

$$\frac{2}{\text{(trade size of larger raceway)}} \times 6 = \underline{12} \text{ in.}$$

© Cengage Learning 2012

Raceways Entering Opposite Removable Covers

Ⓐ Where angle pulls are made, the distance between each raceway entry into the box and the opposite wall of the box must be at least six times the trade size (metric designator) of the largest raceway ≫*314.28(A)(2)*≪. Where no other raceways enter the same wall of the box, no additional raceway diameters are added.

Ⓑ Where a raceway or cable enters the wall of a box (or conduit body) opposite a removable cover, the distance from the entry wall to the cover can be determined by the distance requirements for one wire per terminal found in Table 312.6(A) ≫*314.28(A)(2) Exception*≪.

Ⓒ The minimum distance between raceways enclosing the same conductor(s) is six times the trade size (metric designator) of the largest raceway ≫*314.28(A)(2)*≪.

Raceways or Cables Entering Boxes Opposite from Removable Covers		
Wire Size (AWG or kcmil)	Minimum Distance from Wall to Cover	
	in.	mm
4–3	2	50.8
2	2½	63.5
1	3	76.2
1/0–2/0	3½	88.9
3/0–4/0	4	102
250	4½	114
300–350	5	127
400–500	6	152
600–700	8	203
750–900	8	203
1000–1250	10	254
1500–2000	12	305

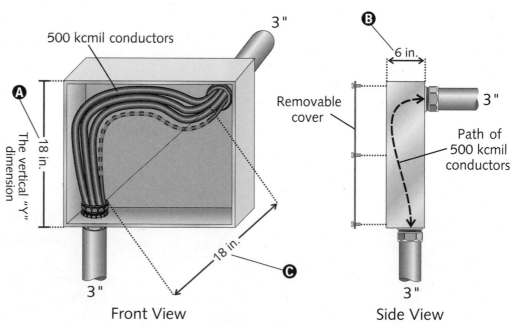

Front View

Side View

Angle Pull for "Y" Dimension

$$\underline{\quad 3 \quad} \times 6 + \underline{\quad 0 \quad} = \underline{\quad 18 \quad}\ \text{in.}$$
(trade size of largest raceway)   (all other raceways in the same row, on the same wall)

Raceways Enclosing the Same Conductors

$$\underline{\quad 3 \quad} \times 6 = \underline{\quad 18 \quad}\ \text{in.}$$
(trade size of larger raceway)

Boxes and Conduit Bodies Not Meeting 314.28 and Chapter 9

Ⓐ Smaller-size conduit bodies can generally hold the same number and sizes of conductors (6 AWG and smaller) as the raceway entering the conduit body. Conduit bodies (and boxes) are manufactured that are smaller than those required by 314.28(A)(1) and (2). These may be used if approved and permanently marked showing the maximum number and size conductors allowed »*314.28(A)(3)*«.

Ⓑ Three 250 kcmil conductors are the maximum number and size permitted in this conduit body.

Ⓒ According to Chapter 9 and Table C8, four 500 kcmil THHN conductors can be installed in a 3-in. rigid metal conduit.

Ⓓ If a conduit body is durably and legibly marked by the manufacturer with the volume, it can contain splices, taps, or devices »*314.16(C)(2)*«.

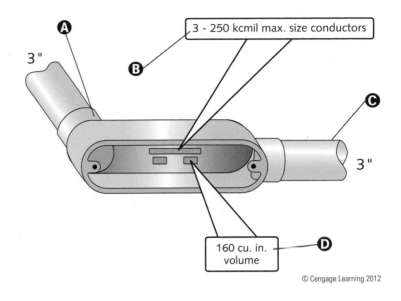

3 - 250 kcmil max. size conductors

160 cu. in. volume

© Cengage Learning 2012

WARNING

Conduit bodies do not have to be large enough to contain the same size and number of conductors permitted in the raceway that enters the conduit body. Some conduit bodies are marked with the maximum size and number of conductors.

Summary

- Limitations apply to the size and number of conductors permitted in boxes (junction, pull, etc.) and conduit bodies.
- One strap (yoke) counts as two of the largest conductors connected to the device.
- Nonmetallic boxes may list the maximum number of conductors permitted in the box, but that number must be reduced if switches, receptacles, etc. are installed in the box.
- Plaster rings, raised covers, extension rings, etc. can provide additional cubic-inch capacity to boxes.
- Conduit bodies can contain splices, taps, or devices if the conduit body is durably and legibly marked by the manufacturer with the volume.
- The minimum length of free conductor (6 in. [150 mm]) is measured from the point in the box where it emerges from its raceway or cable sheath.

- Except as permitted in 250.112(l), all metal boxes shall be grounded and bonded in accordance with Parts I, IV, V, VI, VII, and X of Article 250 as applicable.
- Boxes and conduit bodies must remain accessible.
- In suspended ceilings, boxes can be secured by support wires that are installed in addition to the ceiling grid support wires.
- Where boxes enclose 4 AWG and larger conductors that are required to be insulated, different calculation methods apply to straight pulls than to angle pulls.
- There is a minimum distance required between raceways enclosing the same conductors (4 AWG and larger) within a pull or junction box.
- Conduit bodies may not allow the same size and number of conductors as is permitted in the conduit (or tubing) that enters the conduit body.

Unit 3 Competency Test

NEC Reference	Answer

_____   _____   1. In pull boxes or junction boxes having any dimension over _____ in., all conductors shall be cabled or racked up in an approved manner.

         a) 6 b) 12 c) 36 d) 72

_____   _____   2. A nonmetallic extension can be run in any direction from an existing outlet, but shall not be run on the floor or within _____ in. from the floor.

_____   _____   3. What are the minimum dimensions for "X" and "Y" in the drawing below?

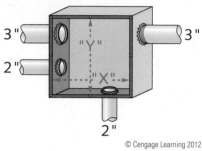

© Cengage Learning 2012

_____   _____   4. Outlet boxes that do not enclose devices or utilization equipment shall have a minimum internal depth of _____ in.

_____   _____   5. A 4¹¹⁄₁₆-in. square box that is 2⅛ in. deep already contains two receptacles, two internal cable clamps, four 12 AWG THHN copper conductors (two black and two white), two grounding conductors, three wire nuts, two pigtails, and one equipment bonding jumper. (A flat plaster ring was used to secure the receptacles to the box.) How many more 12 AWG THHN copper conductors can be added to this box?

_____   _____   6. In damp or wet locations, surface type enclosures (within the scope of Article 312) shall be so placed or equipped as to prevent moisture or water from entering and accumulating within the cabinet or cutout box and shall be mounted so there is at least _____ in. airspace between the enclosure and the wall or other supporting surface.

_____   _____   7. The minimum thickness in inches for a steel box measuring 6 in. × 4 in. × 3½ in. is _____ in. thick.

_____   _____   8. Covers of outlet boxes and conduit bodies having holes through which flexible cord pendants may pass shall be provided with approved _____ or shall have smooth, well-rounded surfaces on which the cord may bear.

_____   _____   9. A weatherproof metal junction box measuring 4 in. × 4 in. × 6 in. has been installed to support a luminaire. Two rigid metal conduits have been threaded wrenchtight into the threaded entries of the enclosure. The box has not yet been secured to the brick wall, but both conduits have been strapped to the wall 16 in. from the box. What additional support (from the following list) is required for this box?

    I. Two metal screws with plastic anchors

    II. Two toggle bolts

    III. Two drive pins

        a) none b) I or II only c) I or III only d) I, II, or III

NEC **Reference**   **Answer**

_____ _____ 10. Where permanent barriers are installed in a junction box, each section shall be considered as a(n) _____.

_____ _____ 11. What is the maximum number of 12 AWG THW conductors permitted in a 4-in. octagon box that is 1½ in. deep? (The box contains a fixture stud and a hickey.)

_____ _____ 12. A means must be provided in each metal box for the connection of a(n) _____.

_____ _____ 13. In walls or ceiling of noncombustible material, boxes shall be installed so that the front edge of the box will not be set back of the finished surface more than _____ in.

_____ _____ 14. Nonmetallic boxes shall be suitable for the lowest _____ conductor entering the box.

_____ _____ 15. An electrician needs to install a surface-mounted, nonmetallic, weatherproof cabinet on the outside of a concrete block building. Since the cabinet must be mounted in a wet location, it must be mounted so there is at least _____ in. of airspace between the cabinet and the wall.

_____ _____ 16. How many 14 AWG THW conductors are permitted in a 3 in. × 2 in. × 2½ in. device box?

_____ _____ 17. Nonmetallic surface extensions must be secured in place by approved means at intervals not exceeding _____ in.

_____ _____ 18. A 2½-in. rigid metal conduit enters the back of a pull box with a removable cover on the opposite side. The raceway encloses four 4/0 AWG THHN copper conductors and one 4 AWG equipment grounding conductor. The minimum depth (distance from the entry wall to the cover) for this pull box is _____ in.

_____ _____ 19. Where nonmetallic boxes are used with open wiring or concealed knob-and-tube wiring, the conductors must enter the box through _____.

_____ _____ 20. Luminaires weighing no more than _____ pounds can be supported by boxes (such as device boxes) not specifically designed to support luminaires, provided the luminaire, or its supporting yoke, is secured to the box with at least two No. 6 or larger screws.

_____ _____ 21. For straight pulls, the length of the box shall not be less than _____ the outside diameter, over sheath, of the largest shielded conductor or cable entering the box on systems over 600 volts, nominal.

U N I T 4

Cables

Objectives

After studying this unit, the student should:

▶ know that cables must be installed at least 1¼ in. (32 mm) from the nearest edge of wood framing members, unless a steel plate (or bushing) has been installed.

▶ understand that nonmetallic-sheathed cable passing through metal framing must be protected by bushings (or grommets) covering all metal edges.

▶ be aware that openings around electrical penetrations through fire-resistant-rated construction must be sealed using approved methods to maintain the fire-resistant rating.

▶ be able to determine what cables are permitted in spaces used for environmental air-handling purposes.

▶ know the support requirements for MC, AC, and nonmetallic-sheathed cable.

▶ be aware that a minimum bending radius must be maintained with cables.

▶ understand that cables must be protected from physical damage.

▶ be familiar with both general and specific installation provisions for MC, AC, and nonmetallic-sheathed cable.

▶ understand conductor identification and the permissible reidentification of certain conductors.

▶ have a good grasp of underground installation provisions.

▶ be introduced to flat conductor, integrated gas-spacer, mineral-insulated, and medium-voltage cables.

Introduction

Unit 4 contains regulations for cable systems that are used often (such as metal-clad cable and nonmetallic-sheathed cable), as well as cable systems that are used rarely (such as integrated gas-spacer cable and flat conductor cable). A key provision found in most of the cable articles (and some of the raceway articles) states that the cable (or raceway) must not be installed where subject to physical damage. Cable protection can be achieved by several methods, including installing the cable a minimum distance from the outside edge of a framing member; installing a steel plate over the cable; or installing the cable in an approved raceway system. Cables installed in attics have different provisions depending on the type of attic entrance. Minimum support distances (from box or enclosure to the first support, or between supports) are included in this unit. Conductor identification (and permissible reidentification) for cables is also presented in this unit.

The cable articles, found in Chapter 3 of the *NEC* have sections titled "Uses Permitted" and "Uses Not Permitted." These sections (*XXX.10* and *XXX.12*) give locations (some specific) where the cable system can (or cannot) be installed. Since most of these provisions are clearly understandable, this book does not repeat much of this information. Also, be aware that state and local jurisdictions restrict the usage of certain cables in some (if not all) types of occupancies.

GENERAL INSTALLATION

Setback for Bored Holes

A Holes must be bored so that the edge of the hole is at least 1¼ in. (32 mm) from the nearest edge of the wood member »*300.4(A)(1)*«.

B The 1¼-in. (32-mm) setback applies to all locations (concealed and exposed).

C The 1¼-in. (32-mm) setback applies to studs, joists, rafters, etc.

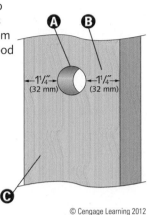

© Cengage Learning 2012

N O T E

The largest hole that can be bored in a 3½-in. wood stud without using a steel plate (clip or sleeve) is 1 in. (provided the drill bit cuts straight through the center of the stud). The 1¼-in. (32-mm) setback must be maintained from both edges (front and back); 3½ in. minus 2½ in. (1¼ setback, two edges) leaves a remainder of 1 in.

Metal Framing Members

A Nonmetallic-sheathed cable passing through holes (or slots) in metal framing must be protected by listed bushings (or grommets) covering all metal edges and securely fastened in the opening prior to cable installation »*300.4(B)(1)*«.

B Section 300.4 applies to all locations (concealed and exposed).

C Openings (slots or holes) can be punched (either factory or field), cut, or drilled into the metal members »*300.4(B)(1)*«.

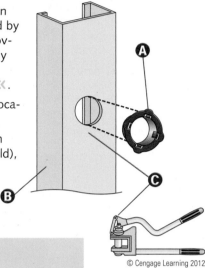

© Cengage Learning 2012

N O T E

Where nails (or screws) are likely to penetrate nonmetallic-sheathed cable (or electrical nonmetallic tubing), a steel plate (clip or sleeve) at least 1/16 in. (1.6 mm) thick shall be used to protect the cable or tubing »***300.4(B)(2)***«.

Steel Plates

A Where the bored hole is less than 1¼ in. (32 mm) from the edge, the cable (or raceway-type wiring method) shall be protected by a steel plate(s) or bushing(s) from penetration by screws or nails »*300.4(A)(1)*«.

B Cables, installed in a groove, covered by wallboard, paneling, carpeting, etc., shall be protected by 1/16-in. (1.6-mm) thick steel plate, sleeve, or equivalent or by at least 1¼ in. (32 mm) free space for the full length of the groove in which the cable is installed »*300.4(F)*«.

C Where there is no potential of weakening building structure, cables (or raceways) can be laid within notches in wood studs, joists, rafters, etc. »*300.4(A)(2)*«.

D The steel plate(s) or bushing(s) must be at least 1/16 in. (1.6 mm) thick and of appropriate length and width to adequately cover the wiring »*300.4(A)(1)*«.

E The steel plate must be at least 1/16 in. (1.6 mm) thick and of appropriate length and width installed to cover the area of the wiring. The steel plate must be installed before the building finish is installed »*300.4(A)(2)*«.

F Requirements for notched wood members apply to all locations (concealed and exposed).

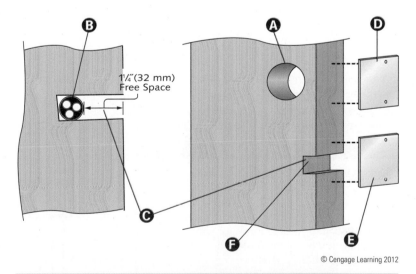

1¼" (32 mm) Free Space

© Cengage Learning 2012

N O T E

A listed and marked steel plate that provides equal or better protection against nail or screw penetration shall be permitted, even if it is less than 1/16 in. (1.6 mm) thick »***300.4(A)(2) Exception No. 2***«.

Parallel to Framing Members and Furring Strips

Ⓐ Cables installed parallel to framing members (studs, joists, etc.) or installed parallel to furring strips shall be installed and supported so that the nearest outside surface of the cable is at least 1¼ in. (32 mm) from the nearest edge of the framing member or furring strip where nails (or screws) are likely to penetrate »300.4(D)«.

Ⓑ If a 1¼-in. (32-mm) setback is not possible, the cable must be protected from penetration by nails (or screws) by a minimum ¹⁄₁₆-in. (1.6-mm) thick steel plate (sleeve, etc.) »300.4(D)«. A listed and marked steel plate less than ¹⁄₁₆ in. (1.6 mm) thick that provides equal or better protection against nail or screw penetration can be installed »300.4(D) Exception No. 3«.

> **NOTE**
>
> For concealed work in finished buildings or finished panels for prefabricated buildings, where such support is impracticable, cables can be fished between access points »***300.4(D) Exception No. 2***«.

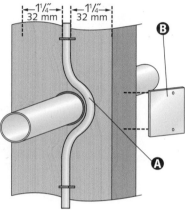

© Cengage Learning 2012

Maintaining the Integrity of Fire-Resistant-Rated Construction

Ⓐ Electrical installation openings that penetrate into or through fire-resistant-rated structures (walls, partitions, floors, ceilings, etc.) must be firestopped using approved methods that maintain the fire-resistance rating »300.21«.

> **CAUTION**
>
> Some state and local jurisdictions may require that all penetrations (fire-rated and non-fire-rated) be sealed.

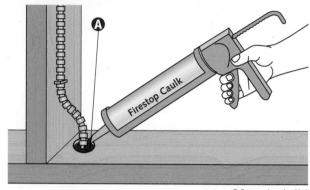

© Cengage Learning 2012

> **NOTE**
>
> In hollow spaces, vertical shafts, and ventilation (or air-handling) ducts, electrical installations must not substantially increase the possible spread of fire or products of combustion »***300.21***«.

Wiring in Ducts, Plenums, and Other Air-Handling Spaces

Ⓐ Only Type MI and MC cables, employing a smooth or corrugated impervious metal sheath without an overall nonmetallic covering, can be installed in ducts specifically fabricated to transport environmental air »300.22(B)«. Section 300.22(B) also lists other raceways permitted in ducts of this type.

Ⓑ Section 300.22(C) applies to spaces not specifically fabricated for environmental air-handling purposes but used for air-handling purposes as a plenum. This section shall not apply to habitable rooms or areas of buildings, the prime purpose of

> **CAUTION**
>
> Ducts used to transport dust, loose stock, or flammable vapors shall not contain wiring systems of any type. No wiring system (of any type) shall be installed within a duct or shaft containing only such ducts used for vapor removal or for ventilation of commercial-grade cooking equipment »***300.22(A)***«.

> **NOTE**
>
> Metallic manufactured wiring systems (without nonmetallic sheath) having listed prefabricated cable assemblies are permitted in this type of installation »***300.22(C)(1)***«.

which is not air handling. Types AC, MI, MC (without an overall nonmetallic covering), or other factory-assembled multiconductor cables (control or power) listed specifically for the use within an air-handling space must be installed in these spaces. All other types of cables and conductors must be installed in one of the raceways (or wireways) named in 300.22(C)(1).

Ⓒ The space over a suspended ceiling used for environmental air-handling purposes is an example of the type of other space to which 300.22(C) applies »300.22(C) Informational Note No. 1«.

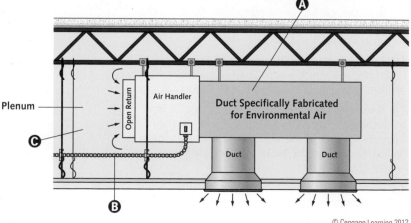

© Cengage Learning 2012

Wiring within Air-Handling Spaces in Dwelling Units

Ⓐ Section 300.22 does not apply to **dwelling unit** joist or stud spaces where wiring passes perpendicular to the long dimension of such spaces ⟫*300.22(C) Exception*⟪.

Ⓑ Conductors must remain at least 1¼ in. (32 mm) from the nearest edge of a wood member ⟫*300.4(A)(1)*⟪.

Ⓒ Joist or stud spaces, used for environmental air-handling purposes, shall not contain nonmetallic-sheathed cable that runs along the long dimension.

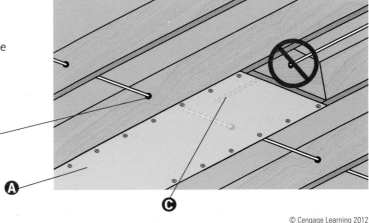

© Cengage Learning 2012

Securing Cables

Generally, all cables must be secured to the box, cabinet, etc. ⟫*314.17(B) and (C)*⟪.

Staples, cable ties, straps, etc. must be designed to secure cables and shall be installed so that cables are not damaged.

Ⓐ Type MC cable must be supported and secured at intervals not exceeding 6 ft (1.8 m) ⟫*330.30*⟪.

Ⓑ Type AC cable must be supported and secured at intervals not exceeding 4½ ft (1.4 m) ⟫*320.30*⟪.

Ⓒ Nonmetallic-sheathed cable must be supported and secured at intervals not exceeding 4½ ft (1.4 m) ⟫*334.30*⟪.

Ⓓ Type MC cables containing no more than four conductors, size 10 AWG or smaller, must be secured within 12 in. (300 mm) of every box, cabinet, fitting, etc. ⟫*330.30*⟪.

Ⓔ Type AC cable must be secured within 12 in. (300 mm) of every box, cabinet, or fitting ⟫*320.30*⟪.

Ⓕ Nonmetallic-sheathed cable (secured to the box) must be secured within 12 in. (300 mm) of every box, cabinet, or fitting ⟫*334.30*⟪.

Ⓖ Nonmetallic-sheathed cable *not* secured to a single-gang box must be secured within 8 in. (200 mm) ⟫*314.17(C) Exception*⟪.

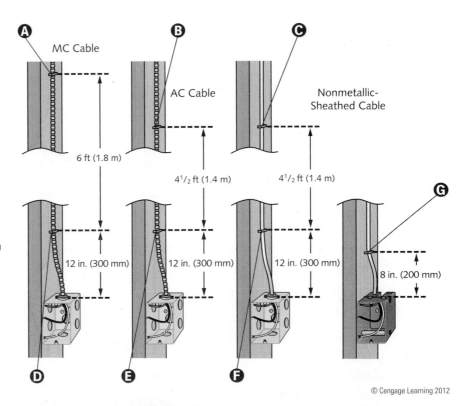

© Cengage Learning 2012

NOTE

Cables fished between access points, where concealed in finished buildings (or structures) and where support is impracticable, can remain unsupported and unsecured ⟫*320.30(D)(1), 330.30(D)(1), and 334.30(B)(1)*⟪.

Cables Passing through Framing Members

A Cables running horizontally (or diagonally) are considered supported and secured when passing through a framing member (wood, metal, etc.), unless the support intervals exceed those listed for the specified cable. Cables installed in notches and protected by a ¹⁄₁₆-in. (1.6-mm) steel plate are also considered secured »320.30(A), 330.30(A), and 334.30(A)«.

B Cables must be secured within 12 in. (300 mm) of every box, cabinet, fitting, etc.

C This cable is not "secured." The support interval exceeds the maximum distance permitted.

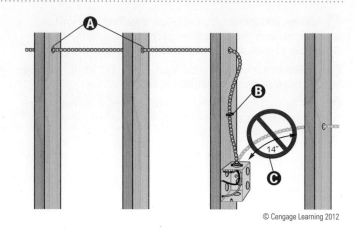

© Cengage Learning 2012

Attics without Permanent Stairs or Ladders

A Attics and roof spaces not accessible by permanent stairs or ladders require protection only within 6 ft (1.8 m) of the nearest edge of the scuttle hole or attic entrance »320.23(A), 330.23, and 334.23«.

B Protection is required for cables located within 6 ft (1.8 m) (measured both vertically and horizontally) of the attic entrance.

© Cengage Learning 2012

Bending Radius

Type AC cable must have a bending radius at least five times the diameter of the cable »320.24«.

Type MC cable (interlocked-type or corrugated sheath) has a bending radius of seven times the external diameter of the metallic sheath »330.24(B)«.

Nonmetallic-sheathed cable has a minimum bending radius of five times the cable diameter »334.24«.

A A curve radius is measured from the inner edge of the bend.

Example: If the outside diameter of Type MC cable (interlocked-type) is ½ (0.5) in. (13 mm), then the radius will need a measurement of 3½ in. (89 mm) (0.5 in. × 7 = 3.5 in.).

CAUTION

All bends shall be made so that the cable will not be damaged.

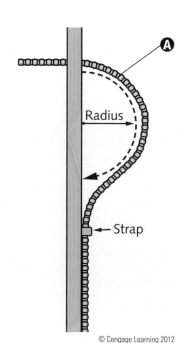

© Cengage Learning 2012

Attics with Permanent Stairs or Ladders

A Cables within 7 ft (2.1 m) of the floor (or floor joist) can run through the studs if meetng the requirements of 300.4(D). Cables more than 7 ft (2.1 m) above the floor (or floor joist) can run across the face of framing members.

B If cables are installed across the face of rafters or studding and they are located within 7 ft (2.1 m) of the floor (or floor joist) in attics or roof spaces that are accessible, the cable must be protected by substantial guard strips that are at least as high as the cable ≫*320.23(A)*≪.

C Cables running across the top of floor joists must be protected by substantial guard strips that are of sufficient height to adequately protect the cable ≫*320.23(A)*≪.

D Cable installed parallel to the sides of rafters, studs, or floor joists does not require guard strips or running boards; however, the installation must also comply with 300.4(D) ≫*320.23(B)*≪.

E Cables not installed on the face (or surface) do not require guard strips or running boards.

F Cables installed in attics (and roof spaces) accessible by permanent stairs (or ladders) must meet 320.23 provisions.

> **NOTE**
> Type MC cable and nonmetallic-sheathed cable must also comply with 320.23 ≫*330.23* and *334.23*≪.

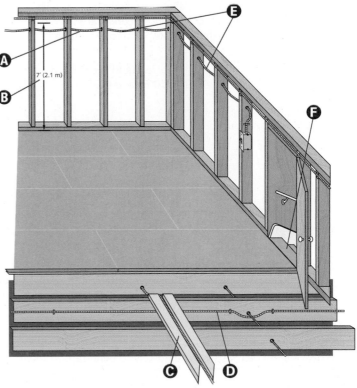

© Cengage Learning 2012

Insulating (Antishort) Bushings

A All armor termination points of AC cable shall have a fitting to protect the wires from abrasion, unless the outlet boxes (or fittings) are designed to afford equivalent protection. In addition, an insulating bushing (or its equivalent protection) shall be provided between the conductors and the armor ≫*320.40*≪.

B Type AC cable shall have a flexible metal tape armor ≫*320.100*≪.

C The connector or clamp that fastens Type AC cable to boxes or cabinets must be designed so that the insulating bushing (or its equivalent) is visible for inspections ≫*320.40*≪.

D Type AC cables shall have an internal bonding strip (copper or aluminum) in intimate contact with the armor for its entire length ≫*320.100*≪.

E Some insulating (antishort) bushings are manufactured so that part of the bushing extends past the connector or clamp (once installed), effectively acting as a flag. This flag increases the visibility of the bushing after installation.

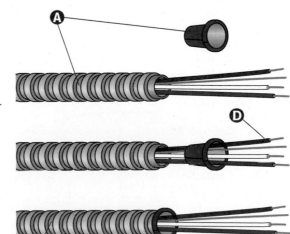
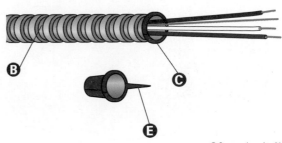

> **NOTE**
> Insulating bushings in Type MC cable are optional rather than required. Although Article 330 does not require an insulating bushing between the conductors and the armor, it is a good practice to use one.

> **NOTE**
> Fittings used for connecting Type MC cable to boxes, cabinets, or other equipment shall be listed and identified for such use ≫*330.40*≪.

© Cengage Learning 2012

Exposed Runs of Type AC and MC Cables under Joists

Ⓐ Exposed runs of Type AC cable installed on the underside of joists must be supported (and secured) at *every* joist and must be located so that physical damage is avoided ≫*320.15*≪.

Ⓑ Type MC cable must be supported (and secured) at intervals of 6 ft (1.8 m) or less ≫*330.30(B)* and *(C)*≪.

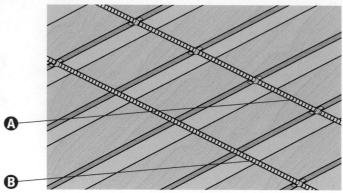

© Cengage Learning 2012

Exposed Nonmetallic-Sheathed Cable in Unfinished Basements and Crawl Spaces

Ⓐ Exposed nonmetallic-sheathed cable (smaller than 8 AWG if three-conductor or 6 AWG if two-conductor) running at angles with joists in unfinished basements and crawl spaces must either be run through bored holes in the joists or on running boards ≫*334.15(C)*≪.

Ⓑ The nearest outside surface of installed and supported cable must be at least 1¼ in. (32 mm) from the nearest edge of the framing member where nails or screws are likely to penetrate ≫*300.4(A)(1)*≪.

Ⓒ Three-conductor 8 AWG, or two-conductor 6 AWG, or larger, can be secured directly to the lower edges of the joists ≫*334.15(C)*≪.

Ⓓ Where current-carrying conductors in multiconductor cables are bundled or stacked longer than 24 in. (600 mm) without maintaining spacing, reduce the allowable ampacity of each conductor as shown in Table 310.15(B)(3)(a) ≫*310.15(B)(3)(a)*≪.

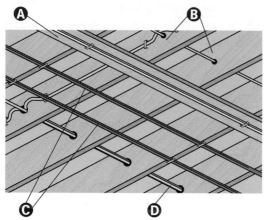

© Cengage Learning 2012

Exposed Nonmetallic-Sheathed Cable Passing through a Floor

Cables entering or exiting conduit (or tubing) used for support or protection against physical damage require fittings on the conduit (or tubing) ends to prevent cable abrasion ≫*300.15(C)*≪.

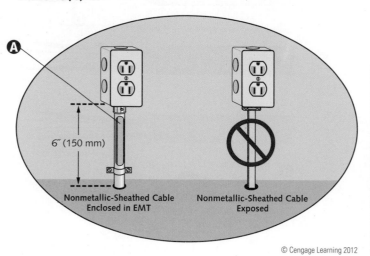

Nonmetallic-Sheathed Cable
Enclosed in EMT

Nonmetallic-Sheathed Cable
Exposed

6″ (150 mm)

© Cengage Learning 2012

Ⓐ Nonmetallic-sheathed cable passing through a floor must be enclosed in rigid (or intermediate) metal conduit, electrical metallic tubing, Schedule 80 PVC conduit, Type RTRC marked with the suffix -XW, or other approved means that extends at least 6 in. (150 mm) above the floor ≫*334.15(B)*≪.

NOTE

Raceway (or cable) openings in a fire-resistant-rated floor must be firestopped using approved methods to maintain the fire-resistance rating ≫*300.21*≪.

If subject to physical damage, conductors, raceways, and cables must be protected ≫*300.4*≪. Nonmetallic-sheathed cable can be protected by rigid (or intermediate) metal conduit, electrical metallic tubing, Schedule 80 PVC conduit, Type RTRC marked with the suffix -XW, or other approved means ≫*334.15(B)*≪.

CONDUCTOR IDENTIFICATION

General Conductor Identification Provisions

Ⓐ Generally, a conductor with a continuous white or gray covering shall be used only as a grounded-circuit conductor ≫ *200.7* ≪.

Ⓑ Equipment grounding conductors can be bare, covered, or insulated. Individually covered (or insulated) equipment grounding conductors must have a continuous outer finish that is either green or green with yellow stripe(s) ≫ *250.119* ≪.

Ⓒ Conductors used as ungrounded (hot) conductors, whether single conductors or in multiconductor cables, must be finished in a way that clearly distinguishes them from grounded and grounding conductors ≫ *310.110(C)* ≪. Ungrounded (hot) conductors (except for a **high-leg** conductor) can be any color other than white, gray, green, or green with yellow stripe(s).

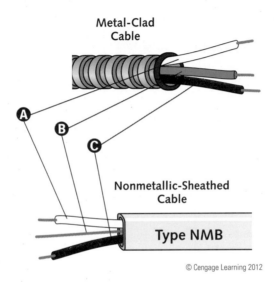

Metal-Clad Cable

Nonmetallic-Sheathed Cable

Type NMB

© Cengage Learning 2012

Three-Phase Conductor Identification

Ⓐ Generally, ungrounded (hot) conductors can be any color except white, gray, green, or green with yellow stripe(s). A widely accepted practice is to identify 3-phase ungrounded (hot) conductors as black, red, and blue in 208/120 volt, 4-wire, wye-connected systems; and brown, orange, and yellow in 480/277 volt, 4-wire, wye-connected systems.

Ⓑ Interlocking-armor Type MC cable requires an equipment grounding conductor.

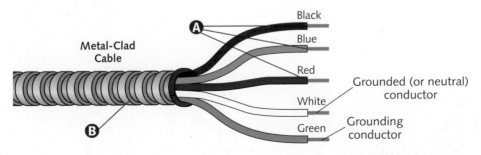

Metal-Clad Cable

Black
Blue
Red
Grounded (or neutral) conductor
White
Green
Grounding conductor

© Cengage Learning 2012

White Conductor Used as Ungrounded Switch Leg (Loop)

A A cable assembly's white or gray conductor can be used as a switch loop (leg) in single-pole, three-way, and four-way switch installations, even though it is an ungrounded (hot) conductor »200.7(C)(1)«.

B The white or gray conductor's new use as an ungrounded (hot) conductor must be permanently reidentified by marking tape, painting, or other effective means at its termination and at each location where the conductor is visible and accessible. Identification shall encircle the insulation and shall be a color other than white, gray, or green »200.7(C)(1)«.

C Red marking tape has been wrapped around the white conductor, reidentifying it as an ungrounded (hot) conductor.

D The white or gray conductor can be used to feed a switch or can be a traveler in three-way (or four-way) switch installations. The white or gray conductor shall not be used as a return conductor from the switch to the outlet »200.7(C)(1)«.

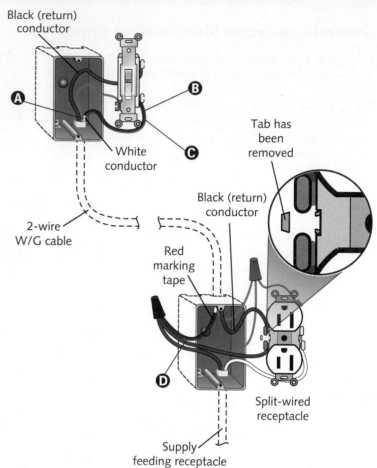

Black (return) conductor

White conductor

2-wire W/G cable

Red marking tape

Black (return) conductor

Tab has been removed

Split-wired receptacle

Supply feeding receptacle

© Cengage Learning 2012

> **CAUTION**
>
> Where switches control lighting loads that are supplied by a grounded general-purpose branch circuit, the grounded circuit conductor for the controlled lighting circuit shall be provided at the switch location. The grounded conductor shall be permitted to be omitted from the switch enclosure where meeting the exception »404.2(C)«.

White Conductor Used as an Ungrounded (Hot) Conductor

A The white or gray conductor can be used as an ungrounded (hot) conductor if it is part of a cable assembly. The insulation must be permanently reidentified as an ungrounded conductor by marking tape, painting, or other effective means at its termination and at each location where the conductor is visible and accessible »200.7(C)(1)«.

> **WARNING**
>
> A white or gray conductor in a conduit (or raceway) shall not be used (or reidentified) as an ungrounded conductor.

> **NOTE**
>
> Identification must encircle the insulation and shall be a color other than white, gray, or green »**200.7(C)(1)**«.

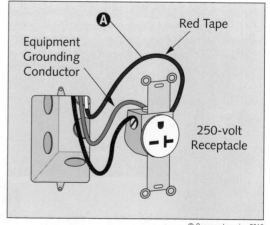

Equipment Grounding Conductor

Red Tape

250-volt Receptacle

© Cengage Learning 2012

GROUNDED CONDUCTORS PROVIDED AT SWITCH LOCATIONS

A Where switches control lighting loads that are supplied by a grounded general-purpose branch circuit, the grounded circuit conductor for the controlled lighting circuit shall be provided at the switch location ≫404.2(C)≪. The grounded conductor shall be permitted to be omitted from the switch enclosure where meeting the exception to 404.2(C).

B Switching in three-way and four-way configurations is done only in the ungrounded (hot) circuit conductor ≫404.2(A)≪.

WARNING

A grounding conductor (green, green with one or more yellow stripes, or bare) cannot be used (or reidentified) as an underground (hot) or a grounded (white) conductor.

NOTE

The grounded circuit conductor shall be permitted to be omitted from the switch enclosure where either of the following conditions in (1) or (2) apply:
(1) Conductors for switches controlling lighting loads enter the box through a raceway. The raceway shall have sufficient cross-sectional area to accommodate the extension of the grounded circuit conductor of the lighting circuit to the switch location whether or not the conductors in the raceway are required to be increased in size to comply with 310.15(B)(2)(a).
(2) Cable assemblies for switches controlling lighting loads enter the box through a framing cavity that is open at the top or bottom on the same floor level, or through a wall, floor, or ceiling that is unfinished on one side ≫404.2(C) *Exception*≪.

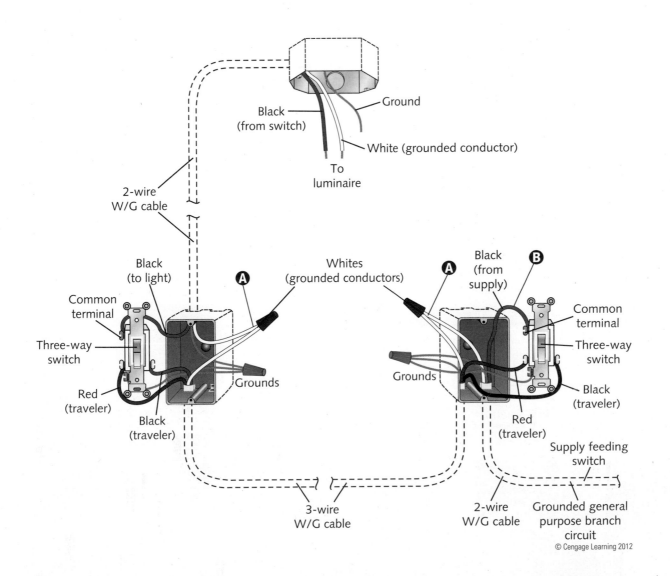

© Cengage Learning 2012

GENERAL PROVISIONS

Suspended (Drop) Ceilings

A Raceways can be supported by independent (additional) support wires, secured at both ends. Support wires and associated fittings must provide adequate support »*300.11(A)*«.

B Boxes can be secured by attaching independent (additional) support wires at both ends. Secure support must be provided by the support wires and associated fittings »*300.11(A) and 314.23(D)(2)*«.

C Ceiling grid support wires shall not be used to support raceways.

D Certain boxes can also be mounted to suspended ceiling framing members »*314.23(D)(1)*«.

E EMT conduit must be fastened securely within 3 ft (900 mm) of all boxes (outlet, junction, device, etc.) »*358.30(A)*«.

F Suspended ceiling system framing members used to support luminaires must be securely fastened to one another as well as to the building structure at appropriate intervals. Luminaires must be securely fastened to the ceiling framing member by mechanical means (bolts, screws, or rivets, etc.). Listed clips, identified for use with the type of ceiling framing member(s) and luminaire(s), are also permitted »*410.36(B)*«.

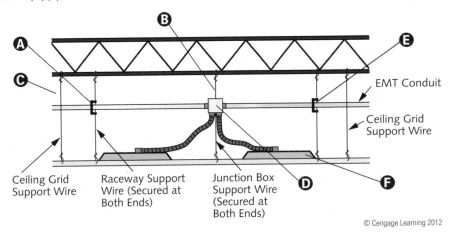

EMT Conduit

Ceiling Grid Support Wire

Ceiling Grid Support Wire

Raceway Support Wire (Secured at Both Ends)

Junction Box Support Wire (Secured at Both Ends)

© Cengage Learning 2012

Maximum Bends in One Run

A The equivalent of four quarter bends (360° total) is the maximum allowed between pull points, for example, conduit bodies and boxes. Because the total bends in this conduit run is 340°, this installation falls within *NEC* specifications.

B The bend maximum of 360° applies to the following raceways: IGS (326.26), IMC (342.26), RMC (344.26), FMC (348.26), LFMC (350.26), PVC (352.26), HDPE (353.26), NUCC (354.26), RTRC (355.26), LFNC (356.26), EMT (358.26), and ENT (362.26).

C Generally, raceway installation must be complete between outlet, junction, or splicing points prior to the installation of conductors »*300.18(A)*«.

D All bends are counted, even those located immediately adjacent to the pull box (or termination). A box offset with two 10° bends counts as 20°.

> **NOTE**
>
> Metal raceways must not be supported, terminated, or connected by welding unless specifically permitted by design or *Code* specifications »*300.18(B)*«.

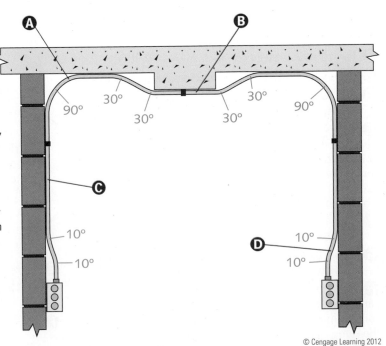

© Cengage Learning 2012

Insulated Fittings

Ⓐ An insulated fitting is not required if a smoothly rounded (or flared) entry for conductors is provided by threaded hubs (or bosses) that are an integral part of a cabinet, box enclosure, or raceway ≫300.4(G) Exception≪.

Ⓑ Where raceways containing 4 AWG or larger insulated circuit conductors enter a cabinet (box, enclosure, or raceway), the conductors must be protected by an identified fitting that provides a smoothly rounded insulating surface, unless the conductors are separated from the fitting (or raceway) by other securely attached identified insulating material ≫300.4(G)≪.

Ⓒ Conduit bushings constructed completely of insulating material shall not be used to secure a fitting or raceway ≫300.4(G)≪. An insulating (plastic, thermoplastic, etc.) bushing shall not replace a locknut.

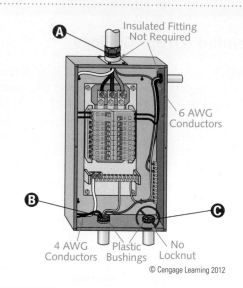

© Cengage Learning 2012

Raceways Supporting Raceways

Ⓐ Conduits (not used as raceways) may support raceways if fastened securely in place with approved fittings ≫300.11(B)≪.

Ⓑ Raceways *shall not* be used to support other raceways, cables, conductors, or nonelectric equipment unless identified for that purpose ≫300.11(B)(1)≪.

Ⓒ This conduit contains power supply conductors for HVAC unit.

Ⓓ Raceways containing power supply conductors for electrically controlled equipment can support Class 2 circuit conductors (or cables) used solely for connection to the equipment control circuits ≫300.11(B)(2)≪.

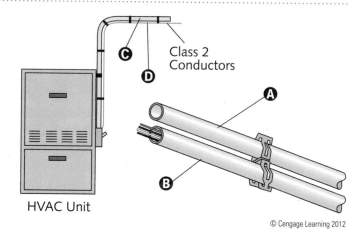

HVAC Unit

© Cengage Learning 2012

Conduit Thickness

Ⓐ Internal diameters for each electrical trade size conduit and tubing are listed in Table 4 of Chapter 9.

Ⓑ Ten 10 AWG THHN conductors are permitted in ¾-in. EMT.

Ⓒ Eleven 10 AWG THHN conductors are permitted in ¾-in. IMC.

Ⓓ Ten 10 AWG THHN conductors are permitted in ¾-in. RMC.

Ⓔ Annex C (preceding the index in the back of the *Code* book) can be used to find the maximum number of conductors permitted in each electrical trade size conduit or tubing. The conductors must be the same size (total cross-sectional area including insulation) when using Annex C.

Ⓕ Nine 10 AWG THHN conductors are permitted in ¾-in. schedule 40 PVC.

Ⓖ Seven 10 AWG THHN conductors are permitted in ¾-in. schedule 80 PVC.

Ⓗ The internal diameters of different types of conduit vary. Therefore, a group of conductors that fit into one conduit may not fit into another type, even though it is the same electrical trade size.

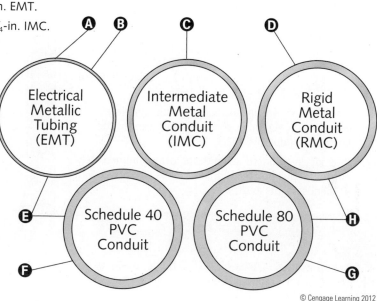

© Cengage Learning 2012

Bending Radius

A Bends must be made so that the conduit or tubing remains undamaged with its internal diameter basically undiminished. For any field bend, the radius of the curve to the centerline of the conduit must not be less than indicated in Table 2 of Chapter 9. Raceways permitted to use the "One Shot and Full Shoe Benders" column include IMC ≫*342.24*≪, RMC ≫*344.24*≪, and EMT ≫*358.24*≪.

B The bending radius of certain other raceways must not be less than shown in the column titled "Other Bends." They include
FMC ≫*348.24*≪,
LFMC ≫*350.24*≪,
PVC ≫*352.24*≪,
LFNC ≫*356.24*≪, and
ENT ≫*362.24*≪.

© Cengage Learning 2012

Table 2 (Chapter 9) Radius of Conduit and Tubing Bends		
Conduit Size Trade Size	**One Shot and Full Shoe Benders** Bending Radius (in in.)	**Other Bends** Bending Radius (in in.)
½	4	4
¾	4½	5
1	5¾	6
1¼	7¼	8
1½	8¼	10
2	9½	12
2½	10½	15
3	13	18
3½	15	21
4	16	24
5	24	30
6	30	36
	A	**B**

NONFLEXIBLE CONDUIT (AND TUBING)

Rigid Metal Conduit: Type RMC

A Rigid metal conduit (RMC) is a raceway of circular cross section. RMC is manufactured in both ferrous (such as steel) and nonferrous (such as aluminum) metal. Other special use types include red brass and stainless steel ≫*344.2*≪.

B RMC is the heaviest (thickest-walled) classification of metal conduit.

C Threadless couplings and connectors used with conduit must be made tight. Those buried in masonry (or concrete) must be the concrete-tight type. If installed in wet locations, they must comply with 314.15 ≫*344.42(A)*≪.

D The minimum approved electrical trade size for RMC is ½ in. ≫*344.20(A)*≪.

E The maximum approved electrical trade size for RMC is 6 in. ≫*344.20(B)*≪.

F Galvanized steel and stainless steel RMC can be used under all atmospheric conditions, within all types of occupancies ≫*344.10(A)(1)*≪.

G Contact of dissimilar metals (except for the combination of aluminum and steel) should be avoided wherever possible to lessen the potential for galvanic action ≫*344.14*≪.

H RMC usually ships in standard lengths of 10 ft (3 m), including the coupling. Normally one coupling is furnished with each length ≫*344.130*≪.

I Coupled with listed fittings, RMC provides electrical continuity and, therefore, can serve as an equipment grounding conductor ≫*344.2 and 344.60*≪.

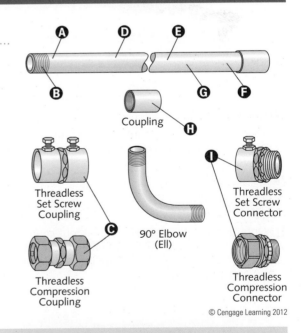

Coupling

Threadless Set Screw Coupling

Threadless Compression Coupling

90° Elbow (Ell)

Threadless Set Screw Connector

Threadless Compression Connector

© Cengage Learning 2012

N O T E

Galvanized steel, stainless steel, and red brass RMC, elbows, couplings, and fittings can be installed in concrete, in direct contact with the earth, or in areas subject to severe corrosive influences where corrosion protection is provided and where judged suitable for the condition ≫*344.10(B)(1)*≪.

Intermediate Metal Conduit: Type IMC

A The minimum approved electrical trade size for IMC is ½ in. ≫342.20(A)≪.

B The maximum approved electrical trade size for IMC is 4 in. ≫342.20(B)≪.

C The definition for intermediate metal conduit (IMC) and rigid metal conduit (RMC) is essentially the same ≫342.2≪. However, as the name implies, IMC is lighter in weight and is constructed with thinner walls than RMC. Unlike RMC, IMC is only manufactured of steel that provides protective strength equivalent to thicker-walled conduits.

D Coupled with listed fittings, IMC provides electrical continuity; therefore, it can serve as an equipment grounding conductor ≫342.2 and 342.60≪.

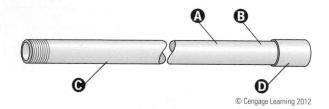
© Cengage Learning 2012

N O T E

For other similarities between IMC and RMC, read Article 342.

Cutting, Reaming, and Threading

A Electrical metallic tubing must not be threaded. Factory threaded integral couplings can be used ≫358.28(B)≪.

B All EMT cut ends must be reamed (or otherwise finished) to remove rough edges ≫358.28(A)≪.

C All cut ends of IMC and RMC must be reamed (or otherwise finished) to remove rough edges ≫342.28 and 344.28≪.

D Running threads shall not be used on conduit for coupling connections ≫342.42(B) and 344.42(B)≪.

E Threading conduit in the field requires a standard cutting die with a ¾-in. taper per ft (1 in 16) ≫342.28 and 344.28≪.

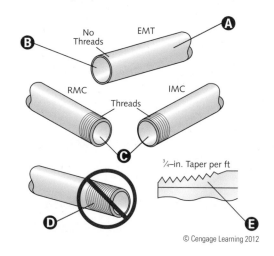
© Cengage Learning 2012

RMC, IMC, and EMT Support Requirements

A The maximum support interval for RMC, IMC, and EMT is 10 ft (3 m) ≫342.30(B)(1), 344.30(B)(1), and 358.30(A)(1)≪.

B In addition, each conduit (or tube) must be securely fastened within 3 ft (900 mm) of each conduit termination (outlet box, junction box, device box, cabinet, conduit body, etc.) ≫342.30(A)(1), 344.30(A), and 358.30(A)≪.

C If structural members are not available within 3 ft (900 mm), a distance of 5 ft (1.5 m) is acceptable for IMC and RMC ≫342.30(A)(2) and 344.30(A)≪.

D Unbroken lengths of EMT, i.e., without coupling, can be fastened within 5 ft (1.5 m) where structural members do not readily permit fastening within 3 ft (900 mm) ≫358.30(A) Exception No. 1≪.

N O T E

RMC, IMC, and EMT must be installed as a complete system before installing conductors ≫342.30, 344.30, and 358.30≪. It is not required (where approved) that RMC and IMC be securely fastened within 3 ft (900 mm) of the service head for above-the-roof mast termination ≫342.30(A)(3) and 344.30(A)≪.

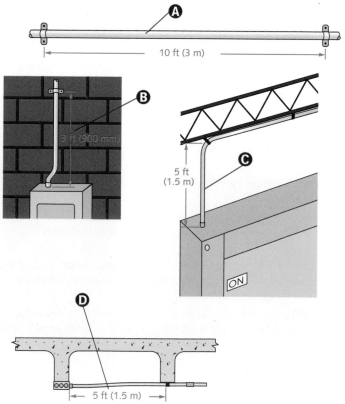
© Cengage Learning 2012

RMC and IMC with Threaded Couplings

A Straight runs of RMC and IMC made up with threaded couplings can be supported in accordance with Table 344.30(B)(2), provided such supports prevent transmission of stresses to termination where conduit is deflected between supports 〉〉 *344.30(B)(2)* 〈〈 .

B The distance between supports increases as the conduit size increases.

C The distance between supports can be increased to 20 ft (6 m) for exposed vertical risers from industrial machinery or fixed equipment, provided (1) the conduit is made up with threaded couplings; (2) the conduit is supported and securely fastened at the top and bottom of the riser; and (3) no other means of intermediate support is readily available 〉〉 *344.30(B)(3)* 〈〈 .

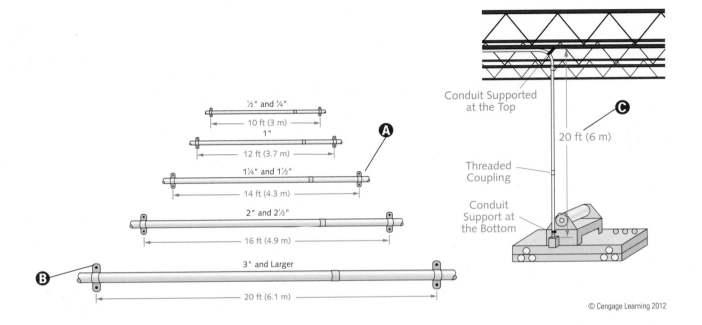

½" and ¾"
10 ft (3 m)

1"
12 ft (3.7 m)

1¼" and 1½"
14 ft (4.3 m)

2" and 2½"
16 ft (4.9 m)

3" and Larger
20 ft (6.1 m)

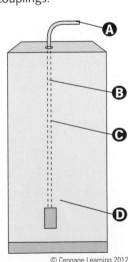

Conduit Supported at the Top

20 ft (6 m)

Threaded Coupling

Conduit Support at the Bottom

© Cengage Learning 2012

Horizontal Runs through Framing Members

A Horizontal runs of RMC, IMC, and EMT that are supported by openings through framing members (at intervals not greater than 10 ft [3 m]) and are fastened securely within 3 ft (900 mm) of termination points, are permitted 〉〉 *342.30(B)(4), 344.30(B)(4), and 358.30(B)* 〈〈 .

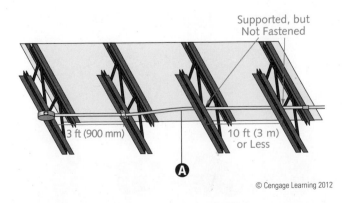

Supported, but Not Fastened

3 ft (900 mm)

10 ft (3 m) or Less

© Cengage Learning 2012

EMT Fished in Walls

A For concealed work in finished buildings (or prefinished wall panels) where standard securing is impracticable, unbroken lengths (without coupling) of electrical metallic tubing can be fished 〉〉 *358.30(A) Exception No. 2* 〈〈 .

B To comply with this exception, the fished portion of tubing in the wall must not have any couplings.

C Normally, EMT must be fastened within 3 ft (900 mm) of device boxes.

D Finished wall provides no access to secure tubing.

© Cengage Learning 2012

EMT Used as an Equipment Grounding Conductor

Ⓐ EMT can serve as an equipment grounding conductor ≫*250.118(4)* and *358.60*≪.

Ⓑ A raceway used as the equipment grounding conductor, as provided in 250.118 and 250.134(A), must comply with 250.4(A)(5) or 250.4(B)(4) ≫*250.122(A)*≪.

Ⓒ EMT must be supported according to 358.30 provisions.

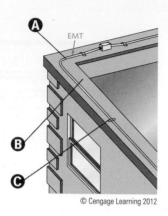

© Cengage Learning 2012

Electrical Metallic Tubing: Type EMT

Ⓐ Electrical metallic tubing (EMT) is an unthreaded thin-wall raceway of circular cross section designed for the physical protection and routing of conductors and cables and for use as an equipment grounding conductor when appropriate fittings are installed ≫*358.2*≪. EMT is also referred to as thin wall.

Ⓑ EMT, the thinnest-walled classification of metal nonflexible raceways, provides protection from all but severe physical damage. Read 358.10 and 12 for additional information on uses (permitted and not permitted).

Ⓒ The minimum approved electrical trade size for EMT is ½ in. ≫*358.20(A)*≪.

> **NOTE**
>
> The number of conductors permitted in EMT must not exceed the percentage fill specified in Table 1, Chapter 9 ≫*358.22*≪.

Ⓓ The maximum approved electrical trade size for EMT is 4 in. ≫*358.20(B)*≪.

Ⓔ All EMT cut ends must be reamed (or otherwise finished) to remove rough edges ≫*358.28(A)*≪.

Ⓕ Couplings and connectors used with tubing must be made tight. Buried in masonry (or concrete), they must be the concrete-tight type. Installed in wet locations, they must comply with 314.15 ≫*358.42*≪.

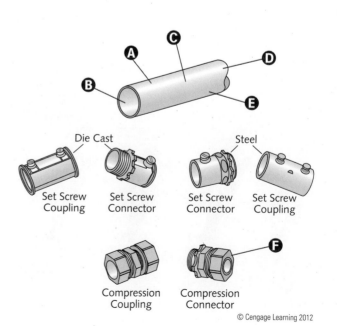

Die Cast

Steel

Set Screw Coupling   Set Screw Connector   Set Screw Connector   Set Screw Coupling

Compression Coupling   Compression Connector

© Cengage Learning 2012

Rigid Polyvinyl Chloride Conduit: Type PVC

NEC identifies five types of rigid PVC conduit:

1. Schedule 80 PVC is an extra-heavy-walled raceway with a wall thickness conforming to Schedule 80-Iron Pipe Size (IPS) dimensions.
2. Schedule 40 PVC is a heavy-walled raceway with a wall thickness conforming to Schedule 40-IPS dimensions.
3. Type A PVC is a thin-walled raceway with wall thickness conforming to Schedule A-IPS dimensions. Limited to underground installations, Type A PVC conduit must be laid with its entire length in concrete.
4. Type EB PVC is a thin-walled raceway with wall thickness designed to achieve a minimum pipe stiffness of 20 lbs./in./in. Type EB PVC conduit, limited to underground installations, must be laid with its entire length in concrete in outdoor trenches.
5. HDPE Schedule 40 is a high-density polyethylene raceway with a wall thickness conforming to Schedule 40-IPS dimensions. HDPE Schedule 40 conduit, also limited to underground installations, can be direct buried with or without being encased in concrete.

A Rigid polyvinyl chloride (PVC) conduit is a rigid nonmetallic conduit of circular cross section, with integral or associated couplings, connectors, and fittings for the installation of electrical conductors and cables ≫ *352.2* ≪.

B All joints between lengths of conduit, and between conduit and couplings, fittings, and boxes, must be made by an approved method ≫ *352.48* ≪.

C All cut ends must be trimmed inside and out to remove rough edges ≫ *352.28* ≪.

D Expansion fittings must be provided for PVC conduit to compensate for thermal expansion and contraction where the length change is expected to be 0.25 in. (6 mm) or greater, in accordance with Table 352.44, in a straight run between securely mounted items such as boxes, cabinets, elbows, or other conduit terminations ≫ *352.44* and *300.7(B)* ≪.

E The minimum approved electrical trade size for PVC conduit is 1/2 in. ≫ *352.20(A)* ≪.

F The maximum approved electrical trade size for PVC conduit is 6 in. ≫ *352.20(B)* ≪.

G Expansion and contraction problems generally do not arise in underground PVC conduit applications.

H Only listed factory elbows and associated fittings shall be used with PVC conduit ≫ *352.6* ≪.

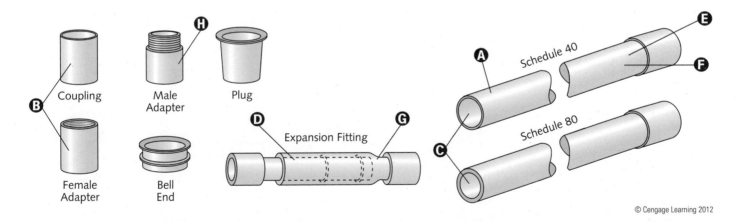

B Coupling
H Male Adapter
Plug
Female Adapter
Bell End
D Expansion Fitting **G**
A Schedule 40 **E** **F**
C Schedule 80

© Cengage Learning 2012

NOTE

Where a raceway crosses a structural joint intended for expansion, contraction, or deflection, used in buildings, bridges, parking garages, or other structures, a listed expansion/deflection fitting or other approved means shall be used ≫ *300.4(H)* ≪.

CAUTION

Where conductors or cables are rated at a temperature higher than the listed temperature rating of PVC conduit, it shall be permissible to install those conductors or cables in PVC conduit, but those conductors or cables must not be operated at a temperature higher than the listed temperature rating of the PVC conduit ≫ *352.10(I)* ≪.

NOTE

Read 352.10 and 12 for a description of uses (permitted and not permitted) of rigid PVC conduit.

Securing Rigid PVC Conduit

Ⓐ Each conduit must be fastened securely within 3 ft (900 mm) of all termination points ≫ *352.30(A)* ≪.

Ⓑ Table 352.30 support provisions must be followed for PVC conduit ≫ *352.30(B)* ≪.

Ⓒ PVC must be fastened so that movement from thermal expansion or contraction is permitted ≫ *352.30* ≪.

> **NOTE**
>
> Horizontal runs of PVC that are supported by openings through framing members (at intervals not greater than those in Table 352.30) and are securely fastened within 3 ft (900 mm) of termination points are permitted ≫ *352.30(B)* ≪.
> PVC conduit, listed for securing at other than 3 ft (900 mm), can be installed in accordance with the listing ≫ *352.30(A)* ≪.

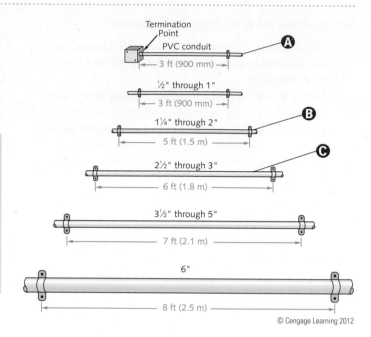

© Cengage Learning 2012

Bending Rigid PVC Conduit

Ⓐ PVC bends must be made so that the conduit remains undamaged and the internal diameter of the conduit is not reduced ≫ *352.24* ≪.

Ⓑ The conduit must not be damaged.

Ⓒ Field bends must be made only with bending equipment identified for the purpose. The radius of the curve to the centerline of such bends must not be less than shown in Table 2 of Chapter 9 ≫ *352.24* ≪.

Ⓓ Installing PVC plugs in the ends of larger conduits (2 to 6 in.) can prevent conduit collapses or other deformities.

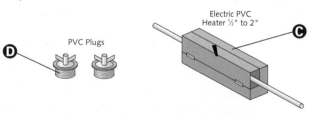

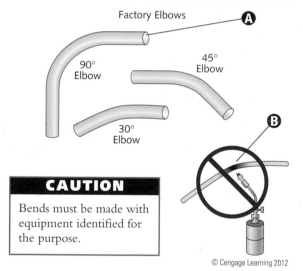

> **CAUTION**
>
> Bends must be made with equipment identified for the purpose.

© Cengage Learning 2012

Securing Electrical Nonmetallic Tubing (ENT)

Ⓐ The equivalent of four quarter bends (360° total) is the maximum between pull points, for example, conduit bodies and boxes ≫ *362.26* ≪.

Ⓑ Electrical nonmetallic tubing must be secured every 3 ft (900 mm) or less ≫ *362.30(A)* ≪.

Ⓒ Bends must be made so that the tubing is undamaged and the tubing's internal diameter is not reduced. Although bends can be made manually (without auxiliary equipment), the radius of the curve of the inner edge of each bend must not be less than shown in Table 2 of Chapter 9 and using the column titled "Other Bends" ≫ *362.24* ≪.

Ⓓ ENT must be fastened securely within 3 ft (900 mm) of each outlet box, device box, junction box, cabinet, or other termination point ≫ *362.30(A)* ≪.

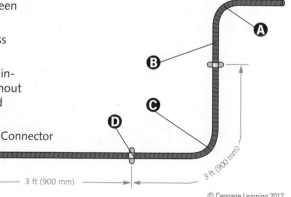

© Cengage Learning 2012

Electrical Nonmetallic Tubing: Type ENT

For the complete listing of ENT uses (permitted and not permitted), read 362.10 and 12.

A Electrical nonmetallic tubing (ENT) is a pliable corrugated raceway of circular cross section with integral (or associated) couplings, connectors, and fittings listed for the installation of electrical conductors. It is composed of a material that is flame-retardant as well as resistant to moisture and chemical atmospheres ≫362.2≪.

B All cut ends must be trimmed inside and out to remove rough edges ≫362.28≪.

C The minimum approved electrical trade size for ENT is ½ in. ≫362.20(A)≪.

D The maximum approved electrical trade size for ENT is 2 in. ≫362.20(B)≪.

E A pliable raceway can be bent by hand with reasonable force, but without other assistance ≫362.2≪.

F Outside diameters are such that standard rigid PVC conduit couplings and connectors can be used on ENT of PVC construction. ENT installation instructions outline the procedure to follow when installing PVC conduit fittings that are cemented in place. Specific cement requirements and application methods are provided.

G An approved method must be used for all joints between lengths of tubing and between tubing and couplings, fittings, and boxes ≫362.48≪.

CAUTION
ENT must not be stored or installed where exposed to direct sunlight, unless identified as "sunlight resistant" ≫362.12(8)≪.

Snap-in Connector

Male Adapter

Coupling

Schedule 40 PVC Male Adapter

© Cengage Learning 2012

NOTE
ENT must comply with 300.4 protection requirements.

ENT through Framing Members

A If the bored hole is less than 1¼ in. (32 mm) from the edge of the framing member, the raceway must be protected from penetration (by screws, nails, etc.) by a steel plate(s) or bushing(s). The steel plate must be at least 1/16 in. (1.6 mm) thick and of appropriate length and width to adequately cover the wiring ≫300.4(A)(1)≪.

B Holes must be bored so that the edge of the hole is at least 1¼ in. (32 mm) from the nearest edge of the wood member ≫300.4(A)(1)≪.

C ENT must be securely fastened in place within 3 ft (900 mm) of all termination points ≫362.30(A)≪.

D Horizontal runs of ENT can be supported by openings through framing members at intervals not greater than 3 ft (900 mm) ≫362.30(B)≪.

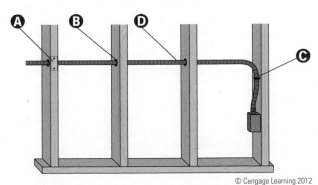
© Cengage Learning 2012

ENT Luminaire Whips

A ENT must be secured within 3 ft (900 mm) of all termination points ≫362.30(A)≪.

B Securing is not required for ENT in lengths not more than 6 ft (1.8 m) from a luminaire terminal connection (for tap connections to luminaires) ≫362.30(A) Exception No. 1≪.

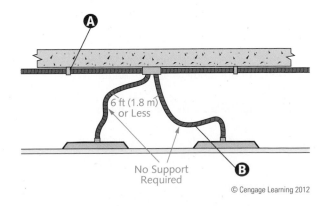

6 ft (1.8 m) or Less

No Support Required

© Cengage Learning 2012

NOTE
Securing is not required for ENT in lengths not exceeding 6 ft (1.8 m) from the last point of support for connections within an accessible ceiling to luminaire(s) or other equipment ≫362.30(A) Exception No. 2≪.

FLEXIBLE CONDUIT

Flexible Metal Conduit: Type FMC

Ⓐ Flexible metal conduit (FMC) is a raceway of circular cross section made of helically wound, formed, and interlocked metal strips ≫348.2≪. FMC must be listed and can be used in both exposed and concealed locations ≫348.6 and 348.10≪.

Ⓑ The minimum electrical trade size for FMC is ½ in., unless a 348.20(A) provision is met.

Ⓒ Flexible metal conduit is often referred to as *Greenfield*, or simply *flex*.

Ⓓ Fittings used with FMC must be listed ≫348.6≪.

Ⓔ The maximum approved electrical trade size for FMC is 4 in. ≫348.20(B)≪.

Ⓕ The equivalent of four quarter bends (360° total) is the maximum between pull points, for example, conduit bodies and boxes ≫348.26≪.

Ⓖ Bends must be made so that the conduit is not damaged and the conduit's internal diameter is not effectively reduced. The radius of the curve of the inner edge of any field bend must not be less than shown in Table 2 of Chapter 9 using the column titled "Other Bends" ≫348.24≪.

Ⓗ All cut ends must be trimmed (or otherwise finished) to remove rough edges, except where fittings are used that thread into the convolutions ≫348.28≪.

Ⓘ Angle connectors shall not be used for concealed raceway installations ≫348.42≪.

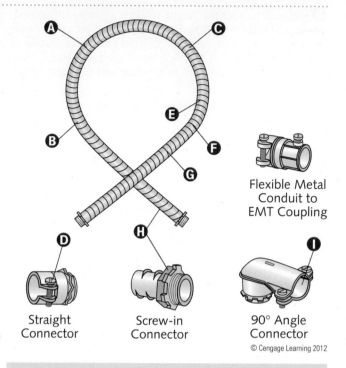

Flexible Metal Conduit to EMT Coupling

Straight Connector

Screw-in Connector

90° Angle Connector

© Cengage Learning 2012

> **NOTE**
>
> For areas where FMC is not allowed, see 348.12.

FMC Support

Support is not required for fished FMC ≫*348.30(A) Exception No. 1*≪.

Ⓐ FMC must be fastened securely in place (by an approved means) at intervals of 4½ ft (1.4 m) or less ≫348.30(A)≪.

Ⓑ FMC must be secured within 12 in. (300 mm) of each box, cabinet, conduit body, or other conduit termination ≫348.30(A)≪.

Ⓒ Refer to Table 348.22 for the maximum number of conductors permitted in ⅜ in. flex.

Ⓓ If the length of FMC from a luminaire terminal for tap connections, as permitted in 410.117(C), to luminaires is 6 ft (1.8 m), or less, supporting is not required ≫348.30(A) Exception No. 3≪.

Ⓔ FMC of ⅜ in. electrical trade size can be used (1) for enclosing the leads of motors as permitted in 430.245(B); (2) in lengths not in excess of 6 ft (1.8 m) as part of a listed assembly, for tap connections to luminaires as permitted in 410.117(C), or for utilization equipment; (3) for manufactured wiring systems as permitted in 604.6(A); (4) in hoistways, as permitted in 620.21(A)(1); or (5) as part of a listed assembly to connect wired luminaire sections as permitted in 410.137(C) ≫348.20(A)≪.

> **NOTE**
>
> Horizontal runs of FMC can be supported by openings through framing members (at intervals not greater than 4½ ft [1.4 m]), if securely fastened within 12 in. (300 mm) of each termination point ≫*348.30(B)*≪.

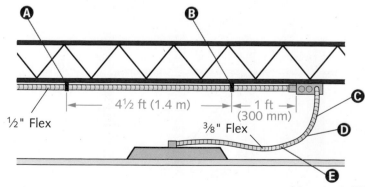

½" Flex   4½ ft (1.4 m)   1 ft (300 mm)   ⅜" Flex

© Cengage Learning 2012

FMC Installation

A Equipment grounding conductors are required for circuits over 20 amperes.

B For lengths of 3 ft (900 mm) or less requiring flexibility, the 12-in. (300-mm) securing distance can be waived »*348.30(A) Exception No. 2*«.

C If an equipment bonding jumper is required around FMC, it must be installed in accordance with 250.102 »*348.60*«.

D Listed FMC can serve as a grounding means if (1) the conduit is terminated in listed fittings; (2) the circuit conductors contained therein are protected by overcurrent devices rated at 20 amperes or less; (3) the total length in any ground-fault current path is 6 ft (1.8 m) or less; and (4) the conduit is not installed where flexibility is necessary to minimize the transmission of vibration from equipment or to provide flexibility for equipment that requires movement »*250.118(5)*«.

E FMC must be secured within 12 in. (300 mm) of each box, cabinet, conduit body, or other conduit termination »*348.30(A)*«.

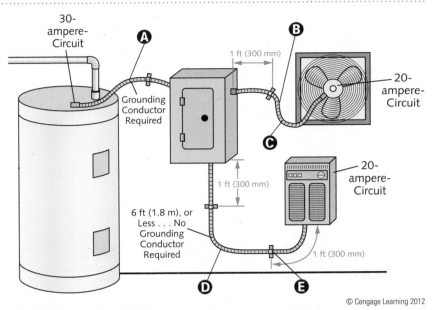

© Cengage Learning 2012

CAUTION

An equipment grounding conductor must be installed in FMC used to connect equipment where flexibility is necessary to minimize the transmission of vibration from equipment or to provide flexibility for equipment that requires movement »*348.60*«.

Liquidtight Flexible Metal Conduit: Type LFMC

The equivalent of four quarter bends (360° total) is the maximum allowed between pull points, for example, conduit bodies and boxes »*350.26*«.

A Liquidtight flexible metal conduit (LFMC) is a raceway of circular cross section having an outer liquidtight, nonmetallic, sunlight-resistant jacket over an inner flexible metal core with associated couplings, connectors, and fittings and approved for the installation »*350.2*«.

B The minimum electrical trade size for LFMC is ½ in., except as provided in 348.20(A) »*350.20(A)*«. The number of conductors allowed in ⅜ in. conduit must not exceed the limit set in Table 348.22, "Fittings Outside Conduit" columns »*350.22(B)*«.

C LFMC and associated fittings must be listed »*350.6*«.

D Angle connectors shall not be concealed »*350.42*«.

E The maximum approved electrical trade size for LFMC is 4 in. »*350.20(B)*«.

F LFMC is often referred to as *Sealtite* (a registered trademark).

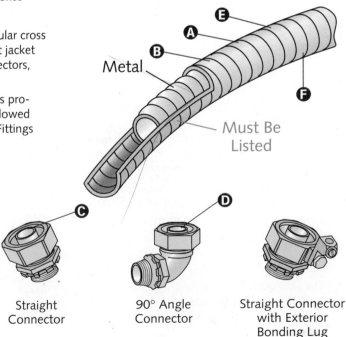

Metal

Must Be Listed

Straight Connector

90° Angle Connector

Straight Connector with Exterior Bonding Lug

© Cengage Learning 2012

NOTE

Securing and support requirements for LFMC are listed in 350.30.

Grounding Liquidtight Flexible Metal Conduit

Ⓐ Listed LFMC, ³⁄₈ in. through 1¼ in., can be used as a grounding means if (1) the total length of flexible conduit in any ground-fault current path is not more than 6 ft (1.8 m); (2) the conduit is terminated in listed fittings; and (3) the circuit conductors contained therein are protected by overcurrent devices rated at 20 amperes or less for ³⁄₈-in. and ½-in. electrical trade sizes and 60 amperes or less for ¾-in. through 1¼-in. electrical trade sizes ≫ *250.118(6)* ≪ .

Ⓑ LFMC can serve as a grounding means as covered in 250.118(6). If an equipment bonding jumper is required around LFMC, it must be installed in accordance with 250.102 ≫ *350.60* ≪ .

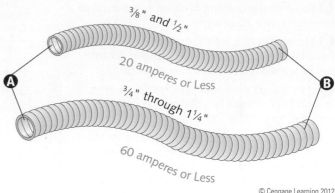

³⁄₈ " and ½ "

20 amperes or Less

¾ " through 1¼ "

60 amperes or Less

© Cengage Learning 2012

Liquidtight Flexible Nonmetallic Conduit: Type LFNC

The equivalent of four quarter bends (360° total) is the maximum allowed between pull points, for example, conduit bodies and boxes ≫ *356.26* ≪ .

Ⓐ Liquidtight flexible nonmetallic conduit (LFNC) is a raceway of circular cross section of various types, including FNMC-A, FNMC-B, and FNMC-C ≫ *356.2* ≪ .

Ⓑ Type LFNC-A has a smooth seamless inner core surrounded by reinforcement layer(s) and bonded to a smooth seamless cover ≫ *356.2(1)* ≪ .

Ⓒ Type LFNC-B has a smooth inner surface having integral reinforcement within the conduit wall ≫ *356.2(2)* ≪ . (Outside appearance is similar to LFMC.)

Ⓓ Type LFNC-C has a corrugated internal and external surface having no integral reinforcement within the conduit wall ≫ *356.2(3)* ≪ . (Appearance is similar to ENT, except more flexible.)

Ⓔ LFNC and associated fittings must be listed ≫ *356.6* ≪ .

Ⓕ Angle connectors shall not be used for concealed raceway installations ≫ *356.42* ≪ .

Ⓖ The maximum approved electrical trade size for LFNC is 4 in. ≫ *356.20(B)* ≪ .

Ⓗ The minimum electrical trade size for LFNC is ½ in., unless a 356.20(A) provision applies.

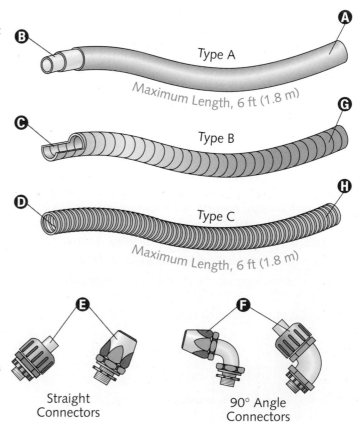

Type A

Maximum Length, 6 ft (1.8 m)

Type B

Type C

Maximum Length, 6 ft (1.8 m)

Straight Connectors

90° Angle Connectors

© Cengage Learning 2012

Liquidtight Flexible Nonmetallic Conduit Installation

Strapping is not required for LFNC lengths of 6 ft (1.8 m) or less from a luminaire terminal connection for tap conductors to luminaires as permitted in 410.117(C) ›› *356.30(2)* ‹‹ .

Support is not required for fished LFNC ›› *356.30(2)* ‹‹ .

Horizontal runs of LFNC can be supported by openings through framing members [at intervals not greater than 3 ft (900 mm)], if securely fastened within 12 in. (300 mm) of each termination point ›› *356.30(3)* ‹‹ .

Securing and supporting is not required for LFNC-B where installed in lengths not exceeding 6 ft (1.8 m) from the last point of support for connections within an accessible ceiling to luminaire(s) or other equipment ›› *356.30(4)* ‹‹ .

Ⓐ LFNC must be securely fastened at intervals not greater than 3 ft (900 mm) ›› *356.30(1)* ‹‹ .

Ⓑ LFNC must be secured within 12 in. (300 mm) of each connection to every outlet box, junction box, cabinet, or fitting ›› *356.30(1)* ‹‹ .

Ⓒ Where flexibility is necessary, LFNC can be secured within 3 ft (900 mm) of the termination ›› *356.30(2)* ‹‹ .

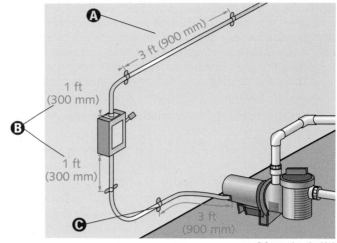

© Cengage Learning 2012

NOTE

If an equipment grounding conductor is required for the circuits installed in LFNC, it can be installed either inside or outside of the conduit. Where installed on the outside, the length of the equipment grounding conductor must not exceed 6 ft (1.8 m) and must be routed with the raceway ›› *250.102(E)* and *(E)(2)* ‹‹ .

OTHER RACEWAYS

Surface Nonmetallic Raceways

Where surface nonmetallic raceways are used in combination for both signaling and for lighting and power circuits, the different wiring systems must be run in separate compartments identified by stamping, imprinting, or color coding of the interior finish ›› *388.70* ‹‹ .

Ⓐ Surface nonmetallic raceway construction must be visibly distinguishable from other raceways. Surface nonmetallic raceways and their fittings must be designed so that sections can be mechanically coupled together and installed without subjecting the wires to abrasion ›› *388.100* ‹‹ .

Ⓑ The size and number of conductors installed in any raceway must not exceed the raceway's design limitations ›› *388.21* and *388.22* ‹‹ .

Ⓒ Splices and taps are permitted within surface nonmetallic raceway having a removable cover that remains accessible once installed. The conductors, at the point of splices and taps, must not fill the raceway to more than 75% of its area. Splices and taps in surface nonmetallic raceways without removable covers must be made only in boxes. All splices and taps must be made using approved methods ›› *388.56* ‹‹ .

Ⓓ Surface nonmetallic raceways can be installed in dry locations ›› *388.10(1)* ‹‹ . NEC 388.12 lists the locations where these raceways shall not be used.

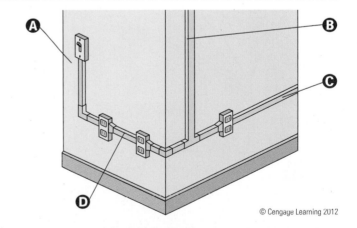

© Cengage Learning 2012

NOTE

Unbroken lengths of surface nonmetallic raceways can pass transversely through dry walls, partitions, and floors. Conductors must be accessible on both sides of the wall, partition, or floor ›› *388.10(2)* ‹‹ .
Where equipment grounding is required, a separate equipment grounding conductor must be installed within the raceway ›› *388.60* ‹‹ .

Surface Metal Raceways

A Surface metal raceway construction must be distinguishable from other raceways. Surface metal raceways and their fittings must be designed so that the sections can be electrically and mechanically coupled together and installed without subjecting the wires to abrasion. Nonmetallic covers and accessories can be used on surface metal raceways only if identified for such use »386.100«.

B Uses (permitted and not permitted) are located in 386.10 and 386.12.

C The number and size of conductors installed in any raceway must not exceed the raceway's design limitations »386.21 and 386.22«.

D The adjustment factors of 310.15(B)(3)(a) do not apply to conductors installed in surface metal raceways where all of the following conditions are met: (1) the cross-sectional area of the raceway exceeds 4 in.² (2500 mm²); (2) the current-carrying conductors do not exceed 30 in number; and (3) the sum of the cross-sectional areas of all contained conductors does not exceed 20% of the interior cross-sectional area of the surface metal raceway »386.22«.

E Unbroken lengths of surface metal raceway can pass transversely through dry walls, dry partitions, and dry floors. Access to the conductors must be maintained on both sides of the wall, partition, or floor »386.10(4)«.

F Where surface metal raceways are used in combination for both signaling and for lighting and power circuits, the different wiring systems must be run in separate compartments identified by stamping, imprinting, or color coding of the interior finish »386.70«.

G Splices and taps are permitted within surface metal raceway having a removable cover that remains accessible after installation. At the point of splices and taps, the conductors must not fill the raceway to more than 75% of its area. Splices and taps in surface metal raceways without removable covers can be made only in boxes. Use only approved methods for splices and taps »386.56«.

H Multioutlet assemblies are covered in Article 380.

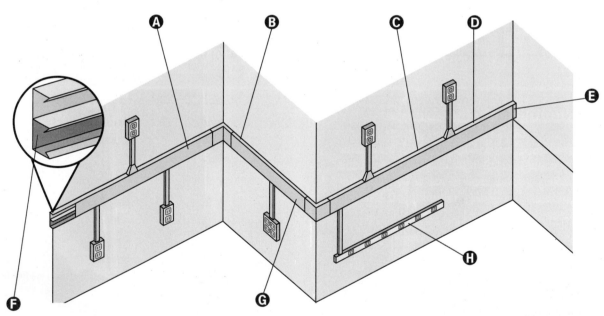

© Cengage Learning 2012

NOTE

If a surface metal raceway enclosure provides a transition from another wiring method, it must have a means to connect an equipment grounding conductor
»386.60«.

Strut-Type Channel Raceways

Use Table 384.22 to determine the maximum number of conductors permitted in strut-type channel raceway. Apply the appropriate Chapter 9 Tables for the cross-sectional area of the type and size of wire used ≫*384.22*≪.

The adjustment factors of 310.15(B)(3)(a) do not apply to conductors installed in strut-type channel raceways where all of the following conditions are met: (1) the cross-sectional area of the raceway exceeds 4 in.² (2500 mm²); (2) the current-carrying conductors do not exceed 30 in number; and (3) the sum of the cross-sectional areas of all contained conductors does not exceed 20% of the interior cross-sectional area of the strut-type channel raceway ≫*384.22*≪.

Conductors larger than that for which the strut-type channel raceway is listed must not be used ≫*384.21*≪.

A surface mount strut-type channel raceway must be secured to the mounting surface with external retention straps at intervals not exceeding 10 ft (3 m), and within 3 ft (900 mm) of each raceway termination (outlet box, cabinet, junction box, etc.) ≫*384.30(A)*≪.

A Strut-type channel raceways, closure strips, and accessories must be listed and identified for such use ≫*384.6*≪.

B Splices and taps are permitted in raceways that provide access after installation via a removable cover. At any point of splices or taps, the conductors must not fill the raceway to more than 75%. All splices and taps must be made by approved methods ≫*384.56*≪.

C Uses (permitted and not permitted) are covered in 384.10 and 384.12.

D Strut-type channel raceway enclosures providing a transition to (or from) other wiring methods must accommodate the connection of an equipment grounding conductor. A strut-type channel raceway can be used as an equipment grounding conductor in accordance with 250.118(13) ≫*384.60*≪.

E Strut-type channel raceways can be suspended in air provided an approved method (designed for the purpose) is applied at intervals of not more than 10 ft (3 m) ≫*384.30(B)*≪.

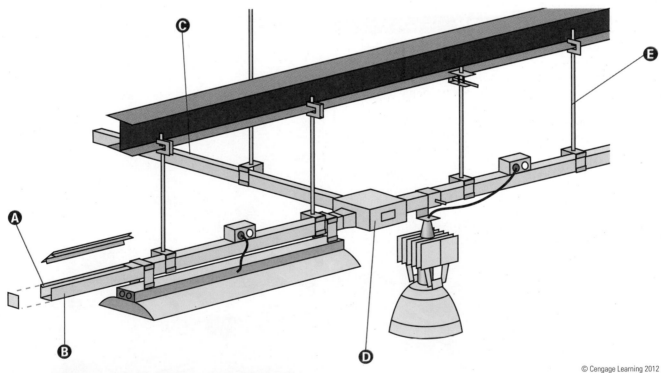

© Cengage Learning 2012

NOTE

Unbroken lengths of strut-type channel raceway can extend through walls, partitions, and floors provided closure strips are removable from either side and the portion within the wall, partition, or floor remains covered ≫*384.10(7)*≪.

Underfloor Raceways

An underfloor raceway is defined as a raceway and associated components designed and intended for installation beneath or flush with the surface of a floor for the installation of cables and electrical conductors.

A Connections between raceways and distribution centers and wall outlets must be made by approved fittings or by any of the wiring methods in Chapter 3, where installed according to the provisions of the respective articles »390.15«.

B Underfloor raceways can be installed beneath a concrete (or other flooring material) surface. In office occupancies, installations flush with the concrete floor and covered with linoleum (or equivalent covering) are acceptable »390.3(A)«.

C The combined cross-sectional area of all conductors or cables must not exceed 40% of the interior cross-sectional area of the raceway »390.6«.

D The size of conductors installed must not be larger than that for which the underfloor raceway is designed »390.5«.

E Inserts must be leveled and sealed to prevent the entrance of concrete. Metal raceway inserts must also be metal and must be electrically continuous with the raceway »390.14«.

F Seal and level junction boxes to the floor grade to prevent entrance of water or concrete. Underfloor metal raceway junction boxes must also be metal and must be electrically continuous with the raceway »390.13«.

G Splices and taps are acceptable only within junction boxes. Continuous, unbroken conductor connecting the individual outlets (so-called loop wiring) is not considered a splice or tap »390.7«.

H Underfloor raceways must be laid so that a straight line from the center of one junction box to the center of the next junction box coincides with the centerline of the raceway system. Raceways must be held firmly in place to prevent misalignment during construction »390.9«.

I Raceway dead ends must be closed »390.11«.

J Install a suitable marker at, or near, each end of straight raceway runs to locate the last insert »390.10«.

CAUTION

When an outlet is abandoned, discontinued, or removed, the supplying circuit conductors must be removed from the raceway. Splices or reinsulated conductors, such as would occur in the case of abandoned outlets on loop wiring, are not allowed in raceways »390.8«.

NOTE

390.3(B) lists areas where underfloor raceways are not permitted.

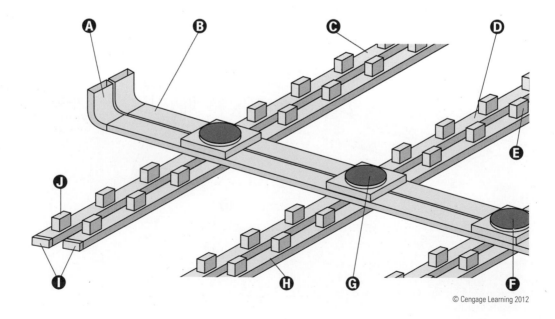

© Cengage Learning 2012

Underfloor Raceway Covering

A Half-round and flat-top raceways not over 4 in. (100 mm) in width must be covered by ¾ in. (20 mm) or more of concrete (or wood) ≫ *390.4(A)* ≪.

B Flat-top raceways greater than 4 in. (100 mm) but not more than 8 in. (200 mm) wide, with a minimum of 1-in. (25-mm) spacing between the raceways, must be covered with at least 1 in. (25 mm) of concrete ≫ *390.4(B)* ≪.

C Trench-type flush raceways having removable covers can be laid flush with the floor's surface. Such approved raceways shall be designed so that the cover plates provide adequate mechanical protection and rigidity equivalent to junction box covers ≫ *390.4(C)* ≪.

D In office occupancies, approved flat-top metal raceways (of 4 in. [100 mm] or less in width) can be flush with the concrete floor surface, provided they are covered with a minimum ¹⁄₁₆-in. (1.6-mm) floor covering, such as linoleum. Where more than one (but fewer than four) single raceways are installed flush with the concrete, they must be contiguous with one another and be joined forming a rigid assembly ≫ *390.4(D)* ≪.

E Flat-top raceways greater than 4 in. (100 mm) but not more than 8 in. (200 mm) wide that are spaced less than 1 in. (25 mm) apart must be covered with at least 1½ in. (38 mm) of concrete ≫ *390.4(B)* ≪.

F Splices and taps are permitted in trench-type flush raceways whose removable covers are accessible after installation. At the point of any splices or taps, the conductors must not fill more than 75% of the raceway's area ≫ *390.7 Exception* ≪.

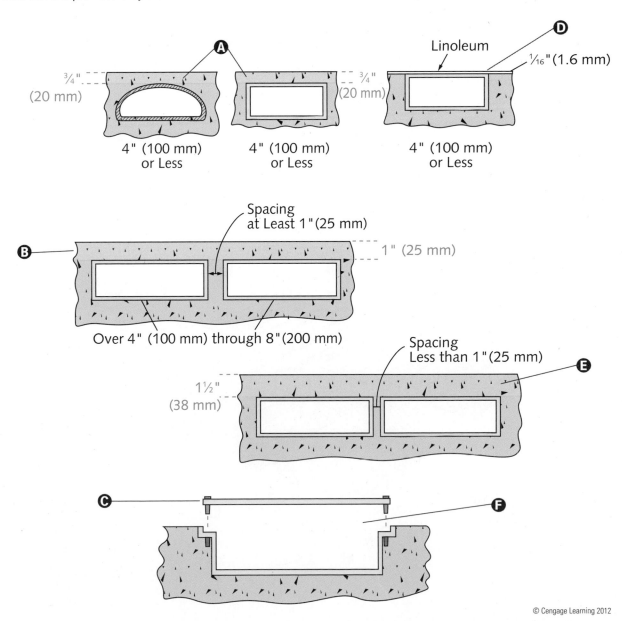

Summary

- Raceways shall not be supported by ceiling grid support wires, but can be supported by independent (additional) support wires.
- Raceways shall not support other raceways, cables, conductors, or nonelectric equipment.
- The maximum total of conduit bends, between pull points, is four quarter bends (360°).
- RMC is a heavy-walled metal raceway that can be threaded.
- IMC has thinner walls than does RMC, and it can also be threaded.
- Unless made up with threaded couplings, RMC and IMC support requirements are the same as EMT.
- EMT, the thinnest-walled classification of metal nonflexible raceways, provides protection from all but severe physical damage.
- The distance between PVC supports increases as conduit size increases.
- Certain raceways, permitted as luminaire whips, do not require support if installed in lengths of 6 ft or less.

- Wireways are troughs with hinged or removable covers for housing and protecting conductors and cables.
- Wireways can pass transversely through walls if the length passing through the wall is unbroken and if conductors can be accessed on both sides of the wall.
- Raceway fill can be calculated from Tables 4 and 5, located in Chapter 9.
- Conduit (and tubing) nipples can be filled to 60% of their cross-sectional area.
- Certain conductor properties are listed in Table 310.104(A).
- Conductor temperature limitations must be considered when determining overcurrent protection.
- Ambient temperature, the number of current-carrying conductors, and continuous loads can alter maximum conductor ampacity or overcurrent protection.

Unit 5 Competency Test

NEC Reference	Answer	
_____	_____	1. Where exposed to the weather, raceways shall be:

    a) rainproof and arranged to drain.

    b) watertight and arranged to drain.

    c) weatherproof and arranged to drain.

    d) suitable for use in wet locations and arranged to drain.

_____	_____	2. Most conduit and tubing type raceways have a maximum equivalent of four _____ bends between pull points, for example, conduit bodies and boxes.
_____	_____	3. The cross-sectional area of 2-in. EMT is _____ in.^{2}
_____	_____	4. All cut ends of conduits shall be reamed or otherwise finished to remove rough edges. Where conduit is threaded in the field, a standard cutting die with a _____-in. taper per ft (1 in 16) shall be used.
_____	_____	5. Multioutlet assemblies shall not:

    I. be installed in hoistways.

    II. run within dry partitions.

    III. run through dry partitions.

      a) I only   b) III only   c) I and II only   d) I, II, and III

| _____ | _____ | 6. Splices and taps shall be permitted within a wireway provided they are accessible. The conductors, including splices and taps, shall not fill the wireway to more than _____ of its area at that point. |

NEC **Reference**   **Answer**

_____ _____ 7. A _____ shall be defined as a transverse raceway for electric conductors, providing access to predetermined cells of a cellular metal floor, thereby permitting the installation of electric conductors from a distribution center to the cells.

_____ _____ 8. In both exposed and concealed locations, where a cable or raceway-type wiring method is installed through bored holes in joist, rafters, or wood members, holes shall be bored so that the edge of the hole is not less than _____ in. from the nearest edge of the wood member.

_____ _____ 9. How many 14 AWG THHN conductors, including an equipment grounding conductor, can be installed in a ⅜-in. flexible metal conduit using inside fittings?

_____ _____ 10. What is the maximum distance (in ft) between supports for a straight run of 2-in. IMC made up with threaded couplings?

_____ _____ 11. The sum of cross-sectional areas of all contained conductors at any cross section of a wireway shall not exceed _____ fill.

_____ _____ 12. Where conductors carrying alternating current are installed in ferrous metal raceways, they shall be so arranged as to avoid heating the surrounding metal by _____.

_____ _____ 13. A _____ is a type of surface, flush, or freestanding raceway designed to hold conductors and receptacles, assembled in the field or at the factory.

_____ _____ 14. Where practicable, contact between dissimilar metals anywhere in the system shall be avoided to eliminate the possibility of _____.

_____ _____ 15. What is the maximum number of 4 AWG THHN conductors permitted in 1½-in. rigid metal conduit?

_____ _____ 16. Where the same 4 AWG conductor enters and then exits a wireway through conduit or tubing, the distance between those raceway entries shall not be less than _____ times the trade diameter of the larger raceway.

_____ _____ 17. All components of an exposed wiring system, installed where walls are frequently washed, must be mounted with a minimum of _____ in. airspace between components (boxes, fittings, conduits, etc.) and the wall (supporting surface).

_____ _____ 18. Where an equipment bonding jumper is installed on the outside of a raceway, the length shall not exceed _____ ft and shall be routed with the raceway or enclosure.

_____ _____ 19. Connections from headers to cabinets and other enclosures, in cellular concrete floor raceways, shall be made by means of:

    I. listed metal raceways.

    II. listed nonmetallic raceways.

    III. listed fittings.

      a) I only b) I and II only c) I and III only d) I, II, and III

_____ _____ 20. ENT shall be secured at least every _____ ft.

_____ _____ 21. IMC encased in a concrete slab, on the first floor of an office building, is considered a _____ location.

_____ _____ 22. When an outlet from an underfloor raceway is discontinued, the sections of circuit conductors supplying the outlet:

    a) shall be permitted to be spliced.

    b) shall be removed from the raceway.

    c) shall be permitted to be reinsulated.

    d) shall be handled like abandoned outlets on loop wiring.

_____ _____ 23. RMC, elbows, couplings, and fittings shall be permitted to be installed in concrete, in direct contact with the earth, or in areas subject to severe corrosive influences where protected by _____ and judged suitable for the condition.

_____ _____ 24. Where installed in raceways, conductors _____ and larger, not specifically permitted or required elsewhere in the *NEC* to be solid, shall be stranded.

_____ _____ 25. In vertical raceways, 3/0 AWG aluminum conductors must be supported if the vertical rise is greater than _____ ft.

_____ _____ 26. Where raceways contain _____ or larger insulated circuit conductors, and these conductors enter a cabinet, a box, an enclosure, or a raceway, the conductors shall be protected by an identified fitting providing a smoothly rounded insulating surface, unless the conductors are separated from the fitting or raceway by identified insulating materials that are securely fastened in place.

_____ _____ 27. Nonmetallic wireways shall be supported where run horizontally at intervals not to exceed _____ ft, and at each end or joint, unless listed for other support intervals.

_____ _____ 28. Horizontal runs of IMC supported by openings through framing members at intervals not exceeding _____ ft and securely fastened within _____ ft of termination points shall be permitted.

_____ _____ 29. If a 1¼-in. EMT raceway containing three conductors is already filled to 20%, what is the raceway's cross-sectional area?

_____ _____ 30. Expansion fittings and telescoping sections of metal raceways shall be made electrically continuous by _____ or other means.

_____ _____ 31. RMC shall be securely fastened within _____ ft of each outlet box, junction box, device box, cabinet, conduit body, or other conduit termination.

_____ _____ 32. The maximum distance between supports for 4-in. PVC is _____ ft.

_____ _____ 33. When calculating the maximum number of conductors permitted in a conduit or tubing, all of the same size (total cross-sectional area including insulation), the next-higher whole number shall be used to determine the maximum number of conductors permitted when the calculation results in a decimal of _____ or larger.

_____ _____ 34. Where insulated conductors are deflected within a wireway, either at the ends or where conduits, fittings, or other raceways or cables enter or leave the wireway, or where the direction of the wireway is deflected greater than _____, dimensions corresponding to one wire per terminal in Table 312.6(A) shall apply.

ONE-FAMILY DWELLINGS

section 2

UNIT 6

General Provisions

Objectives

After studying this unit, the student should:

▶ be able to calculate the minimum number of 15- and 20-ampere branch circuits in a one-family dwelling.

▶ know the requirements for single receptacles on individual branch circuits.

▶ understand the branch-circuit ratings allowed for general-purpose receptacles.

▶ know how to lay out general-purpose receptacles in a dwelling.

▶ know the receptacle ratings allowed on various size branch circuits.

▶ understand the requirements for receptacle boxes.

▶ have a good understanding of split-wire receptacles.

▶ know the requirements for wet bar receptacles.

▶ be familiar with the provisions concerning the minimum length of free conductors inside boxes.

▶ know the receptacle replacement requirements.

▶ understand the general requirements for lighting and switches.

▶ be familiar with the use of a white conductor as an ungrounded conductor.

▶ understand general requirements for devices and luminaire boxes.

▶ know the provisions for outdoor receptacles.

▶ be familiar with the provisions concerning illuminating outdoor entrances and exits.

▶ understand the requirements for attaching receptacles or lighting to vegetation (such as trees).

Introduction

Unit 6 contains provisions concerning general areas both inside and outside of one-family dwellings. A one-family dwelling is a building consisting solely of one dwelling unit ≫ *Article 100* ≪. Learning codes that pertain to one-family dwellings is of great importance because these codes are the foundation for all residential wiring. One-family dwellings are built in all shapes and sizes. Some general codes apply to every dwelling, such as the placement of receptacles in habitable rooms.

Nonmetallic-sheathed cable is the most common wiring type installed in one-family dwellings. Article 334 covers the use, installation, and construction specifications of nonmetallic-sheathed cable (Types NM, NMC, and NMS). Uses permitted for nonmetallic-sheathed cable are covered in 334.10 and uses not permitted are in 334.12. (See Unit 4 of this text for *Code* requirements pertaining to nonmetallic-sheathed cable.)

Prior to the 2008 edition of the *NEC*, only 120-volt, single-phase, 15- and 20-ampere branch circuits supplying outlets installed in dwelling unit bedrooms were required to be arc-fault circuit-interrupter protected. Now all 120-volt, single-phase, 15- and 20-ampere branch circuits supplying outlets installed in dwelling unit family rooms, dining rooms, living rooms, parlors, libraries, dens, bedrooms, sunrooms, recreation rooms, closets, hallways, or similar rooms or areas shall be protected by a listed arc-fault circuit interrupter, combination-type, installed to provide protection of the branch circuit.

Another major change in the 2008 *NEC* pertains to the type of receptacles installed in dwelling units. Listed tamper-resistant receptacles must be installed in all areas specified in 210.52 that require 125-volt, 15- and 20-ampere receptacles.

ELECTRICAL FLOOR PLAN (BLUEPRINT)

Electrical blueprints (floor plans) may be optional on a one-family dwelling. Sometimes it is the responsibility of the electrician to design and install the electrical system. The accompanying electrical floor plan shows receptacles, lighting, switches, and other items that might be found on a residential plan. The *NEC* references (shown here in red), are, of course, not present on general plans.

This chapter covers everything in a one-family dwelling, from a single receptacle in an individual branch circuit to illumination of entrances and exits. Branch circuits are explained briefly in this unit and in greater detail in later units. Receptacles have both general and specific codes. General codes are explained in this unit, while specific codes for rooms and areas with special receptacle requirements are explained in Unit 7. This unit also includes general requirements for lighting and switches, while specific requirements can be found in Unit 7.

CAUTION

Some state and local jurisdictions may not allow the use of nonmetallic-sheathed cable in any dwelling. Obtain a copy of any additional rules and regulations for your area.

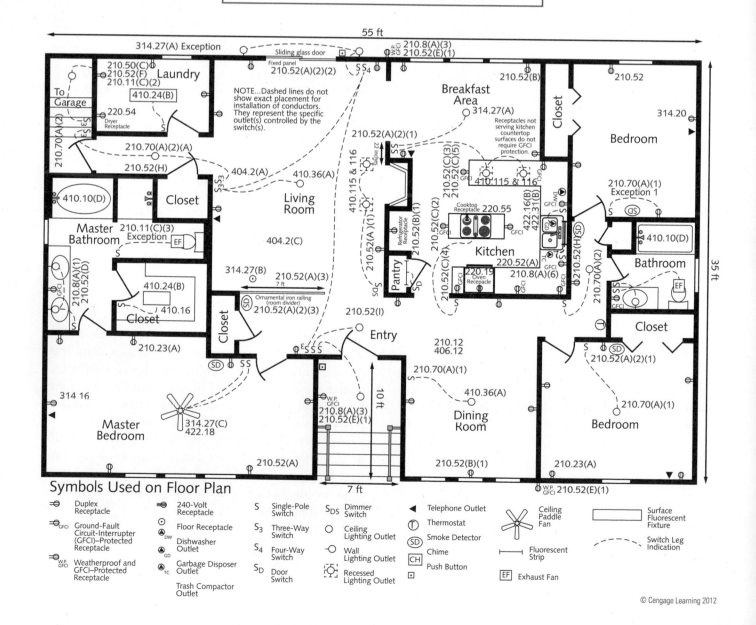

BRANCH CIRCUITS

AFCI Protection

Ⓐ An arc-fault circuit interrupter (AFCI) is a device intended to provide protection from the effects of arc faults by recognizing characteristics unique to arcing and by functioning to de-energize the circuit when an arc fault is detected ≫ *Article 100* ≪ .

Ⓑ All 120-volt, single-phase, 15- and 20-ampere branch circuits supplying outlets installed in dwelling unit family rooms, dining rooms, living rooms, parlors, libraries, dens, bedrooms, sunrooms, recreation rooms, closets, hallways, or similar rooms or areas shall be protected by a listed arc-fault circuit

interrupter, combination-type, installed to provide protection of the branch circuit. ≫ *210.12(A)* ≪ .

Ⓒ In any of the areas specified in 210.12(A), where branch-circuit wiring is modified, replaced, or extended, the branch circuit shall be protected by one of the following: (1) a listed combination-type AFCI located at the origin of the branch circuit, or (2) a listed outlet branch-circuit type AFCI located at the first receptacle outlet of the existing branch circuit ≫ *210.12(B)* ≪ .

Arc-Fault Circuit Interrupter (AFCI)

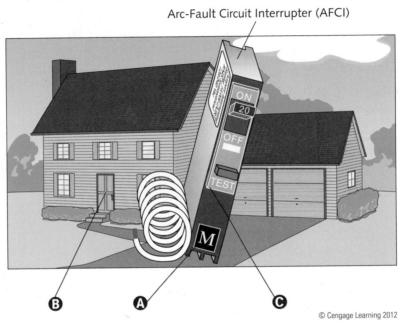

Ⓑ Ⓐ Ⓒ

© Cengage Learning 2012

Tamper-Resistant Receptacles in Dwelling Units

Ⓐ In all areas specified in 210.52, all nonlocking-type 125-volt, 15- and 20-ampere receptacles shall be listed tamper-resistant receptacles ≫ *406.12* ≪ .

Ⓑ Tamper-resistant receptacles are identified by the letters "TR" or the words "Tamper Resistant." After the receptacle has been installed, the identification is only required to be visible with the cover plate removed. See UL (Underwriter Laboratories) White Book, category: Receptacles for Plugs and Attachment Plugs (RTRT).

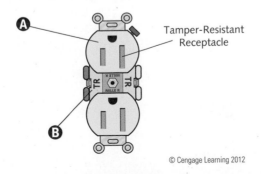

Ⓐ

Tamper-Resistant Receptacle

Ⓑ

© Cengage Learning 2012

NOTE

It is not required to install tamper-resistant receptacles in the following areas:

1. Receptacles located more than 5½ ft (1.7 m) above the floor.

2. Receptacles that are part of a luminaire or appliance.

3. A single receptacle or a duplex receptacle for two appliances located within dedicated space for each appliance that, in normal use, is not easily moved from one place to another and that is cord-and-plug connected in accordance with 400.7(A)(6), (A)(7), or (A)(8).

4. Nongrounding receptacles used for replacements as permitted in 406.4(D)(2)(a) ≫ *406.12 Exception* ≪ .

General-Purpose Branch Circuit

A general-purpose branch circuit may feed lights, receptacles, or both.

A General-purpose branch-circuit overcurrent protection shall not exceed 15 amperes for 14 AWG copper; 20 amperes for 12 AWG copper; and 30 amperes for 10 AWG copper ≫240.4(D)≪.

B Branch-circuit conductors shall have an ampacity not less than the maximum load served ≫210.19(A)(1)≪.

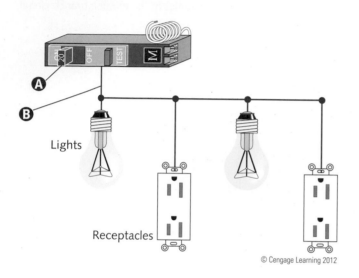

Lights

Receptacles

© Cengage Learning 2012

Required Branch Circuits

A A minimum of two 20-ampere small appliance branch circuits are required ≫210.11(C)(1) and 210.52(B)(1)≪.

B At least one 20-ampere laundry branch circuit is required ≫210.11(C)(2) and 210.52(F)≪.

C A minimum of one 20-ampere bathroom branch circuit is required ≫210.11(C)(3) and 210.52(D)≪.

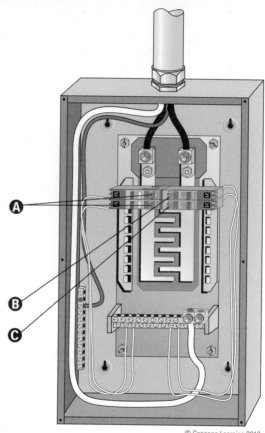

© Cengage Learning 2012

Calculating 15-Ampere Branch Circuits

A Calculation to find the minimum number of 15-ampere branch circuits:

• Calculate the general lighting and receptacle load by using Table 220.12.

• First, multiply 1400 ft² by 3 volt-amperes:

$1400 \times 3 = 4200$ volt-amperes

• Next, divide the total volt-amperes by 120 volts to find the total amperes:

$4200 \div 120 = 35$ amperes

• Finally, divide 35 amperes by 15 (for a 15-ampere circuit) to find the minimum number of circuits: $35 \div 15 = 2.33$. (Round up to the next whole number if the result of the calculation is not a whole number.)

• If 15-ampere circuits are installed for general lighting and receptacles, then at least three circuits are required.

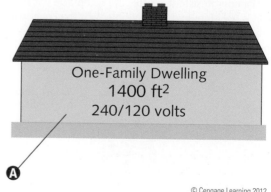

One-Family Dwelling
1400 ft²
240/120 volts

© Cengage Learning 2012

Calculating 20-Ampere Branch Circuits

Ⓐ Calculation to find the minimum number of 20-ampere branch circuits:

- Calculate the general lighting and receptacle load by using Table 220.12.

- First, multiply 1400 ft² by 3 volt-amperes:

  $1400 \times 3 = 4200$ volt-amperes

- Next, divide the total volt-amperes by 120 volts to find the total amperes: $4200 \div 120 = 35$ amperes

- Finally, divide 35 amperes by 20 (for a 20-ampere circuit) to find the minimum number of circuits: $35 \div 20 = 1.75$. (Round up to the next whole number if the result of the calculation is not a whole number.)

- If 20-ampere circuits are installed for general lighting and receptacles, then at least two circuits are required.

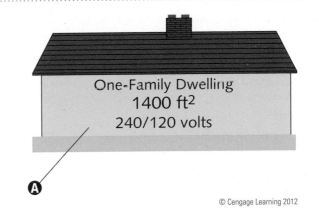

One-Family Dwelling
1400 ft²
240/120 volts

Ⓐ

© Cengage Learning 2012

N O T E

At least four 20-ampere branch circuits are required (in addition to any installed for general lighting and receptacles): two small appliance branch circuits, one laundry branch circuit, and one bathroom branch circuit.

Individual Branch Circuit for a Water Heater

Ⓐ Calculation to find the maximum overcurrent protective device:

- The overcurrent protection shall not exceed the rating marked on the appliance. If the rating is not marked and the appliance is rated over 13.3 amperes, the overcurrent protection shall not exceed 150% of the rated current 》*422.11(E)(3)*《: $18.75 \times 150\% = 28.13$.

- If the calculated rating does not correspond to a standard size fuse or breaker, as found in 240.6(A), the next higher standard rating shall be permitted 》*422.11(E)(3)*《. The next standard size fuse or breaker higher than the calculated rating of 28.13 amperes is 30 amperes.

- The maximum overcurrent protective device (fuse or breaker) is 30 amperes.

Ⓑ The minimum conductor size is 10 AWG copper 》*Table 310.15(B)(16)*《. Because the overcurrent protection shall not exceed 20 amperes for 12 AWG copper, 12 AWG conductors are not permitted 》*240.4(D)*《.

Ⓒ A branch circuit supplying a fixed storage-type water heater (120-gallon capacity or less) shall be considered a continuous load and, therefore, must have a rating not less than 125% of the water heater nameplate rating 》*422.13 and 422.10(A)*《.

Ⓓ Calculation to find the minimum circuit ampacity:

- First, divide the wattage by the voltage to find amperage: $4500 \div 240 = 18.75$

- Next, multiply the amperage by 125% as required by 422.13: $18.75 \times 125\% = 23.44$

- The minimum ampacity required for this water heater is 23.44 amperes.

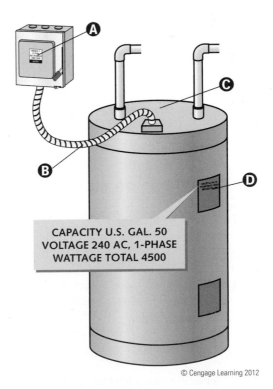

Ⓐ

Ⓒ

Ⓑ

Ⓓ

CAPACITY U.S. GAL. 50
VOLTAGE 240 AC, 1-PHASE
WATTAGE TOTAL 4500

© Cengage Learning 2012

Ampere Rating of Receptacles

Receptacle branch circuits must have a rating of 20 amperes for laundry areas, bathrooms, kitchens (except for refrigeration equipment supplied from an individual branch circuit rated 15 amperes or greater), dining rooms, pantries, breakfast rooms, and similar areas. Throughout the remainder of a one-family dwelling, 15-ampere receptacle branch circuits are allowed.

Lighting and receptacles can share the same branch circuit, except for small-appliance receptacles, bathroom receptacles (unless the circuit supplies a single bathroom), and laundry receptacles ≫*210.23(A)*≪. See Unit 7 for additional information concerning receptacles and lighting in these specific areas.

Ⓐ Receptacles installed on 15-ampere circuits must have an ampere rating of not more than 15 amperes ≫*Table 210.21(B)(3)*≪.

Ⓑ A 20-ampere duplex receptacle shall not be installed on a 15-ampere circuit.

Ⓒ Receptacles installed on 20-ampere circuits can have an ampere rating of either 15 or 20 amperes ≫*Table 210.21(B)(3)*≪.

NOTE

Branch circuits for receptacles shall not be smaller than 14 AWG ≫*210.19(A)(4)*≪. Generally, 15-ampere circuits require 14 AWG and 20-ampere circuits require 12 AWG copper conductors. Larger conductors may be needed to compensate for voltage drop or ambient temperature, or where more than three current-carrying conductors exist in a raceway or cable.

A Single Receptacle on an Individual Branch Circuit

Ⓐ A single receptacle installed on a branch circuit with no other device or outlet shall have an ampere rating not less than the rating of that circuit ≫*210.21(B)(1)*≪.

Ⓑ Although installing two or more 20-ampere receptacles or outlets on a 15-ampere circuit is not permitted, there is no provision that prohibits installing a 20-ampere single receptacle on a 15-ampere circuit. See Section 210.21(B)(1).

Ⓒ A 15-ampere single receptacle must not be installed on a 20-ampere individual branch circuit.

Ⓓ A duplex receptacle is not a single receptacle. As defined in Article 100, a single receptacle is a single contact device with no other contact device on the same yoke.

Ⓔ Receptacles on 20-ampere circuits can have a rating of either 15 or 20 amperes ≫*Table 210.21(B)(3)*≪.

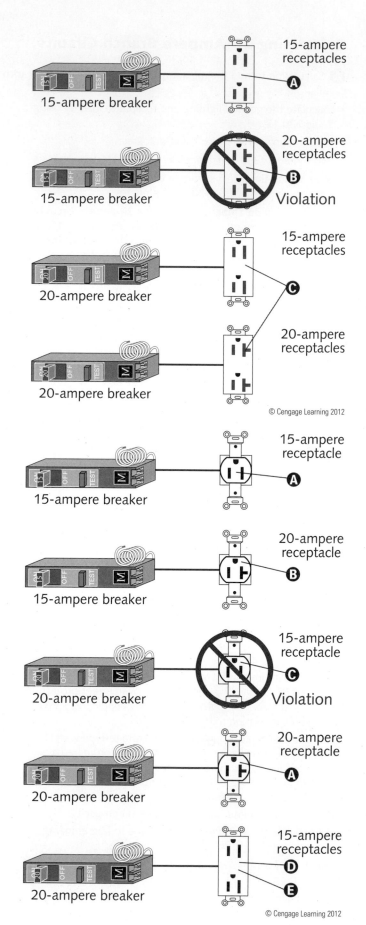

15-ampere breaker — 15-ampere receptacles Ⓐ

15-ampere breaker — 20-ampere receptacles Ⓑ Violation

20-ampere breaker — 15-ampere receptacles Ⓒ

20-ampere breaker — 20-ampere receptacles Ⓒ

© Cengage Learning 2012

15-ampere breaker — 15-ampere receptacle Ⓐ

15-ampere breaker — 20-ampere receptacle Ⓑ

20-ampere breaker — 15-ampere receptacle Ⓒ Violation

20-ampere breaker — 20-ampere receptacle Ⓐ

20-ampere breaker — 15-ampere receptacles Ⓓ Ⓔ

© Cengage Learning 2012

RECEPTACLES

General Receptacle Placement

Wall space determines the minimum number of receptacles in a given dwelling. Receptacle outlets shall be installed in kitchens, family rooms, dining rooms, living rooms, parlors, libraries, dens, sunrooms, bedrooms, recreation rooms, or similar rooms or areas in accordance with the provisions specified in 210.52(A).

A Receptacles shall be installed so that no point measured horizontally along the floor line of any wall space is more than 6 ft (1.8 m) from a receptacle outlet ≫ *210.52(A)(1)* ≪.

B The maximum distance between receptacles is 12 ft (3.6 m).

C General receptacle placement requirements for 125-volt, 15- and 20-ampere receptacle outlets are in 210.52.

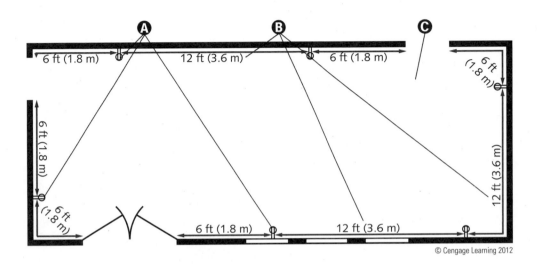

© Cengage Learning 2012

CAUTION

The receptacles required by 210.52(A) through (H) shall be in addition to any receptacle that is (1) part of a luminaire or appliance; (2) controlled by a wall switch in accordance with 210.70(A) Exception No. 1; (3) located within cabinets or cupboards; or (4) located more than 5½ ft (1.7 m) above the floor ≫ *210.52* ≪.

NOTE

Dwelling unit receptacle outlet general provisions (210.52) apply to any part of a basement containing habitable rooms, such as a den, recreational room, etc. ≫ *210.52(G)* ≪.

Wall Spaces 2 ft (600 mm) in Width

A A receptacle is required for any wall space 2 ft (600 mm) or more in width (including space measured around corners), unbroken along the floor line by doorways and similar openings, fireplaces, and fixed cabinets ≫ *210.52(A)(2)(1)* ≪.

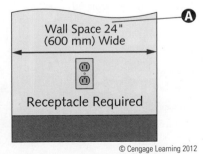

© Cengage Learning 2012

Maximum Distance to a Receptacle

Ⓐ An easy way to understand the placement of dwelling receptacles is to imagine having a floor lamp with a 6-ft (1.8-m) cord. Anywhere this lamp is placed around the wall, there should be a receptacle within reach, without using an extension cord. Even when placed beside a door opening, an outlet should be within reach. If the lamp is placed next to a wall that is at least 24 in. (600 mm) wide, an outlet should be available within that wall space.

Ⓑ The maximum distance to any receptacle, along the floor line of any wall space, measured horizontally, shall be 6 ft (1.8 m) 》210.52(A)(1)《.

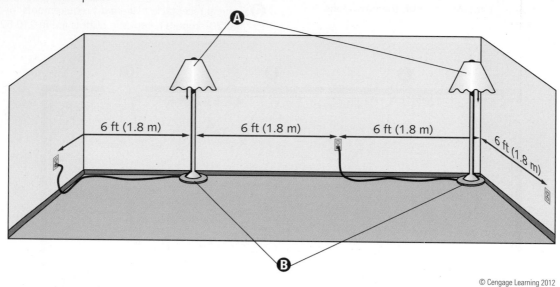

© Cengage Learning 2012

Space Measured around Corners

Ⓐ The maximum distance **between receptacles** along the floor line of any wall space measured horizontally shall be 12 ft (3.6 m) 》210.52(A)(1)《.

Ⓑ Wall space includes space measured around corners 》210.52(A)(2)(1)《.

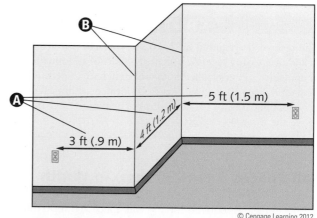

© Cengage Learning 2012

Fixed Panels

Ⓐ Glass door fixed panels in exterior walls are counted as wall space 》210.52(A)(2)(2)《.

Ⓑ Sliding panels in exterior walls are not counted as wall space 》210.52(A)(2)(2)《.

Ⓒ The maximum distance to any receptacle along the floor line measured horizontally shall be 6 ft (1.8 m) 》210.52(A)(1)《.

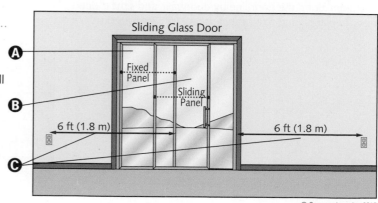

© Cengage Learning 2012

Fixed Room Dividers

A The space afforded by fixed room dividers, such as railings or freestanding bar-type counters, shall be counted as wall space »*210.52(A)(2)(3)*«.

B Receptacle outlets in floors are permitted. Receptacles located more than 18 in. (450 mm) from the wall (or room divider) may not be counted as required receptacles »*210.52(A)(3)*«.

> ### N O T E
>
> Not all types of receptacle boxes are suitable for floor installation. Different types of boxes may be required for different types of floor construction, that is, wood or concrete. Receptacle floor boxes must be listed specifically for the type of floor in which they are installed »*314.27(B)*«.

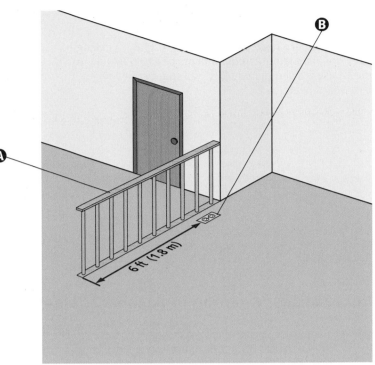

© Cengage Learning 2012

Miscellaneous Receptacle Requirements

Luminaires or appliance(s) with built-in receptacle(s) are permitted, but these receptacles do not count as required receptacles »*210.52*«.

A Although receptacles located more than 5½ ft (1.7 m) above the floor are permitted, they are not counted as required receptacles »*210.52*«.

B Although receptacle outlets within cabinets or cupboards are permitted, they are not counted as required receptacles »*210.52*«.

> ### N O T E
>
> Height requirements for wall receptacles are not defined.

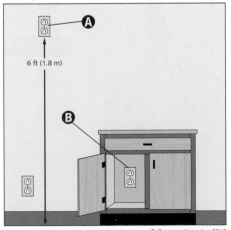

© Cengage Learning 2012

Balcony Handrail

A A receptacle floor box must be listed specifically for the type of floor in which it is installed »*314.27(B)*«.

B A floor receptacle may be required if a balcony handrail is longer than 6 ft (1.8 m) and the area is one listed in 210.52(A).

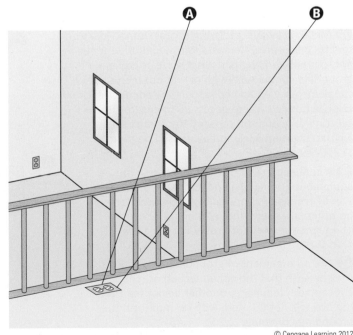

© Cengage Learning 2012

Electric Baseboard Heaters

A A baseboard heater more than 12 ft (3.6 m) in length does not eliminate the requirements of 210.52(A)(1). A receptacle is still required for a wall space containing a baseboard heater.

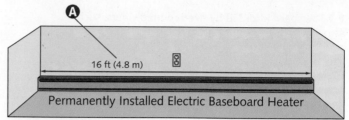

16 ft (4.8 m)

Permanently Installed Electric Baseboard Heater

© Cengage Learning 2012

> **NOTE**
>
> Listed or labeled equipment must be installed (and used) per any instructions included in the listing or labeling ≫*110.3(B)*≪.

> **CAUTION**
>
> Listed baseboard heaters include instructions that may not permit their installation below receptacle outlets ≫*210.52 Informational Note and 424.9 Informational Note*≪.

Receptacles Mounted in Baseboard Heaters

A Permanently installed electric baseboard heaters equipped with factory-installed outlets or outlets provided as a separate assembly by the manufacturer shall be permitted as the required outlet(s) for the wall space utilized by such permanently installed heaters ≫*210.52 and 424.9*≪.

B The receptacle outlet(s) shall not be connected to the heater circuit ≫*210.52 and 424.9*≪.

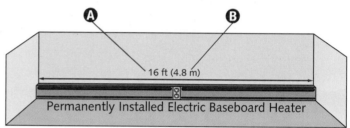

16 ft (4.8 m)

Permanently Installed Electric Baseboard Heater

© Cengage Learning 2012

Receptacle Boxes

Receptacle boxes shall comply with Article 314. An expanded description of boxes, including box fill calculations, can be found in Unit 3 of this guidebook.

A Metal raceways, cable trays, cable armor, cable sheath, enclosures, frames, fittings, and other metal non-current-carrying parts that serve as equipment grounding conductors (with or without the use of supplementary equipment grounding conductors) shall be bonded where necessary to ensure electrical continuity and the capacity to conduct safely any fault current likely to be imposed on them ≫*250.96(A)*≪.

B A connection shall be made between the equipment grounding conductor(s) and a metal box by means of a grounding screw used for no other purpose. Other grounding devices or equipment listed for grounding are allowed ≫*250.148(C)*≪.

C The arrangement of grounding connections shall be such that the disconnection or removal of a receptacle, luminaire, or other device fed from the box will not interfere with (or interrupt) the grounding continuity ≫*250.148(B)*≪.

Grounding Clip

Grounding Screw

Thread-Forming Screw that Engages Less than Two Threads

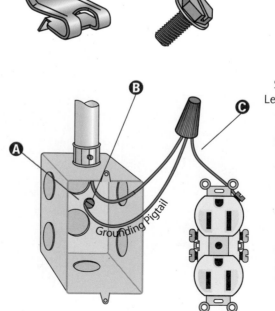

Grounding Pigtail

> **CAUTION**
>
> Thread-forming machine screws that do not engage at least two threads in the enclosure shall not be used as grounding screws ≫*250.8*≪.

© Cengage Learning 2012

Grounding-Type Receptacles

Whereas 14 AWG copper conductors are required for 15-ampere circuits, 20-ampere circuits require 12 AWG ≫*240.4(D)*≪.

Ⓐ Nongrounding-type receptacles may only be used to replace existing nongrounding receptacles (see "Receptacle Replacements" later in this unit).

Ⓑ Grounding-type receptacles shall be used on 15- and 20-ampere branch circuits ≫*406.4(A)*≪.

Ⓒ For 15-, 20-, and 30-ampere circuits, the equipment grounding conductor shall be the same size as the current-carrying conductors ≫*Table 250.122*≪. The size grounding conductor for a 15-ampere circuit is 14 AWG copper conductor; for a 20-ampere circuit is 12 AWG; and for a 30-ampere circuit is 10 AWG.

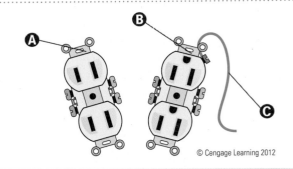

© Cengage Learning 2012

> **N O T E**
>
> Where receptacles have equipment grounding conductor contacts, those contacts shall be grounded by connection to the equipment grounding conductor of the circuit that supplies the receptacle ≫*406.4(B) and (C)*≪.

Split-Wire Receptacles

Ⓐ A switch has been installed to control one of the multiwire branch circuits.

Ⓑ Each multiwire branch circuit must be provided with a means that simultaneously disconnects all ungrounded (hot) conductors at the point where the branch circuit originates ≫*210.4(B)*≪. This is accomplished through the use of either one double-pole breaker or two single-pole breakers with identified handle ties.

Ⓒ A split-wire receptacle receiving power from a single source (one breaker or one fuse) is not a multiwire receptacle.

Ⓓ Switch-controlled, split-wire duplex receptacle(s) are sometimes installed in lieu of a lighting outlet ≫*210.70(A)(1) Exception No. 1*≪.

Ⓔ The tab has been removed so one receptacle can be controlled from the switch and the other receptacle can remain live whether the switch is on or off.

Ⓕ One-half of the duplex receptacle is controlled by a wall switch, while the other half is a typical receptacle.

> **WARNING**
>
> In multiwire branch circuits, the continuity of a grounded conductor shall not be dependent on the device ≫*300.13(B)*≪. If breaking the grounded conductor at the receptacle breaks the circuit down the line, then the grounded conductors must *not* be connected to the receptacle. Simply splice the grounded conductors and install a jumper wire to the receptacle.

> **N O T E**
>
> For additional information concerning multiwire branch circuits, see the definition located in Unit 2.

Split-Wired Receptacles Supplied from a Multiwire Branch Circuit

Split-Wired Receptacles Supplied from a Single Branch Circuit

Switch in "Off" Position

Tab Has Been Removed

120 Volts — Top Outlet Always On

0 Volts — Bottom Outlet Controlled by Switch

© Cengage Learning 2012

Wet Bar Receptacles

If located outside the kitchen, pantry, breakfast room, dining room, or similar area, wet bar countertop receptacle placement is not specified »*210.52(C)*«.

Ⓐ Regardless of whether the receptacle serves countertop space or not, ground-fault circuit-interrupter (GFCI) protection is required if the receptacle is within 6 ft (1.8 m) of the outside edge of the sink »*210.8(A)(7)*«.

Ⓑ GFCI protection is required where receptacles are installed within 6 ft (1.8 m) of the outside edge of the sink »*210.8(A) (7)*«.

Ⓒ For cord-and plug-connected appliances, an accessible, separable connector or an accessible plug and receptacle can serve as the disconnecting means. Where the separable connector (or plug and receptacle) are not readily accessible, cord-and plug-connected appliances shall have a disconnecting means in accordance with 422.31 »*422.33(A)*«.

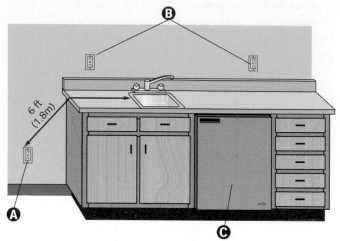

© Cengage Learning 2012

Room Air Conditioner Receptacle

Ⓐ If supplied by an individual branch circuit, the rating of a cord- and attachment plug–connected room air conditioner can be no more than 80% of the circuit's ampere rating »*210.23(A)(1)* and *440.62(B)*«.

Ⓑ Where other receptacles, lighting units, or appliances are also supplied, the rating of a cord- and attachment plug–connected room air conditioner shall not exceed 50% of the branch-circuit ampere rating »*210.23(A)(2)* and *440.62(C)*«.

Ⓒ The attachment plug can serve as the disconnecting means »*440.13*«.

Ⓓ The length of the supply cord shall not exceed 10 ft (3.0 m) for a 120-volt or 6 ft (1.8 m) for a 208- or 240-volt room air conditioner »*440.64*«.

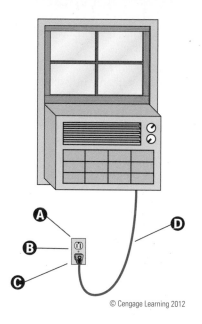

> ### N O T E
>
> For additional provisions pertaining to room air conditioners, see Part VII of Article 440.

Length of Free Conductor

Ⓐ At least 6 in. (150 mm) of free conductor, measured from the point in the box where it emerges from its raceway or cable sheath, shall be left at each outlet, junction, and switch point »*300.14*«.

Ⓑ Conductors must extend a minimum of 3 in. (75 mm) outside of the box opening where the opening to the box is less than 8 in. (200 mm) in any dimension »*300.14*«.

> ### N O T E
>
> No minimum length is specified for conductors that are not spliced or terminated at the outlet, junction, or switch point
> »*300.14 Exception*«.

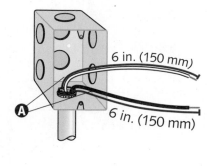

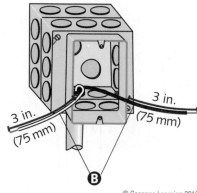

© Cengage Learning 2012

RECEPTACLE REPLACEMENTS

Grounding Means Present or Installed in the Enclosure

A A grounding-type receptacle shall be installed in any receptacle enclosure having a grounding means ⟫*406.4(D)(1)*⟪.

B If an equipment grounding conductor is installed and connected to the grounding electrode system in accordance with 250.130(C), a grounding-type receptacle shall be installed ⟫*406.4(D)(1)*⟪.

C A grounding-type receptacle shall be connected to the equipment grounding conductor in accordance with 406.4(C) or 250.130(C).

Replace with...

© Cengage Learning 2012

> **NOTE**
>
> An existing two-wire receptacle may be attached to a metal receptacle enclosure. Just because the box is metal does not guarantee that it is grounded to the grounding electrode system.

Receptacles Requiring GFCI Protection

A Because of changes in GFCI-protection requirements, some old receptacles must now be replaced with GFCI-protected receptacles ⟫*406.4(D)(3)*⟪.

B All receptacles that serve kitchen countertop surfaces shall have GFCI protection ⟫*210.8(A)(6)*⟪.

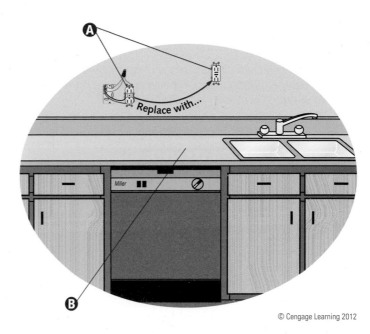

Replace with...

© Cengage Learning 2012

No Grounding Means Present . . . Nongrounding-Type Replaces Nongrounding-Type

A Where attachment to an equipment grounding conductor does not exist in the receptacle enclosure, a nongrounding-type receptacle can replace an existing nongrounding-type receptacle ⟫*406.4(D)(2)(a)*⟪.

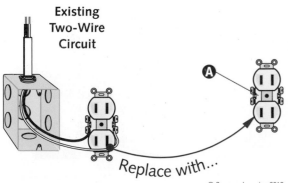

Existing Two-Wire Circuit

Replace with...

© Cengage Learning 2012

No Grounding Means Present . . . GFCI Replaces Nongrounding-Type

A Where attachment to an equipment grounding conductor does not exist in the receptacle enclosure, a GFCI receptacle can replace the old receptacle ⟫*406.4(D)(2)(b)*⟪.

B This GFCI receptacle must be labeled **"No Equipment Ground"** ⟫*406.4(D)(2)(b)*⟪.

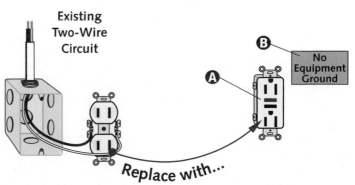

Existing Two-Wire Circuit

No Equipment Ground

Replace with...

© Cengage Learning 2012

No Grounding Means Present . . . GFCI and Grounding-Type Replaces Nongrounding-Type

A This GFCI receptacle must be labeled **"No Equipment Ground"** ≫ *406.4(D)(2)(b)* ≪.

B Where attachment to an equipment grounding conductor does not exist in the receptacle enclosure, a GFCI receptacle can replace an existing nongrounding-type receptacle ≫ *406.4(D)(2)(b)* ≪.

C A grounding-type receptacle may replace a nongrounding-type receptacle where the circuit is ground-fault protected. These receptacles shall be labeled **"GFCI Protected"** and **"No Equipment Ground"** ≫ *406.4(D)(2)(c)* ≪.

D Do not connect an equipment grounding conductor between the nongrounding-type receptacle and the grounding-type receptacle ≫ *406.4(D)(2)(c)* ≪.

CAUTION

An equipment grounding conductor shall not be connected from the GFCI-type receptacle to any outlet supplied from the GFCI receptacle ≫ *406.4(D)(2)(b)* ≪.

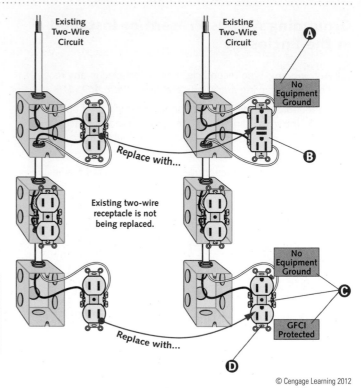

© Cengage Learning 2012

No Grounding Means Present . . . Grounding-Type Replaces Nongrounding-Type

A A grounding-type receptacle may replace a nongrounding-type receptacle where the circuit is ground-fault protected.

B These receptacles shall be labeled **"GFCI Protected"** and **"No Equipment Ground"** ≫ *406.4(D)(2)(c)* ≪.

C Do not connect an equipment grounding conductor between the nongrounding-type receptacle and the grounding-type receptacle ≫ *406.4(D)(2)(c)* ≪.

NOTE

Consumers should be alerted to the fact that a receptacle is not grounded. This is especially important as more goods (such as personal computers) require grounded receptacles.

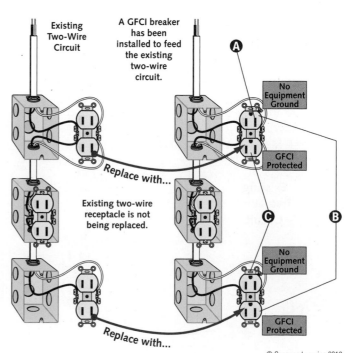

© Cengage Learning 2012

RECEPTACLES REQUIRING AFCI PROTECTION

Ⓐ Where a receptacle outlet is supplied by a branch circuit that requires arc–fault circuit–interrupter (AFCI) protection as specified elsewhere in the *NEC,* a replacement receptacle at this outlet shall be one of the following:

(1)   A listed outlet branch circuit–type arc–fault circuit–interrupter receptacle.

(2)   A receptacle protected by a listed outlet branch circuit–type arc–fault circuit interrupter–type circuit receptacle.

(3)   A receptacle protected by a listed combination–type arc–fault circuit interrupter–type circuit breaker.

This requirement becomes effective January 1, 2014 ›› *406.4(D)(4)* ‹‹ .

Ⓑ Requirements for arc–fault circuit–interrupter protection are in 210.12.

© Cengage Learning 2012

OTHER CONSIDERATIONS WHEN REPLACING RECEPTACLES

Ⓐ Listed tamper-resistant receptacles shall be provided where replacements are made at receptacle outlets that are required to be tamper-resistant elsewhere in the *NEC* ›› *406.4(D)(5)* ‹‹ . In all areas specified in 210.52, all nonlocking-type 125-volt, 15- and 20-ampere receptacles shall be listed tamper-resistant receptacles ›› *406.12* ‹‹ .

Ⓑ Tamper-resistant receptacles are identified by the letters "TR" or the words "Tamper Resistant." After the receptacle has been installed, the identification is only required to be visible with the cover-plate removed. See UL (Underwriter Laboratories) White Book, category: Receptacles for Plugs and Attachment Plugs (RTRT).

Ⓒ Weather-resistant receptacles shall be provided where replacements are made at receptacle outlets that are required to be so protected elsewhere in the *NEC* ›› *406.4(D)(6)* ‹‹ . All 15- and 20-ampere, 125- and 250-volt nonlocking-type receptacles installed in damp and wet locations shall be listed weather-resistant type ›› *406.9(A)* and *(B)* ‹‹ .

Ⓓ Weather-resistant receptacles are identified by the letters "WR" or the words "Weather Resistant." After the receptacle has been installed, the identification must be visible with the cover plate secured in place. See UL (Underwriter Laboratories) White Book, category: Receptacles for Plugs and Attachment Plugs (RTRT).

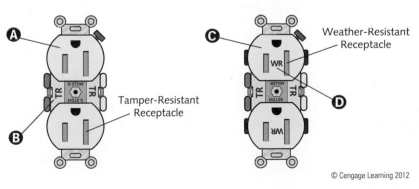

© Cengage Learning 2012

LIGHTING AND SWITCHING

Outdoor Entrances and Exits

A At least one wall switch–controlled lighting outlet shall be installed in every habitable room of a dwelling »*210.70(A)(1)*«.

B At least one wall switch–controlled lighting outlet is required to provide exterior side illumination of outdoor entrances or exits having grade-level access »*210.70(A)(2)(b)*«.

> **NOTE**
>
> Remote, central, or automatic lighting control is permitted for outdoor entrances »***210.70(A)(2) Exception***«.

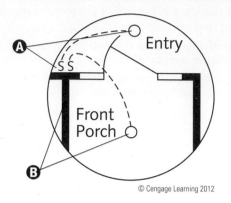

© Cengage Learning 2012

General Lighting

All switches shall be located so that they may be operated from a readily accessible place, not more than 6 ft, 7 in. (2.0 m), from the floor to the center of the switch operating handle »*404.8(A)*«**. No other height requirements are stipulated for wall switches.**

A Dwelling hallways require a minimum of one wall switch–controlled lighting outlet »*210.70(A)(2)(a)*«.

B At least one wall switch–controlled lighting outlet shall be installed in every habitable room and bathroom of a dwelling »*210.70(A)(1)*«.

C Except for kitchens and bathrooms, every habitable room is permitted one or more wall switch–controlled receptacle(s) in lieu of a lighting outlet »*210.70(A)(1) Exception No. 1*«. Switch–controlled receptacles allow for cord-connected lighting.

D At least one wall switch–controlled lighting outlet shall be installed in every bathroom of a dwelling »*210.70(A)(1)*«.

> **NOTE**
>
> Occupancy sensors are permitted to control lighting outlets in lieu of wall switches. One of two requirements must be met in order to use occupancy sensors: either a regular wall switch must be present in addition to the sensor, or the sensor must be equipped with a manual override that allows the sensor to function as a switch. Either type of wall switch shall be located at a customary location »***210.70(A)(1) Exception No. 2***«.

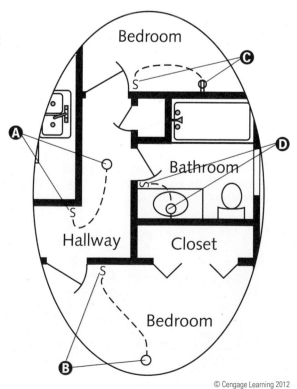

© Cengage Learning 2012

Switches Controlling Lighting Loads

Ⓐ Where switches control lighting loads supplied by a grounded general-purpose branch circuit, the grounded circuit conductor for the controlled lighting circuit shall be provided at the switch location ≫*404.2(C)*≪.

Ⓑ The provision for a (future) grounded conductor is to complete a circuit path for electronic lighting control devices ≫*404.2(C) Informational Note*≪.

> **N O T E**
>
> The grounded circuit conductor shall be permitted to be omitted from the switch enclosure where either of the following conditions in (1) or (2) apply:
> (1) Conductors for switches controlling lighting loads enter the box through a raceway. The raceway shall have sufficient cross-sectional area to accommodate the extension of the grounded circuit conductor of the lighting circuit to the switch location whether or not the conductors in the raceway are required to be increased in size to comply with 310.15(B)(2)(a).
> (2) Cable assemblies for switches controlling lighting loads enter the box through a framing cavity that is open at the top or bottom on the same floor level, or through a wall, floor, or ceiling that is unfinished on one side ≫*404.2(C) Exception*≪.

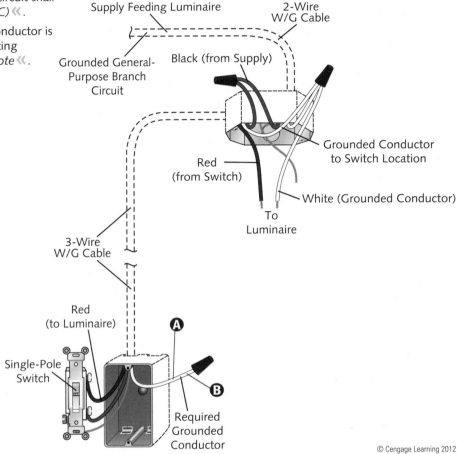

© Cengage Learning 2012

Ceiling-Suspended (Paddle) Fans

Include any light kit or accessory when determining the total weight of the fan.

Ⓐ Outlet boxes or outlet box systems used as the sole support of a ceiling-suspended (paddle) fan shall be listed, shall be marked by their manufacturer as suitable for this purpose, and shall not support ceiling-suspended (paddle) fans that weigh more than 70 pounds (32 kg). For outlet boxes or outlet box systems designed to support ceiling-suspended (paddle) fans that weigh more than 35 pounds (16 kg), the required marking must include the maximum weight that can be supported ≫*314.27(C)*≪.

© Cengage Learning 2012

> **WARNING**
>
> Even if a ceiling-suspended (paddle) fan will not be installed initially, it may be necessary to install a box (ceiling fan box) that is listed to support a ceiling-suspended (paddle) fan. In accordance with 314.27(C), where spare, separately switched, ungrounded conductors are provided to a ceiling-mounted outlet box, in a location acceptable for a ceiling-suspended (paddle) fan in single- or multifamily dwellings, the outlet box or outlet box system shall be listed for sole support of a ceiling-suspended (paddle) fan.

> **N O T E**
>
> Ceiling-suspended (paddle) fans must be supported independently of an outlet box or by listed outlet box or outlet box systems identified for the use and installed in accordance with 314.27(C) ≫*422.18*≪.

Cables Installed to Feed Switches

No provision permits the installation of a smaller conductor as a switch loop. Switch loops (legs) that are part of a 20-ampere branch circuit cannot be smaller than 12 AWG copper conductors. Table 210.24 requires 12 AWG conductors throughout a 20-ampere branch circuit, except for taps. Taps and switch loops are not the same.

A white conductor in a cable can be used as an ungrounded conductor when supplying power to a switch, but not as a return conductor from the switch to the outlet. The conductor shall be permanently reidentified to indicate its use by marking tape, painting, or other effective means at its terminations and at each location where the conductor is visible and accessible ≫ *200.7(C)(2)* ≪. The reidentified conductor can be any color except white, gray, or green.

A Metal switch boxes shall be connected to an equipment grounding conductor as specified in Part IV of Article 250 ≫ *404.12* ≪.

B Where switches control lighting loads supplied by a grounded general-purpose branch circuit, the grounded circuit conductor for the controlled lighting circuit shall be provided at the switch location ≫ *404.2(C)* ≪.

C Snap switches, including dimmer and similar control switches, shall be connected to an equipment grounding conductor and shall provide a means to connect metal faceplates to the equipment grounding conductor, whether or not a metal faceplate is installed. Snap switches shall be considered to be part of an effective ground-fault current path if either of the following conditions is met: (1) the switch is mounted with metal screws to a metal box or metal cover that is connected to an equipment grounding conductor or to a nonmetallic box with integral means for connecting to an equipment grounding conductor; or (2) an equipment grounding conductor or equipment bonding jumper is connected to an equipment grounding termination of the snap switch ≫ *404.9(B)* ≪.

D Where circuit conductors are spliced within a box, or terminated on equipment within or supported by a box, any equipment grounding conductor(s) associated with those circuit conductors shall be connected within the box or to the box with devices suitable for the use in accordance with 250.148(A) through (E) ≫ *250.148* ≪.

> **N O T E**
>
> An outlet box used exclusively for lighting can support a luminaire or lampholder weighing no more than 50 pounds (23 kg), unless the box is listed and marked for the maximum weight to be supported. A separate means for supporting a luminaire (independent of the outlet box) is also permitted ≫ *314.27(A)(2)* ≪.

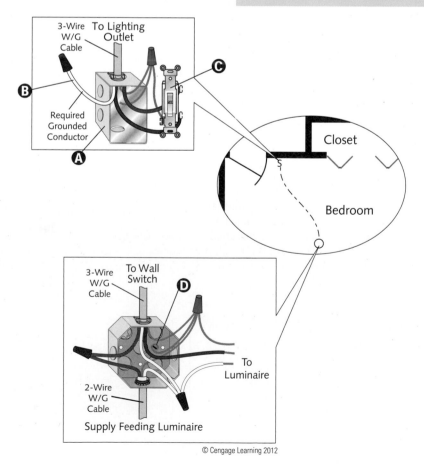

OUTDOOR RECEPTACLES AND LIGHTING

Required Outdoor Receptacles

A One-family dwellings require at least one receptacle outlet installed at the front and back of the dwelling. Each receptacle must be accessible while standing at grade level and located not more than 6 ft, 6 in. (2.0 m) above grade ≫*210.52(E)(1)*≪.

B *Each* grade level unit of a two-family dwelling requires at least one receptacle outlet installed at the front and back of the dwelling. Each receptacle must be accessible while standing at grade level and located not more than 6 ft, 6 in. (2.0 m) above grade ≫*210.52(E)(1)*≪.

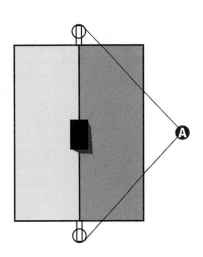

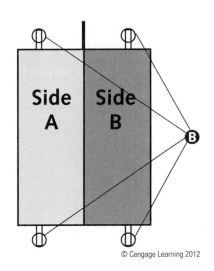

© Cengage Learning 2012

Balconies, Decks, and Porches

A Balconies, decks, and porches that are accessible from inside the dwelling unit shall have at least one receptacle outlet installed within the perimeter of the balcony, deck, or porch. The receptacle shall not be located more than 6-½ ft (2.0 m) above the balcony, deck, or porch surface ≫*210.52(E)(3)*≪.

CAUTION

All balconies, decks, and porches that are accessible from inside the dwelling unit must have the required receptacle outlet regardless of size. There is no exception for small balconies, decks, or porches. For example, a balcony with an area of 10 ft² is on the second floor of a new dwelling. The balcony is outside, but it is accessible from inside the dwelling. Although this balcony is small, a receptacle outlet must be installed within the perimeter of this balcony.

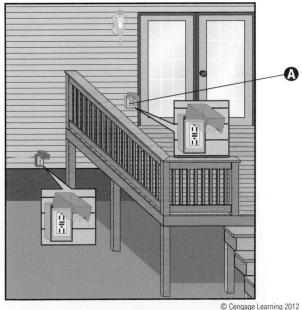

© Cengage Learning 2012

Receptacles in Damp and Wet Locations

(A) An outdoor receptacle, in a location protected from the weather or in other damp locations, requires an enclosure for the receptacle that is weatherproof when the receptacle is covered (attachment plug cap not inserted and receptacle covers closed). Receptacle locations protected from the weather include areas such as under roofed open porches, canopies, marquees, etc., that are not subjected to a beating rain or water runoff 》406.9(A)《.

(B) The enclosure for a receptacle installed in a flush-mounted outlet box in a finished surface requires the use of a weatherproof faceplate assembly that provides a watertight seal between the plate and the finished surface 》406.9(E)《.

(C) An installation suitable for wet locations shall also be considered suitable for damp locations 》406.9(A)《.

(D) All 15- and 20-ampere, 125- and 250-volt receptacles installed in a wet location must have an enclosure that is weatherproof whether or not the attachment plug cap is inserted 》406.9(B)(1)《.

(E) All 15- and 20-ampere, 125- and 250-volt nonlocking receptacles shall be a listed weather-resistant type 》406.9(A) and (B)《.

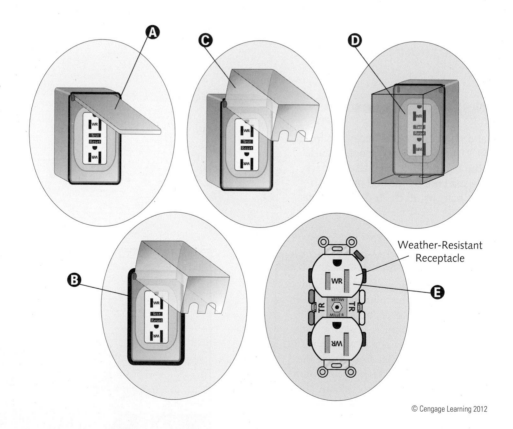

Weather-Resistant Receptacle

© Cengage Learning 2012

NOTE

All 15- and 20-ampere, 125- through 250-volt receptacles installed in a wet location and subject to routine high-pressure spray washing shall be permitted to have an enclosure that is weatherprooof when the attachment plug is removed 》*406.9(B)(1) Exception*《.

Receptacles More than 6 ft 6 in. (2.0 m) Above Grade

Ⓐ At least one receptacle outlet, accessible while standing at grade level and not more than 6 ft, 6 in. (2.0 m) above grade, shall be installed at the front *and* back of the dwelling ≫*210.52(E)(1)*≪.

Ⓑ Balconies, decks, and porches that are accessible from inside the dwelling unit shall have at least one receptacle outlet installed within the perimeter of the balcony, deck, or porch. The receptacle shall not be located more than 6½ ft (2.0 m) above the balcony, deck, or porch surface ≫*210.52(E)(3)*≪.

> **NOTE**
>
> GFCI protection is not required for receptacles that are not readily accessible and are supplied by a branch circuit dedicated to electric snow melting–, deicing-, or pipeline- and vessel-heating equipment. The installation must comply with 426.28 or 427.22, as applicable ≫**210.8(A) (3) Exception**≪. (See 426.28 and 427.22 for ground-fault protection of equipment.) Outdoor receptacles that are not readily accessible (such as under an eave) require GFCI protection.

> **CAUTION**
>
> Outdoor receptacles require GFCI protection ≫*210.8(A)(3)*≪.

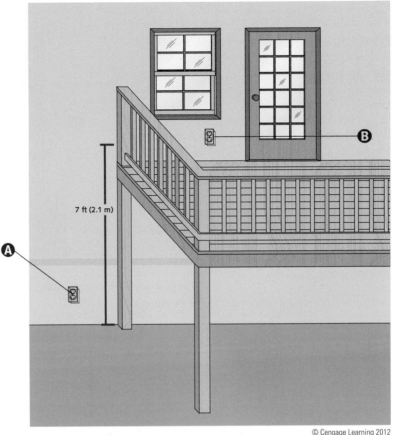

7 ft (2.1 m)

© Cengage Learning 2012

Equipment Outlet

Ⓐ A 125-volt, single-phase, 15- or 20-ampere-rated receptacle outlet shall be installed at an accessible location for the servicing of heating, air-conditioning, and refrigeration equipment. The receptacle shall be located on the same level and within 25 ft (7.5 m) of the heating, air-conditioning, and refrigeration equipment ≫*210.63*≪.

Ⓑ At least one receptacle outlet, accessible while standing at grade level and not more than 6½ ft (2.0 m) above grade, shall be installed at the front and back of the dwelling ≫*210.52(E)(1)*≪.

Ⓒ If installed in accordance with both 210.52(E) and 210.63, only one receptacle outlet is required.

> **NOTE**
>
> A receptacle outlet shall not be required at one- and two-family dwellings for the service of evaporative coolers ≫**210.63 Exception**≪.

> **CAUTION**
>
> The receptacle outlet shall not be connected to the load side of the equipment disconnecting means ≫*210.63*≪.

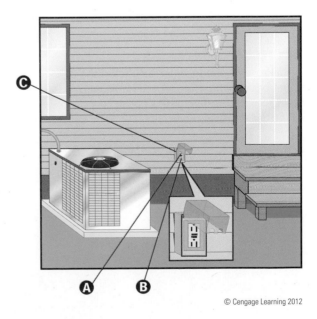

© Cengage Learning 2012

Support for Receptacle Enclosures

A As a general rule, a single conduit shall not support an enclosure that contains a device ≫ *314.23(F)* ≪.

B Rigidly and securely fasten in place all boxes and raceways ≫ *300.11(A)* and *314.23(A)* ≪.

C Supporting an enclosure from grade requires rigid support in the form of conduit or a brace (metal, polymeric, or wood) ≫ *314.23(B)* ≪. Wood brace cross sections must be at least 1 in. × 2 in. (25 mm × 50 mm). Wood braces must be treated to withstand the conditions when used in wet locations ≫ *314.23(B)(2)* ≪.

D An enclosure containing devices can be supported by two conduits under the conditions found in 314.23(F): (1) the box shall not exceed 100 in.^{3} (1650 cm^3); (2) the box has either threaded entries or hubs identified for the purpose; (3) the box shall be supported by two or more conduits threaded wrenchtight into the enclosure or hubs; and (4) each conduit shall be secured within 18 in. (450 mm) of the enclosure.

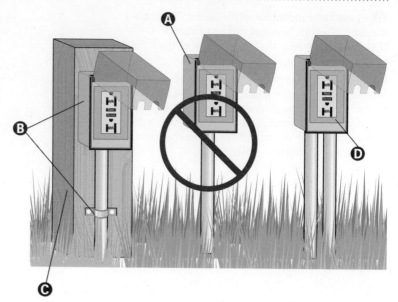

© Cengage Learning 2012

> **NOTE**
>
> Dwelling-unit outdoor receptacles require GFCI protection for personnel ≫ *210.8(A)(3)* ≪.

Illumination of Entrances and Exits

A Install at least one wall switch–controlled lighting outlet to provide illumination on the exterior side of outdoor entrances and exits (doorways) ≫ *210.70(A)(2)(b)* ≪. It is not required that the luminaire be located adjacent to the doorway, as long as illumination around the doorway is provided.

B Install at least one receptacle outlet at the front and back of the dwelling ≫ *210.52(E)(1)* ≪. Outdoor receptacles require GFCI protection ≫ *210.8(A)(3)* ≪.

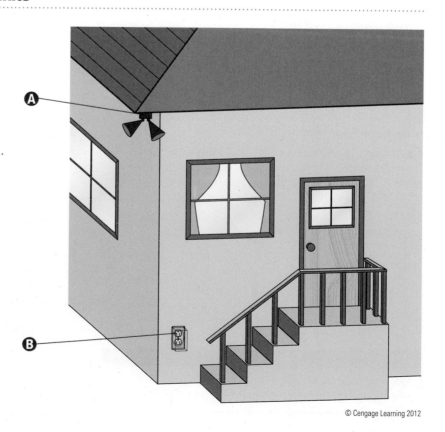

© Cengage Learning 2012

Wiring in Trees

Ⓐ Outdoor luminaires and associated equipment can be supported by trees ≫*410.36(G)*≪.

Ⓑ Vegetation (such as trees) shall not be used to support overhead conductor spans ≫*225.26*≪.

> **NOTE**
>
> Direct-buried conductors and cables emerging from grade and specified in columns 1 and 4 of Table 300.5 shall be protected by enclosures or raceways that extend from the minimum cover distance below grade required by 300.5(A) to a point 8 ft (2.5 m) or more above finished grade ≫***300.5(D)(1)***≪.

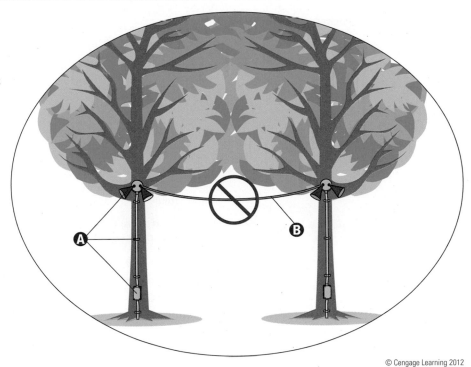

© Cengage Learning 2012

Summary

- All 120-volt, single-phase, 15- and 20-ampere branch circuits supplying outlets installed in dwelling-unit family rooms, dining rooms, living rooms, parlors, libraries, dens, bedrooms, sunrooms, recreation rooms, closets, hallways, or similar rooms or areas shall be protected by a listed arc-fault circuit interrupter, combination-type, installed to provide protection of the branch circuit.
- All nonlocking-type 125-volt, 15- and 20-ampere receptacles, in all areas specified in 210.52, shall be listed tamper-resistant receptacles.
- Balconies, decks, and porches that are accessible from inside the dwelling unit shall have at least one receptacle outlet installed within the perimeter of the balcony, deck, or porch.
- General-purpose branch circuits may feed lights, receptacles, or any combination of those items.
- An individual branch circuit feeds only one piece of equipment.
- The maximum distance to any receptacle measured horizontally along the floor line is 6 ft (1.8 m).
- A receptacle is required for any wall space 2 ft (600 mm) or wider.
- Where connected to a branch circuit supplying two or more receptacles or outlets, receptacles rated 20 amperes are not permitted on a 15-ampere branch circuit.
- Both 15- and 20-ampere receptacles are permitted on 20-ampere branch circuits.
- GFCI-protected receptacles may replace nongrounding-type receptacles where the receptacle enclosure is without a grounding means.
- GFCI-protected receptacles on nongrounded systems must be marked in accordance with 406.4(D)(2) provisions.
- A means to simultaneously disconnect all ungrounded conductors must be provided on multiwire branch circuits.
- A switch-controlled lighting outlet shall be installed in every habitable room of a dwelling, including bathrooms, hallways, and stairways.
- Where switches control lighting loads supplied by a grounded general-purpose branch circuit, the grounded circuit conductor for the controlled lighting circuit shall be provided at the switch location.
- Boxes are permitted to support luminaires weighing 50 pounds (23 kg) or less.
- Listed boxes are permitted to support ceiling fans weighing no more than 35 pounds (16 kg).
- One-family dwellings require at least one exterior GFCI-protected receptacle outlet at the front and back of the dwelling.
- Outdoor entrances and exits must have at least one wall switch–controlled lighting outlet.
- Although lighting and receptacles can be supported by trees, trees shall not support overhead conductor spans.

Unit 6 Competency Test

NEC Reference   Answer

_____   _____   1. A duplex receptacle rated 20 amperes can be installed on a _____ branch circuit.

       a) 15-ampere   b) 20-ampere

       c) 15- or 20-ampere   d) 20- or 25-ampere

_____   _____   2. The continuity of a grounded conductor shall not be dependent on the device in _____.

       a) branch circuits not having a grounded conductor

       b) multiwire branch circuits

       c) individual branch circuits

       d) branch circuits

_____   _____   3. Receptacles located more than _____ ft above the floor are not counted in the required number of receptacles along the wall.

_____   _____   4. At least _____ in. of free conductor, measured from the point in the box where it emerges from its raceway or cable sheath, shall be left at each outlet, junction, and switch point for splices or the connection of luminaires (lighting fixtures) or devices.

_____   _____   5. In nonmetallic-sheathed cable, the equipment grounding conductor for 15-, 20-, and 30-ampere branch circuits _____.

       a) is required only with aluminum or copper-clad aluminum cable

       b) must be the same size as the insulated circuit conductors

       c) may be one size smaller than the insulated circuit conductors

       d) may be two sizes smaller than the insulated circuit conductors

_____   _____   6. Receptacles installed for the attachment of portable cords shall be rated at not less than 15 amperes, 125 volts, or _____ amperes, 250 volts, and shall be of a type not suitable for use as lampholders.

_____   _____   7. A luminaire that weighs more than 6 pounds (3 kg) or exceeds _____ in. in any dimension shall not be supported by the screw shell of a lampholder.

_____   _____   8. Which of the following is not a standard classification for a branch circuit supplying several loads?

       a) 20 amperes   b) 25 amperes   c) 30 amperes   d) 50 amperes

_____   _____   9. A cord connector that is supported by a permanently installed cord pendant shall be considered a(n) _____ outlet.

_____   _____   10. Grounding-type receptacles shall be installed only on circuits of the _____ for which they are rated, except as provided in Tables 210.21(B)(2) and (B)(3).

       I. voltage class

       II. wattage

       III. current

       a) I only   b) I and III only   c) I and II only   d) I, II, and III

_____   _____   11. Outlet boxes or outlet box systems used as the sole support of a ceiling-suspended (paddle) fan shall be listed, shall be marked by their manufacturer as suitable for this purpose, and shall not support ceiling-suspended (paddle) fans that weigh more than _____ pounds.

_____   _____   12. Receptacle outlets in floors shall not be counted as part of the required number of receptacle outlets unless located within _____ in. of the wall.

_____ _____ 13. Luminaires shall be wired with conductors having insulation suitable for the environmental conditions, _____, _____, and _____ to which the conductors will be subjected.

_____ _____ 14. A luminaire that weighs more than 50 pounds (23 kg) shall be supported _____.

_____ _____ 15. A duplex receptacle rated 15 amperes can be installed on a _____ ampere general-purpose branch circuit.

_____ _____ 16. A branch circuit that supplies only one utilization equipment is known as a(n) _____ branch circuit.

_____ _____ 17. The maximum distance between receptacles in a one-family dwelling is _____ ft.

_____ _____ 18. A nongrounding-type receptacle has been replaced with a new grounding-type duplex receptacle. The 15-ampere circuit breaker feeding the circuit has been replaced with a 15-ampere ground-fault circuit breaker. The new receptacle must be marked _____.

    I. "Two-Wire Circuit"

   II. "No Equipment Ground"

  III. "GFCI Protected"

     a) III only   b) I and III only   c) II and III only   d) I, II, and III

_____ _____ 19. An outlet where one or more receptacles are installed is called a(n) _____.

_____ _____ 20. What is the maximum distance that a receptacle wall box can be set back from the finished surface of a ¼-in. wood paneling wall?

     a) 0.0625 in.   b) 0.125 in.   c) 0.25 in.   d) 0.0 in.

_____ _____ 21. Switch-controlled receptacles (in lieu of a lighting outlet) are permitted in all but which of the following?

     a) Bedroom   b) Library   c) Dining room   d) Hallway

_____ _____ 22. A single receptacle rated 50 amperes can be installed on a _____-ampere individual branch circuit.

_____ _____ 23. A(n) _____ is a system or circuit conductor that is intentionally grounded.

_____ _____ 24. The definition of a branch circuit is _____.

    a) the circuit conductors between the service and the subpanel

    b) the circuit conductors prior to the final overcurrent device protecting the circuit

    c) the circuit conductors between the final overcurrent device protecting the circuit and the outlet(s)

    d) the circuit conductors between the final overload device protecting the circuit and the outlet(s)

_____ _____ 25. In dwelling units, a duplex receptacle fed from a multiwire branch circuit must have _____ as a means of disconnect.

    I. two single-pole circuit breakers without identified handle ties

   II. one double-pole circuit breaker

  III. two single-pole circuit breakers with identified handle ties

     a) I only   b) I or II only   c) II only   d) II or III only

BATHROOMS

Bathroom Area

The general provisions for receptacle placement by wall space do not apply to bathrooms.

Ⓐ GFCI protection for personnel is required for every 125-volt, 15- and 20-ampere receptacle located in the bathroom area ≫ *210.8(A)(1)* ≪ .

Ⓑ Bathroom Definition: An area including a basin (lavatory or sink) with one or more of the following: a toilet, a urinal, a tub, a shower, a bidet, or similar plumbing fixtures ≫ *Article 100—Definitions* ≪ . A bathroom is an **area** and not necessarily a single room.

Ⓒ One or more lighting outlets controlled by a wall switch are required in bathrooms ≫ *210.70(A)(1)* ≪ .

> ### N O T E
>
> Service disconnecting means shall not be located in bathrooms ≫*230.70(A)(2)*≪ . Overcurrent devices, other than supplementary overcurrent protection, shall not be installed in bathrooms ≫*240.24(E)*≪ . Supplementary overcurrent protection is not branch-circuit overcurrent protection. It is an additional overcurrent protection usually installed within luminaires, appliances, and other equipment. It is not required that supplementary overcurrent protection be readily accessible ≫*240.10*≪.

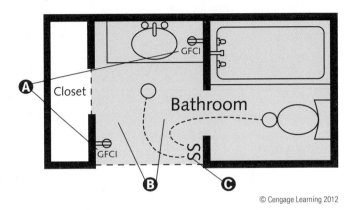

© Cengage Learning 2012

Receptacle within 36 in. (900 mm) of Sink

Ⓐ At least one receptacle shall be located within 36 in. (900 mm) of the outside edge of each basin (lavatory or sink) ≫ *210.52(D)* ≪ .

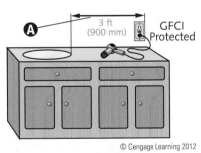

© Cengage Learning 2012

Bathroom Branch-Circuit Rating

Ⓐ Bathroom receptacle outlets shall be supplied by at least one 20-ampere branch circuit ≫ *210.11(C)(3)* ≪ .

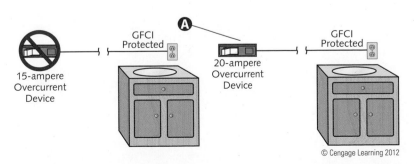

© Cengage Learning 2012

Bathroom Receptacles

Receptacles are not permitted in a face-up position in countertops or similar work surfaces ≫ *406.5(E)* ≪.

A At least one receptacle shall be located within 36 in. (900 mm) of the outside edge of each basin (lavatory or sink) ≫ *210.52(D)* ≪.

B Receptacles may have an individual rating of either 15 or 20 amperes, but must be supplied from a 20-ampere branch circuit ≫ *210.11(C)(3)* ≪. GFCI protection for personnel is required for all bathroom receptacles. The ground-fault circuit interrupter must be installed in a readily accessible location ≫ *210.8(A)(1)* ≪.

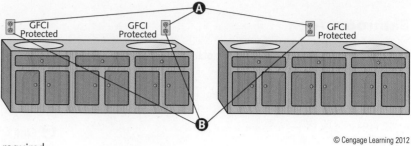

© Cengage Learning 2012

NOTE

Receptacle outlet assemblies listed for the application shall be permitted to be installed in the countertop ≫*210.52(D)*≪.

CAUTION

The receptacle outlet shall be located on a wall or partition that is adjacent to the basin or basin countertop, located on the countertop, or installed on the side or face of the basin cabinet not more than 12 in. (300 mm) below the countertop ≫*210.52(D)*≪.

Bathroom

A A branch circuit providing power to a bathroom receptacle may also provide power to other bathroom receptacles, whether in the same bathroom or in different bathrooms ≫ *210.11(C)(3)* ≪.

B A branch circuit providing power to a bathroom receptacle may also provide power to other equipment, such as lighting and exhaust fans, but only within the same bathroom ≫ *210.11(C)(3) Exception* ≪. If the branch circuit provides power to a bathroom receptacle and other equipment, the circuit shall not provide power to any other bathroom.

C A branch circuit providing power to bathroom receptacles shall not provide power to any receptacle or lighting outside of bathrooms ≫ *210.11(C)(3)* ≪.

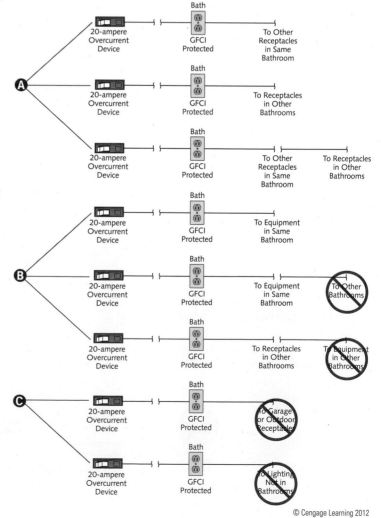

© Cengage Learning 2012

Bathtub and Shower Zone

Ⓐ Luminaire permitted (not in zone)

Ⓑ Luminaire not permitted

Ⓒ No parts of cord-connected luminaires, chain-, cable-, or cord-suspended luminaires, lighting track, pendants, and ceiling-suspended (paddle) fans are permitted within a certain zone of a bathtub 》*410.10(D)*《. The bathtub zone measures 3 ft (900 mm) horizontally and 8 ft (2.5 m) vertically from the top of the bathtub rim or shower stall threshold and includes the space directly over the tub.

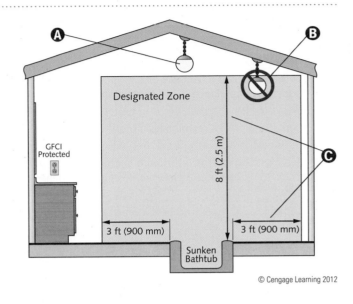

© Cengage Learning 2012

WARNING

Luminaires located within the actual outside dimension of the bathtub or shower to a height of 8 ft (2.5 m) vertically from the top of the bathtub rim or shower threshold shall be marked for damp locations, or marked for wet locations where subject to shower spray 》*410.10(D)*《.

Ⓐ Recessed lights, surface-mounted lights, and exhaust fans are permitted within the bathtub zone. Exposed, normally non-current-carrying metal parts must be connected to an equipment grounding conductor in accordance with 250.110.

Ⓑ Chain-, cable-, or cord-suspended luminaires, cord-connected luminaires, lighting track, pendants, and ceiling-suspended (paddle) fans are permitted only *outside* the zone.

Ⓒ The bathtub zone measures 3 ft (900 mm) horizontally and 8 ft (2.5 m) vertically from the top of the bathtub rim or shower stall threshold. The zone is all-encompassing and includes the space directly over the tub or shower stall 》*410.10(D)*《.

CAUTION

A receptacle shall not be installed within or directly over the bathtub or shower stall 》*406.9(C)*《.

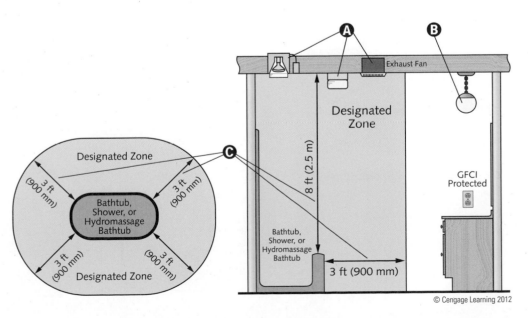

© Cengage Learning 2012

BASEMENTS AND GARAGES

Garage Receptacles

A Whether a duplex receptacle or a single receptacle is installed for an appliance, GFCI protection is required ≫ *210.8(A)(2)* ≪.

B Laundry equipment receptacles are not counted as required garage receptacles ≫ *210.52(G)* ≪.

C At least one receptacle is required in an attached garage ≫ *210.52(G)* ≪. (Receptacle placement is not determined by wall space.)

D Receptacles not readily accessible must have GFCI protection ≫ *210.8(A)(2)* ≪.

E All receptacles installed in garages must have GFCI protection 210.8(A)(2).

F If a duplex receptacle is installed for two appliances, GFCI protection is required. ≫ *210.8(A)(2)* ≪.

G A single receptacle installed on an individual 20-ampere branch circuit must have a rating of 20 amperes ≫ *210.21(B)(1)* ≪.

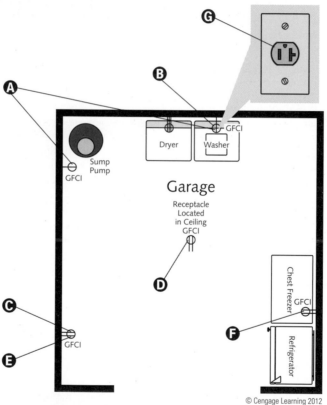

© Cengage Learning 2012

GFCI Receptacles in a Garage

A If a duplex receptacle is installed, GFCI protection is required ≫ *210.8(A)(2)* ≪.

B If a single receptacle is installed, GFCI protection is required. ≫ *210.8(A)(2)* ≪.

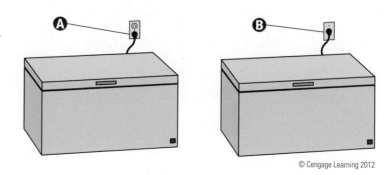

© Cengage Learning 2012

Lighting

A Basements and attached garages require at least one receptacle each ⟫ *210.52(G)* ⟪ . (Receptacle placement is not determined by wall space.)

B At least one wall switch–controlled lighting outlet is required to provide illumination on the exterior side of an outside entrance or exit with grade-level access ⟫ *210.70(A)(2)(b)* ⟪ .

C A vehicle garage door is not considered an outside entrance or exit and therefore does not require a wall switch–controlled lighting outlet ⟫ *210.70(A)(2)(b)* ⟪ .

D A lighting outlet shall be installed at, or near, equipment that may require servicing ⟫ *210.70(A)(3)* ⟪ .

E At least one wall switch–controlled lighting outlet is required for basements and attached garages ⟫ *210.70(A)(2) and (3)* ⟪ .

F Interior stairways with six or more steps shall have a wall switch located at each floor level and landing that includes an entryway ⟫ *210.70(A)(2)(c)* ⟪ .

G A lighting outlet installed to provide illumination for the general area (basement, garage, etc.) may also serve as the equipment lighting, provided it is located at or near the equipment.

H All 125-volt, single-phase, 15- and 20-ampere receptacles installed in unfinished basements shall have GFCI protection for personnel ⟫ *210.8(A)(5)* ⟪ .

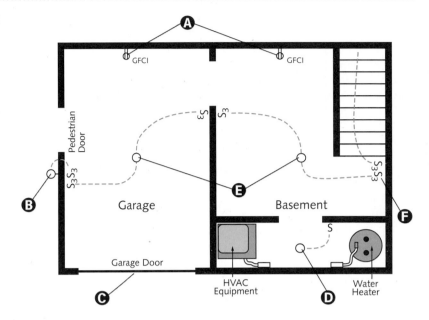

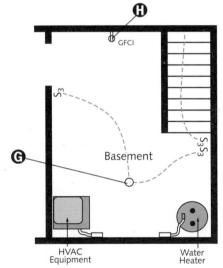

© Cengage Learning 2012

NOTE

A receptacle in an unfinished basement supplying only a permanently installed fire alarm or burglar alarm system shall not be required to have GFCI protection ⟫***210.8(A)(5) Exception***⟪. Receptacles installed under this exception shall not be considered as meeting the requirements of 210.52(G).

NOTE

Unfinished basements are defined as portions or areas of the basement not intended as habitable rooms and limited to storage areas, work areas, and the like ⟫***210.8(A)(5)***⟪ .

CAUTION

Where part of the basement is finished into one or more habitable rooms, each separate unfurnished portion requires at least one receptacle ⟫*210.52(G)*⟪.

Disconnecting Means

A A disconnecting means is not required if the branch-circuit switch or circuit breaker is within 50 ft (15 m) and can be seen while working on the appliance ≫ *422.31(B)* ≪.

B A disconnecting means is required unless the branch-circuit switch or circuit breaker can be locked in the open (off) position. The provision for locking or adding a lock to the disconnecting means shall be installed on or at the switch or circuit breaker used as the disconnecting means and must remain in place whether the lock is installed or not ≫ *422.31(B)* ≪.

C In this illustration, the branch-circuit switch or circuit breaker cannot be seen while working on the appliance.

D A permanently connected appliance rated over 300 volt-amperes requires a means to simultaneously disconnect all ungrounded (hot) conductors from the appliance ≫ *422.30* ≪.

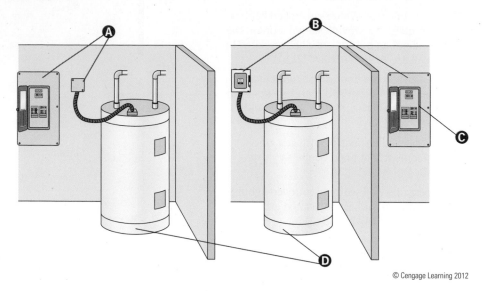

© Cengage Learning 2012

Detached Garages

A At least one receptacle is required in each detached garage with electric power ≫ *210.52(G)* ≪.

B All receptacles installed in detached garages must have GFCI protection, unless installed under one of the exceptions found in *210.8(A)(2)*.

C At least one wall switch–controlled lighting outlet is required for detached garages with electric power ≫ *210.70(A)(2)(a)* ≪.

D A detached garage with electric power requires at least one wall switch–controlled lighting outlet to provide illumination on the exterior side of an outside entrance or exit with grade-level access ≫ *210.70(A)(2)(b)* ≪.

© Cengage Learning 2012

> ### NOTE
> Lighting and receptacles are not required in detached garages. There are no provisions to provide electric power to detached garages. However, when electric power is provided, the provisions for attached garages must be met ≫*210.52(G)*≪.

> ### CAUTION
> In all areas specified in 210.52, all nonlocking-type 125-volt, 15- and 20-ampere receptacles shall be listed tamper-resistant receptacles ≫*406.12*≪.

Accessory Buildings

A All receptacles installed in accessory buildings having a floor located at or below grade level not intended as habitable rooms and limited to storage areas, work areas, and areas of similar use must have GFCI protection ≫*210.8(A)(2)* ≪.

B Lighting and receptacles are not required in accessory buildings. There are no provisions to provide electric power to detached garages.

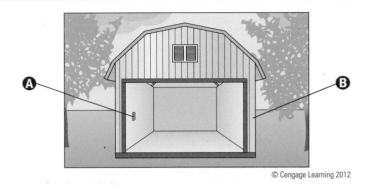

© Cengage Learning 2012

LAUNDRY AREAS

Receptacles and Lighting

A The clothes dryer outlet must have an insulated grounded (neutral) conductor and an equipment grounding conductor ≫*250.138* ≪.

B A lighting outlet is required for spaces containing equipment that requires servicing ≫*210.70(A)(3)* ≪. A lighted area immediately adjacent to a laundry area (such as a hallway) may provide sufficient light for both areas.

C Laundry receptacle outlet(s) must be fed from a 20-ampere branch circuit ≫*210.11(C)(2)* ≪.

D At least one receptacle is required for the laundry area ≫*210.52(F)* ≪.

> **NOTE**
>
> Electric clothes dryers connected to existing branch circuits are permitted to follow 250.140.

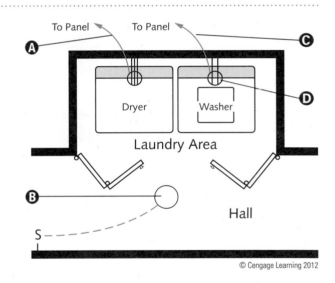

© Cengage Learning 2012

Receptacles and Lighting

A Laundry receptacle outlet(s) must be fed from a 20-ampere branch circuit ≫*210.11(C)(2)* ≪.

B Multiple receptacles are permitted on the laundry circuit as long as all of the outlet(s) are within the laundry area ≫*210.11(C)(2)* ≪.

C A 240-volt receptacle outlet for a clothes dryer is not a requirement (the dryer could be a gas dryer).

D Utility rooms require a lighting outlet ≫*210.70(A)(3)* ≪.

E Receptacle outlet(s) outside of the laundry area are not permitted on a laundry circuit ≫*210.11(C)(2)* ≪.

> **NOTE**
>
> A laundry room/area is not subject to the general provisions for receptacle placement found under 210.52(A). Although additional laundry area receptacles are permitted, only one receptacle outlet is required ≫*210.52(F)*≪.

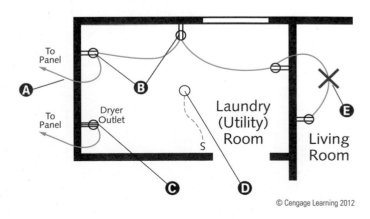

© Cengage Learning 2012

Receptacles and Lighting *(continued)*

A receptacle outlet installed for a specific appliance, such as laundry equipment, shall be installed within 6 ft (1.8 m) of the intended location of the appliance 》*210.50(C)*《.

A The clothes dryer outlet must have an insulated grounded (neutral) conductor *and* an equipment grounding conductor 》*250.138*《.

B Laundry receptacle outlet(s) must be fed from a 20-ampere branch circuit 》*210.11(C)(2)*《. A duplex receptacle installed on an individual 20-ampere branch circuit may have either a 15- or 20-ampere rating 》*210.21(B)(2)*《.

C Height requirements for laundry receptacle outlet(s) are not specified, except that they shall not be located more than 5½ ft (1.7 m) above the floor 》*210.52*《.

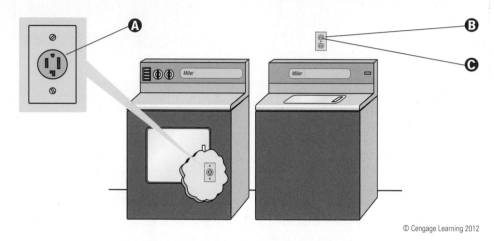

© Cengage Learning 2012

ATTIC AND CRAWL SPACES

Attic Spaces

A receptacle is not required for attic spaces that do not contain equipment that may require servicing.

Attic spaces not used for storage or attics that do not contain equipment that may require servicing do not require lighting outlets.

A Attic spaces used for storage or containing equipment that may require servicing must have at least one lighting outlet 》*210.70(A)(3)*《.

B At least one switch shall be located at the usual entry and exit to the attic space 》*210.70(A)(3)*《. If the luminaire contains a switch and is located at the usual point of entry, a separate switch may not be required.

C Cables not installed within framing members may need protection up to a height of at least 7 ft (2.1 m) 》*320.23(A), 330.23,* and *334.23*《.

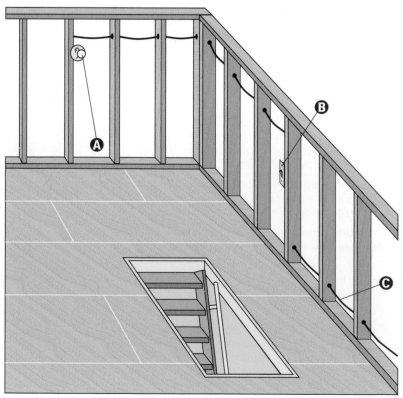

© Cengage Learning 2012

Crawl and Underfloor Spaces

A Crawl spaces with lighting outlet(s) require at least one switch located at the usual entry and exit to the crawl space ❯❯ *210.70(A)(3)* ❮❮. If the luminaire contains a switch and is located at the usual point of entry, a separate switch may not be required.

B A 125-volt, single-phase, 15- or 20-ampere rated receptacle outlet shall be installed at an accessible location for the servicing of equipment. The receptacle shall be located on the same level and within 25 ft (7.5 m) of the equipment. The receptacle shall not be connected to the load side of the equipment disconnecting means ❯❯ *210.63* ❮❮.

C Receptacle outlet(s) require GFCI protection where installed in a crawl space that is not above grade level ❯❯ *210.8(A)(4)* ❮❮.

D Underfloor spaces used for storage containing equipment that may require servicing must have at least one lighting outlet. A lighting outlet shall be located at or near equipment that may require servicing ❯❯ *210.70(A)(3)* ❮❮.

E A disconnecting means must be provided for HVAC equipment ❯❯ *440.3(B), 422.30, and 424.19* ❮❮.

No lighting outlets are required for underfloor spaces that are not used for storage or contain no equipment that may require servicing.

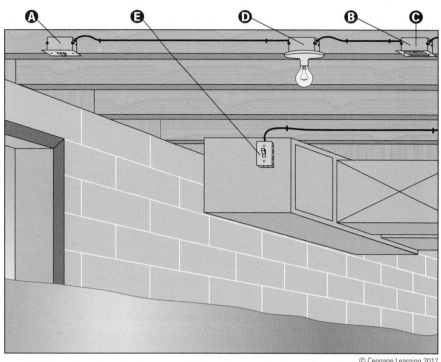

© Cengage Learning 2012

CAUTION

Where cable is run at angles with joists in crawl spaces, it shall be permissible to secure cables not smaller than two 6 AWG or three 8 AWG conductors directly to the lower edges of the joists. Smaller cables must be run either through bored holes in joists or on running boards ❯❯ *334.15(C)* ❮❮.

Summary

- Receptacle branch circuits rated 20 amperes are required for small-appliance branch circuits in kitchens, pantries, dining rooms, breakfast rooms, and similar areas.
- The maximum distance to any countertop receptacle, along the wall line measured horizontally, is 24 in. (600 mm).
- General provisions for countertop receptacle placement do not apply to islands and peninsulas.
- A minimum of two circuits is required for receptacles serving kitchen countertops.
- Receptacles located in kitchens, pantries, dining rooms, breakfast rooms, and similar areas also require a minimum of two circuits.
- All receptacles installed to serve kitchen countertops shall have GFCI protection.

- Some appliances can be cord and plug connected.
- Permanently connected as well as cord- and plug-connected appliances require a disconnecting means.
- Branch-circuit conductors installed for ranges and clothes dryers must have an insulated grounded (neutral) conductor and a grounding means.
- Hallways measuring 10 ft (3.0 m) or more in length require only one receptacle.
- Clothes closets have dedicated space where luminaires are not permitted.
- Only certain types of luminaires are permitted in the dedicated space within bathrooms.
- Receptacles in bathrooms must be GFCI protected and be supplied by 20-ampere branch circuit(s).
- All garage receptacles require GFCI protection.

- Lighting is required at or near equipment that may require servicing.
- At least one laundry receptacle outlet is required and must be fed from a 20-ampere branch circuit.
- Under certain conditions, attics and crawl spaces may require a lighting outlet and receptacle.
- A receptacle is required on the same level and within 25 ft (7.5 m) of HVAC equipment that may require servicing.

Unit 7 Competency Test

NEC Reference	Answer
_____	_____

1. The maximum distance between kitchen countertop receptacles is _____ ft.

2. Hanging luminaires located directly above any part of the bathtub shall be installed so that the luminaire is not less than _____ ft above the top of the bathtub rim.

3. A 15-ampere rated duplex receptacle may be installed on a _____ branch circuit.

   a) 15-ampere   b) 20-ampere

   c) 15- or 20-ampere   d) 15-, 20-, or 25-ampere

4. The minimum size THHN copper neutral conductor permitted for an 8¾ kW, 240-volt, 3-wire household electric range is _____.

   a) 12 AWG   b) 10 AWG   c) 8 AWG   d) 6 AWG

5. Luminaires shall be constructed or installed so that adjacent combustible material will not be subjected to temperatures in excess of _____ °Fahrenheit.

6. A one-family dwelling has a front entrance on the east side of the house, an attached garage with two 10-ft wide doors on the south side, and a back entrance door on the west side of the house. This one-family dwelling requires _____ lighting outlet(s) for these outdoor entrances.

7. Overcurrent devices shall not be located in the vicinity of easily ignitible material such as in _____.

8. A single receptacle installed on an individual branch circuit shall have an ampere rating not less than _____% of the rating of the branch circuit.

   a) 125   b) 100   c) 80   d) 50

9. Appliance receptacle outlets installed for specific appliances, such as laundry equipment, shall be placed within _____ ft of the intended location of the appliance.

10. Tap conductors for household cooking equipment supplied from a 50-ampere branch circuit shall have an ampacity of not less than _____ amperes.

11. One cooktop and two ovens are connected to one branch circuit in a kitchen of a one-family dwelling. The cooktop has a nameplate rating of 4 kW at 240 volts, while each oven has a nameplate rating of 5.5 kW at 240 volts. The minimum load calculation for this branch circuit is _____ watts.

12. The rating of a single cord- and plug-connected utilization equipment shall not exceed _____% of the branch-circuit ampere rating.

13. A recessed incandescent luminaire with a completely enclosed light source installed in the ceiling of a clothes closet must have a minimum clearance of _____ in. between the luminaire and the nearest point of the closet storage space.

14. Where the *NEC* specifies that one equipment shall be "within sight" of another equipment, the specified equipment shall be visible and not more than _____ ft distant from the other.

_____ _____ 15. In a dwelling unit, a hallway measuring 21½ ft in length requires a minimum of _____ receptacle outlet(s).

_____ _____ 16. A permanently connected dishwasher has a nameplate rating of 780 volt-amperes. The circuit breaker is permitted to serve as the disconnecting means where it is:

    I. within sight from the dishwasher.

    II. capable of being locked in the open position.

    III. capable of being locked in the closed position.

      a) I only   b) I or III only   c) I or II only   d) I, II, or III

_____ _____ 17. Interior stairway lighting outlets shall be controlled by a wall switch at each floor level, where the difference between levels is _____ steps or more.

_____ _____ 18. Supplementary overcurrent devices shall not be required to be _____.

_____ _____ 19. The maximum length cord permitted on an electrically operated trash compactor is _____ in.

_____ _____ 20. For a one-family dwelling, at least one receptacle outlet shall be installed in each:

    I. basement.

    II. attached garage.

    III. detached garage.

      a) I only   b) I and II only   c) II and III only   d) I, II, and III

_____ _____ 21. A refrigerator receptacle can be fed from a:

    I. 15-ampere individual branch circuit.

    II. 20-ampere individual branch circuit.

    III. 20-ampere small appliance branch circuit.

      a) II only   b) III only   c) II or III   d) I, II, or III

_____ _____ 22. A receptacle installed on the laundry branch circuit having no other receptacles can be a:

    I. 15-ampere single receptacle.

    II. 15-ampere duplex receptacle.

    III. 20-ampere duplex receptacle.

      a) III only   b) I or III   c) II or III   d) I, II, or III

_____ _____ 23. At least one GFCI-protected receptacle shall be located within _____ ft from the outside edge of each bathroom sink.

_____ _____ 24. Receptacles are permitted under an overhanging countertop, but are not counted as required countertop receptacles, where the countertop extends more than _____ in. beyond its support base.

_____ _____ 25. A branch circuit providing power to a bathroom receptacle may also provide power to:

    I. two other receptacles, two luminaires, and an exhaust fan in the same bathroom.

    II. two other receptacles in the same bathroom and receptacles in two additional bathrooms.

    III. one luminaire in the same bathroom and one luminaire in another bathroom.

      a) I only   b) I or II only   c) II or III only   d) I, II, or III

UNIT 8

Load Calculations

Objectives

After studying this unit, the student should:

▶ be able to calculate the general lighting load in a one-family dwelling.

▶ know the minimum volt-ampere (VA) requirements for small-appliance and laundry branch circuits.

▶ know how to apply demand factors to the general lighting load.

▶ be able to apply demand factors to fastened-in-place appliances.

▶ be able to calculate feeder-demand loads for household clothes dryers.

▶ know how to calculate feeder-demand loads for household cooking equipment.

▶ be able to calculate heating and air-conditioning feeder-demand loads.

▶ be able to calculate a one-family dwelling service or feeder using the standard method.

▶ be able to calculate a one-family dwelling service or feeder using the optional method.

▶ know how to size service and feeder conductors.

▶ be able to calculate and choose the appropriate size neutral conductor.

▶ understand how the grounding electrode conductor is selected.

Introduction

Load calculations must be performed in order to determine the size of services and feeders. Service conductors are the conductors between the power provider and the disconnecting means, whether a main breaker or main lug panel. A feeder is defined as all circuit conductors between the service disconnecting means and the panelboard containing fuses or breakers that feed branch circuits. Additional load calculations are needed for dwellings with panelboards that are not part of the service. For example, a separate panelboard might be installed near the middle of the house to help eliminate voltage drop in branch-circuit conductors. Since the remote panelboard (subpanel) does not carry the total load, an additional calculation is needed to size the feeder and panelboard.

This unit simplifies the standard and optional load calculation methods for one-family dwellings. A blank form is provided at the beginning of each method. The floor plan of the one-family dwelling being calculated is found on page 106 while the specifications are on page 155. Both calculation methods use the same specifications. Each line on each form is explained in detail using that information. The completed form follows the explanations.

COMPILING INFORMATION ESSENTIAL TO LOAD CALCULATIONS

Total Floor Area Square Footage

A Open porches are not included in the calculated floor area of dwelling units ≫ *220.12* ≪. Although this porch has a roof, it is considered open and, therefore, is not included in the calculation.

B Scale rulers are also useful in determining the location of outlets (receptacles, lights, switches, etc.).

C Before a scale ruler can be used to determine dimensions, the scale used to produce the blueprint (floor plan) must be known. (Then the area of an exterior porch, for example, is simple to calculate.)

D Scale rulers are useful in determining the total square footage of a structure (house, building, etc.) that has been drawn on a set of blueprints (floor plans).

E A regular tape measure (ruler, yard stick, etc.) can be used, but the use of a scale ruler makes the job much easier.

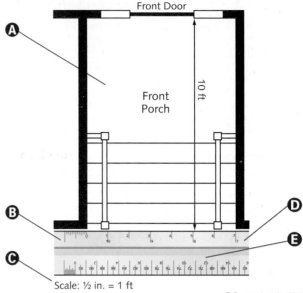

Scale: ½ in. = 1 ft

© Cengage Learning 2012

Gathering Information

Gathering certain information is necessary to accurately perform load calculations. All the essential data can be identified by simply answering the questions found on the load calculation form, either standard or optional. Enter the information on the appropriate line of the load calculation forms provided with this textbook.

A What is the dwelling's total square-foot (ft²) area, using the outside dimensions?

B What fastened-in-place appliances will be installed and what is the volt-ampere load of each?

C How many small appliance branch circuits will be installed?

D How many laundry circuits will be installed?

E If an electric clothes dryer will be installed, what is the volt-ampere load?

F What household cooking equipment will be installed and what is the volt-ampere load of each?

G Will there be an air-conditioning system? If so, what is the total volt-ampere load, including the compressor and fan motors? If an electric heating system will be installed, what is the total volt-ampere load, including the strip heat and blower motor?

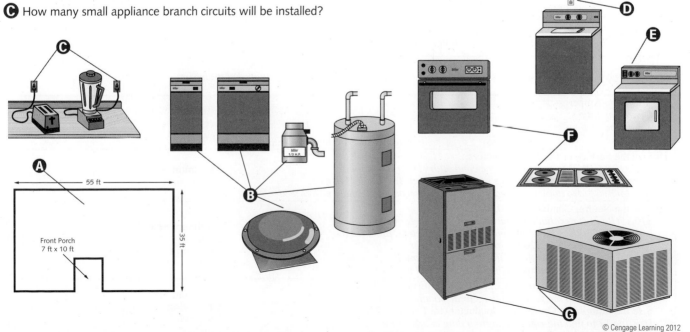

© Cengage Learning 2012

STANDARD METHOD: ONE-FAMILY DWELLINGS

Standard Method Load Calculation for One-Family Dwellings

1 General Lighting and Receptacle Loads 220.12 *Do not include open porches, garages, or unused or unfinished spaces not adaptable for future use.*		$3 \times$ __1855__ (sq ft using outside dimensions) $=$	**1**	5565
2 Small-Appliance Branch Circuits 220.52(A) *At least two small-appliance branch circuits must be included. 210.11(C)(1)*		$1500 \times$ __4__ (minimum of two) $=$	**2**	6000
3 Laundry Branch Circuit(s) 220.52(B) *At least one laundry branch circuit must be included. 210.11(C)(2)*		$1500 \times$ __2__ (minimum of one) $=$	**3**	3000

4 Add lines 1, 2, and 3	**4** 14,565	Lines 5 through 8 utilize the demand factors found in *Table 220.42.*	

5 __14,565__ (line 4) $- 3000 =$	**5** (if 117,000 or less, skip to line 8)	**6** _____ (line 5, if more than 117,000) $- 117,000 =$	**6**
7 _____ (line 6) $\times 25\% =$	**7**	**8** __11,565__ (smaller of line 5 or 117,000) $\times 35\% =$	**8** 4048

9 Total General Lighting and Receptacle Load $\quad 3000 +$ _____ (line 7) $+$ __4048__ (line 8) $=$	**9**	7048

10 Fastened-In-Place Appliances 220.53 *Use the nameplate rating. Do not include electric ranges, clothes dryers, space-heating equipment, or air-conditioning equipment.*	water heater / 4500	dishwasher / 1260	disposer / 1127	
	compactor / 900	3 attic fans / 1512	/	
	/	/	/	
If fewer than four units, put total volt-amperes on line 10. If four or more units, multiply total volt-amperes by 75%.	__9239__ (volt-amps of four or more) $\times 75\% =$		**10**	6929

11 Clothes Dryers 220.54 *(If present; otherwise skip to line 12.) Use 5000 watts or the nameplate rating, whichever is larger. The neutral demand load is 70% for feeders. 220.61(B)*	**11**	5500
12 Ranges, Ovens, Cooktops, and Other Household Cooking Appliances Over 1750 Watts 220.55 *(If present; otherwise skip to line 13.) Use Table 220.55 and all of the applicable Notes. The neutral demand load is 70% for feeders. 220.61(B)*	**12**	8450
13 Heating or Air-Conditioning System (Compare the heat and A/C, and omit the smaller.) 220.60 *Include the air handler when using either one. For heat pumps, include the compressor and the maximum amount of electric heat that can be energized while the compressor is running.*	**13**	15368
14 Largest Motor (one motor only) 220.50 and 430.24 *Multiply the volt-amperes of the largest motor by 25%.* __1127__ (volt-amps of largest motor) $\times 25\% =$	**14**	282

15 Total Volt-Ampere Demand Load: *Add lines 9 through 14 to find the minimum required volt-amperes.*	**15**	43,577

16 Minimum Amperes *Divide the total volt-amperes by the voltage.* __43,577__ (line 15) $\div$ __240__ (voltage) $=$	**16** 182 (minimum amperes)	**17** Minimum Size Service or Feeder 240.6(A)	**17**	200
18 Size the Service or Feeder Conductors. *Use 310.15(B)(7) to find the service conductors up to 400 amperes. Ratings in excess of 400 amperes shall comply with Table 310.15(B)(16) 310.15(B)(7) also applies to feeder conductors serving as the main power feeder.*	Minimum Size Conductors	**18**	2/0 Awg copp. 4/0 Awg Alum	
19 Size the Neutral Conductor. 220.61 *310.15(B)(7) states that the neutral service or feeder conductor can be smaller than the ungrounded (hot) conductors, provided the requirements of 215.2, 220.61, and 230.42 are met. 250.24(C)(1) states that the neutral shall not be smaller than the required grounding electrode conductor specified in Table 250.66.*	Minimum Size Neutral Conductor	**19**	3 copper 2 Alum.	
20 Size the Grounding Electrode Conductor (for Service). 250.66 *Use line 18 to find the grounding electrode conductor in Table 250.66.* Size the Equipment Grounding Conductor (for Feeder). 250.122 *Use line 17 to find the equipment grounding conductor in Table 250.122. Equipment grounding conductor types are listed in 250.118.*	Minimum Size Grounding Electrode Conductor	**20**	4 copper 2 Alum.	

Sample One-Family Dwelling Load Calculation

Assume water heater, clothes dryer, counter-mounted cooking unit, wall-mounted oven, and electric heat kilowatt (kW) ratings equivalent to kilovolt-ampere (kVA).

Dwelling outside dimension . . . . 35 ft × 55 ft
Front porch (included within outside dimensions) . . . . . 7 ft × 10 ft
Small-appliance branch circuits . . . . four
Laundry branch circuits . . . . two
Water heater . . . . 4.5 kW, 240 volt
Dishwasher . . . . 10 amperes, 120 volt
Waste (garbage) disposer . . . . ½HP, 115 volt
Trash compactor . . . . 7.5 amperes, 120 volt
Three attic fans (4.2 amperes each) . . . . 12.6 amperes, 120 volt
Clothes dryer . . . . 5.5 kW, 240 volt
Counter-mounted cooking unit (cooktop) . . . . 7 kW, 240 volt
Wall-mounted oven . . . . 6 kW, 240 volt
Electric heat (three banks at 5 kW each) . . . . 15 kW, 240 volt
Air handler (blower motor) . . . . 3.2 amperes, 115 volt
Air-conditioner compressor . . . . 16.6 amperes, 230 volt
Condenser fan motor . . . . 2 amperes, 115 volt

Line 1—General Lighting and Receptacle Loads

A In Table 220.12 the general lighting loads are listed according to the type of occupancy and are determined by requiring a minimum lighting load for each square foot of floor area.

B The lighting load for residential dwelling units is 3 volt-amperes (VA) per square foot.

C The dwelling floor plan on page 106 has an outside dimension of 35 ft × 55 ft (1925 ft²), but there is an open porch with a dimension of 7 ft × 10 ft (70 ft²). Since open porches are not included in the total area, 70 is deducted from 1925, leaving 1855 ft².

D The floor area for each floor shall be computed using the outside dimensions. The total floor area does not include open porches, garages, or unused (including unfinished) spaces that are not adaptable for future use ≫220.12≪.

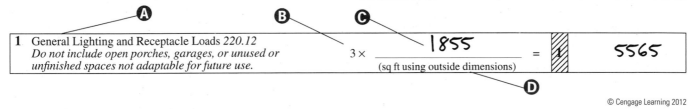

A	**B**	**C**

1   General Lighting and Receptacle Loads *220.12*
    Do not include open porches, garages, or unused or   3 × ____1855____ = 5565
    unfinished spaces not adaptable for future use.   (sq ft using outside dimensions)

D

© Cengage Learning 2012

Line 2—Small-Appliance Branch Circuits

A Small-appliance branch circuits must be included when calculating a dwelling unit service ≫220.52(A)≪.

B Each small-appliance branch circuit is calculated at no less than 1500 volt-amperes ≫220.52(A)≪.

C A dwelling unit must have at least two small-appliance branch circuits ≫210.11(C)(1)≪.

D These loads can be included with the general lighting load and subjected to the demand factors provided in Table 220.42 ≫220.52(A)≪.

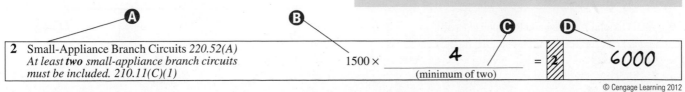

A	**B**	**C**	**D**

2   Small-Appliance Branch Circuits *220.52(A)*
    *At least **two** small-appliance branch circuits*   1500 × ____4____ = 6000
    must be included. 210.11(C)(1)   (minimum of two)

© Cengage Learning 2012

Line 3—Laundry Branch Circuits

Ⓐ Laundry branch circuits must be included when calculating a dwelling unit service ≫ *220.52(B)* ≪.

Ⓑ Each laundry branch circuit is calculated at no less than 1500 volt-amperes ≫ *220.52(B)* ≪.

Ⓒ At least one laundry branch circuit is required per dwelling unit ≫ *210.11(C)(2)* ≪.

Ⓓ These loads can be included with the general lighting load and subjected to the demand factors provided in Table 220.42 ≫ *220.52(B)* ≪.

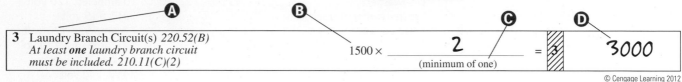

| 3 | Laundry Branch Circuit(s) *220.52(B)*
At least one laundry branch circuit
must be included. 210.11(C)(2) | 1500 × | **2**
(minimum of one) | = 3 | **3000** |

© Cengage Learning 2012

Lines 4 through 8—Applying Demand Factors Found in Table 220.42

Ⓐ Line 4 is simply the total of lines 1 through 3.

Ⓑ Lines 5 through 8 outline the procedure that derates by using demand factors provided in Table 220.42.

Ⓒ Line 5 is the result of subtracting 3000 from the number in line 4.

Ⓓ The first 3000 (or less) volt-amperes must remain at 100% ≫ *Table 220.42* ≪.

Ⓔ If line 5 is 117,000 or less, then lines 6 and 7 can be skipped.

Ⓕ If Line 4 is 120,000 or less, then lines 6 and 7 will remain empty.

Ⓖ Insert the smaller of line 5 or 117,000.

Ⓗ The next 117,000 (from 3001 to 120,000) is multiplied by 35% ≫ *Table 220.42* ≪.

Ⓘ The result found on line 8 has been rounded up from 4047.75 to the next whole number, thus eliminating the decimal.

> **NOTE**
>
> Generally, one-family dwelling load calculations will not use lines 6 and 7. (For example, a one-family dwelling with a total floor area of 25,000 ft², twenty small-appliance circuits and ten laundry branch circuits will not need lines 6 and 7.)

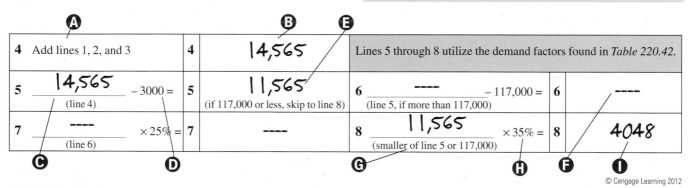

4	Add lines 1, 2, and 3	4	**14,565**	Lines 5 through 8 utilize the demand factors found in *Table 220.42.*		
5	**14,565** (line 4) − 3000 =	5	**11,565** (if 117,000 or less, skip to line 8)	6	---- (line 5, if more than 117,000) − 117,000 =	6	----
7	---- (line 6) × 25% =	7	----	8	**11,565** (smaller of line 5 or 117,000) × 35% =	8	**4048**

© Cengage Learning 2012

Line 9—Total General Lighting (and Receptacle) Load

Ⓐ Line 9 is the total of general lighting and general-use receptacles, small-appliance branch circuits, and laundry branch circuits after derating.

Ⓑ If line 7 was skipped (left blank), leave this space blank also.

Ⓒ This shaded block draws attention to the first of six lines (boxes) that will be added together to give the total volt-ampere demand load for the one-family dwelling.

Ⓓ If performing a load calculation for a feeder (and panel) that supplies less than 1000 ft² of floor area and does not supply small-appliance or laundry branch circuits, the result could be less than 3000. For example, if a feeder is installed to supply only 800 ft² of floor area and will not supply any small appliance or laundry branch circuits, then line 9 will be 2400 (3 VA per ft² × 800 ft² = 2400).

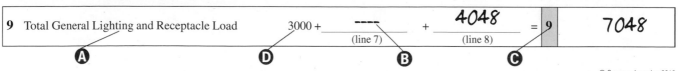

| 9 | Total General Lighting and Receptacle Load | 3000 + | ----
(line 7) | + | **4048**
(line 8) | = 9 | **7048** |

© Cengage Learning 2012

Line 10—Fastened-In-Place Appliances

Ⓐ The term **appliance** designates utilization equipment commonly built in standardized types and sizes, and installed as a unit to perform specific function(s) »*Article 100*«.

Ⓑ For the purpose of this load calculation, a kW rating will be the same as a kVA rating.

Ⓒ Multiplying voltage by amperage produces volt-amperes (VA).

Ⓓ Horsepower ratings must be converted to volt-amperes (VA) before they can be added to this form. The full load current ratings for single-phase motors are found in Table 430.248. Multiply the amperes (9.8) by the rated voltage (115) to find the volt-amperes (1127).

Ⓔ No derating is allowed when there are only one, two, or three fastened-in-place appliances.

Ⓕ If the feeder being calculated contains at least four fastened-in-place appliances, the combined volt-ampere rating of those appliances is multiplied by 75% and placed on line 10 »*220.53*«.

Ⓖ Space is provided for additional fastened-in-place appliances.

> **NOTE**
>
> Electric ranges, dryers, space-heating equipment, and air-conditioning equipment are not included as fastened-in-place appliances »***220.53***«. Household cooking appliances individually rated in excess of 1750 watts are derated under 220.55 provisions; see Line 12.

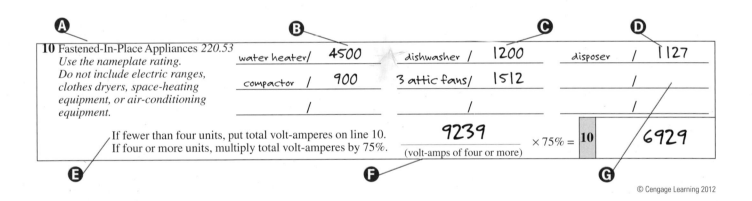

© Cengage Learning 2012

Line 11—Clothes Dryers

Ⓐ A clothes dryer is not a requirement for a load calculation. Skip this line if there is no clothes dryer.

Ⓑ If one of the circuits on the feeder being calculated is a clothes dryer, the rating for the dryer must be at least 5000 watts (volt-amperes) »*220.54*«.

Ⓒ A clothes dryer neutral load on a feeder can be calculated at 70% »*220.61(B)*«.

Ⓓ If the nameplate rating is more than 5000 watts (volt-amperes), the larger number is used »*220.54*«.

Ⓔ 5.5 kW is equal to 5500 watts (volt-amperes).

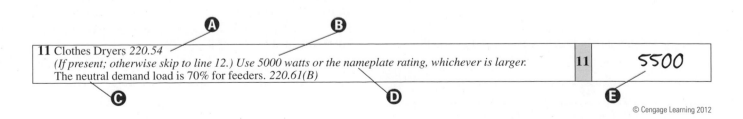

© Cengage Learning 2012

Line 12—Household Cooking Appliances

Ⓐ Household cooking appliances (ranges, wall-mounted ovens, counter-mounted cooking units, etc.) are not required in a load calculation. Skip this line if there are no cooking appliances rated over 1¾ kW.

Ⓑ Individual household cooking appliances rated more than 1750 watts (volt-amperes) can be derated by using Table 220.55 demand factors (and all of the applicable notes).

Ⓒ The neutral load on a feeder can be calculated at 70% for household electric ranges, wall-mounted ovens, and counter-mounted cooking units ≫ 220.61(B) ≪.

Ⓓ A 7-kW counter-mounted cooking unit (cooktop) and a 6-kW wall-mounted oven are included in this calculation. Both units fall within the parameters of Column B. The demand factor percentage found in that column for 2 units is 65%. Multiply the total kW (13) by the demand factor percentage (65%) to find the derated load (8.45 kW); 8.45 kW is equal to 8450 watts (volt-amperes).

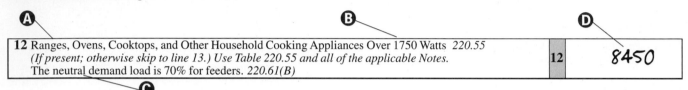

| Ⓐ | Ⓑ | Ⓓ |

12 Ranges, Ovens, Cooktops, and Other Household Cooking Appliances Over 1750 Watts *220.55*
(If present; otherwise skip to line 13.) Use Table 220.55 and all of the applicable Notes.
The neutral demand load is 70% for feeders. 220.61(B)

12 *8450*

Ⓒ

© Cengage Learning 2012

Line 13—Heating or Air-Conditioning System

Ⓐ The smaller of two (or more) **noncoincident loads** can be omitted, as long as they are never energized simultaneously ≫ 220.60 ≪. By definition, noncoincident means not occurring at the same time. A dwelling's electric heating system and air-conditioning system may be noncoincident loads.

Ⓑ The air handler (blower motor) has a rating of 368 volt-amperes (3.2 × 115 = 368). Since both loads are energized simultaneously, add the air handler to the 15 kW of electric heat.

Ⓒ Fixed electric space heating loads are calculated at 100% of the total connected load ≫ 220.51 ≪.

Ⓓ The air handler (blower) works with either the heating or the air conditioning. Add it to both calculations.

Ⓔ The air-conditioner compressor (16.6 × 230 = 3818 VA), condenser fan motor (2 × 115 = 230 VA), and blower motor (3.2 × 115 = 368 VA) have a combined load of 4416 volt-amperes. Because this total is less than the heating load, omit the air-conditioner compressor and the condenser fan motor.

> **N O T E**
>
> A heat pump with supplementary heat is not considered a noncoincident load. Add the compressor full-load current to the maximum amount of heat that can be energized while the compressor is running. Remember to include all associated motors—blower, condenser, etc.

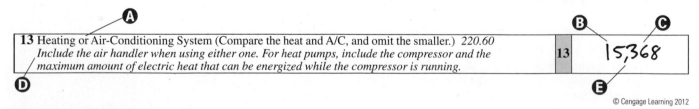

Ⓐ   Ⓑ   Ⓒ

13 Heating or Air-Conditioning System (Compare the heat and A/C, and omit the smaller.) *220.60*
Include the air handler when using either one. For heat pumps, include the compressor and the
maximum amount of electric heat that can be energized while the compressor is running.

13 *15,368*

Ⓓ   Ⓔ

© Cengage Learning 2012

Line 14—Largest Motor

Ⓐ Multiply the largest motor in the dwelling calculation by 25% ≫ 220.50 and 430.24 ≪.

Ⓑ The largest motor is usually the air-conditioner compressor. If the air-conditioner load has been omitted, use the

second largest motor. In this case, use the ½-horsepower garbage disposer motor.

Ⓒ The result of 281.75 has been rounded up, thus eliminating the decimal.

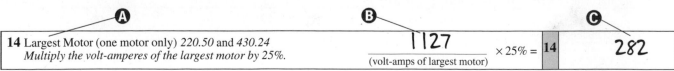

Ⓐ   Ⓑ   Ⓒ

14 Largest Motor (one motor only) *220.50* and *430.24*
Multiply the volt-amperes of the largest motor by 25%.

$$\frac{1127}{\text{(volt-amps of largest motor)}} \times 25\% =$$ **14** *282*

© Cengage Learning 2012

Line 15—Total Demand Load

Ⓐ Add lines 9 through 14 to find the service's minimum volt-ampere load.

Ⓐ

15 Total Volt-Ampere Demand Load: *Add lines 9 through 14 to find the minimum required volt-amperes.*	15	43,577

Lines 16 and 17—Minimum Service or Feeder

Ⓐ Place the total volt-ampere amount found in line 15 here.

Ⓑ Write down the source voltage that will supply the feeder.

Ⓒ It is permissible to round calculations to the nearest whole ampere. Fractions of an ampere 0.5 and higher are rounded up, while fractions less than 0.5 are dropped ≫ *220.5(B)* ≪.

Ⓓ The service (or feeder) overcurrent protection must be higher than the number found in line 16. A list of standard ampere ratings for fuses and circuit breakers is provided in 240.6(A).

Ⓔ Find the amperage by dividing the volt-amperes by the voltage.

Ⓕ This is the minimum amperage rating required for the service or feeder being calculated.

Ⓖ The next standard size fuse or breaker above 182 amperes is 200 ≫ *240.6(A)* ≪.

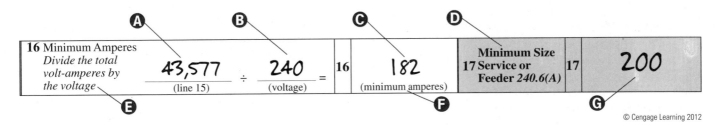

Line 18—Minimum Size Conductors

Ⓐ Use 310.15(B)(7) to find service entrance and service lateral conductors.

Ⓑ Section 310.15(B)(7) also applies to feeder conductors that serve as the main power feeder to a dwelling unit and are installed in a raceway or cable (with or without an equipment grounding conductor). It is not required that the feeder conductors be larger than the service-entrance conductors ≫ *310.15(B)(7)* ≪.

Ⓒ The overcurrent device rating must be 400 amperes or less.

Ⓓ Table 310.15(B)(16) requires 3/0 AWG (75°C [167°F]) copper conductors for 200 amperes. However, since this is a dwelling service, use Table 310.15(B)(7), which allows 2/0 AWG copper conductors.

Ⓔ The main power feeder is the feeder(s) that supplies the lighting and appliance branch-circuit panelboard(s) ≫ *310.15(B)(7)* ≪.

Ⓕ Table 310.15(B)(7) provides sizes for both copper and aluminum conductors. Copper-clad aluminum conductors are listed in the column with aluminum.

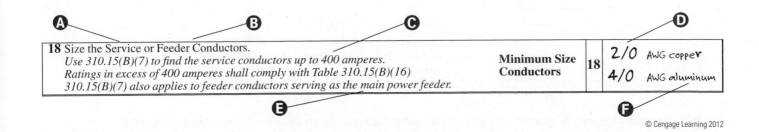

Line 19—Neutral Conductor

(A) No neutral conductor is connected to the water heater in this calculation.

(B) All fastened-in-place appliances utilizing a grounded conductor must be included.

(C) The electric heat and air-conditioner compressor are 240-volt loads (no neutral).

(D) If the largest motor is 120 (115) volts, use the motor load in line 14.

(E) For the purpose of this load calculation, the terms **neutral** and **grounded** are synonymous.

(F) The feeder (or service) neutral load is the maximum un-balance of the load determined by Article 220 »220.61(A)«.

(G) The neutral (grounded) conductor can be smaller than the ungrounded (hot) conductors provided certain requirements in 215.2, 220.61 and 230.42 are met »310.15(B)(7)«.

(H) All numbers are shown as volt-amperes.

(I) Since all of the general lighting and receptacle loads have a rating of 120 volts, the total volt-ampere rating (from line 9) must be included in the neutral calculation.

(J) A demand factor of 75% can be applied to the nameplate rating load of four or more fastened-in-place appliances »220.53«.

(K) Multiply the clothes dryer load (line 11) by 70% to determine the neutral load »220.61(B)«.

(L) Multiplying line 12 by 70% provides the neutral cooking appliances load »220.61(B)«.

(M) Because both of these motors are energized simultaneously, thereby contributing to the neutral load, they must be included in the neutral calculation.

(N) The total neutral volt-ampere load (21,247) divided by the voltage (240) renders the minimum neutral amperes (89).

(O) Size the neutral by finding the maximum unbalanced load.

(P) A 3 AWG (75°C [167°F]) copper conductor is required for 89 amperes »Table 310.15(B)(16)«.

(Q) A 2 AWG (75°C [167°F]) aluminum conductor is required for 89 amperes »Table 310.15(B)(16)«.

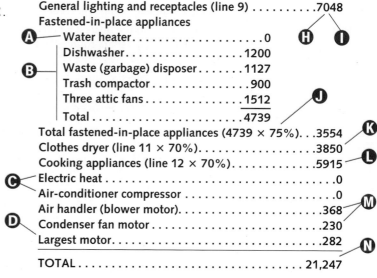

General lighting and receptacles (line 9) 7048
Fastened-in-place appliances
  Water heater 0
  Dishwasher 1200
  Waste (garbage) disposer 1127
  Trash compactor 900
  Three attic fans 1512
  Total 4739
Total fastened-in-place appliances (4739 × 75%) . . . 3554
Clothes dryer (line 11 × 70%) 3850
Cooking appliances (line 12 × 70%) 5915
Electric heat 0
Air-conditioner compressor 0
Air handler (blower motor) 368
Condenser fan motor 230
Largest motor 282

TOTAL 21,247

19 Size the Neutral Conductor 220.61
310.15(B)(7) states that the neutral service or feeder conductor can be smaller than the ungrounded (hot) conductors, provided the requirements of 215.2, 220.61, and 230.42 are met. 250.24(C)(1) states that the neutral shall not be smaller than the required grounding electrode conductor specified in Table 250.66.

| Minimum Size Neutral Conductor | 19 | 3 copper |
| | | 2 aluminum |

Line 20—Grounding Electrode Conductor

(A) Use 310.15(B)(7) to find service entrance and service lateral conductors.

(B) The minimum size grounding electrode conductor is 4 AWG copper (or 2 AWG aluminum) »Table 250.66«.

(C) In outdoor applications, aluminum (or copper-clad aluminum) grounding electrode conductors must not be installed within 18 in. (450 mm) of the earth »250.64(A)«.

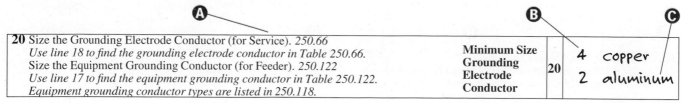

20 Size the Grounding Electrode Conductor (for Service). 250.66
Use line 18 to find the grounding electrode conductor in Table 250.66.
Size the Equipment Grounding Conductor (for Feeder). 250.122
Use line 17 to find the equipment grounding conductor in Table 250.122. Equipment grounding conductor types are listed in 250.118.

| Minimum Size Grounding Electrode Conductor | 20 | 4 copper |
| | | 2 aluminum |

The following page shows the completed one-family dwelling load calculation according to the standard method.

Standard Method Load Calculation for One-Family Dwellings

1 General Lighting and Receptacle Loads *220.12* *Do not include open porches, garages, or unused or* *unfinished spaces not adaptable for future use.*		$3 \times$ __**1855**__ (sq ft using outside dimensions)	= **1**	**5565**
2 Small-Appliance Branch Circuits *220.52(A)* *At least **two** small-appliance branch circuits* *must be included. 210.11(C)(1)*		$1500 \times$ __**4**__ (minimum of two)	= **2**	**6000**
3 Laundry Branch Circuit(s) *220.52(B)* *At least **one** laundry branch circuit* *must be included. 210.11(C)(2)*		$1500 \times$ __**2**__ (minimum of one)	= **3**	**3000**

4 Add lines 1, 2, and 3	**4**	**14,565**	Lines 5 through 8 utilize the demand factors found in *Table 220.42*.

5 __**14,565**__ $- 3000 =$ (line 4)	**5**	**11,565** (if 117,000 or less, skip to line 8)	**6** __**----**__ $- 117,000 =$ (line 5, if more than 117,000)	**6**	**----**
7 __**----**__ $\times 25\% =$ (line 6)	**7**	**----**	**8** __**11,565**__ $\times 35\% =$ (smaller of line 5 or 117,000)	**8**	**4048**

9 Total General Lighting and Receptacle Load	$3000 +$ __**----**__ $+$ __**4048**__ $=$ (line 7) (line 8)	**9** **7048**

10 Fastened-In-Place Appliances *220.53* *Use the nameplate rating.* *Do not include electric ranges,* *clothes dryers, space-heating* *equipment, or air-conditioning* *equipment.*	water heater/ **4500** dishwasher / **1200** disposer / **1127** compactor / **900** 3 attic fans/ **1512** / / / /		
If fewer than four units, put total volt-amperes on line 10. If four or more units, multiply total volt-amperes by 75%.	**9239** $\times 75\% =$ (volt-amps of four or more)	**10**	**6929**

11 Clothes Dryers *220.54* *(If present; otherwise skip to line 12.) Use 5000 watts or the nameplate rating, whichever is larger.* The neutral demand load is 70% for feeders. *220.61(B)*	**11**	**5500**
12 Ranges, Ovens, Cooktops, and Other Household Cooking Appliances Over 1750 Watts *220.55* *(If present; otherwise skip to line 13.) Use Table 220.55 and all of the applicable Notes.* The neutral demand load is 70% for feeders. *220.61(B)*	**12**	**8450**
13 Heating or Air-Conditioning System (Compare the heat and A/C, and omit the smaller.) *220.60* *Include the air handler when using either one. For heat pumps, include the compressor and the* *maximum amount of electric heat that can be energized while the compressor is running.*	**13**	**15,368**
14 Largest Motor (one motor only) *220.50 and 430.24* *Multiply the volt-amperes of the largest motor by 25%.* __**1127**__ $\times 25\% =$ (volt-amps of largest motor)	**14**	**282**

15 Total Volt-Ampere Demand Load: *Add lines 9 through 14 to find the minimum required volt-amperes.*	**15**	**43,577**

16 Minimum Amperes *Divide the total* *volt-amperes by* *the voltage*	__**43,577**__ $\div$ __**240**__ $=$ (line 15) (voltage)	**16** **182** (minimum amperes)	**Minimum Size 17 Service or Feeder 240.6(A)** **17** **200**

18 Size the Service or Feeder Conductors. *Use 310.15(B)(7) to find the service conductors up to 400 amperes.* *Ratings in excess of 400 amperes shall comply with Table 310.15(B)(16)* *310.15(B)(7) also applies to feeder conductors serving as the main power feeder.*	**Minimum Size Conductors** **18**	**2/0** AWG copper **4/0** AWG aluminum
19 Size the Neutral Conductor *220.61* *310.15(B)(7) states that the neutral service or feeder conductor* *can be smaller than the ungrounded (hot) conductors, provided the* *requirements of 215.2, 220.61, and 230.42 are met.* *250.24(C)(1) states that the neutral shall not be smaller than the* *required grounding electrode conductor specified in Table 250.66.*	**Minimum Size Neutral Conductor** **19**	**3** copper **2** aluminum
20 Size the Grounding Electrode Conductor (for Service). *250.66* *Use line 18 to find the grounding electrode conductor in Table 250.66.* Size the Equipment Grounding Conductor (for Feeder). *250.122* *Use line 17 to find the equipment grounding conductor in Table 250.122.* *Equipment grounding conductor types are listed in 250.118.*	**Minimum Size Grounding Electrode Conductor** **20**	**4** copper **2** aluminum

OPTIONAL METHOD: ONE-FAMILY DWELLINGS

Optional Method Load Calculation for One-Family Dwellings

1 General Lighting and Receptacle Loads *220.82(B)(1)*
*Do not include open porches, garages, or unused or
unfinished spaces not adaptable for future use.*

$3 \times$ _____ = **1**
(sq ft using outside dimensions)

2 Small-Appliance Branch Circuits *220.82(B)(2)*
*At least **two** small-appliance branch circuits
must be included. 210.11(C)(1)*

$1500 \times$ _____ = **2**
(minimum of two)

3 Laundry Branch Circuit(s) *220.82(B)(2)*
*At least **one** laundry branch circuit
must be included. 210.11(C)(2)*

$1500 \times$ _____ = **3**
(minimum of one)

4 Appliances *220.82(B)(3) and (4)*
*Use the nameplate rating of **all**
appliances (fastened in place,
permanently connected, or
connected to a specific circuit),
ranges, ovens, cooktops, motors,
and clothes dryers.
Convert any nameplate rating
given in amperes to volt-amperes
by multiplying the amperes
by the rated voltage.*

*Do not include any heating
or air-conditioning
equipment in this section.*

Total volt-amperes
of all appliances
LISTED BELOW **4**

water heater / _____   clothes dryer / _____   range / _____

dishwasher / _____   disposer / _____   _____ / _____

_____ / _____   _____ / _____   _____ / _____

_____ / _____   _____ / _____   _____ / _____

_____ / _____   _____ / _____   _____ / _____

5 Apply *220.82(B)* demand factor to the total of lines 1 through 4.

_____ $- 10{,}000 =$ _____ $\times 40\% =$ _____ $+ 10{,}000 =$ **5**
(total of lines 1 through 4)

6 Heating or Air-Conditioning System *220.82(C)*
*Use the nameplate ratings in volt-amperes for
all applicable systems in lines **a** through **e**.*

a) Air-conditioning and cooling systems, including heat pumps without
any supplemental electric heating:

_____ $\times 100\% =$ **a)**

b) Electric thermal storage and other heating systems where
the usual load is expected to be continuous at full nameplate
value. *Systems qualifying under this selection shall not be
figured under any other selection in 220.82(C).*

_____ $\times 100\% =$ **b)**

c) Supplemental electric heating equipment for heat-pump systems. Include the
heat-pump compressor(s) at 100%. *If the heat-pump compressor is prevented
from operating with the supplemental heat,
omit the compressor.*

_____ $\times 65\% =$ **c)**

d) Electric space-heating equipment, if fewer than four
separately controlled units:

_____ $\times 65\% =$ **d)**

e) Electric space-heating equipment, if four or more
separately controlled units:

_____ $\times 40\% =$ **e)**

7 Total Volt-Ampere
Demand Load:

_____ $+$ _____ = **7**
(largest VA rating from lines 6a through 6e) (line 5)

8 Minimum Amperes
*Divide the total
volt-amperes
by the voltage.*

_____ $\div$ _____ = **8**
(line 7) (voltage) (minimum amperes)

9 Minimum Size
Service or
Feeder *240.6(A)* **9**
(minimum is 100 amperes)

10 Size the Service or Feeder Conductors.
*Use 310.15(B)(7) to find the service conductors up to 400 amperes.
Ratings in excess of 400 amperes shall comply with Table 310.15(B)(16)
310.15(B)(7) also applies to feeder conductors serving as the main power feeder.*

**Minimum Size
Conductors** **10**

11 Size the Neutral Conductor. *220.61*
Note: There is no optional method for calculating the neutral conductor.
*310.15(B)(7) states that the neutral service or feeder conductor
can be smaller than the ungrounded (hot) conductors, provided the
requirements of 215.2, 220.61, and 230.42 are met.
250.24(C)(1) states that the neutral shall not be smaller than the
required grounding electrode conductor specified in Table 250.66.*

**Minimum Size
Neutral
Conductor** **11**

12 Size the Grounding Electrode Conductor.
Use line 10 to find the grounding electrode conductor in Table 250.66.
Size the Equipment Grounding Conductor (for Feeder). *250.122*
*Use line 9 to find the equipment grounding conductor in Table 250.122.
Equipment grounding conductor types are listed in 250.118.*

**Minimum Size
Grounding
Electrode
Conductor** **12**

Lines 1 through 3—General Lighting and Receptacle Loads

A In the **optional method,** lines 1, 2, and 3 are calculated exactly as described in the **standard method.** (See explanations on pages 155 and 156).

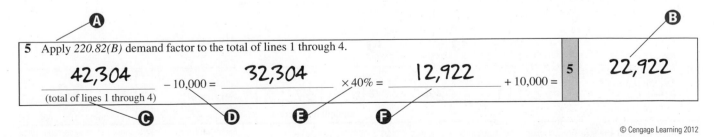

1 General Lighting and Receptacle Loads *220.82(B)(1)* *Do not include open porches, garages, or unused or* *unfinished spaces not adaptable for future use.*	3 ×	**1855** (sq ft using outside dimensions)	= 1	**5565**
2 Small-Appliance Branch Circuits *220.82(B)(2)* *At least **two** small-appliance branch circuits* *must be included. 210.11(C)(1)*	1500 ×	**4** (minimum of two)	= 2	**6000**
3 Laundry Branch Circuit(s) *220.82(B)(2)* *At least **one** laundry branch circuit* *must be included. 210.11(C)(2)*	1500 ×	**2** (minimum of one)	= 3	**3000**

© Cengage Learning 2012

Line 4—Appliances

A This section includes appliances (fastened in place, permanently connected, or connected to a specific circuit), ranges, wall-mounted ovens, counter-mounted cooking units, clothes dryers, and water heaters ≫ *220.82(B)(3)* ≪. Include all permanently connected motors not already included ≫ *220.82(B)(4)* ≪.

B Heating and air-conditioning systems are *not* included in this calculation.

C Use the exact nameplate rating of the clothes dryer, even if less than 5000 volt-amperes.

D Do not apply the demand factors in Table 220.55 to household cooking equipment (ranges, cooktops, and ovens). List the nameplate ratings as they appear.

4 Appliances *220.82(B)(3) and (4)* *Use the nameplate rating of **all** appliances (fastened in place, permanently connected, or connected to a specific circuit), ranges, ovens, cooktops, motors, and clothes dryers.* *Convert any nameplate rating given in amperes to volt-amperes by multiplying the amperes by the rated voltage.*	*Do not include any heating or air-conditioning equipment in this section.* water heater / **4500** dishwasher / **1200** compactor / **900** / /	Total volt-amperes of all appliances LISTED BELOW clothes dryer / **5500** disposer / **1127** 3 attic fans / **1512** / /	range / cooktop / **7000** oven / **6000** / /	4 **27,739**

© Cengage Learning 2012

Line 5—Applying Demand Factors to the Total of Lines 1 through 4

A This demand factor is found in 220.82(B).

B This is the newly calculated load including everything except the heating and air-conditioning systems.

C (5565 + 6000 + 3000 + 27,739)

D Because the first 10,000 volt-amperes are calculated at 100%, subtract 10,000 here.

E The remainder of the load is calculated at 40%.

F The result on line 5 has been rounded up from 12,921.6.

5 Apply *220.82(B)* demand factor to the total of lines 1 through 4.					
42,304 (total of lines 1 through 4)	− 10,000 =	**32,304**	× 40% =	**12,922**	+ 10,000 =
					5 **22,922**

© Cengage Learning 2012

Line 6—Heating or Air-Conditioning Systems

A The air-conditioner compressor (16.6 × 230 = 3818 VA), condenser fan motor (2 × 115 = 230 VA), and blower motor (3.2 × 115 = 368 VA) have a combined load of 4416 volt-amperes.

B The electric heat (3 × 5000 = 15,000) added to the blower motor (3.2 × 115 = 368) is 15,368 volt-amperes.

> **NOTE**
>
> The total volt-ampere rating of one, two, or three separately controlled heating units is multiplied by 65%. The total volt-ampere rating of four (or more) separately controlled heating units is multiplied by 40%.

A

B

6	Heating or Air-Conditioning System *220.82(C)* *Use the nameplate ratings in volt-amperes for all applicable systems in lines **a** through **e**.*

a) Air-conditioning and cooling systems, including heat pumps without any supplemental electric heating:

4416 _____ × 100% = | **a)** 4416

b) Electric thermal storage and other heating systems where the usual load is expected to be continuous at full nameplate value. *Systems qualifying under this selection shall not be figured under any other selection in 220.82(C).*

_____ × 100% = | **b)**

c) Supplemental electric heating equipment for heat-pump systems. Include the heat-pump compressor(s) at 100%. *If the heat-pump compressor is prevented from operating with the supplemental heat, omit the compressor.*

_____ × 65% = | **c)**

d) Electric space-heating equipment, if fewer than four separately controlled units:

15,368 _____ × 65% = | **d)** 9989

e) Electric space-heating equipment, if four or more separately controlled units:

_____ × 40% = | **e)**

© Cengage Learning 2012

Line 7—Total Volt-Ampere Demand Load

A The largest volt-ampere rating of the heating or air-conditioning system(s), after application of demand factors.

B The volt-ampere demand load from line 5.

C The total volt-ampere load calculated by the optional method. (For comparison, this one-family dwelling, calculated by the standard method, is 43,577 volt-amperes.)

A   **B**   **C**

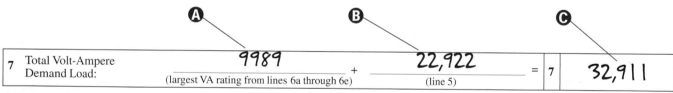

7	Total Volt-Ampere Demand Load:	9989 (largest VA rating from lines 6a through 6e)	+	22,922 (line 5)	=	7	32,911

© Cengage Learning 2012

Lines 8 and 9—Minimum Service or Feeder

A The volt-ampere load from line 7

B The source voltage

C The fraction of an ampere (.13) has been dropped.

D The overcurrent protection chosen for the service (or feeder) must be higher than the number found on line

8. Standard ampere ratings for fuses and circuit breakers are listed in 240.6(A).

E The next standard size fuse or breaker above 137 amperes is 150. (By the standard method, this same dwelling requires a 200-ampere service.)

A   **B**   **C**   **D**   **E**

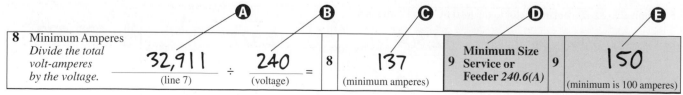

8	Minimum Amperes *Divide the total volt-amperes by the voltage.*	32,911 (line 7)	÷	240 (voltage)	=	8	137 (minimum amperes)	9	**Minimum Size Service or Feeder** *240.6(A)*	9	150 (minimum is 100 amperes)

© Cengage Learning 2012

Line 10—Minimum Size Conductors

A Use 310.15(B)(7) to find service conductors.

B Section 310.15(B)(7) also applies to feeder conductors that serve as the main power feeder to a dwelling unit and are installed in a raceway or cable (with or without an equipment grounding conductor). It is not required that the feeder conductors be larger than the service-entrance conductors »*310.15(B)(7)*«.

C The overcurrent device rating must be 400 amperes or less.

D Table 310.15(B)(16) requires 1/0 AWG (75°C [167°F]) copper conductors for 150 amperes. However, because this is a dwelling service, use Table 310.15(B)(7), which allows 1 AWG copper conductors.

E The main power feeder is the feeder(s) that supplies the lighting and appliance branch-circuit panelboard(s) »*310.15(B)(7)*«.

F Table 310.15(B)(7) provides copper and aluminum (and copper-clad aluminum) conductor sizes.

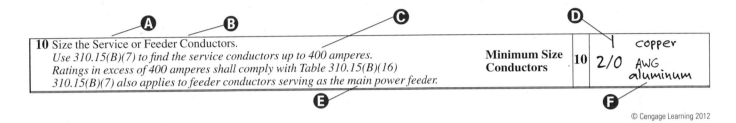

© Cengage Learning 2012

Line 11—Neutral Conductor

A The neutral conductor must be calculated by the standard method.

B Review the complete neutral conductor explanation on page 160, since the calculation method is the same.

N O T E

There is no optional method for calculating the neutral conductor.

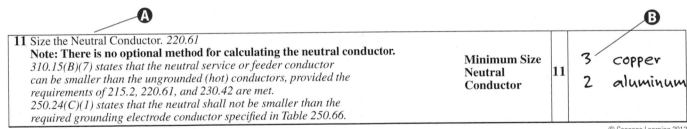

© Cengage Learning 2012

Line 12—Grounding Electrode Conductor

A The minimum size grounding electrode conductor is 6 AWG copper (or 4 AWG aluminum) »*Table 250.66*«.

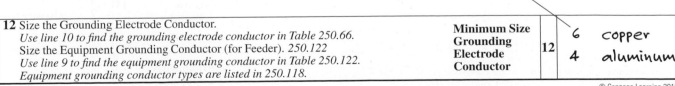

© Cengage Learning 2012

The following page shows the completed one-family dwelling load calculation according to the optional method.

Optional Method Load Calculation for One-Family Dwellings

1 General Lighting and Receptacle Loads *220.82(B)(1)* *Do not include open porches, garages, or unused or unfinished spaces not adaptable for future use.*	$3 \times$ ___**1855**___ = (sq ft using outside dimensions)	**1** **5565**
2 Small-Appliance Branch Circuits *220.82(B)(2)* *At least **two** small-appliance branch circuits must be included. 210.11(C)(1)*	$1500 \times$ ___**4**___ = (minimum of two)	**2** **6000**
3 Laundry Branch Circuit(s) *220.82(B)(2)* *At least **one** laundry branch circuit must be included. 210.11(C)(2)*	$1500 \times$ ___**2**___ = (minimum of one)	**3** **3000**

4 Appliances *220.82(B)(3) and (4)*
*Use the nameplate rating of **all** appliances (fastened in place, permanently connected, or connected to a specific circuit), ranges, ovens, cooktops, motors, and clothes dryers. Convert any nameplate rating given in amperes to volt-amperes by multiplying the amperes by the rated voltage.*

Do not include any heating or air-conditioning equipment in this section.

Total volt-amperes of all appliances LISTED BELOW

4 **27,739**

water heater /	4500	clothes dryer /	5500	range /	
dishwasher /	1200	disposer /	1127	cooktop /	7000
compactor /	900	3 attic fans /	1512	oven /	6000
/		/		/	
/		/		/	

5 Apply *220.82(B)* demand factor to the total of lines 1 through 4.

___**42,304**___ $- 10,000 =$ ___**32,304**___ $\times 40\% =$ ___**12,922**___ $+ 10,000 =$ **5** **22,922**
(total of lines 1 through 4)

6 Heating or Air-Conditioning System *220.82(C)*
*Use the nameplate ratings in volt-amperes for all applicable systems in lines **a** through **e**.*

a) Air-conditioning and cooling systems, including heat pumps without any supplemental electric heating:

___**4416**___ $\times 100\% =$ **a)** **4416**

b) Electric thermal storage and other heating systems where the usual load is expected to be continuous at full nameplate value. *Systems qualifying under this selection shall not be figured under any other selection in 220.82(C).*

_____ $\times 100\% =$ **b)**

c) Supplemental electric heating equipment for heat-pump systems. Include the heat-pump compressor(s) at 100%. *If the heat-pump compressor is prevented from operating with the supplemental heat, omit the compressor.*

_____ $\times 65\% =$ **c)**

d) Electric space-heating equipment, if fewer than four separately controlled units:

___**15,368**___ $\times 65\% =$ **d)** **9989**

e) Electric space-heating equipment, if four or more separately controlled units:

_____ $\times 40\% =$ **e)**

7 Total Volt-Ampere Demand Load:

___**9989**___ $+$ ___**22,922**___ $=$ **7** **32,911**
(largest VA rating from lines 6a through 6e)   (line 5)

8 Minimum Amperes *Divide the total volt-amperes by the voltage.*	___**32,911**___ $\div$ ___**240**___ = (line 7) (voltage)	**8** **137** (minimum amperes)	**9** Minimum Size Service or Feeder *240.6(A)*	**9** **150** (minimum is 100 amperes)	

10 Size the Service or Feeder Conductors.
Use 310.15(B)(7) to find the service conductors up to 400 amperes. Ratings in excess of 400 amperes shall comply with Table 310.15(B)(16) 310.15(B)(7) also applies to feeder conductors serving as the main power feeder.

Minimum Size Conductors — **10** — 1 copper / 2/0 AWG aluminum

11 Size the Neutral Conductor. *220.61*
Note: There is no optional method for calculating the neutral conductor.
310.15(B)(7) states that the neutral service or feeder conductor can be smaller than the ungrounded (hot) conductors, provided the requirements of 215.2, 220.61, and 230.42 are met. 250.24(C)(1) states that the neutral shall not be smaller than the required grounding electrode conductor specified in Table 250.66.

Minimum Size Neutral Conductor — **11** — 3 copper / 2 aluminum

12 Size the Grounding Electrode Conductor.
Use line 10 to find the grounding electrode conductor in Table 250.66. Size the Equipment Grounding Conductor (for Feeder). 250.122 Use line 9 to find the equipment grounding conductor in Table 250.122. Equipment grounding conductor types are listed in 250.118.

Minimum Size Grounding Electrode Conductor — **12** — 6 copper / 4 aluminum

Summary

- A dwelling unit load calculation, for general lighting and receptacles, is determined by total square footage.
- Table 220.12 requires a unit load of 3 volt-amperes per square foot.
- At least one laundry and two small-appliance branch circuits are required when performing a service (or main power feeder) calculation.
- Laundry and small-appliance branch circuits are calculated using a rating of at least 1500 volt-amperes each.
- Table 220.42 demand factors are applied to the general lighting, small appliance, and laundry loads.
- The total volt-ampere rating of four or more fastened-in-place appliances is multiplied by 75%.
- Demand loads for household cooking appliances (over 1¾ kW rating) are found in Table 220.55.
- The heating and air-conditioning loads are compared, and the larger of the two is used.
- For heat pumps, include the compressor and the maximum amount of electric heat that can be energized while the compressor is running.
- Two load calculation methods are provided in Article 220, standard and optional.
- The neutral conductor can be smaller than the ungrounded (hot) conductors, provided the requirements of 215.2, 220.61, and 230.42 are met.
- Table 250.66 is used to size grounding electrode conductors.

Unit 8 Competency Test

NEC Reference	Answer	
_____	_____	1. It shall be permissible to apply a demand factor of _____% to the nameplate rating load of _____ or more appliances fastened in place, other than electric ranges, clothes dryers, space-heating equipment, or air-conditioning equipment, that are served by the same feeder in a one-family dwelling.
_____	_____	2. What is the lighting demand load (before derating) for a house with outside dimensions of 30 ft × 48 ft on the first floor and 22 ft × 42 ft on the second floor?
_____	_____	3. A homeowner wants to add twelve general-purpose receptacle outlets to the electrical drawings before the house is built. What additional load, in volt-amperes, will they add to the service-load calculation?
_____	_____	4. In each dwelling unit, the feeder load shall be computed at _____ volt-amperes for each 2-wire small-appliance branch circuit required by 210.11(C)(1).
_____	_____	5. What is the demand load for the service for two 3½-kW wall-mounted ovens and one 5-kW counter-mounted cooking unit? All of the appliances are supplied from a single branch circuit and are located in the same room of a one-family dwelling. a) 12 kW b) 9.6 kW c) 8 kW d) 6.6 kW
_____	_____	6. A 4.5-kVA, 240-volt clothes dryer contributes _____ amperes to the neutral load, when calculating the service by the standard method.
_____	_____	7. A one-family dwelling contains the following appliances: a 1-kVA, 115-volt dishwasher; a ¼-HP, 115-volt waste (garbage) disposer; and a ⅓-HP, 115-volt trash compactor. Using the standard method, what is the load contribution, in volt-amperes, for these appliances?
_____	_____	8. For one-family dwellings, the service disconnecting means must have a rating of at least _____ amperes, 3-wire.
_____	_____	9. A one-family dwelling has a 175-ampere, 240-volt service that is fed with 75°C (167°F) conductors. What is the minimum size copper grounding electrode conductor required?

NEC Reference   Answer

_____ _____ 10. A one-family dwelling has six 3-kW electric wall heaters (with individual thermostats) and five room air conditioners. Two air conditioners are rated 10.5 amperes at 230 volts, and the others are rated 7.2 amperes at 115 volts. A service calculation is being performed, using the optional method. How many volt-amperes should be included (after demand factors) for the heating and air conditioning? (Assume heater kW ratings equivalent to kVA.)

_____ _____ 11. In each dwelling unit, a feeder load of at least _____ volt-amperes must be included for each 2-wire laundry branch circuit installed as required by 210.11(C)(2).

_____ _____ 12. A 12-kW, 240-volt range contributes _____ watts to the load when calculating the service by the standard method.

Questions 13 through 21 are based on a 120/240-volt, 3-wire, single-phase one-family dwelling containing the following:

Floor area . . . . 2500 ft²	Clothes dryer . . . . 4 kW, 240-volt
Range . . . . 12 kW, 240-volt	Electric heat (two banks at 3 kW each) . . . . 6 kW, 240-volt
Water heater . . . . 4 kW, 240-volt	Air handler (blower motor) . . . . ¼ HP, 115-volt
Dishwasher . . . . 1.5 kW, 120-volt	Air-conditioner compressor . . . . 5 HP, 230-volt
Waste (garbage) disposer . . . . ⅓ HP, 115-volt	Condenser fan motor . . . . ⅙ HP, 115-volt

Assume water heater, clothes dryer, range, and electric heat kW ratings equivalent to kVA.

Using Part B (the standard method) of Article 220:

_____ __132__ 13. What is the minimum ampere rating for the service?

_____ _____ 14. What is the minimum size service?

_____ _____ 15. What is the minimum size THWN copper conductor that can be installed as the service (ungrounded) conductor?

_____ _____ 16. What is the minimum size grounding electrode conductor?

Using the Optional Method:

_____ _____ 17. What is the minimum ampere rating for the service?

_____ _____ 18. What is the minimum size service?

_____ _____ 19. What is the minimum size THWN copper conductor that can be installed as the service (ungrounded) conductor?

_____ _____ 20. What is the minimum size grounding electrode conductor?

Finding the Neutral Load:

_____ __|4__ 21. What is the minimum size THWN copper conductor that can be installed as the neutral conductor?

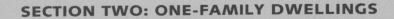

UNIT 9

Services and Electrical Equipment

Objectives

After studying this unit, the student should:

▶ be able to determine adequate strength for a mast supporting service-drop conductors.

▶ understand service-entrance cable provisions.

▶ know the definition of a service lateral and understand the applicable provisions.

▶ be familiar with minimum wiring clearance requirements (vertical, horizontal, etc.) for service and outside wiring.

▶ have a good understanding of the amount of three-dimensional working space required around service equipment, panelboards, electric equipment, etc.

▶ thoroughly understand panelboards, cabinets, and cutout boxes.

▶ be familiar with the multitude of provisions relating to circuit breakers and fuses.

▶ know and understand different aspects of service equipment and panelboard installations.

▶ be able to identify the appropriate table [310.15(B)(7) or 310.15(B)(16)] for conductor sizing.

▶ understand that electric equipment must be installed in a neat and professional manner.

▶ have a detailed understanding of grounding and bonding procedures.

▶ be able to properly position grounded and grounding conductors in remote panelboards (subpanels).

▶ have an extensive understanding of the grounding system as a whole.

▶ understand how to ground and bond panelboards on the supply side as well as the load side of the service disconnecting means.

▶ be able to prevent objectionable current flow in grounding conductors.

▶ understand the grounding requirements for panelboards installed in separate buildings or structures.

Introduction

Because the service is the heart of the electrical system, the importance of understanding this unit is enormous. Many of the regulations learned in this unit are applicable in all types of occupancies, not merely single-family dwellings. Unit 9 is divided into five sections. The first, "Service-Entrance Wiring Methods," addresses both overhead and underground service entrance provisions. The section entitled "Service and Outside Wiring Clearances" covers the clearances required above roofs and final grade. Other clearances (horizontal, vertical, and diagonal) are shown for windows, doors, balconies, platforms, etc. Next, the "Working Space around Equipment" section illustrates common working space requirements. "Service Equipment and Panelboards" explains panelboards, cutout boxes, and cabinets. Specific provisions pertaining to circuit breakers, fuses, and circuit breaker panels are also covered. "Grounding," the last section, explains in detail Article 250 provisions relating to service equipment and panelboards. Refer to Unit 9 often when studying (or installing) services, whether one-family or multifamily dwellings, or commercial and even industrial buildings.

Since many local jurisdictions and electric utility companies have supplemental requirements, exercise caution in compiling a complete set of service installation requirements. Examples of these requirements include, but are not limited to, restrictions on the type of conduit used for service mast; minimum conduit trade size; specific strapping methods; restrictions on the use of service-entrance cables; special underground service provisions; limitations on the maximum distance service-entrance conductors can run within a building or structure; and various grounding provisions. Obtain a copy of these additional rules (if any) for your area.

SERVICE-ENTRANCE WIRING METHODS

Service Mast as Support

A Service-entrance and overhead service conductors shall be arranged so that water shall not enter the service raceway or equipment ≫ *230.54(G)* ≪.

B It is not required (where approved) that rigid (and intermediate) metal conduit be securely fastened within 3 ft (900 mm) of the service head for above-the-roof termination of a mast ≫ *342.30(A)(3)* and *344.30(A)* ≪.

C Open conductors must be attached to fittings identified for use with service conductors or to noncombustible, nonabsorbent insulators securely attached to the building or other structure ≫ *230.27* ≪.

D A service mast used to support service-drop conductors must be of adequate strength or be supported by braces (or guys) to safely withstand the strain imposed by the service drop ≫ *230.28* ≪.

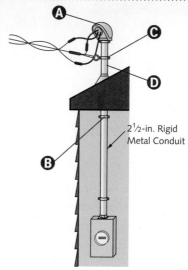

2½-in. Rigid Metal Conduit

© Cengage Learning 2012

Service Heads (Weather Heads)

A Service raceways must be equipped with a service head at the point of connection to service-drop or overhead service conductors. The service head shall be listed for use in wet locations ≫ *230.54(A)* ≪.

B Raceway-type service masts require raceway fittings that are identified for use with service masts ≫ *230.28* ≪.

C Conductors of different potential must be brought out of service heads through separately bushed openings ≫ *230.54(E)* ≪.

D An insulated grounded conductor 4 AWG or larger must be identified either by a continuous white or gray outer finish or by three continuous white stripes on other than green insulation along its entire length or by a distinctive white marking at its terminations during installation. This marking must completely encircle the conductor or insulation ≫ *200.6(B)* ≪.

E Conductors must have adequate mechanical strength and sufficient ampacity to carry the current for the load (as computed in accordance with Article 220) ≫ *230.23(A)* ≪.

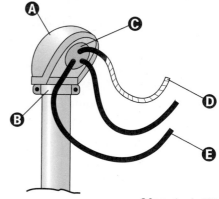

© Cengage Learning 2012

Service Mast Attachments

A Service drop is defined as the overhead conductors between the utility electric supply system and the service point ≫ *Article 100* ≪.

B Nothing except power service-drop conductors can be attached to the service mast ≫ *230.28* ≪.

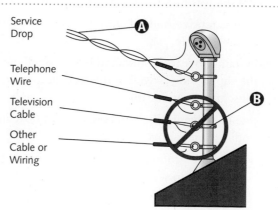

Service Drop

Telephone Wire

Television Cable

Other Cable or Wiring

© Cengage Learning 2012

Service Drops Attached to Buildings

A Open conductors must be attached to fittings identified for use with service conductors, or to noncombustible, nonabsorbent insulators that are securely attached to the building (or other structure) ≫230.27≪.

B Electrical metallic tubing (EMT) couplings and connectors shall be made up tight. If installed in wet locations, they shall be listed for use in wet locations ≫358.42 and 314.15≪.

C Service heads must be located above the point where service-drop or overhead service conductors are attached to the building or other structure ≫230.54(C)≪.

D Where it is impracticable to locate the service head above the point of attachment, the service head must be located within 24 in. (600 mm) of that point ≫230.54(C) Exception≪.

E Because this service mast does not support service-drop conductors, another wiring method (EMT) is used. Other allowable service-entrance methods for 600 volts, nominal, or less are listed in 230.43.

F Electric equipment must be firmly secured to the surface on which it is mounted. Wooden plugs driven into holes in masonry, concrete, plaster, etc., are not acceptable ≫110.13(A)≪.

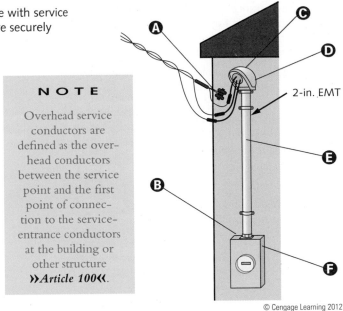

NOTE

Overhead service conductors are defined as the overhead conductors between the service point and the first point of connection to the service-entrance conductors at the building or other structure ≫*Article 100*≪.

2-in. EMT

© Cengage Learning 2012

Support of Overhead Conductors

A Vegetation (such as trees) shall not be used to support overhead conductor spans, except for temporary wiring in accordance with Article 527 ≫225.26≪.

B Drip loops must be formed on each individual conductor. To prevent moisture penetration, service-entrance conductors are connected to the service-drop or overhead service conductors either (1) below the level of the service head or (2) below the level of the termination of the service-entrance cable sheath ≫230.54(F)≪.

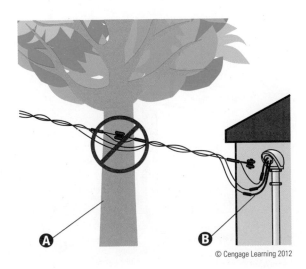

© Cengage Learning 2012

Goosenecks in Service-Entrance Cables

A Bends in service-entrance cable must be made so that the cable is not damaged. In addition, the radius of the curve of the inner edge of any bend must be at least five times the diameter of the cable ≫338.24≪.

B Goosenecks in service-entrance cables must be located above the point of attachment of the service-drop or overhead service conductors to the building (or other structure) ≫230.54(C)≪.

C Type SE cable can be formed in a gooseneck and taped with a self-sealing weather-resistant thermoplastic ≫230.54(B) Exception≪.

D Drip loops must be formed on all individual conductors ≫230.54(F)≪.

Cable Strap

© Cengage Learning 2012

Service-Entrance Cable

Ⓐ Service-entrance cables must be fitted with a raintight service head, except for Type SE cable that has been formed into a gooseneck and taped with a self-sealing, weather-resistant thermoplastic ≫*230.54(B)*≪.

Ⓑ If Type SE or USE cable consists of at least two conductors, one can be uninsulated ≫*338.100*≪.

Ⓒ Service-entrance cable is a single conductor or multiconductor assembly (with or without an overall covering), primarily used for services. Type SE has a flame-retardant, moisture-resistant covering ≫*338.2*≪.

Ⓓ Service-entrance cables must be held securely in place ≫*230.54(D)*≪.

Ⓔ Service head conductors of different potential must be brought out through separately bushed openings ≫*230.54(E)*≪.

Ⓕ Service-entrance cables must be supported by straps (or other approved means) within 12 in. (300 mm) of every service head or gooseneck ≫*230.51(A)*≪.

Ⓖ Entrance cables must be supported at intervals not to exceed 30 in. (750 mm) ≫*230.51(A)*≪.

Ⓗ Entrance cables must be supported within 12 in. (300 mm) of every raceway or enclosure connection ≫*230.51(A)*≪.

Ⓘ Service-entrance and overhead service conductors must be arranged so that water will not enter service raceway or equipment. ≫*230.54(G)*≪.

> **CAUTION**
>
> Where subject to physical damage, service cables must be appropriately protected ≫*230.50*≪.

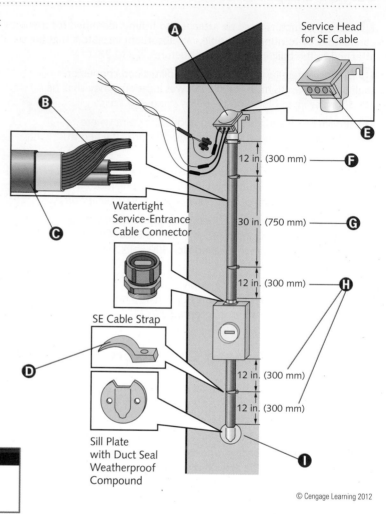

Service Head for SE Cable

12 in. (300 mm) — **Ⓕ**

30 in. (750 mm) — **Ⓖ**

12 in. (300 mm) — **Ⓗ**

12 in. (300 mm)

12 in. (300 mm)

Ⓘ

Watertight Service-Entrance Cable Connector

SE Cable Strap

Sill Plate with Duct Seal Weatherproof Compound

© Cengage Learning 2012

Conductors Considered Outside of a Building

Ⓐ Building or structure interior wall

Ⓑ An interior service disconnecting means must be installed as close as possible to the point of entrance of the service conductors and must be readily accessible. A raceway be-neath a 2-in. (50-mm) concrete slab lies outside the building. Under this condition, the service disconnecting means could be installed on (or in) an interior wall of the building. (See Caution.)

Ⓒ Conductors installed under 2 in. (50 mm) or more of concrete beneath a building (or other structure) are considered outside ≫*230.6(1)*≪.

> **CAUTION**
>
> Although not stipulated in the *NEC*, some local jurisdictions have adopted specific distance requirements for service conduc-tors. (For example, the length for each service conductor between the meter socket enclosure and the service disconnecting means could be limited to only 6 ft [1.8 m]).

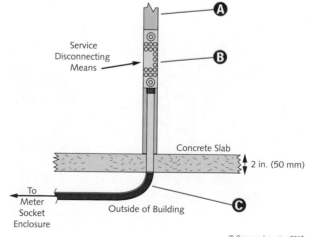

Service Disconnecting Means

Ⓐ

Ⓑ

Concrete Slab

2 in. (50 mm)

To Meter Socket Enclosure

Outside of Building

Ⓒ

© Cengage Learning 2012

Underground Services

Ⓐ Service-lateral conductors must be insulated for the applied voltage ≫*230.30*≪. Grounded conductors qualifying under 230.30 Exception can be uninsulated (bare).

Ⓑ Metal raceways containing service conductors must be connected to the grounded system conductor if the electrical system is grounded ≫*250.80*≪.

Ⓒ Wiring methods permitted for services of 600 volts, nominal, or less are listed in 230.43.

Ⓓ Underground service conductors are defined as the underground conductors between the service point and the first point of connection to the service-entrance conductors in a terminal box, meter, or other enclosure, inside or outside the building wall ≫*Article 100*≪. Where there is no terminal box, meter, or other enclosure, the point of connection is considered to be the point of entrance of the service conductors into the building ≫*Informational Note to Service Conductors, Underground*≪.

Ⓔ Direct-buried conduit (or other raceways) must be installed in adherence with Table 300.5 minimum cover requirements ≫*300.5(A)*≪.

> ### NOTE
> Underground service conductors must have adequate mechanical strength and sufficient ampacity to carry the current for the load (as calculated in accordance with Article 220) ≫***230.31(A)***≪.

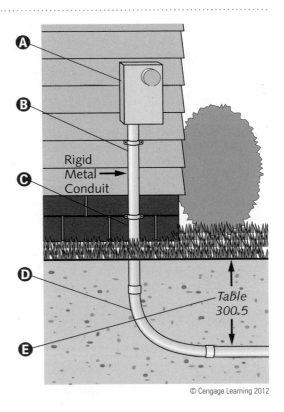

© Cengage Learning 2012

Underground Service-Entrance Cable

Although Type USE cable identified for underground use has a moisture-resistant covering, a flame-retardant covering is not required ≫*338.2*≪.

If Type USE cable contains at least two conductors, one can be uninsulated ≫*338.100*≪.

Ⓐ Underground service conductors must be protected against damage in accordance with 300.5. Service conductors entering a building or other structure must be installed in accordance with 230.6 or must be protected by an approved raceway wiring method identified in 230.43 ≫*230.32*≪.

Ⓑ Where the conductors or cables emerge as a direct-burial wiring method, a bushing (or fitting) must be installed to protect conductors from abrasion on the end of the conduit (or tubing) that terminates underground. A seal providing the same level of protection can be used instead of a bushing ≫*300.5(H)* and *300.15(C)*≪.

Ⓒ Type USE cable used for service laterals can emerge aboveground at outside terminations (in meter bases or other enclosures) provided 300.5(D) protection requirements are met ≫*338.12(B)(2)*≪.

Ⓓ When installed, direct-buried cable must meet Table 300.5 minimum cover requirements ≫*300.5(A)*≪.

Ⓔ Cabled, single-conductor, Type USE constructions, recognized for underground use, may have a bare copper conductor cabled with the assembly. Underground-approved Type USE single, parallel, or cabled conductor assemblies may have a bare copper concentric conductor applied. An outer overall covering is not required for these constructions ≫*338.100*≪.

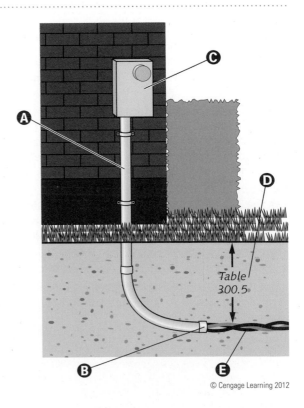

© Cengage Learning 2012

Wiring Methods

A Service-entrance conductors must be installed according to applicable *Code* requirements for the type of wiring method used and limited to the following methods: (1) open wiring on insulators; (2) Type IGS cable; (3) RMC; (4) IMC; (5) EMT; (6) ENT; (7) service-entrance cables; (8) wireways; (9) busways; (10) auxiliary gutters; (11) PVC; (12) cablebus; (13) Type MC cable; (14) mineral-insulated, metal-sheathed cable; (15) FMC (or LFMC) not longer than 6 ft (1.8 m) between raceways, or between raceway and service equipment, having equipment bonding jumper routed with the FMC (or LFMC) according to 250.102(A), (B), (C), and (E) provisions; (16) LFNC; (17) high-density polyethylene conduit (HDPE); (18) nonmetallic underground conduit with conductors (NUCC); or (19) reinforced thermosetting resin conduit (RTRC) ≫ *230.43* ≪.

> ### N O T E
> The wiring method of choice must be installed according to provisions for that particular method. For example, Type rigid metal conduit (RMC) must be installed according to Article 344 provisions.

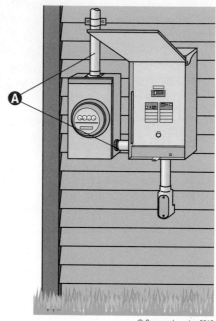

© Cengage Learning 2012

SERVICE AND OUTSIDE WIRING CLEARANCES

Accessibility to Pedestrians

A The point of attachment of the service-drop conductors to a building (or other structure) must meet 230.9 and 230.24 minimum clearances. In all cases, this point of attachment must be at least 10 ft (3.0 m) above finished grade ≫ *230.26* ≪.

B Overhead service conductors, accessible only to pedestrian traffic, must have a minimum 10-ft (3.0-m) vertical clearance above finished grade, sidewalks, platforms, or projections from which they might be reached. The voltage must not exceed 150 to ground ≫ *230.24(B)(1)* and *225.18(1)* ≪.

C The 3-ft (900-mm) minimum requirement does not apply to conductors run above the top level of a window ≫ *230.9(A) Exception and 225.19(D)(1) Exception* ≪.

D The 3-ft (900-mm) clearance from windows found in 230.9 does not apply to raceways and service equipment.

E A drip loop's lowest point must have a minimum vertical clearance of 10 ft (3.0 m) ≫ *230.24(B)(1)* ≪.

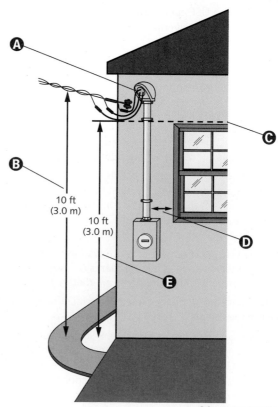

© Cengage Learning 2012

Vertical Clearances

A A 10-ft (3.0-m) minimum vertical clearance is required from any platform or projection from which overhead conductors (of 150 volts, or less, to ground) might be reached »230.24(B)(1) and 225.18(1)«.

B A minimum 12-ft (3.7-m) vertical clearance is required over residential property and driveways, and over commercial areas (not subject to truck traffic) provided conductor voltage does not exceed 300 volts to ground »230.24(B)(2) and 225.18(2)«.

C Conductor voltage exceeding 300 volts to ground has a minimum vertical clearance of 15 ft (4.5 m) »230.24(B)(3) and 225.18(3)«.

D Public streets, alleys, roads, parking areas subject to truck traffic, driveways on nonresidential property, and other land traversed by vehicles (such as cultivated, grazing, forest, and orchard) require a minimum 18-ft (5.5-m) vertical clearance »230.24(B)(4) and 225.18(4)«.

> **NOTE**
>
> Swimming pool overhead conductor clearances are listed in 680.8.

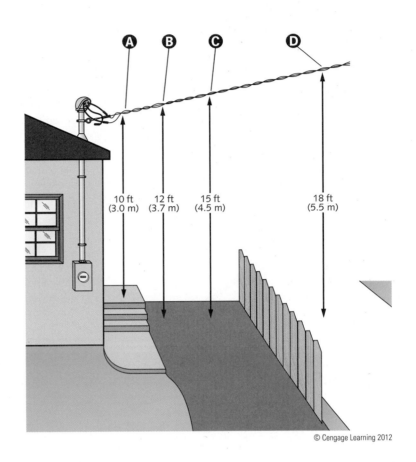

© Cengage Learning 2012

Clearance from Windows and Accessible Areas

A Service conductors installed as open conductors or multiconductor cable (having no overall outer jacket) must have a clearance of at least 3 ft (900 mm) from windows (designed to open), doors, porches, balconies, ladders, stairs, fire escapes, and similar locations »230.9(A) and 225.19(D)(1)«.

B The 3-ft (900-mm) clearance requirement does not apply to conductors run above the top level of a window »230.9(A) Exception and 225.19(D)(1) Exception«.

C The 3-ft (900-mm) clearance is not required for windows that are not designed to open.

D Except for the area above the window, the 3-ft (900-mm) clearance applies to the entire perimeter of windows, doors, etc.

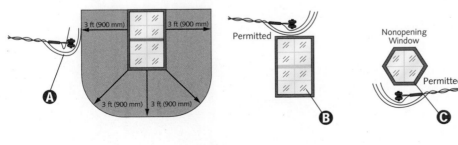
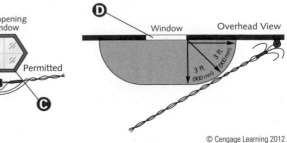

© Cengage Learning 2012

Conductors Obstructing Openings

Ⓐ Overhead conductors must not obstruct building entrances and must not be installed beneath openings designed for passage of materials, such as openings in farm and commercial buildings ≫ *230.9(C)* and *225.19(D)(3)* ≪.

> ### N O T E
>
> A minimum 18-ft (5.5-m) vertical clearance is required over land routinely traversed by vehicles (such as cultivated, grazing, forest, and orchard) **≫ *230.24(B)(4)* and *225.18(4)* ≪**.

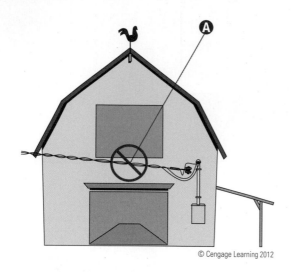

© Cengage Learning 2012

Conductors above Overhanging Portions of Roofs

Ⓐ A maximum of 6 ft (1.8 m) of overhead service conductors pass over the roof.

Ⓑ Conductors terminate in a through-the-roof raceway (or other approved support).

Ⓒ The vertical clearance for overhead service conductors can be reduced to 18 in. (450 mm) provided all 230.24(A) Exception No. 3 requirements are met.

Ⓓ The voltage between conductors does not exceed 300 volts.

Ⓔ The horizontal overhead service conductor measurement shall not exceed 4 ft (1.2 m).

Ⓕ This reduction in clearance applies to conductors passing above roof overhang only.

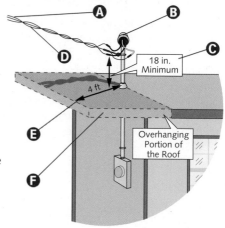

© Cengage Learning 2012

> ### N O T E
>
> If all the requirements of 225.19(A) Exception No. 3 are met, the vertical clearance for the overhead spans of open conductors, including multiconductor cables, can be reduced to 18 in. (450 mm).

Conductor Clearance above Flat Roofs

Ⓐ Conductors must have a vertical clearance of at least 8 ft (2.4 m) above the roof surface ≫ *230.24(A)* and *225.19(A)* ≪.

Ⓑ Although overhead service conductors must not be readily accessible, they must comply with 230.24(A) through (E) for services not over 600 volts, nominal ≫ *230.24* ≪.

Ⓒ A service mast supporting service-drop conductors must be of adequate strength or be supported by braces (or guys) to safely withstand the strain imposed by the service drop ≫ *230.28* ≪.

Ⓓ The vertical clearance above roof level must be maintained for a distance of at least 3 ft (900 mm) from all edges of the roof ≫ *230.24(A)* and *225.19(A)* ≪.

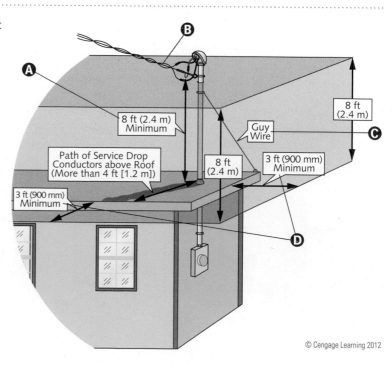

© Cengage Learning 2012

Conductors above Sloped Roofs

Ⓐ The voltage between the ungrounded (hot) conductors is 240 volts.

Ⓑ Where the voltage between conductors does not exceed 300, and the roof has a slope of not less than 4 in. in 12 in. (100 mm in 300 mm), a 3-ft (900-mm) clearance is permitted ≫*230.24(A) Exception No. 2* and *225.19(A) Exception No. 2* ≪.

Ⓒ This roof, as denoted by this symbol, has a slope (or slant) of 6 in. in 12 in., which is greater than 4 in. in 12 in.

Ⓓ Unlike 230.24(B), which stipulates that "vertical clearance" also includes the drip loop, 230.24 provisions mention only the service-drop conductor. Because the end of the service-drop conductors could be part (or all) of the drip loop, caution is advised.

Ⓔ The horizontal service-drop measurement is less than 4 ft (1.2 m). However, the conductors pass over more than just the overhanging portion of this roof. Therefore, the clearance shall not be reduced to 18 in. (450 mm) ≫*230.24(A) Exception No. 3* and *225.19(A) Exception No. 3* ≪.

Ⓕ Service equipment rated at 600 volts or less must be marked as suitable for use as service equipment. All service equipment shall be listed. Individual meter socket enclosures are not considered service equipment ≫*230.66*≪.

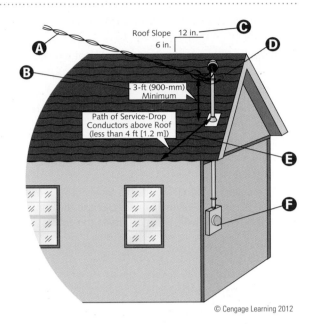

© Cengage Learning 2012

Various Roof Designs

Ⓐ Overhead service conductors above a roof with a slope of at least 4 in. in 12 in. (100 mm in 300 mm) have a minimum clearance of 3 ft (900 mm) ≫*230.24(A) Exception No. 2*≪.

Ⓑ This roof has a slope of 4 in. in 12 in.

Ⓒ The point of attachment is usually the lowest point of the service drop. If, however, the conductors run above the roof's highest point (ridge or peak), a taller service mast may be required.

Ⓓ This roof has a slope of 6 in. in 12 in. (more than 4 in. in 12 in.).

Ⓔ The supply voltage for all three overhead service conductor illustrations is 240 volts.

Ⓕ A service mast supporting service-drop conductors must be of adequate strength or be supported by braces (or guys) to safely withstand the strain imposed by the service drop ≫*230.28*≪.

Ⓖ Overhead service conductors above a roof with a slope less than 4 in. in 12 in. (100 mm in 300 mm) shall have a minimum clearance of 8 ft (2.5 m) ≫*230.24(A)*≪.

Ⓗ This roof has a slope of 3 in. in 12 in. (less than 4 in. in 12 in.).

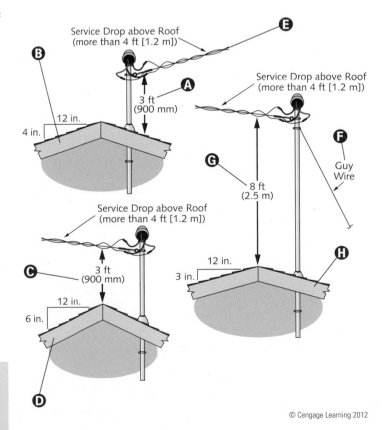

© Cengage Learning 2012

NOTE

Section 225.19 lists the vertical clearance for the overhead span of open conductors and open multiconductor cables. Because each of the illustrated service drops has a horizontal measurement of more than 4 ft (1.2 m), the amount of slope determines the minimum clearance requirement (either 3 ft [900 mm] or 8 ft [2.5 m]).

Panelboards

A All panelboards shall have a rating not less than the minimum feeder capacity required for the load calculated in accordance with Part III, IV, or V of Article 220, as applicable ≫*408.30*≪.

B In addition to the requirement of 408.30, a panelboard shall be protected by an overcurrent protective device having a rating not greater than that of the panelboard unless meeting one of the exceptions in 408.36.

C An individual overcurrent protective device is not required for a panelboard used as service equipment with multiple disconnecting means in accordance with 230.71 ≫*408.36 Exception No. 1*≪.

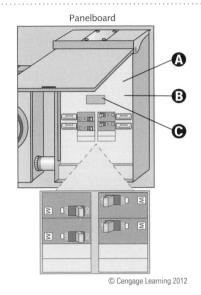

Panelboard

© Cengage Learning 2012

> **NOTE**
>
> In panelboards protected by three or more main circuit breakers or sets of fuses, the circuit breakers or sets of fuses shall not supply a second bus structure within the same panelboard assembly ≫**408.36 Exception No. 1**≪.

A In addition to the requirement of 408.30, a panelboard shall be protected by an overcurrent protective device having a rating not greater than that of the panelboard. This overcurrent protective device shall be located within or at any point on the supply side of the panelboard ≫*408.36*≪.

B The front edge of cabinets (panelboards) situated in walls constructed of noncombustible material (concrete, tile, etc.) must be within ¼ in. (6 mm) of the finished surface ≫*312.3*≪.

C Panelboards equipped with snap switches rated at 30 amperes or less shall have overcurrent protection of 200 amperes or less ≫*408.36(A)*≪.

D A grounded conductor shall not be connected to normally non-current-carrying metal parts of equipment, to equipment grounding conductor(s), or be reconnected to ground on the load side of the service disconnecting means except as otherwise permitted in Article 250 ≫*250.24(A)(5)*≪.

Raceway containing feeder conductors

Ungrounded (hot) Conductors

Grounding Conductor

Neutral Conductor

Panelboard

© Cengage Learning 2012

> **NOTE**
>
> Individual protection shall not be required for a panelboard protected on its supply side by two main circuit breakers or two sets of fuses having a combined rating not greater than that of the panelboard. A panelboard constructed or wired under this exception shall not contain more than 42 overcurrent devices. For the purposes of determining the maximum of 42 overcurrent devices, a 2-pole or a 3-pole circuit breaker shall be considered as two or three overcurrent devices, respectively ≫**408.36 Exception No. 2**≪.

> **CAUTION**
>
> Cabinets in walls constructed of combustible material (wood, etc.) must be flush with or extend beyond the finished surface ≫*312.3*≪.

> **NOTE**
>
> For existing panelboards, individual protection shall not be required for a panelboard used as service equipment for an individual residential occupancy ≫**408.36 Exception No. 3**≪.

Common-Trip and Single-Pole Circuit Breakers

A Circuit breakers must open all ungrounded conductors of the circuit both manually and automatic unless permitted in 240.15(B)(1) through (4) » *240.15(B)* «.

B Individual single-pole circuit breakers, with identified handle ties, are permitted as protection for each ungrounded conductor of multiwire branch circuits serving only single-phase, line-to-neutral loads » *240.15(B)(1)* «. In accordance with 210.4(B), each multiwire branch circuit must be provided with a means that will simultaneously disconnect all ungrounded (hot) conductors at the point where the branch circuit originates. There are no exceptions to this rule.

C In grounded systems, individual single-pole circuit breakers, rated 240 volts alternating current (ac), with identified handle ties are permitted as protection for each ungrounded conductor for line-to-line connected loads for single-phase circuits » *240.15(B)(2)* «.

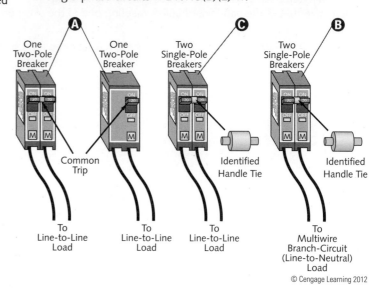

© Cengage Learning 2012

> ### NOTE
>
> For line-to-line loads in 4-wire, 3-phase systems or 5-wire, 2-phase systems, individual single-pole circuit breakers rated 120/240 volts ac with identified handle ties shall be permitted as the protection for each ungrounded conductor, if the systems have a grounded neutral point and the voltage to ground, does not exceed 120 volts **»** *240.15(B)(3)* **«**.

Cartridge Fuses and Fuseholders

Cartridge fuses and fuseholders are classified according to voltage and amperage ranges. Fuses rated 600 volts, nominal, or less can be used for voltages at or below their ratings » *240.61* «.

A Fuseholders are designed so that it is difficult to put a fuse of any given class into a fuseholder intended for a current lower, or voltage higher, than that of the class to which the fuse belongs » *240.60(B)* «.

B Fuses must be plainly marked (by printing on or a label attached to the fuse barrel), showing the following: (1) ampere rating, (2) voltage rating, (3) interrupting rating if other than 10,000 amperes, (4) "current-limiting" where applicable, and (5) the name or trademark of the manufacturer. The interrupting rating is not required on fuses used for supplementary protection » *240.60(C)* «.

C Fuseholders for current-limiting fuses must not permit insertion of non-current-limiting fuses » *240.60(B)* «.

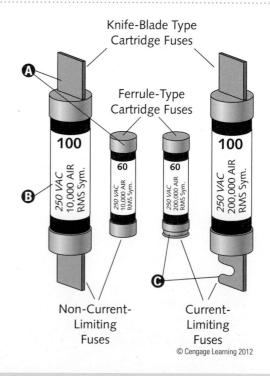

© Cengage Learning 2012

> ### NOTE
>
> Cartridge fuses and fuseholders with a 300-volt rating can be used in the following: (1) circuits not exceeding 300 volts between conductors and (2) single-phase, line-to-neutral circuits supplied from a 3-phase, 4-wire solidly grounded neutral source with line-to-neutral voltage not exceeding 300 volts **»** *240.60(A)* **«**.

> ### NOTE
>
> Class H cartridge fuses of the renewable type are only permitted as replacements in existing installations where there is no evidence of overfusing or tampering **»** *240.60(D)* **«**.

Conductor Sizing

A For individual dwelling units of one-family, two-family, and multifamily dwellings, conductors, as listed in Table 310.15(B)(7), shall be permitted as 120/240-volt, 3-wire, single-phase service-entrance conductors, service-lateral conductors, and feeder conductors that serve as the main power feeder to each dwelling unit and are installed in raceway or cable (with or without an equipment grounding conductor) »*310.15(B)(7)*«.

B The minimum size service-entrance conductors for this 200-ampere disconnect are 2/0 AWG copper or 4/0 AWG aluminum (or copper-clad aluminum) »*Table 310.15(B)(7)*«.

C As 310.15(B)(7) specifies, the main power feeder is the feeder between the main disconnect and the panelboard that supplies, either by branch circuits or by feeders, or by both, all loads that are part or associated with the dwelling unit

NOTE

The grounded (neutral) conductor can be smaller than the ungrounded (hot) conductors, provided 215.2, 220.61, and 230.42 requirements are met »*310.15(B)(7)*«.
The grounded conductor must not be smaller than the required grounding electrode conductor specified in Table 250.66 »*250.24(B)(1)*«.
The feeder conductors to a dwelling unit shall not be required to have an allowable ampacity rating greater than the service-entrance conductors »*310.15(B)(7)*«.

»*310.15(B)(7)*«. In this illustration, it is not permissible to select conductors from Table 310.15(B)(7) to supply power to the indoor panelboard. The indoor panelboard is not the main power feeder.

D Article 440 outlines provisions relating to disconnecting means, branch-circuit overload protection, and branch-circuit conductors for air-conditioning and refrigeration equipment.

E Conductor ampacities are found in Table 310.15(B)(16).

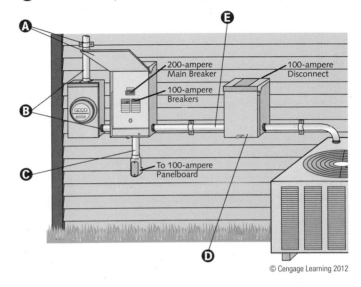

© Cengage Learning 2012

Installation

A Electric equipment must be installed in a neat and professional manner »*110.12*«.

B All electric equipment internal parts (busbars, wiring terminals, insulators, etc.) must remain undamaged and uncontaminated by foreign materials (paint, plaster, cleaners, abrasives, corrosive residues, etc.). Equipment parts that are broken, bent, cut, corroded, impaired due to chemical action or heat, or otherwise damaged in such a way as to adversely affect safe operation or mechanical strength must not be used »*110.12(B)*«.

C Sections 312.10 and 312.11 itemize construction specifications for cabinets, cutout boxes, and meter socket enclosures.

D Cabinets and cutout boxes must have space to sufficiently accommodate (without crowding) all installed conductors »*312.7*«.

E Conductor sizes are expressed in American Wire Gage (AWG) or in circular mils »*110.6*«.

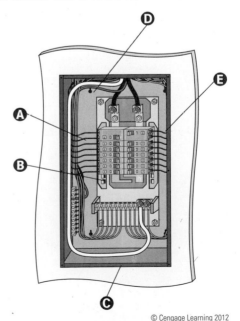

© Cengage Learning 2012

NOTE

The wiring space of enclosures for switches or overcurrent devices shall be permitted for conductors feeding through, spliced, or tapping off to other enclosures, switches, or overcurrent devices where all of the following conditions are met: (1) the total of all conductors installed at any cross section of the wiring space does not exceed 40% of the cross-sectional area of that space; (2) the total area of all conductors, splices, and taps installed at any cross section of the wiring space does not exceed 75% of the cross-sectional area of that space; and (3) a warning label is applied to the enclosure that identifies the closest disconnecting means for any feed-through conductors »*312.8*«.

Plug Fuses, Fuseholders, and Adapters

(A) Plug fuses of 15-ampere and lower rating are identified by a hexagonal configuration in a prominent location (such as window cap or cap) to distinguish them from fuses of higher ampere ratings 》*240.50(C)*《.

(B) Type S adapters must fit Edison-base fuseholders 》*240.54(A)*《.

(C) Once inserted into a fuseholder, Type S adapters cannot be removed 》*240.54(C)*《.

(D) Type S fuses are classified at not over 125 volts, and 0 to 15 amperes, 16 to 20 amperes, or 21 to 30 amperes 》*240.53(A)*《.

(E) Fuseholders of the Edison-base type shall be installed only where they are made to accept Type S fuses by the use of adapters 》*240.52*《.

(F) Plug fuses rated 16 to 30 amperes are identified by means other than a hexagonal configuration.

(G) Type S fuseholders and adapters are designed so that either the fuseholder itself or the fuseholder with a Type S adapter inserted can be used only for a Type S fuse 》*240.54(B)*《.

(H) Type S fuses of an ampere classification specified in 240.53(A) are not interchangeable with a lower-ampere classification. They can be used only in a Type S fuseholder or a fuseholder with a Type S adapter inserted 》*240.53(B)*《.

(I) Type S fuses, fuseholders, and adapters are designed to make tampering or shunting (bridging) difficult 》*240.54(D)*《.

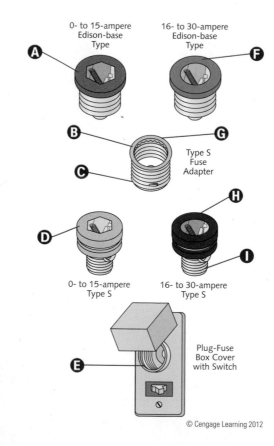

0- to 15-ampere Edison-base Type

16- to 30-ampere Edison-base Type

Type S Fuse Adapter

0- to 15-ampere Type S

16- to 30-ampere Type S

Plug-Fuse Box Cover with Switch

© Cengage Learning 2012

NOTE

The screw shell of a plug-type fuseholder must be connected to the circuit's load side 》*240.50(E)*《.

WARNING

Plug fuses of the Edison-base type can be used only as replacements in existing installations exhibiting no evidence of overfusing or tampering 》*240.51(B)*《.

GROUNDING

Grounded (Neutral) Conductor in the Service Disconnecting Means

Ⓐ Equipment grounding conductors, grounding electrode conductors, and bonding jumpers shall be connected by one of the following means: (1) listed pressure connectors; (2) terminal bars; (3) pressure connectors listed as grounding and bonding equipment; (4) exothermic welding process; (5) machine screw-type fasteners that engage not less than two threads or are secured with a nut; (6) thread-forming machine screws that engage not less than two threads in the enclosure; (7) connections that are part of a listed assembly; or (8) other listed means ≫ *250.8* ≪.

Ⓑ An ac system grounded at any point and operating at less than 1000 volts must have a grounded conductor that is routed with the ungrounded conductors to each service disconnecting means and connected to each service disconnecting means grounded conductor(s) terminal or bus. A main bonding jumper shall connect the grounded conductor(s) to each service disconnecting means enclosure ≫ *250.24(C)* ≪.

Ⓒ A grounded system must have an unspliced main bonding jumper connecting the equipment grounding conductor(s) and the service-disconnect enclosure to the grounded conductor within each service disconnect enclosure in accordance with 250.28 ≫ *250.24(B)* ≪.

Ⓓ A single bar in the service-disconnect enclosure may serve as the neutral bar (or bus) and the equipment grounding terminal bar (or bus).

Ⓔ The grounded conductor shall not be smaller than the required grounding electrode conductor specified in Table 250.66, and is not required to be larger than the largest ungrounded service-entrance conductor(s) ≫ *250.24(C)(1)* ≪.

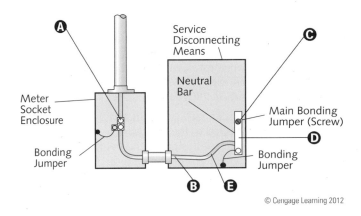

© Cengage Learning 2012

> **NOTE**
>
> The bonding jumper (screw, strap, etc.) is installed only in service equipment and not in subpanels.

Main Bonding Jumper

Ⓐ A main bonding jumper is the connection between the grounded circuit conductor (neutral) and the equipment grounding conductor at the service ≫ *Article100* ≪.

Ⓑ Main bonding jumpers and system bonding jumpers must be connected in the manner specified by the applicable provisions of 250.8 ≫ *250.28(C)* ≪.

Ⓒ A grounded system must have an unspliced main bonding jumper connecting the equipment grounding conductor(s) and the service-disconnect enclosure to the grounded conductor within each service disconnect enclosure ≫ *250.24(B)* ≪.

Ⓓ In cases where the main bonding jumper or a system bonding jumper is a screw only, it must be identified with a green finish that remains visible after installation ≫ *250.28(B)* ≪.

Ⓔ Main bonding jumpers and system bonding jumpers must be made of copper or other corrosion-resistant material; a wire, bus, screw, or similar suitable conductor is acceptable ≫ *250.28(A)* ≪.

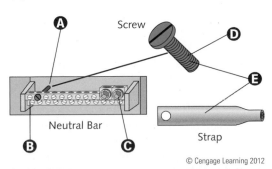

© Cengage Learning 2012

> **NOTE**
>
> The main bonding jumper and system bonding jumpers shall not be smaller than the sizes shown in Table 250.66 ≫ *250.28(D)* ≪.
> (Listed main bonding jumpers furnished with panelboards meet the provisions of 250.28.)

> **CAUTION**
>
> Panelboards listed as suitable for use as service equipment are furnished with a main bonding jumper that has not yet been installed. When using the panelboard as service equipment, install the main bonding jumper (screw, strap, etc.). When the panelboard is used for other purposes, such as a subpanel, do not install the main bonding jumper.

Remote Panelboards (Subpanels)

A Unless grounded by connection to the grounded circuit conductor (permitted by 250.32, 250.140, and 250.142), non-current-carrying metal parts of equipment, raceways, and other enclosures if grounded, must be connected to an equipment grounding conductor by one of the following methods: (A) by connecting to any of the equipment grounding conductors permitted by 250.118, or (B) by connecting it to an equipment grounding conductor contained within the same raceway or cable or otherwise run with the circuit conductors »250.134(A) and (B)«.

B Equipment grounding conductors can be bare, covered, or insulated. Individually covered or insulated equipment grounding conductors must have a continuous outer finish, either green or green with yellow stripe(s), except as otherwise permitted by Article 250, Part VI »250.119«.

C Only in service disconnecting means can the neutral terminal bar be connected to the enclosure or equipment grounding terminal bar. At this point, the neutral bar is isolated from the equipment grounding system.

D A grounded circuit conductor shall not be used for grounding non-current-carrying metal parts of equipment on the load side of the service disconnecting means, unless an exception has been met »250.142(B)«.

> **NOTE**
>
> The bonding jumper (screw, strap, etc.) is installed only in the service disconnecting means and not in subpanels.

E Panelboard cabinets and panelboard frames, if metal, must be in physical contact with one another and must be connected to an equipment grounding conductor. Equipment grounding conductors must not be connected to a terminal bar provided for grounded conductors or neutral conductors unless the bar is identified for that purpose and is located where interconnection between equipment grounding conductors and grounded circuit conductors comply with Article 250 »408.40«.

F A grounding connection must *not* be connected to normally non-current-carrying metal parts of equipment or to equipment grounding conductor(s) or be reconnected to ground on the load side of the service disconnecting means except as otherwise allowed in Article 250 »250.24(A)(5)«.

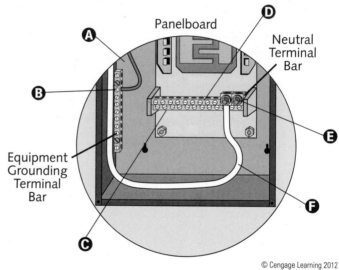

© Cengage Learning 2012

Grounding Electrode Conductor Connections

A The size of the grounding electrode conductor at the service, at each building or structure where supplied by a feeder(s) or branch circuit(s), or at a separately derived system of a grounded or ungrounded ac system shall not be less than given in Table 250.66, except as permitted in 250.66(A) through (C) »250.66«.

B A premises wiring system supplied by a grounded ac service must have a grounding electrode conductor connected to the grounded service conductor, at each service, in accordance with 250.24(A)(1) through (5) »250.24(A)«.

C A grounding electrode conductor must connect the equipment grounding conductors, the service-equipment enclosures, and, where the system is grounded, the grounded service conductor to the grounding electrode(s) as required by Part III of Article 250 »250.24(D)«.

> **NOTE**
>
> The grounding electrode conductor connection shall be made at an accessible point from the load end of the service drop (or service lateral), to and including the terminal (or bus) to which the grounded service conductor is connected at the service disconnecting means **»250.24(A)(1)«**.

D Splices in wire-type grounding electrode conductors are acceptable only if by means of irreversible compression-type connectors (listed as grounding and bonding equipment) or by the exothermic welding process »250.64(C)«.

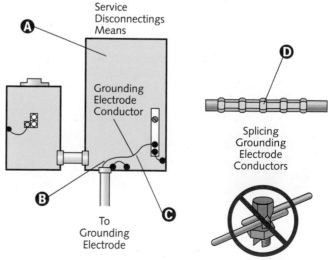

© Cengage Learning 2012

Methods of Bonding at the Service

Ⓐ One method is to bond equipment to the grounded service conductor in a 250.8-approved manner 》 *250.92(B)(1)* 《.

Ⓑ Connections using threaded couplings or threaded hubs on enclosures are permitted if made up wrenchtight 》 *250.92(B)(2)* 《.

Ⓒ Listed devices, such as bonding-type locknuts, bushings, or bushings with bonding jumpers are also permitted to ensure electrical continuity at service equipment 》 *250.92(B)(4)* 《.

Ⓓ Standard locknuts or bushings shall not be the sole means for bonding as required by 250.92(B), but shall be permitted to be installed to make a mechanical connection of the raceway(s) 》 *250.92(B)* 《.

Ⓔ Threadless couplings and connectors are approved if made up tight for metal raceways and metal-clad cables. Standard locknuts and bushings shall not be used to bond these items 》 *250.92(B)(3)* 《.

Ⓕ Bonding jumpers, which meet other Article 250 requirements, shall be used around impaired connections, such as reducing washers or oversized, concentric, or eccentric knockouts 》 *250.92(B)* 《.

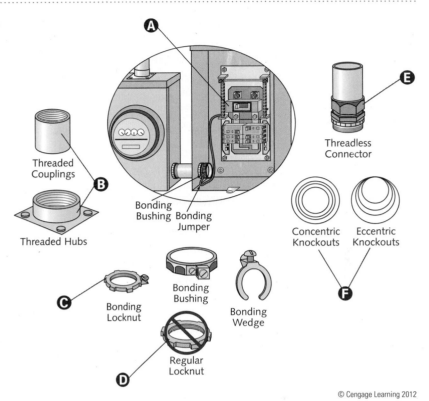

Threaded Couplings

Threaded Hubs

Threadless Connector

Bonding Bushing Bonding Jumper

Concentric Knockouts Eccentric Knockouts

Bonding Locknut

Bonding Bushing

Bonding Wedge

Regular Locknut

© Cengage Learning 2012

Bonding at the Service

Ⓐ Bonding is connected to establish electrical continuity and conductivity 》 *Article 100* 《.

Ⓑ Threaded hubs are acceptable when bonding service equipment enclosures to threaded conduits or threadless connectors 》 *250.92(B)(2) and (3)* 《.

Ⓒ All normally non-current-carrying metal parts of service equipment (such as raceways, enclosures containing service conductors, meter fittings, metal raceway, or armor enclosing a grounding electrode conductor) shall be bonded together 》 *250.92(A)* 《.

Ⓓ Bonding, where necessary, must be provided to ensure not only electrical continuity but also ample capacity to safely conduct any likely fault current 》 *250.90* 《.

Ⓔ Electrical continuity at service equipment, service raceways, and service conductor enclosures must be accomplished by one of the approved methods in 250.92(B).

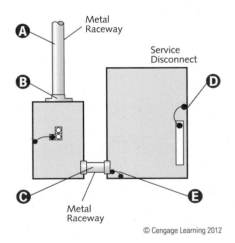

Metal Raceway

Service Disconnect

Metal Raceway

© Cengage Learning 2012

Grounding Electrode System

Grounding electrodes covered in 250.52 include: (1) metal underground water pipe, (2) metal frame of the building or structure, (3) concrete-encased electrode, (4) ground ring, (5) rod and pipe electrodes, (6) other listed electrodes, (7) plate electrodes, and (8) other local metal underground systems or structures. Although some of these grounding electrodes are described on this page, other electrodes from 250.52 are described on the following pages.

Exposed structural metal that is interconnected to form a metal building frame and is not intentionally grounded or bonded and is likely to become energized shall be bonded to the service equipment enclosure; the grounded conductor at the service; the disconnecting means for buildings or structures supplied by a feeder or branch circuit; the grounding electrode conductor, if of sufficient size; or to one or more grounding electrodes used. The bonding jumper(s) shall be sized in accordance with Table 250.66 and installed in accordance with 250.64(A), (B), and (E). The points of attachment of the bonding jumper(s) shall be accessible unless installed in compliance with 250.68(A), Exception No. 2 **》250.104(C)《**.

A The metal frame of the building or structure must be bonded to the grounding electrode system if it is connected to the earth by one or more of the following methods:

(1) At least one structural metal member that is in direct contact with the earth for 10 ft (3.0 m) or more, with or without concrete encasement.

(2) Hold-down bolts that secure the structural steel column and that are connected to a concrete-encased electrode that complies with 250.52(3) and is located in the support footing or foundation. The hold-down bolts shall be connected to the concrete-encased electrode by welding, exothermic welding, the usual steel tie wires, or other approved means **》250.52(A)(2)《**.

B A ground ring, which encircles the building or structure in direct contact with the earth at a depth of at least 2½ ft (750 mm) below the surface, consisting of at least 20 ft

(6.0 m) of bare copper conductor not smaller than 2 AWG, is allowed **》250.52(A)(4)** and *250.53(F)《*.

C A concrete-encased electrode shall be encased by at least 2 in. (50 mm) of concrete, located horizontally within that portion of a concrete foundation or footing that is in direct contact with the earth or within vertical foundations or structural components or members that are in direct contact with the earth. The electrode must consist of one or more bare or zinc galvanized or other electrically conductive coated steel reinforcing bars or rods, each at least ½ in. (13 mm) in diameter and 20 ft (6.0 m) continuous length or consisting of at least 20 ft (6.0 m) of bare copper conductor not smaller than 4 AWG. Multiple bars or rods can be connected together by the usual steel tie wires, exothermic welding, welding, or other effective means to create a 20 ft (6.0 m) or greater length **》250.52(A)(3)《**.

D Grounding electrode conductors and bonding jumpers shall be permitted to be connected to the structural frame of a building that is directly connected to a grounding electrode as specified in 250.52(A)(2) or 250.68(C)(2)(a), (b), or (c) shall be permitted as a bonding conductor to interconnect electrodes that are part of the grounding electrode system, or as a grounding electrode conductor. Permitted methods include: (1) connecting the structural metal frame to the reinforcing bars of a concrete-encased electrode, as provided in 250.52(A)(3), or ground ring as provided in 250.52(A)(4); (2) bonding the structural metal frame to one or more of the grounding electrodes, as specified in 250.52(A)(5) or (A)(7), that comply with (2); and (3) other approved means of establishing a connection to earth **》250.68(C)(2)《**.

WARNING

A concrete foundation or footing is not considered to be in "direct contact" with the earth if the concrete is installed with insulation, vapor barriers, films, or similar items that separate the concrete from the earth **》250.52(A)(3)** Informational Note《.

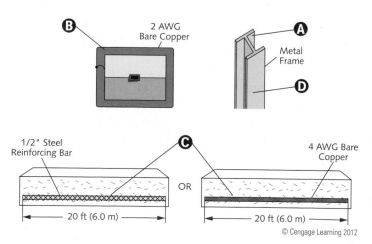

© Cengage Learning 2012

Metal Water Pipe Electrodes

Ⓐ A metal underground water pipe must be in direct contact with the earth for a minimum of 10 ft (3.0 m) (including any metal well casing effectively bonded to the pipe) and electrically continuous (or made so by bonding around insulating joints or insulating pipe) to the points of connection of the grounding electrode conductor and the bonding conductor(s) or jumper(s), if installed ≫ *250.52(A)(1)* ≪.

Ⓑ Grounding path continuity, or the bonding connection to interior piping, must not rely on water meters, filtering devices, or similar equipment ≫ *250.53(D)(1)* ≪.

Ⓒ Bonding jumper(s) shall be installed in accordance with 250.64(A), (B), and (E), shall be sized in accordance with 250.66, and shall be connected as specified in 250.70 ≫ *250.53(C)* ≪.

Ⓓ Although the interior metal water piping system is not a permitted grounding electrode, it can be used as a conductor to interconnect electrodes that are part of the grounding electrode system, but only if located not more than 5 ft (1.52 m) from the point of entrance to the building ≫ *250.68(C)(1)* ≪. There is an exception for industrial, commercial, and institutional buildings or structures.

Ⓔ A metal underground water pipe shall be supplemented by an additional electrode of a type specified in 250.52(A)(2) through (A)(8). If the supplemental electrode is of the rod, pipe, or plate type, it shall comply with 250.52(A). The supplemental electrode shall be bonded to one of the following: (1) grounding electrode conductor; (2) grounded service-entrance conductor; (3) nonflexible grounded service raceway; (4) any grounded service enclosure; and (5) as provided by 250.32(B) ≫ *250.53(D)(2)* ≪.

> **NOTE**
>
> A metal underground water pipe shall be supplemented by an additional electrode of a type specified in 250.52(A)(2) through (A)(8). If the supplemental electrode is of the rod, pipe, or plate type, it shall comply with 250.52(A). The supplemental electrode shall be bonded to one of the following: (1) grounding electrode conductor; (2) grounded service-entrance conductor; (3) nonflexible grounded service raceway; (4) any grounded service enclosure; or (5) as provided by 250.32(B) ≫ *250.53(A)(2)* ≪.

> **NOTE**
>
> The grounding electrode conductor can be run to any convenient grounding electrode available in the grounding electrode system where the other electrode(s), if any, is connected by bonding jumpers that are installed in accordance with 250.53(C). Grounding electrode conductor(s) can also be run to one or more grounding electrode(s) individually. It must be sized for the largest grounding electrode conductor required among all the electrodes being connected ≫ *250.64(F)* ≪. Bonding jumper(s) from grounding electrode(s) can also be connected to an aluminum or copper busbar where installed in accordance with 250.64(F)(3).

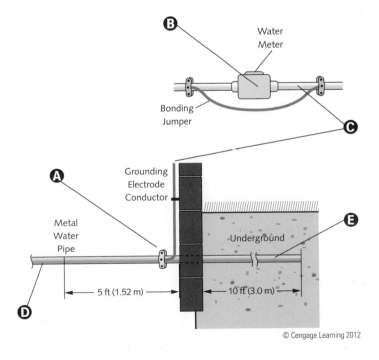

© Cengage Learning 2012

Rod, Pipe, and Plate Electrodes

If none of the grounding electrodes specified in 250.52(A)(1) through (A)(7) exist, one or more of the grounding electrodes specified in 250.52(A)(4) through (A)(8) must be installed and used ≫*250.50*≪.

Pipe or conduit electrodes shall not be smaller than trade size ¾-in., and, if steel, shall have a galvanized outer surface (or shall be otherwise metal-coated or corrosion-protected) ≫*250.52(A)(5)(a)*≪.

If practicable, rod, pipe, and plate electrodes shall be embedded below permanent moisture level. Rod, pipe, and plate electrodes shall be free from nonconductive coatings such as paint or enamel ≫*250.53(A)(1)*≪.

Aluminum grounding electrodes are not permitted ≫*250.52(B)(2)*≪.

Ⓐ The electrode's upper end must be flush with or below ground level unless the aboveground end and the grounding electrode conductor attachment are adequately protected against physical damage as specified in 250.10 ≫*250.53(G)*≪.

Ⓑ Rod-type grounding electrodes of stainless steel and copper or zinc-coated steel must be at least ⅝ in. (15.87 mm) in diameter unless listed ≫*250.52(A)(5)(b)*≪.

Ⓒ In multiple electrode configurations of the type specified in 250.52(A)(5) or (A)(7), each electrode of one grounding system (including that used for strike termination devices) must be at least 6 ft (1.83 m) from any other electrode of another grounding system. Two or more grounding electrodes bonded together are considered a single grounding electrode system ≫*250.53(B)*≪.

Ⓓ In accordance with 250.53(A)(2), if a single rod, pipe, or plate electrode is installed, it must be supplemented by an additional electrode. But, if the single rod, pipe, or plate electrode has a resistance to earth of 25 ohms or less, the supplemental electrode is not required ≫*250.53(A)(2) Exception*≪.

Ⓔ A metal underground gas piping system *shall not* be used as a grounding electrode ≫*250.52(B)*≪.

Ⓕ At least 8 ft (2.44 m) of electrode length must be in contact with the soil ≫*250.53(G)*≪.

Ⓖ Where rock bottom is encountered, the electrode can be driven at an oblique angle not to exceed 45° from vertical ≫*250.53(G)*≪.

Ⓗ Where rock bottom is encountered, the electrode can be buried in a trench that is at least 2½ ft (750 mm) deep ≫*250.53(G)*≪.

Ⓘ Each plate electrode must expose at least 2 ft² (0.186 m²) of surface to exterior soil ≫*250.52(A)(7)*≪. (One square foot of surface area on each side of a 1 ft × 1 ft plate equals 2 square feet.)

Ⓙ If multiple rod, pipe, or plate electrodes are installed to meet the requirements of 250.53(A)(2), they shall not be less than 6 ft (1.8 m) apart ≫*250.53(A)(3)*≪.

The paralleling efficiency of rods is increased by spacing them twice the length of the longest rod ≫*250.53(A)(3) Informational Note*≪.

Ⓚ Electrodes of bare or conductively coated iron or steel plates must be at least ¼ in. (6.4 mm) thick, while solid, uncoated nonferrous metal plates must be at least 0.06 in. (1.5 mm) thick ≫*250.52(A)(7)*≪.

Ⓛ Plate electrodes must be installed at least 2½ ft (750 mm) below the earth's surface ≫*250.53(H)*≪.

> ### NOTE
>
> A single rod, pipe, or plate electrode shall be supplemented by an additional electrode of a type specified in 250.52(A)(2) through (A)(8). If the supplemental electrode is of the rod, pipe, or plate type, it shall comply with 250.52(A). The supplemental electrode shall be permitted to be bonded to one of the following: (1) rod, pipe, or plate electrode; (2) grounding electrode conductor; (3) grounded service-entrance conductor; (4) nonflexible grounded service raceway; or (5) any grounded service enclosure ≫**250.53(A)(2)**≪.

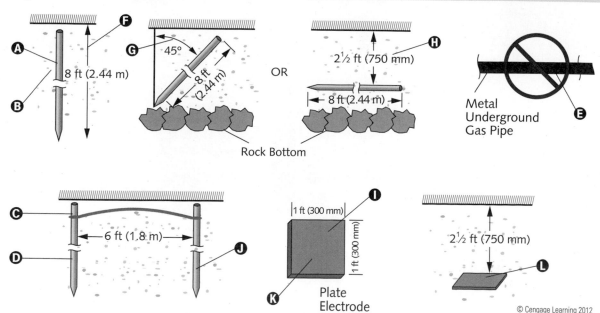

Rock Bottom

Metal Underground Gas Pipe

Plate Electrode

Grounding Electrode Conductor

The grounding electrode conductor must be made of copper, aluminum, or copper-clad aluminum. The material selected shall be inherently resistant to corrosive conditions existing at the site of installation or shall be protected against corrosion. The conductor can be solid (or stranded), insulated, covered, or bare 》*250.62* 《.

Bare aluminum or copper-clad aluminum grounding electrode conductors must not be used in direct contact with masonry or earth or where subject to corrosive conditions. If used outside, aluminum or copper-clad aluminum grounding electrode conductors must not be installed within 18 in. (450 mm) of the earth 》*250.64(A)* 《.

Ⓐ A grounding electrode conductor must be used to connect the equipment grounding conductors, the service-equipment enclosures, and, in a grounded system, the grounded service conductor to the grounding electrode(s) as required by Part III of Article 250. The conductor shall be sized in accordance with 250.66 》*250.24(D)* 《.

Ⓑ The grounding electrode conductor must be installed in one continuous length (without a splice or joint), unless as permitted in 250.30(A)(5) and (A)(6), 250.30(B)(1), and 250.68(C) 》*250.64(C)* 《.

Ⓒ Where exposed, a grounding electrode conductor (or its enclosure) must be securely fastened to the surface on which it is carried 》*250.64(B)* 《.

Ⓓ If a raceway is used as protection for a grounding electrode conductor, the installation must comply with appropriate raceway article requirements 》*250.64(E)* 《.

Ⓔ Ferrous metal raceways that enclose grounding electrode conductors must be bonded on each end 》*250.64(E)* 《.

Ⓕ Ferrous metal enclosures for grounding electrode conductors must be electrically continuous from the point of cabinet (or equipment) attachment to the grounding electrode and must be fastened securely to the ground clamp (or fitting). Ferrous metal enclosures not physically continuous from cabinet (or equipment) to the grounding electrode must be made electrically continuous by bonding each end of the raceway or enclosure to the grounding electrode conductor 》*250.64(E)* 《.

Ⓖ The grounding conductor must be connected to the grounding electrode by exothermic welding or by listed means, such as lugs, pressure connectors, clamps, etc. Connections depending on solder shall not be used 》*250.70* 《.

Ⓗ Only one conductor can be connected to the grounding electrode by a single clamp or fitting, unless it is listed for multiple conductors 》*250.70* 《.

Ⓘ This is one variety of ground-rod clamp listed for direct burial.

Ⓙ Ground clamps must be listed for the grounding electrode and grounding electrode conductor materials and, if used on pipe (rod, or other buried electrodes), must also be listed for direct soil burial or concrete encasement 》*250.70* 《.

Ⓚ The bonding jumper for a grounding electrode conductor raceway or cable armor must be the same size (or larger) than the required enclosed grounding electrode conductor 》*250.64(E)* 《.

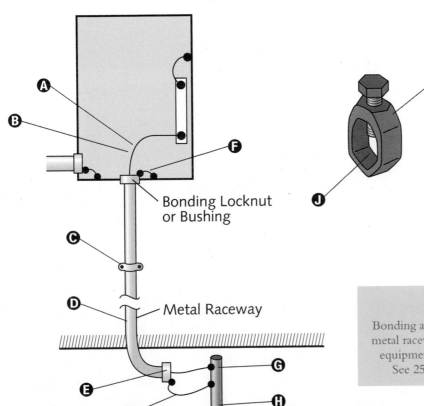

Bonding Locknut or Bushing

Metal Raceway

> **NOTE**
>
> Bonding applies to each end and to all intervening ferrous metal raceways, boxes, and enclosures between the service equipment and the grounding electrode 》**250.64(E)**《.
> See 250.92(B) for bonding methods at the service.

© Cengage Learning 2012

Grounding Electrode Conductor Sizing

Where exposed, a grounding electrode conductor or its enclosure shall be securely fastened to the surface on which it is carried. A 4 AWG or larger grounding electrode conductor (copper or aluminum) must be protected if exposed to physical damage. A 6 AWG grounding electrode conductor not exposed to physical damage can run along the surface of the building construction without metal covering or protection, provided it is securely fastened to the construction. Otherwise, it must be protected in RMC, IMC, PVC, RTRC, EMT, or cable armor ≫*250.64(B)*≪.

Grounding electrode conductors smaller than 6 AWG shall be protected in RMC, IMC, PVC, RTRC, EMT, or cable armor ≫*250.64(B)*≪.

Ⓐ The connection of a grounding electrode conductor at the service, at each building or structure where supplied by a feeder(s) or branch circuit(s), or at a separately derived system and associated bonding jumper(s) shall be made as specified 250.68(A) through (C) ≫*250.68*≪.

Ⓑ A 4 AWG copper (or 2 AWG aluminum or copper-clad aluminum) grounding electrode conductor is required if the service-entrance conductors are 2/0 AWG or 3/0 AWG copper ≫*Table 250.66*≪.

Ⓒ The interior metal water piping system can be used as a conductor to interconnect electrodes that are part of the grounding electrode system, but only if located not more than 5 ft (1.52 m) from the point of entrance to the building ≫*250.68(C)(1)*≪.

Ⓓ To ensure an effective grounding path for a metal piping system used as a grounding electrode, bonding must be provided as necessary around insulated joints as well as around any equipment likely to be disconnected for repairs or replacement. Bonding jumpers shall be of sufficient length to permit removal of such equipment while retaining the integrity of the grounding path ≫*250.68(B)*≪.

Ⓔ If the grounding electrode conductor is connected to rod, pipe, or plate electrodes as permitted in 250.52(A)(5) or (A)(7), that portion of the conductor serving as the sole connection to the grounding electrode is not required to be larger than 6 AWG copper wire or 4 AWG aluminum wire ≫*250.66(A)*≪.

Ⓕ Where the grounding electrode conductor is connected to a concrete-encased electrode as permitted in 250.52(A)(3), that portion of the conductor serving as the sole connection to the grounding electrode is not required to be larger than 4 AWG copper wire ≫*250.66(B)*≪.

Ⓖ If, as 250.52(A)(4) permits, the grounding electrode conductor is connected to a ground ring, that portion of the conductor serving as the sole connection to the grounding electrode does not have to be larger than the ground ring conductor ≫*250.66(C)*≪.

NOTE

Grounding electrode conductors can be installed on or through framing members ≫*250.64(B)*≪.

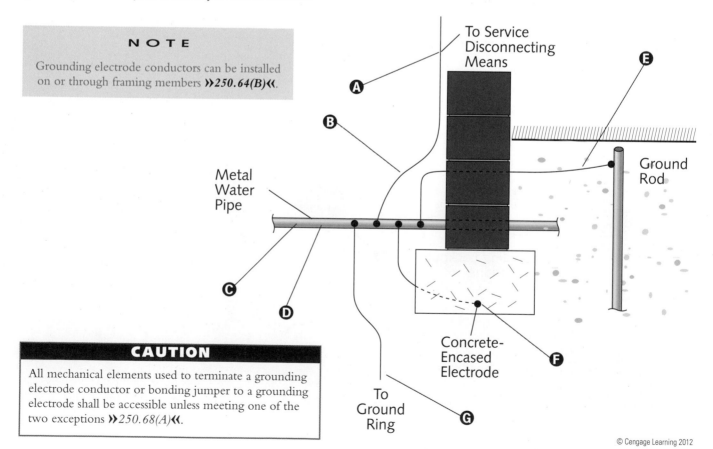

CAUTION

All mechanical elements used to terminate a grounding electrode conductor or bonding jumper to a grounding electrode shall be accessible unless meeting one of the two exceptions ≫*250.68(A)*≪.

Supply-Side Bonding Jumper

Ⓐ Grounding electrode conductor and equipment bonding jumper sizes on the supply side of the service are determined by service-entrance conductor sizes.

Ⓑ Unit 8 explains grounded (neutral) conductor sizing.

Ⓒ The size of the grounding electrode conductor at the service, at each building or structure where supplied by a feeder(s) or branch circuit(s), or at a separately derived system of a grounded or ungrounded ac system shall not be less than given in Table 250.66, except as permitted in 250.66(A) through (C) 》*250.66*《.

Ⓓ Bonding jumpers on the supply side of the service shall not be smaller than the sizes shown in Table 250.66 for grounding electrode conductors 》*250.102(C)*《.

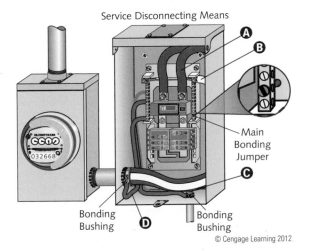

Service Disconnecting Means

Main Bonding Jumper

Bonding Bushing

Bonding Bushing

© Cengage Learning 2012

CAUTION

Metal piping system(s), including gas piping, with the potential to become energized must be bonded to the service equipment enclosure, the grounded conductor at the service, the grounding electrode conductor (if of sufficient size), or to one or more grounding electrode(s) used. The bonding conductor(s) or jumper(s) must be sized in accordance with Table 250.122 by using the rating of the circuit that is likely to energize the piping system(s). The equipment grounding conductor of this circuit can serve as the bonding means. The points of attachment of the bonding jumper(s) shall be accessible 》*250.104(B)*《.

NOTE

The interior metal water piping system must be bonded either to the service equipment enclosure, the grounded conductor at the service, the grounding electrode conductor (if of sufficient size), or to the one or more grounding electrodes used. The bonding jumper must be sized in accordance with Table 250.66 and installed in accordance with 250.64(A), (B), and (E). The bonding jumper's point of attachment must be accessible 》*250.104(A) and (A)(1)*《.

Equipment Bonding Jumper on the Load Side of an Overcurrent Device

The equipment bonding jumper on the load side of an overcurrent device(s) shall be sized, in accordance with 250.122 》*250.102(D)*《.

Ⓐ A panelboard (on the load side of an overcurrent device) protected by a 100-ampere overcurrent protection device (circuit breaker or fuse) requires an 8 AWG copper equipment grounding conductor 》*Table 250.122*《.

Ⓑ Wire-type copper, aluminum, or copper-clad aluminum equipment grounding conductors must not be less than shown in Table 250.122, but in no case are they required to be larger than the circuit conductors supplying the equipment. Where a raceway, cable armor, or sheath is used as the equipment grounding conductor (as provided in 250.118 and 250.134[A]), it must comply with 250.4(A)(5) or (B)(4) 》*250.122(A)*《.

Ⓒ Metal panelboard cabinets and frames must be connected to an equipment grounding conductor and in physical contact with each other. Where the panelboard is used with nonmetallic raceway (or cable), or where separate grounding conductors are provided, a terminal bar for the grounding conductors must be secured within the cabinet. The terminal bar must be bonded to the metal cabinet and panelboard frame. Otherwise it shall be connected to the equipment grounding conductor that is run with the conductors feeding the panelboard 》*408.40*《.

Ⓓ Equipment grounding conductor and equipment bonding jumper sizes (on the load side of an overcurrent device) are determined by the size of the overcurrent device that protects the equipment.

Ⓔ Unit 8 explains grounded (neutral) conductor sizing.

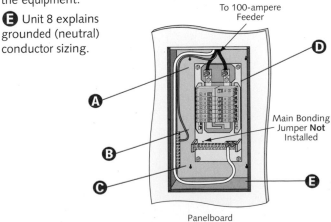

To 100-ampere Feeder

Main Bonding Jumper **Not** Installed

Panelboard

© Cengage Learning 2012

NOTE

Where ungrounded conductor sizes are adjusted to compensate for voltage drop, equipment grounding conductors, where installed, must be adjusted proportionately according to circular mil area of the ungrounded conductors 》*250.122(B)*《.

An equipment grounding conductor run with (or enclosing) the circuit conductors must be one of those listed in 250.118.

Separate Building or Structure – Grounding Electrode Not Required

Besides other requirements in the National Electrical Code, installations in separate buildings and structures must meet requirements in Article 225. Requirements in Article 225 cover outside branch circuits and feeders.

Although a disconnecting means is required and it must be suitable for use as service equipment, there is an exception for garages and outbuildings on residential property. For garages and outbuildings on residential property, a snap switch or a set of three-way or four-way snap switches shall be permitted as the disconnecting means ≫ *225.36 Exception* ≪.

A building is defined as a structure that stands alone or that is cut off from adjoining structures by fire walls with all openings therein protected by approved fire doors ≫ *Article 100* ≪.

Ⓐ A structure is simply defined as that which is built or constructed ≫ *Article 100* ≪.

Ⓑ A grounding electrode shall not be required where only a single branch circuit, including a multiwire branch circuit, supplies the building or structure, and the branch circuit includes an equipment grounding conductor for grounding the normally non–current-carrying metal parts of equipment ≫ *250.32 Exception* ≪.

Ⓒ If a one-family dwelling has a detached garage or accessory building with electric power, at least one wall switch–controlled lighting outlet shall be installed to provide illumination on the exterior side of outdoor entrances or exits with grade level access. A vehicle door in a garage shall not be considered as an outdoor entrance or exit ≫ *210.70(A)(2)(b)* ≪.

Ⓓ Where a one-family dwelling has a detached garage or accessory building with electric power, at least one receptacle outlet, in addition to those for specific equipment, shall be installed ≫ *210.52(G)(1)* ≪.

> **N O T E**
>
> At least one wall switch-controlled lighting outlet shall be installed in detached garages with electric power ≫*210.70(A)(2)(a)*≪.

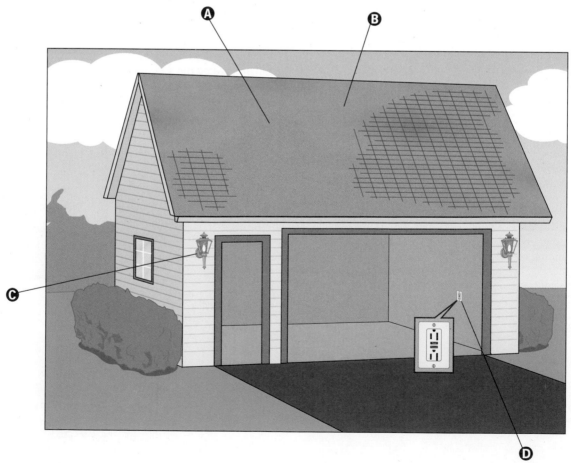

Separate Buildings or Structures

Besides other requirements in the NEC, installations in separate buildings and structures must meet requirements in Article 225. Requirements in Article 225 cover outside branch circuits and feeders.

A Buildings or structures supplied by feeders or branch circuits must have a grounding electrode or grounding electrode system installed in accordance with Part III of Article 250. The grounding electrode conductors must be installed in accordance with 250.32(B) for grounded systems, or (C) for ungrounded systems. If there is no existing grounding electrode, the grounding electrode required in 250.50 must be installed 》250.32(A) 《.

B Means shall be provided for disconnecting all ungrounded conductors that supply or pass through the building or structure 》225.31 《.

C The disconnecting means shall be installed either inside or outside of the building or structure served or where the conductors pass through the building or structure. The disconnecting means shall be at a readily accessible location nearest the point of entrance of the conductors 》225.32 《.

D The disconnecting means specified in 225.31 shall be suitable for use as service equipment 》225.36 《.

E The building or structure disconnecting means shall plainly indicate whether it is in the open or closed position 》225.38(D) 《.

F An equipment grounding conductor, as described in 250.118, shall be run with the supply conductors and connected to the building or structure disconnecting means and to the grounding electrode(s). The equipment grounding conductor shall be used for grounding or bonding or equipment, structures, or frames required to be grounded or bonded. The equipment grounding conductor must be sized in accordance with 250.122 》250.32(B)(1) 《.

G Any installed grounded conductor shall not be connected to the equipment grounding conductor or to the grounding electrode(s) 》250.32(B)(1) 《.

H The size of the grounding electrode conductor to the grounding electrode(s) shall not be smaller than given in 250.66, based on the largest ungrounded supply conductor. The installation shall comply with Part III of Article 250 》250.32(E) 《.

NOTE

There is an exception for installations made in compliance with previous editions of the *NEC* that permitted alternative connections. See the exception to 250.32(B)(1).

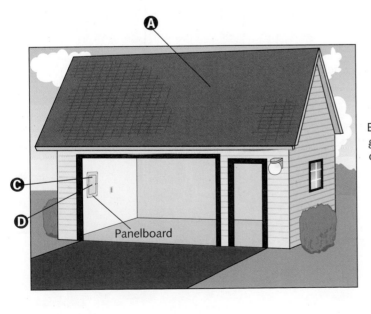

Panelboard

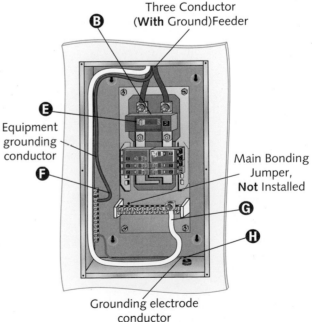

Three Conductor **(With** Ground)Feeder

Equipment grounding conductor

Main Bonding Jumper, **Not** Installed

Grounding electrode conductor

© Cengage Learning 2012

Preventing Objectionable Current

Normally non-current-carrying electrically conductive materials that are likely to become energized must be connected together and to the electrical supply source in a manner that establishes an effective ground-fault current path ≫*250.4(A)(4)*≪.

Temporary currents resulting from abnormal conditions, such as ground faults, are not classified as objectionable current for the purpose specified in 250.6(A) and (B) ≫*250.6(C)*≪.

Ⓐ Normally non-current-carrying conductive materials enclosing electrical conductors (or equipment), or forming part of such equipment, must be connected to earth so as to limit the voltage to ground on these materials ≫*250.4(A)(2)*≪.

Ⓑ If the use of multiple grounding connections results in objectionable current, one or more of the following

alterations in 250.6(B)(1) through (4) are permitted, if the requirements of 250.4(A)(5) or (B)(4) are met: (1) discontinue one or more, but not all, of such grounding connections; (2) change the location of the grounding connections; (3) interrupt the continuity of the conductor (or conductive path) causing the objectionable current; and (4) take other suitable remedial and approved action ≫*250.6(B)*≪.

Ⓒ The grounding of electric systems, circuit conductors, surge arresters, surge-protective devices and conductive normally non-current-carrying materials (and equipment) must be installed and arranged in a manner that prevents objectionable current ≫*250.6(A)*≪.

CAUTION

Connecting a grounded (neutral) and grounding conductor in parallel creates objectionable current on the grounding conductor, because the unbalanced current flows through both the grounded and grounding conductor. Should the grounded conductor lose its continuity (become disconnected), the grounding conductor would then carry all of the unbalanced (neutral) current. A hazard would exist if the grounding conductor's ampacity rating is less than the current flowing through it.

NOTE

Normally non-current-carrying conductive materials enclosing electrical conductors or equipment, or forming part of such equipment, shall be connected together and to the electrical supply source in a manner that establishes an effective ground-fault current path ≫*250.4(A)(3)*≪.

NOTE

Electrical equipment and wiring and other electrically conductive material likely to become energized shall be installed in a manner that creates a low-impedance circuit facilitating the operation of the overcurrent device or ground detector for high-impedance grounded systems. It shall be capable of safely carrying the maximum ground-fault current likely to be imposed on it from any point on the wiring system where a ground fault may occur to the electrical supply source. The earth shall not be considered as an effective ground-fault current path ≫*250.4(A)(5)*≪.

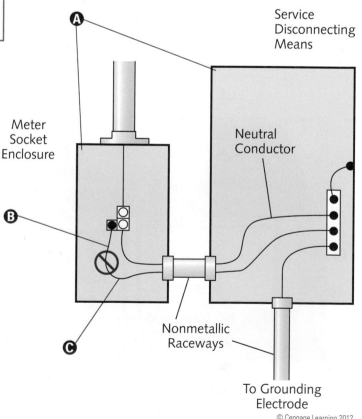

Service Disconnecting Means

Meter Socket Enclosure

Neutral Conductor

Nonmetallic Raceways

To Grounding Electrode

Summary

- A service mast must safely withstand the strain imposed by service-drop conductors.
- Nothing except electrical service-drop conductors can be attached to the service mast.
- Wiring methods permitted for services are listed in 230.43.
- Service-drop conductor vertical ground clearances are found in 230.24(B)
- Service-drop conductor roof clearances are in 230.24(A).
- A minimum of 6½ ft (2.0 m) of workspace headroom is required around service equipment and panelboards.
- A minimum frontal workspace width is 30 in. (762 mm) for service equipment and panelboards; the depth of this workspace must be at least 3 ft (914 mm).
- Panelboards are mounted in cabinets or cutout boxes.
- Each service disconnect must be permanently marked identifying it as a service disconnect.
- The service disconnecting means must be installed at a readily accessible location whether inside or outside.
- Two to six circuit breakers or sets of fuses can serve as the overcurrent device, providing overload protection.
- Table 310.15(B)(7) can be used to size conductors that serve as the main power feeder to a dwelling.
- Conductors not serving as the main power feeder are sized from Table 310.15(B)(16).
- Electric equipment must be installed in a neat and professional manner.
- Grounding and bonding conductors must be connected by listed means.
- The grounded (neutral) conductor is isolated from the equipment grounding conductor in subpanels.
- Grounding electrode conductors and bonding jumpers on the service supply side are sized from 250.66 and Table 250.66.
- Equipment grounding conductors and bonding jumpers, on the load side of the service, are sized according to 250.122 and Table 250.122.
- All non-current-carrying metal parts of service equipment must be bonded together.
- Grounding electrode systems (and conductors) are located in Part III of Article 250.
- Panelboards in separate buildings or structures must be installed according to 250.32 provisions.

Unit 9 Competency Test

NEC Reference   **Answer**

_____   _____   1. The point of attachment of the service-drop conductors to a building must not be less than _____ ft above finish grade.

_____   _____   2. The supply-side bonding jumper shall not be smaller than the sizes shown in Table _____ for grounding electrode conductors.

_____   _____   3. Service conductors run above the top level of a window shall be:

   a) 8 ft above a window.

   b) accessible.

   c) 3 ft above a window.

   d) considered out of reach.

_____   _____   4. Every circuit breaker having an interrupting rating other than _____ amperes shall have its interrupting rating shown on the circuit breaker.

_____   _____   5. Energized parts of service equipment that are not enclosed shall be installed on a _____ and guarded in accordance with 110.18 and 110.27.

   I. switchboard

   II. panelboard

   III. control board

      a) II only   b) I or II only   c) II or III only   d) I, II, or III

_____   _____   6. In addition to the requirement of 408.30, a panelboard shall be protected by an overcurrent protective device having a rating not greater than _____.

Panelboards Supplying Individual Units

A Non-current-carrying metal parts of equipment, raceways, and other enclosures, if grounded, must be connected to an equipment grounding conductor by one of the following methods: (A) by any of the equipment grounding conductors permitted by 250.118, or (B) by an equipment grounding conductor contained within the same raceway or cable, or otherwise run with the circuit conductors ≫ *250.134* ≪.

B Install the bonding jumper (screw, strap, etc.) only in the service disconnecting means, not in subpanels.

C At this point, the neutral bar is isolated from the equipment grounding system.

D The front edge of cabinets (panelboards) situated in walls constructed of noncombustible material (concrete, tile, etc.) must be within ¼ in. (6 mm) of, or extend beyond, the finished surface ≫ *312.3* ≪.

E If all of the qualifications are met, Table 310.15(B)(7) can be used to size feeder conductors.

F A grounded circuit conductor shall not be used for grounding non-current-carrying metal parts of equipment on the load side of the service disconnecting means, unless an exception has been met ≫ *250.142(B)* ≪.

G A grounded conductor shall not be connected to normally non-current-carrying metal parts of equipment or to equipment grounding conductor(s) or be reconnected to ground on the load side of the service disconnecting means except as otherwise permitted in Article 250 ≫ *250.24(A)(5)* ≪.

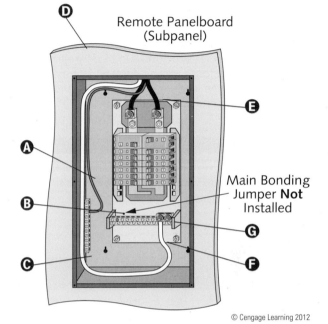

Remote Panelboard (Subpanel)

Main Bonding Jumper **Not** Installed

© Cengage Learning 2012

WARNING

All switchboards and panelboards supplied by a feeder in other than one- or two-family dwellings shall be marked to indicate the device or equipment where the power supply originates ≫ *408.4(B)* ≪.

CAUTION

Cabinets in walls constructed of combustible material must be flush with or extend beyond the finished surface ≫ *312.3* ≪.

NOTE

A circuit directory must be affixed to the face (or inside) of the panel door(s) indicating the purpose of all circuits and any circuit modifications ≫ *408.4(A)* ≪.

Rooftop Heating and Air-Conditioning Equipment

A All 125-volt, single-phase, 15- and 20-ampere dwelling unit outdoor receptacles must have GFCI protection ≫ *210.8(A)(3)* ≪.

B A 125-volt, single-phase, 15- or 20-ampere-rated receptacle outlet must be installed at an accessible location for the servicing of heating, air-conditioning, and refrigeration equipment ≫ *210.63* ≪.

C The receptacle must be located on the same level as, and within 25 ft (7.5 m) of the heating, air-conditioning, and refrigeration equipment ≫ *210.63* ≪. The provision does not stipulate that a receptacle must be located at every unit. One centrally located receptacle could meet the 210.63 requirement for all pieces of equipment located within the 25-ft (7.5-m) radius.

D Article 440 contains provisions pertaining to air-conditioning and refrigeration equipment.

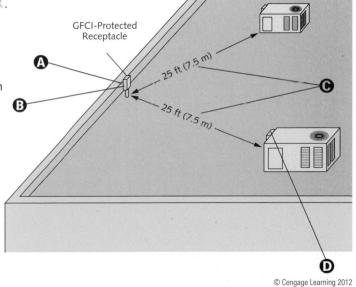

GFCI-Protected Receptacle

25 ft (7.5 m)

25 ft (7.5 m)

© Cengage Learning 2012

CAUTION

The receptacle outlet shall not be connected to the load side of the equipment disconnecting means ≫ *210.63* ≪.

Feeder Conductors

Ⓐ Table 310.15(B)(7) can be used to size 120/240, 3-wire, single-phase feeder conductors serving as the main power feeder to a dwelling unit ≫ *310.15(B)(7)* ≪.

Ⓑ If each unit contains a 100-ampere panelboard, the feeders can be 4 AWG copper (or 2 AWG aluminum) conductors ≫ *Table 310.15(B)(7)* ≪.

Ⓒ Load calculations are computed for each individual unit having its own panelboard. Although located in a multifamily dwelling, each unit is calculated by one of the one-family methods. It is incorrect to perform a load calculation on multiple units and then divide by the number of units.

Ⓓ Standard and optional one-family load calculations are explained in Unit 8 of this book.

Ⓔ The AHJ may require a diagram showing feeder details prior to installation. Such a diagram must show the area in square feet of the building (or other structure) supplied by each feeder, the total calculated load before applying demand factors, the demand factors used, the calculated load after applying demand factors, and the size and type of conductors that will be used ≫ *215.5* ≪.

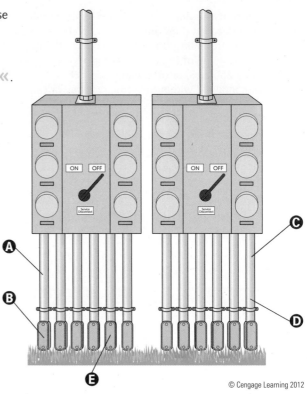

© Cengage Learning 2012

CAUTION

On long runs, it may be necessary to increase the feeder conductors' size to compensate for voltage drop ≫ *215.2(A)(4) Informational Note No. 2* ≪.

BRANCH CIRCUITS

Receptacles

Ⓐ For multifamily dwellings, each dwelling unit that is located at grade level and provided with individual exterior entrance/egress must have at least one receptacle outlet accessible from grade level and not more than 6½ ft (2.0 m) above grade ≫ *210.52(E)(2)* ≪.

Ⓑ Dwelling-unit branch circuits shall supply only loads within, or associated only with, that dwelling unit ≫ *210.25* ≪.

Ⓒ In a multifamily dwelling where laundry facilities are provided on the premises and available to all building occupants, a laundry receptacle is not required in each individual unit ≫ *210.52(F) Exception No. 1* ≪.

Ⓓ In other than one-family dwellings without laundry facilities, a laundry receptacle is not required ≫ *210.52(F) Exception No. 2* ≪.

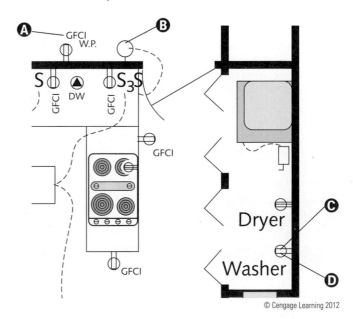

© Cengage Learning 2012

NOTE

Balconies, decks, and porches that are accessible from inside the dwelling unit shall have at least one receptacle outlet installed within the perimeter of the balcony, deck, or porch. The receptacle shall not be located more than 6½ ft (2.0 m) above the balcony, deck, or porch surface ≫ *210.52(E)(3)* ≪. There is no exception for balconies, decks, and porches that have small usable areas.

Receptacles *(continued)*

Ⓐ The maximum distance to any receptacle, measured horizontally along the wall line, is 24 in. (600 mm) ⟫*210.52(C)(1)*⟪.

Ⓑ Dwelling-unit branch circuits shall supply only loads within, or associated only with, that dwelling unit ⟫*210.25*⟪.

Ⓒ Receptacles must be installed so that no point measured horizontally along the floor line of any wall space is more than 6 ft (1.8 m) from a receptacle outlet ⟫*210.52(A)(1)*⟪.

Ⓓ *All 125-volt, 15- and 20-ampere receptacles serving kitchen countertops must have GFCI protection* ⟫*210.8(A)(6)*⟪.

Ⓔ Kitchen receptacles not serving countertops (such as receptacles behind refrigerators) do not require GFCI protection.

Ⓕ All receptacles in the kitchen, pantry, breakfast room, dining room, or similar areas must be supplied from 20-ampere small-appliance branch circuits (except for refrigeration equipment) ⟫*210.52(B)(1)*⟪.

Ⓖ Circuits feeding receptacles in kitchens, pantries, breakfast rooms, dining rooms, or similar areas shall not feed receptacles outside these areas ⟫*210.52(B)(2)*⟪.

Ⓗ GFCI protection is required for every 125-volt, 15- and 20-ampere receptacle located in a bathroom area ⟫*210.8(A)(1)*⟪.

Ⓘ A receptacle is required for any wall space 2 ft (600 mm) or more in width (including space measured around corners), unbroken along the floor line by doorways and similar openings, fireplaces, and fixed cabinets ⟫*210.52(A)(2)(1)*⟪.

Ⓙ Locate at least one receptacle within 36 in. (900 mm) of the outside edge of each basin (lavatory or sink). The receptacle outlet must be located on a wall or partition adjacent to the basin or basin countertop, located on the countertop, or installed on the side or face of the basin cabinet not more than 12 in. (300 mm) below the countertop. Receptacle outlet assemblies listed for the application shall be permitted to be installed in the countertop ⟫*210.52(D)*⟪.

Ⓚ A receptacle is required for each peninsular counter space (at least 12 by 24 in. [300 × 600 mm] in size) that is separated from other counter space by a range top, refrigerator, or sink ⟫*210.52(C)(3) and (4)*⟪.

Ⓛ A circuit providing power to bathroom receptacles shall not provide power to any receptacles (or lighting) outside the bathroom, unless meeting an exception ⟫*210.11(C)(3)*⟪.

> **NOTE**
>
> Only a few differences exist between one-family and multifamily dwelling receptacle requirements. Refer to Units 6 and 7 for more information pertaining to general as well as specific receptacle provisions.

> **CAUTION**
>
> In all areas specified in 210.52, all nonlocking-type 125-volt, 15- and 20-ampere receptacles shall be listed tamper-resistant receptacles ⟫*406.12*⟪.

> **WARNING**
>
> All 120-volt, single-phase, 15- and 20-ampere branch circuits supplying outlets installed in dwelling unit family rooms, dining rooms, living rooms, parlors, libraries, dens, bedrooms, sunrooms, recreation rooms, closets, hallways, or similar rooms or areas shall be protected by a listed arc-fault circuit interrupter, combination-type, installed to provide protection of the branch circuit ⟫*210.12(A)*⟪.

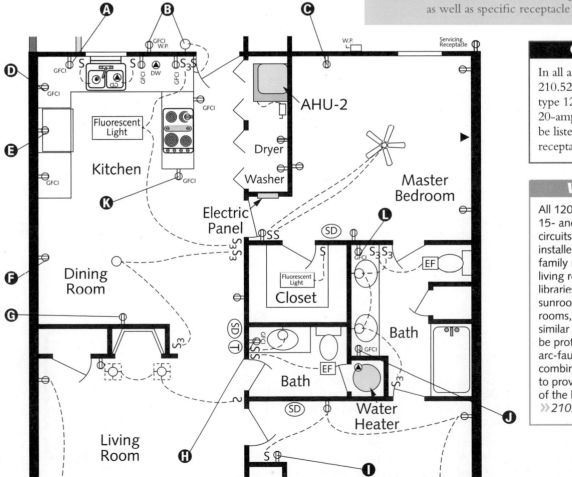

© Cengage Learning 2012

General Lighting

A minimum of one wall switch–controlled lighting outlet is required for dwelling hallways »210.70(A)(2)(a)«.

A At least one wall switch–controlled lighting outlet must be installed in every habitable room of a dwelling »210.70(A)(1)«.

B Clothes closet lighting outlet provisions are found in 410.16.

C At least one wall switch–controlled lighting outlet must be installed in every dwelling bathroom »210.70(A)(1)«.

D Except for kitchens and bathrooms, every habitable room is allowed one or more wall switch–controlled receptacle(s) in lieu of a lighting outlet »210.70(A)(1) Exception No. 1«.

E In hallways, stairways, and outdoor entrances, control of lighting can be remote, central, or automatic »210.70(A)(2) Exception«.

CAUTION

Where switches control lighting loads supplied by a grounded general-purpose branch circuit, the grounded circuit conductor for the controlled lighting circuit shall be provided at the switch location »**404.2(C)**«. The grounded circuit conductor shall be permitted to be omitted from the switch enclosure where meeting one of the two conditions in 404.2(C) Exception.

NOTE

A listed box is required for a ceiling-suspended (paddle) fan where the box provides the only support »**314.27(C)**«.
Only a few differences exist between one-family and multifamily dwelling lighting requirements. Refer to Units 6 and 7 for more information pertaining to general as well as specific lighting provisions.

F Branch circuits installed for the purpose of lighting, central alarm, signal, communication, or other purposes for public or common areas of a two-family or multifamily dwelling shall not be provided from equipment that supplies an individual dwelling unit or tenant space »210.25(B)«.

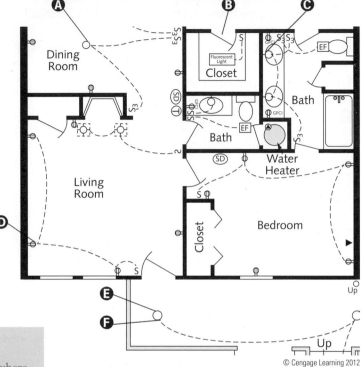

© Cengage Learning 2012

Appliance Disconnecting Means

A A permanently connected appliance, rated over 300 volt-amperes or ⅛ horsepower, must have a means to simultaneously disconnect all ungrounded (hot) conductors from the appliance »422.30 and 422.31«.

B An appliance switch marked with an "off" position that effectively disconnects all ungrounded conductors can serve as the disconnecting means required by Article 422 where other means for disconnection are provided in 422.34(A) through (D) »422.34«.

C For permanently connected appliances rated over 300 volt-amperes, a disconnecting means is not required if the branch-circuit switch or circuit breaker can be locked in the open (off) position »422.31(B)«.

D In multifamily dwellings, the other appliance disconnecting means (as described in 422.34) must be within the dwelling unit or on the same floor as the dwelling unit in which the appliance is installed and can also control lamps and other appliances »422.34(A)«.

E A branch circuit supplying a fixed storage-type water heater with a capacity of 120 gallons (450 L) or less is considered a continuous load and, therefore, must have a rating of at least 125% of the water heater's nameplate rating »422.13 and 422.10(A)«.

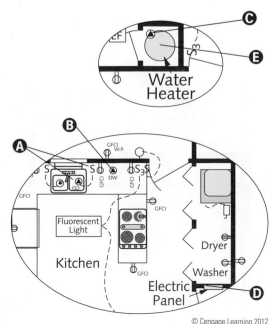

© Cengage Learning 2012

Heating and Air-Conditioning Equipment

(A) For a hermetic refrigerant motor compressor, the rated-load current marked on the equipment nameplate in which the motor compressor is employed must be used in determining the rating or ampacity of the disconnecting means, the branch-circuit conductors, the controller, the branch-circuit short-circuit and ground-fault protection, and the separate motor overload protection ≫ *440.6(A)* ≪.

(B) The disconnecting means for air-conditioning or refrigerating equipment must be readily accessible and within sight of the equipment ≫ *440.14* ≪.

(C) All electric equipment must be surrounded by sufficient unobstructed space to allow ready and safe equipment operation and maintenance ≫ *110.26* ≪. Working space is mandatory for equipment likely to require examination, adjustment, servicing, or maintenance while energized ≫ *110.26(A)* ≪.

(D) Fixed electric space-heating equipment and motors shall be considered continuous load when sizing the branch circuit ≫ *424.3(B)* ≪.

(E) A hermetic refrigerant motor compressor consists of a compressor and motor, both enclosed in the same housing, with no external shaft or shaft seals, and the motor operating in the refrigerant ≫ *440.2* ≪.

(F) On long runs, it may be necessary to increase the branch-circuit conductor's size to compensate for voltage drop ≫ *210.19(A)(1) Informational Note No. 4* ≪.

(G) Means must be provided to simultaneously disconnect all ungrounded conductors from the heater, motor controller(s), and supplementary overcurrent protective device(s) of all fixed electric space-heating equipment ≫ *424.19* ≪.

(H) In multifamily dwellings, the other disconnecting means, as described in 424.19(C), must be within the dwelling unit or on the same floor as the dwelling unit in which the fixed heater is installed and can also control lamps and other appliances ≫ *424.19(C)(1)* ≪.

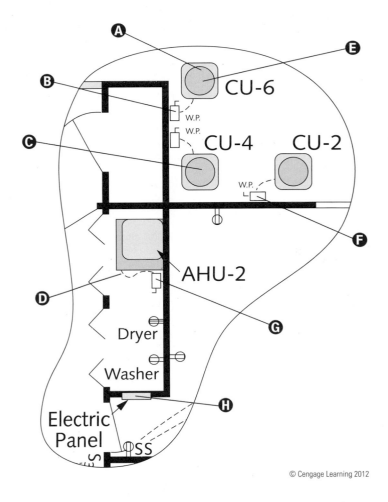

© Cengage Learning 2012

VOLTAGE DROP

Conductor Properties (Chapter 9, Tables 8 and 9)

While skin effect and induction change the resistance in alternating-current (ac) circuits, they do not affect direct-current (dc) circuits. The resistance of a conductor is slightly higher in an ac circuit. Table 9 contains the resistance of conductors in PVC, aluminum, and steel raceways. The factors that change resistance in an ac circuit, such as skin effect, are negligible in smaller conductors.

Ⓐ The larger the circular mil area, the smaller the resistance.

Ⓑ As listed in Table 8, 6 AWG has an area of 26,240 circular mils.

Ⓒ Size 3/0 AWG has an area of 167,800 circular mils and contains 19 strands.

Ⓓ The abbreviated term "kcmil" stands for 1000 (k) circular (c) mills (mil).

Ⓔ Each conductor size larger than 4/0 AWG is actually the circular mil size. A 250-kcmil conductor has a 250,000 circular mil area. A 500-kcmil conductor has a circular mil area of 500,000.

Ⓕ Conductor overall diameter is listed in Table 8. This diameter is the actual wire and excludes conductor insulation.

Ⓖ Conductor strand quantities are listed in Table 8; 6 AWG contains seven strands.

Ⓗ Table 8 lists dc resistance values (in ohms per 1000 ft) at an ambient temperature of 75°C (167°F).

Ⓘ Size 500-kcmil conductors have a quantity of 37 strands. The overall diameter is 0.813 in., with each strand having a diameter of 0.116 in.

Ⓙ The dc resistance for 1000 ft of 6 AWG copper is 0.491 ohms.

Ⓚ The longer the conductor, the higher the resistance.

Ⓛ The dc resistance for 100 ft of 6 AWG copper is 0.0491 ohms (0.491 ÷ 1000 = 0.000491 × 100 = 0.0491).

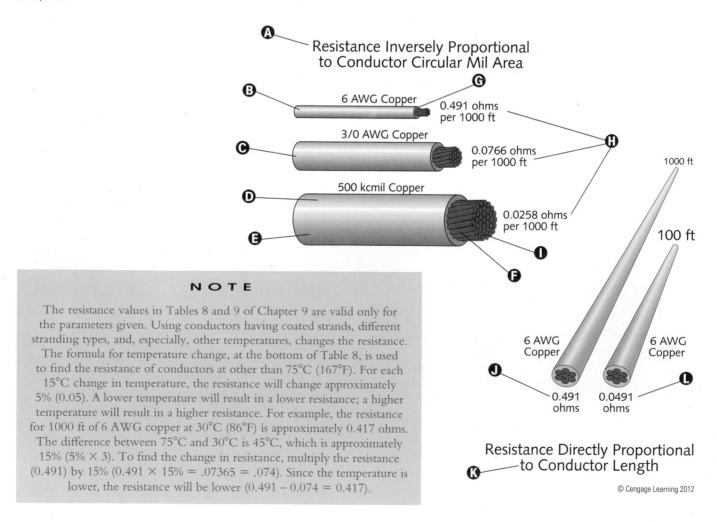

Ⓐ Resistance Inversely Proportional to Conductor Circular Mil Area

Ⓖ

6 AWG Copper — 0.491 ohms per 1000 ft

3/0 AWG Copper — 0.0766 ohms per 1000 ft

500 kcmil Copper — 0.0258 ohms per 1000 ft

Ⓗ

1000 ft

100 ft

6 AWG Copper — 0.491 ohms **Ⓙ**

6 AWG Copper — 0.0491 ohms **Ⓛ**

Resistance Directly Proportional to Conductor Length **Ⓚ**

© Cengage Learning 2012

N O T E

The resistance values in Tables 8 and 9 of Chapter 9 are valid only for the parameters given. Using conductors having coated strands, different stranding types, and, especially, other temperatures, changes the resistance. The formula for temperature change, at the bottom of Table 8, is used to find the resistance of conductors at other than 75°C (167°F). For each 15°C change in temperature, the resistance will change approximately 5% (0.05). A lower temperature will result in a lower resistance; a higher temperature will result in a higher resistance. For example, the resistance for 1000 ft of 6 AWG copper at 30°C (86°F) is approximately 0.417 ohms. The difference between 75°C and 30°C is 45°C, which is approximately 15% (5% × 3). To find the change in resistance, multiply the resistance (0.491) by 15% (0.491 × 15% = .07365 = .074). Since the temperature is lower, the resistance will be lower (0.491 − 0.074 = 0.417).

Voltage-Drop Recommendation

A Except for sensitive electronic equipment in 647.4(D) and fire pumps in 695.7, voltage-drop considerations are only recommendations; compliance is optional.

B The recommended maximum voltage drop for the combined feeder and branch circuit is 5%. However, the voltage drop for feeders is not necessarily 2%. If the branch circuit is 3%, the feeder is 2%, but if the branch circuit is 1%, the feeder can be 4%. Any combination is possible, as long as the branch circuit does not exceed 3%, and the combined branch circuit and feeder does not exceed 5%.

C There is no recommended maximum voltage drop for service conductors.

D The conductor voltage that is dropped is a percentage of the source voltage.

E The recommended voltage drop for a branch circuit is 3% or less. For example, the maximum allowable voltage drop for a 120-volt branch circuit is 3.6 volts (120 × 3%), and the maximum allowable for a 240-volt branch circuit is 7.2 volts (240 × 3%).

F The higher the resistance through a conductor, the higher the voltage drop. Such a conductor voltage drop could result in a reduction of voltage supplying the load.

G A single-phase feeder (or branch circuit) conductor will have a total resistance twice that of one conductor. For example, the length of one conductor must be doubled to find the total resistance of the circuit. The total length for a three-phase circuit is found by multiplying the length of one conductor by the square root of 3 (1.732).

H Branch-circuit conductors, as defined in Article 100, sized to prevent a voltage drop exceeding 3% at the farthest outlet of power, heating, and lighting loads (or combinations of such loads) and where the maximum total voltage drop on both feeders and branch circuits to the farthest outlet does not exceed 5% will provide reasonable efficient operation *» 210.19(A)(1) Informational Note No. 4 and 215.2(A)(4) Informational Note No. 2 «*.

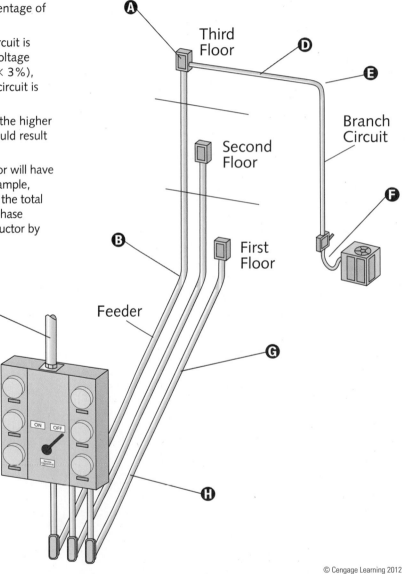

© Cengage Learning 2012

NOTE

Not all electrical installations have feeder conductors.

Single-Phase Voltage-Drop Formulas

Formula Definitions:

V_D = Volts dropped from a circuit.

2 = Multiplying factor for single-phase (the 2 represents the conductor length in a single-phase circuit).

K = Resistivity of the conductor material. The resistance value (measured in ohms) is based on a mil foot at a given temperature. A mil foot is a piece of wire 1 ft long and one mil in diameter. Each conductor resistivity (K) factor can be found by multiplying the circular mil area (cmil) by the resistance (R) for 1 ft. For example, the K factor for a 6 AWG copper conductor at 75°C (167°F) is 12.88384, because 26,240 (area circular mills) × 0.000491 (ohms per ft) = 12.88384. At 75°C (167°F), the approximate K for copper is 12.9 and for aluminum is 21.2.

L = Length, *one way* only: The distance from the voltage source to the load.

I = Actual current used by the load. Do not use 125% for motors and continuous loads.

cmil = Circular mil area of the conductor (see Chapter 9, Table 8).

R = Conductor resistance for 1 ft. *Note:* The resistance values, listed in Chapter 9, Tables 8 and 9, are for 1000 ft. To find the resistance for 1 ft, simply divide the resistance by 1000. Example: The resistance for 1 foot of 6 AWG copper (at 75°C [167°F] is 0.000491 (0.491 ÷ 1000 = 0.000491).

Ⓐ This is one formula used to find voltage drop in a single-phase circuit.

Ⓑ The conductor voltage that is dropped is a percentage of the source voltage. To find the percentage, divide V_D by the source voltage. Example: 2.4 volts dropped from a 120-volt circuit is 2% of the source voltage (2.4 ÷ 120 = 0.02 = 2%).

Ⓒ Here is another formula for finding voltage drop in a single-phase circuit. This method uses the Ohm's law formula. Resistance (for 1 ft of the conductor) is used instead of the K factor and circular mil area.

Ⓓ Use this formula to find the maximum length (distance) from the source to the load. Because of the "2" in the formula, the length is **one way.**

Ⓔ This Ohm's law formula finds the maximum length from the source to the load.

Ⓕ Conductor size can be found using this formula. The calculation provides the minimum circular mil wire size that must be installed to remain below the V_D that was input into the formula.

Ⓖ This formula applies Ohm's law to find the conductor size. The result is the minimum conductor resistance for 1 ft; this keeps the voltage drop below the V_D used in the formula.

Ⓗ This formula calculates the maximum current in amperes.

Ⓘ Use this Ohm's law formula to find the current in amperes.

Ⓙ Since the conductor size is unknown, the exact K cannot be calculated. For copper, at 75°C (167°F), use **12.9** (approximate K). For aluminum, at 75°C (167°F), use **21.2** (approximate K).

Ⓚ V_D represents the actual volts that can drop from the circuit. The maximum (recommended) percentage for a branch circuit is 3%. Be careful not to place "3%" in the V_D position. If the voltage is 120, then 3.6 is the actual volts that can drop in the branch circuit. For 240 voltage, the actual volts that can drop in the branch circuit is 7.2.

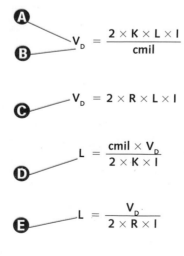

$$\text{Ⓐ} \quad \text{Ⓑ} \qquad V_D = \frac{2 \times K \times L \times I}{cmil}$$

$$\text{Ⓙ} \qquad \text{Ⓕ} \qquad cmil = \frac{2 \times K \times L \times I}{V_D} \qquad \text{Ⓚ}$$

$$\text{Ⓒ} \qquad V_D = 2 \times R \times L \times I$$

$$\text{Ⓖ} \qquad R = \frac{V_D}{2 \times L \times I}$$

$$\text{Ⓓ} \qquad L = \frac{cmil \times V_D}{2 \times K \times I}$$

$$\text{Ⓗ} \qquad I = \frac{cmil \times V_D}{2 \times K \times L}$$

$$\text{Ⓔ} \qquad L = \frac{V_D}{2 \times R \times I}$$

$$\text{Ⓘ} \qquad I = \frac{V_D}{2 \times R \times L}$$

Three-Phase Voltage-Drop Formulas

(A) The multiplying factor for three-phase is "1.732." The square root of 3 (1.732) represents the conductor length in a three-phase circuit. The only difference between the single-phase and three-phase formulas is that "1.732" has replaced "2."

(B) These formulas are used to find voltage drop in a three-phase circuit.

(C) Use these formulas to find the maximum length (distance) from the source to the load in a three-phase circuit. (Because of the "1.732" in the formula, the length is **one way.**)

(D) These are variations of three-phase formulas.

(E) This formula calculates the conductor size in a three-phase circuit.

(F) This formula is used to determine the resistance of the conductor in a three-phase circuit.

(G) The maximum current in amperes in a three-phase circuit is calculated using this formula.

(H) The single-phase formula can be changed to a three-phase formula by placing "0.866" in the line containing the "2." The purpose of putting "0.866" in the same line as "2" is simple: $2 \times 0.866 = 1.732$. (Refer to the definitions in the previous section—Single-Phase Voltage-Drop Formulas.)

(A)

(B)

$$V_D = \frac{1.732 \times K \times L \times I}{cmil}$$

$$V_D = 1.732 \times R \times L \times I$$

(C)

$$L = \frac{cmil \times V_D}{1.732 \times K \times I}$$

$$L = \frac{V_D}{1.732 \times R \times I}$$

(E)

$$cmil = \frac{1.732 \times K \times L \times I}{V_D}$$

(F)

$$R = \frac{V_D}{1.732 \times L \times I}$$

(G)

$$I = \frac{cmil \times V_D}{1.732 \times K \times L}$$

$$I = \frac{V_D}{1.732 \times R \times L}$$

(D)

$$V_D = \frac{2 \times K \times L \times I \times 0.866}{cmil}$$

$$L = \frac{cmil \times V_D}{2 \times K \times I \times 0.866}$$

(H)

Single-Phase Voltage-Drop Example

At 75°C (167°F), what size conductors are required to feed a 2-hp, 230-volt, single-phase motor that is 150 ft from the source? (Do not exceed *NEC* recommendations.)

(A) Both the supply and load side of this equipment disconnecting means are branch-circuit conductors; therefore, the maximum recommended voltage drop is 3% of the source voltage.

(B) Table 430.248 lists full-load current (in amperes) for single-phase ac motors.

(C) This is the voltage drop formula used to find the minimum size conductor.

(D) This is the approximate K for copper at 75°C (167°F).

(E) This is the current in amperes for a 2-hp, 230-volt, single-phase motor 》 *Table 430.248* 《.

(F) This is the minimum circular mil area required. Notice that a 12 AWG conductor (6530 circular mils) is too small for this installation.

(G) This is the minimum size conductor recommended for this installation.

(H) This is the maximum amount of voltage drop on a 230-volt branch circuit that remains within the 3% recommendation (230 × 3% = 6.9).

(I) This is an alternative formula equally effective in determining the minimum size conductor.

(J) In multiplying the 1 ft value by 1000, the resistance values will correspond with Tables 8 and 9, which contain ohms per 1000 ft values.

(K) This is the maximum conductor resistance for 1 ft.

(L) The conductor chosen shall not exceed this resistance number. Both solid and stranded 12 AWG conductors have a higher resistance; therefore, 10 AWG conductors (solid or stranded) must be used.

NOTE

If the total distance of the branch circuit is less than 145 ft (44.2 m), a 12 AWG copper conductor could be installed.

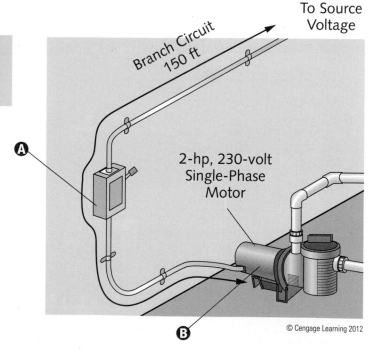

© Cengage Learning 2012

$$\text{cmil} = \frac{2 \times K \times L \times I}{V_D} = \frac{2 \times 12.9 \times 150 \times 12}{6.9} = 6730 = 10 \text{ AWG copper}$$

$$R = \frac{V_D}{2 \times L \times I} = \frac{6.9}{2 \times 150 \times 12} = 0.001917 \times 1000 = 1.917 = 10 \text{ AWG copper}$$

© Cengage Learning 2012

Summary

- Overall receptacle installation requirements, with few exceptions, are the same for both one-family and multifamily dwellings.
- Outdoor receptacle requirements for multifamily dwellings are not the same as requirements for one-family dwellings.
- Under certain conditions, a laundry receptacle is not required.
- A multifamily clubhouse (or portion thereof) designed for the assembly of more than 99 persons must comply with Article 518 provisions.
- Generally, a building is supplied by only one service.
- There can be no more than six disconnects per service grouped in any single location.
- Where separate services supply a building and a grounding electrode is required, the same electrode must be used.

- Separate service laterals, grouped in one location, constitute one service.
- Use Table 310.15(B)(7) to size 120/240, 3-wire, single-phase service-entrance conductors, service-lateral conductors, and feeder conductors serving as the dwelling's main power feeder.
- Service and open conductor clearances pertain to all dwellings.
- Conductor properties are found in Chapter 9, Tables 8 and 9.
- Voltage-drop compliance is discretionary.
- The recommended voltage drop for a branch circuit is 3% or less.
- The recommended voltage drop for combined feeder and branch circuits is 5% or less.
- Voltage-drop formulas, complete with explanations, are found near the end of this unit.

Unit 10 Competency Test

NEC Reference   Answer

_____   _____   1. _____ is a general term including material, fittings, devices, appliances, luminaires, apparatus, machinery, and the like used as a part of, or in connection with, an electrical installation.

_____   _____   2. Where a building is supplied by more than one service, or combination of branch circuits, feeders and services, a permanent _____ or _____ shall be installed at each service disconnect location denoting all other services, feeders, and branch circuits supplying that building and the area served by each.

_____   _____   3. Where the overcurrent device is rated over _____ amperes, the ampacity of the conductors it protects shall be equal to or greater than the rating of the overcurrent device.

_____   _____   4. A(n) _____ is a device, or group of devices, or other means by which the conductors of a circuit can be disconnected from their source of supply.

_____   _____   5. A(n) _____ is a device intended to provide protection from the effects of arc faults by recognizing characteristics unique to arcing and by functioning to de-energize the circuit when an arc fault is detected.

_____   _____   6. Service-drop conductors shall have a vertical clearance of not less than _____ ft above the roof surface.

_____   _____   7. What size copper equipment grounding conductor is required for a circuit having a 40-ampere overcurrent device?

_____   _____   8. Where a change occurs in the size of the _____, a similar change shall be permitted to be made in the size of the grounded conductor.

_____   _____   9. _____ in each dwelling unit shall supply only loads within that dwelling unit or loads associated only with that dwelling unit.

NEC Reference	Answer
_____	_____

10. A metal elbow that is installed in an underground installation of nonmetallic raceway and is isolated from possible contact by a minimum cover of _____ in. to any part of the elbow shall not be required to be connected to the grounded system conductor or grounding electrode conductor.

11. Conductors shall be considered outside of a building or other structure where installed under not less than _____ in. of concrete beneath a building or other structure.

12. What is the service demand load (in kW) for an apartment complex containing ten each of the following: 15-kW ranges, 13-kW ranges, 11-kW ranges, and 9-kW ranges? (The service is 120/240 single-phase.)

13. In _____, remote, central, or automatic control of lighting shall be permitted.

14. Service conductors installed as open conductors shall have a clearance of not less than _____ ft from fire escapes.

15. A grounded circuit conductor shall be permitted to ground non-current-carrying metal parts of equipment on the _____ side of the ac service disconnecting means.

16. Each unit of a thirty-unit apartment building has a 4.5-kW clothes dryer. What is the service demand load contribution (in kW) for these clothes dryers? (The service is 120/240 single-phase.)

17. The maximum distance between receptacle outlets in a multifamily dwelling is _____ ft.

18. Overcurrent devices shall not be located in the vicinity of _____, such as in clothes closets.

19. Cabinets and cutout boxes shall have _____ to accommodate all conductors installed in them without crowding.

20. Where conductors carrying alternating current are installed in ferrous metal enclosures or metal raceways, they shall be arranged so as to avoid heating the surrounding metal by _____.

21. _____ is the highest current at rated voltage that a device is identified to interrupt under standard test conditions.

22. Where ungrounded conductors are increased in size to compensate for voltage drop, equipment grounding conductors, where installed, shall be increased in size proportionately according to:

_____

23. Enclosures for overcurrent devices shall be mounted in a _____ position.

24. A metal pole supporting a luminaire, 18 ft above grade, must have a handhole of at least _____ in.

25. Fittings and connectors shall be used only with the specific wiring methods for which they are _____.

26. _____ is a combination consisting of a compressor and motor, both of which are enclosed in the same housing, with no external shaft or shaft seals, and the motor operating in the refrigerant.

27. For permanently connected appliances rated over _____ volt-amperes, the branch-circuit switch or circuit breaker shall be permitted to serve as the disconnecting means where the switch or circuit breaker is within sight from the appliance or is capable of being locked in the open position.

NEC Reference   **Answer**

_____ _____ 28. Fixed electric space heating equipment and motors shall be considered _____ when sizing the branch circuit.

_____ _____ 29. _____ is the necessary equipment, usually consisting of a circuit breaker(s) or switch(es) and fuse(s) and their accessories, connected to the load end of service conductors to a building or other structure, or an otherwise designated area, which is intended to constitute the main control and cutoff of the supply.

_____ _____ 30. No hanging luminaire parts can be located within a zone measured _____ ft vertically from the top of the bathtub rim and _____ ft vertically from the top of the shower stall threshold.

_____ _____ 31. What is the ac resistance of 500 feet of 1000 kcmil aluminum wire in a steel conduit?

_____ _____ 32. At 75°C (167°F), what size copper conductors are required (without exceeding *NEC* recommendations) to feed a ¼-horsepower, 115-volt, single-phase motor located 230 ft from the source?

_____ _____ 33. Interior metal water piping located not more than _____ ft from the point of entrance to the building shall be permitted to be used as a conductor to interconnect electrodes that are part of the grounding electrode system.

_____ _____ 34. What is the minimum neutral demand load (in kW) for twelve apartments, each containing an 8-kW range?

_____ _____ 35. What is the voltage-drop percentage on two 10 AWG THW copper, stranded, branch-circuit conductors, 120 ft long, supplying a 21-ampere, 240-volt load?

Load Calculations

Objectives

After studying this unit, the student should:

▶ know that the number of dwelling units is essential in performing a multifamily calculation.

▶ be able to calculate the general lighting load in a multifamily dwelling.

▶ correctly identify minimum volt-ampere requirements for small-appliance branch circuits.

▶ thoroughly understand the exceptions pertaining to optional laundry branch circuits.

▶ know how to apply demand factors to the general lighting load, as well as to fastened-in-place appliances.

▶ be able to calculate demand loads for household clothes dryers, cooking equipment, and heating and air-conditioning systems.

▶ understand the standard method for calculating a multifamily dwelling service.

▶ successfully calculate a multifamily dwelling service using the optional method.

▶ be able to calculate a feeder for one unit in a multifamily dwelling using either method.

▶ know how to size service and feeder conductors.

▶ be familiar with paralleled conductor provisions.

▶ correctly calculate and select the appropriate size neutral conductor.

▶ understand how grounding electrode conductors, as well as equipment grounding conductors, are selected.

Introduction

Strong similarities exist between multifamily dwelling load calculations and one-family dwelling load calculations. Both can be performed by a standard method as well as an optional method. In fact, the similarities are so strong that this is reflected in the very design of the load calculation forms. It is, therefore, obviously beneficial to have a clear understanding of one-family dwelling load calculations before studying this unit (see Unit 8). It is absolutely essential to these calculations to know the total number of dwelling units being supplied by the service. To illustrate this point: Two main service disconnecting means supplying power to twelve units must be calculated on the basis of six units per service. Performing a service calculation on twelve units and then dividing the final figure by two would render inaccurate results.

The multifamily dwelling load calculations performed in this unit are based on the floor plan found in Unit 10. The statistical information for each individual dwelling unit remains unchanged for the purpose of load calculation. This data can be found in the floor plan diagram immediately following this introduction. Examples include a multifamily dwelling load calculation for both a twelve-unit and a six-unit service. Each will be calculated by the standard method as well as the optional. Feeder and panelboard sizing for individual units is demonstrated by a standard one-family dwelling calculation. For comparison, the optional method load calculation for one unit of a multifamily dwelling is shown after the optional multifamily dwelling computation.

COMPILING LOAD CALCULATION INFORMATION

Load Calculation Information for Each Unit

Ⓐ The smaller of two (or more) noncoincident loads can be omitted, as long as they are never energized simultaneously ≫ *220.60* ≪.

Ⓑ Although a clothes dryer is not a requirement for a load calculation, be sure to include a dryer load in units containing clothes dryer outlets.

Ⓒ A laundry branch circuit is optional in multifamily dwellings ≫ *210.52(F) Exception No. 1 and 2* ≪.

Ⓓ Gather all load calculation information needed to calculate each service. For a service consisting of twelve units (apartment or condominium), compile the essential information for all twelve units. If the service consists of only six units, gather the data for those six units. Since most multifamily dwellings have a limited number of floor plans, compile the information pertaining to each "unit type" (style, floor plan, etc.). Be sure that each unit grouped in a unit type contains the same information, that is, total square feet, small-appliance branch circuits, laundry branch circuits, appliances, etc. For ease of demonstration in this section, each unit is identical in size and content.

Ⓔ Calculate the floor area using the outside dimensions ≫ *220.12* ≪.

Ⓕ Include household cooking appliances rated over 1¾ kW.

Ⓖ Include all fastened-in-place appliances.

Ⓗ Include at least two small-appliance branch circuits ≫ *210.11(C)(1)* ≪.

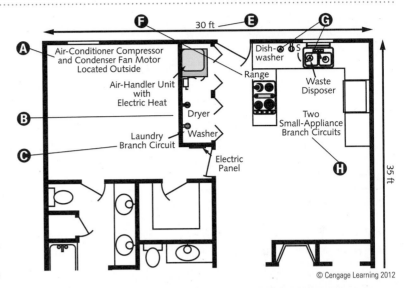

© Cengage Learning 2012

Ⓓ

Dwelling outside dimensions	30′ × 35′
Small-appliance branch circuits	two
Laundry branch circuit	one
Water heater	4.5 kW, 240 volt
Dishwasher	10 amperes, 120 volt
Microwave oven	10 amperes, 120 volt
Waste (garbage) disposer	7.5 amperes, 120 volt
Clothes dryer	5 kW, 240 volt
Range	12 kW, 240 volt
Electric heat	5 kW, 240 volt
Air handler (blower motor)	3 amperes, 115 volt
Air-conditioner compressor	14 amperes, 230 volt
Condenser fan motor	2 amperes, 115 volt

Assume water heater, clothes dryer, range, and electric heat kW ratings equivalent to kVA.

STANDARD METHOD: MULTIFAMILY DWELLINGS

Load Calculation for Twelve Units

Ⓐ The first multifamily load calculation form is based on twelve units. Each unit is identical, as previously described.

Ⓑ In a multiple-occupancy building, each occupant must have access to the unit's service disconnecting means ≫ *230.72(C)* ≪.

Ⓒ There must not be more than six disconnects (switches or circuit breakers) per service grouped in a single location ≫ *230.71(A)* ≪.

Ⓓ One service disconnecting switch controls all twelve units.

Ⓔ Each unit's feeder (and overcurrent protection) must be calculated individually, using the one-family dwelling form (standard or optional method).

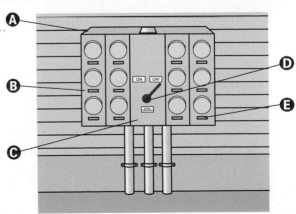

© Cengage Learning 2012

Standard Method Load Calculation for Multifamily Dwellings

1 General Lighting and Receptacle Loads *220.12* *Do not include open porches, garages, or unused or* *unfinished spaces not adaptable for future use.*	$3 \times$ _____ $\times$ _____ $=$ (sq ft outside dimensions) (number of units)	**1**
2 Small-Appliance Branch Circuits *220.52(A)* *At least **two** small-appliance branch circuits* *must be included.* *210.11(C)(1)*	$1500 \times$ _____ $\times$ _____ $=$ (minimum of two) (number of units)	**2**
3 Laundry Branch Circuit(s) *220.52(B)* *Include at least **one** laundry branch circuit *unless* *meeting 210.52(F) Exception No. 1 or 2.* *210.11(C)(2)*	$1500 \times$ _____ $\times$ _____ $=$ *(minimum of one) (number of units)	**3**

4 Add lines 1, 2, and 3	**4**		Lines 5 through 8 utilize the demand factors found in *Table 220.42*.
5 _____ $- 3000 =$ (line 4)	**5**	(if 117,000 or less, skip to line 8)	**6** _____ $- 117,000 =$ **6** (line 5, if more than 117,000)
7 _____ $\times 25\% =$ (line 6)	**7**		**8** _____ $\times 35\% =$ **8** (smaller of line 5 or 117,000)

9 Total General Lighting and Receptacle Load $3000 +$ _____ $+$ _____ $=$ (line 7) (line 8)		**9**
10 Fastened-In-Place Appliances *220.53* *Use the nameplate rating.* *Do not include electric ranges,* *clothes dryers, space-heating* *equipment, or air-conditioning* *equipment.* water heaters/ _____ dishwashers / _____ disposers / _____ _____ / _____ _____ / _____ _____ / _____ _____ / _____ _____ / _____ _____ / _____ If fewer than four units, put total volt-amperes on line 10. If four or more units, multiply total volt-amperes by 75%. _____ $\times 75\% =$ (volt-amps of four or more)		**10**
11 Clothes Dryers *220.54* *(If present; otherwise skip to line 12.) Use 5000 watts or the nameplate rating, whichever is larger.* The neutral demand load is 70% for feeders. *220.61(B)*		**11**
12 Ranges, Ovens, Cooktops, and Other Household Cooking Appliances Over 1750 Watts *220.55* *(If present; otherwise skip to line 13.) Use Table 220.55 and all of the applicable Notes.* The neutral demand load is 70% for feeders. *220.61(B)*		**12**
13 Heating or Air-Conditioning System (Compare the heat and A/C, and omit the smaller.) *220.60* *Include the air handler when using either one. For heat pumps, include the compressor and the* *maximum amount of electric heat that can be energized while the compressor is running.*		**13**
14 Largest Motor (one motor only) *220.50 and 430.24* *Multiply the volt-amperes of the largest motor by 25%.* _____ $\times 25\% =$ (volt-amps of largest motor)		**14**
15 Total Volt-Ampere Demand Load: *Add lines 9 through 14 to find the minimum required volt-amperes.*		**15**

16 Minimum Amperes *Divide the total* *volt-amperes by* *the voltage.* _____ $\div$ _____ $=$ (line 15) (voltage)	**16** _____ (minimum amperes)	**Minimum Size** **17 Service or** **Feeder** *240.6(A)*	**17**
18 Size the Service or Feeder Conductors. *Use 310.15(B)(7) to find the service conductors up to 400 amperes.* *Ratings in excess of 400 amperes shall comply with Table 310.15(B)(16)* *310.15(B)(7) also applies to feeder conductors serving as the main power feeder.*		**Minimum Size** **Conductors**	**18**
19 Size the Neutral Conductor. *220.61* *310.15(B)(7) states that the neutral service or feeder conductor* *can be smaller than the ungrounded (hot) conductors, provided the* *requirements of 215.2, 220.61, and 230.42 are met.* *250.24(C)(1) states that the neutral shall not be smaller than the* *required grounding electrode conductor specified in Table 250.66.*		**Minimum Size** **Neutral** **Conductor**	**19**
20 Size the Grounding Electrode Conductor (for Service). *250.66* *Use line 18 to find the grounding electrode conductor in Table 250.66.* Size the Equipment Grounding Conductor (for Feeder). *250.122* *Use line 17 to find the equipment grounding conductor in Table 250.122.* *Equipment grounding conductor types are listed in 250.118.*		**Minimum Size** **Grounding Electrode** **Conductor . . . or . . .** **Equipment Grounding** **Conductor**	**20**

Line 1—General Lighting and Receptacle Loads

A The residential dwelling unit's lighting load is 3 volt-amperes (VA) per square foot ⟩⟩ *Table 220.12* ⟨⟨.

B Each multifamily dwelling unit has an outside dimension of 30 ft × 35 ft (1050 ft²).

C Insert the number of units (apartments or condominiums) that constitute one service. Additional space will be needed for computations if the units have different square footage dimensions.

D Each unit's floor area shall be calculated using the outside dimensions. The total floor area does not include open

porches, garages, or unused (including unfinished) spaces that are not adaptable for future use ⟩⟩ *220.12* ⟨⟨.

> **NOTE**
>
> All 15- or 20-ampere general-use receptacle outlets (except for small-appliance and laundry) are considered part of the general lighting load. The "a" footnote at the bottom of Table 220.12 refers to 220.14(J), which states that no additional load calculations are required for these outlets.

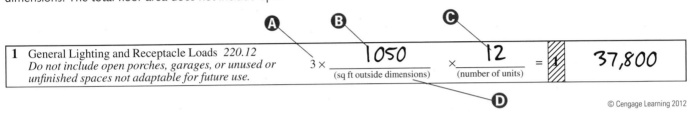

© Cengage Learning 2012

Line 2—Small-Appliance Branch Circuits

A Include small-appliance branch circuits when calculating a dwelling unit service ⟩⟩ *220.52(A)* ⟨⟨.

B Each small-appliance branch circuit is calculated at no less than 1500 volt-amperes ⟩⟩ *220.52(A)* ⟨⟨.

C If any unit(s) has a different number of small appliance branch circuits, calculate each separately.

D Each dwelling unit must have at least two small-appliance branch circuits ⟩⟩ *210.11(C)(1)* ⟨⟨.

E These loads can be included with the general lighting load and are subject to Table 220.42 demand factors ⟩⟩ *220.52(A)* ⟨⟨.

> **NOTE**
>
> A refrigeration equipment individual branch circuit (permitted by 210.52(B)(1) Exception No. 2) can be excluded from this calculation ⟩⟩ *220.52(A) Exception* ⟨⟨.

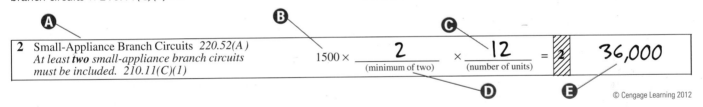

© Cengage Learning 2012

Line 3—Laundry Branch Circuit(s)

A Include laundry branch circuit(s) when calculating a dwelling unit service ⟩⟩ *220.52(B)* ⟨⟨.

B Each laundry branch circuit is calculated at no less than 1500 volt-amperes ⟩⟩ *220.52(B)* ⟨⟨.

C Include only the number of units having a laundry branch circuit. If only six of twelve units contain a laundry branch circuit, put six as the number of units. In this calculation, each unit has a laundry branch circuit.

D In a multifamily building where laundry facilities are provided on the premises, available to all occupants, a laundry

receptacle is not required in each individual unit ⟩⟩ *210.52(F) Exception No. 1* ⟨⟨.

E A laundry receptacle is not required even in multifamily dwellings without common laundry facilities ⟩⟩ *210.52(F) Exception No. 2* ⟨⟨.

F Unless one of the exceptions is met, include at least one laundry branch circuit ⟩⟩ *210.11(C)(2)* ⟨⟨.

G These loads can be included with the general lighting load and are subject to the Table 220.11 demand factors ⟩⟩ *220.52(B)* ⟨⟨.

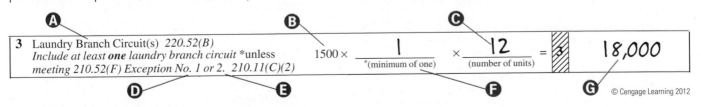

© Cengage Learning 2012

Lines 4 through 8—Applying Demand Factors Found in Table 220.11

A Line 4 represents the total of lines 1, 2, and 3.

B Lines 5 through 8 outline the derating procedure, using Table 220.42 demand factors.

C Line 5 is the result of subtracting 3000 from the number in Line 4.

D The first 3000 (or less) volt-amperes must remain at 100% *» Table 220.42 «*.

E If line 5 is 117,000 or less, skip lines 6 and 7.

F If line 4 is 120,000 or less, then lines 6 and 7 remain empty.

G Insert the smaller of line 5 or 117,000.

H Multiply the next 117,000 (from 3001 to 120,000) by 35% *» Table 220.42 «*.

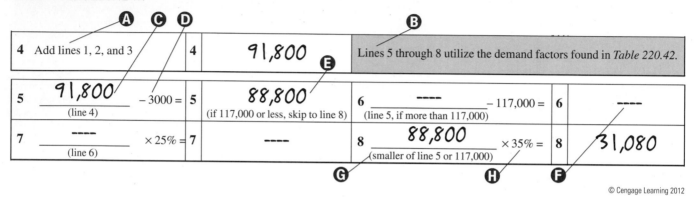

© Cengage Learning 2012

Line 9—Total General Lighting (and Receptacle) Load

A Line 9 is the total of general lighting, general-use receptacles, small-appliance branch circuits, and laundry branch circuit(s) after derating.

B If line 7 is blank, leave this blank also.

C Insert the result of line 8, not the number from line 5.

D This shaded block draws attention to the first of six lines (boxes) that will be added together resulting in the total volt-ampere demand load for the one-family dwelling.

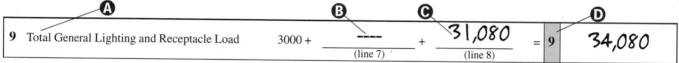

© Cengage Learning 2012

Line 10—Fastened-in-Place Appliances

A The term **appliance** designates utilization equipment (commonly built in standardized types and sizes) installed as a unit to perform specific function(s) *» Article 100 «*.

B For the purpose of this load calculation, a kW rating is the same as a kVA rating.

C Additional space may be needed to calculate total appliance volt-amperes; (1200 × 12 = 14,400) and (900 × 12 = 10,800).

D Derating is allowed for a total of four (or more) fastened-in-place appliances. It is not necessary that the four fastened-in-place appliances be of different types. This derating factor can be used even if all units do not contain four appliances.

E If the calculation contains at least four fastened-in-place appliances, the combined volt-ampere rating of those appliances is multiplied by 75% and placed on Line 10 *» 220.53 «*.

> **NOTE**
>
> Do not include electric ranges, dryers, space-heating equipment, and air-conditioning equipment as fastened-in-place appliances *» 220.53 «*. Household cooking appliances individually rated in excess of 1750 watts are derated under 220.55 provisions.

10 Fastened-In-Place Appliances *220.53*					
Use the nameplate rating.	water heaters / **54,000**		dishwashers / **14,400**		disposers / **10,800**
Do not include electric ranges, clothes dryers, space-heating equipment, or air-conditioning equipment.	microwave ovens / **14,400**		/		/
	/		/		/

D If fewer than four units, put total volt-amperes on line 10. If four or more units, multiply total volt-amperes by 75%.

93,600 (volt-amps of four or more) × 75% = **10** | **70,200**

© Cengage Learning 2012

Line 11—Clothes Dryers

A A clothes dryer is not a requirement for a load calculation. Skip this line if there is no clothes dryer.

B The dryer rating must be at least 5000 watts (volt-amperes) »220.54«.

C Table 220.54 can be used to derate five (or more) clothes dryer loads. First, find the demand factor percentage across from the number of dryers. In this case the percentage is 46 (47 − 1 = 46%). Next, multiply the total dryer load by that percentage and put the result in line 11 (5000 × 12 = 60,000 × 46% = 27,600).

D A clothes dryer neutral load on a feeder is calculated at 70% »220.61(B)«.

E If the nameplate rating exceeds 5000 watts (volt-amperes), use the larger number »220.54«.

> **NOTE**
>
> For four (or fewer) clothes dryers, the demand is 100%.

11 Clothes Dryers *220.54*
(If present; otherwise skip to line 12.) Use 5000 watts or the nameplate rating, whichever is larger.
The neutral demand load is 70% for feeders. 220.61(B)
| **11** | **27,600** |

© Cengage Learning 2012

Line 12—Household Cooking Appliances

A Household cooking appliances (ranges, wall-mounted ovens, counter-mounted cooking units, etc.) are not required in a load calculation. If no cooking appliances are rated over $1\frac{3}{4}$ kW, skip this line.

B Individual household cooking appliances rated more than 1750 watts (volt-amperes) can be derated using Table 220.55 demand factors (and all applicable notes).

C The demand for twelve 12 kW ranges comes from Table 220.55, Column C. First, look at the "Number of Appliances" column and find the number 12. Next, follow that row across to the last column (Column C) and find the kW demand load, which is 27. Finally, multiply this number by 1000 and place in line 12. Because each range is 12 kW, Columns A and B cannot be used.

D For household electric ranges, wall-mounted ovens, and counter-mounted cooking units, the neutral load on a feeder is calculated at 70% »220.61(B)«.

12 Ranges, Ovens, Cooktops, and Other Household Cooking Appliances Over 1750 Watts *220.55*
(If present; otherwise skip to line 13.) Use Table 220.55 and all of the applicable Notes.
The neutral demand load is 70% for feeders. 220.61(B)
| **12** | **27,000** |

© Cengage Learning 2012

Line 13—Heating or Air-Conditioning System

A The smaller of two (or more) **noncoincident loads** can be omitted, as long as they are never energized simultaneously »220.60«. By definition, noncoincident means not occurring at the same time. A dwelling's electric heating system and air-conditioning system may be noncoincident loads.

B The air handler (blower motor) has a rating of 345 volt-amperes (3 × 115 = 345). Because both loads are energized simultaneously, add the air handler to the 5 kW of electric heat.

C Fixed electric space-heating loads are calculated at 100% of the total connected load »220.51«.

D Because the air handler (blower) works with either the heating or the air conditioning, add it to both calculations.

E Each unit contains an air-conditioner compressor (14 × 230 = 3220 VA), condenser fan motor (2 × 115 = 230 VA),

and blower motor (3 × 115 = 345 VA). The combined load is 3795 volt-amperes. Because this is less than the heating load, omit the air-conditioner compressor and the condenser fan motor. Multiply each unit's heat load by the number of units (5345 × 12 = 64,140).

> **NOTE**
>
> A heat pump with supplementary heat is not considered a noncoincident load. Add the compressor full-load current to the maximum amount of heat that can be energized while the compressor is running. Remember to include all associated motor(s), that is, blower, condenser, etc.

13 Heating or Air-Conditioning System (Compare the heat and A/C, and omit the smaller.) *220.60*
Include the air handler when using either one. For heat pumps, include the compressor and the
maximum amount of electric heat that can be energized while the compressor is running.
| **13** | **64,140** |

© Cengage Learning 2012

Line 14—Largest Motor

A Multiply the largest motor in the dwelling calculation by 25% »220.50 and 430.24«.

B This means a total of one motor, not one motor per unit.

C The largest motor is usually the air-conditioner compressor. If the air conditioner load has been omitted, use the second largest motor. In this case, use the 7.5-ampere garbage disposer motor (7.5 × 120 = 900).

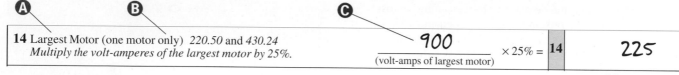

14 Largest Motor (one motor only) 220.50 and 430.24 *Multiply the volt-amperes of the largest motor by 25%.*	$\dfrac{900}{\text{(volt-amps of largest motor)}} \times 25\% =$	14	**225**

© Cengage Learning 2012

Line 15—Total Demand Load

A Find the minimum volt-ampere load by adding lines 9 through 14.

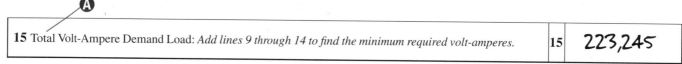

15 Total Volt-Ampere Demand Load: *Add lines 9 through 14 to find the minimum required volt-amperes.*	15	**223,245**

© Cengage Learning 2012

Lines 16 and 17—Minimum Service or Feeder

A Place the total volt-ampere figure found in line 15 here.

B Write down the source voltage supplying the service equipment.

C Fractions of an ampere 0.5 and higher are rounded up to the nearest whole ampere, and fractions less than 0.5 are dropped »220.5(B)«.

D The service (or feeder) overcurrent protection must be higher than the number in line 16. A list of standard ampere ratings for fuses and circuit breakers is provided in 240.6(A).

E Divide the volt-amperes by the voltage to determine the amperage.

F This is the minimum amperage rating required for the service or feeder being calculated.

G The next standard size fuse or breaker above 930 amperes is 1000 »240.6(A)«.

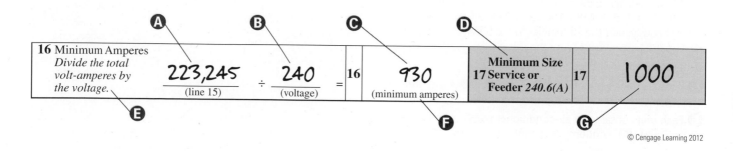

16 Minimum Amperes *Divide the total volt-amperes by the voltage.*	$\dfrac{223,245}{\text{(line 15)}}$ ÷ $\dfrac{240}{\text{(voltage)}}$ =	16	$\dfrac{930}{\text{(minimum amperes)}}$	**Minimum Size** 17 Service or Feeder *240.6(A)*	17	**1000**

© Cengage Learning 2012

Line 18—Minimum Size Conductors

A Use 310.15(B)(7) to find service-entrance and service-lateral conductors.

B Section 310.15(B)(7) also applies to feeder conductors serving as the dwelling unit's main power feeder »*310.15(B)(7)*«.

C Use Table 310.15(B)(7) to size conductors up to a 400-ampere rating.

D When running **three** sets of paralleled copper conductors (for a 1000 ampere overcurrent device), the minimum size is 400 kcmil, unless the equipment is listed and identified for use with 90°C (194°F) conductors. Even if a 90°C (194°F) conductor (such as THHN) is installed, the ampacity rating shall not exceed the 75°C (167°F) ampacity, which is 335 »*110.14(C)(2)*«. Because the overcurrent protection is rated over 800 amperes, the conductor ampacity must match (or exceed) the 1000 ampere rating (1000 ÷ 3 = 333.3 minimum amperes, each conductor) »*240.4(C)*«.

E Other parallel conductor combinations are possible, such as four sets of 250 kcmil copper (Cu), four sets of 350 kcmil aluminum (Al), five sets of 3/0 AWG Cu, five sets of 250 kcmil Al, etc. The smallest conductor that can be run in parallel is 1/0 AWG »*310.10(H)(1)*«.

F Since the rating is more than 400 amperes, use Table 310.15(B)(16) to find the minimum size conductors.

G The number and type of paralleled conductor sets is a design consideration, not necessarily a *Code* issue. Exercise

extreme care when designing a paralleled conductor installation, without violating provisions such as 110.14(A), 110.14(C), 240.4(C), 250.66, 250.122(F), 300.20(A), 310.10(H), etc.

H 1/0 AWG and larger conductors can be connected in parallel (electrically joined at both ends to form a single conductor) »*310.10(H)(1)*«.

> **CAUTION**
>
> Conductors carrying alternating current and installed in ferrous metal enclosures or *metal raceways* must be arranged to avoid heating of the surrounding metal by induction »*300.20(A)*«.

> **N O T E**
>
> The paralleled conductors in each phase, polarity, neutral, grounded circuit conductor, equipment grounding conductor, or equipment bonding jumper must share the same characteristics »*310.10(H)(2)*«.
> For example, all paralleled, Phase A conductors must:
> (1) be the same length,
> (2) consist of the same conductor material,
> (3) be the same size in circular mil area,
> (4) have the same insulation type, and
> (5) be terminated in the same manner.

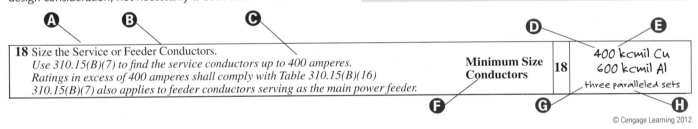

| 18 Size the Service or Feeder Conductors.
Use 310.15(B)(7) to find the service conductors up to 400 amperes.
Ratings in excess of 400 amperes shall comply with Table 310.15(B)(16)
310.15(B)(7) also applies to feeder conductors serving as the main power feeder. | **Minimum Size Conductors** | 18 | 400 kcmil Cu
600 kcmil Al
three paralleled sets |

© Cengage Learning 2012

Line 19—Neutral Conductor

A For the purpose of this load calculation, the terms **neutral** and **grounded** are synonymous.

B The feeder (or service) neutral load is the maximum unbalance of the load determined by Article 220 »*220.61*«.

C The neutral (grounded) conductor can be smaller than the ungrounded (hot) conductors provided certain requirements in 215.2, 220.61, and 230.42 are met »*310.15(B)(7)*«.

D Size the neutral by finding the maximum unbalanced load.

E Although the neutral conductor requires only 152 amperes each (for three paralleled sets), it shall not be smaller than the appropriate grounding electrode conductor (see line 20).

> **N O T E**
>
> The smallest paralleled grounded (neutral) conductor is 1/0 AWG »*250.24(C)(2)*«.

> **CAUTION**
>
> The grounded conductor must not be smaller than the required grounding electrode conductor specified in Table 250.66 »*250.24(C)(1)*«.

| 19 Size the Neutral Conductor. *220.61*
310.15(B)(7) states that the neutral service or feeder conductor can be smaller than the ungrounded (hot) conductors, provided the requirements of 215.2, 220.61, and 230.42 are met.
250.24(C)(1) states that the neutral shall not be smaller than the required grounding electrode conductor specified in Table 250.66. | **Minimum Size Neutral Conductor** | 19 | 3/0 Cu
250 kcmil Al
three paralleled sets |

© Cengage Learning 2012

Line 19—Neutral Conductor *(continued)*

Ⓐ No neutral conductor is connected to the water heaters in this calculation.

Ⓑ All fastened-in-place appliances using a grounded conductor must be included.

Ⓒ The electric heat and air-conditioner compressor are 240-volt loads (no neutral).

Ⓓ Because all of these motors can be energized simultaneously, thereby contributing to the neutral load, include them in the neutral calculation.

Ⓔ To convert to amperes, simply divide volt-amperes by voltage.

Ⓕ The minimum conductor ampacity for three paralleled neutral conductors is 152 amperes. Although the minimum size copper conductor at 75°C (167°F) is 2/0 AWG, the neutral conductor cannot be smaller than the required grounding electrode conductor.

Ⓖ All numbers are shown as volt-amperes.

Ⓗ Since all of the general lighting and receptacle loads have a rating of 120 volts, the total volt-ampere rating (from line 9) must be included in the neutral calculation.

Ⓘ A demand factor of 75% can be applied to the nameplate rating load of four (or more) fastened-in-place appliances ≫ *220.53* ≪.

Ⓙ Multiply the clothes dryer load (line 11) by 70% to determine the neutral load ≫ *220.61(B)* ≪.

Ⓚ Multiplying line 12 by 70% provides the neutral cooking appliances load ≫ *220.61(B)* ≪.

Ⓛ Multiply the largest 120- (115-) volt motor (one motor only) by 25% and include in the calculation.

Ⓜ The minimum neutral load is 109,125 volt-amperes.

General lighting and receptacles (line 9)	34,080
Fastened-in-place appliances	
Water heaters	0
Dishwashers (1200 × 12)	14,400
Waste disposers (7.5 × 120 × 12)	10,800
Microwave ovens (1200 × 12)	14,400
Total	39,600
Total fastened-in-place appliances (39,600 × 75%)	29,700
Clothes dryers (line 11 × 70%)	19,320
Ranges (line 12 × 70%)	18,900
Electric heat	0
Air-conditioner compressors	0
Air handlers (3 × 115 × 12)	4140
Condenser fan motors (2 × 115 × 12)	2760
Largest motor (900 × 25%)	225
TOTAL	**109,125**

109,125 ÷ 240 = 454.7 = 455 minimum neutral ampacity

455 ÷ 3 = 152 minimum amperes per neutral conductor

Line 20—Grounding Electrode Conductor

Ⓐ Table 250.66 has two headings—service conductor size and grounding electrode conductor size. Each heading contains two columns: one for copper and one for aluminum (or copper-clad aluminum). Because of the four columns, take extreme care in selecting the correct grounding electrode conductor.

Ⓑ The grounding electrode conductor is determined by the largest service-entrance conductor (or the equivalent area) if the service-entrance conductors are paralleled. The equivalent area for three parallel sets in this calculation is 1200 kcmil copper (3 × 400) or 1800 kcmil aluminum (3 × 600).

Ⓒ The minimum size grounding electrode conductor is 3/0 AWG copper (or 250 kcmil aluminum) ≫ *Table 250.66* ≪.

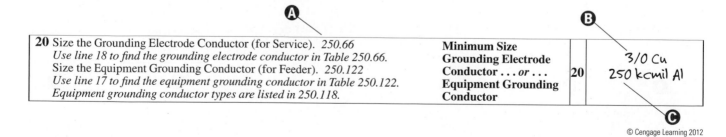

20 Size the Grounding Electrode Conductor (for Service). *250.66* *Use line 18 to find the grounding electrode conductor in Table 250.66.* Size the Equipment Grounding Conductor (for Feeder). *250.122* *Use line 17 to find the equipment grounding conductor in Table 250.122.* *Equipment grounding conductor types are listed in 250.118.*	**Minimum Size** **Grounding Electrode** **Conductor ... or ...** **Equipment Grounding** **Conductor** **20**	3/0 Cu 250 kcmil Al

The following page shows the completed standard method load calculation for a twelve-unit multifamily dwelling, having all units combined in a single service.

Standard Method Load Calculation for Multifamily Dwellings

1	General Lighting and Receptacle Loads *220.12* *Do not include open porches, garages, or unused or* *unfinished spaces not adaptable for future use.*	$3 \times \underline{\quad 1050 \quad}$ (sq ft outside dimensions)	$\times \underline{\quad 12 \quad}$ (number of units) =	**1** **37,800**
2	Small-Appliance Branch Circuits *220.52(A)* *At least **two** small-appliance branch circuits* *must be included. 210.11(C)(1)*	$1500 \times \underline{\quad 2 \quad}$ (minimum of two)	$\times \underline{\quad 12 \quad}$ (number of units) =	**2** **36,000**
3	Laundry Branch Circuit(s) *220.52(B)* *Include at least **one** laundry branch circuit *unless* *meeting 210.52(F) Exception No. 1 or 2. 210.11(C)(2)*	$1500 \times \underline{\quad 1 \quad}$ *(minimum of one)	$\times \underline{\quad 12 \quad}$ (number of units) =	**3** **18,000**

4	Add lines 1, 2, and 3	**4** **91,800**	Lines 5 through 8 utilize the demand factors found in *Table 220.42*.

5 $\underline{\quad 91,800 \quad}$ $- 3000 =$ (line 4)	**5** **88,800** (if 117,000 or less, skip to line 8)	**6** $\underline{\quad ---- \quad} - 117,000 =$ (line 5, if more than 117,000)	**6** **----**
7 $\underline{\quad ---- \quad} \times 25\% =$ (line 6)	**7** **----**	**8** $\underline{\quad 88,800 \quad} \times 35\% =$ (smaller of line 5 or 117,000)	**8** **31,080**

9	Total General Lighting and Receptacle Load	$3000 + \underline{\quad ---- \quad} + \underline{\quad 31,080 \quad} =$ (line 7) (line 8)	**9** **34,080**

10	Fastened-In-Place Appliances *220.53* *Use the nameplate rating.* *Do not include electric ranges,* *clothes dryers, space-heating* *equipment, or air-conditioning* *equipment.*	water heaters/ **54,000** microwave ovens / **14,400** /	dishwashers / **14,400** / /	disposers / **10,800** / /
	If fewer than four units, put total volt-amperes on line 10. If four or more units, multiply total volt-amperes by 75%.	**93,600** $\times 75\% =$ (volt-amps of four or more)	**10** **70,200**	

11	Clothes Dryers *220.54* *(If present; otherwise skip to line 12.) Use 5000 watts or the nameplate rating, whichever is larger.* The neutral demand load is 70% for feeders. *220.61(B)*	**11** **27,600**
12	Ranges, Ovens, Cooktops, and Other Household Cooking Appliances Over 1750 Watts *220.55* *(If present; otherwise skip to line 13.) Use Table 220.55 and all of the applicable Notes.* The neutral demand load is 70% for feeders. *220.61(B)*	**12** **27,000**
13	Heating or Air-Conditioning System (Compare the heat and A/C, and omit the smaller.) *220.60* *Include the air handler when using either one. For heat pumps, include the compressor and the* *maximum amount of electric heat that can be energized while the compressor is running.*	**13** **64,140**
14	Largest Motor (one motor only) *220.50 and 430.24* *Multiply the volt-amperes of the largest motor by 25%.* $\underline{\quad 900 \quad} \times 25\% =$ (volt-amps of largest motor)	**14** **225**
15	Total Volt-Ampere Demand Load: *Add lines 9 through 14 to find the minimum required volt-amperes.*	**15** **223,245**

16	Minimum Amperes *Divide the total* *volt-amperes by* *the voltage.*	$\dfrac{223,245}{(line\ 15)} \div \dfrac{240}{(voltage)} =$	**16** **930** (minimum amperes)	**Minimum Size** **17 Service or** **Feeder** *240.6(A)*	**17** **1000**

18	Size the Service or Feeder Conductors. *Use 310.15(B)(7) to find the service conductors up to 400 amperes.* *Ratings in excess of 400 amperes shall comply with Table 310.15(B)(16)* *310.15(B)(7) also applies to feeder conductors serving as the main power feeder.*	**Minimum Size** **Conductors**	**18** 400 kcmil Cu 600 kcmil Al three paralleled sets
19	Size the Neutral Conductor. *220.61* *310.15(B)(7) states that the neutral service or feeder conductor* *can be smaller than the ungrounded (hot) conductors, provided the* *requirements of 215.2, 220.61, and 230.42 are met.* *250.24(C)(1) states that the neutral shall not be smaller than the* *required grounding electrode conductor specified in Table 250.66.*	**Minimum Size** **Neutral** **Conductor**	**19** 3/0 Cu 250 kcmil Al three paralleled sets
20	Size the Grounding Electrode Conductor (for Service). *250.66* *Use line 18 to find the grounding electrode conductor in Table 250.66.* Size the Equipment Grounding Conductor (for Feeder). *250.122* *Use line 17 to find the equipment grounding conductor in Table 250.122.* *Equipment grounding conductor types are listed in 250.118.*	**Minimum Size** **Grounding Electrode** **Conductor . . . or . . .** **Equipment Grounding** **Conductor**	**20** 3/0 Cu 250 kcmil Al

SIX-UNIT MULTIFAMILY DWELLING CALCULATION

Two Meter Centers, Each Supplying Six Units

Ⓐ Each service drop, set of overhead service conductors, set of underground service conductors, or service lateral supplies only one set of service-entrance conductors, unless two to six service disconnecting means (in separate enclosures) are grouped at one location and supply separate loads from one service drop 》230.40 Exception No. 2 《.

Ⓑ Because service equipment installations can vary greatly, the arrangement must be known before a load calculation is performed. In this configuration, each service (conductors and equipment) must be able to carry the calculated load for six dwelling units.

Ⓒ The following multifamily dwelling, standard method, load calculation is based on six units with identical configurations. Turn to page 231 for dwelling unit details.

Ⓓ Service-entrance conductors must be able to carry the ampacity determined in accordance with Article 220 》230.42(A) 《.

Ⓔ No more than six disconnects per service can be grouped in one location 》230.71(A) 《.

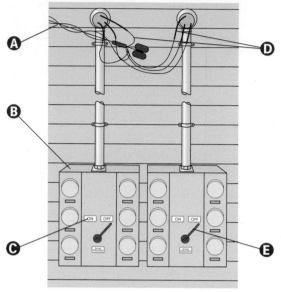

© Cengage Learning 2012

Lines 1 through 9—General Lighting and Receptacle Load

Ⓐ Fill in the first three lines using six dwelling units instead of twelve.

Ⓑ Insert the result of line 8, not the number from line 5.

Ⓒ The general lighting and receptacle load for these six dwelling units is 18,015 volt-amperes. Compare this line 9 with the line 9 for twelve units (34,080). Obviously, this is not half of line 9 for twelve units; therefore, a calculation must be performed for each different application.

Ⓓ Multiply the result of line 5 by 35% and place on line 8.

1 General Lighting and Receptacle Loads *220.12* *Do not include open porches, garages, or unused or unfinished spaces not adaptable for future use.*	3 × <u>1050</u> (sq ft outside dimensions)	× <u>6</u> (number of units)	= 1	**18,900**
2 Small-Appliance Branch Circuits *220.52(A)* *At least **two** small-appliance branch circuits must be included. 210.11(C)(1)*	1500 × <u>2</u> (minimum of two)	× <u>6</u> (number of units)	= 2	**18,000**
3 Laundry Branch Circuit(s) *220.52(B)* *Include at least **one** laundry branch circuit *unless meeting 210.52(F) Exception No. 1 or 2. 210.11(C)(2)*	1500 × <u>1</u> *(minimum of one)	× <u>6</u> (number of units)	= 3	**9000**

4 Add lines 1, 2, and 3	**4**	**45,900**	Lines 5 through 8 utilize the demand factors found in *Table 220.42*.
5 <u>45,900</u> − 3000 = **5** (line 4)	**42,900** (if 117,000 or less, skip to line 8)	**6** <u>----</u> − 117,000 = **6** (line 5, if more than 117,000)	**----**
7 <u>----</u> × 25% = **7** (line 6)	**----**	**8** <u>42,900</u> × 35% = **8** (smaller of line 5 or 117,000)	**15,015**
9 Total General Lighting and Receptacle Load 3000 + <u>----</u> + <u>15,015</u> = **9** (line 7) (line 8)			**18,015**

© Cengage Learning 2012

Lines 11 and 12—Clothes Dryers and Ranges

Ⓐ Use Table 220.54 to derate five (or more) clothes dryer loads. First, find the demand factor percentage across from the number of dryers, in this case 75%. Next, multiply the total dryer load by that percentage and record the result on line 11 (5000 × 6 = 30,000 × 75% = 22,500).

Ⓑ The demand for six 12-kW ranges comes from Table 220.55, Column C. First, look at the "Number of Appliances" column and find the number 6. Next, follow that row across to Column C and find the kW demand load, which is 21. Finally, multiply this number by 1000 and place in line 12. Since each range is 12 kW, Columns A and B cannot be used.

Ⓐ

11 Clothes Dryers *220.54* *(If present; otherwise skip to line 12.) Use 5000 watts or the nameplate rating, whichever is larger.* The neutral demand load is 70% for feeders. *220.61(B)*	**11**	**22,500**
12 Ranges, Ovens, Cooktops, and Other Household Cooking Appliances Over 1750 Watts *220.55* *(If present; otherwise skip to line 13.) Use Table 220.55 and all of the applicable Notes.* The neutral demand load is 70% for feeders. *220.61(B)*	**12**	**21,000**

Ⓑ

© Cengage Learning 2012

Lines 15 through 17—Minimum Amperes

Ⓐ The minimum volt-ampere load for these six dwelling units is 128,910.

Ⓑ The service-entrance conductors and equipment must have a rating of at least 537 amperes.

Ⓒ The next standard size fuse or circuit breaker above 537 is 600 amperes ⟫ *240.6(A)* ⟪.

Ⓐ

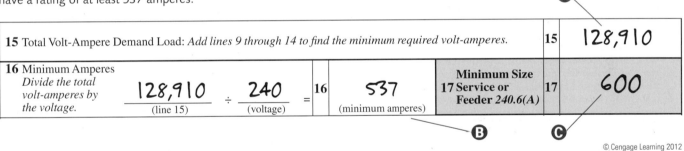

15 Total Volt-Ampere Demand Load: *Add lines 9 through 14 to find the minimum required volt-amperes.*	**15**	**128,910**

| **16** Minimum Amperes
 Divide the total volt-amperes by the voltage. | $\dfrac{128,910}{\text{(line 15)}} \div \dfrac{240}{\text{(voltage)}} =$ | **16** | **537**
 (minimum amperes) | **Minimum Size**
 17 Service or
 Feeder *240.6(A)* | **17** | **600** |

Ⓑ **Ⓒ**

© Cengage Learning 2012

Line 18—Minimum Size Conductors

Ⓐ At 75°C (167°F), the minimum size copper conductors for two parallel sets matching or exceeding 537 amperes are 300 kcmil. Because the overcurrent protection is less than 800 amperes, the conductor ampacity can be less than the 600-ampere rating. The next higher standard overcurrent device rating (above the ampacity of the conductors being protected) shall be permitted to be used, provided all of the following three conditions are met: (1) the conductors being protected are not part of a branch circuit supplying more than one receptacle for cord- and plug-connected portable loads, (2) the ampacity of the conductors does not correspond with the standard ampere rating of a fuse or a circuit breaker without overload trip adjustments above its rating (but that shall be permitted to have other trip or rating adjustments), and (3) the next higher standard rating selected does not exceed 800 amperes ⟫ *240.4(B)* ⟪. The combined rating of two 300-kcmil copper conductors is 570 amperes. Because the combined rating of 250-kcmil copper conductors is only 510 amperes, which is below the minimum required conductor ampacity of 531 amperes, 250-kcmil conductors are not permitted.

Ⓑ Other parallel conductor combinations are possible, such as three sets of 3/0 AWG Cu and three sets of 4/0 AWG Al.

Ⓐ

18 Size the Service or Feeder Conductors. *Use 310.15(B)(7) to find the service conductors up to 400 amperes.* *Ratings in excess of 400 amperes shall comply with Table 310.15(B)(16)* *310.15(B)(7) also applies to feeder conductors serving as the main power feeder.*	**Minimum Size** **Conductors**	**18**	**300 kcmil Cu** **400 kcmil Al** two paralleled sets

Ⓑ

© Cengage Learning 2012

Line 19—Neutral Conductor

A The minimum neutral load is 66,990 volt-amperes.

B The minimum conductor ampacity for two paralleled neutral conductors is 140 amperes. At 75°C (167°F), the minimum size conductor is 1/0 AWG copper *or* 3/0 AWG aluminum.

> ### NOTE
>
> Even with a lower neutral ampacity, the conductors must remain this size because the neutral conductor shall not be smaller than the required grounding electrode conductor ≫*250.24(C)(1)*≪.

General lighting and receptacles (line 9)	18,015
Fastened-in-place appliances	
Water heaters 0	
Dishwashers (1200 × 6) 7200	
Waste disposers (7.5 × 120 × 6). 5400	
Microwave ovens (1200 × 6) 7200	
Total 19,800	
Total fastened-in-place appliances (19,800 × 75%) . .	14,850
Clothes dryers (line 11 × 70%)	15,750
Ranges (line 12 × 70%)	14,700
Electric heat	0
Air-conditioner compressors	0
Air handlers (3 × 115 × 6)	2070
Condenser fan motors (2 × 115 × 6)	1380
Largest motor (900 × 25%)	225
TOTAL	**66,990**

A

66,990 ÷ 240 = 279.13 = 279 minimum neutral ampacity
279 ÷ 2 = 139.5 = 140 minimum amperes per neutral conductor

B

19 Size the Neutral Conductor. *220.61* *310.15(B)(7) states that the neutral service or feeder conductor can be smaller than the ungrounded (hot) conductors, provided the requirements of 215.2, 220.61, and 230.42 are met.* *250.24(C)(1) states that the neutral shall not be smaller than the required grounding electrode conductor specified in Table 250.66.*	Minimum Size Neutral Conductor	19	1/0 Cu 3/0 Al two paralleled sets

© Cengage Learning 2012

Line 20—Grounding Electrode Conductor

A The equivalent area for two parallel sets of service entrance conductors, in this calculation, is 600 kcmil copper (2 × 300) . . . or . . . 800 kcmil aluminum (2 × 400).

B The minimum size grounding electrode conductor is 1/0 AWG copper *or* 3/0 AWG aluminum ≫*Table 250.66*≪.

A

20 Size the Grounding Electrode Conductor (for Service). *250.66* *Use line 18 to find the grounding electrode conductor in Table 250.66.* Size the Equipment Grounding Conductor (for Feeder). *250.122* *Use line 17 to find the equipment grounding conductor in Table 250.122.* *Equipment grounding conductor types are listed in 250.118.*	Minimum Size Grounding Electrode Conductor . . . *or* . . . Equipment Grounding Conductor	20	1/0 Cu 3/0 Al

B

© Cengage Learning 2012

The following page shows the completed standard method load calculation for a six-unit multifamily dwelling.

Standard Method Load Calculation for Multifamily Dwellings

1	General Lighting and Receptacle Loads *220.12* *Do not include open porches, garages, or unused or* *unfinished spaces not adaptable for future use.*	3 × __1050__ (sq ft outside dimensions)	× __6__ (number of units)	= 1		**18,900**
2	Small-Appliance Branch Circuits *220.52(A)* *At least **two** small-appliance branch circuits* *must be included.* *210.11(C)(1)*	1500 × __2__ (minimum of two)	× __6__ (number of units)	= 2		**18,000**
3	Laundry Branch Circuit(s) *220.52(B)* *Include at least **one** laundry branch circuit *unless* *meeting 210.52(F) Exception No. 1 or 2.* *210.11(C)(2)*	1500 × __1__ *(minimum of one)	× __6__ (number of units)	= 3		**9000**

4	Add lines 1, 2, and 3	**4**	**45,900**	Lines 5 through 8 utilize the demand factors found in *Table 220.42.*

5	__45,900__ − 3000 = (line 4)	**5**	**42,900** (if 117,000 or less, skip to line 8)	**6** __----__ − 117,000 = (line 5, if more than 117,000)	**6**	**----**
7	__----__ × 25% = (line 6)	**7**	**----**	**8** __42,900__ × 35% = (smaller of line 5 or 117,000)	**8**	**15,015**

9	Total General Lighting and Receptacle Load	3000 + __----__ + __15,015__ (line 7) (line 8)	= **9**	**18,015**

10	Fastened-In-Place Appliances *220.53* *Use the nameplate rating.* *Do not include electric ranges,* *clothes dryers, space-heating* *equipment, or air-conditioning* *equipment.*	water heaters/ **27,000** microwave ovens / **7200** /	dishwashers / **7200** / /	disposers / **5400** / /		
	If fewer than four units, put total volt-amperes on line 10. If four or more units, multiply total volt-amperes by 75%.	**46,800** × 75% = (volt-amps of four or more)		**10**	**35,100**

11	Clothes Dryers *220.54* *(If present; otherwise skip to line 12.) Use 5000 watts or the nameplate rating, whichever is larger.* *The neutral demand load is 70% for feeders.* *220.61(B)*	**11**	**22,500**
12	Ranges, Ovens, Cooktops, and Other Household Cooking Appliances Over 1750 Watts *220.55* *(If present; otherwise skip to line 13.) Use Table 220.55 and all of the applicable Notes.* *The neutral demand load is 70% for feeders.* *220.61(B)*	**12**	**21,000**
13	Heating or Air-Conditioning System (Compare the heat and A/C, and omit the smaller.) *220.60* *Include the air handler when using either one. For heat pumps, include the compressor and the* *maximum amount of electric heat that can be energized while the compressor is running.*	**13**	**32,070**

14	Largest Motor (one motor only) *220.50 and 430.24* *Multiply the volt-amperes of the largest motor by 25%.*	__900__ × 25% = (volt-amps of largest motor)	**14**	**225**

15	Total Volt-Ampere Demand Load: *Add lines 9 through 14 to find the minimum required volt-amperes.*	**15**	**128,910**

16	Minimum Amperes *Divide the total* *volt-amperes by* *the voltage.*	__128,910__ ÷ __240__ = (line 15) (voltage)	**16** **537** (minimum amperes)	**Minimum Size** **17** Service or **Feeder** *240.6(A)*	**17** **600**
18	Size the Service or Feeder Conductors. *Use 310.15(B)(7) to find the service conductors up to 400 amperes.* *Ratings in excess of 400 amperes shall comply with Table 310.15(B)(16)* *310.15(B)(7) also applies to feeder conductors serving as the main power feeder.*			**Minimum Size** **Conductors**	**18** **300 kcmil Cu** **400 kcmil Al** two paralleled sets
19	Size the Neutral Conductor. *220.61* *310.15(B)(7) states that the neutral service or feeder conductor* *can be smaller than the ungrounded (hot) conductors, provided the* *requirements of 215.2, 220.61, and 230.42 are met.* *250.24(C)(1) states that the neutral shall not be smaller than the* *required grounding electrode conductor specified in Table 250.66.*			**Minimum Size** **Neutral** **Conductor**	**19** **1/0 Cu** **3/0 Al** two paralleled sets
20	Size the Grounding Electrode Conductor (for Service). *250.66* *Use line 18 to find the grounding electrode conductor in Table 250.66.* Size the Equipment Grounding Conductor (for Feeder). *250.122* *Use line 17 to find the equipment grounding conductor in Table 250.122.* *Equipment grounding conductor types are listed in 250.118.*			**Minimum Size** **Grounding Electrode** **Conductor . . . or . . .** **Equipment Grounding** **Conductor**	**20** **1/0 Cu** **3/0 Al**

STANDARD LOAD CALCULATION FOR EACH UNIT OF A MULTIFAMILY DWELLING

Calculating Feeders for Individual Dwelling Units

Ⓐ A load calculation on an individual unit in a multifamily dwelling must be calculated in accordance with one of the one-family dwelling load-calculation methods (standard or optional).

Ⓑ The service disconnecting means must have a rating of at least the calculated load, determined in accordance with Article 220 》230.79《.

Ⓒ If the service disconnecting means consists of more than one switch or circuit breaker (permitted by 230.71), the combined ratings of all switches or circuit breakers used must not be less than that required by 230.79 》230.80《.

Ⓓ A load calculation must be performed on each unique unit, that is, different from any unit already calculated.

Ⓔ A grounded circuit conductor (neutral) shall not be used for grounding non-current-carrying metal equipment on the load side of the service disconnecting means 》250.142(B)《. In other words, the neutral must be isolated from the equipment ground in a remote panelboard (subpanel).

Ⓕ Use Table 310.15(B)(7) to size the dwelling unit's main power feeder(s) 》310.15(B)(7)《.

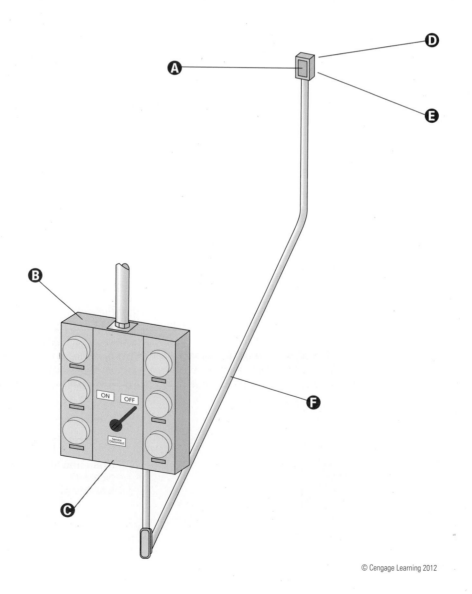

© Cengage Learning 2012

Standard Method—One Unit

A Each identically configured unit—that is, square footage dimensions, small-appliance and laundry branch circuits, fastened-in-place appliances, etc.—results in the same size feeder.

B Although located in a multifamily dwelling, this dwelling unit contains one feeder and one panelboard. It is, therefore, calculated in accordance with one of the one-family dwelling methods.

C A load calculation must be performed on each dissimilar unit.

D Using the standard method, the minimum required volt-amperes for this single unit is 29,048.

> **NOTE**
>
> Load calculations are calculated for each individual unit containing a panelboard (subpanel). Although located in a multifamily dwelling, calculate each unit by one of the methods for one-family dwellings **》Article 220《**. Performing a load calculation on multiple units and then dividing by the number of units will give an incorrect result.

Standard Method Load Calculation for One-Family Dwellings

1 General Lighting and Receptacle Loads *220.12* *Do not include open porches, garages, or unused or unfinished spaces not adaptable for future use.*	$3 \times$ **1050** (sq ft outside dimensions)	= **1**		**3150**
2 Small-Appliance Branch-Circuits *220.52(A)* *Include at least **two** small-appliance branch circuits must be included. 210.11(C)(1)*	$1500 \times$ **2** (minimum of two)	= **2**		**3000**
3 Laundry Branch Circuit(s) *220.52(B)* *Include at least **one** laundry branch circuit *unless meeting 210.52(F) Exception No. 1 or 2. 210.11(C)(2)*	$1500 \times$ **1** *(minimum of one)*	= **3**		**1500**
4 Add lines 1, 2, and 3	**4** **7650**	Lines 5 through 8 utilize the demand factors found in *Table 220.42*.		
5 **7650** (line 4) $- 3000 =$ **5**	**4650** (if 117,000 or less, skip to line 8)	**6** **----** (line 5, if more than 117,000) $- 117,000 =$ **6**		**----**
7 **----** (line 6) $\times 25\% =$ **7**	**----**	**8** **4650** (smaller of line 5 or 117,000) $\times 35\% =$ **8**		**1628**
9 Total General Lighting and Receptacle Load	$3000 +$ **----** (line 7) $+$ **1628** (line 8)	= **9**		**4628**
10 Fastened-In-Place Appliances *220.53* *Use the nameplate rating. Do not include electric ranges, clothes dryers, space-heating equipment, or air-conditioning equipment.*	water heater/ **4500** dishwasher / **1200** disposer / **900** compactor / microwave oven / **1200** / / / /			
	If fewer than four units, put total volt-amperes on line 10. If four or more units, multiply total volt-amperes by 75%. **7800** (volt-amps of four or more) $\times 75\% =$	**10**		**5850**
11 Clothes Dryers *220.54* *(If present; otherwise skip to line 12.) Use 5000 watts or the nameplate rating, whichever is larger. The neutral demand load is 70% for feeders. 220.61(B)*		**11**		**5000**
12 Ranges, Ovens, Cooktops, and Other Household Cooking Appliances Over 1750 Watts *220.55* *(If present; otherwise skip to line 13.) Use Table 220.55 and all of the applicable Notes. The neutral demand load is 70% for feeders. 220.61(B)*		**12**		**8000**
13 Heating or Air-Conditioning System (Compare the heat and A/C, and omit the smaller.) *220.60* *Include the air handler when using either one. For heat pumps, include the compressor and the maximum amount of electric heat that can be energized while the compressor is running.*		**13**		**5345**
14 Largest Motor (one motor only) *220.50 and 430.24* *Multiply the volt-amperes of the largest motor by 25%.*	**900** (volt-amps of largest motor) $\times 25\% =$	**14**		**225**
15 Total Volt-Ampere Demand Load: *Add lines 9 through 14 to find the minimum required volt-amperes.*		**15**		**29,048**

Minimum Size Feeder and Overcurrent Protection

A Feeder conductors must have an ampacity not less than required to supply the load as calculated in Article 220, Parts II, III, and IV. The minimum feeder conductor size before the application of any adjustment or correction factors must have an allowable ampacity equal to, or greater than, the noncontinuous load plus 125% of the continuous load »215.2(A)«.

B Feeders must be protected against overcurrent in accordance with the Article 240, Part I provisions »215.3«.

C The minimum ampere rating for this one unit is 121.

D Use Table 310.15(B)(7) to determine the minimum size feeder conductors serving as the dwelling unit's main power feeders »310.15(B)(7)«.

16 Minimum Amperes *Divide the total volt-amperes by the voltage.* $\dfrac{29{,}048}{\text{(line 15)}} \div \dfrac{240}{\text{(voltage)}} =$ 16	121 (minimum amperes)	**Minimum Size** 17 **Service or Feeder** *240.6(A)*	17	125
18 Size the Service or Feeder Conductors. *Use 310.15(B)(7) to find the service conductors up to 400 amperes. Ratings in excess of 400 amperes shall comply with Table 310.15(B)(16) 310.15(B)(7) also applies to feeder conductors serving as the main power feeder.*		**Minimum Size Conductors**	18	2 copper 1/0 aluminum

© Cengage Learning 2012

Minimum Size Neutral and Equipment Grounding Conductors

A The minimum neutral-conductor ampacity is 74.

B At 75°C (167°F), the minimum size conductor is 4 AWG copper *or* 3 AWG aluminum.

C If a feeder supplies branch circuits requiring equipment grounding conductors, it must include (or provide) a grounding means to which the equipment grounding conductors of the branch circuits shall be connected, in accordance with 250.134 provisions »215.6«.

D Copper, aluminum, or copper-clad aluminum equipment grounding conductors of the wire type must not be smaller than shown in Table 250.122, but do not have to be larger than the circuit conductors supplying the equipment »250.122(A)«.

NOTE

A raceway or cable sheath acting as the equipment grounding conductor, as provided in 250.118 and 250.134(A), must comply with 250.4(A)(5) or (B)(4) »*250.122(A)*«.

General lighting and receptacles (line 9) 4628
Fastened-in-place appliances
      Water heater.   0
      Dishwasher. 1200
      Waste (garbage) disposer.   900
      Microwave oven 1200
      Total 3300

Total fastened-in-place appliances (3 units = 100%) 3300
Clothes dryer (line 11 × 70%). 3500
Range (line 12 × 70%) 5600
Electric heat   0
Air-conditioner compressor   0
Air handler (3 × 115). 345
Condenser fan motor (2 × 115). 230
Largest motor (900 × 25%). 225

TOTAL 17,828

17,828 ÷ 240 = 74.28 minimum neutral-conductor ampacity

19 Size the Neutral Conductor. *220.61* *310.15(B)(7) states that the neutral service or feeder conductor can be smaller than the ungrounded (hot) conductors, provided the requirements of 215.2, 220.61, and 230.42 are met. 250.24(C)(1) states that the neutral shall not be smaller than the required grounding electrode conductor specified in Table 250.66.*	**Minimum Size Neutral Conductor**	19	4 copper 3 aluminum
20 Size the Grounding Electrode Conductor. *250.66* *Use line 18 to find the grounding electrode conductor in Table 250.66.* Size the Equipment Grounding Conductor (for Feeder). *250.122* *Use line 17 to find the equipment grounding conductor in Table 250.122. Equipment grounding conductor types are listed in 250.118.*	**Minimum Size Grounding Electrode Conductor . . . *or* . . . Equipment Grounding Conductor**	20	6 copper 4 aluminum

© Cengage Learning 2012

The following page shows the completed one-family dwelling load calculation for one multifamily dwelling-unit feeder and remote panelboard (subpanel), according to the standard method.

Standard Method Load Calculation for One-Family Dwellings

1	General Lighting and Receptacle Loads *220.12* *Do not include open porches, garages, or unused or unfinished spaces not adaptable for future use.*	$3 \times$ __1050__ (sq ft outside dimensions)	=	**1**	**3150**
2	Small-Appliance Branch-Circuits *220.52(A)* *Include at least **two** small-appliance branch circuits must be included. 210.11(C)(1)*	$1500 \times$ __2__ (minimum of two)	=	**2**	**3000**
3	Laundry Branch Circuit(s) *220.52(B)* *Include at least **one** laundry branch circuit *unless meeting 210.52(F) Exception No. 1 or 2. 210.11(C)(2)*	$1500 \times$ __1__ *(minimum of one)	=	**3**	**1500**

4	Add lines 1, 2, and 3	**4**	**7650**	Lines 5 through 8 utilize the demand factors found in *Table 220.42*.

5 __7650__ (line 4) $-3000 =$	**5** **4650** (if 117,000 or less, skip to line 8)	**6** __----__ (line 5, if more than 117,000) $- 117,000 =$	**6** **----**
7 __----__ (line 6) $\times 25\% =$	**7** **----**	**8** __4650__ (smaller of line 5 or 117,000) $\times 35\% =$	**8** **1628**

9	Total General Lighting and Receptacle Load	$3000 +$ __----__ (line 7) $+$ __1628__ (line 8) $=$	**9**	**4628**

10	Fastened-In-Place Appliances *220.53* *Use the nameplate rating.* *Do not include electric ranges, clothes dryers, space-heating equipment, or air-conditioning equipment.*	water heater / 4500 compactor / /	dishwasher / 1200 microwave oven / 1200 /	disposer / 900 / /	
	If fewer than four units, put total volt-amperes on line 10. If four or more units, multiply total volt-amperes by 75%.	__7800__ (volt-amps of four or more) $\times 75\% =$		**10**	**5850**

11	Clothes Dryers *220.54* *(If present; otherwise skip to line 12.) Use 5000 watts or the nameplate rating, whichever is larger. The neutral demand load is 70% for feeders. 220.61(B)*		**11**	**5000**
12	Ranges, Ovens, Cooktops, and Other Household Cooking Appliances Over 1750 Watts *220.55* *(If present; otherwise skip to line 13.) Use Table 220.55 and all of the applicable Notes. The neutral demand load is 70% for feeders. 220.61(B)*		**12**	**8000**
13	Heating or Air-Conditioning System (Compare the heat and A/C, and omit the smaller.) *220.60* *Include the air handler when using either one. For heat pumps, include the compressor and the maximum amount of electric heat that can be energized while the compressor is running.*		**13**	**5345**
14	Largest Motor (one motor only) *220.50 and 430.24* *Multiply the volt-amperes of the largest motor by 25%.*	__900__ (volt-amps of largest motor) $\times 25\% =$	**14**	**225**

15	Total Volt-Ampere Demand Load: *Add lines 9 through 14 to find the minimum required volt-amperes.*		**15**	**29,048**

16	Minimum Amperes *Divide the total volt-amperes by the voltage.*	__29,048__ (line 15) $\div$ __240__ (voltage) $=$	**16**	__121__ (minimum amperes)	**Minimum Size** **17 Service or** **Feeder** *240.6(A)* **17** **125**

18	Size the Service or Feeder Conductors. *Use 310.15(B)(7) to find the service conductors up to 400 amperes. Ratings in excess of 400 amperes shall comply with Table 310.15(B)(16). 310.15(B)(7) also applies to feeder conductors serving as the main power feeder.*	**Minimum Size Conductors**	**18**	2 copper 1/0 aluminum
19	Size the Neutral Conductor. *220.61* *310.15(B)(7) states that the neutral service or feeder conductor can be smaller than the ungrounded (hot) conductors, provided the requirements of 215.2, 220.61, and 230.42 are met. 250.24(C)(1) states that the neutral shall not be smaller than the required grounding electrode conductor specified in Table 250.66.*	**Minimum Size Neutral Conductor**	**19**	4 copper 3 aluminum
20	Size the Grounding Electrode Conductor. *250.66* *Use line 18 to find the grounding electrode conductor in Table 250.66.* Size the Equipment Grounding Conductor (for Feeder). *250.122* *Use line 17 to find the equipment grounding conductor in Table 250.122. Equipment grounding conductor types are listed in 250.118.*	**Minimum Size Grounding Electrode Conductor . . . or . . . Equipment Grounding Conductor**	**20**	6 copper 4 aluminum

OPTIONAL METHOD: MULTIFAMILY DWELLINGS

Optional Method Load Calculation for Multifamily Dwellings

1 General Lighting and Receptacle Loads *220.84(C)(1)*
Do not include open porches, garages, or unused or unfinished spaces not adaptable for future use.

$3 \times$ _____ $\times$ _____ $=$ **1**
(sq ft outside dimensions)   (number of units)

2 Small-Appliance Branch Circuits *220.84(C)(2)*
*At least **two** small-appliance branch circuits must be included. 210.11(C)(1)*

$1500 \times$ _____ $\times$ _____ $=$ **2**
(minimum of two)   (number of units)

3 Laundry Branch Circuit(s) *220.84(C)(2)*
*Include at least **one** laundry branch circuit *unless meeting 210.52(F) Exception No. 1 or 2. 210.11(C)(2)*

$1500 \times$ _____ $\times$ _____ $=$ **3**
*(minimum of one)   (number of units)

4 through 11

Appliances and Motors
220.84(C)(3) and (4)

*Use the nameplate rating of **all** appliances (fastened in place, permanently connected, or connected to a specific circuit), ranges, wall-mounted ovens, counter-mounted cooking units, motors, water heaters, and clothes dryers.*

Convert any nameplate rating given in amperes to volt-amperes by multiplying the amperes by the rated voltage.

Do not include any heating or air-conditioning equipment in this section.

water heater   / _____ $\times$ _____ $=$ **4**
(volt-amperes each)   (number)

dishwashers   / _____ $\times$ _____ $=$ **5**
(volt-amperes each)   (number)

disposers   / _____ $\times$ _____ $=$ **6**
(volt-amperes each)   (number)

clothes dryers   / _____ $\times$ _____ $=$ **7**
(volt-amperes each)   (number)

ranges   / _____ $\times$ _____ $=$ **8**
(volt-amperes each)   (number)

microwave ovens   / _____ $\times$ _____ $=$ **9**
(volt-amperes each)   (number)

/ _____ $\times$ _____ $=$ **10**
(volt-amperes each)   (number)

/ _____ $\times$ _____ $=$ **11**
(volt-amperes each)   (number)

12 Heating or Air-Conditioning System (Compare the heat and A/C, and omit the smaller.) *220.84(C)(5)*
Include the air handler when using either one.
For heat pumps, include the compressor and the maximum amount of electric heat that can be energized while the compressor is running.

_____ $\times$ _____ $=$ **12**
(volt-amperes each)   (number)

13 Total Volt-Ampere Demand Load:

Multiply total VA by Table 220.84 demand factor percentage.

_____ $+$ _____ $=$ **13**
(total volt-amperes from lines 1 through 12)   (*Table 220.84* demand factor)

14 House Load *(If present; otherwise skip to line 15)*
Calculate in accordance with Article 220, Part III.
Do not include Table 220.84 demand factors.   **14**

15 Minimum Amperes
Divide the total volt-amperes by the voltage.

_____ $\div$ _____ $=$ **15** _____
(lines 13 and 14)   (voltage)   (minimum amperes)

16 Minimum Size Service or Feeder *240.6(A)*   **16**

17 Size the Service or Feeder Conductors.
Use 310.15(B)(7) to find the service conductors up to 400 amperes.
Ratings in excess of 400 amperes shall comply with Table 310.15(B)(16)
310.15(B)(7) also applies to feeder conductors serving as the main power feeder.

Minimum Size Conductors   **17**

18 Size the Neutral Conductor. *220.61*
Note: There is no optional method for calculating the neutral conductor.
310.15(B)(7) states that the neutral service or feeder conductor can be smaller than the ungrounded (hot) conductors, provided the requirements of 215.2, 220.61, and 230.42 are met.
250.24(C)(1) states that the neutral shall not be smaller than the required grounding electrode conductor specified in Table 250.66.

Minimum Size Neutral Conductor   **18**

19 Size the Grounding Electrode Conductor. *250.66*
Use line 17 to find the grounding electrode conductor in Table 250.66.
Size the Equipment Grounding Conductor (for Feeder). *250.122*
Use line 16 to find the equipment grounding conductor in Table 250.122.
Equipment grounding conductor types are listed in 250.118.

Minimum Size Grounding Electrode Conductor ... or ... Equipment Grounding Conductor   **19**

Lines 1 through 3—General Lighting and Receptacle Load

Ⓐ In the **Optional Method,** lines 1, 2, and 3 are calculated exactly as described in the **Standard Method.** (See explanations on page 233.)

Ⓑ The feeder or service multifamily dwelling load can be calculated in accordance with Table 220.84 (instead of Article 220, Part III) where all of the following conditions are met: (1) no dwelling unit is supplied by more than one feeder; (2) each dwelling unit is equipped with electric cooking equipment; and (3) each dwelling unit is equipped with either electric space-heating or air-conditioning, or both ≫*220.84(A)*≪.

Ⓒ This optional load calculation is calculated on the same twelve-unit multifamily dwelling used for the standard method (located in the first part of this unit).

> **N O T E**
>
> When the calculated load for multifamily dwellings, without electric cooking, in Article 220, Part III, exceeds that calculated under Part IV for the identical load, plus electric cooking (based on 8 kW per unit), use the lesser of the two loads ≫*220.84(A)(2) Exception*≪.

Optional Method Load Calculation for Multifamily Dwellings

1 General Lighting and Receptacle Loads *220.84(C)(1)* *Do not include open porches, garages, or unused or* *unfinished spaces not adaptable for future use.*	3 × $\underline{1050}$ _(sq ft outside dimensions)	× $\underline{12}$ _(number of units)	=	**37,800**
2 Small-Appliance Branch Circuits *220.84(C)(2)* *At least **two** small-appliance branch circuits* *must be included. 210.11(C)(1)*	1500 × $\underline{2}$ _(minimum of two)	× $\underline{12}$ _(number of units)	=	**36,000**
3 Laundry Branch Circuit(s) *220.84(C)(2)* *Include at least **one** laundry branch circuit *unless* *meeting 210.52(F) Exception No. 1 or 2. 210.11(C)(2)*	1500 × $\underline{1}$ _{*(minimum of one)}	× $\underline{12}$ _(number of units)	=	**18,000**

Lines 4 through 11—All Appliances

Ⓐ This section includes appliances (fastened in place, permanently connected, or connected to a specific circuit), ranges, wall-mounted ovens, counter-mounted cooking units, clothes dryers, and water heaters ≫220.84(C)(3)≪.

Ⓑ Low-power-factor loads and motors (except air-conditioning motors) are also included ≫220.84(C)(4)≪.

Ⓒ Use the exact clothes dryer nameplate rating, if any, even if less than 5000 volt-amperes. Do not apply the demand factors in Table 220.55 to household cooking equipment (ranges, cooktops, ovens, etc.); instead, list the nameplate ratings as they appear.

Ⓓ Insert the number of appliances (such as water heaters) having the same rating, which may not necessarily be the number of dwelling units. Here, all dwelling units contain identical equipment, so the number of each type of appliance is the same as the number of dwelling units. In another application, if only half of the units are equipped with laundry hookups, the number of units is not the same as the number of a given type of appliance.

Ⓔ Heating and air-conditioning systems are not included in this computation.

Ⓕ Additional lines have been provided for listing appliances.

Ⓖ Inserting numbers in all of the lines is not necessary. However, it is advisable to insert dashes, or some other indicator, to show that the line is intentionally blank.

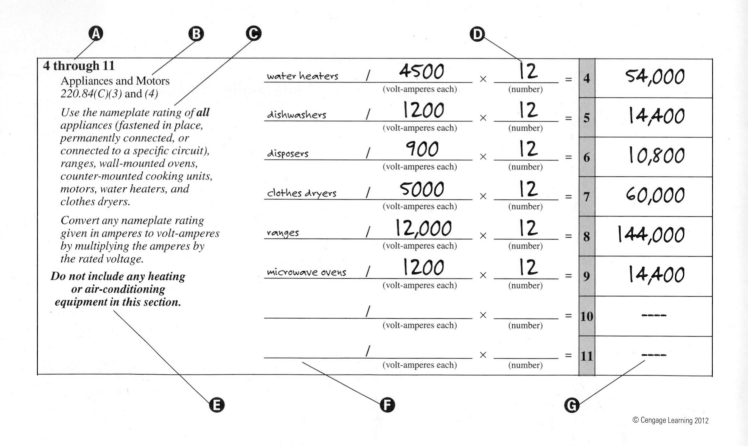

© Cengage Learning 2012

Line 12—Heating or Air-Conditioning System

Ⓐ Include only the larger of the heating or air-conditioning loads (except for heat pumps).

Ⓑ Electric heating loads (including associated motors) are calculated at 100% of the total connected load. Because the air handler (blower) works with either the heating or the air conditioning, add it to both calculations.

Ⓒ Air-conditioning loads (including associated motors) are calculated at 100% of the total connected load. No derating is allowed. Each unit contains an air-conditioner compressor ($14 \times 230 = 3220$ VA), condenser fan motor ($2 \times 115 = 230$ VA), and blower motor ($3 \times 115 = 345$ VA). The combined load is 3795 volt-amperes. Because this is less than the heating load, omit the A/C compressor and the condenser fan motor.

Ⓓ The air handler (blower motor) has a rating of 345 volt-amperes ($3 \times 115 = 345$). Because both loads are energized simultaneously, add the air handler to the 5 kW of electric heat ($345 + 5000 = 5345$ volt-amperes).

> **N O T E**
>
> A heat pump with supplementary heat is not considered a noncoincident load. Add the compressor full-load current to the maximum amount of heat that can be energized while the compressor is running. Remember to include all associated motor(s), that is, blower, condenser, etc.

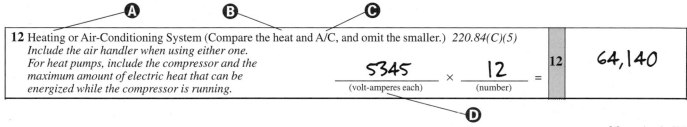

12 Heating or Air-Conditioning System (Compare the heat and A/C, and omit the smaller.) *220.84(C)(5)*
Include the air handler when using either one.
For heat pumps, include the compressor and the
maximum amount of electric heat that can be
energized while the compressor is running.

$$\underset{\text{(volt-amperes each)}}{5345} \times \underset{\text{(number)}}{12} = \boxed{12} \quad 64{,}140$$

© Cengage Learning 2012

Line 13—Total Volt-Ampere Demand Load

Ⓐ Adding lines 1 through 12 results in the volt-ampere load before derating.

Ⓑ Table 220.84 contains demand factors (percentages) for derating three (or more) multifamily dwelling units. Find the number of dwelling units in the first column and follow that row across to the demand factor. The demand factors listed in the second column are percentages. The demand factor for a twelve-unit multifamily dwelling is 41 (41%).

Ⓒ This is the total calculated load excluding house loads (if any).

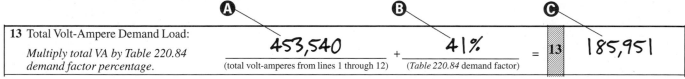

13 Total Volt-Ampere Demand Load:
Multiply total VA by Table 220.84
demand factor percentage.

$$\underset{\text{(total volt-amperes from lines 1 through 12)}}{453{,}540} + \underset{\text{(\textit{Table 220.84} demand factor)}}{41\%} = \boxed{13} \quad 185{,}951$$

© Cengage Learning 2012

Line 14—House Load

Ⓐ House loads must be calculated as stipulated in Article 220, Part III, and must be in addition to the dwelling-unit loads calculated in accordance with Table 220.84 »*220.84(B)*«.

Ⓑ House loads include areas such as clubhouse, office, hallway and stairway lighting, parking lot lighting, etc.

Ⓒ Insert a line (or dashes) in spaces left empty intentionally.

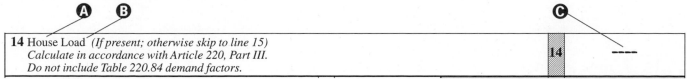

14 House Load *(If present; otherwise skip to line 15)*
Calculate in accordance with Article 220, Part III.
Do not include Table 220.84 demand factors.

$\boxed{14}$ — — — —

© Cengage Learning 2012

Lines 15 and 16—Minimum Service or Feeder

(A) Place the sum of lines 13 and 14 (total volt-amperes) here. If there is no house load, insert only line 13.

(B) Fill in the source voltage supplying the service equipment.

(C) Fractions of an ampere 0.5 and greater are rounded up, while fractions less than 0.5 are dropped (185,951 ÷ 240 = 774.8 = 775) ≫ *220.5(B)* ≪. The minimum ampere rating required for conductors and overcurrent protection, whether for the service or feeder, is 775.

(D) The service (or feeder) overcurrent protection must be higher than the number found in line 15. Standard ampere ratings for fuses and circuit breakers are listed in 240.6(A).

(E) The next standard size fuse or breaker above 775 amperes is 800 ≫ *240.6(A)* ≪.

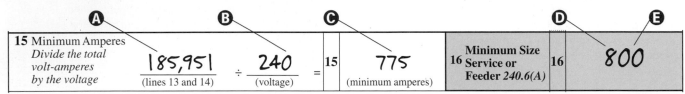

| 15 Minimum Amperes
*Divide the total
volt-amperes
by the voltage* | 185,951
(lines 13 and 14) | ÷ | 240
(voltage) | = |15 | 775
(minimum amperes) | 16 Minimum Size
Service or
Feeder *240.6(A)* | 16 | *800* |

© Cengage Learning 2012

Line 17—Minimum Size Conductors

(A) The total combined rating of paralleled conductors must meet or exceed the minimum calculated load.

(B) At 75°C (167°F), the minimum size copper conductors for three parallel sets matching or exceeding 775 amperes are 300 kcmil. Although three paralleled sets of 250-kcmil copper conductors (at 75°C [167°F]) are sufficient for an 800-ampere overcurrent protective device, they are not sufficient for the 775-ampere calculated load. (Three times 255 is only 765 amperes, short of the necessary 775 rating.)

| 17 Size the Service or Feeder Conductors.
Use 310.15(B)(7) to find the service conductors up to 400 amperes.
Ratings in excess of 400 amperes shall comply with Table 310.15(B)(16)
310.15(B)(7) also applies to feeder conductors serving as the main power feeder. | **Minimum Size
Conductors** | 17 | 300 kcmil Cu
400 kcmil Al
three paralleled sets |

© Cengage Learning 2012

Line 18—Minimum Size Neutral Conductors

(A) There is no optional method for neutral conductor calculation. This neutral calculation is performed in accordance with Article 220, Parts II and III.

(B) The loads for clothes dryers and ranges have already been calculated and are in the "Standard Method Load Calculation for One-Family Dwellings" form, Lines 11 and 12. As permitted in 220.61(B)(1), apply a 70% demand factor to these loads.

(C) The minimum calculated volt-ampere load is 108,705.

(D) The minimum neutral ampacity is 453.

(E) The minimum rating for three paralleled sets of neutral conductors is 151 amperes each.

(F) The loads for general lighting and receptacles have already been calculated and are in the "Standard Method Load Calculation for One-Family Dwellings" form, Line 9.

(G) At 75°C (167°F), the minimum size copper conductor is 2/0 AWG, with an individual rating of 175 amperes ≫ *Table 310.15(B)(16)* ≪.

(H) At 75°C (167°F), the minimum size aluminum conductor, if determined by ampacity alone, would be 3/0 AWG, with a rating of 155 amperes each. However, 3/0 AWG would not be acceptable because the neutral shall not be smaller than the required grounding electrode conductor, which in this example is 4/0 AWG ≫ *250.24(C)(1)* ≪.

General lighting and receptacles (line 9) 34,080
Fastened-in-place appliances
    Water heaters 0
    Dishwashers (1200 × 12) 14,400
    Waste disposers (7.5 × 120 × 12) . . 10,800
    Microwave ovens (1200 × 12) 14,400
    Total 39,600

Total fastened-in-place appliances (39,600 × 75%) . 29,700
Clothes dryers (line 11 × 70%) 18,900
Ranges (line 12 × 70%) 18,900
Electric heat 0
Air-conditioner compressors 0
Air handlers (3 × 115 × 12) 4140
Condenser fan motors (2 × 115 × 12) 2760
Largest motor (900 × 25%) 225
TOTAL 108,705

108,705 ÷ 240 = 452.9 = 453 minimum neutral ampacity
453 ÷ 3 = 151 minimum amperes per neutral conductor

18 Size the Neutral Conductor 220.61 **Note: There is no optional method for calculating the neutral conductor.** *310.15(B)(7) states that the neutral service or feeder conductor can be smaller than the ungrounded (hot) conductors, provided the requirements of 215.2, 220.61, and 230.42 are met. 250.24(C)(1) states that the neutral shall not be smaller than the required grounding electrode conductor specified in Table 250.66.*	Minimum Size Neutral Conductor	18	2/0 Cu 4/0 Al three paralleled sets

© Cengage Learning 2012

Line 19—Grounding Electrode Conductor

(A) The grounding electrode conductor size is determined by the largest service-entrance conductor (or the equivalent area) if the service-entrance conductors are paralleled. The equivalent area for three parallel sets in this calculation is 900-kcmil copper (3 × 300) *or* 1200-kcmil aluminum (3 × 400).

(B) The minimum size grounding electrode conductor is 2/0 AWG copper *or* 4/0 AWG aluminum ≫ *Table 250.66* ≪.

19 Size the Grounding Electrode Conductor. *250.66* *Use line 17 to find the grounding electrode conductor in Table 250.66.* Size the Equipment Grounding Conductor (for Feeder). *250.122* *Use line 16 to find the equipment grounding conductor in Table 250.122. Equipment grounding conductor types are listed in 250.118.*	Minimum Size Grounding Electrode Conductor . . . *or* . . . Equipment Grounding Conductor	19	2/0 Cu 4/0 Al

© Cengage Learning 2012

The following page shows the completed optional method for a twelve-unit multifamily dwelling, having all units combined into a single service.

Optional Method Load Calculation for Multifamily Dwellings

1	General Lighting and Receptacle Loads *220.84(C)(1)* *Do not include open porches, garages, or unused or unfinished spaces not adaptable for future use.*	3 × **1050** (sq ft outside dimensions)	× **12** (number of units)	=		**37,800**
2	Small-Appliance Branch Circuits *220.84(C)(2)* *At least two small-appliance branch circuits must be included.* *210.11(C)(1)*	1500 × **2** (minimum of two)	× **12** (number of units)	=		**36,000**
3	Laundry Branch Circuit(s) *220.84(C)(2)* *Include at least one laundry branch circuit *unless meeting 210.52(F) Exception No. 1 or 2.* *210.11(C)(2)*	1500 × **1** *(minimum of one)	× **12** (number of units)	=		**18,000**

4 through 11 Appliances and Motors *220.84(C)(3) and (4)*	water heaters	/ **4500** (volt-amperes each)	× **12** (number)	=	4	**54,000**
*Use the nameplate rating of **all** appliances (fastened in place, permanently connected, or connected to a specific circuit), ranges, wall-mounted ovens, counter-mounted cooking units, motors, water heaters, and clothes dryers.*	dishwashers	/ **1200** (volt-amperes each)	× **12** (number)	=	5	**14,400**
	disposers	/ **900** (volt-amperes each)	× **12** (number)	=	6	**10,800**
Convert any nameplate rating given in amperes to volt-amperes by multiplying the amperes by the rated voltage.	clothes dryers	/ **5000** (volt-amperes each)	× **12** (number)	=	7	**60,000**
	ranges	/ **12,000** (volt-amperes each)	× **12** (number)	=	8	**144,000**
Do not include any heating or air-conditioning equipment in this section.	microwave ovens	/ **1200** (volt-amperes each)	× **12** (number)	=	9	**14,400**
		/ (volt-amperes each)	× (number)	=	10	-----
		/ (volt-amperes each)	× (number)	=	11	-----

12	Heating or Air-Conditioning System (Compare the heat and A/C, and omit the smaller.) *220.84(C)(5)* *Include the air handler when using either one. For heat pumps, include the compressor and the maximum amount of electric heat that can be energized while the compressor is running.*	**5345** (volt-amperes each)	× **12** (number)	=	12	**64,140**
13	Total Volt-Ampere Demand Load: *Multiply total VA by Table 220.84 demand factor percentage.*	**453,540** (total volt-amperes from lines 1 through 12)	+ **41%** (*Table 220.84* demand factor)	=	13	**185,951**
14	House Load *(If present; otherwise skip to line 15)* *Calculate in accordance with Article 220, Part III. Do not include Table 220.84 demand factors.*				14	-----

15	Minimum Amperes *Divide the total volt-amperes by the voltage*	**185,951** (lines 13 and 14)	÷ **240** (voltage)	=	15	**775** (minimum amperes)	**16** Minimum Size Service or Feeder *240.6(A)*	16	**800**

17	Size the Service or Feeder Conductors. *Use 310.15(B)(7) to find the service conductors up to 400 amperes. Ratings in excess of 400 amperes shall comply with Table 310.15(B)(16) 310.15(B)(7) also applies to feeder conductors serving as the main power feeder.*	**Minimum Size Conductors**	17	**300 kcmil Cu** **400 kcmil Al** three paralleled sets
18	Size the Neutral Conductor *220.61* **Note: There is no optional method for calculating the neutral conductor.** *310.15(B)(7) states that the neutral service or feeder conductor can be smaller than the ungrounded (hot) conductors, provided the requirements of 215.2, 220.61, and 230.42 are met. 250.24(C)(1) states that the neutral shall not be smaller than the required grounding electrode conductor specified in Table 250.66.*	**Minimum Size Neutral Conductor**	18	**2/0 Cu** **4/0 Al** three paralleled sets
19	Size the Grounding Electrode Conductor. *250.66* *Use line 17 to find the grounding electrode conductor in Table 250.66. Size the Equipment Grounding Conductor (for Feeder). 250.122 Use line 16 to find the equipment grounding conductor in Table 250.122. Equipment grounding conductor types are listed in 250.118.*	**Minimum Size Grounding Electrode Conductor ... or ... Equipment Grounding Conductor**	19	**2/0 Cu** **4/0 Al**

SIX-UNIT MULTIFAMILY DWELLING CALCULATION— OPTIONAL METHOD

Lines 1 through 12

Ⓐ This optional method calculation is based on six units instead of twelve.

Ⓑ Since everything is calculated at 100%, lines 1 through 12 are exactly half of that calculated for twelve units.

Ⓐ

Optional Method Load Calculation for Multifamily Dwellings

1 General Lighting and Receptacle Loads *220.84(C)(1)* *Do not include open porches, garages, or unused or* *unfinished spaces not adaptable for future use.*	3 ×	**1050** (sq ft outside dimensions)	×	**6** (number of units)	= **1**	**18,900**
2 Small-Appliance Branch Circuits *220.84(C)(2)* At least **two** small-appliance branch circuits *must be included. 210.11(C)(1)*	1500 ×	**2** (minimum of two)	×	**6** (number of units)	= **2**	**18,000**
3 Laundry Branch Circuit(s) *220.84(C)(2)* Include at least **one** laundry branch circuit *unless* *meeting 210.52(F) Exception No. 1 or 2. 210.11(C)(2)*	1500 ×	**1** *(minimum of one)*	×	**6** (number of units)	= **3**	**9000**
4 through 11 Appliances and Motors *220.84(C)(3) and (4)*	water heaters /	**4500** (volt-amperes each)	×	**6** (number)	= **4**	**27,000**
Use the nameplate rating of all *appliances (fastened in place,* *permanently connected, or* *connected to a specific circuit),*	dishwashers /	**1200** (volt-amperes each)	×	**6** (number)	= **5**	**7200**
ranges, wall-mounted ovens, *counter-mounted cooking units,* *motors, water heaters, and* *clothes dryers.*	disposers /	**900** (volt-amperes each)	×	**6** (number)	= **6**	**5400**
	clothes dryers /	**5000** (volt-amperes each)	×	**6** (number)	= **7**	**30,000**
Convert any nameplate rating *given in amperes to volt-amperes* *by multiplying the amperes by* *the rated voltage.*	ranges /	**12,000** (volt-amperes each)	×	**6** (number)	= **8**	**72,000**
Do not include any heating **or air-conditioning** **equipment in this section.**	microwave ovens /	**1200** (volt-amperes each)	×	**6** (number)	= **9**	**7200**
	/	(volt-amperes each)	×	(number)	= **10**	----
	/	(volt-amperes each)	×	(number)	= **11**	----
12 Heating or Air-Conditioning System (Compare the heat and A/C, and omit the smaller.) *220.84(C)(5)* *Include the air handler when using either one.* *For heat pumps, include the compressor and the* *maximum amount of electric heat that can be* *energized while the compressor is running.*		**5345** (volt-amperes each)	×	**6** (number)	= **12**	**32,070**

Ⓑ

© Cengage Learning 2012

Line 13—Total Volt-Ampere Demand Load

Ⓐ Add lines 1 through 12 to find the volt-ampere load before derating.

Ⓑ Find the demand factor, located in Table 220.84, and insert here. The demand factor for a six-unit multifamily dwelling is 44 (44%).

Ⓐ **Ⓑ**

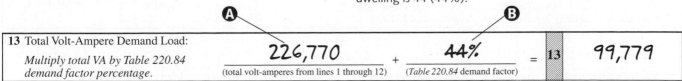

13 Total Volt-Ampere Demand Load: *Multiply total VA by Table 220.84* *demand factor percentage.*	**226,770** (total volt-amperes from lines 1 through 12)	+	**44%** *(Table 220.84 demand factor)*	= **13**	**99,779**

© Cengage Learning 2012

Lines 15 and 16—Minimum Service or Feeder

Ⓐ Place the sum of lines 13 and 14 (total volt-amperes) here. If there is no house load, insert only line 13.

Ⓑ Insert the source voltage supplying the service equipment.

Ⓒ The minimum amperage rating required for conductors and overcurrent protection is 416 (99,779 ÷ 240 = 415.75 = 416).

Ⓓ The minimum service (or feeder) determined by the optional method for these six units is 450 amperes.

Ⓔ The next standard size fuse or breaker above 416 amperes is 450 ≫ *240.6(A)* ≪ .

> **N O T E**
>
> The same six units calculated by the standard method require a rating of 600 amperes.

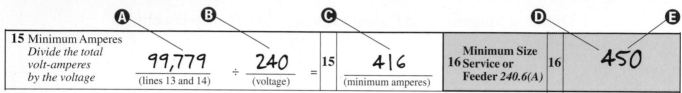

| 15 Minimum Amperes *Divide the total volt-amperes by the voltage* | 99,779
 (lines 13 and 14) | ÷ | 240
 (voltage) | = | 15 | 4\|6
 (minimum amperes) | **Minimum Size**
 16 Service or
 Feeder *240.6(A)* | 16 | *450* |

© Cengage Learning 2012

Line 17—Minimum Size Conductors

Ⓐ Ensure that the total combined rating of paralleled conductors meets or exceeds the minimum calculated load.

Ⓑ At 75°C (167°F), the minimum size conductors for two parallel sets matching or exceeding 416 amperes are 4/0 AWG copper or 300-kcmil aluminum. The minimum rating for each conductor is 208 amperes.

| 17 Size the Service or Feeder Conductors.
 Use 310.15(B)(7) to find the service conductors up to 400 amperes.
 Ratings in excess of 400 amperes shall comply with Table 310.15(B)(16)
 310.15(B)(7) also applies to feeder conductors serving as the main power feeder. | **Minimum Size**
 Conductors | 17 | 4/0 Cu
 300 kcmil Al <br> two paralleled sets |

© Cengage Learning 2012

Lines 18 and 19—Minimum Size Neutral and Grounding Conductors

Ⓐ Since there is no optional method for the neutral conductor calculation, refer to page 242, which gives the neutral for six units. The result requires a minimum rating of 279 amperes, or 140 amperes each for two paralleled conductors.

Ⓑ At 75°C (167°F), the minimum size paralleled conductors are 1/0 AWG copper (with a rating of 150 amperes) *or* 3/0 AWG aluminum (with a rating of 155 amperes) ≫ *Table 310.15(B)(16)* ≪ .

Ⓒ The equivalent area for two paralleled conductors in this calculation is 423.2-kcmil copper (2 × 211,600 ÷ 1000) *or* 600-kcmil aluminum (2 × 300). The minimum size grounding electrode conductor is 1/0 AWG copper *or* 3/0 AWG aluminum ≫ *Table 250.66* ≪ .

| 18 Size the Neutral Conductor *220.61*
 Note: There is no optional method for calculating the neutral conductor.
 310.15(B)(7) states that the neutral service or feeder conductor
 can be smaller than the ungrounded (hot) conductors, provided the
 requirements of 215.2, 220.61, and 230.42 are met.
 250.24(C)(1) states that the neutral shall not be smaller than the
 required grounding electrode conductor specified in Table 250.66. | **Minimum Size**
 Neutral
 Conductor | 18 | 1/0 Cu
 3/0 Al <br> two paralleled sets |
| 19 Size the Grounding Electrode Conductor. *250.66*
 Use line 17 to find the grounding electrode conductor in Table 250.66.
 Size the Equipment Grounding Conductor (for Feeder). *250.122*
 Use line 16 to find the equipment grounding conductor in Table 250.122.
 Equipment grounding conductor types are listed in 250.118. | **Minimum Size**
 Grounding Electrode
 Conductor . . . or . . .
 Equipment Grounding
 Conductor | 19 | 1/0 Cu
 3/0 Al |

© Cengage Learning 2012

The following page shows the completed optional method for a six-unit multifamily dwelling load calculation.

Optional Method Load Calculation for Multifamily Dwellings

1	General Lighting and Receptacle Loads *220.84(C)(1)* *Do not include open porches, garages, or unused or unfinished spaces not adaptable for future use.*	$3 \times$	**1050** (sq ft outside dimensions)	$\times$	**6** (number of units)	= **1**	**18,900**
2	Small-Appliance Branch Circuits *220.84(C)(2)* *At least **two** small-appliance branch circuits must be included. 210.11(C)(1)*	$1500 \times$	**2** (minimum of two)	$\times$	**6** (number of units)	= **2**	**18,000**
3	Laundry Branch Circuit(s) *220.84(C)(2)* *Include at least **one** laundry branch circuit *unless* meeting 210.52(F) Exception No. 1 or 2. 210.11(C)(2)*	$1500 \times$	**1** *(minimum of one)	$\times$	**6** (number of units)	= **3**	**9000**

4 through 11 Appliances and Motors *220.84(C)(3)* and *(4)*	water heaters /	**4500** (volt-amperes each)	$\times$ **6** (number)	= **4**	**27,000**
*Use the nameplate rating of **all** appliances (fastened in place, permanently connected, or connected to a specific circuit),*	dishwashers /	**1200** (volt-amperes each)	$\times$ **6** (number)	= **5**	**7200**
ranges, wall-mounted ovens, counter-mounted cooking units,	disposers /	**900** (volt-amperes each)	$\times$ **6** (number)	= **6**	**5400**
motors, water heaters, and clothes dryers.	clothes dryers /	**5000** (volt-amperes each)	$\times$ **6** (number)	= **7**	**30,000**
Convert any nameplate rating given in amperes to volt-amperes by multiplying the amperes by the rated voltage.	ranges /	**12,000** (volt-amperes each)	$\times$ **6** (number)	= **8**	**72,000**
Do not include any heating or air-conditioning equipment in this section.	microwave ovens /	**1200** (volt-amperes each)	$\times$ **6** (number)	= **9**	**7200**
	/	(volt-amperes each)	$\times$ (number)	= **10**	-----
	/	(volt-amperes each)	$\times$ (number)	= **11**	-----

12	Heating or Air-Conditioning System (Compare the heat and A/C, and omit the smaller.) *220.84(C)(5)* *Include the air handler when using either one. For heat pumps, include the compressor and the maximum amount of electric heat that can be energized while the compressor is running.*	**5345** (volt-amperes each)	$\times$ **6** (number) =	**12**	**32,070**

13	Total Volt-Ampere Demand Load: *Multiply total VA by Table 220.84 demand factor percentage.*	**226,770** (total volt-amperes from lines 1 through 12)	+ **44%** (*Table 220.84* demand factor)	= **13**	**99,779**

14	House Load *(If present, otherwise skip to line 15) Calculate in accordance with Article 220, Part III. Do not include in Table 220.84 demand factors.*	**14** -----

15	Minimum Amperes *Divide the total volt-amperes by the voltage*	**99,779** (lines 13 and 14) $\div$ **240** (voltage) = **15**	**416** (minimum amperes)	**16** Minimum Size Service or Feeder *240.6(A)*	**16**	**450**

17	Size the Service or Feeder Conductors. *Use 310.15(B)(7) to find the service conductors up to 400 amperes. Ratings in excess of 400 amperes shall comply with Table 310.15(B)(16). 310.15(B)(7) also applies to feeder conductors serving as the main power feeder.*	**Minimum Size Conductors**	**17**	4/0 Cu 300 kcmil Al two paralleled sets
18	Size the Neutral Conductor *220.61* **Note: There is no optional method for calculating the neutral conductor.** *310.15(B)(7) states that the neutral service or feeder conductor can be smaller than the ungrounded (hot) conductors, provided the requirements of 215.2, 220.61, and 230.42 are met. 250.24(C)(1) states that the neutral shall not be smaller than the required grounding electrode conductor specified in Table 250.66.*	**Minimum Size Neutral Conductor**	**18**	1/0 Cu 3/0 Al two paralleled sets
19	Size the Grounding Electrode Conductor. *250.66* *Use line 17 to find the grounding electrode conductor in Table 250.66.* Size the Equipment Grounding Conductor (for Feeder). *250.122* *Use line 16 to find the equipment grounding conductor in Table 250.122. Equipment grounding conductor types are listed in 250.118.*	**Minimum Size Grounding Electrode Conductor . . . or . . . Equipment Grounding Conductor**	**19**	1/0 Cu 3/0 Al

OPTIONAL LOAD CALCULATION FOR EACH UNIT OF A MULTIFAMILY DWELLING

Optional Method—One Unit

A The first three lines of both the optional and standard methods of one-family dwelling calculations are identical.

B Although located in a multifamily dwelling, this unit contains one feeder and one panelboard. Therefore, it is calculated in accordance with a one-family dwelling method.

C Under certain conditions, a laundry branch circuit is optional in multifamily dwellings ≫ *210.52(F) Exception No. 1 and 2* ≪.

B

Optional Method Load Calculation for One Multifamily Dwelling Unit

1 General Lighting and Receptacle Loads *220.82(B)(1)* *Do not include open porches, garages, or unused or unfinished spaces not adaptable for future use.*	3 × ___**1050**___ (sq ft outside dimensions)	= 1	**3150**
2 Small-Appliance Branch Circuits *220.82(B)(2)* *At least **two** small-appliance branch circuits must be included. 210.11(C)(1)*	1500 × ___**2**___ (minimum of two)	= 2	**3000**
3 Laundry Branch Circuit(s) *220.82(B)(2)* *Include at least **one** laundry branch circuit *unless meeting 210.52(F) Exception No. 1 or 2. 210.11(C)(2)*	1500 × ___**1**___ *(minimum of one)	= 3	**1500**

© Cengage Learning 2012

Line 4—Appliances

A This section includes appliances (fastened in place, permanently connected, or connected to a specific circuit), ranges, wall-mounted ovens, counter-mounted cooking units, clothes dryers, and water heaters ≫ *220.82(B)(3)* ≪.

B Motors (except air-conditioning motors) are also included in this section ≫ *220.82(B)(4)* ≪.

C Heating and air-conditioning systems are **not** part of this calculation.

D Use the exact nameplate rating of the clothes dryer, even if less than 5000 volt-amperes.

> **NOTE**
>
> Do not apply the demand factors in Table 220.55 to household cooking equipment (ranges, cook tops, and ovens). Instead, list the nameplate ratings as they appear.
>
> Do not increase motor loads by 25% ≫*220.82(B)(4)*≪.

A   **B**   **C**   **D**

4 Appliances *220.82(B)(3) and (4)* *Use the nameplate rating of **all** appliances (fastened in place, permanently connected, or connected to a specific circuit), ranges, ovens, cooktops, motors, and clothes dryers.* *Convert any nameplate rating given in amperes to volt-amperes by multiplying the amperes by the rated voltage.*	*Do not include any heating or air-conditioning equipment in this section.*		Total volt-amperes of all appliances LISTED BELOW	4	**24,800**
	water heater/ **4500**	clothes dryer / **5500**	range / 12,000		
	dishwasher / **1200**	disposer / **900**	microwave oven / 1200		
	/	/	/		
	/	/	/		
	/	/	/		

© Cengage Learning 2012

Line 5—Applying Demand Factors to Lines 1 through 4

A This demand factor is found in 220.82(B).

B The newly calculated load includes everything except the heating and air-conditioning systems (3152 + 3000 + 1500 + 24,800).

C Because the first 10,000 volt-amperes are calculated at 100%, 10,000 is subtracted here.

D The remainder of the load is calculated at 40%.

E The result on line 5 will be part of line 7's calculation.

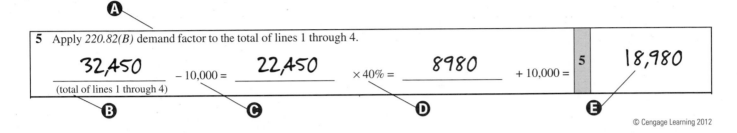

5   Apply *220.82(B)* demand factor to the total of lines 1 through 4.

$$\underset{\text{(total of lines 1 through 4)}}{32,450} - 10,000 = \underline{22,450} \times 40\% = \underline{8980} + 10,000 = \boxed{5} \quad 18,980$$

© Cengage Learning 2012

Line 6—Heating or Air-Conditioning Systems

A The air-conditioner compressor (14 × 230 = 3220 VA), condenser fan motor (2 × 115 = 230 VA), and blower motor (3 × 115 = 345 VA) have a combined load of 3795 volt-amperes. Calculate the air-conditioning system at 100%.

B The electric heat (5000) added to the blower motor (3 × 115 = 345) is 5345 volt-amperes. The heating system is multiplied by 65% and the result placed on line 6d.

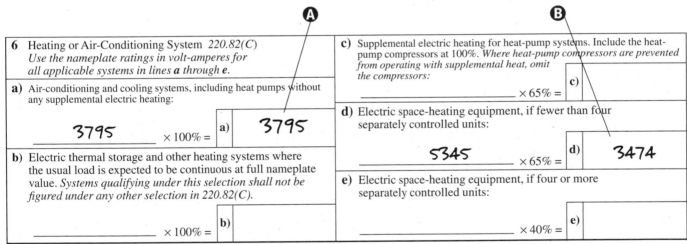

6   Heating or Air-Conditioning System *220.82(C)*
Use the nameplate ratings in volt-amperes for all applicable systems in lines a through e.

a) Air-conditioning and cooling systems, including heat pumps without any supplemental electric heating:

$$\underline{3795} \times 100\% = \boxed{\text{a)} \quad 3795}$$

b) Electric thermal storage and other heating systems where the usual load is expected to be continuous at full nameplate value. *Systems qualifying under this selection shall not be figured under any other selection in 220.82(C).*

$$\underline{\quad} \times 100\% = \boxed{\text{b)}}$$

c) Supplemental electric heating for heat-pump systems. Include the heat-pump compressors at 100%. *Where heat-pump compressors are prevented from operating with supplemental heat, omit the compressors:*

$$\underline{\quad} \times 65\% = \boxed{\text{c)}}$$

d) Electric space-heating equipment, if fewer than four separately controlled units:

$$\underline{5345} \times 65\% = \boxed{\text{d)} \quad 3474}$$

e) Electric space-heating equipment, if four or more separately controlled units:

$$\underline{\quad} \times 40\% = \boxed{\text{e)}}$$

© Cengage Learning 2012

Line 7—Total Volt-Ampere Demand Load

A This is the largest volt-ampere rating of the heating or air-conditioning system(s), after application of demand factors.

B This is the volt-ampere demand load from line 5.

C This is the total volt-ampere load calculated by the optional method. (For comparison, this one-family dwelling calculated by the standard method is 29,048 volt-amperes.)

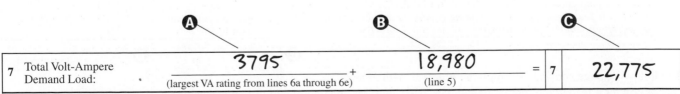

7   Total Volt-Ampere Demand Load:

$$\underset{\text{(largest VA rating from lines 6a through 6e)}}{3795} + \underset{\text{(line 5)}}{18,980} = \boxed{7 \quad 22,775}$$

© Cengage Learning 2012

Lines 8 and 9—Minimum Feeder

A This is the volt-ampere load from line 7.

B This is the source voltage.

C Because the fraction is more than 0.5, the number 94.9 is rounded up to 95.

D The overcurrent protection chosen for this feeder must be higher than the number found on line 8. Standard ampere ratings for fuses and circuit breakers are listed in 240.6(A).

E This dwelling unit, calculated in accordance with the optional method, requires a 100-ampere feeder and panelboard.

F A 100-ampere minimum restriction has been placed on this optional method for both services and feeders ≫ *220.82(A)* ≪ . Feeders calculated in accordance with Article 220, Part III, are not restricted to a minimum rating of 100 amperes.

> **N O T E**
>
> For comparison, this same dwelling unit calculated by the standard method requires a minimum of 125 amperes.

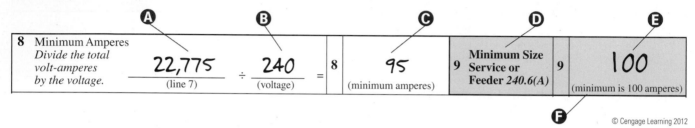

© Cengage Learning 2012

Line 10—Minimum Size Conductors

A Use 310.15(B)(7) to select feeder conductors serving as the main power feeder.

B The minimum size conductors for this dwelling unit are 4 AWG copper *or* 2 AWG aluminum ≫ *Table 310.15(B)(7)* ≪ .

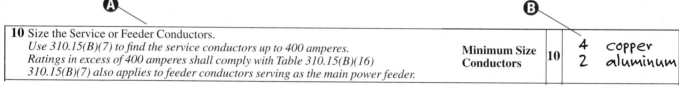

© Cengage Learning 2012

Lines 11 and 12—Minimum Size Neutral and Equipment Grounding Conductors

A Since there is no optional method for neutral calculation, refer to page 246 for a detailed analysis.

B At 75°C (167°F), the minimum size conductor is 4 AWG copper *or* 3 AWG aluminum.

C Because these are feeder, not service, conductors, use Table 250.122 to size the equipment grounding conductor.

D The minimum size equipment grounding conductor for a 100-ampere overcurrent protective device is 8 AWG copper *or* 6 AWG aluminum ≫ *Table 250.122* ≪ .

11 Size the Neutral Conductor. *220.61* **Note: There is no optional method for calculating the neutral conductor.** *310.15(B)(7) states that the neutral service or feeder conductor* *can be smaller than the ungrounded (hot) conductors, provided the* *requirements of 215.2, 220.61, and 230.42 are met.* *250.24(C)(1) states that the neutral shall not be smaller than the* *required grounding electrode conductor specified in Table 250.66.*	Minimum Size Neutral Conductor	11	4 copper 3 aluminum
12 Size the Grounding Electrode Conductor. Table *250.66* *Use line 10 to find the grounding electrode conductor in 250.66.* Size the Equipment Grounding Conductor (for Feeder). *250.122* *Use line 9 to find the equipment grounding conductor in Table 250.122.* *Equipment grounding conductor types are listed in 250.118.*	Minimum Size Grounding Electrode Conductor ... *or* ... Equipment Grounding Conductor	12	8 copper 6 aluminum

© Cengage Learning 2012

The following page shows the completed optional method load calculation for a feeder and remote panelboard (subpanel) for one unit of a multifamily dwelling.

Optional Method Load Calculation for One Multifamily Dwelling Unit

1	General Lighting and Receptacle Loads *220.82(B)(1)* *Do not include open porches, garages, or unused or unfinished spaces not adaptable for future use.*	$3 \times$ ____**1050**____ (sq ft outside dimensions)	= **1**	**3150**
2	Small-Appliance Branch Circuits *220.82(B)(2)* *At least **two** small-appliance branch circuits must be included. 210.11(C)(1)*	$1500 \times$ ____**2**____ (minimum of two)	= **2**	**3000**
3	Laundry Branch Circuit(s) *220.82(B)(2)* *Include at least **one** laundry branch circuit *unless meeting 210.52(F) Exception No. 1 or 2. 210.11(C)(2)*	$1500 \times$ ____**1**____ *(minimum of one)	= **3**	**1500**

4	Appliances *220.82(B)(3) and (4)* *Use the nameplate rating of **all** appliances (fastened in place, permanently connected, or connected to a specific circuit), ranges, ovens, cooktops, motors, and clothes dryers. Convert any nameplate rating given in amperes to volt-amperes by multiplying the amperes by the rated voltage.*	*Do not include any heating or air-conditioning equipment in this section.*	Total volt-amperes of all appliances **LISTED BELOW** **4** **24,800**

water heater / **4500**		clothes dryer / **5500**		range / **12,000**	
dishwasher / **1200**		disposer / **900**		microwave oven / **1200**	
/		/		/	
/		/		/	
/		/		/	

5	Apply *220.82(B)* demand factor to the total of lines 1 through 4. ____**32,450**____ $- 10,000 =$ ____**22,450**____ $\times 40\% =$ ____**8980**____ $+ 10,000 =$ (total of lines 1 through 4)	**5** **18,980**

6 Heating or Air-Conditioning System *220.82(C)* *Use the nameplate ratings in volt-amperes for all applicable systems in lines **a** through **e**.*	**c)** Supplemental electric heating for heat-pump systems. Include the heat-pump compressors at 100%. *Where heat-pump compressors are prevented from operating with supplemental heat, omit the compressors:* _____ $\times 65\% =$ **c)**
a) Air-conditioning and cooling systems, including heat pumps without any supplemental electric heating: ____**3795**____ $\times 100\% =$ **a)** **3795**	**d)** Electric space-heating equipment, if fewer than four separately controlled units: ____**5345**____ $\times 65\% =$ **d)** **3474**
b) Electric thermal storage and other heating systems where the usual load is expected to be continuous at full nameplate value. *Systems qualifying under this selection shall not be figured under any other selection in 220.82(C).* _____ $\times 100\% =$ **b)**	**e)** Electric space-heating equipment, if four or more separately controlled units: _____ $\times 40\% =$ **e)**

7 Total Volt-Ampere Demand Load:	____**3795**____ $+$ ____**18,980**____ $=$ (largest VA rating from lines 6a through 6e) (line 5)	**7** **22,775**

8 Minimum Amperes *Divide the total volt-amperes by the voltage.*	____**22,775**____ $\div$ ____**240**____ $=$ **8** (line 7) (voltage)	**95** (minimum amperes)	**9** Minimum Size Service or Feeder *240.6(A)* **9** **100** (minimum is 100 amperes)

10 Size the Service or Feeder Conductors. *Use 310.15(B)(7) to find the service conductors up to 400 amperes. Ratings in excess of 400 amperes shall comply with Table 310.15(B)(16). 310.15(B)(7) also applies to feeder conductors serving as the main power feeder.*	**Minimum Size Conductors** **10**	**4** copper **2** aluminum
11 Size the Neutral Conductor. *220.61* **Note: There is no optional method for calculating the neutral conductor.** *310.15(B)(7) states that the neutral service or feeder conductor can be smaller than the ungrounded (hot) conductors, provided the requirements of 215.2, 220.61, and 230.42 are met. 250.24(C)(1) states that the neutral shall not be smaller than the required grounding electrode conductor specified in Table 250.66.*	**Minimum Size Neutral Conductor** **11**	**4** copper **3** aluminum
12 Size the Grounding Electrode Conductor. Table *250.66* *Use line 10 to find the grounding electrode conductor in 250.66.* Size the Equipment Grounding Conductor (for Feeder). *250.122* *Use line 9 to find the equipment grounding conductor in Table 250.122. Equipment grounding conductor types are listed in 250.118.*	**Minimum Size Grounding Electrode Conductor ... or ... Equipment Grounding Conductor** **12**	**8** copper **6** aluminum

Summary

- Multifamily dwelling calculations are a progression of the one-family dwelling calculations (standard and optional).
- Some of the information needed for each individual dwelling unit includes total square-foot area, the number of small-appliance branch circuits and laundry branch circuits (if any), appliance ratings, dryer ratings (if any), cooking equipment ratings, and heating and air-conditioning loads.
- Identifying the number of dwelling units supplied by each service or disconnecting means is essential to the performance of multifamily load calculations.
- In certain instances, the laundry branch circuit may be omitted from both the dwelling unit and the calculation.
- Laundry (if installed) and small-appliance branch circuits are calculated using a rating of at least 1500 volt-amperes each.
- Table 220.42 demand factors are applied to general lighting, small-appliance, and laundry loads.
- The total volt-ampere rating of four (or more) fastened-in-place appliances is multiplied by 75% in the standard method calculation.

- Demand factors for household electric clothes dryers are found in Table 220.54.
- Table 220.55 lists the demand loads for household cooking appliances (over 1¾-kW rating).
- The heating and air-conditioning loads are compared, and the larger of the two is used.
- For heat pumps, include the compressor and the maximum amount of electric heat that can be energized while the compressor is running.
- Two multifamily load calculation methods are provided in Article 220: **Standard** and **Optional.**
- The neutral conductor can be smaller than the ungrounded (hot) conductors, provided the requirements of 215.2, 220.61, and 230.42 are met.
- Table 250.66 is used to size grounding electrode conductors.
- Remote panelboards (subpanels) require equipment grounding conductors, which can be one, more, or a combination of the types listed in 250.118.
- Equipment grounding conductors are sized in accordance with Table 250.122.

Unit 11 Competency Test

NEC Reference	Answer	
_____	_____	1. One unit in a multifamily dwelling has a 125-ampere, 240-volt panelboard fed with 75°C (167°F) conductors. What is the minimum size aluminum equipment grounding conductor required?
_____	_____	2. What is the dryer demand load (in kW) for a twenty-five-unit multifamily dwelling with a 4.5-kW clothes dryer in each unit? (The service is 120/240-volt, single-phase.)
_____	_____	3. A four-unit apartment has the following ranges: a 15 kW, a 14 kW, a 10 kW, and a 9 kW. What is the kW demand load added to the service by these ranges?
_____	_____	4. An eighteen-unit multifamily dwelling contains the following appliances in each unit: a 1-kVA, 115-volt dishwasher; a ⅓-HP, 115-volt waste (garbage) disposer; and a 4500-watt, 230-volt water heater. Using the standard method, what is the service neutral load contribution, in volt-amperes, for these appliances? (Assume water heater watt rating equivalent to volt-ampere.)
_____	_____	5. A multifamily dwelling's service-entrance conductors consist of four paralleled sets of 3/0 AWG THHN copper conductors. What size copper grounding electrode conductor is required?
_____	_____	6. A 5.4-kVA, 240-volt clothes dryer will contribute _____ amperes to the neutral load, when calculating the service by the standard method.
_____	_____	7. What is the minimum kW service demand load for twenty 6.5-kW ranges in a multifamily dwelling?

NEC Reference   Answer

_____ _____   8. An apartment has 3000 watts allocated for general lighting and receptacles. How many 15-ampere circuits are required? (The apartment contains laundry facilities.)

_____ _____   9. Two paralleled sets of 500-kcmil copper service-entrance conductors supply a multifamily dwelling disconnecting means. What is the minimum size aluminum grounding electrode conductor required?

_____ _____   10. A fifty-unit apartment building has a 4.5-kW clothes dryer in each apartment. By using the optional method, what is the service demand load?

Questions 11 through 18 are based on a 120/240-volt, 3-wire, single-phase, eight-unit multifamily dwelling. The eight identical units contain the following:

Floor area . . . . 1200 ft²   Electric heat . . . . 4.2 kW, 240 volt
Range. 8¾ kW, 240 volt   Air handler (blower motor) . . . . ¼ hp, 115 volt
Water heater . . . . 4 kW, 240 volt   Air-conditioner compressor . . . . 3 hp, 230 volt
Dishwasher . . . . 1 kW, 120 volt   Condenser fan motor. . . . . ⅙ hp, 115 volt
Clothes dryer . . . . 5 kW, 240 volt

Assume water heater, clothes dryer, range, and electric heat kW ratings equivalent to kVA.

Using Article 220, Parts II and III (the standard method):

_____ _____   11. What is the service demand load for the clothes dryers?

_____ _____   12. What is the service demand load for the cooking appliances?

_____ _____   13. Of the heating or air-conditioning (and associated motors), which is omitted?

_____ _____   14. What is the minimum rating (in amperes) for the service overcurrent device?

_____ _____   15. A parallel run (two sets) of service-entrance conductors will be installed in two raceways. What is the minimum size THWN copper ungrounded conductors that can be used?

_____ _____   16. What is the minimum rating (in amperes) for the neutral conductors?

_____ _____   17. What is the minimum size THWN copper neutral (grounded) conductors that can be installed?

_____ _____   18. What is the minimum size copper grounding electrode conductor?

Questions 19 through 22 are based on a 120/240-volt, 3-wire, single-phase, six-unit multifamily dwelling. The six identical units contain the following:

Floor area . . . . 1350 ft²   Clothes dryer . . . . 4 kW, 240 volt
Range. 10.6 kW, 240 volt   Electric heat (two banks at 3 kW each). . 6 kW, 240 volt
Water heater . . . . 4.2 kW, 240 volt   Air handler (blower motor) . . . . ⅓ hp, 115 volt
Dishwasher . . . . 1.2 kW, 120 volt   Air-conditioner compressor . . . . 3 hp, 230 volt
Garbage disposer . . . . ⅓ hp, 115 volt   Condenser fan motor. . . . . ⅙ hp, 115 volt

Assume water heater, clothes dryer, range, and electric heat kW ratings equivalent to kVA.

Using the Optional Method:

_____ _____   19. What is the minimum rating (in amperes) for the service overcurrent device?

_____ _____   20. What is the minimum size THWN copper ungrounded conductors that can be installed? (Do not parallel the conductors.)

_____ _____   21. What is the minimum size THWN copper neutral (grounded) conductor that can be installed?

_____ _____   22. What is the minimum acceptable size copper grounding electrode conductor?

UNIT 12

General Provisions

Objectives

After studying this unit, the student should:

▶ know that commercial occupancy receptacle placement differs from that of one-family and multifamily dwellings.

▶ understand that commercial bathrooms do not require receptacle outlets.

▶ be aware that each commercial building (or occupancy) accessible to pedestrians must have at least one sign outlet.

▶ be familiar with Article 430 motor provisions.

▶ know that air-conditioning and refrigeration provisions are found in Article 440.

▶ be able to determine receptacle volt-ampere ratings for single, duplex, quad, etc.

▶ know the maximum number of receptacles permitted on 15- and 20-ampere branch circuits.

▶ be aware that at least two receptacle outlets must be readily accessible in guest rooms of hotels, motels, and similar occupancies.

▶ thoroughly understand showcase and show window provisions.

▶ be able to determine an occupancy's general lighting load based on square-foot area.

▶ be familiar with fluorescent, HID, recessed, and track-lighting provisions.

▶ understand that while certain luminaires can be used as raceways, the number of branch circuits permitted therein is limited.

▶ know that a metal pole supporting a luminaire(s) requires a handhole, unless an exception is met.

Introduction

The broad topic of commercial wiring encompasses many types of structures—office buildings, restaurants, stores, schools, and warehouses, to name a few. In fact, most of the occupancies found in Table 220.12 are indeed commercial. Many of the electrical requirements that apply to one-family and multifamily dwellings also apply to commercial and industrial locations. Because this overlap of requirements is common, it is especially important to begin with a solid understanding of not only some but all of the preceding material. Of particular importance are Units 3 through 5 of Section 1, which contain fundamental principles applicable to all types of occupancies. In addition, Unit 9—Services and Electrical Equipment explains one-family dwelling provisions that extend into the realm of commercial wiring systems. Unit 12—General Provisions likewise covers overlapping topics, such as branch circuits, receptacles, and lighting. Because it would be very difficult, if not impossible, to cover such a large field as commercial wiring in the framework of this text, only a small but representative portion is presented. Unit 13—Nondwelling Load Calculations explains nondwelling (inclusive of commercial) load calculations, which are helpful in determining service and feeder loads. Complete subsequent units, and portions of others, apply to commercial wiring as well.

The inception of most commercial electrical projects includes multifaceted plans (blueprints) and detailed specifications. As a reference, illustrations for a retail store's electrical and lighting floor plans are provided. Various general provisions (branch circuits, receptacles, lighting, etc.) and numerous specific provisions (required receptacle outlets, show windows, showcases, etc.) are discussed. Proper receptacle placement is demonstrated through the use of a hotel/motel guest room floor plan, including furniture placement. Receptacle and lighting branch-circuit load calculations are also part of this unit.

While this unit is by no means a complete reference for commercial electrical wiring, taken together with the extensive information presented throughout this text, it does provide a substantial foundation toward understanding commercial electrical wiring systems.

BRANCH CIRCUITS

Required Sign Outlet

The disconnecting means must be within sight of the sign or outline lighting system that it controls. If out of the line of sight from any section that is able to be energized, the disconnecting means must be capable of locking in the open position **》600.6(A)(1)《**.

Signs or outline lighting systems operated by external electronic or electromechanical controllers can have a disconnecting means located within sight of the controller or within the controller enclosure. The disconnecting means must disconnect both the sign (or outline lighting system) and the controller from all ungrounded supply conductors. It must be designed so that no pole operates independently and it must be capable of locking in the open position **》600.6(A)(2)《**.

> ### NOTE
>
> Service hallways or corridors are not considered accessible to pedestrians **》600.5(A)《**.
>
> Switches, flashers, and similar devices controlling transformers and electronic power supplies must either be rated for controlling inductive loads or have a current rating not less than twice the transformer's current rating **》600.6(B)《**.

Ⓐ Each commercial building and occupancy open to pedestrians must have at least one accessible outlet at every entrance to each tenant space for sign or outline lighting systems use **》600.5(A)《**.

Ⓑ The outlet(s) must be supplied by a branch circuit rated 20 amperes or more and that supplies no other load **》600.5(A)《**.

Ⓒ Each sign and outline lighting system, feeder or branch circuit supplying a sign, outline lighting system, or skeleton tubing must be controlled by an externally operable switch (or circuit breaker) that opens all ungrounded conductors and controls no other load, unless (1) the sign is an exit directional sign located within a building or (2) the sign is cord-connected with an attachment plug. The switch or circuit breaker shall open all ungrounded conductors simultaneously on multiwire branch circuits in accordance with 210.4(B) **》600.6《**.

Ⓓ Sign and outline lighting outlets must be calculated at a minimum of 1200 volt-amperes per required branch circuit specified in 600.5(A) **》220.14(F)《**.

> ### CAUTION
>
> The provision for locking or adding a lock to the disconnecting means must remain in place at the switch or circuit breaker whether the lock is installed or not. Portable means for adding a lock to the switch or circuit breaker shall not be permitted **》600.6(A)(1) and (A)(2)(3)《**.

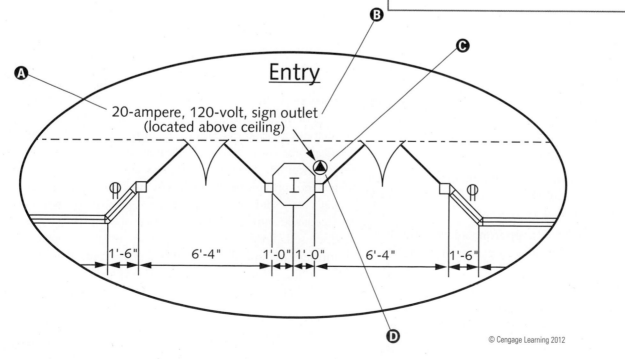

Commercial (Retail) Occupancy

Branch circuits recognized by Article 210 must be rated in accordance with the maximum permitted ampere rating (or setting) of the overcurrent device. Circuits, other than individual branch circuits, must be rated 15, 20, 30, 40, and 50 amperes. If higher ampacity conductors are used for any reason, the ampere rating (or setting) of the specified overcurrent device determines the circuit rating ≫*210.3*≪.

Branch-circuit conductors must have an ampacity not less than the maximum load served. In a branch circuit supplying continuous loads, or any combination of continuous and noncontinuous loads, the minimum branch-circuit conductor size (before the application of any adjustment or correction factors) must have an allowable ampacity equal to or greater than the noncontinuous load plus 125% of the continuous load ≫*210.19(A)(1)*≪.

Equipment and branch-circuit conductors must be protected by overcurrent protective devices rated in compliance with 210.20(A) through (D) ≫*210.20*≪.

Outlet devices must have an ampere rating not less than the load served and must comply with 210.21(A) and (B) ≫*210.21*≪.

The requirements for circuits that have two or more outlets or receptacles, other than the receptacle circuits of 210.11(C)(1), (C)(2), and (C)(3), are summarized in Table 210.24 ≫*210.24*≪.

The minimum number of branch circuits is determined from the total computed load and the size (or rating) of the circuits used. In all installations, the number of circuits must be sufficient to supply the load served. In no case can the load on any circuit exceed the maximum specified by 220.18 ≫*210.11(A)*≪.

Article 210 covers branch circuits with the exception of branch circuits supplying only motor loads. These are covered in Article 430. Articles 210 and 430 provisions apply to branch circuits that have combination loads ≫*210.1*≪.

A A unit load at least equal to that shown in Table 220.12 for a specified occupancy constitutes the minimum lighting load for each square foot of floor area. Floor area (for each floor) is calculated using the outside dimensions of the building, dwelling unit, or other area involved. The minimum general lighting load for a store is 3 volt-amperes per square foot ≫*220.12*≪. The minimum general lighting load for this retail space is 3726 volt-amperes (27 × 46 = 1242 × 3 = 3726).

B No receptacle wall placement provisions exist for commercial occupancies. The "6-ft rule," which is the maximum distance to a receptacle (measured horizontally along the wall), applies only to dwelling units ≫*210.52(A)*≪.

C Receptacles are not required in nondwelling bathrooms. If installed, however, they must be GFCI protected ≫*210.8(B)(1)*≪.

D Where the premises wiring system has branch circuits supplied from more than one nominal voltage system, each ungrounded (hot) conductor of a branch circuit must be identified by phase or line and system at all termination, connection, and splice points. The identification method can be separate color coding, marking tape, tagging, or other approved means. The method utilized for conductors originating within each branch-circuit panelboard or similar branch-circuit distribution equipment must be documented in a manner that is readily available or must be permanently posted at each branch-circuit panelboard on similar branch-circuit distribution equipment ≫*210.5(C)*≪.

> **NOTE**
>
> Refer to 210.2 for a list of other articles (and sections) pertaining to branch-circuit requirements. The provisions for branch circuits supplying equipment in that list amend or supplement Article 210 provisions and apply to the referenced branch circuits ≫*210.2*≪.

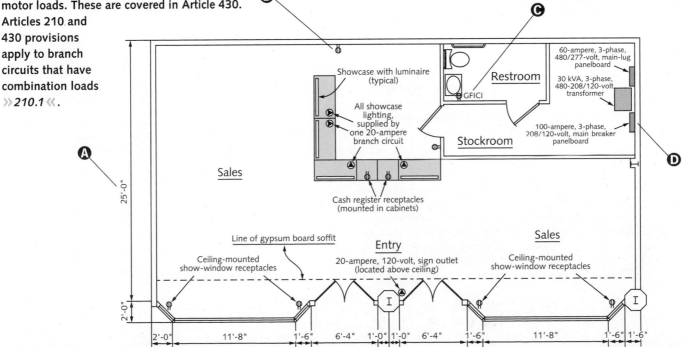

© Cengage Learning 2012

Showcases

Ⓐ Individual moveable showcases can be connected by flexible cord to permanently installed receptacles. Groups of not more than six such showcases can be coupled together (by flexible cord and separable locking-type connectors) provided one of the group is connected (by flexible cord) to a permanently installed receptacle. The installation must comply with 410.59(A) through (E) ≫*410.59*≪.

Ⓑ Flexible cords must be secured to showcase undersides so that (1) wiring will not be exposed to physical damage; (2) cases cannot separate more than 2 in. (50 mm), nor can the first case extend more than 12 in. (300 mm) from the supply receptacle; and (3) the free lead at the end of the showcase group has a female fitting that does not extend beyond the case ≫*410.59(C)*≪.

Ⓒ In cord-connected showcases, the secondary circuit(s) of each electric-discharge lighting ballast is (are) limited to one showcase ≫*410.59(E)*≪.

Ⓓ Flexible cord must be hard-service type, have conductors not smaller than the branch-circuit overcurrent device, and have an equipment grounding conductor ≫*410.59(A)*≪.

Ⓔ Receptacles, connectors, and attachment plugs must be of a listed grounding type, rated 15 or 20 amperes ≫*410.59(B)*≪.

Ⓕ Unless used in wiring of chain-supported luminaires or as supply cords for portable

lamps and other merchandise being displayed or exhibited, flexible cords used in showcases and show windows must be Type S, SE, SEO, SEOO, SJ, SJE, SJEO, SJEOO, SJO, SJOO, SJT, SJTO, SJTOO, SO, SOO, ST, STO, STOO, SEW, SEOW, SEOOW, SJEW, SJEOW, SJEOOW, SJOW, SJOOW, SJTW, SJTOW, SJTOOW, SOW, SOOW, STW, STOW, or STOOW ≫*400.11*≪.

> **NOTE**
>
> Other equipment must not be electrically connected to showcases ≫*410.59(D)*≪.

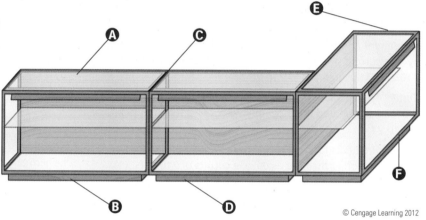

© Cengage Learning 2012

Motor Loads

Article 430 covers motors, motor branch-circuit and feeder conductors and their protection, motor overload protection, motor control circuits, motor controllers, and motor control centers ≫*430.1*≪.

Ⓐ Motor load outlets must be calculated in accordance with 430.22, 430.24, and 440.6 ≫*220.14(C)*≪.

Ⓑ If a circuit supplies only motor-operated loads, apply Article 430 ≫*220.18(A)*≪.

Ⓒ Branch-circuit conductors supplying a single motor, used in a continuous duty application, must have an ampacity of not less than 125% of the motor full-load current rating as determined by 430.6(A)(1), or not less than specified in 430.22(A) through (G) ≫*430.22*≪.

> **NOTE**
>
> Conductors for a motor used in a short-time, intermittent, periodic, or varying-duty application must have an ampacity of not less than the percentage of the motor nameplate current rating shown in Table 430.22(E), unless the AHJ grants special permission for lower ampacity conductors ≫*430.22(E)*≪. Any motor application is considered continuous duty unless the nature of the apparatus driven is such that the motor will not operate continuously with load under any condition of use ≫*Note under Table 430.22(E)*≪.

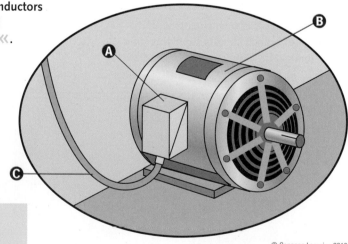

© Cengage Learning 2012

Motor-Operated and Combination Loads

A For circuits supplying loads consisting of motor-operated utilization equipment (fastened in place with a motor larger than $\frac{1}{8}$ hp) in combination with other loads, the total calculated load must be based on 125% of the largest motor load plus the sum of the other loads ≫ *220.18(A)* ≪.

B Because equipment such as room air-conditioners, household refrigerators and freezers, drinking water coolers, and beverage dispensers are considered appliances, Article 422 provisions also apply ≫ *440.3(C)* ≪.

C For cord- and plug-connected appliances, an accessible, separable connector or an accessible plug and receptacle can serve as the disconnecting means. Where the separable connector or plug and receptacle are not accessible, cord- and plug-connected appliances must be provided with a disconnecting means in accordance with 422.31 ≫ *422.33(A)* ≪.

D The rating of a receptacle or a separable connector must not be less than the rating of any connected appliance ≫ *422.33(C)* ≪.

E This is a branch circuit, consisting of two duplex receptacles.

F If supplied by a 20-ampere circuit, this drinking fountain's maximum rating is 10 amperes (20 × 50%). If supplied by a 15-ampere circuit, the maximum rating is 7.5 (15 × 50%).

G This is a receptacle outlet for cord- and plug-connected, non-fastened-in-place utilization equipment.

H The receptacle outlet is fed from a dedicated branch circuit.

I If supplied by a 20-ampere circuit, the maximum rating for this copy machine is 16 amperes (20 × 80%). If supplied by a 15-ampere circuit, the maximum rating is 12 amperes (15 × 80%).

J For cord-connected equipment such as room air-conditioners, household refrigerators (and freezers), drinking water coolers, and beverage dispensers, a separable connector or an attachment plug and receptacle can serve as the disconnecting means ≫ *440.13* ≪.

NOTE

A 15- or 20-ampere branch circuit can supply lighting units, other utilization equipment, or a combination of both. The rating of any one cord- and plug-connected utilization equipment that is not fastened in place must not exceed 80% of the branch-circuit ampere rating. The total rating of utilization equipment fastened in place (other than luminaires) cannot exceed 50% of the branch-circuit ampere rating in the event that lighting units, cord- and plug-connected utilization equipment not fastened in place, or both are also supplied ≫ *210.23(A)* ≪.

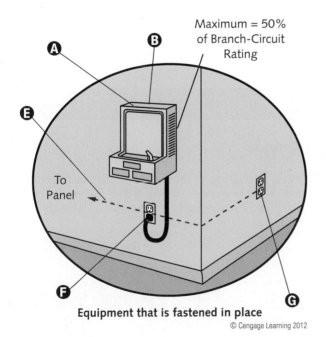

Equipment that is fastened in place
© Cengage Learning 2012

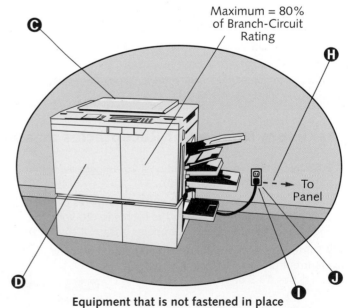

Equipment that is not fastened in place
© Cengage Learning 2012

Air-Conditioning and Refrigeration Equipment

Article 440, Part II, provisions require a means capable of disconnecting air-conditioning and refrigerating equipment (including motor compressors and controllers) from the circuit conductors ≫ *440.11* ≪.

The provisions of Article 440, Part III, specify devices intended to protect the branch-circuit conductors, control apparatus, and motors in circuits supplying hermetic refrigerant motor compressors against overcurrent due to short circuits and ground faults. These provisions amend or supplement those in Article 240 ≫ *440.21* ≪.

Article 310 and Article 440, Part IV, provisions specify conductor ampacities required to carry the motor current (without overheating) under the conditions specified, except as modified in 440.6(A), Exception No. 1 ≫ *440.31* ≪.

Article 440, Part VI, specifies devices intended to protect the motor compressor, the motor-control apparatus, and the branch-circuit conductors against excessive heating due to motor overload and failure to start ≫ *440.51* ≪.

A Motor load outlets must be calculated in accordance with the requirements in 430.22, 430.24, and 440.6 ≫ *220.14(C)* ≪.

B Where a circuit supplies only air-conditioning equipment, refrigeration equipment, or both, apply Article 440 ≫ *220.18(A)* ≪.

C Disconnecting means must be located within sight and readily accessible from the air-conditioning or refrigerating equipment. The disconnecting means can be installed on or within the equipment ≫ *440.14* ≪.

D For a hermetic refrigerant motor compressor, the rated-load current marked on the nameplate of the equipment in which the motor compressor is employed must be used in determining the rating or ampacity of the disconnecting means, the branch-circuit conductors, the controller, the branch-circuit

short-circuit and ground-fault protection, and the separate motor overload protection. Where no rated-load current is shown on the equipment nameplate, use the rated-load current shown on the compressor nameplate ≫ *440.6(A)* ≪.

E Article 440 provisions apply to electric motor-driven air-conditioning and refrigerating equipment, and to their branch circuits and controllers. It provides the special considerations necessary for circuits supplying hermetic refrigerant motor compressors and for any air-conditioning or refrigerating equipment supplied from a branch circuit that also supplies a hermetic refrigeration motor compressor ≫ *440.1* ≪.

> **CAUTION**
>
> The disconnecting means must not be located on panels that are designed to allow access to the air-conditioning or refrigeration equipment or to obscure the equipment name plate(s) ≫ *440.14* ≪.

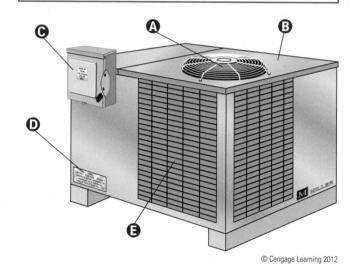

© Cengage Learning 2012

RECEPTACLES

Maximum Number of Receptacles on a Branch Circuit

A Ten receptacles are permitted on a 15-ampere overcurrent protective device ($15 \div 1.5 = 10$).

B Receptacles are calculated at 180 volt-amperes per strap ≫ *220.14(I)* ≪. Therefore, when the source is 120 volts, the rating of each receptacle is 1.5 amperes ($180 \div 120 = 1.5$).

C Thirteen receptacles are permitted on a 20-ampere overcurrent protective device ($20 \div 1.5 = 13.3$ or 13).

D A load having the maximum level of current sustained for three hours or more is referred to as a continuous load. A general-purpose receptacle is not a continuous load ≫ *Article 100* ≪.

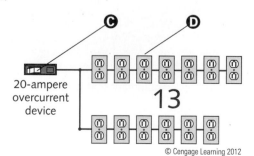

© Cengage Learning 2012

Nondwelling Receptacle Placement

Ⓐ Dwelling unit receptacles must be installed so that no point along the floor line in any wall space is more than 6 ft (1.8 m), measured horizontally, from a receptacle outlet in that space »*210.52(A)(1)*«.

Ⓑ Receptacle outlets in hotels, motels, sleeping rooms in dormitories, and similar occupancy must be installed in accordance with 210.52(A) and (D). Guest rooms or guest suites provided with permanent provisions for cooking shall have receptacle outlets installed in accordance with all of the applicable rules in 210.52 »*210.60(A)*«.

Ⓒ Although no provisions pertain to nondwelling general receptacle placement (except hotel and motel guest rooms and suites), certain requirements exist for specific occupancies or areas. Examples include but are not limited to show windows »*210.62*«; rooftop, attic, and crawl space receptacle outlets for servicing heating, air-conditioning, and refrigeration equipment »*210.63*«; and health care patient bed location receptacles »*517.18(B)*«.

Ⓓ Generally speaking, there are no receptacle placement provisions for nondwelling occupancies.

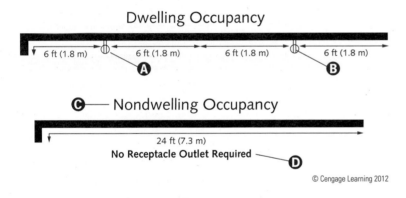

© Cengage Learning 2012

Bathroom Receptacles

Ⓐ Nondwelling bathrooms do not require receptacles. A bathroom receptacle is required only in dwelling units, hotel or motel guest rooms, and sleeping rooms in dormitories »*210.52(D)* and *210.60(A)*«.

Ⓑ Where installed, 125-volt, single-phase, 15- and 20-ampere bathroom receptacles must have GFCI protection for personnel »*210.8(B)(1)*«.

> **N O T E**
>
> GFCIs are designed to trip when a 4– through 6-milliampere (0.004– through 0.006-ampere) difference between the ungrounded (hot) conductor and grounded conductor occurs.

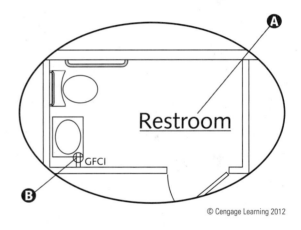

© Cengage Learning 2012

Fixed Multioutlet Assemblies

Ⓐ Where appliances are unlikely to be used simultaneously, each 5 ft (1.5 m) or fraction thereof (of separate and continuous length) shall be considered one outlet of not less than 180 volt-amperes »*220.14(H)(1)*«.

Ⓑ Because fixed multioutlet assemblies used in dwelling units or hotel and motel guest rooms and suites are included in the general lighting load calculation, no additional load calculation is required »*220.14(H)*«.

Ⓒ Where appliances are likely to be used simultaneously, each 1 ft (300 mm) or fraction thereof shall be considered one outlet of not less than 180 volt-amperes »*220.14(H)(2)*«.

Ⓓ It is not stipulated that each receptacle be rated 180 volt-amperes. This illustration shows one receptacle per foot; therefore, each receptacle is rated 180 volt-amperes. Multioutlet assemblies with two receptacles per ft (6 in. [150 mm] on center) have a rating of 180 volt-amperes for two receptacles.

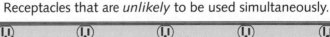

Receptacles that are *unlikely* to be used simultaneously.

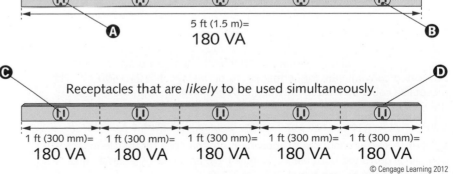

Receptacles that are *likely* to be used simultaneously.

© Cengage Learning 2012

Receptacle Volt-Ampere Rating

A Except as covered in one-, two-, and multifamily dwellings, and in hotel and motel guest rooms and suites, receptacle outlets must be computed at not less than 180 volt-amperes for each single or multiple receptacle on one yoke >> *220.14(I)* <<.

B A single piece of equipment (consisting of four or more receptacles) must be calculated at not less than 90 volt-amperes per receptacle >> *220.14(I)* <<.

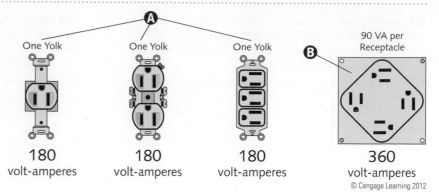

180
volt-amperes

180
volt-amperes

180
volt-amperes

360
volt-amperes

© Cengage Learning 2012

Provisions for Hotel and Motel Guest Rooms and Suites

When performing service (or feeder) calculations, use Table 220.42 to derate hotel and motel (include apartment houses without cooking equipment) guest room lighting and receptacle loads. Do not apply Table 220.42 demand factors to areas where all lighting will probably be used at one time. Examples include but are not limited to office, lobby, restaurant, hallway, and parking areas.

A GFCI protection is required for every 125-volt bathroom receptacle >> *210.8(A)(1)* <<.

B Hallways of less than 10 ft (3.0 m) in length do not require a receptacle >> *210.52(H)* <<.

C At least one wall switch–controlled lighting outlet or receptacle must be installed in hotel, motel, or similar occupancy guest rooms or suites >> *210.70(B)* <<.

D Receptacles must be installed so that no point along the floor line of any wall space is more than 6 ft (1.8 m), measured horizontally, from an outlet in that space >> *210.52(A)(1)* <<. (See 210.60(B) provisions allowing a greater distance due to permanent luminaire layout.)

E Guest rooms or suites in hotels, motels, sleeping rooms in dormitories, and similar occupancies must have receptacle outlets installed in accordance with 210.52 (dwelling unit receptacle provisions) >> *210.60(A)* <<. (See Units 6 and 7 in this book for dwelling unit receptacle requirements.)

F Locate at least one wall receptacle within 36 in. (900 mm) of the outside edge of each basin (lavatory or sink). The receptacle outlet must be located on a wall adjacent to the basin >> *210.52(D)* <<.

G Section 410.10(D) contains bathtub and shower area lighting provisions. (See the illustrated explanation in Unit 7 of this book.)

H Receptacles installed behind the bed must either be positioned so that the bed does not contact any installed attachment plug, or the receptacle must include a suitable guard >> *210.60(B)* <<.

I The total number of receptacle outlets must comply with the minimum number of receptacles provision of 210.52(A). These receptacle outlets can be located conveniently for permanent furniture layout >> *210.60(B)* <<. This receptacle could be located between the beds, even though the distance to the receptacle behind the desk exceeds 12 ft (3.7 m).

J At least two receptacle outlets must be readily accessible >> *210.60(B)* <<.

K Branch-circuit conductors supplying more than one receptacle for cord-and plug-connected portable loads must have an ampacity at least equal to the rating of the branch circuit >> *210.19(A)(2)* <<.

NOTE

Hotels, motels, and similar occupancies having guest kitchen facilities must meet 210.52(B) and (C) provisions. It is not required that occupants in hotel/motel guest rooms or suites that are intended for transient occupancy have ready access to all overcurrent devices protecting conductors supplying their room >> *240.24(B)(1)* <<.

CAUTION

In dwelling units, dormitories, and guest rooms or guest suites, overcurrent devices (other than supplementary overcurrent protection) shall not be located in bathrooms as defined in Article 100 >> *240.24(E)* <<.

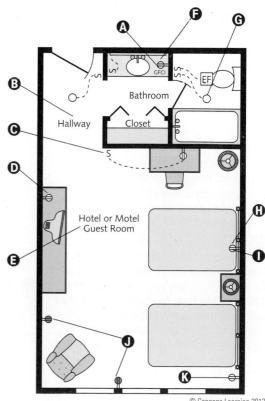

Bathroom

Hallway   Closet

Hotel or Motel
Guest Room

© Cengage Learning 2012

Show Windows

A *show window* is any window designed or used for the display of goods or advertising material, whether it is fully or partly enclosed or entirely open at the rear, and whether or not it has a platform raised higher than the street floor level » *Article 100* «.

Unless used in wiring of chain-supported luminaires, or as supply cords for portable lamps and other merchandise being displayed or exhibited, flexible cords used in showcases and show windows must be Type S, SE, SEO, SEOO, SJ, SJE, SJEO, SJEOO, SJO, SJOO, SJT, SJTO, SJTOO, SO, SOO, ST, STO, STOO, SEW, SEOW, SEOOW, SJEW, SJEOW, SJEOOW, SJOW, SJOOW, SJTW, SJTOW, SJTOOW, SOW, SOOW, STW, STOW, or STOOW » *400.11* «.

A Show-window branch-circuit loads must be calculated either by (a) the unit load per outlet as required by other provisions of 220.14 or (b) at 200 volt-amperes per linear foot » *220.14(G)* «.

B At least one receptacle outlet must be installed within 18 in. (450 mm) of the top of a show window for each 12 linear ft (3.7 m)—or major fraction thereof—of window area measured horizontally at its widest point » *210.62* «.

C The second method for calculating show-window branch-circuit loads is to multiply each show-window linear foot (or major fraction thereof) by 200 volt-amperes (2 + 11.5 + 2 = 15.5 = 16 linear ft . . . 16 × 200 = 3200 volt-amperes) » *220.14(G)* «.

D One of two methods for calculating show-window branch-circuit loads is to multiply each receptacle by 180 volt-amperes (180 × 2 = 360 volt-amperes) » *220.14(G)* and *(I)* «.

E Complete show-window feeder and/or service loads using a minimum rating of 200 volt-amperes for each linear ft of window, measured horizontally along its base (16 × 200 = 3200 volt-amperes) » *220.43(A)* «.

CAUTION

Where receptacles are installed in the floor, the boxes that house the receptacles must be listed specifically for the application » *314.27(B)* «.

NOTE

Where the AHJ judges them free from likely exposure to physical damage, moisture, and dirt, boxes located in **elevated floors of show windows** and similar locations can be other than those listed for floor applications. Receptacles and covers must be listed as an assembly for this type of location » *314.27(B) Exception* «.

Electric signs (including neon tubing) and associated wiring within show windows must comply with Article 600.

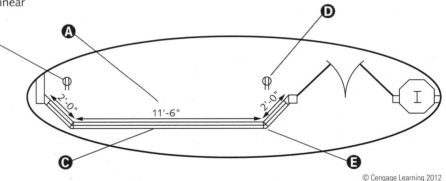

© Cengage Learning 2012

LIGHTING

Lampholder Installations

A Lampholders of the screw shell type shall be installed for use as lampholders only » *410.90* «.

B If the supply circuit has a grounded conductor, the grounded conductor must be connected to the screw shell » *410.90* «.

NOTE

Lampholders installed in wet locations shall be listed for use in wet locations. Lampholders installed in damp locations shall be listed for damp locations or shall be listed for wet locations » *410.96* «.

WARNING

Lampholders shall be constructed, installed, or equipped with shades or guards so that combustible material is not subjected to temperatures in excess of 90°C (194°F) » *410.97* «.

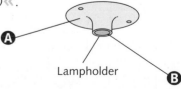

Lampholder

© Cengage Learning 2012

Reflective Ceiling/Lighting Plan

Branch circuits recognized by Article 210 must be rated in accordance with the maximum permitted overcurrent device ampere rating (or setting) ⟩⟩*210.3*⟨⟨.

Branch circuits for lighting and appliances (including motor-operated appliances) shall be provided to supply the loads calculated in accordance with 220.10 ⟩⟩*210.11*⟨⟨.

Branch-circuit conductor ampacity must meet or exceed the maximum load being served. Where a branch circuit supplies continuous loads, or any combination of continuous and noncontinuous loads, the minimum *branch-circuit conductor* size before the application of any adjustment or correction factors shall have an allowable ampacity equal to or greater than the noncontinuous load plus 125% of the continuous load ⟩⟩*210.19(A)(1)*⟨⟨.

Where a branch circuit supplies continuous loads, or any combination of continuous and noncontinuous loads, the rating of the *overcurrent device* must not be less than the noncontinuous load plus 125% of the continuous load ⟩⟩*210.20(A)*⟨⟨.

A 15- or 20-ampere branch circuit can supply lighting units or other utilization equipment, or a combination of both ⟩⟩*210.23(A)*⟨⟨.

Wall switch–controlled lighting outlets are not required in commercial occupancies, except for attic and underfloor spaces containing equipment that requires servicing ⟩⟩*210.70(C)*⟨⟨.

A unit load meeting Table 220.12 specifications for listed occupancies constitutes the minimum lighting load for each square foot of floor area. The area for each floor must be calculated using the outside dimensions of the building, dwelling unit, or other area involved ⟩⟩*220.12*⟨⟨.

Supplementary overcurrent protection used for luminaires, appliances, and other equipment (including internal circuits and components) must not be used as a substitute for required branch-circuit overcurrent devices or in place of the branch-circuit protection. Ready accessibility is not required for supplementary overcurrent devices ⟩⟩*240.10*⟨⟨.

A 30-, 40-, or 50-ampere branch circuit can supply fixed lighting units with heavy-duty lampholders in other than dwelling unit(s) ⟩⟩*210.23(B) and (C)*⟨⟨.

Lighting outlet loads must not be supplied by branch circuits larger than 50 amperes ⟩⟩*210.23(D)*⟨⟨.

A For circuits of over 250 volts to ground, the electrical continuity of metal raceways and cables with metal sheaths containing any conductor other than service conductors shall be ensured by one or more of the methods specified for services in 250.92(B) except for (B)(1) ⟩⟩*250.97*⟨⟨.

B Circuit breakers used as switches in 120-volt and 277-volt fluorescent lighting circuits shall be listed and shall be marked SWD or HID ⟩⟩*240.83(D)*⟨⟨. All switches and circuit breakers used as switches must be located so that they are operable from a readily accessible place. The center of the operating-handle grip of the switch or circuit breaker when in its highest position must not be more than 6 ft, 7 in. (2.0 m) above the floor or working platform ⟩⟩*404.8(A)*⟨⟨.

CAUTION

Wiring located within the cavity of a floor–ceiling or roof–ceiling assembly shall not be secured to, or supported by, the ceiling assembly, including the ceiling support wires. An independent means of secure support shall be provided and shall be permitted to be attached to the assembly. Where independent support wires are used, they shall be distinguishable by color, tagging, or other effective means ⟩⟩*300.11(A)(1) and (2)*⟨⟨.

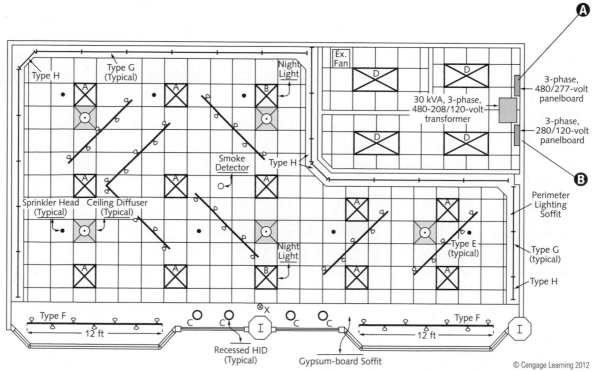

Luminaire Schedule

The minimum number of branch circuits is determined from the total calculated load and the size (or rating) of the circuits used. In all installations, the number of circuits must be sufficient to supply the load served. In no case shall the load on any circuit exceed the maximum specified by 220.18 》*210.11(A)*《.

The load calculated on a volt-ampere per square-foot (or per square-meter) basis must be adequately served by the wiring system up to and including the branch-circuit panelboard(s). This load must be evenly proportioned among multioutlet branch circuits within the panelboard(s). Branch circuits and overcurrent devices must only be installed to serve the connected load 》*210.11(B)*《.

Ⓐ Conductors of alternating-current (ac) and direct-current (dc) circuits, rated 600 volts, nominal or less, can occupy the same equipment wiring enclosure, cable, or raceway. The conductors' insulation rating must equal or exceed the maximum circuit voltage applied to any conductor within the enclosure, cable, or raceway 》*300.3(C)(1)*《.

Ⓑ For lighting units that have ballasts, transformers, or autotransformers or LED drivers, the supply circuit's calculated load is based on the total ampere ratings of such units, not on the lamps' total wattage 》*220.18(B)*《. Obtain the ampere rating from the manufacturer or from the information listed on the ballast. If the luminaire contains more than one ballast, add the ampere ratings. Multiply the total ampere rating by the voltage to find the luminaire's volt-ampere rating.

Ⓐ

Ⓑ

LUMINAIRE SCHEDULE

Type	Manufacturer	Volts	Catalog Number	Comments
A	Lighthouse	277	P622-232U277	2′ × 2′ lay-in fluorescent deep cell parabolic
B	Lighthouse	277	P622-232U277-EM	emergency light
C	Lighthouse	120	10R-CM70MH120	10″ recessed, 70W metal halide
D	Lighthouse	277	RT24–432EB277	2′ × 4′ lay-in fluorescent
E	Lighthouse	120	8001BK/HT308	8′ lighting track with 5 heads
F	Lighthouse	120	8001BK/HT308	12′ lighting track with 7 heads
G	Lighthouse	120	SL48-32EB120	4′ single lamp fluorescent strip
H	Lighthouse	120	SL24-20EB120	2′ single lamp fluorescent strip
X	Lighthouse	120	EX7B1LEDR	Exit light with battery

LAMP SCHEDULE

Lamps per Luminaire	Watts per Lamp	Lamp Size
2	32	F32-T8-U
2	32	F32-T8-U
1	70	MH70/C/U/M
4	32	F32-T8
5	75	75W-PAR30FL
7	75	75W-PAR30FL
1	32	F32-T8
1	20	F20-T8

Lamps are included in the luminaire.

NOTE

The ampacity of branch-circuit conductors must not be less than the maximum load served. Where the branch circuit supplies continuous loads, or any combination of continuous and noncontinuous loads, the minimum branch-circuit conductor size before the application of any adjustment or correction factors must have an allowable ampacity not less than the noncontinuous load plus 125% of the continuous load 》*210.19(A)(1)*《.
Most commercial lighting is considered continuous.

Fluorescent Luminaires

Luminaires shall be equipped with shades (or guards) and constructed or installed so that combustible material will not be subjected to temperatures exceeding 90°C (194°F) »*410.11*«.

Securely support all luminaires, lampholders, and receptacles »*410.30(A)*«.

Exposed metal parts shall be connected to an equipment grounding conductor or insulated from the equipment grounding conductor and other conducting surfaces or be inaccessible to unqualified personnel. Grounding is not required for lamp tie wires, mounting screws, clips, and decorative bands on glass spaced at least 1½ in. (38 mm) from lamp terminals shall not be required to be grounded »*410.42*«.

Raceway fittings supporting a luminaire(s) shall be capable of supporting the combined weight of the luminaire assembly and lamp(s) »*410.36(E)*«.

A Suspended-ceiling system framing members used to support luminaires must be securely fastened to each other and to the building structure at appropriate intervals. Luminaires must be fastened securely to the ceiling framing member by mechanical means such as bolts, screws, or rivets. Listed clips identified for use with the type of ceiling framing member(s) and luminaire(s) are also permitted »*410.36(B)*«.

B Branch circuits recognized by Article 210 can be used as multiwire circuits. A multiwire branch circuit can be thought of as multiple circuits. All conductors must originate from the same panelboard or similar distribution equipment »*210.4(A)*«. Unless an exception is met, multiwire branch circuits can only supply line-to-neutral loads »*210.4(C)*«.

C A 3-phase, 4-wire, wye-connected power system supplying nonlinear loads may necessitate a design allowing for the possibility of high harmonic neutral currents on the neutral conductor »*210.4(A) Informational Note*«.

D Luminaires and equipment shall be mechanically connected to an equipment grounding conductor as specified in 250.118 and sized in accordance with 250.122 »*410.46*«.

E Wiring on or within luminaires must be neatly arranged and must not be exposed to physical damage. Avoid excess wiring. Arrange conductors so they are not subjected to temperatures greater than those for which they are rated »*410.48*«.

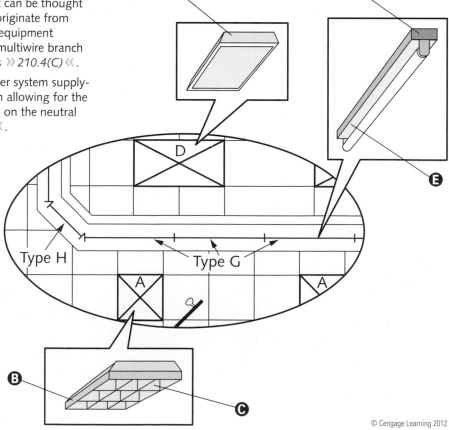

Show-Window and Track Lighting

Heavy-duty lighting track is identified for use exceeding 20 amperes. Each fitting attached to a heavy-duty lighting track shall have individual overcurrent protection »*410.153*«.

A Lighting track is a manufactured assembly designed to support and energize luminaires that are capable of being readily repositioned along the track. Its length may be altered by the addition or subtraction of track sections »*410.2*«.

B Lighting track shall be permanently installed as well as permanently connected to a branch circuit. Install only lighting track fittings on the lighting track. Fittings equipped with general-purpose receptacles shall not be used on lighting track »*410.151(A)*«.

C Lighting track shall be securely mounted so that each fastening suitably supports the maximum weight of luminaires that can be installed. Unless identified for greater support intervals, a single section 4 ft (1.2 m) or less in length shall have two supports. If installed in a continuous row, each individual section of not more than 4 ft (1.2 m) in length shall have one additional support »*410.154*«.

D Lighting track shall be grounded in accordance with Article 250. Track sections shall be securely coupled to maintain continuity of the circuitry, polarization, and grounding throughout »*410.155(B)*«.

E Track system ends shall be insulated and capped »*410.155(A)*«.

F The load connected to a lighting track shall not exceed the track's rating. The rating of the branch circuit that supplies lighting track shall not exceed the track rating »*410.151(B)*«.

G Fittings identified for use on lighting track shall be designed specifically for the track on which they are installed. They shall be securely fastened to the track, maintain polarization and connection to the equipment grounding conductor, and be designed to be suspended directly from the track »*410.151(D)*«.

H When computing feeder or service track lighting in nondwelling units or hotel/motel guest rooms, include an additional load of 150 volt-amperes for every 2 ft (600 mm) of lighting track or fraction thereof »*220.43(B)*«.

I No externally wired luminaire except chain-supported shall be used in show windows »*410.14*«.

J When calculating feeder or service show-window lighting, include a unit load of not less than 200 volt-amperes per linear foot of show window, measured horizontally along the base »*220.43(A)*«
(2 + 11.5 + 2 = 15.5 = 16 × 200 = 3200 volt-amperes).

NOTE

Do not install lighting track in the following locations:

1. Where physical damage is likely
2. In wet or damp locations
3. Where subject to corrosive vapors
4. In storage battery rooms
5. In hazardous (classified) locations
6. Where concealed
7. Where extended through walls or partitions
8. Less than 5 ft (1.5 m) above the finished floor except where protected from physical damage or where the track operates at less than 30 volts root-mean-square (rms) open-circuit voltage
9. Where prohibited by 410.10(D) **»*410.151(C)*«**.

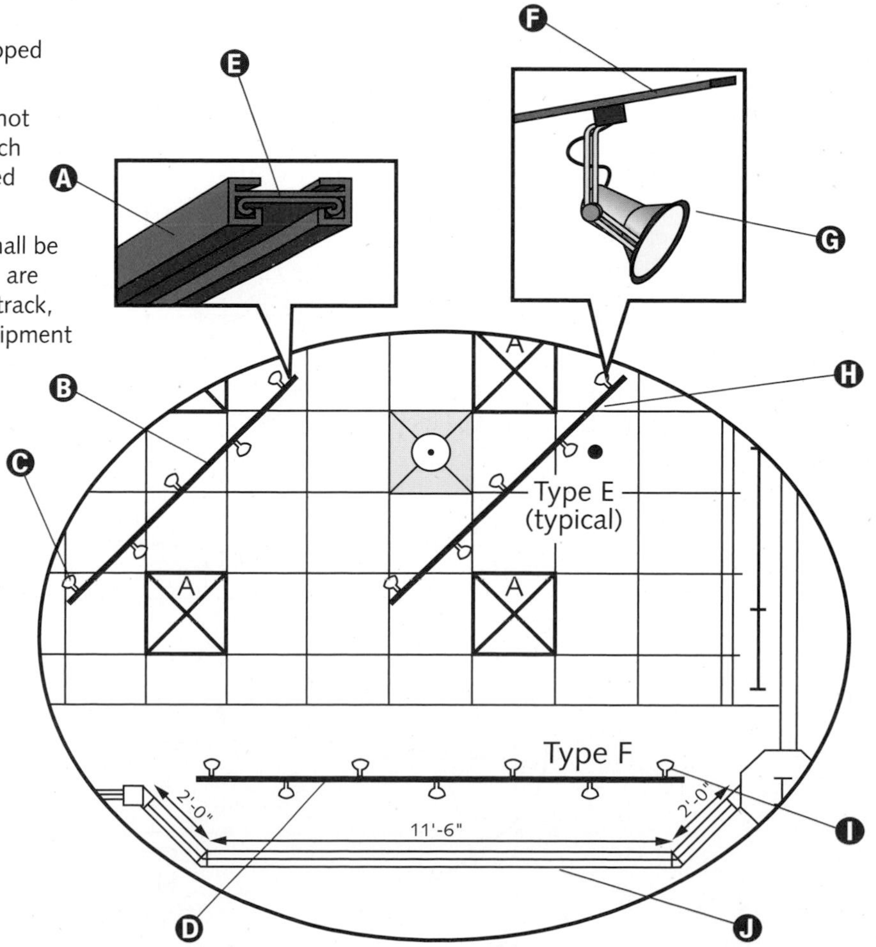

Recessed Luminaires

A recessed luminaire not identified for contact with insulation shall have all recessed parts spaced at least ½ in. (13 mm) from combustible materials. Support points and the trim finishing off the openings in the ceiling, wall, or other finished surface can be in contact with combustible materials ≫*410.116(A)(1)*≪.

A recessed luminaire identified for contact with insulation, Type IC, can contact combustible materials at recessed parts, points of support, and portions passing through or finishing off the structural opening ≫*410.116(A)(2)*≪.

A recessed HID luminaire identified for use and installed in poured concrete does not require thermal protection ≫*410.130(F)(3)*≪.

Ⓐ A luminaire can be recessed in fire-resistant material in a building of fire-resistant construction, subject to temperatures between 90°C (194°F) and 150°C (302°F), provided the luminaire is plainly marked as listed for that service ≫*410.115(B)*≪.

Ⓑ Install luminaires so that adjacent combustible material will not be subjected to temperatures greater than 90°C (194°F) ≫*410.115(A)*≪.

Ⓒ Luminaires installed in recessed cavities in walls or ceilings, including suspended ceilings, shall comply with 410.115 through 410.122 ≫*410.110*≪.

Ⓓ Thermal insulation shall not be installed above a recessed luminaire or within 3 in. (75 mm) of the recessed luminaire's enclosure, wiring compartment, ballast, transformer, LED driver, or power supply unless the luminaire is identified as Type IC for insulation contact ≫*410.116(B)*≪.

Ⓔ High-intensity discharge (HID) luminaires supply power to HID lamps. HID lamps produce light from gaseous discharge arc tubes and include mercury lamps, metal halide lamps, and high-pressure sodium lamps.

Ⓕ A recessed remote ballast for a HID luminaire shall have integral thermal protection and be identified as such ≫*410.130(F)(4)*≪.

Ⓖ Recessed high-intensity luminaires designed for installations in wall or ceiling cavities shall have thermal protection and be identified as such ≫*410.130(F)(1)*≪. Thermal protection is not required in a recessed high-intensity luminaire whose design, construction, and thermal performance characteristics are equivalent to a thermally protected luminaire and are identified as inherently protected ≫*410.130(F)(2)*≪.

> **N O T E**
>
> Luminaires that have exposed ballasts, transformers, LED drivers, or power supplies shall be installed such that ballasts, transformers, LED drivers, or power supplies shall not be in contact with combustible material unless listed for such condition ≫*410.136(A)*≪.

> **WARNING**
>
> Circuit breakers used as switches in 120-volt and 277-volt fluorescent lighting circuits shall be listed and shall be marked SWD or HID. Circuit breakers used as switches in high-intensity discharge lighting circuits shall be listed and shall be marked as HID ≫ *240.83(D)* ≪.

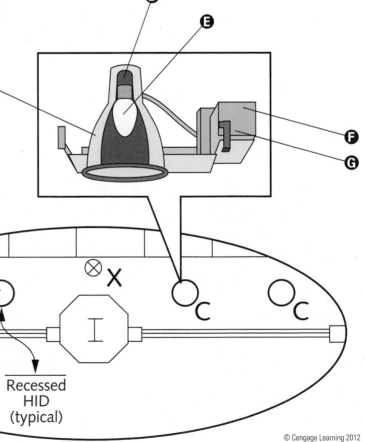

Recessed
HID
(typical)

Exit Luminaires and Egress Luminaires

A ballast in a fluorescent exit luminaire shall not have thermal protection »*410.130(E)(3)*«.

Ⓐ Framing members of suspended ceiling systems used to support luminaires shall be securely fastened to each other and to the building structure at appropriate intervals. Luminaires shall be securely fastened to the ceiling framing member by mechanical means such as bolts, screws, or rivets. Listed clips identified for use with the type of ceiling framing member(s) and luminaires are also permitted »*410.36(B)*«.

Ⓑ The ballast of a fluorescent luminaire installed indoors shall have integral thermal protection. Replacement ballasts shall also have similar thermal protection integral with the ballast »*410.130(E)(1)*«.

Ⓒ A fluorescent luminaire ballast used for egress lighting, energized only during a failure of the normal supply, shall not have thermal protection »*410.130(E)(4)*«.

Ⓓ An exit directional sign located within a building does not require a disconnecting means »*600.6 Exception No. 1*«.

> ### NOTE
>
> Article 700 provisions apply to the electrical safety of emergency systems installation, operation, and maintenance. These systems consist of circuits and equipment intended to supply, distribute, and control electricity for facility illumination, power, or both whenever the normal electrical service is interrupted »*700.1*«. Emergency systems are defined as those systems legally required and classed as emergency by municipal, state, federal, or other codes, or by any governmental agency having jurisdiction. The purpose of these systems is to automatically supply illumination, power, or both to designated areas and equipment in the event of failure of the normal supply, or in the event of accidental damage to systems elements intended to supply, distribute, and control power and illumination essential for safety to human life »*700.2*«.

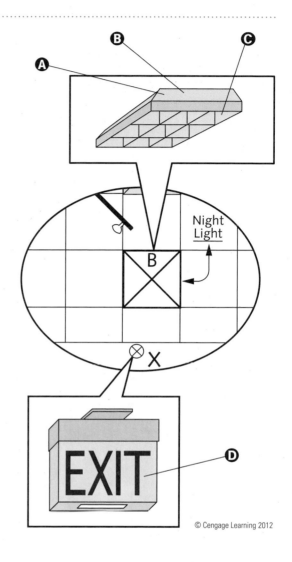

© Cengage Learning 2012

Adjustable Luminaires

Ⓐ Two conduits can support an enclosure containing a device under the conditions found in 314.23(F): (1) the box shall not exceed 100 in.³ (1650 cm³); (2) the box has either threaded entries or hubs identified for the purpose; (3) the box must be supported by two or more conduits threaded wrenchtight into the enclosure or hubs; and (4) each conduit must be secured within 18 in. (450 mm) of the enclosure, provided all entries are on the same side.

Ⓑ Equipment grounding conductors that are part of flexible cords with the largest circuit conductor 10 AWG or smaller or used with luminaire wires in accordance with 240.5 shall not be smaller than 18 AWG copper and not smaller than the circuit conductors »*250.122(E)*«.

Ⓒ A wet location receptacle where the product plugged in is unattended while in use requires an enclosure that is weatherproof at all times (plug inserted or not) »*406.9(B)(2)(a)*«.

Ⓓ Luminaires that require adjusting or aiming after installation do not require an attachment plug or cord connector,

provided the exposed cord is of the hard or extra-hard usage type and is not longer than that required for maximum adjustment. The cord shall not be subject to strain or physical damage »*410.62(B)*«.

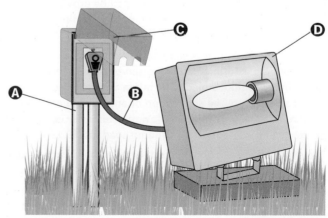

© Cengage Learning 2012

Switches Controlling Lighting Loads

Ⓐ Where switches control lighting loads supplied by a grounded general-purpose branch circuit, the grounded circuit conductor for the controlled lighting circuit shall be provided at the switch location ≫*404.2(C)* ≪.

Ⓑ The grounded circuit conductor shall be permitted to be omitted from the switch enclosure where conductors for switches controlling lighting loads enter the box through a raceway. The raceway shall have sufficient cross-sectional area to accommodate the extension of the grounded circuit conductor of the lighting circuit to the switch location

whether or not the conductors in the raceway are required to be increased in size to comply with 310.15(B)(2)(a) ≫*404.2(C) Exception* ≪.

Ⓒ The provision for a (future) grounded conductor is to complete a circuit path for electronic lighting control devices ≫*404.2(C) Informational Note* ≪.

> ### NOTE
>
> The grounded circuit conductor shall be permitted to be omitted from the switch enclosure where cable assemblies for switches controlling lighting loads enter the box through a framing cavity that is open at the top or bottom on the same floor level, or through a wall, floor, or ceiling that is unfinished on one side ≫*404.2(C) Exception*≪.

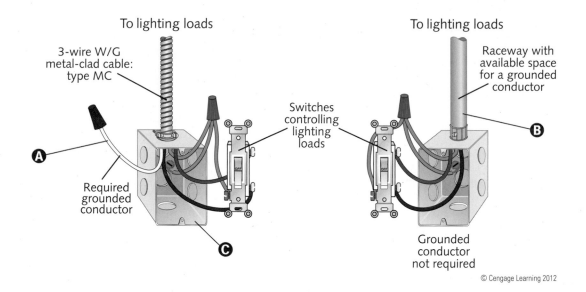

To lighting loads

3-wire W/G metal-clad cable: type MC

Switches controlling lighting loads

Ⓐ

Required grounded conductor

Ⓒ

To lighting loads

Raceway with available space for a grounded conductor

Ⓑ

Grounded conductor not required

© Cengage Learning 2012

Luminaires Used as Raceways

In a completed installation, a cover shall be provided for each outlet box, unless covered by means of a luminaire canopy, lampholder, receptacle, or similar device ≫*410.22* ≪.

Branch-circuit conductors shall have an ampacity at least equal to the maximum load being served. In a branch circuit supplying continuous loads, the minimum branch-circuit conductor size (before the application of any adjustment or correction factors) shall have an allowable ampacity equal to or greater than 125% of the continuous load ≫*210.19(A)(1)* ≪.

The overcurrent device on a branch circuit supplying continuous loads shall be rated at least 125% of the load ≫*210.20(A)* ≪.

Auxiliary equipment for electric-discharge lamps shall be enclosed in noncombustible cases and be treated as heat sources ≫*410.104(A)* ≪.

Ⓐ Luminaires designed for end-to-end connection, thereby forming a continuous assembly, or luminaires connected by recognized wiring methods, are permitted to contain the conductors of a 2-wire branch circuit or one multiwire branch circuit supplying the connected luminaires and need not be listed as a raceway ≫*410.64(C)* ≪.

Ⓑ One additional 2-wire branch circuit separately supplying one or more of the connected luminaires is also permitted ≫*410.64(C)* ≪.

Ⓒ Feeder and branch-circuit conductors within 3 in. (75 mm) of a ballast, LED driver, power supply, or transformer shall have an insulation temperature rating no lower than 90°C (194°F) unless supplying a luminaire marked as suitable for a different insulation temperature ≫*410.68* ≪.

Luminaires Used as Raceways *(continued)*

D Luminaires shall not be used as a raceway for circuit conductors unless listed and marked for use as a raceway ≫*410.64(A)* ≪.

E Luminaires identified for through-wiring, as permitted by 410.21, shall be permitted to be used as a raceway ≫*410.64(B)* ≪.

> **NOTE**
>
> Electric-discharge and LED luminaires supported independent of the outlet box shall be connected to the branch circuit through metal raceway, nonmetallic raceway, Type MC cable, Type AC cable, Type MI cable, or nonmetallic-sheathed cable, or by flexible cord as permitted in 410.62(B) or (C) ≫*410.24(A)*≪.

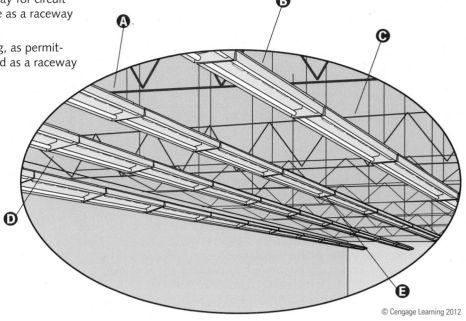

© Cengage Learning 2012

Cord-Connected Lampholders and Luminaires

The inlet of a metal lampholder attached to a flexible cord shall be equipped with an insulating bushing that, if threaded, is not smaller than nominal ³⁄₈-in. pipe size. The cord hole shall be of an appropriate size, and all burrs/fins must be removed, providing a smooth bearing surface for the cord ≫*410.62(A)* ≪.

A Electric-discharge luminaires provided with mogul-base, screw shell lampholders can be connected to branch circuits of 50 amperes or less by cords that comply with 240.5. While receptacles and attachment plugs can be of a lower ampere rating than the branch circuit, they shall not be less than 125% of the luminaire full-load current ≫*410.62(C)(2)* ≪.

B A luminaire or a listed assembly can be cord connected if the following conditions apply:

1. The luminaire is located directly below the outlet or busway.

2. The flexible cord meets all the following:

   a. Is visible for its entire length outside the luminaire.

   b. Is not subject to strain or physical damage.

   c. Is terminated in a grounding-type attachment plug cap or busway plug, or is a part of a listed assembly incorporating a manufactured wiring system connector in accordance with 604.6(C), or has a luminaire assembly with a strain relief and canopy having a maximum 6-in. (152-mm) long section of raceway for attachment to an outlet box above a suspended ceiling ≫*410.62(C)(1)* ≪.

C For circuits that supply lighting units with ballasts, transformers, autotransformers, or LED drivers, the computed load shall be based on the total ampere rating of such units and not on the total lamp(s) wattage ≫*220.18(B)* ≪.

D A load expected to continue at maximum current for 3 hours or more is a continuous load ≫*Article 100* ≪.

E Electric-discharge luminaires having a flanged surface inlet can be supplied by cord pendants equipped with cord connectors. Inlets and connectors can be of a lower ampere rating than the branch circuit but not less than 125% of the luminaire load current ≫*410.62(C)(3)* ≪.

F Cord-connected luminaires shall be located directly below the outlet box or busway ≫*410.62(C)(1)(1)* ≪.

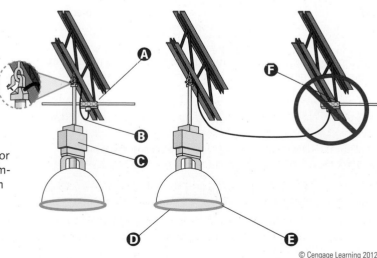

© Cengage Learning 2012

Portable Lamps

A Portable lamps must be wired with flexible cord, recognized by 400.4, and a polarized or grounding-type attachment plug ≫ *410.82(A)* ≪.

B Where used with Edison-base lampholders, the grounded conductor shall be identified and attached to the screw shell as well as the attachment plug's identified blade ≫ *410.82(A)* ≪.

C In addition to the provisions of 410.82(A), portable handlamps shall comply with 410.82(B)(1) through (5):

1. Metal shell, paper-lined lampholders must not be used.
2. Handlamps must be equipped with a handle of molded composition or other insulating material.
3. Handlamps must be equipped with a substantial guard attached to the lampholder or handle.
4. Metallic guards must be grounded by means of an equipment grounding conductor run with circuit conductors within the power-supply cord.
5. Portable handlamps supplied through an isolating transformer with an ungrounded secondary of not over 50 volts do not require grounding ≫ *410.82(B)* ≪.

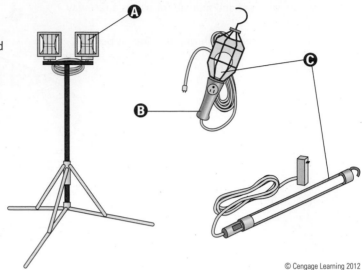

© Cengage Learning 2012

Required Handhole in a Metal Pole

A This metal pole is more than 8 ft (2.5 m) tall abovegrade.

B Metal raceways or other equipment grounding conductors shall be bonded to the pole by means of an equipment grounding conductor recognized by 250.118 and sized in accordance with 250.122 ≫ *410.30(B)(5)* ≪.

C Support conductors in vertical metal poles used as raceway, as provided in 300.19 ≫ *410.30(B)(6)* ≪.

D A pole shall have a handhole not less than 2 in. × 4 in. (50 mm × 100 mm) with a cover suitable for use in wet locations to provide access to the supply terminations within the pole or pole base ≫ *410.30(B)(1)* ≪.

E A metal pole with a handhole must have an equipment grounding terminal accessible from the handhole ≫ *410.30(B)(3)(a)* ≪.

F Direct-buried cable, conduit, or other raceways must meet Table 300.5 minimum cover requirements ≫ *300.5(A)* ≪.

> ### NOTE
>
> Where conductor size is adjusted to compensate for voltage drop, equipment grounding conductors shall be adjusted proportionately according to circular mil area **≫250.122(B)≪** .

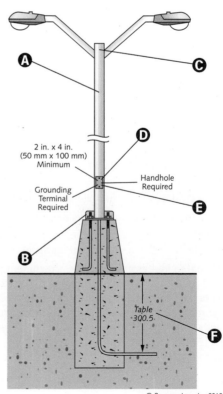

2 in. x 4 in. (50 mm x 100 mm) Minimum

Handhole Required

Grounding Terminal Required

Table 300.5

© Cengage Learning 2012

Hinged Metal Poles, 20 ft (6.0 m) or Less, Supporting Luminaires

A A hinged-base pole longer than 20 ft (6.0 m) supporting a luminaire(s) requires a handhole ≫ *410.30(B)(1)* ≪.

B A metal pole shall have an accessible grounding terminal within the base ≫ *410.30(B)(3)(b)* ≪.

C A metal pole 20 ft (6.0 m) or less in height above grade that has a hinged base does not require a handhole ≫ *410.30(B)(1) Exception No. 2* ≪.

D If equipped with a hinged base, the pole and base must be bonded together ≫ *410.30(B)(4)* ≪.

E Metal raceways or other equipment grounding conductors shall be bonded to the pole by means of an equipment grounding conductor recognized by 250.118 and sized in accordance with 250.122 ≫ *410.30(B)(5)* ≪.

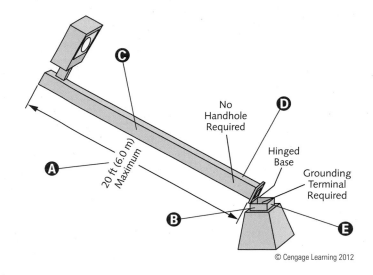

© Cengage Learning 2012

Metal Poles, 8 ft (2.5 m) or Less, Supporting Luminaires

A No handhole is required in a pole no more than 8 ft (2.5 m) in height (abovegrade) where the supply wiring method continues without splice or pull point and where the pole interior and splices are accessible by removing the luminaire ≫ *410.30(B)(1) Exception No. 1* ≪.

B Splices must remain accessible.

C The wiring method must continue without splice to the luminaire termination point.

D A pole longer than 8 ft (2.5 m) supporting a luminaire(s) requires a handhole ≫ *410.30(B)(1)* ≪.

E No grounding terminal is required in a pole 8 ft (2.5 m) or less in height abovegrade where the supply wiring method continues without splice or pull point and where the pole interior and splices are accessible by luminaire removal ≫ *410.30(B)(3) Exception to (3)* ≪.

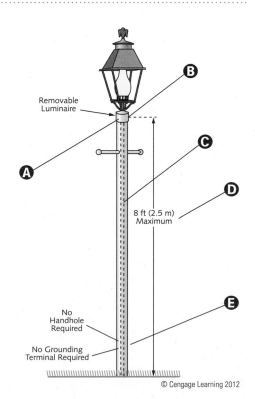

© Cengage Learning 2012

> ### NOTE
>
> A receptacle installed in a pole supporting a luminaire may require GFCI protection (see 210.8). All 15- and 20-ampere, 125- and 250-volt receptacles installed in a wet location must have an enclosure that is weatherproof whether or not the attachment plug cap is inserted. For other than one- or two-family dwellings, an outlet box hood installed for this purpose shall be listed, and where installed on an enclosure supported from grade as described in 314.23(B) or as described in 314.23(F) shall be identified as "extra-duty." All 15- and 20-ampere, 125- and 250-volt nonlocking-type receptacles shall be listed weather-resistant type ≫ *406.9(B)(1)* ≪.

Line 13—Motor Loads

Where one or more of the motors of the group are used for short-time, intermittent, periodic, or varying duty, the ampere rating of such motors used in the summation shall be determined in accordance with 430.22(E). For the highest-rated motor, the greater of either the ampere rating from 430.22(E) or the largest continuous-duty motor full-load current multiplied by 1.25 shall be used in the summation ≫ *430.24 Exception No. 1* ≪.

Where interlocked circuitry prevents simultaneous operation of selected motors or other loads, the conductor ampacity shall be permitted to be based on the summation of the currents of the motors and other loads being operated simultaneously resulting in the highest total current ≫ *430.24 Exception No. 3* ≪.

A The ampacity of the conductors supplying multimotor and combination-load equipment shall not be less than the minimum circuit ampacity marked on the equipment per 430.7(D). If the individual equipment nameplates are visible

(per 430.7[D][2]), but the equipment is not factory wired, use 430.24 to determine conductor ampacity ≫ *430.25* ≪.

B Where conductor heating is reduced as a result of motors operating on duty cycle, intermittently, or from all motors not operating at one time, the AHJ may grant permission for feeder conductors to have an ampacity less than specified in 430.24, provided the conductors have sufficient ampacity for the number of motors supplied and the nature of their loads and duties ≫ *430.26* ≪.

C Conductors supplying several motors or a motor(s) and other load(s) must have an ampacity not less than the sum of each of the following:
(1) 125% of the full-load current rating of the highest rated motor, as determined by 430.6(A)
(2) Sum of the full-load current ratings of all the other motors in the group, as determined by 430.6(A)
(3) 100% of the noncontinuous nonmotor load
(4) 125% of the continuous nonmotor load ≫ *430.24* ≪.

A   **B**

| 13 Motor Loads *220.18(A), 430.24, 430.25, 430.26,* and *Article 440*
 Motor-driven air-conditioning and refrigeration equipment is found in Article 440.
 Multiply the largest motor (one motor only) by 25% and add it to the load. | **13** | |

C

© Cengage Learning 2012

Line 14—All Other Loads

A This line is a catchall for loads not falling into one of the previous categories.

B Calculate all noncontinuous loads (not yet input) at 100% of their volt-ampere rating.

C Total all continuous loads (not yet calculated) and multiply by 125%. Add the result of the continuous loads to that for noncontinuous loads and put the total on line 14.

A   **B**

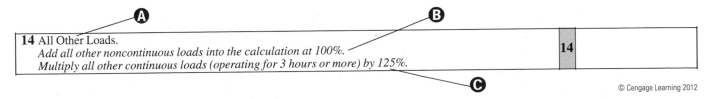

| 14 All Other Loads.
 Add all other noncontinuous loads into the calculation at 100%.
 Multiply all other continuous loads (operating for 3 hours or more) by 125%. | **14** | |

C

© Cengage Learning 2012

Line 15—Total Volt-Ampere Demand Load

A Add all volt-ampere loads listed in lines 3 through 14 and place the result in line 15.

A

| 15 Total Volt-Ampere Demand Load: *Add lines 3 through 14 to find the minimum required volt-amperes.* | **15** | |

© Cengage Learning 2012

Lines 16 and 17—Minimum Size Service or Feeder

A Place the total volt-ampere amount found in line 15 here.

B Write down the source voltage that supplies the feeder/service.

C Fractions of an ampere 0.5 and higher are rounded up, while fractions less than 0.5 are dropped ≫ *220.5(B)* ≪.

D The service (or feeder) overcurrent protection must be higher than the number found in line 16. Refer to 240.6(A) for a list of fuse and circuit breaker standard ampere ratings.

E Divide the volt-amperes by the voltage to find the amperage.

F Three-phase voltage is found by multiplying the voltage (single-phase) by 1.732. For example, the source voltage for 208-volt, 3-phase is 360 (208 × 1.732).

G The result on line 16 is the minimum amperage rating required for the service or feeder being calculated.

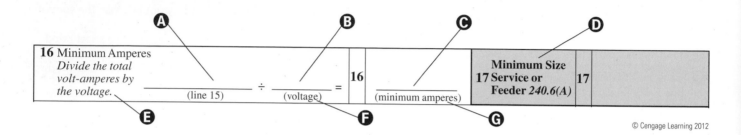

© Cengage Learning 2012

Line 18—Minimum Size Conductors

Conductors 1/0 AWG and larger can be connected in parallel (electrically joined at both ends to form a single conductor) ≫ *310.10(H)(1)* ≪.

The number and type of paralleled conductor sets is a design consideration, not necessarily a *Code* issue. Exercise extreme care when designing a paralleled conductor installation without violating provisions such as 110.14(A), 110.14(C), 240.4(C), 250.66, 250.122(F), 300.20(A), 310.10(H), etc.

A Using Tables 310.15(B)(16) through 310.15(B)(21), choose a conductor size that equals (or exceeds) line 16's minimum ampacity rating. The conductor's ampacity rating does not have to equal or exceed the overcurrent device rating unless its rating exceeds 800 amperes ≫ *240.4(B)* ≪.

B Ampacity adjustment (correction) factors for more than three current-carrying conductors are located in Table 310.15(B)(3)(a).

> **N O T E**
>
> The paralleled conductors in each phase, polarity, neutral, grounded circuit conductor, equipment grounding conductor, or equipment bonding jumper shall share the same characteristics ≫ *310.10(H)(2)* ≪. For example, all paralleled, Phase A conductors must:
> (1) be of the same length,
> (2) consist of the same conductor material,
> (3) be the same size in circular mil area,
> (4) have the same insulation type, and
> (5) be terminated in the same manner.

> **WARNING**
>
> For overcurrent devices rated over 800 amperes, the ampacity of the conductors protected shall equal or exceed the rating of the overcurrent device per 240.6 ≫ *240.4(C)* ≪. Do not exceed the temperature limitations outlined in 110.14(C).

18 Size the Service or Feeder Conductors. *Tables 310.15(B)(16) through 310.15(B)(21) Use the tables along with 310.15(B)(1) through (6) to determine conductor size. If the overcurrent device is rated more than 800 amperes, the conductor ampacity must be equal to, or greater than, the rating of the overcurrent device. 240.4(C)*

Minimum Size Conductors	18

© Cengage Learning 2012

Line 19—Neutral Conductor

Include all lighting and receptacle loads having a 120-volt rating in the neutral calculation.

All appliances, equipment, motors, etc. utilizing a grounded conductor are included in the neutral calculation.

Ⓐ For the purpose of this load calculation, the terms **neutral** and **grounded** are synonymous.

Ⓑ The feeder (or service) neutral load is the maximum unbalance of the load determined by Article 220 ⟫ *220.61* ⟪.

Ⓒ In addition to 220.61 demand factors, a 70% demand factor is permitted for that portion of the unbalanced load above 200 amperes ⟫ *220.61(B)* ⟪.

Ⓓ The neutral is sized by finding the maximum unbalanced load.

> **NOTE**
>
> The grounded conductor shall not be smaller than the required grounding electrode conductor specified in Table 250.66 ⟫*250.24(C)(1)*⟪ .

> **CAUTION**
>
> Reduction of neutral capacity is not permitted for that portion of the load consisting of nonlinear loads supplied from a 4-wire, wye-connected, 3-phase system nor the grounded conductor of a 3-wire circuit consisting of 2-phase wires and the neutral of a 4-wire, 3-phase, wye-connected system ⟫*220.61(C)*⟪.

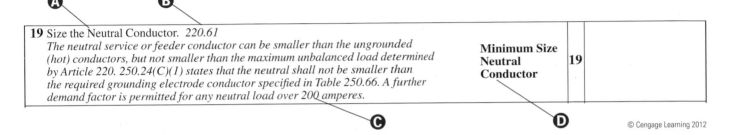

19 Size the Neutral Conductor. *220.61*
The neutral service or feeder conductor can be smaller than the ungrounded (hot) conductors, but not smaller than the maximum unbalanced load determined by Article 220. 250.24(C)(1) states that the neutral shall not be smaller than the required grounding electrode conductor specified in Table 250.66. A further demand factor is permitted for any neutral load over 200 amperes.

| | Minimum Size Neutral Conductor | 19 | |

© Cengage Learning 2012

Line 20—Grounding Conductor

Where the grounding electrode conductor connects to rod, pipe, or plate electrodes and that conductor portion is the sole grounding electrode connection, the maximum size required is 6 AWG copper or 4 AWG aluminum ⟫*250.66(A)* ⟪.

For a grounding electrode conductor connected to a concrete-encased electrode and serving as the only grounding electrode connection, the maximum size required is 4 AWG copper ⟫*250.66(B)* ⟪.

If the grounding electrode conductor is connected to a ground ring and that conductor portion is the sole connection to the grounding electrode, the maximum size required is the size used for the ground ring ⟫*250.66(C)* ⟪.

Ⓐ Grounding electrode conductor size is based on the largest service-entrance conductor or equivalent area for parallel conductors ⟫ *Table 250.66* ⟪. (The minimum size service-entrance conductors were determined on line 18.)

Ⓑ While Table 250.66 is used for service installations, it is also used in other wiring applications, such as separately derived systems ⟫ *250.30(A)(2)* ⟪ and connections at separate buildings or structures ⟫ *250.32* ⟪.

Ⓒ Equipment bonding jumpers on the load side of an overcurrent device(s) shall be sized in accordance with Table 250.122 ⟫ *250.102(D)* ⟪.

Ⓓ The equipment grounding conductor size is based on the rating (or setting) of the circuit's automatic overcurrent device ahead of equipment, conduit, and so on ⟫ *Table 250.122* ⟪.

20 Size the Grounding Electrode Conductor (for Service). *250.66*
Use line 18 to find the grounding electrode conductor in Table 250.66.
Size the Equipment Grounding Conductor (for Feeder). *250.122*
Use line 17 to find the equipment grounding conductor in Table 250.122.
Equipment grounding conductor types are listed in 250.118.

| | Minimum Size Grounding Electrode Conductor ... or ... Equipment Grounding Conductor | 20 | |

© Cengage Learning 2012

SAMPLE LOAD CALCULATION—STORE

Load Calculation Information

A This is the load calculation data for a small retail store.

B Calculate the floor area from the outside dimensions. In this example, the square-foot area is already provided.

C A 3-phase transformer steps down the voltage from 480 to 208Y/120 volts.

A

B

Store's area (in ft²) . . . . .1200 ft²
Receptacles 10
Lighting track. . . . . .80 ft
Two sign circuits . . . . .14.5 amperes, 120 volt (each)
Show window . . . . .32 ft
Water heater . . . . .2 kW, 120 volt
Electric heat . . . . .15 kW, 480 volt, 3-phase
Air handler (blower motor). . . . . .1.8 amperes, 480 volt, 3-phase
Air-conditioner compressor . . . . . .8.5 amperes, 480 volt, 3-phase
Condenser fan motor . . . . .0.8 amperes, 480 volt, 3-phase

Assume water heater and electric heat kW ratings equivalent to kVA.

The electric supply consists of a 480-volt, 3-phase, 4-wire service.

© Cengage Learning 2012

C

Lines 1 and 2

A The different style of box on line 1 (unlike lines 3 through 14) indicates that the load will become part (if not all) of line 3. Line 1 is not included in line 15's total volt-ampere demand load.

B Since there are ten receptacles, the calculated load is 1800 volt-amperes (10 × 180).

C As with line 1, line 2 has a different style box from lines 3 through 14 because the load (if any) becomes part of line 3. Line 2 is not included in line 15's total volt-ampere demand load.

D Because this store has no fixed multioutlet assembly, a dashed line occupies line 2.

A   **B**

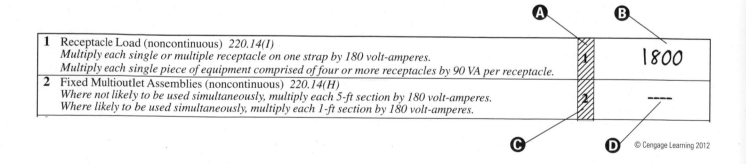

| 1 | Receptacle Load (noncontinuous) *220.14(I)*
Multiply each single or multiple receptacle on one strap by 180 volt-amperes.
Multiply each single piece of equipment comprised of four or more receptacles by 90 VA per receptacle. | 1 | 1800 |
| 2 | Fixed Multioutlet Assemblies (noncontinuous) *220.14(H)*
Where not likely to be used simultaneously, multiply each 5-ft section by 180 volt-amperes.
Where likely to be used simultaneously, multiply each 1-ft section by 180 volt-amperes. | 2 | –––– |

C   **D** © Cengage Learning 2012

Lines 3 and 4

A Line 3 is the first of 12 lines whose values are combined to determine the total volt-ampere demand load.

B Because there is no multioutlet assembly and the receptacle load is less than 10 kVA, the 1800 volt-ampere load from line 1 is inserted in line 3.

C The dashed line indicates line 4 is intentionally blank, because it only applies to banks and office buildings.

D The dashed line indicates line 4 is intentionally blank, because it only applies to banks and office buildings.

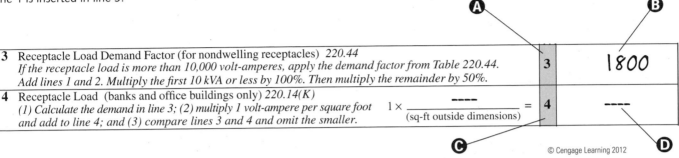

3	Receptacle Load Demand Factor (for nondwelling receptacles) *220.44* *If the receptacle load is more than 10,000 volt-amperes, apply the demand factor from Table 220.44.* *Add lines 1 and 2. Multiply the first 10 kVA or less by 100%. Then multiply the remainder by 50%.*	**3**	1800
4	Receptacle Load (banks and office buildings only) *220.14(K)* *(1) Calculate the demand in line 3; (2) multiply 1 volt-ampere per square foot* $1 \times \dfrac{\text{----}}{\text{(sq-ft outside dimensions)}} =$ *and add to line 4; and (3) compare lines 3 and 4 and omit the smaller.*	**4**	----

© Cengage Learning 2012

Lines 5 and 6

A The volt-ampere unit load for a store is 3 ≫ *Table 220.12* ≪.

B Since the store's square-foot area is provided, no calculation is required.

C Store lighting loads are continuous. The result of line 5 becomes part of the continuous volt-ampere load calculation (line 10).

D Use line 6 only for certain portions of hospitals, hotels, motels, storage warehouses, and apartment houses without provisions for cooking.

E The marking in line 6 indicates that it has intentionally been left blank.

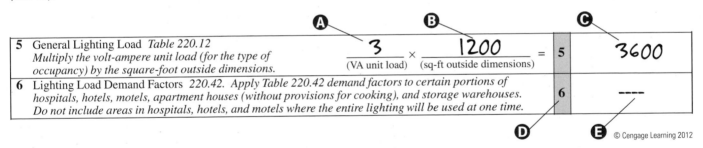

5	General Lighting Load *Table 220.12* *Multiply the volt-ampere unit load (for the type of occupancy) by the square-foot outside dimensions.*	$\dfrac{3}{\text{(VA unit load)}} \times \dfrac{1200}{\text{(sq-ft outside dimensions)}} =$ **5**	3600
6	Lighting Load Demand Factors *220.42. Apply Table 220.42 demand factors to certain portions of hospitals, hotels, motels, apartment houses (without provisions for cooking), and storage warehouses. Do not include areas in hospitals, hotels, and motels where the entire lighting will be used at one time.*	**6**	----

© Cengage Learning 2012

Lines 7 and 8

A Except for dwelling units or hotel/motel guest rooms, track lighting loads are additional to Table 220.12's general lighting loads ≫ *220.43(B)* ≪.

B This store contains 80 ft of lighting track.

C Base the calculation on every 2 ft, or fraction thereof, of track.

D A store's track lighting load is continuous. Line 7's result becomes part of the continuous volt-ampere load calculation (line 10).

E At least one outlet having a minimum rating of 1200 volt-amperes is required.

F This store's actual sign load is 3420 volt-amperes (2 × 14.5 × 120). This store has two sign circuits.

G Since a store's sign load is continuous, the result of line 8 becomes part of the continuous volt-ampere load calculation (line 10).

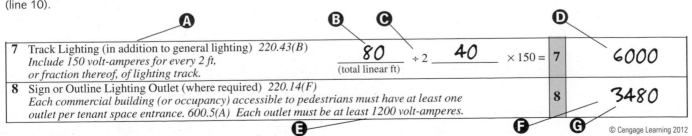

7	Track Lighting (in addition to general lighting) *220.43(B)* *Include 150 volt-amperes for every 2 ft,* *or fraction thereof, of lighting track.*	$\dfrac{80}{\text{(total linear ft)}} \div 2 \ \underline{40} \times 150 =$ **7**	6000
8	Sign or Outline Lighting Outlet (where required) *220.14(F)* *Each commercial building (or occupancy) accessible to pedestrians must have at least one outlet per tenant space entrance. 600.5(A) Each outlet must be at least 1200 volt-amperes.*	**8**	3480

© Cengage Learning 2012

Line 9

Ⓐ Not all commercial occupancies have show windows.

Ⓑ The store in this example has 32 linear ft of show window.

Ⓒ Because show-window load is continuous, the result of line 9 becomes part of the continuous volt-ampere load calculation (line 10).

9 Show-Window Lighting *220.43(A)* *Include at least 200 volt-amperes for each linear foot,* *measured horizontally along the show window's base.*	$\dfrac{32}{\text{(total linear ft of show window)}} \times 200 =$ **9**	**6400**

© Cengage Learning 2012

Lines 10 and 11

Ⓐ Lines 5, 7, 8, and 9 represent the store's continuous loads.

Ⓑ 3600 + 6000 + 3480 + 6400 = 19,480

Ⓒ An additional 25% volt-ampere load has been added because of the continuous loads.

Ⓓ The marking in line 11 indicates a lack of kitchen equipment.

10 Continuous Loads *215.2(A), 215.3,* and *230.42(A)* *Multiply* *the continuous load volt-amperes (listed above) by 25%.* *(General-purpose receptacles are not considered continuous.)*	$\dfrac{19{,}480}{\text{(total continuous load volt-amperes)}} \times 25\% =$ **10**	**4870**
11 Kitchen Equipment *220.56* *Multiply three or more pieces of equipment by the Table 220.56 demand factor (%).* Use *Table 220.55* for household cooking equipment used in instructional programs. *Table 220.55,* Note 5	**11**	**----**

© Cengage Learning 2012

Lines 12 and 13

Ⓐ Because the combined electric heat and air-handler load is larger than the combined compressor, condenser fan motor, and air handler, omit the compressor and condenser fan motor load.

Ⓑ Find the largest motor. In this example, that would be the air-handler motor (1.8 × 480 × 1.732 = 1,496.45). Increase the largest motor by 25% (1,496.45 × 25% = 374).

12 Noncoincident Loads *220.60. The smaller of two (or more) noncoincident loads can be omitted, as* *long as they will never be energized simultaneously (such as certain portions of heating and A/C systems).* *Calculate fixed electric space-heating loads at 100% of the total connected load. 220.51*	**12**	**16,456**
13 Motor Loads *220.18(A), 430.24, 430.25, 430.26,* and *Article 440* *Motor-driven air-conditioning and refrigeration equipment is found in Article 440.* *Multiply the largest motor (one motor only) by 25% and add it to the load.*	**13**	**374**

© Cengage Learning 2012

Lines 14 and 15

Ⓐ The only load not previously calculated is the water heater. A water heater is a noncontinuous load when calculating a feeder or service. Add noncontinuous loads to the calculation at 100%.

Ⓑ Add lines 3 through 14 to find the minimum volt-ampere load (lines 4, 6, and 11 are blank).

14 All Other Loads. *Add all other noncontinuous loads into the calculation at 100%.* *Multiply all other continuous loads (operating for 3 hours or more) by 125%.*	**14**	**2000**
15 Total Volt-Ampere Demand Load: *Add lines 3 through 14 to find the minimum required volt-amperes.*	**15**	**44,980**

© Cengage Learning 2012

Lines 16 and 17

A Insert the volt-ampere load from line 15 on this line.

B The total voltage for a 480-volt, 3-phase system is 831 (480 × 1.732).

C The minimum ampacity for a 480-volt, 3-phase service is 54 amperes.

D The next-higher standard size fuse (or breaker) above 54 amperes is 60 》 *240.6(A)* 《.

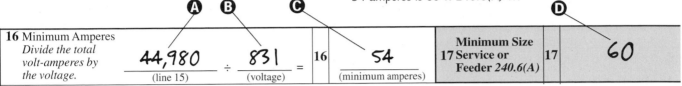

| 16 Minimum Amperes *Divide the total volt-amperes by the voltage.* | 44,980 (line 15) ÷ 831 (voltage) = | 16 | 54 (minimum amperes) | **Minimum Size** 17 **Service or Feeder** *240.6(A)* | 17 | 60 |

© Cengage Learning 2012

Line 18

A The minimum 60/75°C (140/167°F) copper service conductor is 6 AWG 》 *Table 310.15(B)(16)* 《.

B The minimum 60/75°C (140/167°F) aluminum service conductor is 4 AWG 》 *Table 310.15(B)(16)* 《.

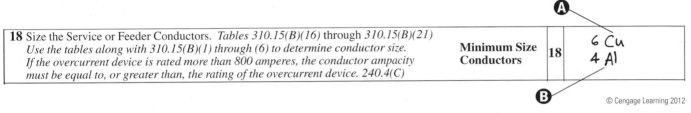

| 18 Size the Service or Feeder Conductors. *Tables 310.15(B)(16)* through *310.15(B)(21)* *Use the tables along with 310.15(B)(1) through (6) to determine conductor size.* *If the overcurrent device is rated more than 800 amperes, the conductor ampacity must be equal to, or greater than, the rating of the overcurrent device. 240.4(C)* | **Minimum Size Conductors** | 18 | 6 Cu 4 Al |

© Cengage Learning 2012

Line 19

A Although there will be little (if any) load on the neutral, a neutral conductor is required. Where an ac system (operating at less than 1000 volts) is grounded at any point, the grounded conductor(s) shall be routed with the ungrounded conductors to each service disconnecting means and shall be connected to each disconnecting means grounded conductor(s) terminal or bus 》 *250.24(C)* 《.

B While the grounded conductor shall not be smaller than the required grounding electrode conductor specified in Table 250.66, it does not have to be larger than the largest ungrounded service-entrance conductor(s) 》 *250.24(C)(1)* 《.

C Since the minimum size copper grounding electrode conductor is 8 AWG, the neutral must also be 8 AWG.

D Because the minimum size aluminum grounding electrode conductor is 6 AWG, the neutral must also be 6 AWG.

| 19 Size the Neutral Conductor. *220.61* *The neutral service or feeder conductor can be smaller than the ungrounded (hot) conductors, but not smaller than the maximum unbalanced load determined by Article 220. 250.24(C)(1) states that the neutral shall not be smaller than the required grounding electrode conductor specified in Table 250.66. A further demand factor is permitted for any neutral load over 200 amperes.* | **Minimum Size Neutral Conductor** | 19 | 8 Cu 6 Al |

© Cengage Learning 2012

Line 20

A The grounding electrode conductor's size is based on the service-entrance conductor 》 *Table 250.66* 《.

B The minimum size copper grounding conductor is 8 AWG.

C The minimum size aluminum grounding conductor is 6 AWG.

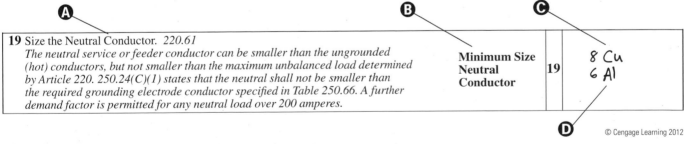

| 20 Size the Grounding Electrode Conductor (for Service). *250.66* *Use line 18 to find the grounding electrode conductor in Table 250.66.* Size the Equipment Grounding Conductor (for Feeder). *250.122* *Use line 17 to find the equipment grounding conductor in Table 250.122.* *Equipment grounding conductor types are listed in 250.118.* | **Minimum Size Grounding Electrode Conductor . . . or . . . Equipment Grounding Conductor** | 20 | 8 Cu 6 Al |

© Cengage Learning 2012

The following page shows the store's completed load calculation.

Nondwelling Feeder/Service Load Calculation

1 Receptacle Load (noncontinuous) *220.14(I)* *Multiply each single or multiple receptacle on one strap by 180 volt-amperes.* *Multiply each single piece of equipment comprised of four or more receptacles by 90 VA per receptacle.*	1	1800
2 Fixed Multioutlet Assemblies (noncontinuous) *220.14(H)* *Where not likely to be used simultaneously, multiply each 5-ft section by 180 volt-amperes.* *Where likely to be used simultaneously, multiply each 1-ft section by 180 volt-amperes.*	2	----
3 Receptacle Load Demand Factor (for nondwelling receptacles) *220.44* *If the receptacle load is more than 10,000 volt-amperes, apply the demand factor from Table 220.44.* *Add lines 1 and 2. Multiply the first 10 kVA or less by 100%. Then multiply the remainder by 50%.*	3	1800
4 Receptacle Load (banks and office buildings only) *220.14(K)* *(1) Calculate the demand in line 3; (2) multiply 1 volt-ampere per square foot* $1 \times \underline{\quad ---- \quad}$ = *and add to line 4; and (3) compare lines 3 and 4 and omit the smaller.* (sq-ft outside dimensions)	4	----
5 General Lighting Load *Table 220.12* *Multiply the volt-ampere unit load (for the type of* $\underline{\quad 3 \quad} \times \underline{\quad 1200 \quad}$ = *occupancy) by the square-foot outside dimensions.* (VA unit load) (sq-ft outside dimensions)	5	3600
6 Lighting Load Demand Factors *220.42.* Apply Table 220.42 demand factors to certain portions of *hospitals, hotels, motels, apartment houses (without provisions for cooking), and storage warehouses.* *Do not include areas in hospitals, hotels, and motels where the entire lighting will be used at one time.*	6	----
7 Track Lighting (in addition to general lighting) *220.43(B)* *Include 150 volt-amperes for every 2 ft,* $\underline{\quad 80 \quad} \div 2 \underline{\quad 40 \quad} \times 150$ = *or fraction thereof, of lighting track.* (total linear ft)	7	6000
8 Sign or Outline Lighting Outlet (where required) *220.14(F)* *Each commercial building (or occupancy) accessible to pedestrians must have at least one* *outlet per tenant space entrance. 600.5(A) Each outlet must be at least 1200 volt-amperes.*	8	3480
9 Show-Window Lighting *220.43(A)* *Include at least 200 volt-amperes for each linear foot,* $\underline{\quad 32 \quad} \times 200$ = *measured horizontally along the show window's base.* (total linear ft of show window)	9	6400
10 Continuous Loads *215.2(A), 215.3,* and *230.42(A)* *Multiply* *the continuous load volt-amperes (listed above) by 25%.* $\underline{\quad 19,480 \quad} \times 25\%$ = *(General-purpose receptacles are not considered continuous.)* (total continuous load volt-amperes)	10	4870
11 Kitchen Equipment *220.56* *Multiply three or more pieces of equipment by the Table 220.56 demand factor (%).* *Use Table 220.55 for household cooking equipment used in instructional programs. Table 220.55, Note 5*	11	----
12 Noncoincident Loads *220.60.* *The smaller of two (or more) noncoincident loads can be omitted, as* *long as they will never be energized simultaneously (such as certain portions of heating and A/C systems).* *Calculate fixed electric space-heating loads at 100% of the total connected load. 220.51*	12	16,456
13 Motor Loads *220.18(A), 430.24, 430.25, 430.26,* and *Article 440* *Motor-driven air-conditioning and refrigeration equipment is found in Article 440.* *Multiply the largest motor (one motor only) by 25% and add it to the load.*	13	374
14 All Other Loads. *Add all other noncontinuous loads into the calculation at 100%.* *Multiply all other continuous loads (operating for 3 hours or more) by 125%.*	14	2000
15 Total Volt-Ampere Demand Load: *Add lines 3 through 14 to find the minimum required volt-amperes.*	15	44,980

16 Minimum Amperes *Divide the total* *volt-amperes by* $\underline{\quad 44,980 \quad} \div \underline{\quad 831 \quad}$ = *the voltage.* (line 15) (voltage)	16	$\underline{\quad 54 \quad}$ (minimum amperes)	**Minimum Size** **17 Service or** **Feeder** *240.6(A)*	17	60
18 Size the Service or Feeder Conductors. *Tables 310.15(B)(16) through 310.15(B)(21)* *Use the tables along with 310.15(B)(1) through (6) to determine conductor size.* *If the overcurrent device is rated more than 800 amperes, the conductor ampacity* *must be equal to, or greater than, the rating of the overcurrent device. 240.4(C)*			**Minimum Size** **Conductors**	18	6 Cu 4 Al
19 Size the Neutral Conductor. *220.61* *The neutral service or feeder conductor can be smaller than the ungrounded* *(hot) conductors, but not smaller than the maximum unbalanced load determined* *by Article 220. 250.24(C)(1) states that the neutral shall not be smaller than* *the required grounding electrode conductor specified in Table 250.66. A further* *demand factor is permitted for any neutral load over 200 amperes.*			**Minimum Size** **Neutral** **Conductor**	19	8 Cu 6 Al
20 Size the Grounding Electrode Conductor (for Service). *250.66* *Use line 18 to find the grounding electrode conductor in Table 250.66.* *Size the Equipment Grounding Conductor (for Feeder). 250.122* *Use line 17 to find the equipment grounding conductor in Table 250.122.* *Equipment grounding conductor types are listed in 250.118.*			**Minimum Size** **Grounding Electrode** **Conductor . . . or . . .** **Equipment Grounding** **Conductor**	20	8 Cu 6 Al

SAMPLE LOAD CALCULATION—BANK

Load Calculation Information

A Use the information below to calculate the service load of this bank.

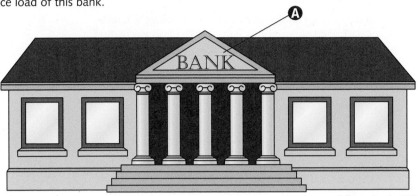

© Cengage Learning 2012

Bank's outside dimensions.	50′ × 100′
Actual inside connected lighting load .	16,200 volt-amperes
Receptacles	unknown
Sign	9 amperes, 120 volt
Show window	none
Parking lot lighting	57 amperes, 120 volt
Water heater	4 kW, 208 volt
Electric heating unit #1	6 kW, 208 volt, 3-phase
Electric heating unit #2	10 kW, 208 volt, 3-phase
Air handler (blower motor) #1	4 amperes, 208 volt, 3-phase
Air handler (blower motor) #2	4 amperes, 208 volt, 3-phase
Air-conditioner compressor #1.	22 amperes, 208 volt, 3-phase
Air-conditioner compressor #2.	22 amperes, 208 volt, 3-phase
Condenser fan motor #1	2.5 amperes, 208 volt, 3-phase
Condenser fan motor #2	2.5 amperes, 208 volt, 3-phase

Assume water heater and electric heat kW ratings equivalent to kVA.

The electric supply consists of a 208-volt, 3-phase, 4-wire service.

> **NOTE**
>
> Because the actual number of receptacles is unknown, line 1 does not contain a number.
>
> Line 2 will not contain a number since the bank has no fixed multioutlet assemblies.

Lines 3 and 4

A Since lines 1 and 2 are blank, line 3 also does not contain a number. A dashed line has been drawn in line 3 showing that it has been left blank intentionally.

B A bank (or office building) with an unknown number of general-purpose receptacle outlets requires a rating of 1 volt-ampere per square foot.

C Since the bank is 5000 ft² (50 × 100), the receptacle load is 5000 volt-amperes.

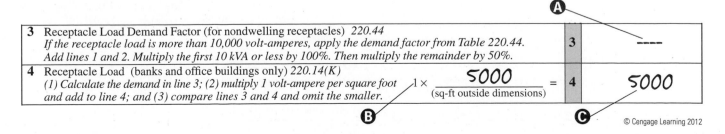

3	Receptacle Load Demand Factor (for nondwelling receptacles) *220.44* *If the receptacle load is more than 10,000 volt-amperes, apply the demand factor from Table 220.44.* *Add lines 1 and 2. Multiply the first 10 kVA or less by 100%. Then multiply the remainder by 50%.*	**3**	––––
4	Receptacle Load (banks and office buildings only) *220.14(K)* *(1) Calculate the demand in line 3; (2) multiply 1 volt-ampere per square foot* *and add to line 4; and (3) compare lines 3 and 4 and omit the smaller.* $1 \times \dfrac{5000}{\text{(sq-ft outside dimensions)}} =$	**4**	5000

© Cengage Learning 2012

Lines 5 and 6

A The volt-ampere unit load for a bank is 3.5
»*Table 220.12*«.

B This bank, with outside dimensions of 50 ft × 100 ft, has a total calculated area of 5000 ft².

C A bank's lighting load is continuous. The result of line 5 becomes part of the continuous volt-ampere load calculation (line 10).

D Because line 6 does not apply to this occupancy, a dashed line has been drawn showing that it has been left blank intentionally.

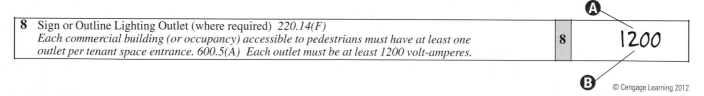

5 General Lighting Load *Table 220.12* *Multiply the volt-ampere unit load (for the type of* *occupancy) by the square-foot outside dimensions.*	$\dfrac{\textbf{3.5}}{\text{(VA unit load)}} \times \dfrac{\textbf{5000}}{\text{(sq-ft outside dimensions)}} =$	**5**	**17,500**
6 Lighting Load Demand Factors *220.42. Apply Table 220.42 demand factors to certain portions of* *hospitals, hotels, motels, apartment houses (without provisions for cooking), and storage warehouses.* *Do not include areas in hospitals, hotels, and motels where the entire lighting will be used at one time.*		**6**	————

© Cengage Learning 2012

Line 8

A Although the bank's actual sign load is 1080 volt-amperes (9 × 120), each sign outlet must have a minimum rating of 1200 volt-amperes. Use the actual sign or outline load(s) only if the rating is greater than the required minimum.

B This bank's sign load is continuous. Therefore, the rating is part of the continuous volt-ampere load calculation (line 10).

8 Sign or Outline Lighting Outlet (where required) *220.14(F)* *Each commercial building (or occupancy) accessible to pedestrians must have at least one* *outlet per tenant space entrance. 600.5(A) Each outlet must be at least 1200 volt-amperes.*	**8**	**1200**

© Cengage Learning 2012

Line 10

A This store's continuous loads are found on lines 5 and 8.

B 17,500 + 1200 = 18,700

C An additional 25% volt-ampere load is added to the calculation because of the continuous loads.

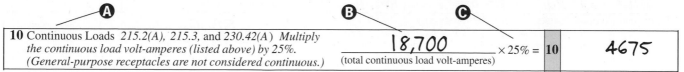

10 Continuous Loads *215.2(A), 215.3,* and *230.42(A) Multiply* *the continuous load volt-amperes (listed above) by 25%.* *(General-purpose receptacles are not considered continuous.)*	$\dfrac{\textbf{18,700}}{\text{(total continuous load volt-amperes)}} \times 25\% =$	**10**	**4675**

© Cengage Learning 2012

Lines 12 and 13

Each air-handler load is 1441 volt-amperes (4 × 208 × 1.732). Each condenser-fan motor load is 901 volt-amperes (2.5 × 208 × 1.732). Each compressor motor load is 7926 volt-amperes (22 × 208 × 1.732).

The total combined compressor, condenser-fan motor, and air-handler load is 20,536 volt-amperes (7926 + 7926 + 901 + 901 + 1441 + 1441).

The total combined electric heat and air-handler load is 18,882 (6000 + 10,000 + 1441 + 1441).

A Because the combined compressor, condenser-fan motor, and air-handler load is larger than the combined electric heat and air handler, omit the electric heat and air-handler load.

B Find the largest motor. In this example, that is the compressor motor (22 × 208 × 1.732 = 7,925.63). Increase the largest motor by 25% (7,925.63 × 25% = 1981).

12 Noncoincident Loads *220.60. The smaller of two (or more) noncoincident loads can be omitted, as long as they will never be energized simultaneously (such as certain portions of heating and A/C systems). Calculate fixed electric space-heating loads at 100% of the total connected load. 220.51*	12	20,536
13 Motor Loads *220.18(A), 430.24, 430.25, 430.26, and Article 440 Motor-driven air-conditioning and refrigeration equipment is found in Article 440. Multiply the largest motor (one motor only) by 25% and add it to the load.*	13	1981

© Cengage Learning 2012

Lines 14 and 15

A At this point, two loads have not been calculated: one continuous and one noncontinuous load. Because parking-lot lighting is continuous, multiply by 125% (57 × 120 × 125% = 8550 volt-amperes). The water heater is a noncontinuous load. These two loads have a combined total rating of 12,550 volt-amperes (8550 + 4000).

B Add lines 3 through 14 to determine the minimum volt-ampere load (lines 3, 6, 7, 9, and 11 are blank).

14 All Other Loads. *Add all other noncontinuous loads into the calculation at 100%. Multiply all other continuous loads (operating for 3 hours or more) by 125%.*	14	12,550
15 Total Volt-Ampere Demand Load: *Add lines 3 through 14 to find the minimum required volt-amperes.*	15	63,442

© Cengage Learning 2012

Lines 16 and 17

A Insert the total volt-ampere demand load from line 15.

B The total voltage for a 208-volt, 3-phase system is 360 (208 × 1.732).

C The minimum ampacity for a 208-volt, 3-phase service is 176 amperes.

D The next higher standard size fuse (or breaker) above 176 amperes is 200 » *240.6(A)* « .

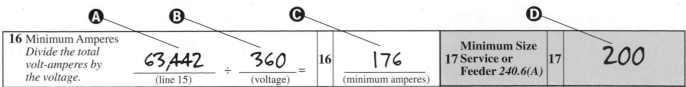

| **16** Minimum Amperes *Divide the total volt-amperes by the voltage.* | 63,442 (line 15) | ÷ | 360 (voltage) | = | 16 | 176 (minimum amperes) | **Minimum Size 17 Service or Feeder** *240.6(A)* | 17 | 200 |

© Cengage Learning 2012

Line 18

Ⓐ The minimum 75°C (167°F) copper service conductor is 3/0 AWG ⟫ *Table 310.15(B)(16)* ⟪.

Ⓑ The minimum 75°C (167°F) aluminum service conductor is 4/0 AWG ⟫ *Table 310.15(B)(16)* ⟪.

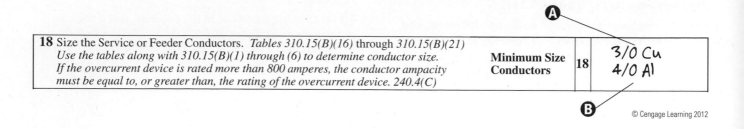

18 Size the Service or Feeder Conductors. *Tables 310.15(B)(16) through 310.15(B)(21)* *Use the tables along with 310.15(B)(1) through (6) to determine conductor size. If the overcurrent device is rated more than 800 amperes, the conductor ampacity must be equal to, or greater than, the rating of the overcurrent device. 240.4(C)*	**Minimum Size Conductors** **18**	3/0 Cu 4/0 Al

© Cengage Learning 2012

Line 19

Ⓐ The neutral conductor calculation requires only loads having a neutral or grounded conductor termination. In this example, include lines 4, 5, 8, 10, and part of line 14. Line 14's neutral load calculation is 8550 volt-amperes (57 × 120 × 125%). The total neutral load is 36,925 volt-amperes (5000 + 17,500 + 1200 + 4675 + 8550). The minimum required neutral rating is 103 amperes (36,925 ÷ 360).

Ⓑ The minimum 75°C (167°F) copper neutral conductor is 2 AWG ⟫ *Table 310.15(B)(16)* ⟪.

Ⓒ The minimum 75°C (167°F) aluminum neutral conductor is 1/0 AWG ⟫ *Table 310.15(B)(16)* ⟪.

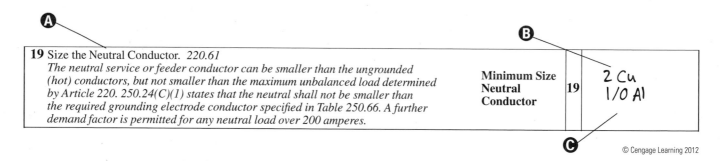

19 Size the Neutral Conductor. *220.61* *The neutral service or feeder conductor can be smaller than the ungrounded (hot) conductors, but not smaller than the maximum unbalanced load determined by Article 220. 250.24(C)(1) states that the neutral shall not be smaller than the required grounding electrode conductor specified in Table 250.66. A further demand factor is permitted for any neutral load over 200 amperes.*	**Minimum Size Neutral Conductor** **19**	2 Cu 1/0 Al

© Cengage Learning 2012

Line 20

Ⓐ The grounding electrode conductor's size is based on the service-entrance conductor ⟫ *Table 250.66* ⟪.

Ⓑ The minimum size copper grounding conductor is 4 AWG.

Ⓒ The minimum size aluminum grounding conductor is 2 AWG.

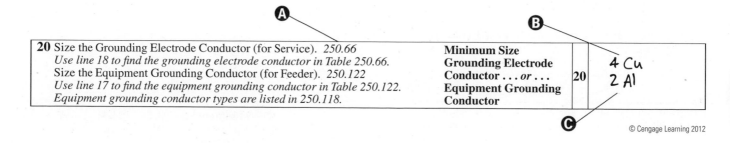

20 Size the Grounding Electrode Conductor (for Service). *250.66* *Use line 18 to find the grounding electrode conductor in Table 250.66.* Size the Equipment Grounding Conductor (for Feeder). *250.122* *Use line 17 to find the equipment grounding conductor in Table 250.122. Equipment grounding conductor types are listed in 250.118.*	**Minimum Size Grounding Electrode Conductor . . . or . . . Equipment Grounding Conductor** **20**	4 Cu 2 Al

© Cengage Learning 2012

The following page shows the bank's completed load calculation.

Nondwelling Feeder/Service Load Calculation

1	Receptacle Load (noncontinuous) *220.14(I)* *Multiply each single or multiple receptacle on one strap by 180 volt-amperes.* *Multiply each single piece of equipment comprised of four or more receptacles by 90 VA per receptacle.*	1	----
2	Fixed Multioutlet Assemblies (noncontinuous) *220.14(H)* *Where not likely to be used simultaneously, multiply each 5-ft section by 180 volt-amperes.* *Where likely to be used simultaneously, multiply each 1-ft section by 180 volt-amperes.*	2	----
3	Receptacle Load Demand Factor (for nondwelling receptacles) *220.44* *If the receptacle load is more than 10,000 volt-amperes, apply the demand factor from Table 220.44.* *Add lines 1 and 2. Multiply the first 10 kVA or less by 100%. Then multiply the remainder by 50%.*	3	----
4	Receptacle Load (banks and office buildings only) *220.14(K)* *(1) Calculate the demand in line 3; (2) multiply 1 volt-ampere per square foot* *and add to line 4; and (3) compare lines 3 and 4 and omit the smaller.* $1 \times \underline{\quad 5000 \quad}$ = (sq-ft outside dimensions)	4	5000
5	General Lighting Load *Table 220.12* *Multiply the volt-ampere unit load (for the type of* $\underline{\quad 3.5 \quad} \times \underline{\quad 5000 \quad}$ = *occupancy) by the square-foot outside dimensions.* (VA unit load) (sq-ft outside dimensions)	5	17,500
6	Lighting Load Demand Factors *220.42.* Apply *Table 220.42* demand factors to certain portions of *hospitals, hotels, motels, apartment houses (without provisions for cooking), and storage warehouses.* *Do not include areas in hospitals, hotels, and motels where the entire lighting will be used at one time.*	6	----
7	Track Lighting (in addition to general lighting) *220.43(B)* *Include 150 volt-amperes for every 2 ft,* $\underline{\quad ---- \quad} \div 2 \underline{\quad ---- \quad} \times 150 =$ *or fraction thereof, of lighting track.* (total linear ft)	7	----
8	Sign or Outline Lighting Outlet (where required) *220.14(F)* *Each commercial building (or occupancy) accessible to pedestrians must have at least one* *outlet per tenant space entrance. 600.5(A) Each outlet must be at least 1200 volt-amperes.*	8	1200
9	Show-Window Lighting *220.43(A)* *Include at least 200 volt-amperes for each linear foot,* $\underline{\quad ---- \quad} \times 200 =$ *measured horizontally along the show window's base.* (total linear ft of show window)	9	----
10	Continuous Loads *215.2(A), 215.3,* and *230.42(A)* *Multiply* *the continuous load volt-amperes (listed above) by 25%.* $\underline{\quad 18,700 \quad} \times 25\% =$ *(General-purpose receptacles are not considered continuous.)* (total continuous load volt-amperes)	10	4675
11	Kitchen Equipment *220.56* *Multiply three or more pieces of equipment by the Table 220.56 demand factor (%).* Use *Table 220.55* for household cooking equipment used in instructional programs. *Table 220.55,* Note 5	11	----
12	Noncoincident Loads *220.60. The smaller of two (or more) noncoincident loads can be omitted, as* *long as they will never be energized simultaneously (such as certain portions of heating and A/C systems).* *Calculate fixed electric space-heating loads at 100% of the total connected load. 220.51*	12	20,536
13	Motor Loads *220.18(A), 430.24, 430.25, 430.26,* and *Article 440* *Motor-driven air-conditioning and refrigeration equipment is found in Article 440.* *Multiply the largest motor (one motor only) by 25% and add it to the load.*	13	1981
14	All Other Loads. *Add all other noncontinuous loads into the calculation at 100%.* *Multiply all other continuous loads (operating for 3 hours or more) by 125%.*	14	12,550
15	Total Volt-Ampere Demand Load: *Add lines 3 through 14 to find the minimum required volt-amperes.*	15	63,442

16 Minimum Amperes *Divide the total* *volt-amperes by* *the voltage.*	$\dfrac{63,442}{\text{(line 15)}} \div \dfrac{360}{\text{(voltage)}} =$ 16	$\dfrac{176}{\text{(minimum amperes)}}$	**Minimum Size** **17 Service or** **Feeder** *240.6(A)*	17	**200**
18 Size the Service or Feeder Conductors. *Tables 310.15(B)(16) through 310.15(B)(21)* *Use the tables along with 310.15(B)(1) through (6) to determine conductor size.* *If the overcurrent device is rated more than 800 amperes, the conductor ampacity* *must be equal to, or greater than, the rating of the overcurrent device. 240.4(C)*			**Minimum Size** **Conductors**	18	3/0 Cu 4/0 Al
19 Size the Neutral Conductor. *220.61* *The neutral service or feeder conductor can be smaller than the ungrounded* *(hot) conductors, but not smaller than the maximum unbalanced load determined* *by Article 220. 250.24(C)(1) states that the neutral shall not be smaller than* *the required grounding electrode conductor specified in Table 250.66. A further* *demand factor is permitted for any neutral load over 200 amperes.*			**Minimum Size** **Neutral** **Conductor**	19	2 Cu 1/0 Al
20 Size the Grounding Electrode Conductor (for Service). *250.66* *Use line 18 to find the grounding electrode conductor in Table 250.66.* Size the Equipment Grounding Conductor (for Feeder). *250.122* *Use line 17 to find the equipment grounding conductor in Table 250.122.* *Equipment grounding conductor types are listed in 250.118.*			**Minimum Size** **Grounding Electrode** **Conductor . . . or . . .** **Equipment Grounding** **Conductor**	20	4 Cu 2 Al

Summary

- Article 220 contains load calculation procedures for non-dwelling units.
- Unlike dwelling unit load calculations, receptacle outlets must be included.
- Receptacle loads, including fixed multioutlet assemblies, can be derated if the load is greater than 10,000 volt-amperes.
- If the actual number of receptacle outlets in a bank or office building is unknown, a load of one volt-ampere per square foot must be included.
- Various occupancy types have different volt-ampere unit loads per Table 220.12.
- One similarity between dwelling unit and nondwelling unit load calculations is that a volt-ampere unit load must be multiplied by the square footage using outside dimensions.

- Table 220.42 contains lighting load demand factors for certain portions of hospitals, hotels, motels, storage warehouses, and apartment houses without provisions for cooking.
- Track lighting loads must be included in addition to the general lighting load.
- Some occupancies require a sign or outline lighting outlet.
- Show-window minimum volt-ampere lighting loads are based on a linear footage measurement.
- Continuous load calculations must be increased by an additional 25% volt-ampere rating.
- The volt-ampere rating, calculated in accordance with Article 220, represents only the minimum rating.

Unit 13 Competency Test

NEC Reference   Answer

_____   _____   1. What is the demand load contribution for a commercial laundry with ten 5-kVA clothes dryers and ten 1.5-kVA washing machines?

_____   _____   2. What is the volt-ampere unit load per square foot for a beauty salon?

_____   _____   3. Outlets for heavy-duty lampholders shall be calculated at a minimum of _____ volt-amperes.

_____   _____   4. What is the minimum general lighting load for an 11,750-ft² nightclub with an actual connected lighting load of 22,800 volt-amperes? (For this question, do not apply the continuous load demand factor.)

_____   _____   5. A restaurant contains the following commercial kitchen equipment: two 12-kW ovens, one 10-kW grill, two 8-kW deep fryers, one 1.2-kW disposer, one 1.5-kW dishwasher, one 10-kW booster heater, and one 4.5-kW water heater. What is the feeder calculated load (in kW) for this equipment?

_____   _____   6. For track lighting in a church, a load of not less than _____ shall be included for every _____ ft of lighting track or fraction thereof.

_____   _____   7. What is the receptacle demand load for a 9600-ft² bank with fifty-two receptacles?

_____   _____   8. Where it is unlikely that two or more _____ loads will be in use simultaneously, it shall be permissible to use only the largest load(s) that will be used at one time in calculating the total load of a feeder or service.

_____   _____   9. What is the receptacle load (after demand factors) for an office building with 250 receptacle outlets?

_____   _____   10. What is the minimum general lighting load for an 8000-ft² assembly hall? (Do not apply the continuous load demand factor.)

_____   _____   11. A manufacturing plant has 320 ft of multioutlet assemblies, of which 60 ft will contain equipment subject to simultaneous use. What is the volt-ampere calculated load contribution for these multioutlet assemblies?

NEC Reference   Answer

_____   _____   12. A school home economics class has twelve 8-kW household ranges. The kitchen equipment is supplied by a 230-volt, single-phase panelboard. What is the minimum size THW copper conductors required for this panelboard?

_____   _____   13. A motel has fifty guest rooms, each room measuring 18 ft × 30 ft. Each room contains eight duplex receptacles, of which one is GFCI protected. Exterior hallways have a total area of 3000 ft^2. What is the lighting and receptacle load (after demand factors) for this motel?

_____   _____   14. Fixed electric space-heating loads shall be calculated at _____% of the total connected load; however, in no case shall a feeder or service load current rating be less than the rating of the largest branch circuit supplied.

_____   _____   15. An outlet supplying recessed luminaire(s) shall be calculated based on _____.

_____   _____   16. For circuits supplying loads consisting of motor-operated utilization equipment that is fastened in place and that has a motor larger than ⅛ hp in combination with other loads, the total calculated load shall be based on _____.

_____   _____   17. In a commercial storage garage, duplex receptacle outlets shall be computed at not less than _____.

_____   _____   18. A restaurant contains the following commercial kitchen equipment: one 12-kW range, one 2.8-kW mixer, one 4.2-kW deep fryer, two 0.8-kW soup wells, and one 6-kW water heater. What is the feeder demand load (in kW) for this equipment?

_____   _____   19. A hospital has 150 patient's rooms, each room measuring 15 ft × 25 ft. What is the lighting load (after demand factors) for these rooms?

_____   _____   20. For circuits supplying lighting units that have ballasts, transformers, autotransformers, or LED drivers, the calculated load shall be based on _____.

Questions 21 through 30 are based on an office containing the following:

Office's total sq-ft area.	19,000 ft^2
Receptacle outlets.	200
Multioutlet assemblies.	80 ft
Multioutlet assemblies. . . . . (simultaneously used)	25 ft
Sign.	15 amperes, 120 volt
Track lighting.	48 ft
Water heater.	4 kW, 208 volt
Four electric heating units.	10 kW, 208 volt (each)
Four air handlers (blower motors) . . .	4 amperes, 208 volt, 3-phase (each)
Four air-conditioner compressors. . . .	24.6 amperes, 208 volt, 3-phase (each)
Eight condenser fan motors.	2.2 amperes, 208 volt, 3-phase (each)

Assume water heater and electric heat kW ratings equivalent to kVA.

The electric supply is a 208-volt, 3-phase, 4-wire service.

_____   _____   21. What is the total receptacle (including multioutlet assembly) volt-ampere service load after demand factors are applied?

_____   _____   22. What is the general lighting load for this 19,000-ft^2 office? (For this question, do not apply the continuous load demand factor.)

_____   _____   23. Without applying the continuous load demand factor, what track lighting load (if any) must be contributed to this office calculation?

NEC Reference   **Answer**

_____ _____ 24. What volt-ampere load shall be included for the sign? (For this question, do not apply the continuous load demand factor.)

_____ _____ 25. Which load(s), if any, can be omitted?

_____ _____ 26. What is the volt-ampere load contribution for the heating or air-conditioning system(s)? (Do not include 25% of the largest motor.)

_____ _____ 27. What is the minimum size service overcurrent protective device required for this office?

_____ _____ 28. A parallel run (two sets) of service-entrance conductors will be installed in two raceways. What is the minimum size THWN copper ungrounded conductors that can be used?

_____ _____ 29. What is the minimum size THWN copper neutral (grounded) conductors that can be installed? (The lighting does not consist of nonlinear loads.)

_____ _____ 30. What is the minimum size copper grounding electrode conductor?

UNIT 14

Services, Feeders, and Equipment

Objectives

After studying this unit, the student should:

▶ know the required minimum vertical wiring clearances for each electrical installation.

▶ be aware that other associated equipment, above or below the electrical installation, shall not extend more than 6 in. (150 mm) beyond the front of that electrical equipment.

▶ be familiar with the dedicated space above panelboards, switchboards, and motor control centers.

▶ be aware that a space equal to the equipment's width and depth, above panelboards, switchboards, and motor control centers, must be clear of foreign systems unless protection is provided.

▶ know that working space clearances vary depending on the conditions and voltages.

▶ understand the conditions that require two equipment working space entrances.

▶ know where to connect grounded and grounding conductors on both the service supply side and load side.

▶ understand the conditions that require ground-fault protection of equipment.

▶ have a good understanding of transformer and generator provisions.

▶ know that grounding and bonding connection points shall be made in the same place, at either the panel or the transformer.

▶ have an extensive understanding of busway provisions.

Introduction

Unit 14 contains electrical provisions relative to commercial type occupancies. Before beginning this unit, a review of Unit 9—Services and Electrical Equipment is recommended. Some of the same provisions that apply to one-family dwellings likewise apply to commercial installations. Vertical wiring clearances, found in Articles 225 and 230, apply to all electrical feeder and service installations. Also applicable to both dwelling and commercial areas is 110.26, which contains minimum working space provisions (600 volts or less) above, below, and in front of electrical equipment. Some requirements, such as for equipment rated 1200 amperes or more, over 6 ft (1.8 m) wide, and containing devices (overcurrent, switching, or control), are not included in Unit 9. This unit contains separately derived system provisions that pertain to certain battery, solar photovoltaic, generator, transformer, and converter winding-system installations. Because of space limitations, only transformer illustrations are used to explain these provisions. In addition to the separately derived system provisions, transformers have their own article (450). Although there are some exceptions, Article 450 covers the installation of all transformers see (450.1). Following the transformer material is an illustration briefly touching on generator provisions. Although generators have their own article (445), other generator provisions are found throughout the *Code*. Generators and their associated wiring and equipment must also adhere to applicable provisions of Articles 695, 700, 701, 702, and 705. Busway provisions close this unit. Busways can also be found in multiple occupancy types, that is, multifamily, commercial, and industrial.

Since state and local jurisdictions may modify *NEC* provisions, it is expedient to obtain a copy of local rules and regulations.

Grounding—Load Side of Service

Where ungrounded conductors are increased in size, equipment grounding conductors (where installed) shall be increased in size proportionately, according to the circular mil area of the ungrounded conductors 》》 *250.122(B)* 《《.

A Equipment bonding jumpers on the load side of an overcurrent device(s) shall be sized in accordance with 250.122. A single common continuous equipment bonding jumper shall be permitted to connect two or more raceways or cables if the bonding jumper is sized in accordance with 250.122 for the largest overcurrent device supplying circuits therein 》》 *250.102(D)* 《《.

B A grounded conductor shall not be connected to normally non-current-carrying metal parts of equipment, to equipment grounding conductor(s), or be reconnected to ground on the load side of the service disconnecting means except as otherwise permitted in Article 250 》》 *250.24(A)(5)* 《《.

C Equipment grounding conductors can be bare, covered, or insulated. Individually covered (or insulated) equipment grounding conductors shall have a continuous outer finish, either green or green with yellow stripe(s), unless otherwise permitted by Article 250, Part IV 》》 *250.119* 《《.

D Metal panelboard cabinets and frames shall physically contact each other and shall be connected to an equipment grounding conductor. If the panelboard is used with nonmetallic raceway (or cable), or if separate equipment grounding conductors are provided, secure a terminal bar for the equipment grounding conductors within the cabinet. The terminal bar shall be bonded to the metal cabinet and panelboard frame. Otherwise, connect it to the equipment grounding conductor that is run with the conductors feeding the panelboard 》》 *408.40* 《《.

E While equipment grounding conductors of wire type copper, aluminum, or copper-clad aluminum shall not be less than shown in Table 250.122, they are not required to be larger than the circuit conductors supplying the equipment. A raceway, cable armor, or sheath used as the

equipment grounding conductor (as provided in 250.118 and 250.134[A]), must comply with 250.4(A)(5) or 250.4(B) (4). Equipment grounding conductors shall be permitted to be sectioned within a multiconductor cable, provided the combined circular mil area complies with Table 250.122 》》 *250.122(A)* 《《.

F Unless grounded by connection to the grounded circuit conductor (permitted by 250.32, 250.140, and 250.142), non-current-carrying metal parts of equipment, raceways, and other enclosures, if grounded, shall be connected to an equipment grounding conductor by one of the following methods: (a) by connection to any of the equipment grounding conductors permitted by 250.118; or (b) by connection to an equipment grounding conductor contained within the same raceway, cable, or otherwise run with the circuit conductors 》》 *250.134* 《《.

G Except as permitted in 250.30(A)(1) and 250.32(B) Exception, a grounded circuit conductor shall not be used for grounding non-current-carrying metal equipment parts on the load side of the service disconnecting means, on the load side of a separately derived system disconnecting means, or the overcurrent device for a separately derived system not having a main disconnecting means, unless an exception has been met 》》 *250.142(B)* 《《.

NOTE

Paralleled conductors within multiple raceways or cables, as permitted in 310.10(H), require that the equipment grounding conductors (where used) also be installed in parallel in each raceway or cable. Where conductors are installed in parallel in the same raceway, cable, or cable tray as permitted in 310.10(H), a single equipment grounding conductor shall be permitted. Equipment grounding conductors installed in cable tray shall meet the minimum requirements of 392.10(B)(1)(c). Each equipment grounding conductor shall be sized in compliance with 250.122 》》 *250.122(F)* 《《.

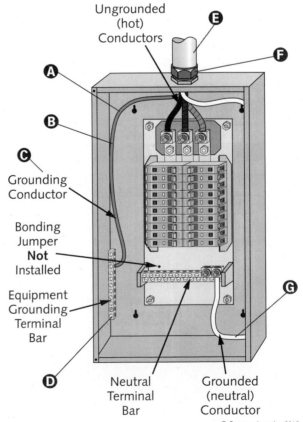

Ungrounded (hot) Conductors — **E**

A

F

B

C Grounding Conductor

Bonding Jumper **Not** Installed

Equipment Grounding Terminal Bar

G

D Neutral Terminal Bar

Grounded (neutral) Conductor

© Cengage Learning 2012

Ground-Fault Protection of Equipment

If a switch and fuse combination is used, the fuses employed shall be capable of interrupting any current higher than the interrupting capacity of the switch when the ground-fault protective system will not cause the switch to open 》》*230.95(B)*《《.

Ground-fault protection that functions to open the service disconnect will afford no protection from faults on the line side of the protective element. It serves to limit damage to conductors and equipment only on the load side of the protective element in the event of an arcing ground fault 》》*230.95(C) Informational Note No. 1*《《.

This added protective apparatus at the service equipment may necessitate a review of the overall wiring system for proper selective overcurrent protection coordination. Additional installations of ground-fault protective equipment may be needed on feeders and branch circuits requiring maximum continuity of electrical service 》》*230.95(C) Informational Note No. 2*《《.

Where ground-fault protection is provided for the service disconnect and another supply system is interconnected by a transfer device, a method may be needed to ensure proper sensing by the ground-fault protection equipment 》》*230.95(C) Informational Note No. 3*《《.

Ⓐ Ground-fault protection of equipment shall be provided for solidly grounded wye electrical services of more than 150 volts to ground but not exceeding 600 volts phase-to-phase for each service disconnect rated 1000 amperes or more. The grounded conductor for the solidly grounded wye system shall be connected directly to ground through a grounding electrode system, as specified in 250.50, without inserting any resistor or impedance device 》》*230.95 and 240.13*《《. See 215.10 for ground-fault protection of equipment for feeders.

Ⓑ The service disconnect rating is considered to be the rating of the largest fuse that can be installed or the highest continuous current trip setting for which the actual overcurrent device installed in a circuit breaker is rated (or can be adjusted) 》》*230.95*《《.

Ⓒ Ground-fault protection systems, when activated, shall cause the service disconnect to open all ungrounded conductors of the faulted circuit. The maximum ground-fault setting is 1200 amperes 》》*230.95(A)*《《.

Ⓓ One second is the maximum time delay for ground-fault currents of 3000 amperes or more 》》*230.95(A)*《《.

Ⓔ **Ground-Fault Protection of Equipment** is a system intended to provide protection of equipment from damaging line-to-ground fault currents by causing the disconnecting means to open all ungrounded conductors of the faulted circuit. This protection is provided at current levels less than those required to protect conductors from damage through the operation of a supply circuit overcurrent device 》》*Article 100*《《.

> **NOTE**
>
> Section 230.95 ground-fault protection provisions do not apply to fire pumps 》》*240.13(3)*《《. The ground-fault protection provisions of 230.95 do not apply to a service disconnect for a continuous industrial process where a nonorderly shutdown introduces additional or increased hazards 》》*230.95 Exception and 240.13(1)*《《.

> **CAUTION**
>
> Bonding for circuits over 250 volts to ground must comply with 250.97.

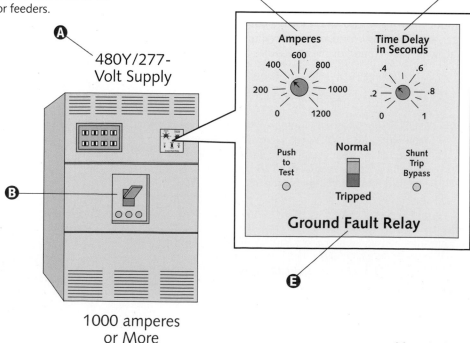

480Y/277-Volt Supply

1000 amperes or More

Ground Fault Relay

SEPARATELY DERIVED SYSTEMS

Transformers

Article 450 covers the installation of all transformers except:

1. Current transformers.

2. Dry-type transformers that constitute a component of other apparatus and comply with these requirements.

3. Transformers that are an integral part of X-ray, high-frequency, or electrostatic-coating apparatus.

4. Transformers used with Class 2 and Class 3 circuits in compliance with Article 725.

5. Sign and outline lighting transformers that comply with Article 600.

6. Transformers for electric-discharge lighting per Article 410.

7. Power-limited fire alarm circuit transformers that comply with Article 760, Part III.

8. Transformers used for research, development, or testing, where effective safeguards protect persons from contacting energized parts »*450.1 Exception Nos. 1 through 8*«.

Article 450 covers the installation of transformers dedicated to supplying power to a fire pump installation as modified by Article 695 »*450.1*«.

Article 450 covers the installation of transformers in hazardous (classified) locations as modified by Articles 501 through 504 »*450.1*«.

Autotransformers are covered in 450.4 and 450.5.

Appropriate provisions shall be made to minimize the possibility of damage to transformers from external causes where the transformers are exposed to such dangers »*450.8(A)*«.

Ⓐ The intended meaning of **transformer** is an individual transformer, single- or polyphase, identified by a single nameplate, unless otherwise indicated by Article 450 »*450.2*«.

Ⓑ Overcurrent protection for transformers over 600 volts, nominal, shall be provided in accordance with Table 450.3(A) »*450.3(A)*«.

Ⓒ Each transformer shall have a nameplate giving the manufacturer's name; rated kilovolt-amperes; frequency;

primary and secondary voltage; impedance of transformers (25 kVA and larger); required clearances for transformers with ventilating openings; and the amount and kind of insulating liquid (where used). In addition, the nameplate of each dry-type transformer shall include the insulation system's temperature class »*450.11*«.

Ⓓ Transformers with ventilation openings shall be installed so that such openings are not blocked by walls or other obstructions. The required clearances shall be legibly marked on the transformer »*450.9*«.

Ⓔ Dry-type transformers rated 600 volts, nominal, or less and not exceeding 50 kVA are permitted in hollow spaces of buildings that are not permanently closed in, provided they meet 450.9 ventilation requirements and 450.21(A) separation from combustible material requirements. Transformers so installed do not have to be readily accessible »*450.13(B)*«.

Ⓕ It is not required that dry-type transformers rated 600 volts, nominal, or less located in the open on walls, columns, or structures be readily accessible »*450.13(A)*«.

Ⓖ Where grounded, exposed non-current-carrying metal parts of transformer installations (fences, guards, and so on), shall be grounded and bonded, under the conditions and in a manner specified for electric equipment and other exposed metal parts in Parts V, VI, and VII of Article 250 »*450.10*«.

NOTE

All transformers and their vaults shall be readily accessible to qualified personnel for inspection and maintenance, or shall otherwise meet 450.13(A) or (B) requirements »*450.13*«.

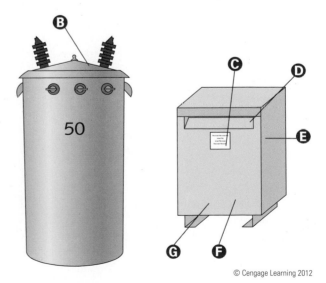

© Cengage Learning 2012

WARNING

Transformers, other than Class 2 or Class 3 transformers, shall have a disconnecting means located either in sight of the transformer or in a remote location. Where the disconnecting means is located in a remote location, it shall be lockable, and the location shall be field-marked on the transformer »*450.14*«.

Transformer—Primary-Only Protection 9 Amperes or More—600 Volts or Less

Conductors supplied by the secondary side of a single-phase transformer having a 2-wire (single-voltage) secondary, or a 3-phase, delta-delta connected transformer having a 3-wire (single-voltage) secondary, can be protected by overcurrent protection situated on the primary (supply) side of the transformer, provided this protection is in accordance with 450.3 and does not exceed the value determined when multiplying the secondary conductor ampacity by the secondary to primary transformer voltage ratio ⟩⟩ *240.21(C)(1)*⟨⟨ .

Ⓐ Where 125% of this current does not correspond to a standard fuse or nonadjustable circuit-breaker rating, the next higher rating (described in 240.6) is permitted ⟩⟩ *Table 450.3(B) Note 1*⟨⟨ .

Ⓑ This represents either a single-phase transformer having a 2-wire (single-voltage) secondary, or a 3-phase, delta-delta connected transformer having a 3-wire (single-voltage) secondary.

Ⓒ No secondary overcurrent protection is required for certain transformers 600 volts, nominal, or less with currents of at least 9 amperes and a maximum primary overcurrent protection of 125% ⟩⟩ *Table 450.3(B)*⟨⟨ . (The absence of secondary protection applies only to certain panelboards. See 408.36(B) Exception.)

Ⓓ Single-phase (other than 2-wire) and multiphase (other than delta-delta, 3-wire) transformer secondary conductors are not thought of as protected by the primary overcurrent protective device ⟩⟩ *240.21(C)(1)*⟨⟨ .

Ⓔ Overcurrent protection for transformers rated 600 volts, nominal, or less must be provided in accordance with Table 450.3(B), unless the transformer is installed as a motor-control circuit transformer in accordance with 430.72(C)(1) through (6) ⟩⟩ *450.3(B)*⟨⟨ .

WARNING

Although Table 450.3(B) does not require secondary overcurrent protection if the primary overcurrent protection is limited to 125%, 408.36(B) requires secondary overcurrent for most panelboards. Where a panelboard is supplied through a transformer, locate the overcurrent protection in 408.36 on the transformer's secondary side ⟩⟩ *408.36(B)*⟨⟨ . A panelboard supplied by the secondary side of a transformer is considered as protected by the overcurrent protection provided on the transformer's primary side, where that protection complies with 240.21(C)(1) ⟩⟩ *408.36(B) Exception*⟨⟨ .

Overcurrent Protection

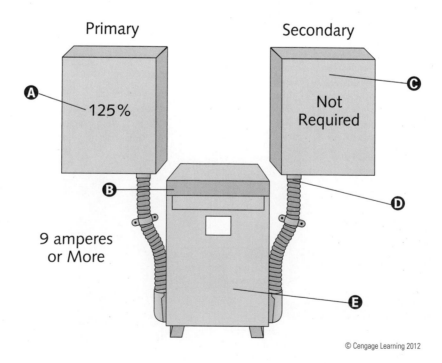

Primary

Secondary

Ⓐ 125%

Ⓒ

Not Required

Ⓑ

Ⓓ

9 amperes or More

Ⓔ

© Cengage Learning 2012

Transformer—Primary and Secondary Protection
9 Amperes or More—600 Volts or Less

A Unlike Note 1 that permits the next standard rating above 125%, the **maximum** rating or setting is 250%.

B A transformer equipped with coordinated thermal overload protection (by the manufacturer) and arranged to interrupt the primary current can have primary overcurrent protection rated (or set) at a current value not more than six times the rated current of transformers having not more than 6% impedance and not more than four times the rated current of transformers having more than 6%, but not more than 10%, impedance ≫ *Table 450.3(B) Note 3* ≪ .

C Overcurrent protection for transformers rated 600 volts, nominal, or less must be provided according to Table 450.3(B), unless the transformer is installed as a motor-control circuit transformer per 430.72(C)(1) through (6) ≫ *450.3(B)* and *Exception* ≪ .

D Where 125% of this current does not correspond to a standard fuse or nonadjustable circuit breaker rating, the next higher rating described in 240.6 is permitted ≫ *Table 450.3(B) Note 1* ≪ .

E If secondary overcurrent protection is required, these devices are permitted to consist of no more than six circuit breakers (or six sets of fuses) grouped in one location. Where multiple overcurrent devices are implemented, the total of all the device ratings must not exceed the single overcurrent device allowed value ≫ *Table 450.3(B) Note 2* ≪ .

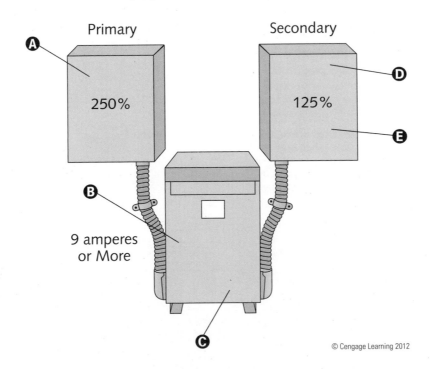

Overcurrent Protection

© Cengage Learning 2012

Grounding and Bonding—Terminating in the Panel

Premises wiring (system) is defined as interior and exterior wiring, including power, lighting, control, and signal circuit wiring together with all their associated hardware, fittings, and wiring devices, both permanently and temporarily installed. This includes (a) wiring from the service point or power source to the outlets or (b) wiring from and including the power source to the outlets where there is no service point. Such wiring does not include wiring internal to appliances, luminaires, motors, controllers, motor control centers, and similar equipment ≫ *Article 100* ≪.

A grounded circuit conductor can be used to ground non-current-carrying metal parts of equipment, raceways, and other enclosures on the supply side or within the enclosure of the main disconnecting means (or overcurrent devices) of a separately derived system as permitted by 250.30(A)(1) ≫ *250.142(A)(3)* ≪.

Ⓐ An unspliced system bonding jumper shall comply with 250.28(A) through (D). This connection shall be made at any single point on the separately derived system from the source to the first system disconnecting means (or overcurrent devices) or shall be made at the source of a separately derived system that has no disconnecting means or overcurrent devices, in accordance with 250.30(A)(1)(a) or (b). The system bonding jumper shall remain within the enclosure where it originates. If the source is located outside the building or structure supplied, a system bonding jumper shall be installed at the grounding electrode connection in compliance with 250.30(C) ≫ *250.30(A)(1)* ≪.

Ⓑ A grounding electrode conductor for a single separately derived system shall be sized in accordance with 250.66 for the derived ungrounded conductors. It shall be used to connect the grounded conductor of the derived system to the grounding electrode as specified in 250.30(A)(4). This connection shall be made at the same point on the separately derived system where the system bonding jumper is connected unless one of the exceptions is met ≫ *250.30(A)(5)* ≪.

Ⓒ For vertically operated circuit-breaker handles, the "up" position of the handle shall be the "on" position ≫ *240.81* ≪.

Ⓓ A grounded separately derived ac system shall comply with 250.30(A)(1) through (8), unless it is an impedance grounded neutral system installed as specified in 250.36 or 250.186, as applicable ≫ *250.30(A)* ≪.

CAUTION

Except as otherwise permitted in Article 250, a grounded conductor shall not be connected to normally non–current–carrying metal parts of equipment, be connected to equipment grounding conductors, or be reconnected to ground on the load side of the system bonding jumper ≫ *250.30(A)* ≪.

Ⓔ Size the equipment grounding conductor in accordance with 250.122. The equipment grounding conductor must be of the types listed in 250.118.

Ⓕ A system bonding jumper at both the source and the first disconnecting means is permitted, if doing so does not establish a parallel path for the grounded conductor. While grounded conductors used in this manner shall not be smaller than the size specified for the system bonding jumper, they do not have to be larger than the ungrounded conductor(s). In applying this exception, connection through the earth does not qualify as providing a parallel path ≫ *250.30(A)(1) Exception No. 2* ≪.

Ⓖ Grounding (and bonding) terminations made at the system disconnecting means or overcurrent device require that the transformer's grounded (neutral) bus be insulated from the transformer enclosure. If the neutral bus is bonded to the enclosure and the raceway to the panelboard is metallic, then part of the neutral current flows on the raceway. Section 250.6(A) prohibits objectionable current flow over grounding paths or grounding conductors.

NOTE

Transformers, which are only one type of separately derived system, are used to illustrate and explain 250.30.

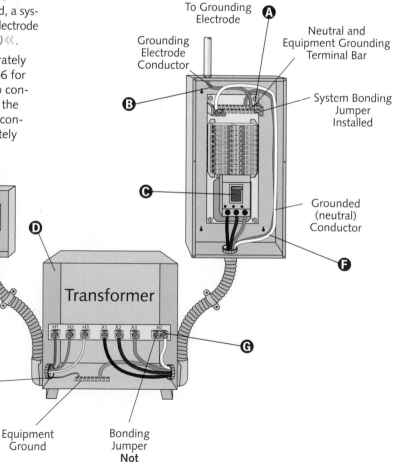

To Grounding Electrode **Ⓐ**

Grounding Electrode Conductor

Neutral and Equipment Grounding Terminal Bar

System Bonding Jumper Installed

Ⓑ

Ⓒ

Grounded (neutral) Conductor

Ⓕ

Ⓓ

Transformer

H1 H2 H3 X1 X2 X3 X0

Ⓔ Equipment Grounding Conductor

Equipment Ground

Bonding Jumper **Not** Installed

Ⓖ

Grounding and Bonding—Terminating in the Transformer

While a 3-phase separately derived system is used for this illustration, the same rules apply to single-phase systems.

A system supplying power to a Class 1, Class 2, or Class 3 circuit having the power derived from a transformer rated 1000 volt-amperes or less must have a system bonding jumper sized no smaller than the derived ungrounded conductors. The smallest size allowed is 14 AWG copper or 12 AWG aluminum »*250.30(A)(1) Exception No. 3*«.

A system that supplies a Class 1, 2, or 3 circuit and is derived from a transformer rated no more than 1000 volt-amperes does not require a grounding electrode conductor, provided the grounded conductor is bonded to the transformer frame (or enclosure) by means of a jumper sized in accordance with 250.30(A)(1), Exception No. 3, and the transformer frame (or enclosure) is grounded by one of the means specified in 250.134 »*250.30(A)(5) Exception No. 3*«.

A If the grounding (and bonding) terminations are made at the transformer, the system disconnecting means (or overcurrent device) grounded (neutral) terminal bar must be insulated from both the panelboard enclosure and the equipment grounding conductor. If the neutral terminal bar is bonded to the enclosure as well as the equipment grounding conductor, part of the neutral current will flow through the raceway (if metallic) and the equipment grounding conductor. Section 250.6(A) strictly prohibits such a condition.

B Except as permitted in 250.30(A)(1) and 250.32(B) Exception, a grounded circuit conductor shall not be used for grounding non-current-carrying metal equipment parts on the load side of a separately derived system disconnecting means (or the overcurrent devices) for a separately derived system having no main disconnecting means »*250.142(B)*«.

C The system bonding jumper connection can be made at any point on the separately derived system, that is, in either the panel or transformer »*250.30(A)(1)*«.

D A grounding electrode conductor for a single separately derived system shall be sized in accordance with 250.66 for the derived ungrounded conductors. It shall be used to connect the grounded conductor of the derived system to the grounding electrode as specified in 250.30(A)(41). This connection shall be made at the same point on the separately derived system where the system bonding jumper is connected »*250.30(A)(5)*«.

E Use an unspliced system bonding jumper that complies with 250.28(A) through (D) to connect the equipment grounding conductors of the separately derived system to the grounded conductor »*250.30(A)(1)*«.

F The grounding electrode conductor installation must comply with 250.64(A), (B), (C), and (E) »*250.30(A)(7)*«.

G If the system bonding jumper specified in 250.30(A)(1) is a wire or busbar, it shall be permitted to connect the grounding electrode conductor to the equipment grounding terminal, bar, or bus, provided the equipment grounding terminal, bar, or bus is of sufficient size for the separately derived system »*250.30(A)(5) Exception No. 1*«.

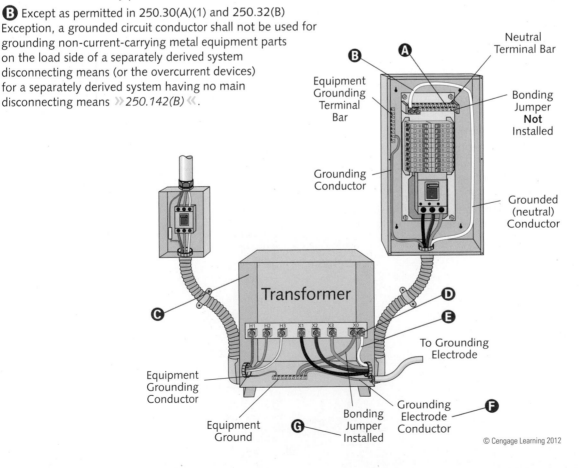

© Cengage Learning 2012

Grounding Electrode and Grounding Electrode Conductor

If a separately derived system originates in listed equipment suitable for use as service equipment, the service (or feeder) equipment's grounding electrode can serve as the separately derived system's grounding electrode ≫ *250.30(A)(4) Exception No. 2* ≪.

Ⓐ The grounding electrode shall be as near as practicable to, and preferably in the same area as, the grounding electrode conductor connection to the system. The grounding electrode shall be the nearest one of the following:

1. Metal water pipe grounding electrode as specified in 250.52(A)(1).
2. Structural metal grounding electrode as specified in 250.52(A)(2) ≫ *250.30(A)(4)* ≪.

Ⓑ Ferrous metal enclosures for grounding electrode conductors shall be electrically continuous from the point of attachment to cabinets or equipment to the grounding electrode and shall be securely fastened to the ground clamp or fitting. Nonferrous metal enclosures shall not be required to be electrically continuous. Ferrous metal enclosures that are not physically continuous from cabinets or equipment to the grounding electrode shall be made electrically continuous by bonding each end of the raceway or enclosure to the grounding electrode conductor. Bonding methods in compliance with 250.92(B) for installations at service equipment locations and with 250.92(B)(2) through (B)(4) for other than service equipment locations shall apply at each end and to all intervening ferrous raceways, boxes, and enclosures between the cabinets or equipment and the grounding electrode. The bonding jumper for a grounding electrode conductor raceway or cable armor shall be the same size as, or larger than, the enclosed grounding electrode conductor. If a raceway is used as protection for a grounding electrode conductor, the installation shall comply with the requirements of the appropriate raceway article ≫ *250.64(E)* ≪.

Ⓒ A grounding electrode conductor for a single separately derived system shall be sized according to 250.66 for the derived ungrounded conductors. It shall be used to connect the grounded conductor of the derived system to the grounding electrode as specified in 250.30(A)(4). This connection shall be made at the same point on the separately derived system where the system bonding jumper is connected ≫ *250.30(A)(5)* ≪.

Ⓓ All mechanical elements used to terminate a grounding electrode conductor or bonding jumper to a grounding electrode shall be accessible ≫ *250.68(A)* ≪.

Ⓔ Each separately derived system's grounded conductor shall be bonded to the nearest available point of interior metal water piping system(s) in the area served by each separately derived system. This connection shall be made at the same point on the separately derived system as the grounding electrode conductor connection. Size the bonding jumper per Table 250.66 based on the largest ungrounded conductor of the separately derived system ≫ *250.104(D)(1)* ≪.

Ⓕ Equipment requiring grounding and having a nonconductive coating (such as paint, lacquer, and enamel) shall have the coating removed from threads and other contact surfaces to ensure good electrical continuity (unless connected by fittings that are designed so as to make the removal unnecessary) ≫ *250.12* ≪.

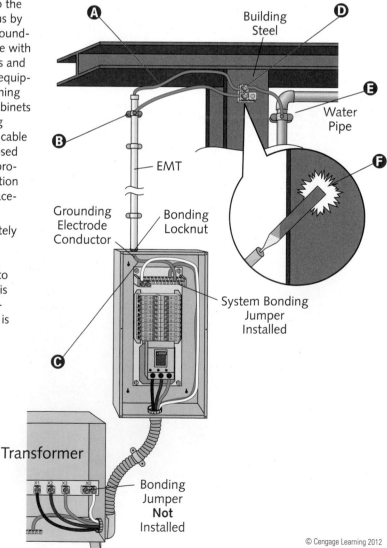

Generators

Article 445 contains installation and other requirements for generators ≫ *445.1* ≪.

Live generator parts operating at more than 50 volts to ground shall not be exposed to accidental contact by unqualified persons ≫ *445.14* ≪.

While legally required standby system requirements for generators and associated equipment are located in Article 701, optional standby system provisions are found in Article 702.

Ⓐ The conductor ampacity from the generator terminals to the first distribution device(s) containing overcurrent device shall not be less than 115% of the generator's nameplate current rating ≫ *445.13* ≪.

Ⓑ An alternate ac power source, such as an on-site generator, is not a separately derived system if the grounded conductor is solidly interconnected to a service-supplied system grounded conductor. An example of such a situation is where alternate source transfer equipment does not include a switching action in the grounded conductor and allows it to remain solidly connected to the service-supplied grounded conductor when the alternate source is operational and supplying the load served ≫ *250.30 Informational Note No. 1* ≪.

Ⓒ Generator provisions are also covered in Articles 695, 700, 701, 702, and 705.

Ⓓ The type of generator used shall be suitable for the installed location. The motor requirements in 430.14 shall also be met ≫ *445.10* ≪.

Ⓔ Depending on the generator type, overcurrent protection must meet 445.12 specifications.

Ⓕ Generators shall be equipped with disconnect(s), lockable in the open position, by means of which the generator, all protective devices, and control apparatus can be entirely disconnected from the circuits supplied by the generator, except where (1) the generator's driving means can be readily shut down and (2) the generator is not arranged to operate in parallel with another generator or other source of voltage ≫ *445.18* ≪.

Ⓖ Where wires pass through an enclosure, conduit box, or barrier opening, a bushing shall protect the conductors from any sharp edges. The bushing surfaces shall be smooth and well-rounded where they may contact the conductors. If oils, grease, or other contaminants are present, the bushing shall be made of a material not harmfully affected ≫ *445.16* ≪.

Ⓗ Each generator shall have a nameplate identifying the manufacturer; the rated frequency; power factor; number of phases (if of alternating current); the subtransient and impedances; the rating in kilowatts or kilovolt amperes; the normal volts and amperes corresponding to the rating; rated revolutions per minute; insulation system class and rated ambient temperature (or rated temperature rise); and time rating ≫ *445.11* ≪.

NOTE

Portable and vehicle-mounted generators must be grounded in accordance with 250.34.
A generator meeting the qualifications of a separately derived system must be grounded per 250.30 specifications.

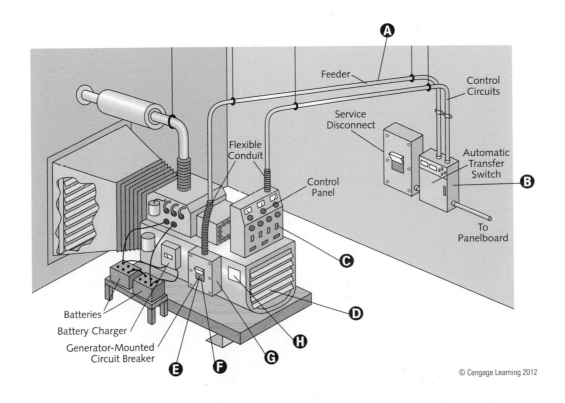

Feeder
Control Circuits
Service Disconnect
Flexible Conduit
Automatic Transfer Switch
Control Panel
To Panelboard
Batteries
Battery Charger
Generator-Mounted Circuit Breaker

BUSWAYS

General Installation Provisions

Busways shall not be installed as follows: (1) where subject to severe physical damage or corrosive vapors; (2) in hoist-ways; (3) in any hazardous (classified) location, unless specifically approved for such use; and (4) outdoors or in wet or damp locations unless identified for such use ⟫*368.12(A)* through *(D)*⟪.

Cord and cable installations must comply with 368.56(B) and (C).

Overcurrent protection is required where busways are reduced in ampacity, unless the industrial establishment exception is met ⟫*368.17(B)*⟪.

A busway used as a branch circuit shall be protected against overcurrent in accordance with 210.20 ⟫*368.17(D)*⟪.

Ⓐ Article 368 covers the service-entrance, feeder, branch-circuit busways, and associated fittings ⟫*368.1*⟪. A busway is a grounded metal enclosure containing factory-mounted, bare, or insulated conductors of copper or aluminum bars, rods, or tubes ⟫*368.2*⟪.

Ⓑ Busways must be securely supported at no more than 5-ft (1.5-m) intervals unless otherwise designed and so marked ⟫*368.30*⟪.

Ⓒ Where a busway serves as a feeder, devices or plug-in connections for tapping off feeder or branch circuits from the busway shall consist of an externally operable circuit breaker or fusible switch. If such devices contain a disconnecting means and are mounted out of reach, a suitable means (ropes, chains, sticks, etc.) shall be provided to facilitate operation of the disconnecting means from the floor ⟫*368.17(C)*⟪. (This section also contains three exceptions.)

Ⓓ A busway shall be protected against overcurrent in accordance with the busway's allowable current rating, unless applying the applicable provisions of 240.4 ⟫*368.17(A)*⟪.

Ⓔ Unbroken busway lengths can extend through dry walls ⟫*368.10(C)(1)*⟪.

Ⓕ A busway's dead end shall be closed ⟫*368.58*⟪.

> **NOTE**
>
> Lighting and trolley busways shall not be installed less than 8 ft (2.5 m) above the floor (or working platform), unless provided with a cover and identified for the purpose ⟫*368.12(E)*⟪.

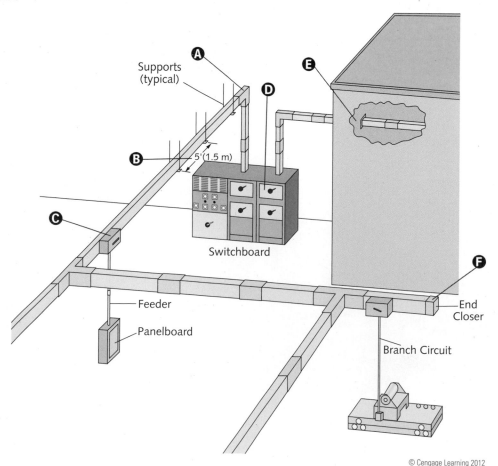

Vertical Installation Provisions

Branches from busways shall be permitted to use any of the following wiring methods:

(1) Type AC (armored cable)

(2) Type MC (metal-clad cable)

(3) Type MI (mineral-insulated, metal-sheathed cable)

(4) Type IMC (intermediate metal conduit)

(5) Type RMC (rigid metal conduit)

(6) Type FMC (flexible metal conduit)

(7) Type LFMC (liquidtight flexible metal conduit)

(8) Type PVC (rigid polyvinyl chloride conduit)

(9) Type RTRC (reinforced thermosetting resin conduit)

(10) Type LFNC (liquidtight flexible nonmetallic conduit)

(11) Type EMT (electrical metallic tubing)

(12) Type ENT (electrical nonmetallic tubing)

(13) Busways

(14) Strut-type channel raceway

(15) Surface metal raceway

(16) Surface nonmetallic raceway

Where a separate equipment grounding conductor is used, connection of the equipment grounding conductor to the busway shall comply with 250.8 and 250.12 》》*368.56*《《.

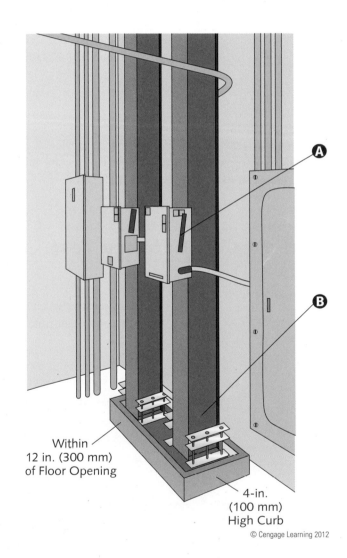

A Busways and busway taps shall be protected against overcurrent in accordance with 368.17 》》*240.21(E)*《《.

B Section 368.10(C)(2) requires that floor penetrations comply with (a) and (b):

(a) Vertical busways can extend through dry floors if totally enclosed (unventilated) where passing through, and for a minimum distance of 6 ft (1.8 m) above the floor, providing adequate physical damage protection.

(b) In other than industrial establishments, where a vertical riser penetrates multiple dry floors, a minimum 4-in. (100-mm) high curb shall be installed around all busway riser floor openings to prevent liquid penetration. The curb shall be installed within 12 in. (300 mm) of the floor opening. Locate electrical equipment so that it is not likely to be damaged by curb-retained liquids.

Within
12 in. (300 mm)
of Floor Opening

4-in.
(100 mm)
High Curb

© Cengage Learning 2012

NOTE

Implement electrical installations in hollow spaces or vertical shafts so that the possible spread of fire, or products of combustion, will not be substantially increased. Openings around electrical penetrations into or through fire-resistant-rated walls, partitions, floors, or ceilings shall be firestopped by approved methods to maintain the fire resistance rating 》》*300.21*《《.

Summary

- Sections 225.18 and 230.24(B) contain minimum vertical wiring clearance provisions.
- Except for meters that are installed in meter sockets, associated equipment located above or below electrical equipment shall not extend more than 6 in. (150 mm) beyond the electrical equipment's front.
- A space equal to the width and depth of the equipment (panelboards, switchboards, and motor control centers), extending from the floor to a height of 6 ft (1.8 m) above the equipment (or to the structural ceiling, whichever is lower) must be dedicated to the electrical installation.
- The space equal to the width and depth of the equipment above panelboards, switchboards, and motor control centers must be clear of foreign systems unless protection is provided to avoid damage from condensation, leaks, or breaks.
- Working space clearances vary, depending on conditions and voltage.
- For equipment rated 1200 amperes or more and over 6 ft (1.8 m) wide containing overcurrent devices, switching devices, or control devices, there shall be an entrance at each end of the working space.
- In switchboards and panelboards, every circuit and circuit modification must be legibly identified as to its clear, evident, and specific purpose or use.
- On the supply side of the service, the grounded circuit conductor and grounding conductors are connected together.
- All switchboards and panelboards supplied by a feeder in other than one- or two-family dwellings shall be marked to indicate the device or equipment where the power supply originates.
- A grounding connection must not be made to any grounded circuit conductor on the load side of the service disconnecting means except as otherwise allowed by Article 250.
- Transformer provisions are located in Article 450.
- Section 250.30 contains separately derived system grounding provisions.
- An alternate ac power source (such as an on-site generator) is not a separately derived system if the grounded conductor is solidly interconnected to a service-supplied grounded conductor.
- Article 368 covers service-entrance, feeder, and branch-circuit busways and associated fittings.

Unit 14 Competency Test

NEC Reference	Answer	
_____	_____	1. A separately derived system's grounding electrode conductor connection can be made at any point from the source to the _____ system disconnecting means or overcurrent device.
_____	_____	2. For the purposes of Article 408, a 3-pole circuit breaker shall be considered _____ overcurrent device(s).
_____	_____	3. Internal parts of electrical equipment, including busbars, wiring terminals, insulators, and other surfaces, shall not be _____ by foreign materials such as paint, plaster, cleaners, abrasives, or corrosive residues.
_____	_____	4. An alternate ac power source such as an on-site generator is not a separately derived system if the _____ is solidly interconnected to a service-supplied system _____.
_____	_____	5. For equipment rated 1200 amperes or more and over 6 ft wide that contains overcurrent devices, switching devices, or control devices, there shall be _____ entrance(s).
_____	_____	6. A 480-volt transformer, equipped with coordinated thermal overload protection by the manufacturer and arranged to interrupt the primary current, shall be permitted to have primary overcurrent protection rated or set at a current value that is not more than _____ the rated current of the transformer for a transformer having 8% impedance.
_____	_____	7. The width of the working space in front of the electric equipment shall be the width of the equipment or _____ in., whichever is greater.

NEC Reference   **Answer**

_____   _____   8. Where wires pass through an opening in an enclosure, conduit box, or barrier, a _____ shall be used to protect the conductors from the edges of an opening having sharp edges within generators.

_____   _____   9. On a switchboard or panelboard supplied from a 4-wire, delta-connected system where the midpoint of one phase winding is grounded, that phase busbar or conductor having the higher voltage to ground shall be durably and permanently marked by an outer finish that is _____ in color or by other effective means.

_____   _____   10. Ground-fault protection of equipment shall be provided for solidly grounded wye electrical systems of more than 150 volts to ground, but not exceeding 600 volts phase-to-phase for each individual device used as a building or structure main disconnecting means rated _____ or more.

_____   _____   11. The _____ conductor of each separately derived system shall be bonded to the nearest available point of the interior metal water piping system(s) in the area served by each separately derived system.

_____   _____   12. Busways shall be securely supported at intervals not exceeding _____ ft unless otherwise designed and marked.

_____   _____   13. What is the minimum vertical clearance (in ft) for 208Y/120-volt, 3-phase overhead service conductors in a commercial area subject to minimal truck traffic?

_____   _____   14. Covered, shielded, fenced, enclosed, or otherwise protected by means of suitable covers, casings, barriers, rails, screens, mats, or platforms to remove the likelihood of approach or contact by persons or objects to a point of danger is the definition of _____.

_____   _____   15. Where the overcurrent device is rated over _____ amperes, the ampacity of the conductors it protects shall be equal to or greater than the rating of the overcurrent device as defined in 240.6.

_____   _____   16. The enclosure for a panelboard shall have the top and bottom wire-bending space sized in accordance with _____ for the largest conductor entering or leaving the enclosure.

_____   _____   17. A(n) _____ is a premises wiring system whose power is derived from source of electric energy other than a service, and that has no direct connection from circuit conductors of one system to circuit conductors of another system, other than connections through the earth, metal enclosures, metallic raceways, or equipment grounding conductors.

_____   _____   18. Dry-type transformers 600 volts, nominal, or less and not exceeding _____ shall be permitted in hollow spaces of buildings not permanently closed in by structure.

_____   _____   19. Where rear access is required to work on nonelectrical parts on the back of enclosed equipment, a minimum horizontal working space of _____ in. shall be provided.

_____   _____   20. The ampacity of the conductors from the generator terminals to the first distribution device(s) containing overcurrent protection shall not be less than _____ % of the nameplate current rating of the generator.

_____   _____   21. Where exposed to the weather, raceways enclosing service-entrance conductors shall be suitable for use in wet locations and _____.

_____   _____   22. For industrial establishments only, omission of overcurrent protection shall be permitted at points where busways are reduced in ampacity, provided that the length of the busway having the smaller ampacity does not exceed _____ ft and has an ampacity at least equal to one-third the rating or setting of the overcurrent device next back on the line, and provided that such busway is free from contact with combustible material.

_____   _____   23. Circuit breakers shall be marked with their ampere rating in a manner that will be _____ after installation.

Wiring Methods—Class I, Division 2 *(continued)*

E Bonding jumpers or conductors and equipment bonding jumpers shall be permitted to be installed inside or outside of a raceway or an enclosure.

(1) Inside a Raceway or an Enclosure. If installed inside a raceway, equipment bonding jumpers and bonding jumpers or conductors shall comply with the requirements of 250.119 and 250.148.

(2) Outside a Raceway or an Enclosure. If installed on the outside, the length of the bonding jumper or conductor or equipment bonding jumper shall not exceed 6 ft (1.8 m) and shall be routed with the raceway or enclosure ≫ *250.102(E)* ≪.

Conduit and Cable Seals—Class I, Divisions 1 and 2

A Seals in conduit and cable systems, within Class I, Divisions 1 and 2 shall comply with 501.15(A) through (F) ≫ *501.15* ≪.

B In a seal, the conductors' cross-sectional area shall not exceed 25% of the cross-sectional area of an RMC of the same trade size, unless it is specifically identified for a higher percentage of fill ≫ *501.15(C)(6)* ≪.

C If a probability exists that liquid or other condensed vapor may be trapped within control equipment enclosures, or at any point in the raceway system, install approved means to prevent accumulation or to permit periodic draining ≫ *501.15(F)(1)* ≪.

D Conduit/cable system seals minimize the passage of gas/vapors and prevent the passage of flames from one portion of the electrical installation to another through the conduit ≫ *501.15 Informational Note No. 1* ≪.

E In a completed seal, the sealing compound's minimum thickness shall at least equal the trade size of the sealing fitting and shall be in no case less than ⅝ in. (16 mm) ≫ *501.15(C)(3)* ≪.

F Sealing compound shall (1) provide a seal against passage of gas/vapors through the seal fitting; (2) not be affected by surrounding atmosphere or liquids; and (3) have a melting point of 93°C (200°F) or higher ≫ *501.15(C)(2)* ≪.

G Install a conduit seal in each conduit run leaving a Class I, Division 1 (or Division 2) location. The conduit seal is permitted on either side, and within 10 ft (3.05 m) of such location's boundary, and must be designated and installed to minimize the amount of gas/vapor within the Division 1 (or Division 2) portion of the conduit from being communicated to the conduit beyond the seal ≫ *501.15(A)(4)* and *501.15(B)(2)* ≪.

H Except for listed explosionproof reducers at the conduit seal, there must be no union, coupling, box, or fitting between the conduit seal and the point at which the conduit leaves the Division 1 or 2 location ≫ *501.15(A)(4)* and *501.15(B)(2)* ≪.

CAUTION

Sealing fittings shall be listed for use with one or more specific compounds and shall be accessible ≫ *501.15(C)(1)* ≪.

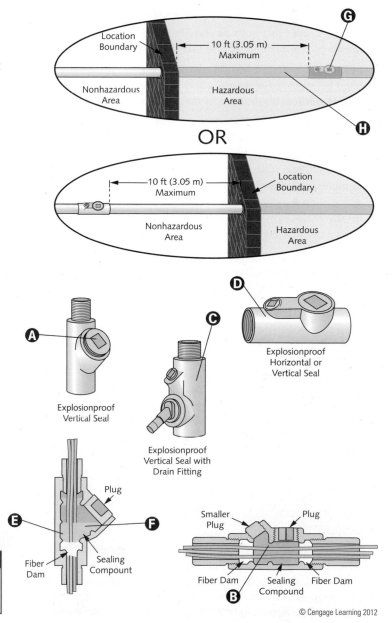

NOTE

Study 501.15 carefully, because many exceptions and informational notes are contained therein.

© Cengage Learning 2012

Conduit and Cable Seals—Class I, Divisions 1 and 2 *(continued)*

Type MI cable termination fittings shall contain sealing compound that excludes moisture/fluids from the cable insulation »*501.15*«.

In Class I, Division 1 locations, conduit seals shall be placed in each conduit entry into an explosionproof enclosure where either (1) the enclosure contains apparatus, such as switches, circuit breakers, fuses, relays, or resistors, that may produce arcs, sparks, or high temperatures that are an ignition source in normal operation or (2) the entry is trade size 2 or larger and the enclosure contains terminals, splices, or taps »*501.15(A)(1)*«.

Class I, Division 2 connections to required explosionproof enclosures shall have a conduit seal in accordance with 501.15(A)(1)(1) and (A)(3). The entire conduit run or nipple between the seal and such enclosure shall comply with 501.10(A) »*501.15(B)(1)*«.

Splices/taps shall not be made inside fittings intended only for sealing with compound, nor can other fittings that contain splices/taps be filled with compound »*501.15(C)(4)*«.

Commercial Garages, Repair, and Storage

Article 514 requirements apply to fuel-dispensing units (other than liquid petroleum gas, which is prohibited) located within buildings »*511.4(B)(1)*«.

Within Class I locations as classified in 511.3, wiring shall conform to applicable Article 501 provisions »*511.4(A)*«.

Seals conforming to 501.15 and 501.15(B)(2) provisions shall be provided and shall apply not only to horizontal but also to vertical boundaries of the defined Class I locations »*511.9*«.

Equipment less than 12 ft (3.7 m) above the floor level that may produce arcs, sparks, or hot metal particles (such as cutouts, switches, charging panels, generators, motors, or other equipment and excluding receptacles, lamps, and lampholders) having make-or-break or sliding contacts, shall be of the totally enclosed type or constructed to prevent the escape of sparks or hot metal particles »*511.7(B)(1)(a)*«.

A Areas adjacent to classified locations in which flammable vapor release is unlikely (such as stock rooms, switchboard rooms, and similar locations), shall be unclassified where (1) mechanically ventilated at a rate of four (or more) air changes per hour; (2) designed with positive air pressure; or (3) effectively separated by walls or partitions »*511.3(E)(1)*«.

B A **major repair garage** is a building or portions of a building where major repairs, such as engine overhauls, painting, body and fender work, and repairs that require draining of the motor vehicle fuel tank are performed on motor vehicles, including associated floor space used for offices, parking, or showrooms »*511.2*«.

C Article 511 occupancies include those used for service and repair of self-propelled vehicles (including, but not limited to, passenger automobiles, buses, trucks, and tractors) that use volatile flammable liquids or flammable gases for fuel or power »*511.1*«.

D For pendants, flexible cord suitable for the type of service and listed for hard usage shall be used »*511.7(A)(2)*«.

E In major repair garages, unless there is mechanical ventilation meeting the specifications in 511.3(C)(1)(a), the entire floor area up to a level of 18 in. (450 mm)

above the floor shall be classified as Class I, Division 2 »*511.3(C)(1)(b)*«.

F The pit area shall be a Class I, Division 2 location where there is mechanical ventilation providing a minimum of six air changes per hour »*511.3(C)(3)(a)*«.

G Fixed lighting lamps and lampholders that are located over lanes through which vehicles are commonly driven or that may otherwise be exposed to physical damage shall be located at least 12 ft (3.7 m) above floor level, unless totally enclosed or constructed to prevent the escape of sparks or hot metal particles »*511.7(B)(1)(b)*«.

H In major repair garages, unless there is mechanical ventilation meeting the specifications in 511.3(C)(3)(a), the pit or depression below floor level and extending up to the floor level shall be a Class I, Division 1 location »*511.3(C)(3)(b)*«.

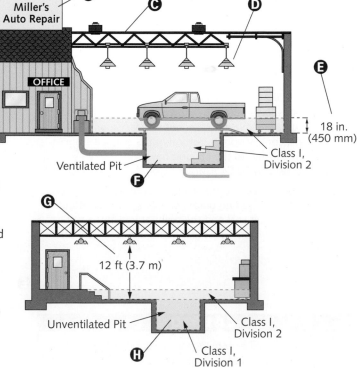

Miller's Auto Repair

OFFICE

18 in. (450 mm)

Ventilated Pit

Class I, Division 2

12 ft (3.7 m)

Unventilated Pit

Class I, Division 2

Class I, Division 1

Commercial Garages, Repair, and Storage *(continued)*

CAUTION

All 125-volt, single-phase, 15- and 20-ampere receptacles in areas where electrical diagnostic equipment, electrical hand tools, or portable lighting equipment are used shall have GFCI protection for personnel 》*511.12*《.

NOTE

The floor area shall be unclassified where there is mechanical ventilation providing a minimum of four air changes per hour or 1 cfm/ft² (0.3 m³/min/m²) of exchanged air for each square foot of floor area. Ventilation shall provide for air exchange across the entire floor area, and exhaust air shall be taken at a point within 12 in. (0.3 m) of the floor 》*511.3(C)(1)(a)*《.

Any circuit in a Class I location supplying portables (or pendants) that include a grounded conductor (per Article 200) shall have receptacles, attachment plugs, connectors, and similar devices of the grounding type, and the flexible cord's grounded conductor shall either be connected to the screw shell of any lampholder or to the grounded terminal of any utilization equipment supplied. Equipment grounding conductor continuity (between the fixed wiring system and the non-current-carrying metal portions of pendant luminaires, portable lamps, and portable utilization equipment) shall be maintained via approved means 》*511.16(B)(1) and (2)*《.

Battery chargers, their control equipment, and batteries being charged shall not be located within areas classified in 511.3 》*511.10(A)*《.

All metal raceways, the metal armor or metallic sheath on cables, and all non-current-carrying metal parts of fixed/portable electrical equipment, regardless of voltage, shall be grounded 》*511.16(A)*《.

Ⓐ All fixed wiring above Class I locations shall be placed within metal raceways, PVC, ENT, FMC, LFMC, or LFNC; or it shall be Type MC, AC, MI, manufactured wiring systems, PLTC cable in accordance with Article 725, or Type TC cable or Type ITC cable in accordance with Article 727 》*511.7(A)(1)*《.

Ⓑ A **minor repair garage** is a building or portions of a building used for lubrication, inspection, and minor automotive

NOTE

Where ventilation is provided to exhaust the pit area at a rate of not less than 1 cfm/ft² (0.3 m³/min/m²) of floor area at all times that the building is occupied or when vehicles are parked in or over this area and where exhaust air is taken from a point within 12 in. (300 mm) of the floor of the pit, belowgrade work area, or subfloor work area, the pit shall be unclassified 》*511.3(D)(3)(a)*《.

maintenance work, such as engine tune-ups, replacement of parts, fluid changes (e.g., oil, antifreeze, transmission fluid, brake fluid, or air-conditioning refrigerants), brake system repairs, tire rotation, and similar routine maintenance work, including associated floor space used for offices, parking, or showrooms 》*511.2*《.

Ⓒ The floor area up to a level of 18 in. (450 mm) above any unventilated pit, belowgrade work area, or subfloor work area and extending a distance of 3 ft (900 mm) horizontally from the edge of any such pit, belowgrade work area, or subfloor work area, shall be classified as Class I, Division 2 》*511.3(D)(1)(b)*《.

Ⓓ In minor repair garages, unless there is ventilation meeting the specifications in 511.3(D)(3)(a), any pit or depression below floor level and extending up to the floor level shall be a Class I, Division 2 location 》*511.3(D)(3)(b)*《.

Ⓔ Where lighter-than-air gaseous fuels (such as natural gas or hydrogen) will not be transferred, such locations shall be unclassified 》*511.3(D)(2)*《.

NOTE

Floor areas in minor repair garages without pits, belowgrade work areas, or subfloor work areas shall be unclassified. Where floor areas include pits, belowgrade work areas, or subfloor work areas in lubrication or service rooms, the classification rules in (a) or (b) shall apply 》*511.3(D)(1)*《.

The entire floor area shall be unclassified where there is mechanical ventilation providing a minimum of four air changes per hour or 1 cfm/ft² (0.3 m³/min/m²) of exchanged air for each square foot of floor area. Ventilation shall provide for air exchange across the entire floor area, and exhaust air shall be taken at a point within 12 in. (0.3 m) of the floor 》*511.3(D)(1)(a)*《.

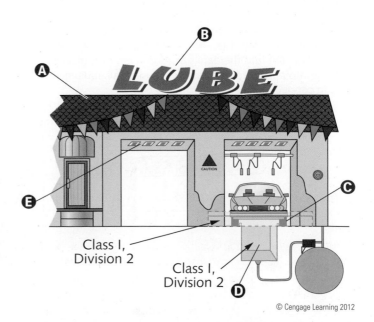

Class I, Division 2

Class I, Division 2

© Cengage Learning 2012

Parking Garages

For further information, see *Standard for Parking Structures, NFPA 88A-2011*, and *Code for Motor Fuel Dispensing Facilities and Repair Garages, NFPA 30A-2008* »*511.3(A) Informational Note*«.

Ⓐ Garages used for parking or storage are permitted to be unclassified »*511.3(A)*«.

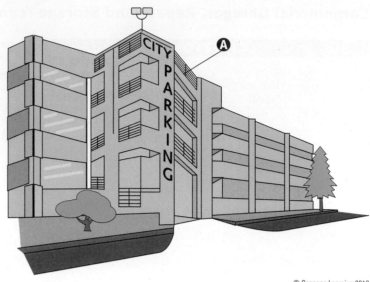

© Cengage Learning 2012

Motor Fuel Dispensing Facilities

Article 514 covers requirements applicable to motor fuel dispensing facilities, marine/motor fuel dispensing facilities, motor fuel dispensing facilities located inside buildings, and fleet vehicle motor fuel dispensing facilities »*514.1*«.

If the AHJ can satisfactorily determine that flammable liquids having a flash point below 38°C (100°F), such as gasoline, will not be handled, such location does not require a hazardous classification »*514.3(A)*«.

A Class I location does not extend beyond any unpierced wall, roof, or other solid partition »*514.3(B)(1)*«.

All metal raceways, the metal armor or metallic sheath on cables, and all non-current-carrying metal parts of fixed/portable electrical equipment, regardless of voltage, shall be grounded and bonded. Grounding and bonding in Class I locations shall comply with 501.30 »*514.16*«.

Ⓐ A **motor fuel dispensing facility** is that portion of a property where motor fuels are stored and dispensed from fixed equipment into fuel tanks of motor vehicles, marine craft, or into approved containers, including all equipment used in connection with motor fuel »*514.2*«.

Ⓑ Wiring and equipment above Class I locations classified in 514.3 shall comply with 511.7 »*514.7*«.

Ⓒ All electrical equipment/wiring within Class I locations classified in 514.3 shall comply with the applicable provisions of Article 501 »*514.4*«.

> ### N O T E
>
> Table 514.3(B)(1) shall be used where Class I liquids are stored, handled, or dispensed and to delineate and classify motor fuel dispensing facilities as well as any other location storing, handling, or dispensing Class I liquids »*514.3(B)(1)*«.

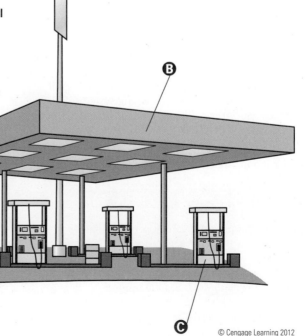

© Cengage Learning 2012

Dispensing Devices

Unattended self-service motor fuel dispensing facility emergency controls as specified in 514.11(A) shall be installed at a location acceptable to the AHJ, such location being more than 20 ft (6 m) but less than 100 ft (30 m) from dispensers. Additional emergency controls shall either be installed on each group of dispensers or on the outdoor equipment controlling the dispensers. Emergency controls shall completely shut off power to all of the station's dispensing equipment. Controls shall be manually reset only in a manner approved by the AHJ 》*514.11(C)*《.

Attended self-service motor fuel dispensing facility emergency controls, as specified in 514.11(A), shall be installed at a location acceptable to the AHJ and not more than 100 ft (30 m) from dispensers 》*514.11(B)*《.

Additional seals apply to horizontal as well as vertical boundaries of the Class I locations 》*514.9(B)*《.

A Within 18 in. (450 mm) horizontally, extending in all directions from grade to the dispenser enclosure, or that portion of the dispenser enclosure containing liquid handling components, is a Class I, Division 2 location 》*Table 514.3(B)(1)*《.

B The space inside the dispenser enclosure is classified as covered in *Power Operated Dispensing Devices for Petroleum Products,* ANSI/UL 87-1995 》*Table 514.3(B)(1)*《.

C Each circuit leading to (or through) dispensing equipment, including all associated power, communications, data, and video circuits, and equipment for remote pumping systems, shall have a clearly identified, readily accessible switch (or other approved means), located away from the dispensing devices, to simultaneously disconnect all circuit conductors (including the grounded conductor, if any) from the supply source. Single-pole breakers utilizing handle ties shall not be permitted 》*514.11(A)*《.

D From grade level up to a height of 18 in. (450 mm) within 20 ft (6.0 m) horizontally of any enclosure edge, is a Class I, Division 2 location 》*Table 514.3(B)(1)*《.

E All or part of any pit, box, or space below grade level within a Division 1 or 2 (or Zone 1 or 2) classified location is designated Class I, Division 1 》*Table 514.3(B)(1)*《.

F A listed seal shall be provided in each conduit run entering/leaving a dispenser or any cavities (or enclosures) in direct communication with the dispensing area. The sealing fitting shall be the first fitting after the conduit emerges from the earth or concrete 》*514.9(A)*《.

G Underground wiring shall be installed either in threaded RMC or threaded steel IMC. Any portion of electrical wiring below the surface of a Class I, Division 1 or 2 location shall be sealed within 10 ft (3.05 m) of the point of emergence above grade. Except for listed explosionproof reducers, at the conduit seal there shall be no union, coupling, box, or fitting between the conduit seal and the point of emergence above grade 》*514.8*《.

> **N O T E**
>
> Each dispensing device shall be provided with a means to remove all external voltage sources, including power, communications, data, and video circuits and including feedback, during periods of maintenance and service of the dispensing equipment. The location of this means shall be permitted to be other than inside or adjacent to the dispensing device. The means shall be capable of being locked in the open position 》*514.13*《.

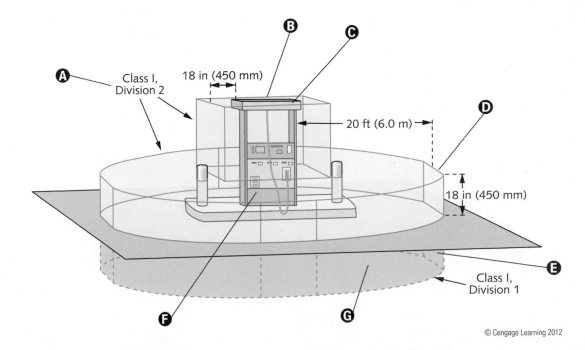

© Cengage Learning 2012

Aircraft Hangars

Mobile Equipment: Equipment having electric components designed for movement via mechanical aids, or having wheels to facilitate movement by person(s) or powered devices ≫*513.2*≪.

Portable Equipment: Equipment with electric components that can be moved by a single person without using mechanical aids ≫*513.2*≪.

All wiring and equipment intended for installation that is installed or operated within any of the 513.3 defined Class I locations shall comply with the applicable provisions of Article 501 or Article 505 for the division or zone in which they are used ≫*513.4(A)*≪.

Attachment plugs and receptacles in Class I locations shall either be identified for Class I locations or designed so that they shall not be energized during connection/disconnection ≫*513.4(A)*≪.

All fixed wiring in a hangar not within a Class I location as defined in 513.3 shall be (1) installed in metal raceways or (2) Type MI, TC, or MC cable ≫*513.7(A)*≪.

Portable utilization equipment and luminaires require flexible cord suitable for the type of service and identified for extra-hard usage. Such cords shall include a separate equipment grounding conductor ≫*513.10(E)(1) and (2)*≪.

Adjacent areas in which flammable liquids or vapors are not likely to be released (stock rooms, electrical control rooms, etc.) shall be unclassified, provided such areas are adequately ventilated and effectively cut off from the hangar itself by walls or partitions ≫*513.3(D)*≪.

Portable utilization equipment that can be, or is, used within a hangar shall be of a type suitable for use in Class I, Division 2 or Zone 2 locations ≫*513.10(E)(2)*≪.

Seals shall be provided in accordance with 501.15 or 505.16, as applicable. Sealing requirements specified apply both to horizontal and vertical Class I location boundaries ≫*513.9*≪.

All metal raceways, the metal armor or metallic sheath on cables, and all non-current-carrying metal parts of fixed/portable electrical equipment, regardless of voltage, shall be grounded. Grounding in Class I locations shall comply with 501.30 or 505.25 ≫*513.16(A)*≪.

Ⓐ Article 513 applies to buildings/structures or parts thereof inside which aircraft (containing Class I liquids or Class II liquids whose temperatures exceed their flash points) are housed, stored, serviced, repaired, or altered. It does not apply to locations used exclusively for aircraft that do not now, nor have ever, contained fuel ≫*513.1*≪.

Ⓑ The area within 5 ft (1.5 m) horizontally from aircraft power plants or fuel tanks is a Class I,

Division 2 or Zone 2 location extending upward from the floor to a level 5 ft (1.5 m) above the upper surface of wings and engine enclosures ≫*513.3(C)(1)*≪.

Ⓒ Any pit or depression below the hangar floor level is a Class I, Division 1 or Zone 1 location that extends up to floor level ≫*513.3(A)*≪.

Ⓓ The hangar's entire area, including any adjacent and communicating areas not suitably separated from the hangar, is designated as a Class I, Division 2 or Zone 2 location up to a level 18 in. (450 mm) above the floor ≫*513.3(B)*≪.

> **NOTE**
>
> In locations above those described in 513.3, equipment less than 10 ft (3.0 m) above aircraft wings and enclosures, which may produce arcs, sparks, or particles of hot metal (such as lamps and lampholders for fixed lighting, cutouts, switches, receptacles, charging panels, generators, motors, or other equipment having make-or-break or sliding contacts), shall be of the totally enclosed type or by construction shall prevent the escape of sparks or hot metal particles ≫*513.7(C)*≪.

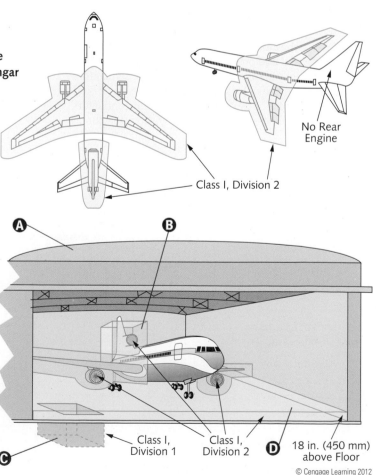

No Rear Engine

Class I, Division 2

Class I, Division 1 — Class I, Division 2 — 18 in. (450 mm) above Floor

© Cengage Learning 2012

Bulk Storage Plants

Sealing requirements apply to horizontal as well as vertical boundaries of the defined Class I locations. Raceways buried under a defined Class I area are considered to be within a Class I, Division 1 or Zone 1 location ≫515.9≪.

Underground wiring shall be enclosed in either threaded RMC or threaded steel IMC; if buried under at least 2 ft (600 mm) of cover, Type PVC conduit, Type RTRC conduit (or a listed cable) can be used. If Type PVC conduit or Type RTRC conduit is used, threaded metal conduit (either rigid or steel intermediate) shall be used for not less than the last 2 ft (600 mm) of the conduit run to the conduit point of emergence from the underground location or to the point of connection to an aboveground raceway. Cable, if used, shall also be enclosed in threaded metal conduit (either rigid or steel intermediate) from the point of lowest buried cable to the point of aboveground raceway connection ≫515.8(A)≪.

Where Type PVC conduit, Type RTRC conduit, or cable with a nonmetallic sheath is used, include an equipment grounding conductor to provide electrical continuity of the raceway system and grounding of non-current-carrying metal parts ≫515.8(C)≪.

Where gasoline or other volatile flammable liquids or liquefied flammable gases are dispensed at bulk stations, the appropriate provisions of Article 514 apply ≫515.10≪.

All metal raceways, the metal armor or metallic sheath on cables, and all non-current-carrying metal parts of fixed/portable electrical equipment, regardless of voltage, shall be grounded and bonded as provided in Article 250 ≫515.16≪.

A A **bulk plant** or **terminal** is that portion of a property where liquids are received (by tank vessel, pipelines, tank car, or tank vehicle), stored, or blended in bulk for the purpose of distribution by tank vessel, pipeline, tank car, tank vehicle, portable tank, or container ≫515.2≪.

B Apply Table 515.3 where Class I liquids are stored, handled, or dispensed. Table 515.3 is also used to delineate and classify bulk storage plants. The class location does not extend beyond any floor, wall, roof, or other solid partition that has no communicating openings ≫515.3≪.

C All electrical wiring and equipment within the Class I locations defined in 515.3 shall comply with the applicable provisions of Article 501 or Article 505 for the division or zone in which they are used ≫515.4≪.

D All fixed wiring above Class I locations shall be in metal raceways, Schedule 80 PVC conduit, Type RTRC marked with suffix -XW, or Type MI, Type TC, or Type MC cable, or Type PLTC and Type PLTC-ER cable in accordance with the provisions of Article 725, including installation in cable tray systems or Type ITC and Type ITC-ER cable as permitted in 727.4. The cable shall be terminated with listed fittings. Fixed equipment that may produce arcs, sparks, or particles of hot metal (such as lamps and lampholders for fixed lighting, cutouts, switches, receptacles, motors, or other equipment having make-or-break or sliding contacts), shall either be of the totally enclosed type or otherwise be constructed to prevent the escape of sparks or hot metal particles. Portable luminaires or other utilization equipment and associated flexible cords shall comply with Article 501's or Article 505's requirements for the class of location above which they are connected or used ≫515.7(A), (B), and (C)≪.

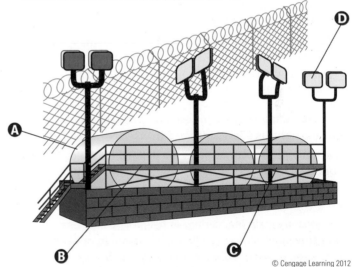

© Cengage Learning 2012

Spray Application, Dipping, and Coating Process

Classification is based on dangerous quantities of flammable vapors, combustible mists, residues, dusts, or deposits ≫516.3≪.

The following spaces are considered Class I, Division I or Class I, Zone 0 as applicable:

1. The interior of any open or closed container of a flammable liquid
2. The interior of any dip tank or coating tank ≫516.3(A)≪

The following spaces are considered Class I or Class II, Division 1 locations or Class I, Zone 1 locations as applicable:

1. Spray booth/room interiors except as specifically provided in 516.3(D)
2. Exhaust duct interiors
3. Any area in the direct path of spray operations
4. For open dipping and coating operations, all space within a 5-ft (1.5-m) radius of the vapor source extending from the surface to the floor. The vapor source is liquid exposed during the process, which includes draining, and any dipped or coated object from which measurable vapor concentrations exceed 25% of the lower flammable limit within 1 ft (300 mm), in any direction, from the object.
5. Sumps, pits, or belowgrade channels within 25 ft (7.5 m) horizontally of the vapor source. The sumps, pits, or belowgrade channels extending beyond 25 ft (7.5 m) must have a vapor stop, without which the entire pit is designated Class I, Division 1.

Spray Application, Dipping, and Coating Process (continued)

6. All space in all directions outside of but within 3 ft (900 mm) of open containers, supply containers, spray gun cleaners, and solvent distillation units containing flammable liquids 》》*516.3(B)*《《

The following spaces are considered Class I or Class II, Division 2 locations or Class I, Zone 2 as applicable:

1. All spaces outside of open spacing, but within 20 ft (6 m) horizontally and 10 ft (3 m) vertically of the Class I, Division 1 location as defined in 516.3(A), and not separated by partitions

2. If spray application operations are conducted within a closed-top, open-face, or open-front booth/room, any electrical wiring or utilization equipment located outside of the booth/room, but within the Division 2 or Zone 2 boundaries shall be suitable for Class I, Division 2; Class I, Zone 2; or Class II, Division 2 locations, whichever is applicable.

3. In open-top spray booth operations, the space 3 ft (900 mm) vertically above the booth and within 3 ft (900 mm) of all other booth openings qualifies as Class I or Class II, Division 2 or Class I, Zone 2.

4. For enclosed spray booth/room operations, the space within 3 ft (900 mm) in all directions from any opening is considered Class I or Class II, Division 2; or Class I, Zone 2 》》*516.3(C)*《《.

The space adjacent to an enclosed dipping (or coating) process/apparatus is unclassified 》》*516.3(D)*《《.

Adjacent locations cut off from the defined Class I or Class II locations by tight partitions without communicating openings, where release of flammable vapors or combustible powders is unlikely, are unclassified 》》*516.3(E)*《《.

Locations using drying, curing, or fusion apparatus having (1) positive mechanical ventilation adequate to prevent accumulation of flammable vapor concentrations and (2) effective interlocks to de-energize all electrical equipment (other than equipment approved for Class I locations) in case of inoperative ventilating equipment are unclassified where the AHJ deems appropriate 》》*516.3(F)*《《.

While fixed electrostatic spraying and detearing equipment requirements are located in 516.10(A), electrostatic handspraying equipment provisions are found in 516.10(B).

All metal raceways, the metal armor or metallic sheath on cables, and all non-current-carrying metal parts of fixed/

portable electrical equipment, regardless of voltage, shall be grounded and bonded. Grounding and bonding shall comply with 501.30, 502.30, or 505.25, as applicable 》》*516.16*《《.

A Article 516 covers the regular (or frequent) spray application of flammable liquids, combustible liquids, and combustible powders, as well as the application of flammable/combustible liquids at temperatures above their flash point, by dipping, coating, or other means 》》*516.1*《《.

B All space within a 5-ft (1.5-m) radius of the vapor source, extending from the surface to the floor, is designated Class I, Division 1; Class II, Division 1; or Class I, Zone 1 》》*516.3(B)(4)*《《.

C A space 3 ft (900 mm) above the floor, extending 20 ft (6 m) horizontally in all directions from the Class I, Division 1; Class I, Zone 1; or Class II, Division 1 location shall be considered Class I, Division 2; Class I, Zone 2; or Class II, Division 2 as applicable 》》*516.3(C)(6)*《《.

D A 3-ft (900-mm) space surrounding the dip tank and drain board's Class I, Division 1 or Class 1, Zone 1 location is considered Class I, Division 2; Class I, Zone 2; or Class II, Division 2 》》*516.3(C)(5)*《《.

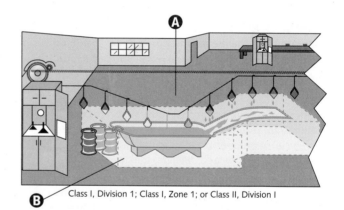

B Class I, Division 1; Class I, Zone 1; or Class II, Division I

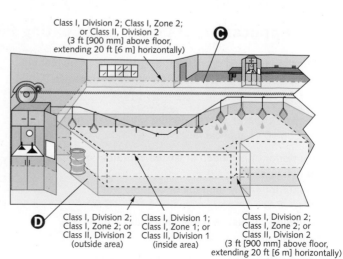

Class I, Division 2; Class I, Zone 2; or Class II, Division 2 (3 ft [900 mm] above floor, extending 20 ft [6 m] horizontally)

D Class I, Division 2; Class I, Zone 2; or Class II, Division 2 (outside area)

Class I, Division 1; Class I, Zone 1; or Class II, Division 1 (inside area)

Class I, Division 2; Class I, Zone 2; or Class II, Division 2 (3 ft [900 mm] above floor, extending 20 ft [6 m] horizontally)

NOTE

Wiring and equipment above Class I and Class II locations must comply with 516.7 specifications.

CLASS II LOCATIONS

Class II, Division 1 Locations

In addition to the requirements found in Article 500, wiring and equipment in Class II locations shall meet Article 502's provisions.

Dust-ignitionproof means equipment enclosed in a manner that excludes dust, and, where installed and protected in accordance with this *Code*, which does not permit arcs, sparks, or heat otherwise generated or liberated inside the enclosure to ignite exterior accumulations or atmospheric suspensions of a specified dust on or near the enclosure »*500.2*«.

The temperature marking for Class II locations, per 500.8(C), shall be less than the ignition temperature of the specific dust to be encountered. For organic dusts that may dehydrate or carbonize, the temperature marking shall not exceed the lower of either the ignition temperature or 165°C (329°F) »*500.8(D)(2)*«.

The type of equipment and wiring defined as explosionproof (in Article 100) is not required and shall not be acceptable for Class II locations unless also identified for such locations »*502.5*«.

In Class II, Division 1 locations, transformers and capacitors containing burnable liquid shall be installed only in vaults compliant with 450.41 through 450.48, in addition to all the following stipulations: (1) openings (doors, etc.) communicating with the Division 1 locations shall have self-closing fire doors on both sides of the wall, carefully fitted and having suitable seals (such as weather stripping) to minimize the entrance of dust into the vault; (2) vent openings and ducts shall connect directly with outside air; and (3) suitable pressure-relief openings to the outside air shall be provided »*502.100(A)(1)*«. Subsequently, transformers and capacitors not containing burnable liquids shall either be installed in vaults complying with 450.41 through 450.48,

or be identified as a complete assembly, including terminal connections »*502.100(A)(2)*«.

No transformer or capacitor shall be installed in a Class II, Division 1, Group E location »*502.100(A)(3)*«.

Equipment listed and marked in accordance with 506.9(C)(2) for Zone 20 locations shall be permitted in Class II, Division 1 locations for the same dust atmosphere, and with a suitable temperature class »*502.6*«.

Ⓐ A Class II, Division 1 location is an area (1) in which combustible dust is airborne under normal operating conditions in quantities sufficient to produce explosive or ignitible mixtures; (2) where mechanical failure or abnormal operation of machinery/equipment might not only produce such explosive or ignitible mixtures, but also provide an ignition source through simultaneous failure of electric equipment, operation of protection devices, or by other causes; or (3) in which Group E combustible dusts may exist in hazardous quantities »*500.5(C)(1)*«.

Ⓑ Because dusts containing magnesium or aluminum are particularly hazardous, extreme precautions are necessary to avoid ignition and explosion »*500.5(C)(1) Informational Note*«.

Ⓒ Class II locations are hazardous because of the presence of combustible dust »*500.5(C)*«.

> **N O T E**
>
> Bonding and grounding must comply with 502.30(A) and (B) provisions.

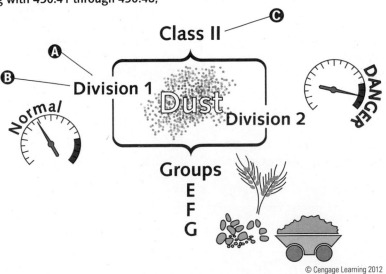

© Cengage Learning 2012

Class II, Division 2 Locations

In Class II, Division 2 locations, transformers and capacitors containing burnable liquid shall be installed within vaults compliant with 450.41 through 450.48 »*502.100(B)(1)*«.

Askarel-containing transformers, rated in excess of 25 kVA, shall have (1) pressure-relief vents; (2) a means for absorbing any gases generated by arcing inside the case, or chimney/flue-connected pressure-relief vents that shall carry such gases outside the building; and (3) at least 6 in. (150 mm) of airspace between the transformer case and any adjacent combustible material »*502.100(B)(2)*«.

Dry-type transformers, operating at not over 600 volts, nominal, shall either be installed in vaults or shall have their windings and terminal connections enclosed in tight metal housings without ventilation or other openings »*502.100(B)(3)*«.

Equipment listed and marked in accordance with 506.9(C)(2) for Zone 20, 21, or 22 locations shall be permitted in Class II, Division 2 locations for the same dust atmosphere and with a suitable temperature class »*502.6*«.

Ⓐ A Class II, Division 2 location is an area (1) where combustible dust due to abnormal operations may be present in the air in quantities sufficient to produce explosive or ignitible mixtures; (2) where combustible dust accumulations typically do not interfere with normal operation of electrical equipment or other apparatus, but may become airborne as a result of infrequent malfunctioning of processing/handling equipment; and (3) where combustible dust accumulations on, in, or near electrical equipment may be sufficient to interfere with safe heat dissipation from said equipment, or may be ignited by abnormal operation or failure of electrical equipment »*500.5(C)(2)*«.

Ⓑ The quantity of combustible dust that may be present and the adequacy of dust removal systems are factors that merit consideration in determining the classification and may result in an unclassified area »*500.5(C)(2) Informational Note No. 1*«.

Ⓒ Where the handling of substances such as seed produces low quantities of dust, the amount of dust deposited may not warrant classification »*500.5(C)(2) Informational Note No. 2*«.

> **NOTE**
>
> Bonding and grounding must comply with 502.30(A) and (B) provisions.

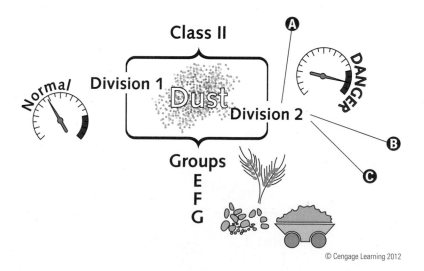

© Cengage Learning 2012

Wiring Methods—Class II, Divisions 1 and 2

Approved wiring methods in Class II, Division 1 locations include threaded RMC, threaded steel IMC, or Type MI cable with termination fittings listed for the location. Type MI cable shall be installed and supported in a manner to avoid tensile stress at the termination fittings ≫*502.10(A)(1)(1)* and *(2)* ≪. In industrial establishments with limited public access, where maintenance and supervision conditions ensure that only qualified persons will service the installation, Class II, Division 1–listed Type MC-HL cable with a gas/vaportight continuous corrugated metallic sheath, an overall jacket of suitable polymeric material, separate equipment grounding conductors (per 250.122), and termination fittings listed for the application are permitted ≫*502.10(A)(1)(3)* ≪.

Class II, Division 1 fittings and boxes shall be provided with threaded bosses for conduit connections or cable terminations and shall be dusttight. Fittings and boxes containing taps, joints, or terminal connections or those that are used in Group E locations shall be identified for Class II locations ≫*502.10(A)(1)(4)* ≪.

Use only (1) dusttight flexible connectors; (2) LFMC with listed fittings; (3) LFNC with listed fittings; (4) interlocked armor Type MC cable having an overall jacket of suitable polymeric material and provided with termination fittings listed for Class II, Division 1 locations; or (5) flexible cord listed for extra-hard usage and terminated with listed dusttight fittings in Class II, Divisions 1 and 2 locations necessitating flexible connections. Any flexible cords used shall comply with 502.140 ≫*502.10(A)(2)* and *(B)(2)* ≪.

Sealing fittings shall be accessible ≫*502.15* ≪.

Unless an exception is met, approved wiring methods in Class II, Division 2 locations include (1) all wiring methods permitted in 502.10(A); (2) RMC, IMC, EMT, dusttight wireways; (3) Type MC or MI cable with listed termination fittings; (4) Type PLTC and Type PLTC-ER cable in accordance with the provisions of

Article 725, including installation in cable tray systems (the cable shall be terminated with listed fittings); (5) Type ITC and Type ITC-ER cable as permitted in 727.4 and terminated with listed fittings; (6) Type MC, MI, or TC cable installed in cable trays (ladder, ventilated trough, or ventilated channel) in a single layer, with a space at least equal to the larger cable diameter between the two adjacent cables; or (7) in industrial establishments with restricted public access where the conditions of maintenance and supervision ensure that only qualified persons service the installation and where metallic conduit does not provide sufficient corrosion resistance, reinforced thermosetting resin conduit (RTRC) factory elbows, and associated fittings, all marked with suffix-XW, and Schedule 80 PVC Conduit, factory elbows, and associated fittings ≫*502.10(B)(1)* ≪.

All Class II, Division 2 boxes and fittings shall be dusttight ≫*502.10(B)(4)* ≪.

In Class II, Division 1 and 2 locations, where a raceway provides communication between an enclosure that is required to be dust-ignitionproof and one that is not, suitable means shall prevent the entrance of dust into the dust-ignitionproof enclosure via the raceway. The following means are permitted: (1) a permanent and effective seal; (2) a horizontal raceway at least 10 ft (3.05 m) long; (3) a vertical raceway not less than 5 ft (1.5 m) long that extends downward from the dust-ignitionproof enclosure; or (4) a raceway installed in a manner equivalent to (2) or (3) that extends only horizontally and downward from the dust-ignitionproof enclosures ≫*502.15* ≪.

Seals are not required where a raceway provides communication between an enclosure that is required to be dust-ignitionproof and an enclosure in an unclassified location ≫*502.15* ≪.

In Class II, Division 1 and 2 locations, explosionproof seals are not required ≫*502.15* ≪.

Ⓐ Class II locations are hazardous because of the presence of combustible dust ≫*500.5(C)* ≪.

CLASS III LOCATIONS

Class III, Division 1 Locations

In addition to Article 500 requirements, wiring and equipment in locations designated Class III must be installed in accordance with provisions in Article 503.

Class III located equipment shall be able to function at full rating without developing surface temperatures high enough to cause excessive dehydration or gradual carbonization of accumulated fibers or flyings. Carbonized or excessively dried organic material is highly susceptible to spontaneous ignition. During operation, the maximum surface temperature shall not exceed 165°C (329°F) for equipment not subject to overloading and 120°C (248°F) for equipment that may be overloaded (such as motors or power transformers) ≫ *503.5* ≪.

Transformers and capacitors in Class III, Division 1 locations shall comply with 502.100(B) ≫ *503.100* ≪.

Equipment listed and marked in accordance with 506.9(C)(2) for Zone 20 locations and with a temperature class of not greater than T120°C (for equipment that may be overloaded) or not greater than T165°C (for equipment not subject to overloading) shall be permitted in Class III, Division 1 locations ≫ *503.6* ≪.

A A Class III, Division 1 location is an area where easily ignitible fibers/flyings are handled, manufactured, or used ≫ *500.5(D)(1)* ≪.

B Easily ignitible fibers/flyings include rayon, cotton (including cotton linters and cotton waste), sisal or

henequen, istle, jute, hemp, tow, cocoa fiber, oakum, baled waste kapok, Spanish moss, excelsior, and other materials of similar nature ≫ *500.5(D)(1) Informational Note No. 2* ≪.

C Class III locations are hazardous because of the presence of easily ignitible fibers or where materials producing combustible flyings are handled, manufactured, or used, even though they are not likely to be airborne in quantities sufficient to produce ignitible mixtures ≫ *500.5(D)* ≪.

> **NOTE**
>
> Bonding and grounding shall comply with 503.30(A) and (B) provisions.

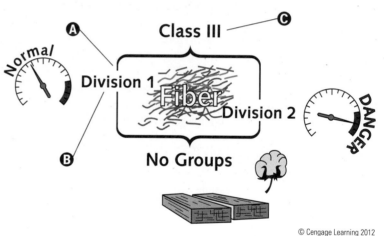

© Cengage Learning 2012

Class III, Division 2 Locations

In Class III, Division 2 locations, transformers and capacitors shall comply with 502.100(B) ≫ *503.100* ≪.

Equipment listed and marked in accordance with 506.9(C)(2) for Zone 20, 21, or 22 locations and with a temperature class of not greater than T120°C (for equipment that may be overloaded) or not greater than T165°C (for equipment not subject to overloading) shall be permitted in Class III, Division 2 location ≫ *503.6* ≪.

A A Class III, Division 2 location is an area in which easily ignitible fibers/flyings are stored or handled other than in the manufacturing process ≫ *500.5(D)(2)* ≪.

> **NOTE**
>
> Bonding and grounding must comply with 503.30(A) and (B) provisions.

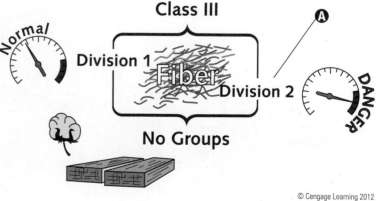

© Cengage Learning 2012

Wiring Methods—Class III, Division 1

In Class III, Division 1 locations, the following wiring methods are permitted: (1) RMC, PVC, RTRC, IMC, EMT, dusttight wireways, or Type MC or MI cable with listed termination fitting; (2) Type PLTC and Type PLTC-ER cable in accordance with the provisions of Article 725 including installation in cable tray systems (the cable shall be terminated with listed fittings); (3) Type ITC and Type ITC-ER cable as permitted in 727.4 and terminated with listed fittings; (4) Type MC, MI, or TC cable installed in ladder, ventilated trough, or ventilated channel cable trays in a single layer, with a space not less than the larger cable diameter between the two adjacent cables ≫ *503.10(A)* ≪. Note, see exception to (4).

All Class III, Division 1 boxes and fittings shall be dusttight ≫ *503.10(A)(2)* ≪.

Where necessary to employ flexible connections, one or more of the following shall be permitted: (1) dusttight flexible connectors, (2) liquidtight flexible metal conduit with listed fittings, (3) liquidtight flexible nonmetallic conduit with listed fittings, (4) interlocked armor Type MC cable having an overall jacket of suitable polymeric material and installed with listed dusttight termination fittings, and (5) flexible cord in compliance with 503.140 ≫ *503.10(A)(3)* ≪. For grounding requirements where flexible conduit is used, see 503.30(B) ≫ *503.10(A)(3) Informational Note* ≪.

Class III, Division 1 and 2 switches, circuit breakers, motor controllers, and fuses (including push buttons, relays, and similar devices), shall have dusttight enclosures ≫ *503.115* ≪.

Class III, Division 1 and 2 flexible cords shall comply with the following: (1) be of a type listed for extra-hard usage; (2) contain, in addition to the conductors of the circuit, a 400.23 compliant equipment grounding conductor; (3) be supported by clamps or other suitable means so that there will be no tension on the terminal connections; and (4) be terminated with a listed dusttight cord and connector ≫ *503.140* ≪.

Class III, Division 1 and 2 receptacles and attachment plugs shall (1) be of the grounding type; (2) be designed to minimize the accumulation (or entry) of fibers/flyings; and (3) prevent the escape of sparks or molten particles ≫ *503.145* ≪. If, in the judgement of the AHJ, only moderate accumulations of lint or flyings are likely to collect in the vicinity of a receptacle, and where such receptacle is readily accessible for routine cleaning, general-purpose grounding-type receptacles (mounted to minimize the entry of fibers/flyings) are permitted ≫ *503.145 Exception* ≪.

Ⓐ Such locations usually include some parts of rayon, cotton, and other textile mills; combustible fibers/flyings manufacturing and processing plants; cotton gins and cotton-seed mills; flax-processing plants; clothing manufacturing plants; woodworking plants; and establishments and industries involving similar hazardous processes or conditions ≫ *500.5(D)(1) Informational Note No. 1* ≪.

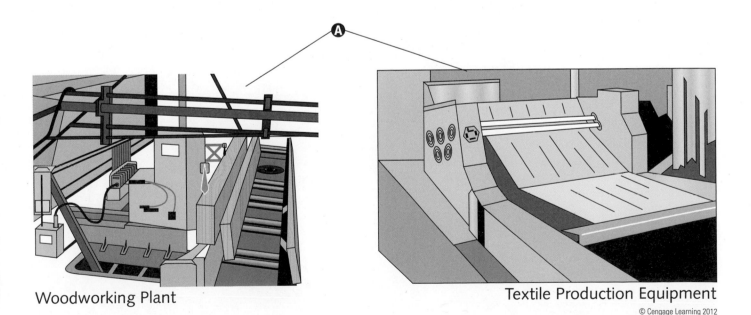

Woodworking Plant

Textile Production Equipment

Wiring Methods—Class III, Division 2

Unless an exception is met, Class III, Division 2 location wiring methods shall comply with 503.10(A) ≫*503.10(B)*≪.

All Class III, Division 2 boxes and fittings shall be dusttight ≫*503.10(A)(2)*≪.

Class III, Division 1 and 2 pendant luminaires shall be suspended by stems of threaded RMC, threaded IMC, threaded metal tubing of equivalent thickness, or by chains with approved fittings. Stems longer than 12 in. (300 mm) shall be permanently and effectively braced against lateral displacement at a level no more than 12 in. (300 mm) above the lower end of the stem, or flexibility in the form of an approved fitting or a flexible connector shall be provided no more than 12 in. (300 mm) from the point of attachment to the supporting box or fitting ≫*503.130(C)*≪.

Class III, Division 1 and 2 portable lighting equipment shall have both handles and substantial guards. Lampholders shall be of the unswitched type, incapable of receiving attachment plugs. There shall be no exposed current-carrying metal parts, and all exposed non-current-carrying metal parts shall be grounded. In all other respects, portable lighting equipment shall comply with 503.130(A) ≫*503.130(D)*≪.

A Class III, Division 1 and 2 luminaires for fixed lighting shall provide enclosures for lamps and lampholders designed to minimize entrance of fibers/flyings and to prevent the escape of sparks, burning material, or hot metal. Each luminaire shall be clearly marked to show the maximum permitted lamp wattage without exceeding an exposed surface temperature of 165°C (329°F) under normal use conditions ≫*503.130(A)*≪.

B A Class III, Division 2 location is a location in which easily ignitible fibers/flyings are stored or handled other than in the process of manufacture ≫*500.5(D)(2)*≪.

> **NOTE**
>
> Class III, Division 1 and 2 luminaires subject to physical damage shall be protected by a suitable guard ≫*503.130(B)*≪.

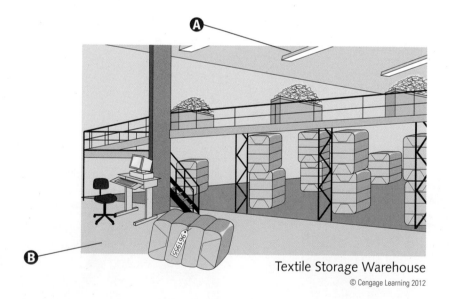

Textile Storage Warehouse

© Cengage Learning 2012

Summary

- Hazardous locations are divided into three classifications (Class I, II, and III); each class is subdivided into two categories (Division 1 and 2).
- While Article 500 covers general requirements for all classes, Articles 501, 502, and 503 provide specific provisions for each class individually.
- Class I locations are those in which flammable gases, flammable liquid-produced vapors, or combustible liquid-produced vapors are or may be present in the air in quantities sufficient to produce explosive or ignitable mixtures.
- Class II locations are hazardous due to the presence of combustible dust.
- Class III locations are hazardous because of the presence of easily ignitible fibers or on material producing combustible flyings, even though they are not likely to be airborne in quantities sufficient to produce ignitible mixtures.
- Under typical operating conditions, Division 1 locations contain ignitible or combustible elements (gases, dust, fibers, etc.) in quantities sufficient to produce explosive (or ignitible) mixtures.
- Locations where ordinarily present quantities of combustible or ignitible elements (gases, dust, fibers, etc.) in the air are insufficient to produce explosive (or ignitible) mixtures are classified as Division 2.
- Article 511 occupancies include those used for service and repair of self-propelled vehicles (including, but not limited to, passenger automobiles, buses, trucks, and tractors) that use volatile flammable liquids for fuel or power.
- Article 513 applies to buildings/structures or parts thereof inside which aircraft (containing Class I or II liquids whose temperatures exceed their flash points) are housed, stored, serviced, repaired, or altered.
- Motor fuel dispensing facility requirements are in Article 514.
- Article 515 provisions address bulk storage plants.
- The regular (or frequent) spray application of flammable liquids, combustible liquids, and combustible powders, as well as the application of flammable/combustible liquids at temperatures above their flash point, by dipping, coating, or other means, are covered by Article 516.

Unit 15 Competency Test

NEC Reference	Answer	
_____	_____	1. In aircraft hangars, any pit or depression below the level of the hangar floor shall be classified as a _____ location that shall extend up to said floor level.
_____	_____	2. Regardless of the classification of the location in which it is installed, equipment that depends on a single compression seal, diaphragm, or tube to prevent flammable or combustible fluids from entering the equipment, shall be identified for a _____ location.
_____	_____	3. A _____ location is a location in which volatile flammable gases, flammable liquid-produced vapors, or combustible liquid-produced vapors are handled, processed, or used, but in which the liquids, vapors, or gases will normally be confined within closed containers or closed systems from which they can escape only in case of accidental rupture or breakdown of such containers or systems or in case of abnormal operation of equipment.
_____	_____	4. All cut ends of rigid metal conduit (RMC) shall be reamed or otherwise finished to remove rough edges. Where conduit is threaded in the field, a standard cutting die with a _____ in. taper per foot shall be used.
_____	_____	5. In bulk storage plants, aboveground tank vents shall be classified as _____ within 5 ft (1.5 m) of the open end, extending in all directions.
_____	_____	6. In Class I, Division 1 locations, NPT threaded entries into explosionproof equipment shall be made up with at least _____ threads fully engaged.
_____	_____	7. In Class II, Division 1 locations, fittings and boxes shall be provided with _____ for connection to conduit or cable terminations, and shall be dusttight.
_____	_____	8. A 1-in. threaded RMC is terminating into a 2-in. sealing fitting. The minimum thickness of the sealing compound shall be _____ in.

NEC **Reference**   **Answer**

_____ _____ 9. In aircraft hangars, the area within _____ ft horizontally from aircraft power plants or aircraft fuel tanks shall be classified as a Class I, Division 2 or Zone 2 location that shall extend upward from the floor to a level _____ ft above the upper surface of wings and of the engine enclosures.

_____ _____ 10. _____ is defined as equipment enclosed in a manner that will exclude dusts and does not permit arcs, sparks, or heat otherwise generated or liberated inside of the enclosure to cause ignition of exterior accumulations or atmospheric suspensions of a specified dust on or in the vicinity of the enclosure.

_____ _____ 11. Class I locations are those in which _____ are or may be present in the air in quantities sufficient to produce explosive or ignitible mixtures.

_____ _____ 12. In commercial garages, lamps and lampholders for fixed lighting that is located over lanes through which vehicles are commonly driven shall be located no less than _____ ft above the floor level.

_____ _____ 13. A _____ location is a location in which easily ignitible fibers/flyings are handled, manufactured, or used.

_____ _____ 14. _____, _____, _____, _____, and _____ are five acceptable hazardous (classified) location protection techniques for electrical and electronic equipment.

_____ _____ 15. A(n) _____ is defined as a circuit other than field wiring in which any arc or thermal effect produced under intended operating conditions of the equipment is not capable, under specified test conditions, of igniting the flammable gas–, vapor–, or dust–air mixture.

_____ _____ 16. In each conduit run passing from a Class I, Division 2 location into an unclassified area, the sealing fitting shall be located within _____ ft of the boundary.

_____ _____ 17. For dipping and coating operations, all space within a _____ ft radial distance from the vapor sources extending from these surfaces to the floor shall be considered a Class I, Division 1 location.

_____ _____ 18. In Class III, Division 2 locations, transformers and capacitors shall comply with *NEC* Section _____.

_____ _____ 19. An outdoor gasoline dispensing device is considered to be a Class I, Division 2 location up to _____ in. abovegrade level within _____ ft horizontally of any edge of the enclosure.

_____ _____ 20. In bulk storage plants, the space between _____ ft and _____ ft from the open end of an aboveground tank vent, extending in all directions, is a Class I, Division 2 or Zone 2 location.

_____ _____ 21. A(n) _____ enclosure is constructed so that dust will not enter the enclosing case under specified test conditions.

_____ _____ 22. For dip tanks and drain boards, the space _____ ft above the floor and extending _____ ft horizontally in all directions from the Class I, Division 1 location, shall be considered a Class I, Division 2 location.

NEC Reference	Answer

23. Aircraft energizers shall be designed and mounted so that all electric equipment and fixed wiring will be at least _____ in. above floor level.

24. A _____ location is a location in which combustible dust is in the air under normal operating conditions in quantities sufficient to produce explosive or ignitible mixtures.

25. For each major repair garage floor, the entire area up to a level of _____ in. above the floor shall be considered to be a Class I, Division 2 location if ventilation is not provided.

26. A ½-in. threaded steel IMC is terminating into a ½-in. sealing fitting. The minimum thickness of the sealing compound shall be _____ in.

27. The entire area of an aircraft hangar, including any adjacent and communicating areas not suitably cut off from the hangar, shall be classified as a Class I, Division 2 or Zone 2 location up to a level _____ in. above the floor.

28. For unattended self-service motor fuel dispensing facilities, emergency controls shall be installed at a location acceptable to the authority having jurisdiction, but the control shall be more than _____ ft but less than _____ ft from the dispensers.

29. _____ is defined as any finely divided solid material that is 420 microns (0.017 in.) or smaller in diameter (material passing a U.S. No. 40 Standard Sieve) and presents a fire or explosion hazard when dispersed and ignited in air.

Health Care

Objectives

After studying this unit, the student should:

▶ have an adequate understanding of health care facility terminology.

▶ be familiar with general as well as specific hospital, nursing home, and limited-care facility requirements.

▶ know the criteria for judging an ambulatory health care facility.

▶ know what area constitutes the patient vicinity.

▶ be familiar with grounding and bonding requirements.

▶ have a good understanding of patient care areas (general care, critical care, and wet locations).

▶ be familiar with general and critical care area branch-circuit and receptacle requirements.

▶ understand the receptacle/receptacle cover tamper-resistance requirements for pediatric areas.

▶ understand the two types of systems (equipment and emergency) as well as the two types of branches (life safety and critical) required by hospitals.

▶ know the required nursing home and limited-care facility branches (life safety and critical).

▶ have a thorough understanding of hazardous (classified) anesthetizing location requirements.

▶ be familiar with X-ray installation provisions, including both fixed (stationary) and mobile equipment.

Introduction

Health care facilities, by definition, are buildings or portions thereof containing, at least in part, occupancies such as hospitals, nursing homes, limited care, supervisory care, clinics, medical/dental offices, and ambulatory care, whether permanent or movable. Electrical installation criteria and wiring methods for health care facilities are far more specialized than for a standard commercial or industrial project. Article 517 of the *NEC* governs electrical installations within health care facilities. Applicable requirements of *NEC* Chapters 1 through 4 must be met, unless specifically modified by Article 517. The provisions of Article 517, Parts II and III, apply not only to single-function buildings, but are also intended for individual application to their respective forms of occupancy within a multifunction structure (for example, 517.10 requirements must be met by a doctor's examining room situated within a limited-care facility). As with any specialized endeavor, a working knowledge of the pertinent terminology is highly recommended. Because most of these terms apply only to health care facilities, 517.2 provides a comprehensive list of the most commonly used words and phrases. Article 517, Part II *(Wiring and Protection)* covers patient care areas throughout the spectrum of health care facilities. *Essential Electrical Systems* (Part III) outlines electrical system requirements for specific occupancies, that is, hospitals, nursing homes, etc. *Inhalation Anesthetizing Location* provisions are presented in Part IV of Article 517. Part V covers *X-Ray Installations* of all varieties: fixed, stationary, portable, and mobile, as well as transportable. In no way is Part V to be construed as specifying safeguards against the useful beam or stray X-ray radiation. As for *Communications, Signaling Systems, Data Systems, Fire Alarm Systems, and Systems Less than 120 Volts, Nominal,* see Part VI for particular provisions. And finally, Article 517, Part VII, applies to the installation of *Isolated Power Systems* that consist of an isolating transformer (or equivalent) and a line isolation monitor with its ungrounded circuit conductors. All in all, Article 517 and the explanations found in this unit offer a reasonably complete picture of health care facility electrical system installations.

GENERAL

Nursing Home and Limited-Care Facility

Requirements in 517.40(C) through 517.44 do not apply to freestanding buildings used as nursing homes and limited-care facilities, provided that:

(a) Admitting and discharge policies are maintained that preclude providing care to any patient (or resident) who may need to be sustained by electrical life-support equipment.

(b) No surgical treatment requiring general anesthesia is offered.

(c) Automatic battery-operated systems or equipment are provided, effective for a minimum of 1½ hours and otherwise in accordance with 700.12. Such a system shall capably supply lighting for exit lights, exit corridors, stairways, nursing stations, medical preparation areas, boiler rooms, and communications areas, as well as power to operate all alarm systems 》*517.40(A) Exception*《.

Nursing homes and limited-care facilities that are contiguous with or adjacent to a hospital can have essential electrical systems supplied by the hospital 》*517.40(C)*《.

Ⓐ **Nursing home:** A building (or part thereof) used for 24-hour housing and nursing care of four or more persons who, because of mental or physical incapacity, may be unable to safely provide for their own needs without assistance 》*517.2*《.

Ⓑ Nursing homes and limited-care facilities are included in the term **health care facilities.**

Ⓒ **Limited-care facility:** A building (or part thereof) used for 24-hour housing of four or more persons incapable of self-preservation because of age; physical limitation, whether due to accident or illness; or limitations, such as mental retardation/developmental disability, mental illness, or chemical dependency 》*517.2*《.

Ⓓ The requirements of Part III, 517.40(C) through 517.44, shall apply to nursing homes and limited-care facilities 》*517.40(A)*《.

Ⓔ Article 517, Part II (Wiring and Protection) requirements shall not apply to areas of nursing homes and limited-care facilities wired in accordance with Chapters 1 through 4 of the *NEC* where these areas are used exclusively as patient sleeping rooms 》*517.10(B)(2)*《.

> **NOTE**
>
> For those nursing home and limited-care facilities that admit patients who need to be sustained by electrical life-support equipment, the essential electrical system from the source to the portion of the facility where such patients are treated shall comply with the requirements of Part III, 517.30 through 517.35 》*517.40(B)*《.

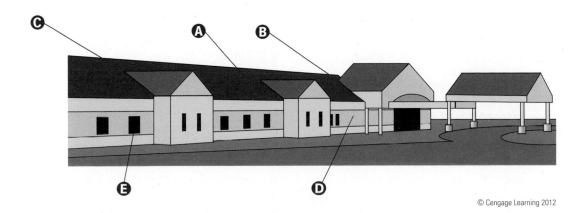

© Cengage Learning 2012

Hospital

The provisions of Article 517 shall apply to electrical construction and installation criteria in health care facilities that provide services to human beings 》*517.1*《.

Article 517 specifies the installation criteria and wiring methods that minimize electrical hazards by maintaining adequately low-potential differences between exposed conductive surfaces that are likely to become energized and are subject to patient contact 》*517.11*《.

Psychiatric hospital: A building used exclusively for 24-hour psychiatric care, with at least four inpatients 》*517.2*《.

Parts II and III requirements apply not only to single-function buildings, but also to their respective forms of occupancy within a multifunction building (for example, a doctor's examining room located within a limited-care facility shall meet 517.10 provisions) 》*517.1*《.

Ⓐ Hospital: A building (or part thereof) used for 24-hour medical, psychiatric, obstetrical, or surgical care of four or more inpatients 》*517.2*《.

Ⓑ Health care facilities: Buildings (or portions thereof) in which medical, dental, psychiatric, nursing, obstetrical, or surgical care is provided. Health care facilities include but are not limited to hospitals; nursing homes; limited-care facilities; clinics; medical and dental offices; and ambulatory care centers, whether permanent or movable 》*517.2*《.

Ⓒ Patient bed location: The location of a patient sleeping bed or the bed (or procedure table) of a critical care area 》*517.2*《.

Ⓓ Article 517, Part II applies to patient care areas of all health care facilities 》*517.10(A)*《.

Ⓔ Patient care area: Any portion of a health care facility wherein patients are intended to be examined or treated. Areas of a health care facility in which patient care is administered are classified as general care areas or critical care areas. The governing body of the facility designates these areas in accordance with the type of patient care anticipated and with the following definitions of the area classification 》*517.2*《.

Ⓕ Business offices, corridors, lounges, day rooms, dining rooms, or similar areas typically are not classified as patient care areas 》*517.2, Patient Care Area Informational Note*《.

N O T E

Article 517, Part II does not apply to the following: (1) business offices, corridors, waiting rooms, and the like in clinics, medical and dental offices, and outpatient facilities and (2) areas of nursing homes and limited-care facilities wired according to Chapters 1 through 4 of the *NEC*, where these areas are used exclusively as patient sleeping rooms 》*517.10(B)*《.
See 517.2 for definitions pertaining to health care facilities.

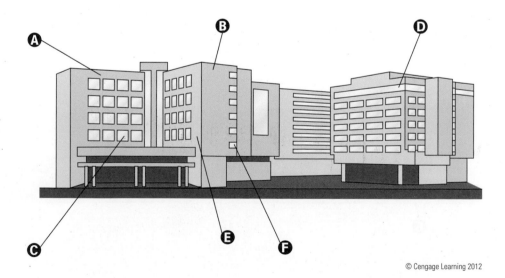

Patient Care Vicinity

A In an area where patient care normally occurs, the **patient care vicinity** is the space having surfaces subject to contact by the patient or by an attendant who may touch the patient. In a patient room, this typically encloses a space within the room no less than 6 ft (1.8 m) beyond the bed's perimeter (in its normal location), and extending vertically no less than 7½ ft (2.3 m) from the floor ≫ 517.2 ≪.

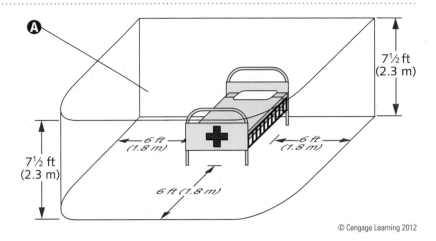

© Cengage Learning 2012

Ambulatory Health Care Occupancy

Where electrical life support equipment is required, the essential electrical distribution shall comply with 517.30 through 517.35 ≫ 517.45(B) ≪.

Where critical care areas are present, the essential electrical distribution shall comply with 517.30 through 517.35 ≫ 517.45(C) ≪.

Battery systems shall be installed per Article 700's requirements, and generator systems shall comply with 517.30 through 517.35 ≫ 517.45(D) ≪.

A Ambulatory health care occupancy: A building (or part thereof) used to provide simultaneous service (or treatment) to four or more patients that provides, on an outpatient basis, one or more of the following: (1) treatment for patients that renders the patients incapable of taking action for self-preservation under emergency conditions without assistance of others; (2) anesthesia that renders the patients incapable of taking action for self-preservation under emergency

conditions without the assistance of others; or (3) emergency or urgent care for patients who, due to the nature of their injury or illness, are incapable of taking action for self-preservation under emergency conditions without the assistance of others ≫ 517.2 ≪.

B The essential electrical distribution system shall be a battery or generator system ≫ 517.45(A) ≪.

C Ambulatory health care occupancy is included in the term **health care facilities.**

NOTE

See NFPA 99-2005, *Standard for Health Care Facilities* ≫ *517.45 Informational Note* ≪.

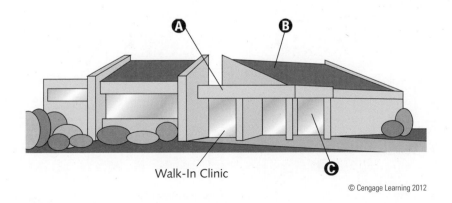

Walk-In Clinic

© Cengage Learning 2012

Electrical System Terminology

Electrical life-support equipment: Electrically powered equipment whose continuous operation is necessary to maintain a patient's life ≫ 517.2 ≪ .

Isolated power system: A system consisting of an isolating transformer (or equivalent) and a line isolation monitor with its ungrounded circuit conductors ≫ 517.2 ≪ . (See related definitions, which include: *hazard current, fault hazard current, monitor hazard current, total hazard current, and line isolation monitor.*)

Isolation transformer: A multiple-winding-type transformer, with physically separated primary and secondary windings which inductively couples its secondary winding(s) to circuit conductors connected to its primary winding(s) ≫ 517.2 ≪ .

A Alternate power source: One or more generator sets (or battery systems, where permitted) to provide power during normal electrical service interruption, or the public utility electrical service intended to provide power during interruption of service normally provided by on-site generating facilities ≫ 517.2 ≪ .

B Life safety branch: An Article 700 compliant subsystem of the emergency system consisting of feeders and branch circuits, providing adequate power to ensure patient and personnel safety, that automatically connects to alternate power sources during interruption of normal power ≫ 517.2 ≪ .

C Critical branch: An emergency subsystem consisting of feeders and branch circuits supplying energy to task illumination, special power circuits, and selected receptacles serving patient care–related areas and functions, that connects to alternate power sources by transfer switch(es) during interruption of the normal power ≫ 517.2 ≪ .

D Emergency system: A system of circuits and equipment intended to supply alternate power to a limited number of prescribed functions vital to the protection of life and safety ≫ 517.2 ≪ .

E Equipment system: A system of circuits and equipment arranged for delayed, automatic, or manual connection to the alternate power source, primarily serving 3-phase power equipment ≫ 517.2 ≪ .

F Essential electrical system: A system comprising alternate power sources and all connected distribution systems (and ancillary equipment), designed both to ensure electrical power continuity to designated areas and functions of a health care facility during disruption of normal power sources and to minimize disruption within the internal wiring system ≫ 517.2 ≪ .

G The essential electrical system for these facilities shall comprise a system capable of supplying a limited amount of lighting and power service, considered essential for life safety and orderly cessation of procedures, during normal electrical service interruption. This includes clinics, medical/dental offices, outpatient facilities, nursing homes, limited-care facilities, hospitals, and other patient-serving health care facilities ≫ 517.25 ≪ .

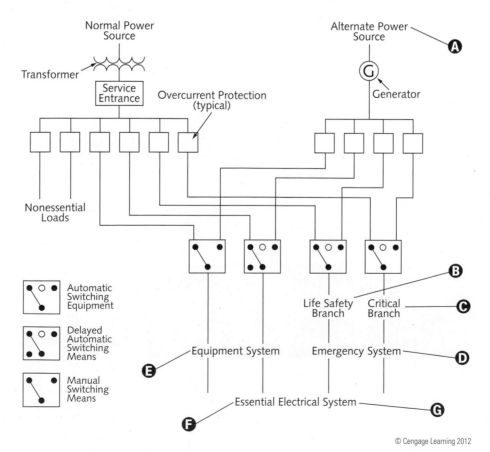

Grounding and Bonding

An insulated equipment bonding jumper that directly connects to the equipment grounding conductor is permitted to connect the box and receptacle(s) to the equipment grounding conductor ≫517.13(B)(1) Exception ≪.

Metal faceplates can be connected to an equipment grounding conductor by means of metal mounting screw(s) securing the faceplate to a grounded outlet box (or grounded wiring device) ≫517.13(B) Exception No. 1 to (B)(3) ≪.

Luminaires more than 7½ ft (2.3 m) above the floor and switches located outside the patient vicinity do not require grounding by an insulated grounding conductor ≫517.13(B) Exception No. 2 to (B)(3) ≪.

Patient equipment grounding point: A jack or terminal bus that serves as the collection point for electric appliance redundant grounding in a patient vicinity, or for grounding other items to eliminate electromagnetic interference problems ≫517.2 ≪.

Reference grounding point: The ground bus of the panelboard or isolated power system panel supplying a patient care area ≫517.2 ≪.

Exposed conductive surfaces: Those unprotected, unenclosed, or unguarded surfaces capable of carrying electric current and permitting personal contact. Paint, anodizing, and similar coatings do not provide suitable insulation unless listed for such use ≫517.2 ≪.

Ⓐ In general care and critical care areas, all patient bed location receptacles shall be listed and identified as "hospital grade" ≫517.18(B) and 517.19(B)(2) ≪.

Ⓑ Receptacles with insulated grounding terminals, as described in 250.146(D), shall not be permitted ≫517.16 ≪.

Ⓒ Normal and essential branch-circuit panelboard equipment grounding terminal buses serving the same individual patient vicinity shall be connected together with an insulated continuous copper conductor no smaller than 10 AWG. Where two or more panelboards serving the same individual patient care vicinity are served from separate transfer switches on the emergency system, the equipment grounding terminal buses of those panelboards shall be connected together with an insulated continuous copper conductor not smaller than 10 AWG. This conductor can be broken in order to terminate on the equipment grounding terminal bus in each panelboard ≫517.14 ≪.

Ⓓ In a patient care area, (1) all receptacle grounding terminals, (2) metal boxes and enclosures containing receptacles, and (3) all non-current-carrying conductive surfaces of fixed electric equipment likely to become energized that are subject to personal contact (operating at over 100 volts) shall be directly connected to an insulated copper equipment grounding conductor that is installed with the branch-circuit conductors in the wiring methods as provided in 517.13(A) ≫517.13(B) ≪.

Ⓔ Equipment grounding conductors and equipment bonding jumpers shall be sized in accordance with 250.122 ≫517.13(B)(2) ≪.

Ⓕ All branch circuits serving patient care areas shall be provided with an effective ground-fault current path by installation in a metal raceway system or a cable having a metallic armor or sheath assembly. The metal raceway system, or metallic cable armor or sheath assembly, shall qualify as an equipment grounding conductor according to 250.118. ≫517.13(A) ≪.

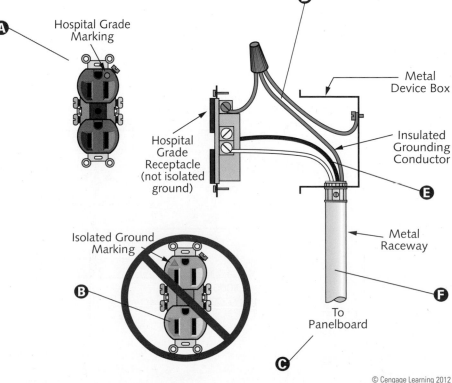

Ⓐ Hospital Grade Marking

Hospital Grade Receptacle (not isolated ground)

Ⓓ

Metal Device Box

Insulated Grounding Conductor

Ⓔ

Metal Raceway

Isolated Ground Marking

Ⓑ

To Panelboard

Ⓕ

Ⓒ

© Cengage Learning 2012

Ground-Fault Protection

Ground-fault protection for the service and feeder disconnecting means operation shall be fully selective so that the feeder device, and not the service device, opens for ground faults on the feeder device's load side. Separation of ground-fault protection time-current characteristics shall conform to manufacturer's recommendations and shall consider all required tolerances and disconnect operating time to achieve 100% selectivity »*517.17(C)*«.

On installation of equipment ground-fault protection, each level shall be performance tested to ensure compliance with 517.17(C) »*517.17(D)*«.

A If ground-fault protection is provided for service disconnecting means (or feeder disconnecting means) operation as specified by 230.95 or 215.10, an additional ground-fault protection step shall be provided in the next level of feeder disconnecting means downstream toward the load. Such protection shall consist of overcurrent devices and current transformers (or other equivalent protective equipment) that cause the feeder disconnecting means to open.

The additional levels of ground-fault protection shall not be installed on the load side of an essential electrical system transfer switch »*517.17(B)*«.

B Ground-fault protection of equipment is defined as a system intended to provide protection of equipment from damaging line-to-ground fault currents by operating to cause a disconnecting means to open all ungrounded conductors of the faulted circuit. This protection is provided at current levels less than those required to protect conductors from damage through the operation of a supply circuit overcurrent device »*Article 100*«.

C Ground-fault protection of equipment shall be provided for solidly grounded wye electric services of more than 150 volts to ground but not exceeding 600 volts phase-to-phase for each service disconnect rated 1000 amperes or more. The grounded conductor for the solidly grounded wye system shall be connected directly to ground through a grounding electrode system, as specified in 250.50, without inserting any resistor or impedance device.

The rating of the service disconnect shall be considered to be the rating of the largest fuse that can be installed or the highest continuous current trip setting for which the actual overcurrent device installed in a circuit breaker is rated or can be adjusted »*230.95*«.

> **NOTE**
>
> The requirements of 517.17 apply to hospitals and other buildings (including multiple-occupancy buildings) with critical care areas or utilizing electrical life-support equipment and buildings that provide the required essential utilities or service for the operation of critical care areas of electrical life-support equipment »*517.17(A)*«.

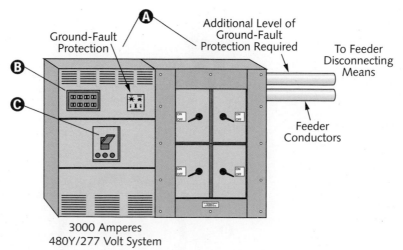

3000 Amperes
480Y/277 Volt System

Wet Procedure Locations

Health care facility patient care areas are classified as *general care areas* or *critical care areas*, either of which may be a *wet procedure location* ≫*517.2*≪.

If an isolated power system is utilized, the isolated power equipment shall be listed as isolated power equipment and the isolated power system shall be designed and installed in accordance with 517.160 ≫*517.20(B)*≪.

Ⓐ **Wet procedure locations:** Those spaces within patient care areas where a procedure is performed and that are normally subject to wet conditions while patients are present. These include standing fluids on the floor or drenching of the work area, either of which condition is intimate to the patient or staff. Routine housekeeping procedures and incidental spillage of liquids do not define a wet procedure location ≫*517.2*≪.

Ⓑ Branch circuits supplying only listed, fixed, therapeutic, and diagnostic equipment can be supplied from a grounded service, single- or 3-phase system, provided that (a) wiring for grounded and isolated circuit wiring does not occupy the same raceway and (b) all conductive equipment surfaces are connected to an isolated copper equipment grounding conductor ≫*517.20(A) Exception*≪.

Ⓒ For requirements for installation of therapeutic pools and tubs, see Part VI of Article 680.

WARNING

Wet procedure location patient care areas shall be provided with special protection against electric shock by one of the following means: (1) power distribution system that inherently limits the possible ground-fault current due to a first fault to a low value, without interrupting the power supply and (2) power distribution system in which the power supply is interrupted if the ground-fault current does, in fact, exceed a value of 6 milliamperes (mA) ≫*517.20(A)*≪.

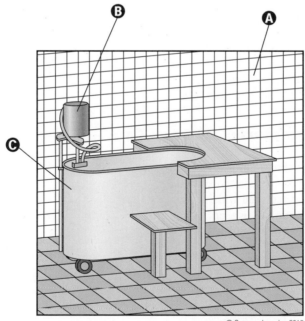

© Cengage Learning 2012

PATIENT CARE AREAS

Patient Bed Location Branch Circuits (General Care Areas)

Section 517.18(A) requirements do not apply to patient bed locations in clinics, medical/dental offices, and outpatient facilities; psychiatric, substance abuse, and rehabilitation hospitals; nursing home sleeping rooms; and limited-care facilities where 517.10(B)(2) requirements are met *≫517.18(A) Exception No. 2≪*.

A Branch circuits serving only special-purpose outlets or receptacles (such as portable X-ray outlets) do not require service from the same distribution panel(s) *≫517.18(A) Exception No. 1≪*.

B Each patient bed location shall be supplied by at least two branch circuits: one from the emergency system and one from the normal system. All normal system branch circuits must originate within the same panelboard *≫517.18(A)≪*.

C If served from two separate emergency system transfer switches, a general care patient bed location does not require circuits from the normal system *≫517.18(A) Exception No. 3≪*.

> **WARNING**
>
> The branch circuit serving patient bed locations shall not be part of a multiwire branch circuit *≫517.18(A)≪*.

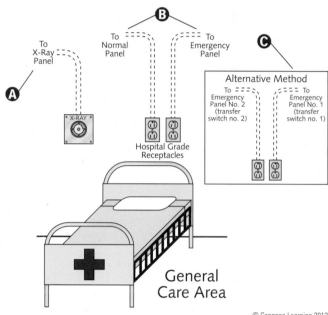

© Cengage Learning 2012

> **N O T E**
>
> **General care areas** are patient bedrooms, examining rooms, treatment rooms, clinics, and similar areas in which it is intended that the patient will come in contact with ordinary appliances such as a nurse call system, electrical beds, examining lamps, a telephone, and entertainment devices *≫517.2≪*.

Patient Bed Location Receptacles (General Care Areas)

A total, immediate replacement of existing non-hospital grade receptacles is not necessary. It is intended, however, that non-hospital grade receptacles be replaced with hospital grade receptacles on modification of use, or during renovation, or as receptacles need replacing *≫517.18(B) Informational Note≪*.

A Special-purpose receptacles are not counted as required receptacles.

B *Each* patient bed location shall be provided with a minimum of four receptacles. They can be either single, duplex, or quadruplex type, or any combination of the three *≫517.18(B)≪*.

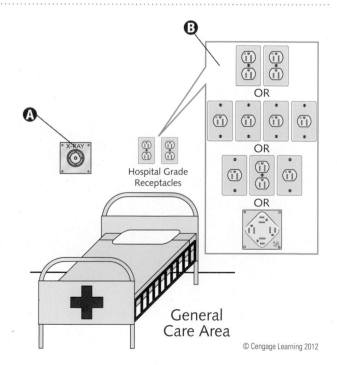

© Cengage Learning 2012

> **N O T E**
>
> All receptacles shall be listed and identified as "hospital grade." The grounding terminal of each receptacle shall be connected to an insulated copper equipment grounding conductor sized in accordance with Table 250.122 *≫517.18(B)≪*.

Pediatric Location Receptacles (General Care Areas)

A Receptacles located within the rooms, bathrooms, playrooms, activity rooms, and patient care areas of designated pediatric locations shall either be **listed** tamper resistant or shall employ a **listed** tamper-resistant cover ≫ *517.18(C)* ≪.

B Tamper-resistant receptacles are identified by the letters "TR" or the words *Tamper Resistant.* After the receptacle has been installed, the identification is only required to be visible with the cover plate removed. See UL (Underwriter Laboratories) White Book, category: Receptacles for Plugs and Attachment Plugs (RTRT).

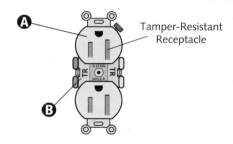
Tamper-Resistant Receptacle

© Cengage Learning 2012

Patient Bed Location Receptacles (Critical Care Areas)

All receptacles shall be listed and identified as "hospital grade." The grounding terminal of each receptacle shall be connected to the reference grounding point by means of an insulated copper equipment grounding conductor ≫ ***517.19(B)(2)*** ≪.

Although not required, a patient care vicinity can have a patient equipment grounding point. Where one is supplied, it can contain one (or more) listed grounding and bonding jacks. An equipment bonding jumper no smaller than 10 AWG shall connect the grounding terminal of all grounding-type receptacles to the patient equipment grounding point. The bonding conductor can be arranged centrically or looped as convenient ≫ ***517.19(C)*** ≪.

Where there is no patient equipment grounding point, it is important that the distance between the reference grounding point and the patient care vicinity be as short as possible to minimize any potential differences ≫ ***517.19(C) Informational Note*** ≪.

A The equipment grounding conductor for special-purpose receptacles (such as the operation of mobile X-ray equipment) shall extend to the branch-circuit reference

grounding points for all locations potentially served from such receptacles. Where an isolated ungrounded system serves such a circuit, the grounding conductor does not have to run with the power conductors; however, the special-purpose receptacle's equipment grounding terminal shall connect to the reference grounding point ≫ *517.19(G)* ≪.

B Each patient bed location shall have a minimum of six receptacles. At least one of the receptacles must be connected to (1) the normal system branch circuit as required by 517.19(A) or (2) an emergency system circuit supplied by a different transfer switch not associated with other receptacles at the same patient bed location ≫ *517.19(B)(1)* ≪.

C The receptacles can be either single, duplex, or quadruplex type, or any combination the three ≫ *517.19(B)(2)* ≪.

NOTE

Where a grounded electrical distribution system is used and metal feeder raceway or Type MC or MI cable that qualifies as an equipment grounding conductor in accordance with 250.118 is installed, grounding of enclosures and equipment, such as panelboards and switchboards, shall be ensured by one of the following bonding means at each termination or junction point of the metal raceway or Type MC or MI cable:

(1) A grounding bushing and a continuous copper bonding jumper, sized according to 250.122, with the bonding jumper connected to the junction enclosure or the panel ground bus.

(2) Connection of feeder raceways or Type MC or MI cables to threaded hubs or bosses on terminating enclosures.

(3) Other approved devices such as bonding-type locknuts or bushings ≫ *517.19(D)* ≪.

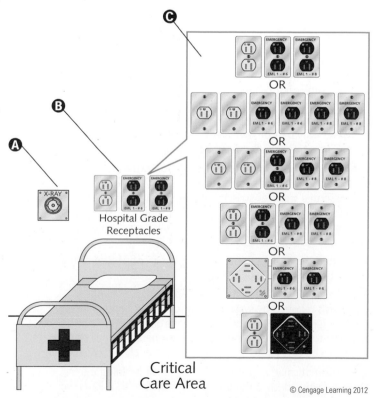

X-RAY

Hospital Grade Receptacles

Critical Care Area

© Cengage Learning 2012

Patient Bed Location Branch Circuits (Critical Care Areas)

Ⓐ Branch circuits serving only special-purpose receptacles or equipment in critical care areas can be served by other panelboards ≫ 517.19(A) Exception No. 1 ≪.

Ⓑ Each patient bed location shall be supplied by at least two branch circuits: one (or more) from the emergency system and one (or more) from the normal system. At least one emergency system branch circuit shall supply outlet(s) at that bed location only ≫ 517.19(A) ≪.

Ⓒ Emergency system receptacles shall be identified and shall also indicate the supplying panelboard and circuit number ≫ 517.19(A) ≪.

Ⓓ Critical care locations served from two separate emergency system transfer switches do not require circuits from the normal system ≫ 517.19(A) Exception No. 2 ≪.

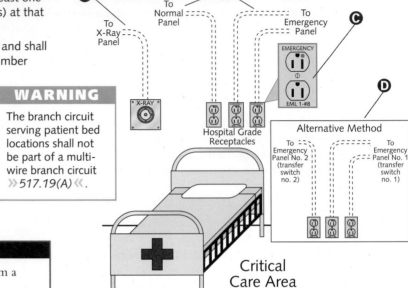

> **NOTE**
>
> **Critical care areas** are those special care units, intensive care units, coronary care units, angiography laboratories, cardiac catheterization laboratories, delivery rooms, operating rooms, and similar areas where patients are subjected to invasive procedures while connected to line-operated electromedical devices ≫**517.2≪**.

> **WARNING**
>
> The branch circuit serving patient bed locations shall not be part of a multiwire branch circuit ≫ 517.19(A) ≪.

> **CAUTION**
>
> All normal system branch circuits shall originate from a single panelboard ≫ 517.19(A)≪.

© Cengage Learning 2012

HOSPITALS

Life Safety Branch

Ⓐ The emergency system life safety branch shall supply power for lighting, receptacles, and equipment as listed in 517.32(A) through (H) ≫ 517.32 ≪.

Ⓑ Illumination of egress means is required, such as lighting for corridors, passageways, stairways, landings at exit doors, and all paths of approach to exits shall be connected to the life safety branch. Switching arrangement to transfer patient corridor lighting from general illumination circuits is permitted, provided only one of two circuits can be selected and both circuits cannot be simultaneously extinguished ≫ 517.32(A) ≪.

Ⓒ Task illumination battery charger for battery-powered lighting unit(s) and selected receptacles at the generator set and essential transfer switch locations shall be connected to the life safety branch ≫ 517.32(E) ≪. Generator set accessories as required for generator performance shall be connected to the life safety branch ≫ 517.32(F) ≪.

Ⓓ Exit and exit directional signs shall be connected to the life safety branch ≫ 517.32(B) ≪.

Ⓔ Alarm and alerting systems, including (1) fire alarms, (2) alarms required by systems used for piping nonflammable medical gases, and (3) mechanical, control, and other accessories required for effective life safety systems operation shall be permitted to be connected to the life safety branch ≫ 517.32(C) ≪.

Ⓕ Automatically operated doors used for building egress shall be connected to the life safety branch ≫ 517.32(H) ≪.

Ⓖ Only functions listed in 517.32(A) through (H) can be connected to the life safety branch of the emergency system ≫ 517.32 ≪.

Ⓗ Hospital communication systems used for issuing instructions during emergency conditions shall be connected to the life safety branch ≫ 517.32(D) ≪.

Ⓘ Elevator cab lighting, control, communications, and signal systems shall be connected to the life safety branch ≫ 517.32(G) ≪.

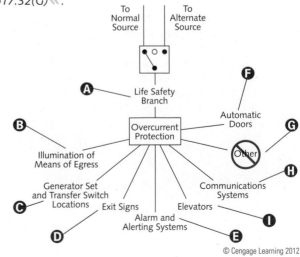

© Cengage Learning 2012

Essential Electrical Systems

(A) Hospital power sources and alternate power sources can serve the essential electrical systems of contiguous, or same-site, facilities ≫*517.30(B)(6)*≪.

(B) Loads served by generating equipment not specifically named in Article 517 shall be served by their own transfer switches so that these loads (1) are not transferred if the transfer will overload the generating equipment and (2) are automatically shed on generating equipment overloading ≫*517.30(B)(5)*≪.

(C) A facility having a maximum essential electrical system demand of 150 kVA can have a single transfer switch serving one or more branches (critical and life safety) or systems (emergency and equipment) ≫*517.30(B)(4)*≪.

(D) Limit the emergency system to only those circuits essential to life safety and critical patient care. These carry the *life safety branch* and *critical branch* designations ≫*517.30(B)(2)* and *517.31*≪.

(E) Emergency system branches shall be installed and connected to the alternate power source so that all functions specified herein are automatically restored to operation within 10 seconds after normal source interruption ≫*517.31*≪.

(F) The equipment system supplies major electrical equipment necessary for patient care and for basic hospital operation ≫*517.30(B)(3)*≪.

(G) The number of transfer switches used is based on reliability, design, and load considerations. Each essential electrical system (emergency and equipment) branch shall be served by transfer switch(es) ≫*517.30(B)(4)*≪.

(H) Essential electrical systems shall comprise two separate systems, both capable of supplying a limited amount of the lighting and power service considered essential for life safety and effective hospital operation during normal electrical service interruption, regardless of cause. These two systems are the *emergency system* and the *equipment system* ≫*517.30(B)(1)*≪.

(I) Demand calculations for generator set(s) sizing shall be based on the following: (1) prudent demand factors and historical data, (2) connected load, (3) Article 220 feeder calculation procedures, or (4) any combination of the preceding ≫*517.30(D)*≪.

(J) The generator set(s) shall have sufficient capacity and be properly rated to meet the demand produced by the essential electrical system(s) load at any given time ≫*517.30(D)*≪.

(K) Feeders shall be sized per Articles 215 and 220 ≫*517.30(D)*≪.

(L) The essential electrical system shall capably meet the demand for the operation of all functions and equipment served by each system and branch ≫*517.30(D)*≪.

(M) The hospital's emergency system wiring shall be mechanically protected. The permitted wiring methods are listed in 517.30(C)(3)(1) through (5) ≫*517.30(C)(3)*≪.

(N) If isolated power systems are installed in any of the areas in 517.33(A)(1) and (A)(2), each system shall be supplied by an individual circuit serving no other load ≫*517.30(C)(2)*≪.

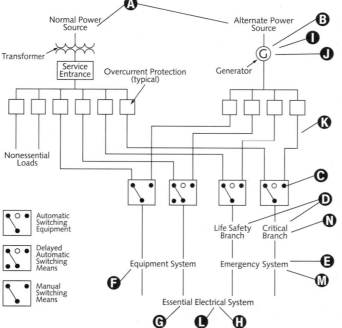

© Cengage Learning 2012

WARNING

The emergency system's life safety branch and critical branch shall remain entirely independent of all other wiring (and equipment) and shall not enter the same raceways, boxes, or cabinets with one another or any other wiring. Life safety branch and critical branch wiring can occupy the same raceways, boxes, or cabinets of other circuits (not part of the branch) where such wiring is:

1. In transfer equipment enclosures, or
2. In exit/emergency luminaries supplied from two sources, or
3. In a common junction box attached to exit/emergency luminaries supplied from two sources, or
4. For multiple emergency circuits supplied from the same branch and same transfer switch.

The equipment system wiring can occupy the same raceways, boxes, or cabinets of other circuits that are not part of the emergency system ≫*517.30(C)(1)*≪.

Receptacle Identification

A Electrical receptacles (or their cover plates) supplied from the emergency system shall be distinctively colored or otherwise marked in a readily identifiable manner ≫ *517.30(E)* ≪.

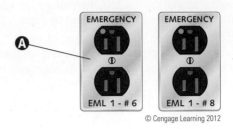

© Cengage Learning 2012

Critical Branch

A The critical branch of the emergency system shall supply power for task illumination, fixed equipment, selected receptacles, and special power circuits serving patient care areas and function as listed in 517.33(A)(1) through (9) ≫ *517.33(A)* ≪.

B Critical care areas that utilize anesthetizing gases, including task illumination, selected receptacles, and fixed equipment shall be connected to the critical branch ≫ *517.33(A)(1)* ≪.

C The isolating power systems in special environments shall be connected to the critical branch ≫ *517.33(A)(2)* ≪.

D Additional specialized patient care task illumination and receptacles, where needed, shall be connected to the critical branch ≫ *517.33(A)(4)* ≪.

E Patient care areas, including task illumination and selected receptacles, in the following: (a) infant nurseries; (b) medication preparation areas; (c) pharmacy dispensing areas; (d) selected acute nursing areas; (e) psychiatric bed areas (omit receptacles); (f) ward treatment rooms; (g) nurses' stations (unless adequately lighted by corridor luminaires) shall be connected to the critical branch ≫ *517.33(A)(3)* ≪.

F Subdividing the critical branch into two or more branches is permitted ≫ *517.33(B)* ≪.

G Additional task illumination, receptacles, and selected power circuits needed for effective hospital operation shall be connected to the critical branch. Single-phase fractional horsepower motors can be connected to the critical branch ≫ *517.33(A)(9)* ≪.

H Task illumination, selected receptacles, and selected power circuits for the following shall be connected to the critical branch: (a) general care beds (at least one duplex receptacle in each patient bedroom); (b) angiographic labs; (c) cardiac catheterization labs; (d) coronary care units; (e) hemodialysis rooms or areas; (f) emergency room treatment areas (selected); (g) human physiology labs; (h) intensive care units; and (i) postoperative recovery rooms (selected) ≫ *517.33(A)(8)* ≪.

I Telephone equipment rooms and closets shall be connected to the critical branch ≫ *517.33(A)(7)* ≪.

J Blood, bone, and tissue banks shall be connected to the critical branch ≫ *517.33(A)(6)* ≪.

K Nurse call systems shall be connected to the critical branch ≫ *517.33(A)(5)* ≪.

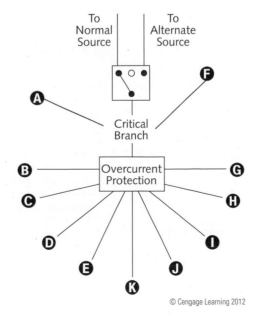

© Cengage Learning 2012

Service Entrance: Six Disconnects

Means shall be provided to disconnect all conductors in a building (or other structure) from the service-entrance conductors ≫ *230.70* ≪.

Install the service disconnecting means at a readily accessible location, either outside of a building/structure or inside nearest the service conductors' entry point ≫ *230.70(A)(1)* ≪.

A set of fuses is considered all the fuses required to protect all of the circuit's ungrounded conductors ≫ *230.90(A)* ≪.

Ⓐ The service disconnecting means for each service (permitted by 230.2), or for each set of service-entrance conductors (permitted by 230.40, Exception Nos. 1, 3, 4, or 5), shall consist of no more than six switches/circuit breakers in a single enclosure, in a group of separate enclosures, or in (or on) a switchboard ≫ *230.71(A)* ≪.

Ⓑ Two to six disconnects, permitted by 230.71, shall be grouped ≫ *230.72(A)* ≪.

Ⓒ Two to six circuit breakers (or sets of fuses) can serve as the overcurrent device providing overload protection. The sum of the circuit breakers' or fuses' ratings can exceed the service conductor's ampacity, provided the calculated load (according to Article 220) does not exceed the ampacity of the service conductors ≫ *230.90(A) Exception No. 3* ≪.

Ⓓ Each service disconnect shall be permanently marked to identify it as a service disconnect ≫ *230.70(B)* ≪.

Ⓔ Where two to six separately enclosed service disconnecting means (supplying separate loads from one service drop, set of overhead service conductors, set of underground service conductors, or service lateral) are grouped at one location, one set of service-entrance conductors can supply each, or several such, service equipment enclosures ≫ *230.40 Exception No. 2* ≪.

Ⓕ Article 376 contains metal wireway provisions.

Ⓖ Service-entrance conductors can be spliced (or tapped) in accordance with 110.14, 300.5(E), 300.13, and 300.15 ≫ *230.46* ≪.

Ⓗ Only service conductors can be installed in the same service raceway or service cable ≫ *230.7* ≪. This provision does not apply to grounding (and bonding) jumpers and load management control conductors having overcurrent protection ≫ *230.7 Exception No. 1* and *No. 2* ≪.

N O T E

Each service disconnect shall simultaneously disconnect all ungrounded service conductors under its control from the premises wiring system ≫*230.74*≪.

Section 230.2 permits one (or more) additional service disconnecting means for fire pumps, emergency systems, and legally required or optional standby services. These additional service disconnecting means shall be installed at a sufficient distance from the normal (one to six) service disconnecting means to minimize the possibility of simultaneous interruption of supply ≫*230.72(B)*≪.

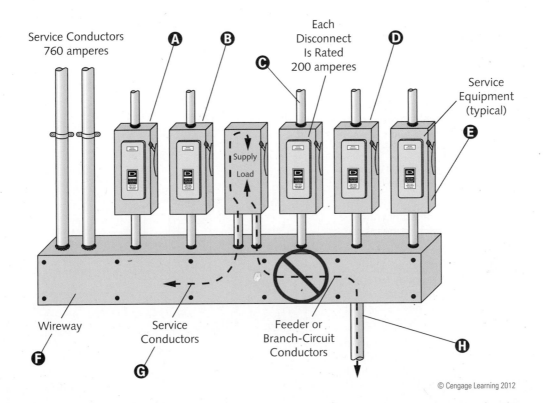

Service Conductors 760 amperes

Each Disconnect Is Rated 200 amperes

Service Equipment (typical)

Supply / Load

Wireway

Service Conductors

Feeder or Branch-Circuit Conductors

© Cengage Learning 2012

Feeder Taps

Because of dissimilar metals' characteristics, devices such as pressure terminal/splicing connectors and soldering lugs shall be identified for the conductor's material, shall be properly installed, and shall be properly used. Conductors of dissimilar metals shall not be intermixed in a terminal (or splicing) connector where physical contact occurs between dissimilar conductors (such as copper and aluminum, copper and copper-clad aluminum, etc.), unless the device is identified for the purpose and conditions of use ≫ *110.14* ≪.

While single-phase system illustrations are used, be aware that the same rules also apply to 3-phase systems.

Ⓐ Tap conductors can be protected against overcurrent in accordance with 210.19(A)(3) and (4), 240.5(B)(2), 240.21, 368.17(B) and (C), 368.17(C), and 430.53(D) ≫ *240.4(E)* ≪.

Ⓑ Conductors can be tapped to a feeder without having overcurrent protection at the tap as specified in 240.21(B)(1) through (5). The provisions of 240.4(B) shall not be permitted for tap conductors ≫ *240.21(B)* ≪.

Ⓒ Per Article 240, a **tap conductor** is a conductor other than a service conductor having overcurrent protection ahead of its point of supply that exceeds the value permitted for

similar conductors protected as otherwise described in 240.4 ≫ *240.2* ≪.

Ⓓ All conductor splices, joints, and free ends shall be covered either with an insulation equivalent to that of the conductors or with an insulating device identified for the purpose ≫ *110.14(B)* ≪.

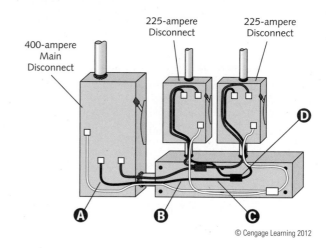

© Cengage Learning 2012

10-ft (3.0-m) Feeder Tap Rule

Ⓐ A 60-ampere rated conductor is the minimum size allowed if the overcurrent protection on the tap conductor's line side is 600 amperes (600 ÷ 10 = 60) ≫ *240.21(B)(1)(4)* ≪.

Ⓑ The tap conductor's ampacity shall not be less than the rating of the device supplied by the tap conductors or less than the overcurrent-protective device rating at the tap conductor's termination ≫ *240.21(B)(1)(1)(b)* ≪.

Ⓒ In addition to the requirement of 408.30, a panelboard shall be protected by an overcurrent protective device having a rating not greater than that of the panelboard. This overcurrent protective device shall be located within or at any point on the supply side of the panelboard ≫ *408.36* ≪.

Ⓓ The tap conductor's ampacity shall not be less than the combined calculated loads on the circuits it supplies ≫ *240.21(B)(1)(1)(a)* ≪.

Ⓔ The tap conductors shall not extend beyond the switchboard, panelboard, disconnecting means, or control devices they supply ≫ *240.21(B)(1)(2)* ≪.

Ⓕ Except where connected to the feeder, tap conductors shall be enclosed in a raceway extending from the tap to the enclosure of an enclosed switchboard, panelboard, or control device, or to the back of an open switchboard ≫ *240.21(B)(1)(3)* ≪.

Ⓖ If the tap conductor's length does not exceed 10 ft (3 m) and all of 240.21(B)(1)(1) through (4) stipulations are satisfied, overcurrent protection at the tap to the feeder is not required ≫ *240.21(B)(1)* ≪.

Ⓗ Field installations with the tap conductors exiting the enclosure (or vault) where the tap is made require that the ampacity of the tap conductors be not less than one-tenth of the rating of the overcurrent device protecting the feeder conductors ≫ *240.21(B)(1)(4)* ≪.

> **NOTE**
>
> Branch–circuit tap conductors meeting the requirements specified in 210.19 shall be permitted to have overcurrent protection as specified in 210.20 ≫*240.21(A)*≪.

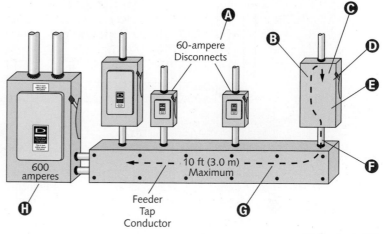

© Cengage Learning 2012

25-ft (7.5-m) Feeder Tap Rule

Ⓐ A 200-ampere rated conductor is the minimum size allowed if the overcurrent protection on the tap conductor's line side is 600 amperes (600 ÷ 3 = 200) 》*240.21(B)(2)(1)*《.

Ⓑ The tap conductors shall terminate in a single circuit breaker (or single set of fuses) that will limit the load of the tap conductor's ampacity. This device can supply unlimited additional load side overcurrent devices 》*240.21(B)(2)(2)*《.

Ⓒ The tap conductors shall be protected from physical damage in an approved manner, such as enclosed in a raceway 》*240.21(B)(2)(3)*《.

Ⓓ If the tap conductor's length does not exceed 25 ft (7.5 m) and all of 240.21(B)(2)(1) through (3) stipulations are satisfied, overcurrent protection at the tap to the feeder is not required 》*240.21(B)(2)*《.

Ⓔ The tap conductors' ampacity shall not be less than one-third of the feeder conductor's overcurrent device rating 》*240.21(B)(2)(1)*《.

> **NOTE**
>
> Tap conductors longer than 25 ft (7.5 m) shall comply with 240.21(B)(4) specifications.

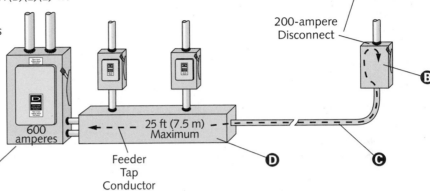

200-ampere Disconnect

600 amperes

25 ft (7.5 m) Maximum

Feeder Tap Conductor

© Cengage Learning 2012

Bonding Service Raceways

Ⓐ The supply-side bonding jumper shall meet Table 250.66 size requirements for grounding electrode conductors. Where the ungrounded supply conductors are larger than 1100-kcmil copper (or 1750-kcmil aluminum), the supply-side bonding jumper shall have an area not less than 12½% of the largest set of ungrounded supply conductor's area, unless the ungrounded supply conductors and the supply-side bonding jumper are of different materials (copper or aluminum) 》*250.102(C)(1)*《.

Ⓑ Here, one supply-side bonding jumper is used to bond *all* service raceways. This supply-side bonding jumper's size is based on the total combined ungrounded supply conductors' area.

Ⓒ Here, a supply-side bonding jumper bonds *each individual* service raceway. Each supply-side bonding jumper is sized according to each individual raceway's ungrounded supply conductors.

Ⓓ Where the ungrounded supply conductors are paralleled in two or more raceways or cables, and an individual supply-side bonding jumper is used for bonding these raceways or cables, the size of the supply-side bonding jumper for each raceway or cable shall be selected from Table 250.66 based on the size of the ungrounded supply conductors in each raceway or cable. A single supply-side bonding jumper installed for

bonding two or more raceways or cables shall be sized in accordance with (C)(1) 》*250.102(C)(1)*《.

Ⓔ The total ungrounded supply conductors' area is 1400 kcmil (350 × 4). The supply-side bonding jumper shall be at least 12½% of that area (1400 × 12.5% = 175 kcmil or 175,000 cmil). In accordance with Chapter 9, Table 8, a 3/0 AWG copper conductor (with a circular mil area of 167,800) is insufficient. Therefore, a 4/0 AWG copper conductor (with a circular mil area of 211,600) meets the minimum size requirement.

Ⓕ The following normally non-current-carrying metal parts of equipment shall be bonded together: (1) all raceways, cable trays, cablebus framework, auxiliary gutters, or service cable armor or sheath that enclose, contain, or support service conductors, except as permitted in 250.80; and (2) all enclosures containing service conductors, including meter fittings, boxes, or the like, interposed in the service raceway or armor 》*250.92(A)(1) and (2)*《.

Ⓖ A supply-side bonding jumper is defined as a conductor installed on the supply side of a service or within a service equipment enclosure(s), for a separately derived system, that ensures the required electrical conductivity between metal parts required to be electrically connected 》*250.2*《.

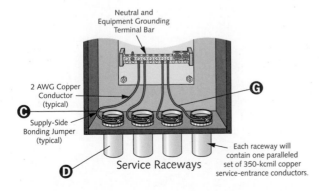

Neutral and Equipment Grounding Terminal Bar

2 AWG Copper Conductor (typical)

Supply-Side Bonding Jumper (typical)

Service Raceways

Each raceway will contain one paralleled set of 350-kcmil copper service-entrance conductors.

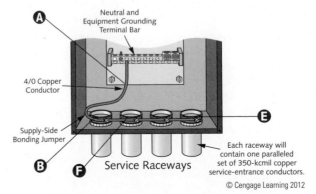

Neutral and Equipment Grounding Terminal Bar

4/0 Copper Conductor

Supply-Side Bonding Jumper

Service Raceways

Each raceway will contain one paralleled set of 350-kcmil copper service-entrance conductors.

© Cengage Learning 2012

Tap Conductors Supplying a Transformer

Ⓐ A transformer's primary conductors shall have an ampacity at least one-third of the feeder conductors' overcurrent device rating »240.21(B)(3)(1)«.

Ⓑ A 100-ampere rated conductor is the minimum size allowed if the overcurrent protection on the tap conductor's line side is 300 amperes (300 ÷ 3 = 100) »240.21(B)(3)(1)«.

Ⓒ Primary and secondary conductors shall be protected from physical damage in an approved manner, such as enclosed in a raceway »240.21(B)(3)(4)«.

Ⓓ Secondary conductors shall terminate in a single circuit breaker or set of fuses that will limit the load current to no more than the conductor ampacity permitted by 310.15 »240.21(B)(3)(5)«.

Ⓔ Conductors supplied by the transformer's secondary shall have an ampacity that is not less than the value of the primary-to-secondary voltage ratio multiplied by one-third of the feeder conductors' overcurrent device rating »240.21(B)(3)(2)«.

Ⓕ The combined length of one primary plus one secondary conductor (excluding any portion of the primary conductor protected at its ampacity) shall not exceed 25 ft (7.5 m) »240.21(B)(3)(3)«.

Ⓖ Conductors supplied from a set of fuses (or circuit breaker) and feeding a transformer are feeder conductors, not feeder tap conductors.

Ⓗ Refer to this book's Unit 14 for transformer provisions (overcurrent protection, grounding, etc.).

Ⓘ Transformer secondary conductor provisions are found in 240.21(C).

WARNING

The provisions of 240.4(B) shall not be permitted for tap conductors »240.21(B)«.

CAUTION

Transformers, other than Class 2 or Class 3 transformers, shall have a disconnecting means located either in sight of the transformer or in a remote location. Where located in a remote location, the disconnecting means shall be lockable, and the location shall be field-marked on the transformer »450.14«.

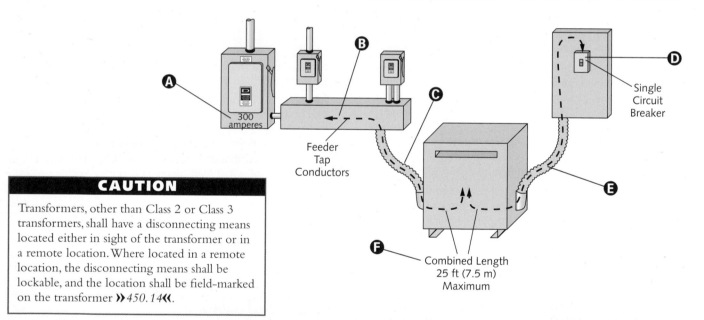

Feeder Tap Conductors

Single Circuit Breaker

Combined Length 25 ft (7.5 m) Maximum

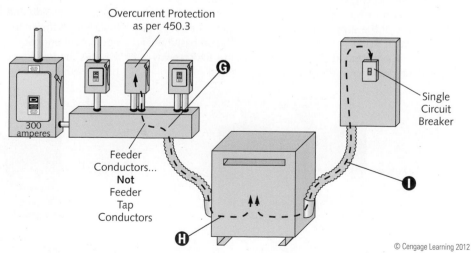

Overcurrent Protection as per 450.3

Feeder Conductors... **Not** Feeder Tap Conductors

Single Circuit Breaker

© Cengage Learning 2012

Transformer Vaults

Wherever such an arrangement is practicable, transformer vaults shall be located so that ventilation to outside air does not rely on flues or ducts ≫ *450.41* ≪.

Where required by 450.9, openings for ventilation shall also comply with 450.45(A) through (F) ≫ *450.45* ≪. That section includes provisions pertaining to location, arrangement, size, covering, dampers, and ducts.

Each doorway from the building interior into the vault shall have a tight-fitting door with a minimum fire rating of three hours, unless the exception is met. The AHJ may require such a door for exterior wall openings, should conditions warrant ≫ *450.43(A)* ≪.

Doors shall be equipped with fully engaged locks, thereby limiting access to qualified persons only ≫ *450.43(C)* ≪.

Personnel doors shall swing out and be equipped with panic bars, pressure plates, or other devices that are normally latched but that open under simple pressure ≫ *450.43(C)* ≪.

Vaults containing more than 100-kVA transformer capacity shall have a drain or other means to carry off any oil or water accumulation, unless local conditions make this impracticable. The vault floor must pitch toward the drain, where provided ≫ *450.46* ≪.

Nonelectrical pipe or duct systems shall neither enter nor pass through a transformer vault. Piping or other facilities providing vault fire protection, or transformer cooling, are allowed ≫ *450.47* ≪.

Ⓐ Vault walls and roofs shall be constructed of materials having adequate structural strength for the conditions and a minimum fire resistance of three hours. For this section's purpose, studs and wallboard construction are not acceptable ≫ *450.42* ≪.

Ⓑ Construction of one hour rating is permitted where transformers are protected with automatic sprinkler, water sprays, carbon dioxide, or halon ≫ *450.42 Exception and 450.43(A) Exception* ≪.

Ⓒ Vault floors in contact with the earth shall be of concrete, no less than 4 in. (100 mm) thick. Where the vault is constructed above a vacant space (or other stories), the floor shall adequately support the load imposed on it and shall have a minimum fire resistance of three hours ≫ *450.42* ≪.

Ⓓ A door sill (or curb) of a sufficient height, at least 4 in. (100 mm), to confine oil from the largest transformer within the vault shall be provided ≫ *450.43(B)* ≪.

NOTE

Entrances to all buildings, rooms, or enclosures containing exposed live parts or exposed conductors operating at over 600 volts, nominal, shall be kept locked, unless such entrances are constantly observed by qualified personnel. Where the voltage exceeds 600 volts, nominal, permanent and conspicuous warning signs shall be posted, reading as follows: *DANGER—HIGH VOLTAGE—KEEP OUT* ≫ *110.34(C)* ≪.

CAUTION

Transformer vaults shall not be used for material storage ≫ *450.48* ≪.

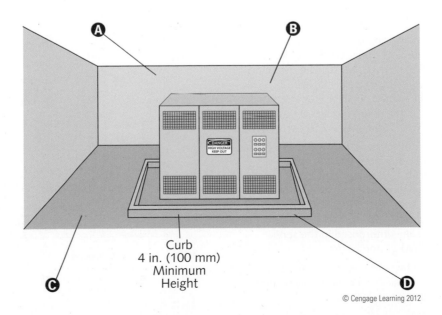

Curb
4 in. (100 mm)
Minimum
Height

© Cengage Learning 2012

Grounding Electrode Conductor Taps

The supply-side bonding jumper shall meet Table 250.66 size requirements for grounding electrode conductors. If the ungrounded supply phase conductors are larger than 1100-kcmil copper (or 1750-kcmil aluminum), the supply-side bonding jumper shall have an area not less than $12\frac{1}{2}\%$ of the largest ungrounded supply conductor's area, unless the ungrounded supply conductors and the bonding jumper are of different materials (copper or aluminum) ≫ *250.102(C)(1)* ≪.

Where the ungrounded supply conductors are paralleled in two or more raceways or cables, and an individual supply-side bonding jumper is used for bonding these raceways or cables, the size of the supply-side bonding jumper for each raceway or cable shall be selected from Table 250.66 based on the size of the ungrounded supply conductors in each raceway or cable. A single supply-side bonding jumper installed for bonding two or more raceways or cables shall be sized in accordance with (C)(1) ≫ *250.102(C)(2)* ≪.

Ⓐ If a service consists of more than a single enclosure as permitted in 230.71(A), grounding electrode connections (taps) shall be made in accordance with 250.64(D)(1), (D)(2), or (D)(3) ≫ *250.64(D)* ≪. A common grounding electrode conductor and grounding electrode conductor taps shall be installed. The common grounding electrode conductor shall be sized in accordance with 250.66, based on the sum of the circular mil area of the largest ungrounded service-entrance conductor(s). If the service-entrance conductors connect directly to a service drop or service lateral, the common grounding electrode conductor shall be sized in accordance with Table 250.66, Note 1. A grounding electrode conductor tap shall extend to the inside of each service disconnecting means enclosure. The grounding electrode conductor taps shall be sized in accordance with 250.66 for the largest service-entrance conductor serving the individual enclosure. The tap conductors shall be connected to the common grounding electrode conductor by one of the following methods in such a manner that the common grounding electrode conductor remains without a splice or joint; (1) exothermic welding, (2) connectors listed as grounding and bonding equipment, (3) connections to an aluminum or copper busbar not less than $\frac{1}{4}$ in. × 2 in. (6 mm × 50 mm). The busbar shall be securely fastened and shall be installed in an accessible location. Connections shall be made by a listed connector or by the exothermic welding process. If aluminum busbars are used, the installation shall comply with 250.64(A) ≫ *250.64(D)(1)* ≪.

Ⓑ The following normally non-current-carrying metal parts of equipment shall be bonded together: (1) all raceways, cable trays, cablebus framework, auxiliary gutters, or service cable armor or sheath that enclose, contain, or support service conductors, except as permitted in 250.80; and (2) all enclosures containing service conductors, including meter fittings, boxes, or the like, interposed in the service raceway or armor ≫ *250.92(A)(1) and (2)* ≪.

Ⓒ Bonding shall be provided where necessary to ensure electrical continuity and the capacity to conduct safely any fault current likely to be imposed ≫ *250.90* ≪.

Ⓓ The grounding electrode conductor shall be of one continuous length (without splice or joint), except as permitted in 250.30(A)(5) and (A)(6), 250.30(B)(1), and 250.68(C). If necessary, splices or connections shall be made as permitted in 250.64(C)(1) through (4) ≫ *250.64(C)* ≪.

Ⓔ Ferrous metal enclosures for grounding electrode conductors shall be electrically continuous from the point of attachment to cabinets or equipment to the grounding electrode and shall be securely fastened to the ground clamp or fitting. Ferrous metal enclosures that are not physically continuous from cabinets or equipment to the grounding electrode shall be made electrically continuous by bonding each end of the raceway or enclosure to the grounding electrode conductor. Bonding methods in compliance with 250.92(B) for installations at service equipment locations and with 250.92(B)(2) through (B)(4) for other than service equipment locations shall apply at each end and to all intervening ferrous raceways, boxes, and enclosures between the cabinets or equipment and the grounding electrode ≫ *250.64(E)* ≪.

Ⓕ A grounding electrode conductor shall be connected to the grounded service conductor(s) in a wireway or other accessible enclosure on the supply side of the service disconnecting means. The connection shall be made with exothermic welding or a connector listed as grounding and bonding equipment. The grounding electrode conductor shall be sized in accordance with 250.66 based on the service-entrance conductor(s) at the common location where the connection is made ≫ *250.64(D)(3)* ≪.

> **NOTE**
>
> A grounding electrode conductor shall be connected between the grounded conductor in each service equipment disconnecting means enclosure and the grounding electrode system. Each grounding electrode conductor shall be sized in accordance with 250.66 based on the service-entrance conductor(s) supplying the individual service disconnecting means ≫ *250.64(D)(2)* ≪.

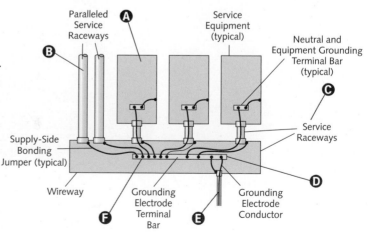

Paralleled Service Raceways — Ⓐ — Service Equipment (typical) — Neutral and Equipment Grounding Terminal Bar (typical) — Ⓒ — Ⓑ — Service Raceways — Supply-Side Bonding Jumper (typical) — Wireway — Grounding Electrode Terminal Bar — Ⓕ — Ⓔ — Grounding Electrode Conductor — Ⓓ

Equipment Grounding Conductors

Where a single equipment grounding conductor is run with multiple circuits in the same raceway, cable, or cable tray, it shall be sized for the largest overcurrent device protecting conductors in the raceway, cable, or cable tray. Equipment grounding conductors installed in cable trays shall meet the minimum requirements of 392.3(B)(1)(c) 》*250.122(C)*《.

While copper, aluminum, or copper-clad aluminum equipment grounding conductors of the wire type shall not be smaller than shown in Table 250.122, in no case, are they required to be larger than the circuit conductors supplying the equipment 》*250.122(A)*《.

Where a raceway, cable tray, or cable armor (or sheath) serves as the equipment grounding conductor, as provided in 250.118 and 250.134(A), it shall comply with 250.4(A)(5) or 250.4(B)(4). Equipment grounding conductors shall be permitted to be sectioned within a multiconductor cable, provided the combined circular mil area complies with Table 250.122 》*250.122(A)*《.

Ⓐ Since the overcurrent protection has a rating of 1200 amperes, the minimum size equipment grounding conductor is 3/0 AWG copper (or 250-kcmil aluminum) 》*Table 250.122*《.

Ⓑ **Each** equipment grounding conductor shall be sized in compliance with 250.122 》*250.122(F)*《.

Ⓒ Equipment grounding conductor provisions are not limited to feeders. For example, an alternative drawing could have shown one piece of equipment supplied by a paralleled set of branch-circuit conductors. Equipment grounding conductor provisions also apply to branch circuits.

Ⓓ Unlike service-equipment bonding jumpers, which can be sized according to each paralleled raceway's service-entrance conductor size, a **full-size** equipment grounding conductor (where used) must be installed in **each** raceway.

Ⓔ For paralleled conductors in multiple raceways (or cables) as permitted by 310.10(H), any equipment grounding conductors installed shall also run in parallel within **each** raceway 》*250.122(F)*《.

Ⓕ If a single raceway supplies the equipment, only one 3/0 AWG copper (or 250-kcmil aluminum) equipment grounding conductor is required.

> **N O T E**
>
> Where ungrounded conductors are increased in size, equipment grounding conductors, where installed, shall be increased in size proportionately according to the circular mil area of the ungrounded conductors 》*250.122(B)*《.

> **WARNING**
>
> An equipment grounding conductor shall not be used as a grounding electrode conductor 》*250.121*《.

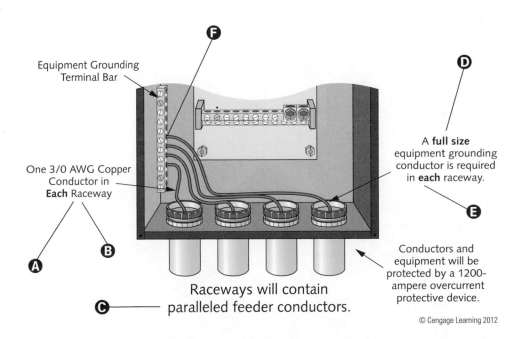

Equipment Grounding Terminal Bar

One 3/0 AWG Copper Conductor in **Each** Raceway

A **full size** equipment grounding conductor is required in **each** raceway.

Conductors and equipment will be protected by a 1200-ampere overcurrent protective device.

Raceways will contain paralleled feeder conductors.

© Cengage Learning 2012

Cable Trays

Cable tray installations are not limited to industrial establishments. Wiring methods in Table 392.10(A) can be installed in cable tray systems under the conditions described in their respective articles and sections ≫*392.10 and 10(A)*≪.

Only in industrial establishments, where maintenance and supervision conditions restrict cable tray system service to qualified personnel, can any of the cables in 392.10(B)(1) and (2) be installed in ladder, ventilated troughs, solid-bottom, or ventilated-channel cable trays ≫*392.10(B)*≪.

Cable tray systems shall be corrosion resistant. If made of ferrous material, the system shall be protected from corrosion per 300.6 ≫*392.100(C)*≪.

Steel or aluminum cable tray systems can be used as equipment grounding conductors provided all 392.60(B)(1) through (4) conditions are met.

While provisions pertaining to the number of multiconductor cables (rated 2000 volts or less) can be found in 392.22(A), 392.22(B) contains single conductor cable provisions.

Ⓐ Cable trays can extend transversely through partitions and walls, or vertically through platforms and floors, in either wet or dry locations where the completed installation meets 300.21 requirements ≫*392.18(D)*≪.

Ⓑ Sufficient space shall be provided and maintained around cable trays to permit adequate access for cable installation and maintenance ≫*392.18(E)*≪.

Ⓒ Cable trays shall be of adequate strength and rigidity to provide support for all contained wiring ≫*392.100(A)*≪.

Ⓓ A cable tray system is a unit (or assembly of units or sections) and associated fittings that together form a structural system used to securely fasten/support cables and raceways ≫*392.2*≪.

Ⓔ Cable trays shall be exposed and accessible except as permitted by 392.10(D) ≫*392.18(E)*≪.

Ⓕ Cable trays shall include fittings or other suitable means to facilitate changes in direction and elevation ≫*392.100(E)*≪.

Ⓖ Cable trays shall have side rails or similar structural members ≫*392.100(D)*≪.

Ⓗ Metallic cable trays can serve as equipment grounding conductors where (1) continuous maintenance and supervision ensures that qualified persons service the installed cable tray system and (2) the cable tray complies with 392.60 provisions ≫*392.60(A)*≪.

Ⓘ Each cable tray run shall be completed before cables are installed ≫*392.18(B)*≪.

CAUTION

Cable trays in hazardous (classified) locations shall contain only the cable types and raceways permitted by other articles in the *NEC* ≫*392.10(C)*≪.

NOTE

Cable tray systems shall not be used in hoistways or where subject to severe physical damage ≫*392.12*≪.

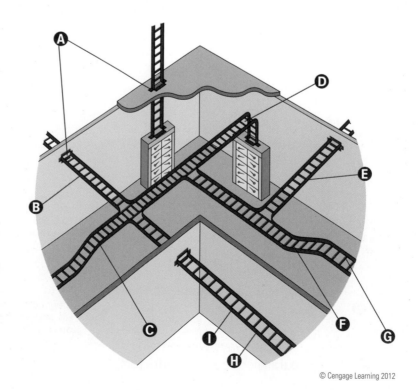

MOTORS

General Motor Provisions

Article 430 covers motors and all of the following as they relate specifically to motors: branch-circuit and feeder conductors and their protection, overload protection, control circuits, controllers, and motor-control centers ≫ *430.1* ≪.

Wires passing through an opening in an enclosure, conduit box, or barrier require a bushing to protect the conductors from any sharp opening edges ≫ *430.13* ≪.

A Article 430, Part V specifies protective devices designed to protect feeder conductors supplying motors against overcurrents due to short circuits or grounds ≫ *430.61* ≪.

B Sections 430.24 through 430.26 contain provisions for conductors supplying multiple motors, or a motor(s) and other load(s). These provisions are applicable to more than feeder conductors.

C Article 430, Part IV specifies devices that are used to protect motor branch-circuit conductors, motor-control apparatus, and motors against overcurrent due to short circuits or ground faults. The rules add to or amend Article 240 provisions ≫ *430.51* ≪.

D Article 430, Part II specifies ampacities of conductors capable of carrying the motor current without overheating, under specified conditions ≫ *430.21* ≪.

E Article 430, Part III specifies overload devices intended to protect motors, motor-control apparatus, and motor branch-circuit conductors against excessive heating due to motor overloads and failure to start ≫ *430.31* ≪.

Overload is defined as operation of equipment in excess of normal, full-load rating, or of a conductor in excess of rated ampacity that, when it persists for a sufficient length of time, would cause damage or dangerous overheating. A fault, such as a short circuit or ground fault, is not an overload ≫ *Article 100* ≪.

F General motor provisions are found in 430.1 through 430.18 (Part I).

G Part XIII of Article 430 addresses the grounding of exposed non-current-carrying metal parts of motor and controller frames that are likely to become energized to prevent a voltage aboveground should accidental contact between energized parts and frames occur. Insulating, isolating, or guarding are suitable alternatives to motor grounding under certain conditions ≫ *430.241* ≪.

H For general motor applications, base current ratings on 430.6(A)(1) and (2): (1) Other than for motors built for low speeds (less than 1200 rpm) or high torques, and for multi-speed motors, use the values given in Tables 430.247 through 430.250 (including notes) to determine conductor ampacity or ampere ratings of switches, branch-circuit short-circuit, and ground-fault protection. Do not use the actual current ratings marked on the motor nameplate unless an exception applies, and (2) Separate motor overload protection is based on the motor nameplate current rating ≫ *430.(6)(A)* ≪.

I Motor disconnecting means provisions are found in 430.101 through 430.113 (Part IX).

> ### NOTE
>
> Motor tables are located in Part XIV of Article 430.

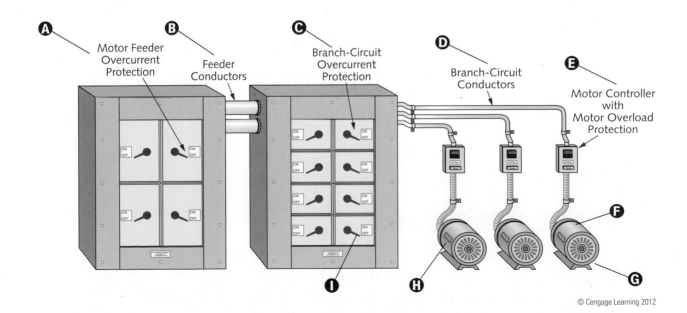

- **A** Motor Feeder Overcurrent Protection
- **B** Feeder Conductors
- **C** Branch-Circuit Overcurrent Protection
- **D** Branch-Circuit Conductors
- **E** Motor Controller with Motor Overload Protection

Motor and Branch-Circuit Overload Protection

Each continuous-duty motor rated 1 hp or less, *not* permanently installed, nonautomatically started, and within sight of the controller can be protected against overloads by the branch-circuit short-circuit and ground-fault device. Comply with branch-circuit overcurrent protection size specifications found in Article 430, Part IV »*430.32(D)*«.

Any automatically started motor, 1 hp or less, must be protected against overload by one of the methods found in 430.32(B)(1) through (4).

A motor controller can serve as an overload device if the number of overload units complies with Table 430.37, and if these units are operative in both the starting and running position (dc motor), or in the running position (ac motor) »*430.39*«.

Overload relays and other devices for motor overload protection incapable of opening short circuits or ground faults shall be protected by fuses (or circuit breakers) rated or set according to 430.52, or by a motor short-circuit protector per 430.52 »*430.40*«.

Overload protection for motors on general-purpose branch circuits (permitted by Article 210) is required and must meet 430.42(A), (B), (C), or (D) specifications.

Ⓐ As an approved method of protecting a motor against overload, 430.32(A)(1) lists a separate overload device responsive to motor current. This device must be selected to trip or shall be rated at no more than the percentage of the motor nameplate full-load current rating shown here:

Motors with a marked service
factor not less than 1.15. . . . . .125%

Motors with a marked temperature
rise not over 40°C. 125%

All other motors 115%

Ⓑ Controllers must be marked according to 430.8 provisions.

Ⓒ Article 430, Part III lists overload devices intended to protect motors, motor-control apparatus, and motor branch-circuit conductors against excessive heating due to motor overloads and failure to start »*430.31*«.

Ⓓ Separate motor overload protection shall be based on the actual motor nameplate current rating, not on the ratings listed in Tables 430.247 through 430.250 »*430.6(A)(2)*«.

Ⓔ Motors (in usual applications) must be marked with the information listed in 430.7(A)(1) through (15).

Ⓕ Each motor used in a continuous-duty application rated more than 1 hp must be protected against overload by a means listed in 430.32(A)(1) through (4).

Ⓖ **Overload** is defined as operation of equipment in excess of normal, full-load rating, or of a conductor in excess of rated ampacity that, when it persists for a sufficient length of time, would cause damage or dangerous overheating. A fault, such as a short circuit or ground fault, is not an overload »*Article 100*«.

CAUTION

A motor overload device, which restarts a motor automatically after overload tripping, shall not be installed if automatic restarting can result in injury to persons »*430.43*«.

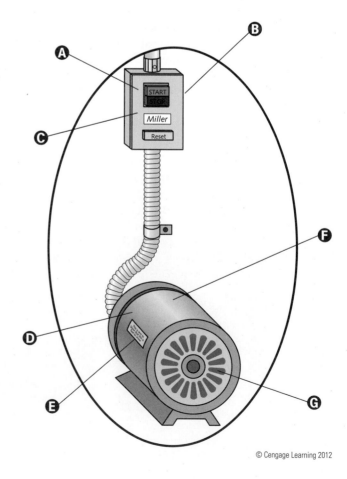

NOTE

Any motor application shall be considered continuous duty unless the driven apparatus, by nature, means the motor shall not, under any conditions, operate continuously with the load »*430.33*«.

WARNING

Section 430, Part III provisions *do not* require overload protection where a power loss would cause a hazard, such as with fire pumps »*430.31*«. For fire pump supply conductor protection, see 695.6.

Motors on General-Purpose Branch Circuits

Where a motor without individual overload protection (as provided in 430.42[A]) is connected to a branch circuit by means of an attachment plug and a receptacle or cord connector, the attachment plug and receptacle or cord connector rating shall not exceed 15 amperes at either 125 or 250 volts. Where individual overload protection is required per 430.42(B) for a motor or motor-operated appliance attached to a branch circuit through an attachment plug and a receptacle or a cord connector, the overload device shall be an integral part of the motor/appliance. The rating of the attachment plug and receptacle or cord connector determines the rating of the circuit to which the motor may be connected, as provided in 210.21(B) ≫*430.42(C)*≪.

The branch-circuit short-circuit and ground-fault protective device of a circuit to which a motor (or motor-operated appliance) is connected shall have a time delay sufficient to start the motor and allow it to accelerate ≫*430.42(D)*≪.

Ⓐ One or more motors without individual overload protection can be connected to a general-purpose branch circuit only if the installation complies with the limiting conditions of 430.32(B) and (D) and 430.53(A)(1) and (A)(2) ≫*430.42(A)*≪.

Ⓑ Motors used on general-purpose branch circuits (as permitted in Article 210) require overload protection per 430.42(A), (B), (C), or (D) specifications ≫*430.42*≪.

Motor Branch-Circuit Conductors

Conductors for motors used in short-time, intermittent, periodic, or varying duty applications shall have an ampacity of no less than the percentage of the motor nameplate current rating shown in Table 430.22(E), unless the AHJ grants special permission for conductors of lower ampacity ≫*430.22(E)*≪.

Where motor circuits contain capacitors, conductors shall comply with 460.8 and 460.9 ≫*430.27*≪.

For a multispeed motor, the selection of branch-circuit conductors on the line side of the controller shall be based on the highest of the full-load current ratings shown on the motor nameplate. The ampacity of the branch-circuit conductors between the controller and the motor shall not be less than 125 percent of the current rating of the winding(s) that the conductors energize ≫*430.22(B)*≪.

Ⓐ Branch-circuit conductors supplying a single motor used in a continuous-duty application shall have an ampacity of at least 125% of the motor's full load current rating as determined by 430.6(A)(1), or not less than specified in 430.22(A) through (G) ≫*430.22(A)*≪.

NOTE

Conductors supplying several motors, or a motor(s) and other load(s), must comply with 430.24.

Ⓒ Motors of larger ratings than specified in 430.53(A) can be connected to general-purpose branch circuits only if each motor has overload protection specifically listed for that motor as specified in 430.32. In the case of more than one motor, both the controller and the motor overload device shall be approved for group installation, and the short-circuit and ground-fault protective device shall be selected according to 430.53 ≫*430.42(B)*≪.

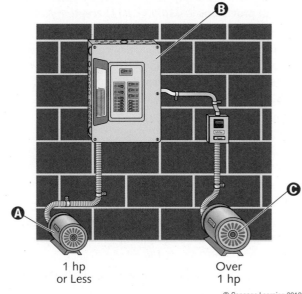

1 hp
or Less

Over
1 hp

© Cengage Learning 2012

Ⓑ Annex D contains a motor application example (Example No. D8).

Ⓒ Placement of motors shall allow adequate ventilation and facilitate maintenance, such as bearing lubrication and brush replacement ≫*430.14(A)*≪.

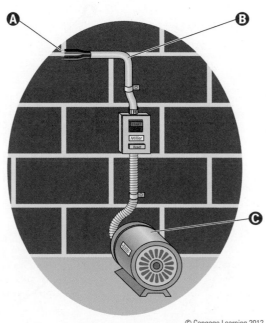

© Cengage Learning 2012

Motor Branch-Circuit Short-Circuit and Ground-Fault Protection

Part IV specifies devices intended to protect the motor branch-circuit conductors, motor-control apparatus, and the motors against overcurrent due to short circuits or ground faults ≫ *430.51* ≪.

Where the rating specified in Table 430.52, or the rating modified by Exception No. 1, is not sufficient for the motor's starting current, apply 430.52(C)(1) Exception No. 2 (a) through (d) provisions ≫ *430.52(C)(1) Exception No. 2* ≪.

Suitable fuses are permitted in lieu of devices listed in Table 430.52 for power electronic devices in a solid-state motor controller system, provided replacement fuse markings are adjacent to the fuses ≫ *430.52(C)(5)* ≪.

A listed self-protected combination controller may be substituted for the devices specified in Table 430.52 ≫ *430.52(C)(6)* ≪.

Torque motor branch circuits shall be protected at the motor nameplate current rating according to 240.4(B) ≫ *430.52(D)* ≪.

The branch-circuit short-circuit and ground-fault protective device rating for multimotor and combination-load equipment shall not exceed the equipment's marked rating in accordance with 430.7(D) ≫ *430.54* ≪.

Where fuses are used for motor branch-circuit short-circuit and ground-fault protection, the fuseholders shall be of adequate size to accommodate the fuses specified by Table 430.52 ≫ *430.57* ≪. (An exception is provided for fuses having a time delay appropriate for the motor's starting characteristics.)

A circuit breaker for motor branch-circuit short-circuit and ground-fault protection shall have a current rating as determined by 430.52 and 430.110 ≫ *430.58* ≪.

Ⓐ Should the values for branch-circuit short-circuit and ground-fault protective devices (determined by Table 430.52) not correspond to a standard size or rating of fuses, non-adjustable circuit breakers, thermal protective devices, or possible settings of adjustable circuit breakers, then the next higher standard size, rating, or possible setting is permitted. This rating or setting shall not exceed the next higher standard ampere rating ≫ *430.52(C)(1) Exception No. 1* ≪.

Ⓑ Use a protective device whose rating (or setting) does not exceed the value calculated according to Table 430.52 ≫ *430.52(C)(1)* ≪.

Ⓒ The motor branch-circuit short-circuit and ground-fault protective device shall comply with 430.52(B) and either (C) or (D), as applicable ≫ *430.52(A)* ≪.

Ⓓ Branch-circuit protective devices shall comply with 240.15 provisions ≫ *430.56* ≪.

> ### N O T E
>
> The motor branch-circuit short-circuit and ground-fault protective device shall be able to carry the motor's starting current ≫ ***430.52(B)*** ≪.

> ### CAUTION
>
> If the maximum branch-circuit short-circuit and ground-fault protective device ratings are shown in the manufacturer's overload relay table (for use with a motor controller), or are otherwise marked on the equipment, they shall not be exceeded even if 430.52(C)(1) allows higher values ≫ *430.52(C)(2)* ≪.

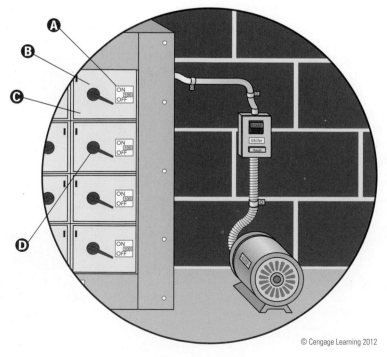

Motor Disconnecting Means

The disconnecting means shall open all ungrounded supply conductors and shall be designed so that no pole operates independently. The disconnecting means can occupy the same enclosure as the controller. The disconnecting means shall be designed so that it shall not be closed automatically ≫ *430.103* ≪ .

The disconnecting means shall plainly indicate whether it is in the open (off) or closed (on) position ≫ *430.104* ≪ .

Motor-control circuits' arrangement shall accommodate disconnection from all supply sources when the disconnecting means is in the open position ≫ *430.75* ≪ .

Where two or more motors are used together or where one or more motors are used in combination with other loads, such as resistance heaters, and where the combined load may be simultaneous on a single disconnecting means, the ampere and horsepower ratings of the combined load shall be determined in accordance with provisions in 430.110(C)(1) though (3).

A switch (or circuit breaker) can serve as both controller and disconnecting means if it complies with 430.111(A) and is one of a type listed in 430.111(B) ≫ *430.111* ≪ .

Every motor-circuit disconnecting means between the feeder's point of attachment and the motor's connection point shall comply with the requirements of 430.109 and 430.110 ≫ *430.108* ≪ .

The disconnecting means shall be a type specified in 430.109(A), unless otherwise permitted in (B) through (G), under the conditions given ≫ *430.109* ≪ .

Ⓐ Motor circuits rated 600 volts, nominal, or less, shall have a disconnecting means with an ampere rating of at least 115% of the motor's full-load current rating ≫ *430.110(A)* ≪ .

Ⓑ According to Article 430, a controller is any switch (or device) normally used to start and stop a motor by making and breaking motor circuit current ≫ *430.2* ≪ .

Ⓒ An individual, fully functional disconnecting means shall be provided for each controller. The disconnecting means shall be located in sight from the controller, unless an exception is met ≫ *430.102(A)* ≪ . The controller disconnecting means required in accordance with 430.102(A) shall be permitted to serve as the disconnecting means for the motor if it is in sight from the motor location and the driven machinery location ≫ *430.102(B)(2)* ≪ .

Ⓓ A disconnecting means shall be located in sight from the motor and driven machinery location ≫ *430.102(B)(1)* ≪ .

Ⓔ Motor branch-circuit and ground-fault protection and motor overload protection can be combined into a single device, where the device's rating (or setting) provides the overload protection required by 430.32 ≫ *430.55* ≪ .

Ⓕ Article 430, Part IX requires a disconnecting means capable of breaking the connection between the motors/controllers and the circuit ≫ *430.101* ≪ .

Ⓖ The phrase "in sight from" indicates that specified items of equipment are visible and are no more than 50 ft (15 m) apart ≫ *Article 100* ≪ .

NOTE

At least one of the disconnecting means shall be **readily** accessible ≫ ***430.107*** ≪ .

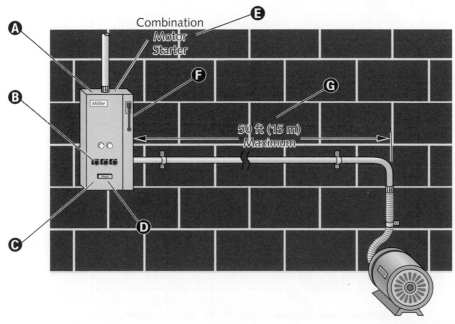

© Cengage Learning 2012

Motor-Control Centers

At motor-control center terminals, minimum wire bending space as well as minimum gutter space shall comply with Article 312 》》*430.97(C)*《《.

Any motor-control center used as service equipment shall be provided with a single main disconnecting means to disconnect all ungrounded service conductors 》》*430.95*《《.

Spacing between motor-control center bus terminals and other bare metal parts shall meet Table 430.97 specifications 》》*430.97(D)*《《.

Barriers are required in all service-entrance motor-control centers to isolate service busbars and terminals from the remainder of the motor-control center 》》*430.97(E)*《《.

Motor-control centers shall be marked according to 110.21, so that the markings remain plainly visible after installation. Common power bus current rating and motor-control center short-circuit rating shall be included in the marking 》》*430.98(A)*《《.

Ⓐ Article 430, Part VIII covers motor-control centers installed for the control of motors, lighting, and power circuits 》》*430.92*《《.

Ⓑ Multisection motor-control centers shall be connected together with an equipment grounding conductor, or an equivalent equipment grounding bus, sized according to Table 250.122. Equipment grounding conductors shall be connected to this equipment grounding bus or to a grounding termination point within a single-section motor-control center 》》*430.96*《《.

Ⓒ Motor-control centers shall have overcurrent protection in accordance with Parts I, II, and VIII of Article 240. The ampere rating or setting of the overcurrent protective device shall not exceed the rating of the common power bus. This protection shall be provided by (1) an overcurrent protective device located ahead of the motor-control center or (2) a main overcurrent protective device in the motor-control center 》》*430.94*《《.

Ⓓ Horizontal travel through vertical sections is acceptable where a barrier isolates the conductors from the busbars 》》*430.97(A) Exception*《《.

Ⓔ Secure busbars firmly in place and provide adequate protection from physical damage. Other than those required for interconnections and control wiring, only the conductors that terminate can be located within that vertical section 》》*430.97(A)*《《.

> ## N O T E
>
> Motor-control units within a motor-control center shall comply with 430.8 》》*430.98(B)*《《.
>
> Motor-control circuit installations must comply with Article 430, Part VI (430.71 through 75).

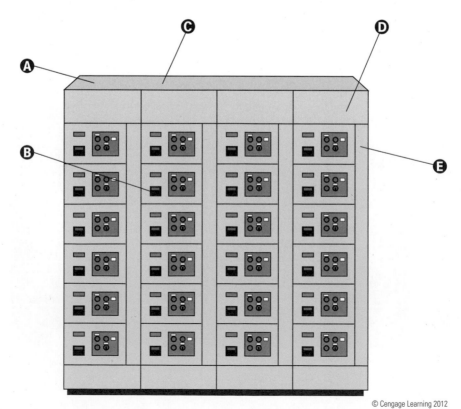

Feeder Conductors

Where one or more of the motors of the group are used for short-time, intermittent, periodic, or varying duty, the ampere rating of such motors (used in the calculation) is determined by 430.22(E). For the highest rated motor, the greater of (1) the ampere rating from 430.22(E) or (2) the largest continuous-duty motor full-load current multiplied by 1.25 is used 》*430.24 Exception No. 1* 《.

The ampacity of conductors supplying motor-operated fixed electric space-heating equipment shall conform to 424.3(B) specifications 》*430.24 Exception No. 2* 《.

Where interlocked circuitry prevents simultaneous operation of selected motors (or other loads), the conductor ampacity can be based on the highest possible total of motor and other load currents to be operated simultaneously 》*430.24 Exception No. 3* 《.

Feeder tap conductors must comply with 430.28 provisions.

> ### N O T E
>
> To ensure compliance with 430.24, 430.53(B), and 430.53(C), the highest rated, or smallest rated, motor shall be based on the rated full-load current selected from Tables 430.247, 430.248, 430.249, and 430.250 》***430.17***《.

A Conductors supplying several motors or a motor(s) and other load(s) shall have an ampacity not less than the sum of each of the following:

(1) 125% of the full-load current rating of the highest rated motor, as determined by 430.6(A),

(2) Sum of the full-load current ratings of all the other motors in the group, as determined by 430.6(A),

(3) 100% of the noncontinuous nonmotor load, and

(4) 125% of the continuous nonmotor load 》*430.24* 《.

In other words, multiply the largest motor full-load current (FLC) rating by 125% and add the FLC ratings of all other motors (or loads) in the group. Note, any nonmotor loads that are continuous shall be added to the calculation at 125%.

B Where reduced heating of the conductors results from duty-cycle operation, intermittent operation, or from all motors not operating at one time, the AHJ may allow a lower feeder-conductor ampacity than that specified in 430.24, provided the conductors' ampacity is sufficient for the maximum load determined according to the size and number of motors supplied and the character of their respective loads and duties 》*430.26* 《.

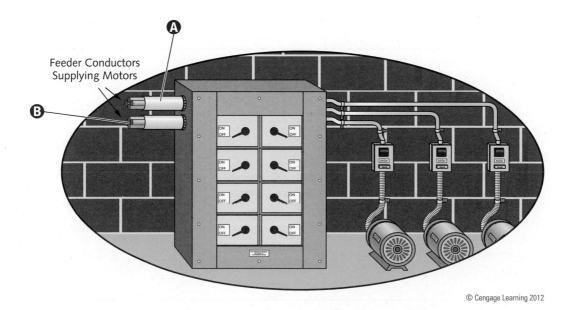

Feeder Conductors
Supplying Motors

© Cengage Learning 2012

Motor Feeder Short-Circuit and Ground-Fault Protection

Where instantaneous trip circuit breaker(s) or motor short-circuit protector(s) are used for motor branch-circuit short-circuit and ground-fault protection, per 430.52(C), the preceding procedure for determining the maximum feeder protective device rating applies with the following provision: For calculation purposes, each instantaneous trip circuit breaker or motor short-circuit protector is assumed to have a rating not exceeding the maximum percentage of motor FLC permitted by Table 430.52 for the type of feeder protective device used ≫*430.62(A) Exception No. 1*≪.

Where the feeder overcurrent protective device also provides overcurrent protection for a motor control center, the provisions of 430.94 shall apply ≫*430.62 Exception No. 2*≪.

Where feeder conductor ampacity is greater than 430.24 requires, the rating (or setting) of the feeder overcurrent protective device can be based on the feeder conductor's ampacity ≫*430.62(B)*≪.

If the same rating (or setting) of the branch-circuit short-circuit and ground-fault protective device is used on multiple branch circuits supplied by the feeder, one of the protective devices is considered the largest for the above calculation ≫*430.62(A)*≪.

Ⓐ A feeder consisting of conductor sizes based on 430.24 that supplies a specific fixed motor load(s) shall have a protective device with a rating (or setting) no greater than the largest rating (or setting) of the branch-circuit short-circuit and ground-fault protective device for any motor supplied by the feeder (based on the maximum permitted value for the specific protective device in accordance with 430.52 or 440.22[A] for hermetic refrigerant motor compressors), plus the sum of the FLCs of the other motors in the group ≫*430.62(A)*≪.

Ⓑ Article 430, Part V specifies devices for protection of feeder conductors supplying motors against overcurrents due to short circuits or grounds ≫*430.61*≪.

N O T E

Where a feeder supplies a motor load and other load(s), the feeder protective device shall have a rating not less than that required for the sum of the other load(s) plus the following:
(1) For a single motor, the rating permitted by 430.52,
(2) For a single hermetic refrigerant motor compressor, the rating permitted by 440.22,
(3) For two or more motors, the rating permitted by 430.62 ≫*430.63*≪.

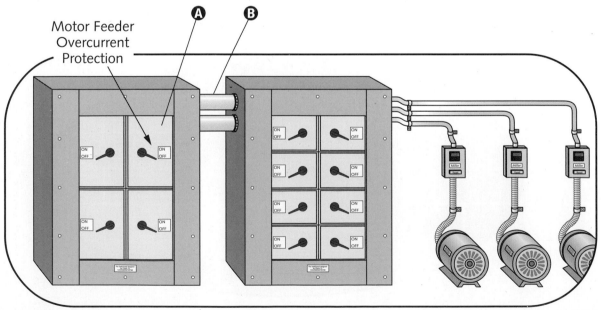

Motor Feeder Overcurrent Protection

© Cengage Learning 2012

SPECIFIC EQUIPMENT

Cranes and Hoists

Conductors shall either be enclosed in raceways or be Type AC cable with insulated grounding conductor, Type MC cable, or Type MI cable, unless 610.11(A) through (E) otherwise permits »*610.11*«.

If a crane, hoist, or monorail hoist operates above readily combustible material, the resistors shall be located as outlined in 610.3(B)(1) and (2) »*610.3(B)*«.

Conductors shall comply with Table 310.104(A) unless otherwise permitted in 610.13(A) through (D) »*610.13*«.

Conductors exiting raceways/cables shall comply with 610.12(A) or (B) »*610.12*«.

Table 610.14(A) dictates the allowable ampacities of conductors »*610.14(A)*«.

Where the secondary resistor and the controller are separate, calculate the minimum size conductors (between controller and resistor) by multiplying the motor secondary current by the appropriate Table 610.14(B) factor, and select a wire from Table 610.14(A) »*610.14(B)*«.

Motor and control external conductors shall not be smaller than 16 AWG, unless otherwise permitted in 610.14(C)(1) and (2) »*610.14(C)*«.

A disconnecting means with a continuous ampere rating not less than that calculated in 610.14(E) and (F) shall be provided between the runway contact conductors and the power supply. Such a disconnecting means shall consist of a motor-circuit switch, circuit breaker, or molded case switch. This switch shall meet 610.31(1) through (4) provisions »*610.31*«.

Leads from crane and monorail hoist runway contact conductors (or other power supply) shall have a motor-circuit switch (or circuit breaker) that can be locked in the open position »*610.32*«.

Section 610.32 requires that the continuous ampere rating of the switch or circuit breaker not be less than 50% of the combined short-time ampere rating of the motors, nor less than 75% of the sum of the short-time ampere rating of the motors required for any single motion »*610.33*«.

Each motor shall have an individual controller unless 610.51(A) or (B) allows otherwise »*610.51*«.

Ⓐ Article 610 covers electrical equipment and wiring installation for use with cranes, monorail hoist, hoists, and all runways »*610.1*«.

Ⓑ All exposed non-current-carrying metal parts of cranes, monorail hoists, hoists, and accessories, including pendant controls, shall be bonded either by mechanical connections or bonding jumpers, where applicable, so that the entire crane or hoist is a ground-fault current path as required or permitted by Article 250, Parts V and VII. Moving parts, other than removable accessories, or attachments that have metal-to-metal bearing surfaces, shall be considered to be electrically bonded to each other through bearing surfaces for grounding purposes. The trolley frame and bridge frame shall not be considered as electrically grounded through the bridge and trolley wheels and its respective tracks. A separate bonding conductor shall be provided »*610.61*«.

Ⓒ Crane, hoist, and monorail hoist overload protection must comply with 610.43.

Ⓓ Crane, hoist, and monorail hoist motor branch circuits shall be protected by fuses or inverse-time circuit breakers that have a rating in accordance with Table 430.52. Where two or more motors operate a single motion, the sum of their nameplate current ratings shall be considered as that of a single motor »*610.42(A)*«.

> ### N O T E
>
> All equipment operating in a hazardous (classified) location shall comply with Article 500 »*610.3(A)*«.

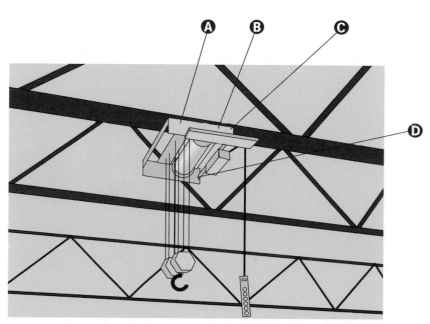

Electric Welders

Each arc welder shall have overcurrent protection rated (or set) at no more than 200% of $I_{1\,max}$. If the $I_{1\,max}$ is not given, the overcurrent protection shall be rated (or set) at no more than 200% of the welder's rated primary current ≫ *630.12(A)* ≪ .

An overcurrent device is not required for an arc welder having supply conductors protected by an overcurrent device rated (or set) at no more than 200% of $I_{1\,max}$, or the welder's rated primary current ≫ *630.12(A)* ≪ .

Supply conductors for an arc welder protected by an overcurrent device rated (or set) at no more than 200% of $I_{1\,max}$ or rated primary welder current do not require a separate overcurrent device ≫ *630.12(A)* ≪ .

A Minimum ampacity of arc welder conductors supplying a group of welders shall be based on individual currents determined in 630.11(A) as the sum of 100% of the two largest welders, plus 85% of the third largest welder, plus 70% of the fourth largest, plus 60% of any other welder ≫ *630.11(B)* ≪ .

B Section 630.12(A) and (B) contain requirements for arc welder overcurrent protection. Where the resulting values do not correspond with 240.6(A) standard ampere ratings, or the rating or setting specified results in unnecessary opening of the overcurrent device, the next higher standard rating or setting is acceptable ≫ *630.12* ≪ .

C Lower percentages are permitted in cases where the work is such that a high-operating duty cycle for individual welders is impossible ≫ *630.11(B) Exception* ≪ .

D Supply conductor ampacity, for a single arc welder shall not be less than the $I_{1\,eff}$ value on the rating plate. If the $I_{1\,eff}$ is not given, the supply conductor ampacity shall meet 630.11 requirements ≫ *630.11(A)* ≪ .

E Conductors supplying one or more arc welders shall have an overcurrent protective device rated (or set) not more than 200% of the conductor ampacity ≫ *630.12(B)* ≪ . (See 630.12[B] Informational Note for calculation explanation.)

F Article 630 covers apparatus for electric arc welding, resistance welding, plasma cutting, and similar welding and cutting process equipment connected to an electric supply system ≫ *630.1* ≪ .

G Conductors used in the secondary circuit of electric welders shall have flame-retardant insulation ≫ *630.41* ≪ .

H Arc welders must have a rating plate with the information listed in 630.14.

> **NOTE**
>
> Resistance welders must comply with Article 630, Part III (630.31 through 630.34) provisions.

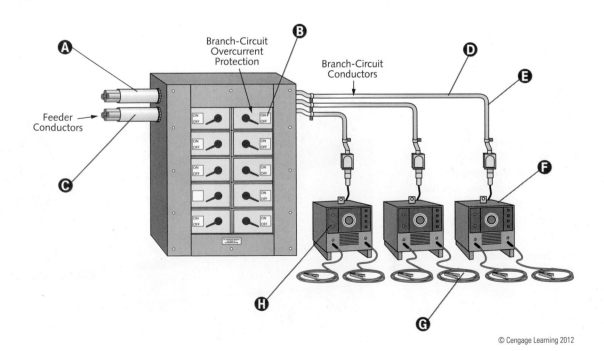

© Cengage Learning 2012

Electroplating

Equipment used in the electroplating process must be specifically identified for such service ⟫ *669.3* ⟪.

Branch-circuit conductors supplying one or more units of equipment shall have an ampacity of at least 125% of the total connected load. Busbar ampacities shall meet 366.23 requirements ⟫ *669.5* ⟪.

The following stipulations apply to conductors connecting the electrolyte tank equipment to the conversion equipment: (A) Insulated conductors in systems not exceeding 50 volts direct current (dc) can be run without insulated support, provided they are protected from physical damage. Bare copper (or aluminum) conductors are permitted where supported on insulators. (B) Insulated conductors in systems exceeding 50 volts direct current can be run on insulated supports, provided they are protected from physical damage. Bare copper (or aluminum) conductors are permitted where (1) supported on insulators and (2) guarded against accidental contact up to the termination point, per 110.27 ⟫ *669.6* ⟪.

Where multiple power supplies serve the same dc system, the dc side of each power supply shall have a disconnecting means ⟫ *669.8(A)* ⟪.

Removable links/conductors can serve as the disconnecting means ⟫ *669.8(B)* ⟪.

Direct-current conductors shall be protected from overcurrent by at least one of the following: (1) fuses or circuit breakers, (2) a current-sensing device that operates a disconnecting means, or (3) other approved means ⟫ *669.9* ⟪.

A Article 669 provisions apply to the installation of the electrical components and accessory equipment that supply the power and controls for electroplating, anodizing, electropolishing, and electrostripping, herein referred to simply as *electroplating* ⟫ *669.1* ⟪.

CAUTION

Warning signs shall be posted to indicate the presence of bare conductors ⟫ *669.7* ⟪.

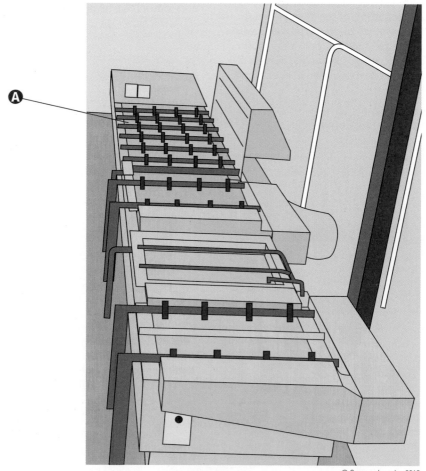

Industrial Machinery

A machine is considered to be an individual unit and, therefore, shall have a disconnecting means. Branch circuits protected by either fuses or circuit breakers can be the disconnecting means. The disconnecting means is not required to incorporate overcurrent protection ≫*670.4(B)*≪.

Where overcurrent protection (single circuit breaker or set of fuses) is furnished as part of the machine, 670.3 required markings shall be used and the supply conductors shall be considered either as feeders (or taps), as covered by 240.21 ≫*670.4(C)*≪.

If the machine has no branch-circuit short-circuit and ground-fault protective device, the overcurrent protective device's rating (or setting) shall be based on 430.52 and 430.53, as applicable ≫*670.4(C)*≪.

Where overcurrent protection is provided, per 670.4(B), the machine shall be marked "overcurrent protection provided at machine supply terminals" ≫*670.3(B)*≪.

A Article 670 covers the definition of, the nameplate data for, and the size and overcurrent protection of supply conductors to industrial machinery ≫*670.1*≪.

B The rating or setting of the overcurrent protective device for the circuit supplying the machine shall not be greater than the sum of the largest rating or setting of the branch-circuit short-circuit and ground-fault protective device provided with the machine, plus 125% of the full-load current rating of all resistance heating loads, plus the sum of the full-load currents of all other motors and apparatus that could be in operation at the same time ≫*670.4(C)*≪.

C Article 110, Part II provisions apply to working space around electrical equipment operating at 600 volts, nominal, or less to ground.

D The overcurrent protective device's rating (or setting) for the circuit supplying the machine must comply with 670.4(C).

E The selected supply conductor size shall have an ampacity not less than 125% of the FLC rating for all resistance heating loads, plus 125% of the highest rated motor's FLC rating, plus the sum of the FLC ratings of all other connected motors and apparatus, based on their duty cycle, that may be simultaneously operated ≫*670.4(A)*≪.

F A permanent nameplate listing supply voltage, number of phases, frequency, FLC, maximum short-circuit and ground-fault protective device ampere rating, largest motor or load ampere rating, short-circuit interrupting rating of the machine overcurrent-protective device, and diagram number(s) shall be attached to the control equipment enclosure/machine, or the number of the index to the electrical drawings, remaining plainly visible after installation ≫*670.3(A)*≪.

G **Industrial machinery (machine)** is defined as a power-driven machine (or a group of machines working together in a coordinated manner), not portable by hand during operation, used to process material by cutting; forming; pressure; electrical, thermal, or optical techniques; lamination; or a combination of these processes. It can include associated equipment used to transfer material or tooling, including fixtures; assemble/disassemble; inspect; test; or package. (Associated electrical equipment, including logic controller[s] and associated software [or logic] together with the machine actuators and sensors, are all part of the industrial machine.) ≫*670.2*≪

> **N O T E**
>
> For information on the workspace requirements for equipment containing supply conductor terminals, see 110.26. For information on the workspace requirements for machine power and control equipment, see NFPA 79–2007, *Electrical Standard for Industrial Machinery* ≫*670.1 Informational Note No. 2*≪.

> **WARNING**
>
> Industrial machinery shall not be installed where the available fault current exceeds its short-circuit current rating as marked in accordance with 670.3(A)(4) ≫*670.5*≪.

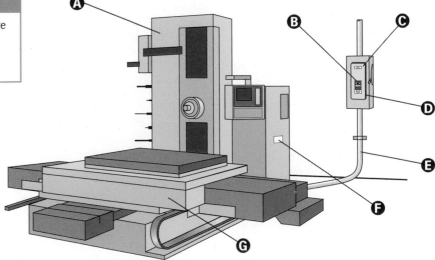

PLACES OF ASSEMBLY

Comprehensive Provisions

The wiring of any such building or area containing a projection booth, stage platform, or area for the presentation of theatrical or musical productions (fixed or portable) shall comply with Article 520. These requirements also apply to associated audience seating and all equipment used in the production, including portable equipment and associated wiring that is not connected to permanent wiring ≫*518.2(C)*≪.

The fixed wiring methods shall be metal raceways, flexible metal raceways, nonmetallic raceways encased in not less than 2 in. (50 mm) of concrete, Type MI, MC, or AC cable. The wiring method shall itself qualify as an equipment grounding conductor according to 250.118 or shall contain an insulated equipment grounding conductor sized in accordance with Table 250.122 ≫*518.4(A)*≪.

ENT and PVC are not approved for use in other spaces used for environmental air in accordance with 300.22(C) ≫*518.4(C)*≪.

Portable switchboards and portable power distribution equipment shall be supplied only from listed power outlets of sufficient voltage and ampere rating. Such power outlets shall be protected by overcurrent devices. Such overcurrent devices and power outlets shall not be accessible to the general public. Provisions for connection of an equipment grounding conductor shall be provided. The neutral conductor of feeders supplying solid-state phase control, 3-phase, 4-wire dimmer systems shall be considered a current-carrying conductor for purposes of ampacity adjustment. The neutral conductor of feeders supplying solid-state sine wave, 3-phase, 4-wire dimming systems shall not be considered a current-carrying conductor for purposes of ampacity adjustment ≫*518.5*≪.

Ⓐ Temporary wiring for display booths within exhibition halls (as in trade shows) shall be permitted to be installed in accordance with Article 590. Flexible cables and cords, approved for hard or extra-hard usage, laid on floors shall be protected from contact by the general public. The GFCI requirements of 590.6 shall not apply. All other GFCI requirements of the *NEC* shall apply.

Where GFCI protection for personnel is supplied by plug and cord connection to the branch circuit or to the feeder, the GFCI protection shall be listed as portable GFCI protection or provide a level of protection equivalent to a portable GFCI, whether assembled in the field or at the factory ≫*518.3(B)*≪.

Ⓑ Where an assembly occupancy forms a portion of a building containing other occupancies, Article 518 applies only to that portion of the building considered an assembly occupancy. Occupancy of any room or space for assembly purposes by less than 100 persons in a building of other

occupancy, and incidental to such other occupancy, shall be classified as part of the other occupancy and subject to the provisions applicable thereto ≫*518.2(B)*≪.

Ⓒ In addition to the wiring methods of 518.4(A), nonmetallic-sheathed cable, Type AC cable, ENT, and PVC can be installed in those buildings (or portions thereof) for which the applicable building code does not require fire-rated construction ≫*518.4(B)*≪.

Ⓓ ENT and PVC can be installed within club rooms, conference and meeting rooms in hotels (or motels), courtrooms, dining facilities, restaurants, mortuary chapels, museums, libraries, and places of religious worship where:

1. The ENT or PVC is concealed within walls, floors, and ceilings where the enclosing structure provides a thermal material barrier having at least a 15-minute finish rating as identified in fire-rated assembly listings.

2. Such tubing or conduit is installed above suspended ceilings where the ceilings act as a thermal material barrier having at least a 15-minute finish rating according to fire-rated assembly listings ≫*518.4(C)*≪.

Ⓔ Except for the assembly occupancies explicitly covered by 520.1, this article covers all buildings or portions of buildings or structures designed or intended for the gathering together of 100 or more persons for such purposes as deliberation, worship, entertainment, eating, drinking, amusement, awaiting transportation, or similar purposes ≫*518.1*≪.

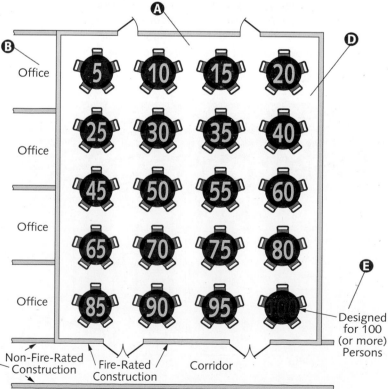

MOTION PICTURE (AND TELEVISION) STUDIOS AND SIMILAR LOCATIONS

Comprehensive Requirements

Portable stage or studio lighting equipment and portable power distribution equipment can be for temporary use outdoors if (1) supervised by qualified personnel while energized and (2) barriered from the general public »530.6«.

Stage or set permanent wiring shall be Type MC cable, Type AC cable containing an insulated equipment grounding conductor sized per Table 250.122, Type MI cable, or approved raceways »530.11«.

The wiring for stage set lighting and other supply wiring not fixed as to location shall be achieved with listed hard usage flexible cords/cables. Where subject to physical damage, such flexible cords/cables shall be of the listed extra-hard usage type. Cable splices or taps are allowed, provided the total connected load does not exceed the cable's maximum ampacity »530.12(A)«.

Stage effects and electrical equipment used as stage properties can be wired with single- or multiconductor listed flexible cords or cables where protected from physical damage and secured to the scenery by approved cable ties or insulated staples. Splices (or taps) can only be made with listed devices in a circuit protected at no more than 20 amperes »530.12(B)«.

Switches used for studio stage set lighting and effects (on the stages and lots and on location) shall be of the externally operable type. Where contactors are used as the disconnecting means for fuses, an individual externally operable switch, suitably rated, for the control of each contactor shall be located at a distance of not more than

6 ft (1.8 m) from the contactor, in addition to remote-control switches. A single externally operable switch shall be permitted to simultaneously disconnect all the contactors on any one location board, where located at a distance of not more than 6 ft (1.8 m) from the location board »530.13«. (Location board is defined in 530.2 definitions.)

Portable luminaires and work lights shall have flexible cords, composition or metal-sheathed porcelain sockets, and substantial guards »530.16«. Portable luminaires used as properties in a motion picture or television stage set, on a studio stage or lot, or on location are, for this purpose, not considered portable luminaires »530.16 Exception«.

Automatic overcurrent protective devices (circuit breakers or fuses) for motion picture studio stage set lighting and associated cables must comply with 530.18(A) through (G).

Ⓐ Article 530 requirements apply to motion picture/television studios using either film or electronic cameras (except as provided in 520.1) as well as exchanges, factories, laboratories, stages, or a building segment in which film or tape wider than $7/8$ in. (22 mm) is exposed, developed, printed, cut, edited, rewound, repaired, or stored »530.1«.

Ⓑ Stage set: A specific area set up with temporary scenery and properties planned for a particular motion picture or television production scene »530.2«.

Ⓒ Television studio or motion picture stage (sound stage): All or part of a building, usually insulated from outside noise and natural light, used by the entertainment industry for motion picture, television, or commercial production purposes »530.2«.

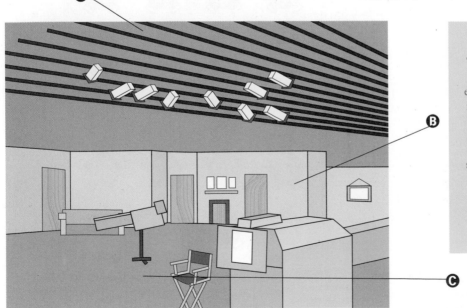

> **NOTE**
>
> Type MC cable, Type MI cable, Type AC cable containing an insulated equipment grounding conductor, metal raceways, and all non-current-carrying metal parts of appliances, devices, and equipment shall be connected to an equipment grounding conductor. This shall not apply to pendant and portable lamps, to portable stage lighting and stage sound equipment, or to other portable and special stage equipment operating at not over 150 volts dc to ground »*530.20*«.

Comprehensive Requirements *(continued)*

The maximum ampacity allowed on a given conductor, cable, or cord size is dictated by the applicable tables of Articles 310 and 400 »*530.18*«.

It shall be permissible to apply Table 530.19(A) demand factors to that portion of the maximum possible connected load for studio or stage set lighting for all permanently installed feeders between substations and stages and to all permanently installed feeders between the main stage switchboard and stage distribution centers (or location boards) »*530.19(A)*«.

Portable feeders can have a demand of 50% of maximum possible connected load »*530.19(B)*«.

Plugs and receptacles, including cord connectors and flanged surface devices, shall be rated in amperes. The voltage rating of plugs and receptacles shall not be less than the nominal circuit voltage. All ac circuit plug and receptacle ampere ratings shall not be less than the feeder (or branch-circuit) overcurrent device ampere rating. Table 210.21(B)(2) shall not apply »*530.21(A)*«.

Any ac single-pole portable cable connectors used shall be listed and of the locking type. Sections 400.10, 406.7, and 406.8 shall not apply to listed single-pole separable connections, or to single-conductor cable assemblies incorporating listed single-pole separable connectors. Paralleled sets of current-carrying single-pole separable connectors acting as input devices shall carry prominent warning labels indicating the presence of internal parallel connections. Single-pole separable connectors shall comply with at least one provision of 530.22(A)(1) through (3) »*530.22(A)*«.

Cellulose Nitrate Film Storage Vaults

A Lamps in cellulose nitrate film storage vaults shall be installed in rigid luminaires of the glass-enclosed and gasketed type »*530.51*«.

B Lamps shall be controlled outside the vault by a switch having a pole in each ungrounded conductor and provided with a pilot light indicating "on" or "off." This switch shall disconnect every ungrounded conductor terminating in any outlet within the vault from any supply source »*530.51*«.

CAUTION
Unless otherwise permitted in 530.51, no receptacles, outlets, heaters, portable lights, or other portable electric equipment are allowed inside cellulose nitrate film storage vaults »*530.52*«.

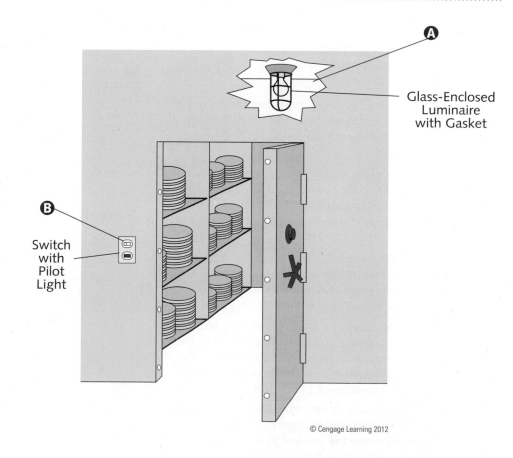

A

Glass-Enclosed Luminaire with Gasket

B

Switch with Pilot Light

© Cengage Learning 2012

MOTION PICTURE PROJECTION ROOMS

General Provisions

Nonprofessional projectors: Any type other than described in 540.2 》*540.2*《. These projectors, including miniature types, employing cellulose acetate (safety) film may be operated without a projection room 》*540.31*《.

Motor-generator sets, transformers, rectifiers, rheostats, and similar equipment for the supply (or control) of current to projection (or spotlight equipment) using nitrate film shall be located in a separate room. If inside the projection room, they shall be located (or guarded) so that arcs/sparks cannot contact film, and the commutator end(s) of motor generator sets shall comply with *one* of the following conditions:

1. Be of the totally enclosed, enclosed fan-cooled, or enclosed pipe-ventilated type.

2. Be enclosed in separate rooms or housings built of noncombustible material constructed so as to exclude flyings or lint with approved ventilation from a source of clean air.

3. Have the motor-generator brush or sliding-contact end enclosed by solid metal covers.

4. Have brushes or sliding contacts enclosed in substantial, tight metal housings.

5. Have the upper half of the brush or sliding-contact end of the motor-generator enclosed by a wire screen (or perforated metal), and the lower half enclosed by solid metal covers.

6. Have wire screens or perforated metal placed at the commutator of brush ends. No dimension of any opening in the wire screen or perforated metal shall exceed 0.05 in. (1.27 mm), regardless of the shape of the opening and of the material used 》*540.11(A)*《.

Extraneous equipment (switches, overcurrent devices, etc.), not normally a part of projection, sound reproduction, flood or other special effect lamps, shall not be placed in projection rooms unless an exception is met 》*540.11(B)*《.

Conductors supplying outlets for arc and xenon projectors (professional-type) shall have an ampacity not less than the projector current rating, but in no case smaller than 8 AWG. Conductors for incandescent-type projectors shall conform to the normal wiring standards of 210.24 》*540.13*《.

Insulated conductors having an operating temperature rating no less than 200°C (392°F) shall be used on all lamps (or other equipment) where the ambient temperature at the installed conductors will exceed 50°C (122°F) 》*540.14*《.

Ⓐ Article 540 provisions apply to motion picture projection rooms, motion picture projectors, and associated equipment, both professional and nonprofessional types, that use incandescent, carbon arc, xenon, or other light source equipment capable of producing hazardous gases, dust, or radiation 》*540.1*《.

Ⓑ Every professional-type projector shall be located within a permanently constructed projection room approved for the type of building in which it is located. All projection ports, spotlight ports, viewing ports, and similar openings shall be completely enclosed by use of glass or other approved material. Such rooms do not qualify as hazardous (classified) locations as defined in article 500 》*540.10*《.

Ⓒ A minimum 30-in. (750-mm) wide working space shall be provided on each side and at the rear of each motion picture projector, floodlight, spotlight, or similar equipment 》*540.12*《. Adjacent pieces of equipment can be served by one such space 》*540.12 Exception*《.

Ⓓ **Professional projector:** Projectors using either (1) 35- or 70-mm film (a minimum of 1⅜ in. [35 mm] wide with 5.4 edge perforations per inch [212 perforations per meter]) or (2) a type using carbon arc, xenon, or other light source equipment producing hazardous gases, dust, or radiation 》*540.2*《.

Ⓔ Projectors and enclosures for arc, xenon, and incandescent lamps and rectifiers, transformers, rheostats, and similar equipment shall be listed 》*540.20*《.

Ⓕ Projectors and other equipment shall be marked with the manufacturer's name (or trademark) as well as the voltage and current for which they are designed, per 110.21 》*540.21*《.

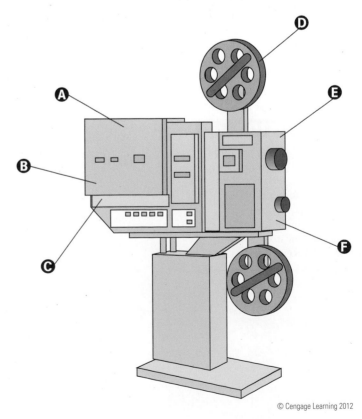

MANUFACTURED BUILDINGS

Manufactured Building Requirements

Fittings and connectors to be concealed at the time of on-site assembly (where tested, identified, and listed to applicable standards) are permitted for on-site module/component interconnection. Such fittings and connectors shall equal the employed wiring method in insulation, temperature rise, and fault-current withstand. They shall also be able to endure the vibration and minor relative motions occurring in the manufactured building components ≫ *545.13* ≪.

In closed construction, cables can be secured only at cabinets, boxes, or fittings where using 10 AWG or smaller conductors and protection against physical damage is provided ≫ *545.4(B)* ≪.

Service-entrance, service-lateral, feeder, or branch-circuit supply conductor routing provisions shall be made to the service or building disconnecting means conductor ≫ *545.5* ≪.

Install service-entrance conductors after the building is site-erected, unless the point of attachment location is known prior to manufacture ≫ *545.6* ≪.

Exposed conductors and equipment shall be protected during manufacturing, packaging, transit, and setup at the building site ≫ *545.8* ≪.

Boxes of dimensions other than those required in Table 314.16(A) can be installed where tested, identified, and listed to applicable standards ≫ *545.9(A)* ≪.

Any box no larger than 100 in.³ (1650 cm³) and intended for closed-construction mounting shall be affixed with anchors (or clamps) to provide a rigid and secure installation ≫ *545.9(B)* ≪.

A receptacle (or switch) with integral enclosure and mounting means can be installed where such is tested, identified, and listed to applicable standards ≫ *545.10* ≪.

Prewired panels and building components shall provide for the bonding, or bonding and grounding, of all exposed metals likely to be energized, per Article 250, Parts V, VI, and VII ≫ *545.11* ≪.

Provisions shall be made to route a grounding electrode conductor from the service, feeder, or branch-circuit supply to the point of attachment to the grounding electrode ≫ *545.12* ≪.

Closed construction: Any building, building component, assembly, or system manufactured in such a manner that concealed parts of manufacture processes cannot be inspected after building site installation without disassembly, damage, or destruction ≫ *545.2* ≫.

Building component: Any subsystem, subassembly, or other system designed for use in, integral with, or as part of a structure. A building component can be structural, electrical, mechanical, plumbing, fire protection, and other health and safety systems ≫ *545.2* ≪.

Building system: Plans, specifications, and documentation for a manufactured building system, or for a type of system building component, such as structural, electrical, mechanical, plumbing, fire protection, and other systems affecting health and safety, including variations thereof specifically permitted by regulation, provided the variations are submitted as part of the building system or as an amendment thereto ≫ *545.2* ≪.

Ⓐ Article 545 covers manufactured building and building components requirements ≫ *545.1* ≪.

Ⓑ **Manufactured building:** Any closed construction building made (or assembled) in manufacturing facilities, whether on or off the building site, for installation, or assembly and installation, on the building site, excluding manufactured homes, mobile homes, park trailers, or recreational vehicles ≫ *545.2* ≪.

Ⓒ All *Code*-approved raceways and cable wiring methods, and such other wiring systems specifically intended and listed for use in manufactured buildings, are permitted with both listed fittings and fittings listed/identified for manufactured buildings ≫ *545.4(A)* ≪.

> **N O T E**
>
> Service equipment shall be installed in accordance with 230.70 ≫ *545.7* ≪.

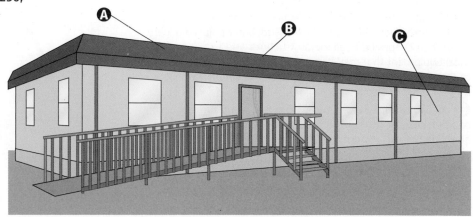

© Cengage Learning 2012

AGRICULTURAL BUILDINGS

Agricultural Building Provisions

Motors and other rotating electrical machinery shall either be totally enclosed or designed to minimize the entrance of dust, moisture, or corrosive particles **》547.7《**.

Equipotential planes shall be connected to the electrical grounding system. The bonding conductor shall be solid copper, insulated, covered or bare, and not smaller than 8 AWG. The means of bonding to wire mesh or conductive elements shall be by pressure connectors or clamps of brass, copper, copper alloy, or an equally substantial approved means. Slatted floors that are supported by structures that are a part of an equipotential plane shall not require bonding **》547.10(B)《**.

For the purpose of 547.10, the term *livestock* does not include poultry **》547.10《**.

Ⓐ This article's provisions apply to agricultural buildings, part of buildings, or adjacent areas of similar nature as specified in (A) or (B).

(A) Agricultural buildings where excessive dust, and dust in combination with water, may accumulate. Included are all areas of poultry, livestock, and fish confinement systems, where litter dust or feed dust (including mineral feed particles) may accumulate.

(B) Agricultural buildings with a corrosive atmosphere. Such buildings include areas where:
   (1) poultry and animal excrement can cause corrosive vapors,
   (2) corrosive particles may mix with water,
   (3) periodic washing for cleaning and sanitizing with water and cleansing agents creates a damp, even wet, environment,
   (4) similar conditions exist **》547.1《**.

Ⓑ The wiring method(s) employed shall be types UF, NMC, copper SE cables, jacketed Type MC cable, PVC, LFNC, or other location-suitable cables/raceways having approved termination fittings. Article 502 wiring methods are permitted for areas described in 547.1(A) **》547.5(A)《**.

Ⓒ An **equipotential plane** is an area where a wire mesh (or other conductive element) is (1) embedded in or placed under concrete; (2) bonded to all metal structures and fixed nonelectrical equipment that may become energized; and (3) connected to the electrical grounding system, thus preventing a voltage difference from developing within the plane **》547.2《**.

Ⓓ All cables shall be secured within 8 in. (200 mm) of each cabinet, box, or fitting. Nonmetallic boxes, fittings, conduit, and cables shall be permitted to be mounted directly to any

building surface covered by this article without maintaining the ¼-in. (6-mm) airspace in accordance with 300.6(D) **》547.5(B)《**.

Ⓔ Luminaires shall comply with all of the following:
   A. By installation, the entrance of dust, foreign matter, moisture, and corrosive material shall be minimized.
   B. If subject to physical damage, shall have a suitably protective guard.
   C. If exposed to moisture, whether from condensation, cleansing water, or solution, shall be listed as suitable for use in wet locations **》547.8《**.

Ⓕ **Indoors:** Equipotential planes shall be installed in confinement areas with concrete floors where metallic equipment is located that may become energized and is accessible to livestock **》547.10(A)(1)《**. **Outdoors:** Equipotential planes shall be installed in concrete slabs where metallic equipment is located that may become energized and is accessible to livestock. The equipotential plane shall encompass the area where the livestock stands while accessing metallic equipment that may become energized **》547.10(A)(2)《**.

Ⓖ Where an equipment grounding conductor is installed within a location falling under the scope of Article 547, it shall be a copper conductor. Where an equipment grounding conductor is installed underground, it shall be insulated or covered copper **》547.5(F)《**.

> ### N O T E
> All 125-volt, single-phase, 15- and 20-ampere general-purpose receptacles installed in areas having an equipotential plane, outdoors, damp or wet locations, and dirt confinement areas for livestock shall have GFCI protection **》547.5(G)《**.

CAUTION

Protect all electrical wiring and equipment subject to physical damage **》547.5(E)《**.

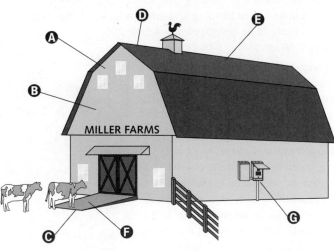

© Cengage Learning 2012

MOBILE HOMES, MANUFACTURED HOMES, AND MOBILE HOME PARKS

General Requirements

Mobile home: A factory-assembled structure transportable in one or more sections, built on a permanent chassis, designed for use as a dwelling having no permanent foundation where connected to the required utilities, and including the plumbing, heating, air-conditioning, and electric systems contained therein ≫550.2≪.

Manufactured home: A structure, transportable in one or more sections, that in traveling mode, is 8 body-ft (2.4 m) or more in width, or 40 body-ft (12.2 m) or more in length, or, when erected on site, is 320 ft² (29.7 m²) or more, built on a permanent chassis and designed for dwelling use (with or without a permanent foundation) when connected therein ≫550.2≪.

At least one receptacle outlet shall be installed outdoors accessible at grade level, and not more than 6½ ft (2.0 m) above grade. A receptacle outlet located in an outside accessible compartment qualifies as an outdoor receptacle. These receptacle outlets shall have GFCI protection for personnel ≫550.13(B) and (D)(8)≪.

If a pipe heating cable outlet is installed, the outlet shall be:

1. Located within 2 ft (600 mm) of the cold water inlet.

2. Connected to an interior branch circuit, other than a small-appliance branch circuit. A bathroom receptacle circuit can be utilized for this purpose.

3. On a circuit where all outlets are on the load side of the ground-fault circuit-interrupter protection for personnel.

4. Mounted on the mobile home's underside, although this is not considered to be the outdoor receptacle outlet required in 550.13 (D)(8) ≫550.13(E)≪.

Use only approved and listed fixed-type wiring methods to join portions of a circuit that must be electrically joined and are located in adjacent mobile home sections after installation on its support foundation. The circuit's junction shall be accessible for disassembly when preparing the home for relocation ≫550.19(A)≪.

A mobile home not intended as a dwelling unit is not required to meet this article's provisions pertaining to the number or capacity of circuits required. Included are those equipped for sleeping purposes only, contractor's on-site offices, construction job dormitories, mobile studio dressing rooms, banks, clinics, or mobile stores, or those intended for the display or demonstration of merchandise or machinery. Such nondwelling units shall, however, meet all other applicable requirements of this article if provided with an electrical installation to be energized from a 120-volt or 120/240-volt ac power supply system. If design or available power supply systems dictate a different voltage, make adjustments in accordance with the appropriate articles/sections for the voltage used ≫550.4(A)≪.

Ⓐ Article 550 provisions cover the electrical conductors and equipment in or on mobile and manufactured homes, mobile and manufactured home electrical supply conductors, and the installation of electrical wiring, luminaires, equipment, and appurtenances related to electrical installations within a mobile home park up to the mobile home service-entrance conductors or, if none, the service equipment ≫550.1≪.

Ⓑ For *Code* purposes (unless otherwise indicated), the term *mobile home* includes manufactured homes ≫550.2 *Mobile Home*≪.

Ⓒ This article's provisions apply to mobile homes designed to connect to a wiring system rated 120/240 volts, nominal, 3-wire ac, with grounded neutral conductor ≫550.4(C)≪.

Ⓓ Outdoor or under-chassis line-voltage (120 volts, nominal, or higher) wiring exposed to moisture or physical damage shall be protected by rigid or IMC, except as provided in 550.15(H) (1) or (2). Conductors shall be suitable for wet locations:

(1) Where closely routed against frames and equipment enclosures, RTRC listed for aboveground use, Type MI cable, EMT, or PVC shall be permitted.

(2) Where extending vertically from a direct-burial depth of at least 18 in. (457 mm) below grade and terminated to a factory-installed conduit or enclosure, Schedule 80 PVC or RTRC listed for exposure to physical damage shall be permitted ≫550.15(H)≪.

CAUTION

All electrical materials, devices, appliances, fittings, and other equipment shall be (1) listed or labeled by a qualified testing agency and (2) connected in an approved manner when installed ≫550.4(D)≪.

NOTE

Mobile homes not installed in mobile home parks shall comply with the provisions of this article ≫550.4(B)≪.

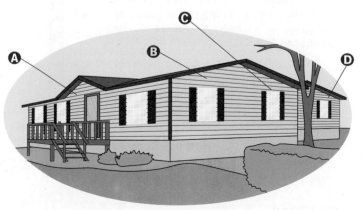

Power Supply

Cords with adapters and pigtail ends, extension cords, and similar items shall not be attached to or shipped with a mobile home ≫*550.10(B)*≪.

A cord passing through walls or floors shall be protected by means of conduits and bushings (or equivalent). The cord can be installed within the walls, provided a continuous raceway (maximum 1¼ in. [32 mm] in size) is installed from the branch-circuit panelboard to the underside of the mobile home floor ≫*550.10(G)*≪.

The power-supply cord's attachment plug cap and any connector cord assembly or receptacle shall be permanently protected against corrosion and mechanical damage, if such devices are externally located while the mobile home is in transit ≫*550.10(H)*≪.

If the calculated load exceeds 50 amperes, or if a permanent feeder is used, the supply shall be by one of the following means:

1. **One mast weatherhead installation, installed per Article 230, containing four continuous, insulated, color-coded feeder conductors, one of which shall be an equipment grounding conductor**

2. **A metal raceway or PVC from the internal disconnecting means to the mobile home's underside, with provisions for attachment to the raceway on the mobile home's underside via a suitable junction box (or fitting) (with or without conductors as in 550.10[I][1])** ≫*550.10(I)*≪.

Ⓐ The attachment plug cap shall not only be a 3-pole, 4-wire, grounding type, rated 50 amperes, 125/250 volts with a configuration as shown in Figure 550.10(C) but also shall be intended for use with a 50-ampere, 125/250-volt receptacle configuration as shown in Figure 550.10(C). It shall be listed, individually or as part of a power-supply cord assembly, for such purpose, and molded to (or installed on) the flexible cord at the point where the cord enters the attachment plug cap ≫*550.10(C)*≪.

Ⓑ In a right-angle cap configuration, the grounding member shall be the farthest from the cord ≫*550.10(C)*≪.

Ⓒ The mobile home power supply shall be a feeder assembly consisting of a single listed 50-ampere mobile home power-supply cord or a permanently installed feeder ≫*550.10(A)*≪.

Ⓓ The power-supply cord shall bear the marking: "FOR USE WITH MOBILE HOMES—40 AMPERES" or "FOR USE WITH MOBILE HOMES—50 AMPERES" ≫*550.10(E)*≪.

Ⓔ The cord shall be a four-conductor listed type. One conductor shall be identified by a continuous green color, or a continuous green color with one or more yellow stripes, for use as the grounding conductor ≫*550.10(B)*≪.

Ⓕ A suitable clamp (or equivalent) shall be provided at the distribution panelboard knockout to afford cord strain relief and effectively prevent strain transmission to the terminals when the power-supply cord is handled as intended ≫*550.10(B)*≪.

Ⓖ A mobile home power-supply cord, if present, shall be permanently attached to the distribution panelboard either directly or via a junction box also permanently connected thereto, with the free end terminating in an attachment plug cap ≫*550.10(B)*≪.

Ⓗ From the end of the power-supply cord (including bared leads) to the face of the attachment plug cap, the cord shall not be less than 21 ft (6.4 m) or more than 36½ ft (11 m) in length. From the face of the attachment plug cap to the mobile home entry point, the cord shall be at least 20 ft (6.0 m) long ≫*550.10(D)*≪.

> ### N O T E
> The feeder assembly shall enter the mobile home through an exterior wall, the floor, or roof ≫*550.10(F)*≪.

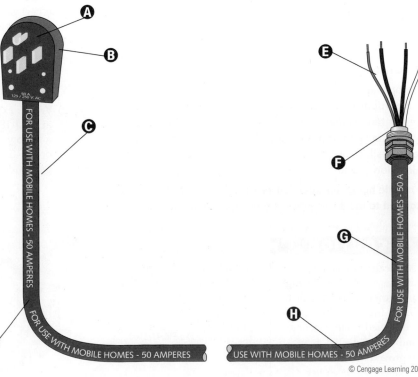

Distribution Panelboards and Branch Circuits

A distribution panelboard shall be rated no less than 50 amperes and employ a two-pole circuit breaker rated 40 amperes for a 40-ampere supply cord, or 50 amperes for a 50-ampere supply cord. A distribution panelboard employing a disconnect switch and fuses shall be rated 60 amperes and employ a single two-pole, 60-ampere fuseholder with 40- or 50-ampere main fuses for 40- or 50-ampere supply cords, respectively. The fuse size shall be plainly marked on the outside of the distribution panelboard ≫*550.11(A)*≪.

Each mobile home shall have branch-circuit distribution equipment that includes circuit breaker or fuse overcurrent protection for each branch circuit. The branch-circuit overcurrent devices shall be rated as follows: (1) not more than the circuit conductors and (2) not more than 150% of a single appliance rated 13.3 amperes (or more) supplied by an individual branch circuit, but (3) not more than the overcurrent protection size and type marked on the air conditioner (or other motor-operated appliance)≫*550.11(B)*≪.

A metal nameplate on the outside adjacent to the feeder assembly entrance shall read:

THIS CONNECTION FOR 120/240-VOLT, 3-POLE, 4-WIRE, 60-HERTZ, _____-AMPERE SUPPLY

Fill in the blank with the correct ampere rating ≫*550.11(D)*≪.

Multiply 3 volt-amperes/ft² (33 volt-amperes/m²) by the outside dimensions of the mobile home (coupler excluded) and divide by 120 volts to determine the number of 15- or 20-ampere lighting circuits ≫*550.12(A)*≪.

There shall be one or more adequately rated circuits in accordance with the following:

1. Ampere rating of fixed appliances not over 50% of circuit rating if lighting outlets (receptacles, other than kitchen, dining area, and laundry, considered as lighting outlets) exist on the same circuit.

2. For fixed appliances on a circuit without lighting outlets, the sum of rated amperes shall not exceed the branch-circuit rating. Motor loads or continuous loads shall not exceed 80% of the branch-circuit rating.

3. The rating of a single cord- and plug-connected appliance on a circuit having no other outlets shall not exceed 80% of the circuit rating.

4. The rating of a range branch circuit shall be based on the range demand as specified in 550.18(B)(5) ≫*550.12(D)*≪.

Ⓐ Each mobile home shall have a single disconnecting means consisting of a circuit breaker, or a switch and fuses, and its accessories installed in a readily accessible location near the supply cord (or conductor's) entry point into the mobile home. The main circuit breakers (or fuses) shall be plainly marked "Main." This equipment shall contain a

solderless-type grounding connector (or bar) with sufficient terminals for all grounding conductors. The terminations of the grounded circuit conductors shall be insulated in accordance with 550.16(A) ≫*550.11(A)*≪.

Ⓑ While the distribution panelboard shall be located in an accessible location, it shall not be located in a bathroom or clothes closet. A clear working space at least 30 in. (750 mm) wide and 30 in. (750 mm) in front of the panelboard shall be provided. This space shall extend from the floor to the top of the distribution panelboard ≫*550.11(A)*≪.

Ⓒ The bottom of the distribution equipment, whether circuit breaker or fused type, shall be at least 24 in. (600 mm) above the mobile home's floor level ≫*550.11(A)*≪.

Ⓓ The distribution equipment shall have a rating not less than the calculated load ≫*550.11(A)*≪.

Ⓔ Where circuit breakers provide branch-circuit protection, 240-volt circuits shall be protected by a 2-pole common or companion trip, or circuit breakers with identified handle ties ≫*550.11(C)*≪.

Ⓕ Determine the required number of branch circuits in accordance with 550.12(A) through (E) ≫*550.12*≪.

Ⓖ The branch-circuit equipment can be combined with the disconnecting means as a single assembly. Such a combination can be designated as a distribution panelboard. If a fused distribution panelboard is used, the maximum fuse size for the mains shall be plainly marked with ¼-in. (6-mm) or taller lettering visible during fuse replacements. If plug fuses and fuseholders are used, they shall be tamper-resistant Type S, enclosed in dead-front fuse panelboards. Electrical distribution panelboards containing circuit breakers shall also be dead-front type ≫*550.11*≪.

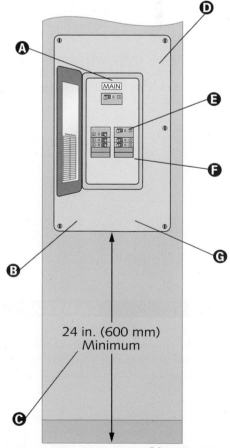

24 in. (600 mm)
Minimum

Grounding

Cord-connected appliances (such as washing machines, clothes dryers, refrigerators, and the electrical system of gas ranges) shall be grounded via a cord having an equipment grounding conductor and grounding-type attachment plug ≫ *550.16(B)(3)* ≪.

Metallic pipes (gas, water, and waste) as well as metallic air-circulating ducts are considered bonded if connected to the chassis terminal by clamps, solderless connectors, or appropriate grounding-type straps ≫ *550.16(C)(3)* ≪.

Any metallic exterior covering is considered bonded if (1) the metal panels overlap one another and are securely attached to the wood or metal frame parts by metallic fasteners and (2) the lower panel of the metallic exterior covering is secured at opposite ends by metallic fasteners at a chassis cross member by two metal straps per mobile home unit (or section). The bonding strap shall be at least 4 in. (100 mm) wide and of the same material as the skin, or of a material of equal or better electrical conductivity. The straps shall be fastened with paint-penetrating fittings such as screws and starwashers or equivalent ≫ *550.16(C)(4)* ≪.

In the electrical system, all exposed metal parts, enclosures, frames, luminaire canopies, etc. shall be effectively bonded to the grounding terminal or enclosure of the distribution panelboard ≫ *550.16(B)(2)* ≪.

A Grounding terminals shall be of the solderless type, listed as pressure-terminal connectors, and recognized for the wire size employed ≫ *550.16(C)(2)* ≪.

B The supply cord or permanent feeder's green-colored insulated grounding wire shall be connected to the grounding bus in the distribution panelboard or disconnecting means ≫ *550.16(B)(1)* ≪.

C The bonding conductor shall be solid or stranded, insulated or bare, but shall be 8 AWG copper minimum, or the equivalent. The bonding conductor routing shall prevent physical damage exposure ≫ *550.16(C)(2)* ≪.

D All potentially energizable exposed, non-current-carrying metal parts shall be effectively bonded to either the grounding terminal or the distribution panelboard's enclosure. A bonding conductor shall be connected between the distribution panelboard and an accessible terminal on the chassis ≫ *550.16(C)(1)* ≪.

E Remove and discard bonding screws, straps, or buses in the distribution panelboard or in appliances ≫ *550.16(A)(1)* ≪.

F The grounded circuit conductor (neutral) shall be insulated from the grounding conductors, from equipment enclosures, and other grounded parts. The grounded circuit terminals in distribution panelboards, ranges, clothes dryers, counter-mounted cooking units, and wall-mounted ovens shall be insulated from the equipment enclosure ≫ *550.16(A)(1)* ≪.

G In a mobile home, grounding of metal parts (both electrical and nonelectrical) shall be accomplished by connection to a distribution panelboard's grounding bus and shall be connected through the green-colored insulated conductor in the supply cord (or the feeder wiring) to the grounding bus in the service-entrance equipment, located adjacent to the mobile home ≫ *550.16* ≪.

NOTE

Connections of ranges and clothes dryers with 120/240-volt, 3-wire ratings shall be made with 4-conductor cord and three-pole, 4-wire, grounding-type plugs or by Type AC cable, Type MC cable, or conductors enclosed in flexible metal conduit ≫ *550.16(A)(2)* ≪.

CAUTION

Neither the mobile home's frame nor any appliance frame shall be connected to the grounded circuit conductor (neutral) in the mobile home ≫ *550.16* ≪.

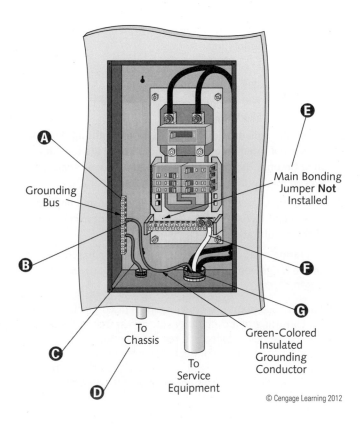

Grounding Bus

Main Bonding Jumper **Not** Installed

To Chassis

To Service Equipment

Green-Colored Insulated Grounding Conductor

© Cengage Learning 2012

Services and Feeders

The mobile home park secondary electrical distribution system supplying mobile home lots shall be single-phase, 120/240 volts, nominal. For Part III purposes, where the park service exceeds 240 volts, nominal, transformers and secondary distribution panelboards shall be treated as services 》》*550.30*《《.

The **manufactured home** service equipment can be installed in or on a manufactured home, provided all of the conditions in 550.32(B) are met 》》*550.32(B)*《《.

Park electrical wiring systems shall be calculated (at 120/240 volts) on the larger of (1) 16,000 volt-amperes for each mobile home lot or (2) the load calculated per 550.18 for the largest typical mobile home that each lot accepts. The feeder or service load can be calculated in accordance with Table 550.31. No demand factor is allowed for any other load, except as provided in this *Code* 》》*550.31*《《.

Feeder conductors shall consist of either a listed cord, factory installed in accordance with 550.10(B), or a permanently installed feeder consisting of four insulated, color-coded conductors that shall be identified by the factory or field marking of the conductors in compliance with 310.110. Equipment grounding conductors shall not be identified by stripping the insulation 》》*550.33(A)(1)*《《. Feeder conductors shall be installed in compliance with 250.32(B) 》》*550.33(A)(2)*《《.

For an existing feeder that is installed between the service equipment and a disconnecting means, as covered in 550.32(A), the equipment grounding conductor can be omitted where the grounded circuit conductor is grounded at the disconnecting means in accordance with 250.32(B) Exception 》》*550.33(A) Exception*《《.

Ⓐ Mobile home service equipment shall be rated no less than 100 amperes at 120/240 volts. A mobile home feeder assembly shall be connected by a permanent wiring method. Power outlets used as mobile home service equipment can also contain receptacles rated up to 50 amperes with appropriate overcurrent protection. Fifty-ampere receptacles shall conform to Figure 550.10(C)'s configuration 》》*550.32(C)*《《.

Ⓑ Additional receptacles are allowed for connection of electrical equipment located outside the mobile home. All such 125-volt, single-phase, 15- and 20-ampere receptacles shall be protected by a listed GFCI 》》*550.32(E)*《《.

Ⓒ Any mobile home service equipment utilizing a 125/250-volt receptacle shall be marked as follows:

> TURN DISCONNECTING SWITCH
> OR CIRCUIT BREAKER OFF BEFORE INSERTING
> OR REMOVING PLUG. PLUG MUST
> BE FULLY INSERTED OR REMOVED.

The marking shall be located adjacent to the service equipment's receptacle outlet 》》*550.32(G)*《《.

Ⓓ The mobile home service equipment shall be located adjacent to, not mounted in or on, the mobile home. It shall be located in sight from and within 30 ft (9.0 m) from the exterior wall of the mobile home it serves. The service equipment can be located elsewhere on the premises, provided a disconnecting means suitable for service equipment is located as stated previously for service equipment and is rated not less than that required for service equipment per 550.32(C). Grounding at the disconnecting means shall be compliant with 250.32 》》*550.32(A)*《《.

Ⓔ Mobile home service equipment or the local external disconnecting means permitted in 550.32(A) shall provide a means for connecting (by a fixed wiring method) an accessory building, structure, or additional electrical equipment located outside the mobile home 》》*550.32(D)*《《.

Ⓕ Outdoor mobile home disconnecting means shall be installed so that the bottom of the disconnecting means enclosure is at least 2 ft (600 mm) above finished grade (or working platform). Installation shall ensure that the center of the operating handle's grip, in the highest position, is no more than 6 ft 7 in. (2.0 m) above the finished grade (or working platform) 》》*550.32(F)*《《.

CAUTION

Mobile home and manufactured home lot feeder circuit conductors shall: (1) have a capacity not less than the loads supplied, (2) be rated at not less than 100 amperes, and (3) be permitted to be sized in accordance with 310.15(B)(7) 》》*550.33(B)*《《.

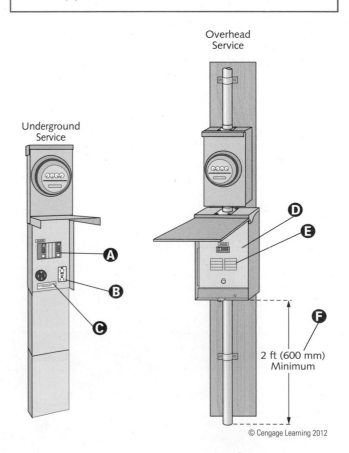

Overhead Service

Underground Service

2 ft (600 mm) Minimum

© Cengage Learning 2012

Manufactured Wiring Systems

Where listed for the purpose, manufactured wiring system assemblies can be used in outdoor locations *≫604.4 Exception No. 2≪*.

Conduit shall be listed FMC, or listed liquidtight flexible conduit, containing nominal 600-volt 8 to 12 AWG copper-insulated conductors, having a copper equipment grounding conductor (bare or insulated) equal in size to the ungrounded conductor *≫604.6(A)(2)≪*. (See Exceptions No. 1 through 3.)

Hard-usage flexible cord (minimum 12 AWG conductors) can be part of a listed factory-made assembly, not exceeding 6 ft (1.8 m) in length, as a transition method between manufactured wiring system components and utilization equipment, not permanently secured to the building structure. The cord must be visible for the entire length, shall not be subject to physical damage, and shall be provided with identified strain relief *≫604.6(A)(3)≪*. (See exception for listed electric-discharge luminaires.)

Ⓐ Article 604 provisions apply to field-installed wiring using off-site manufactured subassemblies for branch circuits, remote control circuits, signaling circuits, and communications circuits in accessible areas *≫604.1≪*.

Ⓑ The type of cable, flexible cord, or conduit shall be clearly marked on each section *≫604.6(B)≪*.

Ⓒ Receptacles and connectors shall be (1) of the locking type, uniquely polarized and identified for the purpose, and (2) part of a listed assembly appropriate for the system *≫604.6(C)≪*.

Ⓓ Manufactured wiring systems shall be secured and supported in accordance with the applicable cable or conduit article for the cable or conduit type employed *≫604.7≪*.

Ⓔ Ceiling grid-supported wires shall not be used to support cables (and raceways). Secure support shall be provided via wires and associated fittings *and* shall be installed in addition to the ceiling grid support wires *≫300.11(A)≪*. (This illustration does not show cable supports.)

Ⓕ A **manufactured wiring system** is a system containing component parts that are assembled in the process of manufacture and cannot be inspected at the building site without damage or destruction to the assembly and used for the connection of luminaires, utilization equipment, continuous plug-in type busways, and other devices *≫604.2≪*.

Ⓖ Cable shall be one of the following:

(1) Listed Type AC cable containing nominal 600-volt, 8- to 12-AWG insulated copper conductors with a bare or insulated copper equipment grounding conductor equivalent in size to the ungrounded conductor.

(2) Listed Type MC cable containing nominal 600-volt, 8- to 12-AWG insulated copper conductors with a bare or insulated copper equipment grounding conductor equivalent in size to the ungrounded conductor.

(3) Listed Type MC cable containing nominal 600-volt, 8- to 12-AWG insulated copper conductors with a grounding conductor and armor assembly listed and identified for grounding in accordance with 250.118(10). The combined metallic sheath and grounding conductor shall have a current-carrying capacity equivalent to the ungrounded copper conductor *≫604.6(A)(1)≪*.

Ⓗ Manufactured wiring systems are permitted in accessible and dry locations, and in ducts, plenums, and other air-handling spaces where listed for this application and installed per 300.22 *≫604.4≪*. In concealed spaces, one end of tapped cable can extend into hollow walls for direct switch/outlet termination points *≫604.4 Exception No. 1≪*.

> ### NOTE
> Manufactured wiring systems shall not be used where limited by the applicable article in Chapter 3 for the wiring method used in its construction *≫604.5≪*.

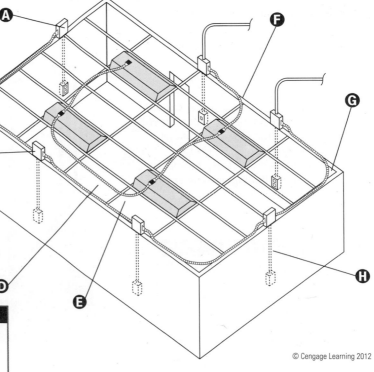

© Cengage Learning 2012

> ### CAUTION
> All connector openings shall be designed to prevent inadvertent contact with live parts or capped to effectively close the connector openings *≫604.6(C)≪*.

Office Furnishings

Freestanding (not fixed) partitions can be permanently connected to the building's electrical system by one of Chapter 3's approved wiring methods ≫*605.7*≪.

Individual freestanding partitions or groups of individual partitions that are electrically connected and mechanically contiguous, not exceeding 30 ft (9.0 m) when assembled, can connect to the building's electrical system by means of a single flexible cord and plug, provided *all* of the following are met:

(A) The flexible power-supply cord shall be of the extra-hard usage type, with 12 AWG or larger conductors, with an insulated equipment grounding conductor, and not more than 2 ft (600 mm) in length.

(B) The receptacle(s) supplying power shall be on a separate circuit serving only panels (no other loads) and shall be located within 12 in. (300 mm) of the partition to which it is connected.

(C) Individual partitions, or groups of interconnected individual partitions, shall contain no more than thirteen 15-ampere, 125-volt receptacle outlets.

(D) Individual partitions or interconnected groups shall not contain multiwire circuits ≫*605.8*≪.

Ⓐ Article 605 covers electrical equipment, lighting accessories, and wiring systems that connect to, are contained within, or are installed on relocatable wired partitions ≫*605.1*≪.

Ⓑ Wiring systems shall be identified as suitable power providers for lighting accessories and appliances in wired partitions. The partitions shall not extend from floor to ceiling, unless the exception is met ≫*605.2*≪.

Ⓒ The electrical connection between partitions shall be either a flexible assembly (identified for wired partition usage) or be of flexible cord, provided *all* of the following conditions are met: (1) the cord is extra-hard usage type with 12 AWG or larger conductors and shall have an insulated equipment grounding conductor; (2) the partitions are mechanically contiguous; (3) the cord, no longer than necessary for maximum partition positioning, is in no case to exceed 2 ft (600 mm); and (4) the cord

terminates at an attachment plug and cord connector with strain relief ≫*605.4*≪.

Ⓓ Lighting equipment listed and identified for wired partition use shall comply with *all* of the following:

(A) A secure attachment or support means is provided.

(B) If cord and plug connection is provided, the cord length, while suitable for the intended application, shall not exceed 9 ft (2.7 m) in length. The cord shall be 18 AWG or larger, shall contain an equipment grounding conductor, and shall be of the hard usage type. Any other means of connection shall be identified as suitable for the existing conditions.

(C) Convenience receptacles are not permitted in lighting accessories ≫*605.5*≪.

Ⓔ All conductors and connections shall be contained within wiring channels (metal or other material) identified as suitable for the conditions of use. These channels shall be free of projections or other conditions that may damage conductor insulation ≫*605.3*≪.

Ⓕ Chapters 5, 6, and 7 supplement or modify the general rules in Chapters 1 through 4. Chapters 1 through 4 apply except as amended by Chapters 5, 6, and 7 for the particular conditions ≫*90.3*≪.

N O T E

Fixed wired partitions (secured to building surfaces) shall be permanently connected to the building electrical system by one of Chapter 3's wiring methods ≫***605.6***≪.

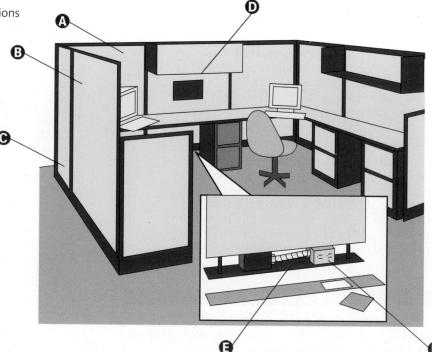

CAUTION

Each multiwire branch circuit shall be provided with a means that will simultaneously disconnect all ungrounded conductors at the point where the branch circuit originates ≫*210.4(B)*≪.

Electric Vehicle Charging Systems

Electric vehicle nonvented storage battery: A hermetically sealed battery comprised of rechargeable electrochemical cells without provisions for excessive gas pressure release, the addition of water (or electrolyte), or external electrolyte specific gravity measurements ≫ *625.2* ≪.

Personnel protection system: A system of personnel protection devices and structural features working together to provide personnel protection against electric shock ≫ *625.2* ≪.

Plug-in hybrid electric vehicle (PHEV): A type of electric vehicle intended for on-road use with the ability to store and use off-vehicle electrical energy in the rechargeable energy storage system, and having a second source of motive power ≫ *625.2* ≪.

Rechargeable energy storage system: Any power source that has the capability to be charged and discharged ≫ *625.2* ≪. Batteries, capacitors, and electromechanical flywheels are examples of rechargeable energy storage systems ≫ *625.2 Informational Note* ≪.

Feeders and branch circuits supplying electric vehicle supply equipment require overcurrent protection, are sized for continuous duty, and shall have a rating of no less than 125% of the maximum electric vehicle equipment load. Where the same feeder or branch circuit supplies noncontinuous loads, the overcurrent device shall have a rating at least equal to the sum of the noncontinuous loads plus 125% of the continuous loads ≫ *625.21* ≪.

Mechanical ventilation is not required where electric vehicle nonvented storage batteries are used, or where the electric vehicle supply equipment is listed/labeled and marked as suitable for charging electric vehicles indoors without ventilation per 625.15(B) ≫ *625.29(C)* ≪.

Ⓐ Unless specifically listed for the purpose and location, the electric vehicle supply equipment's coupling means

> **NOTE**
>
> All electrical materials, devices, fittings, and associated equipment shall be listed or labeled ≫*625.5*≪.

> **WARNING**
>
> Mechanical ventilation (such as a fan) shall be provided where the electric vehicle supply equipment is listed/labeled and marked as suitable for charging electric vehicles that require ventilation for indoor charging, in accordance with 625.15(C). Both supply and exhaust ventilation equipment shall be permanently installed to intake from and vent directly to the outdoors. Positive pressure ventilation systems are only permitted in locations that have been specifically designed and approved for that application. Mechanical ventilation requirements shall be determined using one of the methods found in 625.29(D)(1) through (4) ≫ *625.29(D)* ≪.

shall be situated no less than 18 in. (450 mm) and no more than 4 ft (1.2 m) above floor level ≫ *625.29(B)* ≪.

Ⓑ Article 625 provisions cover the electrical conductors and equipment external to an electric vehicle that connect it to an electrical supply by conductive or inductive means, as well as the installation of equipment and devices related to electric vehicle charging ≫ *625.1* ≪.

Ⓒ Electric vehicle: On-road-worthy automotive-type vehicle (such as a passenger automobile, bus, truck, van, neighborhood electric vehicles, electric motorcycles, and the like) primarily powered by an electric motor drawing current from a rechargeable storage battery, fuel cell, photovoltaic array, or other electric current source. Plug-in hybrid electric vehicles (PHEV) are considered electric vehicles. Article 625 excludes off-road self-propelled electric vehicles (such as industrial trucks, hoists, lifts, transports, golf carts, airline ground support equipment, tractors, boats, etc.) ≫ *625.2* ≪.

Ⓓ Electric vehicle connector: A device (part of the electric vehicle coupler) that, by insertion into an electric vehicle inlet, establishes an electrical connection for the purpose of power transfer and information exchange ≫ *625.2* ≪.

Ⓔ Electric vehicle coupler: A mating electric vehicle inlet and electric vehicle connector set ≫ *625.2* ≪.

Ⓕ Electric vehicle inlet: The electric vehicle device into which the electric vehicle connector is inserted for power transfer and information exchange. For *NEC* purposes, the electrical vehicle inlet is considered part of the vehicle rather than part of the electric vehicle supply equipment ≫ *625.2* ≪.

Ⓖ Electric vehicle supply equipment: Includes the conductors (ungrounded, grounded, and equipment grounding conductors), electric vehicle connectors, attachment plugs, and all other fittings, devices, power outlets, or apparatus purposely installed to transfer energy between the premises wiring and the electric vehicle ≫ *625.2* ≪.

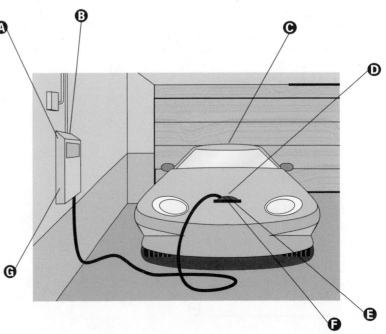

Audio Signal Processing, Amplification, and Reproduction Equipment

Grounding of separately derived systems with *60 volts to ground* shall meet 647.6 requirements »*640.7(B)*«.

Equipment access shall not be denied by accumulated wires and cables that prevent panel removal, including suspended ceiling panels »*640.5*«.

Wireways and auxiliary gutters shall be connected to an equipment grounding conductor(s), to an equipment bonding jumper, or to the grounded conductor where permitted or required by 250.92(B)(1) or 250.142. Where the wireway or auxiliary gutter does not contain power-supply wires, the equipment grounding conductor shall not be required to be larger than 14 AWG copper or its equivalent. Where the wireway or auxiliary gutter contains power-supply wires, the equipment grounding conductor shall not be smaller than specified in 250.122 »*640.7(A)*«.

Isolated grounding-type receptacles are permitted as described in 250.146(D), as well as for the implementation of other Article 250 compliant technical power systems. For separately derived systems with 60 volts to ground, the branch-circuit equipment grounding conductor shall be terminated per 647.6(B) »*640.7(C)*«.

Portable equipment: Equipment fed with portable cords or cables and intended for movement from one place to another »*640.2*«.

Temporary equipment: Portable wiring and equipment used for events of a transient or temporary nature where equipment removal is presumed at the event's conclusion »*640.2*«.

Technical power system (often referred to as *tech power*): An electrical distribution system with grounding in accordance with 250.146(D), where the equipment grounding conductor is isolated from the premises grounded conductor except at a single grounded termination point within a branch-circuit panelboard, at the originating (main breaker) branch-circuit panelboard, or at the premises grounding electrode »*640.2*«.

Grouped (or bundled) insulated conductors of different systems, in close physical contact within the same raceway (or other enclosure), or in portable cords (or cables), shall comply with 300.3(C)(1) »*640.8*«.

Ⓐ Article 640 covers equipment and wiring for audio signal generation, recording, processing, amplification and reproduction; distribution of sound; public address; speech input systems; temporary audio system installations; and electronic musical instruments (including organs). This encompasses audio systems subject to Article 517, Part VI; and Articles 518, 520, 525, and 530 »*640.1*«.

Ⓑ Loudspeaker: Equipment that converts an alternating-current (ac) electric signal into an acoustic signal. The term *speaker* is commonly used to mean loudspeaker »*640.2*«.

Ⓒ Mixer: Equipment used to combine and level-match a multiplicity of electronic signals, as from microphones, electronic instruments, and recorded audio »*640.2*«.

Ⓓ Audio signal processing equipment: Electrically operated equipment that produces or processes electronic signals that, when appropriately amplified and reproduced via loudspeaker, output an acoustic signal within the range of normal human hearing (typically 20 Hz to 20 kHz). Within Article 640, the terms *equipment* and *audio equipment* are equivalent to audio signal processing equipment »*640.2*«.

Ⓔ Audio system: The totality of equipment and interconnected wiring used to fabricate a fully functional audio signal processing, amplification, and reproduction system »*640.2*«.

Ⓕ Equipment rack: A framework for the equipment support or enclosure, either portable or stationary »*640.2*«.

> **N O T E**
>
> Audio signal processing, amplification, and reproduction equipment, cables, and circuits shall be installed in a neat, workmanlike manner »*640.6(A)*«.

> **CAUTION**
>
> Cables installed exposed on the surface of ceilings and sidewalls shall be supported in such a manner that the audio distribution cables will not be damaged by normal building use. Such cables shall be secured by straps, staples, cable ties, hangers, or similar fittings designed and installed so as not to damage the cable. The installation shall conform to 300.4 and 300.11(A) »*640.6(B)*«.

Information Technology Equipment

Ⓐ An approved means shall be provided to disconnect power to all electronic equipment in the information technology equipment room or in designated zones within the room. There shall also be a similar approved means to disconnect the power to all dedicated HVAC systems serving the room or designated zones and shall cause all required fire/smoke dampers to close. Unless the disconnecting means is a critical operations data system as covered in 645.10(B), the disconnecting means shall be implemented by the following methods:

(1) Remote disconnect controls shall be located at approved locations readily accessible in case of fire to authorized personnel and emergency responders.

(2) The remote disconnect controls for the control of electronic equipment power and HVAC systems shall be grouped and identified. A single means to control both systems shall be permitted.

(3) Where multiple zones are created, each zone shall have an approved means to confine fire or products of combustion to within the zone.

(4) Additional means to prevent unintentional operation of remote disconnect controls shall be permitted ≫ *645.10 and 645.10(A)* ≪.

Ⓑ Article 645 covers equipment, power-supply wiring, and equipment interconnected wiring, as well as grounding of information technology equipment and systems in an information technology equipment room ≫ *645.1* ≪.

Ⓒ Article 645 shall be permitted to provide alternate wiring methods to the provisions of Chapters 1 through 4 for power wiring provided that listed information technology equipment is installed ≫ *645.4(3)* ≪.

Ⓓ Information technology equipment shall be permitted to be connected to a branch circuit by a power-supply cord:

(1) Power-supply cords shall not exceed 15 ft (4.5 m).

(2) Power cords shall be listed and a type permitted for use on listed information technology equipment or shall be constructed of listed flexible cord and listed attachment plugs and cord connectors of a type permitted for information technology equipment ≫ *645.5(B)* ≪.

Ⓔ The branch-circuit conductors supplying one or more units of information technology equipment shall have an ampacity not less than 125% of the total connected load ≫ *645.5(A)* ≪.

Ⓕ Cables (power, communications, connecting, and interconnecting), cord and plug connections, and receptacles associated with the information technology equipment are permitted under a raised floor, provided 645.5(E)(1) through (6) requirements are met ≫ *645.5(E)* ≪.

Ⓖ Uninterruptible power supply (UPS) systems installed within the information technology equipment room, and their supply and output circuits, shall comply with 645.10 unless: (1) the installation qualifies under the provisions of Article 685, or (2) the power source is limited to 750 volt-amperes or less derived either from UPS equipment or from battery circuits integral to electronic equipment. The disconnecting means shall also disconnect the battery from its load ≫ *645.11* ≪

Ⓗ Article 645 does apply when a dedicated HVAC system (separate from other occupancy areas) exclusively serves the information technology equipment. Any HVAC system serving other occupancies can also serve the information technology equipment room if fire/smoke dampers exist at room boundary penetration points. Such dampers shall operate both on activation of smoke detectors and by disconnecting means operation as required by 645.10 ≫ *645.4(2)* ≪.

Ⓘ All exposed non-current-carrying metal parts of an information technology system shall either be bonded to the equipment grounding conductor (per Article 250) or be double-insulated. Power systems (derived within listed information technology equipment) supplying information technology systems through receptacles (or cable assemblies) that are part of this equipment are not considered separately derived for the purpose of applying 250.20(D). Signal reference structures, where installed, shall be bonded to the equipment grounding conductor provided for the information technology equipment ≫ *645.15* ≪.

Ⓙ It is not necessary to secure in place cables (power, communications, connecting, and interconnecting) and associated boxes, connectors, plugs, and receptacles that are listed as part of, or for, information technology equipment ≫ *645.5(F)* ≪.

> **NOTE**
>
> Article 645 shall be permitted to provide alternate wiring methods to the provisions of Chapters 1 through 4 for power wiring, 725.154 for signaling wiring, and 770.113(C) and Table 770.154(A) for optical fiber cabling, provided **all** of the conditions listed in 645.4(1) through (6) are met ≫ *645.4* ≪.

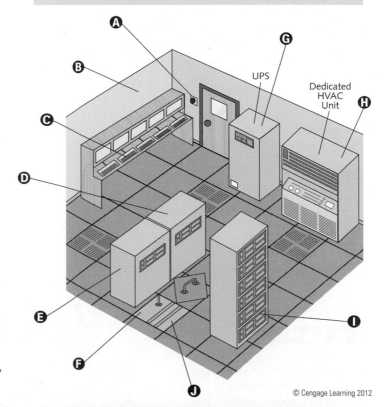

> **WARNING**
>
> Where exposed to physical damage, supply circuits and interconnecting cables shall be protected ≫ *645.5(D)* ≪.

SENSITIVE ELECTRONIC EQUIPMENT

Technical Power-System Receptacles

A Article 647 covers the installation and wiring of sensitive electronic equipment that is connected to a separately derived system operating at 120 volts line-to-line and 60 volts to ground ≫ *647.1* ≪.

> **NOTE**
>
> While isolated ground receptacles are permitted as described in 250.146(D), the branch-circuit equipment grounding conductor shall be terminated per 647.6(B) ≫ *647.7(B)* ≪.

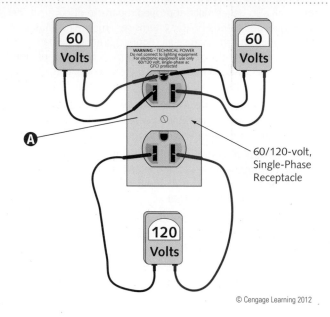

60/120-volt, Single-Phase Receptacle

© Cengage Learning 2012

Receptacle Installation

A All receptacle outlet strips, adapters, receptacle covers, and faceplates shall be marked as required by 647.7(A)(2):

> WARNING—TECHNICAL POWER
>
> Do not connect to
>
> lighting equipment.
>
> For electronic equipment use only.
>
> 60/120 V 1ø ac
>
> GFCI protected.

B All 125-volt receptacles used for 60/120-volt technical power shall be uniquely configured and identified for use with this class of system ≫ *647.7(A)(4)* ≪.

C All 15- and 20-ampere receptacle outlets shall be GFCI protected ≫ *647.7(A)(1)* ≪.

D A 125-volt, single-phase, 15- or 20-ampere-rated receptacle having one of its current-carrying poles connected to a grounded circuit conductor shall be located within 6 ft (1.8 m) of all permanently installed 15- or 20-ampere-rated 60/120-volt technical power-system receptacles ≫ *647.7(A)(3)* ≪.

> **NOTE**
>
> Receptacles used for equipment connection shall meet 647.7(A)(1) through (4) conditions ≫ *647.7(A)* ≪.

> **CAUTION**
>
> Clear markings on all junction box covers shall indicate the distribution panel and the system voltage ≫ *647.4(B)* ≪.

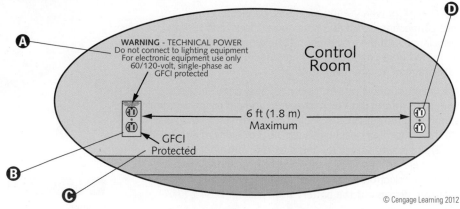

WARNING - TECHNICAL POWER
Do not connect to lighting equipment
For electronic equipment use only
60/120-volt, single-phase ac
GFCI protected

Control Room

6 ft (1.8 m) Maximum

GFCI Protected

© Cengage Learning 2012

Separately Derived Systems with 60 Volts to Ground

A Standard single-phase panelboards and distribution equipment with higher voltage ratings can be used ≫ *647.4(A)* ≪.

B The system shall be grounded per 250.30 as a separately derived single-phase, 3-wire system ≫ *647.6(A)* ≪.

C A separately derived 120-volt, single-phase, 3-wire system with 60 volts on each of two ungrounded conductors to a grounded neutral conductor can be used to reduce objectionable noise in sensitive electronic equipment locations provided that (1) the system is installed only in commercial or industrial occupancies, (2) the system's use is restricted to areas under close supervision by qualified personnel, and (3) all requirements in 647.4 through 647.8 are met ≫ *647.3* ≪.

D Common-trip, two-pole circuit breakers or a combination two-pole fused disconnecting means that are identified for use at the system voltage shall be provided for both ungrounded conductors in all feeders and branch circuits ≫ *647.4(A)* ≪.

E Branch circuits and feeders shall be provided with a means to simultaneously disconnect all ungrounded conductors ≫ *647.4(A)* ≪.

F The system shall be clearly marked on the panel's face or inside the panel's door ≫ *647.4(A)* ≪.

G Permanently wired utilization equipment and receptacles shall be grounded via an equipment grounding conductor, run with the circuit conductors, to an equipment grounding bus (prominently marked "Technical Equipment Ground") in the originating branch-circuit panelboard. The grounding bus shall be connected to the grounded conductor on the line side of the separately derived system's disconnecting means. The grounding shall be sized as specified in Table 250.122 and be run with the feeder conductors. The technical equipment grounding bus need not be bonded to the panelboard enclosure ≫ *647.6(B)* ≪.

> **N O T E**
>
> All feeders and branch-circuit conductors installed under 647.4 shall be identified as to system at all splices and terminations by color, marking, tagging, or equally effective means. The means of identification shall be posted at each branch-circuit panelboard and at the building's disconnecting means ≫ *647.4(C)* ≪.

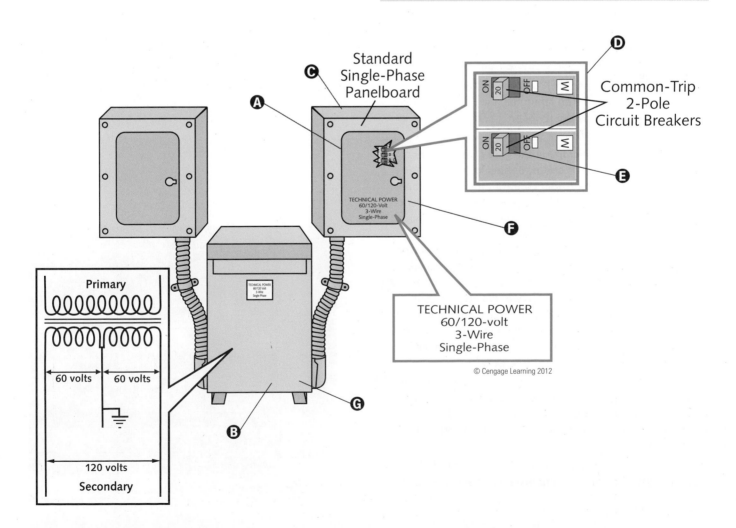

Standard Single-Phase Panelboard

Common-Trip 2-Pole Circuit Breakers

TECHNICAL POWER 60/120-volt 3-Wire Single-Phase

Primary

60 volts   60 volts

120 volts

Secondary

© Cengage Learning 2012

Fire Pumps

Electric motor-driven fire pumps shall have a reliable power source ≫695.3≪. See 695.3(A) for individual source requirements and 695.3(B) for multiple source requirements.

A fire pump can be supplied by a separate service ≫230.2(A) and 695.3(A)(1)≪.

If service or system voltage differs from the fire pump motor's utilization voltage, one or more transformers (protected by disconnecting means and overcurrent protective devices) can be installed between the system supply and the fire pump controller in accordance with 695.5(A) and (B), or with (C). Only transformers covered in (C) can supply loads unrelated to the fire pump system ≫695.5≪.

Power circuits and wiring methods shall comply with the requirements in 695.6(A) through (J), and, as permitted in 230.90(A), Exception No. 4; 230.94, Exception No. 4; 240.13; 230.208; 240.4(A); and 430.31 ≫695.6≪.

The location of electric motor-driven fire pump controllers and power transfer switches shall be within sight from and as close as practicable to the motors they control ≫695.12(A)≪. Engine-driven fire pump controllers shall be located as close as practical to and within sight from the engines they control ≫695.12(B)≪.

Fire pump controllers and power transfer switches, by location or protection, shall remain undamaged by water escaping from pumps or pump connections ≫695.12(E)≪.

The disconnecting means shall be marked "Fire Pump Disconnecting Means." The minimum 1-in. (25-mm)-high letters shall be visible without opening enclosure doors or covers ≫695.4(B)(3)(b)≪.

Fire pump supply conductors on the load side of the final disconnecting means and overcurrent device(s) permitted by 695.4(B), or conductors that connect directly to an on-site standby generator, shall be kept entirely independent of all other wiring. The conductors shall supply only loads that are directly associated with the fire pump system, and they shall be protected from potential damage by fire, structural failure, or operational accident. Where routed through a building, the conductors shall (1) be encased in at least 2 in. (50 mm) of concrete or (2) be protected by a fire-rated assembly listed to achieve a minimum fire rating of 2 hours and dedicated to the fire pump circuit(s) or (3) be a listed electrical circuit protective system with a minimum 2-hour fire rating ≫695.6(A)(2)≪.

Automatic protection against overloads is not allowed on power circuits. Except for protection of transformer primaries provided in 695.5(C)(2), branch-circuit and feeder conductors shall be protected against short circuits only ≫695.6(C)≪.

All engine controller/battery wiring shall be protected against physical damage, being installed in accordance with the controller and engine manufacturer's instructions ≫695.6(F)≪.

Ⓐ All wiring from the controllers to the pump motors shall be in RMC, IMC, EMT, LFMC, or LFNC Type LFNC-B, listed Type MC cable with an impervious covering, or Type MI cable ≫695.6(D)≪.

Ⓑ Conductors supplying fire pump motor(s), pressure maintenance pumps, and associated accessory equipment shall have a minimum rating of 125% of the sum of the fire pump motor(s) and pressure maintenance motor(s) full-load current(s), plus 100% of the associated fire pump accessory equipment ≫695.6(B)(1)≪. Conductors supplying only fire pump motor(s) shall have a minimum rating in accordance with 430.22. Larger conductors may be necessary to comply with 395.7 ≫695.6(B)(2)≪.

Ⓒ Article 695 covers the installation of (1) electric power sources and interconnecting circuits and (2) switching and control equipment dedicated to fire pump drivers ≫695.1(A)≪.

> ### N O T E
>
> Article 695 does not cover (1) performance, maintenance, and acceptance testing of the fire pump system and the system components' internal wiring or (2) pressure maintenance (jockey or makeup) pumps ≫695.1(B)≪.
>
> Taps used to supply fire pump equipment, if provided with service equipment and installed per service-entrance conductor requirements, can be connected to the supply side of the service disconnecting means ≫230.82(5)≪.

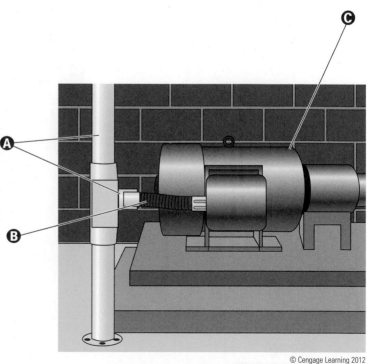

ELEVATORS, DUMBWAITERS, ESCALATORS, MOVING WALKS, PLATFORM LIFTS, AND STAIRWAY CHAIRLIFTS

General

Control system: Overall system governing starting, stopping, direction of motion, acceleration, speed, and retardation of the moving member »*620.2*«.

Motion controller: Electrical device(s) for that portion of the control system governing acceleration, speed, retardation, and stoppage of the moving member »*620.2*«.

Motor controller: The control system's operative units, that is, the starter device(s) and power conversion equipment that drive an electric motor, or the pumping unit used to power hydraulic control equipment »*620.2*«.

Operation controller: Electric device(s) for that portion of the control system that initiates starting, stopping, and direction of motion in response to an operating device's signal »*620.2*«.

Door operator controller and door motor branch circuits, as well as feeders to motor controllers, driving machine motors, machine brakes, and motor-generator sets shall have a circuit voltage of 600 volts or less »*620.3(A)*«.

Operating device: Devices used to activate the operation controller, such as the car switch, push buttons, key, or toggle switch(es) »*620.2*«.

Conductors and optical fibers within hoistways, escalator and moving walk wellways, platform lifts, stairway chairlift runways, machinery spaces, control spaces, in/on cars, and machine/control rooms (exclusive of traveling cables connecting the car or counterweight and hoistway wiring) shall be installed in RMC, IMC, EMT, PVC, or wireways; or shall be Type MC, MI, or AC cable unless otherwise permitted in 620.21(A) through (C) »*620.21*«.

Ⓐ Working space shall be provided around controllers, disconnecting means, and other electrical equipment. The minimum working space shall meet 110.26(A) specifications. Where maintenance and supervision conditions ensure that only qualified persons will examine, adjust, service, and maintain the equipment, 110.26(A) clearance requirements can be waived per 620.5(A) through (D) »*620.5*«.

Ⓑ Circuit voltage of heating/air-conditioning equipment branch circuits located on the elevator car shall not exceed 600 volts »*620.3(C)*«.

Ⓒ Lighting circuits shall comply with Article 410 requirements »*620.3(B)*«.

Ⓓ The minimum conductor size for traveling cables that feed lighting circuits is 14 AWG copper. Provided the ampacity equals or surpasses that of 14 AWG copper, 20 AWG (or larger) copper conductors are permitted in parallel. For traveling cable circuits, other than lighting, 20 AWG copper is the minimum size »*620.12(A)*«.

Ⓔ The motor controller rating shall comply with 430.83. When the controller is marked as power limited, thereby limiting the available power to the motor, the rating of the controller can be less than the nominal rating of the elevator motor »*620.15*«.

Ⓕ Article 620 covers the installation of electric equipment and wiring relating to elevators, dumbwaiters, escalators, moving walks, platform lifts, and stairway chairlifts »*620.1*«.

Ⓖ All live parts of electrical apparatus in (and around) elevator and dumbwaiter hoistways, landings, and cars; escalator and moving walk wellways or landings; and machinery space runways of platform lifts and stairway chairlifts shall be enclosed to guard against accidental contact »*620.4*«.

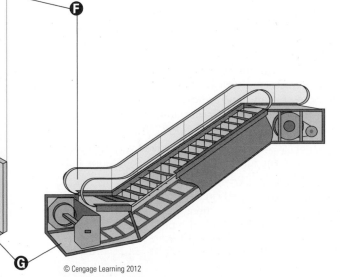

© Cengage Learning 2012

Elevator Wiring

Flexible cords and cables that are components of listed equipment used in circuits operating at 30 volts rms (or less) or 42 volts dc (or less) are permitted in lengths not exceeding 6 ft (1.8 m) provided the cords and cables are (1) supported and protected from physical damage and (2) of a jacketed and flame-retardant type *»620.21(A)(2)(c)«*.

Motor generators, machine motors, or pumping unit motors and valves that are located adjacent to, or underneath, control equipment and provided with extra-length terminal leads and are no longer than 6 ft (1.8 m) can be connected directly to controller terminal studs without regard to the carrying-capacity requirements of Articles 430 and 445. Auxiliary gutters are permitted in machine/control rooms between controllers, starters, and similar apparatus *»620.21(A)(3)(b)«*.

Existing or listed equipment conductors can be grouped together (taped or corded) without being installed in a raceway. Such cable groups should by location be protected from physical damage, being supported at intervals of 3 ft (900 mm) or less *»620.21(A)(3)(d)«*.

Ⓐ FMC, LFMC, or LFNC of ⅜ in. nominal trade size or larger and no longer than 6 ft (1.8 m) can be installed between control panels and machine motors, machine brakes, motor-generator sets, disconnecting means, and pumping unit motors and valves *»620.21(A)(3)(a)«*. LFNC, as defined in 356.2(2), can be installed in lengths exceeding 6 ft (1.8 m) *»620.21(A)(3)(a) Exception«*.

Ⓑ FMC, LFMC, or LFNC of ⅜ in. nominal trade size (or larger) and not exceeding 6 ft (1.8 m) in length, allowed for installation on cars, shall be securely fastened in an oil-free location *»620.21(A)(2)(a)«*. LFNC of ⅜ in. nominal trade size or larger, as defined by 356.2(2), is permitted in lengths greater than 6 ft (1.8 m) *»620.21(A)(2)(a) Exception«*.

Ⓒ Hard-service cords and junior hard-service cords conforming to Article 400 (Table 400.4) requirements are permitted as flexible connections between the car's fixed wiring and the car door/gate devices. Only hard-service cords are permitted as flexible connections for top-of-car operating devices or car-top work lights. Devices or luminaires shall be grounded via an equipment grounding conductor run with the circuit conductors. Cables having smaller conductors as well as other insulation (jacket) types and thicknesses can serve as flexible connections between the car's fixed wiring and the car door/gate devices, if specifically listed for this use *»620.21(A)(2)(b)«*.

Ⓓ FMC, LFMC, or LFNC can be installed within hoistways between risers and limit switch interlocks, operating buttons, and similar devices *»620.21(A)(1)(a)«*.

Ⓔ Class 2 power-limited circuit cables installed in hoistways between risers, signal equipment, and operating devices shall be of a jacketed flame-retardant type, securely supported and protected from physical damage *»620.21(A)(1)(b)«*.

Ⓕ The following wiring methods shall be permitted on the counterweight assembly and on the car assembly in lengths not to exceed 6 ft (1.8 m): (1) flexible metal conduit; (2) liquidtight flexible metal conduit; (3) liquidtight flexible nonmetallic conduit; and (4) flexible cords and cables, or conductors grouped together and taped or corded, shall be permitted to be installed without a raceway. They shall be located to be protected from physical damage and shall be of a flame-retardant type and shall be part of the following:

a. Listed equipment

b. A driving machine, or

c. A driving machine brake *»620.21(A)(2)(d)* and *620.21(A)(4)«*.

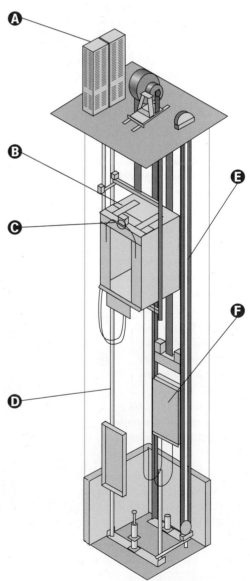

Escalator and Moving Walks Wiring

A FMC, LFMC, or LFNC are acceptable in escalator and moving walk wellways. FMC or liquidtight flexible conduit of ⅜ inch nominal trade size is permitted in lengths of 6 ft (1.8 m) or less ≫ *620.21(B)(1)* ≪. LFNC of ⅜ in. nominal trade size or larger, as defined in 356.2(2), can be installed in lengths greater than 6 ft (1.8 m) ≫ *620.21(B)(1) Exception* ≪.

B Class 2 power-limited circuit cables can be installed within escalators and moving walkways provided the cables are (1) supported and protected from physical damage and (2) of a jacketed and flame-retardant type ≫ *620.21(B)(2)* ≪.

> **NOTE**
>
> Platform lift and stairway chairlift raceways shall be installed according to 620.21(C) provisions. Escalators, moving walks, platform lifts, and stairway chairlifts shall comply with Article 250 ≫*620.84*≪.

C Hard-service cords conforming to Article 400 (Table 400.4) requirements are permitted as flexible connections on escalator and moving walk control panels and disconnecting means where the entire control panel and disconnecting means can be removed from machine spaces per 620.5 ≫ *620.21(B)(3)* ≪.

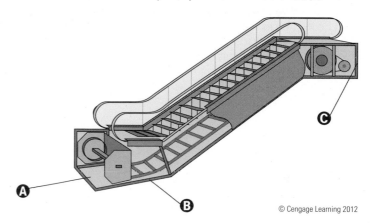

© Cengage Learning 2012

Conductor Installation

Auxiliary gutters are not subject to the length restrictions of 366.12(2), or to the number of conductors per 366.22 ≫*620.35*≪.

A Only electric wiring, raceways, and cables used in direct connection with the elevator or dumbwaiter are permitted inside the hoistway, machine rooms, control rooms, machinery spaces, and control spaces. Wiring for signals; for communication with the car; for lighting, heating, air conditioning, and ventilating the elevator car; for fire-detecting systems; for pit sump pumps; and for lighting and ventilating the hoistway are allowed ≫ *620.37(A)* ≪.

B Cables or raceway supports in a hoistway, escalator/moving walk wellway, or platform lift and stairway chairlift runway shall be securely fastened to the guide rail, escalator/moving walk truss, or the hoistway, wellway, or runway construction ≫ *620.34* ≪.

C Optical fiber cables and conductors for operating devices, operation and motion control, power, signaling, fire, alarm, lighting, heating, and air-conditioning circuits of 600 volts (or less) can run in the same traveling cable (or raceway) system if (1) all conductors are insulated for the maximum voltage applied to any conductor within the cable (or raceway) system and (2) all live parts of the equipment are insulated from ground for the same maximum voltage. Such a traveling cable (or raceway) can also include shielded conductors or coaxial cable(s), if insulated for the maximum voltage applied to any conductor within the cable (or raceway) system. Conductors can be suitably shielded for telephone, audio, video, or higher frequency communications circuits ≫ *620.36* ≪.

D Bonding of elevator rails (car or counterweight) to a lightning protection system grounding-down conductor(s) is permitted. The lightning protection system shall be located outside the hoistway. Elevator rails or other hoistway equipment shall

not be used as the grounding-down conductor for lightning protection systems ≫ *620.37(B)* ≪.

E Main feeders supplying elevator and dumbwaiter power shall be installed outside the hoistway unless (1) by special permission, elevator feeders are permitted within an existing hoistway containing no spliced conductors or (2) feeders are permitted inside the hoistway for elevators with driving machine motors located in the hoistway, on the car, or on the counterweight ≫ *620.37(C)* ≪.

F The cross-sectional area's sum of the individual conductors in a wireway shall be no more than 50% of the wireway's interior cross-sectional area. Vertically run wireways shall be securely supported at intervals of 15 ft (4.5 m) or less and shall have a maximum of one joint between supports. Adjoining wireway sections shall be securely fastened together to form a rigid joint ≫ *620.32* ≪.

> **CAUTION**
>
> Electrical equipment and wiring used for elevators, dumbwaiters, escalators, moving walks, platform lifts, and stairway lifts in garages shall comply with Article 511 requirements ≫*620.38*≪.

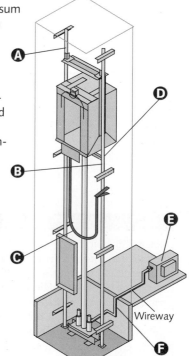

Wireway

© Cengage Learning 2012

Branch Circuits and Traveling Cables

A Each machine room or control room and machinery space or control space requires at least one 125-volt, single-phase, 15- or 20-ampere duplex receptacle 》620.23(C)《.

B A separate branch circuit shall supply each elevator car's lights, receptacle(s), auxiliary lighting power source, and ventilation. The branch circuit's overcurrent protective device shall be located in the elevator machine room or control room/machinery space or control space 》620.22(A)《. A dedicated branch circuit is required for each elevator car's air-conditioning/heating unit. Locate this branch circuit's overcurrent protective device in the elevator machine room or control room/machinery space or control space 》620.22(B)《.

C Traveling cables shall be suspended at both the car and hoistway ends (or counterweight end if applicable), thereby reducing the strain on individual copper conductors to a minimum. Support traveling cables by any one of the following means:

1. Steel supporting member(s)

2. Looping the cables around supports for unsupported lengths less than 100 ft (30 m)

3. Suspending from the supports by a means that automatically tightens around the cable with increased tension, for unsupported lengths up to 200 ft (60 m) 》620.41《

D Careful location of traveling cable supports can reduce to a minimum the possibility of damage due to cables contacting hoistway construction/equipment. Provide suitable guards where necessary to protect the cables against damage 》620.43《.

E Each hoistway pit shall have at least one 125-volt, single-phase, 15- or 20-ampere duplex receptacle 》620.24(C)《.

F A separate branch circuit shall supply the machine room or control room/machinery space or control space lighting and receptacle(s). Required lighting shall not be connected to a GFCI's load side 》620.23(A)《. Locate the lighting switch at the machine room or control room/machinery space or control space point of entry 》620.23(B)《.

G Metal raceways and cables of Types MC, MI, or AC attached to an elevator car shall be bonded to the metal parts of the car that are bonded to the equipment grounding conductor 》620.81《.

H Traveling cables that are suitably supported and protected from physical damage shall be permitted to be run without the use of a raceway in either or both of the following:

(a) When used inside the hoistway, on the elevator car, hoistway wall, counterweight, or controllers and machinery that are located inside the hoistway, provided the cables are in the original sheath.

(b) From inside the hoistway, to elevator controller enclosures and to elevator car and machine room, control room, machinery space, and control space connections that are located outside the hoistway for a distance not exceeding 6 ft (1.8 m) in length as measured from the first point of support on the elevator car or hoistway wall, or counterweight where applicable, provided the conductors are grouped together and taped or corded, or in the original sheath. These traveling cables shall be permitted to be continued to this equipment 》620.44《.

I Hoistway pit lighting and receptacle(s) shall be supplied by a separate branch circuit. In no case should required lighting be connected to the load side of a GFCI 》620.24(A)《. The lighting switch's location shall be readily accessible from the pit access door 》620.24(B)《.

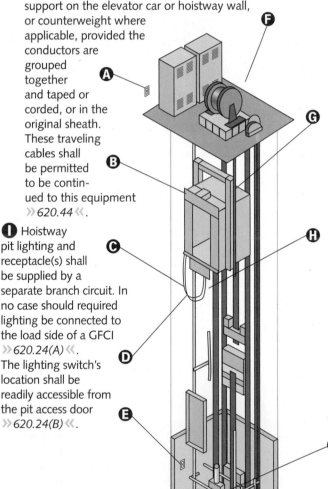

© Cengage Learning 2012

CAUTION

Each 125-volt, single-phase, 15- and 20-ampere receptacle installed in pits or hoistways, on elevator car tops, and in escalator and moving walk wellways shall be of the GFCI type. All 125-volt, single-phase, 15- and 20-ampere receptacles installed in machine rooms and machinery spaces shall have GFCI protection for personnel. A single receptacle supplying a permanently installed sump pump does not require GFCI protection 》620.85《.

NOTE

For electric elevators, all motor frames, elevator machines, controllers, and metal electrical-equipment enclosures in (or on) the car or in the hoistway shall be bonded per Article 250, Parts V and VII 》620.82《.

Protection and Control

Each unit shall have a single means for disconnecting all ungrounded main power supply conductors that is designed so that no pole operates independently. Where multiple driving machines are connected to a single elevator, escalator, moving walk, or pumping unit, a single means shall be provided to disconnect the motor(s) and control valve operating magnets ≫ *620.51* ≪.

The location of the disconnecting means shall be readily accessible to qualified persons ≫ *620.51(C)* ≪. Depending on the application, the location must comply with 1, 2, 3, or 4 in 620.51(C).

Where there are multiple driving machines in a machine room, the disconnecting means shall be numbered to correspond with the identifying number of the driving machine being controlled. The disconnecting means shall have a sign identifying the location of the supply side overcurrent protective device ≫ *620.51(D)* ≪.

Each elevator car shall have a single means for disconnecting all ungrounded car light, receptacle(s), and ventilation power-supply conductors. The disconnecting means shall be an enclosed externally operable fused motor-circuit switch or circuit breaker capable of locking in the open position and shall be located in that elevator car's machine/control room. The provision for locking or adding a lock to the disconnecting means shall be installed on or at the switch or circuit breaker used as the disconnecting means and shall remain in place with or without the lock installed. Portable means for adding a lock to the switch or circuit breaker shall not be permitted as the means required to be installed at and remain with the equipment. Where there is no machine room or control room, the disconnecting means shall be located in a machinery space or control space outside the hoistway that is readily accessible to only qualified persons. Each disconnecting means shall be numbered to correspond with the identifying number of the car whose light source it controls. The disconnecting means shall have a sign identifying the location of the supply side overcurrent protective device ≫ *620.53* ≪.

Operating devices and control/signaling circuits shall be protected against overcurrent according to 725.23 and 725.24. Class 2 power-limited circuits shall be protected against overcurrent in accordance with the requirements of Chapter 9, Notes to Tables 11(A) and 11(B) ≫ *620.61(A)* ≪.

Duty on elevator and dumbwaiter driving machine motors and driving motors of motor generators (used with generator field control) is rated as *intermittent*. Such motors shall be permitted to be protected against overload per 430.33 ≫ *620.61(B)(1)* ≪.

Duty on escalator and moving walk driving machine motors is rated as *continuous*. Protect such motors against overload in accordance with 430.32 ≫ *620.61(B)(2)* ≪. Escalator and moving walk driving machine motors, and driving motors of motor-generator sets, shall be protected against running overload as provided in Table 430.37 ≫ *620.61(B)(3)* ≪.

Platform lift and stairway chairlift driving machine motor duty is rated as *intermittent*. Such motors can be protected against overload according to 430.33 ≫ *620.61(B)(4)* ≪.

Ⓐ Elevator, dumbwaiter, escalator, and moving walk driving machines; motor-generator sets; motor controllers; and disconnecting means shall be installed in a room or space dedicated for that purpose, unless otherwise permitted in 620.71(A) or (B). The room or enclosure shall be secured against unauthorized access ≫ *620.71* ≪.

> ### NOTE
> Elevator emergency and standby power systems must comply with 620.91.

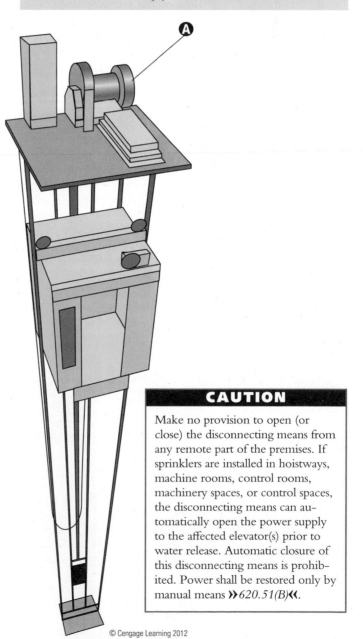

> ### CAUTION
> Make no provision to open (or close) the disconnecting means from any remote part of the premises. If sprinklers are installed in hoistways, machine rooms, control rooms, machinery spaces, or control spaces, the disconnecting means can automatically open the power supply to the affected elevator(s) prior to water release. Automatic closure of this disconnecting means is prohibited. Power shall be restored only by manual means ≫ *620.51(B)* ≪.

© Cengage Learning 2012

SWIMMING POOLS, FOUNTAINS, AND SIMILAR INSTALLATIONS

General

All electrical equipment installed in the water, walls, or decks of pools, fountains, and similar applications shall comply with the provisions of Article 680 **»680.4«**.

Except as modified by this article, wiring and equipment in or adjacent to pools and fountains shall comply with other applicable requirements of the *Code* including provisions identified in Table 680.3 **»680.3«**.

Storable pool provisions are located in Article 680, Part III (680.30 through 34).

The provisions of Article 680, Part I and Part VI shall apply to therapeutic pools and tubs in health care facilities, gymnasiums, athletic training rooms, and similar areas **»680.60«**.

Hydromassage bathtub requirements are located in Article 680, Part VII.

A Article 680 provisions apply to the electrical wiring construction (and installation) and for equipment in or adjacent to all swimming, wading, therapeutic, and decorative pools, fountains, hot tubs, spas, and hydromassage bathtubs, whether permanently installed or storable, as well as to similar metallic auxiliary equipment (such as pumps, filters, etc.). The term *body of water* used throughout Part I applies to all bodies of water covered in this scope unless otherwise amended **»680.1«**.

B Fountain: Includes fountains, ornamental pools, display pools, and reflection pools, but drinking fountains are not included **»680.2«**.

C Part I and Part V provisions apply to all permanently installed fountains as defined in 680.2. Fountains that have water common to a pool shall additionally comply with the requirements in Part II of Article 680. Part V does not cover self-contained, portable fountains. Portable fountains shall comply with Parts II and III of Article 422 **»680.50«**.

D Permanently installed decorative fountains and reflection pools: Those that are constructed in or on the ground, or in a building so that the fountain cannot be readily disassembled, with or without electrical circuits of any nature. These units are constructed primarily for their aesthetic value and are not intended for swimming or wading **»680.2«**.

E Spa or hot tub: A hydromassage pool or tub for recreational or therapeutic use, not located in health care facilities, designed for immersion of users, and usually having a filter, heater, and motor-driven blower. It may be installed either indoors or out and on or in the ground or supporting structure. Generally, a spa or hot tub is not designed to be drained after each use **»680.2«**.

F Spa and hot tub requirements can be found in Article 680, Part IV (680.40 through 44).

G Equipotential bonding provisions for permanently installed pools are located in 680.26.

H Pool: Manufactured or field-constructed equipment designed to contain water on a permanent or semipermanent basis, and used for swimming, wading, immersion, or therapeutic purposes **»680.2«**.

I Permanently installed pool underwater luminaire requirements are located in 680.23.

J Permanently installed swimming, wading, immersion, and therapeutic pools: Those that are constructed totally or partially in the ground, all others with depth capacities greater than 42 in. (1.0 m), and all pools installed inside of a building, regardless of water depth, whether or not served by electrical circuits of any nature **»680.2«**.

K Permanently installed pools must comply with Article 680, Part II.

> ### NOTE
>
> Swimming pool overhead conductor clearance requirements are located in 680.8 and Table 680.8.

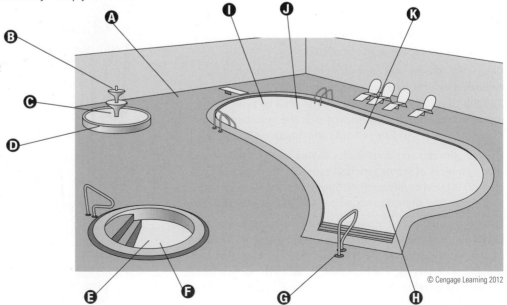

Definitions

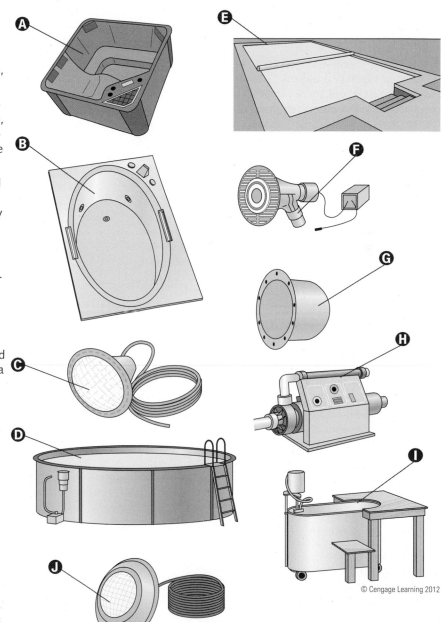

(A) Self-contained spa or hot tub: Factory-fabricated unit consisting of a spa or hot tub vessel having integrated water-circulating, heating, and control equipment. Equipment may include pumps, air blowers, heaters, lights, controls, sanitizer generators, etc. ≫ *680.2* ≪.

(B) Hydromassage bathtub: A permanently installed bathtub with recirculation piping, pump, and associated equipment. It is designed to accept, circulate, and discharge water at each use ≫ *680.2* ≪.

(C) Wet-niche luminaire: A luminaire intended for installation in a pool or fountain structure's forming shell, where completely surrounded by water ≫ *680.2* ≪.

(D) Storable swimming, wading, or immersion pool: Those constructed on or above the ground having a maximum water depth capacity of 42 in. (1.0 m), or a pool with nonmetallic, molded polymeric walls (or inflatable fabric walls) regardless of dimension ≫ *680.2* ≪.

(E) Pool cover, electrically operated: Motor-driven equipment designed to cover and uncover the pool's water surface by means of a flexible sheet or rigid frame ≫ *680.2* ≪.

(F) Cord- and plug-connected lighting assembly: A lighting assembly consisting of a luminaire intended for installation in the wall of a spa, hot tub, or storable pool, having a cord- and plug-connected transformer ≫ *680.2* ≪.

(G) Forming shell: A support structure designed for a wet-niche luminaire assembly and intended for pool or fountain structure mounting ≫ *680.2* ≪.

(H) Packaged spa or hot tub equipment assembly: A factory-fabricated unit consisting of water-circulating, heating, and control equipment mounted on a common base and that operates as a spa or hot tub. Equipment may include pumps, air blowers, heaters, lights, controls, sanitizer generators, etc. ≫ *680.2* ≪.

(I) Self-contained therapeutic tubs or hydrotherapeutic tanks: A factory-fabricated unit consisting of a therapeutic tub or hydrotherapeutic tank with integrated water-circulating, heating, and control equipment. Equipment may include pumps, air blowers, heaters, lights, controls, sanitizer generators, etc. ≫ *680.2* ≪.

(J) No-niche luminaire: A luminaire intended for above or below water installation without a niche ≫ *680.2* ≪.
Note: Not to be mistaken for a dry-niche luminaire.

Dry-niche luminaire: A luminaire intended for installation in the floor or wall of a pool, spa, or fountain in a niche that is sealed against water entry ≫ *680.2* ≪.

© Cengage Learning 2012

Conductive Pool Shells and Perimeter Surfaces

The equipotential bonding required by 680.26 shall be installed to reduce voltage gradients in the pool area ≫ *680.26(A)* ≪.

Ⓐ The parts specified in 680.26(B)(1) through (B)(7) shall be bonded together using solid copper conductors, insulated covered, or bare, not smaller than 8 AWG or with rigid metal conduit of brass or other identified corrosion-resistant metal. Connections to bonded parts shall be made in accordance with 250.8. An 8 AWG or larger solid copper bonding conductor provided to reduce voltage gradients in the pool area shall not be required to be extended or attached to remote panelboards, service equipment, or electrodes ≫ *680.26(B)* ≪.

Ⓑ Bonding to conductive pool shells shall be provided as specified in 680.26(B)(1)(a) or 680.26(B)(1)(b). Poured concrete, pneumatically applied or sprayed concrete, and concrete block with painted or plastered coatings shall all be considered conductive materials due to water permeability and porosity. Vinyl liners and fiberglass composite shells shall be considered to be nonconductive materials ≫ *680.26(B)(1)* ≪.

Ⓒ Unencapsulated structural reinforcing steel shall be bonded together by steel tie wires or the equivalent. Where structural reinforcing steel is encapsulated in a nonconductive compound, a copper conductor grid shall be installed in accordance with 680.26(B)(1)(b) ≫ *680.26(B)(1)(a)* ≪. A copper conductor grid shall be provided and shall: (1) be constructed of minimum 8 AWG bare solid copper conductors bonded to each other at all points of crossing (the bonding shall be in accordance with 250.8 or other approved means), (2) conform to the contour of the pool, (3) be arranged in a 12-in. × 12-in. (300-mm × 300-mm) network of conductors in a uniformly spaced perpendicular grid pattern with a tolerance of 4 in. (100 mm), and (4) be secured within or under the pool no more than 6 in. (150 mm) from the outer contour of the pool shell ≫ *680.26(B)(1)(b)* ≪.

Ⓓ The perimeter surface shall extend for 3 ft (1 m) horizontally beyond the inside walls of the pool and shall include unpaved surfaces as well as poured concrete surfaces and other types of paving. Perimeter surfaces less than 3 ft (1 m) separated by a permanent wall or building 5 ft (1.5 m) in height or more shall require equipotential bonding on the pool side of the permanent wall or building. Bonding to perimeter surfaces shall be provided as specified in 680.26(B)(2)(a) or 680.26(B)(2)(b) and shall be attached to the pool reinforcing steel or copper conductor grid at a minimum of four (4) points uniformly spaced around the perimeter of the pool. For nonconductive pool shells, bonding at four points shall not be required ≫ *680.26(B)(2)* ≪.

(a) Structural reinforcing steel shall be bonded in accordance with 680.26(B)(1)(a).

(b) Where structural reinforcing steel is not available or is encapsulated in a nonconductive compound, a copper conductor(s) shall be utilized where the following requirements are met:

(1) At least one minimum 8 AWG bare solid copper conductor shall be provided.

(2) The conductors shall follow the contour of the perimeter surface.

(3) Only listed splices shall be permitted.

(4) The required conductor shall be 18 to 24 in. (450 to 600 mm) from the inside walls of the pool.

(5) The required conductor shall be secured within or under the perimeter surface 4 to 6 in. (100 to 150 mm) below the subgrade ≫ *680.26(B)(2)(a) and (b)* ≪.

> **NOTE**
>
> All metallic parts of the pool structure, including reinforcing metal not addressed in 680.26(1)(a), shall be bonded. Where reinforcing steel is encapsulated with a nonconductive compound, the reinforcing steel shall not be required to be bonded ≫ *680.26(B)(3)* ≪.

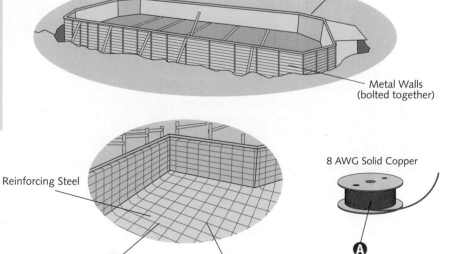

Ⓓ

Metal Walls (bolted together)

Reinforcing Steel

8 AWG Solid Copper

Ⓐ

Ⓑ   Ⓒ

© Cengage Learning 2012

Receptacles

Ⓐ Receptacles that provide power for water-pump motors or for other loads directly related to the circulation and sanitation system shall be located at least 10 ft (3.0 m) from the inside walls of the pool or not less than 6 ft (1.83 m) from the inside walls of the pool if they meet all of the following conditions: (1) consist of single receptacles; (2) employ a locking configuration; (3) are of the grounding type; and (4) have GFCI protection ≫*680.22(A)(1)*≪.

Ⓑ A dwelling unit's permanently installed pool shall have at least one 125-volt 15- or 20-ampere receptacle on a general-purpose branch circuit that is located a minimum of 6 ft (1.83 m), but no more than 20 ft (6.0 m), from the pool's inside wall. This receptacle shall not be more than 6 ft, 6 in. (2.0 m) above the floor, platform, or grade level serving the pool ≫*680.22(A)(3)*≪.

CAUTION

Fifteen- and 20-ampere, 125- and 250-volt receptacles installed in a wet location shall have an enclosure that is weatherproof whether or not the attachment plug cap is inserted. For other than one- or two-family dwellings, an outlet box hood installed for this purpose shall be listed, and where installed on an enclosure supported from grade as described in 314.23(B) or as described in 314.23(F) shall be identified as "extra-duty." All 15- and 20-ampere, 125- and 250-volt nonlocking-type receptacles shall be listed weather-resistant type ≫*406.9(B)(1)*≪.

Ⓒ Where receptacles providing power for water-pump motors or for other loads directly related to the circulation and sanitation system do not meet all the conditions in 680.22(A)(1)(1) through (4), they must be located at least 10 ft (3.0 m) from the inside walls of the pool.

NOTE

All 15- and 20-ampere, single-phase, 125-volt receptacles located within 20 ft (6.0 m) of the pool's inside walls shall be protected by a GFCI ≫*680.22(A)(4)*≪. This distance is determined by measuring the shortest path that the appliance supply cord (connected to the receptacle) would follow without piercing a floor, wall, ceiling, hinged or sliding panel doorway, window opening, or other effective permanent barrier ≫*680.22(A)(5)*≪.

NOTE

Other receptacles shall be not less than 6 ft (1.83 m) from the inside walls of a pool ≫*680.22(A)(2)*≪.

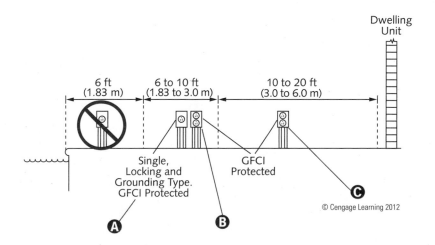

6 ft (1.83 m)

6 to 10 ft (1.83 to 3.0 m)

10 to 20 ft (3.0 to 6.0 m)

Dwelling Unit

Single, Locking and Grounding Type. GFCI Protected

GFCI Protected

Ⓐ Ⓑ Ⓒ

© Cengage Learning 2012

Equipotential Bonding

The parts specified in 680.26(B)(1) through (B)(7) shall be bonded together using solid copper conductors, insulated, covered, or bare, not smaller than 8 AWG or with rigid metal conduit of brass or other identified corrosion-resistant metal. Connections to bonded parts shall be made in accordance with 250.8. An 8 AWG or larger solid copper bonding conductor provided to reduce voltage gradients in the pool area shall not be required to be extended or attached to remote panelboards, service equipment, or electrodes ≫ *680.26(B)* ≪.

All metallic parts of the pool structure, including reinforcing metal not addressed in 680.26(1)(a), shall be bonded ≫ *680.26(B)(3)* ≪.

Ⓐ All fixed metal parts shall be bonded including, but not limited to, metal-sheathed cables and raceways, metal piping, metal awnings, metal fences, and metal door and window frames ≫ *680.26(B)(7)* ≪. Fixed metal parts that are not required to be bonded include: (1) those separated from the pool by a permanent barrier that prevents contact by a person, (2) those greater than 5 ft (1.5 m) horizontally of the inside walls of the pool, and (3) those greater than 12 ft (3.7 m) measured vertically above the pool's maximum water level, or as measured vertically above any observation stands, towers, or platforms, or any diving structures ≫ *680.26(B)(7) Exception No. 1, 2 and 3* ≪.

Ⓑ Bond all metal forming shells and mounting brackets of no-niche luminaires, unless a listed low-voltage lighting system is used that does not require bonding ≫ *680.26(B)(4)* ≪.

Ⓒ Bond any diving structure, observation stands, towers, or platforms unless one of the exceptions in 680.26(B)(7) is met ≫ *680.26(B)(7)* ≪.

Ⓓ Bond all metal fittings within or attached to the pool structure ≫ *680.26(B)(5)* ≪.

Ⓔ Isolated parts not more than 4 in. (100 mm) in any dimension that do not penetrate the pool's structure more than 1 in. (25 mm) do not require bonding ≫ *680.26(B)(5)* ≪.

Ⓕ Bonding to conductive pool shells shall be provided as specified in 680.26(B)(1)(a) or 680.26(B)(1)(b)

≫ *680.26(B)(1)* ≪ (See section in this text titled "Conductive Pool Shells and Perimeter Surfaces.")

Ⓖ Bond all metal fittings within or attached to the pool structure ≫ *680.26(B)(5)* ≪. Note: Each ladder/handrail anchor must be bonded unless not over 4 in. (100 mm) in any dimension.

Ⓗ Bond all metal parts of equipment associated with pool covers, including electric motors ≫ *680.26(B)(6)* ≪.

Ⓘ Bond metal parts of electrical equipment associated with the pool water circulating system, including pump motors. (Metal parts of listed equipment incorporating an approved system of double insulation and providing a means for grounding internal inaccessible, non-current-carrying metal parts shall not be bonded) ≫ *680.26(B)(6)* ≪.
Note: Pool equipment must be bonded to the equipotential bonding grid regardless of the intervening distance or location to the pool.

Ⓙ Where reinforcing steel is encapsulated with a non-conductive compound, the reinforcing steel shall not be required to be bonded ≫ *680.26(B)(3)* ≪.

Ⓚ Unencapsulated structural reinforcing steel shall be bonded together by steel tie wires or the equivalent ≫ *680.26(B)(1)(a)* ≪.

Ⓛ Bonding to perimeter surfaces shall be provided as specified in 680.26(B)(2)(a) or 680.26(B)(2)(b) and shall be attached to the pool reinforcing steel or copper conductor grid at a minimum of four (4) points uniformly spaced around the perimeter of the pool. The perimeter surface shall extend for 3 ft (1 m) horizontally beyond the inside walls of the pool and shall include unpaved surfaces as well as poured concrete surfaces and other types of paving. Perimeter surfaces less than 3 ft (1 m) separated by a permanent wall or building 5 ft (1.5 m) in height or more shall require equipotential bonding on the pool side of the permanent wall or building ≫ *680.26(B)(2)* ≪.

Ⓜ For pool water heaters rated at more than 50 amperes and having specific instructions regarding bonding and grounding, only those parts designated to be bonded shall be bonded and only those parts designated to be grounded shall be grounded ≫ *680.26(B)(6)(b)* ≪.

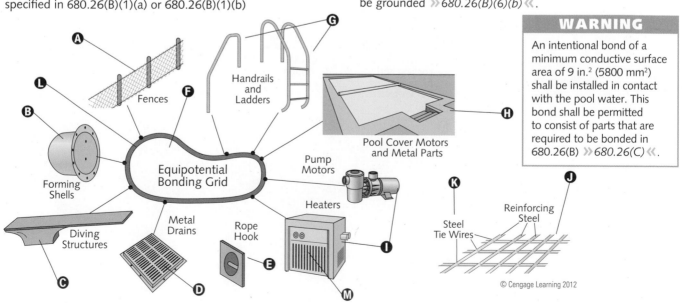

WARNING

An intentional bond of a minimum conductive surface area of 9 in.² (5800 mm²) shall be installed in contact with the pool water. This bond shall be permitted to consist of parts that are required to be bonded in 680.26(B) ≫ *680.26(C)* ≪.

Handrails and Ladders
Fences
Forming Shells
Equipotential Bonding Grid
Pump Motors
Pool Cover Motors and Metal Parts
Diving Structures
Metal Drains
Rope Hook
Heaters
Steel Tie Wires
Reinforcing Steel

© Cengage Learning 2012

Luminaires, Lighting Outlets, and Ceiling-Suspended (Paddle) Fans

For installations in indoor pool areas, the clearances shall be the same as for outdoor areas unless modified as provided in this paragraph. If the branch circuit supplying the equipment is protected by a GFCI, the following equipment shall be permitted at a height not less than 7 ft 6 in. (2.3 m) above the maximum pool water level: (1) totally enclosed luminaires; and (2) ceiling-suspended (paddle) fans identified for use beneath ceiling structures such as provided on porches or patios 》*680.22(B)(2)*《.

Cord- and plug-connected luminaires shall meet the same 680.7 specifications, where installed within 16 ft (4.9 m) of any point along the water's surface, measured radially 》*680.22(B)(5)*《.

The provisions of this section shall apply to all pool deck areas, including a covered pool, where electrically operated comfort heating units are installed within 20 ft (6.0 m) of the inside wall of the pool.

(1) **Unit heaters:** Unit heaters shall be rigidly mounted to the structure and shall be of the totally enclosed or guarded type. Unit heaters shall not be mounted over the pool or within the area extending 5 ft (1.5 m) horizontally from the inside walls of a pool.

(2) **Permanently wired radiant heaters:** Radiant electric heaters shall be suitably guarded and securely fastened to their mounting device(s). Heaters shall not be installed over a pool or within the area extending 5 ft (1.5 m) horizontally from the inside walls of the pool and shall be mounted at least 12 ft (3.7 m) vertically above the pool deck unless otherwise approved.

(3) **Radiant heating cables not permitted:** Radiant heating cables embedded in or below the deck shall not be permitted 》*680.27(C)*《.

Ⓐ For new installations in outdoor pool areas, luminaires, lighting outlets, and ceiling-suspended (paddle) fans shall not be installed over the pool, or over the area extending 5 ft (1.5 m) horizontally from the pool's inside walls, unless located not less than 12 ft (3.7 m) above the maximum water level 》*680.22(B)(1)*《.

Ⓑ Existing luminaires and lighting outlets located less than 5 ft (1.5 m), measured horizontally from the pool's inside walls, shall be (1) at least 5 ft (1.5 m) above the maximum water level surface; (2) rigidly attached to the existing structure; and (3) protected by a GFCI 》*680.22(B)(3)*《.

Ⓒ Luminaires and lighting outlets, and ceiling-suspended (paddle) fans installed in the area extending between 5 ft (1.5 m) and 10 ft (3.0 m) horizontally from a pool's inside walls shall be protected by a GFCI, unless 5 ft (1.5 m) above the maximum water level and rigidly attached to the pool's adjacent (or enclosing) structure 》*680.22(B)(4)*《.

N O T E

Locate all switching devices on the property at least 5 ft (1.5 m) horizontally from a pool's inside walls, unless separated from the pool by a solid fence, wall, or other permanent barrier. A switch listed as being acceptable for use within 5 ft (1.5 m) is also permitted 》*680.22 (C)*《.

CAUTION

Other outlets shall be not less than 10 ft (3.0 m) from the inside walls of the pool. Measurements shall be determined in accordance with 680.22(A)(5) 》*680.22(D)*《. Other outlets may include, but are not limited to, remote-control, signaling, fire alarm, and communications circuits 》*680.22(D) Informational Note*《.

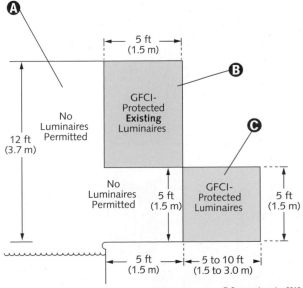

© Cengage Learning 2012

Underwater Luminaires (Permanently Installed Pools)

Requirements for luminaires installed below the pool's normal water level are covered in 680.23(A) through (F).

Wet-niche luminaire requirements are covered in 680.23(B)(1) through (6).

The equipment grounding conductor terminals of a junction box or transformer/other enclosure in the supply circuit to a wet-niche or no-niche luminaire and the field-wiring chamber of a dry-niche luminaire shall be connected to the panelboard's equipment grounding terminal. This terminal shall be directly connected to the panelboard enclosure ≫ *680.24 (F)* ≪.

A Luminaires mounted in walls shall be installed so that the top of the luminaire lens is at least 18 in. (450 mm) below the pool's normal water level, unless the luminaire is listed and identified for use at a depth of not less than 4 in. (100 mm) below the pool's normal water level ≫ *680.23(A)(5)* ≪.

B The 8 AWG bonding conductor termination in the forming shell shall be covered or encapsulated in a listed potting compound to protect it from the possibly deteriorating effect of pool water ≫ *680.23(B)(2)(b)* ≪.

C The luminaire shall be bonded and secured to the forming shell by a positive locking device that ensures a low-resistance contact, and which can only be removed from the forming shell by use of a tool. Luminaires listed for the application and having no non-current-carrying metal parts do not require bonding ≫ *680.23(B)(5)* ≪.

D Other than listed low-voltage luminaires not requiring grounding, all through-wall lighting assemblies, wet-niche, dry-niche, or no-niche luminaires shall be connected to an insulated 12 AWG or larger equipment grounding conductor sized per Table 250.122 ≫ *680.23(F)(2)* ≪.

NOTE

Conductors on the load side of a GFCI or transformer, used to comply with 680.23(A)(8) provisions, shall not occupy raceways, boxes, or enclosures containing other conductors, unless the other conductors are either protected by GFCIs or are grounding conductors. Feed-through type GFCI supply conductors can occupy the same enclosure. GFCIs are permitted in a panelboard containing circuits protected by means other than GFCIs ≫ *680.23(F)(3)* ≪.

CAUTION

All wet-niche luminaires shall be removable from the water for inspection, relamping, or other maintenance. The forming shell location and length of cord in the forming shell shall permit personnel to place the removed luminaire on the deck or other dry location for such maintenance. The luminaire maintenance location shall be accessible without entering or going in the pool water ≫ *680.23(B)(6)* ≪.

E All metal forming shells shall be bonded to an equipotential bonding grid with a solid copper conductor (insulated, covered, or bare) no smaller than 8 AWG ≫ *680.26(B)(4)* ≪.

F A junction box connected to a conduit extending directly to a forming shell or mounting bracket of a no-niche luminaire must comply with 680.24(A)(1), (2), and (3).

G The equipment grounding conductor shall be (1) an insulated copper conductor and (2) installed along with the circuit conductors ≫ *680.23(F)(2)* ≪.

H A GFCI shall be installed in the branch circuit supplying luminaires operating at more than the low voltage contact limit such that there is no shock hazard during relamping. The installation of the GFCI shall be such that there is no shock hazard with any likely fault-condition combination that involves a person in a conductive path from any ungrounded part of the branch circuit or the luminaire to ground ≫ *680.23(A)(3)* ≪. Low voltage contact limit is defined as a voltage not exceeding the following values: (1) 15 volts (RMS) for sinusoidal ac, (2) 21.2 volts peak for nonsinusoidal ac, (3) 30 volts for continuous dc (4) 12.4 volts peak for dc that is interrupted at a rate of 10 to 200 Hz ≫ *680.2* ≪.

I Conduit shall extend from the forming shell to a junction box (or other enclosure) conforming to the requirements as provided in 680.24. Conduit must be RMC, IMC, LFNC, or PVC. Metal conduit shall be approved and shall be made of brass or other approved corrosion-resistant metal ≫ *680.23(B)(2) and (B)(2)(a)* ≪.

J When using nonmetallic conduit, an 8 AWG insulated copper bonding jumper (solid or stranded) shall be installed in the conduit with provisions for terminating in the forming shell, junction box/transformer enclosure, or GFCI enclosure, unless using a listed low-voltage lighting system that does not require grounding ≫ *680.23(B)(2)(b)* ≪.

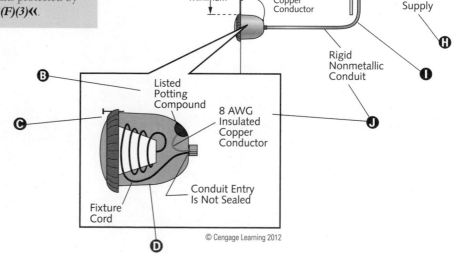

18 in. (450 mm) Minimum

8 AWG Solid Copper Conductor

To GFCI-Protected Supply

Rigid Nonmetallic Conduit

Listed Potting Compound

8 AWG Insulated Copper Conductor

Conduit Entry Is Not Sealed

Fixture Cord

© Cengage Learning 2012

Junction Boxes for Underwater Lighting

A junction box connected to a conduit that extends directly to a forming shell or mounting bracket of a no-niche luminaire shall meet the requirements of 680.24(A) through (F).

An enclosure for a transformer, GFCI, or a similar device connected to a conduit extending directly to a forming shell or mounting bracket of a no-niche luminaire must comply with 680.24(B) requirements.

Junction boxes, transformer and power-supply enclosures, and GFCI enclosures connected to a conduit extending directly to a forming shell or mounting bracket of a no-niche luminaire shall have a number of grounding terminals that exceeds the number of conduit entries by at least one 》*680.24(D)* 《.

Strain relief shall be provided for the termination of an underwater luminaire's flexible cord within a junction box, transformer enclosure, GFCI, or other enclosure 》*680.24(E)* 《.

A Locate the junction box at least 4 ft (1.2 m) from the pool's inside wall, unless separated from the pool by a solid fence, wall, or other permanent barrier 》*680.24(A)(2)(b)* 《.

B A junction box connected to a conduit extending directly to a forming shell or mounting bracket of a no-niche luminaire must comply with 680.24(A)(1)(1) through (3).

C The junction box shall be listed as a swimming pool junction box 》*680.24(A)(1)* 《.

D The junction box shall be comprised of copper, brass, suitable plastic, or other approved corrosion-resistant material 》*680.24(A)(1)(2)* 《.

E The junction box shall have electrical continuity (between every connected metal conduit and the grounding terminals) by means of copper, brass, or other approved corrosion-resistant metal that is integral with the box 》*680.24(A)(1)(3)* 《.

F Measured from the inside of the bottom of the box, the junction box shall be located at least 8 in. (200 mm) above the maximum pool water level 》*680.24(A)(2)(a)* 《. (Note: The bottom of the junction box must not be less than 4 in. (100 mm) above the ground level or pool deck.)

G The junction box shall be equipped with threaded entries/hubs or a nonmetallic hub 》*680.24(A)(1)(1)* 《.

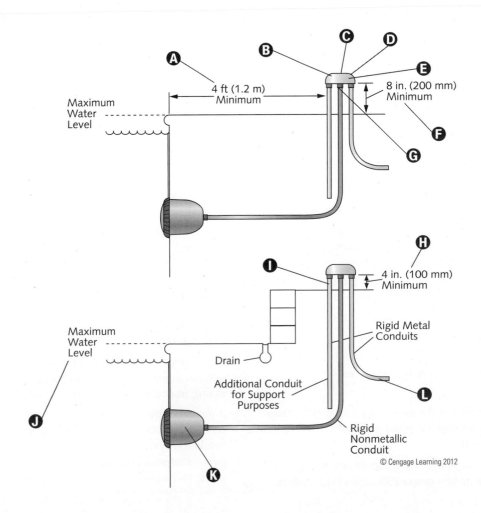

© Cengage Learning 2012

Junction Boxes for Underwater Lighting *(continued)*

H Measured from the inside of the bottom of the box, the junction box shall be located no less than 4 in. (100 mm) above the ground level, or pool deck »*680.24(A)(2)(a)* «. (Note: The bottom of the junction box must not be less than 8 in. [200 mm] above the maximum pool water level.)

I A swimming pool junction box must comply with 314.23(E) support provisions. It must be supported by *two* or more conduits (rigid or intermediate metal conduit only) threaded wrenchtight into the enclosure or hubs. Secure each conduit within 18 in. (450 mm) of the enclosure since all entries are on the same side. Note: PVC is not permitted for swimming pool junction box support.

J Maximum water level is defined as the highest level that water can reach before it spills out »*680.2* «.

> ### N O T E
>
> Branch-circuit wiring on the supply side of enclosures and junction boxes connected to conduits run to wet-niche and no-niche luminaires, and the field wiring compartments of dry-niche luminaires, shall be installed using RMC, IMC, LFNC, PVC conduit, or RTRC. Where installed on buildings, EMT shall be permitted, and where installed within buildings, ENT, Type MC cable, EMT, or Type AC cable shall be permitted. In all cases, an insulated equipment grounding conductor sized in accordance with Table 250.122 but not less than 12 AWG shall be required »*680.23(F)(1)*«.
> (See exception for connecting to transformers.)

K Forming shells shall be installed for the mounting of all wet-niche underwater luminaires and shall be equipped with provisions for conduit entries. Metal parts of the luminaire and forming shell in contact with the pool water shall be of brass or other approved corrosion-resistant metal. All forming shells used with nonmetallic conduit systems, other than those that are part of a listed low-voltage lighting system not requiring grounding, shall include provisions for terminating an 8 AWG copper conductor »*680.23(B)(1)* «.

L The equipment grounding conductor terminals of a junction box, transformer enclosure, or other enclosure in the supply circuit to a wet-niche or no-niche luminaire and the field-wiring chamber of a dry-niche luminaire shall be connected to the equipment grounding terminal of the panelboard. This terminal shall be directly connected to the panelboard enclosure »*680.24(F)* «.

> ### CAUTION
>
> Junction boxes and enclosures mounted above the grade of the finished walkway around the pool shall not be located in the walkway unless afforded additional protection, such as by location under diving boards, adjacent to fixed structures, and the like »*680.24(C)*«.

Equipment and Feeders

The following equipment shall be grounded in accordance with Parts V, VI, an VII of Article 250 and connected by wiring methods of Chapter 3, except as modified by Article 680:

1. Through-wall lighting assemblies and underwater luminaires, other than those low-voltage lighting products listed for the application without a grounding conductor

2. All electrical equipment located within 5 ft (1.5 m) of the inside wall of the specified body of water

3. All electrical equipment associated with the recirculating system of the specified body of water

4. Junction boxes

5. Transformer and power-supply enclosures

6. GFCIs

7. Panelboards (not part of the service equipment) that supply any electrical equipment associated with the specified body of water »*680.6* «

A separate building's panelboard can supply swimming pool equipment if the feeder meets 250.32(B)(1) grounding requirements. If an equipment grounding conductor is installed in other than existing feeders covered in 680.25(A), Exception, it shall be an insulated conductor »*680.25(B)(2)* «.

Branch circuits for pool-associated motors in the interior of dwelling units, or in the interior of accessory buildings associated with a dwelling unit, can be installed in any of Chapter 3's wiring methods where meeting the requirements of this section. Where run in a cable assembly, the equipment grounding conductor can be uninsulated, but it shall be enclosed within the cable assembly's outer sheath »*680.21(A)(4)* «.

Electric equipment shall not be installed in rooms (or pits) without adequate drainage to prevent water accumulation during normal operation or filter maintenance »*680.11* «.

A permanently installed pool can have listed cord- and plug-connected pool pumps that incorporate an approved double insulation system and provide a grounding means for the pump's internal and inaccessible, non-current-carrying metal parts. This listed cord- and plug-connected pool pump shall

Equipment and Feeders *(continued)*

be connected to any wiring method recognized in Chapter 3 that is suitable for the location. **Where the bonding grid is connected to the equipment grounding conductor of the motor circuit in accordance with the second sentence of 680.26(B)(6)(a), the branch-circuit wiring shall comply with 680.21(A)** ≫ *680.21(B)* ≪ .

Ⓐ The branch circuits for pool-associated motors shall be installed in RMC, IMC, PVC, or Type MC cable listed for the location. Other wiring methods and materials are permitted in specific locations or applications as covered in this section. Any wiring method employed shall contain an insulated copper equipment grounding conductor sized per 250.122 but not smaller than 12 AWG ≫ *680.21(A)(1)* ≪ . Where installed on or within buildings, EMT is permitted ≫ *680.21(A)(2)* ≪ .

Ⓑ One or more means to simultaneously disconnect all ungrounded conductors shall be provided for all utilization equipment other than lighting. Each means shall be readily accessible and within sight from its equipment and shall be located at least 5 ft (1.5 m) horizontally from the inside walls of a pool, spa, or hot tub unless separated from the open water by a permanently installed barrier that provides a

5-ft (1.5-m) reach path or greater. This horizontal distance is to be measured from the water's edge along the shortest path required to reach the disconnect ≫ *680.12* ≪ .

Ⓒ Section 680.25 provisions apply to any feeder on the supply side of panelboards supplying branch circuits for pool equipment covered in Part II and on the load side of the service equipment or the source of a separately derived system ≫ *680.25* ≪ . Feeders shall be installed in RMC or IMC. If not subject to physical damage, the following wiring methods shall be permitted: (1) LFNC, (2) PVC, (3) RTRC, (4) EMT where installed on or within a building, (5) ENT where installed within a building, and (6) Type MC cable where installed within a building and if not subject to corrosive environment ≫ *680.25(A)* ≪ .

Ⓓ Where connections must be flexible at (or adjacent to) the motor, LFMC or LFNC with approved fittings are permitted ≫ *680.21(A)(3)* ≪ .

N O T E

The only underground wiring permitted under the pool or within the area extending 5 ft (1.5 m) horizontally from the pool's inside wall is the wiring necessary to supply pool equipment (permitted by this article). Where space limitations prevent wiring outside the 5-ft (1.5-m) restricted area, such wiring is permitted if installed in complete raceway systems of RMC, IMC, or a nonmetallic raceway system. All metal conduit shall be corrosion resistant and suitable for the location ≫ *680.10* ≪ . Minimum burial depths are provided in Table 680.10.

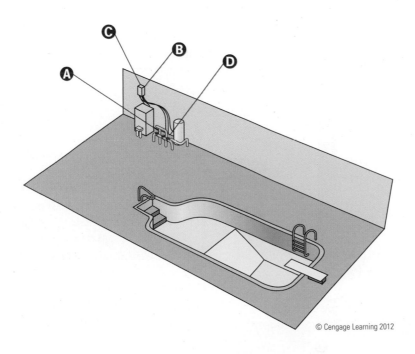

© Cengage Learning 2012

Storable Pools

A luminaire installed in or on a storable pool's wall shall be part of a cord- and plug-connected lighting assembly. This assembly shall be listed as an assembly for the purpose, and have the following construction features:

1. No exposed metal parts

2. A luminaire lamp that is suitable for use at the supplied voltage

3. An impact-resistant polymeric lens, luminaire body, and transformer enclosure

4. A transformer or power supply meeting 680.23(A)(2) requirements with a primary rating not over 150 volts ⟩⟩ *680.33(A)* ⟨⟨

A lighting assembly (without a transformer or power supply) whose luminaire lamp(s) operate at 150 volts or less can be cord- and plug-connected where the assembly is listed as an assembly for the purpose. The installation shall comply with 680.23(A)(5), and the assembly shall have the following construction features:

1. No exposed metal parts

2. An impact-resistant polymeric lens and luminaire body

3. A GFCI with open neutral conductor protection as an integral part of the assembly

4. A permanent connection to the GFCI with open-neutral protection

5. Compliance with 680.23(A) requirements ⟩⟩ *680.33(B)* ⟨⟨

(A) Storable swimming, wading, or immersion pool: Those that are constructed on or above the ground and are capable of holding water to a maximum depth of 42 in. (1.0 m), or a pool with nonmetallic, molded polymeric walls or inflatable fabric walls regardless of dimension ⟩⟩ *680.2* ⟨⟨ .

(B) All 15- and 20-ampere, 125- and 250-volt receptacles installed in a wet location shall have an enclosure that is weatherproof whether or not the attachment plug cap is inserted. For other than one- or two-family dwellings, an outlet box hood installed for this purpose shall be listed, and where installed on an enclosure supported from grade as described in 314.23(B) or as described in 314.23(F) shall be identified as "extra-duty." All 15- and 20-ampere, 125- and 250-volt nonlocking-type receptacles shall be listed weather-resistant type ⟩⟩ *406.9(B)(1)* ⟨⟨ .

(C) A cord-connected pool filter pump shall incorporate an approved system of double insulation or its equivalent and shall be provided with means for grounding only the internal and nonaccessible non-current-carrying metal parts of the appliance. The means for grounding shall be an equipment grounding conductor run with the power-supply conductors in the flexible cord that is properly terminated in a grounding-type attachment plug having a fixed grounding contact member. Cord-connected pool filter pumps shall be provided with a GFCI that is an integral part of the attachment plug or located in the power-supply cord within 12 in. (300 mm) of the attachment plug ⟩⟩ *680.31* ⟨⟨ .

(D) Receptacles shall not be located less than 6 ft (1.83 m) from the inside walls of a pool. In determining these dimensions, the distance to be measured shall be the shortest path the supply cord of an appliance connected to the receptacle would follow without piercing a floor, wall, ceiling, doorway with hinged or sliding door, window opening, or other effective permanent barrier ⟩⟩ *680.34* ⟨⟨ .

CAUTION

All electrical equipment, including power-supply cords, used with storable pools shall be protected by ground-fault circuit interrupters. All 125-volt, 15- and 20-ampere receptacles located within 20 ft (6.0 m) of the inside walls of a storable pool shall be protected by a GFCI. In determining these dimensions, the distance to be measured shall be the shortest path the supply cord of an appliance connected to the receptacle would follow without piercing a floor, wall, ceiling, doorway with hinged or sliding door, window opening, or other effective permanent barrier ⟩⟩ *680.32* ⟨⟨ . If flexible cords are used, see 400.4 ⟩⟩ *680.32 Informational Note* ⟨⟨ .

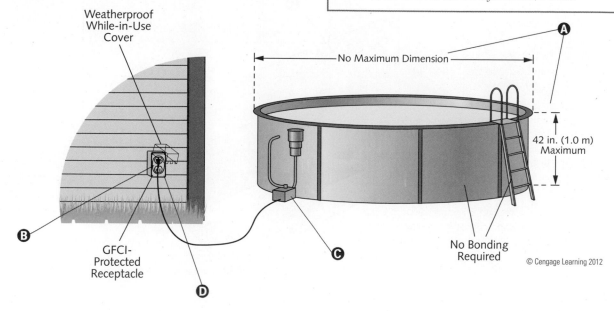

Weatherproof While-in-Use Cover

GFCI-Protected Receptacle

No Maximum Dimension

42 in. (1.0 m) Maximum

No Bonding Required

© Cengage Learning 2012

Spas and Hot Tubs

Receptacles providing spa or hot tub power shall be GFCI protected 》 *680.43(A)(3)* 《.

An indoor spa or hot tub shall comply with Article 680 provisions (Parts I and II) unless modified by 680.43 and shall be connected by a Chapter 3–approved wiring method. Listed spa and hot tub packaged units rated 20 amperes or less can be cord- and plug-connected to facilitate the removal or disconnection of the unit for maintenance and repair 》 *680.43 and Exception No. 1* 《.

The equipotential bonding requirements for perimeter surfaces in 680.26(B)(2) shall not apply to a listed self-contained spa or hot tub installed above a finished floor 》 *680.43 Exception No. 2* 《.

All of the following shall be grounded: (1) electric equipment located within 5 ft (1.5 m) of the spa or hot tub's inside wall and (2) electric equipment associated with the spa or hot tub's circulating system 》 *680.43(F)* 《.

A Luminaires, lighting outlets, and ceiling-suspended (paddle) fans located over the spa/hot tub less than 5 ft (1.5 m) from the spa or hot tub's inside walls shall be a minimum of 7 ft 6 in. (2.3 m) above the maximum water level and shall be GFCI protected unless the mounting height is at least 12 ft (3.7 m) 》 *680.43(B)(1)(b)* 《.

B Luminaires meeting either (1) or (2) of the following requirements *and* protected by a GFCI can be installed less than 7 ft 6 in. (2.3 m) over a spa or hot tub:

1. Recessed luminaires having a glass or plastic lens and nonmetallic or electrically isolated metal trim, suitable for damp location use

2. Surface-mounted luminaires, with a glass or plastic globe, and a nonmetallic body or a metallic body isolated from contact, and suitable for use in damp locations 》 *680.43(B)(1)(c)* 《.

C Luminaires, lighting outlets, and ceiling-suspended (paddle) fans located 12 ft (3.7 m) or more above the maximum water level do not require GFCI protection 》 *680.43(B)(1)(a)* 《.

D Switches shall be located at least 5 ft (1.5 m) measured horizontally from the spa or hot tub's inside walls 》 *680.43(C)* 《.

E A readily accessible, clearly labeled emergency shutoff or control switch for stopping the motor(s) that provide recirculating and jet system power shall be installed at least 5 ft (1.5 m) away, adjacent to, and within sight from the spa or hot tub. Note: This requirement does not apply to single-family dwellings 》 *680.41* 《.

F Receptacles of 125 volts and 30 amperes or less and within 10 ft (3.0 m) of the spa or hot tub's inside walls shall be protected by a GFCI 》 *680.43(A)(2)* 《. Determine this

distance by measuring the shortest path the supply cord of an appliance connected to the receptacle would follow without piercing a building's floor, wall, ceiling, doorway with hinged or sliding door, window opening, or other effective permanent barrier 》 *680.43(A)(4)* 《.

G At least one 125-volt, 15- or 20-ampere general-purpose branch-circuit receptacle shall be located a minimum of 6 ft (1.83 m), and no more than 10 ft (3.0 m), from the inside wall of an indoor spa or hot tub 》 *680.43(A)* 《.

H Locate property receptacles at least 6 ft (1.83 m) measured horizontally from the spa or hot tub's inside walls 》 *680.43(A)(1)* 《.

> **NOTE**
>
> A spa or hot tub installed **outdoors** shall comply with Article 680, Part I and II provisions unless otherwise permitted in the following: (A) listed packaged units utilizing a factory-installed assembly control panel or panelboard can be connected with 6 ft (1.8 m) or less of liquidtight flexible conduit external to the spa or hot tub enclosure in addition to the length needed within the enclosure to make the electrical connection, or can be cord- and plug-connected with a cord no longer than 15 ft (4.6 m), if protected by a GFCI; (B) bonding by metal-to-metal mounting on a common frame or base is permitted. The metal bands or hoops used to secure wooden staves do not require bonding as stipulated in 680.26 》 *680.42(A) and (B)* 《.

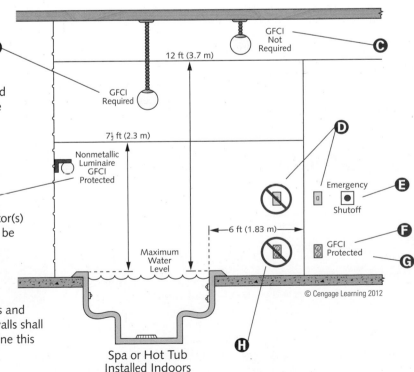

Spa or Hot Tub
Installed Indoors

© Cengage Learning 2012

Pools and Tubs for Therapeutic Use

Outlet(s) supplying the following shall be protected by a GFCI: (1) self-contained therapeutic tub or hydrotherapeutic tank; (2) packaged therapeutic tub or hydrotherapeutic tank; or (3) field-assembled therapeutic tub or hydrotherapeutic tank ≫ *680.62(A)* ≪.

A listed self-contained unit or listed packaged equipment assembly marked to indicate that integral GFCI protection is provided for all electrical parts within the unit or assembly (pumps, air-blowers, heaters, lights, controls, sanitizer generators, wiring, etc.), does not require that the outlet supply be GFCI protected ≫ *680.62(A)(1)* ≪.

A therapeutic tub or hydrotherapeutic tank rated greater than 250 volts or rated 3-phase or with a heater load exceeding 50 amperes does not require supply protection by means of a GFCI ≫ *680.62(A)(2)* ≪.

All receptacles within 6 ft (1.83 m) of a therapeutic tub shall be protected by a GFCI ≫ *680.62(E)* ≪.

Ⓐ Article 680, Part I and Part VI provisions apply to therapeutically used pools and tubs in health care facilities, gymnasiums, athletic training rooms, and similar areas. Portable therapeutic appliances shall comply with Parts II and III of Article 422 ≫ *680.60* ≪.

Ⓑ All tub-associated metal parts shall be bonded by any of the following methods: (1) interconnection of threaded metal piping and fittings; (2) metal-to-metal mounting on a common frame or base; (3) suitable metal clamp connections; or (4) the provision of a solid copper bonding jumper (insulated, covered, or bare) no smaller than 8 AWG ≫ *680.62(C)* ≪.

Ⓒ Tubs used for the therapeutic submersion and treatment of patients, which during normal use are not easily moved from place to place, or which are fastened or secured at a given location (including associated piping systems), shall conform to Part VI of Article 680 ≫ *680.62* ≪.

Ⓓ All of the following shall be connected to an equipment grounding conductor: (1) electrical equipment located within 5 ft (1.5 m) of the tub's inside wall and (2) electrical equipment associated with the tub's circulating system ≫ *680.62(D)(1)* ≪.

Ⓔ The following parts shall be bonded together:

1. All metal fittings within, or attached to, the tub structure.
2. Metal parts of electrical equipment associated with the tub's water circulating system, including pump motors.
3. Metal-sheathed cables and raceways and metal piping within 5 ft (1.5 m) of the tub's inside walls and not separated from the tub by a permanent barrier.
4. All metal surfaces within 5 ft (1.5 m) of the tub's inside walls not separated by a permanent barrier.
5. Electrical devices and controls unrelated to the therapeutic tubs shall either be located at least 5 ft (1.5 m) away from such units, or be bonded to the therapeutic tub system ≫ *680.62(B)* ≪.

Ⓕ Therapeutic pools constructed in or on the ground or within a building in such a manner that the pool cannot be readily disassembled shall comply with Article 680, Parts I and II ≫ *680.61* ≪. The limitations of 680.22(B)(1) through (C)(4) do not apply if all luminaires are of the totally enclosed type ≫ *680.61 Exception* ≪.

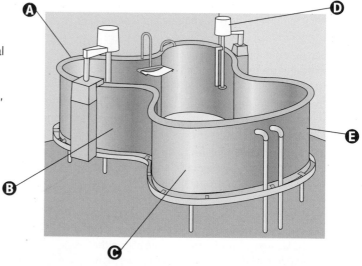

> # CAUTION
>
> All luminaires used in therapeutic tub areas shall be of the totally enclosed type ≫ *680.62(F)* ≪.

> ### NOTE
>
> Small conductive surfaces not likely to become energized, such as air and water jets and drain fittings not connected to metallic piping, and towel bars, mirror frames, and similar nonelectrical equipment not connected to metal framing, shall not be required to be bonded ≫ *680.62(B) Exception* ≪.

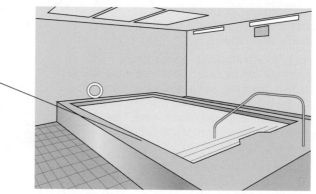

Hydromassage Bathtubs

Hydromassage bathtubs as defined in 680.2 shall comply with Part VII of this article. They shall not be required to comply with other parts of this article 》*680.70*《.

Ⓐ All bathroom receptacles shall have GFCI protection for personnel 》*210.8(A)(1) and (B)(1)*《.

Ⓑ All 125-volt, single-phase receptacles not exceeding 30 amperes and located within 6 ft (1.83 m) measured horizontally of the inside walls of a hydromassage tub shall be protected by a ground-fault circuit interrupter 》*680.71*《.

Ⓒ Hydromassage bathtubs and their associated electrical components shall be on an individual branch circuit(s) and protected by a readily accessible ground-fault circuit interrupter 》*680.71*《.

Ⓓ All metal piping systems and all grounded metal parts in contact with the circulating water shall be bonded together using a solid copper bonding jumper, insulated, covered, or bare, not smaller than 8 AWG. The bonding jumper shall be connected to the terminal on the circulating pump motor that is intended for this purpose. The bonding jumper shall not be required to be connected to a double-insulated circulating pump motor. The 8 AWG or larger solid copper bonding jumper shall be required for equipotential bonding in the area of the hydromassage bathtub and shall not be required to be extended or attached to any remote panelboard, service equipment, or any electrode. The 8 AWG or larger solid copper bonding jumper shall be long enough to terminate on a replacement non-double-insulated pump motor and shall be terminated to the equipment grounding conductor of the branch circuit of the motor when a double-insulated circulating pump motor is used 》*680.74*《.

Ⓔ Hydromassage bathtub electrical equipment shall be accessible without damage to the building structure or finish. Where the hydromassage bathtub is cord- and plug-connected with the supply receptacle accessible only through a service access opening, the receptacle shall be installed so that its face is within direct view and not more than 1 ft (300 mm) of the opening 》*680.73*《.

NOTE

Luminaires, switches, receptacles, and other electrical equipment located in the same room, and not directly associated with a hydromassage bathtub, shall be installed in accordance with the requirements of Chapters 1 through 4 in the *NEC* covering the installation of that equipment in bathrooms 》*680.72*《.

CAUTION

A receptacle shall not be installed within a bathtub or shower space 》*406.9(C)*《.

WARNING

The GFCI protecting the hydromassage bathtub branch circuit shall be readily accessible 》*680.71*《.

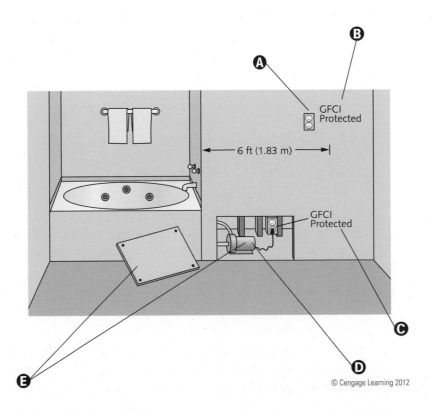

© Cengage Learning 2012

Summary

- Article 600 covers the conductor and equipment installation for electric signs and outline lighting (including neon and skeleton tubing).
- Manufactured wiring system provisions are located in Article 604.
- Article 605 ("Office Furnishings") covers electrical equipment, lighting accessories, and wiring systems used to connect, or contained within, wired partitions.
- Electric vehicle charging system provisions are located in Article 625.
- Audio signal processing, amplification, and reproduction equipment requirements can be found in Article 640.
- Article 645 covers information technology equipment.
- Electrically operated pipe organ circuits and components employed for sounding apparatus and keyboard control are located in Article 650.
- Article 695 ("Fire Pumps") covers the installation of electric power sources and interconnecting circuits as well as switching and control equipment dedicated to fire pump drivers.
- Elevator, dumbwaiter, escalator, moving walk, platform lift, and stairway chairlift provisions are contained in Article 620.

- Article 680 provisions apply to the construction and installation of electrical wiring and equipment in or near all swimming, wading, therapeutic, and decorative pools, fountains, hot tubs, spas, and hydromassage bathtubs, whether permanently installed or storable, as well as to metallic auxiliary equipment (such as pumps, filters, etc.).
- The parts specified in 680.26(B)(1) through (B)(7) shall be bonded together using solid copper conductors, insulated, covered, or bare, not smaller than 8 AWG or with rigid metal conduit of brass or other identified corrosion-resistant metal.
- Very specific and detailed receptacle and lighting (including underwater) requirements are stipulated in Article 680.
- While Article 680, Part II covers permanently installed pools, storable pool requirements are found in Part III.
- Indoor spa and hot tub installations are covered in 680.43(A) through (G).
- Article 680, Part VI provisions apply to pools and tubs for therapeutic use in health care facilities, gymnasiums, athletic training rooms, and similar areas.
- Hydromassage bathtubs (and associated electrical components) are covered in Article 680, Part VII.

Unit 19 Competency Test

NEC Reference	Answer	
_____	_____	1. Storable swimming pools are capable of holding water to a maximum depth of _____ in.
_____	_____	2. Overcurrent protection for feeders and branch circuits supplying electric vehicle supply equipment shall be sized for _____ duty and shall have a rating of not less than _____% of the maximum load of the electric vehicle supply equipment.
_____	_____	3. A clearly labeled emergency shutoff or control switch for the purpose of stopping the motor(s) that provide power to the recirculation system and jet system shall be installed at a point readily accessible to the users and at least _____ ft away, adjacent to, and within sight from the spa or hot tub.
_____	_____	4. Transformers and power supplies used for the supply of underwater luminaires shall incorporate either a transformer of the isolated winding type with an ungrounded secondary that has a _____ between the primary and secondary windings.
_____	_____	5. Duty on elevator driving machine motors shall be rated as _____.
_____	_____	6. Not more than _____ ft of high-voltage cable shall be permitted in nonmetallic conduit from a high-voltage terminal of a neon transformer (over 1000 volts, nominal) supply to the first neon tube.
_____	_____	7. All fixed metal parts that are within _____ ft horizontally of the inside walls of a permanently installed swimming pool and within _____ ft above the pool's maximum water level shall be bonded.

NEC Reference	Answer

_____ _____ 8. Electrically operated pipe organ circuits shall be arranged so that 26 and 28 AWG conductors shall be protected by an overcurrent device rated at not more than _____.

_____ _____ 9. All live parts of electrical apparatus in the hoistways, at the landings, in or on the cars of elevators and dumbwaiters, in the wellways or the landings of escalators or moving walkways, or in the runways and machinery spaces of platform lifts and stairway chairlifts shall be _____.

_____ _____ 10. Unless specifically listed for the purpose and location, the coupling means of electric vehicle supply equipment shall be stored or located at a height of not less than _____ in. and not more than _____ ft above an outdoor parking surface.

_____ _____ 11. A(n) _____ is a structure designed to support a wet-niche luminaire assembly and intended for mounting in a pool or fountain structure.

_____ _____ 12. Switches, flashers, and similar devices controlling transformers and electronic power supplies shall be rated for controlling inductive loads or have a current rating not less than _____ of the current rating of the transformer.

    a) 80% b) 100% c) 125% d) 200%

_____ _____ 13. Audio system equipment supplied by branch-circuit power shall not be placed laterally within _____ ft of the inside wall of a pool, spa, hot tub, or fountain, nor within _____ ft of the prevailing or tidal high water mark.

_____ _____ 14. Where a permanently installed pool is installed at a dwelling unit(s), at least one 125-volt, 15- or 20-ampere receptacle on a general-purpose branch circuit shall be located a minimum of _____ ft from and not more than _____ ft from the inside wall of the pool.

_____ _____ 15. The voltage at a fire pump controller's line terminals shall not drop more than _____ below normal (controller-rated voltage) under motor starting conditions.

_____ _____ 16. Luminaires located over a spa or within 5 ft (1.5 m) from the inside walls of the spa shall be permitted to be not less than _____ ft above the maximum water level where protected by a GFCI.

_____ _____ 17. Traveling cables that are suitably supported and protected from physical damage shall be permitted to be run without the use of a raceway from inside the hoistway, to elevator controller enclosures and to elevator car and machine room, control room, machinery space, and control space connections that are located outside the hoistway for a distance not exceeding _____ ft in length as measured from the first point of support on the elevator car or hoistway wall, or counterweight where applicable, provided the conductors are grouped together and taped or corded, or in the original sheath.

_____ _____ 18. Underground wiring shall not be permitted under the pool or within the area extending _____ ft horizontally from the inside wall of the pool unless this wiring is necessary to supply pool equipment permitted by Article 680.

_____ _____ 19. Hydromassage bathtub electrical equipment shall be _____ without damaging the building structure or building finish.

_____ _____ 20. All 15- and 20-ampere, single-phase 125-volt receptacles located within _____ ft of the inside wall of the pool shall be protected by a GFCI.

_____ _____ 21. Manufactured wiring system cable shall be listed Type AC cable or listed Type MC cable containing nominal 600-volt _____ AWG copper-insulated conductors with a bare or insulated copper equipment grounding conductor equivalent in size to the ungrounded conductor.

_____ _____ 22. Luminaires mounted in permanently installed swimming pool walls shall be installed with the top of the luminaire lens at least _____ in. below the normal water level of the pool.

NEC Reference   Answer

_____   _____

23. Sign or outline lighting system equipment shall be at least _____ ft above areas accessible to vehicles unless protected from physical damage.

24. Existing luminaires and lighting outlets located less than _____ ft measured horizontally from the inside walls of a pool shall be at least _____ ft above the surface of the maximum water level, shall be rigidly attached to the existing structure, and shall be protected by a GFCI.

25. A fixed or stationary electric sign installed inside a fountain shall be at least _____ ft inside the fountain measured from the outside edges of the fountain.

26. The conductors to the hoistway door interlocks from the hoistway riser shall be flame retardant and suitable for a temperature of not less than _____.

27. In new outdoor pool areas, ceiling-suspended (paddle) fans shall not be installed above the pool or over the area extending _____ ft horizontally from the inside walls of the pool unless no part of the fan is less than _____ ft above the maximum water level.

28. The branch-circuit conductors supplying one or more units of information technology equipment shall have an ampacity not less than _____ of the total connected load.

29. A junction box connected to a conduit that extends directly to a forming shell shall be provided with a number of grounding terminals that shall be _____.

30. Electric vehicle supply equipment shall be provided with a(n) _____ that de-energizes the electric vehicle connector and its cable whenever the electric connector is uncoupled from the electric vehicle.

31. Branch circuits that supply neon tubing installations shall not be rated in excess of _____.

32. The termination of the 8 AWG bonding jumper in a permanently installed swimming pool forming shell shall be covered with or encapsulated in a(n) _____ to protect the connection from the possible deteriorating effect of pool water.

33. Conductors supplying a fire pump motor(s), pressure maintenance pumps, and associated fire pump accessory equipment shall have a rating not less than _____ of the sum of the fire pump motor(s) and pressure maintenance motor(s) full-load current(s), and _____ of the associated fire pump accessory equipment.

34. Switching devices shall be located at least _____ ft horizontally from the inside walls of a pool unless separated from the pool by a solid fence, wall, or other permanent barrier.

35. Article _____ covers electrical equipment, lighting accessories, and wiring systems used to connect, contained within, or installed on relocatable wired partitions.

36. A junction box connected to a conduit that extends directly to a forming shell shall be located not less than _____ in., measured from the inside of the bottom of the box, above the ground level, or pool deck, or not less than _____ in. above the maximum pool water level, whichever provides the greater elevation.

Index